# The
# Constitution
## in the
# Supreme Court

# The
# Constitution
# in the
# Supreme Court

The Second Century

# 1888–1986

## David P. Currie

The University of Chicago Press • Chicago and London

DAVID P. CURRIE is the Harry N. Wyatt Professor of Law
at the University of Chicago.

The University of Chicago Press, Chicago 60637
The University of Chicago Press, Ltd., London
© 1990 by The University of Chicago
All rights reserved. Published 1990
Printed in the United States of America

99  98  97  96  95  94  93  92  91  90        5 4 3 2 1

Library of Congress Cataloging in Publication Data

Currie, David P.
    The Constitution in the Supreme Court : the second century,
1888–1986 / David P. Currie.
        p.   cm.
    ISBN 0-226-13111-4 (alk. paper)
    1. United States—Constitutional law—Interpretation and
construction.   2. United States. Supreme Court.   3. United States—
Constitutional history.   I. Title.
KF4550.C873   1990
342.73′029—dc20
[347.30229]                                        90-34143
                                                   CIP

⊗The paper used in this publication meets the minimum requirements of
the American National Standard for Information Sciences—Permanence of Paper
for Printed Library Materials, ANSI Z39.48-1984.

# Contents

# Introduction

This volume is a sequel to *The Constitution in the Supreme Court: The First Hundred Years*, which traced the course of constitutional decision in the highest court of the United States from its establishment in 1789 until the death of Chief Justice Morrison Waite in 1888.[1] As in the earlier study, my aim is not simply to tell the story of how the Justices interpreted the Constitution but also to analyze and criticize their work from a lawyer's point of view.

Substantial portions of this volume originally appeared in the form of articles in various law journals, to all of which thanks are extended for permission to reprint. *See* Currie, *The Constitution in the Supreme Court: The Protection of Economic Interests, 1889-1910*, 52 U. CHI. L. REV. 324 (1985), © 1985 by The University of Chicago; *Full Faith and the Bill of Rights, 1889-1910*, 52 U. CHI. L. REV. 867 (1985), © 1985 by The University of Chicago; *1910-1921*, DUKE L.J. 1111 (1985), ©1985 by the Duke Law Journal; *1921-1930*, DUKE L.J. 65 (1986), ©1986 by the Duke Law Journal; *The New Deal, 1931-1940*, 54 U. CHI. L. REV. 504 (1987), © 1987 by The University of Chicago; *Civil Rights and Liberties, 1930-1941*, DUKE L.J. 800 (1987), © 1987 by the Duke Law Journal; *The Second World War, 1941-1946*, 37 CATH. U. L. REV. 1 (1987), © 1988 by The Catholic University of America; *The Preferred-Position Debate, 1941-1946*, 37 CATH. U. L. REV. 1 (1987), © 1988 by The Catholic University of America; *1946-1953*, 37 EMORY L.J. 249 (1988), © 1988 by the Emory Law Journal; *Bankruptcy Judges and the Independent Judiciary*, 16 CREIGHTON L. REV. 441 (1983), © 1983 by Creighton University School of Law; *Sovereign Immunity and Suits against Government Officers*, SUP. CT. REV. 149 (1984), © 1985 by The University of Chicago; *The Distribution of Powers after Bowsher*, SUP. CT. REV. 19 (1986), © 1987 by The University of Chicago. I should also like to thank the Catholic University Law School, where portions of this study formed the basis of the Pope John XXIII Lecture in April of 1987, as well as the late Ruth Wyatt Rosenson, the D. Francis Bustin Educational Fund for the Law School, the Sonnenschein Fund, and the Jerome S. Weiss Faculty Research Fund for helping to make this study possible; Katherine Goodman, Karla Kraus, and Richard Levy for valuable research assistance; Mitchell Daffner, Mary Beth Gose, Michael Cochrane, and Michael Faris for taming the computer; and Albert Alschuler, Gerhard Casper, Frank Easterbrook, Richard Helmholz, Philip B. Kurland, Michael McConnell, Phil C. Neal, Richard Posner, Carol Rose, Stephen J. Schulhofer, Geoffrey R. Stone, David Strauss, Cass R. Sunstein, Alan O. Sykes, and William Van Alstyne for their advice and encouragement.

[1]D. CURRIE, THE CONSTITUTION IN THE SUPREME COURT: THE FIRST HUNDRED YEARS (1985) [hereafter cited as THE FIRST HUNDRED YEARS].

There is of course no single lawyers' point of view. My own starting point, as I explained in the earlier volume, is the conviction that the Constitution is, as it says, the law of the land, which binds the judges no less than the other officials whose actions they review. It follows that the judges may neither disregard limitations that the Constitution contains nor invent others that it does not. I do not pretend that the Framers answered all questions of constitutional interpretation, or most of them. I do maintain that it is inappropriate for a judge or for any other official to substitute his or her judgment for that of the "People of the United States" in any case in which the latter can fairly be ascertained.

In its first hundred years the Supreme Court had firmly established itself as ultimate interpreter of the Constitution. Most notably under the inspired leadership of John Marshall, it had fleshed out the spare provisions of the Constitution with generous interpretations of federal authority and of the few original limitations on the states. In the closing years of the first century the Justices had also begun to grapple with the great issues raised by the three amendments adopted in response to the Civil War.

The present volume continues the story through the ensuing century, to the retirement of Chief Justice Warren Burger in 1986. This period extends from Grover Cleveland's first term in the White House to Ronald Reagan's second, from the death of Sitting Bull to the birth of Star Wars. It embraces two world wars, the Great Depression, and the civil rights revolution. It contains half the history of the United States.

The Supreme Court's second century can be neatly divided into two parts. From 1888 until 1941, under Chief Justices Melville W. Fuller, Edward Douglass White, William Howard Taft, and Charles Evans Hughes, the Justices addressed themselves above all to the constitutionality of regulatory and spending programs adopted to ameliorate the hardships of the Industrial Revolution as the Court faced the challenge of the welfare state.

This confrontation was characterized by two constitutional turning points of great significance. The period began with the Court's transformation of the fourteenth amendment from an instrument of racial equality into one of laissez-faire; it ended with the abandonment of both written and unwritten limitations on government control of the economy. These two revolutions in constitutional interpretation are the central focus of the first four parts of this volume.

As the Court of the 1930s dismantled the constitutional apparatus of the old order, it began to exhibit increased concern for civil rights and liberties. Justice Harlan F. Stone summed it up in a prescient footnote in the first *Carolene Products* case that charted the Court's course for the next half century: henceforth the Justices would scrutinize most closely those measures affecting interests protected by the specific provisions of the Bill of Rights, endangering the integrity of the political process, or disadvantaging discrete and insular minorities.[2]

For the rest of the century covered by this volume, the Court under Chief Justices Stone, Fred M. Vinson, Earl Warren, and Burger devoted itself principally to the agenda of civil rights and liberties that Stone had traced in 1938. The last four parts of this book tell the story of that period.

---

[2] United States v. Carolene Products Co., 304 U.S. 144, 152 n.4 (1938).

# Part One

Chief Justice Fuller
1888–1910

# Introduction to Part One

The Supreme Court's first hundred years virtually ended with the death of Chief Justice Morrison Waite in 1888. Shortly before leaving the White House for the first time, Grover Cleveland, the only Democratic President to leave office between Fort Sumter and Sarajevo,[1] appointed his longtime friend and adviser, Chicago lawyer Melville W. Fuller, to fill the vacancy. Like his predecessor, Fuller was little known nationally, and his appointment was a surprise.[2]

Within six years Fuller presided over an essentially new Court. All of Waite's brethren save John M. Harlan, Horace Gray, and Stephen J. Field had left the Bench, and the last of these three had long passed the peak of his powers.[3] There were five new faces in addition to Fuller's: David J. Brewer, Henry Billings Brown, George Shiras, Howell E. Jackson, and Edward Douglass White.[4]

It was not long before Jackson and Field gave way to Rufus W. Peckham and Joseph McKenna, Shiras and Gray to William R. Day and the immortal Oliver Wendell Holmes. William H. Moody and Horace R. Lurton served briefly at the end of Fuller's term, and another massive turnover accompanied Fuller's death in 1910. Although twenty Justices sat during these twenty-two years, eleven of them did most of the work: Har-

---

[1] Buchanan's term ended a month before Fort Sumter fell; Woodrow Wilson took office in 1913.

[2] *See* W. KING, MELVILLE WESTON FULLER, ch. 8 (1950); THE FIRST HUNDRED YEARS at 361 (discussing the appointment of Chief Justice Waite).

[3] *See* C. SWISHER, STEPHEN J. FIELD, CRAFTSMAN OF THE LAW 443-45 (1930); W. KING, *supra* note 2, at 222-27. Deputed to suggest it was time Field resigned, Justice Harlan asked whether the latter recalled a similar errand he had run in the case of Justice Grier. Field is said to have retorted "Yes! And a dirtier day's work I never did in my life!" *See* C. E. HUGHES, THE SUPREME COURT OF THE UNITED STATES 76 (1928).

[4] For conflicting evidence as to the spelling of White's middle name see M. KLINKHAMER, EDWARD DOUGLAS [*sic*] WHITE, CHIEF JUSTICE OF THE UNITED STATES 1 n.1 (1943). *Cf.* Currie, *The Most Insignificant Justice: A Preliminary Inquiry,* 50 U. CHI. L. REV. 466, 468 (discussing the case of Justice Duval[l]).

3

lan, Gray, Fuller, Brewer, Brown, Shiras, White, Peckham, McKenna, Holmes, and Day.[5]

Most of these Justices are not household names, but their decisions are. Under Fuller, the Court first employed the due process clause to invalidate state legislation in such cases as *Allgeyer v. Louisiana*,[6] *Smyth v. Ames*,[7] and *Lochner v. New York*.[8] It struck down barriers to the sale of out-of-state liquor under the commerce clause in *Leisy v. Hardin*.[9] It invalidated the federal income tax in *Pollock v. Farmers' Loan & Trust Co.*[10] and held that manufacturing was not "commerce" in *United States v. E. C. Knight Co.*[11] It made constitutional limits on state action more easily enforceable by limiting the immunity of state officers in a series of decisions culminating in *Ex parte Young*.[12]

Yet it would be a mistake to brand the Fuller Court as generally hostile to either state or federal authority. The states' power to enforce racial segregation of trains was upheld in *Plessy v. Ferguson*.[13] Congress was found to have inherent power to exclude and deport aliens,[14] and *In re Debs*[15] upheld the power of a federal court to enjoin a strike that dis-

[5]  JUSTICES OF THE SUPREME COURT DURING THE TIME OF CHIEF JUSTICE FULLER

| Justice | Tenure | 1890 | 95 | 1900 | 05 | 10 |
|---|---|---|---|---|---|---|
| Samuel F. Miller | (1862-1890) | | | | | |
| Stephen J. Field | (1863-1897) | | | | | |
| Joseph P. Bradley | (1870-1892) | | | | | |
| John M. Harlan | (1877-1911) | | | | | |
| Stanley Matthews | (1881-1889) | | | | | |
| Horace Gray | (1881-1902) | | | | | |
| Samuel Blatchford | (1882-1893) | | | | | |
| Lucius Q. C. Lamar | (1888-1893) | | | | | |
| Melville W. Fuller | (1888-1910) | | | | | |
| David J. Brewer | (1889-1910) | | | | | |
| Henry B. Brown | (1890-1906) | | | | | |
| George Shiras | (1892-1903) | | | | | |
| Howell E. Jackson | (1893-1895) | | | | | |
| Edward D. White | (1894-1921) | | | | | |
| Rufus W. Peckham | (1895-1909) | | | | | |
| Joseph McKenna | (1898-1925) | | | | | |
| Oliver W. Holmes | (1902-1932) | | | | | |
| William R. Day | (1903-1922) | | | | | |
| William H. Moody | (1906-1910) | | | | | |
| Horace R. Lurton | (1909-1914) | | | | | |

SOURCE: G. GUNTHER, CASES AND MATERIALS ON CONSTITUTIONAL LAW app. B (11th ed. 1985).

[6] 165 U.S. 578 (1897).
[7] 169 U.S. 466 (1898).
[8] 198 U.S. 45 (1905).
[9] 135 U.S. 100 (1890).
[10] 157 U.S. 429, *modified on rehearing*, 158 U.S. 601 (1895).
[11] 156 U.S. 1 (1895).
[12] 209 U.S. 123 (1908).
[13] 163 U.S. 537 (1896).
[14] The Chinese Exclusion Case, 130 U.S. 581 (1889); Fong Yue Ting v. United States, 149 U.S. 698 (1893).
[15] 158 U.S. 564 (1895).

rupted commerce, although no statute had granted such authority. The *Insular Cases*[16] authorized Congress to govern possessions acquired after the Spanish-American War without regard to various constitutional limitations. In fact the Court under Fuller employed a wide variety of techniques to protect economic interests, including both broad and narrow construction of federal authority and procedural as well as substantive aspects of due process.

The Fuller Court's activism in protecting economic interests contrasts sharply with the judicial restraint of its predecessor, but the differences should not be exaggerated. Most state regulatory laws affecting business passed muster, including limits on the working hours of miners,[17] women,[18] and public works employees.[19] The Sherman Act was found applicable to several business arrangements not falling within a strict definition of interstate or foreign commerce.[20] Congress was allowed to forbid interstate transportation of lottery tickets[21] and to impose prohibitive taxes.[22] The erosion of protection for vested contract rights continued when the Court allowed a state to rescind a grant of submerged land[23] and held that a state could not be sued in federal court by its own citizens when it defaulted on its bonds.[24]

Amid all these politically charged cases, the Court found time to devote itself seriously to the more prosaic problem of distributing judicial authority among the states in a series of full-faith-and-credit decisions that forms the basis of our current law.[25] Moreover, the cases mentioned are but the tip of an iceberg. In these two decades the Court waded through nearly a thousand constitutional controversies—more than in the entire preceding century. A great many of these cases required only the application of settled principle. The discretionary writ of certiorari, introduced in 1891,[26] had enabled the Supreme Court to keep its collective head above the flood of nonconstitutional cases;[27] the extension of certiorari to constitutional cases was long overdue by 1910.[28]

---

[16] See, *e.g.,* Downes v. Bidwell, 182 U.S. 244 (1901).

[17] Holden v. Hardy, 169 U.S. 366 (1898).

[18] Muller v. Oregon, 208 U.S. 412 (1908).

[19] Atkin v. Kansas, 191 U.S. 207 (1903).

[20] *E.g.,* Northern Sec. Co. v. United States, 193 U.S. 197, 325-27 (1904) (creation of a corporation to hold the shares of two competing railroads violates the Sherman Act).

[21] The Lottery Case (Champion v. Ames), 188 U.S. 321 (1903).

[22] McCray v. United States, 195 U.S. 27 (1904).

[23] Illinois Cent. R.R. v. Illinois, 146 U.S. 387 (1892).

[24] Hans v. Louisiana, 134 U.S. 1 (1890).

[25] See, *e.g.* Huntington v. Attrill, 146 U.S. 657 (1892); Clarke v. Clarke, 178 U.S. 186 (1900); Haddock v. Haddock, 201 U.S. 562 (1906); Fauntleroy v. Lum, 210 U.S. 230 (1908); Fall v. Eastin, 215 U.S. 1 (1909).

[26] Act of Mar. 3, 1891, § 6, 26 Stat. 826, 828.

[27] For discussions of the effect of the 1891 Act on the docket see F. FRANKFURTER & J. LANDIS, THE BUSINESS OF THE SUPREME COURT 101-02 (1928); W. KING, *supra* note 2, at 148-51.

[28] For a discussion of the belated achievement of this goal, culminating in the Act of Feb. 13, 1925, 43 Stat. 936, see F. FRANKFURTER & J. LANDIS, *supra* note 27, at 203-16.

Pending publication of the relevant volume in the series HISTORY OF THE SUPREME COURT OF THE UNITED STATES, general historical coverage of the Fuller era remains relatively sparse. Charles Warren's treatment of what was to him a recent period was intentionally sketchy. *See* 2 C. WARREN, THE SUPREME COURT IN UNITED STATES HISTORY chs. 37-38 (rev. ed. 1926). Andrew McLaughlin's discussion was almost as brief. *See* A. McLAUGHLIN, A CONSTITUTIONAL HISTORY OF THE UNITED STATES chs. 50-51 (1935). Biographies of Justices of the time include F. BIDDLE, MR. JUSTICE HOLMES (1942); C. FAIRMAN, MR. JUSTICE MILLER AND THE

SUPREME COURT (1939); M. HOWE, JUSTICE OLIVER WENDELL HOLMES: THE PROVING YEARS, 1870-1882 (1963); M. HOWE, JUSTICE OLIVER WENDELL HOLMES: THE SHAPING YEARS, 1841–1870 (1957); W. KING, *supra* note 2; M. KLINKHAMER, *supra* note 4; F. LATHAM, THE GREAT DISSENTER: JOHN MARSHALL HARLAN, 1833-1911 (1970); M. MCDEVITT, JOSEPH MCKENNA, ASSOCIATE JUSTICE OF THE UNITED STATES (1946); J. MCLEAN, WILLIAM RUFUS DAY (1946); G. SHIRAS, JUSTICE GEORGE SHIRAS JR. OF PITTSBURGH (1953); C. SWISHER, *supra* note 3.

# 1

# The Protection of
# Economic Interests I

### I. THE FURTHER DECLINE OF THE CONTRACT CLAUSE

It seems ironic that the Fuller period, best known for giving life to the questionable doctrine that due process guaranteed the right to make contracts in the future, began with two important decisions that diminished the explicit protection that article I, § 10 provided for contracts already made.

### A. *Hans v. Louisiana*

The eleventh amendment had made enforcement of a state's promises difficult by closing the federal courts to actions against states by citizens of other states or of foreign countries, and the Court had convincingly concluded before Fuller's appointment that a state's immunity could not be evaded either by having another state sue on behalf of its citizens[1] or by suing to require an individual official to discharge the state's debt.[2] But the amendment did not forbid suits against states by their own citizens, and it was the Fuller Court that closed that loophole in the 1890 case of *Hans v. Louisiana*.[3]

Another chapter in the disreputable history of bond repudiation by Southern states after Reconstruction,[4] *Hans* was an action by a Louisiana citizen against his own state for interest due on its bonds. Although the eleventh amendment itself was inapplicable, the Court

---

[1] New Hampshire v. Louisiana, 108 U.S. 76, 91 (1883).

[2] *E.g.*, Hagood v. Southern, 117 U.S. 52, 67-68 (1886); Louisiana v. Jumel, 107 U.S. 711, 720-21 (1883). Despite the questionable conclusion in Osborn v. Bank of the United States, 22 U.S. (9 Wheat.) 738 (1824), that a suit against an officer for restitution or injunction was not a suit against the state, the Court soundly concluded that an officer was not suable when he himself had done no wrong. *See* THE FIRST HUNDRED YEARS at 104-06, 416-28.

[3] 134 U.S. 1 (1890).

[4] *See* THE FIRST HUNDRED YEARS at 420-28.

said its adoption showed that the country had disagreed with the decision in *Chisholm v. Georgia*[5] that article III's provision extending federal judicial power to "Controversies . . . between a State and Citizens of another State" embraced suits against unconsenting states. In its literal application of the words of article III, Justice Bradley concluded, *Chisholm* had ignored the teaching of "history and experience"[6] that "[t]he suability of a State without its consent was a thing unknown to the law."[7] Quoting convincing passages from Hamilton, Madison, and Marshall, the Court emphasized that "[a]ny such power as that of authorizing the federal judiciary to entertain suits by individuals against the States, had been expressly disclaimed, and even resented, by the great defenders of the Constitution whilst it was on its trial before the American people."[8] These views were as applicable to *Hans* as they had been to *Chisholm;* the appeal to the "letter" in both cases was "an attempt to strain the Constitution and the law to a construction never imagined or dreamed of."[9] It would be absurd to allow suits against one's own state while prohibiting those against others; "[t]he truth is, that the cognizance of suits and actions unknown to the law, and forbidden by the law, was not contemplated by the Constitution when establishing the judicial power of the United States,"[10] and the suit could not be maintained.

Some later observers have professed to find that *Hans* "construed" the eleventh amendment itself to apply to suits against the plaintiff's own state;[11] others have written that it invoked a common law principle that could be overridden by statute.[12] But the passages just quoted leave little doubt that the basis of the decision was that article III's provision extending the judicial power to "Cases arising under this Constitution" was subject to an implied exception for suits by individuals against nonconsenting states.[13] In favor of this conclusion, as Bradley noted,[14] were all the arguments that had made *Chisholm* itself questionable.[15] Furthermore, implicit state immunities from the operation of express fed-

[5] 2 U.S. (2 Dall.) 419 (1793), THE FIRST HUNDRED YEARS at 14-20.

[6] *Hans,* 134 U.S. at 14.

[7] *Id.* at 16.

[8] *Id.* at 12.

[9] *Id.* at 15.

[10] *Id.*

[11] *See, e.g.,* C. WRIGHT, LAW OF FEDERAL COURTS 287 & n.6 (4th ed. 1983); Gibbons, *The Eleventh Amendment and State Sovereign Immunity: A Reinterpretation,* 83 COLUM. L. REV. 1889, 1893-94 (1983).

[12] *See, e.g.,* Employees of Dep't of Public Health & Welfare v. Department of Public Health & Welfare, 411 U.S. 279, 313 (1973) (Brennan, J., dissenting); Field, *The Eleventh Amendment and Other Sovereign Immunity Doctrines* (pt. 1), 126 U. PA. L. REV. 515, 537 & n.81 (1977).

[13] *Accord* Employees of Dep't of Pub. Health & Welfare v. Department of Pub. Health & Welfare, 411 U.S. 279, 291-92 (Marshall, J., concurring) (*Hans* made it clear that the eleventh amendment restored "the original understanding" of art. III); *see also id.* at 281 n.1 (Douglas, J., for the Court) (*Hans* dealt with "constitutional constraints on the exercise of the federal judicial power"). Bradley had said in an earlier opinion that the Constitution did not support jurisdiction in such cases. *See* Virginia Coupon Cases, 114 U.S. 269, 337-38 (1885) (Bradley, J., dissenting). Harlan's concurrence observed that, although *Chisholm* had been rightly decided, the suit in *Hans* was "not one to which the judicial power of the United States extends." *Id.* at 21. That Iredell's dissent in *Chisholm,* 2 U.S. (2 Dall.) at 429-50, which *Hans* approved, had been explicitly based on statutory rather than on constitutional grounds does not impair the impact of Bradley's repeated references to the Constitution.

[14] 134 U.S. at 15.

[15] *See* THE FIRST HUNDRED YEARS at 14-20 (discussing the arguments made in *Chisholm*). Indeed, as Harlan seemed to imply in his concurrence, 134 U.S. at 21, the argument for jurisdiction was stronger in *Chisholm* than in *Hans* because, in the former case, the constitutional text expressly extended federal judicial power to contro-

eral authority were no novelty when *Hans* was decided.[16] It is nevertheless noteworthy that a Court destined to give unprecedented protection to certain economic interests opted, in a case that could have gone either way, for an interpretation of the jurisdictional provisions that severely impaired the protection of existing contract rights.[17]

---

versies between a state and citizens of another state. The eleventh amendment may well have been drafted narrowly to modify this offending language and not to allow federal-question suits brought by a citizen against his *own* state.

[16]*See, e.g.,* Collector v. Day, 78 U.S. (11 Wall.) 113, 128 (1871) (Congress may not tax state judge's salary); *cf.* Kentucky v. Dennison, 65 U.S. (24 How.) 66, 103, 107-08 (1861) (Congress may not impose duties on state officer despite implicit authority to implement extradition clause); McCulloch v. Maryland, 17 U.S. (4 Wheat.) 316, 436 (1819) (state may not tax national bank); THE FIRST HUNDRED YEARS at 165-68, 245-47, 355. Less persuasive was Bradley's additional argument in *Hans* that a statute making federal jurisdiction "concurrent" with state jurisdiction meant that the federal court could act only in cases that state courts would hear. 134 U.S. at 18. For the counterargument, see THE FIRST HUNDRED YEARS at 17 n.93.

[17]In Lincoln County v. Luning, 133 U.S. 529, 530 (1890) (Brewer, J.), however, the Court held that a county could be sued on its bonds because a county was not a "state" for eleventh amendment purposes, but a separate corporation with powers of its own. Though in accord with the earlier decision that a county was a "citizen" of a state for diversity purposes, Cowles v. Mercer County, 74 U.S. (7 Wall.) 118, 121-22 (1869), which *Luning* did not cite on this point, this decision is not easy to reconcile with the conclusion in North Am. Cold Storage Co. v. City of Chicago, 211 U.S. 306, 313 (1908), that the fourteenth amendment applied not only to "State[s]" but to the actions of their political subdivisions as well—as the purpose of the amendment seemed to require. Compare the implicit immunity of states from federal regulation proclaimed in National League of Cities v. Usery, 426 U.S. 833, 845 (1976), *infra* pp. 563-68, *overruled,* Garcia v. San Antonio Metro. Transit Auth., 469 U.S. 528 (1985), which apparently extended to political subdivisions.

In the same spirit as *Hans* was the decision in Smith v. Reeves, 178 U.S. 436, 445-49 (1900) (Harlan, J.) (relying on *Hans*), holding that a federal corporation, though not a "Citizen[] of another State" within the eleventh amendment, also could not sue a state in a federal-question case. *Hans* was distinguished, however, in United States v. Texas, 143 U.S. 621, 643-46 (1892) (also written by Harlan), in which the Court allowed the United States to sue a state; judicial resolution of controversies "between these two governments . . . does no violence to the inherent nature of sovereignty," *id.* at 646. Furthermore, Harlan noted, "the permanence of the Union might be endangered if to some tribunal was not entrusted the power to determine [such controversies]. *Id.* at 645. In reaching this convincing result, Harlan appropriately relied on the Court's long-standing practice, derived from an explicit provision of the Articles of Confederation, of entertaining suits by one state against another. *See, e.g.,* Rhode Island v. Massachusetts, 37 U.S. (12 Pet.) 657, 727 (1838) (discussing art. IX of the Articles). The Fuller Court continued this practice, explicitly rejecting the defense of sovereign immunity in such cases. *See, e.g.,* Virginia v. West Virginia, 206 U.S. 290, 318-19 (1907) (Fuller, C. J.); Kansas v. Colorado, 206 U.S. 46, 82-84 (1907) (Brewer, J.); South Dakota v. North Carolina, 192 U.S. 286, 316-18 (1904) (Brewer, J.); *cf. Hans,* 134 U.S. at 15 (discussing interstate suits: "The establishment of this new branch of jurisdiction seemed to be necessary from the extinguishment of diplomatic relations between the States.").

In Kansas v. United States, 204 U.S. 331 (1907) (Fuller, C. J.) (alternative holding), however, the Court unanimously held that *United States v. Texas* was a one-way street: a state could not sue the United States without its consent because "[p]ublic policy forbids that conclusion." 204 U.S. at 342. The public policy in question was not identified, and it would seem that "the permanence of the Union" might be equally "endangered" by the want of a tribunal when the state is a plaintiff as when it is a defendant in a controversy "between these two governments." The Court's question-begging explanation that the state had consented to be sued by joining the union, *id.,* could have been applied as easily to the converse case or to *Hans v. Louisiana.*

That a state could *actually* consent to be sued even by a private party in federal court, *see* THE FIRST HUNDRED YEARS at 427 n.163 (discussing Clark v. Barnard, 108 U.S. 436 (1883)), was reaffirmed in Gunter v. Atlantic Coast Line, 200 U.S. 273, 292 (1906) (White, J.). Smith v. Reeves, 178 U.S. 436 (1900), made it clear, however, that it was not enough for federal jurisdiction that the state had consented to be sued in its *own* courts and added the peculiar qualification—explained only by a cryptic reference to "the supremacy of the Constitution" and of federal laws—that "the final judgment of the highest court of the State in any action brought against

## B.  *Illinois Central* and *Manigault*

Two years after *Hans* the Court undertook a sharp limitation of the substantive protection afforded by the contract clause itself. The Illinois legislature, under shady circumstances,[18] had granted the land under Chicago's harbor to a railroad and then attempted to take it back. The case looked for all the world like *Fletcher v. Peck,*[19] where Marshall had concluded that a state could not rescind its grant. Yet in a lengthy opinion by no less a friend of private property than Justice Field, the Court held that Illinois had validly reclaimed the land.[20]

The key distinction, in Field's view, was that the land in the Illinois case lay under water. Though the state owned submerged land, it did so as trustee for the public interest in navigation, and it had no power to sell in violation of its public trust. Since the original transfer had thus been invalid, no contractual obligation was impaired when the state rescinded the grant.[21]

The words flow easily off the pen; no fancy reasoning is needed to show that a trustee's powers are limited by the terms of his trust. What powers the people of Illinois had given their legislature, however, would appear to depend upon Illinois's constitution, to which Field never referred. In default of Illinois authority, he invoked a number of decisions from other jurisdictions, not one of which, he conceded,[22] had held a legislative grant of

---

it with its consent may be reviewed or reëxamined" in the Supreme Court if the case contains a federal question. *Id.* at 445 (dictum).

Finally, ignoring Marshall's express alternative holding in Cohens v. Virginia, 19 U.S. (6 Wheat.) 264, 393-94 (1821), THE FIRST HUNDRED YEARS at 101, that the Supreme Court's original jurisdiction in cases "in which a State shall be Party" was limited to those cases in which the basis of federal jurisdiction was that a state was a party, the Court in United States v. Texas, 143 U.S. 621 (1892), upheld its original jurisdiction over a suit by the United States against a state, concluding that article III § 2, clause 2, comprehended "all cases mentioned in the preceding clause in which a State may, of right, be made a party defendant." *Id.* at 644. Within three years, the Court underlined the importance of the word "defendant" by reaffirming *Cohens*'s conclusion that the Court had no original jurisdiction of a federal-question suit by a state against its own citizens. California v. Southern Pac. Co., 157 U.S. 229, 257-58 (1895) (apparently restating the rule to allow original jurisdiction whenever federal judicial power was based upon "the character of the parties").

[18] Illinois Cent. R.R. v. Illinois, 146 U.S. 387, 451-52 (1892); *see* 3 B. PIERCE, A HISTORY OF CHICAGO 319 (1957) (reporting that the granting statute "was commonly known as the 'Lake Front Steal' "). Marshall's refusal to investigate legislative motive in the similar circumstances of Fletcher v. Peck, 10 U.S. (6 Cranch) 87 (1810), made it difficult for the Court to invalidate the grant on grounds of bribery or improper influence, though technically the fact that the state was a party would have served to distinguish Marshall's decisive point in *Fletcher,* which was that it would be "indecent, in the extreme" to inquire into legislative corruption when the state was not a party to the suit, *id.* at 131. Nevertheless, one cannot know to what extent the result in *Illinois Central* was influenced by the sense that the deal was less than honest.

[19] 10 U.S. (6 Cranch) 87 (1810), THE FIRST HUNDRED YEARS at 128-36.

[20] Illinois Cent. R.R. v. Illinois, 146 U.S. 387 (1892). The vote was four to three; Fuller and Blatchford did not participate. *Id.* at 476. For the argument that this decision was another manifestation of the same hostility to special privileges that had led to Field's dissent in the Slaughter-House Cases, 83 U.S. (16 Wall.) 36, 83-111 (1873) (THE FIRST HUNDRED YEARS at 342-50), see McCurdy, *Justice Field and the Jurisprudence of Government-Business Relations: Some Parameters of Laissez Faire Constitutionalism, 1863-1897,* in AMERICAN LAW AND THE CONSTITUTIONAL ORDER 246, 258-59 (L. Friedman & H. Scheiber eds. 1978).

[21] 146 U.S. at 452-62.

[22] *Id.* at 455.

submerged land invalid. The leading Supreme Court precedent cited had expressly declined to decide whether the King of England possessed the power, as a trustee for the
British people, to make such a grant and had added that the validity of a grant made by
authority of the people of a state "must . . . be tried and determined by different principles
from those which apply to grants of the British crown. . . ."[23] A New York case heavily
quoted by Field appeared to suggest that even the King could alienate submerged land so
long as the public right of navigation was reserved,[24] as it had been in *Illinois Central*.[25]
In a dictum significantly omitted from Field's opinion, the New York court had added that
the legislature could authorize even the obstruction of navigation.[26] Justice Shiras, in a
brief and telling dissent joined by Gray and Brown, came up with Supreme Court dicta
and state-court holdings sustaining the power to convey.[27]

Apart from precedent, Field's argument from first principles had serious internal difficulties. He attempted throughout to equate the grant of ownership with the relinquishment
of "control" over navigation of the overlying waters.[28] The New York case on which he
relied, however, had emphasized that a grant of submerged land did not imply a surrender
of the public right to navigation or of the state's power to protect that right by legislation.[29]
Moreover, as already mentioned, the *Illinois Central* grant had been made on the express

[23] Martin v. Lessee of Waddell, 41 U.S. (16 Pet.) 367, 410-11 (1842), *cited in Illinois Central*, 146 U.S. at
456. The case held that the "proprietors" of New Jersey, under whom Waddell claimed, had no title to convey
after surrendering back to the crown in 1702 the political powers the King had originally granted them. 41 U.S.
(16 Pet.) at 412-14. Far from claiming that it had no right to convey submerged land, as Justice Thompson
pointed out in dissent, *id.* at 420-21, New Jersey had actually proceeded to do so. *See also* Sax, *The Public Trust
Doctrine in Natural Resource Law: Effective Judicial Intervention*, 68 MICH. L. REV. 471, 476 (1970) ("[T]he
inability of the Sovereign to alienate Crown lands was not a restriction upon government generally, but only upon
the King. . . .").

[24] People v. New York & Staten Island Ferry Co., 68 N.Y. 71, 76-77 (1877), *quoted in Illinois Central*, 146
U.S. at 458.

[25] 146 U.S. at 405 n.1.

[26] People v. New York & Staten Island Ferry Co., 68 N.Y. 71, 77-78 (1877) (citing English authority); *see* B.
WRIGHT, THE CONTRACT CLAUSE OF THE CONSTITUTION 149 n.118 (1938) ("Some of the state cases seem
definitely to contradict [Field's] point of view."). Indeed, a state's power to obstruct navigation seemed implicit
in a long line of Supreme Court cases allowing states to authorize bridges over navigable streams despite their
interference with interstate commerce. *See, e.g.,* Gilman v. Philadelphia, 70 U.S. (3 Wall.) 713 (1866), THE
FIRST HUNDRED YEARS at 331-32. The closest Field could come to real precedent was a dictum in an opinion
signed by one of three participating New Jersey justices but attributed by Field without apparent embarrassment
to "the Supreme Court of New Jersey." Arnold v. Mundy, 6 N.J.L. 1, 78 (1822) (opinion of Kirkpatrick, C. J.),
*quoted in Illinois Central*, 146 U.S. at 456.

[27] 146 U.S. at 464-76 (citing, inter alia, Langdon v. Mayor of New York, 93 N.Y. 129 (1883)). Field responded that general statements in these decisions affirming such power should be "read and construed with
reference to the special facts of the particular cases," that no grant as extensive as the one before him had ever
been sustained, and that the state could convey only "such parcels as are used in promoting the interests of the
public" (*e.g.,* for the construction of piers), "or can be disposed of without any substantial impairment of the
public interest in the lands and waters remaining." 146 U.S. at 453. Even if this served to distinguish the dissenters' cases, it left the majority devoid of authority of its own. Even the foremost modern proponent of the public-
trust doctrine does not argue that *Illinois Central* was supported by precedent. *See* Sax, *supra* note 23, at 489-91.
For a somewhat more sympathetic view, see Selvin, *The Public Trust Doctrine in American Law and Economic
Policy, 1789-1920*, 1980 WIS. L. REV. 1403, 1435.

[28] 146 U.S. at 452-54.

[29] People v. New York & Staten Island Ferry Co., 68 N.Y. 71, 79-80 (1877).

condition that "nothing herein contained shall authorize obstructions to the Chicago harbor, or impair the public right of navigation."[30] Field protested that this clause "placed no impediments upon the action of the railroad company which did not previously exist,"[31] but that only made the dissenters' point stronger: even apart from the explicit limitation, the state had not attempted to relinquish control of navigation.[32]

The Court had already held, building upon a dictum by Marshall in *Fletcher v. Peck,* that a state could not contract away its authority to regulate under the police power.[33] It had done so, under Field's leadership, with as little concern for the state constitution in question as Field exhibited in *Illinois Central.* But in the Illinois case Field pulled out all the stops in a creative effort to extend the precedents, contrary to Marshall's distinction,[34] to a case in which the state had parted only with ownership and not with governmental power, and in which the terms of the grant itself protected the public interest with which the opinion was concerned.

Thirteen years later, in its last significant encounter with the contract clause, the Fuller Court in *Manigault v. Springs*[35] rendered yet another narrow interpretation, upholding a state law authorizing one proprietor to flood another's land despite a preexisting contract in which he had promised not to do so.[36] The police power, wrote Justice Brown, was "paramount to any rights under contracts between individuals. . . . [P]arties by entering into contracts may not estop the legislature from enacting laws intended for the public good."[37] In addition to several inapposite precedents construing particular contracts not to contain promises inconsistent with later legislation,[38] Brown relied on the more nearly relevant decision in *Stone v. Mississippi*[39] that a state could not contract away its police

[30] 146 U.S. at 406 n.1.

[31] *Id.* at 451.

[32] It was also apparent from West River Bridge Co. v. Dix, 47 U.S. (6 How.) 507, 531-32 (1848), that, in making the grant, the state had implicitly reserved the power to retake the land itself for public use upon payment of just compensation. *See* THE FIRST HUNDRED YEARS at 213-15.

[33] Stone v. Mississippi, 101 U.S. 814, 817 (1880); *cf.* Fletcher v. Peck, 10 U.S. (6 Cranch) 87, 135 (1810) (one legislature is always competent to repeal the general legislation of a prior legislature). *See* THE FIRST HUNDRED YEARS at 379-81.

[34] In *Fletcher,* Marshall emphasized that a legislature might repeal the *general* acts of a prior legislature but that a specific sale of land, made on legislative authorization, was an act that could not be "undo[ne]" by subsequent legislation. 10 U.S. (6 Cranch) at 135.

[35] 199 U.S. 473 (1905) (Brown, J.).

[36] Since the statute provided for payment of compensation, 199 U.S. at 486, the Court could have reached this result on the basis of precedents construing sales of government land to individuals as containing an implicit reservation of the power of eminent domain. *See* West River Bridge Co. v. Dix, 47 U.S. (6 How.) 507, 531-32 (1848). But that was not the basis of the Court's decision. *See* Hale, *The Supreme Court and the Contract Clause* (pt. 2), 57 HARV. L. REV. 621, 674 (1944).

[37] 199 U.S. at 480. Justice Holmes made a better known statement to the same effect in Hudson County Water Co. v. McCarter, 209 U.S. 349, 357 (1908): "One whose rights . . . are subject to state restriction, cannot remove them from the power of the State by making a contract about them." This statement was quite unnecessary to the decision, since the contract in question had been made after a law prohibiting such contracts had been passed; as Holmes said, the contract "was illegal when it was made," *id.* at 357.

[38] *See, e.g.,* Charles River Bridge v. Warren Bridge, 36 U.S. (11 Pet.) 420, 548-49 (1837) (statutory charter granted to one bridge company contains no implicit promise not to grant subsequent charter to another bridge company); THE FIRST HUNDRED YEARS at 209-10.

[39] *See* note 33 *supra.*

power. But no state promise was in issue in *Manigault,* and to hold that *private* contracts were implicitly subject to modification whenever required by the police power[40] was perilously close to saying that states could impair contractual obligations whenever they had a good reason.[41] A narrow interpretation of the scope of proper police-power measures might have avoided reading the contract clause out of the Constitution altogether,[42] but *Manigault* was at best a life-threatening precedent.[43]

As one might expect after these decisions, the once mighty contract clause played very little part in striking down state laws during the Fuller period.[44]

[40]

> It is the settled law of this court that the interdiction of statutes impairing the obligation of contracts does not prevent the State from exercising such powers as are vested in it for the promotion of the common weal, or are necessary for the general good of the public, though contracts previously entered into between individuals may thereby be affected.

*Manigault,* 199 U.S. at 480. For a discussion of the difference between public and private contracts in this context, see Hale, *supra* note 36, at 671.

[41] That would be enough to sustain the debtor-relief legislation that had prompted the clause to begin with. *See* Sturges v. Crowninshield, 17 U.S. (4 Wheat.) 122, 204 (1819) (discussing original purpose of the contract clause).

[42] *See* B. WRIGHT, *supra* note 26, at 211-12 (construing cases to limit police-power exception to matters of "unusual public importance").

[43] A few years earlier, the Fuller Court had dealt a similar blow to yet another constitutional provision designed to protect the expectations of creditors—the prohibition in article I, § 10 of the issuance by states of bills of credit. Houston & T.C.R.R. v. Texas, 177 U.S. 66 (1900) (Peckham, J.). The challenged notes were "treasury warrants" issued to state creditors in small denominations and promising future payment. Since the Court had long ago drawn a shaky but necessary line between promissory notes and bills of credit, the notes in *Houston & T.C.R.R.* may have been sustainable on the basis of precedent. *See* Craig v. Missouri, 29 U.S. (4 Pet.) 410, 432-34 (1830), THE FIRST HUNDRED YEARS at 186-89. In upholding the validity of the treasury warrants, however, the Court laid principal stress on its conclusion that they had not been "intended to circulate as money" because "the members of the legislature knew that to issue the warrants to circulate as money would be to condemn them from the start"; it was immaterial that the legislature "may have desired to facilitate the[ir] use" among private persons by agreeing also to accept them in satisfaction of obligations to the state. *Houston & T.C.R.R.,* 177 U.S. at 84. As Justice Brown protested in a separate opinion, this seemed to invite the states to evade the prohibition by a simple exercise in labeling. *See id.* at 102-03 (Brown, J., concurring in the Court's alternative ground that the state was estopped to deny the validity of its own warrants).

[44] For an attempt to explain this phenomenon, see Kainen, *Nineteenth Century Interpretations of the Federal Contract Clause: The Transformation from Vested to Substantive Rights against the State,* 31 BUFFALO L. REV. 381 (1982).

Approximately 250 contract clause cases were decided during Fuller's tenure; in fewer than 10 percent of them was state action found unconstitutional. Over 90 percent of the contract clause cases involved public contracts, and a great many of them concerned the interpretation of particular tax exemptions. Only two not yet mentioned are of interest. One was Crenshaw v. United States, 134 U.S. 99 (1890) (Lamar, J.), which allowed the United States to discharge a naval officer before his term, not on the obvious ground that the contract clause applied only to the states, but because of precedents holding that public officers' agreements were not "contracts" within the meaning of the clause, *id.* at 108; *see, e.g.,* Butler v. Pennsylvania, 51 U.S. (10 How.) 402, 416 (1851), THE FIRST HUNDRED YEARS at 215-17. The other was Douglas v. Kentucky, 168 U.S. 488 (1897) (Harlan, J.), which declared that the Supreme Court was free to disregard state-court decisions *upholding* state authority to make irrevocable grants of lottery privileges, *id.* at 499-500. Harlan, for the Court, relied largely on cases reexamining state-court decisions that had *denied* the existence of a contract, although the Court in such cases had done so to prevent states from evading the contract clause; this consideration is absent when the state court has upheld the contract. *See* THE FIRST HUNDRED YEARS at 218-19 (discussing the Court's approach to such a case in Piqua Branch of State Bank v. Knoop, 57 U.S. (16 How.) 369, 391-92 (1854)). Harlan added, as

## II.  FEDERAL POWER TO PROTECT ECONOMIC INTERESTS

Fuller's accession to the Court essentially coincided with Congress's first major attempts—in the Interstate Commerce and Sherman Acts—to combat perceived abuses of private economic power. Fuller and his brethren, as we shall see, would have ample opportunities to pass upon the scope of federal authority to do so. But federal power was also exercised during this time to *protect* private economic interests, and from the first the Fuller Court construed federal authority broadly to permit such protection.

### A.  The Power to Exclude Aliens

The first example of broad interpretation was Justice Field's 1889 opinion for a unanimous Court in the *Chinese Exclusion Case,*[45] which upheld a federal statute barring the entry of Chinese laborers into the country. Underlying the enactment of this law, as Field observed, was the increasing competition between Chinese and American workers.[46] Acknowledging that denying reentry to individuals who had once lawfully resided in the United States was inconsistent with an earlier treaty, the Court properly invoked precedent indicating that treaties, like statutes, were vulnerable to later contrary congressional action.[47] The argument that the legislation impaired a vested right represented by a reentry certificate issued when the immigrant had left this country was rejected on grounds familiar from contract clause jurisprudence: Congress had no power to promise not to exercise its legislative authority.[48] Most interesting, however, was the ground on which Justice Field defended his central proposition that the exclusion of aliens was among the powers granted to Congress by the Constitution.[49]

A commerce clause argument would have been entirely plausible. Marshall had established in *Gibbons v. Ogden* [50] that the transportation of persons was commerce, and the Court had struck down state laws excluding aliens on the ground that they encroached upon Congress's commercial power.[51] Field elected instead to find the power inherent in

---

the Court had said in Stone v. Mississippi, 101 U.S. 814, 818 (1880), that lottery contracts were not within the clause at all. *Douglas,* 168 U.S. at 504. Support for that interpretation was wanting, however, and most of the *Stone* opinion had dealt with the state's power to contract, which ought to have turned on state law. *See* THE FIRST HUNDRED YEARS at 379-81; *cf. id.* at 150-54 (discussing Ogden v. Saunders, 25 U.S. (12 Wheat.) 213 (1827)).

[45] 130 U.S. 581 (1889).

[46] *Id.* at 594-95.

[47] *Id.* at 600-03 (citing, inter alia, The Head Money Cases, 112 U.S. 580, 599 (1884)).

[48] 130 U.S. at 609; *cf.* Stone v. Mississippi, 101 U.S. 814, 817 (1880) ("[T]he legislature cannot bargain away the police power of a State."), THE FIRST HUNDRED YEARS at 379-81. The Court might have added that there seemed to be no consideration for the promise to readmit and that in any event the contract clause was inapplicable to the United States.

[49] There was no suggestion that the discrimination against Chinese raised any constitutional problem. The equal protection clause by its terms applies only to the states.

[50] 22 U.S. (9 Wheat.) 1, 189-90 (1824), THE FIRST HUNDRED YEARS at 168-76.

[51] *See, e.g.,* Henderson v. Mayor of New York, 92 U.S. 259, 272 (1876), THE FIRST HUNDRED YEARS at 405-08; *cf.* The Head Money Cases, 112 U.S. 580, 600 (1884) (upholding, on the basis of the commerce power, a charge on alien immigrants), THE FIRST HUNDRED YEARS at 431-32; Nishimura Ekiu v. United States, 142 U.S. 651, 659 (1892) (reaffirming the Chinese Exclusion Case and appearing to rest congressional power to

sovereignty, in the teeth of Marshall's confirmation of the well-understood principle that the federal government was one of enumerated powers:[52]

> Jurisdiction over its own territory to that extent is an incident of every independent nation. . . . While under our Constitution . . . the great mass of local matters is controlled by local authorities, the United States, in their relation to foreign countries and their subjects or citizens are one nation, invested with powers which belong to independent nations, the exercise of which can be invoked for the maintenance of its absolute independence and security throughout its entire territory.[53]

These observations were reminiscent of equally unnecessary arguments about the "inherent" powers of Congress previously made by Justice Miller in two cases involving domestic federal authority,[54] neither of which was cited,[55] and they presaged the much later and more famous dicta of Justice Sutherland about foreign-affairs powers in the *Curtiss-Wright* case.[56] Three years after the *Chinese Exclusion Case*, in *Fong Yue Ting v. United States*, Justice Gray extended the inherent-powers concept to include authority to *deport* aliens,[57] which seems harder to fit within the enumerated commerce power: when an alien

---

exclude aliens largely on the commerce clause); L. TRIBE, AMERICAN CONSTITUTIONAL LAW § 5-16, at 277 (1978) (relating the power over aliens to Congress's authority "[t]o establish a uniform Rule of Naturalization" under art. I, § 8); Hesse, *The Constitutional Status of the Lawfully Admitted Permanent Resident Alien: The Pre-1917 Cases,* 68 YALE L.J. 1578, 1582-1609 (1959) (exploring other possible sources, including the war powers). For discussion of the due process question also resolved in the *Nishimura* case, see *infra* p. 43, note 99.

[52] McCulloch v. Maryland, 17 U.S. (4 Wheat.) 316, 405 (1819), THE FIRST HUNDRED YEARS at 160-65.

[53] The Chinese Exclusion Case, 130 U.S. at 603-04. For a recent criticism of this reasoning, see Note, *Constitutional Limits on the Power to Exclude Aliens,* 82 COLUM. L. REV. 957, 967 (1982). By emphasizing other passages of the opinion describing the power over aliens as one "delegated" to Congress, *e.g.,* 130 U.S. at 609, one observer has argued that the Court must have intended to rely on the commerce clause and that the passage quoted in the text "related not to the question of the extent of constitutional power over the people, but rather to the power under international law." Hesse, *supra* note 51, at 1590. This reading seems an exercise in wishful thinking.

[54] United States v. Kagama, 118 U.S. 375, 379-80 (1886) (upholding congressional power to punish crimes committed by Indians on the basis of "the right of exclusive sovereignty which must exist in the National Government, and can be found nowhere else"); *Ex parte* Yarbrough, 110 U.S. 651, 666 (1884) ("waste of time" to look for specific constitutional source of Congress's inherent power to pass laws protecting the right to vote); *see* THE FIRST HUNDRED YEARS at 394-95 n.174, 432-34.

[55] Heavy reliance was placed instead on diplomatic correspondence, much of it irrelevantly recognizing the right of such countries as France or Mexico to exclude aliens without regard to the ticklish federalism issue raised by our own Constitution. The Chinese Exclusion Case, 130 U.S. at 607-08. *See* Henkin, *The Constitution and United States Sovereignty: A Century of Chinese Exclusion and Its Progeny,* 100 HARV. L. REV. 853, 857 (1987).

[56] United States v. Curtiss-Wright Export Corp., 299 U.S. 304, 318 (1936), *infra* p. 231, note 140. The opposing arguments respecting inherent or enumerated powers had been rehearsed in congressional debates on the notorious Alien Act of 1798, 1 Stat. 570. *See* 8 ANNALS OF CONG. 1954-71, 1973-2006 (1851). Field dismissed the relevance of these debates on the unconvincing ground that the 1798 statute had contained provisions going beyond the mere exclusion of aliens. The Chinese Exclusion Case, 130 U.S. at 610-11.

[57] 149 U.S. 698, 707 (1893). Brewer, Field and Fuller dissented. For the procedural issues raised by this case, see *infra* p. 44, note 112.

resides in this country, he is not necessarily part of any "intercourse" with a foreign na-tion.[58] In the context of immigration, at least, the Court could certainly not be described as grudging in its interpretation of federal authority.[59]

## B.   Delegation of Legislative Power

In 1892, in *Field v. Clark*,[60] the Court gave a broad reading to federal *executive* power in upholding another measure designed to protect U.S. economic interests. The Tariff Act of 1890[61] had authorized the President to suspend the free importation of certain goods from any country that he found had imposed "reciprocally unequal and unreasonable" duties on U.S. products. If he did so, a specified tariff schedule would apply.

The problem here was one not of federalism, as in the alien cases, but of the separation of powers between the President and Congress. Justice Lamar put the objection on the right constitutional peg in a separate opinion joined by Chief Justice Fuller: article I vested the legislative power in Congress,[62] and that meant that Congress could not transfer legis-lative authority to anyone else.[63] This, Lamar concluded, was what Congress had done:

[58] *See* C. WARREN, THE SUPREME COURT IN UNITED STATES HISTORY 696 (rev. ed. 1926) (terming *Fong Yue Ting* an "extreme decision" that "seemed to justify the old Alien Law of 1798"). The Court later drew the line at Congress's attempt to punish a citizen for harboring an alien prostitute, concluding that it was not within Con-gress's power "to control all the dealings of our citizens with resident aliens." Keller v. United States, 213 U.S. 138, 148 (1909) (Brewer, J.). Holmes, joined by Harlan and Moody, dissented, employing a very liberal test of the relation between legislative means and the legitimate end of regulating immigration. *Id.* at 150.

[59] Very much in the spirit of the cases about Chinese and Japanese aliens was the dissenting argument of Chief Justice Fuller, joined by the famed civil libertarian Harlan, that children born in this country to Chinese alien parents were not U.S. citizens. United States v. Wong Kim Ark, 169 U.S. 649, 705 (1898) (dissenting opinion). At his most pedantic, Gray took some fifty pages to show for the majority that the law in most of the world was what the fourteenth amendment rather clearly said was our own: "All persons born . . . in the United States, and subject to the jurisdiction thereof, are citizens of the United States. . . ." *Id.* at 702. As Gray said, the natural meaning of this phrase had been confirmed by Yick Wo v. Hopkins, 118 U.S. 356, 369 (1886), which had held that aliens residing in this country were "within [the] jurisdiction" of a state for purposes of the equal protection clause. 169 U.S. at 696. Fuller's best argument was the presumption, supported by two comments made in the debates over the fourteenth amendment, that the amendment was meant to embody the citizenship provision of the 1866 Civil Rights Act, which had excluded persons "subject to any foreign power." *Id.* at 719-22. Gray responded that the language of the amendment was different, cited contrary legislative history, and added the striking assertion that the debates were "not admissible . . . to control the meaning" of the text. *Id.* at 688, 698-99. Ironically it had been Gray who had denied, and Harlan who had supported, citizenship for the children of American Indian tribesmen in the last previous controversy over the meaning of this provision. *See* THE FIRST HUNDRED YEARS at 399-400 n.207 (discussing Elk v. Wilkins, 112 U.S. 94 (1884)).

[60] 143 U.S. 649 (1892).

[61] 26 Stat. 567, 612 (1890).

[62] U. S. CONST. art I, § 1 ("All legislative Powers herein granted shall be vested in a Congress of the United States. . . ."); *id.* § 8 ("The Congress shall have Power To lay and collect Taxes, Duties, Imposts and Ex-cises. . . .").

[63] *Field*, 143 U.S. at 697 (Lamar, J., concurring in the judgment). Since article I speaks only of *federal* legislative power, it is not surprising that the Court has doubted whether the Constitution limits delegations of *state* legislative authority at all. *See* Dreyer v. Illinois, 187 U.S. 71, 83-84 (1902) (Harlan, J.) (fourteenth amend-ment due process clause does not require the separation of state powers). The due process argument, however, was not easily dispatched. The developing notion that due process required whatever the Court might think appropriate, *see infra* pp. 44-50 (discussing Smyth v. Ames, Allgeyer v. Louisiana, and Lochner v. New York), gave some support to the argument. More substantial support could also be found in the historical association of

the statute "extends to the executive the exercise of those discretionary powers which the Constitution has vested in the law-making department."[64]

There are contexts in which those invested with authority may lawfully delegate it to others.[65] As influential a writer as Locke, however, had denied that the legislative power was one of them.[66] Moreover, although in form the President in *Field* was executing a legislative command, indifference to the breadth of discretion left to the executive would run afoul of the accepted wisdom that the reason the Framers placed legislative power in Congress was to assure that fundamental policy decisions be made by elected representatives of the people.[67] Accordingly the majority, speaking through Justice Harlan, conceded without discussion Lamar's formidable premise that the substance of legislative power could not be delegated.[68]

In the majority's view, however, there had been no such delegation. Congress, said Harlan, had made the decision that tariffs should be imposed against any country that charged unequal and unreasonable duties, and Congress had specified what those tariffs

---

the clause with Magna Charta's law-of-the-land requirement, which was clearly designed to preclude executive action without legal sanction—and thus arguably, like article I itself, to require that basic policy decisions be made by the lawmakers. *See* THE FIRST HUNDRED YEARS at 272 & n.268 (discussing Scott v. Sandford, 60 U.S. (19 How.) 393 (1857)). For cases of the Fuller period upholding state laws over delegation objections, see Ohio *ex rel.* Lloyd v. Dollison, 194 U.S. 445, 450 (1904) (McKenna, J.) (even "if a case can exist in which the kind or degree of power given by a State to its tribunals may become an element of due process," a statute need not define such "well known terms" as "wholesale" and "retail" to avoid delegation problem); St. Louis Consol. Coal Co. v. Illinois, 185 U.S. 203, 210-12 (1902) (Brown, J.) (allowing "detail[s]" of mine inspections to be left to an executive, citing *Field* and The Brig Aurora, 11 U.S. (7 Cranch) 382, 387-88 (1813), without addressing the fact that article I is inapplicable to the states).

In Michigan Cent. R.R. v. Powers, 201 U.S. 245, 294 (1906) (Brewer, J.) (dictum), however, the Court left open the question whether a grant of state legislative power to the executive or judiciary might "work an abandonment of a republican form of Government, or be a denial of due process, or equal protection." The relevance of equal protection, despite suggestive precedent, seems doubtful. *See* THE FIRST HUNDRED YEARS at 387 n.134 (discussing Yick Wo v. Hopkins, 118 U.S. 356 (1886)). Further, the Court had not displayed much eagerness to enforce the article IV, § 4 guarantee of "a Republican Form of Government." *See* THE FIRST HUNDRED YEARS at 252-57 (discussing Luther v. Borden, 48 U.S. (7 How.) 1 (1849)); *see also* Taylor v. Beckham, 178 U.S. 548, 578 (1900) (Fuller, C. J.) (alternative holding) (rejecting a guarantee-clause attack on a state legislature's resolution of a contest for Governor with the sweeping observation that *Luther* had "settled that the enforcement of this guarantee belonged to the political department.").

[64] *Field*, 143 U.S. at 699-700.

[65] As early as 1839, the Court had sustained the authority of a President to delegate to his subordinates a congressional authorization to reserve public lands. Wilcox v. Jackson, 38 U.S. (13 Pet.) 498, 513 (1839). Compare the modern trend of allowing trustees to delegate more authority to financial advisers. *See* Langbein & Posner, *Market Funds and Trust-Investment Law*, 1976 AM. B. FOUND. RESEARCH J. 1, 18-24.

[66] J. LOCKE, *Second Treatise of Government* ch. XI, § 141, in TWO TREATISES OF GOVERNMENT (London 1690).

[67] *See, e.g.,* Zemel v. Rusk, 381 U.S. 1, 22 (1965) (Black, J., dissenting) (Congress created on assumption that "enactment of this free country's laws could be safely entrusted [only] to the representatives of the people"); Arizona v. California, 373 U.S. 546, 626 (1963) (Harlan, J., dissenting in part) (antidelegation principle ensures that "fundamental policy decisions" will be made "by the body immediately responsible to the people"); A. BICKEL, THE LEAST DANGEROUS BRANCH 160-61 (1962) (objection to delegation rests largely on notion that the more fundamental the decision, the more democracy requires it to be made by an electorally accountable body); Jaffe, *An Essay on Delegation of Legislative Power* (pt. 1), 47 COLUM. L. REV. 359, 360 (1947) ("[T]he objection to indiscriminate and ill-defined delegation . . . expresses a fundamental democratic concern.").

[68] *Field*, 143 U.S. at 692.

should be. The President's only authority was to "ascertain[] the fact" that unequal and unreasonable duties were being exacted. In so doing he was not making law; he was acting "in execution of the act of Congress."[69] The case was thus governed by *The Brig Aurora*,[70] in which the Marshall Court had unanimously upheld a statute empowering the President to revive an embargo against England or France upon finding that the other country had "cease[d] to violate the neutral commerce of the United States."[71] Adding an impressive list of statutory precedents dating back to 1794, Harlan concluded that such a long-standing "practical construction" by Congress "should not be overruled, unless upon a conviction that such legislation was clearly incompatible with the supreme law of the land."[72]

Lamar was on sound ground in objecting that it was harder to classify the President's job as mere fact-finding in *Field* than it had been in *The Brig Aurora*,[73] since the unreasonableness of a tariff seems less subject to objective verification than the infringement of neutrality.[74] Indeed the neutrality question itself had involved a good deal of independent judgment; the Court's effort to describe the President's duties as ministerial in either case was unconvincing.

Harlan would have done better to argue that the President's power to execute the laws[75] historically and necessarily included more than mere fact-finding. No legislature can be expected to specify how its policy decisions are to be applied to every conceivable fact situation,[76] and the Framers cannot be thought to have demanded the impossible. The 1790 patent law left it to the executive to determine whether an invention was "sufficiently useful and important" to merit protection;[77] the 1795 law authorizing the President to call out the troops left it to him to determine whether or not there was an "imminent danger" of invasion.[78] To label such determinations as merely factual is to obscure the reality that enforcing the laws implies a healthy portion of interstitial policy-making.[79]

---

[69] *Id.* at 692-93.

[70] 11 U.S. (7 Cranch) 382, 388 (1813), *discussed in Field,* 143 U.S. at 682-83; *see* THE FIRST HUNDRED YEARS at 118-19.

[71] Act of Mar. 1, 1809, § 11, 2 Stat. 528, 530-31.

[72] *Field,* 143 U.S. at 683-92. Lamar responded, without supporting argument, that the legislative precedents were distinguishable, *id.* at 700, but they appeared to be squarely on point. His technically accurate protest that the precedents did not bind the Court, *id.,* hardly reflected the Court's established and persuasive practice of giving enactments by early Congresses considerable weight as evidence of the original constitutional understanding. *See* THE FIRST HUNDRED YEARS at 91-92, 160-61 (discussing Martin v. Hunter's Lessee, 14 U.S. (1 Wheat.) 304 (1816), and McCulloch v. Maryland, 17 U.S. (4 Wheat.) 316 (1819)).

[73] *Field,* 143 U.S. at 698-700.

[74] *See* Jaffe, *An Essay on Delegation of Legislative Power* (pt. 2), 47 COLUM. L. REV. 561, 562, 566 (1947) (exercise of judgment in The Brig Aurora "slight"; in *Field* "wide and uncertain").

[75] "He . . . shall take Care that the Laws be faithfully executed. . . ." U. S. CONST. art. II, § 3.

[76] It was on this ground that Locke, who held that legislative power could not be delegated, embraced an even broader conception of executive power than that here suggested. J. LOCKE, *supra* note 66, ch. XIV, § 160 (executive "prerogative" to act for public good even in absence of legal authority).

[77] Act of Apr. 10, 1790, ch. 7, § 1, 1 Stat. 109, 110 (repealed 1793).

[78] Act of Feb. 28, 1795, ch. 36, § 1, 1 Stat. 424, 424; *see* Martin v. Mott, 25 U.S. (12 Wheat.) 19, 29-31 (1827) (holding the President sole judge of a sufficient danger under the act). Additional early examples of delegations by Congress are given in 1 K. DAVIS, ADMINISTRATIVE LAW TREATISE § 3.4 (2d ed. 1978).

[79] *See* Jaffe, *supra* note 67, at 360 ("[E]very statute is a delegation of lawmaking power to the agency appointed to enforce it.").

Twelve years after *Field,* in *Buttfield v. Stranahan,*[80] the Court upheld a delegation to the executive of authority to prescribe "standards of purity, quality and fitness for consumption" of imported tea.[81] Justice White, for a unanimous Court, recast the test in more realistic terms:

> [T]he statute, when properly construed . . . but expresses the purpose to exclude the lowest grades of tea. . . . This, in effect, was the fixing of a primary standard, and devolved upon the Secretary of the Treasury the mere executive duty to effectuate the legislative policy declared in the statute. . . . Congress legislated on the subject as far as was reasonably practicable, and from the necessities of the case was compelled to leave to executive officials the duty of bringing about the result pointed out by the statute.[82]

White's insistence that executive discretion must be interstitial seems a fair reconciliation of executive necessity with the primacy of legislative policy-making.

Judged by this unavoidably slippery standard, the embargo provision in *The Brig Aurora* was not difficult to uphold. Not only had Congress, as in *Field,* specified exactly what was to be done; it had provided the President with an intelligible yardstick to apply in deciding whether to do it, for there was a long history of international practice to help define what Congress had in mind.[83] *Field* and *Buttfield* seem to have been harder cases, for the Court did not make clear whether there were comparable traditions to confine the executive in determining "unreasonable" tariffs or "the lowest grades" of tea.[84]

Even if there were no confining traditions, the Court retained control over future delegations by emphasizing that Congress had made the basic policy decision to protect the producer from hostile tariffs and the consumer from unpalatable brew. Nevertheless, the breadth of the discretion apparently conferred in both cases showed that the Fuller Court was not prepared to fetter federal protection of economic interests by narrowly construing the executive power in the name of protecting legislative prerogatives from the legislature itself.[85]

---

[80] 192 U.S. 470 (1904).

[81] Act of Mar. 2, 1897, § 3, 29 Stat. 604, 605.

[82] 192 U.S. at 496.

[83] *See, e.g.,* VATTEL, THE LAW OF NATIONS, bk. III, ch. VII (anon. trans. Philadelphia 1829) (1st French ed. London 1758) (discussing the principles of neutrality under the law of nations).

[84] *See* Jaffe, *supra* note 74, at 566-67 (finding *Buttfield* "a much easier case" than *Field* because "the settled judgment of the [tea] trade" was available to guide the administrator).

[85] Other Fuller Court cases rejecting delegation arguments include Franklin v. United States, 216 U.S. 559, 568-69 (1910) (Fuller, C. J.) (upholding a statute incorporating existing state laws to define federal crimes on federal enclaves within the states: "There is, plainly, no delegation to the States of authority in any way to change the criminal laws applicable to places over which the United States has jurisdiction."); St. Louis, I. M. & S. Ry. v. Taylor, 210 U.S. 281, 287 (1908) (Day, J.) (relying on *Buttfield* without elaboration to uphold a delegation to a *private association* of power to determine the permissible height of railway couplers under federal law); United States v. Heinszen & Co., 206 U.S. 370, 384-85 (1907) (White, J.) (holding, on the basis of inapposite precedent and without further explanation, that Congress could delegate to the President general legislative authority over the Philippine Islands); Union Bridge Co. v. United States, 204 U.S. 364, 385-87 (1907) (Harlan, J.) (upholding an authorization to order removal of "unreasonable obstructions" to navigation on the ground that it empowered the executive only to ascertain "the facts" to determine "what particular cases came within the rule prescribed by Congress"); Butte City Water Co. v. Baker, 196 U.S. 119, 126 (1905) (Brewer, J.) (upholding a statute leaving

## C.  The Common Law

Possibly more striking than either the alien or the delegation cases was the broad scope the Court afforded to federal executive and judicial powers in the 1895 case of *In re Debs*,[86] in which Justice Brewer, for a unanimous Court, upheld the power of a federal court, at the request of the executive, to enjoin the obstruction of interstate rail traffic during the great Pullman strike of 1894. The subject was federal, Brewer intoned, because article I gave Congress authority to regulate commerce among the states. Since Congress had "assumed jurisdiction" over interstate railroads by passing several laws to regulate them, it was the duty of the federal executive to keep them free from interference. As in the case of any other public nuisance, this executive power included the right not only to abate the obstruction by force but also to seek appropriate judicial relief.[87]

To modern eyes, what may be most startling about *Debs* is the Court's failure to identify the source of the law on which the injunction was based. Presidents have constitutional power to enforce the laws,[88] but not to make them—as Justice Black later emphasized when President Truman seized the steel mills to assure military supply.[89] Brewer nowhere argued that Congress had prohibited private obstructions to interstate rail traffic.

The invocation of public-nuisance cases suggests that the injunction was based upon judge-made law. Only seven years earlier, however, in refusing to allow a federal injunction against a bridge that interfered with interstate and foreign shipping, the Court had

---

it to the states to make "minor and subordinate regulations" respecting mining claims on federal land and noting that the context was "not of a legislative character in the highest sense of the term" but "savors somewhat of mere rules prescribed by an owner of property for its disposal"); *In re* Kollock, 165 U.S. 526, 532-33 (1897) (Fuller, C. J.) (upholding a statute forbidding sales of margarine except in packages "marked, stamped, and branded as the Commissioner of Internal Revenue . . . shall prescribe" on the ground that the statute left to the Commissioner "a mere matter of detail . . . in execution of . . . the law"); Stoutenburgh v. Hennick, 129 U.S. 141, 147 (1889) (Fuller, C. J.) (upholding delegation of lawmaking power to the local legislature of the District of Columbia: "[T]he creation of municipalities exercising local self-government" was sanctioned by "immemorial practice" notwithstanding general rule against delegation of legislative power).

[86] 158 U.S. 564 (1895).

[87] *Id.* at 579-86. The Court also invoked Congress's authority to "establish Post Offices and post Roads," U. S. Const. art, I, § 8, and held that the sixth amendment jury guarantee had not been violated since equity traditionally could enjoin crimes when the legal remedy was inadequate to prevent irreparable harm, 158 U.S. at 594-96. Much of the vigorous criticism of *Debs* centered on this question. *See, e.g.*, Lewis, *A Protest against Administering Criminal Law by Injunction—The Debs' Case*, 33 Am. L. Reg. (n.s.) 879, 881 (1894); Patterson, *Government by Injunction*, 3 Va. L. Reg. 625, 628 (1898). For an approving view, see A. McLaughlin, A Constitutional History of the United States 766 n.10 (1935) ("[T]he mere fact that an act is criminal does not divest the jurisdiction of equity to prevent it by injunction.").

[88] U. S. Const. art. II, § 3.

[89] Youngstown Sheet & Tube Co. v. Sawyer, 343 U.S. 579, 587-88 (1952), pp. 365-69, *infra. See also* Justice Jackson's insistence, concurring in this conclusion, *id.* at 640-41, that the reference to "executive Power" in article II vests the President with only those powers thereafter listed; the President, like Congress, possesses only enumerated powers. Compare *In re* Neagle, 135 U.S. 1, 63-68 (1890) (alternative holding), an uncharacteristically wordy Miller opinion affirming the broad doctrine that the President's duty to execute the laws entitled him to assign an officer to protect a Supreme Court Justice from physical assault while on duty, even absent statutory authorization to do so. *See* 2 C. Warren, The Supreme Court in United States History 697 (rev. ed. 1926) ("This was the broadest interpretation yet given to implied powers of the National Government. . . ."). Neagle had been prosecuted by the state of California for having murdered an assailant of Justice Field. For the lurid facts, see *Neagle*, 135 U.S. at 42-53; C. Swisher, Stephen J. Field, Craftsman of the Law 345-59 (1930).

unanimously held that "there is no common law of the United States which prohibits obstructions and nuisances in navigable rivers. . . ."[90] That case might have been distinguished by arguing that the grant of jurisdiction in cases to which the United States was a party, like that in admiralty cases,[91] gave the courts authority to make law in the face of legislative silence.[92] Yet the Court made no effort either to do so or to distinguish the long-standing precedents holding federal courts without authority to punish nonstatutory crimes.[93] If Brewer meant that the federal executive had authority to enforce *state* common law,[94] he never said so. Neither did he examine the law of any particular state, as this theory would seem to require, or explain why the President's enforcement authority was not limited to federal laws.[95]

Thus in the alien cases the Fuller Court allowed Congress to exercise authority without arguing that it was necessary and proper to any of the enumerated powers. In *Field v. Clark* it allowed Congress to leave to the President a broad range of judgment in determining whether federal taxing power should be asserted. In *Debs* it allowed the executive and the courts to protect federal interests despite the absence of relevant legislation.[96] In short,

[90] Willamette Iron Bridge Co. v. Hatch, 125 U.S. 1, 8 (1888). *Debs* relied on Pennsylvania v. Wheeling & Belmont Bridge Co., 54 U.S. (13 How.) 518 (1852), *see Debs*, 158 U.S. at 588, but as the Court said in *Willamette*, 125 U.S. at 15-16, *Wheeling* had been based on the violation of federal statutes and of an interstate compact, sanctioned by Congress, to preserve free navigation of the Ohio River.

[91] *See infra* p. 36, note 56.

[92] The Court has often found authority to create common law in such cases, though not explicitly on this ground. *See, e.g.,* Clearfield Trust Co. v. United States, 318 U.S. 363, 366-67 (1943) ("The rights and duties of the United States on commercial paper which it issues are governed by federal rather than local law. . . . In the absence of an applicable act of Congress it is for the federal courts to fashion the governing rule of law according to their own standards."). The Fuller Court itself expressly held that the arguably analogous grant of jurisdiction over suits between states contemplated the application of federal common law. Kansas v. Colorado, 206 U.S. 46, 97-98 (1907) (Brewer, J.) (noting that the Court could not appropriately apply the law of either state to resolve a contest between them); Missouri v. Illinois, 200 U.S. 496, 519-20 (1906) (Holmes, J.) (where Congress has provided no substantive law, grant of original jurisdiction to Supreme Court implies Court is to select applicable legal principles). For an approving contemporaneous view, see 21 HARV. L. REV. 132 (1907). On the question of federal common law in *Debs*, see 73 HARV. L. REV. 1228 (1960).

[93] *See* United States v. Coolidge, 14 U.S. (1 Wheat.) 415 (1816); United States v. Hudson, 11 U.S. (7 Cranch) 32, 34 (1812); THE FIRST HUNDRED YEARS at 94-95 n.30. Brewer might have argued that the presence of admiralty jurisdiction in *Coolidge* showed that the difficulty was peculiar to criminal cases, but he did not.

[94] This possibility, which was present in the interstate case of *Wheeling Bridge*, had been unavailable in *Willamette*, where jurisdiction had been based only on the argued existence of a federal common law of nuisance, *see Willamette*, 125 U.S. at 15; *supra* note 90.

[95] At one point, the opinion seemed to flirt with the suggestion that the commerce clause itself forbade the strikers' activities: "If a State with its recognized powers of sovereignty is impotent to obstruct interstate commerce, can it be that any mere voluntary association of individuals within the limits of that State has a power which the State itself does not possess?" *Debs*, 158 U.S. at 581. The radical implication that constitutional provisions limit private as well as official action, theretofore recognized only in respect to the rather unambiguous thirteenth amendment, comports poorly with the language and history of a provision dividing regulatory authority between nation and states, and Brewer did not develop it. If he had, he might have had difficulty explaining why the Court had held that the equal protection clause did not outlaw private discrimination. *See* The Civil Rights Cases, 109 U.S. 3, 11 (1883), THE FIRST HUNDRED YEARS at 398-402.

The Court in *Debs* expressly declined to treat the United States simply as proprietor of the mails suing to protect its property rights. The decision was based in substantial part on the sovereign interest in preventing obstructions to commerce. 158 U.S. at 583-86.

[96] *See also* Baltimore & O.R.R. v. Baugh, 149 U.S. 368, 371-72 (1893) (Brewer, J.) (applying the rule of Swift v. Tyson, 41 U.S. (16 Pet.) 1, 18 (1842), THE FIRST HUNDRED YEARS at 262, to hold, over an impassioned

when the protection of economic interests was at stake, the Court was anything but miserly in its interpretation of federal power.[97]

## III.  Federal Power to Burden Economic Interests

Despite the cases considered in the preceding section, the Fuller Court was by no means uniformly sympathetic to the exercise of federal authority. Indeed, among the decisions for which it is best remembered are two debatably *narrow* interpretations of federal power rendered in the same Term as *Debs:* its holding that the Sherman Act did not apply to the sugar trust and its invalidation of the income tax.

### A.   *United States v. E. C. Knight Co.*

The complaint in the first case sought to undo acquisitions that had given one manufacturer all but 2 percent of the sugar market, on the ground that they constituted a "combination . . . in restraint of trade or commerce among the several States" and a monopolization of such trade.[98] Chief Justice Fuller's answer for the majority was straightforward: manufacturing was not commerce, so the statute did not reach its monopolization.[99] This conclusion was supported with authority of constitutional dimension. The Court had already held that the commerce clause did not prevent state regulation of liquor manufacture, on the express ground that commerce began only after manufacture was completed.[100]

The distinction between manufacturing and commerce was fair enough. Nevertheless, as Justice Harlan protested in a lonely dissent, the complaint attacked not the monopolization of manufacturing as such but rather the concomitant monopolization of interstate sales.[101] By eliminating competition among manufacturers, Harlan argued, the acquisi-

---

dissent by Justice Field, that the scope of the fellow-servant rule in a diversity case was governed by the "general law" despite the Rules of Decision Act, 1 Stat. 73, 92 (1789)). For a defense of Field's position based on the perception that *Swift* had held an action under the law merchant not to be a "trial[] at common law" within the Rules of Decision Act, see Conant, *The Commerce Clause, the Supremacy Clause and the Law Merchant:* Swift v. Tyson *and the Unity of Commercial Law*, 15 J. Mar. L. & Com. 153, 158-59 (1984).

[97] *But see* B. Wright, The Growth of American Constitutional Law 91 (1942) (the more legislation tended to threaten laissez-faire economics, the less liberal was the Court's interpretation of legislative power).

[98] Sherman Act, ch. 647, §§ 1, 2, 26 Stat. 209, 209 (1890) (current version at 15 U.S.C. §§ 1, 2 (1982)).

[99] United States v. E. C. Knight Co., 156 U.S. 1, 12 (1895).

[100] Kidd v. Pearson, 128 U.S. 1, 21 (1888), *quoted in E. C. Knight*, 156 U.S. at 14; *see also* McCready v. Virginia, 94 U.S. 391, 396-97 (1877) (commerce clause does not forbid state regulation of oyster planting: "Commerce has nothing to do with land while producing, but only with the product after it has become the subject of trade."). The Court in *E. C. Knight* also relied on Coe v. Errol, 116 U.S. 517, 527 (1886) (commerce clause does not prohibit a state tax on logs intended for interstate shipment but not yet shipped). 156 U.S. at 13-14.

[101] *E. C. Knight*, 156 U.S. at 34 (Harlan, J., dissenting); *see also id.* at 3-4 (reporter's summary of averments in complaint); Guy, *The Anti-Monopoly Act: A Review of the Decisions Affecting It*, 1 Va. L. Reg. 709, 719 (1896) (calling attention to the lower court's finding, *see* 156 U.S. at 6, that "[t]he object in purchasing the Philadelphia refineries was to obtain a greater influence or more perfect control over the business of refining and selling sugar in this country"); Morawetz, *The Supreme Court and the Anti-Trust Act*, 10 Colum. L. Rev. 687, 706 (1910) ("The only constitutional question was whether Congress could prohibit the purchase of control of competitive businesses . . . when the purpose or effect of the transaction was to monopolize interstate commerce. . . .").

tions had obstructed "freedom in buying and selling articles manufactured to be sold to persons in other States," and "Congress may remove unlawful obstructions, of whatever kind, to the free course of trade among the States."[102]

The necessary and proper clause, which Harlan invoked[103] and the majority ignored, lent him additional support. As construed by Marshall,[104] the clause seemed to authorize Congress to regulate matters that were not themselves commerce in order to effectuate the Framers' purpose of protecting interstate commerce from interference. Indeed over fifty years before the sugar trust case the Taney Court, in upholding a federal statute outlawing the theft of shipwrecked goods, had expressly declared that the commerce power "extends to such acts, done on land, which interfere with, obstruct, or prevent the due exercise of the power to regulate commerce and navigation."[105] If stealing from commerce was subject to congressional prohibition, it is difficult to see why monopolizing it was not. Within four years after *E. C. Knight,* in *Addyston Pipe & Steel Co. v. United States,*[106] the Court unanimously upheld Congress's power to forbid an agreement among manufacturers not to compete in interstate sales; the acquisition of competing sugar refineries in *E. C. Knight* eliminated competition for such sales more effectively than the agreement in *Addyston Pipe.*[107]

Fuller protested that the effect of the sugar acquisitions on commerce was "indirect."[108] Perhaps it was.[109] Behind this characterization, moreover, lay a legitimate concern. As Fuller said, if every effect on interstate commerce were enough to trigger federal authority,

---

[102] 156 U.S. at 33 (Harlan, J., dissenting). *But see* G. SHIRAS, JUSTICE GEORGE SHIRAS, JR. OF PITTSBURGH 147 (1953) (arguing that the government neglected to present available evidence as to the effect on interstate sales); 2 C. WARREN, *supra* note 89, at 733 (blaming the decision on "the unfortunate manner in which the facts were alleged and proved"); *cf.* McCurdy, *The* Knight *Sugar Decision of 1895 and the Modernization of American Corporation Law, 1869-1903,* 53 BUS. HIST. REV. 304, 328 n.94 (1979) (arguing that the Court would have come out the same way even if such evidence had been presented).

[103] 156 U.S. at 39-40 (Harlan, J., dissenting).

[104] McCulloch v. Maryland, 17 U.S. (4 Wheat.) 316, 420-21 (1819), THE FIRST HUNDRED YEARS at 160–65.

[105] United States v. Coombs, 37 U.S. (12 Pet.) 72, 78 (1838), THE FIRST HUNDRED YEARS at 234. *See also* Fuller's own opinion for a unanimous Court in the Danbury Hatters' Case (Loewe v. Lawlor), 208 U.S. 274, 301 (1908), which expressly held immaterial the fact that union members charged with a boycott restraining interstate trade were "not themselves engaged in interstate commerce." For an early argument invoking *Coombs* to sustain congressional power over external restraints on commerce, see Humes, *The Power of Congress over Combinations Affecting Interstate Commerce,* 17 HARV. L. REV. 83, 97 (1903). By requiring only that the prohibited acts be "in restraint of" or "monopoliz[e]" interstate commerce, the Sherman Act itself appeared to apply to actors not themselves in commerce.

[106] 175 U.S. 211, 240 (1899).

[107] Fuller's objection in *E. C. Knight* that "[t]here was nothing in the proofs to indicate any intention to put a restraint upon trade or commerce," 156 U.S. at 17, seems disingenuous, since the effect of the removal of competitors on competition could hardly have escaped the parties. *See id.* at 43-44 (Harlan, J., dissenting). Intent also seems irrelevant to the underlying constitutional issue since, even if the statute implicitly required intent, no reason appears why Congress's power to protect commerce should be limited to the removal of intentional obstructions.

[108] *E. C. Knight,* 156 U.S. at 16.

[109] In *Addyston Pipe,* 175 U.S. at 238-40, Justice Peckham relied on the "directness" criterion in distinguishing *E. C. Knight.* It was fair enough to say that the effect on commerce of an agreement about sale prices was more immediate than that of an acquisition of competing sellers. Just what "indirect" meant, however, was already in some doubt in the wake of decisions upholding state laws impinging "indirectly" on commerce. *See, e.g.,* Peik v. Chicago & N. W. Ry., 94 U.S. 164 (1877); Sherlock v. Alling, 93 U.S. 99 (1876), THE FIRST HUNDRED YEARS at 408-09.

there would be precious little that Congress could not regulate,[110] despite the careful enumeration of limited congressional powers.[111] Fuller was unable to explain, however, why
a distinction between direct and indirect effects on commerce was an appropriate place to
draw the line.[112]

The truth is that there was no logically convincing place to draw it.[113] What logical
extension of the necessary-and-proper argument offends the spirit of enumerated powers
is a question of degree, and thus any line the Court drew would very likely have appeared
arbitrary.[114] Nevertheless *E. C. Knight* found a peculiar place to stop,[115] and the Court's
willingness to insulate a manufacturing combination from congressional grasp[116] contrasts
sharply with its contemporaneous decisions upholding broad federal power to *protect*
American producers.[117]


### B.   *Pollock v. Farmers' Loan & Trust Co.*

The second great 1895 decision narrowly interpreting congressional power, also written
by Chief Justice Fuller, held the federal income tax unconstitutional.[118] The principal

---

[110] *E. C. Knight,* 156 U.S. at 16.

[111] *Id.* at 13. Recall Marshall's insistence in McCulloch v. Maryland, 17 U.S. (4 Wheat.) 316, 421 (1819),
that the necessary and proper clause must be applied with an eye to the "spirit" of the Constitution. *See* THE
FIRST HUNDRED YEARS at 162-64; F. FRANKFURTER, MR. JUSTICE HOLMES AND THE SUPREME COURT 103
(1961) ("[A]s an exercise in ratiocination the commerce clause could absorb the states. But the purposes of our
federalism must be observed, and adjustments struck between state and nation.").

[112] *See* Farage, *That Which "Directly" Affects Interstate Commerce,* 42 DICK. L. REV. 1, 1-2 (1937).

[113] A legislature may set eighteen years as the age at which a person is mature enough to vote; a court would
be embarrassed by its inability to distinguish the seventeen-year-old. Compare the Court's awkward distinction,
under the fourteenth amendment, between juries of five and six members in state criminal trials. Ballew v.
Georgia, 435 U.S. 223, 239 (1978) (rejecting a jury of five members); Williams v. Florida, 399 U.S. 78, 103
(1970) (upholding a jury of six).

[114] T. R. POWELL, VAGARIES AND VARIETIES IN CONSTITUTIONAL INTERPRETATION 34 (1956), argues that
arbitrary lines may be better than none at all: "It may be better for two cases to go in opposite directions than to
have them both go in the same direction and so tip that side of the scales."

[115] *See id.* at 58 (branding the decision a "most unwarranted judicial offense" in "par[ing] the Sherman Act]
down to the minimum that [its] language would warrant").

[116] *See* McCurdy, *supra* note 102, at 308, 335-36 (arguing that, far from representing the triumph of laissez-
faire, *E. C. Knight* was an effort to preserve *state* authority to act against trusts despite the effect of the "dormant"
commerce clause in limiting the states' authority to regulate matters affecting interstate commerce).

[117] *See supra* pp. 14-22. *E. C. Knight* also contrasts sharply with United States v. Gettysburg Elec. Ry., 160
U.S. 668, 681 (1896) (Peckham, J.), in which the Court unanimously upheld the construction of a monument to
the Battle of Gettysburg as necessary and proper to, inter alia, the power to raise armies, essentially because it
would instill feelings of patriotism that would make better soldiers in the future: "The greater the love of the
citizen for the institutions of his country the greater is the dependence properly to be placed upon him for their
defence in time of necessity. . . ." *Id.* at 682; *see* 2 C. WARREN, *supra* note 89, at 706 (*Gettysburg* showed the
Court's support for Congress's power at its broadest). In Felsenheld v. United States, 186 U.S. 126, 132 (1902)
(Brewer, J.), moreover, the Court held, over Peckham's dissent, that Congress could forbid placing advertising
coupons in tobacco packages bearing federal tax stamps for the flimsy reason that people might take the stamp as
a representation that the package contained only tobacco. With reasoning like this there seems little that could
not be brought within congressional authority.

[118] Pollock v. Farmers' Loan & Trust Co., 157 U.S. 429, *modified on rehearing,* 158 U.S. 601 (1895) (invalidating Act of Aug. 27, 1894, ch. 349, §§ 27-37, 28 Stat. 509, 553-60). The first decision struck down the tax
as applied to income from real property, 157 U.S. at 583, and from state or municipal bonds, *id.* at 586. Harlan

ground was that the tax was primarily a direct one not apportioned among the states by population as required by §§ 2 and 9 of article I.[119]

This conclusion must have caused great surprise.[120] Not only had the Justices repeatedly suggested in dicta that only capitation and land taxes were "direct";[121] twice in the preceding twenty-five years they had upheld income taxes, most recently on that precise ground.[122] The dicta were dismissed as such in *Pollock*.[123] The holdings were distinguished because one case had involved an excise tax calculated according to income[124] and the other a taxpayer whose income was derived essentially from professional earnings rather than property,[125] though neither of these facts had been offered as bases for the original decisions.

The tax in *Pollock*, Fuller noted, did apply to income from real and personal property.[126] A tax on personalty was as direct as one on realty, and a tax on the income from property was effectively one on the property itself.[127] The remaining tax on earned income, Fuller concluded, would not have been enacted had Congress known it could not tax property income as well.[128]

---

and White dissented on the former point. Only eight Justices participated—Jackson was ill—and the Court was evenly divided as to the validity of the tax in other respects, *id.* at 586. On rehearing, Jackson having been roused from his sickbed for the last time, the statute was struck down in its entirety, 158 U.S. at 637, though Jackson joined Harlan, White, and Brown in dissent. There has been much insignificant controversy over which Justice deserted the pro-tax forces between the first and second decisions, since otherwise the addition of Jackson would have given them a majority. *See* 2 C. WARREN, *supra* note 89, at 700 (saying it was Shiras); G. SHIRAS, *supra* note 102, at 160-83 (denying it); W. KING, MELVILLE WESTON FULLER 217-21 (1950) (adding that the Justices' votes largely lined up with the per capita wealth of their home states; only Justice Brown of Michigan joined three Southerners in voting to uphold the tax).

[119] *Pollock*, 157 U.S. at 582-83; 158 U.S. at 637.

[120] *See* FRANKFURTER, *supra* note 111, at 93 (decision in *Pollock* "unexpected[]"); A. McLAUGHLIN, *supra* note 87, at 762-63 ("That the law would be upheld . . . appeared to be a reasonable expectation. . . .").

[121] *See* Hylton v. United States, 3 U.S. (3 Dall.) 171, 175 (1796) (opinion of Chase, J.); *id.* at 183 (opinion of Iredell, J.); Pacific Ins. Co. v. Soule, 74 U.S. (7 Wall.) 433, 444-45 (1869); Springer v. United States, 102 U.S. 586, 602 (1881).

[122] Springer v. United States, 102 U.S. 586, 602 (1881); Pacific Ins. Co. v. Soule, 74 U.S. (7 Wall.) 433, 446 (1869); *see* E. CORWIN, COURT OVER CONSTITUTION 204 (1938) ("[T]he decision in the Pollock Case was the most disabling blow ever struck at the principle of *stare decisis* in the field of constitutional law. . . .").

[123] *Pollock*, 157 U.S. at 571-72.

[124] *Id.* at 576.

[125] *Id.* at 578-79.

[126] *Id.* at 580.

[127] *Id.* at 580-81; 158 U.S. at 627-28.

[128] 158 U.S. at 635-37. The intent-based inseparability argument manifests a healthy shift away from the automatic inseparability rule of United States v. Reese, 92 U.S. 214, 221 (1876), THE FIRST HUNDRED YEARS at 393-95. The unanimous additional conclusion that the law could not constitutionally reach the income from state or municipal bonds, 157 U.S. at 583-86, was convincingly based on the intergovernmental-immunity principle of Collector v. Day, 78 U.S. (11 Wall.) 113, 125-26 (1871). Compare the converse case of Weston v. City Council of Charleston, 27 U.S. (2 Pet.) 449, 469 (1829) (striking down state tax on interest from federal obligations); *see* THE FIRST HUNDRED YEARS at 168, 355. Apart from *Pollock*, however, the Court was not inclined to press intergovernmental immunity very far at this time. *See* South Carolina v. United States, 199 U.S. 437, 463 (1905) (Brewer, J.) (United States may tax state liquor business since it is proprietary, not governmental); Snyder v. Bettman, 190 U.S. 249, 254 (1903) (Brown, J.) (United States may tax bequest to state); Plummer v. Coler, 178 U.S. 115, 134-38 (1900) (Shiras, J.) (state may tax bequest of federal bonds); United States v. Perkins, 163 U.S. 625, 630 (1896) (Brown, J.) (state may tax bequest to United States); Reagan v. Mercantile Trust Co., 154

This opinion was clever but not persuasive. To begin with, it was internally inconsistent. In equating taxes on personalty with those on realty, Fuller relied implicitly on a literal interpretation of the word "direct";[129] in equating income with property taxes, he ignored the fact that in the same literal sense an income tax reaches property only indirectly.[130] More important, one cannot determine whether taxes on either income or personalty are constitutionally distinguishable from taxes on land without knowing what it is about the latter that makes them "direct," and this Fuller made no effort to explain. Perhaps most interesting was his failure to rely on the strongest argument for his position— Adam Smith's observation, quoted by Justice Paterson in the carriage-tax case in 1796, that *all* income taxes were "direct": "[T]he state, not knowing how to tax directly and proportionably the revenue of its subjects, endeavors to tax it indirectly, by taxing . . . the consumable commodities upon which it is laid out."[131] Nor, though Fuller referred to foreign authorities that defined income taxes as direct,[132] did he give significant weight to their historically respectable reasoning that direct taxes were those whose burden could not be passed on to someone else in the price of goods or services.[133]

In short, as in its contemporaneous *E. C. Knight* and *Debs* decisions, the Court in *Pollock* went out of its way to protect business or property,[134] this time by another unexpectedly narrow interpretation of congressional authority. In so doing, Fuller made the task unnecessarily difficult by ignoring traditional criteria that would have helped to support his conclusion.

## C.   Later Cases

*E. C. Knight* was not alone among decisions of the period in giving a restrictive interpretation to Congress's power over interstate commerce. In the same spirit were the holdings

---

U.S. 413, 416-17 (1894) (Brewer, J.) (state may regulate rates of railroad, despite federal charter, in absence of express contrary congressional intent). For discussion of these cases, see T. POWELL, *supra* note 114, at 117-18. See also Field's concurrence in *Pollock,* 157 U.S. at 604-05, arguing that the article III ban on reducing judges' salaries forbade taxing the income of federal judges already appointed. For the later fate of this interesting argument, see O'Malley v. Woodrough, 307 U.S. 277, 282 (1939) (taxation of income of federal judge is not an article III diminution), and cases cited therein.

[129] *Pollock,* 158 U.S. at 628. As Harlan observed in dissent, *id.* at 670, Fuller's argument also failed to account for the fact that the carriage tax upheld in Hylton v. United States, 3 U.S. (3 Dall.) 171 (1796), had been a tax on personal property.

[130] *See Pollock,* 157 U.S. at 645 (White, J., dissenting); 158 U.S. at 692-93 (Brown, J., dissenting); E. CORWIN, *supra* note 122, at 186-87; Jones, *Pollock v. Farmers' Loan & Trust Company,* 9 HARV. L. REV. 198, 210 (1895).

[131] A. SMITH, THE WEALTH OF NATIONS 821 (Mod. Lib. reprint 1937, E. Cannan ed. 1904) (1st ed. London 1776), *quoted in* Hylton v. United States, 3 U.S. (3 Dall.) 171, 180 (1796); *see* THE FIRST HUNDRED YEARS at 31-37. Fuller did quote in passing a statement of Albert Gallatin referring to Smith's definition, *Pollock,* 157 U.S. at 569-70, but he did not place any particular weight upon it.

[132] *Pollock,* 157 U.S. at 572 (income taxes classified as "direct" in British law); 158 U.S. at 630-32 (reviewing British and Canadian cases).

[133] *See, e.g.,* J. S. MILL, PRINCIPLES OF POLITICAL ECONOMY 823-29 (W. Ashley ed. 1926) (1st ed. London 1848). At one point Fuller did say that this was the "[o]rdinar[y]" test, but he added that it did not necessarily govern the meaning of article I, and he did not discuss whether the burden of income taxes could be passed on. *Pollock,* 157 U.S. at 558.

[134] For discussion of the hostile reaction to these three decisions, see 2 C. WARREN, *supra* note 89, at 702-04.

that neither a restraint on stockyard sales of out-of-state cattle[135] nor the right of an interstate railway employee to join a union[136] came under Congress's commerce clause powers. The first of these conclusions, however, was effectively abandoned a few years later when Justice Holmes, for a unanimous Court, described stockyard transactions as part of "a current of commerce" from the rancher in one state to the diner in another.[137] The second conclusion was difficult to square with the Court's contemporaneous acknowledgment that Congress could abrogate the fellow-servant rule for railway employees injured in interstate commerce[138] and prevent union members from boycotting goods shipped from one state to another.[139] The "indirect effect" test of *Knight* itself, moreover, seems to have been limited by the divided decision in the *Northern Securities* case, which upheld application of the Sherman Act to the establishment of a holding company that eliminated competition between two interstate railroads.[140] For although, as Justice Harlan stressed, interstate railroading (unlike manufacturing) was itself interstate commerce,[141] the immediate effect of the combination, as in the sugar case, was not on commerce itself but on the ownership

[135] Hopkins v. United States, 171 U.S. 578, 590-91 (1898) (Peckham, J.) (adding nothing to *E. C. Knight's* reasoning).

[136] Adair v. United States, 208 U.S. 161, 178 (1908) (Harlan, J., over dissents by McKenna and Holmes) (alternative holding) ("[W]hat possible legal or logical connection is there between an employé's membership in a labor organization and the carrying on of interstate commerce?"). For criticism, see T. POWELL, *supra* note 114, at 62 (calling the decision "unreason run riot"), 2 C. WARREN, *supra* note 89, at 715.

[137] Swift & Co. v. United States, 196 U.S. 375, 399 (1905); *see* L. BETH, THE DEVELOPMENT OF THE AMERICAN CONSTITUTION, 1877-1917, at 43-44 (1971) ("Holmes . . . did not feel the need to explain why a sugar refinery was not part of a similar flow.").

[138] The Employers' Liability Cases (Howard v. Illinois Cent. R.R.), 207 U.S. 463, 495 (1908) (White, J.) (dictum) ("[W]e fail to perceive any just reason for holding that Congress is without power to regulate the relation of master and servant, to the extent that regulations adopted by Congress on that subject are solely confined to interstate commerce. . . ."); *cf.* Adair v. United States, 208 U.S. 161, 189 (1908) (McKenna, J., dissenting) ("A provision of law which will prevent or tend to prevent the stoppage of every wheel in every car of an entire railroad system [by preventing strikes traceable to the discharge of union members] certainly has as direct influence on interstate commerce as . . . the rule of liability for personal injuries to an employé."). The Court in the *Employers' Liability Cases* went on to hold, rightly enough, that Congress had gone too far in extending its legislative power to injuries of employees whose activities had no relation to interstate commerce apart from the fact that their employer was also engaged in interstate trade, 207 U.S. at 500-01, and it struck down the statute even as to injuries in the course of interstate commerce itself in reliance on the questionable notions of inseparability first announced in United States v. Reese, 92 U.S. 214, 221 (1876). *See supra* note 128.

[139] Loewe v. Lawlor, 208 U.S. 274, 305-09 (1908) (Fuller, C. J.); *see* Adair v. United States, 208 U.S. 161, 186-89 (1908) (McKenna, J., dissenting) (arguing that the ban on firing union members was a means of preventing the "disastrous interruption of commerce" by labor disputes of the kind that the Court, a few pages later, in *Loewe*, would hold Congress could outlaw directly); *see also* B. WRIGHT, *supra* note 97, at 120 (some basis for strongly expressed union belief in Court's unwillingness to uphold prolabor statutes under commerce clause); Roche, *Entrepreneurial Liberty and the Commerce Power: Expansion, Contraction, and Casuistry in the Age of Enterprise*, 30 U. CHI. L. REV. 680, 699 (1963) ("The Supreme Court was only excluding from the commerce-police power pro-labor legislation."); *cf. In re* Garnett, 141 U.S. 1, 12 (1891) (Bradley, J.) (holding that the necessary and proper clause, together with the grant of federal judicial power over maritime cases, empowered Congress to enact a statute protecting American shipowners by limiting their liability); Butler v. Boston & Savannah S. S. Co., 130 U.S. 527, 557 (1889) (Bradley, J.) (same).

[140] Northern Sec. Co. v. United States, 193 U.S. 197, 342-54 (1904) (Harlan, J.) (plurality opinion). Four Justices dissented, and Brewer concurred specially, but he took no issue with this aspect of Harlan's opinion.

[141] *Id.* at 353.

of stock.[142] Even in the context of activities arguably ancillary to actual interstate intercourse, then, the Fuller Court was not uniformly hostile to federal regulatory power in its
interpretation of the commerce clause.

In the 1903 *Lottery Case*,[143] moreover, a bare majority of the Court gave a broad reading to the commerce power in quite a different context, upholding a federal statute that
prohibited interstate transportation of lottery tickets. Except for an ill-considered insurance case that the majority inexcusably failed to discuss,[144] there was no real doubt that
this was literally a regulation of interstate commerce.[145] The serious question was whether
the commerce power could be exercised in order to protect the public morals or was limited, in accordance with its motivating cause, to preventing obstructions to commerce.[146]
The constitutional text suggested that the power was plenary, and Justice Peckham had
already stated as much in *Addyston Pipe:* "The reasons which may have caused the fram-

[142] *See id.* at 368 (White, J., dissenting) ("[T]he question in this case . . . is . . . whether the [commerce]
power extends to regulate the ownership of stock in railroads, which is not commerce at all."). Fuller, Peckham,
and Holmes joined White's dissent, and Holmes added another dissenting opinion.

[143] Champion v. Ames, 188 U.S. 321, 354-55 (1903).

[144] Paul v. Virginia, 75 U.S. (8 Wall.) 168, 183 (1869) (issuing insurance policy not a "transaction of commerce"), THE FIRST HUNDRED YEARS at 352. *Paul* was relied on with some justice by the dissent in the Lottery
Case, 188 U.S. at 367-68. *See* T. POWELL, *supra* note 114, at 62 (criticizing the Lottery Case majority for failing
to address the dissent's reliance on *Paul*).

[145] The objection that prohibition was not regulation, put forth in Fuller's dissent, 188 U.S. at 371-75, and
dismissed by the majority, *id.* at 354-56, had been rejected fifty years earlier in an opinion by Justice Daniel, the
most extreme defender of states' rights ever to grace the Court. United States v. Marigold, 50 U.S. (9 How.),
560, 566-67 (1850) (Congress may prohibit importation of counterfeit coins as a "regulation" of commerce),
THE FIRST HUNDRED YEARS at 234 n.270. Harlan, for the Court, neglected to cite *Marigold*. For approval of the
Court's conclusion, see Parkinson, *Congressional Prohibitions of Interstate Commerce,* 16 COLUM. L. REV.
367, 371-76 (1916). Fuller's argument that power over *foreign* commerce (involved in *Marigold*) was broader
than that over interstate commerce, 188 U.S. at 373, was not dignified by a response. For discussion of the
relationship among the interstate, foreign, and Indian commerce powers, see Cushman, *The National Police
Power under the Commerce Clause of the Constitution,* 3 MINN. L.REV. 289, 300-02 (1919).

[146] In his dissent in the Lottery Case, Fuller argued that "the purpose of Congress . . . was the suppression of
lotteries," 188 U.S. at 364, insisted that the states had not given Congress police powers, *id.* at 365, and declared
it the Court's duty to invalidate laws passed by Congress "under the pretext of executing its powers" but actually
"for the accomplishment of objects not entrusted to the Government," *id.* at 372 (quoting McCulloch v. Maryland, 17 U.S. (4 Wheat.) 316, 423 (1819)). *See* 2 C. WARREN, *supra* note 89, at 736 ("The practical result . . .
was the creation of a Federal police power—the right to regulate the manner of production, manufacture, sale
and transportation of articles and the transportation of persons, through the medium of legislation professing to
regulate commerce between the States."). Marshall's position that the purpose of a *state* law determined whether
it was a regulation of commerce, Gibbons v. Ogden, 22 U.S. (9 Wheat.) 1, 203 (1824) (dictum), THE FIRST
HUNDRED YEARS at 174-75, lent oblique support to the dissenters' position. Fuller's dissent, however, needed to
be squared with his earlier opinion for the Court in *In re* Rapier, 143 U.S. 110, 134 (1892) (upholding the
exclusion of lottery material from the mails: "It is not necessary that Congress should have the power to deal with
crime or immorality within the states in order to maintain that it possesses the power to forbid the use of the mails
in aid of the perpetration of crime or immorality."). *Cf.* United States v. Holliday, 70 U.S. (3 Wall.) 407, 416-18
(1866) (upholding prohibition of liquor sales to Indians); United States v. The William, 28 F. Cas. 614, 621
(C.C.D. Mass. 1808) (No. 16,700) (upholding Jeffersonian embargo on ground that Congress's power over
foreign commerce could be exercised not merely to protect commerce itself but to serve "general policy and
interest"); *cf. also* Cushman, *National Police Power under the Postal Clause of the Constitution,* 4 MINN. L.
REV. 402, 420 (1920) (distinguishing *Rapier* on the ground that government ownership may make the postal
power broader); Cushman, *supra* note 145, at 300-02 (discussing the possible differences among the various
commerce powers).

ers of the Constitution to repose the power to regulate interstate commerce in Congress do not, however, affect or limit the extent of the power itself." [147]

In other contexts, as illustrated by the familiar example of bloodletting in the streets of Bologna, [148] the purpose of a provision has quite reasonably been held to limit its scope. Peckham gave no reason in *Addyston Pipe* for refusing to look to the purposes of the commerce clause, and he inconsistently joined the dissent in the *Lottery Case*. The historical materials do not seem to refute the reasonable textual inference that the Framers' mistrust of the states led them to give Congress control of the whole subject of interstate commerce. [149] But in the face of a challenging dissent, Harlan made essentially no effort to explain. [150]

Just as *E. C. Knight* did not signal a generally narrow approach to the commerce power, the *Pollock* decision did not lead to a general judicial assault on federal taxation. The Fuller Court upheld a variety of federal taxes over the objection that they were direct but unapportioned. [151] In *Knowlton v. Moore* [152] it held that the constitutional requirement

[147] Addyston Pipe & Steel Co. v. United States, 175 U.S. 211, 228 (1899). The question addressed in *Addyston Pipe* was the power to prevent *private* obstructions of commerce; it had been argued that the purpose of the commerce clause was only to prevent obstructions by the states. Compare the controversy over whether the second amendment's "right of the people to keep and bear Arms" is limited by its express explanation that "[a] well regulated Militia" is "necessary to the security of a free State." *See also* THE FIRST HUNDRED YEARS at 43-44 (discussing the ex post facto clauses).

[148] *See, e.g.,* 1 W. BLACKSTONE, COMMENTARIES *60 (reporting that a law forbidding the drawing of blood in the streets was held "not to extend to the surgeon, who opened the vein of a person that fell down in the street with a fit").

[149] *See, e.g.,* Corwin, *Congress's Power to Prohibit Commerce—A Crucial Constitutional Issue,* 18 CORN. L.Q. 477, 482-84, 503-04 (1933) (supporting this conclusion).

[150] Harlan's opinion was filled, in the execrable style of the day, with general quotations from a myriad of commerce clause precedents that had nothing to do with the issues in the case. Bowman v. Chicago & N. W. Ry., 125 U.S. 465 (1888), which Harlan cited only for the inconsequential proposition that liquor was an article of commerce, Lottery Cases, 188 U.S. at 360, had actually given him substantial help by holding that a state could not bar entry of interstate liquor shipments for health reasons because Congress's power over interstate commerce was exclusive, *Bowman,* 125 U.S. at 498-99. *See* THE FIRST HUNDRED YEARS at 415-16 (discussing *Bowman*); T. POWELL, *supra* note 114, at 64-65 ("It might seem that after condemnation of a state law as a regulation of interstate commerce, an identical act of Congress must perforce be . . . held valid. . . .").

[151] Thomas v. United States, 192 U.S. 363, 370-71 (1904) (Fuller, C. J.) (stamp tax on sales of shares of stock); Patton v. Brady, 184 U.S. 608, 621-23 (1902) (Brewer, J.) (tax on tobacco); Knowlton v. Moore, 178 U.S. 41, 83 (1900) (White, J.) (tax on legacies of personal property); Nicol v. Ames, 173 U.S. 509, 518-19 (1899) (Peckham, J.) (stamp tax on sales at board of trade). Most of these taxes, as the Court said of death duties in *Knowlton,* 178 U.S. at 55-56, could be regarded as taxes upon the occurrence of an event rather than upon the ownership of property itself, and all seemed to fit the traditional definitions of duties or excises, which the Constitution distinguished from direct taxes. *See, e.g., Patton,* 184 U.S. at 618; *Knowlton,* 178 U.S. at 78-79. Nevertheless, *Knowlton* seems to depart from the reasoning of *Pollock,* since a legacy tax, though—like an income tax—indirect in form, is effectively a tax on the underlying property. Compare the Court's similar distinction with respect to governmental immunity, permitting state taxation of legacies of government bonds but prohibiting taxation of income from the same bonds. *See supra* note 128. The Court in *Knowlton* had the benefit of a highly relevant precedent, Scholey v. Rew, 90 U.S. (23 Wall.) 331, 346-348 (1875), which had upheld a tax on succession to real property on the ground that a succession tax was no more direct than an income tax, 90 U.S. (23 Wall.) at 347, which, before *Pollock,* was thought to be "indirect" for constitutional purposes. The *Knowlton* Court concluded that *Pollock* had overruled the rationale of *Scholey* but not its ultimate conclusion. 178 U.S. at 79-81.

[152] 178 U.S. 41 (1900) (White, J.).

that indirect taxes be "uniform throughout the United States"[153] did not outlaw progressive taxation, relying persuasively on consistent congressional practice to support the textual inference that the uniformity required was geographical alone.[154] Most significantly, the generous approach to federal authority reflected in the *Lottery Case* prevailed again the following year in *McCray v. United States*,[155] which upheld a cripplingly high tax on colored oleomargarine, relying partly on precedent[156] and partly on the question-begging ground that "a wrongful purpose or motive" was no justification for judicial interference with "the exercise of lawful power."[157] This decision was a far cry from *E. C. Knight,* and it was not surprising that Fuller and two others dissented.[158] After *McCray,* it seemed that Congress could forbid anything under the guise of taxing it,[159] notwithstanding the Framers' plan of a federal government with limited, enumerated powers.[160]

---

[153] U. S. CONST. art. I, § 8, cl. 1. For a detailed analysis of this constitutional provision, see Comment, *The Uniformity Clause,* 51 U. CHI. L. REV. 1193 (1984).

[154] *Knowlton,* 178 U.S. at 83-106 (citing The Head Money Cases, 112 U.S. 580, 594-95 (1884) (dictum)); *cf.* Binns v. United States, 194 U.S. 486, 492-96 (1904) (Brewer, J.) (Congress may lay taxes limited to Alaska to fund local-government expenses under its power to govern the territories; the uniformity clause applies only to taxes raised for national purposes). For further discussion of the scope of the uniformity requirement, see *infra* pp. 61-63 (discussing Downes v. Bidwell, 182 U.S. 244 (1901)).

[155] 195 U.S. 27 (1904) (White, J.).

[156] The Court relied especially on Veazie Bank v. Fenno, 75 U.S. (8 Wall.) 533 (1869), THE FIRST HUNDRED YEARS at 317-20, where, as *McCray* conceded, 195 U.S. at 58, the conclusion relied on had been an alternative holding.

[157] *McCray,* 195 U.S. at 56. *See* Miller, *Public Choice at the Dawn of the Special Interest State: The Story of Butter and Margarine,* 77 CAL. L. REV. 83 (1989).

[158] 195 U.S. at 64 (without opinion). For resolution of another constitutional issue respecting federal taxation, see Twin City Bank v. Nebeker, 167 U.S. 196, 203 (1897) (Harlan, J.) (statute that imposed a tax earmarked for the costs of printing bank notes was not a "Bill[]" for raising Revenue" required by art. I, § 7 to "originate in the House of Representatives": "There was no purpose . . . to raise revenue to be applied in meeting the expenses or obligations of the Government."); *accord* Millard v. Roberts, 202 U.S. 429, 437 (1906) (McKenna, J.) (tax levied to defray cost of building a railroad station not a revenue bill, but merely a "means to the purposes provided by the act").

[159] *See* A. MCLAUGHLIN, *supra* note 115, at 784; 2 C. WARREN, *supra* note 89, at 738; Beck, *Nullification by Indirection,* 23 HARV. L. REV. 441, 442-45 (1910). The only constitutional limits suggested by the *McCray* opinion concerned "freedom and justice" and due process, not federalism. 195 U.S. at 62-64.

[160] The Lottery Case itself had not gone so far; much remains outside congressional power even if the authority to regulate interstate commerce may be exercised for police purposes. *See* Cushman, *The National Police Power under the Taxing Clause of the Constitution,* 4 MINN. L. REV. 247, 249, 255 (1920) (adding the argument that the power "[t]o lay and collect Taxes . . . to . . . provide for the . . . general Welfare," U. S. CONST. art. I, § 8, cl. 1, meant the power to *raise money to be spent* for general welfare).

# 2

# The Protection of
# Economic Interests II

## I. Obstructions to Interstate Commerce

Long before the adoption of the fourteenth amendment, the Supreme Court had developed the debatable thesis that the clause giving Congress power to regulate interstate and foreign commerce implicitly limited state authority to interfere with business that transcended state lines.[1] Since no Justice had ever taken the extreme position that the states lacked authority to affect interstate commerce altogether, a number of conflicting theories had grown up to explain when the states could affect commerce and when they could not. Marshall had distinguished between the regulation of commerce as such and the exercise of the states' reserved police powers;[2] Curtis had concluded that the states could regulate commerce in matters not requiring uniformity;[3] some later Justices had said that the states could pass laws having "indirect" or "incidental" effects on commerce.[4] The failure of Congress to enact legislation had been interpreted sometimes to permit[5] and sometimes to forbid[6] state action.

It was not until after the Civil War that the commerce clause had been unambiguously employed to strike down state legislation, but in the remaining years of the Court's first century it had been wielded with increasing frequency to protect commerce against state interference. Prediction of the fate of any state law had become extremely hazardous. None of the Court's tests suggested clear solutions to particular controversies, and the Justices had compounded the confusion by employing different tests in successive cases.

---

[1] See THE FIRST HUNDRED YEARS at 172-83, 204-06, 222-36, 330-42, 403-16.

[2] Gibbons v. Ogden, 22 U.S. (9 Wheat.) 1, 203-05, 209 (1824).

[3] Cooley v. Board of Wardens, 53 U.S. (12 How.) 299, 319-20 (1852).

[4] See, e.g., Sherlock v. Alling, 93 U.S. 99, 102-04 (1877) (Field, J.).

[5] See, e.g., id. at 104.

[6] See, e.g., Welton v. Missouri, 91 U.S. 275, 282 (1876).

Nor were the results easy to reconcile on any theory; by the time Fuller's term began, there were precedents to justify almost anything the Court might choose to decide.

In the ensuing twenty years the Court added greatly to the stock of decisions in this field. In so doing, without much fanfare, it managed both to shift the overall tendency of the decisions and to make a modest start toward reducing the doctrinal confusion.

## A.   Leisy v. Hardin

Once upon a time John Marshall had said in dictum,[7] and the Court had later held,[8] that state laws passed in the legitimate pursuit of health, safety, or other noncommercial "police power" goals were valid without regard to their impact on interstate commerce.[9] Though an important 1876 Miller opinion[10] had purported to reject this entire theory in favor of the uniformity test first enunciated by Justice Curtis in *Cooley v. Board of Wardens*,[11] the police-power criterion had sprung up again almost immediately[12] and had been the basis of an important 1888 decision upholding state examination and licensing of interstate railway engineers.[13] It had therefore required considerable gymnastic ability for the Court to conclude, just before Fuller's appointment, in the teeth of a forty-year-old decision that had allowed states to bar the sale of liquor imported from other states,[14] that the police power did not justify a state ban on importing such liquor in the first place.[15] It remained for Fuller himself, in one of his first constitutional opinions, to overrule the old precedent and hold that no state could forbid the sale of out-of-state liquor in its original package.[16]

As an omen of what sort of opinions one could expect from the new Chief Justice, *Leisy v. Hardin* was not exactly cheering. The opinion commences with a hackneyed and useless background recitation of the type we have come to associate with legal encyclopedias. After two pages of this, in which he recited Curtis's and Marshall's conflicting theories in consecutive sentences with no apparent appreciation of their incompatibility,[17] Fuller turned to *Brown v. Maryland*.[18] There, in the course of holding that a state could not tax goods imported from foreign countries while still in their original packages,[19] Marshall had added that the same was true of imports from other states. [20] Omitting to note that this dictum had been squarely repudiated in *Woodruff v. Parham*,[21] Fuller pro-

---

[7]Gibbons v. Ogden, 22 U.S. (9 Wheat.) 1, 203-04, 209 (1824) (dictum), THE FIRST HUNDRED YEARS at 172-76.

[8]New York v. Miln, 36 U.S. (11 Pet.) 102, 137-41 (1837), THE FIRST HUNDRED YEARS at 204-06.

[9]In the absence, that is, of any conflicting federal statute. *See Gibbons*, 22 U.S. (9 Wheat.) at 210.

[10]Henderson v. Mayor of New York, 92 U.S. 259, 271-73 (1876), THE FIRST HUNDRED YEARS at 405-08.

[11]53 U.S. (12 How.) 299, 319-20 (1852).

[12]Railroad Co. v. Husen, 95 U.S. 465, 472 (1878), THE FIRST HUNDRED YEARS at 410.

[13]Smith v. Alabama, 124 U.S. 465, 480 (1888).

[14]The License Cases, 46 U.S. (5 How.) 504 (1847).

[15]Bowman v. Chicago & N. W. Ry., 125 U.S. 465, 488-91 (1888), THE FIRST HUNDRED YEARS at 415-16.

[16]Leisy v. Hardin, 135 U.S. 100 (1890).

[17]*Id.* at 108-09.

[18]25 U.S. (12 Wheat.) 419 (1827), *discussed in Leisy*, 135 U.S. at 110-11.

[19]25 U.S. (12 Wheat.) at 445.

[20]*Id.* at 449.

[21]75 U.S. (8 Wall.) 123, 139 (1869), THE FIRST HUNDRED YEARS at 335-37. *Woodruff* flatly held that the imports clause, U.S. CONST. art. I, § 10, cl. 2, which had been the principal basis of *Brown*, was wholly

ceeded to quote hemorrhagically from *Bowman v. Chicago & Northwestern Railway Co.*,[22] the recent decision that had struck down a state ban on the importation of liquor, where the Court had expressly distinguished between importation and sales.[23] Fuller did not explain why the two cases were similar.[24] He did recite, ad nauseam, the arguments that Chief Justice Taney had used to uphold a similar law in the *License Cases*,[25] adding only that Taney had not appreciated the subtleties of the uniformity test developed in later cases[26] but not disclosing why liquor sales required uniform regulation. Instead he launched into a five-page enumeration of the results of previous decisions striking down or upholding various state laws without ever venturing to say which ones *Leisy* resembled or why.[27] There follows the unexplained conclusion that the law was unconstitutional.[28]

Fuller's lamentable opinion notwithstanding, *Bowman*'s heavy reliance on decisions striking down taxes on sales of out-of-state goods[29] made *Leisy* almost a foregone conclusion.[30] *Leisy* thus seemed to suggest not only the primacy of *Cooley*'s uniformity standard but also a continuation of the Waite Court's tendency toward vigorous protection of commerce from state obstruction.[31]

---

inapplicable to imports from other states and declared that the commerce clause forbade only *discriminatory* taxation of sister-state goods even while they remained in their original package. 75 U.S. (8 Wall.) at 140. Contrary to Fuller's statement in *Leisy*, 135 U.S. at 110, the commerce clause itself seems not to have figured significantly in the *Brown* decision. *See* THE FIRST HUNDRED YEARS at 176-81.

[22] 125 U.S. 465 (1888).

[23] *Id.* at 498-99.

[24] *Leisy*, 135 U.S. at 111-15.

[25] *See id.* at 115-18 (citing The License Cases, 46 U.S. (5 How.) 504, 576, 578-79, 586 (1847)).

[26] *See Leisy*, 135 U.S. at 118.

[27] *Id.* at 119-23.

[28] *Id.* at 124-25.

[29] *Bowman*, 125 U.S. at 495-98; *see also id.* at 499 (implicitly casting doubt on the result in the License Cases because "the very purpose . . . of . . . transportation[] is . . . sale").

[30] A wordy dissent by three Justices, none of whom had joined the decision in *Bowman*, suddenly found merit in the unconvincing argument of the *Bowman* majority, 125 U.S. at 498, that, in forbidding importation, the state had attempted to regulate conduct beyond its own borders. *Leisy*, 135 U.S. at 155-56 (Gray, J., joined by Harlan and Brewer, JJ., dissenting). The dissenters' police-power argument, *id.* at 158-60, had been substantially refuted by *Bowman*, and they did not explain their less-than-obvious conclusion that the *Cooley* requirement of uniformity was more significant for importation than for sales, *id.* at 157-58. The dissent could have derived some support from cases allowing state taxation of goods that had come to rest after an interstate journey, *see* Brown v. Houston, 114 U.S. 622, 632-33 (1885), or that had not yet begun one, *see* Coe v. Errol, 116 U.S. 517, 524-25 (1885). Indeed, United States v. E. C. Knight Co., 156 U.S. 1 (1895), *supra* pp. 22-24, coming five years after *Leisy*, cast doubt on the proposition that local sales of out-of-state goods fell within the commerce power at all. Gray's *Leisy* dissent did mention Kidd v. Pearson, 128 U.S. 1 (1888) (Lamar, J.), which had suggestively held that a state could prohibit the distilling of liquor for export on the ground that manufacture preceded commerce, *see id.* at 25-26, but Gray failed to notice its usefulness to his argument. *Leisy*, 135 U.S. at 157 (dissenting opinion). On the other hand, Welton v. Missouri, 91 U.S. 275, 282 (1876), which invalidated a local sales tax that discriminated against sellers of out-of-state goods, showed the danger of this approach. *Cf.* Woodruff v. Parham, 75 U.S. (8 Wall.) 123, 140 (1869) (upholding a nondiscriminatory tax); THE FIRST HUNDRED YEARS at 404-05.

[31] Indeed, in the companion case of Lyng v. Michigan, 135 U.S. 161, 166 (1890) (Fuller, C. J.), the Court applied *Leisy* to hold that a state could not *tax* the sale of sister-state liquor in its original package, on the ground that "no State has the right to lay a tax on interstate commerce in any form." Though the tax in fact discriminated against out-of-state goods, *id.*, the Court did not rest its decision on this fact. The decision thus seemed to undermine the basis of Woodruff v. Parham, 75 U.S. (8 Wall.) 123, 140 (1869), which had upheld a nondiscriminatory tax on the local sale of goods, and which was not cited by the *Lyng* Court.

## B. *Rahrer* and *Plumley*

Near the end of his *Leisy* opinion the Chief Justice tossed off the following remarkable dictum:

> [T]he responsibility is upon Congress, so far as the regulation of interstate commerce is concerned, to remove the restriction upon the State in dealing with imported articles of trade within its limits, which have not been mingled with the common mass of property therein, if in its judgment the end to be secured justifies and requires such action.[32]

Congress snapped at the opportunity in a trice, subjecting all imported liquors to state police-power laws "upon arrival" to the same extent as if they had been locally produced.[33] Though *Cooley* had flatly said that Congress could not empower the states to do what the commerce clause forbade,[34] Fuller and his brethren dutifully upheld Congress's action in *In re Rahrer*[35]—and had the temerity to declare, in plain contradiction of the facts, that the statute "imparted no power to the State not then possessed."[36]

The state law in question had been enacted before Congress spoke, and Justice Curtis had conceded in *Cooley* that Congress might be able to adopt existing state laws as its own.[37] Far from distinguishing *Cooley* on this basis, however, Fuller assumed that the state could have reenacted its law after Congress acted and rejected the argument that it was *required* to do so.[38] Rather, the Chief Justice argued that Congress had enacted a uniform regulation of its own, "divest[ing]" imported beverages of their "character" as "subjects of interstate commerce . . . at an earlier period of time than would otherwise be the case."[39] If this meant that Congress was to be sole judge of the meaning of the commerce clause, it was contrary to *Marbury v. Madison;*[40] if it meant that Congress could authorize state regulations that the Constitution itself forbade, it left the *Cooley* argument unanswered.[41]

---

[32] Leisy v. Hardin, 135 U.S. 100, 123-24 (1890).

[33] Act of Aug. 8, 1890 (Wilson Act), ch. 728, 26 Stat. 313. Rhodes v. Iowa, 170 U.S. 412, 426 (1898) (White, J.), undermined the apparent purpose of the act—which was to return effective control of liquor to the states—by holding that liquor did not "arriv[e]" until received by the consignee, so that while a state could forbid resale in the original package, it could not forbid importation. *See* C. WARREN, THE SUPREME COURT IN UNITED STATES HISTORY 731-32 (rev. ed. 1926). *See also* Scott v. Donald, 165 U.S. 58, 100 (1897) (Shiras, J.) (confirming the apparent statutory requirement that the state not discriminate against foreign liquor); Vance v. W. A. Vandercook Co., 170 U.S. 438, 449-52 (1898) (White, J.) (interpreting the nondiscrimination requirement).

[34] Cooley v. Board of Wardens, 53 U.S. (12 How.) 299, 318 (1852).

[35] 140 U.S. 545 (1891).

[36] *Id.* at 564.

[37] Cooley v. Board of Wardens, 53 U.S. (12 How.) 299, 317-18 (1852).

[38] *Rahrer*, 140 U.S. at 565.

[39] *Id.* at 561-62.

[40] 5 U.S. (1 Cranch) 137, 177-79 (1803); *see* Biklé, *The Silence of Congress*, 41 HARV. L. REV. 200, 209-10 (1927).

[41] Fuller hinted, correctly enough, that, to the extent that the state's inability to act was based on an implicit congressional prohibition, it could be cured by federal statute. *Rahrer*, 140 U.S. at 559-60, 562. Apart from inherent difficulties with the argument from congressional inaction, however, there were too many decisions basing the invalidity of state laws on the commerce clause itself for this explanation to be convincing.

The opinion seemed to be on the right track when it observed that some of the express limits on state authority in article I, § 10 could be removed by Congress.[42] But Fuller failed to develop the argument that, in light of its purpose of permitting Congress to determine the extent to which commerce should be regulated, the implicit commerce clause restriction should be analogized to these removable limitations rather than to those express limitations which are immune from congressional action.[43] Congress, as Fuller said, had made the decision that "the common interests did not require entire freedom in the traffic in ardent spirits,"[44] and this decision seems to have satisfied the Framers' reasons for giving the power to Congress.

Thus, despite the flaws in his reasoning, Fuller seems to have reached a defensible result in *Rahrer*. His opinions in *Leisy* and *Rahrer* together, moreover, show a consistent commitment neither to the police power nor to freedom of commerce but to the more neutral institutional principle that Congress should determine the balance between them.

It is not so easy, however, to find consistency between *Leisy* and the 1894 case of *Plumley v. Massachusetts*,[45] which held that, although Congress had not spoken, a state was free to forbid the sale of out-of-state colored oleomargarine in its original package.[46] Fuller appropriately dissented.[47]

Harlan, who had dissented in *Leisy*, wrote for the Court. The only reason for coloring margarine yellow, he argued, was to deceive buyers into thinking it was butter; preventing such deception fell within the state's police power.[48] This argument might have been persuasive enough before *Leisy*. To distinguish that case Harlan said only that there had been no effort to pass off the beer in that case as anything but beer;[49] he did not say why the state's interest in guarding its citizens from confusing one healthful product with another was more deserving of constitutional protection than its interest in guarding them from substances destructive of health.[50]

---

[42]*Id.* at 560. Article I, § 10 provides, in part, that "[n]o state shall, *without the Consent of Congress,* lay any Duty of Tonnage, Keep Troops, or Ships of War in time of Peace, [or] enter into any Agreement or Compact with another State" (emphasis added).

[43]*See* THE FIRST HUNDRED YEARS at 233-34; T. R. POWELL, VAGARIES AND VARIETIES IN CONSTITUTIONAL INTERPRETATION 161 (1956).

[44]*Rahrer,* 140 U.S. at 561.

[45]155 U.S. 461 (1894).

[46]*Id.* at 478-79.

[47]*Id.* at 480-82. Oddly, he neglected to cite *Leisy.*

[48]*Id.* at 467-68. The dissenters responded with some force that there was no chance of deception since both state and federal law already required explanatory packaging and labeling. *Id.* at 481. But the only precedents suggesting that a state had to exercise its police powers in the manner that was least restrictive of interstate commerce had been in the context of regulations discriminating against foreign goods, *see, e.g.,* Railroad Co. v. Husen, 95 U.S. 465 (1878), while the Massachusetts law was facially neutral: it prohibited the sale of all colored oleomargarine. The Court seemed unconcerned by the possibility that the law might have had the discriminatory effect of protecting the local butter industry from outside competition.

[49]*Plumley,* 155 U.S. at 474.

[50]*See* Carman, *Comments on Federal Trust Legislation,* 12 POL. SCI. Q. 622, 634 (1897) (distinction between *Leisy* and *Plumley* "untenable"). That the Court did not take the health interest lightly had been made clear by the Court's unanimous and ringing depiction of the evils of drink in upholding a prohibition law against due process objections in Mugler v. Kansas, 123 U.S. 623, 662-63 (1887), THE FIRST HUNDRED YEARS at 375-77. *Mugler* makes it hard to explain the contrast between *Plumley* and *Leisy* on the ground that the Justices were an ardent bunch of wets.

The truth was that not one Justice who voted to uphold the state's power over margarine had denied its power over liquor. Four Justices who had voted with the majority in *Leisy* had left the Court,[51] and their successors voted in *Plumley* with two of the *Leisy* dissenters.[52] The distinction between the cases, to borrow Thomas Reed Powell's phrase, seemed to be "the intervening change in the composition of the Court."[53]

## C.   Later Decisions

Although the Court soon suggested that cigarettes were still governed by the *Leisy* rule,[54] later decisions of the Fuller period confirm *Plumley*'s implication that *Leisy* was a misleading indicator of what was to come. In the first place, *Cooley*'s uniformity test, which had figured so prominently in *Leisy* as well as in earlier opinions,[55] practically disappeared for the time being.[56] Furthermore, on balance the new Justices seemed, if anything, less inclined than their predecessors to protect commerce from state obstruction.

---

[51] Miller, Bradley, Blatchford, and Lamar.

[52] The successors, Brown, Shiras, Jackson, and White, voted with Harlan and Gray.

[53] T. POWELL, *supra* note 43, at 110. Justice Brewer, who joined the dissent in *Leisy,* also joined the dissent in *Plumley.* For reasons already suggested, there were several plausible grounds for concluding, as Brewer seems to have done, that *Leisy* was the stronger case for allowing state regulation.

[54] Austin v. Tennessee, 179 U.S. 343, 350 (1900) (Brown, J.). The Court held, however, in order to prevent evasion of state laws, that retail-sized ten-cigarette packets were not "original packages" for purposes of the *Leisy* doctrine, when they had been shipped interstate in large baskets. *Id.* at 360-61. Brewer, Shiras, Peckham, and Fuller dissented. For a perceptive contemporaneous criticism of both the Court's reasoning and the original-package doctrine itself, see Miller, *The Latest Phase of the Original Package Doctrine,* 35 AM. L. REV. 364 (1901).

[55] Two early cases of the period invoking the uniformity rationale were Western Union Tel. Co. v. James, 162 U.S. 650, 660 (1896) (Peckham, J.) (liability for nondelivery of interstate telegrams was not "so extensive and national in character, that it could only be dealt with by Congress"), and Covington & Cincinnati Bridge Co. v. Kentucky, 154 U.S. 204, 221-22 (1894) (Brown, J.) (invalidating state regulation of interstate bridge tolls).

[56] At the same time that the *Cooley* test was disappearing from the commerce clause cases, it cropped up as a test for determining when state laws were preempted by the extension of federal judicial power to "Cases of admiralty and maritime Jurisdiction," U.S. CONST. art. III, § 2. Building in part on Justice Bradley's assertion that there was a federal common law in this field because the Framers had sought "uniformity and consistency," The Lottawanna, 88 U.S. (21 Wall.) 558, 575 (1875), the Fuller Court refused to recognize state laws that immunized municipalities from maritime tort liability, Workman v. New York City, 179 U.S. 552, 557-63 (1900) (White, J.), or that created maritime liens for materials and services provided to an out-of-state vessel at the request of an independent contractor, The Roanoke, 189 U.S. 185, 195-99 (1903) (Brown, J.). In both cases, however, a more obvious ground was also given: the state laws contradicted federal common law. *See* The Roanoke, 189 U.S. at 196; *Workman,* 179 U.S. at 558, 563.

Confusion arose when Justice Holmes failed to deal adequately with either the supremacy or the uniformity criterion in upholding the application of a state wrongful-death statute to a maritime accident. The Hamilton, 207 U.S. 398, 404-06 (1907). The Court had already held that, in the absence of congressional legislation, a state wrongful-death action might apply to a maritime accident without unduly disrupting the freedom of trade guaranteed by the commerce clause. Sherlock v. Alling, 93 U.S. 99, 104 (1876). Thus it was reasonable enough to conclude that such an action might be maintained without offending the similar and equally shaky uniformity thesis that the Court had enunciated under the admiralty clause. The Hamilton, 207 U.S. at 404-05. In his usual breezy way, however, Holmes did not stop to distinguish *Workman* and The Roanoke, though he might have done so on the ground that the absence of a federal common law death remedy reflected not a federal policy opposing such relief but only the traditional notion that such actions could be created only by statute, The Harrisburg, 119 U.S. 199, 213-14 (1886). Another ground of distinction might have been that a state remedy that merely extended liability for the breach of a preexisting federal duty of care did not subject the owner to uncertainty as to his

In 1878, for example, the Court had held that a state law forbidding racial segregation in public conveyances could not be applied to a ship traveling interstate;[57] in 1890 it upheld a state requirement that interstate trains provide separate cars for blacks and whites.[58] Before Fuller's appointment the Court had held that no state could tax the gross receipts of interstate transport;[59] thereafter it displayed increased receptiveness to apportionment formulas that required interstate commerce to pay its way while relieving it of the most obvious multiple burdens.[60] Moreover, while the Court displayed a tendency to proclaim that the states had no power whatever to regulate interstate commerce itself,[61] it managed to uphold a number of significant restrictions of such commerce by labeling them the "indirect" effects of regulating something else.[62]

---

standard of conduct. *See* Currie, *Federalism and the Admiralty: "The Devil's Own Mess,"* 1960 SUP. CT. REV. 158, 172, 186-88.

[57] Hall v. DeCuir, 95 U.S. 485, 488-90 (1878), THE FIRST HUNDRED YEARS at 411.

[58] Louisville, N. O. & T. Ry. v. Mississippi, 133 U.S. 587, 592 (1890) (Brewer, J.). Harlan and Bradley, tripping over their words, sharply dissented: "It is difficult to understand how a state enactment, requiring the separation of the white and black races on interstate carriers of passengers, is a regulation of commerce among the States, while a similar enactment forbidding such separation is not. . . ." *Id.* at 594. The majority responded that the state court had construed the statute to apply only to intrastate commerce, *id.* at 591, but the state court had applied the law to intrastate passengers on interstate trains, which apparently were the only kind that the defendant was running. *See* Louisville, N. O. & T. Ry. v. State, 66 Miss. 662, 675 (1889). The complaining passenger in the 1878 case had been traveling locally as well, and the Court had noted that the "disposition of passengers taken up and put down within the State . . . cannot but affect . . . those taken up without and brought within." Hall v. DeCuir, 95 U.S. 485, 489 (1878). The Court in *Louisville* stressed that the power of the state to require actual segregated seating was not in issue but only the expense of adding a separate car for blacks—an expense no greater than that under "statutes requiring certain accommodations at depots, compelling trains to stop at crossings of other railroads, and a multitude of other matters confessedly within the power of the State." *Louisville,* 133 U.S. at 591. For criticism of the decision, see 9 A. BICKEL & B. SCHMIDT, HISTORY OF THE SUPREME COURT OF THE UNITED STATES 751-52 (1984).

[59] Philadelphia & S.S.S. Co. v. Pennsylvania, 122 U.S. 326, 341-44 (1887) (domestic corporation); Fargo v. Michigan, 121 U.S. 230, 243-44 (1887) (out-of-state corporation); *see* THE FIRST HUNDRED YEARS at 413-14 n.78.

[60] *See, e.g.,* Fargo v. Hart, 193 U.S. 490, 499 (1904) (Holmes, J.) (upholding apportioned tax on express company property); Adams Express Co. v. Ohio State Auditor, 165 U.S. 194, 226 (1897) (Fuller, C. J.) (same); Maine v. Grand Trunk Ry., 142 U.S. 217, 228-29 (1891) (Field, J.) (upholding privilege tax measured by gross receipts apportioned by mileage); Pullman's Palace Car Co. v. Pennsylvania, 141 U.S. 18, 26 (1891) (Gray, J.) (upholding property tax on railroad cars apportioned by mileage). Arguably out of line with the Court's apparent concern for avoiding the competitive disadvantage of multiple burdens was the decision allowing a railroad's home state to tax the total value of its rolling stock, though the above decisions seemed to say that such property was also subject to taxation in other states on an apportioned basis. New York *ex rel.* New York Cent. & H.R.R.R. v. Miller, 202 U.S. 584, 597 (1906) (Holmes, J.) (avoiding the problem by doubting that any cars in question were "so continuously in any other State as to be taxable there"). The holding of the *Grand Trunk* case with respect to privilege taxes was soon qualified by the suggestion that the payment of such a tax could not be made a condition of doing interstate business. Postal Tel. Cable Co. v. Adams, 155 U.S. 688, 698 (1895) (Fuller, C.J.) (dictum).

[61] *See, e.g.,* Crutcher v. Kentucky, 141 U.S. 47, 57-60 (1891) (Bradley, J.).

[62] *See, e.g.,* Rasmussen v. Idaho, 181 U.S. 198, 202 (1901) (Brewer, J.) (upholding temporary ban on importation of sheep from area where disease was prevalent); Erb v. Morasch, 177 U.S. 584, 585 (1900) (Brewer, J.) (upholding six-miles-per-hour speed limit for trains in city); Chicago, M. & St. P. Ry. v. Solan, 169 U.S. 133, 137-38 (1898) (Gray, J.) (upholding ban on railroad's right to contract out of liability for negligent personal injury); New York, N. H. & H.R.R. v. New York, 165 U.S. 628, 631-32 (1897) (Harlan, J.) (upholding prohibition of heating stoves in railroad cars); Hennington v. Georgia, 163 U.S. 299, 308-09, 317-18 (1896) (Harlan,

More interesting than the results was a growing consensus on the applicable criteria. Outside the tax field, the dominant theme was that of the police power.[63] But Marshall's *Gibbons* test[64] had undergone a significant evolution: the Court increasingly insisted that exercises of the police power that affected interstate or foreign commerce be "reasonable."[65] Reasonableness, in turn, tended to depend upon how seriously the measure impinged on commerce and how necessary it was to accomplish the police-power goal. In quarantine cases, for example, where a similar calculus had been applied as early as 1878,[66] the Court continued to inquire whether the state had gone further to restrict commerce than the need justified.[67]

The quarantine cases generally dealt with measures that targeted out-of-state goods for unfavorable treatment. In the Fuller period, however, the Court applied the same test not only to cases in which facially neutral rules had disproportionate effects on outside producers[68] but also to cases in which there was no suggestion of either facial discrimination or disparate impact. In a revealing series of decisions, for example, the Court permitted states to inflict "reasonable" burdens on commerce by requiring some interstate trains to make stops at specified stations,[69] but drew the line whenever it concluded that adequate service had already been provided.[70] And even *Plumley* itself was confined by the Court's determination that deception could be effectively prevented without banning the sale of *all* margarine[71] or requiring that it be colored pink.[72]

---

J.) (upholding ban on running freight trains on Sunday); Louisville & N.R.R. v. Kentucky, 161 U.S. 677, 701 (1896) (Brown, J.) (upholding prohibition on consolidation of in-state with out-of-state railroads).

[63] *See e.g.,* cases cited *supra* note 62; E. FREUND, THE POLICE POWER §§ 136-38 (1904).

[64] *See supra* p. 32.

[65] *E.g.,* Reid v. Colorado, 187 U.S. 137, 152 (1902) (Harlan, J.) (upholding state ban on importation of diseased livestock); Gladson v. Minnesota, 166 U.S. 427, 430-31 (1897) (Gray, J.) (upholding state statute that required intrastate trains to stop at county seats); New York, N. H. & H.R.R. v. New York, 165 U.S. 628, 631 (1897) (Harlan, J.) (upholding state railroad safety regulations); Illinois Cent. R.R. v. Illinois, 163 U.S. 142, 154 (1896) (Gray, J.) (striking down state statute that required fast interstate mail trains to stop at county seats); *see also* cases cited *infra* notes 67-70; Shenton, *Interstate Commerce during the Silence of Congress,* 23 DICK. L. REV. 78 (1919).

[66] Railroad Co. v. Husen, 95 U.S. 465, 473-74 (1878) (striking down overbroad state prohibition of shipment of cattle from area where disease was prevalent), THE FIRST HUNDRED YEARS at 410.

[67] *See, e.g.,* Smith v. St. Louis & S. W. Ry., 181 U.S. 248, 255, 257 (1901) (McKenna, J.) (upholding a temporary ban on importation of cattle from area at risk of disease). Harlan, White, and Brown dissented.

[68] *See, e.g.,* Brimmer v. Rebman, 138 U.S. 78, 82-84 (1891) (Harlan, J.) (striking down requirement of inspection of meat shipped over one hundred miles).

[69] *See, e.g.,* Lake Shore & M. S. Ry. v. Ohio, 173 U.S. 285, 300-03 (1899) (Harlan, J.).

[70] *See, e.g.,* Herndon v. Chicago R. I. & P. Ry., 218 U.S. 135, 156-57 (1910) (Day, J.); Cleveland, C., C. & St. L. Ry. v. Illinois, 177 U.S. 514, 521 (1900) (Brown, J.). This is not to say that the results of these decisions were wholly consistent. *Compare* Illinois Cent. R.R. v. Illinois, 163 U.S. 142, 153-54 (1896) (state cannot require fast interstate mail train to detour seven miles from main line to serve a single county seat), *with* Lake Shore & M. S. Ry. v. Ohio, 173 U.S. 285, 300-03 (1899) (state may require six interstate trains per day to stop at *every* town with three thousand or more inhabitants), *and* Mobile, J. & K.C.R.R. v. Mississippi, 210 U.S. 187, 203 (1908) (McKenna, J.) (state may require a state-chartered railroad company to *construct* an interstate line so as to pass through a county seat).

[71] Schollenberger v. Pennsylvania, 171 U.S. 1, 14-15, 17-18 (1898) (Peckham, J.).

[72] Collins v. New Hampshire, 171 U.S. 30, 33 (1898) (Peckham, J.). These decisions suggest a ground on which *Plumley* and *Leisy* might be reconciled after all: the burden of the ban on yellow margarine was less than that of liquor sales because it did not block access to margarine entirely. *Cf.* Houston & T.C.R.R. v. Mayes, 201

The opinions of the Fuller period did not always acknowledge that the question was one of reasonableness. Justice Brewer protested in at least one concurrence that the reasonableness of a "direct" burden on interstate commerce was irrelevant.[73] An exercise of the state's police power, Justice White said on another occasion, was an impermissible regulation of commerce whenever its effect on interstate commerce was direct.[74] But the "directness" of an effect seemed to have less to do with its immediacy than with its severity. In one of the last decisions of the period, for example, reaffirming its view that the effect of a safety measure determined whether it was a forbidden regulation of commerce, the Court dismissed a challenge to a law that required trains to stop for cross-traffic, because the number of crossings had not adequately been alleged.[75] A large number of stops would have a more serious impact on commerce than a small number, but not, in any literal sense, a more direct one. In short, despite continuing efforts to cloak what was going on in more formalistic terms, the decisions themselves suggest that the Court had agreed in substance to what Justices Harlan and Brown were the most candid in revealing:[76] the test of whether a measure subjected interstate commerce to impermissible burdens was whether the effect on that commerce was unreasonable in light of the state's asserted interest.[77]

---

U.S. 321, 329-31 (1906) (Brown, J.) (acknowledging legitimate police-power purpose in assuring adequate provision of freight cars but holding that absolute requirement of furnishing cars on customers' demand was unreasonable).

[73] Cleveland, C., C. & St. L. Ry. v. Illinois, 177 U.S. 514, 523 (1900) (concurring opinion).

[74] McNeill v. Southern Ry., 202 U.S. 543, 561 (1906) (striking down a state administrative order requiring delivery of railroad cars to a private siding). Justice Peckham had a marked tendency to label the effect on commerce of any law he struck down as "direct." See, e.g., Central of Ga. Ry. v. Murphey, 196 U.S. 194, 203-04, 206 (1905) (striking down requirement that initial carrier trace freight lost by connecting road); Louisville & N.R.R. v. Eubank, 184 U.S. 27, 36 (1902) (striking down statute that prohibited railroads from charging a higher rate for short hauls than for long hauls).

[75] Southern Ry. v. King, 217 U.S. 524, 536-37 (1910) (Day, J.).

[76] See, e.g., Reid v. Colorado, 187 U.S. 137, 148, 151 (1902) (Harlan, J.); Smith v. St. Louis & S. W. Ry., 181 U.S. 248, 262-63 (1901) (Brown, J., dissenting); id. at 260 (Harlan, J., dissenting); Cleveland, C., C. & St. L. Ry. v. Illinois, 177 U.S. 514, 517-18, 522 (1900) (Brown, J.); Lake Shore & M. S. Ry. v. Ohio, 173 U.S. 285, 300 (1899) (Harlan, J.); New York, N. H. & H.R.R. v. New York, 165 U.S. 628, 631-32 (1897) (Harlan, J.).

[77] The Court also continued its effort to avoid the special disadvantage of multiple taxation. See supra note 60. Outright discrimination against interstate operations continued to be struck down in most instances. See, e.g., I. M. Darnell & Son Co. v. City of Memphis, 208 U.S. 113, 125-26 (1908) (White, J.) (property tax exempting local products); Voight v. Wright, 141 U.S. 62, 66-67 (1891) (Bradley, J.) (inspection of out-of-state flour). Indeed, on occasion the Court would look behind a measure that was nondiscriminatory on its face to find an unjustified preference for local interests. See, e.g., Brimmer v. Rebman, 138 U.S. 78, 82-84 (1891) (Harlan, J.) (inspection requirement for meat shipped over a hundred miles); Minnesota v. Barber, 136 U.S. 313, 322-23 (1890) (Harlan, J.) (ban on sale of meat not inspected within state before slaughter). Occasionally, however, the Court was unable to perceive discrimination where in fact it seemed to exist. See, e.g., Williams v. Fears, 179 U.S. 270, 278 (1900) (Fuller, C. J.) (upholding tax on agents hiring persons to work outside state); New York v. Roberts, 171 U.S. 658, 662-63 (1898) (Shiras, J.) (upholding a general corporate franchise tax that exempted corporations that carried on all of their manufacture within the state, on the irrelevant ground that an out-of-state corporation that carried on all of its manufacturing operations within the state would also be exempt). Two famous decisions, moreover, expressly upheld discrimination against interstate commerce on the shaky and unexplained ground that the commodities to be shipped out of state were owned by the people of the state. Hudson County Water Co. v. McCarter, 209 U.S. 349, 357 (1908) (Holmes, J.) (water); Geer v. Connecticut, 161 U.S. 519, 532 (1896) (White, J.) (birds), overruled, Hughes v. Oklahoma, 441 U.S. 322, 325 (1979). For a prior

This is of course the modern test.[78] It makes perfect sense in terms of the Court's long-standing perception that the clause protected the interest in unobstructed trade without denying the states all power to promote their traditional concerns. Very likely, as Justice Stone would later say,[79] the Court had really been balancing state and federal interests in commerce clause cases all along. Stone himself was to make the process far more visible than the Fuller Court had done.[80] Nevertheless, despite the bad start in *Leisy v. Hardin*, the Fuller Court moved significantly, if not always explicitly, in the right direction.

## II. DUE PROCESS AND EQUAL PROTECTION

To modern readers, perhaps the most memorable fourteenth-amendment decision of the Fuller years was Justice Brown's 1896 opinion in *Plessy v. Ferguson*[81] upholding a state law requiring "equal but separate" rail accommodations. At the same time, however, despite Justice Harlan's celebrated and impassioned dissent, the outcome should have appeared pretty well predetermined by the unanimous but oddly enough uncited 1883 decision in *Pace v. Alabama*[82]—which Harlan had joined—endorsing the same principle in the context of interracial sex relations.[83] In any event, *Plessy* was a reliable symbol of the times. The Fuller Court did little to further the fourteenth amendment's central goal of racial justice;[84] it was in the economic arena that Fuller and his brethren made fourteenth amendment history.

---

similar holding under the privileges and immunities clause, see McCready v. Virginia, 94 U.S. 391, 396-97 (1877) (state may limit right to use its oyster beds to its own citizens), THE FIRST HUNDRED YEARS at 404 n.7. The pedigree of the ownership theory was doubtful; as Field observed, dissenting in *Geer*, 161 U.S. at 539-40, many natural-law authorities of the sort cited by the majority seemed to say that wild game was owned by nobody. Moreover, the relevance of ownership to the purposes of the commerce clause was not made clear. For a thorough modern discussion, see Varat, *State "Citizenship" and Interstate Equality*, 48 U. CHI. L. REV. 487 (1981).

[78] *See, e.g.*, Pike v. Bruce Church, Inc., 397 U.S. 137, 142-45 (1970); Southern Pac. Co. v. Arizona, 325 U.S. 761, 781-82 (1945), pp. 327-28 *infra*.

[79] Di Santo v. Pennsylvania, 273 U.S. 34, 44 (1927) (dissenting opinion).

[80] Southern Pac. Co. v. Arizona, 325 U.S. 761, 781-82 (1945).

[81] 163 U.S. 537 (1896).

[82] 106 U.S. 583 (1883), THE FIRST HUNDRED YEARS at 387-90.

[83] For discussion of the relationship between *Pace* and *Plessy*, see Roche, *Civil Liberty in the Age of Enterprise*, 31 U. CHI. L. REV. 103, 112-13 (1963). The fact that *Pace*'s reasoning was not repeated in *Plessy*, taken together with Justice Brown's declaration that the fourteenth amendment had not been intended "to enforce social, as distinguished from political equality," *Plessy*, 163 U.S. at 544, led Schmidt to the interesting conclusion that *Plessy* was not based upon the "equality" of black and white accommodations at all. *See* A. BICKEL & B. SCHMIDT, *supra* note 58, at 755-56. Later in the opinion, however, "social equality" was employed in contrast to "equal rights before the law" in a context suggesting that Brown may have meant only that the state was not responsible for the practical inequality resulting from the attitudes of private citizens. 163 U.S. at 551-52.

[84] *See* Berea College v. Kentucky, 211 U.S. 45 (1908) (Brewer, J.) (ignoring an equal protection argument in upholding a statute forbidding private schools to teach blacks and whites together on the ground of the state's control over its corporations); Hodges v. United States, 203 U.S. 1 (1906) (Brown, J.) (reaffirming that private conspiracy against blacks did not come within the fourteenth amendment); Cumming v. Richmond County Bd. of Educ., 175 U.S. 528 (1899) (Harlan, J.) (refusing to enjoin spending solely for white high school while questioning whether equal protection denied); Williams v. Mississippi, 170 U.S. 213 (1898) (McKenna, J.) (refusing to find that state laws limiting jury service to literate taxpayers discriminated on racial grounds). *But see* Carter v. Texas, 177 U.S. 442 (1900) (Gray, J.) (states may not exclude blacks from grand juries); *cf.* Giles v. Teasley, 193 U.S. 146 (1904), *and* Giles v. Harris, 189 U.S. 475 (1903) (finding procedural roadblocks to damage and injunctive relief, respectively, for the alleged disfranchisement of black voters).

Two of the most significant conclusions of the Court before Fuller's appointment had been that the due process clauses imposed substantive limits on legislative power and that the equal protection clause was not restricted to racial classifications.[85] Neither of these conclusions had been adequately explained, and neither had been applied unequivocally as the Court's sole reason for invalidating government action.[86] Fuller and his brethren never made up for the failure of their predecessors to justify their debatable dicta, but they transformed both conclusions into law. Indeed it is for the aggressive invocation of substantive due process that the Fuller period is best known today. An examination of the entire body of cases, however, reveals that even in those days most laws challenged under the due process and equal protection clauses passed muster; the exceptions should not be taken to have established the rule.

## A.  Rate Regulation

In 1877, in *Munn v. Illinois*,[87] the Court over Justice Field's dissent had upheld state regulation of grain-elevator rates while implying that the regulatory power was limited to businesses "affected with a public interest."[88] A few years later the Court had warned in dicta that "confiscatory" rate regulation would deprive the owners of even such a business of property without due process of law.[89] Under Fuller the Court continued to adhere to *Munn*'s fundamental principle,[90] but for the first time it struck down several state rate provisions on due process grounds.

The story begins with the famous *Milwaukee Road* case,[91] decided only two years after Fuller's appointment. This was apparently the first case in which the Court invalidated a state law under the due process clause. The flaw the Justices perceived was a procedural

---

There were two significant thirteenth amendment cases during this time. In Robertson v. Baldwin, 165 U.S. 275, 281-83 (1897), a learned opinion by Justice Brown relied largely on history and necessity to uphold a statute forbidding desertion by merchant seamen: "[T]he amendment was not intended to introduce any novel doctrine with respect to certain descriptions of service which have always been treated as exceptional. . . ." Brown added more generally and more disturbingly that servitude pursuant to an uncoerced contract was not "involuntary." Justice Harlan dissented. The narrow definition of involuntariness espoused in *Robertson* was abandoned in Clyatt v. United States, 197 U.S. 207, 215 (1905) (Brewer, J.) (upholding a federal statute outlawing "peonage" even where a debtor had agreed to work for his creditor: "peonage, however created, is compulsory service, involuntary servitude"). For general discussion of the Fuller Court's treatment of racial issues, see A. BICKEL & B. SCHMIDT, *supra* note 58, at 751-60, 837-41, 923-27; Schmidt, *Juries, Jurisdiction, and Race Discrimination: The Lost Promise of* Strauder v. West Virginia, 61 TEX. L. REV. 1401, 1462-72 (1983).

[85] *See* THE FIRST HUNDRED YEARS, ch. 11 (discussing, inter alia, Mugler v. Kansas, 123 U.S. 623 (1887); Missouri Pac. Ry. v. Mackey, 127 U.S. 205 (1888)).

[86] For cases in which due process figured in decisions striking down federal laws, see THE FIRST HUNDRED YEARS at 271-72, 320-29 (discussing Scott v. Sandford, 60 U.S. (19 How.) 393 (1857); Hepburn v. Griswold, 75 U.S. (8 Wall.) 603 (1870)).

[87] 94 U.S. 113 (1877), THE FIRST HUNDRED YEARS at 370-73.

[88] *Munn*, 94 U.S. at 130-32.

[89] Railroad Comm'n Cases (Stone v. Farmers Loan & Trust Co.), 116 U.S. 307, 331 (1886).

[90] *See, e.g.*, Budd v. New York, 143 U.S. 517, 543 (1892) (Blatchford, J.), a wordy opinion that illustrates Justice Blatchford's practice of substituting long summaries of prior cases for analysis. Two new Justices—Brewer and Brown—joined Field in arguing *Munn* should be overruled. 143 U.S. at 548-50. *See also* Brass v. North Dakota *ex rel.* Stoeser, 153 U.S. 391, 403, 409-10 (1894) (Shiras, J.) (extending *Munn*, over four dissenters, to a case in which there was no "practical monopoly").

[91] Chicago, M. & St. P. Ry. v. Minnesota, 134 U.S. 418 (1890).

one: the statute made rates set by a commission, without hearing, conclusively reasonable in a judicial proceeding to enforce them. Precisely what was wrong with that Justice Blatchford's brief and conclusory opinion left somewhat unclear. The bulk of the argument seemed to suggest that the due process clause required that a court determine the reasonable rate:

> [The statute] deprives the company of its right to a judicial investigation, by due process of law, under the forms and with the machinery provided by the wisdom of successive ages for the investigation judicially of the truth of a matter in controversy, and substitutes therefor, as an absolute finality, the action of a railroad commission which, in view of the powers conceded to it by the state court, cannot be regarded as clothed with judicial functions or possessing the machinery of a court of justice. . . . The question of the reasonableness of a rate . . . is eminently a question for judicial investigation, requiring due process of law for its determination.[92]

Blatchford failed to identify just what the property was of which the company had been deprived, saying only that it had lost "the lawful use of its property."[93] As to why due process required a judicial investigation, he invoked only the mysterious "wisdom of successive ages"[94]—suggesting the purely historical test that had been repudiated in *Hurtado v. California*[95]—without either citation or supporting reasons. Furthermore, by explaining why the commission could not be "regarded as clothed with judicial functions" he proceeded to cast doubt on whether he really meant that due process required a court decision:

> No hearing is provided for, no summons or notice to the company before the commission has found what it is to find and declared what it is to declare, no opportunity provided for the company to introduce witnesses before the commission, in fact, nothing which has the semblance of due process of law. . . .[96]

In short, the trouble was that the rate had been conclusively determined without a hearing before *any* governmental body;[97] the case holds neither that rates must be set in the first instance by a court nor, as has sometimes been said,[98] that administrative rate-making must always be subject to judicial review.[99]

---

[92]*Id.* at 457-58.

[93]*Id.* at 458.

[94]*Id.* at 457.

[95] 110 U.S. 516, 537 (1884), THE FIRST HUNDRED YEARS at 366-68.

[96] 134 U.S. at 457.

[97]*See* Porter, *That Commerce Shall Be Free: A New Look at the Old Laissez-Faire Court*, 1976 SUP. CT. REV. 135, 148.

[98]*See, e.g.,* L. BETH, THE DEVELOPMENT OF THE AMERICAN CONSTITUTION, 1877–1917, at 179 (1971); G. GUNTHER, CASES AND MATERIALS ON CONSTITUTIONAL LAW 509 n.8 (10th ed. 1980).

[99]*See* Reetz v. Michigan, 188 U.S. 505, 507 (1903) (Brewer, J.) (allowing a state to give an administrative agency final say in medical licensing: "[W]e know of no provision in the Federal Constitution which forbids a

The right to a hearing had frequently been described as essential to due process[100] and could easily have been fitted into the *Hurtado* test of fundamental procedural fairness.[101] Even this narrow reading of the majority opinion, however, received a serious and unanswered challenge in a dissent by that honest former railroad lawyer Bradley: since the state legislature could have set rates without a hearing, why should a different rule apply to a commission?[102]

Forty years later the Court would suggest that the legislature's broad representative basis provided an adequate substitute for the safeguards of an administrative hearing.[103] When administrative action is legislative rather than judicial in character, however, the Court has nevertheless refused to require a hearing.[104] In light of the Court's reasons for this distinction, the action in *Milwaukee Road* was difficult to classify. That the rates applied only to a single railroad reduced the effectiveness of the political checks that constrain legislative rule-making; that many potential customers were affected made it impracticable to give all those interested a quasi-judicial hearing.[105] Blatchford did not go into any of this, and within six years the Court undermined the argument that might have supported him by holding that the setting of rates for a single railroad was beyond the power of the Interstate Commerce Commission because it was a legislative and not a judicial function.[106]

The best explanation of the *Milwaukee Road* decision was suggested by the dependable Miller in a brief concurring opinion.[107] What Blatchford said was "judicial" was not rate making itself but the question whether the rate set was reasonable. An unreasonably low

---

State from granting to a tribunal, whether called a court or a board of registration, the final determination of a legal question. . . . Due process is not necessarily judicial process."); Nishimura Ekiu v. United States, 142 U.S. 651, 660 (1892) (Gray, J.) (unanimously allowing Congress to dispense with judicial review of an executive determination to deny an alien entry to the United States). Other decisions of the period, indeed, tended to establish that the allocation of authority among branches of state government in general was not of federal constitutional concern. *See supra* pp. 16–17 n.63 (discussing delegation of legislative power). For an excellent discussion of the question whether the Constitution requires judicial review of *federal* administrative action, see L. JAFFE, JUDICIAL CONTROL OF ADMINISTRATIVE ACTION ch. 9 (1965).

[100] *See, e.g.,* Davidson v. New Orleans, 96 U.S. 97, 105 (1878) (dictum).

[101] *Hurtado,* 110 U.S. at 535.

[102] *Milwaukee Road,* 134 U.S. at 463-64 (Bradley, J., joined by Gray and Lamar, JJ., dissenting). Within two years, Blatchford himself wrote to uphold legislatively determined rates without justifying the distinction. Budd v. New York, 143 U.S. 517, 546-47 (1892) ("What was said in [*Milwaukee Road*] as to the question of the reasonableness of the rate of charge being one for judicial investigation, had no reference to a case where the rates are prescribed directly by the legislature.")

[103] Southern Ry. v. Virginia, 290 U.S. 190, 197 (1933) ("In theory, at least, the legislature acts upon adequate knowledge after full consideration and through members who represent the entire public.").

[104] Bi-Metallic Inv. Co. v. State Bd. of Equalization, 239 U.S. 441 (1915) (Holmes, J.) (a rule of conduct that applies to "more than a few people" need not be formulated pursuant to judicial-type hearing); *see* B. SCHWARTZ, ADMINISTRATIVE LAW §§ 5.6-5.9 (2d ed. 1984).

[105] In Bi-Metallic Inv. Co. v. State Bd. of Equalization, 239 U.S. 441, 445 (1915), Holmes emphasized the impracticability problem and the effectiveness of the political check. *See also* Anaconda Co. v. Ruckelshaus, 482 F.2d 1301, 1306-07 (10th Cir. 1973) (upholding administrative rule-making applicable to a single company, without quasi-judicial hearing).

[106] ICC v. Cincinnati, N. O. & T. Pac. Ry., 167 U.S. 479, 499, 506, 511 (1897) (Brewer, J.). Only Justice Harlan dissented.

[107] *Milwaukee Road,* 134 U.S. at 459-61 (Miller, J., concurring).

rate, the Court had already announced, would take property without due process.[108] And, said Miller, a court could not be required to enforce a legislatively determined rate without a prior judicial determination of its constitutionality.[109] This conclusion seems compelled by the supremacy clause, which requires state courts to follow the Constitution, "any Thing in the Constitution or Laws of any State to the Contrary notwithstanding";[110] for the state court to accept the commission's determination of that issue was contrary to the principle of *Marbury v. Madison*.[111]

The Court badly mangled the difficult procedural problem presented by the *Milwaukee Road* case, but it still had not struck down a state-set rate on substantive grounds.[112] It did just that in a series of decisions culminating in *Smyth v. Ames*[113] in 1898, a Harlan opinion reaffirming dicta to the effect that a rate not permitting a reasonable return on the value of railroad property was unconstitutional. It did so after a painful reexamination of the complex financial record[114] that boded ill for the future state of the docket. It did so, moreover, without serious consideration of the fundamental question whether the due process clause had anything to do with the reasonableness of rates set by the states for railroads. Substantive due process had come of age without having been properly born.

[108] Railroad Comm'n Cases (Stone v. Farmers Loan & Trust Co.), 116 U.S. 307, 331 (1886).

[109] *Milwaukee Road*, 134 U.S. at 460 (Miller, J., concurring).

[110] U. S. CONST. art. VI, cl. 2.

[111] 5 U.S. (1 Cranch) 137, 178 (1803) ("If, then, the courts are to regard the constitution; and the constitution is superior to any ordinary act of the legislature; the constitution, and not such ordinary act, must govern the case to which they both apply."); *cf.* Yakus v. United States, 321 U.S. 414, 468 (1944) (Rutledge, J., dissenting) ("whenever the judicial power is called into play, it is responsible directly to the fundamental law"); United States v. Klein, 80 U.S. (13 Wall.) 128, 146-47 (1872) (legislature may not forbid the Court "to give the effect to evidence which, in its own judgment, such evidence should have"). *See* THE FIRST HUNDRED YEARS at 308-11 (discussing *Klein*).

[112] In other due process decisions, the Fuller Court did not display a marked tendency to insist upon procedures satisfying modern notions of fair play. *See, e.g.,* Oceanic Steam Navigation Co. v. Stranahan, 214 U.S. 320, 340-43 (1909) (White, J.) (upholding statute authorizing fines to be levied, without a hearing, against companies landing illegal aliens, on the ground that Congress had "absolute power . . . over the right to bring aliens into the United States"); Patterson v. Colorado, 205 U.S. 454, 463 (1907) (Holmes, J.) (allowing judge to try defendant for impugning judge's own honesty through articles and cartoons); Ballard v. Hunter, 204 U.S. 241, 260 (1907) (McKenna, J.) (upholding service of process by publication on a nonresident landowner); Felts v. Murphy, 201 U.S. 123, 129-30 (1906) (Peckham, J.) (holding it permissible to try a deaf person for a crime without repeating testimony into his ear trumpet); Fong Yue Ting v. United States, 149 U.S. 698, 729-30 (1893) (Gray, J.) (upholding a statute placing the burden on a Chinese alien to show he was not deportable and disqualifying Chinese witnesses on the ground that Congress had detected a problem of false testimony among Chinese). The Court had not yet adopted fairness as the test of due process, but neither did it say that all of the above procedures were sanctioned by history. *But see Ex parte* Young, 209 U.S. 123, 145-48 (1908) (Peckham, J.) (holding that the necessity to risk prohibitive penalties in order to test the validity of a rate regulation was the equivalent of denying a hearing entirely); *see also* Lawton v. Steele, 152 U.S. 133 (1894) (Brown, J.), and North Am. Cold Storage Co. v. City of Chicago, 211 U.S. 306 (1908) (Peckham, J.) (upholding, respectively, the seizure of illegal fish nets and the destruction of spoiled foods without prior hearings, relying in the first case on history, in the second on precedent, and in both on necessity, and making clear in both that the owner was entitled to a hearing in a subsequent tort suit against the offending officer).

[113] 169 U.S. 466 (1898). *Smyth* had been preceded by Reagan v. Farmers' Loan & Trust Co., 154 U.S. 362, 397-99 (1894) (Brewer, J.), a diversity case in which the precise source of the law applied was not clarified and in which due process was mentioned only in a quotation from an earlier case, and by Covington & Lexington Turnpike Rd. Co. v. Sandford, 164 U.S. 578, 591-92 (1896) (Harlan, J.), which held it error to dismiss a complaint alleging that rates had been set below costs, and which explicitly invoked due process.

[114] *Smyth*, 169 U.S. at 528-50.

## B.  *Allgeyer v. Louisiana*

The year before *Smyth,* in 1897, the Court had unanimously taken another long step toward giving the due process clause a substantive dimension and had given the term "liberty" in that clause a broad construction in the bargain.[115] The suit was brought by Louisiana to collect a penalty for violation of a statute that prohibited acts within the state to insure property located there through "any marine insurance company which has not complied in all respects with the laws of this State."[116] The act in question was the mailing of a notice advising a New York insurer of a shipment of cotton from New Orleans to be insured pursuant to an existing contract.[117] The opinion consisted of a pair of bare conclusions by Justice Peckham, a newcomer who was to make quite a name for himself in this field. The result was that the state law could not constitutionally be applied.

Peckham first concluded, solely on the basis of prior conclusory dicta, that freedom to give notice under an insurance policy was within the "liberty" protected by the fourteenth amendment:

> The liberty mentioned in that amendment means not only the right of the citizen to be free from the mere physical restraint of his person, as by incarceration, but the term is deemed to embrace the right of the citizen to be free in the enjoyment of all his faculties; to be free to use them in all lawful ways; to live and work where he will; to earn his livelihood by any lawful calling; to pursue any livelihood or avocation, and for that purpose to enter into all contracts which may be proper, necessary and essential to his carrying out to a successful conclusion the purposes above mentioned.[118]

This, of course, is not what was provided in Magna Charta, from which the due process clause had been derived,[119] but Peckham did not pause to justify his momentous and latitudinous interpretation; and thus liberty of contract found its way into the Constitution by bald fiat.[120]

On the question whether the Louisiana statute afforded "due process of law" in depriving the defendants of that liberty, Peckham did no better:

> Such a statute as this in question is not due process of law, because it prohibits an act which under the Federal Constitution the defendants had a right to per-

---

[115] Allgeyer v. Louisiana, 165 U.S. 578 (1897).

[116] *Id.* at 579.

[117] *Id.*

[118] *Id.* at 589.

[119] *See* 2 E. Coke, Institutes 50-55 (London 1642) (discussing the derivation of the term "due process" from Magna Charta); Hand, *Due Process of Law and the Eight-Hour Day,* 21 Harv. L. Rev. 495, 495 (1908) (to construe the term "liberty" to include liberty of contract is "to disregard the whole juristic history of the word"); Shattuck, *The True Meaning of the Term "Liberty" in Those Clauses of the Federal and State Constitutions Which Protect "Life, Liberty, and Property,"* 4 Harv. L. Rev. 365, 372-73 (1891) ("liberty" in Magna Charta referred only to freedom from imprisonment.).

[120] Contrast the Court's almost contemporaneous decision that a public office was not "property" within the due process clause. Taylor v. Beckham, 178 U.S. 548, 576-77 (1900) (Fuller, C. J.) (relying on contract clause precedents).

form. . . . [A]lthough it may be conceded that this right to contract in relation
to persons or property or to do business within the jurisdiction of the State
may be regulated and sometimes prohibited when the contracts or business
conflict with the policy of the State as contained in its statutes, yet the power
does not and cannot extend to prohibiting a citizen from making contracts of
the nature involved in this case outside of the limits and jurisdiction of the
State, and which are also to be performed outside of such jurisdiction; nor can
the State legally prohibit its citizens from doing such an act as writing this
letter of notification, even though the property which is the subject of the
insurance may at the time when such insurance attaches be within the limits
of the State.[121]

One searches the opinion in vain for either reasons or authority in support of this edict.
It is clear enough that what moved the Court was what it perceived as the extraterritorial
application of state law and not the substance of the law itself.[122] Apparently the
due process clause had become the constitutional peg on which to hang Justice Story's
territorialist choice-of-law views,[123] which had occasionally crept into pre-fourteenth-
amendment constitutional decisions without any pretense of textual pedigree.[124] Unfortunately the Court did not say why a theory that limited states to the regulation of acts within
their borders forbade Louisiana to attach consequences to the mailing of a letter from New
Orleans.[125] More important, Peckham never bothered to explain why he thought the due
process clause had anything to do with territorial theory or with choice of law in general.[126]

[121]*Allgeyer,* 165 U.S. at 591-92. The first sentence of this passage is circular, since the due process clause
itself was the only provision invoked as the source of the constitutional right to contract.

[122]In addition to the reservation in the quoted passage *see id.* at 586-88 (distinguishing Hooper v. California,
155 U.S. 648 (1895), in which the Court had upheld a similar law as applied to contracts made within the state).

[123]*See generally* J. STORY, CONFLICT OF LAWS (Boston 1834).

[124]*See, e.g.,* Wilkinson v. Leland, 27 U.S. (2 Pet.) 627, 654-55 (1829) (Story, J.) ("The legislative and
judicial authority of New Hampshire were bounded by the territory of that state, and could not be rightfully
exercised to pass estates lying in another state.").

[125]All that Peckham said was that the mailing of the notice was "collateral" to the contract. *Allgeyer,* 165 U.S.
at 592.

[126]*Allgeyer's* territorial thesis was appropriately invoked, though without citation of the case itself, in explaining the Fuller Court's related principle that due process forbade extraterritorial taxation as well. *See* Union
Refrigerator Transit Co. v. Kentucky, 199 U.S. 194, 204 (1905) (Brown, J.) ("Not only is the operation of state
laws limited to persons and property within the boundaries of the State, but property which is wholly and exclusively within the jurisdiction of another State, receives none of the protection for which the tax is supposed to be
the compensation."). For the latter reason, such a tax was also held to be an uncompensated taking of property.
*Id.* at 202-03. From the standpoint of territorial theory, it is interesting that the Court in *Union Refrigerator*
focused exclusively on the situs of the property, relying in part upon the risk of multiple taxation, in spite of the
fact that the taxpayer was a domestic corporation. *Id.* at 210-11. Justice Holmes's dissent seems, after *Allgeyer,*
to have come too late: "It seems to me that the result reached by the court probably is a desirable one, but I hardly
understand how it can be deduced from the Fourteenth Amendment. . . ." *Union Refrigerator,* 199 U.S. at 211
(Holmes, J., dissenting).

Also of lasting significance was the split decision in Western Union Tel. Co. v. Kansas *ex rel.* Coleman, 216
U.S. 1, 34-38 (1910) (Harlan, J.), which held on the authority of cases respecting surrender of the right to remove
cases to federal court, *e.g.,* Insurance Co. v. Morse, 87 U.S. (20 Wall.) 445 (1874), that a state had no power to
condition the right to do local business on the payment of an extraterritorial tax. Justice Holmes again dissented,
invoking contrary authority and arguing that the company had made a voluntary agreement. *Western Union,* 216

The Court might have made a plausible case by analogy to *Pennoyer v. Neff*,[127] which had said that due process of law incorporated traditional territorial limits on service of process.[128] It might also have made something of the relation between due process and Magna Charta's "law of the land" provision, the text and purpose of which arguably required that cases be decided according to the law applicable at the time and place of the transaction.[129] The point is not that *Allgeyer* was obviously wrong, but that Peckham made not the slightest effort to justify his pathbreaking and by no means inevitable conclusions.[130]

## C.  *Lochner v. New York*

In any event, *Allgeyer* was a choice-of-law decision, not strictly speaking a substantive one. In a series of decisions during the ensuing eight years the Court emphasized the distinction by upholding a great variety of state and federal laws despite the argument that they unduly restricted the newly minted liberty of contract: limitations on the hours to be worked by miners[131] and by employees of public contractors,[132] prohibitions of various contracts in restraint of trade,[133] of charging more for shorter than for longer rail jour-

---

U.S. at 52-56; *cf.* THE FIRST HUNDRED YEARS at 443-44 (discussing the issue of unconstitutional conditions on public employment and Holmes's own famous remark, in McAuliffe v. Mayor of New Bedford, 155 Mass. 216, 220, 29 N. E. 517, 517 (1892), that there was "no constitutional right to be a policeman."); G. HENDERSON, THE POSITION OF FOREIGN CORPORATIONS IN AMERICAN CONSTITUTIONAL LAW 132-47 (1918).

[127] 95 U.S. 714, 733-34 (1878) (dictum), THE FIRST HUNDRED YEARS at 365-66.

[128] The force of this argument, however, had been impaired by rejection of a strict historical test of due process in Hurtado v. California, 110 U.S. 516 (1884), THE FIRST HUNDRED YEARS at 366-68. Dewey v. Des Moines, 173 U.S. 193 (1899) (Peckham, J.), provides an interesting bridge connecting later tax cases like Western Union Tel. Co. v. Kansas ex rel. Coleman, supra note 126, with the established principle that due process restricted the application of judicial power to persons within the state. In *Dewey,* the Court struck down the personal assessment of taxes against a nonresident landowner, citing *Pennoyer* to invalidate the assessment "judgment" and generalizing that "jurisdiction to tax exists only in regard to persons and property or upon the business done within the State." *Dewey,* 173 U.S. at 203.

[129] Both of Peckham's conclusions in *Allgeyer* had been anticipated by the dissenting Justices in Hooper v. California, 155 U.S. 648, 661-63 (1895) (Harlan, J., joined by Brewer and Jackson, JJ., dissenting). These dissenters gave no reason for their conclusions either. For an effort to explain the result in *Allgeyer* in terms of modern governmental-interest analysis while rejecting its "conceptualism," see B. CURRIE, SELECTED ESSAYS ON THE CONFLICT OF LAWS 241-42 (1963).

[130] For the Court's indifference to the plausible argument that due process required application of the law governing at the *time* of the transaction, see United States v. Heinszen & Co., 206 U.S. 370 (1907) (White, J.) (allowing Congress retroactively to ratify a tariff that the President had imposed without authority). Similar considerations of protecting legitimate expectations argue against both extraterritoriality and retroactivity, but to hold that due process barred all retroactive laws would make the ex post facto clause of article I, § 9 redundant. For the argument that, prior to ratification of the fourteenth amendment, state decisions had established that due process limited retroactivity but not extraterritoriality, see Whitten, *The Constitutional Limitations on State Choice of Law: Due Process,* 9 HASTINGS CONST. L. Q. 851, 902-04 (1982). On the ex post facto clauses themselves, see the Court's grisly inquiry into whether a statute that retroactively lengthened the period of imprisonment prior to hanging increased or decreased the punishment in Rooney v. North Dakota, 196 U.S. 319, 325 (1905) (Harlan, J.) (upholding the law).

[131] Holden v. Hardy, 169 U.S. 366 (1898) (Brown, J.).

[132] Atkin v. Kansas, 191 U.S. 207 (1903) (Harlan, J.).

[133] Smiley v. Kansas, 196 U.S. 447, 456-57 (1905) (Brewer, J.) (contract in restraint of trade); Aikens v. Wisconsin, 195 U.S. 194, 204-06 (1904) (Holmes, J.) (conspiracy to injure business maliciously); Addyston Pipe & Steel Co. v. United States, 175 U.S. 211, 228-29 (1899) (Peckham, J.) (market division); United States v. Joint Traffic Ass'n, 171 U.S. 505, 572-73 (1898) (Peckham, J.) (conspiracy to fix rail rates).

neys,[134] of speculation in grain futures[135] and of margin sales,[136] and of paying sailors wages in advance of service.[137] A few relatively trivial state actions, to be sure, were struck down on what were unmistakably substantive due process grounds.[138] As late as 1905, however, that doctrine seemed to pose no great threat to state or federal legislation.[139] Then the Court decided *Lochner v. New York.*[140]

Once again it was Peckham who wrote, reversing Lochner's conviction under a statute that prohibited employing a baker for more than sixty hours in one week. The statute failed as a health measure because the baking trade was not sufficiently unhealthy to justify regulation[141] and as "a purely labor law" because there was "no contention that bakers as a class are not equal in intelligence and capacity to men in other trades . . . or . . . not able to assert their rights and care for themselves."[142]

In light of the precedents it was not surprising that four Justices dissented. Holmes called attention to the decisions sustaining the eight-hour workday for miners and the ban on margin sales, in both of which, as in the ancient example of usury laws, individuals had been protected against the risk of their own improvidence.[143] Harlan, joined by White and Day, graphically demolished the Court's unsubstantiated conclusion on the health

---

[134] Louisville & N.R.R. v. Kentucky, 183 U.S. 503, 510-16 (1902) (Shiras, J.).

[135] Booth v. Illinois, 184 U.S. 425, 430-31 (1902) (Harlan, J.).

[136] Otis v. Parker, 187 U.S. 606, 609-10 (1903) (Holmes, J.).

[137] Patterson v. The Bark Eudora, 190 U.S. 169, 174-75 (1903) (Brewer, J.). The Court had similarly allowed significant restrictions of *property* rights by substantive legislation. *See, e.g.,* St. Louis Consol. Coal Co. v. Illinois, 185 U.S. 203, 207, 209-11 (1902) (Brown, J.) (state may inspect mine at owner's cost); Ohio Oil Co. v. Indiana, 177 U.S. 190, 210-11 (1900) (White, J.) (upholding criminal penalty imposed on owners of gas wells for wasting gas); *cf.* Jacobson v. Massachusetts, 197 U.S. 11, 31 (1905) (Harlan, J.) (upholding compulsory vaccination).

[138] Dobbins v. Los Angeles, 195 U.S. 223, 239-40 (1904) (Day, J.) (invalidating prohibition without reason of gas works authorized by permit); Lake Shore & M. S. Ry. v. Smith, 173 U.S. 684, 698-99 (1899) (Peckham, J.) (invalidating requirement that railroad sell thousand-mile ticket at cut rate); Missouri Pac. Ry. v. Nebraska, 164 U.S. 403, 417 (1896) (Gray, J.) (invalidating order allowing others to build grain elevator on railroad property: "The taking . . . of the private property of one person . . . for the private use of another, is not due process of law. . . ."); *see also supra* p. 44 (discussing the rate cases); *cf.* Norwood v. Baker, 172 U.S. 269 (1898) (Harlan, J.) (invalidating as an uncompensated taking a special assessment not apportioned to benefits, after the Court had held that the due process clause made the taking clause applicable to the states.).

[139] For a survey of pre-*Lochner* state decisions upholding regulations, see Seager, *The Attitude of American Courts towards Restrictive Labor Laws,* 19 POL. SCI. Q. 589 (1904). In Barney v. City of New York, 193 U.S. 430, 437-41 (1904) (Fuller, C. J.), the Court had cut back sharply on the protection afforded by due process by holding, contrary to the thrust of the jury cases of the 1880s, *see* THE FIRST HUNDRED YEARS at 385-87 (discussing Virginia v. Rives, 100 U.S. 313, 318 (1880) (dictum); *Ex parte* Virginia, 100 U.S. 339, 347 (1880)), that action of a state officer unauthorized by state law was not state action for purposes of the fourteenth amendment. *See also* the peculiar and unexplained holdings in Northwestern Nat'l Life Ins. Co. v. Riggs, 203 U.S. 243, 255 (1906) (Harlan, J.), and Western Turf Ass'n v. Greenberg, 204 U.S. 359, 363 (1907) (Harlan, J.), that, although a corporation had long been held a "person" within the fourteenth amendment, it had no "liberty" protected by the due process clause.

[140] 198 U.S. 45 (1905).

[141] *Id.* at 59.

[142] *Id.* at 57. Peckham and Brewer had dissented from Holden v. Hardy, 169 U.S. 366 (1898), where a similar law for miners had been upheld. For an example of contemporaneous approval of *Lochner,* see 21 CENT. L. J. 402, 403 (1905) ("The Supreme Court . . . in exalting the individual's right of contract has once more, indeed, justified its right to be called the great 'bulwark of the liberties of the people.'").

[143] *Lochner,* 198 U.S. at 75. Holmes cited Otis v. Parker, 187 U.S. 606 (1903) (margin sales), and Holden v. Hardy, 169 U.S. 366 (1898) (eight-hour day for miners), and added the famous aphorism, "The Fourteenth

question by documenting the dangers of constant physical exertion under exposure to extreme heat and flour dust and by reporting flatly that bakers " 'seldom live over their fiftieth year.' "[144]

The Court made only the most perfunctory attempt to deal with precedent,[145] and it was obvious that it was applying a far stricter level of scrutiny than it had applied in previous cases.[146] To quibble over the result of the particular case, however, is to miss the main point. Harlan himself had contributed as much as anyone else to the rise of substantive due process with his 1887 opinion upholding a state liquor law only because it was a reasonable exercise of the police power.[147] Once it had been established in dictum that unreasonable laws would offend due process, it was only a matter of opinion which laws were unreasonable.

Thus although on its facts *Lochner* was a notable break with precedent, in the larger sense it was the predictable outgrowth of a long and consistent development. By the time the case was decided nobody argued that due process was not a limitation on the legislature, that it related only to procedure, or that it applied only to punishment for crime.[148] All the Justices agreed that the Constitution made the Court what Miller had so vehemently denied in *Davidson v. New Orleans*[149]—censor of the reasonableness of all laws.[150] They did so, moreover, without ever justifying their improbable conclusion.

It is important to emphasize that *Lochner* did not usher in a reign of terror for social

---

Amendment does not enact Mr. Herbert Spencer's Social Statics." Other precedents allowing similar protection from one's own freedom of contract outside the area of health or safety included Louisville & N.R.R. v. Kentucky, 183 U.S. 503, 510-16 (1902) (upholding prohibition of higher shipping rates for short than for long hauls), and Patterson v. The Bark Eudora, 190 U.S. 169, 174-75 (1903) (upholding prohibition of prepayment of sailors' wages). Peckham attempted to distinguish neither these cases nor *Otis*.

[144] *Lochner*, 198 U.S. at 70-71 (quoting from a study of workers' diseases); *see* Hand, *supra* note 119, at 502 ("It seems very strange that a court should have decided that the limit of eight hours had in fact no such relation" to health.).

[145] Holden v. Hardy, 169 U.S. 366 (1898), which had upheld an eight-hour day for miners, was distinguished on the grounds that the New York law had no emergency provision—an objection Lochner should have lacked standing to raise since he alleged no emergency defense—and that *Holden* had decided only that the nature of mining was such as to make regulation appropriate. Peckham did not say why; presumably he meant mining was more dangerous than baking. Atkin v. Kansas, 191 U.S. 207 (1903), which upheld an eight-hour day for those employed by or on behalf of the state, was distinguished on the conclusory ground that the state had the right to declare the conditions of work done under public contracts. *Lochner*, 198 U.S. at 54-55.

[146] *See* Cushman, *The Social and Economic Interpretation of the Fourteenth Amendment*, 20 MICH. L. REV. 737, 749 (1922) (saying of the decisions of the *Lochner* period, "The time-honored doctrine that laws are presumed to be valid until proved beyond all reasonable doubt to be otherwise seemed to be forgotten or ignored."); Dodd, *The Growth of Judicial Power*, 24 POL. SCI. Q. 193, 194 (1909) (presumption of constitutionality, after *Lochner*, "a mere courteous and smoothly transmitted platitude"). *Compare Lochner* with, *e.g.*, Powell v. Pennsylvania, 127 U.S. 678 (1888) (Harlan, J.) (accepting a flimsy health justification in upholding a ban on the sale of margarine), THE FIRST HUNDRED YEARS at 377-78.

[147] Mugler v. Kansas, 123 U.S. 623 (1887), THE FIRST HUNDRED YEARS at 375-77; *see also* L. BETH, THE DEVELOPMENT OF THE AMERICAN CONSTITUTION, 1877-1917, at 178 (1971) ("after Mugler the Court had accepted the whole concept of substantive due process"). Harlan had also written *Smyth v. Ames*, which struck down railroad rates on substantive due process grounds. *See supra* notes 113-14 and accompanying text.

[148] There were powerful arguments for each of these positions. *See* THE FIRST HUNDRED YEARS at 272, 328, 374 n.63.

[149] 96 U.S. 97, 104-05 (1878), THE FIRST HUNDRED YEARS at 373-75.

[150] *See* Corwin, *The Supreme Court and the Fourteenth Amendment*, 7 MICH. L. REV. 643, 670-71 (1909).

legislation. Apart from Harlan's own conclusion in *Adair v. United States*[151] that a state could not forbid the discharge of an employee for belonging to a union, the Court not only continued to uphold most challenged regulations[152] but went so far as to sustain a maximum-hour law for women in *Muller v. Oregon.*[153] Substantive due process had finally shown that it had teeth,[154] but two serious bites in twenty years should not obscure the fact that most laws passing through its den during the Fuller period did not get bitten at all.[155]

## D.  Suing State Officers

*Lochner* itself reached the Supreme Court on review of a state criminal conviction. To test the constitutionality of a law by violating it, however, is a risky business, rightly com-

[151] 208 U.S. 161, 172-76 (1908) (alternative holding). McKenna and Holmes dissented. The majority opinion contains no reasoning worth mentioning. *Adair*'s alternative commerce-clause holding is discussed *supra* p. 27.

[152] For comments challenging the "laissez-faire" characterization of the Fuller Court, see Dodd, *Social Legislation and the Courts*, 28 POL. SCI. Q. 1, 5 (1913); Porter, *supra* note 97, at 140-41; Warren, *The Progressiveness of the United States Supreme Court*, 13 COLUM. L. REV. 294 (1913). For a statistical summary of the Court's work in this area, see 1 C. WARREN, *supra* note 33, at 741-42. Numbers, of course, do not tell the whole story: "a single decision may decide the fate of many measures." F. FRANKFURTER, MR. JUSTICE HOLMES AND THE SUPREME COURT 106 (1961). Numerous state-court invalidations of social legislation before and after *Lochner* are discussed and criticized in Pound, *Liberty of Contract*, 18 YALE L.J. 454, 462-84 (1909); *see also* Dodd, *supra*, at 16 (Supreme Court "has on the whole been more liberal than the state courts in dealing with new social and industrial legislation").

[153] 208 U.S. 412, 421 (1908) (Brewer, J.) (relying on the "disadvantage" at which "woman's physical structure and . . . maternal functions place her" and the importance of healthy mothers "to preserve the strength and vigor of the race"). This was the case in which the original "Brandeis brief" was filed. Encouraged perhaps by Harlan's use of medical treatises in *Lochner*, it figured prominently in the Court's opinion. *See Muller*, 208 U.S. at 419.

[154] The equal protection clause was more sparingly used. Most attacks on economic classifications were dismissed perfunctorily with, at most, a reference to the reasonableness of the classification. The rare exceptions striking down such laws merely illustrated the capriciousness of the Court's criteria. *Compare* Gulf, C. & S. F. Ry. v. Ellis, 165 U.S. 150 (1897) (Brewer, J.) (state may not impose attorney fees only upon railroads in actions for livestock losses), *with* Atchison, T. & S. F. Ry. v. Matthews, 174 U.S. 96 (1899) (Brewer, J.) (state may impose attorney fees only upon railroads in actions for fires); *compare* Cotting v. Kansas City Stock Yards Co., 183 U.S. 79 (1901) (Brewer, J.) (state may not limit rate regulation to larger stockyards), *with* St. Louis Consol. Coal Co. v. Illinois, 185 U.S. 203 (1902) (Brown, J.) (state may limit inspection to mines employing more than five workers); *compare* Connolly v. Union Sewer Pipe Co., 184 U.S. 540 (1902) (Harlan, J.) (state may not exempt agricultural producers from its antitrust law), *with* Tullis v. Lake Erie & W.R.R., 175 U.S. 348 (1899) (Fuller, C. J.) (state may abolish fellow-servant rule for railroads only). Of over one hundred cases attacking nonracial classifications during the Fuller period, *Ellis, Cotting,* and *Connolly* are virtually the only ones in which a denial of equal protection was found. For the argument that these cases "roughly tracked" the simultaneous development of substantive due process, see Kay, *The Equal Protection Clause in the Supreme Court, 1873-1903*, 29 BUFFALO L. REV. 667, 668 (1980).

[155] One of the most interesting cases not yet mentioned was Sentell v. New Orleans & C.R.R., 166 U.S. 698 (1897) (Brown J.), in which the Court upheld a law that denied a tort remedy against those who killed unlicensed dogs, on the strange ground that dogs, unlike cattle, were not really property. The Court thus seemed to imply that the due process clause imposed an affirmative duty on the state to protect anything that *was* really property. This is an idea of freedom that has made much headway in West German constitutional law but has been basically rejected in our own. *Compare, e.g.,* 39 BVerfG 1 (1975) (interpreting a provision guaranteeing "the right to life"

pared by a later observer to determining whether a mushroom is poisonous by eating it.[156] If substantive due process was to be given full scope, a more adequate remedy had to be found. Brushing aside the maxim that equity would not enjoin criminal proceedings[157] as inapplicable in cases of irreparable harm, the Court found the solution by allowing suits to enjoin government officers from enforcing unconstitutional laws.[158]

The constitutional obstacle to this course was sovereign immunity, embodied in part in the eleventh amendment and, as we have seen, found by the Fuller Court in *Hans v. Louisiana*[159] to be implicit in article III as well.[160] Ever since Marshall, the Court had held these limitations inapplicable to suits against state or federal officers whose actions were such as to make them personally liable for harm.[161] But a series of contract clause decisions in the Waite years had made it clear that an officer could not be sued unless he personally had committed a wrong, and *In re Ayers* had squarely held that the mere filing of suit on an unconstitutional claim was not wrongful.[162]

*Ayers* had been decided in 1887. Within seven years, in *Reagan v. Farmers' Loan & Trust Co.*,[163] the Court began to ignore it.[164] Affirming an injunction against proceedings to enforce rates set by a railroad commission, Justice Brewer argued that the suit was no more against the state than a suit "restraining the collection of taxes,"[165] without acknowledging that *Ayers* had been just such a suit. He reduced the force of this conclusion by

---

as against the state to require that abortion be made in most instances a crime), *with* DeShaney v. Department of Social Services, 109 S. Ct. 998 (1989) (state has no duty to protect child against violent parent).

[156] *See Declaratory Judgments: Hearings on H.R. 5623 before a Subcomm. of the Senate Comm. on the Judiciary*, 70th Cong., 1st Sess. 75 (1928) (statement of Prof. Borchard).

[157] *See, e.g., In re* Sawyer, 124 U.S. 200, 209-11 (1888) (Gray, J.).

[158] *See, e.g., Ex parte* Young, 209 U.S. 123, 161-65 (1908); Smyth v. Ames, 169 U.S. 466, 515-19 (1898). The right to an injunction was significant also because the seventh amendment seemed to preclude de novo reexamination of a jury finding that a prescribed rate was reasonable. *Cf.* Chicago, B. & Q.R.R. v. Chicago, 166 U.S. 226, 242-46 (1897) (Harlan, J.) (jury finding that compensation for taking under eminent domain power was "just" cannot be reexamined on appeal).

[159] 134 U.S. 1 (1890).

[160] *See supra* pp. 7-9.

[161] *See, e.g.,* Osborn v. Bank of United States, 22 U.S. (9 Wheat.) 738 (1824); United States v. Lee, 106 U.S. 196 (1882); Poindexter v. Greenhow, 114 U.S. 270 (1885).

[162] 123 U.S. 443, 504-06 (1887). For discussion of this and earlier cases, see THE FIRST HUNDRED YEARS at 104-07, 416-28.

[163] 154 U.S. 362 (1894).

[164] Indeed, as early as 1891, in reaffirming the governing principle that officers could be sued if they "commit acts of wrong and injury to the rights and property of the plaintiff," the Court unanimously twisted it by upholding an injunction against an officer who was about to sell land that had already been contracted to someone else. Pennoyer v. McConnaughy, 140 U.S. 1 (1891) (Lamar, J.). The ground given was that the officer's acts were "violative of [the plaintiff's] contract," *id.* at 18, though *Ayers* had made clear that an officer could not be liable for breach of the state's contract, to which he was not a party. The result can be reconciled with *Ayers* on the ground that the officer had committed a tort by interfering with the plaintiff's equitable title to the land. *See* THE FIRST HUNDRED YEARS at 353 (discussing the similar case of Davis v. Gray, 83 U.S. (16 Wall.) 203 (1873)).

[165] *Reagan*, 154 U.S. at 390. Brewer added, rightly enough in light of the underlying theory, that it was immaterial whether the statute setting up the commission was constitutional: if the commissioners "go beyond the powers thereby conferred, . . . the fact that they are assuming to act under a valid law will not oust the courts of jurisdiction to restrain their excessive and illegal acts." *Id.* at 391; *see also* Scully v. Bird, 209 U.S. 481, 490 (1908) (McKenna, J.) (allowing an injunction against a state officer in a diversity case, with no mention of any

adding that the state had waived its immunity.[166] Without even citing *Reagan,* however, Justice Harlan followed its broader assertion in the similar 1898 case of *Smyth v. Ames.*[167] With one notable exception,[168] later decisions of the Fuller period continued to follow this line without recognizing its inconsistency with *Ayers,*[169] until the textbook 1908 case of *Ex parte Young.*[170]

*Young* was yet another suit to enjoin a state officer from enforcing allegedly confiscatory rate provisions. This time, in a long and lonely dissent,[171] Justice Harlan rediscovered *In re Ayers.* It was, of course, too late. Harlan had never protested while the Court repeatedly disregarded that decision, and he had written the contrary opinion in *Smyth v. Ames* himself.[172] Forced to justify a position that in time-hallowed fashion he refused to concede was new,[173] Justice Peckham acknowledged that the officer could be sued only if personally liable, but asserted without explanation that the threat of suit under an unconstitutional statute was "equivalent to any other threatened wrong or injury to the property of a plaintiff."[174] The new rule was that officers clothed with enforcement duties "who threaten

---

constitutional claim, on the ground that the officer had acted "in dereliction of duties enjoined by the statutes of the State").

[166] *Reagan,* 154 U.S. at 391-92. Brewer relied on a statute authorizing suit against the commission "in a court of competent jurisdiction in Travis County, Texas," which the Court construed to embrace federal as well as state courts. Later cases would require more explicit consent to be sued in federal courts. *See, e.g.,* Kennecott Copper Corp. v. State Tax Comm'n, 327 US. 573, 577 (1946).

[167] 169 U.S. 466 (1898). Saying only that it was "settled doctrine . . . that a suit against individuals for the purpose of preventing them as officers of a State from enforcing an unconstitutional enactment to the injury of the rights of the plaintiff, is not a suit against the State," *id.* at 518-19, Harlan slid right over the clear distinction drawn in the contract clause cases between seizure of the plaintiff's property, which was a tort, and suit against the plaintiff, which was not.

[168] Fitts v. McGhee, 172 U.S. 516, 525-29 (1899) (Harlan, J.) (following *Ayers*); *see also* Smith v. Reeves, 178 U.S. 436, 445 (1900) (Harlan, J.) (holding suit for a refund from state treasury to be a suit against state because it sought "to compel an officer . . . to perform or comply with the promise of the State").

[169] *See e.g.,* McNeill v. Southern Ry., 202 U.S. 543, 559 (1906) (White, J.); Prout v. Starr, 188 U.S. 537, 542-43 (1903) (Shiras, J.). At the same time, in Belknap v. Schild, 161 U.S. 10, 25 (1896) (Gray, J.), the Court seemed inconsistently to cut back on prior decisions *permitting* officers to be sued by holding that the United States was an indispensable party to a suit to enjoin federal officers from using government property in infringement of a patent, though the Court conceded that the officers could be held personally liable for damages.

[170] 209 U.S. 123 (1908).

[171] *Id.* at 168-204.

[172] He had also dissented in *Ayers,* 123 U.S. at 510.

[173] *Ayers* was distinguished, without revealing its facts or reasoning, on the basis of the misleading half-truth that the relief sought there would have "constitute[d] a performance by the State of the alleged contract of the State," 209 U.S. at 151. This had been equally true in Poindexter v. Greenhow, 114 U.S. 270, 279-80 (1885), where suit had nevertheless been allowed; the true difference was that the seizure of the plaintiff's property in *Poindexter* was a tort and the threatened suit in *Ayers* was not. Fitts v. McGhee, 172 U.S. 516 (1899), the one later decision that followed *Ayers*'s reasoning, was distinguished on the basis of unfortunate language in the *Fitts* opinion that seemed unnecessarily to rest the decision on the fact that the officer sued had no particular duties under the challenged statute. *Young,* 209 U.S. at 156-58; *see* C. WRIGHT, LAW OF FEDERAL COURTS 288 (4th ed. 1983) (*Ayers* "would seem to be decisive of the Young litigation").

[174] 209 U.S. at 158; *see also id.* at 160 ("It would be an injury to complainant to harass it with a multiplicity of suits or litigation generally in an endeavor to enforce penalties under an unconstitutional enactment. . . ."). But even today only *malicious* prosecutions are actionable, and at the time of *Young* the tort had apparently not

and are about to commence proceedings . . . to enforce . . . an unconstitutional act . . . may be enjoined by a Federal court of equity."[175]

The parties in *Young* were not of diverse citizenship; jurisdiction was based on the theory that the case was one arising under the Constitution.[176] To modern eyes this theory seems obviously correct, since the complaint alleged that the defendant threatened to deprive the plaintiff of property without due process of law. In explaining why the suit was not one against the state, however, the court enunciated a thesis wholly inconsistent with this approach:

> If the act which the state Attorney General seeks to enforce be a violation of the Federal Constitution, the officer in proceeding under such enactment comes into conflict with the superior authority of that Constitution, and he is in that case stripped of his official or representative character and is subjected in his person to the consequences of his individual conduct.[177]

If the officer was "stripped of his official . . . character," he could not violate the due process clause, which applies only to state action.[178] Peckham did not attempt to justify this contradiction.[179] The alternative argument that the fourteenth amendment was relevant only to defeat the defense of official authority[180] would have been insufficient to sustain federal jurisdiction under the rule of *Louisville & Nashville Railway v. Mottley*,[181] which held that the federal nature of the case must appear from the plaintiff's statement of his own claim.[182]

Thus Peckham bungled the jurisdictional questions in *Ex parte Young* as badly as he had the more substantive issues in *Allgeyer* and in *Lochner,* and significant new doctrine was established without explanation. And thus the economic decisions of the Fuller Court ended as they had begun, with a ground-breaking pronouncement on the ancillary question of sovereign immunity. As *Hans* had gone beyond the eleventh amendment to help

---

been extended to civil cases at all. *See* W. KEETON, D. DOBBS, R. KEETON & D. OWEN, PROSSER AND KEETON ON THE LAW OF TORTS § 120, at 889-92 (5th ed. 1984) (collecting cases).

[175] 209 U.S. at 156. For the hostile reaction to *Young,* see 2 C. WARREN, *supra* note 33, at 717.

[176] 209 U.S. at 143-45.

[177] *Id.* at 159-60.

[178] The Civil Rights Cases, 109 U.S. 3, 11 (1883), THE FIRST HUNDRED YEARS at 398-402. *See* C. WRIGHT, *supra* note 173, at 289-90; note, 50 HARV. L. REV. 956, 960-61 (1937).

[179] There was no such contradiction in the original theory; the officer was suable not because he had violated the Constitution but because he had committed a common law tort.

[180] This theory may be inferred from the Court's statement that "[t]he State has no power to impart to him any immunity from responsibility to the supreme authority of the United States." *Young,* 209 U.S. at 160.

[181] 211 U.S. 149, 153 (1908). This rule was at least as old as Houston & T.C.R.R. v. Texas, 177 U.S. 66, 78 (1900) (Peckham, J.). *See* Note, *supra* note 178, at 961 n.40 (arguing that *Young* and its progeny may create an implied exception to the *Mottley* rule).

[182] Indeed, in one of the *Virginia Coupon Cases,* the Court had already held that an analytically similar claim invoking the contract clause did not come within the provision of the Civil Rights Act, now 42 U.S.C. § 1983 (1982), that creates a cause of action for deprivation of rights secured by the Constitution. Carter v. Greenhow, 114 U.S. 317, 322-23 (1885), THE FIRST HUNDRED YEARS at 423-24 n.144.

bury an explicit constitutional safeguard for economic interests with which the Court had little sympathy, *Young* rejected sound precedent to help realize a new and more flexible safeguard that the Court had manufactured out of whole cloth.[183]

[183] On the same day *Young* was decided, the Court also held, with Harlan alone protesting, that a state could not invoke sovereign immunity to close *its own* courts to a suit to enjoin an officer from committing a wrong under color of an allegedly unconstitutional statute. General Oil Co. v. Crain, 209 U.S. 211, 228 (1908) (McKenna, J.) ("It being then the right of a party to be protected against a law which violates a constitutional right, . . . a decision which denies such protection gives effect to the law, and the decision is reviewable by this court."). Prior decisions cited by the Court itself, however, had unmistakably held that a want of jurisdiction under state law was an adequate and independent ground for refusing relief and thus precluded Supreme Court review. *Id.* at 221-24; *cf. id.* at 232-34 (Harlan, J., concurring); Murdock v. City of Memphis, 87 U.S. (20 Wall.) 590, 634-35 (1875) (enunciating independent-and-adequate-state-ground rule). The *Crain* Court supported its conclusion with an argument from intolerable consequences: "If a suit against state officers is precluded in the national courts by the Eleventh Amendment . . . , and may be forbidden by a State to its courts, . . . an easy way is open to prevent the enforcement of many provisions of the Constitution. . . ." 209 U.S. at 226. The most obvious flaw in this contention was that *Young* had just reaffirmed that a federal suit was *not* precluded; even if the substantive constitutional provisions invoked by the plaintiff implied that some court must be open to grant an injunction, they seemed satisfied by the availability of a federal remedy. *See* Fletcher, *A Historical Interpretation of the Eleventh Amendment*, 35 STAN. L. REV. 1033, 1096 (1983). Moreover, the notion that the Constitution gave a "right . . . to be protected" by injunction was a giant step beyond Marbury v. Madison, 5 U.S. (1 Cranch) 137 (1803), which had held only that a court had to obey the Constitution when it had jurisdiction. Indeed, the Court had implicitly rejected *Crain*'s thesis in Beers v. Arkansas, 61 U.S. (20 How.) 527 (1858) (holding that a state did not have to permit itself to be sued in its own courts to redress a violation of the contract clause, although sovereign immunity evidently would have barred a federal remedy as well). By emphasizing *Marbury*'s explanation that judicial review was indispensable to the effectuation of constitutional limitations, 5 U.S. (1 Cranch) at 178, and the inadequacy of having to wait to challenge a state law as a defendant in an enforcement proceeding, one might make a respectable argument for overruling *Beers. Cf.* THE FIRST HUNDRED YEARS at 304-05 (discussing *Ex parte* McCardle, 74 U.S. (7 Wall.) 506 (1869)).

# 3

# Full Faith and the Bill of Rights

Apart from the crucial economic controversies considered in the preceding chapters, the constitutional cases of the Fuller period fall into two principal categories. The first consists of decisions interpreting various provisions of the Bill of Rights, the most prominent of which concerned the constitutional status of overseas possessions acquired as a result of the Spanish-American War. The second is an unusually rich collection of decisions applying the article IV command that one state give "full Faith and Credit" to certain acts of another.

## I. THE BILL OF RIGHTS

### A. Domestic Cases

The ringing declarations of the first eight amendments have figured so prominently in the decisions of the late twentieth century that it is surprising how small a part they played in the Court's early history.[1] The number of cases involving the Bill of Rights did increase during the Fuller period, but apart from the substantive due process decisions already discussed it can scarcely be said that the Court took an aggressive view of its responsibilities under those clauses.[2]

Most of the cases can be quickly noted. After *Counselman v. Hitchcock*[3] had sensibly held that the fifth amendment precluded compulsion to give incriminating evidence with-

[1] *See* THE FIRST HUNDRED YEARS *passim.*

[2] *See* Roche, *Civil Liberty in the Age of Enterprise*, 31 U. CHI L. REV. 103, 135 (1963) ("[T]he Constitution had no effective civil liberties content—in the contemporary sense . . . —throughout the period [1870-1920] under analysis.").

[3] 142 U.S. 547 (1892) (Blatchford, J.).

out a grant of immunity as broad as the privilege itself,[4] *Brown v. Walker*[5] predictably allowed compulsion to testify after the witness had been protected from any prosecution related to the transaction in question.[6] *Bradfield v. Roberts*[7] upheld a federal grant to a hospital run by a religious order on the persuasive ground that the hospital's purpose was "purely" secular and that the establishment clause did not require discrimination against those who also practiced religion.[8] *Gibson v. United States*[9] and *Scranton v. Wheeler*[10] established the questionable "navigational servitude" doctrine permitting the United States to cut off access to navigable waters without compensation.[11] Over dissents by

[4]*Id.* at 585-86. The Court also sensibly held that the amendment's purpose required that it be read to protect witnesses before a grand jury as well as in court. *Id.* at 562-63. The opinion is marred by lengthy recitations of barely relevant state-court decisions after the unfortunate fashion of the day. *Cf.* Leisy v. Hardin, 135 U.S. 100 (1890), pp. 32-33 *supra.*

[5]161 U.S. 591 (1896) (Brown, J.). Justices Shiras, Gray, White, and Field dissented.

[6]*Id.* at 610. *But see* Hale v. Henkel, 201 U.S. 43 (1906) (Brown, J.), where the Court invoked British authority in finding it unnecessary that the federal statutory immunity embrace *state* prosecutions because the privilege itself forbade only compulsion to accuse oneself of crimes "arising within the same jurisdiction and under the same sovereignty." The Court unrealistically termed the danger of conviction in another jurisdiction "unsubstantial and remote." *Id.* at 68-69. In *Brown,* 161 U.S. at 606-08, the Court had apparently reached the same conclusion but did not consider it directly relevant since Congress had validly provided for immunity from both federal and state prosecution.

[7]175 U.S. 291 (1899) (Peckham, J.).

[8]*Id.* at 298-99; *see also* Quick Bear v. Leupp, 210 U.S. 50, 81-82 (1908) (Fuller, C. J.) (upholding a grant to sectarian Indian schools). The Court was on shakier ground in extending its holding that the free exercise clause did not protect the rights of Mormons to practice polygamy, Reynolds v. United States, 98 U.S. 145, 165-66 (1879), THE FIRST HUNDRED YEARS at 439-42, to hold that members of the Mormon church could be disenfranchised, Davis v. Beason, 133 U.S. 333, 346-47 (1890) (Field, J.), the church's charter revoked, and its property confiscated because of its advocacy of the crime, Mormon Church v. United States, 135 U.S. 1, 44-48 (1890) (Bradley, J., over the dissent of Fuller, C. J., Field, and Lamar, JJ.). These measures went so far beyond the suppression of actual polygamy as to interfere with the basic right to associate with others of the same religious belief. *See* P. KURLAND, RELIGION AND THE LAW 25 (1962) (concluding that in *Davis* "the alleged crime was adherence to a religious belief"); W. KING, MELVILLE WESTON FULLER 147-48 (1967) (calling Fuller's dissent in the *Mormon Church* case one of his "greatest glories" and noting that Congress later restored the confiscated property); Roche, *supra* note 2, at 133 (arguing that the "core" of Field's dissent in the *Mormon Church* case "was that Congress could do anything it liked with Mormon opinion, but it could not 'confiscate' Mormon property") (quoting 136 U.S. at 66).

[9]166 U.S. 269 (1897) (Fuller, C. J.).

[10]179 U.S. 141 (1900) (Harlan, J.).

[11]*Gibson,* 166 U.S. at 276; *Wheeler,* 179 U.S. at 164-65. The Court seemed to confuse the regulatory power conferred by the commerce clause with a federal property interest. *Cf.* Illinois Central R.R. v. Illinois, 146 U.S. 387 (1892) (creating the public-trust doctrine to limit the protection afforded by the contract clause), pp. 10-13 *supra.* Eldridge v. Trezevant, 160 U.S. 452 (1896), on which the Court in *Gibson* relied, had been based upon a specific Louisiana statute giving the state a proprietary servitude for flood-control purposes. *Id.* at 463-64. In *Scranton,* Justice Shiras, who had written *Eldridge,* dissented from the extension of its holding, pointing out that *Gibson* too had relied on state-court precedents recognizing a servitude under state law. *Scranton,* 179 U.S. at 181-82. But *Gibson* had also expressly said that riparian titles in general were held "subject to the servitude in respect of navigation created in favor of the Federal government by the Constitution." *Gibson,* 166 U.S. at 272. *See also* United States v. Lynah, 188 U.S. 445, 471-74 (1903) (Brewer, J.) (despite the servitude, the government must pay for flooding caused by its navigation improvements); Bedford v. United States, 192 U.S. 217, 225 (1904) (McKenna, J.) (government need not pay when flooding resulted indirectly from improvements that interfered with natural erosion process); Clark v. Nash, 198 U.S. 361, 369-70 (1905) (Peckham, J.) (holding that a taking to irrigate a single plot of private land met the implicit "public use" requirement; Chicago, B. & Q.R.R. v. Chicago, 166 U.S. 226, 247-52 (1897) (Harlan, J.) (allowing nominal compensation for building a road across

Holmes and Brown, *Kepner v. United States*[12] concluded without much reasoning that the double jeopardy clause forbade the United States to appeal an acquittal.[13] Two conclusory 1909 decisions,[14] largely ignoring analogous precedents,[15] allowed Congress to evade fifth and sixth amendment safeguards applicable to criminal cases by labeling penalties for wrongdoing as "civil."[16] *Weems v. United States*,[17] in a good battle over the relevant history, concluded that the eighth amendment's ban on cruel and unusual punishments forbade a sentence disproportionate to the offense.

Two freedom of expression cases deserve somewhat closer attention. Study of this area tends to begin with the great espionage cases of the First World War,[18] but earlier decisions had exhibited an even more grudging attitude toward the first amendment.[19] The Waite Court had mingled notions of immorality with those of property in allowing exclusion of lottery materials from the mails[20] and had upheld restrictions on the political activities of

---

railroad property because there was minimal interference with existing uses, over a sensible Brewer dissent arguing that the proper measure was the market value of the easement).

[12] 195 U.S. 100 (1904) (Day, J.). The case arose under a statute prohibiting double jeopardy in the Philippines. The Court reasonably concluded that the statute imposed the same standards as the fifth amendment itself. *Id.* at 121-24.

[13] *Id.* at 125-32; *see also* Grafton v. United States, 206 U.S. 333, 354-55 (1907) (soldier acquitted by military tribunal cannot be retried in Philippine civil court); *In re* Nielsen, 131 U.S. 176, 190 (1889) (Bradley, J.) (relying on authority and logic to hold that conviction barred trial for lesser included offense). *But cf.* Taylor v. United States, 207 U.S. 120, 127 (1907) (Holmes, J.) (government may appeal dismissal of indictment because as explained in *Kepner,* jeopardy had not yet attached); Trono v. United States, 199 U.S. 521, 533-34 (1905) (Peckham, J.) (another Philippine case, holding on the fictitious basis of waiver that a defendant who appealed his conviction of one offense subjected himself to review of his acquittal of another).

[14] Oceanic Steam Navigation Co. v. Stranahan, 214 U.S. 320, 336-38 (1909) (White, J.) (sustaining administrative penalty without judicial trial), and Hepner v. United States, 213 U.S. 103, 114-15 (1909) (Harlan, J.) (upholding directed verdict for United States despite defendant's right to trial by jury).

[15] *See* Boyd v. United States, 116 U.S. 616, 633-35 (1886) (civil forfeiture proceeding within fifth amendment bar on self-incrimination); *Ex parte* Garland, 71 U.S. (4 Wall.) 333, 376-78 (1867) (finding civil disabilities punishment for purposes of the ex post facto and bill of attainder clauses); Cummings v. Missouri, 71 U.S. (4 Wall.) 277 (1867) (same); THE FIRST HUNDRED YEARS at 292-96, 444-47. In *Hepner,* 213 U.S. at 112, Harlan read *Boyd* as confirming that civil penalty proceedings were constitutional.

[16] *But cf.* Wong Wing v. United States, 163 U.S. 228, 237 (1896) (Shiras, J.) (holding that an alien could not be put to hard labor without an indictment and jury trial). Other jury-trial decisions of the Fuller period include Capital Traction Co. v. Hof, 174 U.S. 1, 37-39 (1899) (Gray, J.) (seventh amendment forbids one civil jury to review another, but a "jury" in a trial conducted by a justice of the peace is not a "jury" for seventh amendment purposes); Thompson v. Utah, 170 U.S. 343, 349 (1898) (Harlan, J.) (sixth amendment preserves traditional requirement that criminal jury consist of twelve persons); American Publishing Co. v. Fisher, 166 U.S. 464, 467-68 (1897) (Brewer, J.) (seventh amendment preserves traditional requirement that civil jury decide unanimously).

[17] 217 U.S. 349 (1910) (McKenna, J.). Justices White and Holmes dissented, and three Justices did not participate.

[18] *E.g.,* Schenck v. United States, 249 U.S. 47 (1919).

[19] *See generally* Rabban, *The First Amendment in Its Forgotten Years,* 90 YALE L.J. 514, 557 (1981) (concluding, after a review of both federal and state decisions, that "[a] general hostility to the value of free expression permeated the judicial system" before the war).

[20] *See Ex parte* Jackson, 96 U.S. 727 (1878), THE FIRST HUNDRED YEARS at 442-43. This holding was reaffirmed in *In re* Rapier, 143 U.S. 110, 134 (1892) (Fuller, C. J.), on the basis of a distinction made much later in the context of abortion: "The circulation of newspapers is not prohibited, but the government declines itself to become an agent in the circulation of printed matter which it regards as injurious to the people." *Compare* Roe v.

federal employees without even discussing the first amendment.[21] The Fuller Court was almost as cavalier.

In 1904, in *United States ex rel. Turner v. Williams*,[22] the Court allowed Congress to exclude an alien from the country on the ground that he was an anarchist. After suggesting that the law was not a limitation on speech at all and that the first amendment did not apply to aliens seeking entry,[23] Chief Justice Fuller declared that it required no argument to show that a person who "believes in or advocates the overthrow of the Government . . . by force" could be denied admission.[24] Moreover, if the word "anarchist" included mere "political philosophers innocent of evil intent," it was enough, "in the light of previous decisions" not identified, that Congress had thought "the tendency of the general exploitation of such views . . . so dangerous" as to justify exclusion: "as long as human governments endure they cannot be denied the power of self-preservation. . . ."[25] No effort was made to reconcile these conclusions with the text, history, or purpose of the first amendment or to explain why, assuming the test was whether a measure impinging on expression was necessary for "self-preservation," it was consistent with *Marbury v. Madison*[26] to let Congress be the sole judge of necessity.[27]

The second case was *Patterson v. Colorado*,[28] where Justice Holmes wrote to sustain a contempt citation for publications that "reflected upon the motives and conduct of the Supreme Court of Colorado in cases still pending."[29] Echoing *Turner*'s concern for coun-

---

Wade, 410 U.S. 113 (1973) (state cannot criminally prohibit abortion in first trimester), *with* Maher v. Roe, 432 U.S. 464 (1977) (state not required to fund constitutionally protected abortions), *and* Harris v. McRae, 448 U.S. 297 (1980) (federal government not required to fund constitutionally protected abortions). *See* pp. 465-75 *infra*.

[21] *See Ex parte* Curtis, 106 U.S. 371 (1882), THE FIRST HUNDRED YEARS at 443-44. Only Justice Bradley, in dissent, considered the first amendment. *Curtis,* 106 U.S. at 376-78.

[22] 194 U.S. 279 (1904) (Fuller, C. J.).

[23] *Id*. at 292: "It is . . . true that . . . he is in fact cut off from . . . speaking or publishing . . . in the country, but that is merely because of his exclusion therefrom. He does not become one of the people to whom these things are secured by our Constitution by an attempt to enter forbidden by law." In an earlier decision, Davis v. Massachusetts, 167 U.S. 43, 47-48 (1897) (White, J.), the Court had not even mentioned freedom of expression in upholding a prohibition on speaking in a public park without a permit, reasoning that the right to exclude everyone from public property "necessarily include[d]" the "lesser" authority to limit use. The Court quoted from Holmes's decision in the court below: "For the legislature absolutely or conditionally to forbid public speaking in a highway or public park is no more an infringement of the rights of a member of the public than for the owner of a private house to forbid it in his house." *Id*. at 47 (quoting from Commonwealth v. Davis, 162 Mass. 510, 511, 39 N.E. 113, 113 (1895) (Holmes, J.)); *cf.* Western Union Tel. Co. v. Kansas, 216 U.S. 1 (1910), *supra* p. 46, note 126, where Holmes dissented from the Court's arguably distinguishable holding that a state could not condition the privilege of doing local business on payment of taxes on out-of-state property, 216 U.S. at 52.

[24] *Turner,* 194 U.S. at 293.

[25] *Id*. at 294. Justice Brewer, concurring, more modestly said the evidence established that Turner "urges and seeks the overthrow by force of all government" and thus it was unnecessary to consider whether Congress could exclude "one who simply entertains and expresses the opinion that all government is a mistake, and that society would be better off without any." *Id*. at 296.

[26] 5 U.S. (1 Cranch) 137 (1803).

[27] *Cf.* McCulloch v. Maryland, 17 U.S. (4 Wheat.) 316, 386-87 (1819) (refusing to reexamine the degree of necessity of a federal statute for purposes of the necessary and proper clause), THE FIRST HUNDRED YEARS at 165. *See also* E. FREUND, THE POLICE POWER § 478 (1904) (arguing that the immigration statute was valid because it did not "restrain the freedom of speech of anarchists residing in the country").

[28] 205 U.S. 454 (1907).

[29] *Id*. at 458-59.

tervailing governmental interests without citing that decision, Holmes invoked state-court and English decisions recognizing a sufficient interest in "preventing interference with the course of justice."[30] Like Fuller in *Turner,* Holmes seemed extremely deferential to someone else's findings regarding the necessity for limiting expression: "if a court regards, as it may, a publication concerning a matter of law pending before it, as tending toward such an interference, it may punish it. . . ."[31]

Indeed Holmes began his discussion of the first amendment by announcing a far more restrictive principle that seemed to make his investigation of the state's interest unnecessary: "the main purpose of such constitutional provisions is 'to prevent all such *previous restraints* upon publications as had been practiced by other governments,' and they do not prevent the subsequent punishment of such as may be deemed contrary to the public welfare."[32] Cited for this momentous proposition, without elaboration, were two decisions construing state constitutions and Blackstone's view of the English common law.[33] Whether the fourteenth amendment made the first applicable to the states at all he expressly left open.[34]

The opinion demonstrated the advantages and disadvantages of Holmes's characteristic brevity: Holmes neither wasted the reader's time nor justified his important and debatable conclusions.

## B.   The Insular Cases

The most interesting and controversial decisions about the Bill of Rights during the Fuller era, however, are found among a series of cases concerning the applicability of various

[30] *Id.* at 463.

[31] *Id.*

[32] *Id.* at 462 (quoting Commonwealth v. Blanding, 20 Mass. (3 Pick.) 304, 313 (1826)) (emphasis in original).

[33] *Blanding,* 20 Mass. at 313; Respublica v. Oswald, 1 Dall. 319, 325 (Pa. 1798). Story had suggested in his treatise that the Constitution preserved the English distinction between prior restraint and subsequent punishment. 3 J. STORY, COMMENTARIES ON THE CONSTITUTION OF THE UNITED STATES § 1878 (1833). Cooley disagreed. T. COOLEY, CONSTITUTIONAL LIMITATIONS, ch. 12 (3d ed. 1874). Harlan also disagreed, assuming his conclusion by declaring that "[t]he public welfare cannot override constitutional privileges." *Patterson,* 205 U.S. at 465 (Harlan, J., dissenting). For the argument that the amendment was meant to confirm the original Constitution's total exclusion of the federal government from the area of speech and press, see Mayton, *Seditious Libel and the Lost Guarantee of a Freedom of Expression,* 84 COLUM. L. REV. 91 (1984). Story recognized but did not comment on this possibility. 3 J. STORY, *supra* § 1885.

[34] 205 U.S. at 462. Justice Harlan, who had previously argued that the fourteenth amendment incorporated other provisions of the Bill of Rights, *see, e.g.,* O'Neil v. Vermont, 144 U.S. 323, 370 (1892) (dissenting opinion); Hurtado v. California, 110 U.S. 516, 538-58 (1884) (dissenting opinion), concluded in dissent that free expression was an "attribute[] of natural citizenship" protected by the privileges or immunities clause against state action and an "essential part[] of every man's liberty" protected by the due process clause as well. *Patterson,* 205 U.S. at 464-65.

During the Fuller years the majority held that the fourteenth amendment did not make applicable to the states the eighth amendment ban on cruel and unusual punishments, *In re* Kemmler, 136 U.S. 436, 448-49 (1890) (Fuller, C. J.), the sixth amendment right to a twelve-member criminal jury, Maxwell v. Dow, 176 U.S. 581, 604-05 (1900) (Peckham, J.), or the fifth amendment privilege against self-incrimination, Twining v. New Jersey, 211 U.S. 78, 113-14 (1908) (Moody, J.). Justice Harlan dissented in both *Maxwell,* 176 U.S. at 605, and *Twining,* 211 U.S. at 114. He was able to write for the Court, however, in feigned reliance on a case that had flatly stated the contrary, that the fourteenth amendment *did* forbid a state to take property without just compensation. *See* Chicago, B. & Q.R.R. v. Chicago, 166 U.S. 226, 235-41 (1897) (citing Davidson v. New Orleans, 96 U.S.

constitutional provisions to the islands acquired from Spain as a result of the Spanish-American War.[35]

The story begins with three 1901 decisions regarding tariffs for goods shipped to or from what was then called Porto Rico. In the course of holding that the island was no longer a "foreign" country within the meaning of the tariff law, *De Lima v. Bidwell*[36] reaffirmed that territory could constitutionally be acquired by treaty[37]—a proposition sanctioned by long practice and unchallenged in the instant case. *Dooley v. United States*[38] followed long-standing precedent[39] in upholding the power of the occupying authorities to

---

97 (1878); *see also* Missouri Pac. R.R. v. Nebraska, 164 U.S. 403, 417 (1896) (Gray, J.) (holding that the due process clause forbade a state to order a railroad to permit the construction of a private grain elevator on its land). *See generally* THE FIRST HUNDRED YEARS at 342-51, 363-64 (discussing earlier fourteenth amendment decisions).

[35] *See generally* 2 C. WARREN, THE SUPREME COURT IN UNITED STATES HISTORY 708 (rev. ed. 1937) (describing these cases as "the most important fact in the Court's history" during the Fuller and White periods); W. KING, *supra* note 8, at 262-77.

[36] 182 U.S. 1 (1901) (Brown, J.). Justices McKenna, Shiras, White, and Gray dissented.

The same term, in Dooley v. United States, 183 U.S. 151 (1901) (Brown, J.), the Court relied on *De Lima* and on Woodruff v. Parham, 75 U.S. (8 Wall.) 123 (1869), THE FIRST HUNDRED YEARS at 335-37, to hold that a tax on goods sent from the United States mainland to Porto Rico was not a tax on "Exports" forbidden by article I, § 9. Four dissenters—Fuller, Harlan, Brewer, and Peckham—stressed the fact that *Woodruff*, which had given a narrow reading to the related clause of article I, § 10, forbidding state taxes on "Imports," had dealt with shipments from one state to another rather than to an overseas possession. *Dooley*, 183 U.S. at 170-72; *see also* Whitney, *The Insular Decisions of December, 1901,* 2 COLUM. L. REV. 79 (1902) (criticizing the decision).

[37] *De Lima,* 182 U.S. at 195-96 (quoting American Ins. Co. v. Canter, 26 U.S. (1 Pet.) 511, 542 (1828) (dictum), THE FIRST HUNDRED YEARS at 120 n.202). In Geofroy v. Riggs, 133 U.S. 258 (1890) (Field, J.), the Court had sensibly interpreted the treaty power to include "any matter which is properly the subject of negotiation with a foreign country." *Id.* at 267. That the subject in question was the right of an alien to inherit land in the United States suggests the breadth of the authority thus recognized. The Court's expansive language is limited somewhat by the facts of the case; because the land at issue was located in the District of Columbia, the Court did not hold that the treaty power extended to subjects over which Congress could not legislate. Four years later, in Wharton v. Wise, 153 U.S. 155 (1894) (Field, J.), the Court suggested a narrow interpretation of what constituted a treaty under the Constitution by holding that an interstate compact respecting fishing rights was not contrary to the provision of the Articles of Confederation forbidding the states to enter into any "treaty, confederation, or alliance" without congressional consent:

> The articles . . . were intended to prevent any union of two or more States, having a tendency to break up or weaken the league between the whole; they were not designed to prevent arrangements between adjoining States to facilitate the free intercourse of their citizens, or remove barriers to their peace and prosperity. . . .

*Id.* at 167. The result in *Wharton* was echoed in United States v. Belmont, 301 U.S. 324, 330-31 (1937), p. 218, note 63 *infra,* where the Court, lent support by the explicit distinction between state "treaties" and "compacts" in the present article I, § 10, held that not every federal agreement with a foreign country required Senate approval under the treaty clause of article II, § 2. More debatable was the decision in Virginia v. Tennessee, 148 U.S. 503 (1893) (Field, J.), that even the compact clause did not require congressional consent for every agreement between states, but only for those "tending to the increase of political power in the States, which may encroach upon or interfere with the just supremacy of the United States." *Id.* at 519. Since this was practically the same definition that the Court would later announce in regard to treaties in *Wharton,* it was just as well that Field added Story's explanation that treaties dealt with "political" matters and compacts with "mere private rights of sovereignty" such as boundaries. *Id.* (quoting 3 J. STORY, *supra* note 33, at § 1403).

[38] 182 U.S. 222 (1901) (Brown, J.).

[39] *E.g.,* Cross v. Harrison, 57 U.S. (16 How.) 164 (1854), *cited in Dooley,* 182 U.S. at 231-33.

impose tariffs on incoming goods as an incident of military government.[40] *Downes v. Bidwell*[41] was another matter; notwithstanding the contemporaneous decision that Porto Rico was not "foreign,"[42] the Court held, over dissents by Fuller, Harlan, Brewer, and Peckham, that the island could be discriminatorily taxed despite the constitutional requirement that duties be "uniform throughout the United States."[43]

Speaking for himself alone, Justice Brown wrote a distressing opinion in which he came close to arguing that nothing in the Constitution applied to any of the territories.[44] As the other eight Justices insisted, the contrary had long been established,[45] and Brown's theory left one wondering how a nation with only the powers given in the Constitution could govern territories at all.[46] The real question, as Justice White argued in an impressive opinion basically joined by the remaining three members of the majority, was whether Porto Rico was a part of "the United States" within the meaning of the uniformity clause.[47]

Brown concluded that no territory was a part of the United States, essentially because, as had been established in Marshall's time, no territory was a state.[48] The "United States,"

[40] The majority held that military authority to tax imports *from the United States* ended when the territory was ceded to this country. *Dooley,* 182 U.S. at 233-34. The Justices who had dissented in *De Lima* on the ground that Porto Rico remained a "foreign country" also dissented from this conclusion. *Id.* at 237-38 (White, Gray, Shiras and McKenna, JJ., dissenting).

[41] 182 U.S. 244 (1901).

[42] *See De Lima,* 182 U.S. at 200. For an early argument that *Downes* was inconsistent with *De Lima*—only Justice Brown sided with the majority in both decisions—see Burgess, *The Decisions of the Supreme Court in the Insular Cases,* 16 Pol. Sci. Q. 486, 494-99 (1901).

[43] U. S. Const. art. I, § 8. The duty was on goods imported to the mainland from Porto Rico. There was no comparable duty on shipments from one state to another, and some Justices contended that imposition of such a duty would be unconstitutional, *Downes,* 182 U.S. at 292 (White, J., concurring), though the Court had struck down state taxes on such shipments on the ground that federal power over interstate commerce was exclusive, *see, e.g.,* Case of the State Freight Tax, 82 U.S. (15 Wall.) 232 (1873), The First Hundred Years at 337-42.

[44] *See Downes,* 182 U.S. at 285-86; *see also* Rassmussen v. United States, 197 U.S. 516, 531-32 (1905) (Brown, J., concurring). Elsewhere in *Downes,* however, he suggested that the ex post facto and bill of attainder clauses did apply, as well as "certain principles of natural justice . . . which need no expression in constitutions." 182 U.S. at 276-77, 280, 282-83.

[45] *See Downes,* 182 U.S. at 291-92 (White, J., concurring); *id.* at 360-63 (Fuller, C. J., dissenting) (citing, inter alia, Scott v. Sandford, 60 U.S. (19 How.) 393 (1857) (power of Congress to legislate regarding territories limited by the Constitution), and Thompson v. Utah, 170 U.S. 343 (1898) (same)). In *Downes,* Brown argued that most of the precedents were distinguishable because Congress had extended the Constitution to the territories in those cases by statute. 182 U.S. at 258, 269-70. But, as the other Justices pointed out, the Court had not always relied on those statutes, and Brown's theory failed to explain why Congress had the power to enact them.

[46] *See* The First Hundred Years at 120, 272 n.265 (discussing American Ins. Co. v. Canter, 26 U.S. (1 Pet.) 511 (1828), and Scott v. Sandford, 60 U.S. (19 How.) 393 (1857)).

[47] *Downes,* 182 U.S. at 287-88, 299 (White, J., joined by Shiras and McKenna, JJ., concurring). Justice Gray agreed "in substance" with White's opinion. *Id.* at 345 (Gray, J., concurring). That the island was no longer "foreign," as held in *De Lima,* was not conclusive. As a textual matter it is entirely conceivable for a U.S. possession to be independent of the influence of other nations without being a part of the United States. *Cf.* Cherokee Nation v. Georgia, 30 U.S. (5 Pet.) 1 (1831), (holding an Indian tribe not a "foreign State" within article III despite a history of separate existence and self-government emphasized by the negotiation of treaties with the United States), The First Hundred Years at 122-24.

[48] *Downes,* 182 U.S. at 250-51, 259, 277, 278. Brown cited, inter alia, New Orleans v. Winter, 14 U.S. (1 Wheat.) 91 (1816), and Hepburn v. Ellzey, 6 U.S. (2 Cranch) 445 (1805), The First Hundred Years at 82-84. *Winter* and *Hepburn* respectively had held that citizens of neither the territories nor the District of Columbia were citizens of a "State" for purposes of diversity jurisdiction.

he argued with some plausibility as an original matter, meant the states themselves; an early draft of the Constitution had placed the uniformity clause among other provisions explicitly protecting states from discrimination.[49] Fuller came up with troubling counter-analogies in dissent,[50] but the great difficulty for Brown was precedent. In upholding Congress's power to impose taxes in the District of Columbia, Chief Justice Marshall had said that the power to tax extended as far as the uniformity clause that limited its exercise, and that the District of Columbia was part of "the United States."[51] Brown responded that the District was different from the territories because it had been formed out of portions of Maryland and Virginia.[52] Whether or not this satisfied his own definition of "the United States,"[53] it had not been the basis for Marshall's conclusion; Marshall had flatly said that the clause's purpose of preventing discrimination was applicable to the entire "American empire," expressly including the territories.[54]

To Chief Justice Fuller and his brethren in dissent, Marshall's decision meant that Porto Rico was part of "the United States."[55] Justice White, for the remaining four Justices, took an imaginative intermediate view: a territory became part of the United States only after it had been "incorporated" by congressional action.[56] Justice Harlan protested that this would leave it to Congress to determine whether or not to abide by constitutional limitations;[57] but the tenor of White's opinion suggested he was speaking, as he should have been, only of provisions limited in their application to "the United States."[58] The British

---

[49] Justice Brown also pointed to the fact that the thirteenth amendment distinguished between "the United States" and "places within [its] jurisdiction." *Downes,* 182 U.S. at 251. But this proved at most that some places subject to U.S. authority were outside the United States, not that Porto Rico was. *Cf.* Neely v. Henkel, 180 U.S. 109, 122-23 (1901) (holding that despite U.S. military occupation, Cuba remained a foreign country), *discussed in Downes,* by White, 182 U.S. at 343-44, and Harlan, *id.* at 387-88 (Harlan, J., dissenting). Fuller went further, describing the amendment's "jurisdiction" clause as having been inserted "out of abundant caution." 182 U.S. at 358 (Fuller, C. J., dissenting). For an earlier argument in support of Brown's position, see Langdell, *The Status of Our New Territories,* 12 HARV. L. REV. 365, 379-91 (1899).

[50] Fuller cited Justice Miller's statement in the Slaughter-House Cases, 83 U.S. (16 Wall.) 36, 74 (1873), that one could be a "citizen of the United States" within the fourteenth amendment without being a citizen of a state. *Downes,* 182 U.S. at 357 (Fuller, C. J., dissenting). Fuller also asserted that it was not clear that the Framers would have wanted to disqualify a territorial resident from the presidency under article II's requirement of fourteen-year residence "in the United States." *Id.; cf.* U. S. CONST. art. III, § 1 ("The Judicial Power of the United States. . . ."). For a strong anticipatory reply to Brown's position on this question, see Lowell, *The Status of Our New Possessions—A Third View,* 13 HARV. L. REV. 155, 157-63 (1899).

[51] Loughborough v. Blake, 18 U.S. (5 Wheat.) 317 (1820), THE FIRST HUNDRED YEARS at 183-84.

[52] *Downes,* 182 U.S. at 260-61.

[53] Brown elsewhere insisted that "the United States" meant the states themselves. *See supra* note 49 and accompanying text. The District was no longer part of a state, *see* Hepburn v. Ellzey, 6 U.S. (2 Cranch) 445 (1805), though an occasional speaker during the ratification debates had argued that it would be, *see* 3 J. ELLIOT, DEBATES IN THE SEVERAL STATE CONVENTIONS ON THE ADOPTION OF THE FEDERAL CONSTITUTION 434-35 (2d ed. 1836) (Mr. Nicholas speaking). *But see id.* at 435 (Mr. Grayson) (arguing the opposite).

[54] *Loughborough,* 18 U.S. (5 Wheat.) at 317.

[55] *Downes,* 182 U.S. at 352-56 (Fuller, C. J., dissenting).

[56] *Id.* at 287-344 (White, J., joined by Shiras and McKenna, JJ., concurring). Justice Gray wrote separately to say he agreed "in substance" with White's opinion. *Id.* at 344-45 (Gray, J., concurring). The incorporation thesis had first been suggested by Lowell, *supra* note 50, at 176.

[57] 182 U.S. at 389 (Harlan, J., dissenting).

[58] *See, e.g, id.* at 292, 299, 341-42 (White, J., concurring). Significantly, White's conclusion appeared applicable to the troublesome question of citizenship, which under the fourteenth amendment extended to most per-

Empire furnishes ample evidence that it is not unusual for a country to have possessions that are not considered part of the country itself, and White cataloged ample reasons why a country might do so.[59] Not only was there no evidence that the framers of the uniformity clause had meant to rule out this traditional distinction, but White impressively mustered history suggesting that early American practice had distinguished between mere acquisition and incorporation.[60] On the subordinate question whether Porto Rico had been incorporated, White was less powerful;[61] but he did seem on respectable ground in concluding that not everything over which the federal government exercised sovereignty was necessarily a part of "the United States."[62]

Three years later, with only Harlan dissenting, the Court held in *Dorr v. United States*[63] that the constitutional provisions requiring juries in criminal trials[64] did not apply to the Philippines. *Downes* had settled, Justice Day began, that unincorporated territories were to be governed by Congress "subject to such constitutional restrictions . . . as are applicable to the situation."[65] On its face this statement applied equally to incorporated territories, since by definition everything Congress does is subject to "applicable" constitutional limitations.[66] Day's emphasis on the fact that the Philippines had not been incorporated,[67] however, suggests that he took *Downes* as having established White's distinction between incorporated and unincorporated areas, although White had not spoken for a majority of participating Justices.[68] Indeed it was only by embracing White's distinction that Day

---

sons born "in the United States." *See id.* at 306, 313. For a sample of the fears conjured up on this score, see Stevenson, *The Relation of the Nation to Its Dependencies,* 36 AM. L. REV. 366, 383-86 (1902).

[59] *Downes,* 182 U.S. at 306-13 (White, J., concurring).

[60] *Id.* at 322-39 (quoting, inter alia, correspondence to show that President Jefferson had never doubted the power to acquire Louisiana by treaty, but only the authority to make it part of the United States). Fuller hardly replied to White's argument. *See id.* at 371-73 (Fuller, C. J., dissenting). Harlan, in a separate dissent, fulminated ineffectually against "monarchical" or "arbitrary" government and professed to find White's distinction incomprehensible. *Id.* at 380-81, 391. For a contemporaneous argument that history did not support White's distinction, see Randolph, *The Insular Cases,* 1 COLUM. L. REV. 436, 451 (1901).

[61] White said essentially only that the treaty itself had not done the trick, *Downes,* 182 U.S. at 339-40 (White, J., concurring); he hardly responded to Harlan's argument, *id.* at 390-91 (Harlan, J., dissenting), that Congress had "incorporated" the territory by enacting a variety of provisions creating, among other things, a permanent civil government. *See also* Randolph, *supra* note 60, at 454-57.

[62] The language of Loughborough v. Blake, 18 U.S. (5 Wheat.) 317 (1820) (discussed *supra* note 51 and accompanying text), was broad enough to cover all U.S. possessions, but the Court there had not addressed the question of incorporation of outlying possessions. *See also Downes,* 182 U.S. at 387-88 (Harlan, J., dissenting) (distinguishing Neely v. Henkel, 180 U.S. 109 (1901), on the ground that there the United States had exercised military control of conquered Cuban territory but had made no claim of sovereignty).

[63] 195 U.S. 138 (1904).

[64] U. S. CONST. art. III, § 2, cl. 3; *id.* amend. VI.

[65] *Dorr,* 195 U.S. at 143.

[66] Day finally settled an ancient controversy by flatly declaring that it was the provision of article IV, § 3, cl. 2 for "Regulations" respecting "the Territory" that gave Congress authority to govern the territories in the first place. *Id.* at 146, 149; *see* THE FIRST HUNDRED YEARS at 268-69 (discussing Scott v. Sandford, 60 U.S. (19 How.) 393 (1857)).

[67] 195 U.S. at 143-44.

[68] It was fair enough to conclude that a majority in *Downes* had held *at least* unincorporated territories not within "the United States," since Justice Brown had said the same of all territories. *See supra* notes 48-49 and accompanying text.

could avoid an earlier decision, which he ignored, that had found it "beyond question" that the jury provisions were applicable in Utah before statehood.[69]

Day was quite right to concede that *Downes* had not held all constitutional limitations inapplicable to unincorporated territories. As White had stressed in his concurring opinion in *Downes*,[70] all that case had purported to settle was that such territories were not subject to a provision limited in terms to "the United States," and the jury provision of article III contained no such limitation.[71] In the intervening case of *Hawaii v. Mankichi*,[72] however, White had written a concurring opinion concluding, without any reference to the compelling distinction he had previously drawn, that *Downes* "controlled" the jury question as well.[73]

Justice White gave no reason in *Mankichi* for concluding that the jury provision applied only in "the United States," beyond an unexplained reference to *In re Ross*,[74] which had suggestively but not decisively held that no jury was required in a consular court in a

---

[69] Thompson v. Utah, 170 U.S. 343, 347 (1898), *cited in Dorr*, 195 U.S. at 155 (Harlan, J., dissenting); *see also* Rassmussen v. United States, 197 U.S. 516, 525-26 (1905) (White, J.) (reaffirming the incorporation thesis in finding the criminal jury requirements violated in Alaska); Binns v. United States, 194 U.S. 486, 490-91 (1904) (Brewer, J.) (holding the uniformity requirement applicable to Alaska because that territory had been incorporated, but holding that the requirement had not been infringed).

[70] *See, e.g.*, 182 U.S. at 292 ("[T]he question which arises is, not whether the Constitution is operative, . . . but whether the provision relied on is applicable."); *supra* note 47 and accompanying text.

[71] U. S. CONST. art. III, § 2, cl. 3 ("The trial of all Crimes . . . shall be by Jury. . . ."). The sixth amendment does speak in its venue provisions only of states, but in light of the accepted impetus for the Bill of Rights it would be perverse to conclude it was meant to diminish the protection afforded by the original Constitution.

[72] 190 U.S. 197 (1903) (Brown, J.).

[73] *Id.* at 219. In *Dorr*, three of the Justices who had dissented in both *Downes* and *Mankichi* thought the latter case had settled the jury question, *Dorr*, 195 U.S. at 153-54 (Peckham, Brewer, JJ., and Fuller, C. J., concurring), but Day did not treat *Mankichi* as decisive, correctly noting that White's statement had appeared in a concurring opinion. *Id.* at 144 (majority opinion). Indeed, the majority in *Mankichi* had oddly contrived not to discuss the constitutional question. After holding that a joint resolution preserving local laws not "contrary to the Constitution" extended only "fundamental" constitutional provisions to the islands, 190 U.S. at 217-18, Justice Brown in *Mankichi* concluded it was unnecessary "to reconsider the questions which arose in the *Insular Tariff* cases regarding the power of Congress to annex territory without at the same time extending the Constitution over it." *Id.* at 218. If the Constitution itself required a jury, of course, it was immaterial whether the resolution also did; the explanation for Day's refusal to discuss the constitutional question seems to be that the case was "argued upon th[e] theory" that the resolution was determinative. *Id.* If the further suggestion that the Court *believed* the resolution decisive, *id.*, meant that the Justices thought *Downes* had settled the inapplicability of the constitutional jury provisions, the Court had some explaining to do, for reasons given in the text. *See* text accompanying notes 70-79.

On the nonconstitutional issue, the majority in *Mankichi* was not persuasive; the resolution did not say that only "fundamental" provisions were extended to the islands, and, as counsel argued, all constitutional requirements were "equally imperative whatever view the court may take of the[ir] relative importance." 190 U.S. at 206. Once again Justice White had a better theory: the resolution merely made clear that nothing in its terms should be read to preserve any laws inconsistent with those "fundamental" constitutional provisions "which were by their own force applicable to the territory with which Congress was dealing." *Id.* at 220-21 (White, J., concurring); *cf.* THE FIRST HUNDRED YEARS at 345-46 (discussing the controversy over whether the fourteenth amendment provision forbidding states to abridge "the privileges or immunities of citizens of the United States" made provisions previously limiting only the United States binding on the states as well).

[74] 140 U.S. 453 (1891) (Field, J.).

foreign country.[75] In *Dorr,* Day essentially said only that the Framers could not have meant to frustrate justice by requiring juries in "a territory peopled by savages."[76] He did not strengthen this conclusion, as he could have, by citing either *Ross* or *Ex parte Milligan's*[77] dictum that military necessity would have justified dispensing with juries in rebel areas during the Civil War. Moreover, even if Day was right that the uncompromising text of the Constitution did not really require the impossible, *Milligan* itself required some showing that jury trials were out of the question in the Philippines before holding the guarantee inapplicable,[78] and Day did not make it. Thus the important question of the geographical scope of the jury provision was decided essentially without explanation, and the dissenters never managed to show why in Justice White's own terms the jury question was different from the uniformity issue decided in *Downes.*[79]

## II.  FULL FAITH AND CREDIT

Article IV's requirement that "Full Faith and Credit shall be given in each State to the public Acts, Records, and judicial Proceedings of every other State"[80] had not figured prominently in Supreme Court decisions of the first hundred years. Two important principles respecting this clause and its implementing statute,[81] however, had been established without much discussion. In general a judgment was to be given the same effect everywhere that it had in the state that had rendered it,[82] but the judgment of a court lacking jurisdiction according to traditional rules of private international law was entitled to no respect.[83] The Court under Fuller took several opportunities to elaborate these principles.

[75] There is language in *Ross* to support both its extension to unincorporated territories and its limitation to foreign countries. *Cf. supra* note 47 (discussing the distinction drawn in *Downes* and *De Lima* between U.S. possessions and foreign countries).

Additional cases cited by White in *Mankichi,* 190 U.S. at 220 (White, J., concurring), holding the Bill of Rights inapplicable to *state* action, *e.g.,* Hurtado v. California, 110 U.S. 516 (1884), were even less clearly relevant, since White did not seem to deny that the action complained of in *Mankichi* was that of agents of the federal government. An argument might have been made that the indigenous authorities, like Indian tribes, were not in fact exercising federal authority, *cf.* Talton v. Mayes, 163 U.S. 376, 382-84 (1896) (White, J.) (grand jury requirement inapplicable to Cherokee Nation because no exercise of federal authority involved), but White did not develop this argument either.

[76] *Dorr,* 195 U.S. at 148. He added with less force that he also did not believe they had meant to require juries where contrary to local customs. *Id.*

[77] 71 U.S. (4 Wall.) 2, 124-27 (1866), THE FIRST HUNDRED YEARS at 288-92.

[78] 71 U.S. (4 Wall) at 127 (martial law justifiable only if there is a real threat, "such as effectually closes the courts and deposes the civil administration").

[79] Justice Peckham did say in *Dorr* that *Downes* was not controlling, but he did not say how the issue was different; he said only that there had been no opinion for the majority. *Dorr,* 195 U.S. at 154 (Peckham, J., concurring).

[80] U. S. CONST. art. IV, § 1.

[81] Act of May 26, 1790, 1 Stat. 122 (codified as amended at 28 U.S.C. § 1738 (1982)).

[82] *See* Mills v. Duryee, 11 U.S. (7 Cranch) 481 (1813), THE FIRST HUNDRED YEARS at 193 n.261.

[83] *See* D'Arcy v. Ketchum, 52 U.S. (11 How.) 165 (1851); *see also* Pennoyer v. Neff, 95 U.S. 714, 729 (1878) (full faith and credit not required when rendering court lacked jurisdiction over parties or subject matter); THE FIRST HUNDRED YEARS at 252 n.119, 365-66.

## A.  *Huntington v. Attrill*

Huntington sued in Maryland to enforce a New York judgment obtained under a statute making directors who had made false statements liable for corporate debts. The Maryland court found the judgment "penal" and refused to enforce it. The Supreme Court, in an 1892 Gray opinion, reversed: it was true that penal judgments fell outside the full faith and credit clause, but this judgment was not penal.[84]

For the first proposition Gray relied on his own recent opinion in *Wisconsin v. Pelican Insurance Co.*,[85] where, in holding its own original jurisdiction limited to civil cases, the Court had said the relevant clause of article III gave jurisdiction only over cases that could otherwise have been brought outside the state whose law was being applied and that full faith would not require one state to enforce the penal judgments of another.[86] The reason given in both cases seemed to be that the rule against enforcing foreign penal laws went to the jurisdiction of the enforcing court; it had long been said that the full faith and credit clause, though making the judgments of other states conclusive, gave no court jurisdiction to enforce them.[87]

This reasoning seemed to invite the states to ignore sister-state judgments by denying their own courts jurisdiction, which would have deprived the clause of much of its effect.[88] An alternative argument would have been that since the clause did not do away with the

---

[84] Huntington v. Attrill, 146 U.S. 657, 683, 686 (1892).

[85] 127 U.S. 265 (1888), *cited in Huntington,* 146 U.S. at 670-72, 685.

[86] 127 U.S. at 289-92. *Pelican Insurance* was influenced by fear that the Supreme Court might be flooded with petty original suits. *Id.* at 300. Gray naturally did not allude to this in *Huntington.*

[87] *See Huntington,* 146 U.S. at 685; *Pelican Insurance,* 127 U.S. at 291-92.

[88] *See infra* notes 96-103 and accompanying text (discussing Fauntleroy v. Lum, 210 U.S. 230 (1908)). However, Gray's principle that the clause did not require the assertion of jurisdiction seemed to be qualified by his sensible caveat that the decision that the law was penal, like the decision that a state had not made a contract it was accused of impairing, must be subject to Supreme Court review to prevent evasion of the full faith requirement. *Huntington,* 146 U.S. at 683-84; *cf.* THE FIRST HUNDRED YEARS at 219 (discussing contract clause cases).

It seemed inconsistent with this insight, and with the similar conclusion reached in Hancock Nat'l Bank v. Farnum, 176 U.S. 640 (1900) (Brewer, J.), for the Court to hold at about the same time that whether one state had misinterpreted another's law did not raise a federal question meriting Supreme Court review. *See* Johnson v. New York Life Ins. Co., 187 U.S. 491 (1903) (Brown, J.); Glenn v. Garth, 147 U.S. 360 (1893) (Fuller, C. J.). There was no suggestion in either of these opinions, as there had been in *Huntington,* 146 U.S. at 683-84, that the clause distinguished between laws and judgments. Indeed, when the decisions were reaffirmed in 1909, the Court expressly stated in dictum that a state constitution was entitled to as much credit as a judgment because it was a "public act[]" within the meaning of the constitutional provisions. Smithsonian Inst. v. St. John, 214 U.S. 19, 28-29 (1909) (Brewer, J.). Moreover, though some language in *Glenn* had suggested that the difficulty lay in the limited categories of federal questions then subject to Supreme Court review under the governing statute, 147 U.S. at 367-68 (distinguishing nonreviewable questions of "construction" from reviewable questions of "validity" of state statutes); *see also* Act of Sept. 24, 1789, § 25, 1 Stat. 73, 85-87 (repealed 1928) (narrowly restricting the Court's power to review highest state-court decisions on writ of error), later decisions went further, *see* *Johnson,* 187 U.S. at 496 (construction issue "not a Federal question"); *Smithsonian,* 214 U.S. at 29 ("[I]t is settled that the mere construction by a state court of the statute of another State, without questioning its validity, does not deny to it the full faith and credit demanded by the constitutional provision."). *But see* B. Currie, *Full Faith and Credit, Chiefly to Judgments: A Role for Congress,* 1964 SUP. CT. REV. 89, 111 (approving the contrary view of some modern cases, *e.g.,* Ford v. Ford, 371 U.S. 187 (1962), that the correctness of the state court's interpretation of the rendering state's law is a federal question).

requirement that the *rendering* court satisfy traditional jurisdictional requirements, it did not do away with other traditional requirements either, including the rule about penal laws.[89] One might in response question whether recognition of traditional exceptions was consistent with a clause designed to make mandatory what had once been a matter of comity;[90] but the same objection could have been leveled against the long-standing jurisdictional exception.[91]

To show that the New York judgment in *Huntington* was not penal, Gray quoted at tiresome length from a flock of decisions, some of which had concluded that "penal" claims did not include private damage actions even though the measure of recovery was not apportioned to the harm the defendant had caused.[92] Unfortunately, however, he had to admit there was a split of authority.[93] That made it impossible to determine what "penal" really meant without understanding the purpose of the rule, and Gray spent so much time quoting other people's conclusions that he never got around to saying what that purpose was. An examination of the reasons usually given to support the rule suggests that Gray was right not to consider the law before him "penal,"[94] but his opinion did not give satisfactory reasons for that conclusion.[95]

---

[89] *See* D'Arcy v. Ketchum, 52 U.S. (11 How.) 165, 175-76 (1851) (discussing the traditional lack of respect for the judgment of a court rendered without service of process: "There was no evil in this part of the existing law, . . . and in our opinion Congress did not intend to overthrow the old rule. . . ."). In support of an exception for penal judgments one might also argue that article IV already provided for enforcement of criminal laws by the distinct means of extradition. This argument would support an even narrower definition of "penal" laws than that taken by the Court in *Huntington*. For a discussion of the different definitions of "penal," see *infra* note 94.

[90] *See* Mills v. Duryee, 11 U.S. (7 Cranch) 481, 485 (1813) (Story, J.) ("Were . . . judgments . . . considered *prima facie* evidence only, this clause in the constitution would be utterly unimportant and illusory."); 3 J. STORY, *supra* note 33, §§ 1303-04; *cf.* Kentucky v. Dennison, 65 U.S. (24 How.) 66, 107-09 (1861) (making similar argument in construing extradition clause of article IV), THE FIRST HUNDRED YEARS at 245-47.

[91] *See supra* note 83 and accompanying text (discussing D'Arcy v. Ketchum, 52 U.S. (11 How.) 165 (1851)). Justice Story, who as indicated was a firm believer that the merits of the rendering court's decision could not be reexamined, argued without explanation that jurisdiction was different. 3 J. STORY, *supra* note 33, § 1307.

[92] 146 U.S. at 666-69, 673-82.

[93] *Id.* at 679 (dismissing contrary cases as having given "no reasons . . . for considering the statute a penal law in the strict, primary and international sense").

[94] *See* RESTATEMENT OF CONFLICT OF LAWS § 611 comment a (1934) (adopting *Huntington's* definition: a penalty is "punishment for a civil wrong," not compensation for loss suffered by injured party); Leflar, *Extrastate Enforcement of Penal and Governmental Claims*, 46 HARV. L. REV. 193, 211, 225 (1932) (explaining the rule largely in terms of provisions requiring local juries and the availability of extradition). There was also a strong argument that the basic reasons for the penal exception were inapplicable to suits for enforcement of judgments. *See* A. EHRENZWEIG, CONFLICT OF LAWS 204-05 (1962); *cf.* Milwaukee County v. M. E. White Co., 296 U.S. 268, 275-77 (1935) (holding a tax judgment entitled to full faith and credit despite the assumption that tax claims not reduced to judgment need not be enforced: "We can perceive no greater possibility of embarrassment [by conflicting interpretations of sister-state laws] in litigating the validity of a judgment for taxes and enforcing it than any other for the payment of money."). The traditional rule seems nevertheless to have embraced such suits. *See* J. STORY, CONFLICT OF LAWS §§ 608-09, 628 (1834). Gray said only that "[t]he essential nature and real foundation of a cause of action are not changed by recovering judgment upon it." *Pelican Insurance*, 127 U.S. at 292.

[95] Fuller dissented, arguing without reasoning that whether the judgment was penal was not a federal question. *Huntington*, 146 U.S. at 688.

## B.  *Fauntleroy v. Lum*

For all its talk about how the full faith and credit clause was not absolute, *Huntington* had required a state to respect a judgment, as did the even more famous 1908 decision in *Fauntleroy v. Lum.*[96]

Fauntleroy had recovered a Missouri judgment on a Mississippi contract respecting cotton futures. A Mississippi court refused to enforce the judgment, and the Supreme Court reversed. Marshall had held that one state must give the judgment of another's competent court the same credit it had at home; the judgment was conclusive in Missouri; and that, said Holmes, was that.[97]

For the four dissenters, Justice White raised two interesting objections. Not only had Gray suggested in *Huntington* and in *Pelican Insurance* that the reason one state need not enforce another's penal judgments was that the full faith clause did not require it to take jurisdiction;[98] as White noted, Holmes himself had written for a unanimous Court in 1903 to hold squarely that a state could decline jurisdiction to enforce an ordinary civil judgment.[99] Holmes responded that the Mississippi law forbidding enforcement of futures contracts in *Fauntleroy* created a "rule of decision" rather than a bar to jurisdiction;[100] he did not explain what earthly significance this distinction had to the terms or purposes of the full faith clause.[101] If Holmes had thought better of his earlier decision, he would have been on firm ground to say so:[102] it is hard to conclude that a state has fulfilled its statutory duty to give a judgment the same credit it would have had where rendered, as the implementing statute requires, when the state refuses to enforce the judgment at all.[103]

---

[96] 210 U.S. 230 (1908).

[97] *Id.* at 236-37 (citing Hampton v. McConnel, 16 U.S. (3 Wheat.) 234 (1818), which had relied on Mills v. Duryee, 11 U.S. (7 Cranch) 481 (1813), *supra* note 83).

[98] *See supra* notes 84-89 and accompanying text.

[99] *See Fauntleroy,* 210 U.S. at 245 (White, J., joined by Harlan, McKenna, and Day, JJ., dissenting) (citing Anglo-American Provision Co. v. Davis Provision Co., 191 U.S. 373 (1903)). The statute in *Anglo-American* had allowed one foreign corporation to sue another only on a local cause of action. 191 U.S. at 373.

[100] 210 U.S. at 234-36.

[101] If Holmes's rationale was that a jurisdictional dismissal would not bar a subsequent suit elsewhere, he drew the wrong line; the question should have been whether the dismissal, jurisdictional or not, was meant to bar only the remedy or the substantive right as well. *Cf.* Bradford Elec. Light Co. v. Clapper, 286 U.S. 145, 160 (1932) (dismissal of foreign cause of action on ground of public policy merely denies a remedy, leaving unimpaired underlying right); Warner v. Buffalo Drydock Co., 67 F.2d 540, 541 (2d Cir. 1933) ("[T]he judgment of the court of a foreign state which dismisses a cause of action because of the statute of limitations of the forum is not a decision upon the merits and is not a bar to a new action upon the identical claim in the courts of another state."). However, in many cases even a dismissal barring only the remedy would leave the judgment holder without practical recourse, just as he would have been before the full faith clause was adopted.

[102] As he later did in Kenney v. Supreme Lodge, 252 U.S. 411, 414-15 (1920), despite an unconvincing attempt to distinguish *Anglo-American* on the basis of "the views about foreign corporations that had prevailed unquestioned since *Bank of Augusta v. Earle* [38 U.S. (13 Pet.) 517 (1839)]": "[A] State cannot escape its constitutional obligations by the simple device of denying jurisdiction . . . to courts otherwise competent."

[103] *See* B. Currie, *supra* note 88, at 119-20; 2 RECORDS OF THE FEDERAL CONVENTION OF 1787, at 447 (M. Farrand rev. ed. 1937) ("Mr. Wilson & Docr. Johnson supposed the meaning to be that Judgments in one state should be the ground of actions in other states. . . .") [hereinafter cited as CONVENTION RECORDS]. The holding that full faith did not require a state to enforce foreign judgments also seems irreconcilable with the almost contemporaneous holding in General Oil Co. v. Crain, 209 U.S. 211 (1908), *supra* p. 54, note 183, that a state could not close its courts on sovereign immunity grounds to suits to enjoin state officers from violating federal

White's other tack was to argue that the clause did not require respect for all valid judgments even if the enforcing court did have jurisdiction.[104] On this point he claimed the authority of the penal exception recognized in *Pelican Insurance*,[105] which Holmes, rather than distinguishing, dismissed as dictum.[106] Dictum in the technical sense it was, though it had been an important part of the Court's explanation for the actual holding; it was also dictum when repeated in *Huntington*,[107] which oddly enough neither side cited at all.

White did not contend that the judgment in *Fauntleroy* was penal. He argued instead that its enforcement would deprive Mississippi of the power to legislate with respect to activities within its own borders; Mississippi had expressed a strong public policy against gambling in cotton futures, and the Court's decision allowed that policy to be frustrated by filing suit in another state.[108] An exception for laws contrary to the public policy of the forum, White suggested, was as much a part of traditional conflict-of-laws doctrine as the penal exception itself.[109] If the full faith and credit clause—which in conformity with his unsympathetic interpretation White kept referring to as the "due faith and credit clause"— did not override traditional exceptions for lack of jurisdiction or for penal claims, parallelism would suggest that it did not override the traditional public policy exception either.[110]

White's concern seemed to raise a substantial doubt: could the Framers have meant to deny a state the power to legislate for its own affairs?[111] The unanimous decision in *Allgeyer v. Louisiana*[112] eleven years before might be thought to have provided an answer: there was no need to distort the full faith and credit clause to avoid reaching absurd results because the state's interest was adequately protected by the ability of the defendant to argue in the original proceeding that due process required the application of Mississippi law.[113]

---

rights. *Cf.* THE FIRST HUNDRED YEARS at 147-48, 211-13 (discussing the extent to which a law abridging a preexisting remedy for breach of contract is an impairment of contracts in violation of article I, § 10).

[104] 210 U.S. at 241-44 (White, J., dissenting).

[105] *Id.* at 242-44. *Pelican Insurance* is discussed *supra* notes 85-88 and accompanying text.

[106] 210 U.S. at 237 (majority opinion). Holmes might have pointed out that Gray had explained the penal exception as part of the general rule that the Constitution did not require a state court to take jurisdiction to enforce foreign judgments. *See supra* notes 85-88 and accompanying text. *But see* Kansas v. Colorado, 206 U.S. 46, 83 (1907) (describing *Pelican Insurance*, in the teeth of Gray's opinion in that case, as "no denial of the jurisdiction of the court, but a decision upon the merits").

[107] *See* 146 U.S. at 670-72, discussed *supra* notes 85-88 and accompanying text.

[108] *See* 210 U.S. at 239-41 (White, J., dissenting).

[109] *Id.* at 241-43. *See* J. STORY, *supra* note 94, §§ 25, 36, 38, 259; 2 J. BEALE, THE CONFLICT OF LAWS § 445.1 (1935).

[110] *See, e.g., Fauntleroy*, 210 U.S. at 242 ("[T]he purpose of the due faith and credit clause was . . . simply to make obligatory that duty which, when the Constitution was adopted rested . . . in comity alone.").

[111] For a more recent version of this argument, see RESTATEMENT (SECOND) OF CONFLICT OF LAWS § 103 comment b (1971) (allowing a public policy exception in "extremely rare" instances involving "too large a sacrifice" of state interests), and see the vigorous response in Ehrenzweig, *The Second Conflicts Restatement: A Last Appeal for Its Withdrawal*, 113 U. PA. L. REV. 1230, 1240 (1965) (advocating strict adherence to *Fauntleroy*).

[112] 165 U.S. 578 (1897), *supra* pp. 45-47.

[113] *See* R. LEFLAR, AMERICAN CONFLICTS LAW § 75 (3d ed. 1977) ("Appeal rather than collateral attack was the losing party's proper remedy. . . .").

The weak spot in this argument is that there seems to have been no such limit on state choice-of-law decisions before the fourteenth amendment was adopted in 1868. The later view that the full faith clause's own reference to "public Acts" required respect for the law of the appropriate state[114] may be out of line with the intentions of the Framers.[115] *Fauntleroy* can thus most effectively be defended on the ground that a public policy exception could easily have destroyed the clause altogether: if a state were free to reject any judgment contrary to its own policy, we would return to the situation the clause was designed to avoid.

Some infringement of one state's interest by another, in other words, may have been the price of full faith and credit. Holmes said none of this; in his lofty way he managed hardly to respond at all to White's provocative challenge.

## C. *Clarke v. Clarke*

Whatever the gaps in Holmes's reasoning, it seemed clear after *Fauntleroy*—with some uncertainty as to the status and nature of the penal exception—that full faith required any court with jurisdiction to give the judgment of another state's court with jurisdiction the same effect it would have had in the state where it was rendered.[116] Most of the Fuller Court's decisions in this field dealt with whether the rendering court had had jurisdiction.

The first such decision came in 1900, when in *Clarke v. Clarke*[117] the Court unani-

---

[114] *See, e.g.,* Bradford Elec. Light Co. v. Clapper, 286 U.S. 145, 154-55 (1932).

[115] The origin of the "public Acts" language was a concern for individual insolvency acts that were similar in effect to judicial judgments. *See* 2 CONVENTION RECORDS, *supra* note 103, at 447 (Messrs. Wilson and Johnson) ("acts of the Legislatures should be included, for the sake of Acts of insolvency &c"); Comment, *Conflict of Laws—Full Faith and Credit as Applied to Statutes,* 51 MICH. L. REV. 267, 269 (1952). Justice Story's influential treatises spoke of full faith and credit only in the context of judgments. J. STORY, *supra* note 94, § 609. He did not suggest that the clause qualified in any way the applicability to states of his general principle that "whatever force and obligation the laws of one country have in another, depends solely on the laws, and municipal regulations of the latter." *Id.* at § 23; *see also* 3 J. STORY, *supra* note 33, §§ 1297-1307. Indeed, Gray had seemed to say in *Huntington* that nothing in the clause required enforcement of foreign claims not reduced to judgment. *See supra* note 88. But suggestions of the opposite theory were already appearing. *See* Atchison, T. & S. F. Ry. v. Sowers, 213 U.S. 55, 66-68 (1909), *infra* note 123; El Paso & N. E. Ry. v. Gutierrez, 215 U.S. 87, 92-93 (1909); Olmsted v. Olmsted, 215 U.S. 386, 394-95 (1910). A notable example is the flat unexplained dictum in Smithsonian Inst. v. St. John, 214 U.S. 19 (1909), relying upon the assumption in an earlier case that "public Acts" included a statute incorporating an individual railroad and finding there had been no denial of full faith and credit. *Id.* at 28-29 (citing Chicago & Alton R.R. v. Wiggins Ferry Co., 119 U.S. 615, 622 (1877) (Waite, C. J.)). In B. CURRIE, SELECTED ESSAYS ON THE CONFLICT OF LAWS (1963), Currie argued that to limit the clause to "legislative decrees of insolvency and divorce . . . not only trivializes the constitutional provision but is in the teeth of clear evidence indicating that the final reference to '*public* Acts' was intended to *exclude* just such legislation from coverage." *Id.* at 198 n.35 (emphasis in original) (citations omitted). The "clear evidence" referred to was Crosskey's speculation that the insertion of the suggestive word "public" was based on the same antipathy to special legislation that induced the Framers to limit Congress to enactment of "uniform" bankruptcy laws. 1 W. CROSSKEY, POLITICS AND THE HISTORY OF THE UNITED STATES 542-44 (1953).

[116] *See* Sistare v. Sistare, 218 U.S. 1 (1910) (White, J.) (reaffirming the holding of Barber v. Barber, 62 U.S. (21 How.) 582 (1859), that alimony decrees were entitled to full faith, reversing Connecticut's reading of New York law, *cf. supra* note 88, and requiring enforcement of past-due sums under an alimony decree though it had been modifiable before the sums fell due); *cf.* Lynde v. Lynde, 181 U.S. 183 (1901) (Gray, J.) (refusing to require enforcement of a similar decree as to *future* installments because the power to modify deprived the decree of binding force even in the rendering state).

[117] 178 U.S. 186 (1900).

mously upheld the refusal of a Connecticut court to honor a South Carolina decree respecting the inheritance of Connecticut land. For the most part, Justice White's opinion reads remarkably like his later dissent in *Fauntleroy:* if Connecticut had to recognize a South Carolina decree, it could not control the ownership of land within its own borders.[118] Since all parties concerned appeared to be from South Carolina,[119] the modern observer may be inclined to take issue with White's conclusion that the substance of the matter was none of South Carolina's business.[120] But the more striking fact is that, despite the similarity of his arguments in the two cases, White did not invoke *Clarke* at all when he dissented from *Fauntleroy* eight years later.

The explanation is that the Court had not held in *Clarke* that a judgment could be collaterally attacked for applying the wrong law; as the last paragraph of the opinion reveals, the decision was based upon "a want of jurisdiction . . . over the particular subject-matter."[121] This conclusion, however, looks at least as peculiar today as the argument that the law of the situs must control. As noted, all the parties seemed to be South Carolinians, and normally the mere fact that foreign law is to be applied does not deprive an otherwise convenient forum of the power to hear the case.[122] Indeed, within nine years after *Clarke* the Court was to hold in *Atchison, Topeka & Sante Fe Railway v. Sowers*[123] that one sovereign could not *prevent* the courts of another from entertaining claims based upon the former's law.[124] The difference between the two cases lay in the traditional distinction between transitory and local actions: an action for personal injuries could be brought anywhere,[125] but actions respecting land could be brought only where the land lay.[126] Modern observers tend to be unsympathetic to the local-action rule at least in its

---

[118]*Id.* at 190-92; *see also* Olmsted v. Olmsted, 216 U.S. 386, 394-95 (1910) (Day, J.) (holding full faith did not require the state where land was situated to recognize a *statute* of another state respecting the right to inherit land: "The full faith and credit clause . . . applies with no more effect to the legislative acts of a foreign State than it does to the judgments of the Courts of such State. . . . The legislature of Michigan had no power to pass an act which would affect the transmission of title to lands located in the State of New York."). For a general statement of the traditional primacy of the law of the situs, see J. STORY, *supra* note 94, § 483.

[119] 178 U.S. at 186.

[120]*See, e.g.,* M. HANCOCK, STUDIES IN MODERN CHOICE-OF-LAW: TORTS, INSURANCE, LAND TITLES chs. 10-12 (1984); Baxter, *Choice of Law and the Federal System,* 16 STAN L. REV. 1, 15-17 (1963).

[121] 178 U.S. at 195.

[122]*See* H. GOODRICH & E. SCOLES, CONFLICT OF LAWS § 96, at 177 (4th ed. 1964); J. STORY, *supra* note 94, § 538.

[123] 213 U.S. 55 (1909) (Day, J.).

[124]*Id.* at 70-71; *cf.* Hughes v. Fetter, 341 U.S. 609, 611-13 (1951) (holding full faith and credit forbade one state to dismiss as contrary to public policy a wrongful-death action based on another's law). The basis of the *Sowers* decision was that, although the place where an accident occurred had power to determine the substantive rights arising out of the occurrence, it could not determine the jurisdiction of a court outside its borders. 213 U.S. at 70. Holmes, whom McKenna joined in dissent, thought the limitation was a "condition to the right" and not a regulation of foreign jurisdiction. *Id.* at 71. For criticism of the decision based on modern interest analysis, see B. CURRIE, *supra* note 115, at 311-26. Of additional significance is the unexplained assumption of all the Justices in *Sowers* that the reference to "public Acts" in the full faith clause and its implementing statute included general statutes. *See supra* note 115 (discussing what was meant by "public Acts").

[125]*See Sowers,* 213 U.S. at 67.

[126]*See, e.g.,* Livingston v. Jefferson, 15 F. Cas. 660 (C.C.D. Va. 1811) (No. 8,411) (action for trespass); 3 J. BEALE, *supra* note 109, § 613.1 ("only the state where the land lies has control over the *res,* and consequently power to affect interests therein").

more extreme applications,[127] but it was firmly established when *Clarke* was decided;[128] that meant that under traditional principles the South Carolina court had lacked jurisdiction.[129]

From today's perspective everything about *Clarke* looks peculiar. It is hard to see why Connecticut should have sole authority to regulate the descent of property among South Carolina citizens. It is hard to see why, even if it has, South Carolina should lack jurisdiction to determine the controversy according to Connecticut law. Finally, it is hard to see why, even if the defect was jurisdictional, the objection should not as a general rule have to be raised in the South Carolina proceeding.[130] All of these things, however, seem to have been pretty standard in 1900.[131] Therefore, though White's lack of explanation and his stress on Connecticut's sole power to *regulate* the transaction seemed to invite a denial of recognition on choice-of-law grounds in *Fauntleroy v. Lum*, the Court in the latter case appears to have recognized *Clarke* for what it really was: a straightforward application according to prevailing jurisdictional principles of the established rule that no credit was due to the judgment of a court without jurisdiction.[132]

---

[127] Most of the criticism has been in the context of actions for trespass to land, where the doctrine has been increasingly discarded. *See, e.g.,* Reasor-Hill Corp. v. Harrison, 220 Ark. 521, 249 S.W.2d 994 (1952); H. GOODRICH & E. SCOLES, *supra* note 122, § 96; *see also* A. EHRENZWEIG, *supra* note 94, at 83 ("Jurisdiction in rem presupposes a situs of the res within the boundaries of the forum state."); *cf.* RESTATEMENT (SECOND), *supra* note 111, § 87 & comment a (preserving the rule when title to land is at stake). The sovereign power rationale that underlies this presupposition, however, *see supra* notes 118, 120, 126, is unpersuasive in a country blessed with a Constitution requiring respect for sister-state judgments. *Cf.* J. STORY, *supra* note 94, § 551 (conceding that the Roman rule allowing land cases to be determined by a domiciliary court made sense in a system in which judgments "would be everywhere respected and obeyed").

[128] *See* J. STORY, *supra* note 94, § 554.

[129] The South Carolina court had attempted to avoid the traditional rule by invoking the fiction that the owner's death had by "equitable conversion" turned the land into personal property; the Supreme Court declined to endorse such a ruse. *Clarke,* 178 U.S. at 191-92; *see* M. HANCOCK, *supra* note 120, at 233 n.26.

[130] The policy of repose underlying full faith and credit is as applicable to jurisdictional questions as it is to the merits, and modern cases have held that even jurisdictional questions can be foreclosed under the full faith and credit clause once actually litigated. *See, e.g.,* Durfee v. Duke, 375 U.S. 106 (1963). For an approving view, see B. Currie, *supra* note 88, at 105. The earlier view was the more formalistic one that a court without jurisdiction had no more power to determine its own jurisdiction than to determine anything else. *See* Thompson v. Whitman, 85 U.S. (18 Wall.) 457, 468 (1873) (Bradley, J.). On top of that, White added in *Clarke* that the party against whom the South Carolina decree was asserted had not been *sui juris* at the time of the South Carolina proceeding (she was a minor) and that no one before the court had had authority to speak for her in respect to out-of-state land. 178 U.S. at 193.

[131] Even at the time of *Clarke,* however, there were so many decisions employing available devices for escaping from the unpalatable consequences of the standard learning that Hancock was able to describe the local-action rule as "a mere textbook aphorism that did not accurately represent . . . practice." M. HANCOCK, *supra* note 120, at 337.

[132] The same is true of the much debated Fall v. Eastin, 215 U.S. 1 (1909), where in an obscure and turgid McKenna opinion the Court over the unexplained dissents of Harlan and Brewer held that Nebraska need not respect a deed to Nebraska land executed by an officer of the state of Washington pursuant to a Washington decree respecting the division of the property of Washington spouses incident to a divorce. Despite the similarity of the case to *Clarke,* the Court acknowledged that the Washington court had had jurisdiction to order the husband to convey the land to his wife and that if he had complied the deed would have been respected. *Id.* at 5-6, 8, 10-11. This suggests that even traditional rules were not so protective of the interests of the situs as *Clarke* might have led one to believe. The trouble was that the Washington officer had attempted to convey the land itself, and that only the situs could exercise jurisdiction to affect the land directly. McKenna seemed to think the distinction as

## D.  *Atherton v. Atherton*

In *Pennoyer v. Neff*,[133] in 1878, the Supreme Court had refused full faith and credit to a judgment for breach of contract on the ground that failure to serve the defendant with process within the state had deprived the rendering court of jurisdiction. In *Atherton v. Atherton*,[134] in 1901, the Court held this rule inapplicable to divorce proceedings, upholding the power of a state where both husband and wife had lived to exercise jurisdiction over an absent spouse who had allegedly abandoned her husband. In two companion cases, however, the Court denied the power of a state in which neither party was domiciled to affect the rights of an absent spouse.[135]

These results are easily explicable in modern terms. *Atherton* was the typical case for which today's long-arm statutes were designed: it seems entirely consonant with the later due process tests of "minimum contacts" and "fair play and substantial justice" to expect an alleged wrongdoer, if actually notified, to litigate at the scene of the wrong.[136] The companion cases presented the other side of the coin: it is unfair to haul a defendant to a forum with which he or she has had no voluntary contact,[137] and a judgment void for want of due process is entitled to no faith anywhere.[138]

Justice Gray, however, did not write in these terms. *Pennoyer* had been based on tradition, not on fairness; due process at that time meant historical process.[139] Indeed Gray did

---

silly as it sounds, but felt bound by it anyway. *See id.* at 11-12. A later commentator, while branding the opinion "undiscriminating, confused, unworthy, reluctant, and ambiguous," has found justification for the distinction in what he thought was the greater interference of a foreign commissioner's deed with the functioning of the recording system. *See* B. Currie, *Full Faith and Credit to Foreign Land Decrees*, 21 U. CHI. L. REV. 620, 639-40, 648 (1954). For questions as to this analysis, see R. CRAMTON, D. CURRIE, & H. KAY, CONFLICT OF LAWS: CASES—COMMENTS—QUESTIONS 641 (4th ed. 1987).

On this point, see also Brown v. Fletcher's Estate, 210 U.S. 82, 94-95 (1908) (Brewer, J.) (holding in accord with traditional understanding that a judgment against an administrator in a suit for an accounting in one state was not binding on an executor of the same decedent elsewhere, on the ground that each state had exclusive jurisdiction to administer property within its borders). For a criticism in modern terms, see D. Currie, *The Multiple Personality of the Dead: Executors, Administrators, and the Conflict of Laws*, 33 U. CHI. L. REV. 429 (1966).

[133] 95 U.S. 714 (1878), THE FIRST HUNDRED YEARS at 365-66.

[134] 181 U.S. 155 (1901).

[135] Bell v. Bell, 181 U.S. 175 (1901); Streitwolf v. Streitwolf, 181 U.S. 179 (1901).

[136] *See* International Shoe Co. v. Washington, 326 U.S. 310, 316 (1945); p. 330 *infra; see also* World-Wide Volkswagen Corp. v. Woodson, 444 U.S. 286 (1980) (adding that the due process clause served also "as an instrument of interstate federalism"); *cf., e.g.*, McGee v. International Life Ins. Co., 355 U.S. 220, 223 (1957) ("It is sufficient for the purpose of due process that the suit was based on a contract which had substantial connection with that State.").

[137] *See* Hanson v. Denckla, 357 U.S. 235, 254 (1958); D. Currie, *The Growth of the Long Arm: Eight Years of Extended Jurisdiction in Illinois*, 1963 U. ILL. L.F. 533, 548-50.

[138] *See* Hanson v. Denckla, 357 U.S. 235, 255 (1958); 28 U.S.C. § 1738 (1982) ("the same full faith and credit in every court . . . as they have . . . in the courts . . . from which they are taken").

[139] The force of tradition had been relaxed before the 1901 cases by Hurtado v. California, 110 U.S. 516 (1884), THE FIRST HUNDRED YEARS at 366-68, which held that the historically requisite grand jury was not part of due process because it was not "fundamental." 110 U.S. at 535. The application of this standard to the particulars of traditional personal-jurisdiction rules had yet to be worked out in detail. An interesting start had been made, however, in the famous case of York v. Texas, 137 U.S. 15 (1890) (Brewer, J.), where the Court held over the unexplained dissents of Bradley and Gray that due process did not require a state to permit a special appear-

not speak of due process at all. Though in holding the judgment entitled to respect he implicitly found it did not offend due process, he was concerned instead with the more ancient principle that, regardless of domestic validity, full faith was not required if traditional jurisdictional standards had not been met.[140]

Just what tradition dictated in the divorce cases was unclear. Gray quoted at pedantic length from a number of state cases upholding jurisdiction over absent spouses in the state where the other lived,[141] added Supreme Court dicta to the same effect,[142] and invoked the authority of influential treatises.[143] As in *Huntington v. Attrill*,[144] however, he had to concede there was contrary state authority.[145] As in *Huntington*, moreover, he resolved the

---

ance to challenge the assertion of jurisdiction over the person. Conceding that the special appearance was sanctified by tradition, the Court said it was enough that the new rule secured "the substance of right . . . without unreasonable burden": the defendant could have protected his right not to be sued in Texas by staying away and attacking the judgment when the plaintiff sued on it in another state. *Id.* at 20-21. Brewer did not acknowledge that he could do so only by forgoing the opportunity to make a defense on the merits in case his jurisdictional attack failed. *Cf.* Fauntleroy v. Lum, 210 U.S. 230 (1908) (forbidding collateral attack on merits), discussed *supra* notes 96-101 and accompanying text. Today it might well be found "unreasonable" to require a defendant to surrender one defense in order to assert another. *See* Note, *Developments in the Law: State-Court Jurisdiction,* 73 HARV. L. REV. 909, 991-97 (1960). The common law, however, was full of such unappetizing choices. For example, the defendant who challenged the legal basis of the plaintiff's case by demurring thereby lost the right to dispute the facts. *See* D. LOUISELL, G. HAZARD, & C. TAIT, CASES AND MATERIALS ON PLEADING AND PROCEDURE 84 (5th ed. 1983); *cf.* Trono v. United States, 199 U.S. 521 (1905) (holding a defendant who appealed a conviction waived double-jeopardy objections to review of his acquittal of another charge in the same case), discussed *supra* note 13. *See also* Roller v. Holly, 176 U.S. 398 (1900) (Brown, J.) (holding five days' notice to a Virginian to defend in Texas not "reasonable" and thus not due process, but evidently by construing the traditional notice requirement as a requirement of reasonable notice).

[140]*See* D'Arcy v. Ketchum, 52 U.S. (11 How.) 165 (1851), discussed *supra* note 83 and accompanying text. Interesting examples of this principle during the Fuller years include Chicago, R. I. & P. Ry. v. Sturm, 174 U.S. 710 (1899) (McKenna, J.), and the well-known case of Harris v. Balk, 198 U.S. 215 (1905) (Peckham, J.), both holding judgments based on so-called foreign attachment entitled to full faith and credit. In both cases the first suit had been brought to collect on an obligation owed by a person beyond the reach of service of process by garnishing a debt owed to the absent person by an individual within the forum state. Without discussing the implicit due process issue, the Court in *Sturm* affirmed the jurisdiction of the court to render a judgment appropriating the garnishee's obligation and discharging him from further liability to the absent party. It did so on the basis partly of historical acceptance, partly of the policy in favor of providing a forum, and partly of physical power over the garnishee. *Sturm,* 174 U.S. at 714-16. In *Sturm* the garnishee had been a resident of the forum state. In *Harris* he was not; though history revealed a lack of consensus on the question, the Court held residence immaterial because any state where the debtor was found had power to extract his money. *Harris,* 198 U.S. at 222.

Under the modern test of fair treatment of the absent party these decisions are quite untenable, and *Harris* has been overruled. *See* Shaffer v. Heitner, 433 U.S. 186 (1977); *see also* D. Currie, *supra* note 137, at 584. Even in terms of power the Court's reasoning in *Harris* seems misguided: although the forum could physically do as it pleased to the unfortunate garnishee, it had no physical power over his absent creditor, and physical power over intangible "property" is pure fiction.

[141]*Atherton,* 181 U.S. at 164-69.

[142]*Id.* at 163-64.

[143]*Id.* at 164, 166 (citing Story, Kent, and Cooley). To the extent that the traditional rule requiring service within the state reflected the supposed futility of entering a judgment that could not be executed—a concern misplaced in a federation with a full faith requirement—divorce cases were distinguishable: the divorce decree would effecively liberate the plaintiff spouse whether or not physical consequences could be visited upon the defendant or his assets.

[144]146 U.S. 657 (1892), discussed *supra* notes 84-95 and accompanying text.

[145]*Atherton,* 181 U.S. at 169-70.

conflict in favor of what he thought the more appropriate rule: "To hold otherwise would make it difficult if not impossible, for the husband to obtain a divorce for the cause alleged, if it actually existed." [146] The companion cases were resolved by mere fiat: "No valid divorce . . . can be decreed on constructive service by the courts of a State in which neither party is domiciled." [147]

Thus the Court seemed to read the full faith and credit clause to require it to develop what was essentially a federal common law of state-court jurisdiction, confected from historical practice and shaped in the mold of public policy. On the facts of *Atherton* and its companion cases the Court by this method and with very little explanation attained results fully in accord with the modern due process calculus of fair play—if one puts to one side the Court's strange indifference to whether the defendant had actually been given notice of the proceeding. [148]

### E.   *Andrews v. Andrews*

Two years later, over three unexplained dissents, Justice White wrote for the Court in *Andrews v. Andrews* [149] to hold that no credit was due to a divorce decreed by a court of a state in which neither party lived even if the defendant did not object to the exercise of jurisdiction. We have discussed the earlier divorce cases in terms of jurisdiction over the person, which can be waived because it relates primarily to the convenience of the litigant. [150] But in *Andrews* the Court explained that *Atherton* and its companion cases had held domicile essential to jurisdiction over the *subject matter*—and a want of subject-matter jurisdiction could not be cured by consent. [151]

Like the decision in *Clarke v. Clarke* that controversies over land titles were not transitory, [152] this characterization was out of line with the practice governing most lawsuits; analogy to tort or contract cases would suggest that any court could divorce a New York couple willing to litigate there so long as New York law was applied. As *Clarke* showed, however, there were exceptions. And, whether or not the exception regarding land made sense, Justice White revealed in *Andrews* why there was a special problem in divorce

---

[146] *Id.* at 173. The dissenters turned this argument around, assuming the facts to be as found by a court in the state to which the wife had moved: "That a husband can drive his wife from his home" and then divorce her there was "at war with sound principle and the adjudged cases." *Id.* at 175 (Peckham, J., joined by Fuller, C. J., dissenting). In voting to sustain the judgment of the wife's state, the dissenters showed that they were by no means hostile to the assertion of jurisdiction over an absent defendant; in their view the jurisdiction of both courts depended on the merits.

[147] Bell v. Bell, 181 U.S. 175, 177 (1901). Streitwolf v. Streitwolf, 181 U.S. 179 (1901), was decided on the authority of *Bell. Id.* at 182-83.

[148] *See Atherton*, 181 U.S. at 171-72 (saying there was a "presumption" that the wife had received an unanswered letter of notification, but finding it irrelevant if she had not because the real question was not actual notice but whether "reasonable steps had been taken to give her notice"). At least one of the cases relied on had said that service by publication would suffice on a defendant whose residence was unknown. *See id.* at 166-67 (citing Ditson v. Ditson, 4 R. I. 87 (1856)). For the modern view of the notice question, see Mullane v. Central Hanover Bank & Trust Co., 339 U.S. 306 (1950).

[149] 188 U.S. 14 (1903). Brewer, Shiras, and Peckham dissented. Holmes, who had taken his seat after argument, took no part. *Id.* at 42.

[150] *See* Note, *supra* note 139, at 997; FED. R. CIV. P. 12(h)(1).

[151] 188 U.S. at 39-41; *cf.* Mansfield, C. & L. M. Ry. v. Swan, 111 U.S. 379 (1884) (lack of diversity jurisdiction not curable by consent of parties); FED. CIV. P. 12(h)(3) (same).

[152] *See supra* notes 117-32 and accompanying text.

cases. The marriage relation was "so interwoven with public policy that the consent of the parties is impotent to dissolve it contrary to the law of the domicil."[153] If the parties could achieve the same result by "perpetrating a fraud" on that law "by temporarily sojourning in another State," then "all efficacious power on the subject of divorce [would] be at an end."[154]

In short, in the ordinary case any interest the state of the tort or contract may have in the application of its own law is to some degree protected by the parties' incentive to insist on application of provisions that favor them;[155] in a state with strict divorce laws both parties are likely to be determined to frustrate state policy. If such laws were not to be evaded at pleasure, some way had to be found to allow the courts to protect the state's interest despite the wishes of the parties, and the label of subject-matter jurisdiction admirably filled the bill. In the first place, it permitted the court in which a divorce was sought to raise the question of domicile on its own motion. Moreover, under the view prevailing at the time of *Andrews,* subject-matter jurisdiction was always open to collateral attack. As in *Andrews* itself, the state of domicile could protect its own interest, even if the other court did not, by refusing to recognize the decree.

With eighty years of hindsight, it may be possible to improve on White's solution to the problem. The jurisdictional label achieved the desired result at the risk of denying the parties a possibly convenient forum; all the Court had to say was that choice-of-law decisions, like some jurisdictional ones, could not be left to the parties in divorce cases.[156] That kind of flexibility, however, was uncommon in turn-of-the-century jurisprudence[157] and did not reflect the traditional rules the Court seemed to think were the measure of full faith and credit. Furthermore, the cases in which it was a hardship for the parties to resort to their own courts must have been relatively rare.[158] *Andrews* came up with an effective solution to the perennial problem of collusive divorce and persuasively explained its reasons.

## F.  *Haddock v. Haddock*

Yet another variation on the divorce problem was presented by the landmark case of *Haddock v. Haddock*[159] in 1906. This time the husband had moved from the marital domicile in New York to Connecticut, where he had procured an ex parte divorce. New York re-

---

[153]*Andrews,* 188 U.S. at 41.

[154]*Id.* at 38, 32; *see also* J. STORY, *supra* note 94, § 226.

[155]Even in such a case, as *Fauntleroy* shows, White argued for protection against the power of the forum to disregard the applicable law. See *supra* notes 104-15 and accompanying text.

[156]*See* D. Currie, *Suitcase Divorce in the Conflict of Laws:* Simons, Rosenstiel *and* Borax, 34 U. CHI. L. REV. 26; 47-48 (1966).

[157]*But cf.* Clark v. Barnard, 108 U.S. 436, 447 (1883) (finding the eleventh amendment's facially absolute ban on the exercise of federal judicial power over certain suits against a state "is a personal privilege which [the state] may waive at pleasure").

[158]*See* Gould v. Gould, 235 N.Y. 14, 138 N. E. 490 (1923) (French divorce of New Yorkers long resident in France under New York law); D. Currie, *supra* note 156, at 48 & n.103 (noting existence of statutes dealing with military personnel). The recognition of the foreign divorce in *Gould* shows that the jurisdictional label affixed in *Andrews* did not necessarily deprive parties of a convenient forum; since the Court did not hold that due process forbade a divorce outside the state of domicile, recognition might still be permitted though not required.

[159]201 U.S. 562 (1906). For a partial list of the copious commentary on this decision, see H. GOODRICH & E. SCOLES, *supra* note 122, at 263 n.53.

fused to recognize the decree, and in another White opinion the Court affirmed over four dissents.[160]

To White the relevant principle was the one he had put forth in *Andrews:* if the Connecticut decree were entitled to recognition, New York could not regulate the marriage relations of her own citizens.[161] To Holmes, dissenting, the case was governed by *Atherton:* if the domicile of one party could grant a divorce, so could the domicile of the other.[162] In modern terms both White and Holmes were wrong.

White was wrong because in *Andrews* the sole state with any interest in the matter was the domicile of both parties, while in *Haddock* Connecticut had as legitimate a concern with the status of its domiciliary as New York had in that of its own. *Andrews* forbade one state to meddle in another's affairs; *Haddock* gave exclusive authority to one state over a matter that was the concern of two.

Holmes was wrong because it was not unfair to require the departing spouse in *Atherton* to return to her earlier home for litigation; it would have been unfair to drag the left-behind spouse in *Haddock* into a forum in a state with which she had had no connection.[163] White's legitimate concern for the choice-of-law problem in *Andrews* had blinded him to the fact that in *Haddock* there was a problem with personal jurisdiction; the traditional insistence on personal service within the state had deafened Holmes to the critical distinction in terms of fair play. In modern terms White reached the right result for the wrong reason, and his failure to articulate the real concern left his decision unnecessarily vulnerable to attack.[164]

---

[160] Justices Brown, Harlan, Brewer, and Holmes dissented. *See id.* at 606 (Brown, J., dissenting).

[161] *Haddock*, 201 U.S. at 573-76.

[162] *Id.* at 629-31 (Holmes, J., dissenting); *cf.* Beale, *Constitutional Protection of Decrees for Divorce*, 19 HARV. L. REV. 586, 596 (1906) (asserting that the decision "astonished the whole bar of the country"). White dressed his conclusion in metaphysical terms by saying the marital "res" was located at the marital domicile, which was where the parties had lived before the husband left the state. *Haddock*, 201 U.S. at 576-78. Since the res was fictitious, its invocation could be neither refuted nor supported, and it did not help his case. *See id.* at 630 (Holmes, J., dissenting).

But for Maynard v. Hill, 125 U.S. 190 (1888), THE FIRST HUNDRED YEARS at 381 n.97, which had held that marriage was not the kind of transaction protected by the contract clause, White might better have argued that Connecticut had impaired the obligation of the marriage contract contrary to article I, § 10 by applying its own law to dissolve a marriage subject in its inception only to the grounds of divorce specified by New York law. *Cf.* McMillan v. McNeill, 17 U.S. (4 Wheat.) 209 (1819), (contract clause offended by application of state insolvency law to contract governed when made by law of another state), THE FIRST HUNDRED YEARS at 154 n.239. An argument could still have been made that it was as unfair to determine the rights of the stay-at-home spouse on the basis of the law of a state with which she had had no connection as to subject her to that state's exercise of judicial power. *See* Sedler, *Judicial Jurisdiction and Choice of Law: The Consequences of* Shaffer v. Heitner, 63 IOWA L. REV. 1031, 1033 (1978); Silberman, Shaffer v. Heitner: *The End of an Era*, 53 N.Y.U. L. REV. 33, 88 (1978) ("To believe that a defendant's contacts with the forum state should be stronger under the due process clause for jurisdictional purposes than for choice of law is to believe that the accused is more concerned with where he will be hanged than whether.")

[163] *See* D. Currie, *supra* note 137, at 548-50. *Compare* McGee v. International Life Ins. Co., 355 U.S. 220 (1957) (allowing judgment to be entered against a nonresident insurance company on a contract that had a substantial connection with the forum state), *with* Hanson v. Denckla, 357 U.S. 235 (1958) (refusing to permit a judgment against a nonresident trust company whose customer became domiciled in the forum state after the transaction had occurred).

[164] *See* Williams v. North Carolina, 317 U.S. 287, 296-301 (1942) (overruling *Haddock*), *infra* pp. 329–30, *id.* at 316-20 (Jackson, J., dissenting) (complaining that *Williams* meant that "settled family relationships may be destroyed by a procedure that we would not recognize if the suit were one to collect a grocery bill").

In terms of the outcome, White's greatest obstacle was *Maynard v. Hill*,[165] in which the Court had upheld a divorce granted by a territorial legislature to a husband who had moved there from the marital domicile despite the absence of the wife. Without attempting to argue that personal jurisdiction requirements were inapplicable to legislative divorces,[166] White distinguished *Maynard* as having held only that the divorce was valid in the territory where it had been rendered, not that it was entitled to respect elsewhere.[167]

The dissenters effectively pointed out the difficulty of reconciling the conclusion that a judgment valid where rendered was not entitled to full faith and credit with the text or purpose of the clause and its implementing statute.[168] *Haddock* itself graphically illustrated the problem: as later Justices were to observe, the result of that decision was that the Haddocks were married in one state and not in another[169]—clearly an intolerable arrangement in a federal system.

Modern analysis would have enabled the Court to avoid the problem by holding that a divorce entered by a court in a state with which an absent defendant had no contact was entitled to no respect anywhere because it deprived the defendant of liberty or property without due process of law.[170] At the time of *Haddock,* however, the distinction between validity at home and respect abroad for decisions not satisfying traditional jurisdictional standards was firmly established;[171] to have reached the due process question would not only have required confronting *Maynard* but would also have gone beyond what was necessary to decide the case.

---

[165] 125 U.S. 190 (1888).

[166] *Cf.* Budd v. New York, 143 U.S. 517, 546-47 (1892); *supra* pp. 42-43. In any event, Allgeyer v. Louisiana, 165 U.S. 578 (1897), had already established that due process limited the territorial scope of substantive state legislation. *See supra* pp. 45-47. If *Maynard* was still law, it thus seemed to dispose of White's concern that Connecticut was meddling with a marriage whose continuation was none of its business.

[167] *Haddock,* 201 U.S. at 574-75.

[168] *Id.* at 626 (Brown, J., dissenting); *id.* at 632-33 (Holmes, J., dissenting). The statute provided that judicial proceedings "shall have such faith and credit . . . in every court . . . as they have . . . in the courts of the State from which they are . . . taken." Act of May 26, 1790, 1 Stat. 122 (codified as amended at 28 U.S.C. § 1738 (1982)).

[169] *See* Williams v. North Carolina, 317 U.S. 287, 299-300 (1942).

[170] *See* D. Currie, *supra* note 156, at 28. As an original question one might have doubted whether marriage rights were either "liberty" or "property" within the due process clause. *See supra* p. 45, discussing Allgeyer v. Louisiana, 165 U.S. 578 (1897). But the Court in holding that the clause protected "liberty of contract" had defined the terms so broadly that the inclusion of marriage should no more have raised eyebrows when *Haddock* was decided than it did when due process was first applied to a divorce case many years later. *See* Alton v. Alton, 207 F.2d 667 (3d Cir. 1953).

[171] Beale, *supra* note 162, at 594, indignantly denied there was any such distinction; but the initial state judgment in D'Arcy v. Ketchum, 52 U.S. (11 How.) 165 (1851) (upholding state's refusal to give full faith to New York judgment rendered without service of process on defendant), discussed *supra* note 83, for example, had been entered in accordance with a statute that the Court did not even suggest was unconstitutional. *See* Schofield, *The Doctrine of* Haddock v. Haddock, 1 ILL. L. REV. 219, 225-29 (1906).

# Conclusion to Part One

"Oh, but there were Giants on the Court in those days." So Fuller is reported to have said of his early years on the Bench,[1] and so there were. Within a short time, however, the three tallest had given way to ordinary mortals as Brown, Shiras, and McKenna replaced Miller, Bradley, and Field. These sad substitutions set the tone for what was to come; in terms of personnel the Fuller period was a drab time in the history of the Court.

In substantive terms it was an important and interesting period. The center of constitutional controversy was the clash of economic interests, and it was characterized by striking contrasts. While the sugar-trust case gave the commerce power an artificially narrow reading, the Court invited Congress to regulate anything it pleased under the guise of a tax, upheld congressional authority over aliens without reference to the enumeration of powers, and allowed the courts to issue injunctions not authorized by statute. The due process clause was employed for the first time to invalidate unreasonable rates, extraterritorial legislation, and the bakers' ten-hour workday; but the Court upheld most similar measures and cut back sharply on the protection afforded by the contract clause. Sovereign immunity was broadened to forbid suits by citizens against their own states and narrowed to permit more suits against state officers.

Some of the apparent inconsistencies suggest a tendency to favor business interests, as when the Court held that the Sherman Act could validly reach labor boycotts but not combinations of manufacturers.[2] As a guardian of business, however, the Fuller Court cannot be described as very successful; the great bulk of business-limiting measures that it addressed were upheld.

No great respect for precedent characterized the decisions of the Fuller years. *Leisy v.*

---

[1] *See* W. KING, MELVILLE WESTON FULLER 125 (1950).

[2] Loewe v. Lawlor, p. 27, *supra;* United States v. E. C. Knight Co., pp. 22-24 *supra. See* R. MCCLOSKEY, THE AMERICAN SUPREME COURT 127 (1960) ("[T]he Court's chief concern was to defend the principle of laissez faire[,] and . . . both nationalist and localist doctrine were being pressed to subserve that end.").

*Hardin* overruled the *License Cases*. *In re Rahrer* evaded *Cooley*'s express declaration that Congress could not allow states to regulate commerce. The *Income Tax Case* essentially overruled two earlier decisions. *Ex parte Young* was inconsistent with *In re Ayers*. And, without fanfare, the Court basically abandoned the uniformity test that had figured so prominently in cases regarding state power over commerce. Typically, the Justices seldom acknowledged that they were departing from precedent. Even *Leisy* blamed the demise of the *License Cases* on an intervening decision—one in which the Court had done its best to pretend that it was not disturbing the prior law.

Of the eleven Justices who did the bulk of the constitutional writing during the Fuller period,[3] only four have a serious claim to eminence in that field. The first is Gray, whose erudition is said to have approached Story's,[4] and who had made a substantial contribution to the work of the Court during the eight years preceding Fuller's appointment. Though he continued to sit for more than half the Fuller era, however, his performance was disappointing. He wrote none of the important economic decisions, nor did he dissent from them. His major constitutional work was in the abstruse fields of full faith and credit and the negative effect of the commerce clause, where he argued for greater state authority and helped rationalize the confused law. His opinions tended to be larded with history, but his use of history was more affected than effective.[5] There was no need to explore all of Western civilization to prove that the fourteenth amendment meant what it said about the children of aliens born in the United States,[6] for example, and history gave conflicting answers to the scope of the penal exception to recognition of judgments, which he resolved in *Huntington v. Attrill* by mere assertion.[7] Despite his promise, in constitutional cases Gray was neither an important voice on the Fuller Court nor distinguished by the quality of his opinions.

The other significant holdover from the Waite days was Harlan, who continued to sit with great vigor throughout the time Fuller was Chief Justice. He wrote over a hundred constitutional opinions during this period, substantially more than any other Justice. He also differed with his brethren far more than anyone else, and he found time to write about fifty dissenting opinions in constitutional cases—three times as many as any of his colleagues.

As foretold by his earlier record, Harlan's work was most noticeably marked by strong support for civil rights and for the police power. In a series of impassioned dissents, he argued for racial equality, for the incorporation of the Bill of Rights in the fourteenth amendment, and for the application of constitutional provisions to the territories. He

---

[3] Matthews, Blatchford, and Lamar, who disappeared early, were hardly missed. Jackson, Moody, and Lurton served too briefly to make much of an impression, though Moody was a much-admired lawyer described as "one of the ablest Justices of his period," *see* W. KING, *supra* note 1, at 308-09, 316-17. Ill health forced his retirement after only four years.

[4] *See, e.g., id.* at 132-33.

[5] "[I]t is this very adherence to the common law and exhaustive historical research which, in the writer's view, deprived Gray of his rightful place in the history of the Supreme Court. . . ." Smith, *Mr. Justice Horace Gray of the United States Supreme Court*, 6 S.D.L. REV. 220, 246 (1961).

[6] *See supra* p. 16, note 59 (discussing United States v. Wong Kim Ark, 169 U.S. 649 (1898)).

[7] "Holmes used to say of Gray that the premise of his opinion and the conclusion stood forth like precipices, with a roaring torrent of precedents between, but he never quite understood how Gray got across. . . ." F. BIDDLE, MR. JUSTICE HOLMES 103 (1942).

wrote for the Court to uphold several important economic measures and dissented from the invalidation of others. While alert to protect interstate activities from practical as well as facial discrimination, he was perhaps the leading exponent of the emerging principle that reasonable police-power measures should be upheld despite their effects on commerce. Yet for all this he was no opponent of substantive due process as such; it may come as a surprise that he was the author of the famous opinions invalidating unreasonable rail rates and the ban on discharge of union members.

Even a brief recitation of Harlan's accomplishments reveals him as a figure of considerable importance in the Court's history, and the country has since come around to many of the views he expressed in often solitary dissents.[8] In several important opinions, moreover—such as the dissents in *Lochner, E. C. Knight,* and *Plessy v. Ferguson*—he put forth persuasive arguments in support of his position. He lacked the incisiveness of Miller or Taney, the learning of Bradley or Story, the magisterial style of Curtis or Marshall, the imagination and theoretical strength of Field.[9] Nevertheless, by any criterion he was one of the standouts of the Fuller period.

The third Justice of note was White, who in sixteen years with Fuller richly earned his unprecedented promotion to succeed the latter as Chief Justice. Though he did not write for the Court in the great economic controversies of the day, he captured attention by the power and originality of his theories in three fields outside the mainstream. It was White who first explained the limits of the nondelegation doctrine in realistic modern terms, who fought tenaciously for an interpretation of the full faith and credit clause that would allow states to regulate their own affairs, and who enunciated the powerful incorporation thesis ultimately adopted to govern the status of territories. White's most conspicuous failing was in *Mankichi,* where he neglected to explain why the argument he had expressly employed only as an interpretation of a clause limited to "the United States" applied to jury-trial provisions containing no such limitation.[10] But he was a major intellectual force on the Court at a time when they were in short supply.

We come at last to Holmes. From the day he arrived, the man with the marvelous mustache displayed dazzling skills that left his more pedestrian colleagues in the shade. In terms of sheer productivity he was prodigious. In eight years he cranked out nearly as many constitutional opinions as the Chief Justice wrote in over twenty, far surpassing even Harlan in constitutional opinions per year. He turned them out with remarkable alacrity; cases in which Holmes wrote were not infrequently decided within two weeks after argument.[11] And his style! His opinions are a breath of fresh air. Gray, Harlan, and White could make good ideas tedious; Holmes made the dullest case a literary adventure.

Yet for all their stylistic appeal, the constitutional opinions of Holmes's first years are substantively not very satisfying. He was adept enough in putting forth interesting ideas,

[8]*See* F. LATHAM, THE GREAT DISSENTER *passim* (1970); Watt & Orlikoff, *The Coming Vindication of Mr. Justice Harlan,* 44 ILL. L. REV. 13 (1949); White, *John Marshall Harlan I: The Precursor,* 19 AM J. LEG. HIST. 1 (1975). For a laudatory assessment at the time of his death, see Brown, *The Dissenting Opinions of Mr. Justice Harlan,* 46 AM. L. REV. 321 (1912).

[9]Holmes once wrote that Harlan's mind was "a powerful vise the jaws of which couldn't be got nearer than two inches to each other." W. KING, *supra* note 1, at 131.

[10]*See supra* pp. 64-65.

[11]*See* W. KING, *supra* note 1, at 290-91 (noting that Holmes often asked for more work and quoting Holmes's observation that "[a] case doesn't generally take more than two days if it does that.").

such as the current-of-commerce theory justifying federal regulation of stockyard sales, but he tended to advance them essentially as unsupported conclusions. His treatment of the serious freedom of expression issues in *Patterson v. Colorado* was indifferent in the extreme.[12] His most celebrated opinion of the time illustrates his inclination to substitute epigrams for analysis: instead of taking *Lochner* as the opportunity to show what the due process clause was all about, Holmes contented himself with the smug assertion that the clause did not "enact Mr. Herbert Spencer's Social Statics."

Like Harlan, Holmes was important because history has embraced his frequent dissenting views. Like no one before him, he was a master of the well-turned phrase. Like Miller, however, he did not always take the trouble to justify his clever conclusions,[13] and he wrote few of the major decisions of the Court while Fuller was Chief Justice.

Fuller, who at the beginning kept for himself such monumental opinions as those on the sugar trust and the income tax, later left the big cases to others to a degree quite foreign to the practice of his four immediate predecessors.[14] He stayed away from the great due process cases, though he joined them; in the politically significant insular cases he found himself in dissent. Indeed, though Fuller wrote dissenting opinions only in major cases, he was recorded as dissenting at least fifty times in constitutional matters—he was far less in control of the outcome than either Taney or Waite had been, not to mention Marshall. Moreover, the quality of his opinions was not high. *Leisy* was a string of unfocused quotations; *E. C. Knight* mischaracterized an indictment respecting interstate sales as one respecting manufacturing; *Pollock* was internally contradictory and neglected strong arguments that would have supported the decision. The contrast between Fuller's conclusions that the sugar trust did not restrain commerce and that the Danbury hat boycott did suggests that he may not have been guided exclusively by neutral legal principles.[15]

Brewer and Peckham were in the forefront of the Court's assault on social legislation. Brewer continued to argue that rate regulation was unconstitutional, took the lead in the few decisions striking down measures on equal protection grounds, and dissented from several decisions rejecting due process objections to state regulatory provisions such as the limitation of miners' hours.[16] Peckham was the Court's chief spokesman for the new liberty of contract and dissented even more frequently than Brewer from decisions upholding state or federal regulation. Peckham was not an effective advocate: *Allgeyer* and *Lochner* were bare conclusions, *Ex parte Young* butchered the law of sovereign immunity, and Peckham almost never bothered to explain his dissenting votes. Brewer's opinions were

---

[12]*Cf.* Rogat, *Mr. Justice Holmes: A Dissenting Opinion* (pt. 2), 15 STAN. L. REV. 254, 308 (1963) (arguing on the basis of decisions respecting aliens and race that "the accepted image of Holmes as uniquely libertarian owes more to the fantasies unloosed by the attractiveness of his personality than to the realities of his career").

[13]*See* Rogat, *Mr. Justice Holmes: A Dissenting Opinion* (pt. 1), 15 STAN. L. REV. 3, 9 (1962); White, *The Integrity of Holmes' Jurisprudence,* 10 HOFSTRA L. REV. 633, 664, 671 (1982) (describing Holmes as "a judge whose principal interest seems to have been in having cases decided, written up, and disposed of" and tracing this attitude to a conviction that judging was largely a matter of arbitrary preferences that could not be satisfactorily explained).

[14]*See* W. KING, *supra* note 1, at 332-33.

[15]Fuller's skills as presiding Justice, however, were widely admired. Miller and Holmes, for example, both of whom served with a number of Chief Justices, were said to have regarded Fuller as the best presiding judge they had encountered. *See* W. KING, *supra* note 1, at 127, 290, 333-34.

[16]For a rather sympathetic modern assessment, see Garner, *Justice Brewer and Substantive Due Process: A Conservative Court Revisited,* 18 VAND. L. REV. 615 (1965).

less obviously flawed, and his commitment to economic rights was coupled with a conspicuous respect for civil liberties, most prominently in cases respecting aliens. But in *Debs* he seemed oblivious to the distinction between congressional and judicial power, and his opinions in general do not make much of an impression.

Four Justices remain: Brown, Shiras, McKenna, and Day. Brown was a relatively important member of the Court, best known today for his callous opinion in *Plessy v. Ferguson,* constructive in the development of commerce clause jurisprudence, and notable for his extreme position that the Constitution applied to none of the territories.[17] Shiras attracted little attention in nearly a dozen years, writing nothing of interest for the Court but providing a few intelligent dissents. Day sat nearly as long as Holmes and left virtually no trace. McKenna, very likely the most inept writer of them all,[18] managed an uncharacteristically effective dissent on the commerce clause issue in the yellow-dog case.

In sum, the Fuller period was a time of important decisions, but it was not on the whole a strong period in the history of the Court.

[17] For a description and criticism of Brown's work as a whole, see Glennon, *Justice Henry Billings Brown: Values in Tension,* 44 U. COLO. L. REV. 553 (1973).

[18] McKenna's appointment prompted two federal trial judges to take the unusual step of writing letters lamenting his unfitness for the post, as evidenced by his performance as a circuit judge. *See* W. KING, *supra* note 1, at 228-30 (adding that McKenna's colleagues "always felt in him some judicial inadequacy" and that "Fuller took care to assign to him the simpler cases").

# Part Two

## Chief Justice White
## 1910–1921

# Introduction to Part Two

The unprecedented promotion[1] of Associate Justice Edward Douglass White to succeed Melville Fuller as Chief Justice in 1910 marked a significant divide in the membership of the Supreme Court. Within a single presidential term (1909-12), William Howard Taft appointed five new Justices: Horace H. Lurton, Charles Evans Hughes, Willis Van Devanter, Joseph R. Lamar, and Mahlon Pitney. Once Pitney had succeeded John M. Harlan in 1912, the only additional changes during White's eleven years as Chief Justice came when President Wilson replaced Lurton, Lamar, and Hughes with James C. McReynolds, Louis D. Brandeis, and John H. Clarke about midway through the period. Joseph McKenna, Oliver Wendell Holmes, and William R. Day were long-standing holdovers who served with White until his death in 1921.[2]

---

[1] Justice Cushing was nominated and confirmed as Chief Justice in 1796, but he declined the promotion. *See* 1 C. WARREN, THE SUPREME COURT IN UNITED STATES HISTORY 139-40 (rev. ed. 1926).

[2]     JUSTICES OF THE SUPREME COURT DURING THE TIME OF CHIEF JUSTICE WHITE

|  |  | 1910 | 12 | 14 | 16 | 18 | 20 |
|---|---|---|---|---|---|---|---|
| John M. Harlan | (1877-1911) | | | | | | |
| Edward D. White | (1894-1921) | | | | | | |
| Joseph McKenna | (1898-1925) | | | | | | |
| Oliver W. Holmes | (1902-1932) | | | | | | |
| William R. Day | (1903-1922) | | | | | | |
| Horace H. Lurton | (1909-1914) | | | | | | |
| Charles E. Hughes | (1910-1916) | | | | | | |
| Willis Van Devanter | (1910-1937) | | | | | | |
| Joseph R. Lamar | (1910-1916) | | | | | | |
| Mahlon Pitney | (1912-1922) | | | | | | |
| James C. McReynolds | (1914-1941) | | | | | | |
| Louis D. Brandeis | (1916-1939) | | | | | | |
| John H. Clarke | (1916-1922) | | | | | | |

SOURCE: Adapted from G. GUNTHER, CASES AND MATERIALS ON CONSTITUTIONAL LAW app. B (11th ed. 1985).

In terms of membership, therefore, the Court over which White presided had an identity rather distinct from that of its predecessor. In terms of constitutional development,
however, the White period was largely a time of continuity. With the striking exception of
*Hammer v. Dagenhart,*[3] the Court continued its general tendency toward broad construction of congressional powers, from the commerce clause in the *Shreveport Rate Case*[4] and
the tax power in *United States v. Doremus*[5] to the war powers in *Hamilton v. Kentucky
Distilleries & Warehouse Co.*[6] and the treaty power in *Missouri v. Holland.*[7] Due process
and equal protection continued to be employed erratically to invalidate occasional economic measures such as the state ban on yellow-dog contracts in *Coppage v. Kansas,*[8]
while the Court receded from its blockade of maximum-hour legislation in *Bunting v.
Oregon.*[9] The Court did pay increasing attention to the Civil War amendments in the field
of racial justice, striking down a peonage law in *Bailey v. Alabama,*[10] a grandfather clause
for voting in *Guinn v. United States,*[11] and a residential segregation ordinance in *Buchanan v. Warley.*[12] A series of decisions beginning with *Southern Pacific Co. v. Jensen*[13]
overshadowed the usual run of cases on the negative effect of the commerce clause by
proclaiming a preemptive force in article III's grant of admiralty jurisdiction far stronger
than that ever attributed to the commerce clause itself. The most interesting and important
aspect of the White years, however, was the famous series of wartime freedom of expression cases beginning with Justice Holmes's opinion for the Court in *Schenck v. United
States,*[14] and concluding with the emergence of a more protective philosophy in his dissent
in *Abrams v. United States*[15] later the same year.[16]

[3] 247 U.S. 251 (1918).
[4] Houston, E. & W. Tex. Ry. v. United States, 234 U.S. 342 (1914).
[5] 249 U.S. 86 (1919).
[6] 251 U.S. 146 (1919).
[7] 252 U.S. 416 (1920).
[8] 236 U.S. 1 (1915).
[9] 243 U.S. 426 (1917).
[10] 219 U.S. 219 (1911).
[11] 238 U.S. 347 (1915).
[12] 245 U.S. 60 (1917).
[13] 244 U.S. 205 (1917).
[14] 249 U.S. 47 (1919).
[15] 250 U.S. 616, 624 (1919) (Holmes, J., dissenting).
[16] The indispensable overall Court history of these years is A. BICKEL & B. SCHMIDT, 9 HISTORY OF THE
SUPREME COURT OF THE UNITED STATES (1984). Standard older histories such as 2 C. WARREN, *supra note* 1,
at 690–756, and A. MCLAUGHLIN, A CONSTITUTIONAL HISTORY OF THE UNITED STATES 760-94 (1935), barely
mention the White period. Biographies of the Justices include F. BIDDLE, MR. JUSTICE HOLMES (1942); M.
HOWE, JUSTICE OLIVER WENDELL HOLMES: THE SHAPING YEARS, 1841-1870 (1957); M. HOWE, JUSTICE
OLIVER WENDELL HOLMES: THE PROVING YEARS, 1870-1882 (1963); M. KLINKHAMER, EDWARD DOUGLAS
[*sic*] WHITE, CHIEF JUSTICE OF THE UNITED STATES (1943); A. MASON, BRANDEIS: A FREE MAN'S LIFE (1946);
M. MCDEVITT, JOSEPH MCKENNA, ASSOCIATE JUSTICE OF THE UNITED STATES (1946); J. MCLEAN, WILLIAM
RUFUS DAY (1946); M. PUSEY, CHARLES EVANS HUGHES (1951); H. WARNER, THE LIFE OF MR. JUSTICE
CLARKE (1959).

# 4

# From Muskrat to Abrams

## I. ENUMERATED POWERS

### A. The Courts

As early as 1792, in *Hayburn's Case,* several Justices had concluded on circuit that article III did not permit federal courts to exercise nonjudicial functions,[1] and the whole Court had seemed to confirm this conclusion the following year in the famous letter declining to give advisory opinions.[2] One of the first problems confronting the Court after White's appointment as Chief Justice was the application of this principle.

In 1902 Congress had provided for allotting to individual members of the Cherokee Nation lands previously belonging to the tribe itself. When later statutes diminished the value of these individual allotments, Congress authorized suits by named beneficiaries of the original provision against the United States "to determine the validity of" the impairing statutes.[3] Citing *Hayburn's Case,* the *Correspondence,*[4] and two later decisions, the Court in *Muskrat v. United States* held that the statute giving it appellate jurisdiction over these suits was invalid for want of a judicial "Case" or "Controversy."[5]

---

[1] 2 U.S. (2 Dall.) 409, 410-14 n.(a) (1792).

[2] Correspondence of the Justices, *reprinted in* H. HART & H. WECHSLER, THE FEDERAL COURTS AND THE FEDERAL SYSTEM 65-67 (3d ed. 1988); *see* THE FIRST HUNDRED YEARS at 11-12.

[3] *See* Muskrat v. United States, 219 U.S. 346, 348-51 (1911). Three separate provisions were challenged: the enlargement of the class of allottees, the lengthening of a time period within which the original allottees were forbidden to alienate their land, and a grant of authority to the federal government to convey pipeline rights of way over the land. *Id.* at 348-49. For further explanation of the legislative background of *Muskrat,* see Gritts v. Fisher, 224 U.S. 640, 642-46 (1912).

[4] *See supra* note 2 and accompanying text.

[5] *Muskrat,* 219 U.S. at 352-61 (citing United States v. Ferreira, 54 U.S. (13 How.) 40 (1852), THE FIRST HUNDRED YEARS at 262 n.197; and Gordon v. United States, 69 U.S. (2 Wall.) 561 (1865), THE FIRST HUNDRED YEARS at 356 n.36). Finding Supreme Court review an essential part of the statutory scheme, the Court ruled the

The opinion, by Justice Day, begins with what appears to be a sweeping denunciation of Congress's purpose as expressed in the jurisdictional statute: "[T]he object and purpose of the suit is wholly comprised in the determination of the constitutional validity of certain acts of Congress; . . . there is neither more nor less in this procedure than an attempt to provide for a judicial determination . . . of the constitutional validity of an act of Congress."[6] If the other requisites of justiciability are met, however, it is difficult to see why a congressional desire for a determination of constitutionality would make the suit any the less a "Case." It would hardly invalidate the general provision for jurisdiction over cases arising under the Constitution, for example, if it were shown that Congress's purpose in enacting it had been to enable the Court to act as a check upon other branches of government.

Indeed the opinion does not rest with its aspersions on legislative motive. The reason why the present effort to obtain a declaration of constitutionality did not present a "Case" or "Controversy," Justice Day continued, was that the United States, though made a defendant by the statute, "has no interest adverse to the claimants."[7] Thus the Court invoked the now standard learning, suggested perhaps by its division over the Attorney General's right to litigate ex officio in *Hayburn's Case*, that a "Case" or "Controversy" requires adverse parties with stakes in the outcome—in order, among other things, to help assure that both sides of the argument are adequately presented.[8]

Just why the government had no adverse interest in *Muskrat*, however, the Court did not say. Nor was it obvious. In the first place, the United States in *Muskrat* arguably had the same type of parens patriae concern that traditionally gives the government a stake in the outcome of criminal prosecutions, and which has led later Congresses to authorize the government to sue for damages on behalf of workers under the Fair Labor Standards Act and to intervene as a party whenever the constitutionality of an act of Congress is challenged.[9] More pointedly, the statutes under attack contemplated various actions by federal

---

review provision inseparable and thus held that the Court of Claims could not exercise original jurisdiction either. *Muskrat*, 219 U.S. at 363. Thus, the Court did not have to decide whether the special status of the Court of Claims excepted it from the rule that article III courts could exercise only judicial functions. *See also* Richardson v. McChesney, 218 U.S. 487, 492 (1910) (Lurton, J.) (refusing to decide a reapportionment claim mooted by an election because "[t]he duty of the court is limited to the decision of actual pending controversies").

[6] *Muskrat*, 219 U.S. at 360-61.

[7] *Id.* at 361.

[8] *See* Hayburn's Case, 2 U.S. (2 Dall.) 409 (1792), THE FIRST HUNDRED YEARS at 6-9. For the modern view and its policy justification, see, *e.g.*, Warth v. Seldin, 422 U.S. 490, 498-99 (1975) ("As an aspect of justiciability, the standing question is whether the plaintiff has 'alleged such a personal stake in the outcome of the controversy' as to warrant *his* invocation of federal-court jurisdiction. . . .") (quoting Baker v. Carr, 369 U.S. 186, 204 (1962)); United States v. Fruehauf, 365 U.S. 146, 157 (1961) (refusing to give "legal judgment upon issues which remain unfocused because they are not pressed before the Court with that clear concreteness provided when a question emerges precisely framed and necessary for decision from a clash of adversary argument").

[9] 29 U.S.C. § 216(c) (1982) (allowing Secretary of Labor to bring suit on behalf of employee claiming violation of Fair Labor Standards Act); 28 U.S.C. § 2403(a) (1982) (allowing intervention by the United States whenever constitutionality of act of Congress is called into question and the United States, its agencies, officers, or employees are not parties to the case). For counterexamples involving the sovereign interest of a *state* government, see Georgia v. Stanton, 73 U.S. (6 Wall.) 50, 77 (1868) (no Supreme Court jurisdiction of suit by state to enjoin execution of Reconstruction Acts), THE FIRST HUNDRED YEARS at 302-04; Oklahoma v. Atchison, T. & S.F. Ry., 220 U.S. 277, 289 (1911) (Harlan, J.) (no original Supreme Court jurisdiction of suit by state to prevent overcharges to citizens).

officials affecting the interests of the plaintiffs. Indeed the very next year, without even discussing justiciability, the Court unanimously entertained a suit by some of the same plaintiffs to enjoin federal officers from carrying out one of the same statutes, on the same constitutional grounds.[10] It is true that the petition in *Muskrat,* while reporting the relevant allegations of the pending injunction suit, had neglected to specify that the same threat of official action made the United States an appropriate defendant in *Muskrat* itself.[11] There is some evidence in the opinion that the Court was seizing upon this failure of phrasing.[12] To have relied wholly on that, however, might have been extremely picky even in 1911.

That something more substantial may have underlain the conclusion that the government was not adverse to the particular petitions filed in *Muskrat* was suggested by the Court's insistence that "the only judgment required is to settle the doubtful character of the legislation. . . . [T]he judgment could not be executed, and amounts in fact to no more than an expression of opinion upon the validity of the acts in question."[13] The implication seems to be that the judicial power did not extend to a complaint seeking only a declaratory judgment—though that was the essence of traditional suits to quiet title or remove a cloud from title, to which Justice Day did not refer.[14]

The statutory provision for payment of the plaintiffs' attorneys' fees "out of the funds in the United States Treasury belonging to the beneficiaries" of the initial allotment legislation, though prominently mentioned in the opinion, was not expressly relied on as a

---

[10]Gritts v. Fisher, 224 U.S. 640, 647-48 (1912) (upholding the addition of new allottees on the ground that the original promise of allotment had created no vested rights). The Secretary of the Interior had ultimate authority to approve additions to the allotment rolls compiled by a federal commission; federal officials were directed to distribute assets to the allottees; and one of the statutes authorized the Secretary to grant rights of way, which he had proceeded to do. Act of July 1, 1902, ch. 1375, §§ 11, 29, 37, 32 Stat. 716, 717, 720-21, 722. *See also* Heckman v. United States, 224 U.S. 413, 438-39 (1912) (Hughes, J.) (upholding authority of United States as guardian of Cherokee rights to sue to enforce the extended restraint on alienation challenged in *Muskrat*).

[11]Record at 9, Muskrat v. United States, 219 U.S. 346 (1911). For similar allegations in the other case decided with *Muskrat,* see Record at 10, Brown v. United States, 219 U.S. 346 (1911).

[12]*See Muskrat,* 219 U.S. at 362 (finding it irrelevant that the petitioners had filed other suits because the statute giving jurisdiction "must depend upon its own terms").

[13]*Id.* at 361-62. The Court added that such a judgment would "not conclude private parties, when actual litigation brings to the court the question of the constitutionality of such legislation." *Id.* at 362. A judgment that binds *nobody* is the essence of an advisory opinion; but there seems no reason to doubt that the judgment authorized would have bound the government as well as the plaintiffs.

[14]*See also id.* at 361 (stressing that the complaint sought no "compensation" from the United States). Chief Justice Taney had said in his 1864 opinion prepared for Gordon v. United States, published posthumously at 117 U.S. 697 (1886), that the award of execution was a necessary ingredient of any judicial judgment. *Gordon,* 117 U.S. at 702. There is no evidence, however, that Taney was speaking for the Court, which had decided the case without opinion some years before. Gordon v. United States, 69 U.S. (2 Wall.) 561 (1865), THE FIRST HUNDRED YEARS at 353 n.10. Nor was Taney's statement necessary to the result in *Gordon,* for the statute there in question had given the Executive the power to redetermine matters decided by the Court of Claims. The legislature's attempt to vest such a power in the Executive had doomed the pension law in *Hayburn* seventy years before. Taney's observations on the judicial power were quoted in *Muskrat,* but his dictum regarding execution was not emphasized. *Muskrat,* 219 U.S. at 354-55. *See generally* Borchard, *The Declaratory Judgment—A Needed Procedural Reform,* 28 YALE L.J. 1, 105 (1918) (giving other examples of purely declaratory remedies and tracing the declaratory judgment itself to both English and Roman law); Sunderland, *A Modern Evolution in Remedial Rights,—The Declaratory Judgment,* 16 MICH. L. REV. 69 (1917) (giving examples of purely declaratory remedies in England and arguing that the contemporary American practice of restricting use of declaratory judgments creates "serious hardship in this country").

basis of the decision.[15] If one party pays the other's expenses, the suspicion may be strong that the suit is collusive—as the Court would emphasize in throwing out a suit on that ground a generation later.[16]

An absolute rule against paying even a losing opponent's costs, however, would go too far. When the government is the one that pays, collusion is not the only permissible inference. In criminal cases publicly financed defense lawyers flourish like rabbits, and there is an increasing tendency to extend the principle of government support to other contexts as well.[17] No one seems to think provisions such as these make a suit collusive. Similarly, the plaintiffs in *Muskrat,* who as original allottees stood to gain something of value and who had demonstrated their apparent good faith by presenting the same claims in another suit without promise of fees, might well have been expected to argue vigorously in support of their position. More important, fees were to be paid only if the plaintiffs won. Far from indicating the absence of an adversary relationship between the parties, this now familiar extension of the traditional assessment of costs actually reinforces such a relationship by increasing the incentive for each party to prevail. Finally, since the fees were to be paid not from the government's own funds but from those it held in trust for the plaintiffs' class, *Muskrat* was not a case of one party's paying the expenses of the other at all.[18]

The fact that the statute singled out named individuals as plaintiffs does raise a red flag: the government's ability to pick its adversary gives it a grand opportunity to choose a patsy. No doubt it is better to have a broad prophylactic rule against that sort of thing than to engage in a subjective and burdensome assessment of the performance of counsel in the particular case—especially since collusion poses a threshold issue that ought to be resolved before there is a record on which to base the decision. This may indeed be the strongest point in favor of the Court's conclusion, but it was not a part of the Court's stated reasoning.

We are thus left wondering whether there was any justifiable basis for the conclusion that the dispute was nonjusticiable, and, if so, just what it was. In hinting at such a number of less than wholly persuasive bases for the decision, Justice Day left us a monument of confusion full of uncertain implications for future litigation.[19] Perhaps the only reliable lesson to be drawn from this episode is that if Congress wants to provide for a test case it should be careful not to invite the conclusion that it has provided instead for an advisory opinion.[20]

[15] *See Muskrat,* 219 U.S. at 351, 360.

[16] United States v. Johnson, 319 U.S. 302, 304-05 (1943); *see also* THE FIRST HUNDRED YEARS at 32 (discussing this issue in connection with Hylton v. United States, 3 U.S. (3 Dall.) 171 (1796), in which the Court may have been unaware of the problem).

[17] *See, e.g.,* 15 U.S.C. § 2605(c)(4)(A) (1982) (attorneys' fees may be awarded to parties who present views that contribute to fair determination in rule-making proceeding, even if they lose).

[18] Perhaps that is why, despite suggestively calling attention to the fee provision, the opinion did not explain the provision's bearing on the decision.

[19] *See* H. HART & H. WECHSLER, *supra* note 2, at 232 ("Complete the following sentence: 'The Supreme Court held that no justiciable controversy was presented in the Muskrat case because. . . .'"). For vehement criticism of no fewer than seven decisional grounds perceived in *Muskrat,* see 3 K. DAVIS, ADMINISTRATIVE LAW TREATISE § 21.01, at 120-24 (1958).

[20] Apart from the unassailable application of the principle of Hans v. Louisiana, 134 U.S. 1 (1890) (article III does not authorize a citizen to sue his own state), pp. 7-9 *supra,* to admiralty cases in *Ex parte* New York, 256 U.S. 490, 497-98 (1921) (Pitney, J.), the most interesting developments respecting the judicial power during the

## B.   Congress

### 1.   The *Shreveport Rate Case*

As early as 1838, in upholding a federal statute outlawing the theft of shipwrecked goods in *United States v. Coombs*,[21] the Supreme Court had held that, in order to protect inter-state commerce from interference, Congress could regulate conduct that was not itself commerce.[22] Although this thesis had received a setback in the 1895 sugar-trust case of *United States v. E. C. Knight Co.*,[23] by 1908 the Fuller Court had returned to the tradi-tional position in upholding the application of the Sherman Act to the Danbury hatters.[24] Under Chief Justice White the Court consistently followed the logic of this position to uphold a number of far-reaching exercises of congressional authority.[25]

In 1911, in one of his first constitutional opinions, the recently appointed Justice Hughes wrote for a unanimous Court to sustain a statute limiting the number of hours a railroad employee engaged in interstate commerce could work even on local trains:

---

White period concerned political questions. In refusing to determine whether a state might constitutionally leg-islate by initiative or referendum, the Court in Pacific States Tel. & Tel. Co. v. Oregon, 223 U.S. 118, 143-51 (1912) (White, C. J.), followed the pattern of the Fuller Court, see Taylor v. Beckham, 178 U.S. 548, 578-81 (1900), *supra* p. 17, note 63, in overgeneralizing from the narrow alternative holding of Luther v. Borden, 48 U.S. (7 How.) 1, 38-47 (1849), THE FIRST HUNDRED YEARS at 252-57, to the flat conclusion that all controversies over the meaning of article IV's guarantee of a republican form of government were nonjusticiable. *Accord* Marshall v. Dye, 231 U.S. 250, 256-57 (1913) (Day, J.) (refusing to decide whether article IV, § 4 guaranteed the right to vote on proposed new state constitution). Interestingly, the Court managed in *Pacific States,* 223 U.S. at 139-41, to dismiss even allegations based on the equal protection clause on the ground that they were essen-tially efforts to raise the guarantee clause claim under another label—a judicial technique repudiated in Baker v. Carr, 369 U.S. 186, 209-10 (1962), pp. 412-14 *infra*, over Justice Frankfurter's emphatic dissent. *See also* Ohio *ex rel.* Davis v. Hildebrant, 241 U.S. 565, 569-70 (1916) (White, C. J.) (disposing similarly of contention that article I, § 4's explicit reference to state "Legislature[s]" forbade state to determine congressional districts by referendum). Later decisions reaching the merits of challenges to procedures for the ratification of constitutional amendments, however, suggested that the White Court was prepared neither to apply this reasoning to every attack on the constitutionality of referenda nor to extend the political-question category to new areas unrelated to the guarantee clause. *See* Hawke v. Smith, 253 U.S. 221, 227 (1920) (Day, J.) (holding state could not make ratification of amendment to United States Constitution dependent on referendum in light of article V provision for ratification by "Legislature"); Dillon v. Gloss, 256 U.S. 368, 375-76 (1921) (Van Devanter, J.) (upholding power of Congress, in light of perceived constitutional policy requiring contemporaneous consensus, to require ratification of constitutional amendment within seven years); *see also* Missouri Pac. Ry. v. Kansas, 248 U.S. 276 (1919) (White, C. J.) (assuming justiciability in reasoning that veto could be overridden under article I, § 7 by two-thirds of members present and voting).

See also Evans v. Gore, 253 U.S. 245 (1920) (Van Devanter, J.) (reasoning cleanly, if somewhat mechani-cally, that a general income tax reduced the compensation of federal judges in violation of article III—a conclu-sion later abandoned, O'Malley v. Woodrough, 307 U.S. 277 (1939), for the expectable reason, given by Holmes and Brandeis in dissent in *Evans,* 253 U.S. at 265, that the generality of the tax reduced its threat to the underly-ing policy of judicial independence, *O'Malley,* 307 U.S. at 281-83); Virginia v. West Virginia, 246 U.S. 565 (1918) (White, C. J.) (Court has authority to enforce judgment against state).

[21] 37 U.S. (12 Pet.) 72 (1838) (Story, J.).

[22] *Id.* at 78-79, THE FIRST HUNDRED YEARS at 234 & n.268.

[23] 156 U.S. 1 (1895), *supra* pp. 22-24.

[24] Loewe v. Lawlor, 208 U.S. 274 (1908).

[25] *See generally* A. BICKEL & B. SCHMIDT, 9 HISTORY OF THE SUPREME COURT OF THE UNITED STATES 200-42, 414-76 (1984).

The length of hours of service has direct relation to the efficiency of the human agencies upon which protection to life and property necessarily depends. . . . [Congress's] power cannot be defeated either by prolonging the period of service through other requirements of the carriers or by the commingling of duties relating to interstate and intrastate operations.[26]

Later the same year, in a brief unanimous opinion by the even more recently appointed Justice Van Devanter, the Court upheld the extension of the Safety Appliance Act to require appropriate couplers on cars traveling locally on interstate railroads, reasoning that interstate and local cars were frequently parts of the same train and that an accident to a local train could impede the passage of an interstate one. The power over interstate commerce, the Court concluded, "may be exerted to secure the safety of the persons and property transported therein and of those who are employed in such transportation, no matter what may be the source of the dangers which threaten it."[27] Similarly, early in 1912, Justice Van Devanter wrote again for a unanimous bench to sustain the application of the Federal Employers' Liability Act to an injury sustained by an employee who was engaged in interstate commerce although the employee who had caused the injury was not: "[S]uch negligence, when operating injuriously upon an employé engaged in interstate commerce, has the same effect upon that commerce as if the negligent employé were also engaged therein."[28]

The culmination of this line of authority came in 1914, in the famous case of *Houston, E. & W. Tex. Ry. v. United States* (the *Shreveport Rate Case*).[29] Finding that low intrastate rates set by the Texas Railroad Commission diverted traffic that would otherwise have traveled between Texas and Shreveport, Louisiana, the Interstate Commerce Commission ordered the affected railroads to equalize their local and interstate rates. Accepting the railroads' contention that compliance might require them to raise local rates, the Court nevertheless upheld the commission's order on the basis of the decisions just noted: "Congress is entitled to keep the highways of interstate communication open to interstate traffic upon fair and equal terms."[30]

This conclusion followed with impeccable logic from prior decisions. Van Devanter had been stating settled law when he said in the coupler case that Congress could protect interstate commerce no matter what the source of the danger. That the danger in the cases before *Shreveport* had been that of physical rather than economic obstruction seemed ir-

---

[26] Baltimore & O.R.R. v. ICC, 221 U.S. 612, 619 (1911).

[27] Southern Ry. v. United States, 222 U.S. 20, 27 (1911).

[28] Second Employers' Liability Cases, 223 U.S. 1, 52 (1912); *see* A. BICKEL & B. SCHMIDT, 9 HISTORY OF THE SUPREME COURT OF THE UNITED STATES 208 n.28 (1984), (suggesting that this decision cast doubt on the earlier conclusion, in First Employers' Liability Cases, 207 U.S. 463 (1908), that Congress could not regulate liability of an interstate carrier for injuries *to* workers not engaged in commerce, because even in the latter case liability might affect interstate commerce). These decisions, together with others discussed *supra* at pp. 27-28, call into question Tribe's assertion that "willingness on the part of the pre-1937 Supreme Court to see the interconnectedness of formally interstate and intrastate activities was unusual," L. TRIBE, AMERICAN CONSTITUTIONAL LAW 235 (1977).

[29] 234 U.S. 342 (1914).

[30] *Shreveport,* 234 U.S. at 353-54. *See also id.* at 355 ("[I]n removing the injurious discrimination against interstate traffic arising from the relation of intrastate to interstate rates, Congress is not bound to reduce the latter below what it may deem to be a proper standard fair to the carrier and to the public.").

relevant to the question of congressional power, and thus the precedents seemed to fit like a glove.[31]

What was perhaps most interesting about the opinion was the subtle way in which Justice Hughes modified the standard learning even as he applied it to what may have been the most extreme case yet decided.[32] Whereas Van Devanter had said the source of the threat was irrelevant, as it surely was to the scope of the federal interest in protecting commerce, Hughes chose to focus on the fact that the carriers whose local rates had been challenged were also engaged in interstate operations: "Congress . . . may . . . requir[e] that *the agencies of interstate commerce* shall not be used in such manner as to cripple, retard or destroy it."[33]

Possibly, like the careful jurist he was, Justice Hughes was only trying to avoid prejudging future controversies. In light of the unexplained dissenting votes of Justices Lurton and Pitney, however, the conspicuous repetition of the fact that the railroads before him were instrumentalities of interstate commerce may suggest that Hughes was attempting to find some way to limit the implications of his decision. As Chief Justice Fuller had emphasized in essaying a different but equally unsatisfying limitation in the sugar-trust case, the argument that Congress may protect commerce from any interference seemed likely to push the Court to the untenable position that Congress could regulate just about anything it liked—for there is scarcely anything in a mobile society that cannot be plausibly argued to affect interstate commerce.[34]

---

[31] For an effort to distinguish the coupler case, see Coleman, *The Evolution of Federal Regulation of Intrastate Rates: The Shreveport Rate Cases,* 28 HARV. L. REV. 34, 69-70 (1914). For a defense of the rate decision, see Biklé, *Federal Control of Intrastate Railroad Rates,* 63 U. PA. L. REV. 69 (1914). The argument that the common law against whose background the commerce clause had been adopted forbade trespasses but not competition suggests that Congress could not limit competition even in commerce itself and is hard to square with the purpose for which the clause was adopted—to prevent otherwise lawful state taxes. Indeed, the result in *Shreveport* had been foretold the preceding year in the Minnesota Rate Cases, 230 U.S. 352, 417, 432-33 (1913) (Hughes, J.) (refusing to strike down similar state rates in the absence of federal legislation).

In the same spirit as the decisions discussed in the text was United States v. Ferger, 250 U.S. 199 (1919) (White, C. J.) (Congress may protect interstate commerce from false bills of lading).

[32] *See also* Wilson v. New, 243 U.S. 332 (1917) (White, C. J.) (upholding requirement that railroad workers be paid ten hours' wages for eight hours' work to prevent strike interrupting commerce); United States v. Chandler-Dunbar Water Power Co., 229 U.S. 53, 72-74 (1913) (Day, J.) (allowing Congress to provide for sale of power produced by navigation dam), *discussed in* A. BICKEL & B. SCHMIDT, *supra* note 28, at 221 (describing the decision as "[t]he most ungrudging legitimation of federal power" during the White years); ICC v. Goodrich Transit Co., 224 U.S. 194, 214 (1912) (Day, J.) (perfunctorily upholding requirement that interstate carriers file reports covering even local operations), *discussed in* A. BICKEL & B. SCHMIDT, *supra* note 28, at 214-15 (arguing that the case should have gone even further).

[33] *Shreveport,* 234 U.S. at 351 (emphasis added). Numerous other examples of such qualifying language are found in *id.* at 351-55.

[34] See Jefferson's early demonstration of the need to find some limiting principle, quoted in G. GUNTHER, CASES AND MATERIALS ON CONSTITUTIONAL LAW 87 (11th ed. 1985). For Fuller's efforts, see United States v. E. C. Knight Co., 156 U.S. 1, 13 (1895). Fuller's distinction between "direct" and "indirect" injuries to commerce might plausibly have been employed to preclude federal regulation in *Shreveport,* because the immediate effect of a low state rate was on those who shipped locally; the concomitant loss to interstate business could fairly be described as secondary. Unfortunately, this line of reasoning fails to distinguish the safety appliance case, in which Van Devanter had relied in part on the existence of a potential secondary effect—obstruction of interstate traffic—caused by an accident disabling a local train. Moreover, the direct/indirect distinction seems quite irrelevant to the inquiry at hand.

If that was what troubled Justice Hughes, he deserves some credit for a modest attempt to slow the juggernaut. The line he attempted to draw, however, was an unconvincing one that had been rejected three-quarters of a century before when the Taney Court held that Congress could provide for punishing a thief who was not an agency of commerce.[35]

## 2.  Hammer v. Dagenhart

If Justice Hughes in the *Shreveport* case was trying to limit the logical growth of the commerce power, he managed to uphold a striking exercise of that power in the process. Just the year before, moreover, in *Hoke v. United States*,[36] the Court had followed the implications of yet another Fuller Court precedent in holding that Congress could outlaw the interstate transportation of women for immoral purposes. As in the *Lottery Case*,[37] wrote Justice McKenna without provoking a dissent, it was no objection to the validity of Congress's enactment that the purpose and effect of the statute were to promote morality rather than to prevent obstructions to commerce: "Congress['s] . . . power over transportation 'among the several States' . . . is complete in itself," and rules adopted under it "may have the quality of police regulations."[38]

However, when Congress predictably took advantage of this reasoning to discourage child labor by prohibiting interstate shipment of goods made in factories employing children, a divided Court executed a sharp about-face. The statute, said Justice Day in *Hammer v. Dagenhart*,[39] "in a twofold sense is repugnant to the Constitution. It not only

---

[35] For decisions of the White years broadly construing Congress's power to ensure the enforceability of measures regulating interstate commerce itself, see McDermott v. Wisconsin, 228 U.S. 115, 136 (1913) (Day, J.) (upholding power to require that labels remain on goods after interstate shipment to facilitate inspection for previous violation), and Hipolite Egg Co. v. United States, 220 U.S. 45, 58 (1911) (McKenna, J.) (upholding power to seize adulterated food after illegal interstate shipment). For further evidence of the contrasting fear of construing the commerce clause too broadly, see the Pipe Line Cases, 234 U.S. 548 (1914) (Holmes, J.) (taking a surprisingly grudging line in reaching the easy conclusion that economic regulation under the Interstate Commerce Act could be extended to interstate oil pipelines); A. BICKEL & B. SCHMIDT, *supra* note 28, at 232-38 (revealing the extent to which Holmes was forced to tone down the opinion).

[36] 227 U.S. 308 (1913).

[37] 188 U.S. 321 (1903), *supra* pp. 28-29.

[38] *Hoke,* 227 U.S. at 321, 323. *See also* Caminetti v. United States, 242 U.S. 470, 491-92 (1917) (Day, J.) (upholding the same statute as applied to interstate transportation of a woman for personal rather than commercial purposes); Clark Distilling Co. v. Western Md. Ry., 242 U.S. 311, 325-32 (1917) (White, C. J.) (upholding act of Congress prohibiting shipment of liquor into state for sale or use in violation of its laws); Weber v. Freed, 239 U.S. 325, 329-30 (1915) (White, C. J.) (upholding congressional authority to ban import of boxing films); Hipolite Egg Co. v. United States, 220 U.S. 45, 57-58 (1911) (McKenna, J.) (assuming the unchallenged authority of Congress to exclude adulterated food from interstate commerce); A. BICKEL & B. SCHMIDT, *supra* note 28, at 224-32 (finding in *Hoke*'s reference to "immoral" purposes, 227 U.S. at 320, and *Hipolite*'s reference to "illicit" articles, 220 U.S. at 57, ambiguities that might significantly limit the sweep of their reasoning); A. BICKEL & B. SCHMIDT, *supra,* at 433 (castigating *Caminetti*'s wooden approach to statutory construction and adding that, although the Court in *Caminetti* had conceded that "Congress could not simply regulate the conduct that a traveler in interstate commerce intended to engage in once he reached his destination," it "affirmed a power to do precisely that in the case of a man and a woman voluntarily traveling together"); *cf. infra* note 150 (discussing another aspect of *Clark Distilling*).

[39] 247 U.S. 251 (1918).

transcends the authority delegated to Congress over commerce but also exerts a power as to a purely local matter to which the federal authority does not extend."[40]

By this peculiar reference to "twofold" unconstitutionality, Day may only have meant to make the obvious point that a statute Congress was not authorized to pass offended the tenth amendment as well.[41] If he meant that a measure lying within Congress's delegated authority might nevertheless be invalid because the matter was "purely local," however, the statement was quite insupportable. As abler Justices had said before and would say again, the tenth amendment takes nothing from the federal government that other provisions have given; it reserves to the states only those powers *not* granted to the United States.[42]

If Justice Day meant that the tenth amendment showed there must be some significant powers that Congress could not exercise,[43] he was on firmer ground. That Congress's powers are limited, however, does not tell us where to draw the boundary. As an original matter, a respectable argument could have been made that the commerce power should be construed, in light of its purpose, only to authorize measures that removed obstructions to commerce. The difficulty was that this position had been rejected both in the *Lottery Case* and in *Hoke,* neither of which the *Hammer* Court purported to question.[44]

Apart from an otherwise unexplained reference to "the character of the particular subjects dealt with" in earlier cases, the only basis for distinction the Court offered was that in each of the prior cases "the use of interstate transportation was necessary to the accomplishment of harmful results," whereas in the child labor case the harm was over before interstate commerce began.[45] Conspicuously, Justice Day made no effort to say why that mattered. Holmes, who said all the right things in his dissent, thought the difference immaterial: "It is enough that in the opinion of Congress the transportation encourages

---

[40]*Id.* at 276.

[41] The amendment was invoked, *id.* at 274, and erroneously paraphrased, *id.* at 275, as reserving to the states "the powers not *expressly* delegated to the National Government" (emphasis added).

[42] United States v. Darby, 312 U.S. 100, 123-24 (1941) (Stone, J.), p. 238 *infra;* McCulloch v. Maryland, 17 U.S. (4 Wheat.) 316 (1819) (Marshall, C. J.), THE FIRST HUNDRED YEARS at 160-68.

[43]*See Hammer,* 247 U.S. at 276: "[I]f Congress can thus regulate matters entrusted to local authority by prohibition of the movement of commodities in interstate commerce, . . . the power of the States over local matters may be eliminated, and thus our system of government be practically destroyed." *Cf.* McCulloch v. Maryland, 17 U.S. (4 Wheat.) 316, 421 (1819) (insisting that measures adopted under necessary and proper clause be consistent with "spirit" as well as letter of the Constitution), THE FIRST HUNDRED YEARS at 164.

[44] Justice Day protested that both the purpose and the effect of the law prohibiting commerce in child-made goods were to prevent child labor in the factory itself, but both the lottery and white-slave laws had survived similar objections. The suggestion that prohibition was not regulation, *Hammer,* 247 U.S. at 269-70, had been rejected not only in the same two cases but also—in the context of foreign commerce—many years before by one of the most state-minded Justices ever to sit on the Court. *See* THE FIRST HUNDRED YEARS at 234 n.270 (discussing United States v. Marigold, 50 U.S. (9 How.) 560 (1850) (Daniel, J.)).

[45]*Hammer,* 247 U.S. at 270-72. For elaboration of this distinction, see Cushman, *The National Police Power and the Commerce Clause of the Constitution,* 3 MINN. L. REV. 289, 381-400 (1919) (the most comprehensive contemporaneous commentary). Bickel took the reference to the "character of the particular subjects" as harking back to the insistence in *Hoke* and *Hipolite, see supra* note 38, that those cases dealt with "immoral" behavior and "illicit" articles. *See* A. BICKEL & B. SCHMIDT, *supra* note 28, at 447; *id.* at 454-58 (adding that *Hammer* came as a shock to the public and was poorly received by academics). The relevance of an external standard of "immorality," if that was what the Court had in mind, was never made clear.

the evil."[46] It is hard to believe that the majority found its own distinctions persuasive.[47]

### 3. Doremus, Hamilton, and Holland

Any hopes that *Hammer* portended an era of increased protection of state prerogatives, however, were chilled by later decisions. In the very next term, for example, in *United States v. Doremus*,[48] the Court permitted Congress effectively to regulate narcotics sales under the cloak of the federal tax power.[49]

The regulatory aspect of the law was unmistakable: the law required sales to be made on specified forms, and it forbade use of the forms except for legitimate purposes. "In other words," wrote Bickel, "no addicts could be served, whether or not they paid the tax." Moreover, the tax itself was so small—one dollar per year—as to raise serious doubts whether it served any legitimate revenue purpose.[50] If there were cases for invoking Marshall's admonition that federal powers were not to be used as the "pretext" for invading state authority,[51] *Doremus* seemed a strong candidate for inclusion.[52] Without even citing *Hammer*, however, the majority blithely upheld the tax in an opinion looking for all the world like Holmes's dissent in that case, relying on all the precedents establishing that the tax power was no more defeated by a purpose or effect of intruding on local affairs than the commerce clause had been before *Hammer* itself. This time the author was not Holmes but Day, who had so emphatically said the opposite as to the commerce clause in *Hammer* only the year before, and he took Pitney with him.[53]

---

[46] *Hammer*, 247 U.S. at 279-80. For contemporaneous support of this position, see Biklé, *The Commerce Power and* Hammer v. Dagenhart, 67 U. Pa. L. Rev. 21, 28-36 (1919); Brinton, *The Constitutionality of a Federal Child Labor Law*, 62 U. Pa. L. Rev. 487, 502-03 (1914); Gordon, *The Child Labor Law Case*, 32 Harv. L. Rev. 45, 51-54 (1918); Lewis, *The Federal Power to Regulate Child Labor in the Light of Supreme Court Decisions*, 62 U. Pa. L. Rev. 504, 506-08 (1914); Parkinson, *Congressional Prohibitions of Interstate Commerce*, 16 Colum. L. Rev. 367, 370-71 (1916); Powell, *Child Labor, Congress, and the Constitution*, 1 N.C.L. Rev. 61, 62-68 (1922). Both Gordon and Parkinson noted the inability of states to forbid interstate transportation of child-made goods and pointed out the anomaly of interpreting a clause dividing authority between state and nation so as to extinguish authority altogether. *See also* T. Powell, Vagaries and Varieties in Constitutional Interpretation 68 (1956).

[47] The shift cannot be explained in terms of intervening changes in personnel. Of the three Justices appointed between *Hoke* and *Hammer*, Brandeis and Clarke joined Holmes and McKenna (the author of *Hoke*) in the *Hammer* dissent. Day was joined in the majority not only by the newly appointed and implacably conservative McReynolds but also by White, Van Devanter, and Pitney, all of whom, like Day himself, had voted to uphold the white-slave law. Commentators suggested a possible basis for distinction not noted by the Court: that Congress's power may be greater when it acts to reinforce rather than to contradict state policy. *See* Bruce, *Interstate Commerce and Child Labor*, 3 Minn. L. Rev. 89, 95-96 (1919); Cushman, *supra* note 45, at 400-12. *See also infra* pp. 179-80 *discussing* Brooks v. United States, 267 U.S. 432 (1925).

[48] 249 U.S. 86 (1919).

[49] White, Van Devanter, and McReynolds dissented, *id.* at 95. For unexplained reasons, they were joined by Justice McKenna, who had written for the Court to uphold the white-slave law and had dissented from invalidation of the child labor provision.

[50] *See* A. Bickel & B. Schmidt, *supra* note 28, at 435.

[51] *See* McCulloch v. Maryland, 17 U.S. (4 Wheat.) 316, 423 (1819).

[52] *Cf.* Guinn v. United States, 238 U.S. 347 (1915) (holding that grandfather clause violates fifteenth amendment), *discussed infra* at pp. 106-07.

[53] "We cannot agree with the contention that the provisions . . . controlling the disposition of these drugs in the ways described, can have nothing to do with facilitating the collection of the revenue. . . ." *Doremus*, 249

If these Justices were worried about residual state sovereignty, they were highly selective about it. If the distinction was between the tax and commerce powers, it seemed backward: because the commerce power can be used for ulterior ends only to the extent that interstate or foreign intercourse is implicated, exercise of the tax power seems to pose the greater danger. One hopes the explanation is not simply that Day and Pitney liked dope peddling less than child labor.[54]

In 1919, on the basis of unspecified war powers, the Court in *Hamilton v. Kentucky Distilleries & Warehouse Co.*[55] upheld an act of Congress banning the sale of distilled spirits for beverage purposes "until the termination of demobilization."[56] What was remarkable about this result was not that the statute had been enacted after the armistice, for earlier cases had correctly recognized that some of the military powers in the Constitution, such as that respecting the raising and maintenance of armies, were not limited to times of actual hostilities.[57] The striking thing was rather the enormously broad scope the Court was willing, even after *Hammer v. Dagenhart,* to give to such powers during the time they did apply. Indeed Justice Brandeis's opinion does not really address the critical ques-

---

U.S. at 95. Powell, *supra* note 46, at 87, termed this decision "[h]ardly candid." For an effort to distinguish earlier cases on the bizarre ground that prohibition was a more legitimate use of the tax power than was regulation, see Long, *Federal Police Power Regulation by Taxation,* 9 VA. L. REV. 81, 83-94 (1922). The best contemporaneous discussion of the general problem is Cushman, *The National Police Power and the Taxing Clause of the Constitution,* 4 MINN. L. REV. 247, 261-65 (1920) (giving the standard argument for limiting the use of the tax power for regulatory purposes but despairing of the Court's ability to administer meaningful limitations).

[54] Other significant federal tax cases of the White period include LaBelle Iron Works v. United States, 256 U.S. 377 (1921) (Pitney, J.) (holding excess-profits tax consistent with fifth amendment); Merchants' Loan & Trust Co. v. Smietanka, 255 U.S. 509 (1921) (Clarke, J.) (capital gain from stock sale is "income"); Brushaber v. Union Pac. R.R., 240 U.S. 1, 24 (1916) (White, C. J.) (an almost unreadable opinion upholding an unapportioned income tax after passage of the sixteenth amendment, adding the surprising dictum that the effect of that provision was to subject all income taxation to the requirement of geographical uniformity applicable to duties, imposts, and excises under article I, § 8); Flint v. Stone Tracy Co., 220 U.S. 107, 150-52 (1911) (Day, J.) (analogizing from decisions respecting governmental immunity from taxation to conclude rather formalistically, *see* Riddle, *The Supreme Court's Theory of a Direct Tax,* 15 MICH. L. REV. 566, 573 (1917), that an "excise" on doing business in corporate form was not a direct tax requiring apportionment according to population even though measured by income). Most notable was the intuitively appealing conclusion in Eisner v. Macomber, 252 U.S. 189, 202-03 (1920) (Pitney, J., over four dissents), that a stock dividend was not "income" within the sixteenth amendment because it did not increase a shareholder's wealth. Justice Brandeis's learned dissent in *Eisner* cast cold water on this conclusion by suggesting, among other things, that a pro rata share of undistributed corporate profits could have been taxed as income to the stockholder, *id.* at 230-31 (Brandeis, J., dissenting); a perceptive commentator added that cash dividends and wages did not increase the taxpayer's net worth any more than stock dividends, because both involved the mere exchange of one asset for another of equal value. *See* Warren, *Taxability of Stock Dividends as Income,* 33 HARV. L. REV. 885, 887-88 (1920). For defense of the decision, see Clark, Eisner v. Macomber *and Some Income Tax Problems,* 29 YALE L.J. 735 (1920). See also the export-tax decisions noted *infra* note 128.

[55] 251 U.S. 146 (1919).

[56] *Id.* at 153.

[57] *E.g.,* Stewart v. Kahn, 78 U.S. (11 Wall.) 493, 507 (1871), THE FIRST HUNDRED YEARS at 314 n.192: the power to suppress insurrections "is not limited to victories in the field and the dispersion of the insurgent forces. It carries with it inherently the power to guard against the immediate renewal of the conflict, and to remedy the evils which have arisen from its rise and progress." Indeed, like that of Justice Hughes in *Shreveport,* Brandeis's opinion in *Hamilton* was rather modest on this score. Instead of making the broad argument traced in *Stewart v. Kahn,* he insisted only that the wartime emergency had not ended even though some time had passed since the end of the shooting. *Hamilton,* 251 U.S. at 158-63.

tion why the prohibition of liquor was necessary and proper to the exercise of any of the war powers.[58]

The statute stated that its purpose was to "conserv[e] the man power of the Nation, and to increase efficiency in the production of arms, munitions, ships, food, and clothing for the Army and Navy"[59]—apparently on the theory that drunken citizens make poor soldiers and inefficient producers of military supplies.[60] The connection is real, but the implications are staggering: Congress may regulate anything that has an effect on the efficiency of the armed forces. That, like the broad construction of the tax power in *Doremus*, would seem to leave precious little beyond the reach of Congress.[61] And this time not a single Justice disagreed.[62]

Finally, in the 1920 case of *Missouri v. Holland*,[63] the Court over two unexplained dissents upheld a treaty protecting migratory birds, despite the assumption that Congress could not have accomplished the same result by statute.[64] At one point, building upon an error made by Chief Justice Marshall in *Marbury v. Madison*, Holmes's opinion for the Court came close to the horrifying suggestion that the treaty power was not limited by other provisions at all because "Acts of Congress are the supreme law of the land only when made in pursuance of the Constitution, while treaties are declared to be so when made under the authority of the United States."[65] Later in the opinion, however, Holmes

[58] The opinion dealt also with the issue of confiscation, with an issue of statutory construction, and with the impact of the intervening ratification of the eighteenth amendment. *Hamilton*, 251 U.S. at 163-68. The validity of a prohibition statute during actual hostilities seems not to have been contested. *See id.* 160-61.

[59] Act of Nov. 21, 1918, ch. 212, 40 Stat. 1045, 1046.

[60] *See Hamilton*, 251 U.S. at 153. *See also* Woods v. Cloyd W. Miller Co., 333 U.S. 138, 142 (1948) (prohibition not only "conserved manpower and increased efficiency of production" but also "helped to husband the supply of grains and cereals depleted by the war effort").

[61] Indeed, Justice Brandeis went out of his way in *Hamilton*, as had Holmes in his *Hammer* dissent, 247 U.S. at 278-79, and Day in *Doremus*, 249 U.S. at 93-94, to stress that neither the effect on local interests nor the motive of Congress was relevant to the scope of congressional power. *Hamilton*, 251 U.S. at 156, 161.

[62] *See also* Jacob Ruppert v. Caffey, 251 U.S. 264, 299-301 (1920) (Brandeis, J., over four dissents) (allowing Congress to specify for ease of administration that any beverage containing 1/2 per cent of alcohol was intoxicating); Dakota Cent. Tel. Co. v. South Dakota, 250 U.S. 163, 183 (1919) (White, C. J.) (upholding federal authority to take over telecommunications during wartime); McKinley v. United States, 249 U.S. 397, 399 (1919) (Day, J.) (upholding federal prohibition of brothel within five miles of military base as incidental to the raising and support of armies); Selective Draft Law Cases, 245 U.S. 366, 377-88 (1918) (White, C. J.) (impressively invoking history of compulsory military service to uphold military draft); A. BICKEL & B. SCHMIDT, *supra* note 28, at 516-40 (discussing the war power cases).

[63] 252 U.S. 416 (1920).

[64] *Id.* at 431-35; *see also id.* at 435 (Van Devanter and Pitney, J. J., dissenting). Technically speaking, the challenge was to a federal statute implementing the treaty. Since the treaty was upheld, the statute was easily found a necessary and proper means of carrying it out. *Id.* at 432. For the interesting role played by Chief Justice White in the migratory-bird controversy, see A. BICKEL & B. SCHMIDT, *supra* note 28, at 477-79.

[65] *Holland*, 252 U.S. at 433 (adding that "[i]t is open to question whether the authority of the United States means more than the formal acts prescribed to make the convention"). *Cf.* Marbury v. Madison, 5 U.S. (1 Cranch) 137, 180 (1803) (relying in part on the "in Pursuance" language of the supremacy clause, U. S. CONST. art. VI, as support for judicial review of statutes). The reference to laws made in pursuance of "[t]his Constitution," U. S. CONST. art. VI (emphasis added), however, taken in connection with the contrasting mention of treaties made under the authority of the United States, *id.*, suggests, contrary to Holmes's suggestion, that supremacy was to be extended to treaties made under the Articles of Confederation, but not to statutes enacted thereunder. *See* Ware v. Hylton, 3 U.S. (3 Dall.) 199, 237 (1796) (giving supremacy to a preconstitutional treaty); THE FIRST HUNDRED YEARS at 39-41, 72-73; Lofgren, Missouri v. Holland in *Historical Perspective*,

based his holding on the conclusion that the treaty was within federal authority because the subject involved "a national interest of very nearly the first magnitude" that "can be protected only by national action in concert with another power."[66]

It was just as well Holmes did not rest his holding upon the existence of a "national interest" alone; the Framers' careful enumeration of what they considered in the national interest suggested they did not wish to leave it to the judges to decide what powers the central government required.[67] More to the point was Holmes's insistence that the problem could be solved only by international action; the significant fact was that migratory birds were a legitimate matter of *international* concern. In light of tradition, as Justice Field had said in an earlier formulation that Holmes did not bother to quote,[68] that was what the treaty power was all about.

The conclusion that the treaty power was not restricted to matters about which Congress could legislate was reasonable enough in light of this tradition. Moreover, it had been foreshadowed not only by Field's definition but more strikingly by an ancient decision reaching the same conclusion even under the feeble Articles of Confederation.[69] Nevertheless, especially in its inattention to the enunciation of a limiting standard, *Holland* was yet another indication that the Justices were not prepared to do much to ensure the preservation of areas in which the central government could not exercise authority.[70] Rather they were content to surprise the country every now and then, as in *Hammer v. Dagenhart*, with a bolt out of the blue.[71]

---

1975 SUP. CT. REV. 77, 104-12 (showing that both the latter interpretation and the existence of constitutional limits on treaties were confirmed by debates on the Jay Treaty in 1796). Fortunately, Holmes added that "[w]e do not mean to imply that there are no qualifications to the treaty-making power," appending the mysterious qualification that "they must be ascertained in a different way." *Holland*, 252 U.S. at 433.

[66] *Holland*, 252 U.S. at 435.

[67] Compare Governor Randolph's initial resolution proposing that Congress be given authority over all matters that could not be satisfactorily handled by the states, *reprinted* in 1 M. FARRAND, RECORDS OF THE FEDERAL CONVENTION OF 1787, at 21 (rev. ed. 1937).

[68] *See* Geofroy v. Riggs, 133 U.S. 258, 266 (1890): "That the treaty power of the United States extends to all proper subjects of negotiation between our government and the governments of other nations, is clear."

[69] Ware v. Hylton, 3 U.S. (3 Dall.) 199, 231-32 (1796), THE FIRST HUNDRED YEARS at 38-41.

[70] *See generally* 2 C. WARREN, THE SUPREME COURT IN UNITED STATES HISTORY 729-56 (rev. ed. 1926). For a conclusory argument that the treaty power went no further than Congress's legislative authority, see Boyd, *The Treaty-Making Power of the United States and Alien Land Laws in States*, 6 CALIF. L. REV. 279, 280-81 (1918); for the narrower contention that migratory birds were not a proper subject of international concern, see Thompson, *State Sovereignty and the Treaty-Making Power*, 11 CALIF. L. REV. 242, 247 (1923).

[71] In three additional decisions the Court found that Congress had exceeded its enumerated powers. Coyle v. Smith, 221 U.S. 559, 566-68, 580 (1911) (Lurton, J.), was a statesmanlike opinion that relied on tradition and constitutional structure to resolve an issue as old as the Missouri Compromise, *see* THE FIRST HUNDRED YEARS at 272 n.270. By reading the equal-footing doctrine, which originated in the uncited Northwest Ordinance, into article IV's provision for admission of "new States . . . into this Union," the Court in *Coyle* concluded that Congress could not, in admitting Oklahoma, forbid it to move its capital. In United States v. Wheeler, 254 U.S. 281, 298 (1920) (White, C. J.), the Court reaffirmed the Waite Court's conclusion, *see* THE FIRST HUNDRED YEARS at 402, that Congress had no power to punish private interference with civil rights. In the strikingly narrow decision in Newberry v. United States, 256 U.S. 232, 256-58 (1921) (McReynolds, J.), Justice Holmes cast the deciding vote to hold that Congress's power to regulate the "Manner of holding Elections" for members of Congress, U. S. CONST. art. I, § 4, did not allow it to regulate spending in a senatorial primary. Pitney and others persuasively objected that primaries were so closely related to the general election that Congress's power would be frustrated unless they were included. *Newberry*, 256 U.S. at 279-82 (Pitney, J., joined by Brandeis and Clarke,

## II.  CONSTITUTIONAL LIMITATIONS

### A.  The Civil War Amendments

#### 1.  *Economic due process*

Before White became Chief Justice, the Court had made substantive due process a painful reality by striking down a state law limiting bakers' hours in *Lochner v. New York*[72] and a federal law protecting the jobs of union members in *Adair v. United States*.[73] Nevertheless the Court had employed the doctrine quite sparingly.[74] It continued to do so during the White period, and *Lochner* itself was discredited in the process.[75]

---

JJ., concurring in part); *id.* at 258-69 (White, C. J., concurring in part); *see also id.* at 258 (McKenna, J., concurring, reserving the question whether the seventeenth amendment cured the deficiency for future legislation). The rejection in *Newberry* of the argument that Congress's inherent authority over federal elections went beyond article I, § 4—an argument suggested by Justice Miller in *Ex parte* Yarbrough, 110 U.S. 651, 660-64 (1884), THE FIRST HUNDRED YEARS at 394 n.174—contrasts sharply with the conclusion in MacKenzie v. Hare, 239 U.S. 299, 311 (1915) (McKenna, J.), that Congress could treat marriage to an alien as a voluntary relinquishment of citizenship:

> [T]here may be powers implied, necessary or incidental to the expressed powers. As a government, the United States is invested with all the attributes of sovereignty. As it has the character of nationality it has the powers of nationality, especially those which concern its relations and intercourse with other countries.

To which express powers this authority was incidental, the Court did not say. *Cf.* The Chinese Exclusion Case, 130 U.S. 581, 603-04 (1889) (finding Congress's power to exclude aliens inherent in the concept of national sovereignty), *supra* pp. 14-16. *See* Corwin, *Constitutional Law in 1920-21,* 16 AM. POL. SCI. REV. 22, 23-25 (1922) (agreeing with McReynolds that "Manner" of holding elections did not include selection of candidates, but approving the notion of inherent power over primary elections); THE FEDERALIST NO. 60 (A. Hamilton) (denying that "Manner" included "qualifications" for office, which were "fixed in the Constitution"), *quoted in Newberry,* 256 U.S. at 255-56; THE FEDERALIST NO. 59 (A. Hamilton) (defending the grant of power over elections on the ground that *"every government ought to contain in itself the means of its own preservation"*) (emphasis in original); A. BICKEL & B. SCHMIDT, *supra* note 28, at 967-82 (lamenting the "narrow literalism" and "historical rigidity" of the *Newberry* decision.

On the question of intergovernmental immunity as a limit on congressional powers, see Second Employers' Liability Cases, 223 U.S. 1, 55-59 (1912) (Van Devanter, J.), which failed to discuss analogous precedents that limited federal power to regulate or tax state action—*e.g.,* Kentucky v. Dennison, 65 U.S. (24 How.) 66 (1861), THE FIRST HUNDRED YEARS at 245-47; Collector v. Day, 78 U.S. (11 Wall.) 113 (1871), THE FIRST HUNDRED YEARS at 355—in holding that a state court could not refuse on grounds of public policy to entertain an action based on federal law. *Cf.* Kenney v. Supreme Lodge, 252 U.S. 411, 415-16 (1920) (Holmes, J.) (holding, despite an apparently contrary precedent, *see* Anglo-American Provision Co. v. Davis Provision Co., 191 U.S. 373, 375 (1903), *supra* p. 68, that the full faith and credit clause required one state to entertain a suit on another's judgment). For a ferocious application of *McCulloch v. Maryland*'s converse doctrine preventing state interference with federal government functions, see Johnson v. Maryland, 254 U.S. 51, 55 (1920) (Holmes, J.) (state may not require post office driver to obtain operator's license: "The decision in [*McCulloch*] was not put upon any consideration of degree. . . .").

[72] 198 U.S. 45 (1905).

[73] 208 U.S. 161 (1908).

[74] *See generally supra,* pp. 47-50; Bird, *The Evolution of Due Process of Law in the Decisions of the United States Supreme Court,* 13 COLUM. L. REV. 37, 50 (1913) (finding, especially in light of the decision in Muller v. Oregon, 208 U.S. 412 (1908), which upheld a limitation on the working hours of women, little likelihood that the clause would be employed against "soundly progressive legislation").

[75] *See generally* 2 C. WARREN, THE SUPREME COURT IN UNITED STATES HISTORY 729-56 (rev. ed. 1926). The cases are considered in detail in A. BICKEL & B. SCHMIDT, *supra* note 28, at 276-94, 580-609.

Reaffirming *Adair* in *Coppage v. Kansas*[76] in 1915, a six-to-three majority invalidated a state law against contracts not to join unions, arguing that due process had the same meaning in the fourteenth amendment as in the fifth and that neither encouraging unions nor "leveling inequalities of fortune" was a legitimate end of the police power.[77] Apart from *Coppage* and one other striking decision discussed below,[78] however, invalidations on substantive due process grounds during the White years were hard to find. This was not for want of opportunity. In this period the Court upheld against due process objections a great variety of measures ranging from the outlawing of billiard parlors to emergency rent control, from progressive taxes to workers' compensation and other statutes making employers strictly liable for work-related injuries.[79]

Most notably, in 1917, after allowing Congress to require ten hours' wages for eight hours' work,[80] the Court in *Bunting v. Oregon*[81] buried *Lochner* without even citing it, upholding a conviction for employing a worker in a flour mill more than ten hours in a day without paying overtime.[82] Justice McKenna, who had voted with the Court in *Lochner,* made no effort to show that a miller's work was more dangerous than a baker's, or indeed that it was dangerous at all. He found the law a reasonable health measure because the state legislature and courts had found it so, because their judgment was shared by many foreign countries, and because the record did not prove the con-

---

[76] 236 U.S. 1, 11-14 (1915) (Pitney, J.).

[77] *Id.* at 11, 15-19. Holmes dissented on the straightforward ground that both *Adair* and *Lochner* should be overruled. *Id.* at 27 (Holmes, J., dissenting). Joined by Hughes, Day—who had voted with the majority in *Adair*—tried to show in a separate dissent, *id.* at 27-42 (Day, J., dissenting), that there was a decisive distinction between discharging union members, as in the earlier case, and making a promise not to join a union a condition of continued employment.

[78] *See infra* text accompanying notes 104-23 (discussing *Buchanan v. Warley*).

[79] Block v. Hirsh, 256 U.S. 135, 158 (1921) (Holmes, J.) (emergency rent control); Arizona Employers' Liability Cases, 250 U.S. 400, 422-24, 430 (1919) (Pitney, J.) (absolute liability); New York Cent. R.R. v. White, 243 U.S. 188, 204-08 (1917) (Pitney, J.) (workers' compensation); Mountain Timber Co. v. Washington, 243 U.S. 219, 235-46 (1917) (Pitney, J.) (workers' compensation with compulsory insurance); Brushaber v. Union Pac. R.R., 240 U.S. 1, 24-25 (1916) (White, C. J.) (progressive tax); Murphy v. California, 225 U.S. 623, 628-30 (1912) (Lamar, J.) (billiards); *see also* LaBelle Iron Works v. United States, 256 U.S. 377, 392-94 (1921) (Pitney, J.) (excess-profits tax); German Alliance Ins. Co. v. Lewis, 233 U.S. 389 (1914) (McKenna, J.) (regulation of insurance rates). These decisions represent only the tip of a large iceberg; nearly two hundred substantive due process claims were rejected during the White years, while only about a dozen—mostly involving individual rate orders—were sustained. For one relatively significant example of the latter, see the five-to-four decision in Adams v. Tanner, 244 U.S. 590, 596-97 (1917) (McReynolds, J.) (striking down a prohibition on fees charged to job seekers by employment agencies).

[80] Wilson v. New, 243 U.S. 332, 345-46 (1917) (White, C. J.) (stressing that the rule applied only until parties agreed on new contract, and that it would avoid disastrous rail strike). Day, McReynolds, Pitney, and Van Devanter dissented, the last two partly on the basis of substantive due process. *Id.* at 383. The controversy attracted widespread academic attention. *See, e.g.,* Burdick, *The Adamson Law Decision,* 2 CORNELL L.Q. 320 (1917) (suggesting that the Court's rationale would justify a great deal of wage regulation as such); Lauchheimer, *The Constitutionality of the Eight-Hour Railroad Law,* 16 COLUM. L. REV. 554 (1916) (noting absence of any health justification and rejection of analogous argument about interruption of commerce in *Adair,* and concluding that the law served only the "leveling" purpose condemned in *Coppage*); Powell, *The Supreme Court and the Adamson Law,* 65 U. PA. L. REV. 607 (1917).

[81] 243 U.S. 426 (1917) (McKenna, J.).

[82] White, Van Devanter, and McReynolds dissented. *Id.* at 439. For contemporaneous understanding that *Lochner* was dead, see, *e.g.,* Powell, *Decisions of the Supreme Court of the United States on Constitutional Questions II, 1914-1917,* 12 AM. POL. SCI. REV. 427, 430 (1918).

trary.[83] The contention that the overtime provision showed the measure to be a regulation of wages rather than of health—thus serving the goal of "leveling" declared illegitimate in *Coppage*—was dismissed by terming overtime pay a penalty imposed by the legislature to enforce the hour limitation.[84]

As indicated by the repeated dissents of McReynolds, Van Devanter, White, and to a lesser extent McKenna, the concept of substantive due process was far from dead.[85] Like the notion of reserved state powers, however, it was able to rouse itself only on rare and unpredictable occasions.[86]

---

[83] *Bunting*, 243 U.S. at 438-39. *Cf.* Frankfurter, *Hours of Labor and Realism in Constitutional Law*, 29 HARV. L. REV. 353, 370-72 (1916) (arguing that new understanding of industrial dangers had undermined the basis of *Lochner*).

[84] *Bunting*, 243 U.S. at 436-37. Note also the distinction drawn between laws designed to protect health and laws regulating workers' contracts in *Lochner*, 198 U.S. at 57-59. In Wilson v. New, 243 U.S. 332, 342-43 (1917), a law increasing wages had been upheld—over dissents drawing the same distinction—only by emphasizing the separate purpose of preventing a disruptive strike.

[85] All four of these Justices dissented in Block v. Hirsh, 256 U.S. 135, 158 (1921), Arizona Employer's Liability Cases, 250 U.S. 400, 434, 440 (1919), and Mountain Timber Co. v. Washington, 243 U.S. 219, 246 (1917); all but McKenna dissented in *Bunting*, 243 U.S. at 439; Van Devanter, Pitney, McReynolds, and Day— the latter two on commerce clause grounds—dissented in Wilson v. New, 243 U.S. 332, 364, 373, 388 (1917); Van Devanter, White, and Lamar—before McReynolds's appointment—dissented in German Alliance Ins. Co. v. Lewis, 233 U.S. 389, 418 (1914). *See also* Stettler v. O'Hara, 243 U.S. 629 (1917) (affirming—by equally divided Court, Brandeis not participating—decisions upholding minimum wage laws). Agreeing with Powell's contemporaneous speculation in *The Constitutional Issue in Minimum-Wage Legislation*, 2 MINN. L. REV. 1, 1-2 & n.2 (1917), Bickel thought it "quite plain[]" that Pitney had voted with White, Van Devanter, and McReynolds to strike down the minimum-wage law, adding that the vote had been five to four against validity before the death of Lamar. A BICKEL & B. SCHMIDT, *supra* note 28, at 598-602. However, although Pitney had been less receptive than the unpredictable McKenna, *see, e.g., id.* at 285, to social legislation in both Adams v. Tanner, 244 U.S. 590 (1917), and Wilson v. New, 243 U.S. 332 (1917), in other cases McKenna took the more restrictive view. Moreover, it was McKenna who took such pains in *Bunting* to establish that the law there upheld regulated hours rather than wages and who, after Pitney had left the Court, cast the decisive vote to strike down minimum wages in Adkins v. Children's Hospital, 261 U.S. 525 (1923). For these reasons Powell seems right in concluding that the fourth vote against minimum wages in *Stettler* was more probably cast by McKenna. *See* Powell, *The Judiciality of Minimum-Wage Legislation*, 37 HARV. L. REV. 545, 549 (1924). *See generally* A. BICKEL & B. SCHMIDT, *supra* note 28, at 253 (concluding that even during the early White years, when Progressives were hailing the perceived liberality of the Court, "it was in literal truth only that the day of the Brewers and the Peckhams was over. Doctrinally they lived on, and were to flourish again.").
Peckhams was over. Doctrinally they lived on, and were to flourish again.").

[86] Similarly, the overwhelming percentage of economic measures survived challenges under the equal protection, contract, and taking provisions during the White period.

In the equal protection field the most notable exception without civil rights overtones was F. S. Royster Guano Co. v. Virginia, 253 U.S. 412 (1920) (Pitney, J.), finding no plausible basis for a provision exempting companies doing only out-of-state business from a tax on income earned by residents outside the state. Brandeis and Holmes dissented, arguing that the measure was a reasonable means of encouraging incorporation of outside businesses in the state. *Id.* at 418-19 (Brandeis and Holmes, JJ., dissenting). *See also infra* note 123 (discussing *Truax v. Raich*); A. BICKEL & B. SCHMIDT, *supra* note 28, at 294-300, 640-43 (noting a modest revival of the clause, which had essentially been abandoned until 1914).

As foretold by *Manigault v. Springs*, 199 U.S. 473, 480 (1905), *supra* pp. 12-13, the Court over dissents by McKenna, White, Van Devanter, and McReynolds permitted rent control legislation to override an existing contract on the ground that the contract clause had not been meant to interfere with the police power. Marcus Brown Holding Co. v. Feldman, 256 U.S. 170, 198 (1921) (Holmes, J.). Moreover, the old learning that grants would be interpreted to reserve the power of eminent domain, West River Bridge Co. v. Dix, 47 U.S. (6 How.) 507, 531-32 (1848), THE FIRST HUNDRED YEARS at 213-15, was superseded by the view that this power, like the

## 2. Civil rights

There was no doubt that, as Justice Miller had said in the *Slaughter-House Cases*, the central purpose of the Civil War amendments had been to stamp out official discrimination against blacks.[87] Apart from the notable jury-selection cases of the 1880s,[88] however, and the analogous early case of *Yick Wo v. Hopkins*,[89] the Supreme Court had done very little to further this purpose on the few occasions before 1910 that gave it an opportunity to do so.[90] The White years witnessed a modest improvement in this regard.[91]

One of the things the Fuller Court had done was to uphold, as an exercise of Congress's power to enforce the thirteenth amendment, a statute making it a federal crime to return a person forcibly to a state of servitude.[92] In *Bailey v. Alabama*,[93] in 1911, the Court went further in an opinion by Justice Hughes: the state could not make it a crime to break a contract to work.[94]

---

police power, could not be conveyed away. Contributors to the Pa. Hosp. v. City of Philadelphia, 245 U.S. 20, 23-24 (1917) (White, C. J.); *cf.* Stone v. Mississippi, 101 U.S. 814, 817 (1879), THE FIRST HUNDRED YEARS at 379-82. Decisions holding particular contracts impaired, however, were still to be found. *E.g.*, Grand Trunk W. Ry. v. City of South Bend, 227 U.S. 544, 558-59 (1913) (Lamar, J.) (franchise to build tracks); Central of Ga. Ry. v. Wright, 248 U.S. 525 (1919) (Holmes, J.) (tax exemption); *see also* A. BICKEL & B. SCHMIDT, *supra* note 28, at 300-05, 643-48 (finding the principal bite of the clause in public contract cases).

Police power considerations similar to those governing the due process decisions tended also to determine for the White Court the crucial distinction between regulation and the taking of property, for which, under decisions of the Fuller Court, *see supra* p. 59, note 34, the fourteenth amendment required the states to give compensation. On the one hand, for example, Hadacheck v. Sebastian, 239 U.S. 394 (1915) (McKenna, J.), relied on traditional nuisance principles to sustain zoning that kept a brickyard out of an urban area. On the other hand, the Court struck down as an uncompensated taking a requirement that unoccupied upper berths on trains be left closed, concluding that the rule was not a health measure but merely served to promote the convenience of passengers below. Chicago, M. & St. P.R.R. v. Wisconsin, 238 U.S. 491, 498 (1915) (Lamar, J., over dissents by Holmes and McKenna). Finally, the Court continued essentially to equate the implicit requirement that a taking be for a public use with a requirement that it serve a legitimate public *purpose*, thus adding to the trend of making as many constitutional questions as possible depend upon the flexible extraconstitutional notion of the police power. *See, e.g.*, Mt. Vernon-Woodberry Cotton Duck Co. v. Alabama Interstate Power Co., 240 U.S. 30, 32 (1916) (Holmes, J.) (upholding condemnation by private company to generate electric power: "If that purpose is not public we should be at a loss to say what is. The inadequacy of use by the general public as a universal test is established."); Noble State Bank v. Haskell, 219 U.S. 104, 110 (1911) (Holmes, J.) (upholding assessment to set up fund for deposit insurance: "[I]t is established by a series of cases that an ulterior public advantage may justify a comparatively insignificant taking of private property for what, in its immediate purpose, is a private use").

[87] 83 U.S. (16 Wall.) 36, 70-72 (1873), THE FIRST HUNDRED YEARS at 342-43.

[88] Neal v. Delaware, 103 U.S. 370 (1881); Strauder v. West Virginia, 100 U.S. 303 (1880).

[89] Yick Wo v. Hopkins, 118 U.S. 356 (1886).

[90] *See* THE FIRST HUNDRED YEARS at 383-90, 393-402; *supra* p. 40; *see generally* A. BICKEL & B. SCHMIDT, *supra* note 28, at 729-990; Schmidt, *Juries, Jurisdiction, and Race Discrimination: The Lost Promise of* Strauder v. West Virginia, 61 TEX. L. REV. 1041 (1982).

[91] *See* A. BICKEL & B. SCHMIDT, *supra* note 28, at 725-27 (describing decisions of this period as "symbols of hope" and concluding that they "mark the first time . . . that the Supreme Court opened itself in more than a passing way to the promise of the Civil War amendments").

[92] Clyatt v. United States, 197 U.S. 207 (1905) (Brewer, J.), *supra* p. 41, note 85.

[93] 219 U.S. 219 (1911).

[94] The statute nominally required a fraudulent intent at the time of the contract. However, because the mere fact of breach was made prima facie evidence of such intent and there was no practical way to rebut it, the Court treated the case as if the breach itself had been made criminal. *Id.* at 233-38.

The Fuller Court had held it immaterial that the employee had agreed to work; what mattered was that he was compelled to do so against his will at the time of performance.[95] *Bailey* took the next step: "[T]he State could not avail itself of the sanction of the criminal law to supply the compulsion any more than it could use or authorize the use of physical force."[96] That this was no foregone conclusion was brought home by Justice Holmes's dissenting observation that the decision seemed to outlaw all contracts for labor: "If the mere imposition of such consequences as tend to make a man keep to his promise is the creation of peonage when the contract happens to be for labor, I do not see why the allowance of a civil action is not, as well as an indictment ending in fine."[97] The challenge Holmes posed was apt, even if his resolution left too much room for reinstating forced labor; yet the majority did not respond.[98]

The unanimous decision in *Guinn v. United States*,[99] striking down as a proxy for racial qualifications a literacy test applicable only to those whose ancestors had been ineligible to vote in 1866, showed that the Court took the fifteenth amendment as seriously as it had taken the thirteenth in *Bailey*.[100] More generally, *Guinn* ranks with the great test-oath cases

[95] Clyatt v. United States, 197 U.S. 207, 215 (1905); *see also id.* at 216: "This amendment denounces a status or condition, irrespective of the manner or authority by which it is created." The point was reiterated in *Bailey*, 219 U.S. at 242-43. To hold that individuals could sell themselves into slavery would seem to contradict the textual provision that slavery should not "exist within the United States," and "involuntary servitude" takes on color from the adjacent reference to slavery.

[96] *Bailey*, 219 U.S. at 244.

[97] *Id.* at 246 (Holmes, J., joined by Lurton, J., dissenting). There is an obvious connection between this reasoning and Holmes's bad-man theory of the law. *See* O. W. HOLMES, *The Path of the Law*, in COLLECTED LEGAL PAPERS 173-75 (1920) (equating penalties with taxes and arguing that "[t]he duty to keep a contract at common law means a prediction that you must pay damages if you do not keep it—and nothing else").

[98] That damages for breach of a work contract were permissible was acknowledged in both cases. *See Bailey*, 219 U.S. at 242-43; Clyatt v. United States, 197 U.S. 207, 215 (1905); A. BICKEL & B. SCHMIDT, *supra* note 28, at 869, 888-900 (finding Holmes oblivious here both to "the practical consequences" of equating criminal punishment with damages and to "questions of degree, which he liked to say were pretty much all of law," *id.* at 869, and finding support for the decision in the traditional reluctance to criminalize or prohibit the breach of a labor contract, *id.* at 888-900); *see also* United States v. Reynolds, 235 U.S. 133 (1914) (Day, J.) (invalidating use of forced labor to pay off debt incurred when employer paid criminal fine, despite amendment's exception for criminal sanctions).

Notwithstanding these decisions, the Court declined to apply the amendment literally to situations foreign to the purposes of its authors. First, in Butler v. Perry, 240 U.S. 328 (1916) (McReynolds, J.), partly on the basis of an effective survey of practices under the antislavery provisions of the Northwest Ordinance and of state constitutions, the Court unanimously upheld a requirement that able-bodied citizens perform road work, adding that "the term involuntary servitude was intended to cover those forms of compulsory labor akin to African slavery . . . , and certainly was not intended to interdict enforcement of those duties which individuals owe to the State, such as services in the army, on the jury, etc." *id.* at 332-33. As foreshadowed in the passage just quoted, two years later the Court without dissent rejected a thirteenth amendment attack on the military draft. Selective Draft Law Cases, 245 U.S. 366 (1918) (White, C. J.). Similar historical evidence was cited in connection with the distinct question whether the measure fell within the power to raise armies, but the servitude issue was treated as obvious, and the decisive precedent of the *Butler* case was not cited. *Id.* at 390.

[99] 238 U.S. 347 (1915) (White, C. J.).

[100] *Id.* at 363 (a statesmanlike opinion by a former Confederate soldier emphasizing that a contrary holding would make the amendment "wholly inoperative because susceptible of being rendered inapplicable by mere forms of expression . . . resting upon no discernible reason other than the purpose to disregard the prohibitions of the Amendment"). *See generally* A. BICKEL & B. SCHMIDT, *supra* note 28, at 908-90 (showing, inter alia, how the Court strained to resolve a serious remedial question in a way that enabled it to reach the merits); Monnet, *The Latest Phase of Negro Disfranchisement*, 26 HARV. L. REV. 42 (1912) (previewing *Guinn*).

of 1867[101] as healthy evidence that, despite Marshall's understandable qualms about determining legislative motive,[102] the Court will sometimes infer a forbidden purpose when it is unable to perceive a legitimate one—as it must if constitutional limitations are not to be evaded at pleasure.[103] More doctrinally interesting, however, was the 1917 case of *Buchanan v. Warley,* in which the Court gave surprisingly broad scope to the *fourteenth* amendment in this field by unanimously invalidating an ordinance requiring residential segregation by race.[104]

From the modern perspective, *Buchanan* was a peculiar case in two respects. First, the suit was brought not by a black person seeking to live in an area reserved for whites, but by a white landowner seeking to enforce a contract of sale against a recalcitrant black buyer who declined to perform in reliance on the ordinance.[105] Second, the decision was based not on the equal protection clause but on substantive due process: the ordinance took property of the white landowner without due process of law.[106]

At first glance one may be tempted to explain the invocation of due process as a clever means of circumventing the general rule forbidding a litigant to assert the constitutional rights of third parties, for it enabled Justice Day to reject an objection to standing on the express ground that the seller was asserting his own property rights and not the interests of potential black residents.[107] This did not explain, however, why the suit had been brought by a white property owner in the first place.

The fact that the defendant was black and the existence of a contractual provision releasing the buyer from his obligation if he could not occupy the premises suggest collusion to manufacture a case in which the defendant could be relied upon to take a dive.[108] An examination of the precedents, however, reveals an even more pressing reason for choosing such an unlikely plaintiff. Odd as it may seem in retrospect, the seller's chances of prevailing on the merits were substantially better than those of the immediate victims of racial discrimination. The ordinance did not impose disabilities on blacks alone; it forbade members of either race to move onto a block dominated by members of the other.[109] Comparable measures touching sexual relations and transportation having passed muster in the

---

[101] *Ex parte* Garland, 71 U.S. (4 Wall.) 333 (1867); Cummings v. Missouri, 71 U.S. (4 Wall.) 277 (1867). *See* THE FIRST HUNDRED YEARS at 292-96.

[102] *See* Fletcher v. Peck, 10 U.S. (6 Cranch) 87, 129-30, THE FIRST HUNDRED YEARS at 129.

[103] For analogous inferences of impermissible *administrative* purposes, see Neal v. Delaware, 103 U.S. 370, 397 (1881) (uniform absence of blacks from juries), and Yick Wo v. Hopkins, 118 U.S. 356, 374 (1886) (uniform denial of permits to Chinese), both discussed in THE FIRST HUNDRED YEARS at 386-87. Contrast the Court's reluctance to look behind a pretextual exercise of federal tax power in United States v. Doremus, 249 U.S. 86 (1919), *supra* pp. 98-99.

[104] Buchanan v. Warley, 245 U.S. 60 (1917) (Day, J.).

[105] *Id.* at 72-73.

[106] *Id.* at 74-81.

[107] *Id.* at 72-73.

[108] *See id.* at 69-70; A. BICKEL & B. SCHMIDT, *supra* note 28, at 789, 805 (giving additional facts bearing on this question). It was remarkable enough that the Justices did not throw the case out of court, as Holmes came close to suggesting in an undelivered dissent, *reprinted in id.* at folio following p. 592. *Cf.* Lord v. Veazie, 49 U.S. (8 How.) 251, 254-56 (1850) (dismissing collusive action brought by parties who had no real dispute and whose interests were adverse to others not parties to the suit), THE FIRST HUNDRED YEARS at 263 n.197. *But cf.* Fletcher v. Peck, 10 U.S. (6 Cranch) 87, 147 (1810) (reaching decision on the merits, but suggesting that case might have been collusively brought), THE FIRST HUNDRED YEARS at 128-36.

[109] *Buchanan,* 245 U.S. at 70-71.

Supreme Court on the ground that they imposed equal disabilities on both races,[110] an equal protection challenge in *Buchanan* faced almost certain disaster on the rocks of the separate-but-equal doctrine.[111]

The due process attack, at the time, was far more promising. At least since the 1898 rate case of *Smyth v. Ames*[112] it had been the law that any measure arbitrarily impairing property interests offended the due process clause.[113] The right to sell, as the *Buchanan* Court concluded, was a normal concomitant of property.[114] It remained only to demonstrate that the segregation ordinance imposed a limitation on that right not justified by the ubiquitous police power.

A similar attack on a statute forbidding integrated teaching in private schools had failed in *Berea College v. Kentucky* in 1908.[115] The reasoning of that opinion, however, seemed to encourage an attack on the residential segregation in *Buchanan*. The *Berea* Court had taken great care to explain that the complaining school was a corporation, that the state had reserved the right to revise its charter, and that the possible invalidity of the statute as applied to individuals was irrelevant. *Buchanan* emphasized all this in distinguishing *Berea*.[116]

On the police-power question Justice Day was brief. Though the city's professed goal of protecting the public peace by preventing racial conflicts was a legitimate one, it "cannot be promoted by depriving citizens of their constitutional rights and privileges."[117] This was circular; as the Court had often held, if the police-power justification was adequate there was no deprivation of constitutional rights.[118] More to the point was the observation that the ordinance was not well tailored either to achieving racial peace or to preserving property values; it fell far short of forbidding blacks and whites to come into allegedly

[110] Plessy v. Ferguson, 163 U.S. 537 (1896), *supra* p. 40; Pace v. Alabama, 106 U.S. 583 (1883), THE FIRST HUNDRED YEARS at 387-90. Justice Day distinguished *Plessy* on the ground that the measure there involved had not deprived blacks of the right to transportation and had been upheld as separate but equal. *Buchanan*, 245 U.S. at 79.

[111] *See* Hunting, *The Constitutionality of Race Distinctions and the Baltimore Negro Segregation Ordinance*, 11 COLUM. L. REV. 24 (1911); Pollak, *Racial Discrimination and Judicial Integrity: A Reply to Professor Wechsler*, 108 U. PA. L. REV. 1, 9-10 (1959). A few years before *Buchanan*, in McCabe v. Atchison, T. & S. F. Ry., 235 U.S. 151, 161-63 (1914) (Hughes, J.), the Court had taken a step that Schmidt views as a challenge to the whole structure of Jim Crow laws. A. BICKEL & B. SCHMIDT, *supra* note 28, at 775-84. It did so by insisting, in a case ultimately dismissed for want of standing, that separate facilities in fact be equal: if luxury train facilities were provided for whites, they must be provided for blacks as well. *But see* Cumming v. Richmond County Bd. of Educ., 175 U.S. 528 (1899) (Harlan, J.) (refusing to enjoin spending for white high school largely on remedial ground that injunction would not benefit black plaintiffs, but also expressing doubt whether equal protection required that blacks as well as whites have public high school). The argument has been made that *Buchanan* was distinguishable from Pace v. Alabama, 106 U.S. 583 (1883), and Plessy v. Ferguson, 163 U.S. 537 (1896), because segregation was more difficult to justify in the context of residence than in sexual relations or in transportation, *see* Note 18 COLUM. L. REV. 147, 148-50 (1918); that analysis overlooks the fact that separation had been upheld because it was not inequality at all and thus required no justification.

[112] 169 U.S. 466 (1898).

[113] *See supra* pp. 44-50, 102-04.

[114] *Buchanan*, 245 U.S. at 74.

[115] 211 U.S. 45 (1908) (Brewer, J.).

[116] *Buchanan*, 245 U.S. at 79. The essence of the *Berea* holding was thus that the right to teach white and black children together had never been among the corporation's property rights. *See* A. BICKEL & B. SCHMIDT, *supra* note 28, at 731-32.

[117] *Buchanan*, 245 U.S. at 80-81.

[118] *See supra* pp. 44-50, 102-04; THE FIRST HUNDRED YEARS at 369-78.

dangerous proximity,[119] and it allowed property to be "acquired by undesirable white neighbors or put to disagreeable though lawful uses."[120] In short, the Court appears to have held the ordinance invalid because it was a poorly designed means of achieving legitimate ends.[121]

It seems obvious that the Court indulged in stricter scrutiny of the relation between ends and means in *Buchanan* than it had in most other substantive due process or equal protection cases, without saying why.[122] It is remarkable that in 1917 it was prepared to do so unanimously, though obliquely, in the service of racial justice.[123]

---

[119]"[I]t is to be noted . . . that the employment of colored servants is permitted, and nearby residences of colored persons not coming within the blocks . . . are not prohibited." *Buchanan,* 245 U.S. at 81.

[120]*Id.* at 82.

[121]This disposition raised the interesting question whether the segregation ordinance in Plessy v. Ferguson, 163 U.S. 537 (1896), would have survived attack on the ground that it took the railroad's property without due process, but no such case reached the Supreme Court.

[122]*See supra* pp. 44-50, 102-04. The basis of Holmes's aborted dissent, *see* A. BICKEL & B. SCHMIDT, *supra* note 28, at folio following p. 592, was that the ordinance did not infringe the plaintiff's property rights. *See also id.* at 815 (adding that Day himself had dissented from both *Lochner* and *Coppage*). This contrast seems to have escaped the notice of Roche, who explained *Buchanan* on the basis that "entrepreneurial liberty was even more sacrosanct than racism." Roche, *Civil Liberty in the Age of Enterprise,* 31 U. CHI. L. REV. 103, 123 (1963).

[123]*See* A. BICKEL & B. SCHMIDT, *supra* note 28, at 813-17 (arguing from the opinion's pointed references to the racial purpose of the amendment that, whatever the technical basis of *Buchanan,* "it was the element of racial discrimination touching property rights and not a neutral conception of property rights that produced the decision"). *See also* Truax v. Raich, 239 U.S. 33 (1915) (Hughes, J.), which employed the equal protection clause for the first time to strike down discrimination against aliens as such—as contrasted with the narrower discrimination against Chinese in Yick Wo v. Hopkins, 118 U.S. 356 (1886). "The discrimination against aliens in the wide range of employments to which the act relates is made an end in itself. . . ." *Truax,* 239 U.S. at 41. The implication seemed to be that a simple preference for one group over another was an illegitimate goal under the clause. *See* Sunstein, *Naked Preferences and the Constitution,* 84 COLUM. L. REV. 1689, 1712-13 (1984). Later the same term, when a state was allowed to discriminate against aliens in public-works employment on the basis of a decision holding the *Lochner* rule against hour limitations inapplicable to such employees. *Truax* was not mentioned. Heim v. McCall, 239 U.S. 175 (1915) (McKenna, J.) (citing Atkin v. Kansas, 191 U.S. 207 (1903), *supra* p. 47, note 132. For an early recognition that *Atkin* might not be on point see Powell, *Decisions of the Supreme Court of the United States on Constitutional Questions III, 1914-1917,* 12 AM. POL. SCI. REV. 640, 640-41 (1918) (doubting that the result would have been the same if the state had excluded Methodists or Republicans). *Truax* itself, moreover, had ignored a unanimous decision rendered earlier the same year dismissing as "frivolous" a fourteenth amendment attack on a law forbidding aliens to own land. *See* Toop v. Ulysses Land Co., 237 U.S. 580, 582-83 (1915) (White, C. J.). For less progressive approaches to civil rights in the area of race relations see the unanimous decision in Jones v. Jones, 234 U.S. 615, 616-19 (1914) (Lurton, J.) (conclusorily rejecting an equal protection challenge to a limitation on inheritance by former slaves, without identifying any justification for the rule), and *see infra* note 128 (discussing *South Covington & C. S. Ry. v. Kentucky*).

Cutting across both economic and civil liberty categories was the important decision in Home Tel. & Tel. Co. v. City of Los Angeles, 227 U.S. 278, 288-89 (1913) (White, C. J.), which unanimously and painstakingly buried the recurrent notion that actions of state officials who misused authority granted to them by the state were not state action for fourteenth amendment purposes—without mentioning the unanimous and apparently contradictory fifth amendment holding in Hooe v. United States, 218 U.S. 322, 336 (1910) (Harlan, J.), that the unauthorized taking of private property by a federal officer "is not the act of the Government."

In the field of procedural due process, the White Court for the first time held that a state could not delegate legislative authority to private individuals, Eubank v. City of Richmond, 226 U.S. 137, 142-45 (1912) (McKenna, J.) (invalidating authorization of two-thirds of property owners to set building line for entire block); *but cf.* Thomas Cusack Co. v. City of Chicago, 242 U.S. 526, 531 (1917) (Clarke, J.) (allowing neighbors to waive a billboard ban and distinguishing *Eubank* by asserting a distinction between imposing and removing restrictions), and struck down several criminal laws as so vague that they did not give fair warning of what they forbade, *e.g.,* United States v. L. Cohen Grocery Co., 255 U.S. 81, 89-93 (1921) (White, C. J.) ("unreasonable" prices);

## B.   Admiralty and Commerce

In *Southern Pacific Co. v. Jensen*,[124] over four vehement dissents, the Court held that a state workers' compensation law could not constitutionally be applied to a longshoreman

---

International Harvester Co. v. Kentucky, 234 U.S. 216, 221-24 (1914) (Holmes, J.) (sales above "real value"). *See also* Ohio Valley Water Co. v. Ben Avon Borough, 253 U.S. 287, 289 (1920) (McReynolds, J., with three Justices dissenting) (invoking inadequate precedents for the otherwise unexplained conclusion that due process required judicial review by a court exercising "independent judgment as to both law and facts" of a rate order challenged as confiscatory); Dodge v. Osborn, 240 U.S. 118, 122 (1916) (White, C. J.) (conclusorily dismissing a due process objection to a ban on injunctions against collecting federal taxes); Bi-Metallic Inv. Co. v. State Bd. of Equalization, 239 U.S. 441, 445-46 (1915) (Holmes, J.) (giving a thoughtful explanation of why no hearing was required before general increase in property valuation). For discussions of *Ben Avon*, see A. BICKEL & B. SCHMIDT, *supra* note 28, at 609-30 pointing out that the rate had been set, *see supra* pp. 41-44 (discussing Chicago, M. & St. P. Ry. v. Minnesota, 134 U.S. 418 (1890)), without a full quasi-judicial hearing; L. JAFFE, JUDICIAL CONTROL OF ADMINISTRATIVE ACTION 636-53 (1965) (noting that the impact of *Ben Avon* has been greatly mitigated by later decisions); Brown, *The Functions of Courts and Commissions in Public Utility Rate Regulation*, 38 HARV. L. REV. 141, 148-49 (1924) (arguing that despite the "legislative" effect of rates, the agency had afforded an adequate quasi-judicial hearing); Freund, *The Right to a Judicial Review in Rate Controversies*, 27 W. VA. L. Q. & B. 207, 210-11 (1921) (arguing that de novo review entailed judicial assumption of administrative functions).

For the conflict of laws aspects of due process, see International Harvester Co. v. Kentucky, 234 U.S. 579, 582-83 (1914) (Day, J.), and the more elaborate Riverside & Dan River Cotton Mills v. Menefee, 237 U.S. 189, 194-95 (1915) (White, C. J.), both of which read into the due process clause, as a limitation on the personal jurisdiction of state courts over foreign corporations, the "doing business" requirement that had been developed in other contexts. *See also* Flexner v. Farson, 248 U.S. 289 (1919) (Holmes, J.) (holding that service on an individual's former agent was inadequate and more questionably suggesting that an individual might never become suable simply by doing business in the state); Kane v. New Jersey, 242 U.S. 160, 167 (1916) (Brandeis, J.) (relying on a state's interest in public safety to uphold a requirement that a nonresident motorist appoint a local agent to accept service of process); United States v. Bennett, 232 U.S. 299, 304-07 (1914) (White, C. J.) (unanimously holding the territorial limit on taxation that the fourteenth amendment imposes on the states, *see supra* p. 46, note 126, inapplicable to the United States despite the indistinguishable terms of the fifth amendment). Both New York Life Ins. Co. v. Head, 234 U.S. 149, 162-65 (1914) (White, C. J.), and New York Life Ins. Co. v. Dodge, 246 U.S. 357, 373-77 (1918) (McReynolds, J., over a powerful Brandeis dissent for four Justices), applied the territorialist doctrine of Allgeyer v. Louisiana, 165 U.S. 578 (1897), *supra* pp. 45-47, to strike down the application of Missouri law to contracts that the Court found had been made in New York. In sharp and unexplained contrast with the decisions just noted, and with the Court's unexplained and confusing use of the full faith and credit clause as a limitation on choice of law in Supreme Council of Royal Arcanum v. Green, 237 U.S. 531, 541-46 (1915) (White, C. J.) (power of fraternal insurance society to raise rates governed solely by law of its state of incorporation), the Court in Kryger v. Wilson, 242 U.S. 171, 176 (1916) (Brandeis, J., for a unanimous Court), flatly stated that a possibly "mistaken application of doctrines of the conflict of laws in deciding that the cancellation of a land contract is governed by the law of the *situs* instead of the place of making and performance" was "purely a question of local common law . . . with which this court is not concerned." *See* Dodd, *The Power of the Supreme Court to Review State Decisions in the Field of Conflict of Laws*, 39 HARV. L. REV. 533, 556, 560 (1926) (conceding that "it certainly cannot be said there are as yet any settled and sharply defined doctrines as to the relation between constitutional law and conflicts," but adding that the Court had "committed itself to . . . making itself, to some extent, a tribunal for bringing about uniformity in the field of conflicts"). For an excellent discussion of the history of personal jurisdiction over foreign corporations down to the *Riverside* decision see G. HENDERSON, THE POSITION OF FOREIGN CORPORATIONS IN AMERICAN CONSTITUTIONAL LAW 77-87 (1918). For refutation of *Flexner's* suggestion that the power to exclude was the sole basis of a state's power over corporations engaged in business within their borders, see *id.* and Scott, *Jurisdiction over Nonresidents Doing Business within a State*, 32 HARV. L. REV. 871 (1919), both pointing to decisions involving corporations engaged solely in interstate commerce.

[124] 244 U.S. 205 (1917).

who had met his death while unloading an interstate ship on navigable waters.[125] "If New York can subject foreign ships coming into her ports to such obligations as those imposed by her Compensation Statute," wrote Justice McReynolds, "other States may do likewise. The necessary consequence would be destruction of the very uniformity in respect to maritime matters which the Constitution was designed to establish; and freedom of navigation between the States and with foreign countries would be seriously hampered and impeded."[126]

The stress on uniformity in *Jensen* is highly reminiscent of the *Cooley* doctrine, which the Court had recently wakened from a twenty-year slumber[127] as a test for the validity of state laws that arguably infringed Congress's authority to regulate interstate commerce.[128]

---

[125] *Id.* at 217-18; *see also id.* at 218-55 (Holmes and Pitney, JJ., joined by Brandeis and Clarke, JJ., dissenting).

[126] *Id.* at 217.

[127] *See supra* pp. 36-40 (noting the decline during the Fuller years (1889-1910) of the *Cooley* "uniformity" test).

[128] See, for example, Port Richmond & B. P. Ferry Co. v. Board of Chosen Freeholders, 234 U.S. 317 (1914) (Hughes, J.), in which the Court equated the test laid down in Cooley v. Board of Wardens, 53 U.S. (12 How.) 299 (1852) (Curtis, J.) (upholding local pilotage rules because subject did not require uniformity), THE FIRST HUNDRED YEARS at 230-34, with the common distinction between direct and indirect burdens on commerce. Unlike "those subjects which require a general system or uniformity of regulation," the Court held, the question of ferry rates from one state to another "presents a situation essentially local requiring regulation according to local conditions." *Port Richmond,* 234 U.S. at 330, 332. For other examples of similar reasoning, see The Minnesota Rate Cases, 230 U.S. 352, 399-403 (1913) (Hughes, J.) (upholding local railroad rates that arguably diverted interstate traffic), and Pennsylvania Gas Co. v. Public Serv. Comm'n, 252 U.S. 23, 29-31 (1920) (Day, J.) (upholding state regulation of rates charged for gas in interstate sale to ultimate consumer). With the *Port Richmond* case, compare City of Sault Ste. Marie v. International Transit Co., 234 U.S. 333 (1914), also announced by Justice Hughes the same day, which struck down a sanction for operating a ferry across international waters without a license, not because the Court found any difference between foreign and interstate commerce, but because prohibition was a more severe burden on commerce than rate regulation.

The police power, not surprisingly, also continued to play a prominent part in the more than one hundred decisions of the White period respecting the negative effect of the commerce clause upon state laws. For example, in a third case decided on the same day as *Port Richmond* and *City of Sault Ste. Marie,* Justice Hughes spoke essentially in police-power terms when he upheld a state law requiring that locomotives be equipped with electric headlights, resting his decision on "the settled principle that . . . the States are not denied the exercise of their power to secure safety in the physical operation of railroad trains . . . , even though such trains are used in interstate commerce." Atlantic Coast Line R.R. v. Georgia, 234 U.S. 280, 291 (1914); *see also* Hendrick v. Maryland, 235 U.S. 610, 622-24 (1915) (McReynolds, J.) (invoking police power and need for road repair in concluding that requirement of vehicle registration and the attendant fee were not "direct" burdens on commerce). That the police power was not an invariable trump, however, was confirmed when—over three pointed dissents seeming to argue just that—the Court struck down a state safety law that would allegedly have required that an interstate train stop at 124 grade crossings in 123 miles, which would have more than doubled the time of the journey. Seaboard Air Line Ry. v. Blackwell, 244 U.S. 310, 312-13 (1917) (McKenna, J.) (once again terming the burden on commerce "direct"). This decision had been foreshadowed when the Fuller Court dismissed a previous attack on the same law for want of sufficient specificity as to the burden on commerce. Southern Ry. v. King, 217 U.S. 524, 533-34, 537 (1910), *supra* p. 39. *See also* South Covington & C. S. Ry. v. City of Covington, 235 U.S. 537, 547-49 (1915) (Day, J.) (upholding certain safety regulations as applied to interstate streetcars but finding others to be "unreasonable" and thus "direct" burdens); South Covington & C. S. Ry. v. Kentucky, 252 U.S. 399, 403-04 (1920) (McKenna, J.) (requirement that same streetcars be segregated by race was "not a regulation of interstate commerce" because the law applied only to the intrastate portion of the journey—which had been equally true, as Day observed in dissent, in the earlier case). In neither of the *South Covington & C. S. Ry.* cases did the Court discuss whether the regulation of an interstate streetcar serving a single metropolitan area was "local" within the principle of the *Port Richmond* case, 234 U.S. at 330, 332.

A similar understanding of what made a burden on commerce "direct" was suggested by Justice Pitney

The Court based its decision, however, not on the commerce clause but on article III's provision extending federal judicial power to "all Cases of admiralty and maritime Jurisdiction."[129] Under that clause, said McReynolds, "no [state] legislation is valid if it contravenes the essential purpose expressed by an act of Congress or works material prejudice to the characteristic features of the general maritime law or interferes with the proper harmony and uniformity of that law in its international and interstate relations."[130]

*Jensen* was not the first opinion to suggest that the admiralty clause had a limiting effect on state laws. Justice Bradley had laid the foundation for such a conclusion in an 1875 decision—holding that maritime law did not provide a lien for services rendered in a vessel's home port—by announcing that the governing case law was federal:

> The general system of maritime law which was familiar to the lawyers and statesmen of the country when the Constitution was adopted, was most certainly intended and referred to when it was declared in that instrument that the judicial power of the United States shall extend "to all cases of admiralty and maritime jurisdiction." . . .
>
> It certainly could not have been the intention to place the rules and limits of maritime law under the disposal and regulation of the several States, as that would have defeated the uniformity and consistency at which the Constitution aimed on all subjects of a commercial character affecting the intercourse of the States with each other or with foreign states.[131]

Though Bradley had not cited it, there was evidence to support the common-sense inference that uniform laws had been among the goals of the admiralty clause,[132] and the federal courts had looked to international customs in deciding maritime cases since the beginning.[133] Bradley had conceded, however, that there was "quite an extensive field of border

---

outside the police-power context in United States Glue Co. v. Town of Oak Creek, 247 U.S. 321, 329 (1918), holding that an apportioned and nondiscriminatory income tax imposed a less direct burden on commerce than did the comparable gross-receipts taxes, *see, e.g.,* Meyer v. Wells, Fargo & Co., 223 U.S. 298, 302 (1912) (Holmes, J.), that the Court had previously struck down; the latter more seriously deterred commerce because they "affect[] each transaction in proportion to its magnitude and irrespective of whether it is profitable." *United States Glue,* 247 U.S. at 329. *Compare* the analogous decision that a nondiscriminatory income tax could be applied to the export business without infringing the prohibition of export taxes in article I, § 9. William E. Peck & Co. v. Lowe, 247 U.S. 165, 173 (1918) (Van Devanter, J.) (distinguishing a nondiscriminatory tax reaching marine insurance for exported goods as "'so directly and closely' bear[ing] on the 'process of exporting' as to be in substance a tax on the exportation") (citing Thames & Mersey Ins. Co. v. United States, 237 U.S. 19, 25 (1915) (Hughes, J.)).

[129] U. S. CONST. art. III, § 2, cl. 1.

[130] *Jensen,* 244 U.S. at 216.

[131] The Lottawanna, 88 U.S. (21 Wall.) 558, 574-75 (1875), THE FIRST HUNDRED YEARS at 404, 428.

[132] Though Hamilton had explained only that maritime cases "so generally depend on the law of nations, and so commonly affect the rights of foreigners, that they fall within the considerations which are relative to the public peace." THE FEDERALIST NO. 80 (A. Hamilton), Madison and Randolph had both referred to the need for uniformity of decision, 3 THE DEBATES IN THE SEVERAL STATE CONVENTIONS ON THE ADOPTION OF THE FEDERAL CONSTITUTION, AS RECOMMENDED BY THE GENERAL CONVENTION AT PHILADELPHIA, IN 1787, at 532, 571 (J. Elliot 2d ed. 1836), if only in the context of foreign relations.

[133] *E.g.,* The General Smith, 17 U.S. (4 Wheat.) 438 (1819), *cited in* The Lottawanna, 88 U.S. (21 Wall.) at 571; *see* G. GILMORE & C. BLACK, THE LAW OF ADMIRALTY 45-46 (2d ed. 1975).

legislation on commercial subjects (generally local in character) which may be regulated by State laws until Congress interposes," [134] including pilotage laws such as that upheld against commerce clause attack in *Cooley* [135] and home-port liens in the case before him. [136]

Under Chief Justice Fuller the Court had begun to flesh out Bradley's vision, upholding in admiralty suits state wrongful-death statutes but not state laws denying municipal tort liability or creating liens for services rendered to a foreign vessel's independent contractor. [137] Once it was accepted that there was a federal common law of the sea, the last two decisions were easy to explain: in both the Court had found that the state law conflicted with federal. [138] Thus McReynolds was on familiar ground when he declared in *Jensen* that state laws could not "contravene[] the essential purpose expressed by an act of Congress or work[] material prejudice to the characteristic features of the general maritime law." [139] As the dissenters observed, however, the Court had never before followed the logic of Justice Bradley's position to the extent of holding that state law could not be applied to maritime cases brought in state tribunals. [140] Perhaps more important, McReynolds made no attempt to show that workers' compensation contradicted any policy of the maritime law. [141] Rather he based his conclusion squarely upon the third branch of his test: the state law "interfere[d] with the proper harmony and uniformity of [maritime] law in its international and interstate relations." [142]

Originally suggested by Justice Bradley's 1875 dictum, the uniformity criterion of the

[134] The Lottawanna, 88 U.S. (21 Wall.) at 581.

[135] *Cooley*, 53 U.S. (12 How.) at 315-21.

[136] In The Lottawanna, Bradley held that there was no lien as a matter of state law. 88 U.S. (21 Wall.) at 578-79.

[137] The Hamilton, 207 U.S. 398, 403-05 (1907) (Holmes, J.) (wrongful-death statute); The Roanoke, 189 U.S. 185, 194-99 (1903) (Brown, J.) (liens on foreign vessel); Workman v. New York City, 179 U.S. 552, 557-63 (1900) (White, J.); *see supra* p. 36, note 56.

[138] *See* The Roanoke, 189 U.S. 185, 196 (1903); Workman v. New York City, 179 U.S. 552, 558, 563 (1900); *cf.* G. GILMORE & C. BLACK, *supra*, note 133 at 48 ("[S]tate legislation is clearly invalid where it actually conflicts with the established general maritime law or federal statutes."). The supremacy clause speaks only of the Constitution, treaties, and statutes, not of federal common law. If article III provided for a supreme federal law, however, a contrary state rule would arguably offend the Constitution itself, or the statute granting admiralty jurisdiction. This same principle explains the White Court's later conclusions that state law could neither abolish limitations on maritime personal injury liability, Chelentis v. Luckenbach S. S. Co., 247 U.S. 372, 382 (1918) (McReynolds, J.), nor contradict the maritime rule that oral contracts were enforceable, Union Fish Co. v. Erickson, 248 U.S. 308, 312-14 (1919) (Day, J.). In both cases, however, the Court unnecessarily invoked *Jensen's* uniformity doctrine as well. *See Union Fish Co.*, 248 U.S. at 313; *Chelentis*, 247 U.S. at 382.

[139] *Jensen*, 244 U.S. at 216.

[140] *Id.* at 222, 239 (Holmes and Pitney, JJ., dissenting). *See* authorities cited in Currie, *Federalism and the Admiralty: "The Devil's Own Mess,"* 1960 SUP. CT. REV. 158, 161 n.14; Dodd, *The New Doctrine of the Supremacy of Admiralty over the Common Law,* 21 COLUM. L. REV. 647 (1921) (arguing against *Jensen* on essentially the same ground as the dissenters). Nevertheless, the purpose of uniformity that underlay the Court's conclusion that article III envisioned a federal common law demanded the application of that body of law in state courts as well. See Currie, *supra*, at 180-85.

[141] *Compare* The Hamilton, 207 U.S. 398 (1907), where the Court had allowed a state wrongful-death statute to be applied in admiralty after having held that the creation of such a remedy was beyond judicial competence in The Harrisburg, 119 U.S. 199, 213 (1886). Although McReynolds did not do so, he might have argued, by analogy to Chelentis v. Luckenbach S. S. Co., 247 U.S. 372 (1918), that in limiting recovery for personal injury, maritime law reflected a policy that would be contradicted by allowing workers' compensation in a maritime death case.

[142] *Jensen*, 244 U.S. at 216.

test applied in *Jensen* had been an alternative basis for each of the Fuller Court's two decisions adverse to state law.[143] Textually it was more difficult to infer such preemption from a provision granting judicial power than to hold an express grant of lawmaking authority exclusive. In terms of the Framers' purposes, however, it followed as easily as the comparable principle derived from the commerce clause.[144] The primary difficulty in *Jensen* was in applying the uniformity principle.

To begin with, McReynolds had to acknowledge precedent establishing that uniformity was not unduly disrupted by "the right given to recover in death cases,"[145] and *Jensen* itself was a death case. This difficulty was arguably more semantic than real, since the death law previously sustained had merely given an additional remedy for violation of duties already existing; the compensation law, imposing liability without violation of duty, arguably placed the shipowner at a greater disadvantage in planning his conduct. The more serious obstacle was that numerous state laws imposing additional primary duties in the interest of safety had been upheld against challenges based upon the analogous principle of the commerce clause. Most striking of all was the fact that, on the very day *Jensen* was decided, Justice McReynolds had also written for an undivided Court in rejecting a commerce clause objection to applying a state workers' compensation law to a seaman's shipboard injury: "In the absence of congressional legislation the settled general rule is that without violating the Commerce Clause the States may legislate concerning relative rights and duties of employers and employees while within their borders although engaged in interstate commerce."[146] Justices Holmes and Pitney, in separate *Jensen* dissents, found it impossible to explain why the admiralty clause should have a greater preclusive effect than the commerce clause, since both were said to have the same purpose; and McReynolds did not bother to tell them.[147]

The contrast was accentuated three years later in *Knickerbocker Ice Co. v. Stewart*,[148] when the Court held, over the same four dissents, that a state could not give compensation in maritime cases even with congressional consent.[149] In the commerce clause context the Court had held that the constitutional purposes were satisfied by a congressional determi-

[143] The Roanoke, 189 U.S. 185, 195 (1903); Workman v. New York City, 179 U.S. 552, 558 (1900).

[144] *See* G. GILMORE & C. BLACK, *supra* note 133, at 48, 406 (arguing that, although McReynolds had taken the *Lottawanna* quotation out of context, "[i]f there is any sense at all in making maritime law a federal subject, then there must be some limit set to the power of the states to interfere in the field of its working"); Morrison, *Workmen's Compensation and the Maritime Law,* 38 YALE L.J. 472, 476 (1929) (finding difficulties of administering *Jensen* test "offset by the logical and practical advantage of having the rights of the parties . . . determinable by a single standard").

[145] *Jensen,* 244 U.S. at 216 (citing The Hamilton, 207 U.S. 398 (1907)).

[146] Valley S. S. Co. v. Wattawa, 244 U.S. 202, 204 (1917) (citations omitted); *cf., e.g.,* Atlantic Coast Line R.R. v. Georgia, 234 U.S. 280 (1914) (upholding state law requiring locomotive headlights); Smith v. Alabama, 124 U.S. 465 (1888) (upholding state engineer-licensing law as applied to interstate trains). The admiralty clause had not been properly invoked by the employer in *Wattawa. See Jensen,* 244 U.S. at 204-05.

[147] McReynolds might have argued that the availability of a federal forum empowered to apply federal common law in maritime cases made the consequences of preemption less intolerable in admiralty than in commerce, an area where—even before Erie R.R. v. Tompkins, 304 U.S. 64 (1938)—the federal courts could make law only if the parties were of diverse citizenship. Instead he made the apparent inconsistency all the more glaring by invoking the commerce clause precedents to demonstrate the necessity for finding a similar limitation in the admiralty clause, by "the same character of reasoning." *Jensen,* 244 U.S. at 217.

[148] 253 U.S. 149 (1920).

[149] *Id.* at 154-55; *see also id.* at 166-70 (Holmes, Pitney, Brandeis, and Clarke, JJ., dissenting).

nation that the subject did not require uniformity.[150] Evidently uniformity was more important in admiralty than in commerce, but nobody had ever explained why.

## C.  Freedom of Expression

### 1.  Schenck v. United States

Alleged to have helped circulate to draftees a document encouraging them to oppose conscription, Schenck and a fellow defendant were found guilty of conspiring to cause insubordination and to obstruct recruiting, in violation of the Espionage Act of 1917. In an opinion whose reasoning occupied less than two pages, Justice Holmes concluded for a unanimous Court that the convictions did not offend the first amendment.[151]

Contrary to popular rumor, *Schenck* was not the first freedom of expression case decided by the Supreme Court. *Ex parte Jackson*[152] and *In re Rapier*[153] had held that Con-

---

[150] *In re* Rahrer, 140 U.S. 545 (1891) (upholding federal statute allowing states to prohibit sale of liquor in original package after the Court had barred states from doing so on commerce clause grounds), *supra* pp. 34-35. McReynolds had the temerity to cite this decision for the proposition that "Congress cannot transfer its legislative power to the States," *Knickerbocker*, 253 U.S. at 164, as if it supported him. He made no effort to distinguish its holding. *See also* Clark Distilling Co. v. Western Md. Ry., 242 U.S. 311 (1917) (White, C. J., over unexplained dissents by Holmes and Van Devanter) (upholding federal statute forbidding shipment of liquor into state for use in violation of state law). Since the federal statute in *Clark* made the breach of state law unlawful as a matter of federal law, it raised an issue of delegation not settled by *Rahrer*, which had only recognized Congress's authority to remove a constitutional barrier to the effectiveness of state law as such. It was an issue, moreover, that could not be resolved, as more typical delegation questions could, by finding interstitial lawmaking power inherent in the President's executive power. *See* United States v. Grimaud, 220 U.S. 506 (1911) (Lamar, J.) (upholding authority to adopt regulations "to preserve the [national] forests from destruction"); Buttfield v. Stranahan, 192 U.S. 420 (1904) (upholding federal statute authorizing Secretary of Treasury to make regulations to effectuate exclusion of low-grade teas); Field v. Clark, 143 U.S. 649 (1892) (upholding federal statute that allowed President to suspend statutory provisions relating to free introduction of sugar); *supra* pp. 16-19. No doubt because the case had grown out of a state's attempt to enforce its own law—the federal statute oddly having provided for no penalties—the Court in *Clark* found *Rahrer* indistinguishable. *See also* United States v. Hill, 248 U.S. 420 (1919) (Day, J.) (relying on *Clark Distilling* to settle the validity of a *federal* prosecution under a later and more stringent provision, over a dissent by McReynolds and Clarke suggesting that a different question was presented). In *Knickerbocker*, McReynolds, who had concurred in the result in *Clark* without explanation, *Clark*, 242 U.S. at 332, chose to emphasize passages in the earlier opinion stressing that Congress could have banned the shipment of liquor altogether and declared that the admiralty clause was different. Except for the unexplained fact that in admiralty there was a federal common law, the reasons he gave were equally applicable to the commerce clause. *Knickerbocker*, 253 U.S. at 165-66. For early appreciation of the inconsistency, see Corwin, *Constitutional Law in 1919-1920* (pt. 2), 15 AM. POL. SCI. REV. 52, 55-56 (1921). For criticism of *Knickerbocker*, see Morrison, *supra* note 144, at 480 ("The fairer conclusion would seem to be that paramount power to fix and determine the maritime law includes the power to determine the extent to which uniformity of rule is needed"); Currie, *supra* note 140, at 191 ("It is difficult to understand why the federal interest in a free commerce, whether land or sea, is in need of protection from the action of the very body to whose care it is intrusted."). The abundant commentary on the problems raised by *Clark Distilling* and *Hill* includes Cushman, *supra* note 45, at 409-12 (criticizing *Hill* on distinct ground that statute was not legitimate regulation of commerce because Congress had neither determined for itself that liquor was harmful nor limited its action to reinforcing state policy); Orth, *The Webb-Kenyon Law Decision*, 2 CORNELL L.Q. 283 (1917); Rogers, *The Constitutionality of the Webb-Kenyon Bill*, 1 CALIF. L. REV. 499 (1913) (noting that President Taft had vetoed the bill on constitutional grounds).

[151] 249 U.S. 47, 51-52 (1919).

[152] 96 U.S. 727, 736-37 (1878) (Field, J.).

[153] 143 U.S. 110, 135 (1892) (Fuller, C. J.).

gress could exclude lottery materials from the mails. *United States ex rel. Turner v. Williams*[154] had allowed Congress to keep an alien anarchist from entering the country. *Patterson v. Colorado,*[155] assuming without deciding that first amendment principles applied to the states, had upheld a contempt citation for publications found to interfere with judicial proceedings. *Gompers v. Bucks Stove & Range Co.*[156] had permitted punishment of a labor leader for exhorting his comrades to a boycott. *Mutual Film Corp. v. Industrial Commission,*[157] interpreting a state constitution, had upheld movie censorship on the unimaginative ground that motion pictures were not speech. *Fox v. Washington*[158] had upheld a conviction for publishing an article announcing a boycott of those who reported public nudity. Decisions upholding additional measures without even adverting to freedom of expression might also be thought to have cast light upon what the amendment was understood to mean.[159]

The precedents had two interesting features in common: none had upheld a freedom of expression claim, and all had dealt rather cavalierly with the question. Thus it was poetic justice that Holmes dealt cavalierly with *them.* He cited *Patterson* only to cast doubt on one of its more general conclusions, *Gompers* only to show that one could prohibit "words that may have all the effect of force,"[160] and the other precedents not at all. He seemed to place most reliance on a decision upholding an earlier conviction for conspiracy to obstruct the draft, in which, as he admitted, the first amendment issue had not been discussed.[161]

It was not as if the precedents had held little of value for the case at hand. At the very least they had established, as the citation of *Gompers* showed, that the first amendment did not preclude every federal law limiting speech. But they arguably stood for a great deal more. In upholding the exclusion of anarchist aliens, *Turner* had stressed the dangerous "tendency" of anarchist views and added that governments "cannot be denied the

---

[154] 194 U.S. 279, 292 (1904) (Fuller, C. J.).

[155] 205 U.S. 454, 462 (1907) (Holmes, J.).

[156] 221 U.S. 418, 439 (1911) (Lamar, J.).

[157] 236 U.S. 230, 244 (1915) (McKenna, J.).

[158] 236 U.S. 273, 277-78 (1915) (Holmes, J.).

[159] *See* THE FIRST HUNDRED YEARS at 442-44; *supra* pp. 57-59. *See also* Toledo Newspaper Co. v. United States, 247 U.S. 402, 410-11 (1918) (White, C. J.) (applying *Patterson's* conclusion to federal contempt citation); Goldman v. United States, 245 U.S. 474 (1918) (upholding conviction for conspiracy to obstruct the draft without discussing first amendment question); Weber v. Freed, 239 U.S. 325 (1915) (upholding ban on importation of prizefight films without discussing first amendment question); Lewis Publishing Co. v. Morgan, 229 U.S. 288, 314-15 (1913) (White, C. J.) (allowing Congress to condition second class mail privileges on disclosure of the identity of owners of periodicals and identification of materials that were advertisements); Davis v. Massachusetts, 167 U.S. 43 (1897) (upholding standardless permit requirement to speak in public park without discussing freedom of expression after Holmes, on the court below, 162 Mass. 510, 511 (1895), had said there was no constitutional right to speak on public property); Ex parte Curtis, 106 U.S. 371, 375 (1882) (upholding ban on political contributions between federal employees over dissent based on freedom of expression). For fuller treatment of the pre-*Schenck* precedents, see Rabban, *The First Amendment in Its Forgotten Years,* 90 YALE L.J. 514 (1981). *Compare Mutual Film,* 236 U.S. 230, 243-44 (1915) (motion pictures not speech), *with* Burrow-Giles Lithographic Co. v. Sarony, 111 U.S. 53, 56-58 (1884) (photograph is a "Writing[]" under copyright clause), *and* Pensacola Tel. Co. v. Western Union Tel. Co., 96 U.S. 1, 8-10 (1878) (telegraphic communication is within commerce clause).

[160] *Schenck,* 249 U.S. at 52.

[161] *Id.* (discussing Goldman v. United States, 245 U.S. 474 (1918)).

power of self-preservation." [162] *Patterson* had affirmed the power to punish even true statements "tending toward" interference with judicial proceedings. [163] *Fox* had allowed punishment of an author who urged a boycott, on the ground that there was no right to encourage violation of state laws. [164] Technically, all of the precedents could have been distinguished. [165] Nevertheless, they strongly suggested that speech could be prohibited if it tended to cause harm or encouraged violations of the law. And that, as Holmes interpreted the facts, was what Schenck and his codefendant had done. [166]

Nor did Holmes make use of readily available historical sources that would have helped to sustain the convictions. In *Patterson,* with some force, he had invoked Blackstone's assertion that the freedom of the press was nothing more than freedom from *"previous restraints"* such as censorship. [167] The technique of looking to tradition to define constitutional terms was almost as old as the document itself, [168] and there was plenty of other evidence to support Blackstone's view. [169] Yet not only did Holmes in *Schenck* decline to repeat his earlier argument; he went out of his way to repudiate it, without giving any of the available reasons: "It well may be that the prohibition . . . is not confined to previous restraints, although to prevent them may have been the main purpose, as intimated in *Patterson v. Colorado.*" [170]

[162] *Turner,* 194 U.S. at 294.

[163] *Patterson,* 205 U.S. at 462-63.

[164] *Fox,* 236 U.S. at 277-78.

[165] In several of the prior cases, as noted, the speech issue had not been raised. Others rested in part on the ground that the complaining party was claiming a privilege that the government was not obligated to afford to anybody. *Jackson,* 96 U.S. at 732; *Rapier,* 143 U.S. at 133; *Turner,* 194 U.S. at 289-90; *see also id.* at 292 (suggesting that first amendment did not apply to an alien outside the country). Two cases indicated that the words in question did not qualify as speech at all. *Gompers,* 221 U.S. at 439; *Mutual Film,* 236 U.S. at 244. *Fox* and *Patterson,* two of the cases most nearly factually on point, had involved state rather than federal action, *see Fox,* 236 U.S. at 275; *Patterson,* 205 U.S. at 459, and the Court had not yet held that the fourteenth amendment made the first amendment applicable to the states. *Toledo Newspaper Co.,* which had reaffirmed *Patterson* in the federal context, had involved judicial interference with expression, *see* 247 U.S. at 410-11; the amendment on its face limits only Congress.

[166] "Of course the document would not have been sent unless it had been intended to have some effect, and we do not see what effect it could be expected to have upon persons subject to the draft except to influence them to obstruct the carrying of it out." *Schenck,* 249 U.S. at 51.

[167] *Patterson,* 205 U.S. at 462 (emphasis in original); *see* 4 W. BLACKSTONE, COMMENTARIES ON THE LAWS OF ENGLAND 151 (4th ed. 1770).

[168] *See, e.g.,* Calder v. Bull, 3 U.S. (3 Dall.) 386, 389 (1798) (relying on a less conclusive passage from Blackstone as one source for narrow reading of ex post facto clause), THE FIRST HUNDRED YEARS at 41-48; Hylton v. United States, 3 U.S. (3 Dall.) 171, 180-81 (1796) (Justice Paterson powerfully, if selectively, invoking Adam Smith's understanding of the term "direct tax"), THE FIRST HUNDRED YEARS at 31-37.

[169] *See generally* L. LEVY, FREEDOM OF SPEECH AND PRESS IN EARLY AMERICAN HISTORY: LEGACY OF SUPPRESSION (1960) (finding evidence to this effect overwhelming, and citing, inter alia, Milton, Locke, James Wilson's statements in the federal convention, and later views of Story and of many state judges). It is not clear whether state constitutions explicitly providing that the abuse of speech was punishable are evidence of something implicit in the principle itself or of an intention to qualify it. *Cf.* THE FIRST HUNDRED YEARS at 127-59, 439-42 (discussing analogous histories of contract and free exercise clauses).

[170] *Schenck,* 249 U.S. at 51-52. Apart from the question whether the prior restraint doctrine developed in the press context applied to the newly minted freedom of speech as well, *see* T. COOLEY, CONSTITUTIONAL LIMITATIONS *421-22—and whether the circular in *Schenck* involved freedom of speech or of the press—there was a powerful argument to be made for repudiating the *Patterson* conclusion: it was difficult to see why anyone desiring to protect freedom of expression would have wanted to allow subsequent punishment of all speech that

Holmes relied principally on the time-honored argument of absurdity so intimately associated with Marshall: "The most stringent protection of free speech," he wrote in one of the most familiar passages in the reports, "would not protect a man in falsely shouting fire in a theatre and causing a panic."[171] Those who wrote the amendment, he seemed to be saying, were too reasonable to have disabled society from protecting itself against speech that all would agree ought to be prohibited.[172]

This argument is less persuasive than it may seem at first glance. As we know from Marshall's unimpeachable decision in *Barron v. Mayor of Baltimore*,[173] nothing in the Bill of Rights was meant to limit the power of *state* governments to outlaw speech harmful to the public welfare. It is not so difficult to believe that the framers of the amendment meant to keep *Congress* entirely out of the field. In fact, the history of the amendment lends considerable support to that conclusion. The standard argument of the defenders of the Constitution had been that a bill of rights was unnecessary because the document itself gave the central government no authority to regulate such matters as expression; the first amendment, as the ninth confirms, gave Congress no additional powers.[174] Disdaining

---

displeased the government, even though the prohibition of prior restraints did mean the interposition of a jury. Gallatin had made this argument in the Sedition Act debates, 8 ANNALS OF CONG. 2159-60 (1798), and it had been picked up in the major treatises of Thomas Cooley and Ernst Freund. *E.g.*, T. COOLEY, *supra*, at *421 ("[T]he liberty of the press might be rendered a mockery and a delusion . . . if, while every man was at liberty to publish what he pleased, the public authorities might nevertheless punish him for harmless publications."); E. FREUND, THE POLICE POWER §§ 474-475 (1904). As Chafee observed in embracing the Gallatin position, by 1919 numerous state decisions had also gone beyond protecting against previous restraints. Z. CHAFEE, FREE SPEECH IN THE UNITED STATES 11 & n.15 (1941). For a more extensive review of the early state cases, see Anderson, *The Formative Period of First Amendment Theory, 1870-1915*, 24 AM. J. LEGAL HIST. 56 (1980). For early explanations of the reasons free expression was desirable see, *e.g.*, the references to Locke, Milton, and Cato in L. LEVY, *supra* note 169, at 88-125, invoking the search for truth, the improvement of government, the preservation of domestic peace, and the promotion of individual autonomy.

[171] *Schenck*, 249 U.S. at 52.

[172] Holmes repeated this argument with an even better example in Frohwerk v. United States, 249 U.S. 204 (1919), discussed *infra* text accompanying notes 184-89: "We venture to believe that neither Hamilton nor Madison, nor any other competent person then or later, ever supposed that to make criminal the counselling of a murder within the jurisdiction of Congress would be an unconstitutional interference with free speech." *Frohwerk*, 249 U.S. at 206. *Cf.* Marbury v. Madison, 5 U.S. (1 Cranch) 137 (1803) (Marshall, C. J.) (judicial review is implicit, because otherwise the limitations on Congress could be evaded at pleasure—a result so absurd that it could not have been intended); Cohens v. Virginia, 19 U.S. (6 Wheat.) 264 (1821) (Marshall, C. J.) (Supreme Court may review the judgments of state courts; contrary decision would leave limits on states unenforceable). *See* THE FIRST HUNDRED YEARS at 66-74, 96-102.

[173] 32 U.S. (7 Pet.) 243, 247-49 (1833), (fifth amendment prohibition of taking without compensation is inapplicable to states), THE FIRST HUNDRED YEARS at 189-93.

[174] *See, e.g.*, 2 M. FARRAND, *supra* note 67, at 617, 618 (Mr. Sherman, opposing a motion proposed by Mr. Pinkney and Mr. Gerry to provide that "the liberty of the Press should be inviolably observed," stated: "It is unnecessary—the power of Congress does not extend to the Press. . . ."); THE FEDERALIST No. 84 (A. Hamilton). For the development of this argument, see Mayton, *Seditious Libel and the Lost Guarantee of a Freedom of Expression*, 84 COLUM. L. REV. 91, 119-21 (1984). Justice Story, who thought that state free speech guarantees forbade only prior restraints, *see supra* note 169, left open the possibility that the federal government was excluded from the field entirely. 3 J. STORY, COMMENTARIES ON THE CONSTITUTION OF THE UNITED STATES §§ 1874-1886 (1833). On the ninth amendment, see THE FIRST HUNDRED YEARS at 41-49 (discussing *Calder v. Bull*).

available replies to this line of reasoning,[175] Holmes stated his argument so sketchily as to invite easy rebuttal.

From the premise that complete protection of speech would be absurd, Holmes jumped without explanation to the famous conclusion that the constitutional test was "whether the words used are used in such circumstances and are of such a nature as to create a clear and present danger that they will bring about the substantive evils that Congress has a right to prevent."[176] This was by no means the only permissible conclusion. Lower courts, for example, had recently enunciated two quite different standards for determining the punishability of statements under the Espionage Act, one requiring only that the words have a natural and probable tendency to bring about the substantive evil, the other requiring a more or less explicit incitement.[177] Holmes neither explained how his test differed from these nor revealed why it was more appropriate. As Justice Curtis had done in the *Cooley* case,[178] Holmes laid down his test as a matter of mere fiat.[179]

Furthermore, the test was so cryptic as to invite a variety of interpretations. Perhaps in requiring that the danger be "clear and present" Holmes meant that the evil be likely to occur in the near future, but that was not the only possible reading.[180] Worse, again following the *Cooley* example, he made no attempt to show how his test applied to the facts of

---

[175] For example, no state had power to make laws for the District of Columbia; it would be odd to expect states to protect from interference the exercise of federal powers by the military or the federal courts; the copyright clause clearly authorized limitation of speaking and publishing; and the language used in the amendment paralleled that employed by states in which libel laws continued to be enforced. The passage of the Sedition Act in 1798, on the other hand, was so controversial that it arguably should not be taken, like many other actions of early Congresses, *see* Martin v. Hunter's Lessee, 14 U.S. (1 Wheat.) 304 (1816), THE FIRST HUNDRED YEARS at 91-96, as evidence of contemporaneous understanding of the amendment's meaning. *But see* McCulloch v. Maryland, 17 U.S. (4 Wheat.) 316, 402 (1819) (controversial nature of enactment of national bank strengthened its value as precedent by showing that the question had not passed unnoticed), THE FIRST HUNDRED YEARS at 60-68. It is noteworthy in any event that Holmes did not refer to the debates on the Sedition Act, in which interesting arguments had been made. *See* 8 ANNALS OF CONG. 2093-2171 (1798).

[176] *Schenck*, 249 U.S. at 52.

[177] Shaffer v. United States, 255 F. 886, 889 (9th Cir. 1919) (intention to cause "natural and probable consequences" presumed); Masses Publishing Co. v. Patten, 244 F. 535 (S.D.N.Y.) (L. Hand, J.) (incitement), *rev'd*, 246 F. 24 (2d Cir. 1917) (natural and reasonable effect plus intent). Apparently it did not occur to Holmes to interpret the statute itself narrowly, as Hand had done, in order to avoid the constitutional question.

[178] *See* Cooley v. Board of Wardens, 53 U.S. (12 How.) 299, 316 (1852), THE FIRST HUNDRED YEARS at 230-34.

[179] *See* Corwin, *Constitutional Law in 1919-1920,* 14 AM. POL. SCI. REV. 635, 657 (1920) (Holmes's clear-and-present-danger test was "apparently made up out of whole cloth").

[180] Chafee said Holmes's test, although lacking the "administrative advantage" of requiring that the utterance "satisfy an objective standard," lent "much support to the views of Judge Learned Hand [in laying down the incitement standard] in the *Masses* case." Z. CHAFEE, *supra* note 170, at 82. Gunther and Rabban, the former with the benefit of correspondence between Hand and Holmes, equate the *Schenck* standard with the natural-and-probable-tendency test used by other lower courts. Gunther, *Learned Hand and the Origins of Modern First Amendment Doctrine: Some Fragments of History,* 27 STAN. L. REV. 719, 720-21 (1975); Rabban, *supra* note 159, at 589-91; *see also* Rabban, *The Emergence of Modern First Amendment Doctrine,* 50 U. CHI. L. REV. 1205, 1207-08 (1983) (concluding that Holmes's treatment of free speech claims in *Schenck* and its companion cases essentially extended prewar tradition of "judicial hostility" and neglect). The latter inference is strengthened by the interesting fact that Holmes affirmed the conviction rather than remanding the case for a new trial in which the lower court would apply what appears to have been a brand new test.

the case. Had he explained that the power to raise and support armies authorized Congress to protect against the immediate impairment of national defense threatened by Schenck's scarcely veiled invitation to evade the draft, he would have helped both to elucidate his test and to justify his conclusion.[181]

Most sobering of all, perhaps, were the implications of the clear-and-present-danger test for future cases in light of the policies underlying the first amendment. It was reasonable enough to conclude that the authors of that provision had not meant to leave the federal government defenseless against outright incitement to the commission of federal crimes. Unlike Learned Hand's almost contemporaneous formulation,[182] however, Holmes's standard required nothing resembling express incitement; it apparently would suffice that the speaker had made the crime sufficiently probable, and that could be said of many who merely criticized the war.[183] It was difficult to reconcile such a conclusion with any conceivable reason for protecting free expression. On the other hand, as the Second Circuit had intimated in overruling Hand's incitement test, to require express incitement would deny the state any real protection; any clever inciter could escape punishment by avoiding the magic words.[184] Holmes gave no indication that he was aware of this tension.

In short, while *Schenck* gave us the enduring test of clear and present danger, the opinion was a disappointment in virtually every respect. Holmes paid little attention to the text of the first amendment, to the history of its adoption, to the established common law meaning of its terms, or to the rich collection of judicial precedents. He did not explain how the test he articulated followed from his premises, what it meant, how it applied to the case, or how it could be squared with the purposes of the amendment.

## 2.  Later cases

Two other Holmes decisions, both rendered a week after *Schenck,* suggest how far the Court was prepared to go in permitting the suppression of speech that threatened to endanger the war effort. They also increased the already considerable doctrinal uncertainty.

In *Frohwerk v. United States,*[185] in which a war critic had suggested that no one should

---

[181] *See* Z. CHAFEE, *supra* note 170, at 81 (adding that *Schenck* "was one of the few reported prosecutions under the Act where there clearly was incitement to resist the draft").

[182] Masses Publishing Co. v. Patten, 244 F. 535, 540 (S.D.N.Y.), *rev'd,* 246 F. 24 (2d Cir. 1917).

[183] *See* Gilbert v. Minnesota, 254 U.S. 325, 332-33 (1920) (McKenna, J.); Schaefer v. United States, 251 U.S. 466, 478-81 (1920) (McKenna, J., over dissents by Brandeis and Holmes, JJ., and by Clarke, J.); Pierce v. United States, 252 U.S. 239, 245-49 (1920) (Pitney, J., over dissents by Brandeis and Holmes, JJ.) (affirming convictions essentially for mere criticism). For similar decisions in the lower federal courts, see Z. CHAFEE, *supra* note 170, at 51-60. Justice Brandeis's lone dissent in *Gilbert,* while based on state interference with federal functions, is noteworthy for the first appearance of his argument that freedom of expression was within the "liberty" protected from state infringement by the fourteenth amendment's due process clause: "I cannot believe that the liberty guaranteed by the Fourteenth Amendment includes only liberty to acquire and to enjoy property." *Gilbert,* 254 U.S. at 343 (Brandeis, J., dissenting).

[184] Masses Publishing Co. v. Patten, 246 F. 24, 38 (2d Cir. 1917) ("[T]he Beatitudes have for some centuries been considered highly hortatory, though they do not contain the injunction, 'Go thou and do likewise.'"); *see also* Hall, *Free Speech in War Time,* 21 COLUM. L. REV. 526, 531-32 (1921) (spelling out consequences of an incitement test); Z. CHAFEE, *supra* note 170, at 49-50 (Judge Hand "regarded Mark Antony's funeral oration . . . as having counseled violence while it expressly discountenanced it").

[185] 249 U.S. 204 (1919).

blame draft resisters, the Court affirmed a conviction without mentioning the clear-and-present-danger test, admitting that the case was closer than *Schenck* because there had been no "special effort to reach men who were subject to the draft," but nonetheless finding it reasonable to conclude that "the circulation of the paper was in quarters where a little breath would be enough to kindle a flame and that the fact was known and relied upon by those who sent the paper out."[186] For the first time Justice Holmes displayed an awareness that one must be careful not to extend this reasoning too far: "We do not lose our right to condemn either measures or men because the Country is at war."[187] Indeed he restated the holding of *Schenck* in terms that resemble Hand's incitement test more than that of clear and present danger: "[We] have decided in *Schenck* . . . that a person may be convicted of a conspiracy to obstruct recruiting by words of persuasion."[188] This was a fair characterization of the facts of both *Schenck* and *Frohwerk* if one was prepared not to require express words of incitement.[189]

The companion case was *Debs v. United States*,[190] which affirmed the conviction of the well-known labor politician for a speech criticizing the war and praising individuals who had been convicted of obstructing the draft. Once again, although *Schenck* was cited as dispositive, clear and present danger was not mentioned. As in *Frohwerk*, moreover, it might have been difficult to show that the danger was either clear or present. At one point, as in *Frohwerk*, Holmes virtually parroted Hand's incitement test: "[I]f a part or the manifest intent of the more general utterances was to encourage those present to obstruct the recruiting service and if in passages such encouragement was directly given, the immunity of the general theme may not be enough to protect the speech."[191] Further on, however, he seemed to approve yet a third standard in noting with approval that the jury had been instructed that it could not convict unless "the words used had as their natural tendency and reasonably probable effect to obstruct the recruiting service, and unless the defendant had the specific intent to do so."[192] It was thus evident that Holmes did not set much store by the particular formulation; he seemed to think that there was no significant difference between natural and probable tendency, clear and present danger, and encouragement or persuasion. But he was willing to give juries considerable latitude to infer both the speaker's intention and the likelihood of bringing about a result that had not been expressly urged.[193]

The next term, however, when the Court affirmed yet another Espionage Act conviction in *Abrams v. United States*,[194] Holmes and Brandeis dissented.[195] The specific ground of

---

[186] *Id*. at 208-09.

[187] *Id*. at 208.

[188] *Id*. at 206.

[189] *See Schenck*, 249 U.S. at 51. Chafee blamed the *Frohwerk* decision on the failure of counsel adequately to present the facts. Z. CHAFEE, *supra* note 170, at 82-83.

[190] 249 U.S. 211, 216 (1919).

[191] *Debs*, 249 U.S. at 212-13.

[192] *Id*. at 216. *Compare* the cases cited *supra* note 177.

[193] *See* Z. CHAFEE, *supra* note 170, at 84 (arguing that "Debs's utterances are hard to reconcile with the Supreme Court test of 'clear and present danger'"); H. KALVEN, A WORTHY TRADITION 136 (1988) (terming *Debs* "a low point in the Court's performance in speech cases").

[194] 250 U.S. 616, 619 (1919).

[195] *Id*. at 624-31 (Holmes, J., dissenting); *see generally* Z. CHAFEE, *supra* note 170, at 108-40 (discussing *Abrams*).

their disagreement was narrow: charged under a statute requiring an intent to interfere with the war against Germany, the defendants had tried only to impede efforts to suppress the Russian Revolution.[196] What was significant was that Holmes went on both to make intention a part of his constitutional test and to redefine what constituted a sufficient danger.

On the facts, Holmes argued, "nobody can suppose that the surreptitious publishing of a silly leaflet by an unknown man, without more, would present any immediate danger that its opinions would hinder the success of the government arms or have any appreciable tendency to do so."[197] At the same time Holmes firmly proclaimed his continued adherence to *Schenck, Frohwerk,* and *Debs,*[198] although the publications in the first two cases were equally easy to characterize as "silly leaflet[s] by . . . unknown [men]" and unlikely to impede the war. Reconciliation is not impossible: Debs was more dangerous because he was famous and influential, Schenck because he had sent his message directly to draftees, and all three because they had come closer than Abrams to expressly encouraging obstruction of the war. "Publishing [Abrams's] opinions for the very purpose of obstructing," as Holmes argued, "might indicate a greater danger."[199]

Unwilling to rest solely on the greater danger of deliberate incitement, however, Holmes reformulated his test to suggest that, if the requisite intent had been present, no actual danger would have had to be shown: "I do not doubt for a moment that by the same reasoning that would justify punishing persuasion to murder, the United States constitutionally may punish speech that produces *or is intended to produce* a clear and imminent danger. . . ."[200] He thus seemed to be saying that the clear-and-present-danger standard had given too much protection to speech of the kind he thought had been at issue in *Schenck.*

One hint as to why he thought so may be found in his observation that intentional encouragement "would have the quality of an attempt."[201] The suggestion seems to be that the amendment did not disturb the common law of attempted crime. Three pages later, however, on the basis of reactions to the 1798 Sedition Act, he flatly rejected the argument that "the First Amendment left the common law as to seditious libel in force."[202] If attempts could still be punished, it was not because the common law as such was undisturbed.

---

[196] *See Abrams,* 250 U.S. at 628: "An intent to prevent interference with the revolution in Russia might have been satisfied without any hindrance to carrying on the war in which we were engaged." But see H. KALVEN, *supra* note 193, at 142: "Holmes seems on the verge of confusing motive and intent."

[197] *Abrams,* 250 U.S. at 625; *see also id.* at 629 (characterizing the defendants or their pamphlets, or both, as "poor and puny anonymities"). See H. KALVEN, *supra* note 193, at 143: "[I]t seems that Abrams moved Holmes because he was so trivial a critic. Debs should have moved him because he was such an important one."

[198] *Abrams,* 250 U.S. at 627.

[199] *Id.* at 628.

[200] *Id.* at 627 (emphasis added). This passage helps to resolve the question "whether Holmes meant that specific intent to hinder the war effort and a high risk of injurious consequences were alternative bases of criminal liability, or rather that both elements had to be shown." L. TRIBE, AMERICAN CONSTITUTIONAL LAW 611 n.16 (1978); *see also id.* at 610 (appearing to favor the latter interpretation).

[201] *Abrams,* 250 U.S. at 628.

[202] *Id.* at 630. For a contemporaneous rejection of his conclusion and a defense of the majority decision in *Abrams,* see Corwin, *Freedom of Speech and Press under the First Amendment: A Resumé,* 30 YALE L.J. 48, 53–55 (1920).

Greater light on Holmes's distinction may be cast by an example he offered to illustrate the importance of an intention to bring about the substantive evil: "A patriot might think that we were wasting money on aeroplanes . . . and might advocate curtailment with success, yet even if it turned out that the curtailment hindered and was thought by other minds to have been obviously likely to hinder the United States in the prosecution of the war, no one would hold such conduct a crime."[203] To punish all speech that endangered the war effort, he seemed at last to be saying, would cut deeply into the values the first amendment was designed to protect.

Holmes then attempted to identify these values for the first time:

> [W]hen men have realized that time has upset many fighting faiths, they may come to believe . . . that the ultimate good desired is better reached by free trade in ideas—that the best test of truth is the power of the thought to get itself accepted in the competition of the market. . . . That at any rate is the theory of our Constitution.[204]

Holmes cited none of the available evidence to support this important conclusion, but he was on firm ground.[205] He proceeded to deduce from this purpose a new version of the test applicable to "expressions of opinion and exhortations":

> While [the first amendment] is part of our system I think that we should be eternally vigilant against attempts to check the expression of opinions that we loathe and believe to be fraught with death, unless they so imminently threaten immediate interference with the lawful and pressing purposes of the law that an immediate check is required to save the country. . . . Only the emergency that makes it immediately dangerous to leave the correction of evil counsels to time warrants making any exception to the sweeping command, "Congress shall make no law . . . abridging the freedom of speech."[206]

In other words, although the *Schenck* formulation had been too protective of incitement, it had not been protective enough of opinions, which were too valuable to be suppressed except on rare occasions of overwhelming need. In addition to placing new emphasis on the time element by rephrasing a "present" danger as an "immediate" or "imminent" one, Holmes added what appears to have been an entirely new requirement of gravity: apart from intentional encouragement constituting an attempted crime, speech may be punished only where necessary "to save the country."[207]

---

[203] *Abrams*, 250 U.S. at 627.

[204] *Id.* at 630.

[205] *See supra* note 170.

[206] *Abrams*, 250 U.S. at 630-31. Holmes's choice of words in the last sentence quoted was unfortunate. Adherence to the judge's oath would forbid making *any* exceptions to the constitutional command, but Holmes himself had demonstrated in his earlier opinions that "the freedom of speech" was a term of art that reasonable people could not have meant to equate with freedom to say whatever one pleased. Even in *Abrams,* Holmes did not explicitly refute Blackstone's position that freedom of expression meant only freedom from previous restraints, but that position was clearly inconsistent with his stated views as to the purpose of the amendment.

[207] *See also Abrams*, 250 U.S. at 627 (insisting that the danger or intended danger be that the evil occur "forthwith"). Immediacy thus seems to have been part of his test of an "attempt" as well. Near the end of his

Was Holmes taking advantage of the freedom of a dissenter to develop an idea he had been able only to hint at without losing his majority in *Schenck,* or had he experienced a conversion not less remarkable than that of Saul of Tarsus?[208] In either event, although he still answered neither Blackstone nor Hand, he vigorously proclaimed the aspirations of the expression clauses and began the long battle to rescue them from the obscurity to which his earlier opinions had helped to consign them.[209]

---

opinion Holmes added, without explanation, the novel and interesting notion that the first amendment also limited the punishment that could be imposed even for speech not wholly protected: "Even if I am technically wrong and enough can be squeezed from these poor and puny anonymities to turn the color of legal litmus paper; . . . even if what I think the necessary intent were shown; the most nominal punishment seems to me all that possibly could be inflicted. . . ." *Id.* at 629. *See* Van Alstyne, *First Amendment Limitations on Recovery from the Press—An Extended Comment on "The Anderson Solution,"* 25 WM. & MARY L. REV. 793, 802 (1984). For an additional indication of the development of more liberal notions of freedom of expression during the White period, see United States *ex rel.* Milwaukee Social Democratic Publishing Co. v. Burleson, 255 U.S. 407, 430-31 (1921) (Brandeis, J., dissenting) (disagreeing with the prevailing notion that use of the mails was a privilege whose regulation was not subject to the restraints applicable to criminal laws: "Congress may not through its postal police power put limitations upon the freedom of the press which if directly attempted would be unconstitutional."). *Cf.* Z. CHAFEE, *supra* note 170, at 99 ("[E]xclusion from the mails practically destroys the circulation of a book or periodical. . . .").

[208] *See* F. FRANKFURTER, MR. JUSTICE HOLMES AND THE SUPREME COURT 52 (1938) (*Schenck* had "laid down cautionary limits against inroads upon freedom of speech not actually embarrassing the nation's safety"); P. MCCLOSKEY, THE AMERICAN SUPREME COURT 172 (1960) (*Schenck* "had committed the Court to an essentially libertarian formula for determining when speech may be abridged"); Gunther, *supra* note 180, at 741-45 (taking a more skeptical view after reviewing Holmes's correspondence and noting, among other things, the initial appearance of Zechariah Chafee's powerful commentary, Z. CHAFEE, *supra* note 170, between *Schenck* and *Abrams*). For evidence that Holmes's noble sentiments in *Abrams* did not meet with universal approbation, see Wigmore, Abrams v. United States: *Freedom of Speech and Freedom of Thuggery in War-Time and Peace-Time,* 14 ILL. L. REV. 539, 545, 552 (1920) (calling the dissent "shocking in its obtuse indifference to the vital issue at stake in August, 1918," and suggesting that "all principles of normal internal order may be suspended" during war).

[209] Other Bill of Rights decisions of the period include Holt v. United States, 218 U.S. 245, 252-53 (1910) (Holmes, J.) (curtly allowing defendant to be required to model a shirt because fifth amendment's self-incrimination provision "is a prohibition of the use of physical or moral compulsion to extort communications from him, not an exclusion of his body as evidence"); Wilson v. United States, 221 U.S. 361 (1911) (Hughes, J.) (relying on property concepts to uphold an order requiring corporate officer to produce corporation's papers that would incriminate him, over a good dissent by McKenna); National Safe Deposit Co. v. Stead, 232 U.S. 58, 71 (1914) (Lamar, J.) (holding fourth amendment's unreasonable-search principle inapplicable to states); Weeks v. United States, 232 U.S. 383, 393-98 (1914) (Day, J., for a unanimous Court) (distinguishing, on grounds of judicial administration, decisions refusing to investigate source of evidence when offered at trial—including the same Justice's decision, again for a unanimous Court, in Adams v. New York, 192 U.S. 585 (1904)—in holding that Constitution required return of property unlawfully seized upon timely application: "If letters and private documents can thus be seized and held and used in evidence against a citizen accused of an offense, the protection of the Fourth Amendment declaring his right to be secure against such searches and seizures is of no value, and, so far as those thus placed are concerned, might as well be stricken from the Constitution."); Silverthorne Lumber Co. v. United States, 251 U.S. 385, 391-92 (1920) (Holmes, J.) (holding that to allow government after returning property unlawfully seized to reclaim it by subpoena on basis of knowledge gained in the unlawful seizure would "reduce[] the Fourth Amendment to a form of words"); Gouled v. United States, 255 U.S. 298, 305-13 (1921) (Clarke, J.) (holding entry by imposture to be unreasonable search, reaffirming conclusions of Boyd v. United States, 116 U.S. 616 (1886), THE FIRST HUNDRED YEARS at 444-47, that warrant may not issue for mere evidence and that introduction of illegally seized papers offends self-incrimination ban, and extending *Weeks* to require exclusion of unlawfully obtained evidence because "a rule of practice must not be allowed for any technical reason to prevail over a constitutional right"); and Burdeau v. McDowell, 256 U.S. 465, 476 (1921) (Day,

J.) (following logic of *Weeks* in refusing to require government to return property taken by private individuals because fourth and fifth amendments not violated by private action). *See also* Minneapolis & St. L. R.R. v. Bombolis, 241 U.S. 211, 217 (1916) (White, C. J.) (holding seventh amendment requirement of civil jury inapplicable to state court enforcing federal law); Slocum v. New York Life Ins. Co., 228 U.S. 364, 380 (1913) (Van Devanter, J.) (exhaustively reviewing the precedents in concluding, over an equally detailed Hughes dissent for four Justices, *id.* at 400-28, that judgment n.o.v. offended seventh amendment provision that "no fact tried by jury, shall be otherwise re-examined in any Court of the United States, than according to the rules of the common law," *see* U.S. CONST. amend. VII).

*Holt* is defended, and *Gouled* criticized, in 8 J. WIGMORE, EVIDENCE IN TRIALS AT COMMON LAW § 2264 n.4, § 2265 & n.7 (J. McNaughton rev. ed. 1961), on the appealing ground that only compulsory testimony implicates the fundamental policies underlying the self-incrimination provision since only in that situation are "the oath and private thoughts and beliefs of the individual . . . involved." *Id.* § 2263. For a serious defense of *Slocum* on historical grounds, see Schofield, *New Trials and the Seventh Amendment*—Slocum v. New York Life Ins. Co., 8 ILL. L. REV. 287, 381, 465 (1913-14). *But see* A. BICKEL & B. SCHMIDT, *supra* note 28, at 312-14 (arguing, in view of the similarity between judgment n.o.v. and accepted directed-verdict practice, that *Slocum* typified the "fundamental conservatism" of White Court).

# Conclusion to Part Two

It is not easy, without prolixity, to give a comprehensive picture of a period in which over six hundred constitutional cases were decided. It helps that, in those days before the modern expansion of certiorari jurisdiction, the great bulk of the cases required only the application of settled principles. It remains true that even these cases add to our understanding of the Court's approach to constitutional decision-making and of the judicial personalities of its members. Moreover, as the voluminous footnotes designed to flesh out the bare bones of the main story indicate, there are a number of significant constitutional decisions that cannot be discussed at length without running the risk of losing sight of the larger picture. One can only hope that the highly restrictive and idiosyncratic process of selection has produced a series of snapshots that not only explore those aspects of the White years that one observer finds most interesting but also indicate something about the period as a whole.

In numerical terms, by far the greater part of the court's constitutional docket consisted, as in the preceding period, of attacks on state action under four provisions: the due process, equal protection, contract, and commerce clauses. Encouraged by the Court's position that the fourteenth amendment made it the ultimate judge of the reasonableness of official action, litigants seemed willing to ask the Court to overturn just about anything a state might try to do—and state governments were very active during the period. Except in the commerce clause cases, however, the challengers were usually disappointed. The Court went through enormous efforts with very little direct impact on the world around it, and in none of these areas did the White period produce important new doctrine.

Far more interesting were developments in two other areas in which the numbers of cases were far smaller: the extent of enumerated congressional powers and the restraints of the first amendment. The first category presented the Court with the continuing challenge of measuring the deeds of an increasingly active Congress against a Constitution framed under strikingly different conditions. The second demonstrated the stress placed upon first amendment values by a wartime emergency. These pressures posed the critical intellectual challenges to the Court during the White period.

I do not think it can be said that the Court responded heroically to these demands. Its decisions on the scope of enumerated powers reveal an awareness of the tension between the necessary and proper clause and the principle of limited powers but seem wholly capricious in attempting to resolve it. The cases on freedom of expression seem to reflect an extreme insensitivity to the values underlying the amendment, in the face of an eloquent if belated appeal by Holmes and Brandeis.

Like the Waite period,[1] this era was characterized by short opinions. No doubt in both periods this was attributable in part to docket pressures; the Court had a great many cases to decide. In the early years of the White Court, moreover, there was a high degree of unanimity—perhaps in part because there were not many important new issues of principle.[2] Dissents, like important new issues, became much more frequent after 1916—and after Wilson's appointments of McReynolds, Brandeis, and Clarke. Concurring opinions were rare throughout the period. Inconsistency and inadequate explanation, as usual, were not.

Individual Justices, on the other hand, were often highly predictable. Lurton, during his brief stay, tended toward narrow construction of federal powers and civil rights.[3] White, Van Devanter, and McReynolds often dissented from decisions upholding federal authority or rejecting due process claims.[4] Holmes, Brandeis, Hughes, and Clarke were more likely than their colleagues to uphold both state and federal authority,[5] except that the first two developed a heightened sensitivity to first amendment claims after Hughes's departure,[6] and that Clarke displayed a marked antipathy to measures of all kinds that

[1] For a discussion of the Waite Court (1874-1888), see THE FIRST HUNDRED YEARS at 361-452.

[2] See also M. PUSEY, CHARLES EVANS HUGHES 282, 293 (1951) (describing early White years as era of good feeling within Court despite Chief Justice's lack of leadership qualities, and noting Hughes's belief that dissent should rarely be expressed); M. KLINKHAMER, EDWARD DOUGLAS [sic] WHITE, CHIEF JUSTICE OF THE UNITED STATES 61 (1943) ("When White was first made Chief Justice, he was reported to have said that he was 'going to stop this dissenting business,' and it was further alleged that he had stopped it except for Mr. Justice Harlan.").

[3] His two most important opinions for the Court were Coyle v. Smith, 221 U.S. 559, 565 (1911) (Congress could not forbid a new state to move its capital), and Jones v. Jones, 234 U.S. 615, 618-19 (1914) (equal protection did not require state to allow former slaves to inherit property). He dissented from the invalidation of peonage in Bailey v. Alabama and the upholding of congressional power in Shreveport. See also A. BICKEL & B. SCHMIDT, 9 HISTORY OF THE SUPREME COURT OF THE UNITED STATES 74-80, 335-40 (1984) (noting that Lurton had not been operating at peak energy during his brief tenure, and concluding that "his main career had been as a federal circuit judge").

[4] All three dissented, for example, from Doremus, Mountain Timber, Bunting, the Arizona Employers' Liability Cases, and Block. The Chief Justice, however, also dissented from the denial of congressional power over primary elections in Newberry, and argued in Gilbert that federal authority to prevent interference with the war effort was exclusive. Van Devanter had begun by writing two opinions broadly construing the power to regulate matters affecting interstate commerce; in later years he proved hostile to the use of federal powers for police purposes, though he had gone along with the Court's opinion in the white-slave case.

[5] Holmes and Hughes dissented from the invalidation of the yellow-dog law; Holmes, Brandeis, and Clarke dissented from the invalidation of the employment agency and child labor laws and of the tax on stock dividends. Brandeis and Clarke, but not Holmes, dissented from invalidation of the federal primary election law in Newberry as well. See also M. PUSEY, supra note 2, at 289 (describing Holmes and Hughes as the "two leading liberals" of the early White years).

[6] See, e.g., Abrams, Pierce, Schaefer, and Gilbert. Brandeis dissented in all of these cases, Holmes in all but Gilbert. Clarke joined them only in Schaefer and wrote for the Court to uphold the conviction in Abrams.

interfered with the market for alcoholic beverages.[7] McKenna was somewhat more inclined than the majority to invoke substantive due process but took a rather broad view of
congressional powers.[8] Pitney, whose ideas of federal authority were narrower, joined
Holmes, Brandeis, and Clarke in opposition to the aggressive doctrine of admiralty
preemption.[9] Day, who seldom dissented in constitutional cases, was most representative
of the position of the White Court in this field.[10]

Like his immediate predecessor, Chief Justice White played a relatively modest role in
speaking for the Court, and, though he dissented often, almost never wrote a dissenting
opinion. Following long-standing tradition, he did use the prestige of his office to good
advantage in reserving to himself several of the most politically sensitive controversies:
the grandfather clause, the income tax, the military draft, and wartime measures that interfered with private interests in order to assure essential services.[11] His opinion style was
generally impenetrable, and there was little evidence during this period of the originality
that had characterized his earlier opinions on insular possessions and full faith and
credit.[12] Yet he marshaled history effectively in the draft case, and his emphatic application of the fifteenth amendment against the grandfather clause was an impressive achievement.

McKenna, the senior Associate Justice, was again given little of importance to write,
and justified the low expectations of two Chief Justices by having little of interest to say.
Most of his opinions that are not completely forgotten applied settled law without flair,[13]
and his most significant departure—in upholding overtime legislation in *Bunting*—failed
both to distinguish the precedents and to explain the reasonableness of the law.[14] Day, on
the other hand, seemed to get more than his share of important opinions to write, includ-

[7] *See* National Prohibition Cases, 253 U.S. 350, 407-11 (1920) (Clarke, J., dissenting from broad construction of the eighteenth amendment); Jacob Ruppert v. Caffey, 251 U.S. 264, 310 (1920) (Clarke, J., dissenting
from decision upholding congressional power to ban nonintoxicating beer); United States v. Hill, 248 U.S. 420,
428 (1919) (Clarke, J., joining in dissent of McReynolds, J., from decision upholding statute forbidding bringing
liquor into state whose law forbade sale).

[8] McKenna dissented in *Hammer, Block,* the Arizona Employers' Liability Cases, and *Mountain Timber.*

[9] Pitney dissented from the upholding of federal authority in *Shreveport* and *Holland,* but also from the denial
of federal power in *Newberry,* and in the admiralty cases of *Jensen, Chelentis,* and *Knickerbocker.*

[10] Day did dissent both from *Coppage v. Kansas* and from *Eisner v. Macomber. See also* J. McLean, William Rufus Day 65, 116 (1946) (describing Day as strict in his construction of federal authority but tolerant of
state police-power measures).

[11] *See Guinn, Brushaber,* Selective Draft Law Cases, Wilson v. New, and *Dakota Cent. Tel.; see also* Virginia
v. West Virginia, 246 U.S. 565, 591 (1918) (upholding judicial authority to enforce judgment against state);
Home Tel. & Tel. Co. v. City of Los Angeles, 227 U.S. 278, 283-84 (1913) (holding abuse of state authority to
be state action within the fourteenth amendment).

[12] *See supra* ch. 3 (discussing the insular cases, Clarke v. Clarke, 178 U.S. 186 (1900), Fauntleroy v. Lum,
210 U.S. 230 (1908), and Haddock v. Haddock, 201 U.S. 562 (1906)); M. Klinkhamer, *supra* note 2, at 234
("The repetitious prolixity just noted is perhaps the most outstanding quality of a style not intrinsically appealing.").

[13] *E.g., Hadacheck, Blackwell,* and *Hoke.*

[14] He also authored two pedestrian opinions allowing the punishment of war critics—Gilbert v. Minnesota,
254 U.S. 325 (1920), and Schaefer v. United States, 251 U.S. 466 (1920)—and originated the novel but ill-
explained use of due process to strike down a delegation of power to private property owners in Eubank v.
Richmond, 226 U.S. 137, 143-44 (1912). Perhaps his best opinion was a dissent, in Wilson v. United States,
221 U.S. 361, 386-94 (1911) (McKenna, J., dissenting), from the Court's narrow reliance on property concepts
to define self-incrimination.

ing *Muskrat, Hammer, Doremus,* and *Buchanan*—although, as his opinions in those cases suggest, he was not among the more impressive craftsmen on the bench.[15]

Of the five Justices appointed by Taft around the time of White's elevation, Lurton and Lamar made little impression, while the other three showed significant abilities.[16] Hughes was unusually prominent for a newcomer, becoming the Court's leading spokesman on civil rights as well as on the positive and negative aspects of the commerce clause before he left the bench to run for President in 1916.[17] Van Devanter, who had played a rather substantial role at the outset, ended up producing very little; his few significant opinions suggested that he was a thorough and careful thinker, if a narrowly literal one.[18] Pitney, the author of *Coppage,* wrote effectively to sustain a state income tax against commerce clause attack, to strike down a federal tax on stock dividends, and to protest both the extension of maritime uniformity and the denial of federal power over primary elections.[19]

Wilson's three appointees were a mixed bag in terms not only of outlook but of craftsmanship as well. Except for his vote, Clarke was not much of a factor.[20] McReynolds wrote surprisingly little beyond his firm, if one-sided, opinions striking down state laws affecting the admiralty.[21] Brandeis wrote even less for the Court in constitutional matters,

---

[15] He deserves credit, however, for having anchored what later became the exclusionary rule in the need to enforce the fourth amendment, Weeks v. United States, 232 U.S. 383 (1914), and for having balked at the Court's willingness to apply more lenient commerce clause standards to a state segregation law than to other police-power regulations affecting the same streetcars. *See supra* p. 111, note 128 (discussing the two *South Covington* cases).

[16] Lamar sat as long as Hughes but wrote fewer than half as many constitutional opinions. His most significant efforts entailed the application of settled principles, *see, e.g.,* Atchison, T. & S. F. Ry. v. Sowers, 213 U.S. 55 (1909), to strike down a provision seeking to localize a transitory cause of action in Tennessee Coal, Iron & R.R. v. George, 233 U.S. 354, 359 (1914), and the more adventurous extension of precedents, *see* Buttfield v. Stranahan, 192 U.S. 470 (1904); Field v. Clark, 143 U.S. 649 (1892); *see also* A. BICKEL & B. SCHMIDT, *supra* note 3, at 664-65; Foster, *The Delegation of Legislative Power to Administrative Officers,* 7 ILL. L. REV. 397, 403-05 (1913), to uphold a delegation of rule-making power to protect national forests in United States v. Grimaud, 220 U.S. 506 (1911). Justice Harlan died before having the time to contribute significantly to the work of the White years. For a discussion of Lurton, see *supra* note 3 and accompanying text. For a favorable view of all five appointments, see generally A. BICKEL & B. SCHMIDT, *supra* note 3, at 3-85; for an assessment of Lamar's achievements, see *id.* at 357-66.

[17] *See* Bailey v. Alabama, Truax v. Raich, and McCabe v. Atchison, T. & S. F. Ry.; the Shreveport Rate Case and Baltimore & O.R.R. v. ICC, the Minnesota Rate Cases, *Atlantic Coast Line, Port Richmond,* and *Sault Ste. Marie;* A. BICKEL & B. SCHMIDT, *supra* note 3, at 392-406 (calling him one of the few Justices ever to make a significant mark in such a short time); M. PUSEY, *supra* note 2, at 303, 314 (praising Hughes's work and concluding that his "greatest contribution to judicial thinking in this period came in the adaptation of law to the control of national economic policy").

[18] *See* Dillon v. Gloss, *Evans,* and *Slocum;* Southern Ry. v. United States and the Second Employers' Liability Cases; M. PUSEY, *supra* note 2, at 284 (noting that Van Devanter added a great deal in conference but was already showing signs of what Justice Sutherland later called "pen paralysis").

[19] *See United States Glue, Eisner, Jensen,* and *Newberry; see also* M. PUSEY, *supra* note 2, at 284 (stating that Pitney was highly regarded by his brethren).

[20] His most important opinions were his uninspiring limitation of speech in *Abrams,* his ill-justified allowance of private lawmaking in *Cusack,* and his vigorous discarding of precedent to extend the remedies for unreasonable seizures in Gouled v. United States.

[21] *See Jensen, Chelentis,* and *Knickerbocker.* He wrote effectively to sustain compulsory road work in *Butler* and ineffectively to require de novo review of administratively set rates in *Ben Avon,* and wrote to deny federal power over primary elections in *Newberry.* For a fascinating portrait of this Justice—whom Bickel described as very likely "the most difficult man ever to serve" on the Court—see A. BICKEL & B. SCHMIDT, *supra* note 3, at

but displayed strength both in his learned dissents from decisions hostile to regulation and taxes and in his impassioned pleas for free expression.[22]

That leaves Holmes. To posterity, and to many contemporaries, he was the dominant figure of the day. This is partly because of his felicitous way with words and partly because of his positions, which are appealing to the late twentieth-century mind.[23] Though he was a workhorse who wrote more majority opinions in constitutional matters than any of his colleagues, what he wrote for the Court was not uniformly impressive. In *Missouri v. Holland* he was careless as to the scope of the treaty power; in *Fox, Schenck, Frohwerk,* and *Debs* he was cavalier, superficial, and inattentive to the values of free expression.[24] As during the Fuller years, it was chiefly in dissent that Holmes made his mark. His name is associated with articulate protests against most of the White Court's illiberal decisions, including *Coppage, Hammer, Jensen,* the tax case of *Eisner v. Macomber,* and, most important of all, *Abrams v. United States.*[25]

If he had done nothing else in these eleven years, Holmes would still be justly celebrated for the *Abrams* dissent, not least because it suggests an astonishing capacity for growth in a man nearly eighty years old. For nobility of aspiration this opinion ranks with the racial justice of *Bailey, Guinn,* and *Buchanan;* for sheer eloquence and creativity it outshines them all. It took a long time for Holmes's message to sink in. In the long run, however, it effected a profound and lasting change in the country's perception of freedom of expression. The *Abrams* dissent was the supreme achievement of an otherwise largely uninspiring period.

---

341-57 (adding that, though able, McReynolds gave little attention to the writing of opinions, "being affected by a curious notion that opinions were essentially superfluities anyway").

[22] *See Ben Avon, Eisner, Pierce, Schaefer, Gilbert,* and *Milwaukee Publishing Co.* His only important constitutional opinion for the Court was that upholding wartime liquor prohibition in *Hamilton. See also* A. BICKEL & B. SCHMIDT, *supra* note 3, at 367-68 (describing Brandeis as the first Justice representative of a new way of thinking and the celebrated fight over his appointment as one "for the soul of the Supreme Court": "In his opinions would be glimpsed the second half of the twentieth century.").

[23] Compare Felix Frankfurter's contemporaneous paean: "It makes all the difference in the world whether the Constitution is treated primarily as a text for interpretation or as an instrument of government." Frankfurter, *Twenty Years of Mr. Justice Holmes' Constitutional Opinions,* 36 HARV. L. REV. 909, 920 (1923).

[24] More admirable were several of his less celebrated opinions, *e.g.,* his interesting insights into the differences between legislative and judicial procedures in Bi-Metallic Inv. Co. v. State Bd. of Equalization, 239 U.S. 441, 444-45 (1915), his indignant prevention of an end run around the fourth amendment in Silverthorne v. United States, 251 U.S. 385, 391-92 (1920), and his persuasive use of precedent and other arguments to sustain rent control in Block v. Hirsh, 256 U.S. 135, 155-58 (1921). *See* M. PUSEY, *supra* note 2, at 285-86 (describing Holmes's opinions as "short and pungent but sometimes lacking in body and clarity").

[25] *See also* Frank v. Mangum, 237 U.S. 309, 347 (1915) (Holmes, J., joined by Hughes, J., dissenting) (protesting that mob domination rendered trial a deprivation of liberty without due process); Evans v. Gore, 253 U.S. 245, 265-66 (1920) (Holmes, J., dissenting) (taking functional view of protection of judicial compensation in article III); and the less liberal, though challenging, dissent from the invalidation of criminal penalties for quitting work in Bailey v. Alabama.

# Part Three

## Chief Justice Taft
## 1921–1930

# Introduction to Part Three

The selection of William Howard Taft to succeed White as Chief Justice in 1921 was followed by three additional appointments in the next two years: George Sutherland, Pierce Butler, and Edward T. Sanford replaced Day, Pitney, and Clarke. The upshot was something of a reign of terror for state and federal legislation.[1]

White himself had been no great supporter of progressive legislation, and neither Day nor Pitney was in later terms a flaming liberal. The last two, however, had frequently voted with Holmes, Brandeis, and Clarke to sustain social legislation against due process attacks. Sutherland, Buttler, and Sanford, like Taft, tended to cast their lot with Van Devanter, McReynolds, and McKenna, who had been frequent dissenters in substantive due process cases before 1921; thus a vocal minority became a solid majority within a two-year period. The replacement of McKenna by Harlan F. Stone in 1925 merely increased the number of regular dissenters from two to three.[2]

---

[1] See Brown, *Due Process of Law, Police Power, and the Supreme Court*, 40 HARV. L. REV. 943, 944 (1927) ("[I]n the six years since 1920 the Supreme Court has declared social and economic legislation unconstitutional under the due process clauses of either the Fifth or the Fourteenth Amendment in more cases than in the entire fifty-two previous years. . . .").

[2] JUSTICES OF THE SUPREME COURT DURING THE TIME OF CHIEF JUSTICE TAFT

| | | 1920 | 22 | 24 | 26 | 28 | 30 |
|---|---|---|---|---|---|---|---|
| Joseph R. McKenna | (1898-1925) | | | | | | |
| Oliver Wendell Holmes | (1903-1932) | | | | | | |
| William R. Day | (1903-1922) | | | | | | |
| Willis Van Devanter | (1910-1937) | | | | | | |
| Mahlon Pitney | (1912-1922) | | | | | | |
| James C. McReynolds | (1914-1941) | | | | | | |
| Louis D. Brandeis | (1916-1939) | | | | | | |
| John H. Clarke | (1916-1922) | | | | | | |
| William H. Taft | (1921-1930) | | | | | | |

During the Taft years the Court not only wielded due process with unprecedented fe-
rocity to annihilate social measures but extended it to new fields as well, forbidding the
outlawing of foreign languages and of private schools in *Meyer v. Nebraska*[3] and *Pierce
v. Society of Sisters.*[4] The Court assumed in *Gitlow v. New York*[5] and in *Whitney v. California,*[6] and may have held in *Fiske v. Kansas,*[7] that due process protected freedom of
expression or assembly as well, but continued to construe those freedoms narrowly over
famous objections by Holmes and Brandeis. The taking clause of the fifth amendment—
which the Court had long held applicable to the states by virtue of the fourteenth amendment—was given new content by none other than the normally restrained Holmes in
*Pennsylvania Coal Co. v. Mahon.*[8] And federal cases arising largely out of Prohibition
began to develop the contours of fourth amendment search and seizure law.

In matters of federalism the record of the Taft period is mixed. One of the Chief Justice's first opinions departed strikingly from the direction of earlier tax cases by invalidating a federal tax on goods made by child labor, and in another decision the Court held that
baseball was not interstate commerce under the Sherman Act. At the same time, however,
the Court not only gave a broad reading to congressional authority to enforce the prohibition amendment but reaffirmed Holmes's conclusion that stockyards were part of the current of commerce, and seemed to recede from *Hammer v. Dagenhart*[9] by permitting Congress to forbid interstate transportation of stolen cars. Justice McReynolds's pet doctrine
limiting the maritime application of state laws underwent an interesting modification,
while Justice Stone contributed new insights into the recurring problems of commercial
and governmental immunities.

With the possible exception of the due process revolution, the most interesting product
of the Taft years was a series of major decisions respecting the separation of federal powers. The case-or-controversy limitation that had been applied in *Muskrat v. United States*[10]

---

[2]    JUSTICES OF THE SUPREME COURT DURING THE TIME OF CHIEF JUSTICE TAFT (*continued*)

|                      |               | 1920 | 22 | 24 | 26 | 28 | 30 |
|----------------------|---------------|------|----|----|----|----|----|
| George Sutherland    | (1922-1938)   |      | ⊢———————————————— |||||
| Pierce Butler        | (1922-1939)   |      | ⊢———————————————— |||||
| Edward T. Sanford    | (1923-1930)   |      |    | ⊢——————————————⊣ ||||
| Harlan F. Stone      | (1925-1941)   |      |    |    | ⊢—————————— |||

SOURCE: G. GUNTHER, CASES AND MATERIALS ON CONSTITUTIONAL LAW app. B (11th ed. 1985).

Biographies of Justices of this period include M. HOWE, JUSTICE OLIVER WENDELL HOLMES: THE SHAPING
YEARS, 1841-1870 (1957); M. HOWE, JUSTICE OLIVER WENDELL HOLMES: THE PROVING YEARS, 1870-1882
(1963); A. MASON, BRANDEIS: A FREE MAN'S LIFE (1946); A. MASON, HARLAN FISKE STONE: PILLAR OF THE
LAW (1956); A. MASON, WILLIAM HOWARD TAFT: CHIEF JUSTICE (1964); M. MCDEVITT, JOSEPH MCKENNA,
ASSOCIATE JUSTICE OF THE UNITED STATES (1946); J. MCLEAN, WILLIAM RUFUS DAY (1946); J. PASCHAL, MR.
JUSTICE SUTHERLAND: A MAN AGAINST THE STATE (1951); H. PRINGLE, THE LIFE AND TIMES OF WILLIAM
HOWARD TAFT (1939); H. WARNER, THE LIFE OF MR. JUSTICE CLARKE (1959).

[3] 262 U.S. 390 (1923).
[4] 268 U.S. 510 (1925).
[5] 268 U.S. 652 (1925).
[6] 274 U.S. 357 (1927).
[7] 274 U.S. 380 (1927).
[8] 260 U.S. 393 (1922).
[9] 247 U.S. 251 (1918).
[10] 219 U.S. 346 (1911).

was elaborated in *Tutun v. United States*,[11] *Massachusetts v. Mellon*,[12] *Keller v. Potomac Electric Co.*,[13] and a variety of decisions respecting ripeness and declaratory judgments. Judicial independence received a setback when *Ex parte Bakelite Corp.*[14] concluded that the Court of Customs Appeals had been established without regard to article III. The great case of *Myers v. United States*[15] resolved an ancient controversy in upholding the President's authority to fire a subordinate despite a statutory requirement of Senate consent. *Springer v. Philippine Islands*,[16] construing the act setting up a local government, implied important constitutional limitations on legislative powers of appointment. *J. W. Hampton Co. v. United States*[17] upheld yet another broad delegation of discretion to the President. The *Pocket Veto Case*[18] gave a liberal interpretation to the President's power to avoid the overriding of a veto, and *McGrain v. Daugherty*[19] legitimatized the legislative investigation.

It was an exciting time. Let us get directly to the particulars.

[11] 270 U.S. 568 (1926).
[12] 262 U.S. 447 (1923).
[13] 261 U.S. 428 (1923).
[14] 279 U.S. 438 (1929).
[15] 272 U.S. 52 (1926).
[16] 277 U.S. 189 (1928).
[17] 276 U.S. 394 (1928).
[18] 279 U.S. 655 (1929).
[19] 273 U.S. 135 (1927).

# 5

# Liberty, Property, and Equality

## I. Constricting the Social State

### A. Equal Protection

The equal protection clause had played little part in controlling state action before 1921. Not only had the separate-but-equal doctrine—which the Taft Court unanimously reaffirmed—limited the reach of the clause even in the racial field,[1] but in other areas the Court had made clear that equality required only that persons similarly situated be treated alike. Reasonable classifications were permissible; only when the Court could find no justification beyond what one commentator has called a "naked preference"[2] would the clause be invoked.[3] The test, moreover, was a deferential one. An ordinance excluding locomotives from a single street, for example, was upheld on the ground that other streets might have lesser problems, without any proof that they had.[4] Given such an attitude, it was not surprising that the Court had found very few unreasonable classifications.

---

[1] See Gong Lum v. Rice, 275 U.S. 78 (1927) (Taft, C. J.) (upholding state authority to exclude child of Chinese extraction from "white" school because "equal" facilities were provided for nonwhites); cf. THE FIRST HUNDRED YEARS at 387-90 (discussing Pace v. Alabama, 106 U.S. 583 (1883)), and supra p. 40 (discussing Plessy v. Ferguson, 163 U.S. 537 (1896)).

[2] Sunstein, Naked Preferences and the Constitution, 84 COLUM. L. REV. 1689 (1984).

[3] See, e.g., Missouri Pac. Ry. v. Mackey, 127 U.S. 205, 210 (1888) ("[T]he hazardous character of the business of operating a railway would seem to call for special legislation. . . ."); Barbier v. Connolly, 113 U.S. 27, 32 (1885) (equality means equal treatment of those "similarly situated"); and Truax v. Raich, 239 U.S. 33, 41 (1915) ("The discrimination against aliens in the wide range of employments to which the act relates is made an end in itself. . . ."). See generally THE FIRST HUNDRED YEARS at 383-92; supra p. 50, note 154, p. 104, note 56, p. 109, note 123.

[4] Railroad Co. v. Richmond, 96 U.S. 521, 529 (1878) (adding that it was "the special duty of the city authorities to make the necessary discriminations in this particular"); see also Fifth Ave. Coach Co. v. City of New York, 221 U.S. 467, 484 (1911) (allowing city to prohibit advertising on bus exteriors while permitting ads on stairs and structures of elevated railways, saying only "[t]his difference, too, is within the power of classification

Before he had been in office three months, however, Chief Justice Taft, in *Truax v. Corrigan*,[5] found another. Arizona had forbidden injunctions against picketing by striking workers. Similar conduct by a competitor, the Court observed, could have been enjoined, and there was no reasonable basis for the distinction.[6]

Pitney, Holmes, Clarke, and Brandeis vainly protested that the employment relationship had often been singled out for special treatment.[7] Those cases had concerned work-related injuries, Taft retorted, without saying why that was significant.[8] No matter; the question was whether the injunction law was reasonable. The dissenters argued that in the labor field special problems had been encountered with the use of the injunction;[9] the majority ridiculed the suggestion by asking whether the frequency of labor violence would justify exempting strikers from the law of criminal assault.[10]

That the Court was not looking very hard for a justification seems evident. The same critical attitude was reflected a few years later in *Quaker City Cab Co. v. Pennsylvania*,[11] where after decades of indifference to special corporate taxes the Court held, over the usual dissents, that a state could not limit a tax on taxicab receipts to cabs operated by corporations.[12]

---

which the city possesses"); Beers v. Glynn, 211 U.S. 477, 484-85 (1909) (upholding state inheritance tax on nonresident's local personalty only when decedent also owned realty within the state); Florida Cent. & Peninsular R.R. v. Reynolds, 183 U.S. 471 (1902) (allowing state to collect delinquent taxes from railroads while failing to collect from other taxpayers); *see* A. BICKEL & B. SCHMIDT, 9 HISTORY OF THE SUPREME COURT OF THE UNITED STATES 294-300 (1984) (concluding that during the early White years the equal protection clause had been almost explicitly abandoned).

[5]257 U.S. 312 (1921) (Taft, C. J.).

[6]*Id.* at 331-39.

[7]*Id.* at 343 (Holmes, J., dissenting); *id.* at 352-53 (Pitney and Clarke, JJ., dissenting); *id.* at 355-56 (Brandeis, J., dissenting).

[8]*Id.* at 338-39.

[9]*Id.* at 342-43 (Holmes, J., dissenting); *id.* at 352-53 (Pitney, J., dissenting); *cf.* Whitney v. California, 274 U.S. 357, 370 (1927) (Sanford, J.):

> A statute does not violate the equal protection clause merely because it is not all-embracing. . . . A State may properly direct its legislation against what it deems an existing evil without covering the whole field of possible abuses. . . . The statute must be presumed to be aimed at an evil where experience shows it to be most felt, and to be deemed by the legislature coextensive with the practical need; and is not to be overthrown merely because other instances may be suggested to which it also might have been applied; that being a matter for the legislature to determine unless the case is very clear.

[10]*Truax*, 257 U.S. at 339. The majority did not respond to Pitney's powerful argument that the employer had no standing to invoke the constitutional rights of his competitors. *See id.* at 349-50 (Pitney, J., dissenting).

[11]277 U.S. 389 (1928) (Butler, J.).

[12]*Id.* at 400-02. Dissents were entered by Justices Holmes, Brandeis, and Stone. *Id.* at 403-12. *Cf.* Frost v. Corporation Comm'n, 278 U.S. 515 (1929) (Sutherland, J.) (holding over same dissents that cooperatives could not be exempted from public necessity requirement applicable to other cotton gin operators). *But see, e.g.,* Florida C. & P.R.R. v. Reynolds, 183 U.S. 471 (1902) (upholding validity of state law that compelled collection of delinquent taxes from railway companies for certain years, but which contained no similar provision regarding other property owners); *Quaker City Cab*, 277 U.S. at 411-12 (Brandeis, J., dissenting). Even the Taft Court, soon after *Quaker City Cab*, held it permissible to reassess a corporation's taxes without doing the same for individuals. *See* White River Lumber Co. v. Arkansas *ex rel.* Applegate, 279 U.S. 692, 696 (1929) (Sanford, J.), which offered no reason for the discrimination and distinguished *Quaker City Cab* on the insufficient ground that that case had not involved back taxes. Butler, Van Devanter, and Taft dissented. For another example of

Accustomed to a more deferential approach to economic classifications, the late twentieth-century reader may find these decisions quite foreign. Yet there is a very modern ring about the Chief Justice's insistence in *Truax* that a classification affecting "fundamental rights" be subjected to "attentive judgment" and that an earlier decision upholding a classification was distinguishable on the ground that it had dealt only with "economic policy."[13] Later Justices would not agree with his characterization of the employer's business and property interests as fundamental, though it certainly fits the Lockean model.[14] But a later generation would reach a conclusion strikingly similar to that of *Truax* in holding that, in light of the fundamental interest of freedom of speech, discrimination in favor of labor invalidated a ban on residential picketing.[15]

The Taft Court was not consistently vigorous in scrutinizing classifications. Laws forbidding aliens to own land, for example, were emphatically upheld on the basis of the state's concern for security,[16] although the interest in owning property seems at least as "fundamental" as the incident of ownership protected in *Truax*, and although a limitation on alien employment had been struck down during the White years as supported by no legitimate purpose.[17] Indeed, when it came to something less fundamental—the right to operate billiard parlors—the Court upheld a discrimination against aliens with barely a hint of speculation as to why it might be reasonable.[18] At the other extreme, however,

---

exacting equal protection scrutiny by the Taft Court, see Schlesinger v. Wisconsin, 270 U.S. 230 (1926) (McReynolds, J., over the usual dissents by Holmes, Brandeis, and Stone) (state could not tax all gifts made within six years before death to prevent evasion of succession taxes).

[13] *Truax,* 257 U.S. at 335, 338.

[14] *See* J. LOCKE, SECOND TREATISE OF CIVIL GOVERNMENT 56-58 (L. DeKoster ed. 1978): "The great and chief end, therefore, of men's uniting into commonwealths and putting themselves under government is the preservation of their property . . ."—by which Locke meant "their lives, liberties, and estates."

[15] Carey v. Brown, 447 U.S. 455 (1980), *infra* p. 508. The remedial consequences of finding an equal protection violation, however, were quite different in the two cases: while *Truax* held only the labor exception invalid and contemplated that the picketing would be enjoined on remand, *Truax,* 257 U.S. at 341-42, *Carey* held that the entire prohibition on picketing must fall because of the invalid exception, *Carey,* 447 U.S. at 459 n.2.

[16] *E.g.,* Porterfield v. Webb, 263 U.S. 225 (1923) (Butler, J.); Terrace v. Thompson, 263 U.S. 197 (1923) (Butler, J.). In neither case was there dissent on the merits.

[17] *See* Truax v. Raich, 239 U.S. 33, 43 (1915) (striking down ban on alien employment), *supra* p. 109, note 123. In fact, the White Court had drawn much the same distinction, upholding an alien land law with little effort at justification in Toop v. Ulysses Land Co., 237 U.S. 580 (1915). The laws upheld in *Terrace* and in *Porterfield,* however, excluded only those aliens who had not declared their intention to become citizens, or those who were ineligible for citizenship; the Court declined to find in these distinctions a disguised discrimination against Japanese and Chinese, who were not eligible for citizenship. *See Terrace,* 263 U.S. at 220; *see also* Collins, *Will the California Alien Land Law Stand the Test of the Fourteenth Amendment?* 23 YALE L.J. 330 (1914) (arguing that statutory terms were euphemisms for forbidden racial classifications); Powell, *Alien Land Cases in United States Supreme Court,* 12 CALIF. L. REV. 259, 270-74, 273 (1924) (arguing persuasively that justification given to sustain discrimination against those not planning to become citizens showed irrationality of excluding only those who were ineligible: "Mr. Justice Butler's two opinions disclose no satisfactory reasons, since when taken together they destroy the only reason suggested. . . .").

[18] Ohio *ex rel.* Clarke v. Deckebach, 274 U.S. 392, 397 (1927)(Stone, J.) (noting that the ordinance "presupposes that aliens in Cincinnati are not as well qualified as citizens to engage in this business" and adverting to "the view admitted by the pleadings that the associations, experiences and interests of members of the class disqualified the class as a whole from conducting a business of dangerous tendencies"). The contrast between this decision and *Quaker City Cab* suggests in later terms that the Court thought corporations a more suspect classification than aliens.

when Texas excluded blacks from voting in primary elections, the Court seemed unwilling to admit the possibility of any justification:

> [The Fourteenth] Amendment, while it applies to all, was passed, as we know, with a special intent to protect the blacks from discrimination against them. . . . States may do a good deal of classifying that it is difficult to believe rational, but there are limits, and it is too clear for extended argument that color cannot be made the basis of a statutory classification affecting the right set up in this case.[19]

The notion that there might be more than one level of scrutiny in equal protection cases seemed to be well on its way.

### B. The Duty to Protect Property

More interesting still was the distinct and broader rationale that the majority in *Truax v. Corrigan* embraced before it even began to discuss equal protection. Free access to the employer's premises was a part of the employer's property right; picketing interfered with that right, and a "law which operates to make lawful such a wrong . . . deprives the owner of the business and the premises of his property without due process."[20]

There were three difficulties with this cryptic reasoning. First, the Court nowhere referred to Arizona law in determining the extent of the property right in question. Nearly a century before, the Court had established that article 1, § 10 forbade the states to impair only those contractual obligations that were defined by state law.[21] The *Berea College* case seemed to have applied the same principle in defining "property" under the due process clause by holding that a corporation's property rights were limited by its charter.[22] If the law applicable when Truax acquired his property did not give him the right to be free of labor pickets, the denial of a remedy did not deprive him of property.[23]

---

[19]Nixon v. Herndon, 273 U.S. 536, 541 (1927) (Holmes, J., for a unanimous Court). The Court refrained from invoking the facially more obviously applicable fifteenth amendment, which deals explicitly with racial discrimination in voting, presumably because of the narrow construction given similar language respecting congressional authority over federal elections, *see, e.g.,* Newberry v. United States, 256 U.S. 232, 255-58 (1921) (congressional authority under U. S. CONST. art I, § 4 did not reach primary elections), *supra* p. 101, note 71. As an original matter, the applicability of the fourteenth amendment's prohibitions to political matters such as voting had been extremely doubtful not only in light of the alternative remedies for voting discrimination provided elsewhere in the same amendment, but because of the repeated assurances of the sponsors. These arguments had been sidestepped rather than rejected in the jury discrimination cases of the 1880s, which had focused on the defendant's interest in a fair trial. *See* THE FIRST HUNDRED YEARS at 383-85 (discussing Strauder v. West Virginia, 100 U.S. 303 (1880)). Holmes did not address the issue in *Nixon*.

[20]*Truax*, 257 U.S. at 328.

[21]Ogden v. Saunders, 25 U.S. (12 Wheat.) 213 (1827), THE FIRST HUNDRED YEARS at 150-56.

[22]Berea College v. Kentucky, 211 U.S. 45, 56-58 (1908), *supra* p. 108; *see also* Bishop v. Wood, 426 U.S. 341, 344 (1976) ("A property interest in employment can, of course, be created by ordinance, or by an implied contract. In either case, however, the sufficiency of the claim of entitlement must be decided by reference to state law."); Board of Regents v. Roth, 408 U.S. 564, 577-78 (1972), *infra* pp. 540-41; Demorest v. City Bank Co., 321 U.S. 36, 42-43 (1944).

[23]In fact, picketing had been enjoinable in Arizona until passage of the statute at issue in *Truax*, 257 U.S. at 323, but the Court did not rely on that circumstance in explaining that there had been a deprivation of property.

Second, despite frequent statements that the only deprivations of liberty or property compatible with due process of law were those imposed after a criminal trial,[24] a long series of cases had established that both liberty and property were themselves qualified by the police power.[25] In contrast to earlier decisions, the Court made no effort in *Truax* to show why the law immunizing picketing was not a reasonable police-power measure.

Finally, the conclusion that the state had deprived Truax of his property by failing to provide him with judicial protection was of the greatest interest and importance.[26] In the Federal Republic of Germany, the Constitutional Court has held that a constitutional right to life requires that abortion generally be made a crime[27]—although there, as here, the relevant constitutional provisions limit only official and not private action.[28] Yet in the usual abortion case, as in *Truax*, it is not the government but a private individual who has brought about the deprivation. In this country, as Judge Posner wrote in denying that the due process clause required the state to rescue an accident victim, the Constitution is

[24]*See, e.g.,* University of North Carolina v. Foy, 5 N.C. (1 Mur.) 57, 63 (1804) (construing law-of-the-land provision): "The property vested in the trustees must remain for the uses intended for the university, until the judiciary of the country in the usual and common form pronounce them guilty of such acts as will, in law, amount to a forfeiture of their rights or a dissolution of their body." *See also* Powell v. Pennsylvania, 127 U.S. 678, 692 (1888) (Field, J., dissenting) (liberty inviolable "except in punishment for crime"); Corwin, *The Doctrine of Due Process of Law before the Civil War,* 24 HARV. L. REV. 366, 381-84 (1911). The alternative argument that reasonable legislation constituted the due process necessary to justify a deprivation would have explained, as the argument under discussion did not, why taxation was sometimes permitted.

[25]*See, e.g.,* Lochner v. New York, 198 U.S. 45, 53 (1905) ("Both property and liberty are held on such reasonable conditions as may be imposed by the governing power of the State in the exercise of . . . [police] powers."); Holden v. Hardy, 169 U.S. 366, 391 (1898) (upholding maximum hour legislation for miners because the "right of contract . . . is itself subject to certain limitations which the State may lawfully impose in the exercise of its police powers"); Munn v. Illinois, 94 U.S. 113, 145 (1877) (Field, J., dissenting) ("The doctrine that each one must so use his own as not to injure his neighbor . . . is the rule by which every member of society must possess and enjoy his property."); T. COOLEY, CONSTITUTIONAL LIMITATIONS 573 (1868) (quoting Chief Justice Shaw in Commonwealth v. Alger, 7 Cush. 53 (Mass. 1851): "[E]very holder of property . . . holds it under the implied liability that his use of it shall not be . . . injurious to the rights of the community. All property in this Commonwealth is . . . held subject to those general regulations which are necessary to the common good and general welfare.").

[26]As the dissenters argued in *Truax,* 257 U.S. at 349, it was not even clear that the statute forbade all remedies for labor picketing. In terms it forbade only an injunction, leaving open the possibility of both damages and criminal prosecution. Taft grasped at the state court's probably loose statement that the statute made picketing "lawful" and went on to question the adequacy of the criminal law that was arguably applicable. *Truax,* 257 U.S. at 328-29. *See* Frankfurter & Greene, *Congressional Power over the Labor Injunction,* 31 COLUM. L. REV. 385, 408 (1931) (arguing for the constitutionality of a law denying federal jurisdiction to enjoin labor activity, and distinguishing *Truax* on the ground that the Court had viewed the Arizona law as legalizing the conduct itself by removing *all* sanctions).

[27]39 BVerfG 1, 65 (1975).

[28]*Id.* at 42 (concluding that the Basic Law [Grundgesetz] not only "prohibits . . . direct governmental encroachments upon the developing life, but also commands the State . . . to safeguard it from illegal encroachments by others"). *See* GRUNDGESETZ [GG] arts. 1(3), 2(2) (W. Ger. 1949, amended 1956): "The following basic rights shall bind the legislature, the executive and the judiciary. . . . Everyone shall have the right to life and to inviolability of his person." The German court's conclusion was facilitated by article 1's explicit provision that the government shall not only "respect," but also "protect," the "dignity of man." While the court relied in part upon this provision, its primary emphasis was on the right to life provision, which does not include the "protect" language.

generally understood to be "a charter of negative rather than positive liberties"—a guarantee of protection from rather than by the government.[29]

The possible ramifications of Taft's contrary conclusion are considerable: The state deprives an individual of life, liberty, or property whenever it fails to protect those interests from invasion by private parties.[30] The Constitution requires that murder and theft be prohibited. Common law tort remedies may be abolished only if adequate substitutes are provided. Governments must prevent private interference with freedom of expression or religion.

Indeed the German cases have carried this principle further: freedom of telecommunications requires the government to assure public access to broadcasting facilities; freedom of education may require the state to provide schooling.[31] Though Taft would no doubt have been horrified, the logic is forceful: if the state infringes liberty by failing to protect it against third parties, it also does so by failing to remedy a deficiency of funds. The state deprives a woman of freedom to have an abortion if it does not assure that she can afford one and of life if it allows her to starve.[32]

In a series of decisions culminating in the *Civil Rights Cases* in 1883, the Supreme Court had made clear that the fourteenth amendment and various other constitutional limitations applied only to official action.[33] The Taft Court reaffirmed this conclusion in *Corrigan v. Buckley*,[34] unanimously holding that judicial enforcement did not make the gov-

---

[29] Jackson v. City of Joliet, 715 F.2d 1200, 1203 (7th Cir. 1983). *Accord* DeShaney v. Department of Social Services, 109 S. Ct. 998 (1989).

[30] Compare the language of the German court quoted *supra* note 28.

[31] *See* 12 BVerfG 205 (1961) (interpreting the provision of GRUNDGESETZ [GG] art. 5(1) (W. Ger.) that "[f]reedom of the press and freedom of reporting by means of broadcasts and films are guaranteed"):

> Article 5 GG demands . . . that this modern instrument of opinion formation not be handed over either to the state or to any one social group. Broadcast stations must therefore be so organized that all interests worthy of consideration have an influence in their governing council and can express themselves in the overall program. . . .

12 BVerfG at 262-63. *See also* 33 BVerfG 303 (1972) (interpreting the provision of GRUNDGESETZ [GG] art. 12(1) (W. Ger.) that "[a]ll Germans shall have the right freely to choose their . . . place of training"):

> The constitutional protection of basic rights in the field of education is not limited to the protective function against governmental intervention traditionally ascribed to the basic rights. . . . [T]he free choice of the place of education aims, by its nature, at free access to institutions; the right would be worthless without the actual ability to make use of it. Accordingly, the draft of a framework law respecting higher education proceeds from the assumption that every German is entitled to carry out his chosen post-secondary study program if he demonstrates the requisite qualifications. Recognition of this entitlement is not at the discretion of the lawmakers.

33 BVerfG at 330-31 (emphasis omitted).

[32] For rejection of this argument in the abortion context, see *infra* pp. 471-75, *discussing* Maher v. Roe, 432 U.S. 464, 474-75 (1977) (state may favor childbirth over abortion and may implement that decision through its allocation of public funds), and Harris v. McRae, 448 U.S. 297, 316 (1980) ("[A]lthough government may not place obstacles in the path of a woman's exercise of her freedom of choice, it need not remove those not of its own creation."). A distinction might be based on the traditional conception of government duty as one of protection against third parties, *see* J. LOCKE, *supra* note 14, at 56-58, but hardly on the text of the Constitution.

[33] *E.g.*, The Civil Rights Cases, 109 U.S. 3, 11 (1883) (Congress may not forbid private discrimination under fourteenth amendment). *See generally* THE FIRST HUNDRED YEARS at 393-402.

[34] 271 U.S. 323 (1926) (Sanford, J.).

ernment responsible for a privately imposed racial covenant.[35] *Truax* suggests that the state could have been held responsible for the private acts in all these cases simply by pointing out its failure to prevent them. This interpretation would reduce long-standing precedents thought to have established landmark limitations on constitutional rights to technical barriers avoidable by clever pleading.

None of this seems to have occurred to Chief Justice Taft, who cited nothing in support of his crucial conclusion that to deny a remedy for picketing would deprive the owner of his property. The sweeping implications of his position indicate the importance of inquiring into possible analogies to support him.

The question had arisen twenty years before in an obscure case in which it had been argued that a law eliminating liability for harm done to unlicensed dogs deprived the dog owner of his property without due process. In resting its rejection of this argument on the imaginative conclusion that there was no true property right in dogs,[36] the Court seemed to assume a duty to protect other property from private harm.[37] More important than this unstated implication was a long succession of contract clause cases holding that a state impaired the obligation of private contracts if it placed excessive limitations on judicial remedies for breach.[38] The same reasoning supports a similar reading of the taking clause: to deny all remedies for trespass would effectively transfer private property to public use, for the essence of private property is the right to exclude others.[39]

Herein may lie a limiting principle to reconcile *Truax* with the general notion that the Constitution does not require government to take affirmative action. Property and contract are legal constructs that almost by definition entail governmental protection from third parties. Life and liberty are not. A ban on state deprivation of life makes sense if it means only that the government itself shall not kill; a similar statement with regard to contract or property is less convincing. Perhaps theft, but not murder, must be made a crime.

---

[35] The Court later changed its mind on this specific issue, without questioning the requirement of state action. *See* Shelley v. Kraemer, 334 U.S. 1 (1948), *infra* pp. 58-60.

[36] Sentell v. New Orleans & C.R.R., 166 U.S. 698, 701 (1897) ("[P]roperty in dogs is of an imperfect or qualified nature. . . ."), *supra* p. 50, note 155. The Court based its conclusion largely on Louisiana law, *Sentell*, 166 U.S. at 706, and derived this result largely from the argument that dogs, unlike farm animals, generally served only ornamental purposes, *id.* at 701. This hardly seems to distinguish them from jewelry, which one supposes qualifies as "property" under the amendment. *Cf.* Currie, *The Most Insignificant Justice: A Preliminary Inquiry*, 50 U. CHI. L. REV. 466, 475, 478 n.70 (1983) (also disparaging dogs).

[37] Some years later, when a related argument about the sanctity of common law rules was made against workers' compensation, the standard defense was not to deny the premise, but to argue there had been a quid pro quo: what the employer gave up in freedom from strict liability he gained by a limitation of damages. *See, e.g.,* New York Cent. R.R. v. White, 243 U.S. 188, 205 (1917). However, the Supreme Court did not rest entirely with this narrow defense, as emphasized by dissents complaining of the absence of a quid pro quo when the Court later upheld a law imposing unlimited strict liability on the basis of the police power. Arizona Employers' Liability Cases, 250 U.S. 400, 450 (1919) (McReynolds, J., dissenting). Moreover, from the employer's point of view, the problem of state inaction was not in issue in the compensation cases. There was no doubt that the state was responsible for any deprivation that took place, for instead of merely refusing the employer a remedy, the state had imposed on him a duty to pay.

[38] *E.g.,* Bronson v. Kinzie, 42 U.S. (1 How.) 311, 317, 318 (1843), THE FIRST HUNDRED YEARS at 211-13.

[39] That this right might be preserved by allowing the owner to use force to protect his own property suggests only, as the workers' compensation cases illustrated, that the state may have a broad range of choice among means to meet its protection obligation. For the right of self-help would be no better than no property right at all unless the state continued to forbid the use of countervailing force by trespassers.

To state the matter this way makes it look suspect. Moreover, there are substantial arguments for a broader version of the *Truax* principle. The theory of the social contract that underlies our Constitution entails a surrender of the right of self-help in exchange for government protection.[40] This understanding is made explicit by the original meaning of the equal protection clause: if the state protects whites against private violence, it must protect blacks as well.[41] Chief Justice Marshall put the point more broadly: "The very essence of civil liberty certainly consists in the right of every individual to claim the protection of the laws, whenever he receives an injury. One of the first duties of government is to afford that protection."[42] Though Marshall did not invoke the Constitution in this passage, it would not be a huge step beyond his position to argue that because of this understanding the life, liberty, and property guarantees of the due process clauses imply a right to governmental protection.[43]

The problem of government inaction raised by *Truax v. Corrigan* is profoundly troubling. We shall not get to the bottom of it here.[44] But the Court seemed unaware that the problem existed.

## C. Later Due Process Cases

When maximum-hour legislation for factory workers was approved in 1917 without so much as a citation to *Lochner v. New York*,[45] the earlier decision seemed thoroughly dis-

---

[40] *See, e.g.,* J. Locke, *supra* note 14, at 58:

> But though men when they enter into society give up the equality, liberty, and executive power they had in the state of nature, into the hands of the society, . . . yet it remains the intention of everyone the better to preserve himself, his liberty, and his property[;] . . . the power of that society . . . is obliged to secure every one's property. . . .

This passage seems to suggest that government has assumed the obligation of giving more protection than the individual had in a state of nature, not that it can absolve itself of responsibility by restoring the law of the jungle.

[41] *See generally* The First Hundred Years at 342-51, 369-86.

[42] Marbury v. Madison, 5 U.S. (1 Cranch) 137, 163 (1803) ("[I]t is a settled and invariable principle in the laws of England, that every right, when withheld, must have a remedy, and every injury its proper redress.") (quoting 3 W. Blackstone, Commentaries on the Laws of England *109).

[43] Given such a reading, the equal protection clause as originally understood is redundant; but, as Marshall demonstrated, so are the necessary-and-proper clause and the tenth amendment. *See* McCulloch v. Maryland, 17 U.S. (4 Wheat.) 316, 405-09, 419-21 (1819), The First Hundred Years at 160-68. For suggestions of affirmative government duties in other interesting contexts, see Gideon v. Wainwright, 372 U.S. 335, 345 (1963) (holding that fourteenth amendment requires state to provide counsel for indigent criminal defendant), *infra* pp. 446-47; *Ex parte* Young, 209 U.S. 123 (1908) (provision setting fines so high as to discourage violating the law in order to obtain a judicial test of its validity worked a deprivation of property—presumably of the underlying right to charge remunerative rates—without due process), *supra* p. 44, note 112; and the series of public forum cases holding that the first and fourteenth amendments required governments to permit use of certain public properties for speech purposes, *e.g.,* Schneider v. State, 308 U.S. 147 (1939) (invalidating bans on distribution of handbills on streets and sidewalks), *infra* pp. 263-66. The first two examples seem readily distinguishable: in both, the government had taken affirmative action against the individual, either by prosecution or by regulation of rates. Some of the public forum cases also involve prosecution after the fact, but only to enforce the government's asserted right not to contribute its property for the promotion of individual speech.

[44] This problem is further explored in Currie, *Positive and Negative Constitutional Rights*, 53 U. Chi. L. Rev. 864 (1986).

[45] 198 U.S. 45 (1905).

credited.[46] When a minimum wage law for District of Columbia women succumbed to a due process assault in *Adkins v. Children's Hospital*[47] in 1923, however, *Lochner* formed the cornerstone of Justice Sutherland's opinion.[48] Maximum-hour legislation, the Court said, had been upheld only when necessary to preserve health. To the dissenting arguments of Taft, Sanford, and Holmes that minimum wages likewise served to keep women healthy and chaste,[49] Sutherland responded with the improbable observation that "[i]t cannot be shown that well paid women safeguard their morals more carefully than those who are poorly paid,"[50] adding that "the inquiry in respect . . . of the income necessary to preserve health and morals . . . must be answered for each individual considered by herself and not by a general formula prescribed by a statutory bureau."[51] In any event, Sutherland concluded, it was unfair to place the burden of ameliorating the worker's poverty on her employer.[52] The ritually invoked presumption of constitutionality had become a hollow shell.[53]

---

[46] Bunting v. Oregon, 243 U.S. 426 (1917), pp. 103-04 *supra*.

[47] 261 U.S. 525 (1923).

[48] *Id.* at 548-50 (quoting at length from Lochner v. New York, 198 U.S. 45 (1905)); *cf. id.* at 564 (Taft, C. J., dissenting) ("It is impossible for me to reconcile the *Bunting Case* and the *Lochner Case* and I have always supposed that the *Lochner Case* was thus overruled *sub silentio*."). When the minimum wage issue had come up during the White years, the Court had divided four to four after the death of Justice Lamar, who apparently had cast the fifth vote for invalidity in conference. *See* Stettler v. O'Hara, 243 U.S. 629 (1917), *supra* p. 104, note 85; A. BICKEL & B. SCHMIDT, *supra* note 4, at 592-603.

[49] *See Adkins*, 261 U.S. at 566-67. Brandeis did not participate. McKenna, who had written *Bunting*, voted silently with the majority. *See* A. MASON, WILLIAM HOWARD TAFT: CHIEF JUSTICE 264 (1964), which describes Taft's dissenting vote in *Adkins* as an aberration from his conservative values, but attributable to his respect for precedent. Precedent was applicable only for those who believed minimum wage laws to be plausible health measures.

[50] *Adkins*, 261 U.S. at 556.

[51] *Id.*

[52] *Id.* at 557-59. The economically apparent connection between poverty and prostitution was a frequent theme in nineteenth-century literature. *See, e.g.,* T. FONTANE, IRRUNGEN, WIRRUNGEN (H. Fikentscher rev. ed. 1929); V. HUGO, LES MISERABLES (L. Wraxall trans. 1887). The Chief Justice invoked more scientific studies, disclosed in the briefs and records, that found a direct relation between low wages and poor health. *Adkins*, 261 U.S. at 564 (Taft, C. J., dissenting). *See* Brown, *Police Power—Legislation for Health and Personal Safety,* 42 HARV. L. REV. 866, 887, 898 (1929) ("it cannot be denied that starvation wages contribute to sickness and immorality"; *Adkins* stands alone in rejecting a law supported by substantial health or safety considerations). For contrasting academic views at the time the issue first reached the Court, compare Brown, *Oregon Minimum Wage Cases,* 1 MINN. L. REV. 471, 484 (1917) (invoking, among other things, the familiar economic argument that minimum wage laws were bad for workers because they led to curtailment of jobs), with Powell, *The Constitutional Issue in Minimum Wage Legislation,* 2 MINN. L. REV. 1, 16-17 (1917) (defending such laws on ground that, though some workers would lose their jobs, greater number would gain financial security). For the barely civil comments of Powell after *Adkins* was decided, see Powell, *The Judiciality of Minimum-Wage Legislation,* 37 HARV. L. REV. 545, 569, 571 (1924) (arguing that employers should provide a "living wage" because employees must be fed in order to work, and finding *Adkins* opinion "ignorant" or "emotionally obtuse" in overlooking analogous precedents).

[53] *See Adkins*, 261 U.S. at 544; *see also* J. PASCHAL, MR. JUSTICE SUTHERLAND: A MAN AGAINST THE STATE 124 (1951) ("Basically, the decision in the *Adkins* case was an attack on the very idea of government."); Biklé, *Judicial Determination of Questions of Fact affecting the Constitutionality of Legislative Action,* 38 HARV. L. REV. 6, 12-13, 27 (1924) (noting inconsistencies in methods by which the Court ascertained factual premises on which it based its determinations of reasonableness of laws, and urging that, as in *Bunting*, the Court decline to set aside law without record proof that it was unreasonable); Finkelstein, *From Munn v. Illinois to Tyson v. Banton: A Study in the Judicial Process,* 27 COLUM. L. REV. 769, 783 (1927) (concluding, in light of *Truax,*

A law forbidding nighttime employment of women in restaurants passed muster the following Term as a health measure.[54] In its next breath, however, with only Brandeis and Holmes dissenting, the Court extinguished a statute regulating the size of bread loaves in order to combat consumer fraud.[55] A year later six Justices joined in nullifying a law forbidding the use of shoddy in quilt manufacturing.[56] In three successive split decisions Justice Sutherland, writing for the Court, held that neither the resale price of theater tickets, the rates charged by employment agencies, nor the price of gasoline could be regulated, because none of the businesses was "affected with a public interest."[57] Finally, in 1928, over two dissents, the Court struck down a requirement that drugstores be owned by licensed pharmacists: "[M]ere stock ownership in a corporation, owning and operating

---

*Adkins,* and other decisions, that the Court was exercising a "judicial veto" whenever "the court does not think that the legislation ought to have been adopted").

[54] Radice v. New York, 264 U.S. 292 (1924) (Sutherland, J.) (without dissent).

[55] Jay Burns Baking Co. v. Bryan, 264 U.S. 504 (1924) (Butler, J.). *See also id.* at 517 (Brandeis and Holmes, JJ., dissenting). The majority objected particularly to the fixing of a *maximum* loaf size, conceding that a *minimum* might be permissible. Brandeis sensibly responded that the "prohibition of excess weight is imposed in order to prevent a loaf of one standard size from being increased so much that it can readily be sold for a loaf of a larger standard size." *See id.* at 513-17, 519.

[56] Weaver v. Palmer Bros., 270 U.S. 402 (1926) (Butler, J.). The Court distinguished the sharply contrasting decision in Powell v. Pennsylvania, 127 U.S. 678 (1888), THE FIRST HUNDRED YEARS at 377-78, which had upheld the prohibition of oleomargarine despite evidence that the product produced by the litigant was healthful, by noting that the *Powell* Court had assumed that other oleo was dangerous; in contrast, the *Weaver* Court assumed that sterilization would remove the dangers of shoddy. *Weaver,* 270 U.S. at 414; *see also id.* at 415 (Holmes, Brandeis, and Stone, JJ., dissenting) (finding it reasonable for the legislature to conclude that inspection and tagging were inadequate means of protecting the public against unsterilized materials).

[57] Williams v. Standard Oil Co., 278 U.S. 235, 239 (1929); Ribnik v. McBride, 277 U.S. 350, 355 (1928); Tyson & Brother v. Banton, 273 U.S. 418, 430 (1927). Of the four dissenters in the earliest case, Sanford bowed to precedent in the next, and Brandeis and Stone apparently in the last, leaving only the obdurate Holmes. *See Williams,* 278 U.S. at 245; *Ribnik,* 277 U.S. at 359-75; *Tyson,* 273 U.S. at 445-56. According to the majority in these cases, German Alliance Ins. Co. v. Kansas, 233 U.S. 389 (1914), which had upheld regulation of insurance rates, had gone to the verge of constitutionality; the Court explained Block v. Hirsch, 256 U.S. 135 (1921), which had upheld rent control, on the basis of an emergency. *See Tyson,* 273 U.S. at 434-37; p. 103 *supra.* It was not enough, the Court concluded, that a business was large or the public legitimately concerned; the business "must be such . . . as to justify the conclusion that it has been *devoted* to a public use and its use thereby in effect *granted* to the public." *Williams,* 278 U.S. at 240. Protested Stone:

> As I read th[e] decisions, such regulation is within a state's power whenever any combination of circumstances seriously curtails the regulative force of competition, so that buyers or sellers are placed at such a disadvantage in the bargaining struggle that a legislature might reasonably anticipate serious consequences to the community as a whole.

*Ribnik,* 277 U.S. at 360 (Stone, J., dissenting). It may be that this criterion was not met in the gasoline case, *see Williams,* 278 U.S. at 240 (Sutherland, J., denying the existence of a monopoly), but Justice Stone did not explain his concurrence in the result. *See also* J. PASCHAL, *supra* note 53, at 127-30 (noting that original formulation of public interest test had been ambiguous); Rottschaefer, *The Field of Governmental Price Control,* 35 YALE L.J. 438, 451-60 (1926) (arguing that price control of necessaries was reasonable regardless of competition); Hamilton, *Affectation with Public Interest,* 39 YALE L.J. 1089, 1103 (1930) (criticizing reliance on Lord Hale's "affected with a public interest" test to determine the validity of price control, and concluding that decisions of 1920s were "a far cry from the time of Lord Hale, when all trafficking in wares was public"); McAllister, *Lord Hale and Business Affected with a Public Interest,* 43 HARV. L. REV. 759, 786 (1930) (largely agreeing with Hamilton but suggesting that Brandeis and Stone had concurred in *Williams* because "Tennessee had not shown that the business [of selling gasoline] was particularly subject to abuse in the matter of price").

a drug store, can have no real or substantial relation to the public health. . . ."[58] In this climate it was perhaps surprising that residential zoning was upheld by analogy to nuisance laws.[59] Substantive due process had grown teeth such as it had never exhibited before.[60]

## D.   Taking and Regulation

The fifth amendment bars taking property for public use without compensation; it says nothing about regulation. The paradigm case in which compensation is required is the appropriation of private land for the construction of government buildings. In light of historical practice it is hardly credible that, by the apparently narrow and specific language of the amendment, the Framers meant to forbid all regulation of the use of property. Invoking the long-standing precedent of nuisance laws, the Court before the Taft period had upheld such limitations as a ban on the manufacture of liquor and on the making of bricks

---

[58] Louis K. Liggett Co. v. Baldridge, 278 U.S. 105, 113 (1928) (Sutherland, J.); *see also id.* at 114 (Holmes and Brandeis, JJ., dissenting) ("Argument has not been supposed to be necessary in order to show that the divorce between the power of control and knowledge is an evil.").

[59] Village of Euclid v. Ambler Realty Co., 272 U.S. 365 (1926) (Sutherland, J.) (over unelaborated dissents by Van Devanter, McReynolds, and Butler, *id.* at 397). *But see* Nectow v. City of Cambridge, 277 U.S. 183 (1928) (Sutherland, J.) (unanimously striking down a particular zoning boundary as unreasonable). For the suggestion that Sutherland had initially planned to vote against the validity of the zoning law in *Euclid,* see A. Mason, Harlan Fiske Stone: Pillar of the Law 252 (1956) (stressing Stone's role in persuading Sutherland to change his mind); J. Paschal, *supra* note 53, at 127 (adding that "[t]he opinion makes clear that Sutherland saw in the zoning act not the deprivation of property, but its enhancement"); *id.* at 9-20 (recounting Sutherland's affinity for the idea of Spencer and Cooley that government's sole function was to prevent people from injuring others). It may also be significant that zoning laws, unlike others considered in this section, dealt with external harms whose private resolution, as in the nuisance case, would often have entailed high transaction costs. *See* Coase, *The Problem of Social Cost,* 3 J. L. & Econ. 1, 15-18 (1960); Brown, *supra* note 52, at 873 (finding nuisance cases easy because of traditional rule of *sic utere tuo*). *Euclid* was previewed in Bettman, *Constitutionality of Zoning,* 37 Harv. L. Rev. 834, 846-51 (1924), and applauded in Ribble, *The Due Process Clause as a Limitation on Municipal Discretion in Zoning Legislation,* 16 Va. L. Rev. 689, 699 (1930) (noting the Court's tendency to be more tolerant of land use regulations, with the striking exception of the racial segregation case of Buchanan v. Warley, 245 U.S. 60 (1917), *supra* pp. 107-09, than of other purported exercises of the police power).

[60] *See also* Fairmont Creamery Co. v. Minnesota, 274 U.S. 1 (1927) (McReynolds, J., over dissents by Holmes, Brandeis, and Stone) (striking down state law forbidding geographical price discrimination); Chas. Wolff Packing Co. v. Court of Indus. Relations, 262 U.S. 522 (1923) (Taft, C. J.) (unanimously invalidating state law requiring arbitration of wage disputes in meat-packing industry); Frost & Frost Trucking Co. v. Railroad Comm'n, 271 U.S. 583, 594 (1926) (Sutherland, J.) (resoundingly reaffirming doctrine of unconstitutional conditions in holding that state could not condition carrier's use of highways on agreement to serve public generally: "If the state may compel the surrender of one constitutional right as a condition of its favor, it may, in like manner, compel a surrender of all. It is inconceivable that guaranties embedded in the Constitution of the United States may thus be manipulated out of existence."); *cf.* Terral v. Burke Constr. Co., 257 U.S. 529 (1922) (Taft, C. J.) (state may not revoke foreign corporation's license to do local business for exercising federal right to remove case to federal court). For an excellent and approving summary of the development of the unconstitutional conditions principle, see G. Henderson, The Position of Foreign Corporations in American Constitutional Law 110-11, 134-47 (1918).

Procedural due process decisions of the Taft era include Ng Fung Ho v. White, 259 U.S. 276 (1922) (Brandeis, J.), which held that a person who had been ordered deported after an administrative hearing was entitled to a judicial redetermination of his claim to citizenship: "To deport one who so claims to be a citizen, obviously

in a populated area.[61] Though substantive due process cases showed that the right to use one's land was part of the bundle of rights that made up a property interest, Justice Harlan had suggested long before that mere regulation was not a "taking . . . for the public benefit" because the government did not appropriate or use the affected property.[62]

A rigid distinction according to the form of governmental intervention, however, would have destroyed the protective power of the clause. To forbid an owner to exclude the public from his property, for example, would effectively transfer the property to public use.[63] Some more functional test had to be devised to accomplish the purposes of the compensation clause without outlawing regulation altogether.

This was what Justice Holmes sought to do in his opinion for the Court in *Pennsylvania Coal Co. v. Mahon.*[64] Having granted the plaintiffs the right to the surface of its land, the company prepared to exercise its reserved right to remove all the underlying coal. Relying on a later statute forbidding mining that would cause subsidence of other people's houses, the plaintiffs sought an injunction. By an eight-to-one vote the Court held that, as applied to these facts, the statute took the company's property without compensation.

Alert to the danger of the formal distinction suggested by Brandeis's dissenting observation that the state had not "appropriate[d]" or "use[d]" the coal company's property,[65]

---

deprives him of liberty. . . . The difference in security of judicial over administrative action has been adverted to by this court." This was a significant step beyond Ohio Valley Water Co. v. Ben Avon Borough, 253 U.S. 287 (1920), *supra* p. 110, note 123, which had found a right to a de novo judicial determination of the question whether a quasi-legislative utility rate was confiscatory. Deportation of those not claiming to be citizens, which would seem to involve a similar loss of liberty, was distinguished on the nonobvious ground that citizenship was a "jurisdictional fact"; cases holding that a claim of citizenship did not give a person excluded at the border a right to judicial hearing were distinguished without reasons. *See Ng Fung Ho,* 259 U.S. at 282, 284. *See also* Hess v. Pawloski, 274 U.S. 352, 356-57 (1927) (Butler, J.) (indulging the fiction that by using the highways a nonresident motorist appointed a local agent to receive process in auto accident suits, but adding in more modern terms that "[i]n the public interest the State may make and enforce regulations reasonably calculated to promote care on the part of all . . . who use its highways"); Tumey v. Ohio, 273 U.S. 510, 523 (1927) (Taft, C. J.) (holding that judge may not be compensated according to fines imposed); A. B. Small Co. v. American Sugar Ref. Co., 267 U.S. 233, 239-40 (1925) (Van Devanter, J.) (extending void-for-vagueness doctrine to case involving civil sanctions); Moore v. Dempsey, 261 U.S. 86, 90-91 (1923) (Holmes, J.) (expanding the availability of habeas corpus in reaching the unsurprising conclusion that a criminal trial dominated by a mob did not provide due process). *See* Easterbrook, *Substance and Due Process,* 1982 SUP. CT. REV. 85, 105 (describing *Moore* as novel because "reasoned wholly as a matter of natural law" and *Tumey,* while based on history, as "the first case to declare a state law unconstitutional for want of adequate procedures (other than ex parte procedures)").

[61] Hadacheck v. Sebastian, 239 U.S. 394 (1915) (city ordinance banning brickyards in certain areas held valid exercise of police power); Mugler v. Kansas, 123 U.S. 623 (1887) (state legislation banning manufacture of alcoholic beverages valid exercise of police power); *see* THE FIRST HUNDRED YEARS at 375-77; p. 105, note 86 *supra.*

[62] Mugler v. Kansas, 123 U.S. 623, 668-69 (1887). *Mugler* properly distinguished Pumpelly v. Green Bay Co., 80 U.S. (13 Wall.) 166 (1872), which had held the flooding of property by a government dam to be a taking under the Wisconsin constitution, as a case in which the "property was, in effect, required to be devoted to the use of the public" for the storage of surplus water. *Mugler,* 123 U.S. at 668. For examples of the position that the right of use was a property right, see Truax v. Corrigan, 257 U.S. 312, 327 (1921), *supra* pp. 139-43; Munn v. Illinois, 94 U.S. 113, 140 (1877) (Field, J., dissenting).

[63] *See* Sax, *Takings and the Police Power,* 74 YALE L.J. 36, 46-48, 71-73 (1964) (giving inventive examples of actual "regulations" designed to circumvent technical requirement of a "taking").

[64] 260 U.S. 393 (1922).

[65] *Id.* at 417 (Brandeis, J., dissenting).

Holmes protested that the effect was the same as if it had: the regulation practically transferred to the surface owner an easement of support.[66] Although some regulation without
compensation was implicitly permitted because otherwise "[g]overnment hardly could go
on," this "implied limitation must have its limits, or the contract and due process clauses
are gone."[67] Thus it was the "general rule . . . that while property may be regulated to a
certain extent, if regulation goes too far it will be recognized as a taking."[68]

And how was one to determine whether a particular regulation went too far? "One fact
for consideration," said Holmes, "is the extent of the diminution. When it reaches a certain magnitude, in most if not in all cases there must be . . . compensation. . . ."[69] In the
present case "the extent of the taking is great. It purports to abolish what is recognized in
Pennsylvania as an estate in land. . . ."[70] The difference between regulation and taking
was one of degree, not of kind.[71]

Justice Brandeis objected that Holmes had misapplied his own test:

> If we are to consider the value of the coal kept in place by the restriction, we
> should compare it with the value of all other parts of the land. . . . For aught
> that appears the value of the coal kept in place by the restriction may be neg-
> ligible as compared with the value of the whole property, or even as compared
> with that part of it which is represented by the coal . . . which may be ex-
> tracted despite the statute.[72]

Beyond this, as Brandeis also noted, Holmes's test appeared to contradict earlier decisions
that had allowed the complete destruction of property values in liquor and oleomargarine
to protect the public interest.[73] Finally, it is difficult to relate Holmes's test to any conceivable purpose of the taking provision. That the state has taken a small bite rather than a
large one affects the amount of compensation; it does not alter the fact that, as he suggested in the same opinion, it is unfair to place the burden of a public benefit on the
shoulders of the individual owner.[74]

---

[66] "To make it commercially impracticable to mine certain coal has very nearly the same effect for constitutional purposes as appropriating or destroying it." *Id.* at 414.

[67] *Id.* at 413.

[68] *Id.* at 415.

[69] *Id.* at 413.

[70] *Id.* at 414.

[71] *Id.* at 416.

[72] *Id.* at 419. For further criticism along these lines, see Rose, Mahon *Reconstructed: Why the Takings Issue
Is Still a Muddle,* 57 S. Cal. L. Rev. 561, 566-69 (1984); Sax, *supra* note 63, at 60.

[73] *Mahon,* 260 U.S. at 418 (Brandeis, J., dissenting) (citing Powell v. Pennsylvania, 127 U.S. 678, 682
(1888); Mugler v. Kansas, 123 U.S. 623, 668, 669 (1887)).

[74] *See Mahon,* 260 U.S. at 416. When property is actually appropriated for public use, this is clearly the law:
not one square inch of land may be taken without compensation, even if the owner remains in possession of the
incomparably larger remaining portion of his property. *See, e.g.,* Loretto v. Teleprompter Manhattan CATV
Corp., 458 U.S. 419, 438 n.16 (1982) (installation of television cable facilities: "[W]hether the installation is a
taking does not depend on whether the volume of space that it occupies is bigger than a bread box."). The
utilitarian argument that compensation serves to assure the efficiency of government actions by internalizing their
costs does not itself justify Holmes's test; as Michelman has said, it would require compensation for essentially
all government-caused harms. Michelman, *Property, Utility, and Fairness: Comments on the Ethical Foundations
of "Just Compensation" Law,* 80 Harv. L. Rev. 1165, 1181 (1967). For the argument that the magnitude of the

Holmes also suggested that the public interest in forbidding the undermining of homes was not great: The statute "is not justified as a protection of personal safety. That could be provided for by notice."[75] Brandeis responded with a pointed reference to two of Holmes's own earlier opinions stressing the need for deference to reasonable legislative decisions.[76] Indeed it is not easy to reconcile Holmes's second-guessing of the adequacy of less intrusive alternatives with his argument that a state could fairly find sterilization of shoddy insufficient to prevent disease.[77] Elsewhere in the same opinion, moreover, Holmes himself revealed a more fundamental objection to his apparent suggestion that a sufficiently strong public interest would dispense with the need for compensation for what otherwise would amount to a taking:[78] "The protection of private property in the Fifth Amendment presupposes" a valid public purpose "but provides that it shall not be taken for public use without compensation."[79] By implying the use of a balancing test, Holmes seemed to be saying property *could* be taken without compensation if there was sufficient public need.[80]

Holmes's arguments, in short, seem less than convincing. Moreover, Justice Brandeis by no means based his dissent on a formal distinction between taking and regulation. He drew rather on the established theory that had been employed by so ardent a protector of property rights as Justice Field to explain—long before the taking clause was found embodied in the fourteenth amendment—why the prohibition of nuisances was not a deprivation of property without due process: "Coal in place is land; and the right of the owner to use his land is not absolute. He may not so use it as to create a public nuisance; and uses, once harmless, may, owing to changed conditions, seriously threaten the public welfare."[81] Harlan had said the same thing in 1887: "[A]ll property in this country is held

---

taking does relate to the taking clause's tendency to reduce the risk that productive activity may be deterred by the fear of capricious government action, see *id.* at 1229-34.

[75] *Mahon,* 260 U.S. at 414. Nor did the statute protect the safety of lessees of surface rights from coal companies, since it allowed undermining the company's own land. *See id; Rose, supra* note 72, at 571-73.

[76] *Mahon,* 260 US. at 420 (citing Patsone v. Pennsylvania, 232 U.S. 138, 144 (1914) (upholding ban on alien ownership of shotguns); Laurel Hill Cemetery v. San Francisco, 216 U.S. 358, 365 (1910) (upholding ban on burial within city)). Brandeis added: "[I]t seems . . . clear that mere notice of intention to mine would not in this connection secure the public safety." *Id.* at 422.

[77] *See* p. 145 *supra* (discussing Weaver v. Palmer Bros., 270 U.S. 402 (1926)). Like the first amendment (*see* pp. 154-60 *infra,* discussing Gitlow v. New York), and unlike the due process clause as construed by the Court, the taking provision does not prohibit only unreasonable action. For Holmes's explanation of this difference, see Adkins v. Children's Hospital, 261 U.S. 525, 568 (1923) (dissent); *see also* pp. 159-60 *infra.* Like the first amendment, however, the taking clause applies only to the central government; cases involving state takings, as well as state limitations on speech, are governed by the due process clause. *See* Chicago, B. & Q.R.R. v. Chicago, 166 U.S. 226, 235-41 (1897); Barron v. Mayor of Baltimore, 32 U.S. (7 Pet.) 243 (1833), THE FIRST HUNDRED YEARS at 189-93.

[78] "[W]e should think it clear that the statute does not disclose a public interest sufficient to warrant so extensive a destruction of the defendant's constitutionally protected rights." *Mahon,* 260 U.S. at 414; *see also id.* at 415 (distinguishing a requirement that miners leave pillars of coal standing sufficient to prevent flooding as a "requirement for the safety of employees invited into the mine").

[79] *Mahon,* 260 U.S. at 415.

[80] Such a conclusion "baffles" not only "legal commentators who take a neoclassical economic approach," as Rose argues, *see supra* note 72, at 593-94, but also those who believe, as the taking clause seems to indicate, that the Philadelphia Convention adopted the "Benthamite point of view" that the public must pay for the property it acquires. *See id.* at 594.

[81] *Mahon,* 260 U.S. at 417; *cf.* Munn v. Illinois, 94 U.S. 113, 145 (1887) (Field, J., dissenting) ("The doctrine that each one must so use his own as not to injure his neighbor—*sic utere tuo ut alienum non laedas*—is the

under the implied obligation that the owner's use of it shall not be injurious to the community."[82] In the ordinary case the ownership of property does not include the right to undermine a neighbor;[83] thus in the ordinary case no property is taken when undermining is forbidden.[84]

The facts of the *Mahon* case, however, seemed to take the case out of this usual rule. As Holmes insisted, the company in selling surface rights to the plaintiffs had expressly reserved the right to mine all the coal.[85] The terms of the conveyance had negated the normal obligation of support and given the company the extraordinary right to undermine the plaintiffs' land.[86] Thus the argument that would support Brandeis's position in the usual case failed in *Mahon:* the prohibition of undermining *did* deprive the company of a preexisting property right—unless the right to reserve such an interest had been qualified from the outset.

As Brandeis once again neatly pointed out, earlier Holmes decisions suggested that it had been: despite the clause forbidding impairment of contracts, no one could remove a subject from the police power by making a contract about it.[87] Indeed decisions under the taking clause itself had gone beyond permitting the enforcement of duties imposed on landowners by the common law. They had upheld the imposition of new and analogous duties, such as the duty not to make or sell liquor, on the broader theory that the ownership of property, like the right to contract, was limited not only by existing laws but also by a general governmental power to legislate for the prevention of harm.[88]

---

rule by which every member of society must possess and enjoy his property. . . ."). *See* THE FIRST HUNDRED YEARS at 372; T. COOLEY, *supra* note 25, at 573.

[82]Mugler v. Kansas, 123 U.S. 623, 665 (1887).

[83]*See, e.g.,* 1 H. TIFFANY, THE LAW OF REAL PROPERTY AND OTHER INTERESTS IN LAND § 301 (1903).

[84]*Cf.* Rose, *supra* note 72, at 582 ("[N]oxious fumes may be abated without compensation because the property owner never had a right to inflict noxious fumes on his neighbors, and consequently lost nothing by regulation."); B. ACKERMAN, PRIVATE PROPERTY AND THE CONSTITUTION 101-02 (1977) (humble example of the bicycle owner who rides over his neighbor's marigolds); *see also id.* at 150-56 (no compensation required when action is designed to prevent socially unacceptable practices).

[85]*Mahon,* 260 U.S. at 412.

[86]*See* H. TIFFANY, *supra* note 83, § 309 ("[T]he owner of the surface of land may grant or release to the owner of subjacent soil or minerals the right to work or mine the latter, even though this causes a disturbance or sinking of the surface.").

[87]*Mahon,* 260 U.S. at 420-21 (citing Hudson County Water Co. v. McCarter, 209 U.S. 349 (1908)); *see also* pp. 12-13 *supra* (discussing Manigault v. Springs, 199 U.S. 473 (1905)). Without responding directly to Brandeis's invocation of his own earlier opinions, Holmes seemed to limit those opinions by acknowledging for the first time that their reasoning posed a threat to the very existence of the constitutional provision: "As long recognized, some values are enjoyed under an implied limitation and must yield to the police power. But obviously the implied limitation must have its limits, or the contract and due process clauses are gone." *Mahon,* 260 U.S. at 413.

[88]*E.g.,* Mugler v. Kansas, 123 U.S. 623, 665, 669 (1887). Compare Cooley's formulation of the relation between the police power and property under the similarly worded due process clause, quoted *supra* note 25. But for this implicit limitation, the Court might well have had to strike down residential zoning laws as takings without compensation, since they went beyond the analogous law of nuisance. As it was, the Court upheld zoning against a due process attack on the basis of the nuisance analogy without even discussing the taking issue. *See* Village of Euclid v. Ambler Realty Co., 272 U.S. 365 (1926), *supra* p. 146. For the alternative argument that zoning was justified by implicit compensation in kind—though hardly well tailored to the facts of the *Euclid* case, where zoning allegedly reduced the value of the affected land by three-quarters—see *infra* text accompanying notes 89-92.

Brandeis did not explicitly explain how to curtail a police-power qualification before it destroyed the taking clause. In answering the Court's suggestion that a provision requiring that miners leave coal pillars along the property line to prevent flooding of adjacent mines was justified by "an average reciprocity of advantage," [89] however, Brandeis drew a distinction that would serve the purpose:

> Reciprocity of advantage is an important consideration, and may even be an essential, where the State's power is exercised for the purpose of conferring benefits upon the property of a neighborhood, as in drainage projects, . . . or upon adjoining owners, as by party wall provisions. . . . But where the police power is exercised, not to confer benefits upon property owners, but to protect the public from detriment and danger, there is, in my opinion, no room for considering reciprocity of advantage. [90]

"Reciprocity of advantage" is compensation in kind; Brandeis and Holmes both seemed to be saying that it would justify an actual taking. [91] But in Brandeis's view there was a taking only when the owner was required to benefit his neighbor, not when he was forbidden to harm him. It is true that one may suffer economic injury in either case, [92] but nuisance law had distinguished the two for centuries. It is on this distinction that Brandeis built: it is unfair to require an individual property owner to contribute his land for a post office, but it is not unfair to make him stop polluting his neighbors. [93]

Borderline cases will prove refractory on Brandeis's test, and *Mahon* was a borderline case. To undermine the Mahons' land would harm them; to forbid undermining would give them a right to support that they had not paid for. That the Mahons had been compensated for forgoing that right does seem at least to shift the equities; even in Brandeis's terms, a strong case can be made for saying the statute gave the Mahons a benefit for which they had not bargained.

Not long after *Mahon* the Court in *Miller v. Schoene* unanimously upheld, against a taking objection, a statute requiring the destruction of ornamental cedar trees infected with a disease damaging to nearby apple orchards. [94] Holmes was silent, although the diminution in value, which he had so heavily stressed in *Mahon,* was obviously great if the cedars, like the right to undermine houses, were to be considered in isolation. In

---

[89] *Mahon,* 260 U.S. at 415 (citing Plymouth Coal Co. v. Pennsylvania, 232 U.S. 531 (1914)).

[90] *Mahon,* 260 U.S. at 422.

[91] *See* Rose, *supra* note 72, at 581.

[92] *See* Coase, *supra* note 59, at 2 (requiring one to avoid causing injuries to another may inflict economic loss on the enjoined party); Sax, *supra* note 63, at 48-50 ("Actually the problem is not one of noxiousness or harm-creating activity at all; rather it is a problem of inconsistency between perfectly innocent and independently desirable uses.")

[93] *See also* Nashville, C. & St. L. Ry. v. Walters, 294 U.S. 405, 428-29 (1935) (Brandeis, J.) (holding unconstitutional a requirement that railroad pay for elimination of grade crossing where reason was promotion of highway speed rather than safety: "[t]he promotion of public convenience will not justify requiring of a railroad . . . the expenditure of money, unless it can be shown that a duty to provide the particular convenience rests upon it"); Dunham, Griggs v. Allegheny County *in Perspective: Thirty Years of Supreme Court Expropriation Law,* 1962 Sup. Ct. Rev. 63, 73-81. Seen in this light, the taking clause and the police power can comfortably coexist as complementary components of the property owner's general right to be left alone.

[94] 276 U.S. 272 (1928).

Brandeis's terms, while the destruction of the cedars could be said to confer a benefit on the apple growers, the proximity of the case to traditional nuisance law seemed to suggest, as in the zoning case, that the statute should be upheld.

Ignoring *Mahon* altogether, Justice Stone announced a new test that avoided choosing between two equally accurate characterizations:

> [T]he state was under the necessity of making a choice between the preservation of one class of property and that of the other wherever both existed in dangerous proximity. It would have been none the less a choice if, instead of enacting the present statute, the state, by doing nothing, had permitted serious injury to the apple orchards within its borders to go unchecked. When forced to such a choice the state does not exceed its constitutional powers by deciding upon the destruction of one class of property in order to save another. . . . [95]

Elaborating on this reasoning, one leading commentator concluded that no compensation should ever be required when the government arbitrated between conflicting uses of adjacent properties.[96] Like Brandeis's distinction, this test serves to separate the abatement of a nuisance from the construction of a post office, where the landowner's activities do not interfere with the use of government land.[97] Yet Justice Stone's thesis might well permit the government also to favor the *perpetrator* of a nuisance on the ground that to protect the victim is to limit the other's right to use his own property.[98] On the assumption that the nuisance had previously been prohibited, why the transfer of rights involved in this case would be more consistent with the constitutional purpose of avoiding arbitrary imposition of burdens than in the case of the post office is not altogether clear.[99]

The elusiveness of a logically satisfying treatment of the regulations in *Mahon* and *Miller* underscores the refractory nature of the problem. However imperfect their solutions, Holmes, Brandeis, and Stone rendered major services by their provocative exploration of the murky borderland between regulation and taking.

---

[95] *Id.* at 279.

[96] Sax, *Takings, Private Property and Public Rights,* 81 YALE L.J. 149, 165 (1971).

[97] *Cf.* Delaware, L. & W.R.R. v. Town of Morristown, 276 U.S. 182 (1928) (Butler, J.) (striking down as an uncompensated taking a requirement that railroad make its property available for taxi stand). Brandeis, joined by Holmes, concurred in a separate opinion. Decided the same day as *Miller,* this case can be reconciled with *Miller* by employing Sax's distinction, because the terminal did not interfere with the use of the cab owner's property. In the language of Brandeis's dissent in *Mahon,* 260 U.S. at 416, the railroad was required to confer a benefit on the cab owners.

[98] *See* Sax, *supra* note 96, at 164-66 (distinguishing between requiring adjoining owner to put up with airport noise and requiring same owner to surrender land for new runway).

[99] *See* Sunstein, *supra* note 2, at 1726 ("[T]he seeds of a destruction of the eminent domain clause may lie within the *Miller* Court's statement."). In an earlier article, Sax had argued that compensation should be required only if the government acted in an "enterprise" capacity as opposed to reconciling private disputes, on the ground that the risk of arbitrary action that gave birth to the compensation requirement was at its height when the government acted to promote its own interest. Sax, *supra* note 63, at 62-67. As Sax's later example of the new runway seems to acknowledge, however, it is also arbitrary to give one person's property to another without compensation. Sax, *supra* note 96, at 164-66. Indeed, the independent "public use" requirement has been held to forbid such a transfer even if compensation is paid. For criticism of both versions of Sax's test on grounds of unfairness, see Berger, *A Policy Analysis of the Taking Problem,* 49 N.Y.U.L. REV. 165, 177-82 (1974) (urging compensation when justifiable expectations of owner are frustrated by government action).

## II.  CIVIL LIBERTIES

### A.  *Meyer v. Nebraska*

Before the Taft period, the Supreme Court had wielded substantive due process only to protect economic interests such as property and the notorious liberty of contract. The Court's definition of the liberty protected by the due process clauses, however, had always been broader. A vaccination law, for example, had been upheld during the Fuller days only on the ground that it was a reasonable health measure.[100] In two important decisions in the Taft years, the Court took further steps to entrench the amendment's protection of noneconomic liberties.

The first was *Meyer v. Nebraska*,[101] decided in 1923, which set aside a conviction for teaching German to a child who had not completed the eighth grade. Earlier broad definitions of fourteenth amendment "liberty" were elaborated:

> [I]t denotes not merely freedom from bodily restraint but also the right of the individual to contract, to engage in any of the common occupations of life, to acquire useful knowledge, to marry, establish a home and bring up children, to worship God according to the dictates of his own conscience, and generally to enjoy those privileges long recognized at common law as essential to the orderly pursuit of happiness by free men.[102]

The right to teach a foreign language, and the right to engage a language instructor, fell within this definition; "[m]ere knowledge of the German language cannot reasonably be regarded as harmful."[103]

Strictly speaking, the inclusion of the right to educate one's children may have been dictum, since ordinarily the accused teacher would lack standing to argue that the parents' rights had been infringed, and the teacher's own right to teach was an economic liberty of the type that had long been protected.[104] Nevertheless, the Court stressed the parents' right

---

[100] Jacobson v. Massachusetts, 197 U.S. 11, 35 (1905), *supra* p. 48, note 137; *see also* Allgeyer v. Louisiana, 165 U.S. 578, 589 (1897) (dictum):

> The liberty mentioned in [the fourteenth] amendment means not only the right of the citizen to be free from the mere physical restraint of his person, as by incarceration, but the term is deemed to embrace the right of the citizen to be free in the enjoyment of all his faculties; to be free to use them in all lawful ways; to live and work where he will; to earn his livelihood by any lawful calling; to pursue any livelihood or avocation, and for that purpose to enter into all contracts which may be proper, necessary and essential to his carrying out to a successful conclusion the purposes above mentioned.

[101] 262 U.S. 390 (1923) (McReynolds, J.).

[102] *Id.* at 399.

[103] *Id.* at 400.

[104] On the standing point, see, for example, Buchanan v. Warley, 245 U.S. 60, 73, 81 (1917), *supra* pp. 107-09, where the Court carefully noted that the plaintiff was asserting only his own property rights. For the conclusion that *Meyer* involved traditional economic rights, see Warren, *The New "Liberty" under the Fourteenth Amendment,* 39 HARV. L. REV. 431, 454 (1926).

as if it were a part of the holding.[105] This application of the term "liberty" seems neither more nor less justifiable than the original inclusion of "liberty of contract." Once torn from its historical moorings,[106] "liberty" may as well embrace freedom of any kind.

Not even Holmes took issue with that conclusion. His objection, which the usually activist Sutherland joined, was that requiring a youngster to hear only English at school was a reasonable means of assuring that "all the citizens of the United States should speak a common tongue" despite their varied origins.[107] Admitting the hardly disputable legitimacy of the end, the majority found the means too extreme: less intrusive measures could have achieved the goal at a lower cost to liberty.[108]

*Meyer* strikes a responsive chord today. Substantive due process was there for the first time drawn upon to protect an intellectual freedom dear to the modern observer against a ham-handed measure most would now find seriously misguided. Justice Brandeis, a staunch holdout against most economic applications of the doctrine, went along without a murmur. But Holmes was entirely consistent in deferring to a legislative judgment that was rational though benighted; the price of deference to legislative determinations is that bad laws must sometimes be upheld.[109] The doctrinal basis for *Meyer* is as shaky as that of *Lochner* itself, for it is the very same.

## B.   Freedom of Expression

### 1.   *Gitlow v. New York*

Not even Holmes dissented, however, when two years later, in *Pierce v. Society of Sisters,* the *Meyer* principle was applied to forbid the effective outlawing of private schools.[110] Moreover, one week later Holmes and Brandeis were far less deferential to legislative judgment than their brethren when they dissented from the upholding of a conviction for the publication of a revolutionary screed in the famous case of *Gitlow v. New York.*[111]

On the threshold question whether the fourteenth amendment made freedom of expression applicable to the states, Holmes was brief: "The general principle of free speech . . .

---

[105] *Meyer,* 262 U.S. at 401-02 (stressing that ideas favoring state control over upbringing of children are "wholly different from those upon which our institutions rest").

[106] *See* Allgeyer v. Louisiana, 165 U.S. 581, 590-92 (1897) (holding that due process clause embraces liberty of contract), *supra* p. 45; *see also* Shattuck, *The True Meaning of the Term "Liberty" in Those Clauses in the Federal and State Constitutions Which Protect "Life, Liberty, and Property,"* 4 HARV. L. REV. 365, 372-73 (1891) ("liberty" in Magna Charta referred only to freedom from imprisonment).

[107] *Meyer,* 262 U.S. at 412-13.

[108] *Id.* at 401-02.

[109] Deference alone, however, does not seem to account for the evident relish with which Holmes wrote, over the lone and unexplained dissent of Butler, to sustain a law providing for the involuntary sterilization of the feeble-minded: "It is better for all the world, if instead of waiting to execute degenerate offspring for crime, or to let them starve for their imbecility, society can prevent those who are manifestly unfit from continuing their kind. . . . Three generations of imbeciles are enough." Buck v. Bell, 274 U.S. 200, 207 (1927).

[110] 268 U.S. 510 (1925) (McReynolds, J.). As in *Meyer,* although the Court stated flatly that the law "unreasonably interferes with the liberty of parents and guardians to direct the upbringing and education of children," no parent was complaining; the Court specifically added that the law also infringed the schools' right to make profitable use of their property. *See id.* at 534-35 (citing *Meyer*); Warren, *supra* note 104, at 455.

[111] 268 U.S. 652, 672-73 (1925) (Holmes, J., dissenting).

must be taken to be included in the Fourteenth Amendment, in view of the scope that has been given to the word 'liberty' as there used. . . ."[112] Brandeis expanded on this theme in his celebrated concurring opinion two years later in *Whitney v. California:*[113]

> Despite arguments to the contrary which had seemed to me persuasive, it is settled that the due process clause . . . applies to matters of substantive law as well as to matters of procedure. Thus all fundamental rights comprised within the term liberty are protected by the Federal Constitution from invasion by the States. The right of free speech, the right to teach, and the right of assembly are, of course, fundamental rights.[114]

In other words, if you can't lick 'em, join 'em; if your pet rights are protected by the shaky notion of substantive due process, so are mine. Fair enough. But this all goes to show that—apart from the consistently rejected theory that the fourteenth amendment incorporates the entire Bill of Rights—the doctrinal basis for holding the states without power to abridge expression is essentially that of *Lochner v. New York.*[115]

As in earlier cases, the majority in *Gitlow* assumed, without deciding, that freedom of speech fell within the "liberty" protected against state invasion by the due process clause and treated the case as if it had involved a federal prosecution.[116] Earlier decisions, Justice Sanford rightly observed, had established that this freedom was not absolute;[117] it "does

[112]*Id.* at 672 (Holmes, J., dissenting).

[113]274 U.S. 357 (1927).

[114]*Id.* at 373.

[115]For the incorporation theory, see Adamson v. California, 332 U.S. 46, 71-75 (1947) (Black, J., dissenting); Twining v. New Jersey, 211 U.S. 78, 122 (1908) (Harlan, J., dissenting); O'Neil v. Vermont, 144 U.S. 323, 370 (1892) (Harlan, J., dissenting). *Cf.* Hurtado v. California, 110 U.S. 516, 528-29 (1884) (due process included only those common law procedures that were fundamental). *See* THE FIRST HUNDRED YEARS at 345-47, 366-68; pp. 321-22, 362 *infra*. One may argue that freedom of expression is a more fundamental "liberty" than freedom of contract, but the basic difficulties of establishing that the due process clauses impose substantive limitations on legislative authority to limit rights other than life, property, and freedom from imprisonment remain. Meyer v. Nebraska had presaged the inclusion of first amendment liberties in the due process clause despite the potential argument that this made the first amendment redundant: the Court there listed freedom of religion as among the liberties protected against abridgement without due process. *See supra* p. 153.

[116]*Gitlow,* 268 U.S. at 666. For a similar but earlier assumption, see Patterson v. Colorado, 205 U.S. 454, 462 (1907), *supra* p. 59. Just a few years before *Gitlow,* with no objection from Holmes or Brandeis, the Court flatly stated that "the Constitution of the United States imposes upon the States no obligation to confer upon those within their jurisdiction either the right of free speech or the right of silence." Prudential Ins. Co. v. Cheek, 259 U.S. 530, 538 (1922) (Pitney, J.) (holding due process not offended by state law requiring employer to explain why employee left job). For the peculiar conclusion that by assuming that speech was among the liberties protected by the due process clause, the Court in *Gitlow* decided that it was, *see* Z. CHAFEE, FREE SPEECH IN THE UNITED STATES 322 (1941) (the Court was "persuaded . . . to settle the long-vexed issue at last by the unanimous statement that 'we may and do assume that freedom of speech and of the press . . . are among the fundamental personal rights and liberties protected . . . from impairment by the states'"); Warren, *supra* note 104, at 458 (*Gitlow* adopted as law the theory that the due process clause protected noneconomic liberties other than freedom from physical restraint).

[117]*Gitlow,* 268 U.S. at 666-67. In support of this assertion, the Court cited, among others, Fox v. Washington, 236 U.S. 272, 277-78 (1915) (upholding punishment for expression interpreted to encourage indecent exposure); Patterson v. Colorado, 205 U.S. 454, 463 (1907) (upholding punishment for expression interfering with judicial

not deprive a State of the primary and essential right of self preservation." [118] "Utterances inciting to the overthrow of organized government by unlawful means," he continued, "present a sufficient danger of substantive evil to bring their punishment within the range of legislative discretion." [119] And that was what the statute in *Gitlow* forbade: by punishing one who "advocates . . . the duty, necessity or propriety of overthrowing . . . organized government by force or violence," [120] the state had penalized only "the advocacy of action," not "the utterance or publication of abstract 'doctrine' or academic discussion having no quality of incitement to any concrete action." [121]

The resemblance between these passages and Learned Hand's famous formulation in *Masses Publishing Co. v. Patten*[122] is striking. By insisting on actual incitement, both Hand and Sanford, in contrast to *Schenck's* formulation of the clear and present danger test, had made clear that the mere probability of harm would not suffice to make speech punishable.[123] Yet posterity, while generally applauding *Masses*, has dealt harshly with *Gitlow*. There seem to be at least two explanations for this discrepancy.

First, despite its advantages, the incitement test alone, as *Gitlow* demonstrates, is not sufficient to satisfy anyone who believes that encroachments upon the interest in free expression may be justified only when the countervailing concern is overwhelming. Whether or not the Court was correct in concluding that the publication in question employed "the language of direct incitement," [124] Holmes was surely right that "there was no present danger of an attempt to overthrow the government by force on the part of the admittedly small minority who shared the defendant's views." [125] Indeed, as he added, there was ample room for "doubt whether there was any danger that the publication could

---

proceeding); and several of the World War I cases, including Schenck v. United States, 249 U.S. 47, 52-53 (1919) (upholding punishment for encouraging draft resistance). For a discussion of these antecedents, see *supra* p. 115-24.

[118] *Gitlow,* 268 U.S. at 668.

[119] *Id.* at 669.

[120] *Id.* at 654 (quoting N.Y. PENAL LAW § 161 (Consol. 1909)).

[121] *Gitlow,* 268 U.S. at 664-65.

[122] 244 F. 535, 540-42 (S.D.N.Y. 1917), *rev'd,* 246 F. 24 (2d Cir. 1917):

> If one stops short of urging upon others that it is their duty or their interest to resist the law, it seems to me one should not be held to have attempted to cause its violation. . . . The question . . . is . . . : Could any reasonable man say, not that the indirect result of the language might be to arouse a seditious disposition, for that would not be enough, but that the language directly advocated resistance to the draft?

*See supra* p. 119, note 177.

[123] Holmes had taken significant steps in this direction by emphasizing in his later *Abrams* dissent that the constitutional standard was especially strict in the absence of an intention to cause harm, Abrams v. United States, 250 U.S. 616, 630-31 (1919) (Holmes, J., dissenting). Hand's test of incitement, however, seemed more protective in this respect because of its emphasis on the objective meaning of the words used. *See Masses,* 244 F. at 541-42. For discussion of passages in *Gitlow* that suggest the less protective "natural tendency" test, see Z. CHAFEE, *supra* note 116, at 323-24.

[124] *Gitlow,* 268 U.S. at 665. As quoted in *id.* at 656-60 n.2, the publication said that "[r]evolutionary socialism . . . insists . . . that it is necessary to destroy the parliamentary state" and establish "a revolutionary dictatorship of the proletariat . . . by means of revolutionary mass action" building upon "mass industrial revolts," and ended with the declaration that "[t]he Communist International calls the proletariat of the world to the final struggle!"

[125] *Id.* at 673.

produce any result" at all.[126] Having dismissed the *Masses* prosecution for failure to establish incitement, Judge Hand had not had to deal with this problem.

Whatever its weaknesses, the test Holmes had enunciated for the Court in *Schenck v. United States*[127] had required that the danger be both "clear" and "present,"[128] and *Gitlow* could not fairly be said to meet either criterion. Justice Brandeis expanded on the basis for the immediacy requirement in *Whitney:* "If there be time to expose through discussion the falsehood and fallacies, to avert the evil by the processes of education, the remedy to be applied is more speech, not enforced silence."[129] A later Court would combine the more protective features of both the Holmes and Hand tests by requiring incitement to immediate harm.[130] In *Gitlow* the majority approved the refusal of an instruction to this effect and denied that the state was "required to defer the adoption of measures for its own peace and safety until the revolutionary utterances lead to actual disturbances of the public peace or imminent and immediate danger of its own destruction."[131]

The second important difference between *Masses* and *Gitlow* was the explicit holding in the latter case that the statute should be judged only on its face:

> [W]hen the legislative body has determined generally . . . that utterances of a certain kind involve such danger of substantive evil that they may be punished, the question whether any specific utterance coming within the prohibited class is likely, in and of itself, to bring about the substantive evil, is not open to consideration.[132]

This issue had not been reached in *Masses* either, because Hand had there held the statute had not been violated.[133]

Holmes protested that Sanford's holding contradicted the rule of *Schenck* that "the words used" in the particular case must create a clear and present danger.[134] Sanford cleverly responded that there was more reason to defer to legislative judgment when, as in

---

[126] *Id.; see also* Z. CHAFEE, *supra* note 116, at 324: "The terror which these dull and rusty phrases caused our prosecutors and judges would render them the laughing-stock of European conservatives."

[127] 249 U.S. 47 (1919).

[128] *Id.* at 52. In his dissent in Abrams v. United States, Holmes had sharpened the idea by insisting that the danger be immediate in cases to which the test applied, 250 U.S. 616, 630 (1919) (Holmes, J., dissenting). *See supra* pp. 121-24. Holmes was not inconsistent in voting to convict Schenck but not Gitlow, for the two cases raised distinct problems. *Schenck* showed that Holmes was willing to infer an intention to provoke crime though it had not been clearly expressed. *Gitlow* showed that he took seriously the separate requirement that the risk be an imminent one.

[129] Whitney v. California, 274 U.S. 357, 377 (1927) (Brandeis, J., concurring).

[130] *See* Brandenburg v. Ohio, 395 U.S. 444, 447 (1969) ("[T]he constitutional guarantees of free speech and free press do not permit a State to forbid or proscribe advocacy of the use of force or of law violation except where such advocacy is directed to inciting or producing imminent lawless action and is likely to incite or produce such action."); *see* p. 442 *infra.*

[131] *Gitlow,* 268 U.S. at 661, 669. In his dissent in Abrams v. United States, 250 U.S. 616, 627, Holmes had said it would also suffice if the speaker had *intended* to create a present danger. In *Gitlow,* he insisted that the indictment concerned only the publication and not its author's intent to induce an uprising. *Gitlow,* 268 U.S. at 673 (Holmes, J., dissenting).

[132] *Gitlow,* 268 U.S. at 670.

[133] *Masses,* 244 F. at 542.

[134] *Gitlow,* 268 U.S. at 672 (Holmes, J., dissenting) (quoting *Schenck,* 249 U.S. at 52).

*Gitlow,* the lawmakers had focused directly upon the speech issue by enacting a statute specifically limiting expression than when, as in *Schenck,* a statute forbidding the causing of a crime in general terms was interpreted to include speech.[135]

In due process cases, moreover, the need for generality in enacting rules had often persuaded the Court that a law did not have to be tailored precisely to the facts. In *Powell v. Pennsylvania,*[136] for example, the Court had held that the need to protect the public from unwholesome oleomargarine justified the legislature in banning even that oleomargarine which was healthful. In *Village of Euclid v. Ambler Realty Co.,*[137] without objection from Holmes or Brandeis, the Court upheld the exclusion of all industry from residential neighborhoods because many industries were offensive:

> [T]his is no more than happens in respect of many practice-forbidding laws which this Court has upheld although drawn in general terms so as to include individual cases that may turn out to be innocuous in themselves. The inclusion of a reasonable margin to insure effective enforcement, will not put upon a law, otherwise valid, the stamp of invalidity."[138]

If it is permissible to draft a statute broadly enough to embrace inoffensive conduct, then by definition the application of the statute to such conduct is not unconstitutional.

This is not to say, however, that the legislature's decision to extend a prohibition to inoffensive cases was immune to judicial investigation. Deference to the legislature, as Justice Brandeis would soon observe in *Whitney v. California,* had never forbidden inquiry into the reasonableness of a law.[139] On the contrary, the question whether the statute had been drawn too broadly was part of the general inquiry into the reasonableness of the fit between legislative ends and means, even when, as in *Gitlow,* the legislature had explicitly addressed the question whether the interest asserted should be restricted. Not infrequently, indeed, the legislative judgment was found wanting. This was the basis, for example, of the decision the year after *Gitlow* that the state could not forbid all use of shoddy in bedding simply because unsterilized shoddy posed a danger of infection.[140]

The basic question in *Gitlow* thus was whether the legislative judgment to forbid *all* incitement to violent overthrow of the government was reasonable, or whether the statute should have been limited to those incitements that created a clear and present danger of harm. For the majority, Justice Sanford did explain why he thought it was permissible not to limit the statute to immediate threats: "If the State were compelled to wait until the apprehended danger became certain, then its right to protect itself would come into being

---

[135] *Gitlow,* 268 U.S. at 670-71. This argument seems also to distinguish such precedents as Dahnke-Walker Milling Co. v. Bondurant, 257 U.S. 282 (1921) (striking down application of state regulatory statute to interstate transactions), invoked by Brandeis in *Whitney,* 274 U.S. at 378, and Collector v. Day, 78 U.S. (11 Wall.) 113 (1871) (federal income tax law could not constitutionally be applied to salaries of state government officials). Neither in *Dahnke-Walker* nor in *Day* had the legislature directed its attention toward interstate commerce or state officials, respectively.

[136] 127 U.S. 678, 684 (1888), THE FIRST HUNDRED YEARS at 377-78.

[137] 272 U.S. 365 (1926).

[138] *Id.* at 388-89 (citations omitted).

[139] 274 U.S. at 374, 378-79 (Brandeis, J., concurring).

[140] Weaver v. Palmer Bros., 270 U.S. 402, 415 (1926), *supra* p. 145.

simultaneously with the overthrow of the government, when there would be neither prosecuting officers nor courts for the enforcement of the law." [141] He did not say, though, why it was reasonable to prohibit publications as puny as Gitlow's. On the other hand, apart from reliance on a passage from *Schenck* that had admittedly been qualified by later cases, Holmes offered no reason for his contrary position that harmless incitements could not be included.

In retrospect the majority appears to have been, as in the oleomargarine case, very deferential indeed. It is not at all clear why the state thought it necessary to punish incitements posing no substantial danger. The intimidating difficulties of enforcing a more selective measure that had led to the flat ban invalidated in the shoddy case, for example, seemed wholly absent in *Gitlow*. Possibly the Court thought that speech such as Gitlow's was of such low value that it did not take much to make its inclusion in the prohibition reasonable.

Holmes and Brandeis, on the other hand, seemed far less deferential to the legislative judgment in *Gitlow* than was their wont. Ever since his celebrated dissent in *Lochner*, deference had been the hallmark of Holmes's due process jurisprudence. Not only would both he and Brandeis emphatically dissent from invalidation of the shoddy law, where the legislative judgment was arguably more reasonable than that in *Gitlow;* they would repeatedly protest that the majority was substituting its judgment for that of the lawmakers. [142] In *Gitlow*, by contrast, they found the majority too deferential.

It was consistent enough for Holmes and Brandeis to take a less deferential line when *congressional* restrictions of expression were in issue. Their deference in due process matters was a natural result of their substantive position that the clause outlawed only unreasonable legislation; [143] even if Congress was not ousted from the speech field altogether, the first amendment on its face imposed more stringent limitations. [144] Their hardline scrutiny in *Gitlow*, however, cannot be so easily explained, for in their view *Gitlow* was a due process case—only the due process clause limited state authority over expression.

Holmes displayed awareness of this distinction by acknowledging generally that the states might enjoy "a somewhat larger latitude of interpretation than is allowed to Congress by the sweeping language that governs or ought to govern the laws of the United States." [145] Further, he couched his conclusion that Gitlow could not be convicted in terms

[141] *Gitlow*, 268 U.S. at 669-70 (quoting People v. Lloyd, 304 Ill. 23, 35, 136 N.E. 505, 512 (1922)).

[142] *See supra* pp. 143-46.

[143] The same can be said of their deferential position in equal protection cases in light of the accepted learning that the clause forbade only unreasonable classifications. *E.g.,* Quaker City Cab Co. v. Pennsylvania, 277 U.S. 389, 403, 405 (1928) (Holmes, J., dissenting, Brandeis, J., dissenting), p. 137 *supra*; F. S. Royster Guano Co. v. Virginia, 253 U.S. 412, 418 (1920) (Brandeis and Holmes, JJ., dissenting). *See* p. 104, note 86 *supra*.

[144] Thayer's famous argument for deference, however, like the suggestions in early decisions that the Court should never set aside a legislative judgment except in a clear case, *see* THE FIRST HUNDRED YEARS at 33, was based on institutional considerations that transcended the requirements of particular provisions. *See* J. THAYER, LEGAL ESSAYS 9-31 (1908). "It is plain that where a power so momentous as this primary authority to interpret is given [to the legislature], the actual determinations of the body to whom it is intrusted are entitled to a corresponding respect. . . ." *Id.* at 11.

[145] *Gitlow*, 268 U.S. at 672. Without this qualification, the protection of speech against state action would have had the paradoxically illiberal result of strengthening Holmes's *Schenck* argument that the protection of speech against acts of Congress was not absolute: maybe Congress was not meant to have power over people who shout "fire" in crowded theaters, but surely someone was.

that nominally satisfied his usual deferential standard: "[I]t is *manifest* that there was no present danger. . . ."[146] Whether this conclusion really jibed with Holmes's position that a state could reasonably find a ban on foreign-language teaching necessary to assure fluency in English, however, may fairly be doubted.[147] Without spelling out arguments to support such a distinction, Holmes and Brandeis seemed to be moving toward a stricter level of scrutiny in some substantive due process cases than in others. The majority, in contrast, seemed to think speech cases entailed, if anything, more deference than usual.[148]

### 2.   *Whitney* and *Fiske*

*Whitney v. California*[149] was an even weaker case for conviction than *Gitlow*. Ms. Whitney had been convicted not for making a statement, but for helping to establish an organization that espoused it.[150] "The novelty," as Brandeis observed in his separate opinion, "is that the statute aims, not at the practice of criminal syndicalism, nor even directly at the preaching of it, but at association with those who propose to preach it."[151] For the majority, Justice Sanford was unfazed: "That such united and joint action involves even greater danger to the public peace and security than the isolated utterances and acts of individuals, is clear."[152]

As in *Gitlow*, the Court said it could not examine the defendant's actual behavior, deferring this time not explicitly to a legislative judgment but to the judicial factfinder: though couched in constitutional terms, the question whether the defendant had the requisite knowledge of the association's purposes "is one of fact merely which is not open to review in this Court, involving as it does no constitutional question whatever."[153]

Like the question of review of a statute as applied, the problem of deference to the factfinder in constitutional cases is a knotty one. On the one hand, the Court had already held that it could not examine de novo a state-court determination that the compensation awarded for a taking had been adequate.[154] On the other, the Court had also established that, in order to prevent evasion on due process limitations on state tax power, it was not

[146]*Id.* at 673 (Holmes, J., dissenting).

[147]*Cf.* Meyer v. Nebraska, 262 U.S. 390 (1923) (Holmes, J., dissenting), *supra* pp. 153-54.

[148]For the later development of the notion of varying levels of scrutiny see, for example, United States v. Carolene Products Co., 304 U.S. 144, 152-53 n.4 (1938), *infra* p. 244.

[149]274 U.S. 357 (1927).

[150]*Id.* at 360.

[151]*Id.* at 373 (Brandeis, J., concurring). See Z. CHAFEE, *supra* note 116, at 344-45 for a description of the innocence of Whitney's own activities and for the conclusion that she had been convicted for "being at a meeting and nothing more." Both Gitlow and Whitney were pardoned after the Court had upheld their convictions. *See id.* at 324, 352-53.

[152]*Whitney,* 274 U.S. at 372.

[153]*Id.* at 367. In *Gitlow* the question was whether the statements created a constitutionally sufficient danger; the further question in *Whitney* was whether there was a constitutionally sufficient intent. As in *Gitlow,* the Court proceeded on the assumption that the fourteenth amendment made first amendment guarantees applicable to the states, this time without adverting to the question.

[154]*See* Chicago, B. & Q.R.R. v. Chicago, 166 U.S. 226, 242-46 (1897). At least to the extent that "facts" in the historical sense are concerned, this degree of deference may be compelled in civil jury cases by the seventh amendment: "[N]o fact tried by a jury shall be otherwise reexamined in any Court of the United States, than according to the rules of the common law." U. S. CONST. amend. VII.

bound by a state court's finding that the taxes in question had been paid voluntarily.[155] In concluding not only that the jury's resolution of the question had been reasonable but that the issue presented "no constitutional question whatever,"[156] the Court was not necessarily contradicting the latter decision; it may have meant, along the lines suggested in *Gitlow*, that a statute including unsuspecting members of a prohibitable association would be constitutional. Unfortunately, if this is what Sanford had in mind, he neither said so nor defended that rather extreme conclusion.

Joined by Holmes, Brandeis eloquently enlarged upon the former's explanation of the purposes of the first amendment, reaffirmed that the danger of harm must be both immediate and serious, and rejected Sanford's "suggestion . . . that assembling with a political party, formed to advocate the desirability of a proletarian revolution by mass action at some date necessarily far in the future, is not a right within the protection of the Fourteenth Amendment."[157] Nevertheless, Brandeis and Holmes did not dissent; finding "other testimony" supporting "the existence of a conspiracy . . . to commit present serious crimes" that "would be furthered by the activity of the society of which Miss Whitney was a member," they concurred on the ground of her failure to preserve the clear-and-present-danger issue in the lower courts.[158]

What was most remarkable was what Justice Sanford wrote on the same day for an undivided Court in *Fiske v. Kansas*.[159] The statute in issue was much the same as those upheld in *Gitlow* and *Whitney*, and in both those cases the Court had refused to review the facts. In *Fiske* Sanford both said and did the opposite: "[T]his Court will review the finding of facts by a State court where a federal right has been denied as the result of a finding shown by the record to be without evidence to support it. . . ."[160] Though the pamphlets the defendant had distributed indeed sought sweeping social changes, in contrast to *Gitlow* or *Whitney*, there was neither "charge [n]or evidence that the organization in which he secured members advocated any crime, violence or other unlawful acts as a means of effecting" them.[161]

Just how this was to be squared with the reasoning of the earlier cases was left unsaid. Perhaps, in contrast to *Gitlow*, deference to the legislature was unnecessary because that

[155] Ward v. Love County, 253 U.S. 17, 22 (1920) ("Of course, if non-federal grounds, plainly untenable, may be thus put forward successfully, our power to review easily may be avoided."). It is useful to compare *Ward* to the numerous cases reexamining, for the same reason, a state court finding that a contract allegedly impaired had never existed. *See, e.g.*, Piqua Branch of State Bank v. Knoop, 57 U.S. (16 How.) 369, 382 (1854), THE FIRST HUNDRED YEARS at 218-19. In later years, indeed, the Court would insist on reviewing de novo such questions as whether a confession was coerced, a search unreasonable, or a defamatory statement malicious. *See, e.g.*, Monaghan, *Constitutional Fact Review*, 85 COLUM. L. REV. 229 (1985) (discussing Bose Corp. v. Consumers Union of United States, 466 U.S. 485 (1984), and its constitutional requirement that appellate judges review the record to determine whether actual malice was shown in defamation cases).

[156] *Whitney*, 274 U.S. at 367.

[157] *Id.* at 373, 379 (Brandeis, J., joined by Holmes, J., concurring). Holmes's stress on the marketplace of ideas, *see* Abrams v. United States, 250 U.S. 616, 630 (1919) (Holmes, J., dissenting), suggested that freedom of expression was a means to an end. Brandeis, insisting that "[t]hose who won our independence believed that the final end of the State was to make men free to develop their faculties," maintained that "[t]hey valued liberty both as an end and as a means." *Whitney*, 274 U.S. at 375 (Brandeis, J., concurring).

[158] *Whitney*, 274 U.S. at 379 (Brandeis, J., joined by Holmes, J., concurring).

[159] 274 U.S. 380 (1927).

[160] *Id.* at 385.

[161] *Id.* at 387.

body had never determined that statements like Fiske's should be prohibited. Perhaps, in contrast to *Whitney*, the facts were of constitutional magnitude because the fourteenth amendment forbade punishment of those who advocated change by lawful means. But Sanford made no effort to explain.

Sanford reached his conclusion that the statute could not be applied to Fiske, moreover, without even discussing the still unresolved question whether the due process clause made freedom of expression applicable to the states. The most natural inference may be that *Fiske* finally decided that it did.[162] Yet the Court nowhere said that freedom of expression had been infringed; it spoke only in terms of the unspecified "liberty" protected by the due process clause.[163] If by "liberty" the Court meant freedom from a sentence of imprisonment, then *Fiske* may not have been a free speech decision at all, but rather—though the conclusion that "the Act" was unconstitutional as "[t]hus applied" seems to suggest the contrary—an unexplained application of the later-announced general procedural principle that due process forbids conviction without evidence of the offense charged.[164]

However mysterious its basis, *Fiske* seemed to suggest that the persistent hammering by Holmes and Brandeis was beginning to have an effect: for the first time in its history, the Court had struck down an effort to inflict punishment for the expression of ideas.[165]

## C.   Searches and Seizures

Like the other provisions of the Bill of Rights, the fourth amendment's prohibition of "unreasonable searches and seizures" applied only to the central government and not to

---

[162] Fiske's argument had been cast in freedom of expression terms, concluding with the statement that the applicability of speech and press guarantees to the states through the due process clause was not being discussed at length because it had been established in *Gitlow*. Brief for the Plaintiff in Error at 27, Fiske v. Kansas, 274 U.S. 380 (1927).

[163] *Fiske*, 274 U.S. at 387 ("Thus applied the Act is an arbitrary and unreasonable exercise of the police power of the State, unwarrantably infringing the liberty of the defendant in violation of the due process clause of the Fourteenth Amendment.").

[164] *See* Thompson v. Louisville, 362 U.S. 199, 204 (1960). *But cf.* Arrowsmith v. Harmoning, 118 U.S. 194, 196 (1886) ("Certainly a State cannot be deemed guilty of a violation of [the due process clause] simply because one of its courts . . . has made an erroneous decision."). Fiske had in fact been sentenced to imprisonment. *See* Transcript of Record at 3, Fiske v. Kansas, 274 U.S. 380 (1927). The alternative explanation is that the Court understood the state court to have construed the statute not to require unlawful means despite its express terms, and held that the statute so construed invaded freedom of expression. *See* Z. CHAFEE, *supra* note 116, at 352; H. HART & H. WECHSLER, THE FEDERAL COURTS AND THE FEDERAL SYSTEM 615 (2d ed. 1973):

> If a state may not, as a matter of federal constitutional law, punish particular conduct—*e.g.*, simply arguing with a policeman—then it is clearly appropriate for the Supreme Court to review and reverse where there is no evidence of any facts which might take the conduct outside of constitutional protection. This is the teaching of Fiske v. Kansas. . . .

[165] Both Holmes and Brandeis had gone along when the Court, without significant discussion, held that the government of Puerto Rico could constitutionally punish a libel against its Governor in Balzac v. Porto Rico, 258 U.S. 298, 314 (1922). The Court seemed simply to assume that the first amendment limited the Puerto Rico legislature. *See id.* at 314. The Court also reaffirmed the inapplicability of criminal jury guarantees to Puerto Rico, which the Court concluded had still not been "incorporated" into the United States. *See id.* at 304-05; *see also* pp. 59-65 *supra* (discussing earlier decisions on the applicability of various constitutional provisions to insular possessions).

the states.[166] Partly for this reason, and partly because of the long absence of any provision for appellate review of federal convictions,[167] the amendment had not figured prominently in Supreme Court jurisprudence before Taft's appointment in 1921.

The Court had begun by giving the clause a broad construction in *Boyd v. United States* in 1886, holding that it prohibited a court order to produce evidence even though there was no physical invasion of the defendant's premises or person.[168] *Gouled v. United States* had held the amendment applicable to an entry accomplished by fraud and had completed the development of the rule requiring exclusion of evidence unlawfully obtained.[169] In other respects the amendment remained largely unexplored.

The ratification of the prohibition amendment in 1919, however, led to an unprecedented increase in federal criminal enforcement and to a corresponding spate of important search and seizure decisions during the Taft period.

## 1. Open fields

The first case, *Hester v. United States,* was decided in 1924.[170] The evidence objected to had been obtained by revenue agents who had apparently entered private land without permission. Justice Holmes disposed of the fourth amendment objection in two sentences: "[T]he special protection accorded by the Fourth Amendment to the people in their 'persons, houses, papers, and effects,' is not extended to the open fields. The distinction between the latter and the house is as old as the common law."[171]

Cited for the traditional distinction was a passage from Blackstone dealing with the law

---

[166] Smith v. Maryland, 59 U.S. (18 How.) 71 (1856); *see* THE FIRST HUNDRED YEARS at 189-93 (discussing Barron v. City of Baltimore, 32 U.S. (7 Pet.) 243 (1833) (taking clause)). The Court had reaffirmed this conclusion after the adoption of the fourteenth amendment. *See, e.g.,* Weeks v. United States, 232 U.S. 383, 398 (1914).

[167] *See* Evarts Act of March 3, 1891, ch. 517, § 5, 26 Stat. 826, 827 (codified as amended in scattered sections of 28 U.S.C.) ("capital or otherwise infamous crimes"); Act of Feb. 6, 1889, ch. 113, § 6, 25 Stat. 655, 656 (writ of error in capital cases); Judiciary Act of 1789, ch. 20, § 22, 1 Stat. 73, 84 (making final judgments in "civil actions" reviewable in district or circuit court); *see also* H. HART & H. WECHSLER, *supra* note 164, at 1539-41.

[168] 116 U.S. 616 (1886); *see* THE FIRST HUNDRED YEARS at 444-47.

[169] 225 U.S. 298 (1921); *see also* Silverthorne Lumber Co. v. United States, 251 U.S. 385, 391-92 (1920) (refusing to subpoena evidence that had been returned after unlawful search); Weeks v. United States, 232 U.S. 383 (1914) (upholding a search victim's right to recover property unlawfully seized):

> If letters and private documents can thus be seized and held and used in evidence against a citizen accused of an offense, the protection of the Fourth Amendment declaring his right to be secure against such searches and seizures is of no value, and, so far as those thus placed are concerned, might as well be stricken from the Constitution.

*Id.* at 393. In *Gouled* itself, where the principle was extended to require the exclusion of evidence, Justice Clarke relied not on the argument of enforcing the fourth amendment, but on unconvincing dicta in the *Boyd* opinion suggesting that the introduction of evidence unlawfully seized would violate the fifth amendment's ban on compulsory self-incrimination. *Gouled,* 255 U.S. at 306. The fifth amendment ground was repeated regularly in the opinions of the Taft period. *See, e.g.,* Agnello v. United States, 269 U.S. 20, 33-34 (1925).

[170] 265 U.S. 57 (1924).

[171] *Id.* at 59.

of burglary.[172] The law of trespass, as Holmes acknowledged, protected open fields as well,[173] and—unless the text compelled this conclusion—it was not clear why burglary was a more appropriate analogy. The celebrated English case on which *Boyd* had so heavily relied had described permissible searches as an exception to the law of trespass, and *Boyd* itself had said the amendment was designed to protect the "indefeasible right of personal security, personal liberty and private property"[174]—which seemed broad enough to embrace the premises in *Hester*. Since one of the essential prerogatives of the landowner is the right to exclude others, one might well argue that land ownership creates the very sort of legitimate expectation of privacy that the amendment was designed to protect.[175]

The obvious stumbling block is the text. Pointedly quoted by Holmes, it protects not all property but only "persons, houses, papers, and effects," and the last term is generally taken to refer to personal rather than real property.[176] However, as noted by three dissenters when *Hester* was reaffirmed half a century later, a series of decisions beginning in 1967 renounced this literal interpretation in an effort to effectuate the purposes of the provision.[177] It is possible that the House of Representatives' unexplained substitution of the term "effects" for Madison's originally proposed reference to "property" reflected a deliberate judgment that the privacy interest in real property other than "houses" was insufficient to justify further limiting the authority of government to investigate crime.[178] A Court not convinced of this, however, could easily have read the language more broadly after having held that a court order constituted a "search," a regulation of land use a "taking," and a photograph a "writing" within the copyright clause.[179] Since Holmes himself had written the opinion in the taking case less than three years before, it is not obvious that he really found the text decisive, and, as so often was the case, he did not say what else was on his mind.[180]

---

[172] 4 W. BLACKSTONE, COMMENTARIES ON THE LAWS OF ENGLAND *223-26.

[173] *Hester*, 265 U.S. at 58.

[174] 116 U.S. at 630 (citing the "celebrated" case of Entick v. Carrington, 19 Howell's State Trials 1029 (1765)).

[175] *See* Oliver v. United States, 466 U.S. 170, 189-95 (1984) (Marshall, J., dissenting).

[176] *See id.* at 177 n.7 (opinion of the Court).

[177] *Id.* at 186-88 (Marshall, J., dissenting) (citing Katz v. United States, 389 U.S. 347 (1967), *infra* p. 448, which had held electronic surveillance of public telephone booths within fourth amendment and echoing Chief Justice Marshall's insistence in McCulloch v. Maryland, 17 U.S. (4 Wheat.) 316, 407 (1819), that the Constitution should not be read like a detailed code). The majority in *Oliver* explained *Katz* as based upon the amendment's protection of "persons" from unreasonable search. *Oliver*, 466 U.S. at 176 n.6. A literal interpretation of "houses" might exclude not only open fields but also commercial and industrial buildings from the scope of the amendment. Yet Holmes himself had struck down a search of business premises in Silverthorne Lumber Co. v. United States, 251 U.S. 385 (1920), without adverting to any difficulty. Perhaps it sufficed that in *Silverthorne*, as in the usual search of business premises, the objects searched and seized within the building constituted "effects."

[178] *See* Oliver v. United States, 466 U.S. 170, 176-77 (1984); J. LANDYNSKI, SEARCH AND SEIZURE AND THE SUPREME COURT 41 (1966); 1 ANNALS OF CONG. 452 (1789).

[179] *See* Boyd v. United States, 116 U.S. 616 (1886); Pennsylvania Coal Co. v. Mahon, 260 U.S. 393, 413-15 (1922), *supra* pp. 146-51; Burrow-Giles Lithograph Co. v. Sarony, 111 U.S. 53 (1884), THE FIRST HUNDRED YEARS at 435-36, 444-45.

[180] To hold all private property protected by the fourth amendment would not make every observation of activity on such premises an unreasonable search. Much that is done outdoors on private land can be seen from outside its boundaries, and it does not seem unreasonable to allow the government to see what the owner has knowingly exposed to public view. *See infra* text accompanying notes 199-201 (discussing United States v. Lee,

## 2. Vehicles and houses

Whatever the limits of the types of real property protected by the fourth amendment, the Court had no difficulty in treating an automobile as one of the "effects" embraced by the search and seizure provision. The question in the 1925 case of *Carroll v. United States* was what made a search of protected effects "unreasonable."[181]

The opinion was long and tedious, but the holding was clear: a moving automobile could be stopped and searched without a warrant if there was probable cause to believe it was carrying illegal beverages.[182] To a substantial degree this conclusion was based upon a long-standing congressional practice[183] that, as a leading student of the amendment observed,[184] had largely been confined to searches at or near international borders—a context in which the Court acknowledged that the ordinary rules did not apply.[185] More persuasive was the Court's explanation of the basis for the distinction it thought Congress had traditionally drawn: in the case of a vehicle or vessel "it is not practicable to secure a warrant because the vehicle can be quickly moved out of the locality or jurisdiction in which the warrant must be sought."[186]

On the Court's explicit assumption that it was "unreasonable" to search without a warrant whenever it was practicable to get one,[187] the *Carroll* exception made some sense,[188]

---

274 U.S. 559, 563 (1927)). Beyond this, it does not seem unreasonable for an enforcement officer to enter private property that has been opened to the public by the owner, as in the case of many business establishments. *See* Air Pollution Variance Bd. v. Western Alfalfa Corp., 416 U.S. 861, 865 (1974) (inspector not required to have warrant to enter property open to public). The Court did not reach this issue in *Hester* because it held the premises in question wholly outside fourth amendment protection. *Hester*, 265 U.S. at 59; *see* Oliver v. United States, 466 U.S. 170, 193-94 (1984) (Marshall, J., dissenting).

[181] 267 U.S. 132 (1925).

[182] *Id.* at 153-56. McReynolds and Sutherland, in dissent, protested that, among other things, there was no probable cause: "Has it come about that merely because a man once agreed to deliver whisky, but did not, he may be arrested whenever thereafter he ventures to drive an automobile on the road to Detroit!" *Id.* at 174. For similar criticism, see J. LANDYNSKI, *supra* note 178, at 89-90 (citing Black, *A Critique of the Carroll Case*, 29 COLUM. L. REV. 1068 (1929)). For the majority's argument that the prohibition agents in *Carroll* had probable cause, see *Carroll*, 267 U.S. at 159-62.

[183] *See id.* at 150-53 (listing statutes dating from as early as 1789 authorizing warrantless searches of vessels or vehicles and issuance of warrants to search buildings).

[184] J. LANDYNSKI, *supra* note 178, at 90 (citing Black, *supra* note 182, at 1075, and criticizing relevance of Taft's examples).

[185] *Carroll*, 267 U.S. at 154 (explaining that "national self protection" justified searching vehicles at border without even probable cause). The 1789 statute cited in *Carroll* was not strictly limited to ships entering the country, but later cases have extended the notion of somewhat relaxed rules for international travelers miles beyond the actual border, especially when ships are involved. *See* United States v. Villamonte-Marquez, 462 U.S. 579, 588-93 (1983) (upholding high-seas inspection without probable cause and stressing "need to deter or apprehend smugglers"); United States v. Martinez-Fuerte, 428 U.S. 543, 566-67 (1976) (upholding questioning of vehicle occupants by Border Patrol agents at fixed checkpoints without probable cause); *infra* p. 553. Early statutes dealing with liquor in Indian country, *see Carroll*, 267 U.S. at 152-53, may have been based upon similar reasoning, and a statute dealing with searches in Alaska antedated congressional recognition that the Bill of Rights applied to that territory. *See* J. LANDYNSKI, *supra* note 178, at 90 n.12; Black, *supra* note 182, at 1068. In light of the discussion that follows, it may also be significant that the statutes authorizing warrants to search buildings did not expressly forbid searching them without warrants.

[186] *Carroll*, 267 U.S. at 153.

[187] *Id.* at 156.

[188] *See* Alschuler, *Bright Line Fever and the Fourth Amendment*, 45 U. PITT. L. REV. 227, 275-77 (1984), which notes the absence of any basis in *Carroll* for arresting the occupants of the vehicle before the search, and

as did the similarly supported exception for warrantless searches incident to a lawful arrest, which the Court confirmed in dictum in the same opinion.[189] The assumption was itself confirmed a few months later in *Agnello v. United States*,[190] in which a unanimous Court held that "[t]he search of a private dwelling without a warrant is in itself unreasonable and abhorrent to our laws."[191] As Justice Butler wrote, the Court had long assumed that this was so; he made no effort to justify his conclusion as an original matter.[192]

Later observers have explained that the fourth amendment expresses a preference for warrants in order to interpose the judgment of an independent magistrate between the investigator and the citizen.[193] More recently, however, support has been growing for the argument that *Agnello* "stood the fourth amendment on its head": "Far from looking at the warrant as a protection against unreasonable searches, [the Founding Fathers] saw it as an authority for unreasonable and oppressive searches, and sought to confine its issuance and execution in line with the stringent requirements applicable to common-law warrants for stolen goods. . . ."[194]

There is nothing in the text of the amendment to answer the question whether warrantless searches are presumptively unreasonable. Respected Justices have argued, however, that to allow the police to search without a warrant whenever there is probable cause would leave the amendment an empty shell: the limits on the issuance of warrants would do no good if warrants were not required.[195] The factual basis of a counterargument is found in Chief Justice Taft's opinion for the Court in *Carroll:* a warrant "protects the seizing officer against a suit for damages" even if the search is later held unlawful.[196] The

---

comments on the Court's thoughtless extension of *Carroll,* in Chambers v. Maroney, 399 U.S. 42, 52 (1970), to a situation in which a car had been impounded after arrest, on the ground that "mobility of the car . . . still obtained at the stationhouse." Taft's argument is impaired to some degree by the fact that the articles sought may also be removed from a house before a warrant can be obtained.

[189] *Carroll,* 267 U.S. at 158. Applied two years later in United States v. Lee, 274 U.S. 559, 563 (1927) (Brandeis, J.) (alternative holding), this rule has generally been justified on the ground that immediate action is necessary to protect the arresting officer from concealed weapons and to prevent the destruction of evidence. *See, e.g.,* Chimel v. California, 395 U.S.752, 762-63 (1969). Given this rationale, it is not surprising that the Court refused to find that a search of one house was incident to an arrest made in another. Agnello v. United States, 269 U.S. 20, 30-31 (1925) (Butler, J.). For the same reason, however, it does seem surprising that on this theory the same Justices allowed a search of the entire establishment in which the defendant had been arrested, Marron v. United States, 275 U.S. 192, 199 (1927) (Butler, J.). As later cases would recognize, there was no risk that a defendant in custody would employ or destroy items wholly outside his reach. *See Chimel,* 395 U.S. at 762-68.

[190] 269 U.S. 20 (1925).

[191] *Id.* at 32.

[192] *See id.* at 32-33.

[193] *See, e.g.,* New York v. Belton, 453 U.S. 454, 457 (1981) (Stewart, J.); Johnson v. United States, 333 U.S. 10, 13-14 (1948) (Jackson, J.).

[194] T. TAYLOR, TWO STUDIES IN CONSTITUTIONAL INTERPRETATION 23-24, 41 (1969); *see also* Posner, *Rethinking the Fourth Amendment,* 1981 SUP. CT. REV. 49, 72 & n.56. For judicial acknowledgment of this argument, see Robbins v. California, 453 U.S. 420, 438 (1981) (Rehnquist, J., dissenting); Payton v. New York, 445 U.S. 573, 608-11 (1980) (White, J., dissenting); Coolidge v. New Hampshire, 403 U.S. 443, 492 (1971) (Harlan, J., concurring).

[195] *See, e.g.,* Jones v. United States, 357 U.S. 493, 497-98 (1958) (Harlan, J.); Johnson v. United States, 333 U.S. 10, 13-14, 17 (1948) (Jackson, J.). As noted, *supra* note 194, Justice Harlan later acknowledged there were reasons to reexamine this position.

[196] *Carroll,* 267 U.S. at 156. *See* T. COOLEY, CONSTITUTIONAL LIMITATIONS 303 (1868). In other words, one might view the warrant provision as a means of ensuring that warrants were no longer used to undermine the

citizen already had some protection against warrantless searches because the officer was liable in tort for acting unreasonably;[197] the warrant clause served the purpose of limiting the occasions when a warrant could deprive the citizen of this protection. Thus the warrant provision makes ample sense in light of the history of abusive warrants that prompted adoption of the amendment, even if no warrant is ever required, and thus one argument for the Court's conclusion in *Agnello* disappears.

The mere fact that the opposing argument is not absurd, however, does not prove it correct. It would have been entirely consistent for the Framers to seek both to prevent the abuse of warrants and to secure such additional protection as comes from the interposition of a disinterested magistrate—however ephemeral that protection may be or have become in practice. If, as is sometimes said, the reasonableness of some searches and seizures depended upon a warrant at common law,[198] *Agnello* may have been right after all.

### 3. Searchlights and wiretaps

In *United States v. Lee,* in 1927, the Court held the *Carroll* principle permitting warrantless searches of vehicles on probable cause applicable to vessels and reaffirmed *Carroll's* dictum permitting warrantless searches incident to a lawful arrest.[199] More interesting, however, was the unanimous conclusion in the same case that the use of a searchlight to reveal the contents of a boat to persons who were not on it was permissible because it was not a "search" at all.[200] Brandeis's argument was brief: using a searchlight was like using a field glass, and *Hester* was cited by way of unexplained comparison.

At first glance the Court's conclusion seems to follow a fortiori from *Hester:* if one may trespass upon private property to view what is visible there, surely it is less offensive to view it from outside, where one has a right to be. Yet *Hester* was based upon the conclusion that open fields were not "effects" protected by the search provision. Since vessels were assumed to be "effects," *Hester* did not authorize trespassing upon them to discover evidence, and the analogy fails.

Brandeis cited no authority for his conclusion that the term "search" should be narrowly defined, and he did not say why the use of either searchlights or field glasses did not qualify. In the literal sense a search had been made: the officers had examined the deck of the boat in an effort to find contraband. It would have been fair enough to hold that such a search was not "unreasonable," since one who puts his belongings where they can easily

---

common law requirement, written into the amendment's ban on unreasonable searches, that there be probable cause. Taft did not appear to perceive that this cut against his premise that a warrant was required whenever practicable.

[197] *See Carroll,* 267 U.S. at 156 ("In cases where seizure is impossible except without warrant, the seizing officer acts unlawfully and at his peril unless he can show the court probable cause.").

[198] *See, e.g.,* J. SCARBORO & J. WHITE, CONSTITUTIONAL CRIMINAL PROCEDURE—CASES, QUESTIONS, AND NOTES 306-11 (1977). John Adams's notes of the 1761 Massachusetts writs-of-assistance case attribute to James Otis the argument that the home could never be invaded without a warrant, and a 1762 newspaper article, also attributed to Otis, fulminated against general writs even on the express assumption that they provided no immunity from damages for wrongful intrusion, on the ground that they left the decision to every "petty officer." *See* M. SMITH, THE WRITS OF ASSISTANCE CASE 544, 563 (1978).

[199] 274 U.S. 559, 563 (1927).

[200] *Id.* at 563 (alternative holding).

be seen can hardly have a legitimate expectation of keeping them secret. Brandeis's choice of the ostensibly more sweeping ground that there had been no "search" at all may perhaps be defended on the ground that the Framers would not have wanted to subject the police-man watching passersby to the usual paraphernalia of fourth amendment inquiry.[201] By neglecting to specify just why there had been no search in *Lee,* however, Brandeis left the opinion open to the interpretation that there could be no search without physical intrusion into "persons, papers, houses, [or] effects."

The chickens came home to roost the next year in *Olmstead v. United States,* where the Court, over four dissents, allowed the use of evidence obtained by tapping telephone wires without a warrant.[202] Said Chief Justice Taft, after another tiresome recapitulation of irrelevant decisions:[203] *Hester* made clear that the phone company's wires were not among the speaker's protected effects, and *Lee* established that there had been no "search" of the speaker's "person" or "house" because there had been no trespass.[204]

Justice Brandeis's anguished dissent is an eloquent exposition of the values protected by the fourth amendment: "The makers of our Constitution . . . sought to protect Ameri-cans in their beliefs, their thoughts, their emotions and their sensations. They conferred, as against the Government, the right to be let alone—the most comprehensive of rights and the right most valued by civilized men."[205] To effectuate these goals, "every unjustifi-able intrusion by the Government upon the privacy of the individual, whatever the means employed, must be deemed a violation of the Fourth Amendment."[206] The words of the amendment, he insisted, were no barrier: the Court had already construed them liberally by holding them to include, among other things, a court order to produce evidence in *Boyd.*[207]

All of this was persuasive enough as an original matter if one agrees, as Brandeis asserted without substantiation, that the interests protected by the amendment include

---

[201] *See* United States v. Dionisio, 410 U.S. 1, 8, 14-15 (1973) (defining a search as intrusion upon reasonable expectations of privacy); Amsterdam, *Perspectives on the Fourth Amendment,* 58 MINN. L. REV. 349, 395 (1974) (noting that "to subject [a broad range of police practices] to fourth amendment control but exempt them from the warrant or probable cause requirements would threaten the integrity of the structure of internal fourth amendment doctrines"); Stone, *The Scope of the Fourth Amendment: Privacy and the Police Use of Spies, Secret Agents, and Informers,* 1976 AM. B. FOUND. RESEARCH J. 1193, 1211-12. *But see* Terry v. Ohio, 392 U.S. 1 (1968) (holding a stop-and-frisk encounter to be a search and seizure but finding neither warrant nor probable cause required), *infra* p. 451, note 280; Amsterdam, *supra,* at 393 ("[T]o exclude any particular police activity from coverage is essentially to exclude it from judicial control and from the command of reasonableness, whereas to include it is to do no more than say that it must be conducted in a reasonable manner."). *Compare* the question whether every communicative act is "speech" subject to the stringent standards of the first amendment. *See, e.g.,* United States v. O'Brien, 391 U.S. 367, 376 (1968) (burning of draft card), *infra* p. 440-41.

[202] 277 U.S. 438 (1928).

[203] *Cf.* Carroll v. United States, 267 U.S. 132 (1925), *discussed supra* at pp. 165-66.

[204] *Olmstead,* 277 U.S. at 464-66.

[205] *Id.* at 478.

[206] *Id.* For criticism of *Olmstead* on essentially the same grounds, see Stone, *supra* note 201, at 1201-11 (elaborating on nature of privacy protected): "[T]he amendment's protection of privacy should properly be viewed as extending primarily, if not exclusively, to preservation of the individual's interest in keeping informa-tion about him away from the prying hands, eyes, and ears of government." *Id.* at 1209.

[207] *Olmstead,* 277 U.S. at 476; *see also id.* at 472-73 (invoking other examples of broad construction of constitutional provisions).

secrecy as well as freedom from disruption of one's activities.[208] As Taft argued, however, it came a little late. Brandeis and Holmes—who also dissented in *Olmstead* but on other grounds[209]—had laid the foundation for the exclusion of wiretapping by their heedlessly narrow interpretations of "houses," "effects," and "searches" in *Lee* and in *Hester.*[210] Had they based these decisions on the ground that searchlight and open field searches were not "unreasonable," or that a "search" involved the invasion of a reasonable expectation of privacy,[211] wiretapping could easily have been distinguished. Contrary to the Chief Justice's suggestion,[212] it does not seem reasonable to conclude that one who speaks over the telephone intends to broadcast his words to the public generally. Nor should the fact that wiretapping was known to be a technical possibility at the time Olmstead spoke require the opposite conclusion. If it did, as Brandeis noted, new inventions such as x-ray cameras or powerful microphones could obliterate the amendment's protection.[213] After *Lee* had held that the use of a searchlight was not a "search" at all, however, it was necessary to explain why a wiretap was, and if there was no search, one never reached the question whether the officers' action was unreasonable.[214]

---

[208] See the excellent discussion in Posner, *The Uncertain Protection of Privacy by the Supreme Court,* 1979 SUP. CT. REV. 173, 177-90 (citing the colonial concern with the opening of mail as evidence supporting Brandeis's conclusion).

[209] *See Olmstead,* 277 U.S. at 469-70. Holmes agreed with Brandeis's alternative argument, *id.* at 479-85, that on the basis of the equitable clean hands doctrine the courts should exclude evidence obtained by federal officers in violation of state criminal law. Justice Stone agreed with both dissenting arguments, Justice Butler with that based on the fourth amendment. *Id.* at 485-88.

[210] *See* Amsterdam, *supra* note 201, at 381-82.

[211] *See supra* note 201.

[212] "The reasonable view is that one who installs in his house a telephone instrument with connecting wires intends to project his voice to those quite outside. . . ." *Olmstead,* 277 U.S. at 466.

[213]   Ways may some day be developed by which the Government, without removing papers from secret drawers, can reproduce them in court, and by which it will be enabled to expose to a jury the most intimate occurrences of the home. Advances in the psychic and related sciences may bring means of exploring unexpressed beliefs, thoughts and emotions. . . . Can it be that the Constitution affords no protection against such invasions of individual security?

*Id.* at 474 (Brandeis, J., dissenting). *See also* Amsterdam, *supra* note 201, at 384. Compare Holmes's employment of a similar argument to ignore the literal terms of the taking clause in Pennsylvania Coal Co. v. Mahon, 260 U.S. 393 (1922), *supra* pp. 146-48.

[214] Brandeis was notably reticent about *Hester* and *Lee,* explaining unexpectedly that the former had involved "voluntary disclosures by the defendant" (which had not been the Court's basis of decision) and following this statement with the unelaborated direction to "[c]ompare . . . United States v. Lee." *Olmstead,* 277 U.S. at 478 n.11. This passage may have been a belated attempt to say that the earlier cases had involved searches, but that they had been reasonable. Or perhaps Brandeis meant that a "search" was the invasion of a legitimate expectation of privacy. *Cf.* United States v. Place, 462 U.S. 696, 707 (1983) (looking in part to the degree of intrusiveness in concluding that subjecting luggage to a dog trained to sniff out narcotics was not a "search" at all); Katz v. United States, 389 U.S. 347, 351-52 (1967) (stressing expectation of privacy in overruling *Olmstead* and finding warrantless electronic eavesdropping an unreasonable search—without saying whether of persons, papers, houses, or effects).

# 6

# The Distribution of Authority

## I. FEDERALISM

### A. Maritime Cases

As in earlier years, the Court during Taft's tenure was confronted with a flock of cases raising the question whether state law was contrary to the negative implications of the commerce clause. Apart from a dissent by Justice Stone presaging a general recognition that in deciding whether a burden on commerce was "direct" or "indirect" the Court had really been balancing the state's interest in regulation against the national interest in freedom of commerce,[1] these decisions added little to previous understanding of the law.[2]

Of somewhat greater interest were developments in Justice McReynolds's related doctrine that the grant of admiralty jurisdiction implicitly limited state power to regulate maritime transactions.[3] Reaffirming precedent allowing state wrongful-death laws to provide relief in the case of maritime torts, McReynolds explained in *Western Fuel Co. v. Garcia* that the subject was "maritime and local in character" and that use of the state death law would not, in terms of the governing standard, "work material prejudice to the characteristic features of the general maritime law, nor interfere with the proper harmony and uniformity of that law in its international and interstate relations."[4] Why the sub-

---

[1] Di Santo v. Pennsylvania, 273 U.S. 34, 44-45 (1927) (Stone, J., dissenting); *cf.* Southern Pac. Co. v. Arizona, 325 U.S. 761, 783-84 (1945) (Stone, C. J.) ("[T]he state interest is outweighed by the interest of the nation in an adequate, economical and efficient railway transportation service. . . ."), *infra* pp. 327-28.

[2] *See also* Buck v. Kuykendall, 267 U.S. 307, 315-16 (1925) (Brandeis, J.) (state may not refuse license for interstate trucking on ground that existing service is adequate); Pennsylvania v. West Virginia, 262 U.S. 553, 596-97 (1923) (Van Devanter, J.) (reaffirming that state cannot require discrimination against out-of-state customers in sale of natural gas).

[3] *See supra* pp. 110-15 (discussing, for example, Southern Pac. Co. v. Jensen, 244 U.S. 205 (1917)).

[4] Western Fuel Co. v. Garcia, 257 U.S. 233, 242 (1921). As the Court added, it seemed to follow from the fact that recovery for wrongful death was based on state law (despite the traditional rule that normally time

ject was "local," and why there was no impermissible disruption of uniformity, was not explained.

A month later, in *Grant Smith-Porter Ship Co. v. Rohde*,[5] the maritime-but-local doctrine cropped up once again. A carpenter had been injured while completing the construction of a ship on navigable waters; the Court held that his action for damages under the general maritime law was precluded by a state statute making workers' compensation his only remedy. The case, wrote McReynolds, was controlled by *Garcia:* though the tort was maritime, "the application of the local law cannot materially affect any rules of the sea whose uniformity is essential."[6]

Though the terms he employed were the same in both cases, it is clear that what made the matter in *Rohde* "local" was not what had done so in *Garcia*. Rohde's case was "local" because of the nature of his employment: "The contract for constructing 'The Alhala' was nonmaritime, and although the incompleted structure upon which the accident occurred was lying in navigable waters, neither Rohde's general employment, nor his activities at the time had any direct relation to navigation or commerce."[7] Earlier decisions forbidding application of compensation laws to maritime cases, including the seminal *Southern Pacific Co. v. Jensen*,[8] were distinguished because in "each of them the employment or contract was maritime in nature and the rights and liabilities of the parties were prescribed by general rules of maritime law essential to its proper harmony and uniformity."[9] In contrast, it cannot have been the nature of the worker's employment in *Garcia* that made his case "local," for he, like Jensen, had been a stevedore, and the defendant had been the operator of a vessel.[10] It must have been the nature of the wrongful-death law itself that allowed its application to a person whose employment was "direct[ly] relat[ed] to navigation or commerce."[11]

McReynolds did not explain why there was no need for uniformity with regard either

---

limitations were a "procedural" matter governed by the law of the forum, *see* RESTATEMENT OF CONFLICT OF LAWS §§ 604-605 (1934)) that no relief could be granted after expiration of the applicable state statute of limitations. *Garcia*, 257 U.S. at 242-44 (invoking the similar conclusion of The Harrisburg, 119 U.S. 199, 213-14 (1886)). To justify the opposite result would have required finding either that state death laws were utilized in maritime cases only to provide a framework for enforcing a federal policy or that the state time limitation had been intended only to reduce the docket burdens of state courts. *See* D. Currie, *Federalism and the Admiralty: The Devil's Own Mess*, 1960 SUP. CT. REV. 158, 191-93, 192 n. 173.

[5] 257 U.S. 469 (1922).

[6] *Id.* at 477.

[7] *Id.* at 475-76; *see also id.* at 477 ("Here the parties['] . . . rights and liabilities had no direct relation to navigation, and the application of the local law cannot materially affect any rules of the sea whose uniformity is essential."); *accord* Miller's Indem. Underwriters v. Braud, 270 U.S. 59 (1926) (McReynolds, J.) (allowing compensation award in death of diver employed by local shipbuilder). *See* Morrison, *Workmen's Compensation and the Maritime Law*, 38 YALE L. J. 472, 491-99 (1929).

[8] 244 U.S. 205 (1917).

[9] *Rohde*, 257 U.S. at 477.

[10] *See Garcia*, 257 U.S. at 238-39; *Jensen*, 244 U.S. at 207-08.

[11] McReynolds appeared to confirm the two disparate senses of the maritime-but-local concept in allowing a state wrongful-death action on behalf of a repairman who had fallen from a barge: while state compensation law had applied to Rohde because of the local nature of his employment, "[h]ere the circumstances are very different"—though in both cases state law applied—because "the rights and liabilities of the parties are matters which have a direct relation to navigation and commerce." Great Lakes Dredge & Dock Co. v. Kierejewski, 261 U.S. 479, 480-81 (1923).

to wrongful-death laws or to the rights and duties of shipbuilders. We can help him: if the concern is that persons engaged in traffic from one place to another should not be subjected to a variety of confusing or conflicting obligations, it is important that the death law apparently imposed no new rules of conduct and that the shipbuilder and his employee did not travel.[12]

This may explain why state law was permitted to operate in cases such as *Garcia*, in which maritime law expressed no contrary policy. It does not explain, however, why McReynolds was willing to allow the state to deprive Rohde of a right to relief given by federal law. Uniformity was but one aspect of the *Jensen* principle, and the less obvious one at that; before *Rohde* it had been thought fundamental that state law could not take away what maritime law had given, because federal law was supreme.[13]

---

[12] *See* The Roanoke, 189 U.S. 185, 195 (1903) (the master's "position is such that it is almost impossible for him to acquaint himself with the laws of each individual State he may visit, and he has a right to suppose that the general maritime law applies to him and his ship, wherever she may go.") As Brandeis protested when the Court soon afterward refused to extend the maritime-but-local doctrine to a compensation claim on behalf of a longshoreman against his equally stationary employer, the uniformity argument is as weak in such a case as in *Rohde* itself, although a maritime contract as well as a tort is involved: "How can a law of New York, making a New York employer liable to a New York employee for every occupational injury occurring within the State, mar the proper harmony of the assumed general maritime law in its interstate and international relations, when neither a ship, nor a shipowner, is the employer affected . . . ?" Washington v. W. C. Dawson & Co., 264 U.S. 219, 231 (1924) (Brandeis, J., dissenting); *accord* Morrison, *supra* note 7, at 482, 502. McReynolds did not respond; reaffirming his earlier unexpected holding that Congress lacked the power to remove the uniformity requirement that was designed to serve the very federal interests the admiralty and necessary and proper clauses had entrusted to Congress, *see* Knickerbocker Ice Co. v. Stewart, 253 U.S. 149 (1920), *supra* pp. 114-15, he obtusely echoed the inapplicable concern of The Roanoke that "[t]he confusion and difficulty, if vessels were compelled to comply with the local statutes at every port, are not difficult to see." *Washington*, 264 U.S. at 228. *See also* London Guar. & Accident Co. v. Industrial Accident Comm'n, 279 U.S. 109 (1929) (Taft, C. J.) (no state workers' compensation for seaman employed wholly in intrastate commerce); Robins Dry Dock & Repair Co. v. Dahl, 266 U.S. 449 (1925) (McReynolds, J.) (denying application of state scaffolding law in suit by repairman against local employer for injury suffered while repairing ship in navigable waters). Indeed, as Brandeis seemed to suggest, application of the uniformity doctrine under such circumstances had the perverse effect of creating disuniformity by making the obligation to pay compensation depend upon whether the accident occurred on the ship or on the shore. If the accident occurred on shore, it was subject to state law because it was not within the admiralty jurisdiction. *See Washington*, 264 U.S. at 229 (citing State Indus. Comm'n v. Nordenholt Corp., 259 U.S. 263 (1922)).

[13] *See supra* p. 113 (discussing Southern Pac. Co. v. Jensen, 244 U.S. 205 (1917), and other cases). Parallelling the rise of the maritime-but-local doctrine permitting additional state regulation of maritime affairs was the unanimous decision in Metcalf & Eddy v. Mitchell, 269 U.S. 514 (1926) (Stone, J.), which took a fairly relaxed view of intergovernmental immunity by permitting federal taxation of income derived from contracts with a state. *Contrast* Pollock v. Farmers' Loan & Trust Co., 157 U.S. 429, 584 (1895) (holding that United States could not tax income from state securities), *supra* p. 25, note 128; Collector v. Day, 78 U.S. (11 Wall.) 113 (1870) (holding that United States could not tax state officers' salaries), THE FIRST HUNDRED YEARS at 355. On the other hand, split decisions of the Taft period actually *expanded* the converse immunity of the United States from state taxation that had been established in McCulloch v. Maryland, 17 U.S. (4 Wheat.) 316 (1819), THE FIRST HUNDRED YEARS at 160-68. *See* McCallen Co. v. Massachusetts, 279 U.S. 620 (1929) (Sutherland, J.) (effectively overruling Society for Savings v. Coite, 73 U.S. (6 Wall.) 594 (1868), which had permitted a state to include income from federal securities in determining the amount of a privilege tax, on the persuasive ground that constitutional immunities may not be evaded by labeling). *See also* Panhandle Oil Co. v. Mississippi *ex rel* Knox, 277 U.S. 218, 222 (1928) (Butler, J.) (holding sales to the United States immune from state taxation); Long v. Rockwood, 277 U.S. 142 (1928) (McReynolds, J.) (holding tax on patent royalties void). Four Justices dissented from the invalidation of the sales tax in *Panhandle*, two of them joining Holmes's convincing argument that the decision

## B.  Congressional Authority

### 1. The *Child Labor Tax Case*

In 1918, over four dissents, the Court in *Hammer v. Dagenhart* had struck down a congressional attempt to ban the interstate transportation of goods made in factories employing children, finding the federal law an effort to meddle with the subject of manufacturing—an area reserved to the states.[14] Immediately after this decision, Congress imposed a 10 percent tax on the incomes of persons employing child labor; the Court struck down the tax as well.[15]

The obvious effort to circumvent *Hammer v. Dagenhart* made the result less than surprising. Stressing the fact that the tax was payable only for knowing actions and without regard to the number of children employed, Taft argued that "a court must be blind not to see that the so-called tax is imposed to stop the employment of children" and quoted Marshall's famous condemnation of measures adopted by Congress "under the pretext of executing its powers" but "for the accomplishment of objects not intrusted to the [federal] government."[16] "Grant the validity of this law," he concluded,

> and all that Congress would need to do, hereafter, in seeking to take over to its control any one of the great number of subjects of public interest, jurisdiction of which the States have never parted with, and which are reserved to them by the Tenth Amendment, would be to enact a detailed measure of complete regulation of the subject and enforce it by a so-called tax upon departures from it. To give such magic to the word "tax" would be to break down all constitutional limitation of the powers of Congress and completely wipe out the sovereignty of the States.[17]

Amen, Chief Justice Taft. Not even Holmes and Brandeis, dissenters in *Hammer*, took issue with this reasoning.[18] Nor did they explain why they thought the two cases different.

---

was inconsistent with *Metcalf & Eddy*, which had allowed a tax on income from a government contract; in either case there was a chance that the tax might increase the price of government procurement. It was in this dissent that Holmes strongly questioned *McCulloch*'s premise that governments were implicitly immune from nondiscriminatory taxes: "The power to tax is not the power to destroy while this Court sits." *Panhandle*, 277 U.S. at 223 (Holmes, J., joined by Brandeis and Stone, JJ., dissenting). The fourth dissenter was McReynolds, *Id.* at 225. Holmes's dissent in *Long*, analogizing a patent to a grant of federal land, was joined by Brandeis, Stone, and Sutherland. *Long*, 277 U.S. at 148-51. Stone, Holmes, and Brandeis also dissented in *McCallen*, 279 U.S. at 634-38. For a perceptive contemporaneous discussion, see Cohen & Dayton, *Federal Taxation of State Activities and State Taxation of Federal Activities*, 34 YALE L. J. 807 (1925) (urging that government itself should be immune even in proprietary capacity but that nondiscriminatory taxes on government contractors should generally be allowed).

[14] 247 U.S. 251, 276 (1918), *supra* pp. 96-98.

[15] Bailey v. Drexel Furniture Co., 259 U.S. 20, 44 (1922) (the Child Labor Tax Case).

[16] *Id.* at 37, 40 (quoting McCulloch v. Maryland, 17 U.S. (4 Wheat.) 316, 423 (1819)).

[17] *Id.* at 36-40; *see also* Hill v. Wallace, 259 U.S. 44, 68-69 (1922) (Taft, C. J.) (unanimously striking down a federal tax on grain-future transactions not complying with detailed provisions).

[18] Justice Clarke, also a *Hammer* dissenter, dissented from the tax decision alone and without opinion. The Child Labor Tax Case, 259 U.S. at 44.

Nevertheless the cases can respectably be distinguished: because it is not limited to activities affecting interstate or foreign commerce, the tax power is a greater threat to the notion of a limited central government than is the commerce clause.[19] The odd thing was that in the past the Court had seemed to view the matter in precisely the opposite way: *Hammer v. Dagenhart* appeared to subject commerce clause measures to stricter scrutiny than the Court had employed in tax cases.[20] Working his way unconvincingly around precedents that had been indifferent to the dangers of pretextual taxes,[21] Taft seemed to demonstrate that for only the second time in twenty years the Court was prepared to take seriously the Framers' clear instruction that the national government was to have only limited powers.[22]

[19] *See* Powell, *Child Labor, Congress, and the Constitution,* 1 N.C.L. REV. 61 (1922) (approving the Holmes-Brandeis position in both cases); Sutherland, *The Child Labor Cases and the Constitution,* 8 CORNELL L.Q. 338 (1923) (same).

[20] *See supra* pp. 30, 98-99.

[21] The Child Labor Tax Case, 259 U.S. at 40-43. Taft rightly explained that an alternative ground for upholding the prohibitive tax on state bank notes in Veazie Bank v. Fenno, 75 U.S. (8 Wall.) 533 (1869), THE FIRST HUNDRED YEARS at 319, had been that Congress could have accomplished the same goal by regulation. The Child Labor Tax Case, 259 U.S. at 41-42. He distinguished McCray v. United States, 195 U.S. 27 (1904), on the feeble ground that the law imposing a prohibitive tax on oleomargarine did not "show on its face as does the law before us the detailed specifications of a regulation of a state concern and business." The Child Labor Tax Case, 259 U.S. at 42. Taft concluded that United States v. Doremus, 249 U.S. 86 (1919), had upheld the imposition of detailed regulatory requirements on the sale of narcotic drugs on the ground that they had "a reasonable relation to the enforcement of" a nominal tax. The Child Labor Tax Case, 259 U.S. at 43. Despite a dictum by McReynolds in United States v. Daugherty, 269 U.S. 360, 362–63 (1926), questioning the vitality of *Doremus,* it was reaffirmed over dissents by McReynolds and Sutherland, *see* Nigro v. United States, 276 U.S. 332, 351-54 (1928) (Taft, C.J.) (adding that intervening amendments had rendered the revenue collected by the tax substantial). McReynolds himself wrote to uphold a stamp tax on morphine and cocaine sales. Alston v. United States, 274 U.S. 289, 294 (1927) (contested provisions "do not absolutely prohibit buying and selling; have produced substantial revenue; contain nothing to indicate that by colorable use of taxation Congress is attempting to invade the reserved powers of the States").

[22] Determining where to draw the line promised to be a formidable task. Inquiry into legislative motive, as Marshall had long ago warned, was a ticklish affair. Fletcher v. Peck, 10 U.S. (6 Cranch) 87 (1810), THE FIRST HUNDRED YEARS at 128-29. Moreover, the Court rightly acknowledged in the Child Labor Tax Case that an "incidental motive" of discouraging undesirable activities was consistent with the legitimate exercise of federal tax power. 259 U.S. at 38. As the taxpayer had conceded, "Congress could not possibly levy internal excise taxes . . . without some incidental interference with the conduct of citizens in those fields which are directly regulatable only by the States." *Id.* at 31. *Cf.* J.W. Hampton, Jr. & Co. v. United States, 276 U.S. 394, 412 (1928) (Taft, C. J.) (unanimously upholding a protective tariff on the basis of long history: "So long as the motive of Congress and the effect of its legislative action are to secure revenue for the benefit of the general government, the existence of other motives in the selection of the subjects of taxes can not invalidate Congressional action."); Alston v. United States, 274 U.S. 289, 294 (1927), *supra* note 21. Taft might have added that, as in the *Veazie Bank* case, 75 U.S. (8 Wall.) 533, 541-42 (1869), *supra* note 21, the tariff could not be considered a means to an illegitimate end, because Congress could have accomplished its protective goal by direct regulation under the commerce clause. The Court's insistence that the tax serve a legitimate revenue purpose found substantial analogical support in Guinn v. United States, 238 U.S. 347 (1915), *supra* pp. 106-07, which had invalidated a grandfather clause for voting under the fifteenth amendment because it served no conceivable purpose other than the forbidden one of racial discrimination. *See also* Cummings v. Missouri, 71 U.S. (4 Wall.) 277 (1867) (holding a test oath punitive for ex post facto purposes because no legitimate reason appeared for disqualifying former Confederate sympathizers from ministry), THE FIRST HUNDRED YEARS at 292-93.

## 2. The commerce clause

Even as it recognized that federal taxes had to be scrutinized in order to defend the principle of limited federal power, the Court continued to construe rather broadly Congress's authority to regulate commerce among the several states. In 1922, for example, in opinions by the Chief Justice, the Court reaffirmed Congress's power to regulate both stockyard sales of cattle between legs of an interstate journey and intrastate rates that had harmful effects on interstate commerce.[23] In the same year, to be sure, the Court held that Congress could not regulate all grain futures transactions[24] and that the Sherman Act applied to neither professional baseball[25] nor a mine strike.[26] But the first of these decisions was influenced by Congress's failure to limit its rules to transactions affecting interstate or foreign commerce and the last by lack of evidence of an intention to disrupt commerce.[27] When these deficiencies were remedied, the Court sustained the application of federal law.[28]

Most striking in its contrast both with the *Child Labor Tax Case* and with *Hammer v. Dagenhart,* however, was the unanimous 1925 decision in *Brooks v. United States,* upholding a federal statute forbidding interstate transportation of stolen cars.[29] Earlier cases had established, wrote the Chief Justice, that Congress could indeed exercise "the police power . . . within the field of interstate commerce" to prevent "the use of such commerce as an agency to promote immorality, dishonesty or the spread of any evil or harm to the people of other States from the State of origin."[30] Interstate commerce facilitated theft by "help[ing] to conceal the trail of the thieves," and that was enough: "Congress may properly punish such interstate transportation . . . because of its harmful result and its defeat of the property rights of those whose machines against their will are taken into other jurisdictions."[31]

Before *Hammer v. Dagenhart,* all this would have been very plausible, and the *Child Labor Tax Case* could have been distinguished (instead of ignored) on the ground that the commerce power, unlike the power to tax, could safely be exercised solely for police-power ends. But *Hammer* had limited the use of the commerce clause for police purposes,

[23] Stafford v. Wallace, 258 U.S. 495 (1922); Wisconsin R.R. Comm'n v. Chicago, B. & Q.R.R., 257 U.S. 563, 585-86 (1922); *see also* Tagg Bros. & Moorhead v. United States, 280 U.S. 420 (1930) (Brandeis, J.) (regulation of stockyard brokers dealing with livestock traveling interstate); United States v. New York Cent. R.R., 272 U.S. 457, 464 (1926) (Stone, J.) (regulation of local traffic using interstate terminal); Colorado v. United States, 271 U.S. 153 (1926) (Brandeis, J.) (abandonment of local rail line whose unprofitability endangered interstate operations); *cf.* Swift & Co. v. United States, 196 U.S. 375 (1905), *supra* p. 27; Houston, E. & W.T. Ry. v. United States, 234 U.S. 342 (1914) (the Shreveport Rate Case), *supra* pp. 94-96.

[24] Hill v. Wallace, 259 U.S. 44 (1922) (Taft, C. J.).

[25] Federal Baseball Club v. National League, 259 U.S. 200 (1922) (Holmes, J.).

[26] United Mine Workers v. Coronado Coal Co., 259 U.S. 344, 407-13 (1922) (Taft, C. J.).

[27] *Id.;* Hill v. Wallace, 259 U.S. 44, 68 (1922).

[28] Coronado Coal Co. v. United Mine Workers, 268 U.S. 295, 310 (1925) (Taft, C. J.); Board of Trade v. Olsen, 262 U.S. 1, 32-36 (1923) (Taft, C. J., over dissents by McReynolds and Sutherland) (relying on "current of commerce" theory of Stafford v. Wallace, 258 U.S. 495 (1922)).

[29] 267 U.S. 432 (1925) (Taft, C. J.).

[30] *Id.* at 436-37.

[31] *Id.* at 438-39.

distinguishing prior decisions on the ground that goods made by child labor, unlike lottery tickets or adulterated food, were "harmless"; Congress could not forbid interstate transportation simply to discourage the perceived evil of child labor.[32]

Recognizing this distinction, Taft proceeded to misapply it, arguing only that interstate transportation encouraged auto theft—the very argument that he acknowledged had been held insufficient in *Hammer*.[33] He made no effort to show that stolen cars were harmful to anyone in the state to which they were transported.[34] He thus left *Hammer* dangling without visible support and exposed the Court to a serious charge of inconsistency.

Nevertheless there may be more to *Brooks* than a mere judicial conviction that car theft is worse than child labor. In upholding a federal ban on interstate transportation of lottery tickets, the Court had noted that Congress had merely "supplemented" state lottery laws by making clear that "it would not permit the declared policy of the States . . . to be overthrown or disregarded by the agency of interstate commerce."[35] In *Hammer* it had insisted that the commerce power could not be used "to control the States in their exercise of the police power over local trade and manufacture."[36] In *Clark Distilling Co. v. Western Maryland Railway*,[37] on which *Brooks* relied, the Court had upheld a federal statute forbidding the transportation of liquor into a state in which its use was prohibited. The pattern seems clear: it is easier to sustain a federal police measure that reinforces state policy than one that contradicts it. And the federal stolen car law, unlike the child labor law, was in aid of state policy.[38]

That congruence with state policy makes a regulation any more one of interstate commerce in the textual sense is a little difficult to swallow. To the extent that the *Hammer* limitation reflects the need to prevent use of the commerce power to undermine state autonomy, however, the distinction makes perfect sense. Taft did not put it in these terms, but the result he reached in *Brooks* followed logically from the premises that had underlain both of the Court's child labor decisions.

## 3.  Prohibition

The eighteenth amendment, which took effect in 1920, forbade "the manufacture, sale, or transportation of intoxicating liquors within, the importation thereof into, or the exportation thereof from the United States and all territory subject to the jurisdiction thereof for beverage purposes." Its second section gave "Congress and the several States . . . concur-

---

[32] *Hammer*, 247 U.S. at 271-72.

[33] *Brooks*, 267 U.S. at 438.

[34] *See id.* at 438-39. He might have argued, perhaps, that buyers in the receiving state would be injured by the possibility of having to return the vehicles to their rightful owners without compensation, but he did not.

[35] Lottery Case, 188 U.S. 321, 357 (1903).

[36] *Hammer*, 247 U.S. at 273-74.

[37] 242 U.S. 311 (1917), *supra* p. 96, note 38.

[38] For early arguments based on this distinction, see Bruce, *Interstate Commerce and Child-Labor*, 3 MINN. L. REV. 89, 99-100 (1919); Cushman, *The National Police Power under the Commerce Clause of the Constitution*, 3 MINN L. REV. 289, 300-08 (1919). The child labor law, as the Court in *Hammer* noted, had been defended on the ground that the law made it possible for some states to pursue policies against child labor by protecting themselves from outside competition; but it did so by undermining the contrary policy of other states. *See Hammer*, 247 U.S. at 273.

rent power to enforce this article by appropriate legislation."[39] As already noted, this "noble experiment" gave rise to a number of interesting search and seizure questions that the Court uniformly resolved in favor of law enforcement.[40] It also produced a bevy of decisions on more substantive issues, several of which were of lasting significance for their implications as to the interpretation of other grants of congressional power.

Except in two commerce clause decisions near the end of the nineteenth century,[41] the Supreme Court had always displayed a tolerant attitude toward efforts to limit the availability of alcoholic beverages. It had upheld state power to outlaw liquor manufacture even for the maker's own use or for shipment outside the state.[42] Even after overruling its earlier conclusion that the commerce clause allowed the states to forbid sales of out-of-state liquor in the original package,[43] the Court had permitted Congress both to remove the commerce clause barrier to state legislation and to make importation into a dry state a federal crime.[44] Finally, it had upheld a general federal prohibition law on the rather strained ground that it promoted the waging of a war whose fighting had already ended.[45] When the nation decided that previous measures were inadequate and that the Constitution itself should, for only the second time, outlaw private conduct,[46] the Court not only remained tolerant; it seemed to become an enthusiastic partisan.

Immediately before Taft was appointed, the Court in the *National Prohibition Cases* had rejected arguments that the eighteenth amendment exceeded the amending power reserved by article V and that the reference to "concurrent power" required joint state and federal action for the adoption of enforcing legislation.[47] Oddly, the Court pointedly announced only its "conclusions," without professing to supply any supporting reasons. Chief Justice White, who concurred, justly protested and gave a reason of his own for the

[39] U.S. CONST. amend. XVIII (repealed by amend. XXI in 1933). The third section, the constitutionality of which the Court upheld, *see infra* note 48, required that ratification take place within seven years.

[40] *See supra* pp. 162-69.

[41] Leisy v. Hardin, 135 U.S. 100, 118 (1890) (overruling The License Cases, 46 U.S. (5 How.) 504 (1847), which upheld state laws prohibiting sales of out-of-state liquor sold in original package); Bowman v. Chicago & N. Ry., 125 U.S. 465, 500 (1888) (state may not bar importation).

[42] Kidd v. Pearson, 128 U.S. 1, 23-24 (1888) (state may prohibit manufacturing of liquor intended for export); Mugler v. Kansas, 123 U.S. 623, 661-63 (1887) (state prohibition of manufacture of liquor does not infringe any right, privilege, or immunity secured by the Constitution); Bartemeyer v. Iowa, 85 U.S. (18 Wall.) 129, 133 (1847) (ordinary state legislation regulating or prohibiting sale of liquor raises no constitutional issue).

[43] Leisy v. Hardin, 135 U.S. 100, 118 (1890) (overruling The License Cases, 46 U.S. (5 How.) 504 (1847)).

[44] United States v. Hill, 248 U.S. 420, 425 (1919) (Congress may forbid interstate transportation of liquor without reference to the policy or law of any state); Clark Distilling Co. v. Western M. Ry., 242 U.S. 311, 322 (1917) (sustaining state law that forbade shipment or transportation of intoxicating liquor for personal use under Webb-Kenyon Act); *In re* Rahrer, 140 U.S. 545, 564 (1891) (sustaining federal act providing that imported liquor should be subject to state laws as if the liquor had been produced in the state itself).

[45] Hamilton v. Kentucky Distilleries & Warehouse Co., 251 U.S. 146, 163 (1919); Jacob Ruppert Corp. v. Caffey, 251 U.S. 264, 301 (1920).

[46] The only precedent was the thirteenth amendment's ban on slavery.

[47] National Prohibition Cases, 253 U.S. 350, 386-87 (1920) (Van Devanter, J.). Consideration of the explicit limitations on the amending power contained in article V ought to have squelched the argument that the general authority to amend did not mean what it said (despite the clever analogy to implicit sovereignty limits on the tax power drawn by counsel in Leser v. Garnett, 258 U.S. 130, 132 (1922)). The Convention itself had rejected the argument that its authority to propose amendments to the Articles of Confederation was implicitly limited to minor changes. *Compare* 1 THE RECORDS OF THE FEDERAL CONVENTION OF 1787, at 249 (M. Farrand rev. ed.

Court's conclusion: to require joint action would be incompatible with the apparent purpose of providing for effective enforcement.[48]

This conclusion effectively determined the result of the Taft Court's first encounter with
Prohibition: *Vigliotti v. Pennsylvania* held that a state prohibition law survived the adoption of the amendment.[49] The decision in *United States v. Lanza* that prosecution under a
state liquor law did not bar a federal prosecution for the same act was no more surprising,
because it had long been established that double jeopardy meant two prosecutions by the
same sovereign.[50]

---

minor changes. *Compare* 1 THE RECORDS OF THE FEDERAL CONVENTION OF 1787, at 249 (M. Farrand rev. ed.
1937) [hereinafter cited as M. FARRAND] (Lansing argued that "the power of the Convention was restrained to
amendments of a federal nature, and having for their basis the Confederacy in being"), *with id.* at 262 (Randolph
responded that "the whole of the confederation upon revision is subject to *amendment and alteration*") (emphasis
in original), *and* THE FEDERALIST No. 40, at 258-67 (J. Madison) (J. Cooke ed. 1961). *See also* Leser v. Garnett,
258 U.S. 130, 136 (1922) (Brandeis, J.) (rejecting argument that nineteenth amendment exceeded amending
power because admitting women to electorate destroyed states' political autonomy; the analogous fifteenth
amendment, which had extended vote to blacks, had been accepted as valid for half a century). *Leser* added that
state constitutions could not limit the ratification authority given state legislatures by article V and refused to look
behind official certifications to determine whether ratification had been accomplished in accordance with state
legislative procedures, *id.* at 137. For a sampling of arguments for implicit limitations on the amending power,
see Abbot, *Inalienable Rights and the Eighteenth Amendment*. 20 COLUM. L. REV. 183 (1920); Marbury, *Limits
upon the Amendment Power*, 33 HARV. L. REV. 223 (1919); Skinner, *Intrinsic Limits on the Power of Constitutional Amendment*, 18 MICH L. REV. 213 (1920); White, *Is There an Eighteenth Amendment?* 5 CORNELL L.Q.
113 (1920). For a response, see Frierson, *Amending the Constitution of the United States*, 33 HARV. L. REV. 659
(1920).

[48] National Prohibition Cases, 253 U.S. at 388-92. Not only would it have been bizarre to find that an amendment designed to eliminate alcoholic beverages had actually weakened the preexisting authority of state and
federal governments independently to outlaw liquor within their respective spheres, but in neither legislative nor
judicial contexts had "concurrent" traditionally meant (as McKenna and Clarke urged in dissent) "joint." Commerce clause decisions finding concurrent state power had upheld the authority of a state to act on its own, *see*
Needham, *The Exclusive Power of Congress over Interstate Commerce*, 11 COLUM. L. REV. 251, 256-57 (1911),
and the notion that two courts would share jurisdiction over the same case is little short of absurd. The Court's
construction does not deprive the mention of state authority of all force; the "concurrent" power provision both
precludes any implication of exclusive federal power and expands state authority over interstate and international
transactions. *See* United States v. Lanza, 260 U.S. 377, 381 (1922) (Taft, C. J.). Nevertheless, there were
respectable arguments for a surprising variety of alternative interpretations. *See, e.g.*, Cushing, *"Concurrent
Power" in the Eighteenth Amendment*, 8 CALIF. L. REV. 205 (1920); Dowling, *Concurrent Power under the
Eighteenth Amendment*, 6 MINN. L. REV. 447 (1922).

Before Taft's appointment, the prohibition amendment had given rise to two other interesting issues of
amendment procedure. *See* Dillon v. Gloss, 256 U.S. 368, 373, 375 (1921) (Van Devanter, J.) (upholding Congress's power to require ratification within seven years, finding in article V both an intention "to invest Congress
with a wide range of power in proposing amendments" and "a fair implication that [ratification] must be sufficiently contemporaneous . . . to reflect the will of the people in all sections at relatively the same period");
Hawke v. Smith, 253 U.S. 221, 230 (1920) (Day, J.) (holding that article V's provision for ratification by state
"legislatures" precluded states from imposing additional referendum requirement). Since the eighteenth amendment had been ratified within the specified period, it was not clear that there was an actual controversy over the
validity of the time limit. *See Dillon*, 256 U.S. at 369 (appellant argued that time limit "tended to destroy any
deliberation" on amendment). For a good contemporary discussion of these issues, see Dodd, *Amending the
Federal Constitution*, 30 YALE L.J. 321 (1921).

[49] 258 U.S. 403, 409 (1922) (Brandeis, J.). Day and McReynolds dissented without opinion. *Id.*

[50] 260 U.S. 377, 382 (1922) (Taft, C. J.) (citing, for example, Fox v. Ohio, 46 U.S. (5 How.) 410 (1847)). In
Taft's view, state authority to combat liquor was not derived from the amendment, which merely "put an end to

More controversial were the split decisions in *Grogan v. Hiram Walker & Sons, Ltd.*[51] and *Cunard Steamship Co. v. Mellon*[52] that the amendment's unqualified prohibitions of "transportation" and "importation" applied to sealed shipments across the United States and to sealed supples on board domestic and foreign ships in United States waters. Brushing aside the dissenters' precedents as inapposite, Holmes persuasively explained in *Grogan* that the amendment's ban on exportation of liquor suggested both a concern that liquor in transit might be deflected to local use and a desire to keep the country entirely out of the liquor business.[53] In *Cunard* Van Devanter, employing similar arguments as well as invoking *Grogan,* answered the respectable argument that provisions should be presumed not to infringe international law by citing precedents that narrowly defined the traditional immunity of foreign vessels in U.S. harbors.[54]

Most significant for future constitutional litigation, however, were three decisions of the Taft period giving a broad construction to Congress's authority under section 2 of the

---

restrictions upon the State's power arising from the Federal Constitution." Lanza, 260 U.S. at 381. He added a strong reason for the narrow interpretation of double jeopardy:

> If a State were to punish the manufacture, transportation and sale of intoxicating liquor by small or nominal fines, the race of offenders to the courts of that State to plead guilty and secure immunity from federal prosecution for such acts would not make for respect for the federal statute or for its deterrent effect.

*Id.* at 385.

[51] 259 U.S. 80 (1922).

[52] 262 U.S. 100 (1923).

[53] *Grogan,* 259 U.S. at 80-90. United States v. Gudger, 249 U.S. 373, 375 (1919), had held shipment across a state not to be transportation *"into* any State or Territory" within the meaning of an earlier statute, but the eighteenth amendment used the broader term "transportation . . . *within* . . . the United States." Cases giving a narrow interpretation to terms like "importation" for tariff purposes, *e.g.,* The Conqueror, 166 U.S. 110, 115 (1897), can be distinguished as based upon the distinct purposes of the tax laws. The argument for construing the amendment narrowly to avoid conflict with an earlier treaty was rejected by Holmes as a "makeweight[]" argument, insufficient to withstand the language and purpose of the new provision. *Grogan,* 259 U.S. at 88-89 ("The Eighteenth Amendment meant a great revolution in the policy of this country, and presumably and obviously meant to upset a good many things on as well as off the statute book."). That the treaty really authorized what the amendment forbade was not even clear: in allowing the passage of goods through the country without payment of tariffs, it arguably gave only an exemption from the tax laws.

[54] *Cunard,* 262 U.S. at 124-25 (citing The Exchange, 11 U.S. (7 Cranch) 116, 144 (1812) (holding a foreign warship immune from judicial process, but noting that merchant vessels would not be immune), and Wildenhus's Case, 120 U.S. 1, 11 (1887) (upholding punishment of a foreign seaman under U.S. law for killing another foreigner on a foreign ship in U.S. waters)). *See also id.* at 132-33 (Sutherland, J., dissenting). The respectability of Sutherland's premise—that long-standing traditions should be presumed not to have been overthrown—is confirmed by such cases as Hans v. Louisiana, 134 U.S. 1 (1890) (article III grant of judicial power implicitly subject to sovereign immunity), *supra* pp. 7-9; Collector v. Day, 78 U.S. (11 Wall.) 113 (1871) (state judge's salary implicitly immune from federal taxation), THE FIRST HUNDRED YEARS at 393 n. 172. *But cf.* Fitzpatrick v. Bitzer, 427 U.S. 445, 456 (1976), pp. 573-74 *infra.* Because the Court's precedents had shown that application of the amendment to foreign ships was consistent with the traditional rule that purely internal matters were governed by the law of the flag, its decision that the amendment applied to foreign ships in this country did not depend upon the further conclusion that the amendment's reference to "the United States and all territory subject to the jurisdiction thereof" displaced the traditional rule. It was the latter conclusion that led the Court to hold that the amendment did not apply to U.S. ships on the high seas, *Cunard,* 262 U.S. at 123-24, which arguably were of greater concern to U.S. policy than were foreign ships in New York harbor. *Cf.* D. Currie, *Flags of Convenience, American Labor, and the Conflict of Laws,* 1963 SUP. CT. REV. 34.

amendment "to enforce this article by appropriate legislation." In 1924, without dissent, Justice Sanford wrote in *James Everard's Breweries v. Day*[55] to uphold congressional authority to forbid the sale of malt liquors for medicinal purposes. The significant objection was that, like the fourteenth amendment, the eighteenth amendment gave Congress the power only to enforce its own provisions, and the amendment did not outlaw sales for medicinal use.

There were precedents that might appear to support this argument. The enforcement provisions of the fourteenth and fifteenth amendments, for instance, had rightly been held to authorize Congress to prohibit neither private racial discrimination nor the denial of the right to vote on grounds unrelated to race. As Justice Bradley had said in the *Civil Rights Cases,* the fourteenth amendment limited only "state" action, and Congress's sole authority was "to adopt appropriate legislation for correcting the effects of such prohibited State laws and State acts."[56]

Echoing *McCulloch v. Maryland's*[57] broad test for determining whether a measure was "necessary and proper" to the exercise of specific federal powers, Justice Sanford found the prohibition of medicinal beer an appropriate means of preventing beverage use:

> The opportunity to manufacture, sell and prescribe intoxicating malt liquors for "medicinal purposes," opens many doors to clandestine traffic in them as beverages under the guise of medicines; facilitates many frauds, subterfuges and artifices; aids evasion: and, thereby and to that extent, hampers and obstructs the enforcement of the Eighteenth Amendment.[58]

Thought Sanford did not say so, this passage served both to distinguish the fourteenth and fifteenth amendment cases, where the invalidated measures had not served to prevent evasion of the constitutional mandate,[59] and to make analogous the many decisions allowing Congress to regulate matters that were not themselves interstate commerce in order to further the constitutional purpose of keeping that commerce free.[60] He added that the measure could not be said to be arbitrary, in view of the lack of evidence that malt liquor had any significant medicinal value.[61]

---

[55] 265 U.S. 545 (1924).

[56] The Civil Rights Cases, 109 U.S. 3, 11 (1883). *See also* United States v. Harris, 106 U.S. 629 (1883) (invalidating federal law forbidding private denial of equal protection); United States v. Reese, 92 U.S. 214 (1876) (striking down voting rights law as overbroad). *See generally* THE FIRST HUNDRED YEARS at 393–402.

[57] 17 U.S. (4 Wheat.) 316 (1819).

[58] *Day,* 265 U.S. at 561.

[59] *Cf.* Katzenbach v. Morgan, 384 U.S. 641 (1966) (upholding prohibition of English literacy test for voting, in part because of risk that such a requirement might be a cover for racial discrimination), *infra* pp. 425-27; United States v. Price, 383 U.S. 787 (1966) (allowing federal punishment of private persons "jointly engaged" with state officers in killing civil rights workers without due process). The passage in *Day* also served to show, in contrast to the Child Labor Tax Case, *supra* pp. 173-74, that this prohibition was not a pretext for regulating the practice of medicine.

[60] *E.g.,* Houston, E. & W.T. Ry. v. United States, 234 U.S. 342 (1914) (the Shreveport Rate Case), *supra* pp. 93-96. Along the same lines was the conclusion of an undivided Court in United States v. Alford, 274 U.S. 264, 267 (1927) (Holmes, J.) ("Congress may prohibit the [setting of fires] upon privately owned lands that imperil the publicly owned forests," apparently under its article IV authority to make "Rules and Regulations respecting the Territory or other Property belonging to the United States," U. S. CONST. art. IV, § 3, cl. 2).

[61] *Day,* 265 U.S. at 561–62.

This decision seemed to make obvious the later holdings that Congress could both regulate the sale of denatured alcohol[62] and limit the amounts of wine and whiskey that doctors could prescribe.[63] Interestingly, however, four Justices dissented in the latter case, distinguishing *Day* on the ground that whiskey and wine, unlike beer, had real medicinal value.[64] Sanford had indeed mentioned the lack of medicinal value in the earlier case, but that other liquors had such value did not reduce the need to control them in order to avoid frustration of federal policy; no one had denied that the denatured alcohol Congress had unanimously been allowed to regulate had legitimate industrial uses.[65]

I am inclined to think that all the Prohibition decisions discussed in this section were rightly decided. In particular, the decisions respecting congressional power seem to have been substantially in accord with analogous commerce clause doctrine. It remains striking, however, that under the influence of the popular uprising that culminated in the adoption of the amendment, a Court so strict in its scrutiny of legislative means under the innocuous-looking due process clauses[66] would assume such a relaxed attitude in determining the appropriateness of means to achieve limited congressional goals—especially since nothing in the opinions suggested that the Court's principles of broad construction applied only to Prohibition cases.[67]

## II.   THE ALLOCATION OF FEDERAL POWERS

### A.   The Courts

From the beginning the Supreme Court had appeared to treat article III's vesting of "judicial" power to decide enumerated categories of "cases" and "controversies" in the federal

---

[62] Selzman v. United States, 268 U.S. 466, 469 (1925) (Taft, C. J.) ("It helps the main purpose of the Amendment . . . to hedge about the making and disposition of the denatured article every reasonable precaution and penalty to prevent the proper industrial use of it from being perverted to drinking it.").

[63] Lambert v. Yellowley, 272 U.S. 581, 589 (1926) (Brandeis, J.) ("That the limitation upon the amount of liquor which may be prescribed for medicinal purposes, is a provision adapted to promote the purpose of the amendment is clear.").

[64] *Id.* at 600-02 (Sutherland, J., dissenting, joined by McReynolds, Butler, and Stone, JJ.).

[65] Sutherland attempted to distinguish between regulation and prohibition of intoxicants, *id.* at 604-05 (Sutherland, J., dissenting), but the distinction seems at best a poor substitute for the argument, rejected in McCulloch v. Maryland, 17 U.S. (4 Wheat.) 315, 413-15 (1819), that Congress must use the least restrictive means. Moreover, it was not clear that Sutherland applied his own distinction correctly, for Congress had merely limited the amount that could be prescribed, not prohibited it altogether. *Cf.* pp. 28-29 *supra* (discussing The Lottery Case, 188 U.S. 321 (1903)). *Hammer's* notion that the tenth amendment somehow limited the powers granted to Congress, echoes of which appear in the *Lambert* dissent, had been flatly rejected in *Day:* "[I]f the act is within the power confided to Congress, the Tenth Amendment, by its very terms, has no application, since it only reserves to the States 'powers not delegated to the United States by the Constitution.'" James Everard's Breweries v. Day, 265 U.S. 545, 558 (1924).

[66] *See supra* pp. 139-46.

[67] For the most part, the opponents of broad construction of the eighteenth amendment were the traditional enemies of government regulation: Sutherland, McReynolds, and Butler. They were joined in dissent in the medicinal wine case, however, by Stone, who, though normally tolerant of legislative intervention, was said to have been a collector of fine wines. *See* A. MASON, HARLAN FISKE STONE: PILLAR OF THE LAW 726-33 (1956). Less out of line, perhaps, was the presence of Justice Van Devanter among those voting to uphold federal authority. Though a stubborn advocate of substantive due process, he had written some of the Court's broadest commerce clause decisions in his first days on the Court. *See supra* p. 94. Whether either the latter cases or his Prohibition record were consistent with his opinions during the later New Deal days is a matter best addressed after consideration of the latter cases.

courts as implicitly forbidding them to engage in other governmental functions.[68] This conclusion had been resoundingly confirmed in 1913 in *Muskrat v. United States*. There, on a variety of unpersuasive grounds, the Court had struck down a statute authorizing suit to determine the constitutionality of a law as providing in essence for an advisory opinion.[69] The Taft period afforded the Court several opportunities to expand on the definition of a case or controversy and produced a major opinion on judicial independence as well.

### 1. Parties

One aspect of the case-or-controversy limitation on which the Court had relied in *Muskrat* was the elementary requirement that there be two adverse parties—in order, among other things, to help ensure that both sides of the argument be vigorously presented in the interest of a sound decision.[70] In *Muskrat* the Court concluded that the United States, though expressly made a defendant by statute, was not a proper one because it had no interest adverse to that of the plaintiffs. In *Tutun v. United States*,[71] in contrast, the Court suggested that the United States might be a proper defendant in a proceeding to which it had never been made a party.

The question in *Tutun* was whether a person seeking U.S. citizenship could appeal the denial of his petition to a circuit court of appeals.[72] The answer depended upon finding that the naturalization proceeding was a "case" within the meaning of the appeal statute, and that, Justice Brandeis concluded, turned on whether it was a "case" or "controversy" in the constitutional sense.[73]

Practice, as Brandeis noted, yielded an affirmative answer: the federal courts had been passing upon naturalization petitions without objection since 1790.[74] The difficulty, however, was that naturalization was normally an ex parte proceeding. The applicant presented a petition, the court listened to his evidence, and it issued or denied a certificate. There was no requirement that anyone be named as a defendant or appear in opposition.[75]

Justice Brandeis, pointing to a statutory provision permitting the United States to be heard in opposition to any naturalization petition, responded that "[t]he United States is always a possible adverse party."[76] He did not say that the United States had opposed the petition in *Tutun*, and he carefully refrained from limiting his decision to cases in which it had. He appeared to conclude that it was enough that the government *might* oppose a petition if it chose to.

---

[68] *See e.g.*, Gordon v. United States, 69 U.S. (2 Wall.) 561 (1865); Hayburn's Case, 2 U.S. (2 Dall.) 409, 410-14 (1792). *See generally* THE FIRST HUNDRED YEARS at 6-13; Correspondence of the Justices, *reprinted in* H. HART & H. WECHSLER, THE FEDERAL COURTS AND THE FEDERAL SYSTEM 64–66 (2d ed. 1973).

[69] 219 U.S. 346, 361-63 (1911). *See supra* pp. 89-92.

[70] *Muskrat*, 219 U.S. at 361; *see also* Baker v. Carr, 369 U.S. 186, 204 (1962) ("Have the appellants alleged such a personal stake in the outcome of the controversy as to assure that concrete adverseness which sharpens the presentation of issues upon which the court so largely depends for illumination of difficult constitutional questions? This is the gist of the question of standing.").

[71] 270 U.S. 568 (1926).

[72] *Id.* at 574.

[73] *Id.* at 576.

[74] *Id.*

[75] Act of June 29, 1906, ch. 3592, § 11, 34 Stat. 596, 599.

[76] *Tutun*, 270 U.S. at 577 (citing Act of June 29, 1906, ch. 3592, § 11, 34 Stat. 596, 599).

If the United States actually opposes a particular naturalization claim, as it did in *Tutun*,[77] a controversy arises. It is difficult, however, to see how there can be any controversy until it does so. Only two years later the same Justice was to write for the Court in denying that a suit to remove a cloud from title presented a controversy because the allegedly adverse parties had not disputed the rights of the plaintiffs: "No defendant has wronged the plaintiff or has threatened to do so."[78] He did not explain how this conclusion could be reconciled with *Tutun*.[79]

In both *Muskrat* and *Tutun* the arguably missing party had been the defendant; in *Fairchild v. Hughes*[80] and *Massachusetts v. Mellon*[81] it was the plaintiff. In *Fairchild* Justice Brandeis rejected a citizen's challenge to the constitutionality of the procedure by which the nineteenth amendment was being ratified. The argument that a proclamation of the amendment's ratification would lead to invalid elections, said the Court, was not for the plaintiff to make:

> Plaintiff has only the right, possessed by every citizen, to require that the Government be administered according to law and that the public moneys be not wasted. Obviously this general right does not entitle a private citizen to institute in the federal courts a suit to secure by indirection a determination whether . . . a constitutional amendment about to be adopted, will be valid.[82]

In the second case Justice Sutherland wrote to hold that neither a state nor a federal taxpayer had standing to challenge a federal law providing for grants to promote maternal health: the state could neither sue in its sovereign capacity nor represent its citizens' interests against the United States, while the taxpayer's interest "is shared with millions of

[77] *See* Brief for Petitioner at 1, 5, Tutun v. United States, 270 U.S. 568 (1926).

[78] Willing v. Chicago Auditorium Ass'n, 277 U.S. 274, 288, 290 (1928) (Brandeis, J.); *see also* Liberty Warehouse Co. v. Grannis, 273 U.S. 70, 76 (1927) (Sanford, J.) (holding that a federal court had no jurisdiction to issue declaratory judgment). Indeed, along with Justice McReynolds, Brandeis was one of the Court's most vigorous exponents of the principle forbidding decision of unripe disputes. *See* Pennsylvania v. West Virginia, 262 U.S. 553, 603-23 (1923) (McReynolds, J., and Brandeis, J., dissenting in separate opinions); Terrace v. Thompson, 263 U.S. 197, 224 (McReynolds and Brandeis, JJ., dissenting ) (1923). In both cases, Brandeis and McReynolds dissented from decisions finding suits to enjoin the enforcement of state laws ripe. In *Terrace*, the remaining Justices concluded with much force that the threat to enforce a criminal statute against the plaintiffs created a traditional equitable controversy: "They are not obliged to take risk of prosecution, fines and imprisonment and loss of property in order to secure an adjudication of their rights." *Terrace*, 263 U.S. at 216.

[79] Nor did he draw the arguable conclusion that the long tradition of judicial naturalization proceedings showed that *Muskrat* had been wrong in holding adverse parties a requisite of a "case" or "controversy." Cf. Davis, *Standing: Taxpayers and Others*, 35 U. Chi. L. Rev. 601, 607 (1968) ("From the beginning, federal courts have performed many functions in addition to deciding 'questions presented in an adversary context.' Federal courts often decide questions of law and fact and discretion in absence of an adversary context, as they do whey they . . . admit aliens to citizenship when no issue arises. . . .").

[80] 258 U.S. 126 (1922).

[81] 262 U.S. 447 (1923).

[82] *Fairchild*, 258 U.S. at 129-30. Since the plaintiff resided in a state whose constitution already provided for women's suffrage, and since presidential voting is conducted on a state-by-state basis, it would have been hard for him to argue that the amendment would dilute his voting power. *See id.* at 129.

others; is comparatively minute and indeterminable; and the effect upon future taxation, of any payment out of the funds, so remote, fluctuating and uncertain, that no basis is afforded for an appeal to the preventive powers of a court of equity."[83]

The notion that a plaintiff could sue only to redress an injury of his own was by no means new.[84] What may have been new, despite the quoted reference in *Mellon* to "the preventive powers of a court of equity," was the attribution of this rule to the case-or-controversy requirement of article III. Justice Brandeis was unequivocal in *Fairchild:* "In form [this proceeding] is a bill in equity; but it is not a case within the meaning of § 2 of Article III of the Constitution. . . ."[85] In *Mellon* too the Court explicitly invoked article III in holding that the state could not sue, and it ended its opinion with a passage that seemed to say that the Constitution controlled the taxpayer's suit as well: because "the parties plaintiff" had not alleged "direct injury as the result of . . . enforcement" of the challenged measure, to grant them relief "would be not to decide a judicial controversy but to assume a position of authority over the governmental acts of another and co-equal department, an authority which plainly we do not possess."[86]

That article III should require an interested plaintiff follows from the same considerations of optimal decision-making that require an interested defendant. Justice Sutherland's closing comment, moreover, suggested that the standing limitation implicated separation-of-powers concerns as well. "We have no power *per se,*" he had said earlier in the same opinion, "to review and annul acts of Congress on the ground that they are unconstitutional."[87] Judicial review was only the power "of ascertaining and declaring the law applicable to the controversy. It amounts to little more than the negative power to disregard an unconstitutional enactment, which otherwise would stand in the way of the enforcement of a legal right."[88]

It seems clear enough that the case-or-controversy limitation has something to do with separation of powers, and that it serves, among other things, to avoid the decision of unnecessary constitutional questions. It is also true that in describing judicial review as merely the inevitable consequence of deciding cases and controversies Sutherland was echoing something that Marshall had said in justifying the doctrine in *Marbury v. Madison.*[89] Sutherland exhibited no awareness, however, of *Marbury's* equally prominent insistence that judicial review had to be inferred in order that constitutional limitations on Congress be respected: judicial review was no mere incident but an essential element in a system of checks and balances.[90]

In this light, far from reinforcing the result in *Mellon*, *Marbury* gives rise to an argument that the case was wrongly decided: if no one has standing to challenge a federal

---

[83] *Mellon*, 262 U.S. at 487.

[84] *See, e.g.,* Owings v. Norwood's Lessee, 9 U.S. (5 Cranch) 344, 348 (1809).

[85] *Fairchild.* 258 U.S. at 129.

[86] *Mellon*, 262 U.S. at 480–85, 488–89.

[87] *Id.* at 488.

[88] *Id.*

[89] 5 U.S. (1 Cranch) 137, 177-78 (1803) ("Those who apply the rule to particular cases, must of necessity expound and interpret the rule. . . . So, if a law be in opposition to the constitution; . . . the court must determine which of these conflicting rules governs the case. . . .").

[90] *Marbury,* 5 U.S. (1 Cranch) at 178 (to require the courts to "close their eyes on the constitution . . . would be giving to the legislature a practical and real omnipotence, with the same breath which professes to restrict those powers within narrow limits"). *See* THE FIRST HUNDRED YEARS at 66-74.

spending program, there is no way to prevent unconstitutional spending. Of course this argument cannot justify judicial action in the absence of the case or controversy the Constitution requires, but it may help in determining just what a case or controversy is.[91]

That a state could not sue to protect merely sovereign interests was not at all obvious. Not only would such a proceeding assure judicial review of actions that might otherwise go unreviewed, but the state seems a logical defender of the position that state rights have been invaded by federal legislation—and that was the claim in *Mellon*. Unfortunately for Massachusetts, however, the lack of standing on this basis had been established in two major nineteenth-century decisions; despite the striking contrast of an intervening Holmes opinion,[92] it was not surprising that the Court elected to follow them.[93]

The Court's argument with respect to the state's representative claim was shakier. Although the state had been permitted to speak for its citizens in suing other states, said Sutherland, "it is no part of its duty or power to enforce their rights in respect of their relations with the Federal Government. In that field it is the United States, and not the State, which represents them as *parens patriae*. . . ."[94] Neither authority nor argument was offered to support this conclusion, and it seems no less appropriate for the state to represent its citizens against the United States than against anyone else. Nevertheless Sutherland seems to have reached the right result, even if on the wrong ground: since the state's alleged right to sue was based upon representation of its citizens, it could sue only to enforce their rights, and no one had identified any citizen whose rights the federal law infringed.

Most interesting and influential was the final conclusion that Frothingham, the taxpayer, also lacked standing to sue. Her argument was straightforward: if the contested payments were made, "this plaintiff . . . will be subjected to taxation to pay her propor-

[91] *See* J. PASCHAL, MR. JUSTICE SUTHERLAND: A MAN AGAINST THE STATE 149 (1951): "[P]erhaps no other single decision in the Court's history has been fraught with such destructive implications for the idea of limited government," an idea for which Sutherland fought continually in his opinions on the merits. Compare the question whether the critical function of judicial review places implicit limits on Congress's express article III authority to make "exceptions" to the Supreme Court's appellate jurisdiction. *See* THE FIRST HUNDRED YEARS at 304-07 (discussing *Ex parte* McCardle, 74 U.S. (7 Wall.) 506 (1869)).

[92] Missouri v. Holland, 252 U.S. 416, 431 (1920).

[93] *See* Georgia v. Stanton, 73 U.S. (6 Wall.) 50 (1868) *cited in Mellon*, 262 U.S. at 483-84; Cherokee Nation v. Georgia, 30 U.S. 1 (1831); *see also* THE FIRST HUNDRED YEARS at 122-26, 302-04; *accord*, New Jersey v. Sargent, 269 U.S. 328 (1926) (Van Devanter, J.). Shortly before *Mellon*, however, in upholding the standing of a state to challenge a federal treaty, the Court had declined to rest its decision solely upon the government's concession that the state had standing as owner of the migratory birds affected by the treaty. Rather, the Court had emphasized that "it is enough that the bill is a reasonable and proper means to assert the alleged quasi-sovereign rights of a State." Missouri v. Holland, 252 U.S. 416, 431 (1920). *See* Corwin, *Constitutional Law in 1919-1920*, 15 AM. POL. SCI. REV. 52, 54-55 n.52 (1921) (arguing that this decision seemed to undermine *Stanton*). The references to "political" questions in *Mellon*, 262 U.S. at 484-85, like those in *Stanton*, 73 U.S. (6 Wall) at 50, 56, seem to mean that the "rights" asserted by the state were political, not that the issue on the merits was beyond judicial competence.

[94] *Mellon*, 262 U.S. at 485-86. For the state's authority in interstate suits, the Court correctly cited Missouri v. Illinois, 180 U.S. 208, 241 (1901) (suit to abate water pollution), which was reaffirmed immediately after *Mellon* in Pennsylvania v. West Virginia, 262 U.S. 533, 592 (1923) (Van Devanter, J.) (alternative holding). Even in this context, however, the Court tended to be somewhat chary, lest limitations on its original jurisdiction be circumvented. *See, e.g.,* New Hampshire v. Louisiana, 108 U.S. 76, 81 (1883), THE FIRST HUNDRED YEARS at 420 n. 122, *reaff'd in* North Dakota v. Minnesota, 263 U.S. 365, 372-76 (1923) (Taft, C. J.) (allowing state on behalf of its citizens to seek injunction but not damages).

tionate share of such unauthorized payments."[95] Sutherland's reply, already quoted, seemed to make three points: the interest of a federal taxpayer was "shared by millions of others"; it was "minute and indeterminable"; and the effect of payment on future taxation was "remote, fluctuating and uncertain."[96] In all these respects, said Sutherland, Frothingham differed from municipal taxpayers, who had been held to have standing to challenge expenditures.[97]

All of this has been severely criticized. Although Brandeis had noted in *Fairchild* that the right asserted by the plaintiff was one "possessed by every citizen,"[98] he had not said why that mattered. Contrary to Sutherland's suggestion that a flood of lawsuits in such circumstances would be undesirable,[99] one might think it all the more important that the government not get away with violating everybody's rights: one would not expect to find standing to challenge an unreasonable search denied on the ground that the government had unreasonably searched everyone in the country.[100] Sutherland offered no evidence to support his suggestion that the federal tax burden was smaller even in 1923 than the municipal one, and trespass cases were but one indication that the law had long permitted suit by persons suffering trivial harm.[101] More serious was the apparent suggestion that it was not clear whether enjoining the contested payments would reduce the plaintiff's taxes: Congress might have collected the money anyway and put it to some constitutional use. Of course this does not distinguish the municipal taxpayer, who the Court conceded had standing. Nor is it clear why the mere possibility that the plaintiff may not benefit from a decision that reduces the government's need for tax money should be held to destroy the adverse interest needed for sound decision-making—especially since the consequence seems to have been that no one could challenge most federal expenditures at all.

In short, Justice Sutherland seems right that an interested plaintiff was an element of the constitutional case-or-controversy requirement, but he did not satisfactorily explain why a federal taxpayer did not meet that description in the case before him.

## 2.  Finality and rulemaking

Apart from its arguably misplaced concern for a lack of proper parties, the Court in *Muskrat* had expressed concern about the nature of the remedy provided by the challenged

---

[95] *Mellon*, 262 U.S. at 477.

[96] *Id.* at 487 (quoted *supra* text accompanying note 83).

[97] *Id.* at 486-87 (citing Crampton v. Zabriskie, 101 U.S. 601, 609 (1879)). In Williams v. Riley, 280 U.S. 78, 80 (1929) (McReynolds, J.), a divided Court applied the *Frothingham* principle, without discussion, to preclude a taxpayer from challenging a *state* law. More surprisingly, it did so in a case in which the taxpayer appeared to challenge not an expenditure, but the collection of the tax itself. *Id.* at 79. However doubtful it may be that enjoining an expenditure will reduce the plaintiff's tax bill, there seems no doubt that enjoining collection of the tax will reduce the amount the plaintiff pays. The Court had entertained numerous suits to enjoin tax collection in the past and would continue to do so. *E.g.*, Educational Films Corp. v. Ward, 282 U.S. 379 (1931); Allen v. Baltimore & O.R.R., 114 U.S. 311 (1884).

[98] *See Fairchild*, 258 U.S. at 129.

[99] *Mellon*, 262 U.S. at 487.

[100] *See* United States v. SCRAP, 412 U.S. 669, 688 (1973) ("To deny standing to persons who are in fact injured simply because many others are also injured, would mean that the most injurious and widespread Government actions could be questioned by nobody. We cannot accept that conclusion."). The widespread nature of the harm would provide a political check not present when a narrow class or individual is alone damaged, but that would not defeat standing in the search case posed in the text.

[101] *See id.* at 685–90 (giving other examples).

jurisdictional provisions: a mere declaration of rights would not bind private parties.[102] On the facts of the case this argument too seems to have been misplaced: there was no evident reason to doubt that the lower court's decision would be entitled to res judicata effect. In *Postum Cereal Co. v. California Fig Nut Co.*,[103] however, the Court found an instance in which *Muskrat's* concern was apt. The Commissioner of Patents had rejected a request to cancel the registration of a trademark, and the District of Columbia Court of Appeals had refused review. Chief Justice Taft concluded that because the statute provided that a decision in such a proceeding would not "preclude any person interested from the right to contest the validity" of the trademark, the Supreme Court had no jurisdiction over the appeal: "The decision of the Court of Appeals . . . is not a judicial judgment. . . . In the exercise of such [administrative] function it does not enter a judgment binding parties in a case as the term case is used in the third article of the Constitution."[104]

With this decision it is hard to quarrel; a judicial pronouncement that would not bind the parties would literally be an advisory opinion. The difficulty was that in *Tutun v. United States*, decided just the previous year, the Court had held explicitly that the government's right to file a later suit to rescind citizenship did not destroy the justiciability of a naturalization proceeding.[105] Perhaps the decisions are reconcilable on the ground that the denaturalization provision went no further than traditional provisions for relief from illegal judgments,[106] but Taft did not seek to distinguish *Tutun*.

Four years before *Postum*, in *Keller v. Potomac Electric Power Co.*,[107] the Court had refused to review a decision of the District of Columbia appellate court setting aside an administrative order determining the value of utility property for rate purposes. Despite the superficial similarity of the two cases, however, it was not the advisory character of nonbinding decisions that dictated the result in *Keller*. Indeed the statute appeared to make the local court's decision immune from collateral review.[108] Chief Justice Taft called upon a still more fundamental dimension of the case-or-controversy requirement: an article III court may decide only *judicial* cases or controversies. The statute in question, Taft concluded, went beyond conferring on the courts the ordinary power to determine the legality of administrative action; in authorizing the court to "revise the legislative discretion of the Commission by . . . entering the order it deems the Commission ought to have made," Congress had attempted to confer the "legislative" power of "laying down new rules, to change present conditions and to guide future action," not the judicial power of "definition and protection of existing rights."[109] As the case itself illustrated, drawing the line be-

[102] Muskrat v. United States, 219 U.S. 346, 362 (1911).

[103] 272 U.S. 693 (1927) (Taft, C. J.).

[104] *Id.* at 698-99. *See* 35 U.S.C. § 62 (1929), *repealed by* Act of July 19, 1952, Pub. L. No. 593, § 5, 66 Stat. 792, 815.

[105] *Tutun*, 270 U.S. at 579–80. *See* H. HART & H. WECHSLER, *supra* note 68, at 95–97 (comparing the two decisions).

[106] *See Tutun*, 270 U.S. at 579 ("The remedy afforded the Government by [the cancellation provision] is narrower in scope than the review commonly afforded by appellate courts.").

[107] 261 U.S. 428 (1923) (Taft, C. J.).

[108] *See Keller*, 261 U.S. 439-40 ("Paragraph 65 limits the time within which such a proceeding . . . may be begun to 120 days, and thereafter the right to appeal or of recourse to the courts shall terminate absolutely.").

[109] *Id.* at 440,442 (citing Prentis v. Atlantic Coast Line Co., 211 U.S. 210, 226 (1908)). In *Prentis*, the Court had drawn a similar distinction for the different purpose of determining whether a federal challenge to a state rate order pending state-court review was barred either by the ban on enjoining state-court proceedings or by the doctrine of exhaustion of administrative remedies. As to exhaustion of remedies, the dominant consideration

tween judicial and legislative functions was not going to be easy;[110] but the principle that the courts could do only judicial business was certainly sound.


## 3. Declaratory judgments

In connection with its conclusion that the judgment Congress had sought to authorize would not bind the parties, the Court in *Muskrat* had added that "in a legal sense" such a judgment "could not be executed."[111] Against the background of Chief Justice Taney's dictum in *Gordon v. United States* that "[t]he award of execution is . . . an essential part of every judgment passed by a court exercising judicial power,"[112] this language could be read to suggest that no action seeking only a declaration of the rights of the litigants could be a case or controversy because such a judgment, even if binding, would not order anyone to do or refrain from doing anything. Two decisions of the Taft period seemed to lend additional force to this position.

The first was *Liberty Warehouse Co. v. Grannis*,[113] in which the Court unanimously affirmed a federal trial court's refusal to entertain a suit seeking a declaration that a state statute regulating the plaintiffs' tobacco business was unconstitutional. Without saying exactly why, Justice Sanford concluded that the case was governed by *Muskrat*. In listing the elements of an article III case or controversy he noted that there had to be "real parties," a "real case," and the possibility of "pronouncing and carrying into effect a judgment," and in summing up the facts he observed that "no relief of any kind is prayed" against the state officer who had been sued.[114] The second case was *Willing v. Chicago Auditorium Association*.[115] There, in holding that article III precluded a federal court from removing an alleged "cloud" on a lessee's right to replace a building, Justice Brandeis stated flatly that what the plaintiff sought was "simply a declaratory judg-

---

should be whether the state court's decision would be preclusive, for if the court's decision is entitled to res judicata effect, a doctrine designed only to postpone federal litigation will preclude it altogether. *See* Bacon v. Rutland R.R., 232 U.S. 134, 137 (1914); D. CURRIE, FEDERAL COURTS: CASES AND MATERIALS 506 (4th ed. 1990) (citing H. FRIENDLY, FEDERAL JURISDICTION: A GENERAL VIEW 101 (1973)).

[110] Although, in *Keller*, the Court held that article III forbade substitution of a court's judgment for that of an administrative agency, *see supra* notes 107-10 and accompanying text, in Ohio Valley Water Co. v. Ben Avon Borough, 253 U.S. 287, 291 (1920), and in Ng Fung Ho v. White, 259 U.S. 276, 284-85 (1922), the Court had held that due process *required* it. *See supra* p. 110, note 123, and p. 146, note 60. Thus it can hardly have been de novo review, as such, that made the court's function in *Keller* legislative rather than judicial, but rather the nature of the issue the court was to consider. In *Ng Fung Ho*, the question was whether to deport a person claiming to be a citizen, *Ng Fung Ho*, 259 U.S. at 282; in *Ben Avon* it was whether to set aside a utility rate as confiscatory, *Ben Avon*, 253 U.S. at 287-88. In both, in *Keller's* terms, the court had been asked merely to determine existing rights, not to lay down a new rule to govern future controversies.

[111] *Muskrat*, 219 U.S. at 362; *see also id.* at 361 ("The object is not to assert a property right as against the Government, or to demand compensation for alleged wrongs. . . .").

[112] 117 U.S. 697, 702 (draft opinion). The case had been decided without opinion, 69 U.S. (2 Wall.) 561 (1867), after Taney's death, and there is no evidence that the Court had approved his reasoning. Nor was the passage referred to necessary to the result; even Taney based his conclusion on the statutory provision for executive review of the court's decision. *Gordon*, 117 U.S. at 702-03.

[113] 273 U.S. 70 (1927).

[114] *Id.* at 73-74.

[115] 277 U.S. 274 (1928).

ment" and that to "grant that relief is beyond the power conferred upon the federal judiciary."[116]

Concurring in the result in *Willing* on the ground that the suit was not "within the equity jurisdiction conferred" by statute, Justice Stone politely tweaked Brandeis for deciding more than was necessary: "There is certainly no 'case or controversy' before us requiring an opinion on the power of Congress to incorporate the declaratory remedy into our federal jurisprudence."[117] Indeed, apart from Stone's statutory argument, Brandeis's own opinion reveals a narrower ground for his holding: "No defendant has wronged the plaintiff or has threatened to do so."[118] The same was true in *Grannis*, where Justice Sanford had emphasized the absence of any allegation "that the plaintiffs have done or contemplate doing any of the things forbidden by the Act before being advised by the court as to their rights, [or] . . . that the [defendant] has threatened to take or contemplates taking any action against them."[119] Under these circumstances there might well have been in Sanford's terms no "real case" and no "real parties" in either *Grannis* or *Willing*, even if coercive relief had been sought; neither case need be taken to establish that a declaratory judgment was unavailable in an actual dispute between adverse parties.[120]

Just the year before *Willing*, in fact, Justice Stone had written an opinion for the Court that appeared to conclude, in no uncertain terms, that in such circumstances declaratory relief would be entirely consistent with article III.[121] The question was whether a state court decision in a suit by a city to determine the validity of a tax assessment was entitled to res judicata effect; that depended, according to Stone, on whether the state proceeding had satisfied the case-or-controversy requirement.[122] The Court held that it had, although

---

[116]*Willing*, 277 U.S. at 289 (citing *Grannis*, 273 U.S. at 74). Brandeis may have meant only that no statute authorized such relief. *See* Borchard, *The Constitutionality of Declaratory Judgments*, 31 COLUM. L. REV. 561, 600 (1931).

[117]*Willing*, 277 U.S. at 290–91. The Conformity Act, which required federal courts to follow state procedural rules and might have been thought to embrace state-created remedies, applied only to actions at law, and *Willing* was a suit in equity. In equity cases, Congress had, by negative implication, prescribed adherence to federal equity practice. Conformity Act of 1872, ch. 255, § 5, 17 Stat. 196 (1873). *See also Grannis*, 273 U.S. at 76 (rejecting the argument that the Conformity Act justified federal use of Kentucky declaratory judgment statute: former act "relates only to 'practice, pleadings, and forms and modes of procedure'; and neither purports to nor can extend the jurisdiction of the district courts beyond the constitutional limitations").

[118]*Willing*, 277 U.S. at 290. *See also id.* at 288 (explaining that the lessors, although made defendants, had not taken a firm position denying the right the plantiff claimed).

[119]*Grannis*, 273 U.S. at 73. Borchard was sharply critical of this reasoning. *See* Borchard, *supra* note 116, at 585-89. He noted that the defendant had gone so far as to prepare an indictment against the plaintiff, citing the *Euclid* and *Pierce* cases, *supra* pp. 146, 154, in which the Court had enjoined the enforcement of statutes, as evidence that the Court had not generally required a threat of enforcement, and he persuasively argued that "no civilized legal system operating under a constitution" should in effect inform "the prospective victim that the only way to determine whether the suspect is a mushroom or a toadstool is to eat it."

[120]Keenly sensitive to the dangers of deciding premature constitutional issues, Justice Brandeis several times dissented from constitutional decisions of this period on the ground that there was an insufficient threat of harm to justify judicial intervention under article III even when traditional coercive relief was requested. *See supra* note 78. Holmes, however, appeared to think that the invalidity of the declaratory procedure had been settled by *Grannis* and that *Willing* reaffirmed it: "'I do not care to join in the criticism of his [Brandeis's] opinion,' he wrote on his copy of Stone's concurrence [in *Willing*], 'but I also regret his conclusion that we cannot render declaratory judgments—which, however, I thought had been stated heretofore.'" A. MASON, *supra* note 67, at 246.

[121]*See* Fidelity Nat'l Bank & Trust Co. v. Swope, 274 U.S. 123 (1927).

[122]*Id.* at 130-31.

it had resulted only in a declaration that the taxpayers were liable: "While ordinarily a case or controversy results in a judgment requiring award of process of execution to carry it into effect, such relief is not an indispensable adjunct to the exercise of the judicial function."[123] Commendably cited for this conclusion were "suits . . . for the construction of a will," "bills to quiet title," and *Tutun v. United States,* written by Brandeis himself, which had upheld judicial power to issue a certificate of naturalization.[124] The year after *Willing* this language was repeated approvingly in an opinion for the Court by Chief Justice Taft.[125]

In short, as the result of decisions during the Taft period, the contours of the case-or-controversy limitation seemed to be shaping up pretty clearly. Aside from the embarrassing problem of naturalization, there had to be interested parties on both sides; there had to be actual harm or threat of harm; the determination must be of a judicial rather than legislative nature and must be binding on the parties. Despite unnecessarily broad statements in *Muskrat, Grannis,* and *Willing,* the stage seemed to be set for the Court to entertain requests for declaratory judgments that would finally settle ripe and concrete disputes between adverse parties.

## 4. Independence

In the *Keller* and *Postum* cases the Supreme Court held it could not review the decision of a District of Columbia court in a nonjudicial proceeding. At the same time, however, it confirmed the authority of the local courts over the same proceedings. Not all limitations that restricted congressional power to legislate within the states, Taft explained, were applicable to the District. There, by virtue of article I's grant of authority "[t]o exercise exclusive legislation in all cases whatsoever," Congress had all the powers of a state legislature: "Subject to the guaranties of personal liberty in the amendments and in the original Constitution, Congress has as much power to vest courts of the District with a variety of jurisdiction and powers as a state legislature has in conferring jurisdiction on its courts."[126]

It was obvious enough from the text that article I was meant to give Congress the power

---

[123] *Id.* at 132.

[124] *Id.* Also on point were bills to remove existing clouds from titles, which Brandeis had seemed to concede in *Willing* were traditionally cognizable by the courts. *Willing,* 277 U.S. at 288. Unlike Stone's other examples, the naturalization proceeding resulted not simply in a declaration of existing rights, but in a change of status. *See* Borchard, *The Declaratory Judgment—A Needed Procedural Reform,* 28 YALE L.J. 1, 4-5 (1918) (arguing for broader remedy). It was, however, convincing evidence that the existence of a case or controversy did not depend upon the availability of coercive relief.

[125] Old Colony Trust Co. v. Commissioner, 279 U.S. 716, 725 (1929) (alternative holding) (upholding judicial authority to review decision of Board of Tax Appeals approving deficiency assessment). "[I]t is not necessary, in order to constitute a judicial judgment that there should be . . . power to issue formal execution to carry the judgment into effect. . . ." *Id.* Though this statement was qualified by the argument that "[a] judgment is sometimes regarded as properly enforceable through the executive departments instead of through an award of execution by the Court, where the effect of the judgment is to establish the duty of the department to enforce it," the Court went on to cite *Swope* for the more general proposition that "the award of execution is not an indispensable element." *Id.*

[126] Keller v. Potomac Elec. Power Co., 261 U.S. 428, 442-43 (1923); *accord* Postum Cereal Co. v. California Fig Nut Co., 272 U.S. 693, 700 (1927).

to regulate matters of local concern in the District; federalism concerns have no place in territory over which Congress has exclusive jurisdiction. It did not necessarily follow, however, that the District of Columbia provision also did away with limitations, such as the case-or-controversy requirement, that reflected the distinct philosophy of separation of powers. Taft conceded that Congress's power over the District was limited by constitutional "guaranties of personal liberty"; he needed to explain why it was not limited by article III's case-or-controversy requirement as well.

His sole effort to do so was the suggestion in *Postum* that courts of the District were not courts "established under Article III." [127] The implication seemed to be that, under its power to legislate for the District of Columbia, Congress could establish courts that met none of the requirements of article III: neither the limitation to disputes of national significance listed in § 2, nor the case-or-controversy limitation, nor the requirements of tenure and irreducible compensation in § 1. [128]

Like the case-or-controversy limitation, the tenure and salary provisions promote the separation of powers: they assure the litigant the protection of an independent judge. [129] There was no reason as an original matter to think judicial independence less important in the District than elsewhere. The Court had held in Marshall's time, however, that courts could be created in the territories without reference to the requirements for establishing courts within the states. [130] If this was true of the territories, it might also be true of the District, which was in a similarly anomalous position; although the transitoriness of the territories meant that application of the tenure requirement there would have created a problem of surplus judges inapplicable to the District, that had not been Marshall's reason for decision. [131]

None of this was said in *Keller* or in *Postum*. Justice Van Devanter said it, however, in *Ex parte Bakelite Corp.* [132] in 1929, upholding the authority of the Court of Customs Appeals to render what appeared to be an advisory opinion. *Keller, Postum,* and the territorial cases, he announced, had "settled that Article III does not express the full authority of Congress to create courts, and that other Articles invest Congress with powers in the exertion of which it may create inferior courts and clothe them with functions deemed essential or helpful in carrying those powers into execution." [133] Because the Court of Customs Appeals had not been created pursuant to article III, it was not subject to article

---

[127] *Postum,* 272 U.S. at 700.

[128] U. S. CONST. art. III, §§ 1, 2.

[129] *See, e.g.,* THE FEDERALIST NO. 78, at 529 (A. Hamilton) (J. Cooke ed. 1961) ("That inflexible and uniform adherence to the rights of the constitution and of individuals, which we perceive to be indispensable in the courts of justice, can certainly not be expected from judges who hold their offices by a temporary commission."); THE FEDERALIST NO. 79, at 531 (A. Hamilton) (J. Cooke ed. 1961) ("And we can never hope to see realised in practice the complete separation of the judicial from the legislative power, in any system, which leaves the former dependent for pecuniary resources on the occasional grants of the latter.").

[130] American Ins. Co. v. Canter, 26 U.S. (1 Pet.) 511, 546 (1828), THE FIRST HUNDRED YEARS at 119.

[131] *See* O'Donoghue v. United States, 289 U.S. 516, 535-38 (1933) (distinguishing the District on this ground). *But see* Palmore v. United States, 411 U.S. 389, 405-07 (1973) (taking it back), *infra* p. 593, note 243.

[132] 279 U.S. 438 (1929). The statute in question empowered the President to impose sanctions on importers whom he found guilty of unfair practices. The Court of Customs Appeals was authorized to review administrative determinations that were merely recommendations to the President. *Id.* at 446-47. *Cf.* THE FIRST HUNDRED YEARS at 6 (discussing Hayburn's Case, 2 U.S. (2 Dall.) 409 (1792)).

[133] *Bakelite,* 279 U.S. at 449.

III's limitations. It was thus unnecessary to decide whether the business at hand constituted a case or controversy. And in unmistakable dictum the Court added that the judges of the Court of Customs Appeals held office only "for such term as Congress prescribes."[134]

In so concluding, the Court took a giant step beyond the precedents. Both the territorial and District of Columbia cases had expressly relied on the special status of those areas. It was one thing to hold article III inapplicable to areas outside the states. It was quite another to hold that article III could be evaded within the states themselves. Marshall had flatly said in the first territorial case that the latter could not be done: although the territories were subject to a different rule, "admiralty jurisdiction can be exercised in the states in those Courts, only, which are established in pursuance of the third article of the Constitution."[135] This dictum had been resoundingly confirmed when the Court overturned the court-martial conviction of a civilian in *Ex parte Milligan:* "One of the plainest constitutional provisions was, therefore, infringed when Milligan was tried by a court not ordained and established by Congress, and not composed of judges appointed during good behavior."[136]

Apparently alert to the danger that the *Bakelite* decision posed to article III's goal of an independent judiciary, Justice Van Devanter took steps to limit the extent of the damage: "Legislative" courts not enjoying article III protections could be created not in all cases but only—apart from special geographical areas—"to examine and determine various matters, arising between the government and others, which from their nature do not require judicial determination and yet are susceptible of it."[137] This formulation was taken from the 1856 decision in *Murray's Lessee v. Hoboken Land & Improvement Co.,*[138] which had held that article III did not forbid the government to collect its debts by seizing the debtor's property. Customs duties, Van Devanter concluded, could be collected in the same way; thus the collection of customs could be entrusted to a court whose judges lacked the tenure guaranteed by article III.[139]

---

[134]*Id.* at 449-50, 460-61.

[135]American Ins. Co. v. Canter, 26 U.S. (1 Pet.) 511, 546 (1828).

[136]71 U.S. (4 Wall.) 2, 122 (1867) (alternative holding). *See* THE FIRST HUNDRED YEARS at 288. *Milligan* conceded that article III did not forbid the court-martial of military personnel for service-connected crimes, as had been acknowledged in Dynes v. Hoover, 61 U.S. (20 How.) 65, 79 (1858) (dictum). But the fact that article III was held not to have displaced the tradition of extraordinary military trials would hardly have been an excuse for holding that article III imposed no limitation at all. *See* Currie, *Bankruptcy Judges and the Independent Judiciary,* 16 CREIGHTON L. REV. 441, 449 (1983).

[137]*Bakelite,* 279 U.S. at 451.

[138]59 U.S. (18 How.) 272, 284 (1856) ("[T]here are matters, involving public rights, which may be presented in such form that the judicial power is capable of acting on them, and which are susceptible of judicial determination, but which congress may or may not bring within the cognizance of the courts of the United States, as it may deem proper."). *See* THE FIRST HUNDRED YEARS at 272.

[139]*Bakelite,* 279 U.S. at 458. That due process really permitted taxes to be collected without even a subsequent opportunity for hearing on the question whether they were due seems doubtful in light of Ward v. Love County, 253 U.S. 17, 24 (1920): "To say that the county could collect these unlawful taxes by coercive means and not incur any obligation to pay them back is nothing short of saying that it could take or appropriate the property of these Indian allottees arbitrarily and without due process of law." For a valiant effort to explore the limits of the principle that matters not "inherently" judicial could be entrusted to legislative tribunals, see Katz, *Federal Legislative Courts,* 43 HARV. L. REV. 894 (1930). *See also Bakelite,* 279 U.S. at 452-55 (dictum) (concluding that the Court of Claims was a legislative court because government debts had long been paid by legislative or executive action and because government's creditors had no "right to sue . . . unless Congress consents").

The *non sequitur* was glaring. *Murray's Lessee* held only that article III did not require that courts always be used. When they are used, however, article III leaves no doubt about the tenure or salary of their judges.[140]

## B. The Executive and Congress

### 1. *Myers v. United States*

In 1789 Congress had carefully amended a bill establishing the Department of Foreign Affairs to provide not that the Secretary would be "removable by the President," but that his subordinate would assume certain functions "whenever the said principal officer shall be removed from office by the President of the United States"—in order, the sponsor of the amendment said, to avoid any implication that the power of removal was for Congress to give or withhold.[141] In 1867 President Johnson was impeached but not convicted for discharging the Secretary of War in violation of an 1867 statute effectively requiring Senate consent for his removal.[142] In 1926, in *Myers v. United States*,[143] a divided Court held that Congress could not constitutionally require Senate consent for the discharge of a postmaster who had been appointed by the President with the consent of the Senate.

*Myers* was a battle royal. In sharp contrast with most constitutional decisions of the period, the various opinions cover nearly two hundred pages. The depth of historical research on both sides was impressive. Relying heavily on the 1789 incident and dismissing the 1867 statute as an aberration reflecting the excesses of the Reconstruction Congress in a time of crisis, ex-President Taft produced his most prodigious opinion in a case that was obviously close to his heart. The power to remove executive officers, he argued, was an element of the "executive Power" granted the President by article II and "an incident of the power to appoint them," which the same article conferred. Moreover, article II also directed the President to "take Care that the Laws be faithfully executed." This he could do only "by the assistance of subordinates"; it would be unreasonable to conclude that Congress could "fasten[] upon him, as subordinate executive officers, men who by their inefficient service under him, by their lack of loyalty to the service, or by their different view of policy, might make his taking care that the laws be faithfully executed most difficult or impossible."[144]

In separate dissents McReynolds and Brandeis offered an alternative view of history and an alternative interpretation of the constitutional provisions. Removal itself might be an executive act, but determining the conditions for removal was a legislative function committed to Congress under the necessary and proper clause. The executive power

---

[140] Moreover, as the second Justice Harlan pointed out many years later, the fact that Congress might have had power to create a legislative court did not prove it had done so. Glidden Co. v. Zdanok, 370 U.S. 530, 549-51 (1962) (plurality opinion). The premise of *Murray's Lessee*, on which the *Bakelite* Court relied, had been that Congress had a choice whether or not to entrust to a court matters not inherently judicial.

[141] See Myers v. United States, 272 U.S. 52, 111-15 (1926) (quoting 1 ANNALS OF CONG. 370-71, 383, 455, 576, 578-80, 585, 591 (1789); Act of July 27, 1789, ch. 4, § 2, 1 Stat. 28, 29.

[142] See Myers, 272 U.S. at 166; Act of March 2, 1867, ch. 154, 14 Stat. 430 (providing that officers appointed with Senate consent hold office until approval of their successors).

[143] 272 U.S. 52 (1926).

[144] Id. at 117, 131, 161, 175-76. For Justice Stone's substantial role in the reworking of Taft's opinion, see A. MASON, *supra* note 67, at 225-32.

vested in the President was only that which was expressly enumerated. The Reconstruction Congress was not alone in enacting restrictions on removal; the Court had upheld one in *United States v. Perkins* in 1886. The 1789 incident was ambiguous, and nobody doubted that Congress could inhibit a President's control of his subordinates by rejecting his nominees or by prescribing qualifications for office.[145]

As a purely textual matter, a variety of conclusions would have been plausible. At one extreme, the provision for removal upon impeachment for high crimes and misdemeanors[146] might have been taken to imply that otherwise officers were not removable at all. Alternatively, Taft's argument that the power of removal implicitly went along with that of appointment might have led to the conclusion that Senate approval was always required to remove officers whose appointments were subject to Senate consent—whether Congress wanted it that way or not.[147] Finally, there were the contrasting positions embraced by the various Justices: that the manner of removal had been left to Congress by the necessary and proper clause, and that Congress's power was limited by the grants of executive authority in article II.[148]

Taken together, the opinions suggest that history, while rich in relevant materials, yields no clear understanding of the correct interpretation.[149] If that is so, the central question boils down to whether—judicial precedents for the moment to one side—one interpretation or another is more consistent with the general purposes of the Framers. On that issue the Chief Justice seems to have had a strong argument: Presidents cannot effectively carry out their constitutional obligation to see that the laws are faithfully executed if they cannot control their subordinates, and they cannot control them without authority to remove. Senate power to prevent appointments, specifically provided in article II, seems to represent the extent to which the Framers were willing to compromise the President's authority, and it does not require the President to work with those who would contradict his orders.[150] Finally, as the Chief Justice argued,

---

[145] *See Myers,* 272 U.S. at 178-295. Holmes added a brief dissent, *id.* at 177, essentially on the ground that it was up to Congress to decide whether or not to create the office of postmaster.

[146] U. S. CONST. art II, § 4.

[147] *See* THE FEDERALIST NO. 77, at 515 (A. Hamilton) (J. Cooke ed. 1961) ("The consent of that body would be necessary to displace as well as to appoint."). Taft rejected this conclusion on the ground that the consent requirement had been based upon the need to assure small states a voice on the staffing of offices, not on "any desire to limit removals." *Myers,* 272 U.S. at 119-20, 164.

[148] Compare the similarly knotty question whether the President alone may terminate a treaty made with Senate consent under article II, § 2. *See* Goldwater v. Carter, 444 U.S. 996 (1979) (where the majority found a suit attempting to raise this question nonjusticiable).

[149] *See* Corwin, *Tenure of Office and the Removal Power under the Constitution,* 27 COLUM. L. REV. 353 (1927) (painstakingly attacking Taft's view of history).

[150] The latter consideration also serves to distinguish the power of Congress to prescribe qualifications for office, so stressed by Brandeis in dissent. *See Myers,* 272 U.S. at 264-74. For the position that Taft's argument for presidential control was of less force with respect to officials below the Cabinet level, see Corwin, *supra* note 149, at 394-95; Van Alstyne, *The Role of Congress in Determining Incidental Powers of the President and of the Federal Courts: A Comment on the Horizontal Effect of the Sweeping Clause,* LAW & CONTEMP. PROBS., Spring 1976, at 102, 114-15. *Cf.* Branti v. Finkel, 445 U.S. 507, 517 (1980) (dictum) (first amendment does not forbid discharge of certain key officers for political reasons); Elrod v. Burns, 427 U.S. 347;, 366–67 (1976) (dictum) (discharges of policy-making government employees for lack of affiliation with party in power do not violate first amendment). As the later cases suggest, absolute presidential discretion in firing seems less critical at less discretionary levels, but the power to discharge those who disobey orders seems indispensable throughout government.

the creation of a unified executive had been one of the prime purposes of the Constitution.[151]

Precedent, invoked by the dissenters, was not really to the contrary, though Taft did not distinguish it as successfully as he might have. *Marbury v. Madison,* in what Taft with technical accuracy characterized as dictum, had stated without qualification that the President could not in effect dismiss a justice of the peace appointed for a term of years;[152] but control of judicial officers, even where not prohibited by article III,[153] is hardly necessary to the unified exercise of executive power. More nearly on point was *United States v. Perkins,*[154] which had upheld Congress's power to place limitations on the removal of inferior officers appointed by heads of departments. As Taft noted, the Court in reaching this decision had said that the power to provide for such appointments implied the power of limiting removal,[155] but this conclusion seems inconsistent with the Court's argument for executive control in *Myers.*[156]

More to the point was the Chief Justice's further observation that *Perkins* had not held that Congress could "draw to itself, or to either branch of it, the power to remove or the right to participate in the exercise of that power."[157] The statute in *Perkins* had not required Senate consent; it had provided for a court martial. Presumably disobedience of presidential orders would be a ground for court martial; like the civil service laws so loudly invoked by the dissent in *Myers,*[158] the *Perkins* law left the President with ample authority to enforce his policies through discharge of obstructive subordinates.[159]

## 2.   Other cases

In *Myers v. United States,* thanks in part to the influence of ex-President Taft, the Court came down firmly on the side of executive over legislative power. The Court made maximum use of an unusual constellation of cases to establish additional executive prerogatives during the Taft years.

*J. W. Hampton, Jr., & Co. v. United States*[160] was a relatively easy decision. There,

---

[151] *See Myers,* 272 U.S. at 116-17 (citing the Constitutional Convention debates and alluding to "the humiliating weakness of the Congress during the Revolution and under the Articles of Confederation"); 1 M. FARRAND, *supra* note 47, at 64-97; THE FEDERALIST NO. 70, at 472 (A. Hamilton) (J. Cooke ed. 1961); Strauss, *The Place of Agencies in Government: Separation of Powers and the Fourth Branch,* 84 COLUM. L. REV. 573, 599-602 (1984). None of the analogies invoked by Corwin, *supra* note 149, at 384, would divide responsibility for executive functions: "No one would contend that the President could appropriate money, or erect courts, or create offices, or enlarge the military forces, on the justification that such action was necessary to assure the enforcement of the laws."

[152] 5 U.S. (1 Cranch) 137, 162 (1803) ("[A]s the law creating the office, gave the officer a right to hold for five years, independent of the executive, the appointment was not revocable. . . ."). *See Myers,* 272 U.S. at 139-43.

[153] *See supra* pp. 190-93 (discussing *Ex parte* Bakelite Corp., 279 U.S. 438 (1929)).

[154] 116 U.S. 483, 485 (1886).

[155] *See id.* at 485, *noted in Myers,* 272 U.S. at 161.

[156] *See* Corwin, *supra* note 149, at 357-58 ("[T]he decision in the *Myers* case, considered in the light of the reasoning supporting it, endows the President with a power of removal over all executive officers of the United States however appointed, which power Congress cannot control. . . .").

[157] *Myers,* 272 U.S. at 161.

[158] *Id.* at 262-64 (Brandeis, J., dissenting).

[159] *See* Strauss, *supra* note 151, at 607-08.

[160] 276 U.S. 394 (1928).

relying on precedent, the Chief Justice wrote to hold that a law authorizing the President to increase tariffs to make up for lower foreign production costs did not unconstitutionally delegate legislative power, because it merely called upon the President to execute "an intelligible principle" laid down by Congress.[161] More novel was the conclusion in *Springer v. Philippine Islands*[162] that provisions of the Philippine Organic Act vesting legislative power in the legislature and executive power in the Governor General forbade legislative participation in selecting the directors of public corporations.[163] Relying in part on *Myers*, Justice Sutherland concluded that the appointment of nonlegislative officers was an executive rather than a legislative function, and therefore it could not be entrusted to members of the legislature.[164]

Since the provisions on which the Court relied had counterparts in the Constitution, there was reason to think the same fate would have befallen a similar act of Congress. Indeed the case for a similar conclusion is far stronger in the case of the federal government. Article II specifically provides for the appointment of most officers by the President (with or without Senate consent), by the heads of departments, or by the courts.[165] As for the Philippines, not only did Holmes and Brandeis protest rather abstractly that separation of powers was not an absolute concept;[166] there were enough states in which legislatures had been given appointment powers to make questionable the Court's easy conclusion that the appointment of officers was not a legislative task.[167]

More interesting still was the *Pocket Veto Case*, decided in 1929.[168] Nine days after presenting a bill to the President for his signature, the Sixty-ninth Congress adjourned its first session sine die.[169] The President had taken no action on the bill, and the question was whether it had become a law.

To Justice Sanford, writing for a unanimous Court, the question was answered by the text of article I. Section 7 of that article provides that a bill shall become law if it "shall not be returned by the President within ten Days" "to that House in which it shall have originated," "unless the Congress by their Adjournment prevent its Return, in which Case it shall not be a Law." "[T]en days," said the Court, meant calendar (not legislative) days excluding Sundays, the "House" meant the body in session and not its clerk, and "Adjournment" was not limited to the final dispersal before the convening of a new Con-

---

[161] *Id.* at 409-11 (1928) (citing Field v. Clark, 143 U.S. 649 (1892) (upholding grant of authority to retaliate for "unreasonable" foreign tariffs)). *See supra* pp. 16-19. Unlike *Myers*, this case did not present a conflict between the President and Congress, for Congress had sought to grant the President the authority he sought to exercise.

[162] 277 U.S. 189 (1928).

[163] *Id.* at 204-06.

[164] *Id.* at 205.

[165] *See* Buckley v. Valeo, 424 U.S. 1, 109-43 (1976) (holding the Houses of Congress not "Departments" for this purpose), *infra* p. 589.

[166] *See Springer*, 277 U.S. at 209-12 (Holmes, J., joined by Brandeis, J., dissenting).

[167] *See* Corwin, *supra* note 149, at 387 & n.88 ("*The power of appointment is not an inherent executive power but a specific power.* This has always been the controlling principle in the state constitutions; and by accepted canons of construction it is likewise the view of the United States Constitution."). In reaching the additional conclusion that appointment was an executive function, the Court unnecessarily implied that it could not be entrusted to an independent agency either; but in so holding, the Court had the backing of the policy of unified executive control that had also underlain *Myers*.

[168] 279 U.S. 655 (1929).

[169] *Id.* at 672.

gress.[170] Thus, because Congress's adjournment had prevented the President from returning the bill to the House within ten days, it had not become a law.

Apart from reliance on impressive evidence of long-standing legislative and executive understanding,[171] the Court's reasoning was largely textual: the explicit exclusion of Sundays from the ten-day period confirmed the presumption that the words of that provision were "to be taken in their natural and obvious sense";[172] the "House" to which the bill was to be returned was the same that was to "proceed to reconsider it";[173] § 5 of the same article provided that a number less than a quorum could "adjourn from day to day" and that neither House should "adjourn for more than three days" without the other's consent.[174]

Little consideration was given to the question whether such a literal reading was compatible with the purposes of the provisions being construed. The basic principle of the section is to give the President not an absolute veto but one subject to override by a two-thirds vote of both Houses.[175] The requirement that the President return a bill within ten days prevents him from converting a suspensive veto into an absolute one by inaction. The exception for cases in which adjournment prevents timely return of the bill keeps Congress from destroying the veto power altogether by disbanding. To hold that every absence of Congress on the tenth day is an "adjournment" that prevents return of a bill, however, would allow a President to take advantage of every brief recess to circumvent the legislative right to override his veto.[176]

This argument was noted but rejected in the Court's opinion. Since the Constitution deliberately gave the President a full ten days in which to consider the merits of a bill, Sanford concluded, it was improper to blame the death of a bill not returned before adjournment on a presidential plot to avoid override: it was "attributable solely to the action of Congress in adjourning before the time allowed the President for returning the bill had expired."[177]

As the Court suggested, Congress can protect its right to override presidential objections by remaining in session continuously for ten days after passing each bill. The burden of its doing so, however, seems unnecessarily wasteful. As the losing party argued, the relative rights of both the President and Congress could be equally served at lower cost by

---

[170] Id. at 679-83.

[171] See id. at 683-91.

[172] Id. at 679.

[173] Id. at 681.

[174] Id. at 680.

[175]
> If after such Reconsideration two thirds of that House shall agree to pass the Bill, it shall be sent, together with the Objections [of the President], to the other House, by which it shall likewise be reconsidered, and if approved by two thirds of that House, it shall become a Law.

U. S. CONST. art. I, § 7, cl. 2. For insistence that the veto should not be absolute, see 1 M. FARRAND, supra note 47, at 98-104 (Convention debate and vote rejecting absolute veto); THE FEDERALIST NO. 73, at 494-99 (A Hamilton) (J. Cooke ed. 1961).

[176] See Wright v. United States, 302 U.S. 583, 596-97 (1938) (Hughes, C. J.). That a simple majority of Congress could pass a new bill to the same effect as the vetoed one seems not to disparage this conclusion. After a pocket veto, the measure may have to be repassed not once but twice, since it, being a new bill, is subject to another veto. Moreover, Congress's ability to pass the new measure twice is dependent upon the absence of a second pocket veto.

[177] The Pocket Veto Case, 279 U.S. at 676-79.

holding that a return to the agent of an absent House sufficed to keep a bill from immediately becoming law. Congress, if it chose, could then repass the bill when it reconvened, and the basic principle of a suspensive veto would be preserved.[178]

Unfortunately this argument seems to mean that the provision for the death of a bill that cannot be returned was unnecessary, while the Framers clearly contemplated cases in which return would be impossible. Perhaps they merely thought there might be times when not even a congressional clerk could be found, such as after final adjournment. Or perhaps, as Sanford argued, they contemplated that a returned bill would receive immediate reconsideration, rather than lingering "in a state of suspended animation."[179]

The holding was only that the final adjournment of one session of Congress "prevent[ed]" the subsequent return of bills. The Court's textual arguments, however, seemed equally applicable to brief adjournments in the course of a session. In that context, as suggested by Sanford's own concern about "suspended animation," the Court's literal approach would appear to enhance presidential power without serving any legitimate countervailing purpose.[180]

In *McGrain v. Daugherty,*[181] where the executive power was not at risk, the Taft Court gave a boost to legislative authority.[182] There the Court resoundingly affirmed a broad implicit congressional power to investigate matters pertinent to possible legislation,[183] a power that had been placed under a cloud by the hostility displayed in *Kilbourn v. Thompson* some forty years before.[184] In conflicts between executive and legislative power, however, the former invariably prevailed while ex-President Taft was at the helm.

[178] *See id.* at 679 n.6.

[179] *Id.* at 684-85.

[180] Some of the implications of the opinion were repudiated in Wright v. United States, 302 U.S. 583 (1938), in which, over the protest of Justice Stone, the Court held that an adjournment of a single House for not more than three days, as permitted by article I, § 5, was not an adjournment of "Congress" that would stop the running of the ten-day period for returning a bill under § 7. In order to avoid the conclusion that such a recess deprived the President of his veto power entirely, it was necessary to retract Justice Sanford's emphatic conclusion that a return to a clerical employee could never constitute a return to the originating House, for otherwise the President would have no way of returning the bill even though Congress had not adjourned. Stone got around this unacceptable result by construing the reference to an adjournment of "Congress" to mean, in light of its purpose, that of the originating House. *Id.* at 605-09 (concurring opinion). The trouble with that solution was, as suggested in the text, that it unnecessarily gave the President an absolute veto during every brief recess. In holding that delivery to an authorized agent sufficed, Hughes emphasized this problem, thereby raising doubts whether even an adjournment of both Houses that was brief enough not to place a bill in "suspended animation" would be held to "prevent" return within the meaning of § 7. *See id.* at 596-97; Kennedy v. Sampson, 511 F.2d 430, 437 (D.C. Cir. 1974) (holding that no intrasession adjournment "prevented" return); *see also* Barnes v. Kline, 759 F.2d 21, 35-38 (D.C. Cir. 1985) (holding the *Pocket Veto Case* no longer applicable to "modern intersession adjournment" because of decreased length of absences and explicit provision by House for acceptance of return by clerk).

[181] 273 U.S. 135 (1927) (Van Devanter, J.).

[182] *See also* Barry v. United States *ex rel.* Cunningham, 279 U.S. 597 (1929) (upholding Senate power to investigate Senate elections and to compel the appearance of witnesses at hearings during such investigations); Sinclair v. United States, 279 U.S. 263 (1929) (Butler, J.) (upholding the Teapot Dome investigation).

[183] *McGrain,* 273 U.S. at 160-67.

[184] 103 U.S. 168 (1881). *Kilbourn* had not denied the power to investigate for legislative purposes, but had appeared to take a dim view of congressional investigations generally and had found no legitimate legislative purpose for the one in question. *See* THE FIRST HUNDRED YEARS at 437-38. For detailed advocacy of a broad investigative power, see Landis, *Constitutional Limitations on the Congressional Power of Investigation,* 40 HARV. L. REV. 153 (1926).

# Conclusion to Part Three

Chief Justice Taft was a strong leader.[1] Like several of his predecessors, he wrote far more constitutional decisions than did any of his colleagues. He kept for himself not only the Wagnerian separation-of-powers struggle of *Myers v. United States,* but also the bulk of the great issues of federalism in such cases as the *Child Labor Tax Case, Brooks v. United States, Stafford v. Wallace,* and *Olsen v. Board of Trade.* In these matters he set the tone of the period: by no means grudging in interpretation of Congress's enumerated powers, but alert to prevent their misuse to usurp authority not granted.

Though he wrote relatively little in the field of substantive due process, Taft set the tone here too by his strikingly aggressive opinion in *Truax v. Corrigan* and by silent concurrences in most of the great due process decisions of the time. It was in this area, however, that he wrote his sole dissenting opinion in a constitutional case, protesting the invalidation of the minimum wage law in *Adkins v. Children's Hospital.* It was not simply that Taft, like Fuller, generally chose not to highlight his disagreements by writing opinions. Rather, unless he routinely declined even to acknowledge disagreement, he seems to have been in remarkable accord with the decisions of his colleagues; for in nine terms he recorded a dissenting vote in only a handful of constitutional cases. Taft truly appeared to embody the spirit of the Court over which he presided.[2]

---

[1] For an affirmative appraisal of Taft's performance as an administrator, see A. MASON, WILLIAM HOWARD TAFT: CHIEF JUSTICE 299-301 (1964). For his efforts to influence judicial appointments, see *id.* at 162-91. For his leading role in obtaining relief from the oppressive docket, see *id.* at 108-14, and in obtaining authorization for the Court's own building, see *id.* at 133-37 (adding more generally that "Taft's lobbying has no precedent in Supreme Court annals," *id.* at 137).

[2] Taft was a forceful and often powerful opinion writer. *See, e.g.,* in addition to his opinions in *Myers, Adkins, Stafford,* and the Child Labor Tax Case, Cooke v. United States, 267 U.S. 517 (1925) (hearing required to convict for contempt outside courtroom); *Ex parte* Grossman, 267 U.S. 87 (1925) (President may pardon criminal contempt); Tidal Oil Co. v. Flanagan, 263 U.S. 444 (1924) (reaffirming inapplicability of contract clause to judicial action); Balzac v. Porto Rico, 258 U.S. 298 (1922) (reaffirming the inapplicability of criminal jury provisions to unincorporated possessions).

Spokesmen for the Court in the pivotal due process and equal protection cases were Butler, McReynolds, and above all Sutherland, author of *Adkins* and of the three decisions striking down price regulation as well as of the opinion upholding zoning in *Village of Euclid v. Ambler Realty Co.* Butler tended to be somewhat less tolerant of state regulation than his colleagues, Sutherland less tolerant of federal regulation, and McReynolds less tolerant of either.[3] Apart from his virtual monopoly on maritime cases and his prodigious dissent in *Myers,* McReynolds made his mark principally by a strident judicial activism that led him not only to write the famous and much-admired "liberal" decisions in favor of academic freedom in *Meyer v. Nebraska* and *Pierce v. Society of Sisters* but also to dissent more frequently in constitutional cases than anyone but Holmes and Brandeis, usually because the Court had upheld some state or federal regulation.[4]

Van Devanter and Sanford, who wrote relatively little,[5] almost never wrote dissenting opinions. Both generally agreed with the majority, though Van Devanter seemed somewhat more and Sanford somewhat less willing than most to invalidate state legislation.[6] Van Devanter wrote most significantly on such exotic questions as legislative investigations and judicial independence, while Sanford is known principally for his narrow views of free speech in *Gitlow* and *Whitney.*[7]

Fundamentally out of sympathy with the prevailing judicial philosophy, Holmes, Brandeis, and Stone made their names during the 1920s very largely in dissent.[8] For the Court,

---

[3] Butler dissented in both *Euclid* and *Buck v. Bell*, Sutherland in *Lambert v. Yellowley* and *Chicago Bd. of Trade v. Olsen* (as well as, uncharacteristically, in *Meyer v. Nebraska*). McReynolds dissented in *Lambert*, *Stafford v. Wallace*, *Olsen*, and *Euclid*. Paschal gives Sutherland much of the credit for the resurgence of laissez-faire constitutionalism in the 1920s and 1930s, *see* J. PASCHAL, MR. JUSTICE SUTHERLAND: A MAN AGAINST THE STATE 153 (1951), adding that Sutherland "stands apart from his conservative colleagues primarily because he was a man of ideas" who had a well-developed theory of the proper functions of government, *id.* at 241.

[4] Against this background it is interesting that McReynolds also tended to join his substantive adversary Brandeis in protesting what they considered premature judicial intervention. *See supra* p. 183, note 78 (discussing Pennsylvania v. West Virginia and Terrace v. Thompson). Apart from *Myers*, McReynolds's opinions tended to be cursory. *See* A. BICKEL & B. SCHMIDT, 9 HISTORY OF THE SUPREME COURT OF THE UNITED STATES 341-57 (1984) (describing the difficulties of working with McReynolds and adding that he gave little attention to his opinions); A. MASON, *supra* note 1, at 195 (quoting Taft's remark that McReynolds was "always trying to escape work").

[5] *See* A. MASON, *supra* note 1, at 195, 209 (describing Van Devanter as strong in conference but "opinion-shy" and "the slowest member" at writing opinions); 2 H. PRINGLE, THE LIFE AND TIMES OF WILLIAM HOWARD TAFT 971 (1939) (quoting Letter from Taft to Horace Taft, Dec. 26, 1924) (Van Devanter was "[m]y mainstay in the court").

[6] Van Devanter dissented in *Euclid,* Sanford in *Adkins* and in the price-regulation case of Tyson v. Banton, 273 U.S. 418, 454 (1927).

[7] Clarke, Day, Pitney, and McKenna left the Court without making noteworthy contributions to the constitutional jurisprudence of the Taft period. *See* A. MASON, *supra* note 1, at 161, 213-15 (noting Clarke's boredom, Day's advanced age, Pitney's nervous breakdown, and McKenna's senility and the fact that, after his brethren had agreed not to decide any case in which his vote was crucial, McKenna finally retired at Taft's urging).

[8] Just as before Taft's appointment, Brandeis's dissents tended to be learned treatises on the history and background of the provisions in question—designed, like his earlier briefs, to demonstrate, as they so often did, the reasonableness of the laws. For examples, see his dissents in Frost v. Corporation Comm'n, 278 U.S. 515 (1929) (cooperatives); Jay Burns Baking Co. v. Bryan, 264 U.S. 504 (1924) (bread-weight provisions); Missouri *ex rel.* Southwestern Bell Tel. Co. v. Public Serv. Comm'n, 262 U.S. 276 (1923) (rate regulation); Truax v. Corrigan, 257 U.S. 312 (1921) (labor legislation); Frankfurter, *Mr. Justice Brandeis and the Constitution*, 45 HARV. L. REV. 33, 60 (1931). For additional displays of Brandeis's awesome wizardry in dealing with complex financial

Holmes and Brandeis scored liberal gains in the procedural area by writing against mob-dominated trials and for de novo review of citizenship claims respectively. Holmes struck an extreme blow for judicial restraint by upholding involuntary sterilization in *Buck v. Bell*, and Brandeis exercised similar restraint in his disparagement of declaratory relief in *Willing v. Chicago Auditorium Association*. Judicial restraint was the dominant theme of the numerous dissents of all three Justices, especially in substantive due process and equal protection cases. Yet it was Holmes who wrote for the Court to strike down a regulation as a taking in *Pennsylvania Coal Co. v. Mahon*, and all three Justices were more interventionist than the majority in the wiretapping case of *Olmstead v. United States*. Strikingly, Stone parted company with Holmes and Brandeis in their most notable departure from judicial restraint by joining the majority in allowing limitations on speech in *Gitlow* and *Whitney*.

In any event it was Taft's Court, not that of Holmes or Brandeis; activism in support of traditional values was the order of the day.

---

matters, see his majority opinions in Farmers & Merchants Bank v. Federal Reserve Bank, 262 U.S. 649 (1923) (banking); Atlantic Coast Line R.R. v. Daughton, 262 U.S. 413 (1923) (income taxation). Holmes, as usual, tended to be pithy. For an illuminating contrast of the styles of these two allies, see A. MASON, BRANDEIS: A FREE MAN'S LIFE 570-81 (1946) (concluding that "Holmes is the enlightened skeptic; Brandeis, the militant crusader").

# Part Four

## Chief Justice Hughes
## 1930–1941

# Introduction to Part Four

During the 1920s, over repeated dissents by Justices Holmes, Brandeis, and Stone, the Supreme Court under Chief Justice Taft had been unprecedentedly aggressive in striking down social and economic regulation. In 1930, when Taft resigned, President Hoover turned naturally to Charles Evans Hughes, who had distinguished himself not only as Governor of New York and as Secretary of State but also as Associate Justice from 1910 until 1916.[1] In that capacity, Hughes had tended to vote with Holmes to uphold economic regulation, and he had taken a strikingly broad view of the federal commerce power.[2]

The sudden death of Justice Sanford later the same year thus left a Court that could be expected to divide four to four on basic questions of regulatory authority. As the country slid ever deeper into depression, and as legislators and executives turned toward increasingly intrusive regulation as an antidote, the question of Sanford's replacement assumed extraordinary importance.

After liberal senators defeated his first nominee for the crucial ninth seat,[3] President Hoover appointed Owen J. Roberts of Pennsylvania. Having spent virtually his entire

---

[1] See M. PUSEY, CHARLES EVANS HUGHES (1951).

[2] See 2 M. PUSEY, supra note 1, at 660 (noting progressive opposition to Hughes's appointment as Chief Justice based largely on his having represented corporate clients as an attorney: "The strange thing is that men who claimed to be 'liberals' chose as their target one of the greatest champions of human rights in the current century.").

[3] Judge John J. Parker of the Fourth Circuit was rejected partly because he had followed Supreme Court precedent in enforcing a yellow-dog contract and partly because of his 1920 statement that the "participation of the Negro in politics is a source of evil and danger to both races and is not desired by the wise men in either race or by the Republican parts of North Carolina." See C. SWISHER, AMERICAN CONSTITUTIONAL DEVELOPMENT 776-79 (1943).

career in law practice and teaching, Roberts was a largely unknown quantity.[4] In the story of the Supreme Court during the 1930s he was to play a very important role.[5]

The story has three chapters and an epilogue. The first chapter is characterized by greater judicial acceptance of social legislation, over the monolithic objections of Justices Van Devanter, McReynolds, Sutherland, and Butler. The path was not straight, but its direction was unmistakable; the laissez-faire majority of the 1920s had become a minority.[6] Both Hughes and Roberts tended to vote on these matters with Holmes, Brandeis, and Stone, and when the celebrated state-court jurist Benjamin Cardozo took Holmes's place in 1932, he tended to take his predecessor's position, too.

The second chapter lasted only two years, from *Panama Refining Co. v. Ryan* in 1935 to *West Coast Hotel Co. v. Parrish* in 1937.[7] In one of the most dramatic periods in its history, the Court began to demolish President Roosevelt's New Deal and appeared to revitalize substantive limitations on state law as well.[8] None of these decisions, perhaps, was actually inconsistent with what the Court had done before. Several were joined not only by Roberts but by Hughes as well. The most notorious of them all—the "sick chicken" case invalidating the National Industrial Recovery Act—was unanimous.[9] Nevertheless the division of the Court in other cases left no doubt that both Hughes and (especially) Roberts were less tolerant of the new legislation than their earlier decisions seemed to suggest.

The final chapter records the famous "switch in time," the remarkable reversal beginning with the upholding of a minimum wage law in *Parrish* and resulting in the virtual abandonment not only of the judicially created doctrine of substantive due process but also of the Constitution's own basic principle of limited federal power.[10] These revolutionary changes were cemented by the replacement of three of the activist old guard (and of Brandeis and Cardozo) by representatives of the new order: Hugo Black, Stanley Reed, Felix Frankfurter, William O. Douglas, and Frank Murphy.[11] But that was just icing on the cake; the essential change had occurred before any new appointments were made.

---

[4] Roberts had gained some notoriety as special prosecutor in the Teapot Dome cases, however. *See* C. LEONARD, A SEARCH FOR A JUDICIAL PHILOSOPHY: MR. JUSTICE ROBERTS AND THE CONSTITUTIONAL REVOLUTION OF 1937, at 8-10 (1971).

[5] Owen Roberts, wrote Fred Rodell, "was for years the most powerful person in the United States." NINE MEN 221 (1955).

[6] *See* R. McCLOSKEY, THE AMERICAN SUPREME COURT 163-64 (1960); E. CORWIN, THE TWILIGHT OF THE SUPREME COURT 44-45 (1934).

[7] 293 U.S. 388 (1935); 300 U.S. 379 (1937).

[8] *See* B. WRIGHT, THE GROWTH OF AMERICAN CONSTITUTIONAL LAW ch. 9 (1942); McCLOSKEY, *supra* note 6, at 165-68: "for two busy terms the Court waged what is surely the most ambitious dragon-fight in its long and checkered history."

[9] A.L.A. Schechter Poultry Corp. v. United States, 295 U.S. 495 (1935).

[10] *See* McCLOSKEY, *supra* note 6, at 175-87; WRIGHT, *supra* note 8, at ch. 10; E. CORWIN, CONSTITUTIONAL REVOLUTION, LTD. 64-79 (1941).

[11]              JUSTICES OF THE SUPREME COURT DURING THE TIME OF CHIEF JUSTICE HUGHES

|  |  | 1930 | 32 | 34 | 36 | 38 | 40 |
|---|---|---|---|---|---|---|---|
| Oliver Wendell Holmes, Jr. | (1902-1932) | ——┤ | | | | | |
| Willis Van Devanter | (1910-1937) | ———————————┤ | | | | | |
| James C. McReynolds | (1914-1941) | ———————————————————┤ | | | | | |
| Louis D. Brandeis | (1916-1939) | ————————————————┤ | | | | | |

The epilogue is a legacy of decisions expanding civil rights and liberties that foreshadowed the agenda of the future.

JUSTICES OF THE SUPREME COURT DURING THE TIME OF CHIEF JUSTICE HUGHES (continued)

| | | 1930 | 32 | 34 | 36 | 38 | 40 |
|---|---|---|---|---|---|---|---|
| George Sutherland | (1922-1938) | | | | | | |
| Pierce Butler | (1922-1939) | | | | | | |
| Harlan F. Stone | (1925-1946) | | | | | | |
| Charles Evans Hughes | (1930-1941) | | | | | | |
| Owen J. Roberts | (1930-1945) | | | | | | |
| Benjamin N. Cardozo | (1932-1938) | | | | | | |
| Hugo L. Black | (1937-1971) | | | | | | |
| Stanley F. Reed | (1938-1957) | | | | | | |
| Felix Frankfurter | (1939-1962) | | | | | | |
| William O. Douglas | (1939-1975) | | | | | | |
| Frank Murphy | (1940-1949) | | | | | | |

SOURCE: G. GUNTHER, CASES AND MATERIALS ON CONSTITUTIONAL LAW, app. B. (11th ed. 1985).
Biographies of these Justices include PUSEY, *supra* note 1; LEONARD, *supra* note 4; G. HELLMAN, BENJAMIN N. CARDOZO: AMERICAN JUDGE (1940); A. MASON, BRANDEIS: A FREE MAN'S LIFE (1946); J. PASCHAL, MR. JUSTICE SUTHERLAND: A MAN AGAINST THE STATE (1951); A. MASON, HARLAN FISKE STONE: PILLAR OF THE LAW (1956); G. DUNNE, HUGO BLACK AND THE JUDICIAL REVOLUTION (1977); H. THOMAS, FELIX FRANKFURTER: SCHOLAR ON THE BENCH (1960); J. W. HOWARD, MR. JUSTICE MURPHY: A POLITICAL BIOGRAPHY (1968).

# 7

# The New Deal

## I.  By the Dawn's Early Light

From 1930 to 1935, buoyed up by Roberts and Hughes, the Court seemed well on the way to making peace with the modern social state. A series of split decisions culminating with *Nebbia v. New York*[1] and *Home Building & Loan Ass'n v. Blaisdell*[2] significantly relaxed both fourteenth amendment and contract clause limitations on economic legislation. Congressional powers were generously construed, while *Crowell v. Benson* gave a slightly qualified imprimatur to the rise of quasi-judicial administrative tribunals.[3] The 1920s already seemed a long time ago.

## A.  Insurance and Chain Stores

Under Chief Justice Taft the Court had struck down price regulation of theater admissions, employment agencies, and gasoline dealers, strengthening the traditional view that government had no legitimate interest in rectifying the effects of unequal bargaining power except in a narrowly defined category of businesses "affected with a public interest."[4] Under Chief Justice Hughes the Court lost little time in taking a different view.

The first hint of a more tolerant approach came just a few months after the new appointments when, in *O'Gorman & Young, Inc. v. Hartford Fire Ins. Co.*, the Court upheld a

---

[1] 291 U.S. 502 (1934).

[2] 290 U.S. 398 (1934).

[3] 285 U.S. 22 (1932).

[4] Tyson & Brother v. Banton, 273 U.S. 418 (1927) (theater admissions); Ribnik v. McBride, 277 U.S. 350 (1928) (employment agencies); Williams v. Standard Oil Co., 278 U.S. 235 (1929) (gasoline dealers). *See also* p. 145 *supra*. For the origins of the public interest requirement, see THE FIRST HUNDRED YEARS at 370-73, (discussing Munn v. Illinois, 94 U.S. 113 (1877)). For the narrow conception of legitimate governmental ends reflected in the Taft Court decisions, see pp. 47-49, 103-04 *supra*.

state law forbidding the payment of excessive or disuniform commissions to fire insurance agents.[5] As Justice Brandeis emphasized in a brief opinion for the majority, the Court had already allowed states to regulate the rates charged to policyholders because the insurance business was affected with a public interest, and the amounts paid to agents had an obvious effect on those rates.[6] Thus on the surface the case seemed easy; even Van Devanter, who had dissented from the earlier decision, did not deny that insurance was affected with a public interest.[7]

Justices Van Devanter, McReynolds, Sutherland, and Butler nevertheless dissented, arguing that the sole effect of the statute as construed was to prevent paying agents at different rates, not to limit their compensation. Thus, "the restrictions have no immediate or necessary relation" to the cost of insurance; "so far as we can see, this legislation will afford no protection to those who wish to insure."[8]

The decisive difference between the majority and the dissent seemed to concern the appropriate level of scrutiny of the relation between means and ends, and it was brought home by sharply contrasting views as to the burden of proof. While the dissenters insisted that the party seeking to sustain the law must show "special circumstances sufficient to indicate the necessity" for the specific means chosen, Brandeis concluded that "the presumption of constitutionality must prevail in the absence of some factual foundation of record for overthrowing the statute."[9] It was this attitude, more than the result in the particular case, that seemed to augur an easier time for regulation in the years to come.[10]

An equal protection decision rendered later in the same term lent additional force to this expectation. In *State Board of Tax Commissioners v. Jackson*, over the same four dissents, Justice Roberts wrote to uphold a license tax that discriminated against chain stores.[11] Arguing that the advantages attributed to multiple stores actually depended upon the size of the business, Sutherland's dissent tellingly invoked a recent decision invalidating a taxicab tax that had discriminated against corporations.[12] Roberts, whose tedious opinion consisted largely of poorly integrated summaries of earlier decisions, went to some lengths to show that no individual store enjoyed all the advantages of a chain.[13] If Roberts seemed more concerned to show that there was an actual justification for the

---

[5] 282 U.S. 251 (1931).

[6] *Id.* at 257 (citing German Alliance Ins. Co. v. Lewis, 233 U.S. 389 (1914), *supra* p. 103, note 79).

[7] 282 U.S. at 266 (Van Devanter, McReynolds, Sutherland, and Butler, dissenting).

[8] 282 U.S. at 269-70. The dissenters also argued that the law might actually *increase* costs: "in order to operate at all . . . [in some geographic areas], the insurer may find it necessary to pay agents much more than prudent management would require [at other localities], and beyond the real value of their services at such [other] places." Unless the resulting fee was itself illegal, the nondiscrimination provision would require payment of an inflated fee throughout the state. *Id.* at 270.

[9] *Id.* at 269, 257-58. Brandeis's approach seems more in accord with Justice Chase's original perception. *See* Hylton v. United States, 3 U.S. 171, 174 (1796) ("[I]t is unnecessary . . . for me to determine, whether this court, constitutionally possesses the power to declare an act of congress void, on the ground of its being made contrary to . . . the constitution; but if the court have such power, I am free to declare, that I will never exercise it, but in a very clear case."). *See also* THE FIRST HUNDRED YEARS at 33.

[10] On the day *O'Gorman* was decided, wrote Walton Hamilton, "the views of Brandeis" respecting judicial review in general "became 'the opinion of the court and a new chapter in judicial history began to be written.'" Hamilton, *The Jurist's Art*, 31 COLUM. L. REV. 1073, 1073 (1931).

[11] 283 U.S. 527 (1931).

[12] *Id.* at 546-50 (citing Quaker City Cab Co. v. Pennsylvania, 277 U.S. 389 (1928), p. 137 *supra*).

[13] 283 U.S. at 534-36.

challenged measure than Brandeis had been in the insurance case, he also appeared quite willing to find one.

### B.   Monopolies and Milk Prices

That the millennium had not yet arrived was rudely demonstrated the following term when both Hughes and Roberts joined Justice Sutherland's opinion in *New State Ice Co. v. Liebmann,* striking down a law limiting entry into the ice business.[14] Unlike cotton ginning, where the Court had recognized the validity of a similar restriction,[15] the ice business was not, in the majority's view, "charged with a public use."[16] Brandeis's monumental dissent, joined by Stone, coupled judicial restraint with condemnation of wasteful competition, reminded the reader how far the Court had departed from the *Slaughter-House Cases,*[17] and closed with the famous description of the states as "laborator[ies]" able to "try novel social and economic experiments without risk to the rest of the country."[18]

*Liebmann's* echo of the past was drowned out in 1934 by Justice Roberts's celebrated fortissimo in *Nebbia v. New York,* upholding minimum milk prices.[19] The notion that price and entry regulations were permissible only in certain businesses affected with a public interest, Roberts insisted, had been based upon a misunderstanding of the decision sustaining rate regulation in *Munn v. Illinois.*[20] "The phrase 'affected with a public interest' can, in the nature of things, mean no more than that an industry, for adequate reason, is subject to control for the public good." A court's task, he concluded, was "to determine in each case whether circumstances vindicate the challenged regulation as a reasonable exertion of governmental authority or condemn it as arbitrary or discriminatory."[21] This was what Brandeis had said in dissenting from *Liebmann,* which Roberts did not mention, and it left the reader wondering how Roberts and Hughes could have gone along with the contrary decision in that case.[22]

---

[14] 285 U.S. 262 (1932). *See* Howard, *The Supreme Court and State Action Challenged under the Fourteenth Amendment, 1931–1932,* 81 U. PA. L. REV. 505, 514 (1933) (citing *Liebmann* and intervening decisions invalidating state taxes as casting "considerable doubt" on the thesis that *O'Gorman* "was portentous of a more tolerant attitude toward state legislative action challenged under the Fourteenth Amendment").

[15] Frost v. Corporation Commission, 278 U.S. 515 (1929).

[16] 285 U.S. at 277.

[17] 83 U.S. 36 (1873) (holding that Louisiana statute giving partial monopoly of the slaughtering business to one company did not violate the fourteenth amendment). *See* THE FIRST HUNDRED YEARS at 342-50.

[18] 285 U.S. at 285, 292, 303, 311. Holmes had resigned; Cardozo, just appointed, did not participate. Brandeis attacked the requirement that the regulated business be "affected with a public interest" as resting upon "historical error": "the true principle is that the State's power extends to every regulation of any business reasonably required and appropriate for the public protection." *Id.* at 302-03. For criticism of the notion of "wasteful" competition, see R. POSNER, ECONOMIC ANALYSIS OF LAW 590-92 (3d ed. 1986).

[19] 291 U.S. 502 (1934).

[20] 94 U.S. 113 (1877).

[21] 291 U.S. at 536.

[22] 285 U.S. at 285. Hughes later told his biographer that although he had considered *Liebmann* a close case, he thought it reconcilable with *Nebbia* because in the latter case no one had been denied the right to sell milk— i.e., the restriction was less intrusive. Roberts "is said to have paced the floor . . . until the early morning hours" before deciding how to vote in *Nebbia. See* 2 M. PUSEY, CHARLES EVANS HUGHES 700 (1951).

Freed from the necessity to demonstrate that the milk business was affected with a public interest, Roberts was within easy reach of his goal. Reciting legislative findings as to the harmful effects of unrestricted price cutting, he found the challenged measure not "without relation" to the legitimate "purpose to prevent ruthless competition from destroying the wholesale price structure on which the farmer depends for his livelihood, and the community for an assured supply of milk." McReynolds and his three soulmates predictably added an anguished and rambling dissent.[23] Economic due process was unmistakably in retreat; both Hughes and Roberts had come down firmly on the side of tolerance for economic legislation.[24]

## C.  The Mortgage Moratorium

Even more dramatic than what the new Justices did to substantive due process in *Nebbia* was what they had done to the contract clause just a few months earlier in *Home Building & Loan Ass'n v. Blaisdell.*[25] At the depth of the depression, Minnesota had passed a law authorizing up to two years' extension of the redemption period upon foreclosure of preexisting mortgages.[26] As Sutherland wrote for the usual four dissenters in one of his most powerful opinions, debt extensions in economic crises had been among the specific evils the clause was designed to prevent, and the Court had repeatedly struck them down since *Bronson v. Kinzie* nearly a century before.[27] Yet the majority upheld the law in a landmark opinion by Chief Justice Hughes specifically declaring the original understanding irrelevant:

> If by the statement that what the Constitution meant at the time of its adoption
> it means to-day, it is intended to say that the great clauses of the Constitution
> must be confined to the interpretation which the framers, with the conditions
> and outlook of their time, would have placed upon them, the statement carries
> its own refutation.[28]

---

[23] 291 U.S. at 530 (majority opinion of Roberts), 539-59 (dissent of McReynolds).

[24] *See* White, *Constitutional Protection of Liberty of Contract: Does It Still Exist?*, 83 U. PA. L. REV. 425, 440 (1935) (lamenting after *Nebbia* that "the Supreme Court has in effect surrendered its power to declare void acts of legislature on the ground that they infringe liberty of contract").

[25] 290 U.S. 398 (1934).

[26] The statute authorized a court to extend the then existing one-year period of redemption as necessary.

[27] 290 U.S. at 448, 453-71 (citing, among other cases, Bronson v. Kinzie, 42 U.S. 311 (1843), THE FIRST HUNDRED YEARS at 211-13).

[28] 290 U.S. at 442-43. Predictably, the Chief Justice took refuge in Marshall's oracular dictum that " 'it is a *constitution* we are expounding.' " 290 U.S. at 443 (quoting McCulloch v. Maryland, 17 U.S. 316, 407 (1819)). For academic approval of the notion that original meaning is irrelevant, see tenBroek, *Use by the United States Supreme Court of Extrinsic Aids in Constitutional Construction* (part 5), 27 CAL. L. REV. 399 (1939). *But see* Epstein, *Toward a Revitalization of the Contract Clause,* 51 U. CHI. L. REV. 703, 735 (1984) ("This passage contains some of the most misguided thinking on constitutional interpretation imaginable."). Hughes's further suggestion that the Framers might have approved of the decision had they been aware of "the conditions of the later day," 290 U.S. at 443, was hardly credible in light of Sutherland's demonstration that the clause had been adopted precisely to prevent debtor relief in times of economic crisis.

Hughes demonstrated at some length that the Court had often permitted modifications of contract remedies that did not alter the obligation itself.[29] He nowhere said an extension of the redemption period went only to the remedy, and *Bronson* had held it did not. *Bronson* had also confirmed that even remedial changes were forbidden if they " 'materially . . . impair[ed] the rights and interests of the owner,' " as the extension of time seemed clearly to do.[30]

Apart from the matter of remedies, Hughes hastened to add, "the State also continues to possess authority to safeguard the vital interests of its people. . . . [T]he reservation of essential attributes of sovereign power is . . . read into contracts as a postulate of the legal order."[31] As evidence he cited decisions holding that public contracts implicitly reserved the power of condemnation,[32] that states could not bargain away the power to forbid such arguably obnoxious activities as lotteries,[33] and, most pertinently, that private contracts were subject to later exercises of the police power.[34]

Nobody had objected when this last proposition was asserted in an obscure 1905 case involving a promise not to obstruct a creek, and *Blaisdell* seemed to show just how sweeping that conclusion had been.[35] One might have argued there was a difference between a contract to commit murder and one for foreclosure of a mortgage, but Hughes flatly rejected it, and even the earlier decision was arguably on the wrong side of the line.[36] Subjecting private contracts to the police power seemed to reduce the contract clause to the equivalent of substantive due process.[37]

The upshot seemed to be that the mortgage moratorium law was valid, despite its det-

---

[29] 290 U.S. at 429-34.

[30] *Bronson*, 42 U.S. at 315 (quoting Green v. Biddle, 21 U.S. 1, 17 (1823)). Unlike the extension provision in *Bronson*, the law in *Blaisdell* required payment of a reasonable rent during the period of extension. Nevertheless, as Sutherland observed, it deprived the mortgagee of the significant rights of occupancy and sale. 290 U.S. at 480.

[31] 290 U.S. at 434-35.

[32] *Id.* at 435-38 (citing, for example, West River Bridge Co. v. Dix, 47 U.S. 507 (1848)).

[33] Stone v. Mississippi, 101 U.S. 814 (1880).

[34] Manigault v. Springs, 199 U.S. 473 (1905). *See also* THE FIRST HUNDRED YEARS at 213-15; pp. 12-13 *supra*.

[35] *See* Hale, *The Supreme Court and the Contract Clause: II,* 57 HARV. L. REV. 621, 671-74 (1944).

[36] *See* Blaisdell, 290 U.S. at 438-39 (dismissing the argument that "state power may be addressed directly to the prevention of the enforcement of contracts only when these are of a sort which the legislature in its discretion may denounce as being in themselves hostile to public morals, or public health, safety or welfare, or where the prohibition is merely of injurious practices"). Sutherland's manful effort to tie the police-power principle to the established doctrine of implied conditions excusing performance on the ground of supervening illegality fell short of explaining all the precedents. *See id.* at 475-78 (Sutherland, dissenting); B. WRIGHT, THE CONTRACT CLAUSE OF THE CONSTITUTION 211-12 (1938) (reading precedents to subject contract rights between private persons to police power only in cases of "unusual public importance").

[37] *See* Hale, *The Supreme Court and the Contract Clause: III,* 57 HARV. L. REV. 852, 890-91 (1944) ("there is at least a tendency for the contract clause and the due process clause to coalesce"). Holmes had pretty well said as much in 1921 in upholding over four dissents a state law extending housing leases: "contracts are made subject to this exercise of the power of the State when otherwise justifiable, as we have held this [under the due process clause] to be." Marcus Brown Holding Co. v. Feldman, 256 U.S. 170, 198 (1921). Sutherland properly made no serious effort to distinguish this decision, accurately observing that the contract clause question there had "received little, if any, more than casual consideration." 290 U.S. at 478-79. Hughes naturally gave it prominent billing. *Id.* at 440-42.

rimental impact on the obligation, if it was "reasonable."[38] If this was the question, the answer was easy: the relief of debtors in an economic emergency was a legitimate end and the moratorium a reasonable means of attaining it. "If it be determined, as it must be, that the contract clause is not an absolute and utterly unqualified restriction of the State's protective power, this legislation is clearly so reasonable as to be within the legislative competency."[39]

Precedent may have pointed the way to this conclusion, but the Court had never before said quite so blatantly that the prohibition of "any . . . law impairing the obligation of contracts" forbade only those that were unreasonable.[40] One is reminded of the scene from *Animal Farm* in which reexamination of a provision that "[n]o animal shall drink alcohol" reveals it to outlaw drinking *"to excess."*[41]

To narrow the text of a constitutional provision on the basis of its history has a long and respectable pedigree based upon the premise that the Framers' words are only a partial guide to their command.[42] To do so in the teeth of that history seems to give a most unhappy connotation to Hughes's earlier remark that "the Constitution is what the judges say it is."[43]

[38] *See* 290 U.S. at 444 ("The principle of this development is . . . that the reservation of reasonable exercise of the protective power of the State is read into all contracts.").

[39] *Id.* at 447.

[40] See R. McCLOSKEY, THE AMERICAN SUPREME COURT 164 (1960) ("The idea appeared to be that the states could now violate the contract clause so long as they were 'reasonable' about it."). *See also* B. WRIGHT, *supra* note 36, at 112 ("taken in connection with other decisions . . . interpreting . . . the prohibition . . . [of the contract] clause, . . . [*Blaisdell*] appears as merely another step, and not necessarily a long one, in the change of that prohibition from an absolute one to a reasonable one").

[41] "[A] few days later Muriel, reading over the Seven Commandments to herself, noticed that there was yet another of them which the animals had remembered wrong. They had thought the Fifth Commandment was 'No animal shall drink alcohol,' but there were two words that they had forgotten. Actually the Commandment read: 'No animal shall drink alcohol *to excess.*'" GEORGE ORWELL, ANIMAL FARM 120 (illus. ed. 1954) (emphasis in original).

[42] *See* THE FIRST HUNDRED YEARS at 14-20, 41-49 (discussing Chisholm v. Georgia, 2 U.S. 419 (1793), and Calder v. Bull, 3 U.S. 386 (1798)).

[43] *See* 1 M. PUSEY, *supra* note 22, at 204 (quoting the 1907 speech in which Hughes made this remark and indignantly rejecting the suggestion that Hughes had meant to "expose[] the solemn function of judging as a sort of humbuggery").

Contemporaneous decisions respecting intergovernmental immunities also reflected a lenient tendency. *See, e.g.,* Educational Films Corp. v. Ward, 282 U.S. 379, 391 (1931) (Stone, over the expected dissents of Sutherland, Van Devanter, and Butler) (upholding a state corporation tax whose measure included copyright royalties despite an earlier decision invalidating state taxes laid directly upon patent royalties) (Long v. Rockwood, 277 U.S. 142 (1928)) and despite McCallen Co. v. Massachusetts, 279 U.S. 620 (1929) (which seemed to reject precedents allowing a state to *measure* taxes by income it could not tax as such); Fox Film Corp. v. Doyal, 286 U.S. 123 (1932) (Hughes) (unanimously overruling *Long v. Rockwood* in holding that, like land granted to a private party by the United States, copyright royalties themselves were subject to state taxation). The earlier decisions are noted *supra* at p. 172, note 13. The Court demonstrated that it was not yet prepared to make a very great shift in this field, however, by reaffirming that Congress could tax neither sales to local governments, Indian Motocycle Co. v. United States, 283 U.S. 570 (1931) (Van Devanter, over dissents by Stone and Brandeis, and with Holmes acquiescing solely on the basis of precedent), nor the income from a state oil lease, Burnet v. Coronado Oil & Gas Co., 285 U.S. 393 (1932) (McReynolds, over dissents by Stone, Brandeis, Roberts, and Cardozo). Brandeis's opinion in *Coronado Oil* contains a careful argument for limiting stare decisis in cases involving application of the Constitution to particular facts. 285 U.S. at 405-13. For detailed and penetrating

## D.   The Administrative State

Even in Chief Justice Taft's days the Court had read Congress's power to regulate interstate commerce rather broadly,[44] and in the early 1930s it continued to do so. In *Texas &
N.O. R.R. v. Brotherhood of Railway & S. S. Clerks,* in 1930, the Court upheld a provision of the Railway Labor Act protecting the right of rail workers to choose bargaining
representatives, reasoning that "Congress may facilitate the amicable settlement of disputes which threaten the service of the necessary agencies of interstate transportation."[45]
Despite the contrary thrust of the twenty-year-old decision in *Adair v. United States,*[46]
which had struck down a ban on yellow-dog contracts in the face of a similar argument,
no one dissented.[47] The next year, in *Arizona v. California,* the Court held that an act
providing for construction of Boulder Dam fell within the power to "regulate commerce
. . . among the several states," although it involved spending rather than regulation and
despite a plausible argument that the dam would impair rather than promote navigation.[48]

The most significant relaxation of constitutional obstacles to the modern administrative
state, however, came in Chief Justice Hughes's 1932 opinion in *Crowell v. Benson.* The
Longshoremen's and Harbor Workers' Compensation Act, enacted in 1927 to fill gaps in
compensation for injured workers created by decisions limiting state authority over maritime matters, empowered a federal administrative agency to adjudicate maritime workers'
compensation claims, authorizing the courts to set aside agency orders "not in accordance
with law." "Apart from cases involving constitutional rights," wrote Hughes, "the Act
contemplates that, as to questions of fact . . . the findings of the deputy commissioner,
supported by the evidence and within the scope of his authority, shall be final."[49]

Properly disdaining reliance on precedent,[50] the Court found this scheme consistent
with article III's command that federal judicial power be vested in judges with life tenure
and irreducible salary. "[T]here is no requirement that . . . all determinations of fact . . .
be made by judges"; juries and masters made them all the time. "[T]he reservation of full
authority to the court to deal with matters of law provides for the appropriate exercise of
the judicial function in this class of cases."[51]

---

analysis of these and later decisions in this field, see T. POWELL, VAGARIES AND VARIETIES IN CONSTITUTIONAL
INTERPRETATION 118-41 (1956).

[44] *See* pp. 175-76 *supra.*

[45] 281 U.S. 548, 570 (1930) (Hughes).

[46] 208 U.S. 161 (1908) (Harlan). *See* p. 27 *supra.*

[47] McReynolds did not participate. Texas & N. O. R.R., 281 U.S. at 571. *See also* T. POWELL, *supra* note
43, at 78 (arguing that this decision and NLRB v. Jones & Laughlin Steel Corp., 301 U.S. 1 (1937), pp. 236-38
*infra,* "clearly annul Mr. Justice Harlan's absurd commerce clause point in the *Adair* case").

[48] 283 U.S. 423 (1931) (Brandeis). McReynolds alone dissented, *id.* at 464, arguing only that the case should
not be disposed of on a motion to dismiss. *See* Niles, *Arizona v. California,* 10 N.Y.U. L. Q. REV. 188, 194-201
(1932).

[49] 285 U.S. 22, 39-40, 44, 46 (1932).

[50] Earlier cases, as Hughes noted, had allowed Congress to vest civilian adjudicatory authority within the
states in non-article III tribunals only when there was no constitutional right to judicial proceedings of any kind,
as in the payment of government obligations. *See id.* at 50-51 (discussing *Ex parte* Bakelite Corp., 279 U.S. 438
(1929)); pp. 191-93 *supra.*

[51] 285 U.S. at 51, 54. This conclusion echoed the position Hughes had taken as Governor of New York in
1907 in advocating limited judicial review of public utility commissions. *See* 1 M. PUSEY, *supra* note 22, at 203-

In the next section of the opinion, in which he concluded that "fundamental or 'jurisdictional'" fact-findings had to be reviewed de novo, Hughes neatly refuted his own argument. To permit Congress to

> substitute for constitutional courts, in which the judicial power of the United
> States is vested, an administrative agency . . . for the final determination of
> the existence of the facts upon which the enforcement of the constitutional
> rights of the citizen depend . . . would be to sap the judicial power as it exists
> under the Federal Constitution, and to establish a government of a bureau-
> cratic character alien to our system, wherever fundamental rights depend, as
> not infrequently they do depend, upon the facts.[52]

Juries and masters were distinguishable after all, for the former acted "under the constant
superintendance of the trial judge," and the latter's reports were "essentially advisory."[53]

Hughes was right the second time: review of questions of law was inadequate to protect
the rights of the parties. It was this insight that had led the Framers to authorize Congress
to establish lower federal courts.[54] Moreover, as Alexander Hamilton pointed out, constitutional questions are not the only ones that should be decided without fear of reprisal.[55]
In suggesting that essentially appellate review of most administrative decisions would
satisfy article III, the Court seemed to say that the explicit requirements of tenure and
irreducible salary for judges "both of the supreme and inferior courts" applied only to
appellate judges.[56]

---

04. It did seem to suggest that article III required judicial review of questions of law decided by non-article III
tribunals.

[52] 285 U.S. at 56-57. The issues held subject to de novo review were whether the injury occurred on navigable
waters and whether the relation of master and servant existed: "These conditions are indispensable to the application of the statute, not only because the Congress has so provided explicitly . . . but also because the power of
the Congress to enact the legislation turns upon the existence of these conditions." *Id.* at 55. Related to this
conclusion was the reaffirmation in St. Joseph Stock Yards Co. v. United States, 298 U.S. 38 (1936) (Hughes,
over critical concurrences by Brandeis, Stone, and Cardozo), that due process required "an independent judicial
judgment upon the facts" when administratively prescribed rates were attacked as confiscatory. *Id.* at 52. *See*
Ohio Valley Water Co. v. Ben Avon Borough, 253 U.S. 287, 289 (1920), *supra* p. 110, note 123; Chicago, M.
& St. P. Ry. v. Minnesota, 134 U.S. 418 (1890), pp. 41-44 *supra*. For the subsequent fate of these requirements,
see L. JAFFE, JUDICIAL CONTROL OF ADMINISTRATIVE ACTION 636-53 (1965).

[53] 285 U.S. at 61. One may add that juries are explicitly required by the Constitution and are immune from
the presidential and congressional pressures that underlie the tenure and salary provisions.

[54] Osborn v. Bank of the United States, 22 U.S. 738, 822-23 (1824) (noting that without original federal
jurisdiction the litigant would have only "the insecure remedy of an appeal upon an insulated point, after it has
received the shape which may be given to it by another tribunal"). *See also* THE FIRST HUNDRED YEARS at 93
n.24, 104.

[55] "[I]t is not with a view to infractions of the Constitution only that the independence of the judges may be an
essential safeguard." FEDERALIST PAPERS NO. 78, at 470 (A. Hamilton) (Heirloom ed. 1966).

[56] Later commentators have recognized that this, rather than the limited requirement of de novo review that
originally attracted much attention, was the more significant aspect of the decision. *See* L. JAFFE, *supra* note 52,
at 89-90; P. BATOR, P. MISHKIN, D. SHAPIRO, & H. WECHSLER, HART AND WECHSLER'S THE FEDERAL COURTS
AND THE FEDERAL SYSTEM 338 (2d ed. 1973) [hereinafter cited as HART AND WECHSLER]. Justice Brandeis,
joined by Stone and Roberts, would have gone even further, permitting Congress to limit review even of constitutional fact findings, principally because Congress did not have to create lower federal courts at all: "Matters

## II.  Darkness at Noon

By the time 1934 ended, the Court had thus provided strong evidence of a tendency to relax a variety of preexisting limitations on social and economic legislation. For anyone who thought the bad old days were over, however, 1935 was to serve a strong dose of cold water.

## A.  Delegation

### 1.  Hot oil

The National Industrial Recovery Act was a centerpiece of the New Deal, a comprehensive shock treatment designed to cure the economy of its depression. Among other things, the act authorized the President to prohibit interstate and foreign transportation of petroleum and its products "produced or withdrawn from storage in excess of the amount permitted . . . by any state law." In *Panama Refining Co. v. Ryan* the Court held that this provision unconstitutionally delegated to the President legislative power vested in Congress by article I.[57]

The principle the Chief Justice invoked was hoary and respectable, but it had never drawn blood before. Recognizing that the President's article II responsibility to execute the laws entailed interstitial policy-making, the Court had upheld a variety of measures against nondelegation arguments. An executive finding that one nation respected our neutrality could reactivate an embargo against another; executive officers could be empowered to set standards of quality and fitness for imports, to protect national forests from deterio-

---

which may be placed within their jurisdiction may instead be committed to the state courts." 285 U.S. at 86-87. State judges, however, are not subject to the congressional and presidential pressures that prompted adoption of the tenure and salary requirements, and allowing them to decide federal cases serves independent goals of federalism that are absent in the case of federal administrative agencies. *See* Krattenmaker, *Article III and Judicial Independence: Why the New Bankruptcy Courts Are Unconstitutional*, 70 Geo. L. J. 297, 304 (1981); D. Currie, *Bankruptcy Judges and the Independent Judiciary*, 16 Creighton L. Rev. 441, 447 (1983).

Two decisions the following year, without citing *Crowell*, showed there was still life in article III. *See* O'Donoghue v. United States, 289 U.S. 516, 536 (1933) (Sutherland, over three dissents), which distinguished the cases upholding territorial courts, such as American Ins. Co. v. Canter, 26 U.S. 511 (1828), The First Hundred Years at 119-22, on the ground that the territories were "transitory," in holding that article III protected salaries of District of Columbia judges from reduction; Williams v. United States, 289 U.S. 553, 580-81 (1933) (Sutherland, for a unanimous Court), which artificially concluded that suits brought against the United States with its consent were not article III cases, in order to reconcile reduction of the salaries of Court of Claims judges with the principle that article III powers could be exercised only by article III courts: "since Congress . . . may . . . confer upon an executive officer or administrative board, . . . or retain for itself, the power to . . . determine controversies respecting claims against the United States, it follows indubitably that such power . . . is no part of the judicial power vested in the constitutional courts." For precedents less favorable to the independence of the judges, see pp. 191-93 *supra;* for apt criticism of the *Williams* reading of the jurisdictional clauses of article III, see Hart and Wechsler, *supra* note 56, at 398-99.

[57] 293 U.S. 388 (1935) (invalidating the National Industrial Recovery Act of June 16, 1933, Title I, § 9(c), 48 Stat. 195, 200 (1933)). *See* U.S. Const. art. I, § 1 ("All legislative powers herein granted shall be vested in a Congress of the United States.").

ration, and to raise tariffs to compensate for high duties or low production costs abroad.[58] The decisive factor seemed to be that in each case Congress had made the basic policy decision, leaving to the executive only the task of applying a statutory "primary standard" or "intelligible principle."[59]

As Cardozo observed in a lone dissent, the provision at stake in *Panama* left the President no latitude whatever once he decided to act: he was to forbid interstate or foreign commerce in petroleum produced in excess of state limitations. In this respect the law was far more confining than many of those the Court had previously upheld.[60]

What concerned the Court was the absence of any provision limiting the President's discretion whether to act at all:

> Section 9(c) does not state whether, or in what circumstances or under what conditions, the President is to prohibit the transportation of the amount of petroleum . . . produced in excess of the State's permission. . . . Congress has declared no policy, has established no standard, has laid down no rule.[61]

Earlier opinions had not emphasized that the provisions they upheld were mandatory, but Cardozo could not very well deny that whether to ban commerce in "hot" oil was a fundamental policy question. Instead, he found elsewhere in the legislation implicit criteria to direct and confine the President in answering it. "[B]y reasonable implication the power conferred upon the President by § 9(c) is to be read as if coupled with the words that he shall exercise the power whenever satisfied that by doing so he will effectuate the policy of the statute as theretofore declared"—that is, when the effect of transporting hot oil "is to promote unfair competition or to waste the natural resources or to demoralize prices or to increase unemployment or to reduce the purchasing power of the workers of the nation."[62] In declining to follow this path, the other eight Justices seemed to pay little heed to the familiar maxim that statutes should be construed if possible so as to preserve their constitutionality.[63]

[58] *See* The Brig Aurora, 11 U.S. 382, 383 (1813); Buttfield v. Stranahan, 192 U.S. 470 (1904); United States v. Grimaud, 220 U.S. 506 (1911); Field v. Clark, 143 U.S. 649 (1892); J. W. Hampton, Jr. & Co. v. United States, 276 U.S. 394 (1928); THE FIRST HUNDRED YEARS at 118-19; pp. 16-19, 195-96 *supra.*

[59] *See Buttfield,* 192 U.S. at 496; J. W. Hampton, Jr. & Co., 276 U.S. at 409.

[60] *See* 293 U.S. at 434-35. Notwithstanding a lack of persuasive supporting reasons, precedent had essentially disposed of the argument that by allowing state production quotas substantially to determine federal policy the statute invalidly delegated congressional power to the states. *See* United States v. Hill, 248 U.S. 420 (1919); p. 115, note 150 *supra.*

[61] 293 U.S. at 415, 430.

[62] *Id.* at 438, 437. For a view approving this position, see L. JAFFE, *supra* note 52, at 63. For the view that the majority was right but that the limits it placed on delegation were "formal rather than substantial," see Cousens, *The Delegation of Federal Legislative Power to Executive Officials,* 33 MICH. L. REV. 512, 539-40, 544 (1935).

[63] *See* 293 U.S. at 439 (Cardozo, dissenting). For the origins of this venerable principle, see THE FIRST HUNDRED YEARS at 29-30, (discussing Mossman v. Higginson, 4 U.S. 12 (1800)).

No limiting construction was thought necessary, on the other hand, to sustain the delegation of authority to the President to prohibit the sale of arms to Bolivia or Paraguay if he found such a ban "may contribute to the reestablishment of peace between those two countries." United States v. Curtiss-Wright Corp., 299 U.S. 304,

Since the defect the Court had perceived could be mended by a more definitive assertion of congressional will, and since the opinion had been joined by such tolerant Justices
as Brandeis and Stone, the decision did not necessarily display hostility toward regulation
as such, or even toward federal regulation.[64] Nevertheless it portended rough sailing for
other and more important New Deal provisions.

## 2.  Sick chickens

Four months later, in *Schechter Poultry Corp. v. United States*, the Court applied the same
doctrine to cut the heart out of the statute whose extremities the *Panama* decision had
already amputated. Schechter had been prosecuted for violating a "code of fair competition," promulgated by the President for the poultry business under § 3 of the National
Industrial Recovery Act, by failing to comply with the code's minimum-wage and
maximum-hour provisions and by selling "an unfit chicken."[65]

The only flaw in the provision nullified in *Panama*, wrote Chief Justice Hughes, had
been the breadth of presidential discretion in determining whether or not to act. In *Schechter* the difficulty was "more fundamental": there was no "adequate definition of the subject
to which the codes [we]re to be addressed."[66] Apart from antimonopoly and hearing provisions and a requirement that trade associations proposing codes to the President be "representative," the President's discretion in this regard was "virtually unfettered." Unlike the
"unfair methods of competition" forbidden by the Federal Trade Commission Act, codes
of "fair competition" were not limited to anything resembling the established common
law. "Rather, the purpose is clearly disclosed to authorize new and controlling prohibitions

---

312 (1936). Assuming that such a delegation would be invalid "if it were confined to internal affairs," Justice
Sutherland properly observed that it was easier to uphold statutes authorizing the President to act in foreign
matters, since the Constitution itself gave him authority in that field "which does not require as a basis for its
exercise an act of Congress." *Id.* at 315, 319-20. Similar considerations may support the Court's cavalier conclusion in Sibbach v. Wilson & Co., 312 U.S. 1, 9-10 (1941), that Congress could delegate to the Supreme Court
authority to adopt procedural rules with virtually no legislative standards at all. With respect to the authority of
courts to adopt their own procedural rules, see also THE FIRST HUNDRED YEARS at 117-19 (discussing Wayman
v. Southard, 23 U.S. 1 (1825)).

For another interestingly broad view of the President's foreign affairs authority, see United States v. Belmont,
301 U.S. 324, 330-31 (1937) (Sutherland), upholding an executive agreement whereby the United States succeeded to claims of Russian citizens expropriated by the Soviet government. As the Court said, the agreement
was incidental to United States recognition of that government and the establishment of diplomatic relations; it
could therefore plausibly fit within the President's apparently innocuous authority to "receive Ambassadors," art.
II, § 3, which Sutherland did not mention. *See* G. GUNTHER, CASES AND MATERIALS ON CONSTITUTIONAL LAW
368 (11th ed. 1985). More serious was the objection that the treaty clause of article II required Senate consent;
in holding that not every "international compact" was a "treaty" without specifying which ones were (compare
the distinction in art. I, § 10 between state "treaties" that are absolutely forbidden and "compacts" that Congress
may approve), the Court seemed to risk erosion of the Senate's constitutional authority. *See* Berger, *The Presidential Monopoly of Foreign Relations*, 71 MICH. L. REV. 1, 33-48 (1972); Kurland, *The Impotence of Reti-
cence*, 1968 DUKE L. J. 619, 626.

[64] Indeed Congress remedied the defect within six weeks by forbidding interstate transportation of hot oil
outright. Connally Hot Oil Act, 49 Stat. 30 (1935). *See* Stern, *The Commerce Clause and the National Economy,
1933–1946*, 59 HARV. L. REV. 645, 658 (1946).

[65] 295 U.S. 495, 521-22, 528 (1935).

[66] *Id.* at 530-31.

through codes of laws which would embrace what the formulators would propose, and what the President would approve, or prescribe, as wise and beneficient [*sic*] measures for the government of trades and industries in order to bring about their rehabilitation, correction and development."[67]

This time the decision was unanimous, and rightly so. As Cardozo noted in a concurring opinion joined by Stone, the power conveyed was "as wide as the field of industrial regulation. . . . [A]nything that Congress may do within the limits of the commerce clause for the betterment of business may be done by the President . . . by calling it a code. This is delegation running riot."[68] It would no doubt have been impolitic to say so, but it can hardly have escaped the Justices that apart from its limitation to business there was little to distinguish what Congress had attempted from the 1933 legislation authorizing Adolf Hitler to govern Germany by decree.[69] Far from reflecting hostility to federal regulation as such, the delegation decision in *Schechter* was a salutary reminder of the wisdom of the Framers' decision to vest legislative power in a representative assembly.[70]


### 3. Coal miners

The codes of fair competition in *Schechter* had been formulated by private trade associations and approved by the President. The requirement of presidential approval made it unnecessary to decide whether a delegation of legislative authority to private persons also would be unconstitutional,[71] but the opinion left no doubt that it would:

> [W]ould it be seriously contended that Congress could delegate its legislative authority to trade or industrial associations or groups so as to empower them to enact the laws they deemed to be wise and beneficent for the rehabilitation and expansion of their trade or industries? . . . The answer is obvious. Such a delegation of legislative power is unknown to our law and is utterly inconsistent with the constitutional prerogatives and duties of Congress.[72]

The Bituminous Coal Conservation Act of 1935, another New Deal measure, presented the question thus previewed in *Schechter.* Congress had provided in effect that minimum wages and maximum hours agreed upon by the preponderance of coal miners and produc-

---

[67]*Id.* at 533-35, 537. For a prediction that the precedents could sustain even this delegation, see Black, *The National Industrial Recovery Act and the Delegation of Legislative Power to the President,* 19 CORNELL L. Q. 389 (1934).

[68]295 U.S. at 553.

[69]BGBl. 1933, Teil I, S. 141 ("Reichsgesetze können ausser in dem in der Reichsverfassung vorgesehenen Verfahren auch durch die Reichsregierung beschlossen werden." [Imperial statutes may be enacted not only by the procedure provided for in the Constitution of the Empire, but also by the Imperial Executive.]). For a glimpse of the delegation issue in modern Germany through American eyes, see Currie, *Der Vorbehalt des Gesetzes: Amerikanische Analogien,* in GÖTZ, KLEIN, & STARCK, DIE ÖFFENTLICHE VERWALTUNG ZWISCHEN GESETZ-GEBUNG UND RICHTERLICHER KONTROLLE 68 (1985).

[70]*See also* Currie, *The Distribution of Powers after* Bowsher, 1986 SUP. CT. REV. 19, 21-31.

[71]*See Schechter,* 295 U.S. at 552 (Cardozo, concurring) ("The[ir] function is strictly advisory; it is the *imprimatur* of the President that begets the quality of law. . . . When the task that is set before one is that of cleaning house, it is prudent as well as usual to take counsel of the dwellers.").

[72]*Id.* at 537.

ers should bind the entire industry.[73] Speaking through Justice Sutherland in *Carter v. Carter Coal Co.* in 1936, the Court lived up to its promise:

> The power conferred upon the majority is, in effect, the power to regulate the affairs of an unwilling minority. This is legislative delegation in its most obnoxious form; for it is not even delegation to an official or an official body, presumptively disinterested, but to private persons whose interests may be and often are adverse to the interests of others in the same business.

Regulation was "necessarily a governmental function," and a statute attempting to confer regulatory power on private persons was "so clearly arbitrary, and so clearly a denial of rights safeguarded by the due process clause of the Fifth Amendment, that it is unnecessary to do more than refer to decisions of this court which foreclose the question."[74]

Cited for this proposition were not only *Schechter* but also two earlier decisions striking down state laws found to have delegated lawmaking authority to private parties.[75] This was not necessarily to condemn lawmaking by initiative or referendum, whose constitutionality the Court had refused on political-question grounds to determine.[76] The democratic nature of these processes adequately distinguishes them from measures conferring legislative authority on particular interest groups.[77] But the Court's invocation of due process rather than article I to support its convincing conclusion did seem to call into question earlier suggestions that the separation of powers at the state level was of no federal concern. For *Carter* reminds us that due process traditionally meant the executive could act only in accordance with the "law of the land"; the policy behind the prohibition forbids the executive as well as the coal industry to make basic policy.[78]

## B.   The Headless Fourth Branch

William E. Humphrey was a member of the Federal Trade Commission, appointed by President Hoover for a seven-year term and removable by the President "for inefficiency, neglect of duty, or malfeasance in office." In *Humphrey's Executor v. United States* the

---

[73] *See* Bituminous Coal Conservation Act of 1935, Pub. L. No. 402, § 4 pt. III(g), 49 Stat. 991, 1002.

[74] 298 U.S. 238, 311 (1936).

[75] *See* Eubank v. Richmond, 226 U.S. 137, 143 (1912); Seattle Trust Co. v. Roberge, 278 U.S. 116, 121-22 (1928). *See* p. 109, note 123, *supra*. *See also* Old Dearborn Distributing Co. v. Seagram-Distillers Corp., 299 U.S. 183,194 (1936) (Sutherland), (distinguishing *Eubank, Roberge,* and *Carter* in upholding a statute creating a private right of action to recover damages resulting from sales lower than those fixed by "fair trade" (resale price maintenance) agreements to which the defendant need not be a party: "Here, the restriction, already imposed with the knowledge of appellants, ran with the acquisition [of the goods] and conditioned it").

[76] Pacific Telephone Co. v. Oregon, 223 U.S. 118 (1912), *supra* p. 93, note 20.

[77] *See* City of Eastlake v. Forest City Enterprises, Inc., 426 U.S. 668, 675 (1976) (upholding a requirement that zoning changes be approved by referendum: the nondelegation doctrine "is inapplicable where, as here, rather than . . . a delegation of power, we deal with a power reserved by the people to themselves").

[78] *See supra* p. 16-17, note 63 and cases cited therein; THE FIRST HUNDRED YEARS at 272. Nevertheless, the Court unanimously refused, the year after *Carter,* to reexamine its conclusion regarding separation of powers at the state level. Highland Farms Dairy, Inc. v. Agnew, 300 U.S. 608, 612 (1937) (Cardozo) ("How power shall be distributed by a state among its governmental organs is commonly, if not always, a question for the state itself.").

Court held that President Roosevelt had acted unlawfully in removing Humphrey for policy reasons before his term expired.[79]

In *Myers v. United States*, a few years before, the Taft Court had ringingly held that a statutory requirement of Senate consent to discharge a postmaster impaired the President's article II control over executive functions.[80] This principle, wrote Justice Sutherland for a unanimous Court in *Humphrey's Executor*, was inapplicable to the trade commission because it was not an executive agency:

> In administering the provisions of the statute in respect of "unfair methods of competition"—that is to say in filling in and administering the details embodied by that general standard—the commission acts in part quasi-legislatively and in part quasi-judicially . . . To the extent that it exercises any executive function—as distinguished from executive power in the constitutional sense—it does so in the discharge and effectuation of its quasi-legislative or quasi-judicial powers, or as an agency of the legislative or judicial departments of the government.[81]

This was quite remarkable. Previous decisions had upheld delegations of apparently legislative or judicial powers to administrative officers on the ground that the executive function itself embraced the elaboration and application of legislative policy.[82] To deny that the commission's powers were executive was to demonstrate that they could be exercised only by Congress or by the courts.

Even if the Court was right that giving content to the statutory command in deciding cases was not an executive function, the same hardly could be said of the commission's authority to file complaints against offenders. Prosecution is neither legislation nor adjudication but rather a quintessential means of law enforcement.[83] If the President cannot control the prosecutor, he cannot fulfill his constitutional duty to "take care that the laws be faithfully executed."[84] The message of *Humphrey's Executor* thus seemed to be that

[79] 295 U.S. 602 (1935). Strictly speaking, the holding was that Humphrey was entitled to his continuing salary. *See* Miller, *Independent Agencies*, 1986 SUP. CT. REV. 41, 93-95 (arguing for this reason that the decision is not a firm precedent for congressional authority to limit the power of removal).

[80] 272 U.S. 52 (1926), pp. 193-95 *supra*.

[81] Humphrey's Executor, 295 U.S. at 628.

[82] *See, e.g.*, notes 57-64 and accompanying text above (discussing Panama Refining Co. v. Ryan); Murray's Lessee v. Hoboken Land & Improvement Co., 59 U.S. 272 (1856) (extrajudicial distraint procedure held consistent with article III as an executive function); *Ex parte* Bakelite Corp., 279 U.S. 438, 451 (1929) (executive officers may adjudicate "matters . . . which from their nature do not require judicial determination and yet are susceptible of it"). *Humphrey's Executor* itself described the commission as "an administrative body created by Congress to carry into effect legislative policies embodied in the statute." 295 U.S. at 628. *See also* Bowsher v. Synar, 478 U.S. 714, 733 (1986) ("Interpreting a law enacted by Congress to implement the legislative mandate is the very essence of 'execution' of the law.").

[83] *See* Buckley v. Valeo, 424 U.S. 1, 109-43 (1976) (holding that because, among other things, their prosecutorial duties were executive, members of the Federal Election Commission were "Officers of the United States" who consequently could not be appointed by Congress).

[84] U.S. Const. art. II, § 3. *See also* Miller, *supra* note 79, at 44. Hughes himself had made a similar argument at the policy level in arguing for gubernatorial removal of bungling members of public service commissions in 1907. *See* 1 M. PUSEY, *supra* note 22, at 202-03. Unlike the provision condemned in *Myers*, and like the one Hughes had advocated in 1907, the provision upheld in *Humphrey's Executor* permitted the President to discharge

Congress could violate article II if it was willing to violate articles I and III at the same time, as well as the separation of powers.[85]

## C.  Commerce

The nondelegation doctrine only forbade Congress to transfer its authority to others; it cast no doubt on the validity of congressional regulation. Both *Schechter* and *Carter*, however, also made clear that Congress itself could not have enacted the challenged measures, and a third decision rendered shortly before *Schechter* had taken a still more restrictive view.

### 1. Schechter Poultry Corp. v. United States

The defendants bought live poultry, slaughtered it, and sold it to local retailers. Most of the poultry came from other states. However, as the Court in *Schechter* said, the interstate journey ended when the birds reached the slaughterhouse: "Neither the slaughtering nor the sales by defendants were transactions in interstate commerce."[86]

The government argued that the wages and hours of slaughterhouse employees and the quality of birds sold *affected* interstate commerce by influencing the price, quantity, and quality of poultry shipped from one state to another.[87] Chief Justice Hughes, who had written two of the principal decisions on which this argument was based, agreed that Congress had some power to protect interstate commerce from "injury . . . due to the conduct of those engaged in intrastate operations."[88] If Congress could regulate *everything* affecting commerce, however, "there would be virtually no limit to the federal power and for all practical purposes we should have a completely centralized government."[89]

---

a trade commissioner for "inefficiency, neglect of duty, or malfeasance in office." *Humphrey's Executor,* 295 U.S. at 620. Since one of the principal goals of the legislation had been to create a commission independent of the President, however, one could not very well twist these restrictive terms to make the failure to follow presidential orders a ground for removal. *See* 295 U.S. at 624-26, summarizing the legislative history.

[85] *See* Currie, *supra* note 70, at 31-36. The principle that the same person may not be both prosecutor and judge also is reflected in the concept that due process requires fundamentally fair procedure. *See also* Tumey v. Ohio, 273 U.S. 510, 523 (1927) (holding that a judge may not be compensated only when he convicts defendants); L. CARROLL, ALICE'S ADVENTURES IN WONDERLAND ch. 3 (McKibbin ed. 1899). For a comprehensive contemporaneous assessment of *Humphrey's Executor,* see Cushman, *The Constitutional Status of the Independent Regulatory Commissions,* 24 CORNELL L. Q. 13, 163 (1938).

[86] 295 U.S. at 543 (citing, among others, Brown v. Houston, 114 U.S. 622 (1885) (upholding state tax on goods after interstate transportation). *See* THE FIRST HUNDRED YEARS at 414 n.78.

[87] 295 U.S. at 508-10. *See* Stern, *supra* note 64, at 660, concluding that the record respecting any such effects was "meagre" and that "a sounder argument" was the more sweeping one "that depressed business conditions had catastrophically affected all commerce, including interstate, and that a possible remedy was to increase the purchasing power of all wage earners through wage and hour regulation, thereby increasing the demand for products to be shipped in commerce." This argument, Stern conceded, "had . . . little chance of success in the judicial climate of that period." *Id.* at 661.

[88] 295 U.S. at 544 (citing, among others, Houston, E. & W. Tex. Ry. v. United States (Shreveport Rate Case), 234 U.S. 342 (1914) (Hughes) (federal regulation of local rail rates in competition with interstate traffic)). *See also* Baltimore & Ohio R.R. v. Int. Com. Comm., 221 U.S. 612, 619 (1911) (Hughes) (federal limitation of hours worked in local commerce by employee also engaged in interstate commerce); pp. 93-96 *supra.*

[89] 295 U.S. at 548. *See also* Black, *The Commerce Clause and the New Deal,* 20 CORNELL L. Q. 169, 179 (1935) ("Since the depression seriously obstructs the flow of commodities in interstate commerce, it follows that

This was true, and it was refreshing to see the Court acknowledge it, for in some of their more recent pronouncements the Justices had tended to emphasize the effect on commerce without much attention to whether their decision left anything outside the enumeration of limited federal powers.[90] Cardozo put the point with his accustomed elegance in an emphatic concurring opinion: "If centripetal forces are to be isolated to the exclusion of the forces that oppose and counteract them, there will be an end to our federal system."[91]

As always, it was easier to declare that there were limits than to explain why the particular case lay beyond them. Hughes recurred to the tired distinction between "direct" and "indirect" effects on commerce without satisfactorily distinguishing earlier decisions.[92] Cardozo abandoned the illusive quest for objective criteria altogether, stressing that "[t]he law [was] not indifferent to considerations of degree" and concluding without elaboration that "[t]o find immediacy or directness here is to find it almost everywhere."[93]

The candid imprecision of Cardozo's approach reflects the subjective nature of the problem. Surely too he and all his colleagues were right on the facts of the case: to permit Congress to regulate the wages and hours in a tiny slaughterhouse because of remote effects on interstate commerce would leave nothing for the tenth amendment to reserve.

## 2.   *Carter v. Carter Coal Co.*

Five Justices thought *Schechter* governed the commerce clause question in *Carter.* Coal mining was production, not commerce; Congress could no more regulate what preceded interstate trade than what followed it. Any impact of low wages or long hours in the mining industry on commerce, moreover, was "indirect." It mattered not that the companies involved were large and the effect on commerce great: "The word 'direct' . . . connotes the absence of an efficient intervening agency or condition. . . . The distinction between a direct and an indirect effect turns, not upon the magnitude of either the cause or the effect, but entirely upon the manner in which the effect has been brought about."[94] Thus Congress itself could not set minimum wages or maximum hours for coal miners.

---

measures reasonably calculated to free business from the burdens of the depression are regulations which will protect and foster interstate commerce."). *See generally* Powell, *Commerce, Pensions, and Codes, II,* 49 Harv. L. Rev. 193 (1935).

[90] *See* pp. 93-96 *supra* and cases there discussed.

[91] 295 U.S. at 554.

[92] *Id.* at 546-48. *Contrast* with the finding of indirectness in *Schechter,* Baltimore & Ohio R.R. v. Int. Com. Comm., 221 U.S. 612 (1911) (hours worked locally by employee also engaged in interstate commerce); Southern Ry. Co. v. United States, 222 U.S. 20, 27 (1911) (couplers on intrastate cars); Shreveport Rate Case, 234 U.S. 342 (1914) (intrastate rail rates). *See* pp. 22-24, 93-96 *supra.* For criticism of Hughes's distinction, see Corwin, *The Schechter Case—Landmark, or What?,* 13 N.Y.U. L. Q. Rev. 151, 162-70 (1936).

[93] 295 U.S. at 554. *See also* Panhandle Oil Co. v. Knox, 277 U.S. 218, 223 (1928) (Holmes, dissenting) ("most of the distinctions of the law are distinctions of degree").

[94] Carter, 298 U.S. at 307-08. *See* the government's ingenious argument that the enumerated powers should be construed in light of Randolph's initial proposal to authorize Congress "to legislate in all cases to which the separate States are incompetent, or in which the harmony of the United States may be interrupted by the exercise of individual Legislation." *Id.* at 257-58 (oral argument of Mr. Dickinson). This argument, which had been developed in Stern, *That Commerce Which Concerns More States Than One,* 47 Harv. L. Rev. 1335, 1338-40 (1934), was not easy to reconcile with the Convention's rejection of that proposal in favor of an enumeration. *Carter,* 298 U.S. at 292.

While the result was the same as in *Schechter,* the tone of the opinion in *Carter* was quite different. Conspicuously missing from *Carter* was Hughes's insistence that Congress had power to prevent harm to commerce regardless of its source. In accents reminiscent of the discredited decision in *United States v. E. C. Knight Co.,*[95] Sutherland seemed to consider his job essentially done once he had laboriously established the obvious proposition that mining was not itself interstate commerce.[96]

In a separate opinion Hughes agreed that the labor provisions went "beyond any proper measure of protection of interstate commerce." However, following the analysis he had employed in *Schechter,* he suggested that additional provisions setting minimum prices for local coal sales might be permissible in order to prevent discrimination against interstate commerce. Cardozo's dissent, joined by Brandeis and Stone, went further: "Within rulings the most orthodox, the prices for intrastate sales of coal have so inescapable a relation to those for interstate sales that a system of regulation for transactions of the one class is necessary to give adequate protection to the system of regulation adopted for the other."[97]

Both Hughes and Cardozo relied on the *Shreveport Rate Case,* which had upheld federal regulation of local rail rates. The citation was apt; the provisions in both cases prevented the loss of substantial interstate business to local competition. Finding the price and labor provisions inseparable, the majority nullified the price provisions without considering their merits.[98] Cardozo, on the other hand, found the challenge to the labor provisions unripe.[99] The majority thus struck down one provision; the dissenters voted to uphold another.

If precedent was to be respected, the difficult question in *Carter* was whether the effect of the labor provisions was more like that of the rate regulation upheld in *Shreveport* or that of similar wage and hour rules struck down in *Schechter.* In Sutherland's terms it was arguable that the effect of wages on commerce was always more indirect than that of prices. Low local prices attract customers away from interstate markets; low wages reduce production costs and thus tend to lower prices.[100] On the other hand, wages paid by huge coal companies clearly have a greater impact on commerce than those paid by a diminutive butcher, and there was no compelling reason for Sutherland's conclusion that the magnitude of the effect had to be ignored. Hughes, the only Justice to comment on both the price and the labor provisions, did not say why he found one more acceptable than the other.[101]

---

[95] 156 U.S. 1 (1895), pp. 22-24 *supra.*

[96] 298 U.S. at 297-310.

[97] *Id.* at 320 (Hughes), 329 (Cardozo).

[98] 298 U.S. at 312-16. The Court reached this conclusion despite a clause explicitly providing that "[i]f any provision of this Act . . . is held invalid, the remainder of the Act . . . shall not be affected thereby." For the obvious objections, see the separate opinions of Hughes and Cardozo, 298 U.S. at 321-24, 334-38; Stern, *Separability and Separability Clauses in the Supreme Court,* 51 HARV. L. REV. 76 (1937). That Congress had meant what it said was suggested by its prompt reenactment of the price provisions, see Bituminous Coal Act of 1937, Pub. L. No. 48, § 4 pt. II, 50 Stat. 72, which were upheld over McReynolds's dissent in Sunshine Coal Co. v. Adkins, 310 U.S. 381 (1940).

[99] 298 U.S. at 324.

[100] The effect of wages paid in processing goods that are to be shipped or have been shipped from one state to another, however, may be thought more "direct" than that of wages paid in connection with competing local goods.

[101] Hughes's biographer, who paints the Chief Justice as a consistent supporter of broad federal authority, says he objected to the labor provisions "chiefly" on delegation grounds. 2 M. PUSEY, *supra* note 22, at 746. But the

Cardozo pointed out once again that it was a mistake to attempt to encompass the governing principle in the single adjective "direct":

> Strictly speaking, the intrastate rates [in cases like *Shreveport*] have a primary effect upon the intrastate traffic and not upon any other, though the repercussions of the competitive system may lead to secondary consequences affecting interstate traffic also. . . . At times, as in [*Schechter*], the waves of causation will have radiated so far that their undulatory motion, if discernible at all, will be too faint or obscure, too broken by cross-currents, to be heeded by the law. In such circumstances the holding is not directed at prices or wages considered in the abstract, but at prices or wages in particular conditions.[102]

One regrets that Cardozo did not have the opportunity to show how this unavoidably subjective test applied to minimum wages and maximum hours for coal miners.

### 3. *Railroad Retirement Board v. Alton R.R.*

*Carter* may have been a borderline case after *Shreveport,* but Sutherland's emphasis on the distinction between production and commerce seemed to cast doubt on *Shreveport* itself. More startling still was the split decision in *Railroad Retirement Board v. Alton R.R.* that Congress could not establish a retirement and pension system even for railroad workers indisputably engaged in interstate commerce.[103]

As Hughes argued for four Justices in dissent, a long series of decisions had upheld regulations touching interstate railroading. "[N]othing which has a real or substantial relation to the suitable maintenance of [rail] service, or to the discharge of the responsibilities which inhere in it," they argued, "can be regarded as beyond the power of [congressional] regulation."[104] Pension plans could reasonably be found to promote transportation by encouraging retirement of superannuated employees, reducing wage costs attributable to seniority, and improving worker morale.[105]

For the majority, Roberts applied an extremely sharp scalpel to these arguments. The fact that railroads were becoming safer as their workers aged showed that pensions had no effect on safety, and in any event the railroads could retire overage workers without pension. Retirement was irrelevant to cost because pay did not increase with seniority, and morale could not be considered without abandoning all limits on federal power.[106]

---

opinion flatly added that "[t]he provision goes beyond any proper measure of protection of interstate commerce and attempts a broad regulation of industry within the State." 298 U.S. at 318-19.

[102] 298 U.S. at 327–28. "Perhaps," he added, "if one group of adjectives is to be chosen in preference to another, 'intimate' and 'remote' will be found to be as good as any."

[103] 295 U.S. 330 (1935), criticized in Powell, *Commerce, Pensions, and Codes,* 49 HARV. L. REV. 1 (1935).

[104] 295 U.S. at 376 (Hughes, joined by Brandeis, Stone, and Cardozo, dissenting). An example of the decisions upholding regulations affecting interstate railroading is Northern Securities Co. v. United States, 193 U.S. 197, 342-54 (1904) (upholding federal antitrust prosecution for creation of holding company eliminating competition between two interstate railroads). *See also* the railroad cases discussed at pp. 93-96 *supra* and in the *Alton R.R.* opinions, and the irreverent suggestion in T. POWELL, *supra* note 43, at 42, that after *Alton R.R.* "[i]t is a regulation of interstate commerce to help railroads but not to help railroad employees."

[105] 295 U.S. at 378-80.

[106] *Id.* at 362-71. The majority added that workers' compensation was distinguishable because it created an incentive to safety. *Id.* at 370.

Not all of this reasoning was logically flawed.[107] The level of scrutiny it reflected, however, was at opposite poles from the test of necessity and propriety of federal legislation that Marshall had laid down in the national bank case.[108] The tenor of the opinion was inconsistent not only with the judicial restraint exercised with Roberts's concurrence in reviewing insurance regulation in *O'Gorman,* but also with Roberts's own sympathetic search for debatable bases on which to uphold the chain store tax in *Jackson.*[109]

*Schechter* was an obvious case, and *Carter* may have been right even after *Shreveport.* But one would have to go back to the 1908 decision forbidding Congress to protect the union rights of interstate rail workers[110] to find another decision in which the commerce clause was so grudgingly construed as in the case of the Alton Road.[111]

## D.   Taxing

In the *Child Labor Tax Case* in 1922 the Court had invalidated a federal tax as a pretext for regulating a subject Congress could not regulate directly.[112] In 1935 and 1936 the Court invalidated two more.

One of these was in *Carter.* The Bituminous Coal Conservation Act imposed a 15 percent gross receipts tax but largely exempted producers who adhered to the wage and price standards. "It is very clear," wrote Sutherland, "that the 'excise tax' is not imposed for revenue but exacted as a penalty to compel compliance with the regulatory provisions of the act."[113] No Justice took issue with this conclusion, and the prohibitive nature of the exaction supports it. Sutherland did not try to distinguish *McCray v. United States,* which had upheld an equally crippling federal tax on yellow margarine.[114]

The year before, in *United States v. Constantine,* the Court had struck down a federal excise tax on persons selling liquor in violation of state law. That the tax singled out criminals and that the amount was forty times that levied on lawful dealers, wrote Justice Roberts, showed that "the purpose [was] to impose a penalty as a deterrent and punishment of unlawful conduct." Cardozo, joined by Brandeis and Stone, argued in dissent that the higher profits and enforcement costs associated with illegal activities afforded plausible reasons of revenue policy for the discrimination and protested that the Court's search

---

[107] The last argument was refuted by the fact that the measure was confined to an interstate industry, and the increase in safety attributable to technological advances did not disprove the self-evident risks created by elderly workers.

[108] *See* THE FIRST HUNDRED YEARS at 160-65 (discussing McCulloch v. Maryland, 17 U.S. 316 (1819)).

[109] Though different constitutional provisions were involved in these cases, Roberts acknowledged in *Alton R.R.* that, as Justice Harlan had established many years before, Mugler v. Kansas, 123 U.S. 623, 661 (1887), THE FIRST HUNDRED YEARS at 375-77, the due process and necessary and proper clauses both required that legislation be an appropriate means to a legitimate end. 295 U.S. at 347-48 n.5.

[110] Adair v. United States, 208 U.S. 161, 178 (1908), p. 27 *supra.*

[111] *See* Fraenkel, *Constitutional Issues in the Supreme Court, 1934 Term,* 84 U. PA. L. REV. 345, 351 (1936) (arguing that *Alton R.R.* "will probably rank with *Lochner v. New York* and *Adkins v. Children's Hospital* as high-water marks of reaction").

[112] 259 U.S. 20 (1922) (invalidating 10 percent excise tax on employers of child labor), pp. 173-74 *supra. See also* Hill v. Wallace, 259 U.S. 44 (1922) (invalidating tax on grain futures as impermissible effort at regulation).

[113] *See* 298 U.S. at 280-81, 289. *See also id.* at 289 ("The whole purpose of the exaction is to coerce what is called an agreement—which, of course, it is not, for it lacks the essential element of consent. One who does a thing in order to avoid a monetary penalty does not agree; he yields to compulsion precisely the same as though he did so to avoid a term in jail.").

[114] 195 U.S. 27 (1904), p. 30 *supra.*

for Congress's true motive had extended "the process of psychoanalysis . . . to unaccustomed fields."[115]

Even the *Child Labor Tax Case* had confirmed, as Cardozo argued, that an "incidental motive" to influence conduct immune from federal regulation did not condemn otherwise permissible taxes as pretextual; incentives are unavoidable in any tax system.[116] In the past the Court had been unduly reluctant to look behind federal taxes even when they appeared to serve no legitimate federal purpose.[117] Since nothing of the sort could be said of a $1,000 tax on an illegal liquor business, *Constantine* seemed to go too far in the opposite direction.[118]

## E.   Spending

In *Carter* and *Constantine* Congress had attempted to use taxation as a stick to discourage undesirable conduct it could not forbid. In *United States v. Butler* it attempted to use federal grants as carrots to encourage desirable conduct it could not require.[119]

In an effort to reduce surpluses that diminished farm income, the Agricultural Adjustment Act authorized the Secretary of Agriculture to subsidize farmers who agreed to limit their production. Only Stone, Brandeis, and Cardozo voted to sustain the statute, and Roberts wrote for the majority.[120]

Roberts has been widely pilloried for commencing his discussion with the statement that the Court's task was simply "to lay the article of the Constitution which is invoked beside the statute which is challenged and to decide whether the latter squares with the former."[121] This unfelicitous choice of words suggested a mechanical conception of judicial review inconsistent with the open-endedness of the text. Yet Roberts did not deny that the task required the exercise of judicial judgment. The point he was trying to make was a worthy and important one: "This court neither approves nor condemns any legislative policy. Its delicate and difficult office is to ascertain and declare whether the legislation is in accordance with, or in contravention of, the provisions of the Constitution."[122]

The only constitutional provision invoked to support the statute was the opening clause

---

[115] 296 U.S. 287, 295, 297-99 (1935).

[116] *See* Child Labor Tax Case, 259 U.S. at 38; *Constantine,* 296 U.S. at 297-98 (Cardozo, dissenting); Cushman, *Social and Economic Control through Federal Taxation,* 18 MINN. L. REV. 759, 764 (1934).

[117] *See* McCray, 195 U.S. 27 (prohibitive tax on colored margarine); United States v. Doremus, 249 U.S. 86 (1919) ($1 annual tax on persons engaged in the production or distribution of narcotics), pp. 98-99 *supra.*

[118] *See* Fraenkel, *Constitutional Issues in the Supreme Court, 1935 Term,* 85 U. PA. L. REV. 27, 29 (1936) (*Constantine* "marked a departure from earlier cases which had refused to test taxes by their motives.").

[119] 297 U.S. 1 (1936).

[120] The suit was brought by receivers of a corporation that had been assessed a special processing tax to pay for the grants. Taxpayer standing to challenge expenditures in general had been denied in Frothingham v. Mellon, 262 U.S. 447 (1923), because the impact of spending upon the taxpayer was so tenuous. *See* pp. 185-86 *supra. Butler* presented no such difficulty. Since the processing tax was earmarked for the subsidies under attack, if there were no spending there would be no tax either. *See* 297 U.S. at 57-61.

[121] 297 U.S. at 62. *See, e.g.,* A. BICKEL, THE LEAST DANGEROUS BRANCH 90 (2d ed. 1986); Barnett, *Constitutional Interpretation and Judicial Self-Restraint,* 39 MICH. L. REV. 213, 217 (1940); A. SCHLESINGER, THE POLITICS OF UPHEAVAL 458 (1960) ("slot-machine theory of jurisprudence"); T. POWELL, *supra* note 43, at 42-43 ("Try as I will, I cannot bring myself to admire both the candor and the capacity of the men who write such things to be forever embalmed in the official law reports.").

[122] 297 U.S. at 63. *See id.* at 63 ("The only power . . . [the Court] has, if such it may be called, is the power of judgment.").

of article I, § 8, which authorizes Congress "[t]o lay and collect Taxes, Duties, Imposts and Excises, to pay the Debts and provide for the common Defence and general Welfare of the United States." [123] The text can be read to confer one power or four: "to pay the debts . . ." might mean "*and* to pay the debts . . ." or "*in order*" to do so. The structure and history of the Constitution, however, had persuaded even so zealous a nationalist as Story that the clause did not give Congress an independent power to "provide for the . . . general Welfare." The Court unanimously agreed: such a construction would make

> "the government of the United States . . . , in reality, a government of general and unlimited powers, notwithstanding the subsequent enumeration of specific powers." . . . [T]he only thing granted is the power to tax for the purpose of providing funds for payment of the nation's debts and making provision for the general welfare. [124]

This authority to tax and spend for the general welfare, however, was not, as Madison had asserted, "confined to the enumerated legislative fields committed to Congress." [125] Such an interpretation, Roberts argued, would make the general welfare provision "mere tautology, for taxation and appropriation are or may be necessary incidents of the exercise of any of the enumerated legislative powers." Thus, as Hamilton and Story had argued, "Congress . . . has a substantive power to tax and to appropriate, limited only by the requirement that it shall be exercised to provide for the general welfare of the United States" and not "by the direct grants of legislative power found in the Constitution." [126]

It seemed to follow from this conclusion, as Justice Stone argued in dissent, that in a nationwide agricultural depression "the expenditure of public money in aid of farmers" was one for "the general welfare" of the United States. [127] Significantly, Roberts did not

---

[123] The United States did not contend that the act was a valid exercise of the commerce power. *Id.* at 64.

[124] *Id.* at 64 (quoting 1 J. STORY, COMMENTARIES ON THE CONSTITUTION OF THE UNITED STATES § 907 (1833)). For the same position, see Corwin, *The Spending Power of Congress—Apropos the Maternity Act*, 36 HARV. L. REV. 548, 551 (1923), *reprinted in* 1 CORWIN ON THE CONSTITUTION 246, 248 (R. Loss ed. 1981).

[125] *See Butler*, 297 U.S. at 64.

[126] *Id.* at 65, 65-66. *See* Alexander Hamilton, 1791 *Report on the Subject of Manufactures* (1791), reprinted in 10 PAPERS OF ALEXANDER HAMILTON 230, 302-04 (H. C. Syrett ed. 1966); 1 J. STORY, *supra* note 124, at ch. 14; CORWIN, *supra* note 124, at ch. 14, *reprinted in* 1 CORWIN ON THE CONSTITUTION at 249-69. Hughes later wrote that he considered this broad interpretation "the most 'significant and important ruling in the *Butler* case.'" *See* 2 M. PUSEY, *supra* note 22, at 743. In agreement is Holmes, *The Federal Spending Power and State Rights*, 34 MICH. L. REV. 637, 637 (1936), which argues that *Butler* "point[ed] the way toward unprecedented expansion of federal functions."

[127] 297 U.S. at 79. The refusal of an early Congress to provide disaster relief for a single community after debate had raised serious constitutional doubts tends to support Hamilton's insistence that "the object to which an appropriation of money is . . . made [must] be *General* and not *local;* its operation extending in fact, or by possibility, throughout the Union, and not being confined to a particular spot." 10 PAPERS OF HAMILTON, *supra* note 126, at 303 (emphasis in original). *See also* 6 ANNALS OF CONGRESS 1712-27 (1796). Story, who agreed with Hamilton's conclusion, added that expenditures for foreign palaces or for "propagating Mahometanism among the Turks . . . would be wholly indefensible upon constitutional principles." 1 J. STORY, *supra* note 124, at § 922. In fact, even foreign and local conditions may affect the general welfare; modern foreign aid, for example, is not entirely eleemosynary. In any event, the problem to which the farm subsidies were directed was neither foreign nor local. One might have argued that aid for a particular segment of the population, even if nationally distributed, did not serve the "general" welfare. *Compare* Loan Association v. Topeka, 87 U.S. 655 (1875) (striking down municipal aid to private manufacturer for want of public purpose), THE FIRST HUNDRED

deny that it was: "We are not now required to ascertain the scope of the phrase 'general welfare of the United States' or to determine whether an appropriation in aid of agriculture falls within it." Even if it did, "another principle embedded in our Constitution prohibits the enforcement of the Agricultural Adjustment Act. The act invades the reserved rights of the states" because its provisions "are . . . means to [the] unconstitutional end" of "regulat[ing] and control[ling] agricultural production, a matter beyond the powers delegated to the federal government." [128]

With such respect as may be due, as the noncommittal phrase goes, this is nonsense. Having assumed that promoting agriculture was a legitimate end of federal spending, Roberts was in a poor position to argue that it was an unconstitutional one. Having held that the spending power was not limited by the enumeration of other congressional powers, he was hopelessly inconsistent in doing so on the ground that Congress had no independent authority to regulate agriculture. [129] The Court's reliance on Marshall's warning against the pretextual use of federal powers and on such derivative precedents as the *Child Labor Tax Case* was therefore misplaced, for under Roberts's own test the law was not a pretext for the accomplishment of an illegitimate purpose. [130]

Roberts went on to insist that the law was regulatory in effect because it was coercive: "The farmer, of course, may refuse to comply, but the price of such refusal is the loss of benefits. The amount offered is intended to be sufficient to exert pressure on him to agree to the proposed regulation." [131] Stone's response was crushing:

> The power of Congress to spend is inseparable from persuasion to action over which Congress has no legislative control. Congress may not command that the science of agriculture be taught in state universities. But if it would aid the teaching of that science by grants to state institutions, it is appropriate, if not necessary, that the grant be on the condition . . . that it be used for the intended purpose. [132]

Roberts protested that "[t]here is an obvious difference between a statute stating the conditions upon which moneys shall be expended and one effective only upon assumption of

---

YEARS at 381-82. But most expenditures benefit some persons more than others, and it would have been hard to deny that the plight of the farmers posed serious problems for the nation as a whole.

[128] 297 U.S. at 68.

[129] *See* T. POWELL, *supra* note 43, at 82-83 (adding that "Mr. Justice Roberts drew from a major premise what he had expressly excluded from it").

[130] *See* 297 U.S. at 68-70. For the same reason, the Court's invocation of cases applying the doctrine of unconstitutional conditions, *see id.* at 71-72 (citing Frost Trucking Co. v. Railroad Com., 271 U.S. 583 (1926)), also was misplaced. Indeed, Roberts's broad reading of the tax power in *Butler* arguably cast doubt on the *Child Labor Tax Case* itself: if the tax power could be employed for any purpose serving the general welfare, then taxation for the purpose of preventing child labor was for a legitimate purpose. *Butler* need not be read this broadly, however, for Roberts preserved the requirement of a revenue purpose by defining the taxing power as the power to tax "for the purpose of providing funds" with which to promote the general welfare. 297 U.S. at 64. *See* pp. 96-98 *supra* (discussing Hammer v. Dagenhart, 247 U.S. 251 (1918)); text accompanying notes 176-77 *infra* (discussing United States v. Darby, 312 U.S. 100 (1941)).

[131] 297 U.S. at 70-71.

[132] Indeed, he argued, "[e]xpenditures would fail of their purpose and thus lose their constitutional sanction if their terms of payment were not such that by their influence . . . the permitted end would be attained." *Id.* at 83.

a contractual obligation to submit to a regulation which otherwise could not be enforced."[133] The difference was indeed obvious, but so was its irrelevance to the question
of coercion; in either case Congress has exerted powerful economic pressure to comply
with provisions it could not have imposed directly.[134]

All this floundering was motivated by the same concern that had underlain efforts to
limit the commerce power in cases from *E. C. Knight* to *Carter.* If Congress could buy
reductions in acreage, said Roberts, it could buy anything else it liked. It could not be that
the Framers of the Constitution, who "in erecting the federal government, intended sedu-
lously to limit and define its powers, . . . nevertheless by a single clause gave power to
the Congress to tear down the barriers, to invade the states' jurisdiction, and to become a
parliament of the whole people."[135]

The concern was justified, but it was a little late to assert it. Roberts gave the game
away when he accepted Hamilton's argument that Congress could spend for any purpose
that served the general welfare. As Stone pointed out, the power to spend is the power to
make offers that cannot be refused. Such authority is incompatible with the basic premise
of limited federal power.

Roberts's objection to Madison's alternative interpretation of the clause was not convincing. *McCulloch v. Maryland* teaches both that redundancy is not foreign to the Constitution (the necessary and proper clause and the tenth amendment having been added out
of an abundance of caution) and that the power to tax for purposes elsewhere enumerated
would not be redundant (since it "cannot be implied an incidental to other powers").[136] It
would indeed have been astounding for the Framers to leave to the vagaries of implication
their most important departure from the Articles of Confederation.[137]

A glimpse at those Articles, in fact, affords an invaluable clue to the purpose of the
general welfare clause, for the words are taken directly from that document:

> All charges of war, and all other expences that shall be incurred for the com-
> mon defence or general welfare, and allowed by the united states in congress
> assembled, shall be defrayed out of a common treasury, which shall be sup-
> plied by the several states in proportion to the value of all land within each
> state.[138]

This provision granted no authority to spend at all; it merely prescribed how Congress was
to defray such expenses as might be incurred pursuant to authority elsewhere given.

---

[133] *Id.* at 73.

[134] *See id.* at 83-84 (Stone, dissenting) ("It makes no difference that there is a promise to do an act which the
condition is calculated to induce. Condition and promise are alike valid since both are in furtherance of the
national purpose for which the money is appropriated."). Roberts would have been better advised to focus upon
content rather than form. Conditions or promises relating to the use of the granted funds themselves arguably
might have been distinguished from those unrelated to the use of the money, since, if the latter are permitted,
there is indeed no practical limit to federal power. *Cf.* pp. 472-75 *infra* (discussing Maher v. Roe).

[135] *Id.* at 78.

[136] 17 U.S. 316, 406, 409, 411, 420-21 (1819), THE FIRST HUNDRED YEARS at 160-65.

[137] *See* THE FEDERALIST No. 30, at 189 (A. Hamilton) (arguing that the inadequacy of the revenue provisions
of the Articles reduced the Confederation to a condition "which affords ample cause, both of mortification to
ourselves, and of triumph to our enemies").

[138] Articles of Confederation art. VIII (1781).

The only significant change made in this provision in 1789 was the addition of a power to tax. Far from being redundant, the general welfare clause provided that legitimate expenses should be paid out of federal taxes instead of state contributions. There is no evidence that it was meant to expand the purposes for which expenditures might be made.

Justice Roberts therefore may well have reached the right result in striking down the Agricultural Adjustment Act,[139] but by conceding too much he made it seem quite untenable; and that boded poorly for the future of the federal system.[140]

## F.  Minimum Wages

It was not only article I that the Court began to read narrowly in 1935. Other decisions of the same time suggested a return to more restrictive understanding of other limits on both federal and state authority.

The most notable of these was *Morehead v. New York ex rel. Tipaldo,* a five-to-four due process decision striking down yet another minimum wage law on the authority of *Adkins v. Children's Hospital.*[141] After *Nebbia,* the Court might have been expected to come out the other way. By abandoning the requirement that the business be "affected with a public interest," that decision had seemed to mean that what the Court had once dismissed as impermissible "leveling"—the effort to ameliorate the effects of unequal

---

[139] In 1 CORWIN ON THE CONSTITUTION, *supra* note 124, at 253-69, Corwin collected impressive instances of broad construction of the general welfare clause by figures as diverse as Washington and Calhoun, and pointed to numerous federal statutes spending for such purposes as lighthouses, internal improvements, and the promotion of agriculture or education. As Corwin conceded, *id.* at 267, internal improvements had been upheld as necessary and proper to the commerce, postal, and war powers. See THE FIRST HUNDRED YEARS at 275 n.298, 429-30. However, these powers were not the basis of the original argument for their validity, and they fail to explain the grants for agriculture or education. Since this broad interpretation had been controversial, it does not disprove the conclusion as to original intent suggested by the Articles of Confederation; but by 1936 it may have been a little late to deny it respect as what Justice Frankfurter was later to term a "gloss" on the Constitution. *See* Youngstown Sheet & Tube Co. v. Sawyer, 343 U.S. 579, 610 (1952) (concurring opinion) ("Deeply embedded traditional ways of conducting government cannot supplant the Constitution . . . , but they give meaning to the words of a text or supply them."). *See also* Grant, *Commerce, Production and the Fiscal Powers of Congress: II,* 45 YALE L. J. 991, 1000 (1936) (Hamiltonian view too embedded by the "forces of history" to undo).

[140] In striking contrast to the decisions of this period narrowly interpreting domestic federal powers was Justice Sutherland's sweeping conclusion in United States v. Curtiss-Wright Corp., 299 U.S. 304, 315-16 (1936), over a dissent by Justice McReynolds, that the United States possessed plenary authority over foreign affairs without regard to the limited enumeration in article I: "The broad statement that the federal government can exercise no powers except those specifically enumerated in the Constitution, and such implied powers as are necessary and proper to carry into effect the enumerated powers, is categorically true only in respect of our internal affairs." The conclusion that the Framers intended to convey plenary authority over foreign affairs is hard to avoid in light of history; but Sutherland's peculiar argument that "the states severally never possessed international powers," *id.* at 316, has been severely criticized. *See* Goebel, *Constitutional History and Constitutional Law,* 38 COLUM. L. REV. 555, 572 (1938); Lofgren, United States v. Curtiss-Wright Export Corporation: *An Historical Reassessment,* 83 YALE L. J. 1 (1973); Levitan, *The Foreign Relations Power: An Analysis of Mr. Justice Sutherland's Theory,* 55 YALE L. J. 467 (1946); Patterson, In re the United States v. The Curtiss-Wright Corporation, 22 TEX. L. REV. 286 (1944); L. HENKIN, FOREIGN AFFAIRS AND THE CONSTITUTION 23-25 (1972). Since the case involved a regulation of foreign commerce clearly within article I, § 8, Sutherland's remarks went far beyond the necessities of the case.

[141] Morehead v. New York *ex rel.* Tipaldo, 298 U.S. 587 (1936); Adkins v. Children's Hospital, 261 U.S. 525 (1923).

bargaining power—had become a legitimate goal, even if the Justices were not yet prepared to recognize the palpable relation between low wages, ill health, and crime.[142]

Most significantly, as Hughes pointed out in dissent, the law in *Morehead* had been
drafted to meet the objection most stressed in *Adkins*. "The feature of this statute which,
perhaps more than any other, puts upon it the stamp of invalidity," Justice Sutherland had
complained in that case, "is that it exacts from the employer an arbitrary payment for a
purpose and upon a basis having no causal connection with his business. . . . The moral
requirement implicit in every contract of employment, viz, that the amount to be paid and
the service to be rendered shall bear to each other some relation of just equivalence, is
completely ignored."[143]

By contrast, the New York law in *Morehead* forbade only those wages that were "both
less than the fair and reasonable value of the services rendered and less than sufficient to
meet the minimum cost of living necessary for health."[144] The Court had struck down the
law in *Adkins* because it required employers to solve a problem they had not caused; the
law they struck down in *Morehead* cured that defect by imposing on the employer only
the reasonable cost of his business.

Brushing aside the crucial language Hughes quoted from *Adkins*, Justice Butler for the
majority insisted that the decision had invalidated *all* minimum wage laws.[145] More surprisingly still, he refused even to consider whether *Adkins* was still law, on the ground that
the question had not been raised in the petition for review. Justice Stone in a second dissent
pointed tellingly to the petition's statement that " 'the circumstances prevailing under
which the New York law was enacted call for a reconsideration of the *Adkins* case in the
light of the New York act.' " More sweepingly, he attacked the Court's premise: "I know
of no rule or practice by which the arguments advanced in support of an application for
certiorari restrict our choice between conflicting precedents in deciding a question of constitutional law which the petition, if granted, requires us to answer."[146]

The majority's ringing restatement of *Adkins* did little to encourage the hope that the
decision would be overruled even if the question was more explicitly presented; and as in
*Alton* it was Justice Roberts who cast the decisive vote against regulation.[147]

## G.   Other Cases

*Morehead* did not stand alone as evidence of the vitality of extraneous limitations on state
and federal legislation. *Alton* invoked the due process clause of the fifth amendment as a

[142] *See* the discussion of *Nebbia* in notes 19-24 and accompanying text; of *Adkins* at p. 144 *supra;* and of
"leveling" at pp. 47-49, 103-04 *supra*. The modern economic literature insisting that minimum wage laws reduce
employment is summarized in R. POSNER, *supra* note 18, at 28.

[143] *Adkins,* 261 U.S. at 558, *quoted in Morehead,* 298 U.S. at 623-24 (Hughes, dissenting, joined by Brandeis, Cardozo, and Stone).

[144] 298 U.S. at 605, 621.

[145] *Id.* at 610-14. Butler did not explain whether the fault lay in the illegitimacy of the legislature's goals or in
the inappropriateness of the means for attaining them.

[146] *Id.* at 636.

[147] The minimum wage law in *Morehead* applied only to women and children, and there was a foretaste of
modern equal protection analysis in Justice Butler's observation that "prescribing of minimum wages for women
alone would unreasonably restrain them in competition with men and tend arbitrarily to deprive them of employment and a fair chance to find work." *Id.* at 617. The dissenters protested, in terms then viewed as progressive,

second ground for striking down various provisions of the railroad retirement law.[148] Several decisions cited either due process or full faith and credit in imposing territorialist limitations on state taxation and choice of law.[149] *Louisville Bank v. Radford* unanimously invalidated a federal measure for the relief of insolvent farmers as an uncompensated taking of property from creditors.[150] Two unanimous decisions striking down state legislation even showed that, despite *Blaisdell,* there was still some life in the contract clause.[151] *Perry v. United States*[152] invented a spanking new limitation in concluding that

that states were entitled to conclude that women needed special protection. *See id.* at 629-30 (Hughes, dissenting).

[148] 295 U.S. at 348-62 (objecting principally to provisions found to operate retroactively or to treat all railroads "as a single employer" and holding them inseparable). The same four Justices who dissented from the commerce clause holding largely dissented from these conclusions as well, although they agreed with the majority that for Congress to require the extension of pensions to those no longer employed by the railroads was arbitrary and beyond its power. *Id.* at 384-92, 389 (Hughes, dissenting).

[149] *See* Baldwin v. Missouri, 281 U.S. 586 (1930) (McReynolds, over dissents by Holmes, Brandeis, and Stone) (only owner's domicile may tax bank accounts, bonds, and notes); Senior v. Braden, 295 U.S. 422 (1935) (McReynolds, over dissents by Stone, Brandeis, and Cardozo) (state may not tax intangible interest in foreign land); Home Ins. Co. v. Dick, 281 U.S. 397 (1930) (Brandeis) (state may not invalidate clause in foreign contract limiting time for suit); Bradford Elec. Co. v. Clapper, 286 U.S. 145 (1932) (Brandeis) (state of injury must respect exclusivity provision in workers' compensation law of employment state); Hartford Co. v. Delta Co., 292 U.S. 143 (1934) (Roberts) (same as *Dick,* despite more substantial contacts with forum state); Broderick v. Rosner, 294 U.S. 629 (1935) (Brandeis) (shareholder's state must enforce shareholder liability law of state of incorporation); John Hancock Ins. Co. v. Yates, 299 U.S. 178 (1936) (Brandeis) (law of place of contracting determines effect of fraud in insurance application). *See also* Young v. Masci, 289 U.S. 253, 258 (1933) (Brandeis) (allowing New York to make New Jersey automobile owner liable for negligence of bailee in New York) ("Liability for a tort depends upon the law of the place of the injury."). For criticism of this line of cases, see Lowndes, *Spurious Conceptions of the Constitutional Law of Taxation,* 47 HARV. L. REV. 628 (1934); Beale, *Two Cases on Jurisdiction,* 48 HARV. L. REV. 620 (1935).

The Court also appropriately furthered the purposes of the full faith and credit clause by requiring one state to respect another's judgments for child support, Yarborough v. Yarborough, 290 U.S. 202 (1933) (Brandeis, over an emotional dissent by Stone), and for taxes, Milwaukee County v. White Co., 296 U.S. 268 (1935) (Stone) (effectively previewed in Leflar, *Extrastate Enforcement of Penal and Governmental Claims,* 46 HARV. L. REV. 193 (1932)). For earlier decisions in these fields, see pp. 45-47, 65-78, & p. 110, note 123 *supra.*

[150] 295 U.S. 555 (1935) (Brandeis) (invalidating Frazier-Lemke Act). *See also* Nashville, C. & St. L. Ry. v. Walters, 294 U.S. 405 (1935) (Brandeis, with Stone and Cardozo dissenting), which held that a railroad could not be required to pay for a grade separation promoting only convenience and not safety. These holdings followed easily from Brandeis's sensible distinction between forbidding a person to injure others and requiring him to help them. *See* pp. 146-52 *supra* (discussing Pennsylvania Coal Co. v. Mahon, 260 U.S. 393 (1922)).

[151] W.B. Worthen Co. v. Thomas, 292 U.S. 426 (1934) (Hughes) (exemption of insurance benefits from garnishment to satisfy preexisting debts); Worthen Co. v. Kavanaugh, 295 U.S. 56 (1935) (Cardozo) (severe impairment of security for preexisting debts).

[152] 294 U.S. 330 (1935) (Hughes, with Stone declining to reach the issue). The case involved a congressional effort to pay off in depreciated currency obligations expressly stated in terms of gold. *See also id.* at 354 (invoking § 4 of the fourteenth amendment, which provides that "[t]he validity of the public debt of the United States . . . shall not be questioned"); Eder, *A Forgotten Section of the Fourteenth Amendment,* 19 CORNELL L. Q. 1 (1933). The taking clause would have furnished a more traditional basis for the decision; in reducing the value of the obligations, the government had enriched itself without compensating its victim. In a companion case essentially governed by the *Legal Tender* cases, THE FIRST HUNDRED YEARS at 321-29; *see* Dickinson, *The Gold Decisions,* 83 U. PA. L. REV. 715 (1935), the Court held due process was not offended by a similar effort directed toward *private* contracts. Norman v. B. & O. R.R. Co., 294 U.S. 240 (1935) (Hughes, over the expected four dissents). *See also* Dawson, *The Gold Clause Decisions,* 33 MICH. L. REV. 647 (1935), and Collier, *Gold*

the grant of power to borrow implicitly forbade the United States to welsh on its obligations: money can be borrowed only if it will be paid back.

The invalidation of a graduated state sales tax in *Stewart Dry Goods Co. v. Lewis*
showed that equal protection too was alive and well in economic cases despite the chain
store cases.[153] Even the forgotten privileges or immunities clause of the fourteenth amendment was disinterred to strike down a preference for local investment in *Colgate v.
Harvey*.[154] *Baldwin v. G. A. F. Seelig* demonstrated the strength of the negative effect of
the commerce clause by rubbing out a state law designed to place local and out-of-state
milk sellers on an equal footing.[155] The Court seemed rather strict in holding that both
railroading and water distribution were "governmental" functions immune from taxation
by other governments.[156] Finally, in forbidding Congress to allow local governments to

---

*Contracts and Currency Regulation,* 23 CORNELL L. Q. 520 (1938) (both tracing the government's efforts to
article I, § 8's provision empowering Congress to "regulate the value" of money). Moreover, even in *Perry* the
government ultimately got its way because of the Chief Justice's bizarre conclusion (over the same four dissents)
that the bondholders had lost nothing by the enormous depreciation of their rights. *See* 294 U.S. at 354-58; Hart,
*The Gold Clause in United States Bonds,* 48 HARV. L. REV. 1057, 1077-81 (1935); T. POWELL, *supra* note 43,
at 86 ("[H]ow it could be held that Congress may not renege on a national promise to pay in gold of specified
density, and then apply to the bondholder the tort measure of damages instead of the contract one, well nigh
passes comprehension."). Roosevelt had gone so far as to prepare a speech justifying disobedience of judicial
orders for delivery in case of an adverse decision. *See* 2 M. PUSEY, *supra* note 22, at 736.

[153] 294 U.S. 550 (1935) (Roberts, over three dissents).

[154] 296 U.S. 404, 430 (1935) (Sutherland, over dissents of Stone, Brandeis, and Cardozo), building upon the
unpedigreed right to travel recognized in Crandall v. Nevada, 73 U.S. 35 (1868), THE FIRST HUNDRED YEARS at
335, to conclude that "[t]he right . . . to make a lawful loan of money in any state other than that in which the
citizen resides is a privilege equally attributable to his national citizenship." According to Justice Stone, the Court
decided to rely on the privileges or immunities clause only after it became clear that an equal protection challenge
was untenable. *See* A. MASON, HARLAN FISKE STONE: PILLAR OF THE LAW 399-402 (1956). For contemporaneous criticism, see Howard, *The Privileges and Immunities of Federal Citizenship and Colgate v. Harvey,* 87 U.
PA. L. REV. 262 (1939); Fraenkel, *supra* note 118, at 40 (arguing that *Colgate* "illustrates the capacity of the
Court to find in the Constitution language appropriate to every need, at least when property rights are involved").
For the earlier fate of this clause, see THE FIRST HUNDRED YEARS at 342-51, 363-64.

[155] 294 U.S. 511 (1935) (Cardozo). The law forbade sale in New York of milk bought elsewhere at a price
lower than that permitted within the state; it was condemned as an effort to shield New York farmers from outside
competition. *Id.* at 522. Cardozo's analogy of a tariff against out-of-state products, *id.* at 521-22, seemed out of
place, for a tariff is discriminatory. Nevertheless, if both states adopted conflicting regulations on this subject,
interstate commerce could be stifled entirely. *See* THE FIRST HUNDRED YEARS at 337-42 (discussing the Case of
the State Freight Tax, 82 U.S. 232 (1873)).

Other decisions of the mid-thirties reaffirmed congressional power both to remove the commerce clause
barrier to state legislation and to make interstate transportation of goods contrary to state law a federal crime.
Whitfield v. Ohio, 297 U.S. 431 (1936) (Sutherland), and Kentucky Whip & Collar Co. v. Illinois Central R.R.,
299 U.S. 334 (1937) (Hughes) (both involving prison-made goods). For earlier precedents, see pp. 34-35, p.
115, note 150, & pp. 175-76 *supra*. For contemporaneous commentary, see Grant, *State Power to Prohibit
Interstate Commerce,* 26 CAL. L. REV. 34 (1937).

[156] New York *ex rel.* Rogers v. Graves, 299 U.S. 401 (1937) (Sutherland) (employee of Panama Rail Road,
operated as adjunct to Panama Canal, exempt from state income tax); Brush v. Commissioner, 300 U.S. 352
(1937) (Sutherland, over dissents of Brandeis and Roberts) (employee of city water bureau exempt from federal
income tax). *Contrast* South Carolina v. United States, 199 U.S. 437, 458, 463 (1905) (allowing federal tax on
state liquor sales). At the same time, declaring it immaterial whether the activity regulated was governmental or
proprietary, the Court unanimously held that Congress could require automatic couplers on a state-owned railroad. United States v. California, 297 U.S. 175, 183-85 (1936) (Stone). In the converse situation, the Court had
sensibly recognized that state regulation was as great a threat to federal autonomy as was state taxation. *See*
Johnson v. Maryland, 254 U.S. 51 (1920) (state may not require license for post office driver).

discharge their debts in federal court, it perversely employed the immunity doctrine to the detriment of its intended beneficiaries.[157]

By 1937 it was abundantly clear that the measures that many people believed necessary for economic recovery would not survive Supreme Court scrutiny. It was at this point that President Roosevelt decided to attack the Court.

## III. The End of the Tunnel

On February 5, 1937, the President announced his proposal to enlarge the Court to fifteen members. Although he coated the pill with unconvincing arguments about the inefficiency of elderly Justices, he made no secret of his real purpose: to pack the Court with judges more sympathetic to his legislative program.[158]

Had he succeeded, the Court would never have been the same. Recognition of the legitimacy of diluting the votes of obstructive Justices would have severely weakened the Court's ability to enforce the Constitution against other branches, which ever since *Marbury v. Madison* had been accepted as one of its principal functions.[159]

---

[157] Ashton v. Cameron County Water Improv. Dist., 298 U.S. 513 (1936) (McReynolds, over four apt dissents). Contrast Clark v. Barnard, 108 U.S. 436, 447-48 (1883) (state's eleventh amendment immunity from suit "a personal privilege which it may waive at pleasure"), THE FIRST HUNDRED YEARS at 427 n.163; Lincoln County v. Luning, 133 U.S. 529 (1890) (county not "state" within eleventh amendment); United States v. California, 297 U.S. 175 (1936) (suggesting intergovernmental immunity is no limit on commerce power). *See* the sensible criticism in Reuschlein, *Municipal Debt Readjustment: Present Relief and Future Policy,* 23 CORNELL L. Q. 365, 373-82 (1938); Fraenkel, *supra* note 118, at 38 (terming *Ashton* "as clear a case of judicial legislation as has taken place in a long time").

[158] The bill provided for appointing one new judge for each member of the Court who had reached the age of seventy, had sat for ten years, and had neither resigned nor retired within six months thereafter. S.1392, 75th Cong., 1st Sess. (1937). Six of the nine Justices met these criteria when the bill was introduced. Reorganization of the Federal Judiciary, Sen. Rep. No. 711, 75th Cong., 1st Sess. 11 (June 7, 1937). Roosevelt explained his purpose in an address on March 9: "the majority of the court has been assuming the power to pass on the wisdom of . . . acts of the Congress . . . [W]e must take action to save the Constitution from the Court." 81 CONG. REC. app. pt. 9 at 469, 470. *See generally* R. JACKSON, THE STRUGGLE FOR JUDICIAL SUPREMACY (1941); Leuchtenburg, *The Origins of Franklin D. Roosevelt's "Court-Packing" Plan,* 1966 SUP. CT. REV. 347; G. GUNTHER, *supra* note 63, at 129-300. Others more appropriately suggested a constitutional convention to increase federal power. *See, for example,* Haines, *Judicial Review of Acts of Congress and the Need for Constitutional Reform,* 45 YALE L. J. 816 (1936). *See also* Levinson, *Limiting Judicial Review by Act of Congress,* 23 CAL. L. REV. 591 (1935) (advocating statutory requirement of extraordinary majority to invalidate federal statutes under congressional power to make "exceptions" or "regulations" respecting the Court's appellate jurisdiction); McGovney, *Reorganization of the Supreme Court,* 25 CAL. L. REV. 389 (1937) (supporting the packing plan). For a serious proposal to deal by constitutional amendment with the sometimes acute problem of Justices who had lost their mental capacity, see Fairman, *The Retirement of Federal Judges,* 51 HARV. L. REV. 397 (1938).

[159] *See* R. McCLOSKEY, *supra* note 40, at 169 (arguing that passage of the packing plan "would set a precedent from which the institution of judicial review might never recover. . . . [T]he ambiguous and delicately balanced American tradition of limited government was mortally endangered by this bill."). Hughes himself is said to have declared that were the bill to pass, "it would destroy the [C]ourt as an institution." *See* 2 M. PUSEY, *supra* note 22, at 755. Even Stone, who had excoriated the Court for its excesses in *Butler,* wrote privately that the President's "proposal [wa]s too high a price to pay for the correction of some decisions of the Court which I, in common with a great many others, think unfortunate." *See* A. MASON, *supra* note 154, at 449. *See also* the admirable answer to Roosevelt's proposal in Sen. Rep. No. 711, *supra* note 158, at 23 ("a measure which should be so emphatically rejected that its parallel will never again be presented to the free representatives of the free people of America"); Mason, *Politics and the Supreme Court: President Roosevelt's Proposal,* 85 U. PA. L. REV. 659, 676 (1937) (urging instead an amendment to allow Congress by two-thirds vote to override Supreme Court

Happily it never came to that, for the Court dramatically changed its course. The packing plan died of supererogation. Unhappily the price of judicial independence was the death of our federal system.

## A. The Passing of Federalism

On March 29, 1937, less than two months after the President had announced his packing plan and less than a year after *Morehead* had reaffirmed the unconstitutionality of minimum wage laws, *West Coast Hotel Co. v. Parrish* reached the opposite conclusion.[160] Once again the vote was five to four. The difference was attributable to Justice Roberts, who silently joined the majority in both cases.

The common perception that this was the crucial change of heart that saved the Court seems erroneous. To begin with, the critical vote in *Parrish* had been taken before the packing plan was made public; unless there was a leak, the decision does not even seem to have been a response to the proposal.[161] Second, it was not clear that Roberts had actually changed his mind. *Parrish* overruled *Adkins v. Children's Hospital*, which had established the general principle that minimum wage laws were unconstitutional; *Morehead* had carefully said the question of overruling *Adkins* was not before the Court.[162] Finally, due process had never been at the center of the Court's disagreement with the New Deal; until the Court receded from its restrictive interpretation of *federal* power, the President's program remained in mortal peril.

The real breakthrough came on April 12, when in three companion cases the Court by the same five-to-four vote upheld the National Labor Relations Act provision protecting the right of employees not engaged in interstate or foreign commerce to organize for purposes of collective bargaining. The Court took the easiest case first: *Labor Board v. Jones & Laughlin Steel Corp.*, which involved a giant steelmaker that obtained its ores from other states and shipped 75 percent of its products in interstate commerce.[163]

---

decisions); THE FIRST HUNDRED YEARS at 66-74, 304-07 (discussing Marbury v. Madison, 5 U.S. 137 (1803), and *Ex parte McCardle*, 74 U.S. 506 (1869)).

[160] 300 U.S. 379 (1937) (Hughes), finding the statute an admissible means for promoting both "the health of women and their protection from unscrupulous and overreaching employers" and noting—in evident response to the argument that employers should not be made to bear the burden—that " '[i]t is safe to assume that women will not be employed at even the lowest wages allowed unless they earn them.' " *Id.* at 397-98 (quoting Holmes's *Adkins* dissent). The argument of sex discrimination was rejected summarily: women's "relative need in the presence of the evil, no less than the existence of the evil itself, is a matter for the legislative judgment." *Id.* at 400.

[161] *See* Frankfurter, *Mr. Justice Roberts*, 104 U. PA. L. REV. 311 (1955) (quoting a memorandum left by Roberts); 2 M. PUSEY, *supra* note 22, at 757, adding that Hughes himself later insisted that "[t]he President's proposal had not the slightest effect on our decision." On the secrecy surrounding the proposal, see Leuchtenburg, *supra* note 158, at 396.

[162] *See* 300 U.S. at 389. *See also* T. POWELL, *supra* note 43, at 81 n.89: "Mr. Justice Roberts's position in the two cases can be harmonized as the view of one who was unable to distinguish the *Adkins* case but who would accept an opportunity to overrule it." Indeed, *Parrish* seemed more in line with Roberts's views on related issues than did *Morehead*. *See* notes 4-24 and accompanying text (discussing, among others, Nebbia v. New York, 291 U.S. 502 (1934)); 2 M. PUSEY, *supra* note 22, at 771; Frankfurter, *supra* note 161, at 314-15 (quoting the Roberts memorandum)).

[163] 301 U.S. 1, 25-28 (1937).

The author was Hughes, and the rationale was that which he had enunciated in *Shreveport* and *Schechter:* the commerce power "may be exerted to protect interstate commerce 'no matter what the source of the dangers which threaten it.' "[164] As the Court recently had held in upholding similar provisions for railroad workers, "the right of employees to self-organization . . . [was] often an essential condition of industrial peace."[165] Though manufacturing was not itself commerce, "the stoppage of . . . [Jones & Laughlin's] operations by industrial strife would have a most serious effect upon interstate commerce"; congressional protection of the right to organize was "necessary to protect interstate commerce from the paralyzing consequences of industrial war."[166]

Given the established test Hughes employed, this answer was hard to avoid. As he pointed out, an organizing strike at Jones & Laughlin could have had a "catastrophic" impact on interstate commerce in steel.[167] A similar argument had been rejected in *Carter,* however, on the ground that this impact was "indirect."[168] One of the companion cases, moreover, cited *Jones & Laughlin* without discussion to sustain application of the labor law to a small clothing manufacturer with a minuscule share of the interstate market.[169] "The business of the Company is so small," McReynolds objected in dissent, "that to close its factory would have no direct or material effect upon the volume of interstate commerce in clothing."[170] That made the case hard to distinguish from *Schechter,* and thus the decision seemed to leave very little beyond the reach of the commerce power.[171]

This time Roberts and Hughes did seem to have changed their minds, but so had Brandeis, Stone, and Cardozo, all of whom had concurred in *Schechter.*[172] The dissenters had

---

[164] *Id.* at 37.

[165] *Id.* at 42. *See* Texas & N.O.R.R. Co. v. Clerks, 281 U.S. 548 (1930) (Hughes); Virginian Ry. v. System Federation, 300 U.S. 515 (1937) (Stone).

[166] *Jones & Laughlin,* 301 U.S. at 41.

[167] *Id.* at 41. *See also id.* at 42 ("[O]f what avail is it to protect the facility of transportation, if interstate commerce is throttled with respect to the commodities to be transported!"). McReynolds, who wrote the usual dissent, protested that a strike was not inevitable even in the absence of legislation. *Id.* at 99. This, however, had been equally true in the railroad cases.

[168] *Carter,* 298 U.S. at 308 (majority opinion), 317 (Hughes, in separate opinion).

[169] Labor Board v. Clothing Co., 301 U.S. 58 (1937) (Hughes). In this case, the company's total sales in the first ten months of 1935 amounted to $1,750,000. *Id.* at 72. The third case, Labor Board v. Fruehauf Co., 301 U.S. 49 (1937) (Hughes), applied the same reasoning to the country's largest trailer manufacturer.

[170] *Clothing Co.,* 301 U.S. at 94 (dissent).

[171] *See id.* at 99 (McReynolds, dissenting) ("Almost anything—marriage, birth, death—may in some fashion affect commerce.") Powell's attempted distinction between pre- and post-commerce activities (T. POWELL, *supra* note 43, at 80, arguing that *Schechter* involved "local practices after the interstate transportation was completed, with no future extrastate effect to follow") fails to distinguish the coal mining regulations struck down in *Carter,* which many thought had sealed the doom of the statute upheld in the *Labor Board* cases. *See, e.g.,* Stern, *supra* note 64, at 676; Fraenkel, *supra* note 118, at 36. *See also* Mueller, *Businesses Subject to the National Labor Relations Act,* 35 MICH. L. REV. 1286, 1297 (1937), which maintains that both *Schechter* and *Carter* were distinguishable from *Jones & Laughlin* because the effect of a work stoppage on commerce was more immediate than the " 'intricate economic effects of . . . labor costs upon the prices and movement of products in interstate commerce' " (quoting from the government's brief in *Jones & Laughlin*). But this argument had been made and rejected in *Carter.*

[172] The usually tolerant Brandeis reputedly told Thomas Corcoran on the day *Schechter* was decided: "This is the end of this business of centralization, and I want you to go back and tell the President that we're not going to let this government centralize everything." *See* A. SCHLESINGER, *supra* note 121, at 280.

been deftly hoisted by their own petard, for it was Sutherland in the *Carter* case who had so fatefully insisted that the magnitude of the effect on commerce was immaterial.[173]

Other decisions confirmed that the game was over. *Helvering v. Davis* demonstrated the breadth of *Butler's* concession that Congress could spend for any nationwide purpose by upholding the old-age benefits provided through Social Security.[174] *Steward Machine Co. v. Davis* suggested that *Butler* and *Carter* had lost much of their restrictive force by sustaining a federal tax plainly designed to induce states to provide unemployment insurance.[175] *United States v. Darby*[176] explicitly overruled *Hammer v. Dagenhart* in holding that Congress could exclude from interstate commerce goods made by employees paid less than a specified wage and drove yet another nail into *Schechter's* coffin by upholding federal minimum wages for employees engaged in production. Not only did the latter provision, in Stone's view, protect against the adverse effects of low wages on interstate commerce; it was also sustainable on the more sweeping ground that it helped to effectuate the exclusion from interstate trade.[177]

It was shortly after Hughes's retirement that *Wickard v. Filburn* permitted Congress to limit the wheat a farmer grew for his own consumption on the ground that what he could not grow he might buy from another state.[178] But that was only to write the epitaph; constitutional federalism had died in 1937.

---

[173] The Court expressly confirmed that in Labor Board v. Fainblatt, 306 U.S. 601, 606 (1939) (Stone), involving yet another small clothing manufacturer: "[t]he power of Congress to regulate interstate commerce . . . extends to all such commerce be it great or small." With Van Devanter and Sutherland gone, only McReynolds and Butler remained to protest that, as construed by the Court, the commerce power "brings within the ambit of federal control most if not all activities of the Nation" and that "[i]f the possibility of this had been declared the Constitution could not have been adopted." *Id.* at 610.

[174] 301 U.S. 619 (1937) (Cardozo, over dissents by McReynolds and Butler).

[175] Steward Machine Co. v. Davis, 301 U.S. 548 (1937) (Cardozo, over four dissents). The law gave a 90 percent credit for contributions made to an unemployment fund under state law. *Id.* at 574. As the Court noted, there was no contract in *Steward, id.* at 592; but the arrangement was no less coercive as a result. Even Sutherland, however, did not argue that states were coerced into establishing the unemployment fund. *See id.* at 610. *See also* Sonzinsky v. United States, 300 U.S. 506, 514 (1937) (Stone), unanimously upholding a $200 annual tax on dealers in such firearms as machine guns and sawed-off shotguns: "[Courts] will not undertake, by collateral inquiry as to the measure of the regulatory effect of a tax, to ascribe to Congress an attempt, under the guise of taxation, to exercise another power denied by the Federal Constitution." This case closely resembles *Constantine,* 296 U.S. 287 (1935), in all save the result; Powell, *supra* note 43, at 87, termed it "[h]ardly candid."

[176] 312 U.S. 100, 115 (1941) (Stone).

[177] "Congress, having . . . adopted the policy of excluding from interstate commerce all goods . . . which do not conform to the specified labor standards, . . . may choose the means reasonably adapted to the attainment of the permitted end, even though they involve control of intrastate activities." 312 U.S. at 121. Gunther suggests that if this "superbootstrap" argument were taken at face value, congressional "regulation of local activities . . . [could] now be justified *without* any showing of the impact of the local activity on commerce—simply by having the regulatory scheme include a ban on interstate shipments, and then justifying the regulation as a means to effectuate that 'commerce-prohibiting' sanction." G. GUNTHER, *supra* note 63, at 143–44. The tenth amendment, Stone correctly emphasized, "states but a truism that all is retained which has not been surrendered." *Darby,* 312 U.S. at 124. The decision was unanimous, having been rendered two days after the retirement of Justice McReynolds, the last of the old guard.

[178] 317 U.S. 111 (1942) (Jackson). The Court rejected the distinction between direct and indirect effects, holding it irrelevant that "appellee's own . . . demand for wheat may be trivial by itself . . . where, as here, his contribution, taken together with that of many others similarly situated, is far from trivial." *Id.* at 127-28. There was no one left to dissent. When subsidies for the same purpose were struck down in *Butler,* no one had even argued that Congress could directly impose production quotas under the commerce power. *See* R. McCLOSKEY,

## B. Mopping Up

Federalism was not the only victim of the judicial New Deal. Other long-standing constitutional limitations also underwent momentous changes.[179]

The decline of economic due process heralded by *Parrish* continued with the overruling of decisions striking down bans on yellow-dog contracts and regulation of employment agency fees.[180] A state was allowed to legalize peaceful picketing despite the due process and equal protection implications of *Truax v. Corrigan*.[181] In sustaining a ban on interstate shipment of "filled" milk, the famous *Carolene Products* opinion enunciated a "rational basis" test that raised doubts whether any economic regulation would be held to offend due process on substantive grounds.[182] *Olsen v. Nebraska* fueled those doubts by declaring that "the only constitutional prohibitions or restraints which respondents have

---

*supra* note 40, at 185: "It was now evident that Congress could reach just about any commercial subject it might want to reach and could do to that subject just about anything it was likely to want to do." Powell, *supra* note 43, at 83-84, called *Wickard* "an able latitudinarian opinion" by which "formalism has been succeeded by plain common sense" and concluded that "[h]appily . . . the Framers were wise enough . . . to leave room for the judgments of their successors" when drafting the commerce clause. *See also* the approving comments of Stern, *supra* note 64, at 908-09.

[179] *See* Fraenkel, *Constitutional Issues in the Supreme Court, 1937 Term,* 87 U. PA. L. REV. 50, 50 (1938): "The 1937 Term is distinguished . . . by the large number of cases in which the Court reversed earlier positions."

[180] Phelps Dodge Corp. v. Labor Board, 313 U.S. 177, 187 (1941) (Frankfurter), confirming the demise of Adair v. United States, 208 U.S. 161 (1908), and of Coppage v. Kansas, 236 U.S. 1 (1915); Olsen v. Nebraska, 313 U.S. 236, 244 (1941) (Douglas), overruling Ribnik v. McBride, 277 U.S. 350 (1928). *Compare* Wright v. Vinton Branch, 300 U.S. 440 (1937) (Brandeis) (unanimously upholding a revised federal law for the relief of insolvent farmers), *with* Louisville Bank v. Radford, 295 U.S. 555 (1935).

[181] Senn v. Tile Layers Union, 301 U.S. 468, 479-80 (1937) (Brandeis, over four dissents), distinguishing Truax v. Corrigan, 257 U.S. 312 (1921), on the ground that the picketing in that case had not been peaceful. Indeed, the Court would soon hold in Thornhill v. Alabama, 310 U.S. 88 (1940) (Murphy), that peaceful picketing was *protected* from state abridgement by freedom of expression.

[182] United States v. Carolene Products Co., 304 U.S. 144, 152 (1938) (Stone, speaking at this point for four Justices) ("[R]egulatory legislation affecting ordinary commercial transactions is not to be pronounced unconstitutional unless in the light of the facts made known or generally assumed it is of such a character as to preclude the assumption that it rests upon some rational basis within the knowledge and experience of the legislators."). A fifth vote for the result was cast by Justice Black, who had already advanced the startling conclusion that corporations were not "persons" within the fourteenth amendment at all. Connecticut General Co. v. Johnson, 303 U.S. 77, 85 (1938) (dissenting opinion). *See* R. MCCLOSKEY, *supra* note 40, at 186: "It is hard to conceive a law so patently unreasonable that it would fail under [the *Carolene Products*] test, and it is therefore not surprising that the court since 1937 has never encountered one."

The statute defined "filled milk" as skimmed milk "compounded with . . . any fat or oil other than milk fat"—in this case, with coconut oil. 304 U.S. 144, 145 n.1 (1938). A similar state law had been upheld in less tolerant days in Hebe Co. v. Shaw, 248 U.S. 297 (1919) (Holmes, over three dissents on statutory grounds). *See also* Powell v. Pennsylvania, 127 U.S. 678 (1888) (upholding ban on sale of oleomargarine), THE FIRST HUNDRED YEARS at 377-78. The most serious argument in favor of the law upheld in *Carolene* was that because crucial vitamins were removed with the butter fat, children drinking only filled milk might suffer undernourishment and consequent disease. *See* 304 U.S. at 149 n.2. But the Court subsequently sustained application of the law even after the manufacturer remedied this deficiency by adding vitamins, because it was "disputable" whether labeling requirements would counter the risk of confusion. Carolene Products Co. v. U.S., 323 U.S. 18, 22-23, 29 (1944) (Reed, for a unanimous Court). See the devastating account in Miller, *The True Story of Carolene Products,* 1987 SUP. CT. REV. 397, 398: "The statute upheld in the case was an utterly unprincipled example of special interest legislation."

suggested for the invalidation of this legislation are those notions of public policy embedded in earlier decisions of this Court but which, as Mr. Justice Holmes long admonished, should not be read into the Constitution." [183]

Other equal protection landmarks fell, and the recently exhumed privileges or immunities clause of the fourteenth amendment was reburied, when the Court sustained an agricultural exemption from antitrust regulation and upheld a state statute that discriminated against out-of-state deposits. [184] Further inroads were made on the contract clause by allowing states retroactively to limit both deficiency judgments and savings withdrawals. [185] What looked like a delegation of legislative power to private parties was upheld without so much as a reference to *Carter*. [186] Under the deft leadership of Justice Stone, moreover, the Court made drastic revisions in three other areas involving the operation of the federal system. [187]

In the field of intergovernmental immunity the Court retreated from its recent conclusion that local governments could not be permitted to invoke the protection of bankruptcy. [188] It departed from other precedents as well in allowing the taxation of government contractors and governmental salaries. [189] At least where the burden on government was

[183] 313 U.S. 236, 246-47 (1941) (Douglas) (upholding state statute limiting fees charged by private employment agencies). *See* McCloskey, *Economic Due Process and the Supreme Court: An Exhumation and Reburial,* 1962 SUP. CT. REV. 34, 36-40.

[184] Tigner v. Texas, 310 U.S. 141 (1940) (Frankfurter, over one of McReynolds's last dissents), overruling Connolly v. Union Sewer Pipe Co., 184 U.S. 540 (1902); Madden v. Kentucky, 309 U.S. 83, 92-93 (1940) (Reed, over dissents by McReynolds and Roberts) "We think it quite clear that the right to carry out an incident to a trade, business or calling such as the deposit of money in banks is not a privilege of national citizenship."), overruling Colgate v. Harvey, 296 U.S. 404 (1935)).

[185] Honeyman v. Jacobs, 306 U.S. 539, 542 (1939) (Hughes) (stressing that the statute abrogated the right to seek a deficiency judgment only if the value of the land sold at foreclosure had equaled the outstanding debt: "The contract contemplated that the mortgagee should make himself whole, if necessary, out of the security but not that he should be enriched at the expense of the debtor."); Veix v. Sixth Ward Ass'n, 310 U.S. 32 (1940) (Reed). Earlier cases had held that laws suspending contract rights had to be limited to the emergency that necessitated them. *See, e.g.,* W. B. Worthen Co. v. Thomas, 292 U.S. 426, 432 (1934). *Veix* held it irrelevant that the limit on savings withdrawals was "permanent." *See* 310 U.S. at 39-40. *See also* Hale, *The Supreme Court and the Contract Clause: I,* 57 HARV. L. REV. 512, 548-51 (1944) (explaining that the law upheld in *Honeyman* was "designed to prevent a party from getting more by way of remedy than he would get by performance").

[186] United States v. Rock Royal Co-op, 307 U.S. 533, 577-78 (1939) (Reed) (upholding provision for milk marketing orders to be effective upon approval by two-thirds of producers, on the unconvincing ground that "Congress had the power to put this Order into effect without the approval of anyone"). *See* Jaffe, *Law Making by Private Groups,* 51 HARV. L. REV. 201 (1937), for sobering examples of the prevalence of private "lawmaking," from collective bargaining agreements to professional standards to rules of stock exchanges and political parties. The delegation of authority to the Secretary of Agriculture to determine the terms of such an order, which the court also upheld, was fully consistent with the criteria laid down in *Schechter,* for the statute required him, in the Court's words, essentially to establish "the prices that will give the commodity a purchasing power equivalent to that of the base period, considering the price and supply of feed and other pertinent economic conditions affecting the milk market in the area." 307 U.S. at 577.

[187] *See* Dowling, Cheatham, and Hale, *Mr. Justice Stone and the Constitution,* 36 COLUM. L. REV. 351 (1936).

[188] United States v. Bekins, 304 U.S. 27 (1938) (Hughes, over two dissents), overruling Ashton v. Cameron County Water Improv. Dist., 298 U.S. 513 (1936).

[189] James v. Dravo Contracting Co., 302 U.S. 134, 149-61 (1937) (Hughes, over dissents by Roberts, McReynolds, Sutherland, and Butler after Van Devanter had retired), disapproving Panhandle Oil Co. v. Knox, 277 U.S. 218 (1928); Helvering v. Gerhardt, 304 U.S. 405 (1938) (Stone, over two dissents), limiting Collector v.

only indirect, the Court of the late 1930s seemed disinclined to treat the power to tax as the power to destroy unless it was discriminatorily applied.[190]

A similar philosophy underlay Justice Stone's equally creative conclusion that the commerce clause precluded essentially only those state laws discriminating against interstate commerce or subjecting it to multiple burdens.[191] Like the federal and state governments in the field of immunity, interstate commerce was not in his view entitled to special privileges; it was enough that it not be subjected to special burdens.[192]

---

Day, 78 U.S. (11 Wall.) 113 (1871); Graves v. New York *ex rel.* O'Keefe, 306 U.S. 466 (1939) (Stone, over two dissents), overruling both *Day* and New York *ex rel.* Rogers v. Graves, 299 U.S. 401 (1937); Helvering v. Mountain Producers Corp., 303 U.S. 376 (1938) (Hughes), overruling Burnet v. Coronado Oil & Gas Co., 285 U.S. 393 (1932), and Gillespie v. Oklahoma, 257 U.S. 501 (1922), in broadening the ability of Congress to tax state oil lessees. *See also* O'Malley v. Woodrough, 307 U.S. 277, 282 (1939) (Frankfurter, over Butler's dissent) (permitting Congress to tax the salaries of federal judges appointed after the tax law was passed and casting doubt on Evans v. Gore, 253 U.S. 245 (1920), which had forbidden taxation of previously appointed judges whose compensation was expressly protected against diminution by article III). *See generally* Lowndes, *Taxation and the Supreme Court, 1937 Term,* 87 U. PA. L. REV. 1, 2-15 (1938); T. POWELL, *supra* note 43, at 122 (criticizing *Dravo* on the ground that "[f]rom an economic standpoint it makes no difference whether the tax is imposed on the seller or on the buyer, on the builder or on his patron.").

[190] "I have always felt," wrote Stone privately in 1937, "that everything needful would have been accomplished had Marshall merely declared that neither government can adopt a tax which discriminates against the other." Letter to Irving Brant, May 1, 1937, *quoted in* A. MASON, *supra* note 154, at 503. *See also* THE FIRST HUNDRED YEARS at 165-68 (discussing *McCulloch,* 17 U.S. 316 (1819)).

[191] *See, e.g.,* South Carolina State Highway Dept. v. Barnwell Bros., 303 U.S. 177 (1938) (Stone) (upholding state law limiting width and weight of trucks as safety measure despite serious effect on commerce); Western Live Stock v. Bureau of Revenue, 303 U.S. 250 (1938) (Stone) (upholding tax measured by gross receipts no other state could tax); McGoldrick v. Berwind-White Coal Mining Co., 309 U.S. 33, 69 (1940) (Stone) (upholding sales tax on goods delivered from other states over Hughes's dissent invoking Stone's own multiple burden test: "[i]f New York can tax the delivery, Pennsylvania can tax the shipment and New Jersey the transshipment"); California v. Thompson, 313 U.S. 109 (1941) (Stone) (overruling DiSanto v. Pennsylvania, 273 U.S. 34 (1927), in upholding licensing of agent selling interstate transportation).

*See also* Henneford v. Silas Mason Co., 300 U.S. 577 (1937) (Cardozo) (upholding compensatory use tax on goods bought outside the state despite analogy of Baldwin v. G.A.F. Seelig, 294 U.S. 511 (1935)); Milk Board v. Eisenberg Co., 306 U.S. 346 (1939) (Roberts) (upholding power to set minimum prices for milk sold for transportation in interstate commerce after *Baldwin* had removed risk of contradictory law in receiving state). *See generally* Dowling, *Interstate Commerce and State Power,* 27 VA. L. REV. 1, 19-20 (1940) (urging a frank balancing of state and federal interests under the rubric of implicit congressional will); T. POWELL, *supra* note 43, at chs. 5, 6, and especially *id.* at 167-69 (suggesting by analogy to the original package cases, pp. 32-36 *supra,* that *Baldwin* and *Henneford* might be reconcilable on the ground that "prohibition is much more of an intrusion on a free national economy than is an equalizing tax"); Brown, *The Open Economy: Justice Frankfurter and the Position of the Judiciary,* 67 YALE L. J. 219 (1957) (arguing that Stone's emphasis on equality was insufficient to prevent protectionism or exploitation of geographical advantage). Endorsements of Stone's view of multiple taxation include Powell, *New Light on Gross Receipts Taxes,* 53 HARV. L. REV. 909 (1940); Lockhart, *State Tax Barriers to Interstate Trade,* 53 HARV. L. REV. 1253 (1940); Morrison, *State Taxation of Interstate Commerce,* 36 ILL. L. REV. 727 (1942).

[192] *See* Barnwell, 303 U.S. at 184-85 n.2 (invoking the virtual representation argument that Marshall had made in distinguishing state and federal taxes in *McCulloch,* 17 U.S. 316). Stone wrote: "Underlying the stated rule [against discrimination against interstate commerce] has been the thought . . . that when the regulation is of such a character that its burden falls principally upon those without the state, legislative action is not likely to be subjected to those political restraints which are normally exerted on legislation where it affects adversely some interests within the state." The same philosophy seems in part to underlie other provisions assuring that politically weak classes are treated as well as the dominant majority. *See, e.g.,* U. S. CONST. art. IV, § 2 (citizens of other

No less revolutionary was Justice Stone's reformulation of the geographical limitations that the Court had found both due process and full faith and credit to impose on state power to tax or regulate. What mattered in the tax field was no longer the often fictitious location of intangible property but rather whether the taxpayer could fairly be said to receive protection in return for his money.[193] Similarly, in choice of law cases Justice Story's territorialist analysis yielded to the requirement that the application of the law in question serve a legitimate state interest.[194] While this development left unfulfilled the hope that the full faith and credit clause might provide a means of resolving conflicts that interested states could not work out on their own,[195] some have defended it on the ground that the problem is unfit for judicial resolution.[196] In any event the new analysis of state interests seemed more consonant with the constitutional purpose of keeping one state from meddling in another's affairs than did the procrustean rules it supplanted.[197]

Related to the interstate choice of law cases was the stunning decision in *Erie R.R. v. Tompkins*,[198] overruling nearly a hundred years of precedent in holding that federal courts must follow state judge-made law as well as state statutes except where the Constitution or federal statutes otherwise required.[199] That was indeed what the governing statute

---

states entitled to privileges and immunities of local citizens); *id.* amend. XIV, § 1 (equal protection of the laws). *See generally* J. ELY, DEMOCRACY AND DISTRUST 77-88 (1980).

[193] *See* New York *ex rel.* Cohn v. Graves, 300 U.S. 308 (1937) (Stone, over dissents by Butler and Mc-Reynolds) (state may tax income from out-of-state property); First Bank Stock Corp. v. Minnesota, 301 U.S. 234, 240-41 (1937) (Stone) (state of corporation's commercial domicile may tax its shares in foreign corporations); Curry v. McCanless, 307 U.S. 357 (1939) (Stone, over four dissents) (both testator's and trustee's domiciles may tax passage of trust property by will).

[194] *Contrast, e.g.,* Osborn v. Ozlin, 310 U.S. 53 (1940) (Frankfurter, over dissents by Roberts, Hughes, and McReynolds) (upholding requirement that local risks be insured through a local agent, without regard to place contract was made), *with* Allgeyer v. Louisiana, 165 U.S. 578 (1897) (invalidating requirement that insurer qualify to do business in state before taking action there with respect to insuring local risks). *Contrast* Pacific Ins. Co. v. Industrial Accident Comm., 306 U.S. 493 (1939) (Stone) (state of injury may apply own workers' compensation law though employment contract centered elsewhere), *with* Bradford Elec. Co. v. Clapper, 286 U.S. 145 (1932) (Brandeis) (holding law of the place of employment governed). The way to *Pacific Ins. Co.* had been cleared in Alaska Packers Ass'n v. Industrial Accident Comm., 294 U.S. 532 (1935), where Stone had employed his novel interest analysis to reaffirm the *Clapper* conclusion that the state of employment might apply its law as well. *Consider also* Skiriotes v. Florida, 313 U.S. 69 (1941) (Hughes) (upholding state's right to regulate its citizen's gathering of sponges outside territorial limits). The one decision out of line with other developments in this area was Sovereign Camp of the Woodmen of the World v. Bolin, 305 U.S. 66, 75 (1938) (Roberts) (alternative holding), where in reliance on precedent the Court unanimously held that a policyholder's state could not deny that the terms of an insurance contract were ultra vires, because "the rights of membership [in a fraternal benefit society] are governed by the law of the State of incorporation."

[195] *See, e.g.,* Jackson, *Full Faith and Credit—The Lawyer's Clause of the Constitution*, 45 COLUM. L. REV. 1 (1945).

[196] *See* B. CURRIE, SELECTED ESSAYS ON THE CONFLICT OF LAWS ch. 5 (1963).

[197] Both the territorialist approach and Justice Stone's approach to full faith and credit depended on the disputable conclusion that the reference to "public Acts" in that clause was meant to require respect for general laws of other states rather than, as explained in the Convention, for quasi-judicial legislation such as individual acts of bankruptcy. *See* p. 70, note 115 *supra.* As far as due process was concerned, Stone's interest analysis was a natural corollary of the general requirement that laws be reasonably tailored to accomplish legitimate legislative goals.

[198] 304 U.S. 64 (1938) (Brandeis, over dissents by Butler and McReynolds).

[199] The contrary conclusion, with the exception of such "local" matters as those respecting land, had been reached in Swift v. Tyson, 41 U.S. 1 (1842).

seemed to modern eyes to say, and recent scholarship had suggested it reflected the original intention as well.[200] But Justice Brandeis was willing to depart from stare decisis only because he was convinced that the earlier practice was unconstitutional: "Congress has no power to declare substantive rules of common law applicable in a State whether they be local in their nature or 'general,' be they commercial law or a part of the law of torts. And no clause in the Constitution purports to confer such a power upon the federal courts."[201]

It may seem odd that the Court cut back on federal judicial authority at the same time it so greatly expanded the powers of Congress. Perhaps it was still true, as Brandeis argued, that Congress itself could not regulate everything. After the permissive commerce clause decisions of the preceding year, however, there was certainly a strong argument that Congress could have regulated the liability of interstate railroads to trespassers, and that was what *Erie* involved.[202]

Thus on the facts of the case the more serious objection seemed to be one less of federalism than of separation of powers: whether or not Congress could make rules to govern the particular case, it had not done so; and the federal courts had only those powers given them by the Constitution or statute.[203]

The grant of admiralty jurisdiction had long been understood to imply authority to fashion federal common law.[204] Brandeis did not explain why the parallel grant of diversity jurisdiction, which was the basis of the suit in *Erie*, did not imply such authority as well.[205] The answer lies in the differing purposes the Court has found to underlie the two jurisdictional provisions: while one reason for the admiralty grant was apparently to permit the development of a uniform maritime law, the purpose of diversity jurisdiction was only to assure out-of-state litigants an impartial forum.[206]

---

[200] See Judiciary Act of Sept. 24, 1789, § 34, 1 Stat. 73, 92, codified at 28 U.S.C. § 725 ("[T]he laws of the several states, except where the constitution, treaties, or statutes of the United States shall otherwise require or provide, shall be regarded as rules of decision in trials at common law in the courts of the United States in cases where they apply"); Warren, *New Light on the History of the Federal Judiciary Act of 1789,* 37 HARV. L. REV. 49 (1924). Later observers have been less confident of this conclusion. *See* 1 & 2 W. CROSSKEY, POLITICS AND THE CONSTITUTION IN THE HISTORY OF THE UNITED STATES 626-28, 866-71 (1953); Friendly, *In Praise of Erie—And of the New Federal Common Law,* 39 N.Y.U. L. REV. 383, 389-91 (1964).

[201] 304 U.S. at 78. *See* Ely, *The Irrepressible Myth of Erie,* 87 HARV. L. REV. 693, 703 (1974) (practice under *Swift v. Tyson* "was unconstitutional because nothing in the Constitution provided the central government with a general lawmaking authority of the sort the Court had been exercising").

[202] See Ely, *supra* note 201, at 703 n.62; Second Employers' Liability Cases, 223 U.S. 1, 52 (1912) (upholding federal law rendering interstate railroad liable for injuries to employees), p. 94 *supra.* For lingering doubts on this issue, see Jay, *Origins of Federal Common Law: Part Two,* 133 U. PA. L. REV. 1231, 1312 & n.401 (1985).

[203] Viewed in this light, *Erie* and the increased tolerance for federal legislation were wholly consistent manifestations of a general tendency toward restraint in the exercise of federal judicial authority.

[204] See The Lottawanna, 88 U.S. 558, 574-75 (1875), THE FIRST HUNDRED YEARS at 404 n.4; Southern Pacific Co. v. Jensen, 244 U.S. 205, 215 (1917) ("[I]n the absence of some controlling statute the general maritime law as accepted by the federal courts constitutes part of our national law."), pp. 110-15 *supra.*

[205] See McCormick and Hewins, *The Collapse of "General" Law in the Federal Courts,* 33 ILL. L. REV. 126, 135, 141 (1938). This contrast was heightened by Brandeis's unexplained conclusion, the very day *Erie* was decided, that "whether the water of an interstate stream must be apportioned between the two States is a question of 'federal common law' upon which neither the statutes nor the decisions of either State can be conclusive." Hinderlider v. La Plata River & Cherry Creek Ditch Co., 304 U.S. 92, 110 (1938).

[206] See Field, *Sources of Law: The Scope of Federal Common Law,* 99 HARV. L. REV. 881, 915–18 (1986). *See also* Knickerbocker Ice Co. v. Stewart, 253 U.S. 149, 160 (1920) ("To preserve adequate harmony and

Thus the best explanation of the constitutional holding in *Erie* is that, like a state court that has no significant contacts with the matter in controversy, a federal court sitting solely in diversity is a disinterested forum with respect to the merits. And as Justice Stone made clear in the interstate choice of law cases, only an interested forum can apply its own law.[207]

Appropriately, it was Justice Stone—perhaps the principal architect of the whole revolution—who summed it all up in the most clairvoyant and best-known footnote in Supreme Court history. No longer would the Court be much concerned with the controversies over social and economic legislation that had commanded the bulk of its past attention. In suggesting that the presumption of constitutionality might have less force with respect to measures affecting specific guarantees like freedom of speech, disadvantaging "discrete and insular minorities," or obstructing "those political processes which can ordinarily be expected to bring about repeal of undesirable legislation," Stone established the Court's agenda for the next fifty years.[208]

---

appropriate uniform rules relating to maritime matters and bring them within control of the Federal Government was the fundamental purpose [of the admiralty clause]."); D. Currie, *Federalism and the Admiralty: "The Devil's Own Mess,"* 1960 Sup. Ct. Rev. 158, 158-64; Bank of the United States v. Deveaux, 9 U.S. 61, 87 (1809) (attributing diversity jurisdiction to "apprehensions" that state courts might not "administer justice . . . impartially" in cases involving outsiders). Justice Brandeis reaffirmed this understanding of diversity jurisdiction elsewhere in the *Erie* opinion. 304 U.S. at 74.

The citation in *Hinderlider,* 304 U.S. at 110, to Kansas v. Colorado, 206 U.S. 46, 98 (1907), helps to explain the contrast between *Hinderlider* and *Erie. Kansas* was a controversy between states. Since to apply the law of either state in such a case would make one party the judge in its own cause, the jurisdictional grant of jurisdiction over controversies between states has also been held to confer federal common law authority. *See* Texas v. New Jersey, 379 U.S. 674, 677 (1965); Friendly, *supra* note 200, at 383, 394-98. *Hinderlider* was not itself an interstate suit, but the federal common law developed in such suits is supreme and thus applicable in other cases as well. *Compare* Pope & Talbot, Inc. v. Hawn, 346 U.S. 406, 411 (1953) (holding federal maritime law governed in diversity case).

For the argument that *no* grant of judicial power in article III was meant to embrace lawmaking authority, see Stimson, *Swift v. Tyson—What Remains?,* 24 Cornell L. Q. 54, 60-64 (1938) (invoking an earlier draft conveying "jurisdiction" rather than "judicial power").

[207] That a forum with no interest in the merits may have legitimate interests in its own procedure helps to explain how the Court could so easily dismiss possible constitutional objections to the Federal Rules of Civil Procedure after *Erie. See* Sibbach v. Wilson & Co., 312 U.S. 1, 9-10 (1941). For decisions upholding state procedural requirements in related contexts see Wells v. Simonds Abrasive Co., 345 U.S. 514 (1953) (allowing state court to dismiss action based on foreign law in reliance on local statute of limitations); Missouri *ex rel.* Southern Ry. Co. v. Mayfield, 340 U.S. 1 (1950) (allowing state court to dismiss FELA action on grounds of forum non conveniens).

[208] *Carolene Products,* 304 U.S. at 152-53 n.4. *See also* R. McCloskey, *supra* note 40, at 177-79; P. Murphy, The Constitution in Crisis Times, 1918-1969, at 169 (1972).

# 8

# The New Agenda

Amid the thunder of the great economic controversies that destroyed economic due process, the contract clause, and the concept of limited federal power, the Supreme Court of the 1930s quietly began to work on the agenda of the future: criminal procedure, civil rights, and civil liberties.

## I. CRIMINAL PROCEDURE

In *Murray's Lessee v. Hoboken Land & Improvement Co.*,[1] in 1856, The Court had defined due process in essentially historical terms. Unless the challenged procedure conflicted with other provisions of the Constitution, the question was whether it was in accord with "those settled usages and modes of proceeding existing in the common and statute law of England, before the emigration of our ancestors, and which are shown not to have been unsuited to their civil and political condition by having been acted on by them after the settlement of this country."[2] Applying this test, the Court had upheld a statute providing for summary collection of money that a customs collector owed the United States, because such a procedure was sanctioned by practice in both England and the Colonies.[3]

Any implication of the converse proposition—that all procedural rights sanctioned by history were indispensable elements of due process—had been rejected in *Hurtado v. California*[4] in 1884. It was true that "a process of law, which is not otherwise forbidden, must be taken to be due process of law, if it can show the sanction of settled usage both in England and in this country; but it by no means follows that nothing else can be due process of law."[5] Historical acceptance was a sufficient but not a necessary condition of

---

[1] 59 U.S. (18 How.) 272 (1856).
[2] *Id.* at 277.
[3] *Id.* at 281-86. *See* THE FIRST HUNDRED YEARS at 276 n. 304.
[4] 110 U.S. 516 (1884).
[5] *Id.* at 528.

constitutionality; due process required only such established procedures as were "fundamental."[6]

On this basis indictment, jury trial, and the privilege against self-incrimination had all
been held to be outside the scope of the due process requirement and thus inapplicable to
the states.[7] The essence of due process, the Court said, was adequate notice and a hearing
before an unbiased and unintimidated judge with jurisdiction.[8] Under Chief Justice
Hughes, while downplaying the historical dimension of the inquiry, the Court significantly expanded the list of due process requirements.

### A.    *Powell v. Alabama*

The first example of this expansion was *Powell v. Alabama*,[9] a 1932 decision arising out
of the notorious prosecution of seven young blacks—who came to be known as the Scotts-
boro boys—for the rape of two white girls on a freight train. Without reaching claims of
discrimination in jury selection and mob domination of the trial, the Court concluded that
due process required the state to permit the defendants to appear by counsel and to provide
legal assistance for those unable to obtain their own.[10]

The first conclusion was relatively easy. Although English courts had afforded no right
to counsel in serious criminal cases at the time of emigration, the English practice had
been repudiated in the Colonies and thus was not sanctioned by history in the sense of
*Murray's Lessee*. Moreover, given the helplessness of the layman accused of a crime, the
defect was fundamental in the *Hurtado* sense: "The right to be heard would be, in many
cases, of little avail if it did not comprehend the right to be heard by counsel."[11] Finally,

---

[6]*Id*. at 535; THE FIRST HUNDRED YEARS at 366-37.

[7]*Hurtado*, 110 U.S. at 538 (indictment); Maxwell v. Dow, 176 U.S. 581, 604-05 (1900) (twelve-member
jury); Twining v. New Jersey, 211 U.S. 78, 113-14 (1908) (self-incrimination); *see also* Walker v. Sauvinet, 92
U.S. 90, 92-93 (1876) (due process does not embrace the right to jury trial).

[8]*See, e.g.*, Roller v. Holly, 176 U.S. 398, 409 (1900) (notice); Hovey v. Elliott, 167 U.S. 409, 413-15 (1897)
(hearing); Tumey v. Ohio, 273 U.S. 510, 523-32 (1927) (unbiased judge); Moore v. Dempsey, 261 U.S. 86, 90-
91 (1923) (mob domination); Pennoyer v. Neff, 95 U.S. 714, 733 (1878) (dictum) (jurisdiction). Chief Justice
Hughes wrote to refine the notion of bias in United States v. Wood, 299 U.S. 123, 136-51 (1936), concluding
that absent a showing of actual bias the presence of government employees on a criminal jury was forbidden by
neither history nor justice and thus offended neither due process nor the sixth amendment right to an impartial
jury. Both *Wood*, 299 U.S. at 142-49, and Patton v. United States, 281 U.S. 276, 288 (1930) (Sutherland, J.),
which allowed the defendant to waive a twelve-member jury with government consent, stressed that the principle
*Hurtado* had enunciated in the due process context applied to the explicit criminal jury provisions as well; only
the "essential" elements of the common law right were preserved. Although in *Wood* Hughes argued that a similar
test had been employed in applying the seventh amendment provision that jury findings be reviewed only "according to the rules of the common law," 299 U.S. at 143-44 (quoting Baltimore & Carolina Line v. Redman,
295 U.S. 654, 657 (1935)), the decisions under that provision seemed to follow history much more closely, as
the language of the clause itself suggested, *see, e.g.*, Dimick v. Schiedt, 293 U.S. 474, 486-88 (1935) (Sutherland, J.) (five-to-four decision striking down an additur provision for avoiding a new trial for inadequate damages
if the defendant agreed to pay more than the jury had awarded, because the practice had been unknown in
England in 1791); *Redman*, 295 U.S. at 659-61 (upholding a provision for judgment notwithstanding the verdict
after reservation of ruling on motion for directed verdict, because similar practice had existed at common law).

[9]287 U.S. 45 (1932) (Sutherland, J., over dissents by Butler and McReynolds, JJ.).

[10]*Id*. at 68-71. The dissents argued that counsel had actually been provided. *Id*. at 74.

[11]*Id*. at 68-69.

although one of the grounds given in *Hurtado* for holding that due process did not include the right to an indictment had been that a contrary holding would make redundant the specific fifth amendment requirement of a federal grand jury, Justice Sutherland rightly observed in *Powell* that later cases had shown such an overlap not determinative; due process must in any even be given its natural meaning.[12]

The requirement that the state *provide* counsel was another story. Sutherland nowhere asserted that colonial practice had required the government to pay for an attorney; most of the provisions he cited merely recognized the right to employ one.[13] Rather the basis for this decision was simply that the right to appointed counsel, "at least in cases like the present," was "fundamental." Every state required the appointment of counsel at least in capital cases. If this universal practice did not "establish" the right, it surely "reflect[ed]" it. In any event, to condemn an incompetent defendant to death without assigned counsel "would be little short of judicial murder."[14]

Unlike the conclusion that due process required an opportunity to employ counsel, the requirement that the state provide counsel seemed to turn the *Hurtado* test on its head. *Hurtado* had introduced the fundamental-rights test as a means of *denying* rights historically afforded; *Powell* employed it to *grant* rights historically denied.[15]

## B.   Sequels

*Mooney v. Holohan*[16] and *Brown v. Mississippi*,[17] while adding that knowing use of perjured testimony and reliance on a coerced confession were also fundamental flaws, suggested a narrow interpretation of the new test. Like a trial without counsel or dominated by a mob, trial on the basis of coerced or perjured testimony was a mere "pretense."[18] In effect, the Court was saying, the defendants had received no hearing at all, and the right

[12] *See id.* at 60-71 (citing for the last point decisions holding that due process prohibited the states from infringing freedom of speech or press or taking property without compensation).

[13] *See id.* at 61-65. The one apparent exception was a Pennsylvania statute paraphrased as providing that "in capital cases learned counsel should be assigned to the prisoners." It is possible that other provisions such as those granting simply a "right to counsel" had been construed to require the state to provide attorneys, but Sutherland did not say they had.

[14] *Id.* at 72-73. The central argument of the opinion seems equally applicable to any serious criminal case, although the Court's appropriate insistence that it was deciding only the case before it and its observation that counsel was necessary "above all" because the defendants stood "in deadly peril of their lives," *id.* at 71, furnished a handhold for a narrower reading. Nor should the requirement that counsel be provided at state expense be taken to expand the holding of Truax v. Corrigan, 257 U.S. 312 (1921), that a state deprived a person of life or property by its failure to affirmatively protect him, 257 U.S. at 328-30; in *Powell* the state, by virtue of its criminal prosecution, was actively seeking to deprive the defendant of his life, 287 U.S. at 46. *See* pp. 139-43 *supra* (discussing *Truax*); Currie, *Positive and Negative Constitutional Rights*, 53 U. CHI. L. REV. 864, 873-74 (1986).

[15] *See* Easterbrook, *Substance and Due Process*, 1982 SUP. CT. REV. 85, 106 ("*Hurtado* . . . give[s] no support to judicial augmentation of historically recognized procedures.").

[16] 294 U.S. 103, 112 (1935) (per curiam) (perjured testimony).

[17] 297 U.S. 278, 285-86 (1936) (Hughes, C. J.) (confession obtained by physical torture).

[18] In Chambers v. Florida, 309 U.S. 227, 238-39 (1940), Justice Black applied *Brown* to confessions obtained by six days of repeated questioning. There was no suggestion that the same reasoning would apply to a *voluntary* confession, which would render the trial an even more foregone conclusion; the distinction may lie in the realm of waiver.

to a hearing had always been an essential element of due process.[19] Thus, even if there was no historical support for the particular requirements announced in these cases, they might all be viewed as implicit in the historical and fundamental right to a "hearing," and the *Hurtado* test arguably had not been perverted after all.

The trouble with this reasoning is that, at least with regard to the right to assigned counsel, it seems to contradict the historical understanding of what constituted a hearing. The issue of mob domination could have been fitted within the historical requirement of an impartial arbiter, and the common law had excluded coerced confessions.[20] No departure from history was thus required to outlaw them. It was otherwise, however, with the right to assigned counsel. The materials cited in *Powell* suggested that no such right was implicit in the historical concept of a hearing.

In any event, the language of the opinions suggests that the question whether an alleged right was "fundamental" had basically displaced the historical inquiry it had been designed to accompany. In 1937 Justice Cardozo's famous opinion in *Palko v. Connecticut*,[21] permitting the state to appeal an unfavorable criminal judgment, lent force to this conclusion by announcing that due process embraced all requirements of the Bill of Rights that were "implicit in the concept of ordered liberty."[22] Even long-established procedures, it seemed, were now subject to scrutiny for their compatibility with contemporary notions of fair play.[23]

Once *Hurtado* had concluded that the Framers did not mean to burden us with unnecessary anachronisms, one might plausibly have argued they would not have wanted to subject us to unfair ones either. It was true that the particular vice of holding all common law rights protected was that legislatures could not alter them,[24] while nothing in the Constitution appeared to inhibit the states from affording *additional* rights. It might nevertheless be argued that those intent on protecting existing fundamental rights from legislative interference would not have trusted legislators to remedy past inadequacies, though

[19] *See, e.g., Powell,* 287 U.S. at 68.

[20] *See* W. LaFave & J. Israel, Criminal Procedure 264-65 (1985).

[21] 302 U.S. 319 (1937) (over the unexplained dissent of Butler, J.).

[22] *Id.* at 325. *See also id.* at 328 ("Is that kind of double jeopardy to which the statute has subjected [the defendant] a hardship so acute and shocking that our polity will not endure it? . . . The answer surely must be 'no.' "); Snyder v. Massachusetts, 291 U.S. 97, 115 (1934) (Cardozo, J., over a dissent by Roberts, J., joined by Brandeis, Sutherland and Butler, JJ.) (holding that the defendant need not be present when a jury viewed the scene of the crime: "There can be no sound solution without an answer to the question whether in the particular conditions exhibited by the record the enforced absence of the defendant is so flagrantly unjust that the Constitution of the United States steps in to forbid it.").

[23] *See* Nutting, *The Supreme Court, the Fourteenth Amendment and State Criminal Cases,* 3 U. Chi. L. Rev. 244, 254 (1936) (arguing that under decisions of the Hughes period any state measure offended due process "the effect of which is to deprive the accused of what the Supreme Court of the United States may regard as a fair trial"); *cf.* Milliken v. Meyer, 311 U.S. 457, 463 (1940) (Douglas, J.) (undertaking no historical analysis in holding that civil jurisdiction of state court based upon out-of-state service on domiciliary of forum state satisfied "traditional notions of fair play and substantial justice" and noting that "[t]he state which accords him privileges and affords protection to him and his property by virtue of his domicile may also exact reciprocal duties"); Ohio Bell Tel. Co. v. Public Utils. Comm'n, 301 U.S. 292, 300 (1937) (Cardozo, J.) (undertaking no historical analysis in holding that administrative reliance on information not revealed to the parties for possible rebuttal denied a litigant "[t]he fundamentals of a trial").

[24] *Hurtado,* 110 U.S. at 529 ("[T]o hold that [settled usage] is essential to due process of law would be to deny every quality of the law but its age, and to render it incapable of progress or improvement.").

the open-endedness of the resulting judicial authority might have furnished a basis of distinction. What was most noteworthy was that the Court made no attempt to explain or to justify the momentous change it appeared to be making.[25]

## II.  CIVIL RIGHTS

The central purpose of the Civil War amendments, as the Supreme Court stressed in the *Slaughter-House Cases*,[26] was to put an end to state discrimination against blacks.[27] Under Waite and Fuller the Court had condemned the exclusion of blacks from juries and of Chinese from the laundry business and established that equality did not preclude separation.[28] Under Fuller and White it had struck down peonage and grandfather clauses and held that racial zoning, despite its apparent conformity with the separate-but-equal doctrine, deprived landowners of property without due process of law.[29] Under Taft it had held that the state could not exclude blacks from voting in political primaries.[30] In contrast to the whirlwind of activity that had characterized fourteenth amendment litigation in other fields, that was about all the Court had had to say about race before 1930.

### A.   Juries, Grandfathers, and Schools

Under Hughes the Court made modest progress. The Justices exhibited what seemed to be an increased willingness to scrutinize records for proof of discrimination against blacks in the selection of juries.[31] *Lane v. Wilson*[32] belatedly struck down Oklahoma's effort to evade the grandfather clause decision. *Missouri ex rel. Gaines v. Canada*[33] put teeth in

---

[25] *See* Easterbrook, *supra* note 15, at 108-09.

[26] 83 U.S. (16 Wall.) 36, 67-72, 81 (1873).

[27] *See* THE FIRST HUNDRED YEARS at 342-51 (discussing the *Slaughter-House Cases*).

[28] *See, e.g.,* Strauder v. West Virginia, 100 U.S. 303 (1880) (black jurors); Yick Wo v. Hopkins, 118 U.S. 356 (1886) (Chinese laundries); Plessy v. Ferguson, 163 U.S. 537 (1896) (upholding segregated trains); Pace v. Alabama, 106 U.S. 583 (1883) (criminal statute separately defining interracial offense not racially discriminatory where same punishment prescribed for both races). *See* THE FIRST HUNDRED YEARS at 383-90 (discussing *Strauder, Yick Wo,* and *Pace*); p. 40 *supra* (discussing *Plessy*).

[29] *See, e.g.,* Bailey v. Alabama, 219 U.S. 219 (1911) (peonage); Clyatt v. United States, 197 U.S. 207 (1905) (peonage); Guinn v. United States, 238 U.S. 347 (1915) (grandfather clause); Buchanan v. Warley, 245 U.S. 60 (1917) (racial zoning). *See* pp. 105-09 *supra* (discussing *Bailey, Guinn,* and *Buchanan*).

[30] *See, e.g.,* Nixon v. Herndon, 273 U.S. 536 (1927) (white primary), pp. 138-39 *supra*.

[31] *See, e.g.,* Smith v. Texas, 311 U.S. 128 (1940) (Black, J.); Pierre v. Louisiana, 306 U.S. 354 (1939) (Black, J.); Hale v. Kentucky, 303 U.S. 613 (1938) (per curiam); Hollins v. Oklahoma, 295 U.S. 394 (1935) (per curiam); Norris v. Alabama, 294 U.S. 587 (1935) (Hughes, C. J.): Nutting, *supra* note 23, at 250-51. The Chief Justice made clear in *Norris* that Supreme Court review in these cases extended to state-court findings of fact where necessary to ensure that constitutional rights had not been denied. 294 U.S. at 589-90. *See also Pierre,* 306 U.S. at 358 ("[W]hen a claim is properly asserted . . . that a citizen whose life is at stake has been denied the equal protection of his country's laws on account of his race, it becomes our solemn duty to make independent inquiry and determination of the disputed facts. . . .").

[32] 307 U.S. 268 (1939) (Frankfurter, J., over dissents by McReynolds and Butler, JJ.). The new provision required those who had not voted in 1914 to register within twelve days or forever be disenfranchised. "The practical effect . . . was to accord to the member of the negro race . . . not more than 12 days within which to reassert constitutional rights which this Court found in the *Guinn* case to have been improperly taken from them." *Id.* at 276.

[33] 305 U.S. 337 (1938) (Hughes, C. J., over a dissent by McReynolds, J.).

quirement that separate facilities be equal by holding that a state with a law school of its own could not require a black to go beyond its borders to study law, even if it paid his expenses.

Chief Justice Hughes could easily have based this last conclusion on the convincing argument that a legal education outside the state was objectively disadvantageous,[34] but he selected a broader ground. Whether or not opportunities elsewhere were as good as those in Missouri,

> [t]he white resident is afforded legal education within the State; the negro resident having the same qualifications . . . must go outside the State to obtain it. That is a denial of the equality of legal right to the enjoyment of the privilege which the State has set up, and the provision for the payment of tuition fees in another State does not remove the discrimination.[35]

Earlier cases, both in and out of the area of race, had held it sufficient for fourteenth amendment purposes that one class of persons was treated as well as another, even if its members were afforded different privileges.[36] By declining to follow this principle the Court seemed to lay the foundation for an attack on the doctrine of separation itself, which Hughes distinguished on the unpersuasive ground that "the obligation of the State to give the protection of equal laws can be performed only where its laws operate, that is, within its own jurisdiction."[37]

## B.   White Primaries

Equally interesting was the 1932 decision in *Nixon v. Condon*[38] that a black could not be denied the right to vote in a primary election in Texas. An earlier decision so holding had been relatively easy, for the state had excluded blacks from the primary by statute.[39] Thereafter, however, the statute had been amended to permit each party's State Executive Committee to prescribe qualifications for participation in its primaries.[40] It was contended with some force that because it was now a party rule that excluded blacks, the state was no longer responsible; and only the state was forbidden to deny equal protection.[41]

---

[34] *See id.* at 349 (noting "the opportunities for the particular study of Missouri law and for the observation of the local courts" and adverting to "the difference in distances to be traveled"—whose impact in terms of personal and professional contacts, it should be added, is not covered by payment of travel expenses.).

[35] *Id.* at 349-50.

[36] *See, e.g.,* Plessy v. Ferguson, 163 U.S. 537 (1896) (separate railroad cars for different races); Missouri v. Lewis, 101 U.S. 22 (1879) (separate courts for different regions of state with one region having no right of appeal to the state's supreme court); THE FIRST HUNDRED YEARS at 388-89 & n.145 (discussing various meanings of equality).

[37] 305 U.S. at 350. *See* R. MCCLOSKEY, THE AMERICAN SUPREME COURT 211 (1960) ("The *Missouri* decision signalized a new judicial mood toward Negro rights.").

[38] 286 U.S. 73 (1932).

[39] Nixon v. Herndon, 273 U.S. 536, 541 (1927).

[40] *See* 286 U.S. at 82.

[41] *See id.* at 83; *id.* at 89-106 (McReynolds, Van Devanter, Sutherland, and Butler, JJ., dissenting).

The Court's rejection of this argument rested on the fact that the statute had vested in the State Executive Committee a power to act on behalf of the party. The party itself had given its committee no such authority. Thus, the Court concluded, the committee had acted "not as the delegates of the party, but as the delegates of the State."[42]

The possible implications of this reasoning were sweeping. If a special authorization to make rules for the party was enough to make the committee a state agent, the same might arguably be said of general laws recognizing the power of a majority of the members to do so. This could mean that every act of a state-chartered corporation might be held to be that of the state.[43]

Three years later, in *Grovey v. Townsend*,[44] the Court unanimously recoiled from this implication, holding that a resolution of the Democratic party *convention* excluding blacks was not state action despite the existence of state laws providing for the election of convention delegates. Nor was it enough to make the state responsible for the party's discrimination, wrote Justice Roberts, that the state extensively regulated primary elections, that a state officer had refused the petitioner his ballot in reliance on the party resolution, or that "in Texas nomination by the Democratic party [was] equivalent to election."[45]

In making such a nice distinction between the two cases, the Court foreshadowed future difficulties in drawing the line between public and private discrimination. It also made clear that the *Nixon* holding had been much less revolutionary than it might at first have appeared. For the time being, the Southern states remained at liberty to render the fifteenth amendment hollow by allowing the dominant political party to exclude blacks from the only election that mattered.[46]

## III.  CIVIL LIBERTIES

Apart from the economic cases, the most important developments in constitutional law during the 1930s concerned the first amendment freedoms of expression, assembly, and religion.

---

[42]*Id.* at 85.

[43]In response one might argue that the authority of a majority to govern the party came not from the law of voluntary associations, but from the agreement of the members, and that the state was no more responsible for this decision than for any other private agreement it might recognize as legally binding.

[44]295 U.S. 45, 53-54 (1935) (Roberts, J.).

[45]*Id.* at 54. For a contemporaneous argument to the contrary, see Evans, *Primary Elections and the Constitution*, 32 MICH. L. REV. 451, 462 (1934).

[46]Another device commonly employed to disenfranchise blacks survived judicial scrutiny when the Court upheld a statute conditioning the right to vote on payment of a poll tax in Breedlove v. Suttles, 302 U.S. 277 (1937) (Butler, J.). The complaining party in this case was white, and no argument of disguised racial motive was addressed. "Exaction of payment before registration," the Court said, "undoubtedly serves to aid collection from electors desiring to vote." *Id.* at 283. A later generation of judges, still without entering the thicket of legislative motives, would find this an inadequate reason for discriminating among otherwise eligible voters. *See* Harper v. Virginia Bd. of Elections, 383 U.S. 663 (1966), pp. 424-25 *infra*. The exception of nonvoting women from the poll tax, Justice Butler added, was justified by the "burdens necessarily borne by them for the preservation of the race." *Breedlove*, 302 U.S. at 282.

## A.  The First Amendment and the States

The first amendment itself, the Court had held, applied only to the federal government—as its language and history made abundantly clear.[47] In *Meyer v. Nebraska*,[48] however, the Court had declared in dictum that "the right of the individual . . . to worship God according to the dictates of his own conscience" was among the "libert[ies]" protected against state infringement by the fourteenth amendment's due process clause.[49] In *Gitlow v. New York*,[50] the majority had expressly assumed, without deciding, that the same was true of freedom of speech and the press; in *Whitney v. California*,[51] it had rejected a challenge to a state law without alluding to the question. *Fiske v. Kansas*[52] had actually overturned a state conviction that had been attacked on speech grounds, without saying whether the basis of decision was freedom of expression or a procedural requirement of evidence to support the charge.[53] Under Chief Justice Hughes the Court turned these intimations into clear holdings and extended them.[54]

Before his first term was over, Hughes wrote for the Court in *Stromberg v. California*[55] to strike down a state law as an infringement of the freedom of speech. He relied wholly on precedent to show that this guarantee applied to the states: "It has been determined that the conception of liberty under the due process clause of the Fourteenth Amendment embraces the right of free speech."[56] Cited for this conclusion were *Gitlow, Whitney* and *Fiske,* none of which had addressed the issue explicitly. Thus the important and debatable conclusion that the fourteenth amendment protected speech against state abridgement entered the law without ever having been explicitly justified in a majority opinion.

Two weeks later, in *Near v. Minnesota*,[57] Hughes cited the same three precedents, as well as *Stromberg,* as having established that freedom of the press was likewise protected against the states, though only *Gitlow* had so much as mentioned the press. This time he offered something resembling a reason for the conclusion: "It was found impossible to conclude that this essential personal liberty of the citizen was left unprotected by the general guaranty of fundamental rights of person and property."[58]

---

[47]Permoli v. New Orleans, 44 U.S. (3 How.) 589, 609 (1845) (free exercise of religion). The first amendment provides that "*Congress* shall make no law. . . ." U.S. CONST. amend. I (emphasis added); *cf.* Barron v. Baltimore, 32 U.S. (7 Pet.) 243 (1833) (holding that the taking clause of the fifth amendment did not apply to the states). *See* THE FIRST HUNDRED YEARS at 189-93.

[48]262 U.S. 390 (1923).

[49]*Id.* at 399.

[50]268 U.S. 652, 666 (1925). Holmes, in dissent, flatly asserted that the Court's assumption was correct. *Id.* at 672.

[51]274 U.S. 357 (1927). Brandeis, in a separate concurring opinion, reaffirmed the answer Holmes had given in *Gitlow. Id.* at 373.

[52]274 U.S. 380 (1927).

[53]*See* G. STONE, L. SEIDMAN, C. SUNSTEIN & M. TUSHNET, CONSTITUTIONAL LAW 966 (1986). These decisions are discussed at pp. 153-62 *supra.*

[54]*See* Green, *Liberty under the Fourteenth Amendment,* 27 WASH. U. L.Q. 479, 515-16 (1942).

[55]283 U.S. 359 (1931).

[56]*Id.* at 368. Justices McReynolds and Butler, dissenting, did not think it necessary to reach the question. *Id.* at 370-76.

[57]283 U.S. 697 (1931) ("It is no longer open to doubt that the liberty of the press, and of speech, is within the liberty safeguarded by the due process clause of the Fourteenth Amendment from invasion by state action.").

[58]*Id.* at 707.

Justice Sutherland was more explicit in *Grosjean v. American Press Co.*[59] in 1936. *Powell v. Alabama,* he said, had held that due process made those Bill of Rights provisions that were "fundamental" applicable to the states, and speech and press freedoms were as fundamental as the right to counsel. Thus in determining what liberties the clause protected the Court, without explanation, employed the test it had developed for determining what process was due when those liberties were taken away.

*De Jonge v. Oregon*[60] added freedom of assembly to the list of incorporated freedoms in 1937. "The right of peaceable assembly," wrote the Chief Justice, "is a right cognate to those of free speech and free press and is equally fundamental."[61] Finally, in *Cantwell v. Connecticut*[62] in 1940, the Court for the first time invalidated state action as an infringement of religious freedom, citing a speech case for the overbroad conclusion that "[t]he fundamental concept of liberty embodied in [the Fourteenth] Amendment embraces the liberties guaranteed by the First Amendment."[63]

The best explanation for all this remained that given by Justice Brandeis in his concurring opinion in *Whitney:* once "liberty" had been misconstrued to include freedom of contract, there was no reason to exclude other rights that were equally important.[64] Thus the application of the first amendment to the states rested on the same sandy foundation that supported *Lochner v. New York;*[65] yet the Court vigorously extended the former as it dismantled the latter, with little attention to the apparent inconsistency.[66]

## B.  Political Dissent

Most of the freedom of expression cases decided before 1930 had involved political dissent, which Justice Brandeis had suggested lay at the heart of the first amendment.[67] In these decisions, despite varying formulations of the governing standard, the Court had seemed to exercise considerable restraint in reviewing both state and federal convictions

---

[59] 297 U.S. 233, 243-44 (1936).

[60] 299 U.S. 353 (1937).

[61] *Id.* at 364.

[62] 310 U.S. 296 (1940).

[63] *Id.* at 303 (citing Schneider v. State, 308 U.S. 147, 160 (1939)). Justice Butler had declared religious liberties protected in equally conclusory terms in Hamilton v. Regents of the Univ. of Cal., 293 U.S. 245, 262 (1934), in which the challenged requirement was upheld.

[64] 274 U.S. 357, 373 (1927).

[65] 198 U.S. 45 (1905).

[66] As an original matter there was a stronger though not conclusive case for incorporation of the first amendment through the privileges or immunities clause of the fourteenth amendment, but that argument had been decisively rejected half a century before. *See* THE FIRST HUNDRED YEARS at 342-51, 363-64 (discussing the Slaughter-House Cases, 83 U.S. (16 Wall.) 36 (1872), and subsequent decisions).

[67] *See Whitney,* 274 U.S. at 375 (Brandeis, J., concurring) ("Those who won our independence . . . valued liberty both as an end and as a means . . . They believed that freedom to think as you will and to speak as you think are means indispensable to the discovery and spread of political truth. . . ."); *see also* United States v. Carolene Prods. Co., 304 U.S. 144, 152-53 n. 4 (1938) (Stone, C. J.) (assimilating "restraints upon the dissemination of information" to "legislation which restricts those political processes which can ordinarily be expected to bring about repeal of undesirable legislation"); Palko v. Connecticut, 302 U.S. 319, 327 (1937) (Cardozo, J.) (describing freedom of speech and thought as "the matrix, the indispensable condition, of nearly every other form of freedom").

for speech thought to be subversive.[68] The 1930s witnessed the blossoming of speech protections outside this traditional field, as we shall see; but they also produced three decisions suggesting a significant trend toward stricter scrutiny of punishment for allegedly subversive expression.

## 1.  Herndon v. Lowry

The least revolutionary of these decisions, *Herndon v. Lowry,*[69] was the last. Herndon had been convicted of the statutory offense of attempting to incite insurrection.[70] *Gitlow* seemed to establish that such a statute was constitutional whether or not a particular attempt was likely to succeed.[71] Gitlow, however, had been found responsible for distributing a revolutionary "manifesto."[72] Unlike the four dissenters,[73] Justice Roberts reasonably, if rather strictly, concluded that Herndon's mere possession of somewhat similar pamphlets did not prove he had *distributed* them.[74]

On this view of the evidence, Herndon had been convicted for mere solicitation of members for the Communist party. That, Roberts concluded, was not enough to prove him guilty of incitement to insurrection, and thus the conviction was unconstitutional.[75] This technique had been employed in 1927 in *Fiske v. Kansas,*[76] which struck down a conviction for incitement to violent overthrow of government for want of evidence that the organization for which the defendant solicited members had in fact advocated violence. *Fiske* had said only that such a conviction "unwarrantably infring[es] the liberty of the defendant in violation of the due process clause."[77] *Herndon,* without explanation and without citing *Fiske,* based its conclusion squarely on freedom of speech and assembly.[78]

This clarification was an important step, and the Court's willingness to scrutinize the record for inadequate evidence, like that in *Fiske,* contrasted sharply with its refusal to do so in *Whitney.*[79] The Court made clear, however, that it was not saying the state could not

---

[68] *See* cases cited *supra* notes 50-52; pp. 115-24 *supra* (discussing Schenck v. United States, 249 U.S. 47 (1919) and Abrams v. United States, 250 U.S. 616 (1919)).

[69] 301 U.S. 242 (1937).

[70] *Id.* at 243.

[71] *See Gitlow,* 268 U.S. at 669-70 (upholding conviction under statute outlawing advocacy of forcible overthrow of government).

[72] *Id.* at 655-59.

[73] *Herndon,* 301 U.S. at 274-75 (Van Devanter, McReynolds, Sutherland, and Butler, JJ., dissenting).

[74] *Id.* at 259-60.

[75] *Id.* at 261 ("His membership in the Communist Party and his solicitation of a few members wholly fails to establish an attempt to incite others to insurrection.").

[76] 274 U.S. 380, 386-87 (1927).

[77] *Id.* at 387.

[78]   If the evidence fails to show that he did so incite, then, as applied to him, the statute unreasonably
    limits freedom of speech and freedom of assembly . . . In these circumstances, to make member-
    ship in the party and solicitation of members for that party a criminal offense . . . is an unwar-
    ranted invasion of the right of freedom of speech.

301 U.S. at 259-61. The Court added that the statute itself was unconstitutionally vague because it "does not furnish a sufficiently ascertainable standard of guilt." *Id.* at 261.

[79] 274 U.S. at 367 (dismissing an objection to statutorily required finding of knowledge of an organization's subversive goals as "involving . . . no constitutional question whatever," but softening the blow by observing

make mere solicitation for the Communist party a crime. Since the legislature had not done so, there was no occasion for the broad deference to legislative judgment that had been practiced in *Gitlow.*[80] Even if the legislature had specifically prohibited such solicitation, Roberts warned, the punishment inflicted would have to "find its justification in a reasonable apprehension of danger to organized government"; and for this additional limitation he cited the earlier case of *De Jonge v. Oregon.*[81]

## 2. *De Jonge v. Oregon*

De Jonge had been convicted for assisting in the conduct of a meeting called by the Communist party.[82] In contrast to *Herndon,* the legislature had explicitly made this conduct a crime;[83] the Court unanimously held that by doing so the legislature itself had gone too far.

There was nothing in the record in *De Jonge* to indicate that the meeting had been called to further subversive goals. For all that appeared, the defendant might have been convicted for assisting in the conduct of a meeting "to discuss the tariff, or the foreign policy of the Government, or taxation, or relief, or candidacies for the office of President."[84] It was one thing to outlaw actual incitement to revolution, as in *Gitlow,* or knowing assistance in setting up a revolutionary organization, as in *Whitney.*[85] Mere assistance in the conduct of a Communist-run meeting was another matter. "The question . . . is not as to the auspices under which the meeting is held but as to its purpose; not as to the relations of the speakers, but whether their utterances transcend the bounds of the freedom of speech which the Constitution protects."[86] Because "peaceable assembly for lawful discussion cannot be made a crime," the statute was invalid as applied.[87]

As Hughes and Roberts argued, the results in *De Jonge* and *Herndon* were not necessarily irreconcilable with *Gitlow* or *Whitney.* They suggested, however, a new spirit of aggressiveness, in reviewing both legislative and judicial findings affecting expression, that was more reminiscent of the separate views of Holmes and Brandeis in the earlier cases than of the majority opinions they were protesting.

## 3. *Stromberg v. California*

Still more novel and far reaching was the earlier decision in *Stromberg v. California,*[88] which invalidated a state statute forbidding the exhibition of a red flag as a symbol of

---

that the jury finding had been "sustained by the Court of Appeals over the specific objection that it was not supported by the evidence"); *cf.* Norris v. Alabama, 294 U.S. 587, 590 (1935) (aggressive approach to review of state court factfinding relevant to issue of discrimination in jury selection), note 31 *supra.*

[80] *Herndon,* 301 U.S. at 256, 260.

[81] *Id.* at 258-59 (citing De Jonge v. Oregon, 299 U.S. 353 (1937)).

[82] 299 U.S. at 357.

[83] *Id.* at 356-57.

[84] *Id.* at 363.

[85] *Id.*

[86] *Id.* at 365.

[87] *Id.*

[88] 283 U.S. 359 (1931).

opposition to government. As in *De Jonge,* a decision of the legislature itself was struck down, but the reason was far more radical.

Though the Court did not advert to it, there was an important threshold question whether freedom of expression extended beyond the spoken and written word to embrace visual symbols like the red flag. In light of the first amendment's apparent purpose of encouraging the communication of ideas, a powerful argument could have been made for treating every method of communication as speech,[89] leaving the problem of unreasonably obstructive or dangerous means of communication to be worked out along the lines soon to be developed for regulating the time, place, and manner of expression in words.[90] Far from disputing that the display of a red flag was speech, the state had proscribed it only for the message it conveyed; the Court took the state at its word.[91]

The flag in *Stromberg* had been raised at a children's camp in connection with a pledge of allegiance "to the workers' red flag, and to the cause for which it stands; one aim throughout our lives, freedom for the working class."[92] The Court might easily have held, as in *De Jonge,* that the statute could not validly be applied to such an innocuous event as that shown by the record. Yet Chief Justice Hughes selected a broader ground. The statutory language was so sweeping, he wrote, that it might be applied to "peaceful and orderly opposition to government by legal means" and thus to "conduct which [like the peaceable assembly in *De Jonge*] the State could not constitutionally prohibit."[93] A statute "so vague and indefinite as to permit the punishment" of such protected conduct, Hughes concluded without explanation, was "invalid on its face."[94]

Thus both *Stromberg* and *De Jonge* held that the state legislature had invalidly punished constitutionally protected conduct. There, however, the resemblance between the two decisions ends. *De Jonge* set aside a conviction because the record did not show the defendant had done anything that could constitutionally be punished; *Stromberg* did so without examining the record because it would be unconstitutional to apply the statute to someone else.[95]

Even more striking was the contrast with *Gitlow.* In that case the Court had allowed punishment of an act assumed to be innocuous because other prohibited acts might be

---

[89]*See* Henkin, *The Supreme Court,* 1967 *Term—Foreword: On Drawing Lines,* 82 HARV. L. REV. 63, 79-80 (1968) ("If it is intended as expression, if in fact it communicates, . . . it is 'speech.'").

[90]*See* Clark v. Community for Creative Non-Violence, 468 U.S. 288 (1984) (upholding ban on sleeping in park as applied to protest on behalf of homeless); Nimmer, *The Meaning of Symbolic Speech under the First Amendment,* 21 UCLA L. REV. 29, 61 (1973); Alfange, *Free Speech and Symbolic Conduct: The Draft-Card Burning Case,* 1968 SUP. CT. REV. 1, 24-26; *infra* notes 122-51 and accompanying text.

[91]*See* Nimmer, *supra* note 90, at 45 ("The state should not be heard to deny the actor's claim that the conduct in question was intended to communicate if the state acted in order to suppress such a communication.").

[92]283 U.S. at 362.

[93]*Id.* at 369 (citing the state-court opinion below, People v. Mintz, 62 Cal. App. 788, 290 P. 93 (1930)).

[94]*Id.* at 369-70. Justices McReynolds and Butler argued in dissent that the validity of this provision was not properly before the Court. *Id.* at 370-76.

[95]The condemnation of the law as "vague and indefinite" reminds one of earlier decisions outside the speech field striking down vague laws on due process grounds for failure to give fair warning of what they forbade. *E.g.,* United States v. L. Cohen Grocery Co., 255 U.S. 81, 89-93 (1921), *supra* p. 109, note 123. In *Stromberg,* however, the Court spoke not of fair warning, but of the impact of the statute on the constitutionally protected right of political discussion. In the earlier cases, moreover, there was no suggestion that one defendant was released because the law could not constitutionally be applied to another. The overlap between the two doctrines is discussed in Note, *The Void-for-Vagueness Doctrine in the Supreme Court: A Means to an End,* 109 U. PA. L. REV. 67 (1960).

dangerous; in *Stromberg* it forbade punishment of an act assumed to be dangerous because other prohibited acts might be innocuous. Not a word was said to explain why the invalidity of the statute as applied to others was relevant in *Stromberg,* or why the Court sometimes took one approach and sometimes another.

*Gitlow,* however, had not denied that a statute that reached too broadly would be unconstitutional. Because it had found the challenged law valid, the Court in *Gitlow* had not had to face the severability question that *Stromberg* posed: did an overbroad law have to be struck down even as to activities that could validly have been forbidden, or could it be cut down to constitutional size?

*Stromberg*'s unexplained conclusion that the statute could not be pared down echoed the decision in *United States v. Reese,*[96] which had aborted a prosecution for infringing voting rights on racial grounds because the statute improperly forbade all interference with voting.[97] This holding seemed peculiar in itself and has since ceased to be generally followed.[98] Moreover, *Reese* involved a federal statute, *Stromberg* a state one. One would expect severability in the latter case to be a question of state law.[99]

Much later the Court would explain that the overbreadth doctrine, first applied to speech cases in *Stromberg,* served to protect persons from being deterred from protected expression because of the risk that it might be found punishable.[100] If Hughes had something like that in mind he kept it to himself, and he left his novel approach entirely unexplained.

## C.   Freedom of the Press

### 1.   *Near v. Minnesota*

*Herndon, De Jonge,* and *Stromberg* all involved punishment for past expression. *Near v. Minnesota*[101] involved an effort to prevent expression in the future.

---

[96] 92 U.S. 214 (1875).

[97] *Id.* at 221-22.

[98] *See, e.g.,* United States v. Raines, 362 U.S. 17, 24 (1960); THE FIRST HUNDRED YEARS at 393-95.

[99] In commerce clause cases, for example, the Court had frequently struck down the application of state statutes to particular transactions without suggesting that they could no longer be applied at all. *See, e.g.,* Dahnke-Walker Milling Co. v. Bondurant, 257 U.S. 282, 292-93 (1921) (state may not require foreign corporation engaged solely in interstate commerce to qualify to do business). In other cases, moreover, the Court had expressly refused to consider whether a state statute that could validly be applied to the case at bar would be invalid if applied to someone else. *See, e.g.,* Yazoo & M. R.R. v. Jackson Vinegar Co., 226 U.S. 217, 219-20 (1912) (upholding a provision requiring prompt settlement of claims for lost freight as applied: "this court must deal with the case in hand and not with imaginary ones."). *But see* Monaghan, *Overbreadth,* 1981 SUP. CT. REV. 1, 6-14 (distinguishing *Yazoo* as a case that reached the Supreme Court "without any authoritative construction of the statute by the state courts" and arguing that the Court regularly invalidates on their face statutes overbroad as construed, because "a litigant . . . can insist that his conduct be judged in accordance with a rule that is constitutionally valid.").

[100] *See* Gooding v. Wilson, 405 U.S. 518, 521 (1972) ("This is deemed necessary because persons whose expression is constitutionally protected may well refrain from exercising their rights for fear of criminal sanctions provided by a statute susceptible of application to protected expression."); *see also* Note, *The First Amendment Overbreadth Doctrine,* 83 HARV. L. REV. 844, 853 (1970). In equal protection cases it is immaterial whether the conduct in question could have been prohibited by a different statute, but that is because the vice toward which that clause was directed is inequality. A different argument is necessary to justify facial review of statutes challenged on first amendment grounds.

[101] 283 U.S. 697 (1931).

Following a series of colorful articles charging public officials with failure to enforce laws against organized crime, a state court had enjoined the defendants from publishing, distributing, or possessing any newspaper that was "malicious, scandalous and defamatory."[102] In a 1931 opinion by Chief Justice Hughes, the Court held the statute authorizing the injunction unconstitutional as applied. The difficult question in the past, he said, had been whether freedom of speech was protected against subsequent punishments; history showed that protection against "previous restraints" was at the heart of the first amendment.[103]

In what sense, however, was the injunction a previous restraint? It was true that, though based upon a finding that the defendant had published offensive material before,[104] the injunction prohibited future publications on pain of contempt. A criminal statute embodying the same prohibition, however, would likewise have prohibited future conduct, on pain of criminal sanctions; such a statute would be taken to impose a threat of subsequent punishment, not a previous restraint. The Court did not say in what respect the injunction posed a greater threat to freedom of expression than would an ordinary criminal law.

The previous restraint condemned by Blackstone and others on whom the Court relied had consisted of a licensing system forbidding publication without prior official approval.[105] Licensing not only prevents publication of punishable material; it delays publication of inoffensive material as well, as the innocuousness of the publication is no defense to the separate offense of publishing without a license. In a criminal prosecution based upon the offensiveness of the publication itself, in contrast, the defendant can escape punishment by showing that the publication was not prohibited. The principal vice of a previous restraint thus seems to lie in the fact that it delays the publication of protected materials until after their legality has been determined.[106]

In this light, equating an injunction with licensing begins to make sense. Unlike a criminal law, an injunction generally must be obeyed until set aside even if it was invalidly entered, and protected speech may therefore be delayed.[107]

---

[102] *Id.* at 704, 706.

[103] *Id.* at 713-15.

[104] *See id.* at 735-36 (Butler J., joined by Van Devanter, McReynolds, and Sutherland, JJ., dissenting).

[105] *See, e.g., id.* at 734-35 (Butler, J., dissenting) (quoting J. STORY, COMMENTARIES ON THE CONSTITUTION § 1882 (1883)); *see also* Pound, *Equitable Relief against Defamation and Injuries to Personality,* 29 HARV. L. REV. 640, 651 (1916) (arguing that the rule against previous restraints ought not to be taken as precluding injunctions against defamation, because history shows the "main purpose" to be "freedom from a regime of general censorship and license of printing"). For a challenging panoply of arguments why injunctions are less harmful to legitimate speech interests than licensing, see Mayton, *Toward a Theory of First Amendment Process: Injunctions of Speech, Subsequent Punishment, and the Costs of the Prior Restraint Doctrine,* 67 CORNELL L. REV. 245 (1982).

[106] *See* Redish, *The Proper Role of the Prior Restraint Doctrine* in *First Amendment Theory,* 70 VA. L. REV. 53, 55-58 (1984). The purpose of the previous-restraint rule is thus related to that of *Stromberg's* overbreadth doctrine: both prevent certain methods of suppressing even those publications that constitutionally may be prohibited, in order to remove impediments to the publication of protected materials. *See* G. STONE, L. SEIDMAN, C. SUNSTEIN & M. TUSHNET, *supra* note 53, at 1036, 1046.

[107] *See* United States v. United Mine Workers, 330 U.S. 258, 293-95 (1947) (stressing overriding need for respect for judicial orders); Walker v. City of Birmingham, 388 U.S. 307, 315 (1967) (applying this rule in freedom of expression case); *see also* Barnett, *The Puzzle of Prior Restraint,* 29 STAN. L. REV. 539, 552 (1977) (discussing *Walker*).

It is true that the injunction appealed in *Near* had been issued only after a trial.[108] It had not, however, been stayed pending appellate review; therefore it too posed the risk of delaying the publication of information that ultimately might be held to be protected. It is also true that in a contempt proceeding for violating the injunction, the defendants could have defended on the ground that the material published had not been "malicious, scandalous or defamatory" within the meaning of the order. They could not have done so, however, on the ground that those terms were unconstitutionally broad or that conduct falling within them was constitutionally protected. Thus the effect of the injunction, like that of a licensing law, seemed to be to postpone the publication of arguably protected material until after a final determination of its acceptability; the Court was right to treat it as a previous restraint.[109]

Even previous restraints, the Chief Justice hastened to add, were not always forbidden.

> No one would question but that a government might prevent actual obstruction to its recruiting service or the publication of the sailing dates of transports or the number and location of troops. On similar grounds, the primary requirements of decency may be enforced against obscene publications. The security of the community life may be protected against incitements to acts of violence and the overthrow by force of orderly government. The constitutional guaranty of free speech does not "protect a man from an injunction against uttering words that may have all the effect of force." These limitations are not applicable here. Nor are we now concerned with questions as to the extent of authority to prevent publications in order to protect private rights according to the principles governing the exercise of the jurisdiction of courts of equity.[110]

Several of these examples seemed to be, as Hughes argued, "exceptional cases," in which the interests requiring previous restraints could fairly be described as overwhelming. Obscenity, however, hardly seems to fall into that category.[111] The list of exceptions thus left the reader wondering what was left of the supposedly powerful principle against previous restraints and why the publication in question fell within it.

As in *Herndon v. Lowry,* Van Devanter, McReynolds, Sutherland, and Butler dissented.[112] It is interesting that the four Justices most zealous to discover infringements of economic liberties under the due process clause were the least willing to find invasions of freedom of expression under the same provision.

---

[108] 283 U.S. at 735 (Butler, J., dissenting) ("The restraint authorized is only in respect of continuing to do what has been duly adjudged to constitute a nuisance.") Upon filing of the complaint, however, the trial court had also entered an order temporarily forbidding circulation. *Id.* at 704-05.

[109] But see Jeffries, *Rethinking Prior Restraint,* 92 YALE L.J. 409, 431-33 (1983) (arguing that this difficulty might better be addressed by narrowing the occasions on which an invalid injunction must be obeyed).

[110] 283 U.S. at 716 (citations omitted).

[111] The traditional justification for punishing obscenity is the perception that its social value is slight. *See* Chaplinsky v. New Hampshire, 315 U.S. 586, 572 (1942) ("[T]he lewd and obscene, the profane, the libelous, and the insulting or 'fighting' words . . . are no essential part of any exposition of ideas, and are of such slight social value as a step to truth that any benefit that may be derived from them is clearly outweighed by the social interest in order and morality.") The risk of delaying protected publications may be an acceptable cost if the publication arguably endangers national security; it is harder to justify if the publication is arguably worthless.

[112] 283 U.S. at 723-38. *See supra* notes 69-81 and accompanying text (discussing *Herndon*).

## 2. *Grosjean v. American Press Co.*

The press won another great victory in *Grosjean v. American Press Co.*,[113] in which Justice Sutherland wrote for the whole bench in holding invalid a Louisiana tax measured by the gross advertising receipts of newspapers distributing over twenty thousand copies weekly. Taxes on newspapers, Sutherland noted, had been subject to vehement opposition in England and in the Colonies because they were a means of suppressing criticism of the government; they were therefore at the heart of the guarantee of freedom of the press.[114]

The tax in question was especially suspicious in that it applied only to papers of large circulation, "with the plain purpose of penalizing the publishers and curtailing the circulation of a selected group of newspapers."[115] The thrust of the opinion, however, was broader. Although nothing the Court said was "to suggest that the owners of newspapers are immune from any of the ordinary forms of taxation for support of the government," special taxes on the press alone were impermissible.[116]

To the extent that he relied upon an unexpressed purpose to suppress publication,[117] Sutherland seemed to evince an unusual willingness to look behind plausible revenue measures in search of impermissible motives.[118] Apart from motive, however, he seemed on sound ground in terms both of history and of underlying policy in concluding that discriminatory taxes had a forbidden deterrent effect on the press whether or not they picked favorites among publishers.[119]

Not mentioned in *Grosjean* was the Court's departure from its inexplicable conclusion of thirty years before that, although corporations were "persons" within the fourteenth

---

[113] 297 U.S. 233 (1936).

[114] *Id.* at 246-49 (echoing the ancient *Murray's Lessee* decision, *supra* note 1, in insisting that the common law was a guide to the meaning of the Constitution only if "the common-law rule . . . be one not rejected by our ancestors as unsuited to their civil or political conditions").

[115] *Id.* at 251. *See* 2 M. PUSEY, CHARLES EVANS HUGHES 721 (1951) (reflecting the popular understanding that the case involved "Huey Long's tax on the . . . newspapers that were opposing him").

[116] 297 U.S. at 250.

[117] "The tax . . . is bad because, in the light of its history and of its present setting, it is seen to be a deliberate and calculated device in the guise of a tax to limit the circulation of information to which the public is entitled. . . ." *Id.* at 250.

[118] *Cf.* pp. 226-27 *supra* (discussing United States v. Constantine, 296 U.S. 287 (1935), which struck down a federal excise tax on persons selling liquor in violation of state law because the law was based on an improper purpose).

[119] *Cf.* Reynolds v. United States, 98 U.S. 145 (1879) (employing similar nondiscrimination test in applying first amendment ban on federal laws abridging free exercise of religion); THE FIRST HUNDRED YEARS at 439-42. The suggestion that the press enjoyed no blanket exemption from generally applicable laws was borne out by the decision in Associated Press v. NLRB, 301 U.S. 103 (1937) (Roberts, J., over dissents by Sutherland, Van Devanter, McReynolds, and Butler, JJ.) that the Wagner Act's prohibition on firing employees from union activity could constitutionally be applied to a news-gathering service: "[t]he publisher of a newspaper has no special immunity from the application of general laws." *Id.* at 132-33. For justification of the distinction see Minneapolis Star & Tribune Co. v. Minnesota Comm'r of Revenue, 460 U.S. 575, 585 (1983) (reaffirming *Grosjean*) ("We need not fear that a government will destroy a selected group of taxpayers by burdensome taxation if it must impose the same burden on the rest of its constituency. . . . When the State singles out the press, though, the political constraints that prevent a legislature from passing crippling taxes of general applicability are weakened, and the threat of burdensome taxes becomes acute.").

amendment, they enjoyed none of the "liberty" there protected.[120] Justice Black was soon to attack even the accepted wisdom that corporations were "persons";[121] though unwilling to say why, the other Justices were moving in the opposite direction.

### D.   Jehovah's Witnesses

Presbyterians, on the whole, tend to keep their religion pretty much to themselves. Jehovah's Witnesses, on the other hand, feel called upon to convince others that their way is the right one.[122] In doing so, they frequently have come up against general laws enacted to secure privacy, clean and unobstructed streets, and public order. The result has been a series of decisions, beginning in the 1930s, that have helped in no small way to define the limits of constitutional protection of methods of propagating ideas.[123]

### 1.   Permits

The story begins in 1938 with *Lovell v. City of Griffin*,[124] in which the Court unanimously struck down an ordinance that forbade distribution of literature of any kind anywhere in the city without a permit. More clearly than the injunction in *Near*, this was a classic previous restraint.[125] History showed that freedom of the press embraced "pamphlets and leaflets" as well as "newspapers and periodicals" and that "[l]iberty of circulation [was] as essential . . . as liberty of publishing; indeed, without the circulation, the publication would be of little value."[126]

Chief Justice Hughes did not say in *Lovell* why the distribution of leaflets was not one of those "extraordinary" matters with respect to which, he had said in *Near*, previous restraints were permitted. He did point out that the ordinance was neither restricted "with respect to time or place" nor "limited to ways [of circulation] which might be regarded as inconsistent with the maintenance of public order or as involving disorderly conduct, the molestation of the inhabitants, or the misuse of littering of the streets."[127] Whatever the evils the ordinance was designed to prevent, Hughes seemed to be saying, the measure swept altogether too broadly in achieving them.

---

[120] *See, e.g.*, Western Turf Ass'n v. Greenberg, 204 U.S. 359, 363 (1907); Northwestern Nat'l Life Ins. Co. v. Riggs, 203 U.S. 243, 255 (1906); p. 48, note 139 *supra*. Without noticing *Grosjean*, Justice Stone repeated the earlier understanding in Hague v. CIO, 307 U.S. 496, 527 (1939) (separate opinion).

[121] Connecticut Gen. Life Ins. Co. v. Johnson, 303 U.S. 77, 85-90 (1938) (Black, J., dissenting). The initial decision that corporations were "persons" for fourteenth amendment purposes had been made without discussion. *See* Santa Clara County v. Southern Pacific R.R., 118 U.S. 394, 396 (1886); THE FIRST HUNDRED YEARS at 387 n. 133.

[122] *See* Z. CHAFEE, FREE SPEECH IN THE UNITED STATES 399 (1941) (describing Jehovah's Witnesses as "a sect distinguished by great religious zeal").

[123] *See generally* Barber, *Religious Liberty v. Police Power: Jehovah's Witnesses*, 41 AM. POL. SCI. REV. 226 (1947) (discussing the practices of the Witnesses and their frequent conflicts with the law); Waite, *The Debt of Constitutional Law to Jehovah's Witnesses*, 28 MINN. L. REV. 209 (1944).

[124] 303 U.S. 444 (1938).

[125] *Id.* at 451-52.

[126] *Id.* at 452 (quoting *Ex parte* Jackson, 96 U.S. 727, 733 (1877), THE FIRST HUNDRED YEARS at 442-43).

[127] 303 U.S. at 451.

The next year, in *Schneider v. State*,[128] the Court went further, striking down a licensing requirement that applied only to those who distributed literature door to door. Although trespasses and frauds could be forbidden directly, wrote Justice Roberts, the greater efficiency of a permit requirement did not "empower a municipality to abridge freedom of speech and press."[129]

In thus begging the question, the *Schneider* opinion seemed to imply that the marginal benefits of the permit system were insufficient to justify its burdens on legitimate speech. Those burdens included not only the delay that inheres in all previous restraints, but also the risk of discrimination resulting from the broad terms of the ordinance, which in the Court's view gave the police "a discretion . . . to say some ideas may, while others may not, be carried to the homes of citizens."[130]

To this reasoning one might plausibly respond that the Court should wait to intervene until there is actual discrimination. The mere possibility that legislative authority might be misused, for example, does not outlaw its existence. The prophylactic rule adopted in *Schneider,* however, had been employed in the equal protection context fifty years earlier as an alternative ground in *Yick Wo v. Hopkins.*[131] Although this rule had not shown much vitality since *Yick Wo,* it might have been defended in the context of *Schneider* as a corollary of the peculiar constitutional aversion to previous restraints: because of the importance of not delaying legitimate expression, delegations of authority to license speech must be accompanied by unusually precise standards.[132]

The implication that some permit requirements might be constitutional was borne out in *Cox v. New Hampshire,*[133] which upheld the conviction of five Jehovah's Witnesses for parading on the sidewalks without a license. Traffic control, said the Chief Justice, was a legitimate state concern. The possibility of administrative abuse was strictly limited by the state court's holding that the officer issuing the permits was to consider only the effect of the proposed parade on traffic. The requirement that a permit be obtained in advance

---

[128] 308 U.S. 147 (1939). Justice McReynolds dissented without opinion.

[129] *Id.* at 164.

[130] *Id.* The ordinance, as paraphrased by the Court, required the police to refuse a permit upon finding that "the canvasser is not of good character or is canvassing for a project not free from fraud." *Id.* at 158. The risk of discrimination posed by such a broad grant of discretion had figured prominently in a flock of late nineteenth-century state court decisions invalidating parade permit ordinances on state law grounds. *See, e.g., In re* Frazee's Case, 63 Mich. 396, 406-07, 30 N.W. 72, 76 (1886) ("If this were allowed . . . , it would enable a mayor or council to shut off processions of those whose notions did not suit their views or tastes, in politics or religion, or any other matter on which men differ."); G. ABERNATHY, THE RIGHT OF ASSEMBLY AND ASSOCIATION 85-96 (2d ed. 1981).

The unexplained observation in *Schneider* that the opinion was "not to be taken as holding that commercial soliciting and canvassing may not be subjected to such regulation as the ordinance requires," 308 U.S. at 165, was perhaps the Court's first suggestion that commercial speech might not be entitled to the same protection as political or religious speech.

[131] 118 U.S. 356, 366-73 (1886). *See* THE FIRST HUNDRED YEARS at 387 n. 134.

[132] *See* Currie, *Der Vorbehalt des Gesetzes: Amerikanische Analogien,* in V. GOTZ, H. KLEIN, & C. STARCK, DIE ÖFFENTLICHE VERWALTUNG ZWISCHEN GESETZGEBUNG UND RICHTERLICHER KONTROLLE 68, 76-77 (1986).

[133] 312 U.S. 569 (1941).

had "[t]he obvious advantage . . . [of] giving the public authorities notice . . . so as to afford opportunity for proper policing."[134]

The Court thus confirmed the dictum in *Near* that not all previous restraints were forbidden. It also confirmed the inference that the "extraordinary" situations in which such restraints were allowed were not limited to those in which there was a grave threat to national security; it sufficed that previous restraint was reasonably necessary to the impartial reconciliation of competing claims for the use of limited resources by regulation of what the Court felicitously referred to as the "time, place and manner" of expression.[135] Not only are impartial time, place, and manner restrictions likely to serve legitimate interests unrelated to the desire to suppress information; they also leave the speaker free to convey his message in other ways.

## 2. Public Streets

The fact that a regulation impartially limits only the time, place, and manner of expression, however, does not assure its constitutionality; the burden it places on means of communicating protected messages may be out of proportion to the strength of the countervailing governmental concern. This limitation was appropriately illustrated by another aspect of *Schneider v. State*, where the Court also struck down a collection of ordinances forbidding the distribution of handbills on public streets and sidewalks.[136] "[T]he purpose to keep the streets clean and of good appearance" by preventing littering, wrote Justice Roberts, was "insufficient to justify an ordinance which prohibits a person rightfully on a public street from handing literature to one willing to receive it."[137] The unrealistic suggestion that this purpose could be achieved by "punishment of those who actually throw papers on the streets"[138] was surely unnecessary to this conclusion. If the question is whether it is reasonable to weigh the risk of paper in the streets more heavily than the benefits of handbilling, the only conceivable answer is no.[139]

The more interesting question, however, is whether Roberts asked the right question. The city was the owner of the streets, and a generation earlier—before it had held freedom of expression applicable to the states—the Court had held in *Davis v. Massachusetts* that local governments did not have to allow public property to be used for the communication of ideas at all.[140] The government—as Justice Holmes had put it for the state court in

---

[134] *Id.* at 576. *Compare* Kalven, *The Concept of the Public Forum: Cox v. Louisiana*, 1965 SUP. CT. REV. 1, 26 ( describing *Cox* as "symboliz[ing] the ideal of Robert's Rules of Order" for expression in public places) *with* Baker, *Unreasoned Reasonableness: Mandatory Parade Permits and Time, Place, and Manner Regulations*, 78 Nw. U. L. REV. 937 (1983) (taking a more critical view of *Cox*).

[135] 312 U.S. at 575. *See* L. TRIBE, AMERICAN CONSTITUTIONAL LAW 729 (1978) ("The *relative importance* of the government's interests . . . cannot explain the cases.").

[136] 308 U.S. 147, 162–64 (1939).

[137] *Id.* at 162.

[138] *Id. See* Kalven, *supra* note 134, at 17 n.64 ("It is difficult to take seriously so impractical an alternative.").

[139] *See* Z. CHAFEE, *supra* note 122, at 406 ("Handbills are almost the only available way for poor men to express ideas to the public or announce a protest meeting."). *But see* Kalven, *supra* note 134, at 18 (arguing that handbilling is "a method of communication of some annoyance to a majority of people so addressed" and questioning its impact on its audience).

[140] 167 U.S. 43 (1897).

*Davis*—was as free to determine how its property was to be used as any private land-owner.[141]

Holmes's argument clearly went too far. Governments, unlike private parties, are subject to constitutional limitations, and as later decisions correctly recognized, the selective denial of government benefits can both distort the market for ideas and effectively punish the exercise of a constitutional right.[142] That was not what had happened in *Schneider;* the question there was whether the government could impartially deny everyone the use of the streets for the expression of ideas.

Justice Roberts treated the question lightly, saying only that "the streets are natural and proper places for the dissemination of information and opinion."[143] A few months before, in *Hague v. CIO,*[144] Roberts had reached the peculiar conclusion that the nearly forgotten privileges or immunities clause of the fourteenth amendment gave citizens the right to discuss federal legislation on the streets of Jersey City. He had been a little more expansive in *Hague:*

> Wherever the title of streets and parks may rest, they have immemorially been held in trust for the use of the public and, time out of mind, have been used for purposes of assembly, communicating thoughts between citizens, and discussing public questions. Such use of the streets and public places has, from ancient times, been a part of the privileges, immunities, rights, and liberties of citizens.[145]

All this was stated as a bald conclusion. Roberts cited no evidence to support his historical assertion, and the mere fact that the streets had traditionally been used for speech

---

[141] Commonwealth v. Davis, 162 Mass. 510, 511, 39 N. E. 113, 113 (1895), *aff'd,* 167 U.S. 43 (1897); *cf.* McAuliffe v. Mayor of New Bedford, 155 Mass. 216, 220, 29 N. E. 517, 517 (1892) (no constitutional right to be a policeman). *See* THE FIRST HUNDRED YEARS at 442-44 (discussing *Ex parte* Jackson and *Ex parte* Curtis); p. 58, note 23 *supra* (discussing *Davis*).

[142] *See e.g.,* Elrod v. Burns, 427 U.S. 347 (1976) (political test for government employment), pp. 505-06 *infra. See generally* Stone, *Content Regulation and the First Amendment,* 25 WM. & MARY L. REV. 189 (1983).

[143] 308 U.S. at 163.

[144] 307 U.S. 496 (1939).

[145] *Id.* at 515. Only Justices Black and Hughes joined Roberts in this reasoning. *Id.* at 500, 532. Justices Stone and Reed, agreeing with the result, relied on the due process clause instead, without explaining how the right of expression had been infringed, thus appearing to accept Roberts's analysis under a different label. *Id.* at 500, 518-32. *See* Kalven, *supra* note 134, at 13 ("[I]t is not altogether clear for whom Mr. Justice Roberts was speaking. . . ."). Roberts's unorthodox approach seems to have been attributable to the unjustified belief that the relevant jurisdictional statute applied only to "privileges" and "immunities" despite its plain inclusion of "rights." *See* D. CURRIE, FEDERAL COURTS 535-38 (2d ed. 1975). Black's concurrence seems related to his later implication that it might be the privileges or immunities clause that made freedom of expression and other guarantees in the bill of rights applicable to the states. *See* Adamson v. California, 332 U.S. 46, 68-92 (1947) (Black, J., dissenting), pp. 321-22 *infra.*

Despite Roberts's broad language about the public's right to use the streets for speech, *Hague* could have been decided on narrower grounds. First, like the permit decision in *Schneider,* it involved a licensing provision found to convey "arbitrary" power. Second, the court below had found that a facially absolute ban on distributing literature had been administered in a discriminatory manner. *See Hague,* 307 U.S. at 501, 505-06, 516.

does not prove they must continue to be.[146] Whether the streets are "held in trust for the use of the public" would seem in the first instance to be a question of state law, which in *Hague* was to the contrary.[147] Of course it was possible that the Framers of the fourteenth amendment had imposed a public trust for expression purposes that overrode state law, but Roberts's historical explication was not enough to show they had done so.

A more promising approach might have been to argue that the right to speak on public streets was so essential to the effective communication of ideas that a meaningful freedom of expression must be held to include it.[148] The possible implications of this approach, however, are momentous. One might equally argue that the government must subsidize other conduct it cannot prohibit, as all rights are hollow for those who cannot afford to exercise them. If government may not forbid abortions, it must pay for them; if it may not kill a man outright, it may not let him starve.

Some support for these conclusions might be drawn from the unexplained and arresting holding of the Taft Court in *Truax v. Corrigan*[149] that the state must protect property rights from invasion by third parties. In accord with the eighteenth-century conception of the social compact underlying our Constitution, however, the Court has generally refused to extend *Truax* so far. Even if the government may deprive a person of life, liberty, or property by failing to protect him against other individuals, it does not do so by failing to protect him against poverty.[150]

The fact that denial of access to public property takes the form of a traditional prohibition makes it easy to overlook the possible applicability of this distinction. Even if government is only prohibited from actively depriving persons of their rights, that is what it seems to have done by banning the distribution of handbills in the streets. If one looks behind the form, however, it seems clear that, like a law forbidding theft of funds from the state treasury to pay for private publication, the prohibition is a necessary means of protecting the government's right not to subsidize private expression.[151]

The tradition of public use of streets and parks and the aggressive form of the governmental action involved have helped to confine any inroads that *Hague* and *Schneider* may have made into the general understanding that our Constitution is one of negative rather

---

[146]*See* Regina v. Graham, 4 T.L.R. 212, 226 (Cen. Crim. Ct. 1888) "[U]ndoubtedly [Trafalgar] square had been used for public meetings . . . ,[but] his Lordship had to say that he could find no warrant for considering that there was any right to hold meetings in Trafalgar-square, or, indeed, in any other public place.").

[147]*See, e.g.*, Thomas v. Casey, 121 N.J.L. 185, 1 A.2d 866 (1938) (New Jersey Supreme Court) (upholding the same statute). *See also* pp. 10-11 *supra* (criticizing Illinois Cent. R. R. v. Illinois, 146 U.S. 387 (1892), for holding that state could not convey submerged land held in "public trust" without referring to state law).

[148]*See* Stone, *Fora Americana: Speech in Public Places*, 1974 SUP. CT. REV. 233, 238.

[149]257 U.S. 312, 328 (1921), pp. 139-43 *supra*.

[150]*See, e.g.*, Harris v. McRae, 448 U.S. 297, 316 (1980) (government need not pay for abortion), pp. 471-75 *infra;* Currie, *Positive and Negative Constitutional Rights, supra* note 14.

[151]Cox v. New Hampshire, 312 U.S. 569, 576-77 (1941), softened the blow somewhat by holding that the state could impose a reasonable fee to cover policing and other costs incident to private use of public property. For consideration of the problems suggested by this conclusion, see Blasi, *Prior Restraints on Demonstrations*, 68 MICH. L. REV. 1481, 1527-32 (1970); *see also* Goldberger, *A Reconsideration of* Cox v. New Hampshire: *Can Demonstrators Be Required to Pay the Costs of Using America's Public Forums?*, 62 TEX. L. REV. 403, 413 (1983) (because the public as well as the speaker benefits from use of the public forum, "a proper distribution of costs . . . would allocate the costs . . . to the society as a whole.").

than positive liberties. Nevertheless these cases stand with *Truax* as reminders that generalization in this area is a dangerous practice.

### 3. Religious freedom

In 1940, in *Cantwell v. Connecticut*,[152] the Court applied the techniques developed in the speech cases of *Schneider* and *Herndon* to reverse criminal convictions of Jehovah's Witnesses on grounds of religious liberty. Writing for the Court, Justice Roberts appeared to equate the tests for constitutionality of measures impinging on expression and of those impinging on religion. The previous-restraint doctrine applied in *Near* and *Lovell*, however, suggested that the historical understanding of free expression comprehended exemption from regulations that could be validly applied to noncommunicative activities.[153] The history of the free exercise clause, in contrast, was largely one of opposition to discrimination, and the Court had emphasized in its first encounter with that clause in 1898 that it gave no right to exemption from otherwise valid laws—such as those proscribing polygamy.[154] Two decisions in the 1930s respecting conscientious objectors, while arguably distinguishable as involving government privileges, had tended to confirm this analysis.[155]

In striking down one of the two convictions in *Cantwell*, the Court was comfortably within the established framework of free exercise analysis. Cantwell had been convicted for soliciting funds without a permit, and the permit was to be issued only on finding that the applicant represented a bona fide religious or charitable organization. To make the right to solicit dependent upon an administrator's "determin[ation] whether the cause is a religious one," said Roberts, was a "censorship of religion."[156] Like the permit requirement in *Schneider,* this provision posed an undue risk of discriminatory administration, and discrimination is at the heart of the constitutional prohibition.[157]

Less obvious in light of the history of the religion clause was the Court's further conclusion that Cantwell's religious freedom had been infringed by a second conviction for breach of the peace in playing an offensive phonograph record.[158] On one hand, it was

---

[152] 310 U.S. 296 (1940).

[153] *See* Z. CHAFEE, *supra* note 122, at 400 (noting the significance of *Lovell* in light of the fact that "permits . . . must be obtained for all sorts of activities which are thought capable of causing harm to the community").

[154] *See* Reynolds v. United States, 98 U.S. 145, 166-67 (1878), THE FIRST HUNDRED YEARS at 439-42.

[155] In United States v. Macintosh, 283 U.S. 605 (1931) (Sutherland, J.), the Court held that naturalization might be denied on grounds of conscientious objection despite its religious basis. Chief Justice Hughes, dissenting with three others, addressed only the issue of statutory construction. Similarly, in Hamilton v. Regents of Univ. of Cal., 293 U.S. 245 (1934) (Butler, J.), the Court held that a state university might exclude students who refused military education on religious grounds. *See Macintosh,* 283 U.S. at 624 (dictum) ("The privilege of the native-born conscientious objector to avoid bearing arms comes not from the Constitution, but from the acts of Congress.").

[156] *Cantwell,* 310 U.S. at 305.

[157] *Cf. supra* notes 128-30 and accompanying text (discussing *Schneider*).

[158] 310 U.S. at 307-11. The Court distinguished the deferential Gitlow v. New York, 268 U.S. 652 (1925), for want of a statute specifically regulating speech and revived Holmes's clear-and-present-danger test to measure restrictions on both religious freedom and nonpolitical expression:

> Although the contents of the [phonograph] record not unnaturally aroused animosity, we think that, in the absence of a statute narrowly drawn to define and punish specific conduct as constituting a clear and present danger to a substantial interest of the State, the petitioner's communication,

clear that Cantwell had been singled out because of what he had said—others apparently were free to say other things in the streets. On the other hand, it was not the religious content but rather the offensive form of the defendant's statements that had provoked his prosecution; it appears that the state was enforcing a neutral rule forbidding the use of offensive words in expressing any ideas. Thus it could be argued that the Court in *Cantwell* suggested for the first time that freedom of religion not only forbade discrimination against religious activities but also required religious exemptions from generally applicable laws.

It did not come to that in *Cantwell* itself, for the alternative holding that the conviction offended freedom of expression seemed to mean that purveyors of nonreligious messages could not have been convicted for using similarly offensive language either.[159] Any suggestion that persons activated by religion were entitled to special privileges, moreover, was dramatically repudiated two weeks later in *Minersville School District v. Gobitis*,[160] where Justice Frankfurter's first important constitutional opinion concluded that Jehovah's Witnesses could be required to pledge allegiance to the U.S. flag.

If, as in the speech area, the test was whether the governmental interest could be found sufficient to justify the incursion on freedom, Justice Stone was clearly right in protesting that this decision was monstrous.[161] Justice Frankfurter, however, viewed the case as presenting a claim for a special exemption from a general law assumed to be otherwise valid:

> [T]he question remains whether school children, like the Gobitis children, must be excused from conduct required of all the other children in the promotion of national cohesion . . . . That the flag-salute is an allowable portion of a school program for those who do not invoke conscientious scruples is surely not debatable.[162]

The problem, as Justice Jackson would demonstrate when the Court overruled *Gobitis*, was with Frankfurter's assumption that the government's interest in inculcating patriotism was great enough to justify requiring *anyone* to pledge allegiance to the flag.[163] Recognition that freedom of speech embraces the right not to speak would raise interesting line-drawing problems of its own,[164] but the two decisions taken together tended to confirm the

---

considered in the light of the constitutional guarantees, raised no such clear and present menace to public peace and order as to render him liable to conviction of the common law offense in question.

310 U.S. at 311. *See supra* pp. 115-24 (discussing Schenck v. United States, 249 U.S. 47 (1919)); pp. 154-60 (discussing *Gitlow*).

[159] *See Cantwell,* 310 U.S. at 307.

[160] 310 U.S. 586, 600 (1940).

[161] *Id.* at 601-07 (Stone, J., dissenting). For a contemporaneous criticism of the decision, see Fennell, *The "Reconstructed Court" and Religious Freedom: The Gobitis Case in Retrospect,* 19 N.Y.U. L. Q. REV. 31 (1941).

[162] 310 U.S. at 595, 599. For analysis of how Frankfurter's phrasing of the question made the decision seem easier than it was see Danzig, *How Questions Begot Answers—Felix Frankfurter's First Flag Salute Opinion,* 1977 SUP. CT. REV. 257.

[163] West Virginia State Bd. of Educ. v. Barnette, 319 U.S. 624, 634-36 (1943).

[164] *See, e.g.,* Abood v. Detroit Bd. of Educ., 431 U.S. 209 (1977) (compulsory payment of union dues by government employee), pp. 518-22 *infra.*

understanding that freedom of religion did not entitle the religious to special exemptions from otherwise valid laws.[165]

### E.  Thornhill v. Alabama

Justice Murphy's opinion for the Court in *Thornhill v. Alabama*,[166] in 1940, appropriately sums up the civil liberties cases of the Hughes period. There, over the sole and unexplained dissent of Justice McReynolds, the Court struck down a conviction for labor picketing on the ground that the statute under which the defendant had been prosecuted infringed freedom of expression.[167]

First, as in *Stromberg,* the Court condemned the statute as overbroad on its face. An overbroad statute, like the broad permit standard in *Schneider,* "readily lends itself to harsh and discriminatory enforcement" and "sweeps within its ambit other activities that in ordinary circumstances constitute an exercise of freedom of speech or of the press." Moreover, there were "special reasons" for insisting that the statute itself be beyond reproach when freedom of expression was concerned.[168]

Second, as it had done without discussion in the Jehovah's Witnesses cases in holding that freedom of expression extended to religious speech, the Court in *Thornhill* gave broad scope to the types of expression protected. Despite an earlier suggestion that purely commercial speech might be excluded from first amendment protection, the Court held that labor picketing was included because it dealt with matters of public concern.[169]

Third, as in *Schneider,* the Court reaffirmed that the Constitution placed limits even on measures that restricted only the time, place, and manner of conveying messages, repeating *Schneider*'s conclusion that "one is [entitled] not to have the exercise of his liberty of expression in appropriate places abridged on the plea that it may be exercised in some other place."[170] Indeed, as a companion case makes clear, *Thornhill* may also be said to have reaffirmed *Stromberg*'s silent holding that freedom of expression was not limited to the written or spoken word, since picketing entails expression in part through physical presence.[171]

---

[165] *See* P. KURLAND, RELIGION AND THE LAW OF CHURCH AND STATE AND THE SUPREME COURT 37-49 (1962). As Kurland notes, the message of *Barnette* is somewhat ambiguous. *Id.* at 45-47. While "substantially in agreement" with Jackson's "opinion of the Court," Justices Black and Douglas explained their concurrence on freedom of religion grounds. *Barnette,* 319 U.S. at 643-44. Justice Murphy appeared to embrace both theories, 319 U.S. at 644-46, and three dissenters in two different dissents thought the flag salute constitutional, 319 U.S. at 642-43 (Roberts and Reed, JJ., dissenting); 319 U.S. at 646-71 (Frankfurter, J., dissenting).

[166] 310 U.S. 88 (1940).

[167] *Id.* at 101-06.

[168] *Id.* at 97-98 (emphasizing the relation between overbreadth and previous-restraint doctrines).

[169] *See id.* at 102-04 ("Free discussion concerning the conditions in industry and the causes of labor disputes appears to us indispensable to the effective and intelligent use of the processes of popular government to shape the destiny of modern industrial society."). *Compare id. with* Schneider v. State, 308 U.S. 147, 163-65 (1939) (suggesting commercial speech not protected), *supra* note 130.

[170] 310 U.S. at 506 (quoting *Schneider,* 308 U.S. at 163). *See also* Mendelson, *Clear and Present Danger— From* Schenck *to* Dennis, 52 COLUM. L. REV. 313, 318 (1952) ("*Thornhill* . . . made explicit what Mr. Justice Holmes had only implied, namely, that a regulation of the manner of expression may in some circumstances be a serious impediment to ideas themselves.").

[171] *See* Carlson v. California, 310 U.S. 106, 112-13 (1940) (Murphy, J.,) ("The carrying of signs and banners, no less than the raising of a flag, is a natural and appropriate means of conveying information on matters of public concern."); Henkin, *supra* note 89, at 79 ("In picketing, . . . it is not solely or primarily the words that commu-

Fourth, as in *Cantwell*, the Court expressly revived the clear-and-present danger test that Holmes had enunciated for the Court in the political context in *Schenck v. United States*.[172] It did so, moreover, while striking down a statute specifically directed toward speech, contrary to the apparent thrust of *Gitlow v. New York*.[173] In applying that test Justice Murphy reasonably concluded that the danger of violence from labor picketing did not justify a blanket ban, just as the danger of littering had not justified the handbilling prohibition in *Schneider*.[174] By stressing the importance of picketing and the trivial nature of the interest in preventing litter, however, the Court in each case seemed to suggest that the clear-and-present-danger formula did not entirely capture what the Justices were actually doing. In response to the nature of the problem it was attempting to solve, the Court seemed to be weighing the need for regulation against the degree of incursion on the interest in communication; whether the relevant dangers were clear or present was only part of that inquiry.[175]

Finally, Justice Murphy confirmed the obvious impression that measures impinging on freedom of expression were now being scrutinized far more strictly than those limiting purely economic interests,[176] and he explained why: "Abridgement of freedom of speech

---

nicate; the presence of the pickets is itself a communication, and indeed picketing is often effective regardless of what the placards say, because even persons who never read the placards are reluctant to cross a picket line."); *see also* Teller, *Picketing and Free Speech*, 56 HARV. L. REV. 180, 200-08 (1942) (arguing that picketing is not persuasion but "a form of economic pressure"); Dodd, *Picketing and Free Speech: A Dissent*, 56 HARV. L. REV. 513, 517 (1943) (responding that picketing "is generally the only practicable method of communicating the ideas which [labor unions] wish to express to the person to whom they wish to express them").

[172] 310 U.S. at 104-05 ("Abridgement of the liberty of such discussion can be justified only where the clear danger of substantive evils arises under circumstances affording no opportunity to test the merits of ideas by competition for acceptance in the market of public opinion. We hold that the danger of injury to an industrial concern is neither so serious nor so imminent as to justify the sweeping proscription of freedom of discussion embodied in [the statute]."). *See also supra* pp. 266-267, note 158 (discussing *Cantwell*).

[173] *See* 268 U.S. at 670-71; pp. 154-60 *supra*.

[174] *See* 310 U.S. at 105 ("[N]o clear and present danger of destruction of life or property, or invasion of the right of privacy, or breach of the peace can be thought to be inherent in the activities of every person who approaches the premises of an employer and publicizes the facts of a labor dispute involving the latter."). *Cf. supra* notes 136-39 and accompanying text (discussing *Schneider*). In one respect *Thornhill* was the easier of the two cases, for the picketing ban was not neutral as to the content of speech; it forbade picketing only for the purpose of discouraging others from dealing with the owner of the premises or of injuring his business. 310 U.S. at 91.

[175] In the brief time remaining before Chief Justice Hughes left the Court, the Justices began to grapple with the difficult problems presented by labor injunctions under rules more narrowly tailored to preventable evils than was the statute in *Thornhill*. In so doing the Justices revealed disagreements concealed by the relatively easy speech cases of the 1930s that would make the ensuing period one of deep disagreement over the degree of scrutiny of state measures affecting expression. *See* Milk Wagon Drivers Union v. Meadowmoor Dairies, Inc., 312 U.S. 287, 292, 294 (1941) (Frankfurter, J., over dissents by Black, Douglas, and Reed, JJ.) (injunction against peaceful picketing allowed because past picketing had been so "enmeshed with contemporaneously violent conduct" that "it could justifiably be concluded that the momentum of fear generated by past violence would survive even though future picketing might be wholly peaceful"). The contrast with Near v. Minnesota, 283 U.S. 897 (1931), where past publications assumed to be punishable had been held not to justify an injunction even against defamatory publications, was striking. *See* 312 U.S. at 319 (Reed, J., dissenting) ("If the fear engendered by past misconduct coerces storekeepers during peaceful picketing, the remedy lies in the maintenance of order, not in denial of free speech.").

[176] 310 U.S. at 95. *Thornhill* dramatically illustrated the change of focus by holding that the Constitution forbade a limitation on picketing that the Court had once found to be constitutionally required. *See* Truax v. Corrigan, 257 U.S. 312, 328 (1921), pp. 139-43 *supra*.

and of the press . . . impairs those opportunities for public education that are essential to effective exercise of the power of correcting error through the processes of popular government."[177] Fittingly, he cited at this point Justice Stone's celebrated footnote in *United States v. Carolene Products Co.*,[178] which had suggested closer scrutiny of measures limiting participation in the formulation of policy as well as of those touching rights specifically listed in the first eight amendments or affecting discrete and insular minorities.[179] We had not seen the last of this formulation.

[177] 310 U.S. at 95. Justice Murphy added, without a trace of the deference that had characterized recent substantive due process decisions in the economic sphere, *see* pp. 239-40 *supra,* that "[m]ere legislative preference for one rather than another means for combatting substantive evils . . . may well prove an inadequate foundation on which to rest regulations which are aimed at or in their operation diminish the effective exercise of rights so necessary to the maintenance of democratic institutions." 310 U.S. at 95-96.

[178] 304 U.S. 144, 152-53 n.4 (1938); *see* p. 244 *supra.*

[179] For doubts as to the appropriateness of this formulation see Ackerman, *Beyond* Carolene Products, 98 HARV. L. REV. 713, 723-24, 728, 742 (1985) (arguing that while Stone was "right to emphasize the special vulnerability of discrete and insular minorities," "anonymous and diffuse" groups also deserved special consideration because they were "systematically disadvantaged in a pluralist democracy"; the prevalence of farm subsidies illustrated that, "[o]ther things being equal, 'discreteness and insularity' will normally be a source of enormous bargaining advantage"). *See also* Lusky, *Footnote Redux: A* Carolene Products *Reminiscence,* 82 COLUM. L. REV. 1093, 1098 (1982), in which Justice Stone's then law clerk reminds us that the famous footnote was "offered . . . as a starting point for debate" and " 'did not purport to *decide* anything.' "

# Conclusion to Part Four

The Constitution was very different at the end of Hughes's tenure from what it had been at the beginning. The retreat of substantive due process in economic cases was a blessing; the doctrine had been illegitimate from the start. In rewriting the contract clause and eradicating federalistic limitations on national authority, however, the Court seemed to embrace the dangerous principle that constitutional provisions that did not suit contemporary needs could be ignored.

All nine Justices voted to enforce the limitation on congressional power in *Schechter;* two years later five of them voted to disregard it. Why? Had the Court-packing proposal frightened them into making a tactical concession to avoid the greater evil?[1] Had circumstances or public opinion persuaded them that the need for a stronger central government justified taking liberties with the Constitution?[2] Had repeated encounters with refractory factual situations convinced them that there was no tenable place to draw the line? Answers to questions like these are not to be found in judicial opinions.

The revolution was often explained in terms of Justice Holmes's familiar argument of judicial restraint.[3] In cases involving "ordinary commercial transactions," wrote Justice

---

[1] *See, e.g.,* F. RODELL, NINE MEN 250 (1955) ("with childlike clarity, the citizen saw that the Court had nakedly succumbed to political pressure)." Chief Justice Hughes denied not only that the packing plan had any effect, but also that he had ever changed his mind. His biographer rosily attributes the apparent switch in judicial attitude to increased congressional restraint. *See* 2 M. PUSEY, CHARLES EVANS HUGHES 768, 771 (1951).

[2] *See* E. CORWIN, CONSTITUTIONAL REVOLUTION, LTD. 73 (1941) (invoking the 1936 election and industrial unrest). Justice Roberts himself pointed to the coercive effect of public opinion: "it is difficult to see how the Court could have resisted the popular urge for uniform standards . . . for what in effect was a uniform economy. . . . An insistence by the Court on holding federal power to what seemed its appropriate orbit when the Constitution was adopted might have resulted in even more radical changes." O. ROBERTS, THE COURTS AND THE CONSTITUTION 61-62 (1951). *See also* R. MCCLOSKEY, THE AMERICAN SUPREME COURT 225 (1960) ("history, not the Court, made this decision").

[3] *See, e.g.,* Lochner v. New York, 198 U.S. 45, 74-76 (1905) (dissent); Ribble, *Some Aspects of Judicial Self-Restraint,* 26 VA. L. REV. 981 (1940).

Stone in the *Carolene Products* case, "in the absence of statutory findings" supporting the legislative judgment "they would be presumed."[4] This was the deferential approach Brandeis had employed in upholding limits on insurance commissions in 1931,[5] suggesting both a respect for the opinions of other branches and what Judge Cooley had referred to as "conscious[ness] of the fallibility of the human judgment."[6] Similar considerations underlay Brandeis's familiar list in the *Ashwander* case of judicially created doctrines for avoiding the decision of constitutional questions entirely.[7]

Other decisions, however, contained little hint of deference to legislative determinations. Both *Parrish* and the Labor Board cases, like Roberts's earlier opinion upholding graduated chain store taxes,[8] ringingly endorsed the reasonableness of the legislative decision, while the opinion sustaining regulation of employment agency fees cast doubt on the concept of substantive due process itself.[9] It may well be that on average the Justices of the late 1930s took a more modest view of the judicial function in economic cases than some of their predecessors; but they pretty clearly also had a different view of the substantive provisions they were construing. Moreover, the restraint exercised by the new majority was conspicuously confined to economic cases. In the fields of criminal procedure, civil rights, and civil liberties the Court was more aggressive than ever before.[10]

The revolution was basically the work of five judges. Brandeis, Stone, and Cardozo were implacable opponents of substantive due process, generous in their interpretation of federal authority, and sensitive to civil rights and liberties.[11] Hughes and Roberts were with them in most cases. Both defected in the important cases of *Liebmann, Carter,* and *Butler,* and Roberts in *Alton* and *Morehead* as well. Both came back on board to stay, however, in *Parrish* and the *Labor Board Cases* in 1937.[12]

On the other side, until they began leaving the Bench in 1937, were four dependable defenders of the old order: Van Devanter, McReynolds, Sutherland, and Butler. Not only

[4] 304 U.S. at 152-53.

[5] O'Gorman and Young v. Hartford Ins. Co., 282 U.S. 251 (1931).

[6] 1 T. Cooley, Constitutional Limitations 332 (8th ed. 1927).

[7] Ashwander v. TVA, 297 U.S. 288, 345-48 (1936), (concurrence) (quoting 1 T. Cooley, *supra* note 6, at 232. *See also* Coleman v. Miller, 307 U.S. 433 (1939), where over the dissents of Butler and McReynolds the Court refused to decide whether a state could ratify a proposed constitutional amendment after rejecting it and whether it could be ratified thirteen years after its proposal. Three Justices concluded that article V confided the decision of both questions exclusively to Congress; four others thought this was true of the entire amendment process and argued with much force that state legislators who had voted against the amendment had no standing to sue. For criticism of this decision, see Dellinger, *The Legitimacy of Constitutional Change: Rethinking the Amendment Process,* 97 Harv. L. Rev. 386, 397-98, 411 (1983) ("Neither the text of the Constitution nor prior congressional practice nor judicial precedent supports this bestowal of exclusive power on Congress.").

[8] Tax Commissioners v. Jackson, 283 U.S. 527 (1931).

[9] Olsen v. Nebraska, 313 U.S. 236 (1941).

[10] *See* Freund, *Charles Evans Hughes as Chief Justice,* 81 Harv. L. Rev. 4, 42 (1967) ("It can be said compendiously that this period was a watershed in the Court's thinking about the meaning of the Bill of Rights and the fourteenth amendment.").

[11] So, of course, was Holmes; but the grand old man, who was plainly past his peak, was gone by 1932 and played little role in the decisions of the Hughes period. *See* 2 M. Pusey, *supra* note 1, at 681 (noting that Hughes assigned Holmes only easy cases and ultimately persuaded him to leave the Bench).

[12] *See* F. Rodell, *supra* note 1, at 221-23 (concluding that Justice Roberts "was for years the most powerful person in the United States": "[N]ever once in a major case did [Hughes] cast a deciding vote; for never once in a major case was Hughes to the right of Roberts").

did these Justices vote more often than their colleagues to strike down both federal and state regulation of the economy; all four dissented from the recognition of civil rights and liberties in *Nixon v. Condon, Near v. Minnesota,* and *Herndon v. Lowry* as well. In the latter field, however, there were significant differences of opinion among them; only McReynolds and Butler dissented in *Stromberg v. California* and *Powell v. Alabama,* for example, and in the latter case it was Sutherland who wrote the Court's noble opinion.[13]

As in earlier years, Sutherland was the most articulate of the four, stating the traditional position with great power in such cases as *Liebmann, Carter, Parrish,* and *Blaisdell.*[14] On the other side, memorable dissents were written by Brandeis in *Liebmann,* Stone in *Butler,* Cardozo in *Carter,* and Hughes in *Alton* and *Morehead.*[15] As befitted his pivotal position, Roberts was given a number of important opinions to write, including *Nebbia, Alton,* and *Butler.* If the last two of these left something to be desired in terms of both craftsmanship and judgment, Roberts was at the same time an eloquent spokesman for the new majority in such civil liberties cases as *Herndon, Schneider,* and *Cantwell.*

But the authoritative voice of the Hughes Court was Hughes himself, who wrote nearly twice as many majority opinions in constitutional cases as any other member of the Court, including most of the big ones—*Blaisdell, Schechter, Parrish, Jones & Laughlin,* the *Gold Clause Cases, Crowell v. Benson,* and most of the civil liberties decisions not authored by Roberts: *Stromberg, Near, DeJonge,* and *Lovell,* as well as *Missouri ex rel. Gaines v. Canada.*[16] Hughes wrote concisely and admirably, although he was arguably too willing to sacrifice constitutional values in the face of change; like Brandeis, Cardozo, and Stone, if not also Sutherland, he must be counted among the greatest of our judges.[17]

In abandoning the old limits on economic regulation, the Court under Hughes cleared the way for undivided attention to the new agenda that Justice Stone had so astutely drafted in *Carolene Products.* In holding first amendment freedoms applicable to the states, in adding to the procedural components of due process, and in closely scrutinizing allegations of racial discrimination, it made a significant start in dealing with that agenda.[18] In establishing the basic contours of the doctrines of previous restraint, overbreadth, symbolic speech, time, place, and manner regulations, and the public forum, while showing new vigor in protecting dissident political speech, it erected the framework upon which the modern law of free expression rests.

[13] On the philosophical differences among these four Justices see 2 M. Pusey, *supra* note 1, at 670; for Sutherland's concern for civil rights and liberties see J. Paschal, Mr. Justice Sutherland: A Man against the State (1951).

[14] Van Devanter, whose pen paralysis appeared to be progressive, wrote very little, and some of his cases had ultimately to be reassigned to other Justices. *See* 2 M. Pusey, *supra* note 1, at 667. McReynolds, as usual, was given nothing of importance to write for the Court. Butler wrote his share of constitutional opinions, but apart from *Morehead* few were of much significance or interest.

[15] 2 M. Pusey, *supra* note 1, at 671, described Brandeis as the intellectual leader of this bloc, but he left the job of writing dissents largely to Stone and Cardozo.

[16] *See* 2 M. Pusey, *supra* note 1, at 704 (concluding that Hughes wrote more important opinions than any Justice since Marshall).

[17] For Hughes's excellence as a judicial administrator see McElwain, *The Business of the Supreme Court as Conducted by Chief Justice Hughes,* 63 Harv. L. Rev. 5 (1949); 2 M. Pusey, *supra* note 1, at 671-78. For his "singular devotion to civil liberties," *see id.* at 717-29.

[18] *See* R. McCloskey, *supra* note 2, at 169-79.

# Part Five

Chief Justice Stone
1941–1946

# Introduction to Part Five

When Harlan F. Stone was named to succeed Charles Evans Hughes as Chief Justice in 1941, the ballgame was new and so were the players. Dead and buried were the once burning controversies over economic liberties and the scope of enumerated federal powers. While devoting much of their attention to a number of troublesome issues brought about by the Second World War, the Justices were to focus increasingly on the new agenda of civil rights and liberties that Stone had laid out for them in *United States v. Carolene Products Co.*[1] in 1938.

It was altogether fitting that Justice Stone, the prophet of the new order, was elevated to Chief Justice after fifteen distinguished years of intellectual leadership on the Court.[2] The only other familiar face was that of Owen Roberts, who, more than any other single Justice, had helped precipitate the change by abandoning his restrictive view of regulatory authority when he held the balance of power.[3] All the other Justices owed their initial appointments to President Franklin D. Roosevelt, and he had been careful in their selection.

Eldest of those in service was former Senator Hugo Black of Alabama, the "ultra-radical of the Senate" who had shocked the legal world by a series of unrestrained populistic dissents immediately following his appointment[4] and who had spoken out eloquently for the oppressed in voiding a conviction based on a coerced confession in *Chambers v.*

---

[1] *See* pp. 244, 270, *supra*.

[2] "No other President," said former Justice Brandeis when Stone was appointed Chief Justice, "has performed such a signal service." *See* A. Mason, Harlan Fiske Stone: Pillar of the Law 570 (1956).

[3] *See* C. Leonard, A Search for a Judicial Philosophy: Mr. Justice Roberts and the Constitutional Revolution of 1937, *passim* (1971); pp. 216-44 *supra*.

[4] *See, e.g.,* Connecticut General Life Ins. Co. v. Johnson, 303 U.S. 77, 83 (1938) (Black, J., dissenting) (denying after all those years that a corporation was a "person" within the fourteenth amendment); G. Dunne, Hugo Black and the Judicial Revolution 25, 178-79 (1977).

*Florida.*[5] Next in service was former Solicitor General Stanley Reed of Kentucky, who had written several significant and competent opinions reflecting the broad modern view of federal and state authority over the economy and who had authored a strong dissent evincing an even greater degree of constitutional protection for labor picketing than the majority after *Thornhill v. Alabama* was prepared to afford.[6]

Next to Justice Black sat the man who was to be his principal adversary over the next twenty years in one of the epic struggles of U.S. constitutional history, former professor Felix Frankfurter of Harvard. Best known for his controversial opinion denying Jehovah's Witnesses a constitutional exemption from a compulsory flag salute,[7] Justice Frankfurter was to respond to the lesson of *Lochner v. New York*[8] by becoming the Court's foremost exponent of an uncompromising judicial restraint as the press of new issues revealed differences that had been concealed by unanimity on the questions of the 1930s.[9]

The remaining holdovers from the last days of Chief Justice Hughes were destined to be steadfast allies of Justice Black in this coming controversy. The young William O. Douglas, one-time professor and Securities Exchange Commission Chairman, had written the Court's most sweeping condemnation of economic due process.[10] Former Attorney General and Michigan Governor Frank Murphy, father of the expansive protection for picketing in *Thornhill*, was to be even more insistent than Black or Douglas in pressing the claims of civil liberty.[11]

Appointed to fill the vacancies created by the departure of Hughes and McReynolds in 1941 were South Carolina Senator James F. Byrnes and yet another Attorney General, Robert H. Jackson. The former, who served the shortest term of any Justice ever confirmed,[12] left the following year to work for Roosevelt; the latter stayed to become one of history's most illustrious Justices.[13] Byrnes's replacement, former professor and circuit judge Wiley Rutledge, was to do yeoman service as an ally of Black, Douglas, and Murphy in defense of civil liberties. The only other change in membership before Stone's

---

[5] 309 U.S. 227 (1940).

[6] *See, e.g.,* Milk Wagon Drivers Union v. Meadowmoor Dairies, 312 U.S. 287, 317-21 (1941) (Reed, J., dissenting from affirmance of injunction against peaceful picketing against background of violence); United States v. Appalachian Elec. Power Co., 311 U.S. 377, 398 (1940) (upholding Congress's power to impose intrusive conditions on license to dam river that could be made navigable); Veix v. Sixth Ward Bldg. & Loan Ass'n, 310 U.S. 32, 34 (1940) (upholding retroactive state limitation on savings withdrawals); United States v. Rock Royal Coop., Inc., 307 U.S. 533, 539 (1939) (upholding federal minimum prices for milk); *cf. Thornhill,* 310 U.S. 88, 91 (1940) (striking down statute construed to bar all labor picketing at site of dispute), pp. 268-70 *supra.*

[7] Minersville School Dist. v. Gobitis, 310 U.S. 586 (1940), p. 267 *supra.*

[8] 198 U.S. 45 (1905) (invalidating law limiting hours of bakers), pp. 47-50, *supra.*

[9] *See generally* L. BAKER, FELIX FRANKFURTER (1969); H. THOMAS, FELIX FRANKFURTER: SCHOLAR ON THE BENCH (1960).

[10] *See* Olsen v. Nebraska, 313 U.S. 236 (1941), (overruling square precedent in upholding state regulation of employment agency fees), pp. 239-40 *supra.*

[11] For an excellent study, see J. HOWARD, MR. JUSTICE MURPHY (1968).

[12] John Rutledge served only a few months when given a recess appointment as Chief Justice in 1795, but the Senate refused to confirm him. *See generally* Currie, *The Most Insignificant Justice: A Preliminary Inquiry,* 50 U. CHI. L. REV. 466 (1983).

[13] *See generally* E. GERHART, AMERICA'S ADVOCATE: ROBERT H. JACKSON (1958).

death in 1946 was President Truman's appointment of Ohio Senator Harold H. Burton to replace Justice Roberts at the end of the period.[14]

Only two months after Stone took his seat as Chief Justice, Pearl Harbor was bombed and Congress declared war. It was not long before the war effort confronted the Court with a panoply of challenging problems ranging from military trials to price regulation and selective service, as well as the much-lamented internment of citizens of Japanese descent. It is with the war cases that we begin; the remaining decisions of the period are considered in the following chapter.

[14]    JUSTICES OF THE SUPREME COURT DURING THE TIME OF CHIEF JUSTICE STONE

| | | 1941 | 42 | 43 | 45 | 46 |
|---|---|---|---|---|---|---|
| Harlan F. Stone | (1925-1946) | | | | | |
| Owen J. Roberts | (1930-1945) | | | | | |
| Hugo L. Black | (1937-1971) | | | | | |
| Stanley F. Reed | (1938-1957) | | | | | |
| Felix Frankfurter | (1939-1962) | | | | | |
| William O. Douglas | (1939-1975) | | | | | |
| Frank Murphy | (1940-1949) | | | | | |
| James F. Byrnes | (1941-1942) | | | | | |
| Robert H. Jackson | (1941-1954) | | | | | |
| Wiley B. Rutledge | (1943-1949) | | | | | |
| Harold H. Burton | (1945-1958) | | | | | |

SOURCE: G. GUNTHER, CASES AND MATERIALS ON CONSTITUTIONAL LAW, app. B (11th ed. 1985).

# 9

# The Second World War

## I. MILITARY TRIALS

### A. *Ex parte Quirin*

Six months after the bombing of Pearl Harbor, eight German saboteurs equipped with explosives secretly landed on New York and Florida beaches. Apprehended, they were held for trial by a military commission established pursuant to presidential order. Sitting in an extraordinary summer session in July of 1942, the Supreme Court in *Ex parte Quirin*[1] upheld the commission's jurisdiction in a unanimous opinion by Chief Justice Stone.

In *Ex parte Milligan*,[2] in 1866, the Court had courageously held that the military trial of civilians for giving aid to the rebellion offended both the constitutional guarantee of jury trial and article III's requirement that federal judicial power be vested in judges appointed to serve during good behavior. The *Milligan* Court had conceded that military trials might be permissible "on the theatre of active military operations," as a matter of necessity. If "the courts [we]re actually closed" by hostilities, military tribunals were unavoidable if justice was to be dispensed at all.[3] This concession, however, was of no use in *Quirin*. As the Court acknowledged, "ever since petitioners' arrest the state and federal courts in Florida, New York, and the District of Columbia, and in the states in which each of the petitioners was arrested or detained, have been open and functioning normally."[4]

The Court in *Milligan* had also conceded that the explicit exception from the fifth amendment's grand jury requirement for "cases arising in the land or naval forces, or in

---

[1] 317 U.S. 1, 18 (1942) (Justice Murphy did not participate).
[2] 71 U.S. (4 Wall.) 2, 121-22 (1866); *see* THE FIRST HUNDRED YEARS at 288-92.
[3] *Milligan*, 71 U.S. (4 Wall.) at 127.
[4] *Quirin*, 317 U.S. at 23-24.

the [m]ilitia, when in actual service, in time of [w]ar or public danger,"[5] implicitly limited other procedural protections of the criminal defendant as well.[6] Over the objections of four Justices, this exception was appropriately construed in *Milligan* not to embrace prosecutions of civilians for giving comfort to the enemy,[7] and Chief Justice Stone did not rely on it in *Quirin*.[8] Rather, Stone invoked history. Offenses against the laws of war, including "unlawful belligerency," had consistently been tried by military tribunals both before and after the adoption of the Constitution.

> The object [of article III's jury trial provision] was to preserve unimpaired trial by jury in all those cases in which it had been recognized by the common law . . . , but not to bring within the sweep of the guaranty those cases in which it was then well understood that a jury trial could not be demanded as of right.[9]

If Chief Justice Stone was correct about the history of military commissions, he was on firm ground. The tradition of sovereign immunity had been read into the unqualified jurisdictional grants of article III on similar grounds;[10] the tradition of courts-martial for offenses by military personnel had qualified article III's guarantee of tenured judges;[11] the tradition of nonjury trials for petty offenses and for contempt had limited the jury-trial provisions themselves.[12] Thus, while one might have hoped to find that the Constitution limited military trials to cases of strict necessity, it is hard to quarrel with the Court's contrary conclusion.[13] *Quirin* is a salutary reminder that it is not the courts alone that have a responsibility to see that those charged with offenses are afforded appropriate procedural protections.[14]

---

[5] U.S. Const. amend. V.

[6] 71 U.S. (4 Wall.) at 123.

[7] *Id.* at 123-24.

[8] 317 U.S at 41. "We may assume, without deciding, that a trial prosecuted before a military commission . . . is not one 'arising in the land . . . forces,' when the accused is not a member of or associated with those forces." *Id.*

[9] *Id.* at 39. The fifth and sixth amendments, the Court added, "did not enlarge the right to jury trial as it had been established by that Article." *Id.* No challenge based upon the tenure provisons of article III was made; it would have been subject to the same historical argument. *Cf. Milligan,* 71 U.S. (4 Wall.) at 2. The history of military commissions is considered in Kaplan, *Constitutional Limitations on Trials by Military Commissions,* 92 U. Pa. L. Rev. 119 (1943).

[10] *See, e.g.,* Hans v. Lôuisiana, 134 U.S. 1 (1890), *supra* pp. 7-9.

[11] Dynes v. Hoover, 61 U.S. (20 How.) 65, 79 (1858) (dictum).

[12] *See, e.g.,* Schick v. United States, 195 U.S. 65 (1904) (petty offenses); *Ex parte* Terry, 128 U.S. 289, 309 (1888) (contempt). Both cases are cited in *Quirin,* 317 U.S. at 39-40.

[13] In further contrast to *Milligan,* the President had acted pursuant to express statutory authorization in establishing the military commission in *Quirin.* It was unnecessary to decide whether, contrary to the suggestion of Chief Justice Chase in the earlier case, the President had inherent authority to establish such tribunals by virtue of his position as Commander in Chief, in the absence of "controlling necessity." *See Milligan,* 71 U.S. (4 Wall.) at 139-40 (concurring opinion); *Quirin,* 317 U.S. at 29. For a discussion of Chief Justice Stone's doubts whether the proceedings had been in accordance with the Articles of War and his efforts to secure unanimity, see A. Mason, Harlan Fiske Stone: Pillar of the Law 653-66 (1956).

[14] *See* Cushman, Ex parte Quirin *et al.—The Nazi Saboteur Case,* 28 Cornell L.Q. 54, 65 (1941) (finding it "a wholesome and desirable safeguard of civil liberty in time of war" that the Court took jurisdiction at all).

## B. *In re Yamashita*

Nearly four years after *Quirin,* General Yamashita, commander of a Japanese army in the Philippines, was condemned to death for war crimes by another military commission. In *In re Yamashita*[15] the Court once again upheld military jurisdiction in an opinion by Chief Justice Stone, but this time there were dissents by Justices Murphy and Rutledge.[16]

With respect to the jurisdictional question, the most obvious difference between this case and *Quirin* was that the commission in *Yamashita* had been convened after hostilities had ceased. The Court readily found this distinction immaterial. "The war power," wrote Chief Justice Stone, "is not limited to victories in the field, but carries with it the inherent power to guard against the immediate renewal of the conflict, and to remedy . . . the evils which the military operations have produced."[17] This sensible proposition had ample precedential support.[18] Moreover, in the case of punishment for war crimes committed by enemy combatants "the practical administration of the system of military justice under the law of war would fail if such authority were thought to end with the cessation of hostilities. For only after their cessation could the greater number of offenders and the principal ones be apprehended and subjected to trial."[19] No one disagreed with this conclusion.

Justice Murphy's dissenting argument was that, in contrast to *Quirin,* the charge against Yamashita failed to state an offense under the laws of war.[20] Yamashita had been charged not with committing or authorizing atrocities, but with failing to prevent his troops from committing them. At the time of the acts in question, said Murphy, the Japanese army had been so decimated by American attacks that its commander was in no position to control it. "International law," Murphy argued, imposed no "liability under such circumstances for failure to meet the ordinary responsibilities of command,"[21] and thus the proceeding was not within the traditional military jurisdiction.

Justice Rutledge, who agreed with Murphy, added a separate constitutional argument of his own: the procedures followed by the military tribunal were not in accordance with the fifth amendment's requirement of due process of law.[22] The admission of incompetent

---

[15] 327 U.S. 1 (1946).

[16] *See id.* at 26-41 (Murphy, J., dissenting); *id.* at 41-81 (Rutledge, J., dissenting). Justice Jackson, who spent the entire term prosecuting German war criminals before a similar tribunal in Nuremberg, did not participate. *Id.* at 26.

[17] *Id.* at 12. The grant of authority on which Congress had relied, "to define and punish . . . Offenses against the Law of Nations," U. S. CONST. art. I, § 8, certainly does not suggest any limitation to periods of actual hostilities. *See Yamashita,* 327 U.S. at 7.

[18] *See, e.g.,* Stewart v. Kahn, 78 U.S. (11 Wall.) 493, 507 (1871) (suspension of statute of limitations for claims that could not be brought during hostilities), *cited in Yamashita,* 327 U.S. at 12; Hamilton v. Kentucky Distilleries & Whse. Co., 251 U.S. 146 (1919) (postwar ban on liquor manufacture); *see* pp. 99-100 *supra.*

[19] *Yamashita,* 327 U.S. at 12. It was true that the end of hostilities reduced the necessity for employing military courts for this purpose, as the civilian courts could now be reopened. As *Quirin* shows, however, the test of military judicial authority is not necessity but history; the civil courts were open in *Quirin* too.

[20] *Id.* at 26-41.

[21] *Id.* at 35 (Murphy, J., dissenting).

[22] *Id.* at 41-81 (Rutledge, J., dissenting). Finding the procedures followed also inconsistent with statute and treaty, Justice Murphy joined this opinion too. *Id.* at 81. Justice Rutledge further suggested an ex post facto problem that cropped up again at Nuremberg, but he did not develop its application to *Yamashita:* "it is not in our tradition for anyone to be charged with crime which is defined after his conduct, alleged to be criminal, has taken place." *Id.* at 43 (Rutledge, J., dissenting).

evidence, including much hearsay, had made it impossible for Yamashita to rebut the case against him, and he had had insufficient time to prepare a defense to the multifarious allegations.[23]

The Court replied to Rutledge with the traditional argument that habeas corpus lay only to determine the jurisdiction of the sentencing tribunal.[24] Its response to Murphy was a denial that there was any "contention . . . that the commission held petitioner responsible for failing to take measures which were beyond his control."[25]

On this view the Court, as in *Quirin*, may well have been in no position to interfere. If this is so, then *Yamashita* is yet another example of the importance of recognition by the other branches of government of their constitutional and moral obligation to assure a fair trial. As Thomas Paine said in a passage Justice Rutledge quoted with force at the end of his opinion, "'He that would make his own liberty secure must guard even his enemy from oppression; for if he violates this duty he establishes a precedent that will reach to himself.'"[26]

## C.   *Duncan v. Kahanamoku*

On the day Pearl Harbor was bombed, the Governor of Hawaii declared the territory under "'martial law,'" authorizing the Commanding General "'to exercise all the powers normally exercised' by the Governor and by the 'judicial officers and employees of this territory.'"[27] The President, without knowing the exact terms of the order, approved it two days later.[28]

While this order was in effect, Duncan and White were convicted of criminal offenses by military tribunals. Both were civilians, and White's alleged offense—embezzlement from another private citizen—had nothing to do with the military.[29] Both Duncan and

[23] *See id.* at 43-45, 48-61, 78-81 (Rutledge, J., dissenting).

[24] *Id.* at 8-9, 23. For discussion of the traditional limitations on habeas corpus, see Bator, *Finality in Criminal Law and Federal Habeas Corpus for State Prisoners*, 76 HARV. L. REV. 441 (1963); Hart, *Foreword: The Time Chart of the Justices*, 73 HARV. L. REV. 84 (1959). Unwilling to undermine the congressional decision to insulate miltary convictions from direct civilian review, the Court was reluctant to extend to military prisoners the decisions expanding the type of issues cognizable on habeas corpus for civil prisoners beyond the traditional concept of jurisdiction. *See, e.g.,* Johnson v. Zerbst, 304 U.S. 458, 467-68 (1938) (right to counsel); *see also* D. CURRIE, FEDERAL COURTS 629-33 (4th ed. 1990). Justice Murphy, it should be added, drew the opposite conclusion: precisely because those convicted by military tribunals lacked direct recourse to civilian courts, "the judicial review available by habeas corpus must be wider than usual in order that proper standards of justice may be enforceable." *Yamashita*, 327 U.S. at 31 (Murphy, J., dissenting).

[25] *Yamashita*, 327 U.S. at 16; *see* Fairman, *The Supreme Court on Military Jurisdiction: Martial Rule in Hawaii and the* Yamashita *Case*, 59 HARV. L. REV. 833, 869-70 (1946) (arguing that Justice Murphy's conclusions had no support in the record).

[26] *Yamashita*, 327 U.S. at 81 (Rutledge, J., dissenting) (quoting 2 THE COMPLETE WRITINGS OF THOMAS PAINE 588 (Foner ed. 1945)).

[27] Duncan v. Kahanamoku, 327 U.S. 304, 307-308 (1946) (citation omitted).

[28] *See id.* at 308 & n.2. It is perhaps because the President was unaware that the civilian courts had been supplanted that there was no apparent effort to justify the order on the basis of the President's constitutional powers as Commander in Chief.

[29] Duncan, on the other hand, had been convicted of assaulting two marines in violation of a military rule. *See id.* at 309–11.

White sought habeas corpus, and this time, in contrast to *Quirin* and *Yamashita,* the Court held the military tribunal without jurisdiction.[30]

On the constitutional level, *Duncan* differed from *Milligan* in that Hawaii had been subject to a devastating enemy attack that obviously justified some immediate extraordinary measures. On this basis Justice Burton argued in a dissent joined by Justice Frankfurter that the Court should defer to what he viewed as a reasonable exercise of executive discretion to determine the scope of the emergency.[31]

By the time the defendants were tried, however, Justice Murphy argued in an impassioned concurrence, "the territorial courts of Hawaii [like the Indiana courts in *Milligan*] were perfectly capable of exercising their normal criminal jurisdiction had the military allowed them to do so."[32] As *Milligan* itself had made clear, and as the Court unanimously reaffirmed in its decision striking down a Texas governor's use of martial law in 1932, the courts could not simply accept an executive determination as to the existence of an emergency or the measures necessary to meet it.[33]

Without attempting to resolve the constitutional question, Justice Black for the majority chose a narrower ground of decision: the statute authorizing the Governor to declare "martial law," read in light of constitutional traditions, did not authorize military trials of civilians.

> The phrase "martial law" as employed in th[e Hawaii Organic] Act, . . . while intended to authorize the military to act vigorously for the maintenance of an orderly civil government and for the defense of the Islands against actual or threatened rebellion or invasion, was not intended to authorize the supplanting of courts by military tribunals.[34]

History had saved the military trials in *Quirin*; it condemned those in *Duncan.*

Prudently, the Court announced this brave conclusion only after the war was over. Sen-

---

[30] 327 U.S. 304, 324 (1946).

[31] *Id.* at 337-58 (Burton, J., dissenting, joined by Frankfurter, J.); *cf.* Prize Cases, 67 U.S. (2 Black) 635, 670-71 (1862) (upholding presidential blockade of Confederate ports under statute authorizing use of armed forces to suppress insurrections: "The proclamation of blockade is itself official and conclusive evidence to the Court that a state of war existed which demanded and authorized a recourse to such a measure. . . ."), THE FIRST HUNDRED YEARS at 273-75; Martin v. Mott, 25 U.S. (12 Wheat.) 12, 18-20 (1827) (holding statute gave President unreviewable discretion to determine whether imminent danger of invasion existed for purposes of calling out militia).

[32] *Duncan,* 327 U.S. at 327 (Murphy, J., concurring) (stressing right to trial by jury); *see also id.* at 333-34 (Murphy, J., concurring) (rejecting contention that presence of citizens of Japanese descent made jury trials impracticable); *id.* at 313-14 (opinion of the Court) (noting that neither defendant was connected with the military forces or charged with any offense against the laws of war); *id.* at 335-37 (Stone, C. J., concurring).

[33] *See* Sterling v. Constantin, 287 U.S. 378, 402 (1932) (Hughes, C. J.) ("The assertion that such action can be taken as conclusive proof of its own necessity . . . has no support in the decisions of this Court."); Fairman, *supra* note 25, at 856 (arguing that "no convincing reason could have been advanced" why military trial of an embezzlement charge was "necessary to the defense of Hawaii"); Frank, Ex parte Milligan *and the Five Companies: Martial Law in Hawaii,* 44 COLUM. L. REV. 639, 665 (1944) (arguing that *Milligan* applied).

[34] *Duncan,* 327 U.S. at 324. Only once, in the Reconstruction Act, said Justice Black, had Congress "authorized the supplanting of the courts by military tribunals," and its power to do so had been seriously challenged. *Id.* at 323; *see also id.* at 320-21 (noting that the troops sent to put down both Shays' Rebellion and the Whiskey Rebellion in the eighteenth century had been specifically directed to turn over offenders to the civil courts for trial).

sibly, unlike the impetuous Murphy, it declined to reach an unnecessary constitutional question. Nevertheless *Duncan* stands with *Milligan* as an monument to the value of judicial review in protecting the essential liberties of the citizen.

## II.  THE JAPANESE-AMERICAN CASES

### A.  *Hirabayashi v. United States*

On March 24, 1942, Lieutenant General J. L. DeWitt, Military Commander of the Western Defense Command, issued a proclamation requiring "all persons of Japanese ancestry" within a "military area" comprising the entire Pacific coast to "be within their place of residence between the hours of 8:00 P.M. and 6:00 A.M."[35] Hirabayashi, a U.S. citizen of Japanese descent living in Seattle, Washington, was convicted of violating this curfew, and in *Hirabayashi v. United States*[36] the Supreme Court unanimously affirmed.

General DeWitt was not acting entirely on his own. Responding to claims of military necessity, President Roosevelt had issued an Executive Order empowering military commanders to restrict "the right of any person to enter, remain in, or leave" areas to be designated in the interest of preventing espionage and sabotage.[37] Congress had ratified the President's action by enacting criminal penalties for violations of restrictions imposed pursuant to the Executive Order, knowing that a curfew was among the restrictions contemplated.[38] Reading the statute to "authorize[ ] curfew orders . . . for the protection of war resources from espionage and sabotage,"[39] the Court found no forbidden delegation of legislative power:

> The essentials of the legislative function are preserved when Congress authorizes a statutory command to become operative, upon ascertainment of a basic conclusion of fact by a designated representative of the Government. . . . [T]he basic facts . . . were whether th[e] danger [of sabotage] existed and whether a curfew order was an appropriate means of minimizing the danger.[40]

This reasoning seems wholly in accord with the deferential attitude the Justices had displayed toward other delegations since 1937 and in most earlier cases as well.[41]

"The war power of the national government," wrote Chief Justice Stone once again for the Court, "extends to every matter and activity so related to war as substantially to affect its conduct and progress. . . . It embraces every phase of the national defense, including

[35] *See* Hirabayashi v. United States, 320 U.S. 81, 86-88 (1943).

[36] 320 U.S. 81, 83-84 (1943). Douglas, Murphy, and Rutledge wrote separate concurring opinions. *Id.* at 105-14. Justice Murphy's opinion had originally been drafted as a dissent. *See* J. HOWARD, MR. JUSTICE MURPHY 300-09 (1968). In Yasui v. United States, 320 U.S. 115, 117 (1943), the Court sustained the district court's judgment on the authority of *Hirabayashi*.

[37] *Hirabayashi*, 320 U.S. at 85-86.

[38] *See id.* at 85-91. Thus, as in *Quirin* and *Yamashita*, there was no need to decide whether the President could have imposed such a restriction without statutory authorization on the basis of his article II powers as Commander in Chief. *Id.* at 92.

[39] *Id.* at 104; *cf.* Panama Refining Co. v. Ryan, 293 U.S. 388, 437-39 (1935) (Cardozo, J., dissenting) (construing NIRA hot-oil provision, in light of statutory purposes, to limit presidential discretion), pp. 216-18 *supra*.

[40] *Hirabayashi*, 320 U.S. at 104.

[41] *See* pp. 16-19, 195-96, 186 *supra*.

the protection of war materials and the members of the armed forces. . . ."[42] At the time the curfew was imposed, noted Stone, "the danger to our war production by sabotage and espionage in [the Pacific Coast] area seem[ed] obvious."[43] A curfew was "an obvious protection against the perpetration of sabotage most readily committed during the hours of darkness."[44] The Court added that although "racial discriminations [we]re in most circumstances irrelevant," they were not so here: "We cannot close our eyes to the fact, demonstrated by experience, that in time of war residents having ethnic affiliations with an invading enemy may be a greater source of danger than those of a different ancestry."[45] "We cannot say," Stone concluded, "that the war-making branches of the Government did not have ground for believing that in a critical hour [disloyal] persons could not readily be isolated and separately dealt with. . . ."[46] There was accordingly a "rational basis" for the decision to impose the curfew; thus that measure was within the war powers of Congress and did not deprive Hirabayashi of his liberty without due process of law.[47]

John Marshall had said that a measure was "necessary and proper" to the execution of federal authority only if it was an "appropriate" means to a "legitimate" end, and his successors had enunciated a similar test to determine the compatibility of substantive measures with due process.[48] Though some have argued that General De Witt was motivated as much by racial antagonism as by his professed security concerns,[49] the Court has understandably been loath to question the motives behind official action.[50] Furthermore, one could hardly deny that preventing sabotage was a legitimate federal concern. The most pressing question was whether the curfew was closely enough tailored to this end to survive judicial scrutiny.

Even assuming there was a sufficient danger of sabotage to support such a drastic measure as a curfew, the order actually promulgated was curiously broad in one respect and curiously narrow in another. It restricted the liberty of *all* Japanese-Americans on the West Coast because *some* of them might be dangerous; yet it applied neither to those in Hawaii nor to Americans whose forebears had come from Germany or Italy, with which we were also at war.[51] One would not need to revert to the judicial arrogance of *Lochner v. New*

---

[42] *Hirabayashi*, 320 U.S. at 93.

[43] *Id.* at 96.

[44] *Id.* at 99.

[45] *Id.* at 101. The Court buttressed its conclusion that Japanese-Americans presented special dangers with the observation that "social, economic and political conditions"—by which Stone meant official and other forms of discrimination against Japanese-Americans—"have in large measure prevented their assimilation as an integral part of the white population" and "encouraged the[ir] continued attachment . . . to Japan." *Id.* at 96 n.4, 98. This was as indecent as it was true: the Court was saying that one instance of racial discrimination justified another.

[46] *Id.* at 99.

[47] *Id.* at 92-102. For a rare argument in support of this conclusion, see Alexandre, *Wartime Control of Japanese-Americans*, 28 CORNELL L.Q. 385 (1943).

[48] McCulloch v. Maryland, 17 U.S. (4 Wheat.) 316, 421 (1819); Mugler v. Kansas, 123 U.S. 623, 661-62 (1887), THE FIRST HUNDRED YEARS at 375-77.

[49] *See, e.g.*, M. GRODZINS, AMERICANS BETRAYED, POLITICS AND THE JAPANESE EVACUATION 302 (1949) (discussing a later act in the same tragedy: "[T]he evacuation decision was predicated on a racist philosophy, nurtured by regional pressures, and eventually justified by falsehood.").

[50] *See, e.g.*, Fletcher v. Peck, 10 U.S. (6 Cranch) 87, 129-30 (1810) (declining to decide whether land grant resulted from bribery of legislators), THE FIRST HUNDRED YEARS at 129; McCray v. United States, 195 U.S. 27, 59-64 (1904) (upholding prohibitive federal tax on margarine), p. 30 *supra*.

[51] *See* J. TENBROEK, E. BARNHART & F. MATSON, PREJUDICE, WAR, AND THE CONSTITUTION 303-04 (1968) [hereinafter J. TENBROEK].

*York*[52] and *Railroad Retirement Board v. Alton Railroad Co.*[53] to doubt whether a curfew at once so overinclusive and so underinclusive was a reasonably appropriate means of achieving the legislative goal. A Court less deferential to the conclusions of other branches might have found the measure unauthorized by the statute as construed, unnecessary to the exercise of Congress's war powers, and so arbitrary as to deprive those within its reach of their liberty without due process of law.[54]

The principal achievement of the New Deal revolution, however, had been essentially to abandon both of the constitutional doctrines on which such a conclusion could have been based. Except in cases involving application of the "specific" provisions of the Bill of Rights to the states, the Court had not taken an argument of limited federal power or of substantive due process seriously since 1936.[55] As early as 1919, the Justices had accepted an argument of military necessity at least as farfetched as that in *Hirabayashi* in upholding a postwar ban on liquor manufacture as a means to "'conserv[e] the man power of the Nation, and to increase efficiency in the production of arms.'"[56] In 1942 the Court had made a mockery of the tenth amendment by allowing Congress to regulate planting for on-farm consumption because "[h]ome-grown wheat . . . competes with wheat in commerce."[57] Five years before *Hirabayashi*, Justice Stone had written that "the existence of facts supporting the legislative judgment is to be presumed" and that "ordinary commercial" regulation was not to be set aside on due process grounds unless shown not to rest on "some rational basis."[58] Three years later the Court had dismissed substantive due process objections as "notions of public policy . . . which . . . should not be read into the Constitution."[59] *Milligan*, which had more strictly scrutinized a claim of military necessity,[60] was of no help since *Hirabayashi* involved only the discredited doctrines of substantive due process and enumerated powers, not the explicit guarantees of judge and jury.

Subsequent decisions have familiarized us with stricter levels of judicial scrutiny in cases involving either "fundamental rights" or "suspect classifications"—both of which could easily have been found in *Hirabayashi*.[61] Justice Stone himself had pointed the way

[52] 198 U.S. 45 (1905) (finding health risks to bakers insufficient to justify limiting their working hours despite strong evidence to contrary), pp. 47-50 *supra*.

[53] 295 U.S. 330 (1935) (finding pensions for railroad workers not closely enough related to interstate transportation under commerce clause), pp. 225-26 *supra*.

[54] *Cf.* De Jonge v. Oregon, 299 U.S. 353, 365-66 (1973) (holding danger of subversion did not justify punishing mere assistance in conducting meeting called by Communist party), p. 255 *supra*; A.L.A. Schechter Poultry Corp. v. United States, 295 U.S. 495, 551 (1935) (unanimously holding regulation of wages, prices, and product quality in local slaughterhouse beyond commerce power), pp. 222-23, *supra*. *See generally* P. IRONS, JUSTICE AT WAR 278-310 (1983) (documenting the conclusion that the government's brief effectively concealed from the Court evidence of serious doubts within the administration as to the need for discriminatory measures); Rostow, *The Japanese American Cases—A Disaster*, 54 YALE L.J. 489, 505-07 (1945) (arguing that there was no factual basis for the conclusion of military necessity).

[55] *See generally* pp. 236-40 *supra*.

[56] Hamilton v. Kentucky Distilleries & Warehouse Co., 251 U.S. 146, 166-67 (1919), pp. 99-100 *supra; see* Woods v. Cloyd W. Miller Co., 333 U.S. 138, 141-42 (1948) (upholding postwar rent control as exercise of war powers shortly after Justice Stone's death).

[57] Wickard v. Filburn, 317 U.S. 111, 128 (1942).

[58] United States v. Carolene Prods. Co, 304 U.S. 144, 152 (1938) (upholding special-interest measure protecting dairy industry from competition).

[59] Olsen v. Nebraska, 313 U.S. 236, 247 (1941).

[60] *See* J. TENBROEK, *supra* note 51, at 238 (arguing that *Korematsu* was "the exact antithesis" of *Milligan*).

[61] *See, e.g.,* Roe v. Wade, 410 U.S. 113, 152-55 (1973) ("fundamental" right to abortion); Palmore v. Sidoti, 466 U.S. 429, 432-33 (1984) (race as suspect classification).

in his famous footnote in the first *Carolene Products* case, suggesting the possibility of heightened scrutiny of measures disadvantaging "discrete and insular minorities."[62] *Hirabayashi*, unlike *Carolene Products*, involved no "ordinary commercial" measure. Decisions of the Hughes period seemed to confirm that the Court was less deferential in speech and press cases than in those where merely economic interests were involved.[63] Moreover, the year before the curfew case, the Court had expressly exercised "strict scrutiny" in striking down on equal protection grounds a state law providing for sterilization of habitual thieves but not embezzlers, arguing that the statute "involves one of the basic civil rights of man."[64] On the basis of these leads, one might have expected the Court to exercise stricter scrutiny in *Hirabayashi*.[65]

It is easier, however, to find support for these varying levels of deference in political theory[66] than in the due process or war clauses, which were at issue in *Hirabayashi*. It is one thing to conclude that the first amendment's firm declaration that "Congress shall make no law . . . abridging the freedom of speech"[67] imposes more stringent limitations than the "rational basis" requirement the Court had read into due process, or (as Justice Black was soon to suggest) that the privileges or immunities clause makes the same stringent restrictions applicable to the states.[68] It is quite another to conclude that a single clause requires varying degrees of deference because five judges believe some rights more important or some classifications more suspect than others.[69]

The fact of the matter is that *Hirabayashi* was a classic case of racial discrimination, which the Court had consistently held prohibited by the equal protection clause of the

[62] 304 U.S. at 153 n.4.

[63] *See, e.g.*, Thornhill v. Alabama, 310 U.S. 88, 95-96 (1940) ("Mere legislative preference for one rather than another means for combatting substantive evils . . . may well prove an inadequate foundation on which to rest regulations which are aimed at or in their operation diminish the effective exercise of rights so necessary to the maintenance of democratic institutions"). *See generally* pp. 253-70 *supra*.

[64] Skinner v. Oklahoma, 316 U.S. 535, 541 (1942) (Douglas, J.). Chief Justice Stone's concurring opinion in *Skinner* made the due process argument for invalidating the overboard curfew in *Hirabayashi:* "A law which condemns . . . all the individuals of a class to such a harsh measure as the present because some or even many merit condemnation, is lacking in the first principles of due process." *Id.* at 545 (Stone, C. J., concurring).

[65] *See* M. GRODZINS, *supra* note 49, at 354; Dembitz, *Racial Discrimination and the Military Judgment: The Supreme Court's* Korematsu *and* Endo *Decisions,* 45 COLUM. L. REV. 175, 187-88 (1945).

[66] *See generally* J. ELY, DEMOCRACY AND DISTRUST (1980).

[67] U. S. CONST. amend. I.

[68] *See* Adamson v. California, 332 U.S. 46, 71-72 (1947) (Black, J., dissenting).

[69] It would have been easy to distinguish the economic cases if their basis had been the historically attractive argument that "liberty" meant only freedom from restraints on mobility, *see* p. 45 *supra* (discussing Allgeyer v. Louisiana, 165 U.S. 578 (1897)), but it was not. To the extent that the test of due process was the reasonableness of the challenged measure, it did seem to require a balancing of costs and benefits; thus, a greater need might well be required to justify a more serious harm. For example, as Justice Jackson was soon to assert, arguments of military necessity sufficient to sustain a curfew might not suffice for more invasive measures such as exclusion from the entire West Coast. *See infra* text accompanying notes 82-84 (discussing Korematsu v. United States, 323 U.S. 214 (1944)). When the interests affected differ in kind rather than in degree, however, as liberty of contract and of movement do, the determination of relative importance becomes much more subjective.

Any claim of *procedural* due process seems to have been foreclosed by Bi-Metallic Investment Co. v. State Board of Equalization, 239 U.S. 441, 445-46 (1915), which held that due process imposed no requirement of a hearing before adoption of rules of general applicability because the large numbers of persons affected made a hearing impracticable and increased the effectiveness of political checks. As for due process in determining whether an individual was subject to the curfew, the substantive standard left no facts to try except Japanese ancestry, which was conceded.

fourteenth amendment[70]—which applies, alas, only to the *states* and not to the United States. "The Fifth Amendment," said Chief Justice Stone in echo of a myriad of decisions that had once appeared progressive, "contains no equal protection clause."[71] Substantive due process is a shaky enough concept to begin with.[72] To hold that it embraces equal protection would make an explicit clause of the fourteenth amendment redundant, which is hardly the most natural assumption.[73] When the Court ultimately did hold that due process included equal protection, it could only protest that it was "unthinkable" that a Constitution prohibiting state racial classifications "would impose a lesser duty on the Federal Government."[74] It may have been unthinkable, but unfortunately it was true. When the Constitution proves deficient, the proper course is to amend it by the procedure prescribed in article V.

## B.   *Korematsu v. United States*

Less than two months after promulgation of the curfew upheld in *Hirabayashi*, General DeWitt ordered that all persons of Japanese ancestry be excluded from designated West Coast areas including Alameda County, California.[75] Korematsu was convicted of violating this provision. Affirming in a brief opinion by Justice Black, the Court held that the case was governed by *Hirabayashi*.[76] This time, however, the decision was not unanimous. Justices Roberts, Murphy, and Jackson dissented.

Roberts zeroed in on an earlier proclamation prohibiting Japanese-Americans from leaving the area that Korematsu had been convicted for *not* leaving. Thus, in his view, Korematsu "was faced with two diametrically contradictory orders": one "made him a criminal if he left the zone in which he resided," the other "made him a criminal if he did not leave."[77] "I had supposed," said Justice Roberts, "that if a citizen was constrained by two . . . orders . . . and obedience to one would violate the other, to punish him for violation of either would deny him due process of law."[78]

---

[70] *See, e.g.,* Missouri *ex rel.* Gaines v. Canada, 305 U.S. 337 (1938) (exclusion of blacks from state law schools); Nixon v. Herndon, 273 U.S. 536 (1927) (exclusion of blacks from primary election); Yick Wo v. Hopkins, 118 U.S. 356 (1886) (exclusion of Chinese from laundry business); Strauder v. West Virginia, 100 U.S. 303 (1880) (exclusion of blacks from juries). As the Court had said in *Strauder*, racial discrimination was at the heart of the fourteenth amendment, and the Court had never suggested that it could be justified by any showing of alleged necessity. *See id.* at 310; *see also* Slaughter-House Cases, 83 U.S. (16 Wall.) 36, 67-72, 81 (1873), THE FIRST HUNDRED YEARS at 342-50.

[71] *Hirabayashi*, 320 U.S. at 100 (citing Detroit Bank v. United States, 317 U.S. 329, 337-38 (1943)).

[72] *See* pp. 44-50 *supra.*

[73] Overlap between the due process clause and other provisions of the Bill of Rights, however, though once ruled out on similar grounds, *see* Hurtado v. California, 110 U.S. 516, 534-35 (1884) (grand jury indictment), THE FIRST HUNDRED YEARS at 366-68, had since become accepted. *See, e.g.,* Powell v. Alabama, 287 U.S. 45, 60-71 (1932) (right to counsel and cases cited including uncompensated taking and free speech), pp. 246-47 *supra.*

[74] Bolling v. Sharpe, 347 U.S. 497, 500 (1954).

[75] *See* Korematsu v. United States, 323 U.S. 214, 229 (1944) (Roberts, J., dissenting).

[76] 323 U.S. 214, 217 (1944). Hirabayashi had also been convicted of violating an exclusion order. Because his concurrent sentence for curfew violation was upheld, however, it was immaterial whether or not his exclusion conviction was also valid, and the Court did not pass on it. *See Hirabayashi*, 320 U.S. at 85.

[77] *Korematsu*, 323 U.S. at 232 (Roberts, J., dissenting).

[78] *Id.* at 228-29, 232 (Roberts, J., dissenting).

For those who believe in substantive due process, Roberts's statement of the governing principle is certainly appealing. The majority, however, found no such contradiction: the order forbidding Korematsu to leave the area expressly applied only "'until and to the extent that a future proclamation or order should so permit or direct,'" and it had been superseded by the exclusion order.[79]

Justice Jackson waxed eloquent over the unconstitutionality of the exclusion provision itself, although he emphatically refused to decide whether or not it was reasonable.[80] "Korematsu," he stated, "has been convicted of an act not commonly a crime. It consists

---

[79]*Id.* at 220. Justice Roberts further argued that the exclusion order, which he "might" have agreed was constitutional if standing alone, could not be considered in isolation from accompanying provisions requiring those excluded to report to an "Assembly Center"—"a euphemism for a prison"—as part of a scheme "to lock [them] up in a concentration camp." *Id.* at 230-32 (Roberts, J., dissenting). Justice Black fairly responded that the detention issue was not presented because the detention provisons were separable and Korematsu had not been charged with violating them. *Id.* at 221-22.

[80]*Id.* at 248 (Jackson, J., dissenting). Courts were in no position, Jackson argued, to determine the reasonableness of military orders, and military commanders could not be expected to "conform to conventional tests of constitutionality" in emergencies. *Id.* at 244-45 (Jackson, J., dissenting). "I do not suggest that the courts should have attempted to interfere with the Army in carrying out its task. but I do not think they may be asked to execute a military expedient that has no place in law under the Constitution." *Id.* at 248 (Jackson, J., dissenting).

Justice Frankfurter protested in a concurring opinion that this was double-talk: "If a military order . . . does not transcend the means appropriate for conducting war, such action . . . is . . . constitutional. . . ." *Id.* at 225. It is not plain, however, that the Constitution authorized all "reasonable" means of making war. Congress must first declare war, unless the President is acting "to repel sudden attacks." *See* 2 M. FARRAND, RECORDS OF THE CONSTITUTIONAL CONVENTION 318 (rev. ed. 1937). The order must either be authorized by statute or fall within the President's authority as Commander in Chief, *see* Youngstown Sheet & Tube Co. v. Sawyer, 343 U.S. 579 (1952), and it must not offend constitutional limitations such as freedom of speech, the taking clause, or the jury and judge provisions that were enforced in *Milligan*. *See supra* notes 2-7 and accompanying text. Moreover, not only our own revolution but the adoption of the Constitution itself reflected Locke's admonition that obedience to law might properly take second place in extremis. The experience of the totalitarian governments we were fighting when *Korematsu* was decided accentuated his wisdom—though one might wonder whether we really want every soldier to view our republican Constitution the way Jefferson viewed the British colonial system in 1776. *See* J. LOCKE, SECOND TREATISE OF CIVIL GOVERNMENT chs. 18, 19 (C. Sherman ed. 1937) (right of revolution); The Declaration of Independence para. 3 (U.S. 1776) (right of people to alter or abolish bad government); 2 M. FARRAND, *supra*, at 469 (James Wilson: "We must . . . go to the original powers of Society, the House on fire must be extinguished, without a scrupulous regard to ordinary rights."). *See generally* W. SHIRER, THE RISE AND FALL OF THE THIRD REICH (1960). This is perhaps why article I itself explicitly authorizes suspension of the writ of habeas corpus, which effectively precludes determination of the lawfulness of executive actions, during certain emergencies. U. S. CONST. art. I., § 9, cl. 2. Justice Jackson added:

> A military commander may overstep the bounds of constitutionality and it is an incident. But if we review and approve, that passing incident becomes the doctrine of the Constitution. . . . [T]he Court for all time has validated the principle of racial discrimination. . . . The principle . . . lies about like a loaded weapon ready for the hand of any authority that can bring forward a plausible claim of an urgent need.

*Korematsu*, 323 U.S. at 246 (Jackson, J., dissenting); *cf.* A. BICKEL, THE LEAST DANGEROUS BRANCH 139-40 (1962) (arguing that the Court should refuse to "legitimate" deplorable practices it is unable to find unconstitutional lest, in the context of motion picture censorship, it "encourage Comstockian tendencies").

Justice Jackson's argument seems, in fact, the more intellectually respectable; he suggested not that the Court allow a misimpression of the law to prevail in hopes of influencing political choices among legitimate alternative policies, but that the Court refuse to term constitutional that which in his view was not. How the Court was to avoid "interfer[ing] with the Army in carrying out its [arguably reasonable but unconstitutional] task" if an appropriate suit was brought, Jackson did not say. *See Korematsu*, 323 U.S. at 248 (Jackson, J., dissenting).

merely of being present in the state whereof he is a citizen, near the place where he was born, and where all his life he has lived."[81] Moreover, noted Jackson, that act was made criminal only "because his parents were of Japanese birth. . . . [H]ere is an attempt to make an otherwise innocent act a crime merely because this prisoner is the son of parents as to whom he had no choice, and belongs to a race from which there is no way to resign."[82]

All this could have been said with equal force in *Hirabayashi,* where Jackson had been silent. But *Hirabayashi,* he added, was different:

> Now the principle of racial discrimination is pushed from support of mild measures to very harsh ones. . . . Because we said that these citizens could be made to stay in their homes during the hours of dark, it is said we must require them to leave home entirely; and if that, we are told they may also be taken into custody for deportation, and if that, it is argued they may also be held for some undetermined time in detention camps. How far the principle of this case would be extended before plausible reasons would play out, I do not know.[83]

For those who believe that federal authority is limited either by the enumeration of powers itself or by substantive due process, the severity of a deprivation is surely relevant to the question whether it is an appropriate means to its asserted goal. Justice Jackson's refusal to decide whether the exclusion order was reasonable, however, leaves one wondering how he could have found it unconstitutional, since both of the pegs on which that conclusion could have been hung had always been defined in terms of the appropriateness of the challenged action.

Justice Black, writing for the majority, conceded that exclusion was "a far greater deprivation" than curfew.[84] Moreover, without adverting to the "rational basis" standard applied in *Hirabayashi,* he dramatically professed a more demanding one: "[A]ll legal restrictions which curtail the civil rights of a single racial group are immediately suspect. . . . [C]ourts must subject them to the most rigid scrutiny."[85] "Nothing short of apprehension by the proper military authorities of the gravest imminent danger to the public safety" could justify either measure.[86] Yet in Black's view, even the exclusion order met this stringent test: "[E]xclusion from a threatened area, no less than curfew, has a definite and close relationship to the prevention of espionage and sabotage."[87]

We come at last to Justice Murphy, who of the three dissenters was, as usual, the most impassioned. Making no effort to distinguish *Hirabayashi,* Murphy went to the heart of

---

[81] *Korematsu,* 323 U.S. at 243 (Jackson, J., dissenting).

[82] *Id.* at 243 (Jackson, J., dissenting).

[83] *Id.* at 247 (Jackson, J., dissenting).

[84] *Id.* at 218. The hardships inflicted by the exclusion order are detailed in the REPORT OF THE COMMISSION ON WARTIME RELOCATION AND INTERNMENT OF CIVILIANS, PERSONAL JUSTICE DENIED (1982).

[85] *Korematsu,* 323 U.S. at 216. This was to assume the less deferential stance adumbrated by Chief Justice Stone in *Carolene Products* for measures affecting "discrete and insular minorities." *See supra* note 62 and accompanying text.

[86] *Korematsu,* 323 U.S. at 218.

[87] *Id.*

the difficulty with both exclusion and curfew by pointing to the gross overinclusiveness of the orders. Of course there had been individual instances of subversive activities by persons of Japanese descent, Murphy noted, "[b]ut to infer that examples of individual disloyalty . . . justify discriminatory action against the entire group is to deny that under our system of law individual guilt is the sole basis for deprivation of rights."[88] The argument that there was no time to "treat . . . Japanese Americans [like German- or Italian-Americans] on an individual basis by holding investigations and hearings to separate the loyal from the disloyal," he continued, was refuted by the facts:

> [N]early four months elapsed after Pearl Harbor before the first exclusion order was issued; nearly eight months went by until the last order was issued; and the last of these 'subversive' persons was not actually removed until almost eleven months had elapsed. Leisure and deliberation seem to have been more of the essence than speed.[89]

In other words, the exclusion of all Japanese-Americans from the West Coast was a means poorly tailored to the legitimate end of preventing sabotage. For all of Justice Black's protestations, the Court did not seem to be scrutinizing the measure very strictly.[90] Therefore, in Justice Murphy's opinion, "the order deprive[d] all those within its scope of the equal protection of the laws as guaranteed by the Fifth Amendment."[91]

There is only one weakness in this argument: there is no such provision.

## C. *Ex parte Endo*

Pursuant to an exclusion order similar to that upheld in *Korematsu,* Endo was evacuated from Sacramento, California, in May 1942. From then on, until the Supreme Court in an eloquent opinion by Justice Douglas ordered her release in December 1944 in *Ex parte Endo,*[92] she was detained in "relocation centers"—which Justice Roberts in *Korematsu* had labeled concentration camps—against her will.

The government conceded that Endo was "a loyal and law-abiding citizen"; General

---

[88]*Id.* at 240 (Murphy, J., dissenting).

[89]*Id.* at 241 (Murphy, J., dissenting); *see also* J. TENBROEK, *supra* note 51, at 295-96; Rostow, *supra* note 54, at 507.

[90]*See* Dembitz, *supra* note 65 at 182, 195 (arguing that *Korematsu* was actually even more deferential than *Hirabayashi*); J. TENBROEK, *supra* note 51, at 237-38. *Contrast, e.g.,* Craig v. Boren, 429 U.S. 190 (1976), pp. 495-96 *infra,* where, in applying a supposedly less rigorous degree of scrutiny, the Court ruled that the fact that more males than females between the ages of eighteen and twenty-one drove while intoxicated did not justify setting the drinking age higher for men than for women. Indeed, if Justice Black meant to suggest that the "strict" level of scrutiny he professed to apply in *Korematsu* would also govern a case of state racial discrimination under the equal protection clause, he seemed to be not raising but lowering the scrutiny level; for no decision before *Hirabayashi* (which had emphasized, as Justice Black did not, that the latter requirement applied only to the states) had ever suggested that racial discrimination could be justified at all. *See supra* note 70.

[91]*Korematsu,* 323 U.S. at 234-35 (Murphy, J., dissenting). Justice Murphy's additional argument that the failure to conduct individual loyalty hearings offended the requirement of "procedural due process," *id.* at 242, overlooked the fact that under the order individual loyalty was irrelevant. Due process had long been held to impose no procedural restrictions at all on the promulgation of generally applicable rules. *See supra* note 69.

[92]323 U.S. 283, 285 (1944). *Endo* and *Korematsu* were decided on the same day.

DeWitt himself had declared that "military necessity required only that the Japanese population be removed from the coastal area and dispersed in the interior, where the danger of action in concert during any attempted enemy raids . . . would be eliminated."[93] This would appear to eliminate any military justification for detention. As Murphy and Roberts insisted in separate concurring opinions,[94] that was to leave the order defenseless before any applicable requirement of equal protection or substantive due process—and possibly also to render it, even in the permissive climate of the times, neither necessary nor proper to the execution of any congressional power.[95]

Prudently, as in *Duncan,* the Court chose a narrower and entirely convincing ground of decision: neither Congress nor the President had authorized the detention of loyal citizens after their evacuation. Neither the statute nor the Executive Order said a word about detention. "Their single aim," wrote Justice Douglas for the majority, "was the protection of the war effort against espionage and sabotage. . . . [D]etention which has no relationship to that campaign [is unauthorized]."[96]

Thus one of the most deplorable government programs in the history of the United States finally encountered its legal limit. Reading the story is likely to leave one feeling ill. As in the war-crimes cases, it was not principally the judges who let us down—though the decisions underline the cost of their studied indifference to the limited nature of Congress's enumerated powers over the preceding few years.[97] That the evacuation program may not have been unconstitutional under prevailing standards, however, does not prove it was right. The episode is a sobering warning against complacency about government even in this generally free country, and an arresting reminder that the Constitution does not provide a remedy for every wrong.[98]

---

[93] *Id.* at 294-95; *see* J. TENBROEK, *supra* note 51, at 250.

[94] 323 U.S. at 307-08 (Murphy, J., concurring) ("[D]etention in Relocation Centers of persons of Japanese ancestry regardless of loyalty is not only unauthorized by Congress or the Executive but is another example of the unconstitutional resort to racism inherent in the entire evacuation program."); *id.* at 310 (Roberts, J., concurring) ("An admittedly loyal citizen has been deprived of her liberty for a period of years" in violation of "the guarantees of the Bill of Rights . . . and especially the guarantee of due process of law.").

[95] In fact the detention program had admittedly been "'due primarily to the fact that the interior states would not accept an uncontrolled Japanese migration.'" *Id.* at 295-96 (quoting General DeWitt). Racial prejudice, as Justice Black said in *Korematsu,* 323 U.S. at 216, is surely the least acceptable excuse for racial discrimination.

[96] *Endo,* 323 U.S. at 300-02. Justice Roberts's protest that Congress had implicitly ratified the detention plan by voting a general appropriation for the agency that administered it, *id.* at 308-10 (Roberts, J., concurring), seems hardly faithful to the familiar canon that statutes should be construed whenever possible to ensure their validity, *see id.* at 299 (opinion of the Court). Additionally, Justice Douglas was on solid ground in concluding that "a lump appropriation . . . for the overall program of the [Relocation] Authority" did not demonstrate congressional approval of detention of persons whose loyalty was unquestioned: "Congress may support the effort to take care of these evacuees without ratifying every phase of the program." *Id.* at 303 n.24.

[97] A generation after the Japanese-American cases, Justices Black and Frankfurter showed how serious scrutiny of the connection between means and ends could be used to limit the reach of article I war powers in striking down a court-martial of servicemen's spouses in Reid v. Covert, 354 U.S. 1 (1957). *See* pp. 400-03 *infra.*

[98] In later years, lawsuits have been filed seeking to reopen the question of the legality of the evacuation program and to recover damages for the harm caused to its unfortunate victims. Apart from the necessity of showing that the government acted illegally, these actions present troublesome procedural obstacles, not the least of which is the statute of limitations. *See, e.g.,* Hohri v. United States, 586 F. Supp. 769 (D.D.C. 1984), *aff'd,* 847 F. 2d 779 (Fed. Cir. 1988) (rejecting claims on grounds of sovereign immunity, failure to exhaust administrative remedies, and delay in filing suit).

The arguable lawfulness of the action, however, affords no basis for objecting to subsequent congressional

## III. Treason

"Treason against the United States," article III provides, "shall consist only in levying War against them, or in adhering to their Enemies, giving them Aid and Comfort." No one may be convicted of treason "unless on the Testimony of two Witnesses to the same overt Act, or on Confession in open Court," and punishments extending beyond the offender himself are forbidden.[99]

"In the century and a half of our national existence," wrote Justice Jackson in 1945, "not one execution on a federal treason conviction has taken place."[100] Indeed, as James Willard Hurst reported, during that period "less than two score [federal] treason prosecutions" were even "pressed to trial."[101] "We have managed to do without treason prosecutions," Justice Jackson added, "to a degree that probably would be impossible except while a people was singularly confident of external security and internal stability."[102]

Only once before, in *Ex parte Bollman*,[103] an 1807 case growing out of Aaron Burr's mysterious western adventures, had the Supreme Court had occasion to consider charges of treason. In *Cramer v. United States*,[104] where the petitioner had been convicted of assisting two of the enemy saboteurs whose military trials were at issue in *Quirin*, it had another.

*Bollman* had given a narrow interpretation to the clause of article III making it treason to "levy[ ] War" against the United States. A mere conspiracy, Chief Justice Marshall insisted, was not enough; there must be "an actual assembling of men for the treasonable purpose, to constitute a levying of war."[105] *Cramer* gave a similarly restrictive reading to the alternative offense of "adhering to [our] Enemies, giving them Aid and Comfort," and went on to decide an important question respecting the requirement of "two Witnesses to the same overt Act."

"[T]he basic law of treason in this country," Justice Jackson wrote, "was framed by men . . . taught by experience and by history to fear abuse of the treason charge almost as much as they feared treason itself."[106] Responding to this fear of abuse, Jackson contin-

---

efforts to make reparations. *See* the American-Japanese Evacuation Claims Act of 1948, 50 U.S.C. app. §§ 1981-1987 (1982) (providing for satisfying certain claims of property loss), Civil Liberties Act of 1988, 102 Stat. 903 (apologizing for "grave injustice" and "violations of . . . constitutional rights" and authorizing payment of $20,000 per victim). Unlike damages, statutory compensation does not depend upon a finding that the program was unconstitutional, illegal, or even—as with the benefit of hindsight most people seem to believe—misguided. Like draftees, and like those whose property was condemned for military installations, Americans of Japanese descent were required to bear disproportionate burdens for what was viewed as the common good. Although the fifth amendment's guarantee of just compensation of persons in such a position applies only to those called upon to sacrifice property, *see* U. S. Const. amend. V, it furnishes a model to guide Congress in seeking a more equitable distribution of the burden.

[99] U. S. Const. art III, § 3.

[100] Cramer v. United States, 325 U.S. 1, 24 (1945).

[101] J. Hurst, The Law of Treason in the United States 187 (1971). This excellent book grew out of a study commissioned by the Justice Department in connection with the *Cramer* case. *See id.* at vii.

[102] *Cramer,* 325 U.S. at 26 (footnote omitted).

[103] 8 U.S. (4 Cranch) 46 (1807), The First Hundred Years at 82 n.132.

[104] 325 U.S. 1 (1945); *see also supra* text accompanying notes 1-14 (discussing *Quirin*). *See generally* Howard, *Advocacy in Constitutional Choice: The* Cramer *Treason Case, 1942-1945,* 1986 Am. B. Found. Res. J. 375.

[105] *Bollman,* 8 U.S. (4 Cranch) at 126.

[106] *Cramer,* 325 U.S. at 21.

ued, the Framers "adopted every limitation [on treason] that the practice of governments had evolved or that politico-legal philosophy . . . had advanced . . . and added two of their own[:] . . . a prohibition of legislative or judicial creation of new treasons . . . [and the requirement of] two witnesses to the same overt act."[107] By "closely circumscribing the kind of conduct which should be treason," the Constitution diminished the risk of "perversion . . . to repress peaceful political opposition"; by imposing "procedural requirements" it reduced the risk of "conviction of the innocent as a result of perjury, passion, or inadequate evidence."[108]

The clause recognizing treason by "adhering to . . . Enemies, giving them Aid and Comfort," Jackson concluded, stated only one offense, not two. The first phrase required a treasonable intention, the second an act promoting it. Both conditions had to be met before the offense was complete:

> A citizen intellectually or emotionally may favor the enemy and harbor sympathies or convictions disloyal to this country's policy or interest, but so long as he commits no act of aid and comfort to the enemy, there is no treason. On the other hand, a citizen may take actions which do aid and comfort the enemy—making a speech critical of the government or opposing its measures, profiteering, striking in defense plants or essential work, and the hundred other things which impair our cohesion and diminish our strength—but if there is no adherence to the enemy in this, if there is no intent to betray, there is no treason.[109]

Cramer's own testimony showed that he had met with two of the saboteurs, that he had reason to suspect they had arrived clandestinely to further the enemy cause, and that one of them had given him $3,600 in cash for safe keeping.[110] Accepting the money, Justice Jackson conceded, was a highly suspicious act under the circumstances: "That such responsibilities are undertaken and such trust bestowed without the scratch of a pen to show it, implies some degree of mutuality and concert from which a jury could say that aid and comfort was given and was intended."[111] The Court found it unnecessary to decide, however, whether Cramer's testimony qualified as a "Confession in open Court" or as that of one of the two required witnesses, for the government had not submitted this transaction to the jury as one of the requisite "overt Act[s]."[112]

---

[107] *Id.* at 23-24; *cf.* J. HURST, *supra* note 101, at 126, 134 ("The basic policy of the treason clause written into the Constitution emerges from all the evidence available as a restrictive one. . . . [T]he debate . . . seems clearly to establish a general agreement on the wisdom of limiting the scope of the offense in all doubtful cases.").

[108] *Cramer,* 325 U.S. at 27-28. English law had long required two witnesses in treason cases; what was new was the requirement that both testify to "the same overt Act." Dean Wigmore explained the utility of the addition: "[T]he opportunity of detecting the falsity of the testimony, by sequestering the two witnesses . . . and exposing their variance in details, is wholly destroyed by permitting them to speak to different acts." 7 WIGMORE, EVIDENCE § 2037 (3d ed. 1940), *quoted in* J. HURST, *supra* note 101, at 217; *see also* 2 M. FARRAND, *supra* note 80, at 348 ("Docr Franklin wished this amendment to take place—prosecutions for treason were generally virulent; and perjury too easily made use of against innocence").

[109] *Cramer,* 325 U.S. at 29.

[110] *Id.* at 5.

[111] *Id.* at 39.

[112] *Id.* Justice Douglas relied heavily on Cramer's testimony in his dissent, *id.* at 63-67 (Douglas, J. dissenting), but Justice Jackson seems correct that submission of the case to the jury in a way that allowed them to

What the prosecution *had* relied on were the meetings between Cramer and the sabo-teurs—duly observed and testified to by two federal agents, as article III required. Though adequately proved, Justice Jackson concluded, the meetings themselves were not "overt Act[s]" within the meaning of the constitutional provision. Insisting that "[t]he very min-imum function that an overt act must perform in a treason prosecution is that it show sufficient action by the accused, in its setting, to sustain a finding that the accused actually gave aid and comfort to the enemy,"[113] Jackson observed:

> There is no two-witness proof of what they said. . . . There is no showing that Cramer gave them any information whatever of value to their mis-sion. . . . Cramer furnished them no shelter, nothing that can be called suste-nance or supplies, and there is no evidence that he gave them encouragement or counsel, or even paid for their drinks. . . . [Without looking beyond the testimony of the two witnesses] it is difficult to perceive any advantage which this meeting afforded to [the saboteurs] as enemies or how it strengthened Germany or weakened the United States. . . .[114]

This conclusion prompted an irate dissent by Justice Douglas, not generally perceived as hostile to the rights of the outcast, which Chief Justice Stone and Justices Black and Reed joined.[115] The Constitution, they emphasized, requires that two witnesses testify not to every fact necessary to make out the offense of treason, but only to a single "overt Act." As in the law of conspiracy, that "act, standing alone, may appear to be innocent or indif-ferent, such as joining a person at a table, stepping into a boat, or carrying a parcel of food." Thus, according to the dissent, "a meeting with the enemy" sufficed when, as in *Cramer,* other evidence demonstrated its "character and significance."[116]

Justice Douglas was right about the law of conspiracy,[117] and most treason cases before

---

convict on the basis of an "overt Act" not meeting the constitutional standard required reversal. *See id.* at 36 n.45 (explaining the refusal to decide whether an alternative overt act submitted to the jury—false statements to FBI agents after arrest—met the article III standard: "Since it is not possible to identify the grounds on which Cramer was convicted, the verdict must be set aside if any of the separable acts submitted was insufficient.") (citation omitted).

[113]*Id.* at 34 (footnotes omitted).

[114]*Id.* at 37-38. Hurst argued that the Court misapplied its own test since the second meeting "afforded the essential opportunity to transfer [the saboteur's] money" and found it difficult to understand the Court's describ-ing as "an 'apparently commonplace and insignificant act' a prearranged meeting with a known enemy agent for the probable purpose of undertaking the safekeeping of his funds." J. HURST, *supra* note 101, at 208, 216. In all this Hurst, like Justice Douglas in his dissent, *see infra* note 116 and accompanying text, relied on facts about the meeting that were not proved by two witnesses.

[115]*See Cramer,* 325 U.S. at 48-77 (Douglas, J., dissenting).

[116]*Id.* at 61-63 (Douglas, J., dissenting). For an approving view, see E. CORWIN, TOTAL WAR AND THE CONSTITUTION 123-27 (1947).

[117]*See* W. LAFAVE & A. SCOTT, CRIMINAL LAW 547-49 (2d ed. 1986).

> If the agreement has been established but the object has not been attained, virtually any act will satisfy the overt act requirement. Thus . . . an interview with a lawyer, attending a lawful meet-ing, . . . [and] making a phone call . . . have all been held to be overt acts in the context of the criminal object alleged.

*Id.* at 549.

*Cramer* had taken the same position.[118] It follows logically from the perception that the function of the "overt act" requirement is, as Justice Douglas argued, "to preclude punishment for . . . plans or schemes or hopes which have never moved out of the realm of thought or speech," which was plainly one of the principal aims of the Framers.[119]

In a 1919 opinion questioning the applicability of the conspiracy standard, however, Judge Learned Hand had called attention to an additional purpose reflected in the distinctive procedural requirements of the treason provision. "I doubt very much," Hand wrote, "whether that rule has any application to the case of treason, where the requirement affected the character of the pleading and proof, rather than accorded a season of repentance before the crime should be complete."[120] Justice Jackson agreed: "[T]he function we ascribe to the overt act is significant chiefly because it measures the two-witness rule protection to the accused," and this rule was designed in part to prevent "conviction of the innocent as a result of perjury, passion, or inadequate evidence."[121] If the government could "prove by two witnesses an apparently commonplace and insignificant act and from other circumstances create an inference that the act was a step in treason," noted Jackson, this purpose would be poorly served.[122]

Hand and Jackson may have had the better of this interesting dispute. In focusing on the purpose of the requirement that an overt act *occur*, Justice Douglas overlooked the purpose of the requirement that it be *proved* by two witnesses. "One witness shall not rise up against a man for any iniquity," says the Mosaic law; "at the mouth of two . . . [or] three witnesses, shall the matter be established."[123] This formulation required the "iniquity" itself, not simply an "overt act" toward its accomplishment, to be shown by more than one witness. The initial proposal before the Constitutional Convention suggested a comparable requirement: "No person shall be convicted of treason, unless on the testimony of two witnesses."[124] The stated reason for the amendment requiring that both witnesses testify "to the same overt act" was to make conviction more difficult, not less so.[125] Thus the Framers may have meant to require testimony by two witnesses to *the same act of treason*,[126] not to some innocuous act in furtherance of an allegedly treasonable design.

The decision in *Cramer*, rendered over the dissent of two of the Court's most vociferous civil libertarians, was an impressive blow for liberty and tolerance in a time too often characterized, as the cases so far discussed indicate, by their absence.[127] The triumph was

---

[118] *See* J. HURST, *supra* note 101, at 209 ("Such ordinary commercial transactions as purchasing goods, holding money on deposit, provisioning a ship, and borrowing from a bank have been held sufficient overt acts, where they were linked with an intention thereby to give aid and comfort to the enemy.").

[119] *Cramer*, 325 U.S. at 61 (Douglas J., dissenting); *see also* J. HURST, *supra* note 101, at 210 ("As soon as one requires the showing of some act reasonably advanced in the execution of the criminal intention the danger of prosecuting men for their thoughts alone has been met."); W. LAFAVE & A. SCOTT, *supra* note 117 at 548; *supra* text accompanying note 117.

[120] United States v. Robinson, 259 F. 685, 690 (S.D.N.Y. 1919), *quoted in Cramer*, 325 U.S. at 6.

[121] *Cramer*, 325 U.S. at 34, 27.

[122] *Id.* at 34.

[123] *Deuteronomy* 19:15, *quoted in Cramer*, 325 U.S. at 24 n.37.

[124] *See* 2 M. FARRAND, *supra* note 80, at 182, *quoted in Cramer*, 325 U.S. at 22.

[125] *See supra* note 108 (quoting Dr. Franklin).

[126] Jackson himself declined to go quite this far, saying only that this position "would place on the overt act the whole burden of establishing a complete treason." *Cramer*, 325 U.S. at 34.

[127] Not surprisingly, Hurst viewed the decision from the opposite perspective: "[T]he majority opinion . . . has cast such a net of ambiguous limitations about the crime of 'treason' that it is doubtful whether a careful

somewhat muted, however, by the Court's intimation that Cramer might have been punished for some other crime on the same record, if Congress had so provided.[128] In so saying, Justice Jackson echoed Chief Justice Marshall's words of over a century before[129] and quoted Rufus King's observation at the Constitutional Convention that the "controversy . . . might be of less magnitude than was supposed; as the legislature might punish capitally under other names than Treason."[130]

This passage raises questions about the treason provision even more fundamental than those resolved in *Cramer* itself. Surely Justice Jackson was correct in adding that the cherished substantive and procedural protections of article III could not be evaded simply by changing the name of the crime.[131] Surely he was also right in rejecting the position that nothing less than treason was punishable at all.[132] Yet strong arguments have been made that the Framers *did* mean to forbid punishment of mere "treasonable" *words* under

---

prosecutor will ever again chance an indictment under that head." J. HURST, *supra* note 101, at 218. This assessment seemed unduly lugubrious in light of the Court's discussion of the unsubmitted overt act of accepting the saboteur's money, *see supra* text accompanying note 110, and Hurst's later work showed that ten more treason cases arising out of the Second World War were pressed to conviction. *See* J. HURST, *supra* note 101, at 236.

[128] "Of course we do not intimate that Congress could dispense with the two-witness rule merely by giving the same offense another name. But the power of Congress is in no way limited to enact prohibitions of specified acts thought detrimental to our wartime safety." *Cramer*, 325 U.S. at 45.

[129] *See Ex parte* Bollman, 8 U.S. (4 Cranch) 46 (1807).

> Crimes so atrocious as those which have for their object the subversion by violence of those laws and those institutions which have been ordained in order to secure the peace and happiness of society, are not to escape punishment because they have not ripened into treason. The wisdom of the legislature is competent to provide for the case. . . .

*Id.* at 77.

[130] 2 M. FARRAND, *supra* note 80, at 347, *quoted in Cramer*, 325 U.S. at 45.

[131] *See supra* note 128. Chief Justice Marshall seemed to think the important thing was that the legislature formulate specific rules rather than leave the matter to ad hoc judicial interpretation:

> [T]he framers of our constitution . . . must have conceived it more safe, that punishment [in cases not meeting the constitutional definition] should be ordained by general laws, formed upon deliberation, under the influence of no resentments, and without knowing on whom they were to operate, than that it should be inflicted under the influence of those passions which the occasion seldom fails to excite, and which a flexible definition of the crime, or a construction which would render it flexible, might bring into operation.

*Bollman*, 8 U.S. (4 Cranch) at 77. But the Convention also rejected a proposal that would have empowered Congress itself to define treason. *See* 2 M. FARRAND, *supra* note 80, at 136. It seemed for adequate reasons to have trusted Congress no more than the courts.

[132] *See Cramer*, 325 U.S. at 45 ("Congress repeatedly has enacted prohibitions of specific acts thought to endanger our security. . . ."); *see also* J. HURST, *supra* note 101, at 151 ("There is no evidence that the word was used in the Constitution with intent to exclude the creation of all possible varieties and degrees of subversive crime except the levying of war and adherence to enemies."); *Ex parte* Quirin, 317 U.S. 1, 38 (1942) (rejecting on the basis of a not wholly convincing analogy to double jeopardy the contention that attempted sabotage by an American citizen on behalf of an enemy could be prosecuted only as treason), *discussed in* J. HURST, *supra* note 101, at 147-48. Possible reasons suggested by Hurst for forbidding punishment of acts short of the constitutional definition only as treason include "the peculiar intimidation and stigma carried by the mere accusation of treason," "the characteristic severity of the punishment," and the since abandoned view that Congress would have no authority to punish any offenses beyond the few expressly mentioned in the Constitution. *See* J. HURST, *supra* note 101, at 149-50, 155-56, 181-82.

any label; otherwise their central goal of eliminating punishment for acts earlier viewed as "constructive" treason would not have been achieved.[133]

Thus *Cramer* by no means put an end to controversies over the treason provision. But it did an impressive job with the troublesome issues the case itself presented.


## IV. Price Control

Wars create a demand for goods and services and thus tend to increase prices. Less than two months after the bombing of Pearl Harbor, "when it was common knowledge . . . that there was grave danger of wartime inflation,"[134] Congress passed the Emergency Price Control Act, authorizing a new Office of Price Administration (OPA) to fix maximum prices and rents for a limited period.[135]

Emergency price limitation had survived due process scrutiny in much more hostile times,[136] and the revolution of the 1930s seemed to remove any doubts on that score.[137] The World War I precedent upholding federal prohibition of liquor manufacture[138] assured the validity of *federal* price control as a war measure, even if after *Wickard v. Filburn*[139] there was still room to argue it was not necessary and proper to the regulation of interstate and foreign commerce. The interesting constitutional questions concerned the manner in which Congress had sought to achieve its goal.

[133]*See* J. HURST, *supra* note 101, at 141, 152, 166.

> [T]he historic policy restrictive of the scope of "treason" under the Constitution was most con-
> sciously based on the fear of extension of the offense to penalize types of conduct familiar in the
> normal processes of the struggle for domestic political or economic power. . . . [T]he record does
> suggest that the clause was intended to guarantee nonviolent political processes against any theory
> or charge, the burden of which was the allegedly seditious character of the conduct in question.
>
> . . .
>
> The historic background of the treason clause furnishes a basis never yet adequately examined,
> for a reconsideration of the constitutionality of such legislation as the federal Espionage Act and
> state legislation [*sic*] against "criminal syndicalism" insofar as these are directed primarily against
> utterances.

*Id.; see also* Mayton, *Seditious Libel and the Lost Guarantee of a Freedom of Expression,* 84 COLUM. L. REV. 91 (1984). In Frohwerk v. United States, 249 U.S. 204, 210 (1919), Justice Holmes rejected an argument to this effect with the curt observation that "[t]hese suggestions seem to us to need no more than to be stated."

[134]Yakus v. United States, 321 U.S. 414, 432 (1944).

[135]Pub. L. No. 421, 56 Stat. 23 (codified at 50 U.S.C. app §§ 901-946 (Supp. V 1946)); *see also Yakus,* 321 U.S. at 419-21.

[136]*See* Block v. Hirsh, 256 U.S. 135 (1921), p. 79 *supra.*

[137]*See, e.g.,* Olsen v. Nebraska, 313 U.S. 236 (1941) (enunciating permissive standard in upholding limita-tion of employment agency fees); West Coast Hotel Co. v. Parrish, 300 U.S. 379 (1937) (overruling decisions outlawing minimun wage legislation); Nebbia v. New York, 291 U.S. 502 (1934) (eliminating the general re-quirement that the industry regulated be one especially "affected with a public interest" in upholding minimum prices for milk); pp. 236, 239-40 *supra.* In Bowles v. Willingham, 321 U.S. 503, 516-19 (1944) (Douglas, J.), the Court accordingly rejected due process objections to World War II rent control despite the argument that "generally fair and equitable" rents might be unfair "as applied to a particular landlord."

[138]Hamilton v. Kentucky Distilleries & Warehouse Corp., 251 U.S. 146 (1919), pp. 99-100 *supra.*

[139]317 U.S. 111 (1942) (upholding federal limitation of wheat grown for on-farm consumption); *see also* pp. 236-38 *supra.*

## A.  Delegation

The Emergency Price Control Act directed the administrator to establish prices that "in his judgment" were "generally fair and equitable" and "effectuated the purposes of [the] Act," which were set out in detail in section 1(a).[140] In so doing, "[s]o far as practicable," he was to "ascertain and give due consideration to the prices prevailing between October 1 and October 15, 1941" and to "make adjustments for such relevant factors as he may determine and deem to be of general applicability, including . . . general increases or decreases in cost of production, distribution, and transportation."[141]

Alone among the nine Justices in *Yakus v. United States*,[142] Justice Roberts believed the statute unlawfully delegated legislative power vested in Congress by article I. Focusing on the general statements of purpose in §1(a) of the statute, Roberts concluded: "[t]he act sets no limits upon the discretion or judgment of the Administrator. His commission is to take any action with respect to prices which he believes will preserve what he deems a sound economy during the emergency. . . ."[143] In practical effect, Roberts lamented, "*Schechter Corp. v. United States*"[144]—where the Court had struck down a statute read as authorizing the President to do whatever was necessary to bring business out of the depression—"is now overruled."[145]

In contrast to *Schechter,* said Chief Justice Stone for the majority, in the price legislation at issue in *Yakus* Congress had "laid down standards to guide the administrative determination of both the occasions for the exercise of the price-fixing power, and the particular prices to be established."[146] "The directions that the prices fixed shall be fair and equitable, that in addition they shall tend to promote the purposes of the Act, and that in promulgating them consideration shall be given to prices prevailing in a stated base period," he argued, "confer no greater reach for administrative determination" than a flock of provisions the Court had upheld both before and after *Schechter.*[147]

Contrary to popular rumor,[148] *Yakus* is scant evidence of the demise of the salutary nondelegation doctrine. Congress had clearly enunciated the governing policy: price levels prevailing in October 1941 were basically to be preserved, with adjustments for chang-

---

[140] 50 U.S.C. app. §§ 901(a), 902(a) (Supp. V. 1941-1946).

[141] *Id.* § 502(a).

[142] 321 U.S. 414 (1944).

[143] *Id.* at 451 (Roberts, J., dissenting).

[144] 295 U.S. 495 (1935).

[145] *Yakus,* 321 U.S. at 451-52 (Roberts, J., dissenting) (citing Schechter Poultry Corp. v. United States, 295 U.S. 495 (1935) (striking down a grant of authority to promulgate "codes of fair competition" for various industries)), pp. 218-19 *supra; see also* Bowles v. Willingham, 321 U.S. 503, 530-42 (1944) (Roberts, J., dissenting).

[146] *Yakus,* 321 U.S. at 423.

[147] *Id.* at 427; *see also* L. JAFFE, JUDICIAL CONTROL OF ADMINISTRATIVE ACTION 71 (1965) ("There are still differences of degree between the NRA on the one hand . . . and the OPA on the other."). In unnecessarily distinguishing *Schechter* on the additional ground that the "function of formulating the codes" in that case had been delegated to "private individuals," *Yakus,* 321 U.S. at 424, Chief Justice Stone seemed to overlook the fact that the statute had vested the more significant power to *promulgate* the codes in the President.

[148] *See, e.g.,* E. GELLHORN & B. BOYER, ADMINISTRATIVE LAW AND PROCESS IN A NUTSHELL 19-20 (2d ed. 1981).

ing costs.[149] Applying such a legislative policy to the myriad goods and services offered in the market is what the execution of the laws is all about.[150]

Justice Roberts had shown a notable ability to adapt to changing times in voting at last to uphold New Deal measures against federalistic and due process objections.[151] In *Yakus* he showed he was not wholly in tune with the times by voting to strike down a delegation easily sustainable under the criteria applicable even when he was appointed. Five years earlier, in the company of Justices McReynolds and Butler, he had dissented from decisions upholding a very similar delegation to set milk prices.[152] On this issue Roberts was, if nothing else, consistent.

## B.   Judicial Review

The Emergency Price Control Act authorized any person subject to a price regulation or order to file a protest with the administrator within sixty days after its promulgation, or later in the case of grounds arising after the original sixty days expired.[153] Any person aggrieved by the denial of such a protest might within thirty days file a complaint with the Emergency Court of Appeals to enjoin enforcement of the challenged limitation, subject to Supreme Court review. "Except as provided in this section," however, the act added that "no court . . . shall have jurisdiction or power to consider the validity of such regulation, order, or price schedule, or to stay, restrain, enjoin, or set aside . . . any [relevant] provision of this Act. . . ."[154] The Supreme Court took this jurisdictional restriction literally and upheld it against constitutional objections in two interesting opinions by Chief Justice Stone.

The first was *Lockerty v. Phillips*,[155] a suit brought in federal district court to enjoin enforcement of OPA regulations setting maximum wholesale beef prices alleged to be so low as to deprive the plaintiffs of their property without due process of law. Relying on the jurisdictional limitation, the district court dismissed, and the Supreme Court unanimously affirmed.[156]

This was easy. Although Chief Justice Stone's invocation of the compromise that permitted but did not require Congress to create lower federal courts suggested that they

---

[149] *See supra* text accompanying note 141.

[150] Stone's focus upon a court's ability "to ascertain whether the will of Congress has been obeyed" in reviewing a particular price order, *Yakus*, 321 U.S. at 426, seems to miss the main point of the delegation doctrine. A delegation of *all* Congress's power would make it easy to determine whether the agency had exceeded its statutory mandate, but would hardly comport with the Framers' vision that basic policy should be made by elected representatives. *See* pp. 16-19 *supra* (discussing Field v. Clark, 143 U.S. 649 (1892)).

[151] *See* pp. 236-40 *supra*.

[152] *See* United States v. Rock Royal Coop., Inc., 307 U.S. 533, 583-87 (1939) (Roberts, J., dissenting); *see also* H. P. Hood & Sons, Inc. v. United States, 307 U.S. 588, 603-08 (1939) (Roberts, J., dissenting). Chief Justice Stone gave surprisingly little weight to this precedent in *Yakus*, 321 U.S. at 423-27; Justice Douglas gave it appropriate billing in a companion case upholding a similar authorization to fix rents in areas where defense activities had created inflationary pressures. *See* Bowles v. Willingham, 321 U.S. 503, 512-16 (1944).

[153] Pub. L. No. 421, § 203, 56 Stat. 23, 31 (codified at 50 U.S.C. app. §§ 901-946 (Supp. V. 1946)).

[154] *Id.*

[155] 319 U.S. 182, 184-87 (1943).

[156] *Id.* at 189.

might have been closed altogether to such claims,[157] it was unnecessary to go this far. The Emergency Court of Appeals, an article III tribunal whose members were drawn from the regular courts, had jurisdiction under the statute to enjoin unconstitutional regulations, and "[t]here is nothing in the Constitution which requires Congress to confer equity jurisdiction on any particular inferior federal court."[158]

*Yakus,* already discussed in connection with delegation, presented a harder case. The defendant had been criminally prosecuted for violating the wholesale beef regulations, and the district court had refused to hear arguments against their validity.[159] Once again the Supreme Court affirmed, this time over a powerful dissent by Justice Rutledge, which Justice Murphy joined.[160]

"It is one thing," said Rutledge, "for Congress [as in *Lockerty*] to withhold jurisdiction. It is entirely another to confer it and direct that it be exercised in a manner inconsistent with constitutional requirements or, what in some instances may be the same thing, without regard to them."[161] The Constitution may not guarantee that judges can hear cases brought to keep other branches within their constitutional limits, but on even the narrowest view of *Marbury v. Madison*[162] they may not themselves be required to violate the Constitution.[163]

As Henry Hart pointed out in his famous dialogue, the majority did not argue that, by virtue of its power to limit jurisdiction, Congress could order the Court to act unconstitutionally: "*Yakus* . . . dealt directly with the scope of constitutional rights, with no nonsense about any question being foreclosed by the power to regulate jurisdiction."[164] Chief Justice Stone concluded that the statutory review procedure had afforded Yakus an adequate opportunity to obtain judicial review of the validity of the regulations: "No procedural principle is more familiar to this Court than that a constitutional right may be for-

---

[157]*See id.* at 187 ("Article III left Congress free to establish inferior federal courts or not as it thought appropriate. It could have declined to create any such courts, leaving suitors to the remedies afforded by state courts, with such appellate review by this Court as Congress might prescribe." (citation omitted)); *see also* Sheldon v. Sill, 49 U.S. (8 How.) 441 (1850); 1 M. Farrand, *supra* note 80, at 124-25. Chief Justice Stone did not suggest, however, that if Congress had closed the federal courts it could have closed state courts as well. The closing of *all* courts to a constitutional claim, in light of Marbury v. Madison, 5 U.S. (1 Cranch) 137 (1803), arguably would have effectively denied a constitutional right. *See* The First Hundred Years at 27, 304-05.

[158]*Lockerty,* 319 U.S. at 187. For the composition of the Emergency Court, see § 204(c) of the act, 56 Stat. 32 (1942).

[159]*Yakus,* 321 U.S. 414, 418-19 (1944); *see supra* notes 142-52 and accompanying text.

[160]*Id.* at 460-89. Justice Roberts's separate dissent went solely to the issue of delegation. Roberts, J., dissenting); *supra* text accompanying notes 142-45.

[161]*Yakus,* 321 U.S. at 468 (Rutledge, J., dissenting).

[162]5 U.S. (1 Cranch) 137 (1803).

[163]*See id.* at 177-78; Chicago, M. & P. St. Ry. v. Minnesota, 134 U.S. 418 (1890), pp. 41-44 *supra*; United States v. Klein, 80 U.S. (13 Wall.) 128 (1872), The First Hundred Years at 308-11; Hart, *The Power of Congress to Limit the Jurisdiction of Federal Courts: An Exercise in Dialectic,* 66 Harv. L. Rev. 1362, 1378-79 (1953):

> Name me a single Supreme Court case that has squarely held that, in a civil enforcement proceeding, questions of law can be validly withdrawn from the consideration of the enforcement court where no adequate opportunity to have them determined by a court has been previously accorded. When you do, I'm going back to re-think *Marbury v. Madison.*

[164]Hart, *supra* note 163, at 1379.

feited in criminal as well as civil cases by the failure to make timely assertion of the right before a tribunal having jurisdiction to determine it." [165]

Stringent time limits for challenging judicial or quasi-judicial orders have long been common. [166] When the complaining party is singled out as a party to a proceeding and served personally with the resulting order, there is no unfairness in requiring him to challenge it within a short period or not at all. As Justice Rutledge argued, however, it is quite another matter to extend this principle to persons seeking to challenge regulations of general applicability. [167] Not everyone affected by such a regulation will have participated in rule-making proceedings or will hear about the requirement as soon as it is adopted. Indeed, persons who go into the affected business after the time for challenge expires arguably have no opportunity to object at all. [168]

Influenced perhaps by the unfairness of this draconian provision, Congress repealed it after two years. [169] Later Congresses, however, have made wholesale use of the precedent in imposing similar limitations on judicial review of ordinary pollution control regulations. [170] There is not yet a requirement that constitutional challenges to federal statutes be made within sixty days after their enactment. One hopes that, if there were, the Court would limit the harsh decision in *Yakus* to "the urgency and exigencies of wartime price regulation" on which Chief Justice Stone expressly relied. [171]

[165] *Yakus*, 321 U.S. at 444.

[166] *See, e.g.*, 28 U.S.C. § 2107 (1982) (appeal of district-court judgments); 15 U.S.C. § 45(c) (1982) (cease-and-desist orders of Federal Trade Commission).

[167] *Yakus*, 321 U.S. at 472 (Rutledge, J., dissenting) (distinguishing judicial examples on the ground that "the previous opportunity is in an earlier phase of the same proceeding, not as here a separate and independent one of wholly different character"). Yet Justice Rutledge oddly thought the opportunity to institute a "separate and independent" proceeding *was* adequate to preclude judicial review of OPA regulations in *civil* enforcement proceedings. "Since in these cases the rights involved are rights of property, not of personal liberty or life as in criminal proceedings, the consequences, though serious, are not of the same moment under our system, as appears from the fact they are not secured by the same procedural protections in trial." Bowles v. Willingham, 321 U.S. 503, 525 (1944) (Rutledge, J., concurring).

[168] One hopes that the Court in such a case would invoke the statutory provision permitting tardy challenges on "grounds" arising after expiration of the sixty-day period, though the language of the statute seems directed more toward the arguments for invalidity than toward the standing of the complaining party. § 203(a), 56 Stat. 31; *see also* D. CURRIE, AIR POLLUTION: FEDERAL LAW AND ANALYSIS, § 9.15 (1981).

[169] Stabilization Extension Act of 1944, ch. 325, tit. I, § 107, 58 Stat. 639.

[170] *E.g.*, 42 U.S.C. § 7607(b)(1)(1982)(attacks on validity of certain air pollution regulations may be made only by petition in court of appeals within sixty days and not in civil or criminal enforcement proceedings).

[171] *See Yakus*, 321 U.S. at 435. In a less controversial part of the same opinion, Chief Justice Stone appropriately invoked decisions permitting the collection of taxes, Phillips v. Commissioner, 283 U.S. 589 (1931), and the destruction of allegedly contaminated food, North Am. Cold Storage Co. v. Chicago, 211 U.S. 306 (1908), before hearing in sustaining a provision forbidding injunctive relief against unauthorized price regulations until after trial. *See Yakus*, 321 U.S. at 437-43. Justice Rutledge did not quarrel with this conclusion. *Id.* at 466 (Rutledge, J., dissenting); *see also* Bowles v. Willingham, 321 U.S. 503, 519-21 (1944) (reaffirming that no hearing was required before promulgation of rent limitations of general applicability: "To require hearings for thousands of landlords before any rent control order could be made effective might have defeated the program of price control.").

In Case v. Bowles, 327 U.S. 92, 101 (1946), the Court held that OPA price limitations could constitutionally be applied to sales of timber by a state to raise money for educational purposes. Declining the reasonable invitation to invoke precedents permitting federal taxation of proprietary state activities, *see* Allen v. Regents of Univ. System, 304 U.S. 439, 451-52 (1938) (revenue from state-university football games), on the ground that this "criterion . . . has proved to be unworkable," Justice Black said only that "an absence of federal power to fix

## V. SELECTIVE SERVICE

Like wartime price regulation, compulsory military service had long been recognized as constitutional.[172] Like those of the contemporaneous price control law, however, the procedural provisions of the World War II draft law raised troublesome constitutional questions. The difficulties were illustrated by litigation that arose when local draft boards denied the requests of three Jehovah's Witnesses for classification as "ministers of religion" statutorily exempt from all forms of compulsory service.

In *Falbo v. United States*,[173] the board had classified the applicant as a conscientious objector and ordered him to report for alternative civilian service. In a criminal prosecution for disobeying the order, the district court refused to decide whether the board had erred in rejecting the claim for ministerial exemption, and the Supreme Court affirmed.[174]

In the context of "the need which [Congress] felt for mobilizing national manpower in the shortest practicable period," noted Justice Black for the majority, the omission of any provision for judicial review of an order to report for service must have been deliberate: "Against this background the complete absence of any provision for such challenges in the very section providing for prosecution of violations in the civil courts permits no other inference than that Congress did not intend they could be made."[175] Justice Murphy spoke eloquently in construing the statute differently,[176] but none of the Justices suggested there was any constitutional problem.

---

maximum prices for state sales or to control rents charged by a State might result in depriving Congress of ability effectively to prevent the evil of inflation" and render "the constitutional grant of the power to make war . . . inadequate to accomplish its full purpose." *Case,* 327 U.S. at 101-02. In so reasoning, Justice Black was in line with other cases of the period upholding federal regulation of state activities, none of which had stressed the proprietary nature of the regulated activity. *See* California v. United States, 320 U.S. 577, 586 (1944) (Frankfurter, J.) (Shipping Act ban on preferences applied to state-owned marine terminal); United States v. California, 297 U.S. 175, 183-85 (1936) (Stone, J.) (Safety Appliance Act applied to state-owned railroad), p. 234, note 156 *supra.* Justice Black, however, gave no hint that state sovereignty ever implicitly limited federal authority, as had consistently been recognized in decisions involving both suits against and taxes upon the states. *See, e.g.,* New York v. United States, 326 U.S. 572 (1946) (upholding federal tax on state sale of mineral water over a dissent by Douglas in which Black joined, but with all Justices insisting that some state tax immunity remained); Monaco v. Mississippi, 292 U.S. 313 (1934) (foreign nation may not sue state in federal court); Hans v. Louisiana, 134 U.S. 1 (1890), pp. 7-9 *supra*; Collector v. Day, 78 U.S. (11 Wall.) 113 (1871), THE FIRST HUNDRED YEARS at 355. Finding the constitutional question in *Case* to involve "substantial intrusions on the sovereignty of the States," Justice Douglas dissented, opting for a construction of the rather unambiguous statute that would avoid reaching the issue. *See Case,* 327 U.S. at 103 (Douglas, J., dissenting); Hulbert v. Twin Falls County, 327 U.S. 103, 105-06 (1946) (Douglas, J., dissenting).

[172] *See* Selective Draft Law Cases, 245 U.S. 366 (1918) (invoking persuasive historical materials in holding draft within war power and unaffected by thirteenth amendment ban on involuntary servitude), p. 100, note 62 *supra,* & p. 106, note 98.

[173] 320 U.S. 549 (1944).

[174] *Id.* at 549-51.

[175] *Id.* at 554–55

[176] *See id.* at 557, 560-61 (Murphy, J., dissenting):

The power to administer complete justice and to consider all reasonable pleas and defenses must be presumed in the absence of legislation to the contrary. . . .

That an individual should languish in prison for five years without being accorded the opportunity of proving that the prosecution was based upon arbitrary and illegal administrative action is not in keeping with the high standards of our judicial system.

The problem was that to which Justice Rutledge would soon call attention in *Yakus*: here, too, a court was required to punish a man for violating an order whose validity it could not question. Indeed the statute in *Falbo* lacked even the controversial procedure for Emergency Court of Appeals review that had shielded the price control provisions from constitutional attack. Unlike *Yakus*, Falbo had had no previous opportunity whatsoever to challenge in court the order he was charged with violating.

*Estep v. United States,*[177] decided two years after *Falbo,* showed that the Court was not insensitive to this difficulty. Profiting from Falbo's failure, Estep and his fellow petitioner had reported to the induction station after their requests for ministerial classifications were denied, had been accepted for actual service, and only then had refused to be inducted. This time, by a five-to-three vote, the Court held that the validity of the classifications should have been reviewed in the criminal proceedings.[178]

Justice Douglas's majority opinion in *Estep* reads like Justice Murphy's dissent in *Falbo:*

> [T]he silence of Congress as to judicial review is not necessarily to be construed as a denial of the power of the federal courts to grant relief in the exercise of the general jurisdiction which Congress has conferred upon them. . . . We cannot readily infer that Congress departed so far from the traditional concepts of a fair trial . . . as to provide that a citizen of this country should go to jail for not obeying an unlawful order of an administrative agency.[179]

*Falbo* was distinguished on the ground, hinted at in the earlier opinion, that Falbo had not exhausted his administrative remedies by giving the authorities the opportunity to reject him at the induction center.[180]

The tone of each of the two opinions is strikingly different. Nevertheless, in light of *Estep*, the draft registrant did have an opportunity to challenge the classification order without submitting to it after all. Thus the majority did not have to reach the constitutional question.[181]

Relying heavily on a statutory provision making the classification decisions of local boards "final," Chief Justice Stone and Justices Frankfurter and Burton disagreed, without suggesting that their interpretation raised any constitutional problem.[182] "Three Justices of

---

[177] 327 U.S. 114 (1946).

[178] *Id.* at 116-17.

[179] *Id.* at 120, 122.

[180] *See id.* at 123; *see also Falbo,* 320 U.S. at 553.

[181] Later cases would raise the interesting question whether a registrant was entitled to injunctive relief to challenge his classification on the ground that the adverse consequences of a wrong guess made violation of the order an inadequate method of judicial review; but no such contention was made in *Falbo* or *Estep. See* Oestereich v. Selective Serv. Sys., 393 U.S. 233, 240-43 (1968) (Harlan, J., concurring); *cf. Ex parte* Young, 209 U.S. 123, 145-48 (1908) (severe criminal penalties unconstitutionally restricted judicial review of railroad rate order).

[182] *See Estep,* 327 U.S. at 134-46 (Frankfurter, J., concurring in the result on unrelated grounds; Burton, J. & Stone, C. J., dissenting). The majority, noting that the statute made board decisions final only if made "within their respective jurisdictions," argued somewhat artificially that a board acting "in the teeth of the regulations" would "exceed its jurisdiction." *Id.* at 120-21. The result was a rather narrow scope of judicial review: "The decisions . . . made in conformity with the regulations are final even though they may be erroneous. The question

the Supreme Court of the United States," wrote Hart indignantly, "were willing to assume that Congress had power . . . to direct courts created under Article III to employ the judicial power . . . to convict a man of a crime and send him to jail without his ever having had a chance to make his defenses."[183]

Justice Murphy, as usual, protested that such a course would be unconstitutional.[184] Justice Rutledge invoked his dissenting opinion in *Yakus:* if Congress could not "make it a crime . . . to violate an administrative order without affording an *adequate* opportunity to show its constitutional invalidity," a fortiori it could not do so without affording any opportunity for challenge at all.[185]

Rutledge overstated his case somewhat; as the dissenting Justices noted, a registrant could challenge his classification by petitioning for habeas corpus after submitting to induction.[186] Hart protested that to rely on the availability of habeas corpus to justify denial of an earlier hearing "turns an ultimate safeguard of law into an excuse for its violation."[187] There were plenty of examples in which pressing public need had justified postponing a hearing until after the government had acted,[188] but what is good enough for destruction of allegedly contaminated food might arguably be insufficient when personal liberty is at stake.

Insofar as the defenses in *Estep* rested upon *statutory* claims for exemption from compulsory service,[189] the constitutional argument for review by the convicting court was somewhat more complicated than it had been in *Yakus*. When a court convicts without considering a constitutional objection to the order whose violation gave rise to the charge, it arguably offends the substantive provision invoked by the defense. Absent a constitutional objection to the order, however, the most obvious argument is that conviction without entertaining the defense is inconsistent with procedural due process. By modern standards, due process requires *some* opportunity to object to the individualized deprivation of a right to which one is entitled by statute.[190] Less clear, despite limited judicial authority so suggesting, is why a quasi-judicial hearing before the administrative body itself would not satisfy the constitutional standard.[191] To the extent that an attempt is made to satisfy the due process requirement in the administrative process, however, *Crowell v. Benson*[192]

---

of jurisdiction . . . is reached only if there is no basis in fact for the classification. . . ." *Id.* at 122-23. Justice Murphy, concurring, gave the finality provision even less weight: "This merely determines the point of administrative finality, leaving to the courts the ultimate and historic duty of judging the validity of the 'final' administrative orders which they are called on to enforce. . . ." *Id.* at 128.

[183] Hart, *supra* note 163, at 1382.

[184] *Estep,* 327 U.S. at 125 (Murphy, J., concurring) (invoking due process of law).

[185] *Id.* at 133 (Rutledge, J., concurring) (emphasis added).

[186] *See id.* at 146 (Burton, J., dissenting).

[187] Hart, *supra* note 163, at 1382.

[188] *See supra* note 171 (discussing the prohibition of interlocutory relief in *Yakus*).

[189] *See* Hamilton v. Regents of the University of California, 293 U.S. 245 (1934) (although distinguishable, suggesting that there was no valid constitutional claim to exemption).

[190] *See, e.g.,* Goldberg v. Kelly, 397 U.S. 254 (1970) (because welfare benefits are a matter of statutory entitlement, a pretermination hearing is necessary to meet procedural due process requirements), pp. 539-40 *infra*.

[191] *See* Ng Fung Ho v. White, 259 U.S. 276 (1922), (person ordered deported after quasi-judicial hearing entitled to judicial redetermination of citizenship claim), *supra* p. 146, note 60.

[192] 285 U.S. 22 (1932).

suggests a further argument: article III's requirement that federal judicial power be exercised by tenured judges permits quasi-judicial resolution of matters falling within that article only if questions of law are reviewable by an article III court.[193]

The Court's construction of the statute to permit judicial review in *Estep* made it possible to postpone decision of these vexing questions. Like the price control decisions, the draft cases highlighted the absence of any explicit constitutional guarantee of judicial review of administrative action.[194] How far Congress can go in making such action final remains one of the great unanswered questions in U.S. constitutional law.[195]

In short, the war produced a number of governmental actions difficult to reconcile with our libertarian traditions—military trials, deportation and internment of citizens accused of no offenses, and draconian limitations on judicial review of administrative action. In each of these areas the Supreme Court interfered only when the inconsistency with fundamental principles became patent, and even then without invoking the rather hazy limits of the Constitution. By and large, however, it was not the Court but the other branches of government that were less than zealous in protecting our basic liberties.[196]

---

[193] *Id.* at 54 (dictum) ("[T]he reservation of full authority to the court to deal with matters of law provides for the appropriate exercise of the judicial function in this class of cases."); *see* pp. 214-15 *supra*.

[194] *Cf.* Basic Law of the Federal Republic of Germany, art. 19(4) ("Should any person's right be violated by public authority, recourse to the court shall be open to him.").

[195] *See* L. Jaffe, *supra* note 147, at 381-89.

[196] Mason's assessment was rosier still:

> [T]he amazing thing is not that so much freedom was sacrificed on the altar of military necessity during World War II, but that more was not. Even in the time of greatest stress, the Justices upheld the citizen's liberty to think, speak, and act to an extent that the nation at peace has sometimes felt it could ill afford to maintain.

A. Mason, *supra* note 13, at 698. *Contra* J. tenBroek, *supra* note 51, at 220 (arguing that in the Japanese-American cases the Court "carried judicial self-restraint to the point of judicial abdication"); J. Howard, *supra* note 36, at 377-78 ("Despite articulation of a stricter policy of review over military trial of civilians in *Duncan v. Kahanamoku*, the Court did little to dispel the belief that total war had eroded constitutional barriers irrevocably.").

# 10

# The Preferred-Position Debate

While the Supreme Court grappled with questions arising out of the Second World War, ordinary life went on. In a large number of decisions more remote from the emotions and uncertainties of war, the Court cemented the gains of the New Deal revolution and made further progress in defining the contours of civil rights and liberties that it had begun to draw under the leadership of Chief Justice Hughes.

In addressing the familiar economic issues that had dominated the docket before that revolution, the Justices largely confirmed the *Washington Post*'s sunny prediction that " 'for years to come there would be virtual unanimity on the tribunal.' "[1] None of the brethren objected when, in *Wickard v. Filburn*,[2] a congressional limitation of the wheat a farmer could plant for his own use was upheld under the commerce clause, even though the transaction was neither interstate nor commerce.[3] None complained when, after the addition of vitamins had eliminated any legitimate health concern, the second *Carolene*

---

[1] *See* G. DUNNE, HUGO BLACK AND THE JUDICIAL REVOLUTION 204 (1977).

[2] 317 U.S. 111 (1942).

[3] "[I]f we assume that it is never marketed, it supplies a need of the man who grew it which would otherwise be reflected by purchases in the open market. Home-grown wheat in this sense competes with wheat in commerce." *Id.* at 128 (Jackson, J., for a unanimous Court); *see also* A. B. Kirschbaum Co. v. Walling, 316 U.S. 517 (1942) (Frankfurter, J., over a dissent by Roberts, J.) (holding Fair Labor Standards Act's wage and hour regulations applied, inter alia, to elevator operators in building whose tenants manufactured goods for interstate shipment); Dodd, *The Supreme Court and Fair Labor Standards, 1941-1945*, 59 HARV. L. REV. 321, 324-34 (1946); Stern, *The Commerce Clause and the National Economy, 1933–1946* (pt. 2), 59 HARV. L. REV. 883, 901-09 (1946) (applauding the decision).

The Court also unanimously held that Congress could regulate insurance despite three-quarters of a century of unpersuasive precedent that it was not commerce even if interstate. *See* Paul v. Virginia, 75 U.S. (8 Wall.) 168, 183 (1868), THE FIRST HUNDRED YEARS at 352. In a companion case, however, four Justices insisted that Congress could do so only because insurance *affected* interstate commerce, thereby avoiding a disruption of established schemes of state regulation. *See* United States v. South-Eastern Underwriters Ass'n, 322 U.S. 533, 552-53 (1944) (Black, J., writing for four of the seven participating Justices) (holding Sherman Act applied to insurance). *But see id.* at 562-83 (Stone, C. J., dissenting); *id.* at 583-84 (Frankfurter, J., dissenting); *id.* at 584-

*Products* decision rejected due process objections to a ban on interstate transportation of "filled" milk on the ground that it was "disputable" whether mere regulation could remove the danger of confusion with "the natural product."[4] The methods employed in the exercise of congressional powers, wrote Justice Reed in the latter case, "are beyond attack without a clear and convincing showing that there is no rational basis for the legislation."[5]

In the first *Carolene Products* decision, however, Justice Stone had suggested that the Court might more strictly scrutinize measures falling "within a specific prohibition . . . such as those of the first ten amendments," or "restrict[ing] those political processes which can ordinarily be expected to bring about repeal of undesirable legislation," or directed against "discrete and insular minorities."[6] The civil rights and civil liberties decisions of the 1930s seemed to bear out this suggestion.[7] In grappling with cases in Stone's preferred categories, however, great differences of opinion developed among Justices who had been unanimous in upholding ordinary economic legislation.[8]

## I. The Opening of the Rift

### A. Obstructing Justice

Soon after Stone became Chief Justice, differences of opinion among the Justices erupted in *Bridges v. California*,[9] where the Court split five to four over the constitutionality of contempt convictions for statements allegedly interfering with the administration of justice in pending cases. Justice Black wrote for the majority to set aside the convictions on freedom of expression grounds.[10] Justice Frankfurter, joined by Chief Justice Stone and Justices Roberts and Byrnes, wrote for the dissenters.[11] It was a battle of giants and a preview of things to come.

In part the difference between the opinions of Black and Frankfurter lay in their varying assessments of the facts. The President of the International Longshoremen's and Ware-

---

95 (Jackson, J., dissenting); Polish Nat'l Alliance v. NLRB, 322 U.S. 643 (1944) (Frankfurter, J.) (applying the theory of the *South-Eastern* dissenters to uphold application of the National Labor Relations Act to an insurer); Powell, *Insurance as Commerce in Constitution and Statute*, 57 HARV. L. REV. 937 (1944) (agreeing with the dissenters in *South-Eastern*).

When Congress in the McCarran Act intervened to restore any state authority taken away by the *South-Eastern* decision, the Court predictably upheld the statute, *see* Prudential Ins. Co. v. Benjamin, 328 U.S. 408, 423 (1946) (Rutledge, J., noting that to hold otherwise "would invert the constitutional grant into a limitation upon the very power it confers"), as it had upheld similar statutes removing commerce clause barriers to state regulation since the 1890s, *see, e.g., In re* Rahrer, 140 U.S. 545 (1891)), pp. 34-35 *supra*, despite indefensible contrary decisions respecting the analogous limitation found implicit in article III's grant of admiralty jurisdiction, *see, e.g.*, Knickerbocker Ice Co. v. Stewart, 253 U.S. 149 (1920), pp. 114-15 *supra*.

[4]Carolene Products Co. v. United States, 323 U.S. 18, 21-22, 28-29 (1944).

[5]*Id.* at 31-32. Justices Black and Douglas concurred only in the result, presumably because they thought economic due process should have been disowned altogether. *Id.* at 32. *See* Olsen v. Nebraska, 313 U.S. 236 (1941) (Douglas, J., enunciating an even more hands-off approach), p. 239 *supra*.

[6]United States v. Carolene Products Co., 304 U.S. 144, 152 n.4 (1938), p. 244 *supra*.

[7]*See* ch. 8 *supra*.

[8]For statistical demonstration of this fractiousness, see C. PRITCHETT, THE ROOSEVELT COURT: A STUDY IN JUDICIAL POLITICS AND VALUES 1937-1947 (1948).

[9]314 U.S. 252, 258-59 (1941).

[10]*Id.* at 258-78.

[11]*Id.* at 279-305 (Frankfurter, J., dissenting).

housemen's Union had published a telegram warning of a crippling strike if a court order was enforced. The *Los Angeles Times* had published an editorial urging a judge not to place named offenders on probation.[12] To Frankfurter, both publications were "attempt[s] to overawe a judge in a matter immediately pending before him."[13] To Black they were essentially harmless. The *Times* editorial "did no more than threaten future adverse criticism which was reasonably to be expected anyway in the event of a lenient disposition of the pending case," and Bridges's telegram had told the judge nothing he could not be assumed to have known before.[14]

Yet the differences between the majority and dissenting Justices ran deeper. They quarreled, to begin with, over the weight to be given to history in interpreting the speech and press guarantees. Justice Frankfurter insisted that "the power to punish for contempt for intrusions into the living process of adjudication ha[d] been an unquestioned characteristic of English courts and of the courts of this country" for over two hundred years;[15] Black retorted that the first amendment had been adopted in order to disavow "oppressive English restrictions" and that "untested state decisions" were not determinative.[16]

The Justices also differed as to the substantive standard by which the state's action was to be judged. Noting that the contempt citations in *Bridges* rested not upon a legislative determination entitled to deference under *Gitlow v. New York*[17] but on the common law, Justice Black took the occasion to enshrine the famous "clear and present danger" test, which had begun to crop up again in the late 1930s, in its most protective form: "the substantive evil must be extremely serious and the degree of imminence extremely high before utterances can be punished."[18] Justice Frankfurter, who thought it enough, as the state court had held, that the publications had a " 'reasonable tendency to interfere with the orderly administration of justice,' " argued that "[t]he phrase 'clear and present danger' is merely a justification for curbing utterance where that is warranted by the substantive evil to be prevented, . . . and the literary difference between it and 'reasonable tendency' is not of constitutional dimension."[19]

---

[12]*Id.* at 298-302 (Frankfurter, J., dissenting).

[13]*Id.* at 279 (Frankfurter, J., dissenting). "A powerful newspaper brought its full coercive power to bear [on a judge, whose continuance in office was dependent upon securing popular approval within a year], in demanding a particular sentence." *Id.* at 300 (Frankfurter, J., dissenting), adding that it would be "inadmissible dogmatism" to say that publication of the telegram (which the state supreme court regarded "as 'a threat that if an attempt was made to enforce the decision, the ports of the entire Pacific Coast would be tied up' ") could not have "dominated the mind" of the state court judge. *Id.* at 302 (Frankfurter, J., dissenting).

[14]*Id.* at 273, 278.

[15]*Id.* at 285 (Frankfurter, J., dissenting); *see also id.* at 290 (Frankfurter, J., dissenting) (invoking Justice Holmes's decision upholding a similar conviction in Patterson v. Colorado, 205 U.S. 454, 462 (1907)), pp. 58-59 *supra*.

[16]314 U.S. at 265, 268 & n.13 (dismissing Patterson v. Colorado, 205 U.S. 454 (1907), on the ground—which Holmes had refused to take—that the Court had not yet held first amendment limitations applicable to the states); *see Patterson*, 205 U.S. at 462 (expressly assuming that state was forbidden to abridge freedom of expression).

[17]268 U.S. 652 (1925), pp. 154-60 *supra*.

[18]*Bridges*, 314 U.S. at 260-63. For the earlier career of this standard, see pp. 119-24, 154-62, 269 *supra*.

[19]*Bridges*, 314 U.S. at 295-96 (Frankfurter, J., dissenting). Holmes had said much the same thing in *Patterson:* "If a court regards, as it may, a publication concerning a matter of law pending before it, as tending toward such an interference, it may punish it. . . ." 205 U.S. at 463; *see also* Hanson, *The Supreme Court on Freedom of the Press and Contempt by Publication*, 27 Cornell L.Q. 165 (1942) (highlighting this disagreement and applauding Justice Black).

The majority and the dissenters also differed in the relative importance they accorded to the competing values of free speech and fair trial. Black emphasized that punishment of the utterances in question would preclude discussion of matters of great public importance at a crucial time,[20] Frankfurter that "[the] administration of justice by an impartial judiciary" was "basic to our conception of freedom."[21] Finally, while there was no hint of either judicial restraint or federalism in Justice Black's opinion, Justice Frankfurter invoked both "the presumption of validity" and the "duty to give due regard . . . to the state's power to deal with what may be essentially local situations."[22] In short, some of the New Deal Justices seemed much more willing than others to set aside measures affecting freedom of expression, and among the more reluctant in *Bridges* was Chief Justice Stone.[23]

## B. Picketing

In a final burst of near unanimity that closed the Hughes era, Justice Murphy's maiden opinion in *Thornhill v. Alabama*,[24] assimilating freedom of speech to *Carolene Products'* preferred category of devices for the democratic correction of error, had struck down as overbroad a state statute read essentially to forbid all labor picketing.[25] Less than one year later, however, that concord had vanished as Justices Black, Douglas, and Reed dissented in *Milk Wagon Drivers Union v. Meadowmoor Dairies, Inc.*,[26] where the Court upheld an injunction against peaceful picketing that Justice Frankfurter said could justifiably be found coercive because of "the momentum of fear generated by past vio-

[20] *Bridges,* 314 U.S. at 268.

[21] *Id.* at 268-69, 282 (Frankfurter, J., dissenting).

[22] *Id.* at 293 (Frankfurter, J., dissenting), adding that "[w]e must be fastidiously careful not to make our private views the measure of constitutional authority."

[23] *Bridges* also presented interesting technical problems to which Justice Black did not advert, though the dissenters prominently called attention to some of them. *See id.* at 280 (Frankfurter, J., dissenting) (protesting that "[w]e are not even vouchsafed reference to the specific provision of the Constitution" on which the majority relied). Bridges was an alien and the owner of the *Times* was a corporation; neither was a "citizen" protected by the privileges or immunities clause, which Justice Black was later to suggest made the first amendment applicable to the states. *See* Adamson v. California, 332 U.S. 46, 68-123 (1947) (Black, J., dissenting). Earlier decisions had placed freedom of expression within the due process clause. *See* pp. 252-53 *supra.* However, as Justice Frankfurter argued, without adverting to Grosjean v. American Press Co., 297 U.S. 233 (1936) (a case in which the Court had ignored the problem in striking down a tax restricting the press freedom of corporations), there was authority to the effect that corporations—which Black had once iconoclastically denied were "persons" for due process purposes, *see* Connecticut General Life Ins. Co. v. Johnson, 303 U.S. 77, 85-90 (1938) (Black, J., dissenting)—had no "liberty" within the meaning of that clause. Finally, the actions complained of in *Bridges* were those of judges rather than legislators; if the theory was that the fourteenth amendment made the first amendment applicable to the states, it should have been food for thought that the latter ("*Congress* shall make no law") seemed to limit only legislative action.

[24] 310 U.S. 88 (1940), pp. 268-70 *supra.*

[25] *Id.* at 95-96 ("Mere legislative preference for one rather than another means for combatting substantive evils . . . may well prove an inadequate foundation on which to rest regulations which are aimed at or in their operation diminish the effective exercise of rights so necessary to the maintenance of democratic institutions.") *See also* AFL v. Swing, 312 U.S. 321, 326 (1941) (Frankfurter, J., over two dissents arguing only that the issue was not properly presented) (holding without much explanation that the state could not ban all organizational picketing: "The right of free communication cannot . . . be mutilated by denying it to workers, in a dispute with an employer, even though they are not in his employ.").

[26] 312 U.S. 287 (1941).

lence."[27] As in *Bridges,* the disagreement in *Milk Wagon* turned in part upon differing assessments of the facts.[28] Furthermore, Frankfurter once again emphasized deference to the state courts while Black continued to insist on the need to find a "clear and present danger" of harm.[29] Justice Reed went further, arguing that "[i]f the fear engendered by past misconduct coerces storekeepers during peaceful picketing, the remedy lies in the maintenance of order, not in denial of free speech."[30]

This basic disagreement between the Justices flared up again in two picketing cases decided soon after Stone became Chief Justice. *Carpenters & Joiners Union v. Ritter's Cafe,*[31] in another Frankfurter opinion, upheld an injunction against picketing a restaurant in violation of a state antitrust law over dissents by Black, Douglas, Murphy, and Reed. The picketers' only quarrel with the restaurant owner was that he had hired a contractor who employed nonunion labor to construct another building less than two miles away. To hold this picketing constitutionally protected, wrote Frankfurter, "would compel the states to allow the disputants in a particular industrial episode to conscript neutrals having no relation to either the dispute or the industry in which it arose."[32]

However, in *Bakery & Pastry Drivers & Helpers Local 802 v. Wohl,*[33] decided the same day, the Court unanimously set aside an injunction against the picketing of bakeries because of a dispute with "independent jobbers" who purchased their products, delivered them to retailers in their own trucks, and resold them. Effectively distinguishing *Ritter's Cafe* without referring to it, Justice Jackson explained that the jobbers' "mobility and their insulation from the public as middlemen made it practically impossible for [the union] to make known [its] legitimate grievances to the public whose patronage was sustaining the peddler system" without picketing the bakers, and that the picketing was "such as to have slight, if any, repercussions upon the interests of strangers to the issue."[34]

The reference to the impact upon "strangers" seemed to suggest that the bakers, unlike the owner of Ritter's Cafe, were not "neutrals" since the "independent jobbers" were their former deliverymen. In a real sense the dispute was over the bakers' own decision to stop employing union labor.[35] The argument respecting the drivers' mobility, however, was more fundamental. *Thornhill* had established that picketing was an indispensable means

---

[27]*Id.* at 293, 294 (adding that "utterance in a context of violence can lose its significance as an appeal to reason and become part of an instrument of force").

[28]*See id.* at 313-16 (Black, J., joined by Douglas, J., dissenting) ("[I]t is going a long way to say that because of the acts of these few men, six thousand other members of their union can be denied the right to express their opinion. . . ."); *cf. id.* at 294-95 (Frankfurter, J.) (terming the acts of violence "neither episodic nor isolated," quoting the state court's conclusion that " 'in connection with or following a series of assaults or destruction of property, [picketing] could not help but have the effect of intimidating the persons in front of whose premises such picketing occurred,' " and adding that "[w]e can reject such a determination only if we can say that it is so without warrant as to be a palpable evasion of the constitutional guarantee" (citation omitted)).

[29]*See id.* at 313 (Black, J., dissenting).

[30]*Id.* at 319 (Reed, J., dissenting).

[31]315 U.S. 722 (1942).

[32]*Id.* at 728.

[33]315 U.S. 769, 775 (1942).

[34]*Id.* at 775. Justice Douglas, joined by Black and Murphy, added a separate concurring opinion. *Id.* at 775-77 (Douglas, J., concurring).

[35]*See id.* at 770-71 (showing that drivers had been made "independent" to reduce social security and unemployment-insurance costs); *cf.* NLRB v. Hearst Publications, Inc., 322 U.S. 111, 132 (1944) (holding "independent" newsboys newspaper "employees" within National Labor Relations Act).

for bringing "the facts of a labor dispute" to the attention of the public; the risk that it might "persuade some of those reached to refrain from entering into advantageous relationships with the business establishment which is the scene of the dispute" did not justify forbidding it altogether.[36] Similarly, when the mobility of those with whom the picketers dispute makes it impracticable to convey the message by picketing them directly, as in *Wohl,* even "repercussions upon the interests of strangers" may have to be accepted if the message is to be effectively conveyed.[37] The state had a legitimate interest, however, in protecting innocent persons from group boycotts designed to force them to take sides in other people's disputes. Furthermore, the state was entitled to effectuate this interest so long as it left the parties, as in *Ritter's Cafe,* a reasonable opportunity to get their information across at the site of the actual dispute.

Thus there was a strong argument that, unlike the blanket prohibition on picketing in *Thornhill,* the injunction upheld in *Ritter's Cafe* was a reasonable regulation of the place and manner of communicating information.[38] Moreover, the fact that the picketers chose to convey their message at the premises of a person with whom they had no direct dispute suggests that their purpose was in large part to persuade others not to do business with him. If the state can forbid a concerted refusal to deal under these circumstances, it should be able to forbid speech incitng to the commission of the offense—by picketing or otherwise.[39] The decision underlined the growing split on matters of free expression between Frankfurter, Roberts, Byrnes, and Stone on one side and Black, Douglas, Murphy, and Reed on the other, with Justice Jackson holding the balance of power between them.

## II.   JEHOVAH'S WITNESSES—AGAIN

In the 1930s, Jehovah's Witnesses had won significant first amendment victories, from freedom from overbroad or discretionary permit requirements to the right to distribute handbills and protection against abusive enforcement of laws against breaches of the

[36] *See Thornhill,* 310 U.S. 88, 102, 104 (1940) ("The safeguarding of these means is essential to the securing of an informed and educated public opinion. . . ."); *cf.* Schneider v. State, 308 U.S. 147, 162 (1939) (holding risk of littering did not justify total ban on distribution of handbills on sidewalks and streets), p. 263 *supra.*

[37] Thus, for example, picketing the site of the new building in *Ritter's Cafe* might well have been constitutionally protected, although it too might have some tendency to "conscript neutrals," because that was the most logical place to publicize a dispute with the building contractor. Picketing at the building site, Justice Frankfurter noted, had not been enjoined. *Ritter's Cafe,* 315 U.S. at 724.

[38] Congress soon wrote similar distinctions into § 8(b) of the Taft-Hartley Act, Pub. L. No. 86-257, 73 Stat. 519 (codified at 29 U.S.C. § 158(b)(4), (7) (1982)). *Ritter's Cafe* may indeed have been easier to defend than the limitations in Taft-Hartley, which forbade picketing only by labor organizations and only for certain goals, since it was based upon a general antitrust statute that seemed neutrally to forbid *all* speakers to induce third parties to take sides in other people's disputes.

[39] *See* Hughes v. Superior Court, 339 U.S. 460, 469 (1950) (Frankfurter, J., without dissent) (upholding injunction against picketing to induce unlawful racial discrimination in hiring); Giboney v. Empire Storage & Ice Co., 336 U.S. 490, 498 (1949) (Black, J., for a unanimous Court) (upholding injunction against picketing to induce wholesaler to join illegal group boycott of nonunion ice peddlers: "It rarely has been suggested that the constitutional freedom for speech and press extends its immunity to speech or writing used as an integral part of conduct in violation of a valid criminal statute."); Frohwerk v. United States, 249 U.S. 204, 206 (1919) ("We venture to believe that neither Hamilton nor Madison, nor any other competent person then or later, ever supposed that to make criminal the counselling of a murder within the jurisdiction of Congress would be an unconstitutional interference with free speech."); Dodd, *Picketing and Free Speech: A Dissent,* 56 HARV. L. REV. 513, 524

peace.[40] At the end of the Hughes period, however, the Witnesses had been rebuffed in seeking special exemption from a generally applicable flag salute requirement and in attacking a parade permit provision carefully limited to traffic control purposes.[41] Continued reversals during the early days of Chief Justice Stone came to an abrupt halt after Wiley Rutledge replaced Byrnes in 1943.


## A.  Fighting Words

In *Chaplinsky v. New Hampshire,* none of the Justices had any difficulty in concluding that a state could punish a Jehovah's Witness or anyone else for calling a city marshal a " 'God damned racketeer' and 'a damned Fascist.' "[42] It was the libertarian Justice Murphy who wrote to emphasize that "the right of free speech [wa]s not absolute" and that "insulting or 'fighting' words—those which by their very utterance inflict injury or tend to incite an immediate breach of the peace"—were among "certain well-defined and narrowly limited classes of speech" that were not protected—both for historical reasons and because of their "slight social value" when compared with "the social interest in order and morality."[43]

While Justice Black rejected history in *Bridges,* Justice Murphy embraced it in *Chaplinsky.* Posterity was to have difficulty with Murphy's gratuitous assimilation of "the lewd and obscene, the profane, [and] the libelous" to the unprotected categories,[44] as well as with the Court's contemporaneous and wholly conclusory holding that "commercial advertising" was not protected either.[45] Regardless of history, it is always troublesome in

---

(1943). It is noteworthy that the remedy in all the picketing cases was an injunction, which the Court in Near v. Minnesota, 283 U.S. 697 (1931), had condemned as a prior restraint even when the expression enjoined was constitutionally punishable. *See* pp. 257-59 *supra.* Nobody explained why illegal picketing should be an exception to this rule. *See* Teller, *Picketing and Free Speech,* 56 HARV. L. REV. 180, 195-200 (1942) (arguing that *Ritter* and *Wohl* substantially weakened *Thornhill's* equation of picketing with speech).

[40]*See* Cantwell v. Connecticut, 310 U.S. 296 (1940); Schneider v. State, 308 U.S. 147 (1939); Lovell v. Griffin, 303 U.S. 444 (1938).

[41]Minersville School Dist. v. Gobitis, 310 U.S. 586 (1940), *overruled,* Board of Educ. v. Barnette, 319 U.S. 625 (1943); Cox v. New Hampshire, 312 U.S. 569 (1941); *see generally* pp. 261-68 *supra.*

[42]315 U.S. 568, 569-70 (1942) (quoting the complaint in *Chaplinsky*).

[43]Id. at 571-72 (adding that the punishment of speech in such categories had "never been thought to raise any Constitutional problem"); *see also id.* at 574 ("The appellations 'damned racketeer' and 'damned Fascist' are epithets likely to provoke the average person to retaliation, and thereby cause a breach of the peace."). Justice Murphy's biographer, who carefully documented his increasing zeal for protection of civil liberties, termed the *Chaplinsky* opinion "early Murphy." *See* J. HOWARD, MR. JUSTICE MURPHY 256 (1968).

[44]*Chaplinsky,* 315 U.S. at 572; *cf.* New York Times Co. v. Sullivan, 376 U.S. 254 (1964) (limiting the traditional cause of action for libel); Roth v. United States, 354 U.S. 476, 508-14 (1957) (Douglas & Black, JJ., dissenting from decision holding obscene publications punishable). See pp. 382-83, 438-39 *infra.*

[45]Valentine v. Chrestensen, 316 U.S. 52, 54-55 (1942) (Roberts, J.). This debatable decision had been foreshadowed by equally conclusory dictum in Schneider v. State, 308 U.S. 147, 165 (1939), *supra* p. 262, note 130, and it derived support from repeated arguments that the purpose of the first amendment was to permit free discussion of political issues as an instrument of self-government. *See, e.g.,* Whitney v. California, 274 U.S. 357, 375 (1927) (Brandeis & Holmes, JJ., concurring); A. MEIKELJOHN, FREE SPEECH AND ITS RELATIONS TO SELF-GOVERNMENT 15-16, 24-27, 39 (1948); *see also* Chrestensen v. Valentine, 122 F.2d 511, 524 (2d Cir. 1941) (Frank, J., dissenting) ("Such men as Thomas Paine, John Milton and Thomas Jefferson were not fighting for the right to peddle commercial advertising."); Resnick, *Freedom of Speech and Commercial Solicitation,* 30

terms of first amendment policy to limit the content of speech.[46] A neutral ban on fighting words, in contrast, can be defended as a reasonable restriction of the *manner* of expression, since it leaves the speaker free to convey whatever message he likes in less inflammatory terms.[47]

## B. License Taxes

Two months after *Chaplinsky,* differences of opinion boiled up again when the Court, by a five-to-four vote in *Jones v. Opelika,*[48] held that the Constitution granted Jehovah's Witnesses no exemption from taxes on the sale of religious literature. The lineup of Justices was the same as in the picketing case of *Ritter's Cafe,* with two interesting exceptions. This time it was Justice Reed who wrote to reject the constitutional claim, while Chief Justice Stone joined the predictable Black, Douglas, and Murphy in dissent.[49]

Discriminatory taxes on newspapers had been struck down in *Grosjean v. American Press Co.*[50] in 1936, but the taxes upheld in *Jones* applied impartially to purveyors of other goods as well.[51] In *Grosjean* the Court made clear that it did not mean "to suggest that the owners of newspapers are immune from any of the ordinary forms of taxation for the support of the government."[52] A later decision would explain why: "We need not fear that a government will destroy a selected group of taxpayers by burdensome taxation if it must impose the same burden on the rest of its constituency."[53] Justice Reed thought this argument determinative in *Jones:* "The First Amendment does not require a subsidy in the form of fiscal exemption" for either religion or the press.[54]

The Witnesses' setback was temporary, however, for within a year Rutledge had replaced Byrnes, voted with the *Jones* dissenters to grant a rehearing,[55] and joined Justice Douglas's opinion in *Murdock v. Pennsylvania*[56] for a new five-to-four majority reaching

---

CAL. L. REV. 655, 661 (1942). *But see* Virginia Pharmacy Bd. v. Virginia Consumer Council, 425 U.S. 748, 764 (1976) (holding certain advertisements protected: "[S]ociety also may have a strong interest in the free flow of commercial information."), pp. 515-16 *infra.*

Determining what speech was "commercial," in any event, was to prove somewhat challenging. For example, while *Valentine* had held that an advertisement could not be brought under the constitutional umbrella simply by affixing to it a protest against the advertising ban itself, 316 U.S. at 55, Jamison v. Texas, 318 U.S. 413, 416 (1943) (Black, J.), held that distribution of an invitation to a religious meeting could not be prohibited simply because it also invited the purchase of books. Not one Justice suggested that the two cases were indistinguishable.

[46] *See* Stone, *Content Regulation and the First Amendment,* 25 WM. & MARY L. REV. 189, *passim* (1983).

[47] *See Id.* at 242-44 (discussing the related issue of profanity).

[48] 316 U.S. 584 (1942).

[49] *See id.* at 600-24.

[50] 297 U.S. 233 (1936), pp. 260-61 *supra.*

[51] *Jones,* 316 U.S. at 586-92.

[52] 297 U.S. at 250; *cf.* Oklahoma Press Publishing Co. v. Walling, 327 U.S. 186, 192-93 (1946) (Rutledge, J.) (holding the press not immune from Fair Labor Standards Act); Associated Press v. United States, 326 U.S. 1, 19-20 (1945) (Black, J.) (holding the press not immune from antitrust law); Associated Press v. NLRB, 301 U.S. 103, 132-33 (1937) (holding press not immune from generally applicable labor laws).

[53] Minneapolis Star & Tribune Co. v. Minnesota Comm'r of Revenue, 460 U.S. 575, 585 (1983).

[54] 316 U.S. at 599.

[55] Jones v. Opelika, 319 U.S. 103 (1943) (per curiam).

[56] 319 U.S. 105 (1943).

the opposite conclusion.[57] Echoing Stone's dissent in the earlier case, Douglas argued it was not enough that similar taxes had been laid upon commercial enterprises operated for profit; the Constitution had placed freedom of speech, press, and religion "in a preferred position."[58]

Decisions limiting the use of injunctions and permits that could have been employed against other activities did indeed suggest that speech and press, although not religion, were entitled to special constitutional privileges.[59] There were, moreover, respectable arguments to support this distinction. The virtual representation assured by forbidding discrimination may well be sufficient to protect "discrete and insular minorities," which seems to have been the purpose of the free exercise clause. It may nevertheless be inadequate to assure the integrity of the political process, which Stone had rightly suggested was one of the functions of free expression in *Carolene Products*.[60] Justice Murphy seemed to be going very far, however, in suggesting in a second *Jones* dissent that those exercising first amendment freedoms bore no responsibility whatever for helping to defray the common costs of government.[61] Justice Douglas, in *Murdock*, pulled back from this extreme position: "It is one thing to impose a tax on the income or property of a preacher. It is quite another thing to exact a tax from him for the privilege of delivering a sermon."[62]

Douglas's hackneyed argument that "[t]he power to tax the exercise of a privilege is the power to control or suppress its enjoyment" applied equally to the income and property taxes he professed to distinguish.[63] Moreover, there was no contention that the amounts

---

[57] *See* Mendelson, *Clear and Present Danger—From Schenck to Dennis*, 52 COLUM. L. REV. 313, 320 (1952) ("The tenure of Mr. Justice Rutledge marks the era *par excellence* of civil liberties . . . in American jurisprudence.").

[58] *Murdock*, 319 U.S. at 115; *Jones*, 316 U.S. at 608. Stone had also argued in *Jones* that the discretionary power of city officials to revoke a permit for the sale of literature created the same potential for discrimination that had condemned a permit requirement in Lovell v. Griffin, 303 U.S. 444 (1938), pp. 261-63 *supra*. *Jones*, 316 U.S. at 600-03. Justice Reed reaffirmed *Lovell* in Largent v. Texas, 318 U.S. 418, 422 (1943); in *Jones*, he appropriately responded that the revocation provision was not at issue. 316 U.S. at 599-600.

[59] *See* pp. 257-63 *supra*, (discussing Near v. Minnesota, 283 U.S. 697 (1931) and Lovell v. Griffin, 303 U.S. 444 (1938)). *See generally* Minersville School Dist. v. Gobitis, 310 U.S. 586 (1940) (no religious exemption from flag salute rule); Reynolds v. United States, 98 U.S. 145 (1879) (no religious exemption from polygamy laws), THE FIRST HUNDRED YEARS at 439-42. For an early effort to assimilate the criteria for infringements on freedom of religion to those on freedom of expression, see Summers, *The Sources and Limits of Religious Freedom*, 41 ILL. L. REV. 53 (1946).

[60] 304 U.S. 144, 152 n.4 (1938).

[61] Except for fees "commensurate with any expenses entailed by the presence of the Witnesses," Murphy argued, "no tax whatever can be levied on petitioners' activities in distributing their literature or disseminating their ideas." *Jones*, 316 U.S. at 620 (Murphy, J., dissenting) (citing Cox v. New Hampshire, 312 U.S. 569, 577 (1941), for the acceptability of fees to cover expenses caused by a parade); *see* p. 265, note 151 *supra*. *But see Murdock*, 319 U.S. at 131 (Reed, J., dissenting) ("The distributors of religious literature, possibly of all informatory publications, become today privileged to carry on their occupations without contributing their share to the support of the government which provides the opportunity for the exercise of their liberties."); *id*. at 135 (Frankfurter, J., dissenting). Murphy also suggested that the tax had been discriminatorily applied. "[N]o attempt was . . . made to apply the ordinance to ministers functioning in a more orthodox manner than petitioner." *Jones*, 316 U.S. at 617 (Murphy, J., dissenting). A showing of discrimination would of course have condemned the tax, but the Court did not find discrimination in *Murdock*, and Justice Frankfurter insisted that no claim of discrimination had been made. *Murdock*, 319 U.S. at 135 (Frankfurter, J., dissenting).

[62] 319 U.S. at 112.

[63] *Id*. at 112; *see also id*. at 137 (Frankfurter, J., dissenting) (quoting Holmes's aphorism in Panhandle Oil Co. v. Knox, 277 U.S. 218, 223 (1928), that " '[t]he power to tax is not the power to destroy while this Court sits' ");

demanded were oppressive or prohibitive.[64] Nevertheless there were aspects of the privilege tax that arguably justified Douglas's distinction.

First, the taxes in question were "fixed in amount and unrelated to the scope of the activities of petitioners or to their realized revenues."[65] Accordingly, as Chief Justice Stone had said in analogizing to state taxes on persons engaged in interstate commerce, by its form alone "[t]he tax imposed . . . [was] more burdensome and destructive of the activity taxed than any gross receipts tax."[66] Payment of the tax, moreover, was made a condition of the right to sell literature, for the sanction for nonpayment was denial of the right itself.[67] As Justice Douglas also suggested, commerce clause precedents had long insisted that the payment of a tax not unduly burdensome in itself could not be made a condition of exercising the federal right to engage in interstate commerce: while interstate commerce could be required to pay its own way, it could not be prohibited.[68] Finally, the requirement that the speaker obtain a license to speak conjured up visions of the censorship that had been at the heart of the historic opposition to limitations on free expression. Though the requirement left the licensing authority no discretion to deny a permit to anyone tendering payment of the tax, it bore more than a little resemblance to the classic "previous restraint."[69] *Jones* and *Murdock* were anything but easy cases, but they did not hold that speech, press, or religion must be exempted from paying their share of the cost of governing.

## C. Doorbells and Flags

In *Martin v. City of Struthers*,[70] decided the same day as *Murdock* and by the same vote, Jehovah's Witnesses won another great victory as Justice Black wrote to strike down an ordinance forbidding door-to-door distribution of handbills, circulars, and other forms of advertisements.[71] Conceding that "the peace, good order, and comfort of the community

---

*cf.* McCulloch v. Maryland, 17 U.S. (4 Wheat) 316, 431 (1819) ("[T]he power to tax involves the power to destroy."). Justice Jackson added an embarrassing dissent of his own in which Justice Frankfurter joined, fulminating in what seemed a rather injudicious manner against the Witnesses' aggressive methods of spreading their message. *id.* at 166-82 (Jackson, J., dissenting).

[64] *See Murdock*, 319 U.S. at 130 (Reed, J., dissenting); *id.* at 134-35 (Frankfurter, J., dissenting) ("No claim is made that the effect of these taxes, either separately or cumulatively, has been, or is likely to be, to restrict the petitioners' religious propaganda activities in any degree. Counsel expressly disclaim any such contention.").

[65] *Id.* at 113 (Douglas, J.).

[66] *Jones*, 316 U.S. at 609 (Stone, C. J., dissenting) (citing McGoldrick v. Berwind-White Co., 309 U.S. 33, 55-57 (1940) (dictum)); *cf. Berwind-White*, 309 U.S. at 45 n.2 (taxes of a kind that two or more states might impose upon the same transaction forbidden without regard to their amount because they placed interstate trade at a competitive disadvantage).

[67] *See Murdock*, 319 U.S. at 106, 114 ("It is a flat license tax levied and collected as a condition to the pursuit of activities whose enjoyment is guaranteed by the First Amendment.").

[68] *See id.* at 113; *cf., e.g.*, Postal Tel. Cable Co. v. Adams, 155 U.S. 688, 698 (1895) (Fuller, C. J.) (dictum).

[69] *See Murdock*, 319 U.S. at 114 ("[I]t restrains in advance those constitutional liberties of press and religion. . . ."); *cf.* Cox v. New Hampshire, 312 U.S. 569 (1941) (upholding permit requirement limited to traffic concerns); Lovell v. City of Griffin, 303 U.S. 444 (1938) (striking down permit requirement for distribution of literature as previous restraint); pp. 257-63 *supra*.

[70] 319 U.S. 141 (1943).

[71] *Id.* at 142; *see also id.* at 152 (Frankfurter, J. dissenting); *id.* at 154 (Reed, J., dissenting); *id.* at 157, 166, 181-82 (Jackson, J., dissenting). That the ordinance discriminated against speakers and in favor of salesmen made it immediately suspect, but the Court chose a broader ground of decision.

may imperatively require regulation of the time, place and manner of distribution" and that the homeowner's privacy was a legitimate state concern,[72] Black convincingly argued that the means selected to assuage it went too far. "Door to door distribution of circulars," Black asserted, was "essential to the poorly financed causes of little people"; the city had substituted its judgment for that of the householders, some of whom might wish to receive the message.[73] The interest in privacy, he concluded, could be adequately protected by making it an offense "to ring the bell of a householder who has appropriately indicated that he is unwilling to be disturbed."[74] Like the handbilling and picketing decisions, *Martin* seemed to strike an admirable balance between competing interests.[75]

One of the oddest aspects of the license-tax litigation was a separate dissent by Justices Black, Douglas, and Murphy in *Jones* signaling their repentance for having voted in *Minersville School District v. Gobitis*,[76] over Stone's lone dissent, to sustain the requirement that Jehovah's Witnesses salute the flag.[77] Hughes and McReynolds, who also had joined the majority in *Gobitis,* had since given way to Jackson and Rutledge, both of whom joined in a six-to-three opinion by the former in the famous case of *West Virginia State Board of Education v. Barnette*,[78] where the Court reversed itself on this issue too.[79]

Stone's earlier dissent had suggested that those with religious objections were entitled to a special exemption from what he seemed to assume was an otherwise valid requirement, and so had the brief statement of the three converts in *Jones.*[80] Jackson's magnificent "opinion of the Court" in *Barnette,* however, took a broader tack by proclaiming that *no one* could be compelled to salute the flag. Freedom of speech included the freedom not to speak; no state interest in inculcating patriotism justified such an infringement upon individual autonomy.[81]

---

[72]*Id.* at 143.

[73]*Id.* at 146.

[74]*Id.* at 148.

[75]*See supra* notes 24-39 and accompanying text (discussing the picketing cases); *supra* p. 263 (discussing Schneider v. State, 308 U.S. 147 (1939)).

[76]310 U.S. 586 (1940), p. 267 *supra.*

[77]Jones v. Opelika, 316 U.S. 584, 623-24 (1942) (Black, Douglas, & Murphy, JJ., dissenting) (describing both cases as sanctioning "device[s] which . . . suppress[] or tend[] to suppress the free exercise of a religion practiced by a minority group"). *Gobitis* had met with virtually unanimous scholarly criticism. *See* Heller, *A Turning Point for Religious Liberty,* 29 Va. L. Rev. 440, 450-53 (1943) (collecting the authorities).

[78]319 U.S. 624 (1943).

[79]*Id.* at 642; *see also id.* at 642-43 (Roberts & Reed, JJ., dissenting); *id.* at 646-71 (Frankfurter, J., dissenting).

[80]*See supra* note 77.

[81]*See Barnette,* 319 U.S. at 634-35 ("Nor does the issue as we see it turn on one's possession of particular religious views. . . . It is not necessary to inquire whether non-conformist beliefs will exempt from the duty to salute unless we first find power to make the salute a legal duty."); *id.* at 633 n.13 (citing William Tell's legendary refusal to salute a bailiff's hat and William Penn's refusal to uncover his head in deference to civil authority); *id.* at 634 ("To sustain the compulsory flag salute we are required to say that a Bill of Rights which guards the individual's right to speak his own mind, left it open to public authorities to compel him to utter what is not in his mind."); *id.* at 641 ("Ultimate futility of such attempts to compel coherence is the lesson of every such effort from the Roman drive to stamp out Christianity as a disturber of its pagan unity, the Inquisition, as a means to dynastic unity, the Siberian exiles as a means to Russian unity, down to the fast failing efforts of our present totalitarian enemies. . . . To believe that patriotism will not flourish if patriotic ceremonies are voluntary . . . is to make an unflattering estimate of the appeal of our institutions to free minds."). Justices Black, Douglas, and Murphy

In announcing this eminently appropriate assessment of the competing interests, Justice Jackson went out of his way to endorse Stone's suggestion in *Carolene Products* that measures affecting first amendment freedoms were subject to much stricter scrutiny than those in which the due process clause was "applied for its own sake:"

> The test of legislation which collides with the Fourteenth Amendment, because it also collides with the principles of the First, is much more definite than the test when only the Fourteenth is involved. Much of the vagueness of the due process clause disappears when the specific prohibitions of the First become its standard. The right of a State to regulate, for example, a public utility may well include, so far as the due process test is concerned, power to impose all of the restrictions which a legislature may have a "rational basis" for adopting. But freedoms of speech and of press, of assembly, and of worship may not be infringed on such slender grounds. They are susceptible of restriction only to prevent grave and immediate danger to interests which the State may lawfully protect.[82]

Justice Frankfurter's famous dissent left no doubt that he rejected this distinction in toto:

> The admonition that judicial self-restraint alone limits arbitrary exercise of our authority is relevant every time we are asked to nullify legislation. The Constitution does not give us greater veto power when dealing with one phase of 'liberty' than with another. . . . Our power does not vary according to the particular provision of the Bill of Rights which is invoked. . . . [W]henever legislation is sought to be nullified on any ground, . . . responsibility for legislation lies with legislatures, answerable as they are directly to the people, and this Court's only and very narrow function is to determine whether within the broad grant of authority vested in legislatures they have exercised a judgment for which reasonable justification can be offered.[83]

---

wrote separate opinions invoking religious freedom, but they did not disown Jackson's "opinion of the Court." *See id.* at 643 (Black & Douglas, JJ., concurring) ("We are substantially in agreement with the opinion [of Jackson] just read. . . ."); *id.* at 644 (Murphy, J., concurring) ("I agree with the opinion of the Court and join in it."); *see also id.* at 632-33 (Jackson, J.) (reaffirming that freedom of expression embraced communicative actions as well as words: "Symbolism is a primitive but effective way of communicating ideas."); pp. 255-56 *supra* (discussing Stromberg v. California, 283 U.S. 359 (1931)).

The implication of the two flag salute cases that freedom of religion did not require exemptions from generally applicable laws was reinforced the following term when the Court upheld application of child labor laws to the proselytizing activities of Jehovah's Witnesses in Prince v. Massachusetts, 321 U.S. 158, 164 (1944) (Rutledge, J.) (reaffirming that first amendment freedoms made applicable to the states by due process enjoyed a "preferred position in our basic scheme"). Murphy filed the expected dissent. *Id.* at 171-76. Justice Jackson, joined by Roberts and Frankfurter, petulantly concluded that the distinguishable decision in *Murdock,* from which they had dissented, required them to vote to reverse the judgment sustaining the application of the child labor law although they believed it correct. *Id.* at 176-78 (Jackson, J., dissenting).

[82]*Barnette,* 319 U.S. at 639.

[83]*Id.* at 648-49 (Frankfurter, J., dissenting).

In so saying, Justice Frankfurter laid bare the fundamental cause of the unbridgeable abyss that separated New Deal Justices who had all agreed in burying economic due process. Stone, Black, and Jackson were no less adamant than Frankfurter that the catastrophe of *Lochner v. New York*[84] must not be repeated, but they disagreed sharply as to the means of preventing it. The majority of the Justices had a narrow conception of substantive due process; Frankfurter had a narrow conception of judicial review.

The majority had yet to give a satisfactory answer to Frankfurter's question how measures impinging on different "liberties" could be given different levels of scrutiny in applying the due process clause to evaluate state action.[85] His reference to the Bill of Rights and his further insistence that the question was the same as if an act of Congress had been involved,[86] however, made clear that his disagreement with the majority was broader. He seemed to have concluded that the only way to protect against further abuses like *Lochner* was to minimize judicial authority to enforce *any* constitutional provisions.[87]

Justice Jackson recognized in *Barnette* that it was not necessary to stop enforcing limitations that were in the Constitution in order to avoid imposing others that were not. In his sincere concern to keep judges from exceeding their constitutional authority, Justice Frankfurter came perilously close to repudiating that authority itself.[88]

## III.  Criminal Procedure

The basic dispute over the intrusiveness of judicial review that characterized the Stone Court's encounters with the "specific prohibitions" of the first amendment emerged in other fields as well. In *Powell v. Alabama*,[89] for example, where "ignorant" defendants had been sentenced to death for rape, the Court had broken new ground in a noble 1932 opinion by Justice Sutherland by holding that the due process clause required a state to

---

[84] 198 U.S. 45 (1905).

[85] *See* pp. 287-88 *supra*.

[86] *Barnette*, 319 U.S. at 650 (Frankfurter, J., dissenting).

[87] *See id.* at 666 (Frankfurter, J., dissenting):

> The uncontrollable power wielded by this Court brings it very close to the most sensitive areas of public affairs. As appeal from legislation to adjudication becomes more frequent, and its consequences more far-reaching, judicial self-restraint becomes more and not less important, lest we unwarrantably enter social and political domains wholly outside our concern.

For his Spartan view of the judicial function, Justice Frankfurter invoked Justice Holmes, whose pungent dissent in *Lochner* had served more than anything else to call attention to the problem. *See id.* at 649 (quoting Missouri, K. & T. Ry. v. May, 194 U.S. 267, 270 (1904)); *Lochner*, 198 U.S. at 75, pp. 47-50 *supra*). Significantly, however, despite suggestions in his earlier opinions, Holmes himself had abandoned the position for which Frankfurter cited him. Several of his most illustrious opinions attest that his standards for reviewing claims both of free expression and of uncompensated takings were far stricter than those he applied in ordinary substantive due process cases. *See, e.g.*, Gitlow v. New York, 268 U.S. 652, 672-73 (1925) (Holmes, J., dissenting) Pennsylvania Coal Co. v. Mahon, 260 U.S. 393 (1922); Abrams v. United States, 250 U.S. 616, 624-31 (1919) (Holmes, J., dissenting); pp. 121-24, 146-51, 154-60 *supra*. Following Holmes's example in accordance with *Carolene Products'* suggestion respecting "specific prohibitions[s]" of the Constitution, the Court was far from deferential in upholding (over dissents by Justices Black and Burton) a taking claim based on the low flight of airplanes over the plaintiff's land in United States v. Causby, 328 U.S. 256 (1946) (Douglas, J.).

[88] *See* Kalven, Book Review, 37 IND. L.J. 572, 577 (1962) (reviewing W. MENDELSON, JUSTICES BLACK AND FRANKFURTER: CONFLICT IN THE COURT (1961)) ("[W]hy should any one have preferred the setting up of this anemic check to the simplicity of not having judicial review at all?").

[89] 287 U.S. 45, 173 (1932), pp. 246-47 *supra*.

provide lawyers to defendants unable to employ their own: "The right to be heard would be, in many cases, of little avail if it did not comprehend the right to be heard by counsel."[90] Ten years later, in *Betts v. Brady*,[91] a divided Court nevertheless upheld a state robbery conviction although the defendant's request for an assigned attorney had been denied.

In concluding in *Betts* that the right to assigned counsel in such cases was not "fundamental," Justice Roberts relied largely on the absence of such a right in the colonies and in many state constitutions.[92] If practice was to be a guide, however, Justice Black furnished food for thought in noting that thirty-five states provided for appointing counsel in noncapital cases by either constitution, statute, or judicial custom.[93] More important, neither history nor practice had been the basis of *Powell*, and it was equally true in noncapital cases that a trial without counsel was no trial at all.[94]

The Court had displayed neither judical restraint nor concern for state autonomy in *Powell* or in its other criminal procedure decisions of the early 1930s.[95] In 1937, however, in *Palko v. Connecticut*,[96] Justice Cardozo had employed language reminiscent of the hands-off attitude that characterized economic cases of the later Hughes period in arguing that right-minded men could reasonably believe that permitting the state to appeal an acquittal was not "repugnant to the conscience of mankind."[97] In echoing this language, *Betts* showed how miserly such an attitude could be by largely abandoning a right that even the Justices of the early 1930s had rightly deemed fundamental. In order to find that convicting a defendant with no lawyer to defend him was not "offensive to the common and fundamental ideas of fairness and right,"[98] the Justices needed, as Black protested, a very thick skin.[99]

Only Douglas and Murphy joined Black in his dissent in *Betts*; Rutledge had not yet been appointed. It was interesting that Chief Justice Stone voted with the majority after his suggestion in *Carolene Products* of more aggressive review in cases involving "specific prohibition[s] . . . such as those of the first ten amendments, which are deemed equally specific when held to be embraced within the Fourteenth."[100] Apparently, while freedom of speech was made "specific[ally]" applicable to the states because it was so fundamental, the right to assigned counsel was not because it was fundamental only in certain cases.[101]

In rejecting this subtle distinction, Justice Black, who had joined the *Palko* majority,

---

[90] *Id.* at 69.

[91] 316 U.S. 455 (1942) (Roberts, J.).

[92] *Id.* at 465-72.

[93] *See id.* at 477 & n.2 (Black, J., dissenting).

[94] In reliance on *Powell*, the Court had declared that the sixth amendment entitled *every* impoverished federal criminal defendant to assigned counsel. Johnson v. Zerbst, 304 U.S. 458, 462-63, 467 (1938).

[95] For a discussion of the decisions, see pp. 246-49 *supra*.

[96] 302 U.S. 319 (1937).

[97] *Id.* at 323.

[98] Betts v. Brady, 316 U.S. 455, 473 (1942).

[99] *Id.* at 475-76 (Black, J., dissenting).

[100] *See* 304 U.S. 144, 152 n.4 (1938). Other criminal procedure decisions of the Stone period are summarized in Boskey & Pickering, *Federal Restrictions on State Criminal Procedure*, 13 U.Chi. L. Rev. 266 (1946).

[101] *See Betts*, 316 U.S. at 461-62:

> The due process clause of the fourteenth amendment does not incorporate, as such, the specific guarantees found in the Sixth Amendment, although a denial by a State of rights or privileges

first suggested the sweeping doctrine for which his dissent in *Adamson v. California*[102] would soon make him famous. Legislative history showed, Black argued in *Betts,* that the purpose of the fourteenth amendment was "to make secure against invasion by the states the fundamental liberties and safeguards set out in the Bill of Rights," including the right to counsel:[103] "I believe that the fourteenth amendment made the sixth amendment applicable to the states."[104] This position had been rejected before, and there were troublesome arguments against it.[105] However, if the Senate spokesman for the amendment was correct in saying that it made all the protections of the Bill of Rights "privileges or immunities of citizens of the United States" binding the states as well,[106] it was not inconsistent after all to enforce these rights aggressively against the states while essentially abandoning substantive due process, for in this view their applicability to the states did not depend on that discredited doctrine at all.

## IV.  INSULAR MINORITIES AND POLITICAL PROCESSES

### A.  Blacks

*Carolene Products* hinted at strict enforcement not only of "specific" constitutional prohibitions—which should have included the equal protection clause and the fifteenth amendment's ban on racial denial of the vote—but also of provisions protecting "those political processes which can ordinarily be expected to bring about repeal of undesirable legislation" or the rights of "discrete and insular minorities."[107] These two categories coalesced in *Smith v. Allwright,*[108] a case involving a white primary, where the Court delivered one of its greatest blows both for the equality of blacks and for the integrity of our political system.

Although the Court had previously struck down the exclusion of blacks from primary elections whenever it could find the state responsible, it had felt stymied in *Grovey v. Townsend,*[109] where the discriminatory decision had been made by a party convention. Nine years after *Grovey,* in *Smith,* the Court changed its mind. On second thought, the discrimination could be pinned on the state after all.[110]

---

specifically embodied in that and others of the first eight amendments may . . . operate, in a given case, to deprive a litigant of due process of law. . . .

[102] 332 U.S. U.S. 46 (1947).

[103] 316 U.S. at 474 & n.1 (Black, J., dissenting); *cf. Adamson,* 332 U.S. at 68-123 (Black, J., dissenting).

[104] *Betts,* 316 U.S. at 474 (Black, J., dissenting).

[105] *See* THE FIRST HUNDRED YEARS at 342-51, 363-68 (discussing the Slaughter-House Cases, 83 U.S. (16 Wall.) 36 (1873)).

[106] CONG. GLOBE, 39th Cong., 1st Sess. 2764-66 (1866) (remarks of Senator Howard).

[107] *See* United States v. Carolene Products Co., 304 U.S. 144, 152 n.4 (1938).

[108] 321 U.S. 649 (1944).

[109] 295 U.S. 45 (1935). *See* pp. 250-51 *supra.*

[110] Only Justice Roberts, author of *Grovey* and one of the two remaining Justices who had then been on the Court, dissented. *Smith,* 321 U.S. at 666-70. There was irony in his protest against the Court's willingness to overrule precedents, since Roberts himself is best known for voting to overrule decisions invalidating minimum wage laws in West Coast Hotel Co. v. Parrish, 300 U.S. 379 (1937), p. 236 *supra.*

The majority professed to find support for its change of mind in United States v. Classic, 313 U.S. 299 (1941) (Stone, J.), which had repudiated the parsimonious conclusion in Newberry v. United States, 256 U.S. 232

Justice Reed's opinion for the Court relied in substantial part on state regulation of the party, which *Grovey* had found insufficient. State law, said Reed, provided for the election of party officers and delegates to the party convention; state statutes set the fees to be paid by candidates to defray costs of the primary elections; state courts had jurisdiction "to compel party officers to perform their statutory duties."[111] Thus "[p]rimary elections [were] conducted by the party under state statutory authority," and "[t]he party [took] its character as a state agency from the duties imposed upon it by state statutes."[112]

All of this was pretty flimsy, and none of it seemed to distinguish political parties from other associations or individuals whose activities were regulated by state law. Such arguments, if taken at face value, could have largely obliterated the constitutional distinction between public and private action.[113] Not only was the Court, in conformity with Stone's dictum, showing precious little restraint in protecting minorites and the political process;[114] it also seemed to be stretching the Constitution in order to do so.

After Stone's death, the Justices had to find a new rationale for their decision in *Terry v. Adams*[115] that the "Jaybird Democratic Association's" lilywhite preprimary was unconstitutional. As Justice Minton protested in a lone dissent, the preprimary was not regulated by the state at all.[116] Justice Black, joined by Douglas and Burton, seemed to argue that the state was responsible for private discrimination because it had not prohibited it—a thesis that would wholly eliminate the requirement of state action.[117] Justice Frankfurter, in arguing that state officers had "participated in" the discriminatory scheme "by voting in the Jaybird primary," ignored the distinction between public and private acts of state officials on which he himself had most zealously insisted in other cases.[118] Justice Clark,

---

(1921), that Congress's article I authority over federal "elections" did not include primaries. *See* p. 101, note 71 *supra*. *Classic* enabled the Court in *Smith* to base its conclusion on the more obviously relevant fifteenth amendment rather than the equal protection clause, which had been the basis of two earlier cases striking down state exclusion of blacks from primaries. *See* Nixon v. Condon, 286 U.S. 73 (1932); Nixon v. Herndon, 273 U.S. 536 (1927). It was of no direct relevance to the problem that had precluded relief in *Grovey*, however, for *Classic* involved both actions of state officials and a provision that did not require state action. The fifteenth amendment, like the fourteenth, applies to the "State[s]" and also, unlike the latter, to the United States.

[111] *Smith*, 321 U.S. at 663.

[112] *Id.*

[113] *See* THE FIRST HUNDRED YEARS at 398-402 (discussing the Civil Rights Cases, 109 U.S. 3 (1883)).

[114] *See Smith*, 321 U.S. at 662 ("Despite Texas' decision that the exclusion is produced by private or party action, . . . federal courts must for themselves appraise the facts leading to that conclusion."); *see also* p. 249, note 31 *supra* (discussing Norris v. Alabama, 294 U.S. 587 (1935)).

[115] 345 U.S. 461 (1953).

[116] *Id.* at 485 (Minton, J., dissenting).

[117] *Id.* at 469 (opinion of Black, J.) ("For a state to permit such a duplication of its election processes is to permit a flagrant abuse of those processes to defeat the purposes of the Fifteenth Amendment."); *see also id.* at 485 (Minton, J., dissenting) ("As I understand Mr. Justice Black's opinion, he would have this Court redress the wrong even if it was individual action alone.").

[118] *See id.* at 473-77 (opinion of Frankfurter, J.); *id.* at 485 (Minton, J., dissenting) (adding that the record contained no evidence that officials had participated in the primary); *cf.* Snowden v. Hughes, 321 U.S. 1, 17 (1944) (Frankfurter, J., concurring) ("I am unable to grasp the principle on which the State can here be said to deny the plaintiff the equal protection of the laws of the State when the foundation of his claim is that the Board had disobeyed the authentic command of the State."); Monroe v. Pape, 365 U.S. 167, 202-59 (1961) (Frankfurter, J., dissenting) (taking a similar view of the "under color of" state law requirement of 42 U.S.C. § 1983 (1982)).

writing for the remaining four members of the Court, seemed to put his finger on a more promising argument:

> [T]he Jaybird Democratic Association is the decisive power in the county's recognized electoral process. . . . [W]hen a state structures its electoral apparatus in a form which devolves upon a political organization the uncontested choice of public officials, that organization itself, in whatever disguise, takes on those attributes of government which draw the Constitution's safeguards into play.[119]

This argument takes on meaning from Justice Black's opinion in *Marsh v. Alabama*,[120] one of the Court's last pronouncements before Stone's death in 1946. That case followed *Lovell v. City of Griffin*[121] and other precedents in forbidding a municipality to bar the sidewalk distribution of literature or to condition it on a permit that could be denied at will.[122] There was just one difference between *Marsh* and the earlier cases: the municipality in *Marsh* was a company town.

Chickasaw, Alabama, where the case arose, was owned and governed by the Gulf Shipbuilding Corporation.[123] Justice Reed, joined by Stone and Burton, objected in dissent that *Marsh* was "the first case to extend by law the privilege of religious exercises . . . to private places without the assent of the owner."[124] Justice Black demurred, arguing that the corporation's right to control the residents of Chickasaw was not "coextensive with the right of a homeowner to regulate the conduct of his guests."[125] "[A] company-owned town," as Frankfurter succinctly stated in a concurring opinion, "is a town."[126] Except for the question of title, Black added, there was "nothing to distinguish Chickasaw from any other town,"[127] and the public interest in open channels of communication was the same.[128]

Those who govern, in other words, are the "state" within the meaning of the fourteenth amendment. The purposes of the amendment are applicable to all who perform the functions of government, whether they are elected, appointed, or otherwise private persons. That seems to be what Justice Clark was suggesting when he noted in *Terry* that the Jaybird organization had "take[n] on those attributes of government which draw the Consti-

---

[119]*Terry,* 345 U.S. at 484 (Clark, J., concurring); *cf. id.* at 469 (opinion of Black, J.) ("The only election that has counted in this Texas county for more than fifty years has been that held by the Jaybirds from which Negroes were excluded. . . . The Jaybird primary has become an integral part, indeed the only effective part, of the elective process that determines who shall rule and govern in the county.").

[120]326 U.S. 501 (1946).

[121]303 U.S. 444 (1938).

[122]*Marsh,* 326 U.S. at 504 (citing *Lovell,* 303 U.S. 444 (1938), p. 261 *supra*).

[123]*Marsh,* 326 U.S. at 502-03; *id.* at 513 (Reed, J., dissenting) (Company towns "may be essential to furnish proper and convenient living conditions for employees on isolated operations in lumbering, mining, production of high explosives and large-scale farming."). "In the bituminous coal industry alone," Justice Black noted, "approximately one-half of the miners in the United States lived in company-owned houses in the period from 1922-23." *Id.* at 508 n.5.

[124]*Id.* at 512 (Reed, J., dissenting).

[125]*Id.* at 506.

[126]*Id.* at 510 (Frankfurter, J., concurring).

[127]*Id.* at 503.

[128]*Id.* at 507.

tution's safeguards into play." [129] Justice Reed, despite his *Marsh* dissent and his stress on ephemeral traces of state regulation in *Smith,* had intimated the same thing when he commented in that case that "recognition of the place of the primary in the electoral scheme makes clear that state delegation to a party of the power to fix the qualifications of primary elections is delegation of a state function that may make the party's action the action of the State." [130]

Like governing itself, in other words, the election of those who govern is such a central state function that whoever controls it is the "state" within the meaning of constitutional limitations. This test, like most, would present nasty line-drawing problems. Yet it seemed much more faithful to the purposes of the Framers than any of the more sweeping theories that had been offered in an effort to make the fifteenth amendment more than an empty formality. Moreover, it certainly suggested very little in the way of judicial restraint.

## B.   Other Outsiders

Because state regulations affecting interstate commerce often imposed burdens "principally upon those without the state," Justice Stone had noted in *South Carolina Highway Department v. Barnwell Brothers*[131] in 1938, "legislative action [in such cases] is not likely to be subjected to those political restraints which are normally exerted on legislation." In light of these observations it was understandable that Stone cited *Barnwell* in *Carolene Products* along with cases of racial and religious discrimination as an example of the arguable need for "more searching judicial inquiry" in cases involving "discrete and insular minorities." [132]

Since geographical outsiders have no vote, they are in special need of constitutional protection. An efficient way to provide this protection, with relatively modest displacement of the normal political process, is to tie the fate of those who are not represented to that of those who are by forbidding discrimination. [133] The Framers utilized this approach in article IV by requiring one state to afford citizens of another all the privileges and immunities of its own citizens. The same method was employed in the fourteenth, fifteenth, and nineteenth amendments to protect the interests of blacks and later of women. As Justice Stone explained in *Barnwell,* this approach also helps to explain the Court's long-standing insistence that interstate commerce may not be subjected to discriminatory burdens. [134]

---

[129] Terry v. Adams, 345 U.S. 461, 484 (1953) (Clark, J., concurring).

[130] Smith v. Allwright, 321 U.S. 649, 660 (1944); *see also id.* at 664 ("When primaries become a part of the machinery for choosing officials, state and national, . . . the same tests to determine the character of discrimination or abridgement should be applied to the primary as are applied to the general election."). For an approving view, see Cushman, *The Texas "White Primary" Case*—Smith v. Allwright, 30 CORNELL L.Q. 66 (1944).

[131] 303 U.S. 177, 185 n.2 (1938). *See* p. 241 *supra.*

[132] United States v. Carolene Prods. Co., 304 U.S. 144, 152 n.4 (1938). Justice Stone also cited in this connection McCulloch v. Maryland, 17 U.S. (4 Wheat.) 316, 428 (1819), where Justice Marshall had made a similar argument in holding the Bank of the United States immune from state taxation. *See* THE FIRST HUNDRED YEARS at 165-68.

[133] *See* J. ELY, DEMOCRACY AND DISTRUST 81-87 (1980).

[134] *See* 303 U.S. at 185 (dictum) ("The commerce clause, by its own force, prohibits discrimination against interstate commerce, whatever its form or method. . . ."); *see also, e.g.,* Welton v. Missouri, 91 U.S. 275 (1876) (striking down state tax applicable only to out-of-state goods), THE FIRST HUNDRED YEARS at 404-05. Because

*Edwards v. California*,[135] abandoning ancient dicta in holding that the commerce clause forbade a state to exclude paupers in the most important opinion of the short-tenured Justice Byrnes, properly reflected these concerns with the observation that "the indigent non-residents who are the real victims of this statute are deprived of the opportunity to exert political pressure upon the California legislature in order to obtain a change in policy."[136] Douglas, Black, and Murphy, evidently gearing up for an assault on the Court's commerce clause jurisprudence, argued instead that the state's action abridged the mysterious right to travel originally recognized in *Crandall v. Nevada*,[137] which the *Slaughter-House Cases*[138] had described as a privilege or immunity of national citizenship protected by the fourteenth amendment; Jackson basically agreed.[139] Although Douglas mentioned it in passing, none of the Justices relied on the most obvious constitutional basis for the decision: clear discrimination against citizens of other states in violation of the privileges and immunities clause of article IV.[140]

---

local residents with normal political power may also engage in interstate transactions, the analogy to racial minorities is not perfect. Yet the presence of outside interests suggests that the concerns of interstate commerce may be underrepresented in the counsels of any one state.

Marshall's reasoning in the analogous field of intergovernmental immunity in *McCulloch*, 17 U.S. (4 Wheat.) at 428, seemed to go further than this argument required. A ban limited to *discriminatory* taxes, such as that imposed in *McCulloch* itself, would have given the national bank political protection by tying its fate to that of local institutions. Under Chief Justice Stone, recognizing that the United States could protect itself by legislation and that the states were adequately represented in Congress, the Court continued to chip away at intergovernmental immunities. *See, e.g.,* Case v. Bowles, 327 U.S. 92 (1946) (Black, J.) (federal price regulation may apply to state timber sales), *supra* p. 303, note 171; Penn Dairies, Inc. v. Milk Control Comm'n, 318 U.S. 261 (1943) (Stone, C. J.) (upholding application of state minimum price regulations to sale of milk to United States); Alabama v. King & Boozer, 314 U.S. 1 (1941) (Stone, C. J.) (upholding state tax on government contractor's purchase of building materials despite contract clause passing on all costs to United States). Neither Stone nor any other Justice voted, however, to abandon such immunities entirely or to limit that of the United States strictly to discriminatory measures. *See, e.g.,* United States v. Allegheny County, 322 U.S. 174 (1944) (Jackson, J.) (striking down nondiscriminatory tax on government property). The immunity decisions of the period are discussed in Powell, *The Waning of Intergovernmental Tax Immunities*, 58 HARV. L. REV. 633 (1945), and Powell, *The Remnant of Intergovernmental Tax Immunities*, 58 HARV. L. REV. 757 (1945).

[135] 314 U.S. 160 (1941).

[136] *Id.* at 174. *Contra, e.g.,* New York v. Miln, 36 U.S. (11 Pet.) 102, 142-43 (1837) (upholding requirement that ship captains furnish authorities with passenger lists with the observation that states had right to protect themselves against "the moral pestilence of paupers, vagabonds, and possibly convicts"). The question of state authority to exclude paupers had been reserved in Henderson v. Mayor of New York, 92 U.S. 259, 275 (1876), where a bond requirement had been struck down as a means of coercing payment of a forbidden tax. *See* THE FIRST HUNDRED YEARS at 204-06, 405-08.

[137] 73 U.S. (6 Wall.) 35 (1868), THE FIRST HUNDRED YEARS at 355.

[138] 83 U.S. (16 Wall.) 36, 79 (1873).

[139] *See Edwards*, 314 U.S. at 177-81 (Douglas, J., concurring); *id.* at 181-86 (Jackson, J., concurring). Jackson, while conceding that Byrnes's commerce clause ground was "permissible . . . under applicable authorities," also emphasized the *Crandall* argument, reopening a controversy long considered settled, by suggesting that "the migrations of a human being . . . do not fit easily into my notions as to what is commerce." *Id.* at 181-82; *cf.* Passenger Cases, 48 U.S. (7 How.) 283 (1849); Groves v. Slaughter, 40 U.S. (15 Pet.) 449 (1841); THE FIRST HUNDRED YEARS at 168-69 & n.78, 222-30. Byrnes's first draft had reportedly based the decision on the privileges or immunities clause, but Stone talked him out of it by reminding him of the mischief that Old Guard Justices had attempted under that provision. *See* A. MASON, HARLAN FISKE STONE: PILLAR OF THE LAW 578-80 (1956); p. 234 *supra* (discussing Colgate v. Harvey, 296 U.S. 404 (1935)).

[140] "[T]here are expressions in the cases that this right of free movement of persons is an incident of *state* citizenship protected against discriminatory state action by Art. IV, § 2 of the Constitution." *Edwards*, 314 U.S.

In *Barnwell* Justice Stone had come close to saying that the states could regulate commerce so long as they did not discriminate against it.[141] Justice Douglas echoed this position in his dissent in *Southern Pacific Co. v. Arizona*,[142] where the majority struck down a nondiscriminatory provision limiting the length of trains. Justice Black, in a separate dissent in *Southern Pacific*, seemed to question the entire notion that the commerce clause limited state power, suggesting that the Court should be "at least" as deferential to state legislatures in this field as it was in substantive due process cases.[143] The Chief Justice, however, took the occasion to entrench for the majority his original position that the validity of nondiscriminatory state regulations affecting commerce turned on "accommodation of the competing demands of the state and national interests involved."[144]

The dubious safety advantages of the train-length law sufficiently distinguish *Southern Pacific* from *Barnwell*, which had upheld an obviously reasonable limitation of the width of trucks.[145] The tone of the two opinions, however, was significantly different. While *Barnwell* had intimated that even severe burdens on commerce were permissible in the absence of discrimination, *Southern Pacific* declared that the states had wide scope for regulation of matters of local concern "provided it [did] not materially restrict the free flow of commerce across state lines."[146] The contrast between the deferential tone of *Barnwell* and the unabashed activism of *Southern Pacific* suggests that Stone's thinking about the commerce clause had undergone some evolution in the intervening years.

---

at 180 (Douglas, J., concurring) (emphasis in original). The Court had consistently applied this provision according to its purpose of preventing one state from discriminating against citizens of another. *See* THE FIRST HUNDRED YEARS at 348 & n.137. In addition, the Articles of Confederation, from which the clause was taken, had expressly included the right of "free ingress and regress to and from any other State"—not qualified to except "paupers, vagabonds, and fugitives from justice," as was the basic provision itself at the time. Articles of Confederation, art. 4. It seems most unlikely that in omitting the explanatory clause respecting the right of entry, the Framers of the present Constitution, which generally increased the restrictions on state authority, meant to empower one state to deny another's citizens the most fundamental privilege of all.

[141]    In each of these cases regulation involves a burden on interstate commerce. But so long as the state action does not discriminate, the burden is one which the Constitution permits because it is an inseparable incident of the exercise of a legislative authority, which, under the Constitution, has been left to the states.

*Barnwell*, 303 U.S. at 189.

[142] 325 U.S. 761, 795-96 (1945) (Douglas, J., dissenting) ("My view has been that the courts should intervene only where the state legislation discriminated against interstate commerce or was out of harmony with laws which Congress had enacted.").

[143] *Id.* at 792 (Black, J., dissenting).

[144] *Id.* at 769; *see also* Parker v. Brown, 317 U.S. 341, 362 (1943) (Stone, C. J.) (applying same test to uphold state restrictions on marketing of raisins); Di Santo v. Pennsylvania, 273 U.S. 34, 44 (1927) (Stone, J., dissenting).

[145] *See Southern Pacific*, 325 U.S. at 781-82 (the state's "regulation of train lengths, admittedly obstructive to interstate train operation, . . . passes beyond what is plainly essential for safety since it does not appear that it will lessen rather than increase the danger of accident."); *Barnwell*, 303 U.S. at 196 (noting that the use of ninety-six-inch trucks on roads with ninety-six-inch lanes "tends to force other traffic off the concrete surface"); *see also id.* at 191-96 (upholding a gross-weight limitation designed to prevent road damage over the objection that limitations on weight per axle would have sufficed). Chief Justice Stone's explicit basis for distinguishing the two cases—the state's ownership of its highways—seemed less compelling. *Southern Pacific*, 325 U.S. at 783; *cf.* Bibb v. Navajo Freight Lines, 359 U.S. 520 (1959) (striking down highway regulation that exposed interstate truckers to contradictory requirements in different states).

[146] *See Southern Pacific*, 325 U.S. at 770; *Barnwell*, 303 U.S. at 189.

In aggressively applying a balancing test for determining the reasonableness of laws that imposed neither discriminatory nor cumulative burdens on interstate trade, Chief Justice Stone seemed to go beyond *Barnwell*'s explanation that relatively strict scrutiny was necessary to protect politically impotent outsiders from competitive disadvantage. In so doing, however, he merely made explicit what the Court had basically been doing for nearly a century.[147] By stressing the distinct national interest in unimpeded interstate transportation, moreover, he seemed to assimilate the implicit limitation of the commerce clause on state power to those "specific prohibitions" which, like those of the Bill of Rights, were also candidates for less restrained judicial enforcement under *Carolene Products*. In short, like Jackson in *Barnette* and Black in *Betts*, the Chief Justice seemed to make clear in *Southern Pacific* that his objection to the economic activism of the days before 1937 was to substantive due process, not to aggressive judicial review.

## C.   Interstate Relations

Like the privileges and immunities clause of the same article, the full faith and credit clause of article IV was designed to protect unrepresented out-of-state interests in the name of interstate harmony—in this case the legitimate interests of other states in recognition of their governmental acts. In light of his heightened concern for the politically powerless in *Carolene Products,* it seems surprising that Stone's signal contribution to this field was to replace the traditional strict scrutiny of state choice-of-law decisions with a deferential analysis that permitted any interested state to resolve conflicts in its own favor.[148]

Unlike the equally deferential commerce clause views he had expressed in *Barnwell*, this interest analysis continued to determine interstate choice-of-law decisions after Stone's elevation to Chief Justice.[149] Once the rights of the parties had been determined by litigation, however, Stone was faithful to his own prior position that the policy of finality

---

[147] *See* pp. 36-40 *supra.*

[148] *See* Alaska Packers Ass'n v. Industrial Accident Comm'n, 294 U.S. 532 (1935) (Stone, J.); Pacific Employers Ins. Co. v. Industrial Accident Comm'n, 306 U.S. 493 (1939) (Stone, J.) (allowing either state of accident or of contract to apply its own workers' compensation law); pp. 45-47; 110, note 123; & 242 *supra,* discussing the earlier cases. It was understandable that Stone would reject the Procrustean notion that only the state where an event occurred had any legitimate concern in its regulation, but his theory of unrepresented interests might have led him to attempt to determine which state's interest was the greater. *Cf.* Jackson, *Full Faith and Credit—The Lawyer's Clause of the Constitution,* 45 COLUM. L. REV. 1 (1945). *But see* Freund, *Chief Justice Stone and the Conflict of Laws,* 59 HARV. L. REV. 1210, 1235 (1946) ("[P]roblems of choice of law have not lent themselves to satisfactory solution as constitutional questions, and . . . in their nature they cannot be expected to.").

[149] *See* State Farm Mut. Auto Ins. Co. v. Duel, 324 U.S. 154, 158, 160 (1945) (Douglas, J.) (state may determine amount of reserve out-of-state insurer must maintain to satisfy claims by insured residents); Pink v. A.A.A. Highway Express, Inc., 314 U.S. 201, 210-11 (1941) (Stone, C. J.) (state may apply own law to determine whether resident has become member of out-of-state corporation and thus liable for share of its debts); *see also* Freund, *supra* note 148, at 1232 (noting the "notable latitude" left the states by the *Pink* decision: "If choice of law in commercial transactions is to be subjected to some extent to the unifying force of the full faith and credit clause, there could scarcely be a more appropriate matter for such treatment than the relation of a policyholder to his company. . . .").

embodied in the full faith clause required even an interested state to respect another state's judgment.[150]

The critical assumption on which this clause subordinates the interest of one state to another state's interest in finality, however, is that the litigant have a reasonable opportunity to present his case in the forum whose judgment is sought to be enforced.[151] This assumption fails when a judgment is pleaded against one who was not a party to the initial litigation and when the parties have every incentive to frustrate the nonparty's legitimate interest. Thus it was entirely appropriate for the Court in *Williams v. North Carolina*[152] to hold that a foreign divorce decree did not preclude a state from prosecuting for bigamy two of its residents who had remarried after traveling to another state for the sole purpose of evading the strict divorce limitations of their home state.

The Court had shown less concern for the interest of the stay-at-home spouse whose partner had fled to Nevada by holding, in an earlier chapter of the same litigation, that a divorce was valid though the defendant never had any contact with the divorcing state.[153]

---

[150] Magnolia Petroleum Co. v. Hunt, 320 U.S. 430 (1943) (one state's workers' compensation award bars second claim for same injury in second state). Chief Justice Stone distinguished between statutes and judgments and stressed "the clear purpose of the full faith and credit clause to establish throughout the federal system the salutary principle of the common law that a litigation once pursued to judgment shall be as conclusive of the rights of the parties in every other court as in that where the judgment was rendered." *Id.* at 436-39; *see* Freund, *supra* note 148, at 1225-30; Cheatham, *Res Judicata and the Full Faith and Credit Clause:* Magnolia Petroleum Co. v. Hunt, 44 COLUM. L. REV. 330 (1944) (arguing that workers' compensation should be treated as an exceptional case). *See also* Milwaukee County v. M. E. White Co., 296 U.S. 268 (1935) (Stone, J.) (requiring state to respect sister-state judgment for taxes); Yarborough v. Yarborough, 290 U.S. 202 (1933) (forbidding state to grant child support beyond that provided by sister-state decree); Fauntleroy v. Lum, 210 U.S. 230 (1908) (requiring state to respect judgment on gambling contract contrary to its public policy). Stone had let sympathy draw him from this path in *Yarborough,* 290 U.S. at 213-27 (Stone, J., dissenting), but since then he had been the Court's leading spokesman for a strict interstate res judicata policy.

The award given binding effect in *Magnolia* was that of an administrative agency rather than of a court, but, as Stone said, the policy of the clause was unaffected by the label: whether the proceeding was a "judicial" one or its award a "record," the clause required both to be equally respected. 320 U.S. at 443. Justice Black, writing for the four dissenters, made the more serious objection that the first state's tribunal had no jurisdiction to decide claims under any other state's law: "The decision of this Court today, therefore, is tantamount to holding that Texas intended to extinguish a claim against the employer in a proceeding in which . . . liability under Louisiana law was not allowed to be raised." *Id.* at 453. Jurisdiction to decide had always been a condition of full faith and credit. *See* D'Arcy v. Ketchum, 52 U.S. (11 How.) 165 (1851). Unless filing a claim under one state's law fairly can be held an election, there are due process difficulties in allowing a tribunal to destroy rights it has no jurisdiction to enforce. *See* Hansberry v. Lee, 311 U.S. 32 (1940) (Stone, J.) (holding due process forbade enforcing judgment against nonparty).

A few years after *Magnolia,* in Industrial Comm'n v. McCartin, 330 U.S. 622, 627-28 (1947) (Murphy, J.), a unanimous Court sensibly permitted a second state to give further compensation after concluding that the first tribunal had intended to preclude further relief only under its own law. For the subsequent fate of these decisions, see Thomas v. Washington Gas Light Co. 448 U.S. 261 (1980), in which six Justices voted to repudiate *McCartin* and four to overrule *Magnolia* as well.

[151] *See Hansberry,* 311 U.S. at 40-45; pp. 70-78 supra.

[152] 325 U.S. 226 (1945) (Frankfurter, J.). *See also* Lorenzen, *Extraterritorial Divorce*—Williams v. North Carolina II, 54 YALE L.J. 799, 801-02 (1945) ("[A] divorce decree in such circumstances appears more like an interference by Nevada in the marital relations of North Carolinians. . . .").

[153] Williams v. North Carolina, 317 U.S. 287 (1942) (Douglas, J.) (overruling Haddock v. Haddock, 201 U.S. 562 (1906), pp. 76-78 *supra*).

As Justice Jackson succinctly stated in his dissent, the net result was that "settled family relationships may be destroyed by a procedure that we would not recognize if the suit were one to collect on a grocery bill." [154] Unless one concludes that the absent spouse was not substantially harmed because the marriage in question existed in name only, [155] this decision seems hardly reconcilable with the modern standard of "minimum contacts, . . . 'fair play and substantial justice' " that Chief Justice Stone would soon enunciate to determine whether a state's exercise of personal jurisdiction was consistent with due process in *International Shoe Co. v. Washington.* [156]

In *International Shoe,* decided only a few months before his death, Chief Justice Stone did for the law of personal jurisdiction what he had been doing since his appointment for full faith and credit, intergovernmental immunity, extraterritorial taxation, and state laws affecting interstate commerce. [157] He brought order out of chaos, brought out of the closet the functional considerations that had often underlain earlier decisions, and laid down sensible criteria that have governed ever since. [158]

## D.   Representation

The famous 1946 decision in *Colegrove v. Green* [159] involved a challenge by Illinois citizens to the apportionment of congressional seats among various districts within the state. One of the complainants lived in a district containing more than 900,000 people; other districts contained as few as 112,000. [160] The complainant's vote, as Justice Black observed in his dissent, was "only one-ninth as effective . . . as the votes of other citizens." [161]

Joined as usual by Douglas and Murphy, Black argued that "[s]uch discriminatory legislation . . . [was] exactly the kind that the equal protection clause was intended to prohibit." [162] As an original matter this conclusion seems questionable, since the Framers' focus was on racial discrimination and they had expressly disclaimed any intention of affecting the right to vote. [163] By 1946 it was a little late to raise either objec-

---

[154] *Williams,* 317 U.S. at 316 (Jackson, J., dissenting).

[155] *See* D. Currie, *Suitcase Divorce in the Conflict of Laws,* 34 U. CHI. L. REV. 26, 29 (1966). This suggestion was based on Estin v. Estin, 334 U.S. 541, 546-48 (1948), and May v. Anderson, 345 U.S. 528, 534 (1953), which had reduced the impact of an *ex parte* divorce by holding it could not cut off rights to alimony or child custody. *But see* Simons v. Miami Beach First Nat'l Bank, 381 U.S. 81 (1965) (holding *ex parte* divorce extinguished right to dower).

[156] 326 U.S. 310, 316 (1945).

[157] *See* pp. 240-42, 325-29 *supra.*

[158] *See* Cheatham, *Stone on Conflict of Laws,* 45 COLUM. L. REV. 719, 729 (1945). In *International Shoe,* 326 U.S. at 322-26, Justice Black wrote a separate opinion agreeing that the court below had jurisdiction and protesting, as he did repeatedly in other contexts, that the Constitution gave the Court no warrant to determine whether a state's exercise of power was "reasonable" or in accord with "fair play and substantial justice." *See supra* text accompanying notes 142-46 and *infra* p. 362, note 194 (discussing Southern Pacific Co. v. Arizona, 325 U.S. 76 (1945), and Adamson v. California, 332 U.S. 46 (1947)).

[159] 328 U.S. 549 (1946).

[160] *See id.* at 569 (Black, J., dissenting).

[161] *Id.* (Black, J., dissenting).

[162] *Id.* (Black, J., dissenting).

[163] *See* THE FIRST HUNDRED YEARS at 342-51, 384 (discussing the Slaughter-House Cases, 83 U.S. (16 Wall.) 36 (1873), and Strauder v. West Virginia, 100 U.S. 303 (1880)).

tion.[164] Whether there might be justifications for the discrepancy in voting power, however, remained to be seen.[165]

Although the substantive issues raised by the complaint were extremely challenging, the majority did not reach them. Justice Frankfurter, joined by Reed and Burton, concluded that the questions presented were "of a peculiarly political nature and therefore not meet for judicial determination."[166] Rutledge, the only other Justice participating, concluded that the complaint had been properly dismissed "for want of equity."[167] Hence, by a four-to-three vote, the judgment dismissing the complaint was affirmed.

Earlier decisions had occasionally suggested that certain "political" questions were indeed beyond judicial ken.[168] The whole course of constitutional decision, however, demonstrated that the mere fact that an issue was of political significance did not bring it within that category. Though some of the opinions were foggy, the Court seemed largely to have held that certain matters lay within the discretion of other governmental bodies[169] and that the provision of article IV by which the United States guaranteed to each state a republican form of government, as its text suggested, gave the citizen no enforceable rights.[170]

Frankfurter's most concrete argument was that article I gave *Congress* authority to revise state regulations governing the time, place, and manner of congressional elections.[171] Explicit congressional authority to enforce the Civil War amendments,[172] however, had never been held to oust courts of jurisdiction to determine the constitutionality of state action under them. Furthermore, since it was Congress that was allegedly malapportioned, there was a particularly hollow ring to Justice Frankfurter's contention that "[t]he remedy for unfairness in districting" was "to invoke the ample powers of Congress."[173] In fact *Colegrove* was a classic illustration of Stone's wisdom in suggesting a special need for judicial review to assure the proper functioning of "those political pro-

---

[164] *See id.* at 390-92 (discussing the extension of equal protection to nonracial classifications); pp. 138-39 *supra* (discussing its application to voting in Nixon v. Herndon, 273 U.S. 536 (1927)).

[165] Justice Black also invoked article I's requirement that members of the House be "chosen . . . by the People of the several States," U. S. CONST. art. I, § 2, cl. 1, which obviously required some interpretation before it could be said to outlaw the apportionment in question. *See Colegrove*, 328 U.S. at 570 (Black, J., dissenting).

[166] *Colegrove*, 328 U.S. at 552.

[167] *Id.* at 565 (Rutledge, J., concurring).

[168] *See* THE FIRST HUNDRED YEARS at 67 & n.19, 252-57 (discussing Marbury v. Madison, 5 U.S. (1 Cranch) 137, 165-71 (1803), and Luther v. Borden, 48 U.S. (7 How.) 1 (1849)); p. 272, note 7 (discussing Coleman v. Miller, 307 U.S. 433 (1939)).

[169] *E.g.*, Williams v. Suffolk Ins. Co., 38 U.S. (13 Pet.) 415, 421 (1839) (President's authority to recognize foreign sovereignty), THE FIRST HUNDRED YEARS at 253 n.121; *see also Marbury*, 5 U.S. (1 Cranch) at 137. The foggiest decision of all, *Coleman*, 307 U.S. at 433, can be viewed as holding that the Constitution imposed no limit on the time for ratification of an amendment and did not forbid ratification after rejection, though the Court also spoke more vaguely about the lack of judicially manageable standards for decision. *See id.* at 453-55.

[170] *See* U. S. CONST. art. IV, § 4; *see also* Pacific States Tel. & Tel. Co. v. Oregon, 233 U.S. 118, 143-51 (1912); Luther v. Borden, 48 U.S. (7 How.) 1 (1849).

[171] *Colegrove*, 328 U.S. at 554 (citing U. S. CONST. art. 1, § 4, cl. 1).

[172] *See* U. S. CONST. amends. XIII-XV.

[173] *Colegrove*, 328 U.S. at 556. Justice Frankfurter also suggested that voters might "secure State legislatures that will apportion properly," *id.*, but those legislatures were apportioned in the same way and therefore no more likely than Congress to give away the excessive power of their incumbents. *See id.* at 567 (Black, J., dissenting).

cesses which can ordinarily be expected to bring about repeal of undesirable legislation."[174]

Chief Justice Stone died suddenly in April 1946, shortly before *Colegrove* was decided. Someone must have known how he would have voted in the case, since it had been argued before his death. One likes to think he would have voted with Justice Black to determine the case on its merits, since it was he who had pointed out in *Carolene Products* that the integrity of the democratic process was the crucial assumption on which deference to the political branches rested.[175]

Nothing in Justice Frankfurter's brief opinion seems sufficient to justify a refusal to determine the impact of the equal protection clause in such a context. He would make a much more elaborate effort to do so some sixteen years later in *Baker v. Carr.*[176] For now let it suffice that, popular impressions to the contrary notwithstanding, Frankfurter lost on this issue in *Colegrove*. In providing the decisive vote for dismissal on the ground that it might be too late for the petitioners to obtain effective relief before the impending election, Justice Rutledge made clear that he thought precedent established that the questions raised were justiciable.[177]

---

[174]United States v. Carolene Prods. Co., 304 U.S. 144, 152 n.4 (1938). *See also* R. JACKSON, THE STRUGGLE FOR JUDICIAL SUPREMACY 285 (1941).

[175]Justice Murphy's biographer reports that "only one Justice" (not Black, Murphy, or Rutledge) voted to intervene when *Colegrove* was first discussed in conference, and that Justice Black initially had the "assignment" of writing to deny justiciability. *See* J. HOWARD, *supra* note 43, at 484 & n.c.

[176]369 U.S. 186, 266-330 (1962) (Frankfurter, J., dissenting). *See* pp. 412–14 *infra*.

[177]*Colegrove*, 328 U.S. at 564-65 (Rutledge, J., concurring).

# Conclusion to Part Five

Stone's brief tenure as Chief Justice was a time of great Justices—Stone himself, Black, Frankfurter, and Jackson, to name only the most illustrious. Seldom have so many gifted Justices graced the institution at the same time.

It was a time of great victories and of great disappointments. Great blows were struck for freedom in such inspiring opinions as *Duncan v. Kahanamoku* and *Ex parte Endo, Cramer v. United States* and *Estep v. United States, Martin v. City of Struthers* and *West Virginia State Board of Education v. Barnette, Smith v. Allwright* and *Marsh v. Alabama.* Entire fields of law were modernized and clarified by the Chief Justice's fine opinions in *Southern Pacific Co. v. Arizona* and *International Shoe Co. v. Washington.* The Court did what it could to curb the excesses of war; but cases like *Ex parte Quirin, In re Yamashita, Hirabayashi v. United States,* and *Korematsu v. United States* were sobering reminders of both the limits of judicial review and the responsibility of other branches for safeguarding fundamental liberties. *Colegrove v. Green* postponed for a generation the correction of the glaring anomaly of malapportionment, and *Betts v. Brady* prevented for the same period fulfillment of the promise of fair trial the Court had made ten years before.

It was a time of vigorous disagreement among the Justices, most notably over the question of heightened scrutiny of measures affecting "specific" constitutional prohibitions, political processes, and insular minorities that Stone had raised in his perceptive footnote in the first *Carolene Products* case. To a substantial extent Stone's view had already prevailed, though the battle was not to be fully won until Justice Frankfurter's retirement in 1962. As leading spokesmen for the two competing views, Justices Black and Frankfurter, like Field and Miller three-quarters of a century before,[1] squared off in 1946 for another decade and a half of intense controversy over the most fundamental questions of judicial authority.

---

[1] *See* THE FIRST HUNDRED YEARS at 357-58.

It was a time, finally, to celebrate the career of a truly extraordinary member of the Court. In his twenty years on the Bench, Harlan F. Stone had done more perhaps than any other Justice to bring constitutional law into the twentieth century.[2] We are indebted to him for one of the most effective protests against the old order[3] and for the authoritative program of the new. He almost singlehandedly wrote the modern law of intergovernmental immunity, commerce clause preemption, full faith and credit, extraterritorial taxation, and personal jurisdiction.[4] Next to Marshall and Holmes, Stone may well have been the most influential Justice yet to have sat on the Supreme Court.

[2]*See* A. MASON, HARLAN FISKE STONE: PILLAR OF THE LAW 777 (1956): ("In a logical, as well as a chrono-logical, sense Stone was the one who, in both the old and the new Court, carried the Holmes-Brandeis tradition to its fruition.").

[3]*See* United States v. Butler, 297 U.S. 1, 78-88 (1936), pp. 227-31 *supra; see also* Wechsler, *Stone and the Constitution,* 46 COLUM. L. REV. 764, 777 (1945) ("In the battle that followed [the *Butler* dissent] was the standard of attack.").

[4]*See* Cheatham, *Stone on Conflict of Laws,* 45 COLUM. L. REV. 719, 733 (1945) ("[S]ince Story wrote his great treatise over one hundred years ago no member of the court has contributed more than the late Chief Justice to conflict of laws."); Magill, *Stone on Taxation,* 46 COLUM. L. REV. 747, 752, 763 (1945) ("Mr. Justice Stone's operations in the field of state jurisdiction to tax intangibles . . . contributed much to the establishment of sen-sible rules. . . . He put intergovernmental tax relations on a sound basis.").

# Part Six

Chief Justice Vinson
1946–1953

# Introduction to Part Six

Vinson, Burton, Minton, and Clark. Scarcely household names, President Truman's four appointees to the Supreme Court tended to join the more restrained of their senior colleagues to slow down the expansion of civil liberties after the departures of Roberts and Stone at the end of World War II and the premature deaths of Frank Murphy and Wiley Rutledge in 1949.[1]

This period, however, witnessed great strides in the related field of civil rights. The Vinson Court stretched the concept of a state discrimination to outlaw judicial enforcement of racial covenants,[2] put the final nail in the coffin of the obnoxious white primary,[3] and aggressively limited discrimination against aliens[4]—while exhibiting an incongruous indifference toward disadvantageous treatment of women.[5]

While federalism remained in its deep freeze,[6] the Court struck a major blow for the

---

[1] See Frank, *Fred Vinson and the Chief Justiceship*, 21 U. CHI. L. REV. 212, 246 (1954) (describing Vinson as a "symbol of the judicial age which reversed the trend of the Hughes-Stone periods toward judicially enforced civil libert[ies]").

[2] Shelley v. Kraemer, 334 U.S. 1 (1948).

[3] See p. 358 *infra*.

[4] See p. 360 *infra*.

[5] See p. 361 *infra*.

[6] See, e.g., Oklahoma v. Civil Service Comm'n, 330 U.S. 127 (1947) (Reed, J.) (upholding Congress's power to condition federal highway grants on state's acceptance of limitations on political activity of state employees); Testa v. Katt, 330 U.S. 386 (1947) (Black, J.) (upholding power of Congress to require state courts to entertain treble-damage actions under federal price legislation); Woods v. Cloyd W. Miller Co., 333 U.S. 138, 141-44 (1948) (Douglas, J.) (upholding postwar federal rent control to alleviate results of housing deficit caused in part by war); National Mut. Ins. Co. v. Tidewater Transfer Co., 337 U.S. 582 (1949) (no majority opinion) (upholding congressional authority to grant federal court jurisdiction over controversies between citizens of the District of Columbia and citizens of a state); United States v. Sanchez, 340 U.S. 42, 44 (1950) (Clark, J.) (upholding federal tax on marijuana distributors); United States v. Kahriger, 345 U.S. 22 (1953) (Reed, J., over dissents on this point by Frankfurter and Douglas) (upholding federal tax on business of accepting wagers).

separation of powers by invalidating the President's seizure of steel mills in *Youngstown Sheet & Tube Company v. Sawyer.*[7] Moreover, despite its general passivity in the face of the persecution of suspected Communists, the Court drew a brave line in *Wieman v. Updegraff*[8] to limit indirect interference with first amendment freedoms. Indeed the Vinson period began with the incorporation of yet another of those freedoms into the due process clause of the fourteenth amendment; and that is the starting point of our inquiry.[9]

[7]343 U.S. 579 (1952).
[8]344 U.S. 183 (1952).

[9]    JUSTICES OF THE SUPREME COURT DURING THE TIME OF CHIEF JUSTICE VINSON

| | | 1946 | 48 | 50 | 52 | 54 |
|---|---|---|---|---|---|---|
| Hugo L. Black | (1937-1971) | ——————————————————————— | | | | |
| Stanley F. Reed | (1938-1957) | ——————————————————————— | | | | |
| Felix Frankfurter | (1939-1962) | ——————————————————————— | | | | |
| William O. Douglas | (1939-1975) | ——————————————————————— | | | | |
| Frank Murphy | (1940-1949) | ———————————\| | | | | |
| Robert H. Jackson | (1941-1954) | ——————————————————————— | | | | |
| Wiley B. Rutledge | (1943-1949) | ———————————\| | | | | |
| Harold H. Burton | (1945-1958) | ——————————————————————— | | | | |
| Fred M. Vinson | (1946-1953) | \|—————————————————————————————\| | | | | |
| Tom C. Clark | (1949-1967) | | | \|———————————————— | | |
| Sherman Minton | (1949-1956) | | | \|———————————————— | | |

SOURCE: G. GUNTHER, CASES AND MATERIALS ON CONSTITUTIONAL LAW app. B (11th ed. 1985).

*See generally* G. DUNNE, HUGO BLACK AND THE JUDICIAL REVOLUTION (1977); H. THOMAS, FELIX FRANKFURTER: SCHOLAR ON THE BENCH (1960); L. BAKER, FELIX FRANKFURTER (1969); J. HOWARD, MR. JUSTICE MURPHY: A POLITICAL BIOGRAPHY (1968).

# 11

# From Everson to Youngstown

## I.  RELIGION

### A.  School Buses

"Congress shall make no law," reads the first amendment, "respecting an establishment of religion, or prohibiting the free exercise thereof. . . ."[1] By their own terms, these provisions limit only the federal government.[2] While Hughes was Chief Justice, however, the Court had held that religious freedom was part of the "liberty" the fourteenth amendment protected against deprivation without due process of law.[3] In *Everson v. Board of Education* the Court concluded that the due process clause made the establishment provision applicable to the states as well.[4]

There were no dissents on this point, and there was no discussion. The difficulty was that the text did not lend itself to incorporation of the establishment clause. Unlike the provisions earlier held applicable to the states, the clause in question does not speak in terms of "freedom." It was not obvious that an establishment of religion as such would

---

[1] U. S. CONST. amend. I.

[2] *See* Permoli v. New Orleans, 44 U.S. (3 How.) 589 (1845); *cf.* Barron v. Baltimore, 32 U.S. (7 Pet.) 243 (1833) (fifth amendment prohibition of takings without just compensation inapplicable to states). *See* THE FIRST HUNDRED YEARS at 189-93.

[3] Cantwell v. Connecticut, 310 U.S. 296 (1940), p. 253 *supra*.

The only interesting free exercise case decided during the Vinson period was Kedroff v. St. Nicholas Cathedral, 344 U.S. 94 (1952) (Reed, J.), holding over Justice Jackson's dissent that New York could not transfer authority over the Russian Orthodox Church in America to local dissidents to avoid communist influence after the Russian Revolution of 1917. For criticism, see P. KURLAND, RELIGION AND THE LAW 96 (1978) ("Especially difficult to comprehend is the compulsory withdrawal of state power in favor of 'ecclesiastical government' when the very issue in the case was which of two ecclesiastical governments was entitled to make the decision.").

[4] 330 U.S. 1 (1947).

deprive anyone of "life, liberty, or property."[5] Justice Black slid over the problem, as had Roberts in the case of free exercise, with an overbroad invocation of precedent: a free exercise decision was said to have established that "the First Amendment" applied to the states.[6] Earlier incorporation decisions, it is true, had taken comparable liberties with the language. Not once, for example, had the Justices explained the bearing of the limiting phrase "without due process of law" upon state deprivation of freedom of religion, expression, and assembly.

The measure under attack in *Everson* provided government funds to transport pupils to public and parochial schools.[7] The Court upheld it five to four. Along the way, however, Justice Black gave the establishment clause a broad construction going far beyond the prohibition of a national church on the English model that the text suggested.

> Neither a state nor the Federal Government can set up a Church. Neither can pass laws which aid one religion, aid all religions, or prefer one religion over another. . . . No tax in any amount, large or small, can be levied to support any religious activities or institutions. . . . Neither a state nor the Federal Government can . . . participate in the affairs of any religious organizations or groups and *vice-versa*. In the words of Jefferson, the clause . . . was intended to erect 'a wall of separation between church and State.'[8]

For this sweeping interpretation Black relied on the history of opposition to religious taxes in Virginia that lay behind Madison's drafting of the first amendment. Opposing a bill to impose taxes to support teachers of the Christian religion, Madison's famous Memorial and Remonstrance had condemned the state's exaction of even "three pence" for religious purposes. Jefferson's Virginia Bill for Religious Liberty, enacted in response to the Remonstrance, had declared it "sinful and tyrannical" to "compel a man to furnish contributions of money for the propagation of opinions which he disbelieves."[9]

Justice Story had taken a narrower view of the Virginia Bill of Rights, opining in 1815 that an impartial subsidy of all religions would be permissible.[10] Many influential critics

---

[5] *See* Corwin, *The Supreme Court as National School Board,* 14 LAW & CONTEMP. PROBS. 3, 19 (1949); M. HOWE, THE GARDEN AND THE WILDERNESS 72-73, 138 (1965) (adding that the measure in *Everson* might be argued to deprive taxpayers of property but doubting that the fourteenth amendment was meant to deprive states of their historic authority to support religion). *But see* L. LEVY, THE ESTABLISHMENT CLAUSE 168 (1986) ("[F]reedom from an establishment . . . is an indispensable attribute of liberty.").

[6] 330 U.S. at 8 (citing Murdock v. Pennsylvania, 319 U.S. 105 (1946)). *Cf. Cantwell,* 310 U.S. at 303 (citing a speech case for the proposition that liberty in the fourteenth amendment "embraces the liberties guaranteed by the First Amendment").

[7] 330 U.S. at 3.

[8] *Id.* at 15-16 (emphasis in original).

[9] *Id.* at 11-13 (quoting the Preamble of the Virginia Bill for Religious Liberty). *See also id.* at 33-41 (Rutledge, J., dissenting). Both the Remonstrance and the bill it protested are reprinted in full as appendices to Justice Rutledge's opinion; *see id.* at 63-74.

[10] *See, e.g.,* Terrett v. Taylor, 13 U.S. (9 Cranch) 43, 49 (1815) (dictum), THE FIRST HUNDRED YEARS at 140; T. COOLEY, PRINCIPLES OF CONSTITUTIONAL LAW 205 (1880) ("by establishment of religion is meant the setting up or recognition of a state church, or at least the conferring upon one church of special favors and advantages which are denied to others."); R. CORD, SEPARATION OF CHURCH AND STATE 15 (1982); M. HOWE, *supra* note

took the same view of the federal provision. The Court's history, however, suggests a concern that went beyond the mere favoring of one sect over another. Against this background there may be significance in the Framers' decision to ban not merely an "establishment" but all laws "respecting" one,[11] and to define the forbidden establishment as not one of "a religion" but of "religion" in general.[12]

The dissenters thought it followed from the Court's reasoning that the busing provision was unconstitutional.[13] Because the state's assistance could not be attributed only to secular instruction, Justice Black's criteria seemed to fit perfectly:[14] in subsidizing bus rides to places where religious instruction was given, the state "aid[ed] . . . religion" by spending tax money "to support . . . religious activities."[15] [T]he most fitting precedent" for the majority opinion, Justice Jackson suggested, was "that of Julia who, according to Byron's reports, 'whispering "I will ne'er consent,"—consented.' "[16]

In the same sense, however, the state supports religion when it puts out a fire in a church or protects it against thieves.[17] "[W]e must be careful," wrote Justice Black, "that we do not inadvertently prohibit New Jersey from extending its general state law benefits to all its citizens without regard to their religious belief." The first amendment "requires the state to be a neutral in its relations with groups of religious believers and nonbelievers; it does not require the state to be their adversary."[18]

This argument takes on added force when one considers the free exercise clause of the

---

5, *passim;* Corwin, *supra* note 5, at 10-16; Fahy, *Religion, Education, and the Supreme Court,* 14 LAW & CONTEMP. PROBS. 73 (1949); McConnell, *Accommodation of Religion,* 1985 SUP. CT. REV. 1, 20-22; Meiklejohn, *Educational Cooperation between Church and State,* 14 LAW & CONTEMP. PROBS. 61 (1949); Murray, *Law or Prepossessions?,* 14 LAW & CONTEMP. PROBS. 23 (1949).

[11] *See* 330 U.S. at 31 (Rutledge, J., dissenting); L. LEVY, *supra* note 5, at 95; Pfeffer, *Church and State: Something Less Than Separation,* 19 U. CHI. L. REV. 1, 14 (1951). *But see* Corwin, *supra* note 5, at 12 (explaining "respecting" as "a two-edged word, which bans any law *disfavoring as well as any law favoring an establishment of religion*") (emphasis in original).

[12] The reported debates on the establishment clause are meager, but tend to suggest a narrower interpretation. James Madison explained to the House of Representatives that his proposed amendment ("no religion shall be established by law, nor shall the equal rights of conscience be infringed") meant that "Congress should not establish a religion, and enforce the legal observation of it by law, nor compel men to worship God in any manner contrary to their conscience" and said it should quiet fears that "one sect might obtain a pre-eminence, or two combine together, and establish a religion to which they would compel others to conform." 1 ANNALS OF CONG. 757-58 (J. Gales ed. 1789). Levy finds support for the Court's reading in the fact that by 1791 no state "maintained a single or preferential establishment of religion" and in the rejection of three narrow Senate versions of the establishment clause that would have barred Congress from "establishing articles of faith or a mode of worship." *See* L. LEVY, *supra* note 5, at xvi, 82-84. *See also* L. PFEFFER, CHURCH, STATE AND FREEDOM, ch. 5 (rev. ed. 1967); Kurland, *The Origins of the Religion Clauses of the Constitution,* 27 WM. & MARY L. REV. 839 (1986).

[13] *See* 330 U.S. at 18-28 (Jackson, J., joined by Frankfurter, J., dissenting); 330 U.S. at 28-63 (Rutledge, J., joined by Frankfurter, Jackson, and Burton, JJ., dissenting).

[14] *See* 330 U.S. at 29 n.3, 44-49 (Rutledge, J., dissenting).

[15] *Id.* at 16 (Black, J.).

[16] *Id.* at 19 (Jackson, J., dissenting).

[17] *Id.* at 17 (Black, J.).

[18] *Id.* at 16-18. *See also* M. HOWE, *supra* note 5, at 139 (arguing that the decision may have been influenced by "the Court's mounting concern for equality"); Katz, *Freedom of Religion and State Neutrality,* 20 U. CHI. L. REV. 426, 432 (1953).

same amendment. To put out fires for everybody except churches would unconstitutionally discriminate against them.[19]

## B.   Released Time

The following year, in another opinion by Justice Black, the Court employed the tools
fashioned in *Everson* to strike down a state provision that promoted religion alone in
*Illinois ex rel. McCollum v. Board of Education.*[20] The measure released public school
pupils from secular studies to attend religious classes in public classrooms.[21] "[N]ot only
are the state's tax-supported public school buildings used for the dissemination of religious doctrines," wrote Justice Black; "[t]he State also affords sectarian groups an invaluable aid in that it helps to provide pupils for their religious classes through use of the
State's compulsory public school machinery. This is not separation of Church and
State."[22]

Four years later, however, the Court upheld a released-time program by a divided vote
in *Zorach v. Clauson.*[23] "We are a religious people," wrote Justice Douglas in accents that
betrayed no hint of neutrality, "whose institutions presuppose a Supreme Being."[24] The
program in *Zorach* was permissible, he concluded, because religious instruction took
place on private rather than public property. In contrast to *McCollum,* no tax money was
used to promote religion.[25]

But the use of public property was only one of the objections the Court had emphasized
in *McCollum,*[26] and arguably not the more important one. As Justice Jackson pointed out

---

[19] *See* U.S. at 17-18 ("State power is no more to be used so as to handicap religions than it is to favor them").
*See* P. KURLAND, *supra* note 3, at 82; Giannella, *Religious Liberty, Nonestablishment, and Doctrinal Development: Part II. The Nonestablishment Principle,* 81 HARV. L. REV. 513, 520-21 (1968).

The dissenters noted with some force that the measure in question actually provided transportation only for
pupils in public and in Catholic schools, thus raising difficulties of favoritism for a particular religion. 330 U.S.
at 20-21 (Jackson, J., dissenting); 330 U.S. at 61-62 (Rutledge, J., dissenting). Justice Black responded by
arguing that this issue had not properly been raised. 330 U.S. at 4 n.2 ("[A]ppellant does not allege . . . that
there were any children in the township who attended or would have attended, but for want of transportation, any
but public and Catholic schools.").

[20] 333 U.S. 203 (1948).

[21] *Id.* at 205-09.

[22] *Id.* at 212. Frankfurter, joined by the other three Justices who had dissented in *Everson,* wrote a concurring
opinion, 330 U.S. at 212-32, as did Jackson, 330 U.S. at 232-28. While professing to accept the interpretation
of the establishment clause announced in *Everson,* Justice Reed, as the sole dissenter, actually seemed to call it
into question by noting the existence of congressional and military chaplains and Jefferson's approval of religious
instruction at the University of Virginia, adding that "[t]he phrase 'an establishment of religion' may have been
intended . . . to be aimed only at a state church." 330 U.S. at 238, 244 (Reed, J., dissenting).

[23] 343 U.S. 306 (1952).

[24] *Id.* at 313.

[25] *Id.* at 308-09, 315.

[26] Symbolism, though not stressed in the opinion, was another objection: when religious instruction is given
in public buildings, it appears to the public as part of the state's educational program. *See* L. TRIBE, AMERICAN
CONSTITUTIONAL LAW 825 (1978); *cf.* Grand Rapids School Dist. v. Ball, 473 U.S. 373 (1985) (conversely
striking down a shared time and community education program providing for sending public teachers into
parochial schools); Burton v. Wilmington Parking Auth., 365 U.S. 715, 720, 724 (1961) (suggesting analogous
argument in holding state responsible for private decision to serve only white patrons in restaurant built with

in dissent, in both *Zorach* and *McCollum* "schooling . . . serves as a temporary jail for a pupil who will not go to church."[27] The distinction between *Zorach* and *McCollum* was "trivial."[28]

Justices Black and Frankfurter, intellectual leaders of the active and passive wings of the Court, added emphatic dissents of their own.[29] It is food for thought when the Court's three strongest members take issue with its conclusions.[30]


## II.  SPEECH

### A.  Peace and Quiet


### 1.  State power

In *Saia v. New York,* in 1948, the Court struck down an ordinance requiring a permit for the use of loudspeakers that might inconvenience people in public places.[31] In *Kovacs v. Cooper,* a year later, the Court upheld an ordinance forbidding loudspeakers on the streets even though it did not authorize the issuance of permits at all.[32]

Both decisions were five to four; only Chief Justice Vinson thought the cases distinguishable. Justices Black and Jackson, who were on opposite sides in each case, believed that the Court had it backward: the ordinance the Court upheld limited speech more than the one the Court struck down, for the latter authorized the police to waive the restriction.[33]

In so concluding, Black and Jackson took no account of the dangers of discriminatory application that had condemned the permit provision in *Saia.* As Justice Douglas wrote in that case, the ordinance provided "no standards" to guide the determination of whether to authorize a loudspeaker.[34] "The right to be heard is placed in the uncontrolled discretion

---

public funds in connection with parking facility operated by an agency of the state on public property). This difficulty was reduced in *Zorach* by the fact that public property was not involved. *See generally* Marshall, *"We Know It When We See It" : The Supreme Court and Establishment,* 59 S. CAL. L. REV. 495 (1986).

[27] 343 U.S. at 324.

[28] *Id.* at 325 (Jackson, J., dissenting). Douglas's response that there was "no evidence" to support the suggestion of coercion missed the point. *Id.* at 311. Coercion was inherent in the program. *See* Cushman, *Public Support of Religious Education in American Constitutional Law,* 45 Ill. L. Rev. 333, 353 (1950) ("A state which says to a pupil, 'You must study religion or sit in study-hall,' is not taking a neutral attitude toward religion."). Moreover, as Justice Frankfurter noted in dissent, evidence of coercion had been excluded. *Zorach,* 343 U.S. at 321-22 (Frankfurter, J., dissenting). *See* P. KURLAND, *supra* note 3, at 86 ("Most of what *McCollum* had done . . . was undone a few years later in *Zorach* . . .").

[29] 343 U.S. at 315-20 (Black, J., dissenting); 343 U.S. at 320-23 (Frankfurter, J., dissenting).

[30] A further important establishment issue was postponed when the Court, over three dissents, held that a taxpayer had no standing to challenge Bible reading in the public schools. "There is no allegation that this activity . . . adds any sum whatever to the cost of conducting the school." Doremus v. Board of Educ., 342 U.S. 429, 433 (1952) (Jackson, J.).

[31] 334 U.S. 558 (1948) (Douglas, J.).

[32] 336 U.S. 77 (1949).

[33] *Id.* at 98 (Jackson, J., concurring); 336 U.S. at 101 (Black, J., dissenting).

[34] *Saia,* 334 U.S. at 560.

of the Chief of Police."[35] Since the 1930s, the Court had consistently stood firm against such discretionary power to discriminate among potential speakers.[36] The only surprising thing about *Saia* was that Frankfurter, Reed, Jackson, and Burton dissented.[37]

The flat prohibition in *Kovacs,* while more restrictive, avoided this risk of arbitrary enforcement; the question was whether it was a reasonable regulation of the time, place, and manner of speaking. Under Hughes the Court had held that the state could not ban all handbilling or picketing in the streets; under Stone it had held door-to-door solicitation equally protected.[38] Without citing these cases, Justice Black invoked their reasoning in his *Kovacs* dissent: sound trucks were the poor man's press, and barring them stacked the deck in favor of those with more money.[39] As in the solicitation case, Jackson and Frankfurter balanced the opposing interests in favor of privacy.[40] Three Justices, in an opinion by Reed, read the ordinance to forbid only "loud and raucous" noises and voted to uphold it.[41]

As Justice Reed noted, sound trucks are more intrusive than handbills, which the passerby need not read; "[t]he unwilling listener . . . is practically helpless to escape. . . ."[42] They are likewise more intrusive than the solicitor, who the Court had said could be kept away by No Trespassing signs.[43] Black conceded that the state could limit the volume, hours, and location of amplifiers,[44] and Reed agreed that a total ban would "probably" be unconstitutional.[45] They thus seemed to differ only as to the meaning of the statute and of

[35]*Id.* at 560-61.

[36]Schneider v. State, 308 U.S. 147 (1939); Hague v. CIO, 307 U.S. 496 (1939); Lovell v. Griffin, 303 U.S. 444 (1938); *cf.* Cantwell v. Connecticut, 310 U.S. 296 (1940) (administrative authority to determine what constituted religion). *Cf.* Cox v. New Hampshire, 312 U.S. 569 (1941) (upholding permit ordinance limited to determining traffic effect of parades); *see* pp. 261-62 *supra.* The *Saia* rationale was followed in two subsequent cases. *See* Niemotko v. Maryland, 340 U.S. 268, 272-73 (1951) (Vinson, C. J.) (invalidating standardless requirements for park permits); Kunz v. New York, 340 U.S. 290, 293, 295 (1951) (Vinson, C. J., over a dissent by Jackson, J.) (invalidating standardless requirements for street permits).

[37]Ignoring the precedents respecting administrative discretion, the dissenters essentially argued that the city need not allow noise in the parks—a separate issue that the majority did not have to reach. *See* 334 U.S. at 562-66 (Frankfurter, J., joined by Reed and Jackson, JJ., dissenting); 334 U.S. at 566-72 (Jackson, J., dissenting).

[38]Martin v. Struthers, 319 U.S. 141 (1943); Thornhill v. Alabama, 310 U.S. 88 (1940); Schneider v. State, 308 U.S. 149 (1939). *See* pp. 263, 268-70, 317-18 *supra.*

[39]336 U.S. at 102-03 (Black, J., dissenting). *See* Stone, *Content-Neutral Restrictions,* 54 U. Chi. L. Rev. 46, 66 (1987).

[40]*See* 336 U.S. at 89-97 (Frankfurter, J., concurring); 336 U.S. at 97-98 (Jackson, J., concurring); *cf.* Martin v. Struthers, 319 U.S. 141, 152-57 (1943) (Frankfurter, J., dissenting); 319 U.S. at 166-82 (Jackson, J., dissenting).

[41]336 U.S. at 82-89 (opinion of Reed, J., joined by Vinson, C. J., and Burton, J.). Justice Black took Reed to task for interpreting the ordinance more narrowly than it had apparently been understood by the state court and for finding the defendant guilty of an offense with which he had never been charged. The complaint was simply that he had operated a sound truck on the street. 336 U.S. at 98-100 (Black, J., joined by Douglas and Rutledge, JJ., dissenting).

[42]336 U.S. at 86-87. *See* Stone, *Fora Americana: Speech in Public Places,* 1974 Sup. Ct. Rev. 233, 269 (adding that the unwilling listener in the loudspeaker case "is in his home, his 'castle,' where his right to be let alone is at its peak").

[43]336 U.S. at 86. *See Martin,* 319 U.S. 141, 148 (1943).

[44]336 U.S. at 104 (Black, J., dissenting).

[45]*Id.* at 81-82.

the judgment below. Both seemed to strike an appropriate balance between the competing interests,[46] and together they spoke for a clear majority of the Court.[47]

It was nonetheless portentous that the four Justices who had voted with Stone to protect door-to-door solicitation in *Martin v. Struthers* found themselves in dissent in seeking to protect sound trucks. Two years after *Kovacs*, in *Breard v. Alexandria*,[48] *Martin* itself was held inapplicable to salesmen soliciting magazine subscriptions because "selling . . . brings into the transaction a commercial feature" absent in the earlier case.[49] Stone, Rutledge, and Murphy having died, the number of votes to strike down the prohibition on speech grounds was reduced to two,[50] and the majority's opinion seemed to cast doubt on *Martin* itself.[51] The pendulum seemed to have swung away from aggressive protection of expression.

## 2. State duty

In *Kovacs* the Court held the state was *permitted* to protect the unwilling listener against loudspeakers. In *Public Utilities Commission v. Pollak.* two Justices argued it was *required* to do so.[52] The Capital Transit Company, operating in the District of Columbia under a franchise granted by Congress, broadcast radio programs through loudspeakers inside its buses and streetcars. When some passengers protested, the Public Utilities Commission concluded that the broadcasts "tend[ed] to improve the conditions under which the public ride" and thus were "not inconsistent with public convenience, comfort and safety."[53] The Court of Appeals for the District of Columbia held that the complaining passengers had been deprived of their liberty without due process of law.[54] A divided Supreme Court reversed.

[46] *See* Frank, *The United States Supreme Court: 1948-49*, 17 U. Chi. L. Rev. 1, 29 (1949) ("[I]t is hard to find in the Constitution a requirement that anyone . . . can be compelled to hear a message which he does not choose to hear.").

[47] Justice Frankfurter's concurrence in *Kovacs* was largely devoted to an attack on Reed's invocation of the "preferred position" terminology that had characterized recent speech and religion decisions. 336 U.S. at 89-97. *See* 336 U.S. at 88 & n.14 (citing *e.g.*, Murdock v. Pennsylvania, 319 U.S. 105 (1943)). *See* p. 316 *supra*. While condemning such language as "deceptive" and "mechanical," Frankfurter seemed to modify his earlier position considerably by conceding that "those liberties of the individual which history has attested as the indispensable conditions of an open as against a closed society come to this Court with a momentum for respect lacking when appeal is made to liberties which derive merely from shifting economic arrangements." *Kovacs*, 336 U.S. at 95-96. *Compare* West Virginia Bd. of Educ. v. Barnette, 319 U.S. 625, 646-71 (1943) (Frankfurter, J., dissenting), pp. 318-20 *supra*.

[48] 341 U.S. 622 (1951) (Reed, J.).

[49] *Id.* at 642-43.

[50] *See id.* at 649-50 (Black and Douglas, JJ., dissenting). Chief Justice Vinson, joined by Justice Douglas, dissented on the ground that the ordinance unreasonably burdened interstate commerce. *Id.* at 645-49.

[51] *See id.* at 644-45 (balancing the interests in favor of privacy without considering the alternative of posting signs); *id.* at 627 (noting that this alternative "was rejected early as less practical"). For doubts whether the activity in *Breard* was really more "commercial" than that in *Martin* see Schiro, *Commercial Speech: The Demise of a Chimera*, 1976 Sup. Ct. Rev. 45, 54-60.

[52] 343 U.S. 451 (1952).

[53] *Id.* at 454.

[54] 191 F.2d 450 (D.C. Cir. 1951).

Justice Douglas, in dissent, agreed with the lower court that due process had been denied. "Liberty" in the fifth amendment, he argued in a passage that foreshadowed important developments, included "privacy," because "[t]he right to be let alone is indeed the beginning of all freedom."[55] Transit riders were "a captive audience," because many had no alternative means of transportation.[56] Thus the case "involves a form of coercion to make people listen," and "[i]f liberty is to flourish, government should never be allowed to force people to listen to any radio program."[57] For a Justice who had denounced substantive due process arguments only a few years earlier as "notions of public policy" that "should not be read into the Constitution,"[58] this sounded remarkably like *Lochner v. New York.*[59] The majority disagreed on the blandest and narrowest of grounds: most riders enjoyed the broadcasts, and "[t]he liberty of each individual in a public vehicle or public place is subject to reasonable limitations in relation to the rights of others."[60]

Justice Black, who agreed with the Court that the broadcasting of music offended nothing in the Constitution, came up with a more novel objection to other transmissions. "[S]ubjecting . . . passengers to the broadcasting of news, public speeches, views, or propaganda of any kind and by any means would violate the First Amendment."[61] He did not say why, and the majority said only that the issue was not properly presented: "There is no substantial claim that the programs have been used for objectionable propaganda."[62]

Compelling people to listen to propaganda conjures up visions of Orwell's *1984,*[63] but it is not obvious that it has anything to do with freedom of speech. The first amendment's focus is on the right to communicate; even the flag-salute case had relied on the right to determine what one would *say.*[64] A general right not to be spoken to seems more remote from the purposes of free expression.[65]

The most striking aspect of the *Pollak* decision, however, was the willingness of the entire Court to address the first and fifth amendment questions at all, since the decision to play music in the buses and streetcars had been made by a private corporation.[66] Although the fifth amendment speaks in the passive voice without identifying the actors it means to

---

[55] 343 U.S. at 467 (Douglas, J., dissenting).

[56] *Id.* at 468.

[57] *Id.* at 468-69 (Douglas, J., dissenting).

[58] Olsen v. Nebraska, 313 U.S. 236, 247 (1941), pp. 239-40 *supra.*

[59] 198 U.S. 45 (1905), pp. 47-49 *supra.*

[60] 343 U.S. at 465.

[61] *Id.* at 466 (separate opinion of Black, J.).

[62] *Id.* at 463. Since the programs evidently included news broadcasts and other "matters of civic interest," the Court's reasoning does not seem wholly responsive. *Id.* at 461. Justice Black dissented "[t]o the extent, if any," that the Court allowed the broadcast of news or views in *Pollak. Id.* at 466. No Justice argued that the broadcasts were so loud as to interfere with communication among the passengers.

[63] *See* Black, *He Cannot Choose But Hear: The Plight of the Captive Auditor,* 53 COLUM. L. REV. 960 (1953).

[64] West Virginia Bd. of Educ. v. Barnette, 319 U.S. 624 (1943), pp. 318-20 *supra.*

[65] There have been suggestions that compulsory attendance at school prayers, quite apart from establishment problems, would infringe the free exercise of religion. This conclusion would not compel agreement with Justice Black's parallel argument respecting free speech, for the two provisions need not in all respects be congruent. Forced exposure to alien doctrine may easily offend religious tenets without interfering with freedom of expression. *See, e.g.,* Engel v. Vitale, 370 U.S. 421, 423-24 n.2 (1962) (quoting the trial court opinion).

[66] *See* 343 U.S. at 454 ("The Capital Transit Company . . . is a privately-owned public utility corporation. . . .").

limit,[67] history and precedent made clear that, like the rest of the Bill of Rights, it was designed to apply only to the federal government. The parties conceded that neither amendment restricted private actions.[68]

Writing for the Court, Justice Burton nevertheless found "a sufficiently close relation between the Federal Government and the radio service to make it necessary for us to consider those Amendments."[69] This was not because the company held a franchise granted by Congress and not because Congress had given it "a substantial monopoly."[70] It was because the company operated "under the regulatory supervision" of a governmental commission, and particularly because that agency, "after formal public hearings, ordered its investigation dismissed on the ground that the public safety, comfort and convenience were not impaired."[71]

The monopoly argument that Burton disdained seems in fact the strongest argument for holding the government responsible. If the distinction between public and private action means anything at all, it cannot be that a mere refusal to prevent private action—and that is all the dismissal of the investigation had been—activates constitutional limitations applicable only to government. If the government denies to the citizen all other practicable means of transportation, however, it may have to share responsibility for additional limits that the monopolist places upon the citizen's freedom. The government may not have a general duty to feed the people; but if it locks a man up without feeding him, it deprives him of life.[72]

Burton's treatment of the issue was as sketchy as that provided here—perhaps because he did not necessarily mean to resolve it. In the next breath he proceeded to consider the substantive issues, "*assuming* that the action of Capital Transit . . . together with the action of the Commission . . . amounts to sufficient Federal Government action to make the First and Fifth Amendments applicable."[73] With this apparent disclaimer in mind, a second glance at the Court's earlier conclusion reveals a conspicuous flabbiness. Burton wrote that the government's connection to the broadcasting was sufficiently close "to make it necessary for us to consider" the amendments, not to make them applicable.[74] That may have been only to say that the relationship was close enough that the argument of state involvement could not be rejected out of hand; rather than resolve the question, it was preferable to dismiss the less troublesome substantive arguments on the assumption that the government was responsible.[75]

---

[67] U. S. Const. amend. V ("[N]or shall any person . . . be deprived of life, liberty, or property, without due process of law. . . .").

[68] 343 U.S. at 461-62 (citing, *inter alia*, Barron v. Baltimore, 32 U.S. (7 Pet.) 243 (1833), The First Hundred Years at 189-93, which held the taking provision of the fifth amendment inapplicable to the states).

[69] 343 U.S. at 462.

[70] *Id.*

[71] *Id.*

[72] *See* Black, *supra* note 63, at 963-64; Currie, *Positive and Negative Constitutional Rights*, 53 U. Chi. L. Rev. 864, 874 (1986).

[73] 343 U.S. at 462-63 (emphasis added).

[74] *Id.* at 462.

[75] The other Justices were silent on the issue. Black and Douglas, who argued against constitutionality, were implicitly willing to find the government responsible.

Thus *Pollak* was tantalizingly inconclusive on its novel theories of both free speech and government responsibility. The Court's unwillingness to take a firm stand may have reflected only a traditional reluctance to decide more than was necessary, but the seriousness with which it took such arguments suggested we had not heard the last of them.

## B.  The Heckler's Veto

*Terminiello v. Chicago* involved the disorderly conduct conviction of a public speaker who had engendered such strong feelings in his speech as to precipitate a riot.[76] His anti-Communist and anti-Semitic diatribe appealed to some of his listeners' prejudices, and a hostile crowd outside the building threw bricks through the windows. Although present in force, the police were unable to control the situation. The state appellate courts sustained conviction of the speaker on the ground that he had employed "fighting words" calculated to provoke reasonable listeners to violence,[77] which the whole Court had held punishable in *Chaplinsky v. New Hampshire*.[78]

Justice Jackson, who argued for affirmance of the conviction in his dissent, contended more broadly that Terminiello had "provoked a hostile mob and incited a friendly one."[79] Fresh from his extrajudicial labors in prosecuting Nazi war criminals at Nuremberg, Jackson compared what had happened in *Terminiello* to the street battles between Fascists and Communists that had preceded Adolf Hitler's rise to power and argued that Terminiello's speech had created a clear and present danger of rioting that the state had a right to prevent.[80]

To the dismay of Jackson and his fellow dissenters, Justice Douglas's majority opinion avoided these troublesome questions as well as the original issue of fighting words by concluding that the statute as construed below was too broad. The state could not punish people for every speech that "stirs the public to anger, invites dispute, [or] brings about a condition of unrest."[81] It is "a function of free speech under our system to invite dispute."[82] In fact speech "may . . . best serve its high purpose when it induces a condition of unrest, creates dissatisfaction with conditions as they are, or even stirs people to anger."[83] It was irrelevant that Terminiello's speech might have been punished under a different law. Like the red-flag statute struck down in *Stromberg v. California*,[84] the statute under which he had been convicted was invalid because it outlawed speech that created no clear and present danger of substantive harm.[85]

---

[76] 337 U.S. 1 (1949).

[77] 337 U.S. at 2-3 (1949); *id.* at 6-8 (Vinson, C. J., dissenting); *id.* at 14-23 (Jackson, J., dissenting).

[78] 315 U.S. 568 (1942), pp. 314-15 *supra*.

[79] 337 U.S. at 13 (Jackson, J., dissenting).

[80] *Id.* at 23-26 ("It was a local manifestation of a worldwide and standing conflict between two organized groups of revolutionary fanatics, each of which has imported to this country the strong-arm technique developed in the struggle by which their kind has devastated Europe."). *Id.* at 23.

[81] *Id.* at 4.

[82] *Id.*

[83] *Id.*

[84] 283 U.S. 359 (1931), pp. 255-57 *supra*.

[85] 337 U.S. at 4-5. Frankfurter, Vinson, Jackson, and Burton forcefully objected that the breadth of the statute had never been questioned below. *Id.* at 6-13. Douglas irrelevantly responded that Terminiello had raised "both points—that *his speech* was protected . . . [and] that the inclusion of *his speech* within the ordinance" was

The issues Jackson raised in *Terminiello* arose once again in *Feiner v. New York*,[86] after Minton and Clark had replaced Murphy and Rutledge. This time Jackson's views prevailed. Feiner's street-corner speech, the trial judge found, "gave the impression that he was endeavoring to arouse the Negro people against the whites," and "at least one [onlooker] threatened violence if the police did not act."[87] Ultimately, "[b]ecause of the feeling that existed in the crowd both for and against the speaker," the police " 'stepped in to prevent it from resulting in a fight.' "[88] Feiner was convicted of disorderly conduct, and the Supreme Court affirmed.[89]

Quoting *Cantwell v. Connecticut*,[90] Vinson emphasized that the state could punish " 'incitement to riot,' " adding that " '[w]hen clear and present danger of riot, disorder . . . or other immediate threat to public safety, peace, or order, appears, the power of the State to prevent or punish is obvious.' "[91] What had been missing in *Cantwell* was present in *Feiner*:

> It is one thing to say that police cannot be used as an instrument for the suppression of unpopular views, and another to say that, when as here the speaker passes the bounds of argument or persuasion and undertakes incitement to riot, they are powerless to prevent a breach of the peace. . . . The findings of the state courts as to the existing situation and the imminence of greater disorder coupled with petitioner's deliberate defiance of the police officers convince us that we should not reverse this conviction in the name of free speech.[92]

Justice Black, dissenting, said there was no clear and present danger of breach of the peace (as there had been in *Terminiello*): it was "farfetched to suggest" that there was "any imminent threat of riot or uncontrollable disorder."[93] Black made a more fundamental point as well: even if the situation *was* critical, the police should have kept the peace by controlling the crowd, not by silencing the speaker.[94] Douglas and Minton echoed this argument in a separate dissent: if "the police throw their weight on the side of those who would break up the meetings, the police become the new censors of speech."[95]

Like Roberts in *Cantwell* and Jackson in *Terminiello*, the majority in *Feiner* seemed to

---

unconstitutional. *Id.* at 6 (emphasis added). The ground on which the conviction was set aside had nothing to do with Terminiello's own speech.

[86] 340 U.S. 315 (1951).

[87] *Id.* at 317.

[88] *Id.* at 317-18.

[89] *Id.* at 316, 321.

[90] 310 U.S. 296, 308 (1940), pp. 266-67 *supra* (reversing breach of peace conviction for want of sufficient danger).

[91] 340 U.S. at 320 (quoting *Cantwell*, 310 U.S. at 296, 308).

[92] 340 U.S. at 321.

[93] *Id.* at 325 (Black, J., dissenting). Black insisted, as precedent suggested, that the Court had a duty to reassess the facts for itself to determine whether federal rights had been denied. *Id.* at 322 & n.4 (citing Norris v. Alabama, 294 U.S. 587, 589-90 (1935), *supra* p. 249, note 31).

[94] 340 U.S. at 326-27 (Black, J., dissenting).

[95] *Id.* at 331 (Douglas, J., joined by Minton, J., dissenting).

lump together two types of speakers who arguably presented quite different constitutional problems: one who urges his audience to commit crimes and one whose audience wishes to silence him. That the danger of disturbance may be equally clear and present in the two cases merely exposes one of the defects of Holmes's mellifluous phrase as a universal test of the limits of expression.[96] Incitement to crime is not only dangerous but of little social value; the heckler's veto may deprive us of arguments that lie at the heart of first amendment protection.[97] The inciter calls sanctions upon himself by blameworthy conduct; the heckler's veto rewards the enemies of freedom for their misbehavior. Black and Douglas were right: if the crowd refuses to let the speaker speak, it is the crowd that should be punished.

A later Court would recognize this in holding that widespread public opposition did not justify abandoning the constitutional ban on racial exclusion from public school.[98] Although *Feiner* seems to look in the opposite direction, a studied ambiguity surrounds both Vinson's opinion and the passage from *Cantwell* on which he relied. In each case the talk of clear and present danger was coupled with the term "incitement to riot" in such a way as to leave it unclear whether the former was intended as an alternative ground for upholding the conviction[99] or as an additional requirement even in cases of incitement— as the Court would later hold in one of its briefest and greatest opinions.[100] In any event, because the Court concluded that Feiner had incited his hearers to riot, anything the opinion implied as to the hecklers' power was unnecessary to the decision.[101]

## C.　Group Libel

A leaflet distributed in Chicago called upon the city " 'to halt the further encroachment, harassment and invasion of white people, their property, neighborhoods and persons, by

---

[96] *See* P. FREUND, THE SUPREME COURT OF THE UNITED STATES 44 (1961).

[97] This also distinguishes fighting words, which tend to provoke even reasonable people to violence and which can be avoided without suppressing whatever message the speaker wishes to convey.

[98] Cooper v. Aaron, 358 U.S. 1, 19-20 (1958).

[99] In a concurring opinion also applying to *Feiner,* Justice Frankfurter appeared to take this position: "It is not a constitutional principle that, in acting to preserve order, the police must proceed against the crowd, whatever its size and temper, and not against the speaker." Niemotko v. Maryland, 340 U.S. 268, 289 (1951) (Frankfurter, J., concurring).

[100] Brandenburg v. Ohio, 395 U.S. 444 (1969), p. 442 *infra.*

[101] Traditional incitement principles also go far to justify several decisions of the Vinson period upholding the prohibition of picketing whose object was to bring about actions in violation of the law. *See* Local Union No. 10, United Ass'n of Journeymen Plumbers v. Graham, 345 U.S. 192 (1953) (Burton, J.) (violation of right-to-work law); International Bhd. of Elec. Workers v. NLRB, 341 U.S. 694, 705 (1951) (Burton, J.) (secondary boycott); Building Serv. Employees v. Gazzam, 339 U.S. 532 (1950) (Minton, J.) (employer interference with choice of bargaining representative); International Bhd. of Teamsters v. Hanke, 339 U.S. 470 (1950) (no majority opinion) (involuntary union shop); Hughes v. Superior Court, 339 U.S. 460 (1950) (Frankfurter, J.) (racial quota in hiring); Giboney v. Empire Storage & Ice Co., 336 U.S. 490 (1949) (Black, J.) (refusal to deal with nonunion ice peddlers). *See also* Cox, *Strikes, Picketing and the Constitution,* 4 VAND. L. REV. 574, 595 (1951) (" 'Signal picketing' is entitled to no greater constitutional protection than the combination it sets in motion."); Cox, *Some Aspects of the Labor Management Relations Act,* 1947, 61 HARV. L. REV. 1, 26-27 (1947) ("Banning the use of secondary strikes and boycotts as weapons of organization is primarily a prohibition against economic pressures; the interference with freedom of persuasion is relatively slight since all avenues of communication except the picket line are left open."); pp. 311-13 *supra* (discussing *Giboney* as well as earlier picketing cases). For a more critical assessment, see Fraenkel, *Peaceful Picketing—Constitutionally Protected?,* 99 U. PA. L. REV. 1 (1950).

the Negro.' "[102] " 'If persuasion and the need to prevent the white race from becoming mongrelized by the negro will not unite us,' " the leaflet added, " 'then the aggressions . . . rapes, robberies, knives, guns and marijuana of the negro, surely will.' "[103] The distributor of this leaflet was prosecuted under an Illinois statute forbidding certain publications or exhibitions " 'which . . . portray[] depravity, criminality, unchastity, or lack of virtue in a class of citizens, of any race, color, creed or religion . . . [and] expose[] the citizens of any race, color, creed or religion to contempt, derision or obloquy.' "[104] President Truman's four appointees joined Justice Frankfurter's 1952 opinion in *Beauharnais v. Illinois* to uphold the conviction.[105] The other four Roosevelt appointees—Black, Douglas, Reed, and Jackson—dissented.[106]

Frankfurter resolved the case by an exercise in taxonomy. Libel of an individual had always been a crime, which Justice Murphy's dictum in *Chaplinsky* had ranked with fighting words as a "class[] of speech, the prevention and punishment of which ha[s] never been thought to raise any Constitutional problem."[107] It would surely be libelous to brand an individual "a rapist, robber, carrier of knives and guns, and user of marijuana."[108] Furthermore, the state might "warrantably believe that a man's job and his educational opportunities and the dignity accorded him may depend as much on the reputation of the racial and religious group to which he willy-nilly belongs, as on his own merits."[109] Extending the traditional libel law to statements disparaging an entire racial or religious group was thus not "a wilful and purposeless restriction unrelated to the peace and well-being of the State," and no clear and present danger of injury was required since "[l]ibelous utterances" were not "within the area of constitutionally protected speech."[110]

History indeed furnished powerful evidence that punishment of garden-variety defamation had been thought consistent with freedom of expression. As Frankfurter acknowledged, however, the historical record was not so clear as to statements that disparaged entire classes of the population.[111] Moreover, as Justice Black observed in dissent, the differences between individual and group libels were relevant to the reasons why it was appropriate that ordinary libel be denied protection.[112]

At first glance one might think it obvious that defaming an entire race was worse than defaming an individual. Group libel, however, may do less harm to the individual. To call blacks a race of "gun-toting rapists" says little about the habits of any particular black.

[102] Beauharnais v. Illinois, 343 U.S. 250, 252 (1950) (quoting leaflet distributed by the defendant).

[103] *Id.* at 252.

[104] *Id.* at 251 (quoting ILL. REV. STAT. ch. 38, para. 471 (1949)).

[105] *Id.* at 250, 251-67 (1952).

[106] *Id.* at 267-305.

[107] *Id.* at 256 (quoting Chaplinsky v. New Hampshire, 315 U.S. 568, 571-72 (1942)).

[108] *Id.* at 257-58.

[109] *Id.* at 263.

[110] *Id.* at 258-66. On the other hand, when New York attempted to protect religious groups from "contempt, mockery, scorn and ridicule" by requiring a license to exhibit motion pictures, the Court predictably invalidated the scheme as a previous restraint, adding in contrast to *Beauharnais* that "[i]t is not the business of government . . . to suppress real or imagined attacks upon a particular religious doctrine." Joseph Burstyn, Inc. v. Wilson, 343 U.S. 495, 505 (1952) (Clark, J.). Justice Reed concurred in *Burstyn* on the ground that the particular movie at issue was constitutionally protected. *Id.* at 506-07. Justices Frankfurter and Jackson concurred on the ground that the statutory term "sacrilege" was unconstitutionally vague. *Id.* at 507-40.

[111] 343 U.S. at 258.

[112] *Id.* at 272-75 (Black, J., joined by Douglas, J., dissenting).

Although it would be hard to deny the destructive power of group defamation,[113] reduced harm to the individual arguably makes less pressing "the social interest in order and morality" on which Murphy relied in *Chaplinsky.*

More important are the differences between individual and group libel with respect to the other side of Murphy's calculus, the "social value" of the proscribed communication. Traditional libel law, said Black, "confined state punishment of speech and expression to the narrowest of areas involving nothing more than purely private feuds. Every expansion of the law of criminal libel so as to punish discussions of matters of public concern means a corresponding invasion of the area dedicated to free expression by the First Amendment."[114] The leaflet in question presented "arguments on questions of wide public interest and importance";[115] "to petition for and publicly discuss proposed legislation" could not constitutionally be made a crime.[116]

*Kovacs, Breard,* and *Feiner* might perhaps be explained away, but *Beauharnais* left no doubt that freedom of expression was in retreat. To say the state could forbid statements on political topics of general public interest because they exposed a racial group to "obloquy" seemed to cut deeply into first amendment values.[117]

Most ominous was the majority's acceptance of an extremely deferential attitude toward legislative judgments that Frankfurter alone had exhibited in the second flag-salute case.[118] To ask only whether the extension of libel laws to matters of public interest was "wilful and purposeless" seemed inconsistent with Frankfurter's own concession in *Kovacs* that "those liberties . . . which history has attested as the indispensable conditions of an open . . . society come to this Court with a momentum for respect lacking when appeal is made to liberties which derive merely from shifting economic arrangements."[119] As Douglas implied, the Court seemed to be saying expression was as subject to regulation as "factories, slums, apartment houses, [and the] production of oil."[120]

---

[113] *See* Arkes, *Civility and the Restriction of Speech: Rediscovering the Defamation of Groups,* 1974 SUP. CT. REV. 281, 291-92; Riesman, *Democracy and Defamation: Control of Group Libel,* 42 COLUM. L. REV. 727, 728 (1942) ("In the rise of the Nazis to power in Germany, defamation was a major weapon."); Riesman, *Democracy and Defamation: Fair Game and Fair Comment I,* 42 COLUM. L. REV. 1085 (1942) (describing the Nazi strategy).

[114] 343 U.S. at 272 (Black, J., dissenting).

[115] *Id.* at 273.

[116] *Id.* at 275. Jackson's dissent, echoing Black's concern for "the right to comment upon matters of public interest," stressed the absence of any showing of clear and present danger, adding that the trial judge had excluded evidence of truth and submitted only the issue of publication to the jury. *Id.* at 299-305. Justice Reed thought the vague statutory terms "virtue," "derision," and "obloquy" included speech that could not constitutionally be punished. *Id.* at 280-84. Justice Douglas waved the flag. *Id.* at 284-87. There was no suggestion that Beauharnais had incited anyone to the commission of crime, provoked a hostile audience to endanger the public peace, or addressed fighting words to any individual within fighting range. *See id.* at 272-73, 302 (Black and Jackson, JJ., dissenting). For an argument against letting juries decide the "truth" of racial slurs, see Arkes, *supra* note 113, at 301-02.

[117] *See* H. KALVEN, THE NEGRO AND THE FIRST AMENDMENT 50-51 (1965).

[118] *See* pp. 318-20 *supra* (discussing West Virginia Bd. of Educ. v. Barnette, 319 U.S. 624 (1943)); Frank, *The United States Supreme Court: 1951-52,* 20 U. CHI. L. REV. 1, 27 (1952).

[119] Kovacs v. Cooper, 336 U.S. 77, 95 (1949) (Frankfurter, J., concurring).

[120] 343 U.S. at 286 (Douglas, J., dissenting). *See also id.* at 269 (Black, J., dissenting) ("Today's case degrades First Amendment freedoms to the 'rational basis' level."). Justice Jackson went to some lengths in his dissent to embrace Holmes's suggestion in *Gitlow* that the limits the fourteenth amendment imposed on state

## D.  The Witch Hunt

A distressing series of decisions upholding measures designed to protect against subversion revealed the full extent of the retreat. World War II had produced its share of questionable limitations on freedom,[121] but restrictions of speech and assembly had not figured prominently among them. Any inference that this was attributable to the educational value of earlier wartime excesses,[122] however, was rudely dispelled by a rising tide of repressive legislation once the crisis was past. Soviet Russia, our former ally, was now perceived as working actively to undermine our government. Communists were imagined under every bed; Senator Joe McCarthy was the man of the hour.[123]

### 1.  Dennis v. United States

"[S]elf-preservation," wrote Justice Frankfurter, "is the most pervasive aspect of sovereignty."[124] Obviously, said the Chief Justice, Congress can "protect the Government of the United States from armed rebellion."[125] It followed, for six of the eight participating Justices, that leaders of the Communist party could be jailed under the Smith Act[126] for conspiring to "organize" a society to "advocate" the violent overthrow of the government.[127]

There was no doubt that the Smith Act served a compelling governmental interest. The question, as Vinson noted, was whether the statute was an appropriate means for achieving that goal.[128] Congress had not been content to forbid only rebellion itself, or even its incitement; conspiring to organize persons to advocate overthrow was three steps removed from the substantive crime.

The *Whitney* and *Gitlow* opinions of the 1920s,[129] which went far to sustain the statute, had been discredited.[130] Yet the case for conviction in *Dennis,* Frankfurter rightly ob-

---

restrictions of speech might be less stringent than those the first amendment imposed on the United States. *Beauharnais,* 343 U.S. at 287-95. *See* Gitlow v. New York, 268 U.S. 652, 672 (1925) (Holmes, J., dissenting). For criticism of this conclusion, see H. KALVEN, *supra* note 117, at 33-34.

[121] *See* ch. 9 *supra.*

[122] *See* pp. 115-24 *supra* (discussing the World War I Espionage Act cases).

[123] *See generally* R. MCCLOSKEY, THE AMERICAN SUPREME COURT 196 (1960) ("Growing national awareness of the totalitarian threat in the years after 1945 generated a national mood toward 'subversion' that sometimes approached hysteria"); Emerson & Helfeld, *Loyalty among Government Employees,* 58 YALE L. J. 1 (1948); O'Brian, *Loyalty Tests and Guilt by Association,* 61 HARV. L. REV. 592 (1948); D. CAUTE, THE GREAT FEAR (1978).

[124] Dennis v. United States, 341 U.S. 494, 519 (1951) (Frankfurter, J., concurring).

[125] *Id.* at 501 (opinion of Vinson, C. J.).

[126] 18 U.S.C. §§ 2385, 2387 (1982).

[127] *See* 341 U.S. at 496-97. Justice Clark, who had previously been in charge of Smith Act prosecutions as Attorney General, did not sit. *Id.* at 517.

[128] *Id.* at 501.

[129] Whitney v. California, 274 U.S. 357 (1927); Gitlow v. New York, 268 U.S. 652 (1925); *see* pp. 154-62 *supra.*

[130] *See* 341 U.S. at 507 (Vinson, C. J.) (noting that later decisions had "inclined toward" the views expressed by Justices Holmes and Brandeis in separate opinions). Justice Frankfurter, in his concurring opinion, stated that "it would be disingenuous to deny that the dissent in *Gitlow* has been treated with the respect usually accorded to a decision." *Id.* at 541.

served, was much stronger. It would require "excessive tolerance of the legislative judg-ment" to believe that what Holmes had referred to as the "puny anonymities" in *Gitlow* "could justify serious concern." [131] In Frankfurter's view, however, Congress could reason-ably have found that a tightly organized party of sixty thousand members with subversive goals posed "a substantial danger to national security." [132]

Douglas and Black protested that there was no clear and present danger of rebellion. [133] Professing to accept this test, Vinson seemed to read out of it the requirement that the danger be "present." "Obviously, the words cannot mean that . . . the Government . . . must wait until the *putsch* is about to be executed. . . ." [134] Lost in the shuffle was Bran-deis's appealing insight that suppression was impermissible while there was time for dis-cussion. [135] Jackson insisted that the first amendment did not forbid punishment of conspir-acy, [136] giving no weight to the fact that the conspiracy charged was one not to overthrow the government but to organize a group to advocate its overthrow. If the association itself could not be punished, focusing on the more remote conspiracy should not have made conviction any easier. [137] Frankfurter's argument that it was basically up to Congress to determine the limits of its own power [138] seemed to confirm the impression left by his dissent in *West Virginia Sate Board of Education v. Barnette* that he took a dim view of judicial review in general. [139] As John Marshall had said, the Framers did not mean to leave the fox in charge of the chickens. [140]

Vinson spoke for four Justices. Despite the contrary views of Frankfurter and Jackson, clear and present danger had become the test of convictions even under statutes specifi-cally directed to subversive speech, [141] but it had lost its protective power. [142]

[131] 341 U.S. at 541.

[132] *Id.* at 547. *See also id.* at 510 (Vinson, C. J.) ("The situation with which Justices Holmes and Brandeis were concerned in *Gitlow* was a comparatively isolated event, bearing little relation, in their minds, to any substantial threat to the safety of the community."). *See* Meiklejohn, *What Does the First Amendment Mean?*, 20 U. Chi. L. Rev. 461 (1953) (sharply criticizing Justice Frankfurter's opinion).

[133] 341 U.S. at 579 (Black, J., dissenting), 341 U.S. at 581 (Douglas, J., dissenting).

[134] *Id.* at 509. *See* Frank, *The United States Supreme Court: 1950-51*, 19 U. Chi. L. Rev. 165, 189-90 (1952) ("[T]he Vinson opinion claims a lineage from Holmes and Brandeis which it does not have. The voice is Jacob's voice, but the hands are the hands of Esau.").

[135] Whitney v. California, 274 U.S. 357, 376-77 (1927) (Brandeis, J., concurring) (quoted in *Dennis*, 341 U.S. at 585-86 (Douglas, J., dissenting)). For a reply to the argument that application of the clear-and-present-danger test would leave the government powerless to protect itself, see Nathanson, *The Communist Trial and the Clear-and-Present-Danger Test*, 63 Harv. L. Rev. 1167 (1950).

[136] 341 U.S. at 561-79 (Jackson, J., concurring).

[137] See the excellent analysis in H. Kalven, A Worthy Tradition 190-210 (1988) (arguing that the Court in *Dennis* failed to confront the basic question of the extent to which "conspiracy doctrine can be used . . . to enlarge the jurisdiction of the censor").

[138] 341 U.S. at 525-27, 550-52 (Frankfurter, J., concurring).

[139] West Virginia Bd. of Educ. v. Barnette, 319 U.S. 624, 646-71 (1943) (Frankfurter, J., dissenting), pp. 318-20 *supra*.

[140] *See* Marbury v. Madison, 5 U.S. (1 Cranch) 137, 178 (1803), The First Hundred Years at 66-74.

[141] *Compare* Gitlow v. New York, 268 U.S. 652, 670-71 (1925) *with* Dennis v. United States, 341 U.S. at 516-17.

[142] *See* R. McCloskey, *supra* note 123, at 197; Mendelson, *Clear and Present Danger—From Schenck to Dennis*, 52 Colum. L. Rev. 313, 330 (1952) ("The remoteness element . . . is the heart of the danger test. . . .").

## 2. The privilege doctrine

Criminal penalties were not the only tools employed in the rush to shore up national security. Suspect organizations were blacklisted by the Attorney General; their members were excluded from government jobs, from union offices, and even—if they were aliens—from the country itself. The Supreme Court went along with most of this, but in the last of such cases during the Vinson period it firmly drew the line.

The tale begins with cases having nothing to do with subversion. In a notorious opinion for the Supreme Judicial Court of Massachusetts, Justice Holmes had denied that the dismissal of a police officer for political activity raised any freedom of expression question because there was "no constitutional right to be a policeman." [143] The Supreme Court had already recognized, however, that to condition the grant of such a "privilege" on surrender of a constitutional right could effectively abridge the right itself. Thus a foreign corporation could not be required to surrender its right to litigate in federal court or to submit to otherwise unconstitutional taxation or regulation as a condition of doing business within a state. [144] Similarly, when the Vinson Court, by a four-to-three vote in *United Public Workers v. Mitchell*, [145] upheld the Hatch Act's [146] drastic limitation of the political activity of civil service employees, it did not rest on the ground that there was no right to government employment. Acknowledging that Congress could not exclude Republicans or practicing Catholics from federal jobs, Justice Reed frankly, if deferentially, found the restriction justified by the government's interest in keeping politics out of the civil service. [147]

Consequently, when in 1950 the Justices in *American Communications Association v. Douds* [148] passed upon a Taft-Hartley Act provision denying access to the National Labor Relations Board to unions whose officers declined to swear they were not Communists, Chief Justice Vinson did not simply brand access to the board as a "privilege" that could

---

[143] McAuliffe v. Mayor of New Bedford, 155 Mass. 216, 220, 29 N. E. 517, 517 (1892).

[144] Frost & Frost Trucking Co. v. Railroad Comm'n, 271 U.S. 583, 594 (1926); Western Union Tel. Co. v. Kansas, 216 U.S. 1, 34-38 (1910); Insurance Co. v. Morse, 87 U.S. (20 Wall.) 445 (1874). *See* THE FIRST HUNDRED YEARS at 413 n.74; p. 46, note 126 & p. 146, note 60 *supra*. Justice Holmes never seemed to get the point; he dissented in both *Western Union*, 216 U.S. at 52-56, and *Frost*, 271 U.S. at 600-02.

[145] 330 U.S. 75 (1947).

[146] 5 U.S.C. §§ 7324-7327 (1982 & Supp. III 1985).

[147] 330 U.S. 75, 94-104 (1947); *cf. Ex parte* Curtis, 106 U.S. 371 (1881) (upholding ban on one civil servant's acceptance of political contribution from another), THE FIRST HUNDRED YEARS at 443-44. Justices Black and Douglas, dissenting in *Mitchell*, seemed correct in asserting that to deny such fundamental rights to public workers was an extreme means of protecting them from pressure from their superiors. 330 U.S. at 105-15 (Black, J., dissenting); *id.* at 115-26 (Douglas, J., dissenting). *See also* H. KALVEN, *supra* note 137, at 303-08. Justice Douglas also criticized the Court for concluding that employees who had not yet violated the act had no standing to challenge it, arguing convincingly that the risk of prosecution for activities they would otherwise engage in created an actual controversy within the meaning of article III. Otherwise, as Borchard had argued, "the only way to determine whether the suspect is a mushroom or a toadstool is to eat it"—scarcely an acceptable course in a "civilized legal system." Borchard, *The Constitutionality of Declaratory Judgments*, 31 COLUM. L. REV. 561, 585-89 (1931). *See* pp. 188-90 *supra* (discussing earlier decisions respecting anticipatory relief).

[148] 339 U.S. 382 (1950).

be denied or limited at will.[149] Rather, he set forth an exemplary framework for determining when conditioning government benefits on surrender of a constitutional right should be treated as a denial of the right itself.[150]

"Men who hold union offices," wrote Vinson, "often have little choice [under the Act] but to renounce Communism or give up their offices."[151] "By exerting pressures on unions to deny offices to Communists . . . [the statute] has the . . . necessary effect of discouraging the exercise of political rights protected by the First Amendment"[152]—for not even in *Dennis* would the Court say it could be made a crime simply to be a member of the Communist party.

To Justice Black this was enough to make the oath requirement unconstitutional.[153] Vinson was correct, however, that the government need not open all its doors to everyone it cannot put behind bars. On the one hand, the effect of the oath provision on protected conduct was less severe than that of a criminal prohibition. The statute "touches only a relative handful of persons . . . [a]nd it leaves those few who are affected free to maintain their affiliations . . . subject only to possible loss of positions."[154] On the other hand, the government's interest was greater because union officers were in a unique position to precipitate crippling political strikes.[155] Greater restrictions might be placed on "a general with five hundred thousand men at his command" than on the "village constable."[156] The first amendment requires that one "be permitted to believe what he will" and usually to advocate it, but not "to be the keeper of the arsenal."[157]

That the balance of interests was more favorable to a measure limited to union officers than to a general prohibition, however, did not compel Vinson's conclusion that the Taft-Hartley provision was constitutional. The statute swept quite broadly, disqualifying unions whose officers were Communist party members regardless of whether they shared

[149] Indeed Vinson acknowledged that the provision limited some interests that could not fairly be characterized as privileges, such as the right to enter into union shop contracts or engage in certain strikes or boycotts. *Douds,* 339 U.S. at 389-90 & n.6. *See generally* Van Alstyne, *The Demise of the Right-Privilege Distinction in Constitutional Law,* 81 HARV. L. REV. 1439 (1968); Note, *Unconstitutional Conditions,* 73 HARV. L. REV. 1595 (1960) (both tracing the development of limits on the "privilege" doctrine).

[150] 339 U.S. at 382, 393-412 (1950).

[151] *Id.* at 393.

[152] *Id.*

[153] *Id.* at 445-53 (Black, J., dissenting). Douglas, Clark, and Minton did not participate. *See id.* at 415.

[154] *Id.* at 404.

[155] *Id.* at 391.

[156] *Id.* at 409.

[157] *Id.* at 412. "[T]he problem," said Vinson, "is one of weighing the probable effects of the statute upon the free exercise of the right of speech and assembly against the congressional determination . . . that Communists . . . pose continuing threats to th[e] public interest when in positions of union leadership." *Id.* at 400. In citing for this test a decision dealing with content-neutral regulation of the time, place, or manner of speaking, Schneider v. State, 308 U.S. 147, 161 (1939), p. 263 *supra,* Chief Justice Vinson seemed to make it easier than it should have been to uphold the restriction; for even an indirect burden laid only upon those professing a particular point of view has a more distorting effect on public debate than any neutral limitation. *See generally* Stone, *Content Regulation and the First Amendment,* 25 WM. & MARY L. REV. 189 (1983) (supporting a sharp distinction between content-based and content-neutral restrictions on expression). Nevertheless, McCloskey's conclusion that Vinson's opinion "suggested . . . that Congress could use the commerce power to interfere with free speech and association without fear of constitutional hindrance" seems to overstate the point. R. MCCLOSKEY, *supra* note 123, at 197.

or even knew of the party's goals. As the Court would soon recognize, mere party membership might be entirely innocent. The statute seemed to limit the liberty of far more persons than was necessary to protect commerce from interruption.[158]

Three cases decided soon after *Douds* followed its implications by upholding various measures designed to exclude subversives from candidacy for public office, from municipal employment, and from teaching in public schools.[159] In 1952 the majority went so far as to permit the deportation of long-time resident aliens for mere membership in the Communist party in the distant past.[160] In the meantime, however, four of eight participating Justices had found constitutional defects in the Attorney General's blacklisting of "subversive" organizations.[161] In *Wieman v. Updegraff*, decided just a few months before Vinson's death, the Court unanimously found the limit.[162]

Oklahoma had denied public employment to anyone unwilling to swear that he was not a member of any organization on the Attorney General's list.[163] Without once again facing the divisive issues surrounding the list itself, the Court distinguished its earlier public employment decisions on the ground that the restrictions upheld in those cases had all

[158] Frankfurter and Jackson joined Black in objecting to the additional requirement that union officers swear that they did not "believe in . . . the overthrow of the United States Government by force or by any illegal or unconstitutional methods." *See* 339 U.S. at 419-22 (Frankfurter, J., dissenting in part); 339 U.S. at 435-44 (Jackson, J., dissenting in part). Since Douglas, Minton, and Clark did not participate, the Court was equally divided on this issue. *See id.* at 415. See generally H. KALVEN, *supra* note 137, at 332-39 (agreeing that *Douds* "makes a remarkable contribution to the mapping of the partial sanction issue" but that "the balancing should somehow be done with a First Amendment thumb on the scales.").

[159] Adler v. Board of Educ., 342 U.S. 485, 492, 494 & n.8 (1952) (Minton, J.) (upholding provision construed to require dismissal of teachers for knowing membership in an organization advocating the violent overthrow of the government); Garner v. Board of Pub. Works, 341 U.S. 716, 723-24 (1951) (Clark, J., over four dissents) (upholding a provision understood to require that municipal employees swear that they did not advocate and were not knowing members of a group that advocated such overthrow); Gerende v. Board of Supervisors, 341 U.S. 56, 56-57 (1951) (per curiam) (unanimously upholding a requirement that a candidate swear he was not engaged " 'in the attempt to overthrow the government *by force or violence*' " (quoting Shub v. Simpson, 196 Md. 177, 192, 76 A.2d 332, 338 (1950)) (emphasis in original).

Justices Black and Douglas dissented on the merits in *Adler,* 342 U.S. at 496-97 (Black, J., dissenting); *id.* at 508-11 (Douglas, J., dissenting). Frankfurter powerfully argued that the plaintiffs lacked standing. "These teachers do not allege that they have engaged in proscribed conduct or that they have any intention to do so." *Id.* at 504. In upholding a further requirement that public employees *disclose* whether they were or had been members of the Communist party, *Garner* gave a foretaste of the great controversies over legislative investigations that would occupy the Justices after the appointment of Vinson's successor. *Garner,* 341 U.S. at 720.

[160] Harisiades v. Shaughnessy, 342 U.S. 580, 581, 591-92 (1952) (Jackson, J.). For criticism of the Court's long-standing reluctance to interfere with exercises of Congress's power over immigration see Logomsky, *Immigration Law and the Principle of Plenary Congressional Power,* 1984 SUP. CT. REV. 255; Henkin, *The Constitution and the Sovereignty of the United States: A Century of Chinese Exclusion and Its Agency,* 100 HARV. L. REV. 853, 858-62 (1987).

[161] Joint Anti-Fascist Refugee Comm. v. McGrath, 341 U.S. 123 (1951). Justices Black, *id.* at 142-149, Frankfurter, *id.* at 160-74, Douglas, *id.* at 174-83, and Jackson, *id.* at 186-87, all found a denial of procedural due process. Black added first amendment and bill of attainder arguments as well. *Id.* at 143-46. Burton concurred on nonconstitutional grounds. *Id.* at 124-42. Reed, joined by Vinson and Minton, voted to uphold the order. *Id.* at 199-213; Clark, who as Attorney General had promulgated the challenged list, did not vote. *Id.* at 142.

[162] 344 U.S. 183 (1952) (Clark, J.). Justice Burton concurred only in the result. Justice Jackson did not participate. *See id.* at 192.

[163] 344 U.S. at 186-87.

been read to apply only to those who participated knowingly in proscribed organizations or *personally* sought to destroy the government by force.[164] Mere membership in a subversive organization could not be made conclusive.[165] Thus the Oklahoma provision excluded too many innocent persons.[166]

This was true enough, though it distinguished neither *Douds* nor the deportation case. Nevertheless the Court seemed to have changed its tone if not its tune; individual responsibility had not been stressed much in the schoolteacher decision. Repeated exposure to provisions of this sort and to press reports of witch hunting seemed to have heightened the Court's awareness of the dangers that unbridled concern for national security held for first amendment freedoms.[167]

## III.   Equality and Process

### A.   Race

As noted in an earlier chapter, the Vinson Court put the final kibosh on the exclusion of blacks from primary elections in *Terry v. Adams* in 1953.[168] This decision was as predictable as it was creative, for the period had begun as it ended in *Terry*—with a bold decision holding the state responsible for discrimination by persons with no official governmental power.

*Shelley v. Kraemer* involved two suits to enjoin violations of restrictive covenants forbidding the occupancy of land by persons not of "the Caucasian race."[169] Without dissent, the Supreme Court set the injunctions aside on the ground that they denied black purchasers equal protection of the laws.[170]

Because the equal protection clause limits only the states, Vinson conceded that the private agreements not to permit black occupancy were not themselves unconstitutional.[171] In *Shelley,* however, the property owners had been willing to disobey their agreements; "but for the active intervention of the state courts, supported by the full panoply of state power, petitioners would have been free to occupy the properties in question."[172] Ever since the jury discrimination cases of 1880 it had been clear that the fourteenth amend-

---

[164]*Id.* at 188-89.

[165]*Id.* at 190 ("A state servant may have joined a proscribed organization unaware of its activities and purposes").

[166]*See id.* at 191 ("Indiscriminate classification of innocent with knowing activity must fall as an assertion of arbitrary power."). The opinion did not explicitly mention freedom of speech or assembly, concluding only that "[t]he oath offends due process." *Id.* Van Alstyne considers *Wieman* based essentially upon the concept of equality, although the equal protection clause was nowhere mentioned. Van Alstyne, *supra* note 149, at 1454-55. *Cf.* Niemotko v. Maryland, 340 U.S. 268 (1951).

[167]*See* Kalven, *Upon Rereading Mr. Justice Black on the First Amendment,* 14 U.C.L.A. L. Rev. 428, 438 (1967) (describing *Wieman* as "an impressive victory at a time when few anti-subversive measures were being found wanting").

[168]345 U.S. 461 (1953), pp. 323-25 *supra.*

[169]334 U.S. 1, 4-7 (1948).

[170]Reed, Jackson, and Rutledge did not participate. 334 U.S. at 23.

[171]*Id.* at 13 (citing Corrigan v. Buckley, 271 U.S. 323 (1926)).

[172]*Id.* at 19.

ment limited state judicial as well as legislative action;[173] and that, said Vinson, was that.[174]

Of course, as the Court so laboriously demonstrated, there had been state action. The serious question was whether that action had denied equal protection of the laws.[175] The parties to the covenants, not the state, had made the decision to discriminate on racial grounds. The state's policy was the racially neutral one of enforcing private agreements. The decision appeared to mean the police could no longer enforce a householder's decision to invite only whites to his cocktail party.[176] It rings hollow to proclaim private rights while denying the state's power to protect them; *Shelley* seemed to deprive the constitutional distinction between public and private action of much of its significance.[177]

In other cases of the period, the Court continued to insist that separate schooling for blacks in fact be equal.[178] A crucial passage in *Shelley,* however, seemed to foretell the demise of racial segregation itself. It was immaterial, Vinson argued, whether the states would enforce racial covenants that excluded whites as well as those directed against blacks. "The rights created by the first section of the Fourteenth Amendment are, by its terms, guaranteed to the individual. . . . It is, therefore, no answer to these petitioners to say that the courts may also be induced to deny white persons rights of ownership and

[173] *Id.* at 14-18 (citing, *e.g.,* Virginia v. Rives, 100 U.S. 313, 318 (1880), THE FIRST HUNDRED YEARS at 385-86 (equal protection clause forbids judicial officers to exclude blacks from juries).

[174] For approving views see Ming, *Racial Restrictions and the Fourteenth Amendment: The Restrictive Covenant Cases,* 16 U. CHI. L. REV. 203, 214 (1949); Frank, *The United States Supreme Court: 1947-48,* 16 U. CHI. L. REV. 1, 23 (1948) ("[I]t would have been hair-splitting indeed to say that a state may do through its courts what it may not do through its legislature.").

In a companion case from the District of Columbia, the Court reached the same result on statutory and public-policy grounds without reaching the question whether the fifth amendment's due process clause imposed limitations on Congress similar to those the equal protection clause imposed on the states. Hurd v. Hodge, 334 U.S. 24 (1948) (Vinson, C. J.). *See* pp. 285-93 *supra* (discussing the Japanese-American cases).

[175] *See* Henkin, *Shelley v. Kramer: Notes for a Revised Opinion,* 110 U. PA. L. REV. 473, 481 (1962).

[176] *See* Wechsler, *Toward Neutral Principles of Constitutional Law,* 73 HARV. L. REV. 1, 29 (1959). Earnest efforts have been made to limit *Shelley* to cases in which the state assists individuals in coercing third parties, Pollak, *Racial Discrimination and Judicial Integrity,* 108 U. PA. L. REV. 1, 13 (1959), or is not constitutionally barred from interfering with the private discriminatory decision, Henkin, *supra* note 175, at 498. Neither of these arguments answers the basic objection that the state's position was racially neutral in *Shelley,* and neither explains how the state can be said to be any more responsible for the private decision in one case than in the other. Analytically more attractive is the effort in Lewis, *The Meaning of State Action,* 60 COLUM. L. REV. 1083, 1115-16 (1960), which assimilates *Shelley* to the white-primary cases, *supra* note 168, by arguing that private covenants were a private exercise of the public function of zoning. This ordinary use of private ordering, however, seems a far cry from control of the machinery for choosing state officials or from the comprehensive exercise of governmental functions by the company town in Marsh v. Alabama, 326 U.S. 501 (1946), pp. 324-25 *supra.*

[177] When *Shelley* was applied to forbid the grant of damages for violation of a racial covenant in Barrows v. Jackson, 346 U.S. 249 (1953) (Minton, J.), Vinson dissented alone, 346 U.S. at 260-69, although on the crucial issue of state action the cases seemed indistinguishable. More interesting was the Court's conclusion in *Barrows,* 346 U.S. at 254-59, that a white seller being sued for violating the covenant had standing to assert the constitutional rights of black purchasers. The general principle that even injured parties may assert only their own rights was a judicially developed "rule of self-restraint," not a constitutional requirement; it should be relaxed in *Barrows* because in such a case "it would be difficult if not impossible for those persons whose rights are asserted to present their grievance before any court." *Id.* at 257.

[178] McLaurin v. Oklahoma State Regents, 339 U.S. 637 (1950) (Vinson, C. J.); Sweatt v. Painter, 339 U.S. 629 (1950) (Vinson, C. J.); Sipuel v. Board of Regents, 332 U.S. 631 (1948) (per curiam).

occupancy on grounds of race or color. Equal protection of the laws is not achieved through indiscriminate imposition of inequalities." [179]

Two wrongs, in other words, do not make a right; both whites and blacks are denied equal protection if each is denied what the other receives. *Brown v. Board of Education*, held over for reargument, was not decided until after Vinson's death,[180] but the Justices would have some explaining to do if the separate-but-equal doctrine was to survive.

## B.  Other Classifications

As early as 1915 the Court had held that equal protection precluded the states from limiting the number of aliens a willing employer could hire.[181] In 1948 it added that aliens could not be excluded from commercial fishing.[182] A few months earlier the Court had even made a substantial dent in the oppressive alien land laws it had unhesitatingly upheld in earlier years,[183] striking down discrimination against a minor citizen who held paper title on the ground that his father was an alien ineligible for citizenship.[184] *Niemotko v. Maryland* employed the equal protection clause rather than the free exercise clause to strike down religious discrimination in the issuance of park permits.[185] In other respects, however, the Vinson Court was most unreceptive to arguments that equal protection had been denied.

*Kotch v. Pilot Commissioners* upheld a state law prescribing rank nepotism in the selection of river pilots;[186] *Railway Express Agency v. New York* made only the feeblest effort to explain why it might be reasonable to exempt an owner's own messages from a ban on

---

[179] 334 U.S. at 22. *See also* Roche, *Education, Segregation and the Supreme Court—A Political Analysis*, 99 U. Pa. L. Rev. 949, 952 (1951) (finding similar significance in a passage from *Sweatt v. Painter:* "The Chief Justice stated in so many words that *separate legal education cannot be equal*. . . .") (emphasis in original).

[180] 345 U.S. 972 (1953), pp. 377-79 *infra*. The Court had earlier taken the unusual step of inviting petitions for certiorari before a decision had been rendered in a case pending before the Court of Appeals for the District of Columbia raising the same question under the due process clause of the fifth amendment. *See* Brown v. Board of Educ., 344 U.S. 1, 3 (1952) (per curiam).

[181] Truax v. Raich, 239 U.S. 33 (1915), p. 109, note 123 *supra*.

[182] Takahashi v. Fish & Game Comm'n, 334 U.S. 410 (1948) (Black, J., over a dissent by Justice Reed). *Cf.* Toomer v. Witsell, 334 U.S. 385, 395-403 (1948) (Vinson, C. J.) (reaching the same conclusion as to citizens of other states under the more explicit privileges and immunities clause of article IV).

The law struck down in *Takahashi* applied only to aliens "ineligible to citizenship," 334 U.S. at 418, and thus the case has been argued to present the easier case of *racial* discrimination against alien Japanese. Yet the Court's opinion deals basically with the law as if it excluded all aliens, going to some lengths to refute the state's argument that the limitation to persons ineligible for citizenship *justified* an otherwise impermissible discrimination. *Takahashi*, 334 U.S. at 420. *See* Rosberg, *The Protection of Aliens from Discriminatory Treatment by the National Government*, 1977 Sup. Ct. Rev. 275, 297-98; *cf.* Yick Wo v. Hopkins, 118 U.S. 356, 374 (1886), The First Hundred Years at 387.

[183] *See, e.g.*, Terrace v. Thompson, 263 U.S. 197 (1923); *see* p. 138, note 17 *supra*.

[184] Oyama v. California, 332 U.S. 633 (1948) (Vinson, C. J.). Reed, Burton, and Jackson dissented, 332 U.S. at 674-89, the last objecting that "[i]f California has power to forbid certain aliens to own its lands, it must have incidental power to prevent evasion of that prohibition by use of an infant's name to cloak a forbidden ownership." *Id.* at 684. Black, Douglas, Murphy, and Rutledge concurred, arguing that the prohibition on alien ownership was itself invalid. *Id.* at 647-74.

[185] 340 U.S. 268, 272-73 (1951) (Vinson, C. J.) (alternative holding).

[186] 330 U.S. 552 (1947) (Black, J., with Rutledge, Reed, Douglas, and Murphy, JJ., dissenting). The allegations of the complaint, accepted as true for purposes of a motion to dismiss, were that only "relatives and friends" of established pilots were accepted into an apprenticeship program that was a prerequisite to state employment.

advertising on the exterior of vehicles.[187] *MacDougall v. Green* summarily dismissed a challenge to a requirement that new political parties seeking to nominate candidates for office obtain petition signatures in at least fifty counties,[188] though *Carolene Products* had suggested that restrictions on the political process might be subjected to unusually strict scrutiny.[189] Most vividly, *Goesaert v. Cleary* gave the back of the judicial hand to a challenge to the virtual exclusion of women from bartending.[190] The contrast with the alien cases was striking. Despite the obvious political weakness of foreigners,[191] one might have thought sex a more suspect classification than alienage. It seems fair to assume that

---

*Id.* at 555. Citing "the advantages of early experience under friendly supervision . . . , the benefits to morale and *esprit de corps* which family and neighborly tradition might contribute," and "the close association in which pilots must work and live," Justice Black concluded that the measure was not "unrelated" to the legitimate objective of securing "the safest and most efficiently operated pilotage system practicable." *Id.* at 563-64 (emphasis in original).

[187] 336 U.S. 106, 110 (1949) (Douglas, J.) ("The local authorities may well have concluded that those who advertise their own wares on their trucks do not present the same traffic problem in view of the nature or extent of the advertising which they use."); *cf.* 336 U.S. at 114-15 (Jackson, J., concurring) ("There is not even a pretense here that the traffic hazard created by the advertising which is forbidden is in any manner or degree more hazardous than that which is permitted."). Justice Jackson also made the interesting argument that the Court should be less deferential in passing upon equal protection than due process claims because a holding that the state had unconstitutionally discriminated left it free to reenact the law in more general form. "The framers of the Constitution knew . . . that there is no more effective practical guaranty against arbitrary and unreasonable government than to require that the principles of law which officials would impose upon a minority must be imposed generally." *Id.* at 111-12. For development of Jackson's theme see Gunther, *Foreword: In Search of Doctrine on a Changing Court: A Model for a Newer Equal Protection*, 86 HARV. L. REV. 1 (1972).

[188] 335 U.S. 281, 283 (1948) (per curiam) ("To assume that political power is a function exclusively of numbers is to disregard the practicalities of government."). Douglas, Black, and Murphy dissented. 335 U.S. at 287-91. Justice Rutledge argued, as he had in Colegrove v. Green, 328 U.S. 549, 564-66 (1946), pp. 330-32 *supra*, that the short period before the next election made equitable relief improper. 335 U.S. at 284-87.

[189] United States v. Carolene Prods. Co., 304 U.S. 144, 152 n.4 (1938), p. 244 *supra*. *See also* Skinner v. Oklahoma, 316 U.S. 535 (1942), p. 288 *supra* (strict scrutiny of classification affecting "fundamental" right of reproduction). South v. Peters, 339 U.S. 276 (1950) (per curiam, over dissent of Douglas and Black, JJ.), decided after the deaths of Murphy and Rutledge, refused even to consider the merits of an equal protection attack on Georgia's county-unit system for statewide elections despite the system's obvious departure from equal electoral power for voters in heavily populated counties, saying only that "[f]ederal courts consistently refuse to exercise their equity powers in cases posing political issues arising from a state's geographical distribution of electoral strength among its political subdivisions." 339 U.S. at 277. Cited for this ambiguous conclusion were both *McDougall*, where the merits had been reached, and *Colegrove*, where three of the majority Justices had termed the issue "political" and the fourth (since deceased) had relied on particular timing problems that the Court did not suggest were present in *Peters*. *See also* Chicago & S. Air Lines, Inc. v. Waterman S.S. Corp., 333 U.S. 103, 111 (1948) (Jackson, J.), where the Court employed political-question terminology to support the conclusion that the decision whether to allow an airline to operate international flights was unreviewable, essentially because the matters were committed to the President's discretion. The opinion also reaffirmed the conclusion of three circuit courts in Hayburn's Case, 2 U.S. (2 Wall.) 409 (1792), THE FIRST HUNDRED YEARS at 6-9, that judicial decisions could not constitutionally be subjected to executive review. 333 U.S. at 113-14.

[190] 335 U.S. 464 (1948) (Frankfurter, J., over a dissent by Rutledge, Douglas, and Murphy, JJ.). "Michigan could, beyond question, forbid all women from working behind a bar." *Id.* at 465. The question actually presented was the constitutionality of an exemption for wives and daughters of bar owners. *Id.* The widespread lack of concern over sex discrimination at the time was exemplified by the observation of John P. Frank, normally a fervent advocate of civil rights and liberties, that *Goesaert* "illustrates that equal protection is far indeed from being a serious control over state economic legislation." Frank, *supra* note 46, at 26.

[191] *See* Rosberg, *supra* note 182, at 301-08.

the citizenship clause of the fourteenth amendment was meant to confer something of value.[192]

## C. Procedure

It was not long after Vinson's appointment, in *Adamson v. California,* that Justice Black made his most ambitious effort to establish that the fourteenth amendment made the entire Bill of Rights applicable to the states.[193] Though joined by Douglas, Murphy, and Rutledge,[194] he fell one vote short. Reaffirming that the privileges or immunities clause protected only rights "inherent in national citizenship" and due process only those " 'implicit in the concept of ordered liberty,' "[195] the majority, in an opinion by Justice Reed, adhered to the conclusion reached in *Twining v. New Jersey* that state prosecutors and judges might constitutionally comment on the refusal of a criminal defendant to take the stand.[196]

---

[192] History indeed suggests that citizens were to be protected generally against state discrimination under the privileges and immunities clause of the same amendment. The original sense of equal protection was the narrower one of protection against the wrongs of third parties. *See* THE FIRST HUNDRED YEARS at 342-51 (discussing the Slaughter-House Cases, 83 U.S. (16 Wall.) 36 (1873)). Dissenters during the Vinson period revived the related argument that the equal protection clause was wholly inapplicable to corporations. *See* Wheeling Steel Corp. v. Glander, 337 U.S. 562, 576-81 (1949) (Douglas and Black, JJ., dissenting).

Substantive due process, not surprisingly, enjoyed equally little favor. *See, e.g.,* Day-Brite Lighting Co. v. Missouri, 342 U.S. 421 (1952) (Douglas, J., over a dissent by Jackson, J.) (upholding requirement that employer pay for time off taken by employee to vote); Lincoln Fed. Labor Union v. Northwestern Iron & Metal Co., 335 U.S. 525, 536 (1949) (Black, J.) (upholding state' right-to-work law):

> This Court beginning at least as early as 1934 . . . has steadily rejected the due process philosophy enunciated in the *Adair-Coppage* line of cases. In doing so it has consciously returned closer and closer to the earlier constitutional principle that states have power to legislate against what are found to be injurious practices in their internal commercial and business affairs, so long as their laws do not run afoul of some specific federal constitutional prohibition, or of some valid federal law.

Even the explicit guarantee of compensation for a federal taking of property was read narrowly in United States v. Caltex, Inc., 344 U.S. 149 (1952) (Vinson, C. J.) (allowing an uncompensated destruction of property to prevent it from falling into enemy hands during World War II). As Douglas and Black objected in dissent, the fact that public necessity justified destroying the property meant only that it could be destroyed *with* compensation. *Id.* at 156 (Douglas, J., joined by Black, J., dissenting). The fifth amendment's basis is that when property must be sacrificed for the common good, "the public purse, rather than the individual, should bear the loss." *Id.* A better basis for the decision might have been that, given the presence of the enemy, the value of the property to its owners was close to zero.

[193] 332 U.S. 46, 68-123 (1947) (Black, J., dissenting). The classic response to Black's thesis is Fairman, *Does the Fourteenth Amendment Incorporate the Bill of Rights?,* 2 STAN. L. REV. 5 (1949). *See also* pp. 321-22 *supra.*

[194] 332 U.S. at 92 (Douglas, J., joining Black's dissent); 332 U.S. at 123-24 (Murphy, J., joined by Rutledge, J., dissenting).

[195] 332 U.S. at 53-54. *See* Slaughter-House Cases, 83 U.S. (16 Wall.) 36 (1873), THE FIRST HUNDRED YEARS at 342-51; Palko v. Connecticut, 302 U.S. 319, 323, p. 248 *supra.*

[196] "It seems quite natural that when a defendant has opportunity to deny or explain facts and determines not to do so, the prosecution should bring out the strength of the evidence by commenting upon the defendant's failure to explain or deny it." 332 U.S. at 56. *See also id.* at 60 (Frankfurter, J., concurring) ("Sensible and just-minded men, in important affairs of life, deem it significant that a man remains silent when confronted with serious and responsible evidence against himself which it is within his power to contradict."); Twining v. New Jersey, 211 U.S. 78 (1908); Friendly, *The Fifth Amendment Tomorrow: The Case for Constitutional Change,* 37 U. CIN. L. REV. 671, 700 (1968).

The fifth amendment itself was narrowly construed to permit the United States to require the keeping and production of incriminating records, Shapiro v. United States, 335 U.S. 1 (1948) (Vinson, C. J., over four

Justice Black's famous response is commonly cited as evidence of his expansive view both of the fourteenth amendment and of the judicial function. But there was a restrictive aspect to his argument as well as an expansive one, and it was equally central to his philosophy: "I think [the *Twining*] decision and the 'natural law' theory of the Court upon which it relies degrade the constitutional safeguards of the Bill of Rights and simultaneously appropriate for this Court a broad power which we are not authorized by the Constitution to exericse."[197] For Justice Black it was no more appropriate for judges to invent constitutional limitations than to ignore them.

Two years later, in *Wolf v. Colorado,* the Court held six to three that the fourteenth amendment did not require a state court to exclude evidence obtained by unreasonable search or seizure.[198] "The security of one's privacy against arbitrary intrusion by the police," Justice Frankfurter acknowledged, was "basic to a free society" and thus "enforceable against the States through the Due Process Clause."[199] There was room for honest difference of opinion, however, whether the exclusion of relevant evidence was an indispensable means of securing it.[200] "[M]ost of the English-speaking world" did not so regard it.[201] The great Cardozo, noting that the exclusionary rule required "[t]he criminal . . . to go free because the constable has blundered," had rejected it for New York.[202] Moreover, the rule perversely served to give greatest protection to "those upon whose person or premises something incriminating has been found. We cannot, therefore, regard it as a departure from basic standards" to remit search victims "to the remedies of private action and such protection as the internal discipline of the police, under the eyes of an alert public opinion, may afford."[203]

Black agreed. Even in federal courts the "exclusionary rule is not a command of the Fourth Amendment but is a judicially created rule of evidence which Congress might negate."[204] The Justices who had joined him in *Adamson,* however, dissented. "Self-scrutiny is a lofty ideal," said Murphy, but it was visionary to "expect a District Attorney to prosecute himself or his associates for well-meaning violations of the search and seizure clause. . . ."[205] Damage actions were beset with so many difficulties—from the requirement of malice to the difficulty of proving physical harm and the limits of an officer's finances—that they provided a wholly "illusory" deterrent.[206] As the Court had said in announcing the exclusionary rule for federal prosecutions in *Weeks v. United States,* if

---

dissents), and the registration of those engaged in illegal gambling, United States v. Kahriger, 345 U.S. 22, 32-33 (1953) (Reed, J., with two dissents on this issue). *See generally* Meltzer, *Required Records, the McCarran Act, and the Privilege against Self-Incrimination,* 18 U. CHI. L. REV. 687 (1951).

[197] 332 U.S. at 70. *See also id.* at 69, 91-92. Murphy and Rutledge, however, rejected the restrictive aspect of Black's interpretation: "Occasions may arise where a proceeding falls so far short of conforming to fundamental standards of procedure as to warrant constitutional condemnation in terms of due process despite the absence of a specific provision in the Bill of Rights." *Id.* at 124 (Murphy, J., dissenting).

[198] 338 U.S. 25 (1949).

[199] *Id.* at 27-28.

[200] *Id.* at 28-29.

[201] *Id.* at 29.

[202] *Id.* at 31. *See* People v. Defore, 242 N.Y. 13, 21, 150 N. E. 585, 587 (1926) (Cardozo, J.).

[203] 338 U.S. at 31.

[204] *Id.* at 39-40 (Black, J., concurring).

[205] *Id.* at 42 (Murphy, J., dissenting).

[206] *Id.* at 42-44 (Murphy, J., dissenting).

evidence unlawfully seized could be introduced at trial, " 'the Fourth Amendment . . . might as well be stricken from the Constitution.' "[207]

*Wolf* notwithstanding, it was Justice Frankfurter who concluded for a unanimous Court in the 1952 case of *Rochin v. California* that due process forbade a state court to consider evidence obtained by pumping the defendant's stomach against his will.[208] Defensively insisting that the "vague contours" of the prevailing criteria did not "make due process of law a matter of judicial caprice,"[209] Frankfurter concluded that the conduct of the police in *Rochin* "shocks the conscience."[210] "[T]o sanction th[is] brutal conduct . . . would be to afford brutality the cloak of law. Nothing would be more calculated to discredit law and thereby to brutalize the temper of a society."[211]

This was all very persuasive, but it seemed equally applicable to *Wolf*, where Frankfurter had reached the opposite conclusion. That pumping the defendant's stomach was "shocking" only made it, like any other unreasonable search, unconstitutional. That was not enough, *Wolf*, had held, to forbid introducing its fruits as evidence; "[h]ow such arbitrary conduct should be checked" was up to the states.[212] Frankfurter's argument that the numerous decisions excluding coerced confessions were not based solely upon their unreliability only accentuated the tension.[213] If confessions had to be excluded whenever the methods by which they were obtained "offend[ed] the community's sense of fair play and decency,"[214] it seemed to follow that the fruits of an unreasonable search should be excluded too.[215]

As a result of the expansive decisions of the 1930s, the docket was increasingly swollen with other criminal cases, most of which raised only factual questions of no general interest. Shortly before Vinson's death, the Justices took a meat ax to the habeas corpus statute in an effort to relieve themselves of the burden.[216]

---

[207] *Id.* at 42 (quoting *Weeks*, 232 U.S. 383, 393 (1914)). *See also* 338 U.S. at 40-41 (Douglas, J., dissenting); *id.* at 47-48 (Rutledge, J., dissenting). For agreement with the dissenters, see Allen, *The Wolf Case: Search and Seizure, Federalism, and the Civil Liberties,* 45 ILL. L. REV. 1 (1950); Frank, *supra* note 46, at 32 ("The parade was magnificent, but the enemy remained unscathed."). *But see* Posner, *Rethinking the Fourth Amendment,* 1981 SUP. CT. REV. 49, 55-56 (branding the exclusionary rule "an exceptionally crude deterrent device" that discourages "much lawful and proper police work" by imposing "social costs . . . greatly disproportionate to the actual harm" caused by illegal searches).

[208] 342 U.S. 165 (1952).

[209] *Id.* at 170-72.

[210] *Id.* at 172.

[211] 342 U.S. at 173-74. Black and Douglas concurred, proffering an unconvincing self-incrimination argument even though the Court had long since made clear that the purposes of the fifth amendment provision applied only to *testimonial* compulsion. *Id.* at 174-75 (Black, J., concurring); *see also id.* at 177-79 (Douglas, J., concurring). Justices Murphy and Rutledge were no longer on the Court. *See* Holt v. United States, 218 U.S. 245, 252-53 (1910), p. 124, note 209 *supra*.

[212] *Wolf,* 338 U.S. at 28.

[213] 342 U.S. at 172-73 (citing, *inter alia,* Brown v. Mississippi, 297 U.S. 278 (1936), pp. 247-48 *supra*).

[214] 342 U.S. at 173.

[215] *See* Allen, *Due Process and State Criminal Procedures: Another Look,* 48 Nw. U. L. REV. 16, 26-27 (1953); Perlman, *Due Process and the Admissibility of Evidence,* 64 HARV. L. REV. 1304, 1308-11 (1951). Equally difficult to reconcile with *Rochin* was the unanimous decision reaffirming that the kidnapping of a defendant by state officers was no ground for voiding his conviction. Frisbie v. Collins, 342 U.S. 519, 522 (1952) (Black, J.) (reaffirming Ker v. Illinois, 119 U.S. 436, 444 (1886)). *See* Allen, *supra,* at 27-28.

[216] *See, e.g.,* Brown v. Allen, 344 U.S. 443 (1953) (permitting federal court on habeas corpus to reexamine nonjurisdictional issues decided by state court); Hart, *The Time Chart of the Justices,* 73 HARV. L. REV. 84 (1959) (tracing evolution of Court's habeas corpus jurisdiction with emphasis on *Brown*).

## IV. THE STEEL SEIZURE CASE

On April 5, 1952, at the height of the Korean War, the Steelworkers' Union gave notice of a nationwide strike. Three days later, to assure continued production of essential war materials, President Truman directed the Secretary of Commerce to take possession of the steel mills. In *Youngstown Sheet & Tube Company v. Sawyer* the Supreme Court held that he had acted beyond his power.[217]

Four of the six Justices in the majority concluded that Congress had forbidden the seizure. An amendment to the Taft-Hartley Act that would have authorized seizure in national emergency cases had been rejected in favor of a provision for enjoining the strike itself. "The authoritatively expressed purpose of Congress to disallow such power to the President," said Justice Frankfurter, "could not be more decisive if it had been written into . . . the Labor Management Relations Act."[218]

---

Among the more interesting procedural decisions of the Vinson era in noncriminal matters were United States *ex rel.* Knauff v. Shaughnessy, 338 U.S. 537 (1950) (Minton, J.) (holding that an alien could be denied entry into the United States without a hearing if admission would be prejudicial to the interests of the United States), and Shaughnessy v. United States *ex rel.* Mezei, 345 U.S. 206 (1953) (Clark, J.) (allowing indefinite detention of an alien without a hearing at the discretion of the Attorney General on a confidential finding that entry would be prejudicial to the security of the United States).

The basis for these conclusions seemed to be that the admission of aliens was a "privilege" rather than a "right." *Knauff,* 338 U.S. at 542. Thus, the alien's admission was apparently neither "liberty" nor "property" under the due process clause. As Jackson observed in a dissent in *Mezei,* it was hard to deny that a person confined to Ellis Island had been deprived of liberty. 345 U.S. at 220-21 (Jackson, J., joined by Frankfurter, J., dissenting). Justices Black and Douglas also dissented. 345 U.S. at 216-18. Contrast the solicitude shown by the Court during the same period for resident aliens subjected to discriminatory treatment by state law. *See supra* text accompanying notes 181-84; *see also* the criticism of *Knauff* and *Mezei* in Henkin, *The Constitution and United States Sovereignty: A Century of Chinese Exclusion and Its Progeny,* 100 HARV. L. REV. 853, 858-63 (1987).

At the same time, limiting its earlier distressing conclusion that personal jurisdiction over the defendant was not necessary in divorce cases, *see* Williams v. North Carolina, 317 U.S. 287 (1942), pp. 329-30 *supra,* the Justices held that a court without personal jurisdiction could not cut off a spouse's right to alimony, Estin v. Estin, 334 U.S. 541 (1948) (Douglas, J.), or to child custody, May v. Anderson, 345 U.S. 528 (1953) (Burton, J.). The Court exhibited less regard for the interests of the parties' home state than for those of the parties themselves, holding that the appearance of the defendant precluded a collateral attack on a divorce judgment, even by third parties, for lack of domicile. Cook v. Cook, 342 U.S. 126 (1951) (Douglas, J.); Johnson v. Muelberger, 340 U.S. 581 (1951) (Reed, J.); Sherrer v. Sherrer, 334 U.S. 343 (1948) (Vinson, C. J.). *See generally* D. Currie, *Suitcase Divorce in the Conflict of Laws:* Simons, Rosenstiel, *and* Borax, 4 U. CHI. L. REV. 26 (1966) (exploring the problems of *ex parte* and collusive divorce proceedings).

The Court deviated from the general trend toward permitting any interested state to apply its own law to decide a controversy, pp. 242, 328-29 *supra,* when it held that the full faith and credit clause required a policy-holder's state to defer to the law of the state of incorporation in determining the validity of a clause in a fraternal insurance policy limiting the time for suit. Order of United Commercial Travelers v. Wolfe, 331 U.S. 586 (1947) (Burton, J., over four dissents). *See also* Hughes v. Fetter, 341 U.S. 609 (1951) (Black, J.) (holding that state where both parties resided could not refuse to entertain a wrongful-death action based on law of the place of the wrong but stressing that the forum had not attempted to apply its own law). *See generally* B. CURRIE, SELECTED ESSAYS ON THE CONFLICT OF LAWS 253-58, 283-311 (1963); Harper, *The Supreme Court and the Conflict of Laws,* 47 COLUM. L. REV. 883, 895-900 (1947); Reese, *Full Faith and Credit to Statutes: The Defense of Public Policy,* 19 U. CHI. L. REV. 339 (1952).

[217] 343 U.S. 579, 582-83 (1952). For background, see M. MARCUS, TRUMAN AND THE STEEL SEIZURE CASE (1977).

[218] 343 U.S. at 602 (Frankfurter, J., concurring); *see also id.* at 634, 639 (Jackson, J., concurring) ("Congress has not left seizure of private property an open field but has covered it by three statutory policies inconsistent

It may have been stretching things to find a prohibition in mere failure to authorize seizure, but Justice Jackson was correct that the President's power is "at its lowest ebb" when he acts contrary to "the expressed or implied will of Congress."[219] Although the Constitution grants the President authority that Congress cannot take from him,[220] no one denied that Congress could limit any presidential power to seize private property.[221] Article II's command that the President "take care that the laws be faithfully executed" and article VI's designation of federal statutes as "supreme law of the land" confirm the implication that the laws which article I empowers Congress to enact bind the President as well as everyone else.[222]

Justice Black's "opinion of the Court," however, took a broader approach. No statute, he wrote, justified the President's action; his authority as Commander in Chief did not reach so far;[223] and the order could not be sustained on the basis of the "several constitutional provisions that grant executive power to the President":

> [T]he President's power to see that the laws are faithfully executed refutes the idea that he is to be a lawmaker. The Constitution limits his functions in the

---

with this seizure."); *id.* at 655, 660 (Burton, J., concurring) ("Congress . . . has prescribed for the President specific procedures, exclusive of seizure, for . . . meeting the present type of emergency."); *id.* at 660, 662 (Clark, J., concurring in the judgment) ("where Congress has laid down specific procedures to deal with the type of crisis confronting the President, he must follow those procedures"). For approving views of this line of reasoning see Corwin, *The Steel Seizure Case: A Judicial Brick without Straw,* 53 COLUM. L. REV. 53, 65 (1953); Kauper, *The Steel Seizure Case: Congress, the President, and the Supreme Court,* 51 MICH. L. REV. 141, 180 (1952).

[219] 343 U.S. at 637. Other decisions of the Vinson period tended to confirm Jackson's converse principle that executive power "is at its maximum" when exercised in accordance with congressional authorization. *See, e.g.,* Lichter v. United States, 334 U.S. 742, 784-86 (1948) (Burton, J.) (invoking the purpose and "factual background" of the statute (including practice under prior legislation) to supply adequate standards for the recovery of "excessive profits" from government contractors); Fahey v. Mallonee, 332 U.S. 245, 250 (1947) (Jackson, J.) (upholding delegation of authority to appoint conservators for failing banks because the "accumulated experience of supervisors" acting under state law had "established well-defined practices" to guide the executive decision); United States *ex rel.* Knauff v. Shaughnessy, 338 U.S. 537, 542-43 (1950) (upholding authorization to exclude alien whose entry, as characterized by the United States Attorney General, "would be prejudicial to the interests of the United States" because the right to exclude aliens "is inherent in the executive power to control . . . foreign affairs"). *Cf.* United States v. Curtiss-Wright Export Corp., 299 U.S. 304 (1936) (upholding congressional delegation of foreign policy matter to the President), p. 217, note 63 *supra.*

[220] *Ex parte* Milligan, 71 U.S. (4 Wall.) 2, 139-40 (1866) (Chase, C. J., concurring). *See generally* W. TAFT, OUR CHIEF MAGISTRATE AND HIS POWERS 128-29 (1916); THE FIRST HUNDRED YEARS at 292 n.31.

[221] *See Youngstown,* 343 U.S. at 643 (Jackson, J., concurring) (stressing that article I empowered Congress "to raise and support armies" and "to provide and maintain a navy"); *id.* at 660-61 (Clark, J., concurring) (quoting Little v. Barreme (*The Flying Fish*), 6 U.S. (2 Cranch) 170 (1804) (enforcing congressional limitation on seizure of vessels to enforce laws against trading with French ports). *See also* U.S. Const. art I, § 8, cl. 18 ("The Congress shall have power . . . To make all Laws which shall be necessary and proper for carrying into execution the foregoing powers, and all other powers vested by this Constitution in the Government of the United States, or in any department or officer thereof.").

[222] *See* Marbury v. Madison, 5 U.S. (1 Cranch) 137, 154-62 (1803) (emphasizing the executive's amenability to congressional enactments by concluding that an act of Congress required the Secretary of State to deliver Marbury's commission).

[223] *See also* Jackson's concurrence, 343 U.S. at 641-46.

lawmaking process to the recommending of laws he thinks wise and the veto-
ing of laws he thinks bad. And the Constitution is neither silent nor equivocal
about who shall make laws which the President is to execute.[224]

In Black's view, more was involved than the President's duty to obey statutes actually
passed by Congress: apart from the Constitution's own grants of authority over foreign
affairs and the armed forces, the President may act only on the basis of legislation. Both
the grant of legislative authority to Congress and the enumeration of executive powers
suggest this conclusion, and the history of the Constitution supports it. Congress was
empowered to raise and support armies, for example, so that the Executive would not do
so.[225] Jackson added another powerful argument, juxtaposing the President's duty to execute the laws with an early understanding of the due process clause. "One [provision]
gives a governmental authority that reaches so far as there is law, the other gives a private
right that authority shall go no farther. These signify about all there is of the principle that
ours is a government of laws, not of men. . . ."[226]

Chief Justice Vinson, speaking also for Reed and Minton, seemed to suggest in dissent
that the President's authority was not limited to commanding the armed forces and executing the laws: article II gave him the entire "executive power" of the United States.[227] If
Vinson meant to embrace the Solicitor General's argument that the President's powers
were not, like those of Congress and the courts, limited by the enumeration that followed,[228] Jackson had an answer for him. "If that be true, it is difficult to see why the
forefathers bothered to add several specific items, including some trifling ones."[229] Al-

[224] 343 U.S. at 587. Justice Clark, concurring in the judgment on the ground that Congress had forbidden the
seizure, expressly disagreed with Black's broader conclusion: "[T]he Constitution does grant to the President
extensive authority in times of grave and imperative national emergency." *Id.* at 662.

[225] *See* THE FEDERALIST NOS. 24, 26, 28 (A. Hamilton); Currie, *The Distribution of Powers after Bowsher*,
1986 SUP. CT. REV. 19, 21-26; *cf. Youngstown*, 343 U.S. at 644 (Jackson, J., concurring) ("While Congress
cannot deprive the President of the command of the army and navy, only Congress can provide him an army or
navy to command."). Justice Douglas made the analogous argument that a seizure not authorized by statute would
undermine the express constitutional requirement of a congressional appropriation for the expenditure of federal
funds: "The branch of government that has the power to pay compensation for a seizure is the only one able to
authorize a seizure. . . ." *Id.* at 631 (Douglas, J., concurring) (referring to U. S. CONST. art I, § 9).

[226] 343 U.S. at 646 (Jackson, J., concurring). *See also* THE FIRST HUNDRED YEARS at 272 n.268; Corwin,
*The Doctrine of Due Process of Law before the Civil War*, 24 HARV. L. REV. 366 (1911). Without commenting
on Jackson's use of due process, Corwin criticized Justice Black's argument as "a purely arbitrary construct
created out of hand for the purpose of disposing of this particular case . . . altogether devoid of historical verification." Corwin, *supra* note 218, at 64-65. *But see* Taft, *supra* note 220, at 139-47 (taking issue with Theodore
Roosevelt's view that the President might "do anything that the needs of the Nation demanded unless such action
was forbidden by the Constitution or by the laws": "The President can exercise no power which cannot be fairly
and reasonably traced to some specific grant of power or justly implied and included within such express grant as
proper and necessary to its exercise.").

[227] 343 U.S. at 681 (Vinson, C. J., dissenting).

[228] *See id.* at 640 (Jackson, J., concurring) (quoting from the government's brief).

[229] *Id.* at 640-41 (Jackson, J., concurring) (adding that "[t]he example of such unlimited executive power that
must have most impressed the forefathers was the prerogative exercised by George III, and the description of its
evils in the Declaration of Independence leads me to doubt that they were creating their new Executive in his
image"). *Id.* at 641. *See also* 1 THE RECORDS OF THE FEDERAL CONVENTION OF 1787, at 65-66 (M. Farrand rev.
ed. 1937) ("Mr. Wilson . . . did not consider the Prerogatives of the British Monarch as a proper guide in defining

though the text of article II is not as explicit on this point as are articles I and III,[230] Jackson was aided by evidence of the Framers' purposes in concluding that the vesting of "executive power" in the President was not "a grant in bulk of all conceivable executive power," but rather "an allocation to the presidential office of the generic powers thereafter stated."[231]

Vinson's principal argument was that, in seizing the steel mills, the President had acted within his constitutional authority to execute statutes providing both for military procurement and for combating inflation. None of these statutes provided explicitly for the seizure of private property in order to accomplish their purposes. In Vinson's view, however, article II empowered the President to employ all suitable means of enforcing the laws that Congress had not forbidden.[232]

Past decisions lent some credence to this contention. The Court had hinted in *Little v. Barreme* (*The Flying Fish*) that the President might have enforced the trade laws by seizure if Congress had been silent;[233] *In re Neagle* had upheld presidential authority to appoint marshals to protect federal judges who applied the laws;[234] *In re Debs* had sustained the President's right to seek an injunction against a strike that threatened to interrupt commerce and the mails.[235] Black did not respond to the invocation of these precedents. Even if one concedes that the President may not be limited strictly to enforcement methods spelled out by statute, however, a line must be drawn somewhere if anything is to remain of the principle that only Congress shall make the laws.[236]

The greater part of Vinson's dissenting opinion was devoted to an ambitious effort to demonstrate a historical understanding that the President might take emergency action

---

the Executive powers. . . . The only powers he conceived strictly Executive were those of executing the laws, and appointing officers. . . ."); Kauper, *supra* note 218, at 175-77 (reading Vinson as basing his opinion solely on the President's authority to execute the laws).

[230] *See* U. S. CONST. art. I, § 1 ("[a]ll legislative Powers *herein granted* shall be vested in a Congress of the United States. . . ."); U. S. CONST. art. III, § 1 ("The judicial Power of the United States, shall be vested in one supreme Court, and in such inferior Courts as the Congress may from time to time ordain and establish."); U. S. CONST. art. III, § 2 ("The judicial Power *shall extend to* [certain enumerated classes of cases and controversies]"); 7 WORKS OF ALEXANDER HAMILTON 80 (1951) (arguing that the "different modes of expression in regard to the [executive and legislative] powers confirm the inference that the authority vested in the President is not limited to the specific cases of executive power delineated in Article II").

[231] 343 U.S. at 641 (Jackson, J., concurring). *See, e.g.,* THE FEDERALIST Nos. 24, 26, 28 (A. Hamilton); Corwin, *supra* note 218, at 53 ("The records of the Constitutional Convention make it clear that the purposes of this clause were simply to settle the question whether the executive branch should be plural or single and to give the executive a title.").

[232] 343 U.S. at 701-02 (Vinson, C. J., dissenting).

[233] 6 U.S. (2 Cranch) 170, 177-78 (1804) (quoted in *Youngstown,* 343 U.S. at 660 (Clark, J., concurring in the judgment)).

[234] 135 U.S. 1, 63-68 (1890), p. 20, note 89 *supra.*

[235] 158 U.S. 564 (1895), pp. 20-21 *supra.* Vinson relied on both *Neagle* and *Debs,* 343 U.S. at 687-88, 702 (Vinson, C. J., joined by Reed and Minton, JJ., dissenting).

[236] *See* Kauper, *supra* note 218, at 150 (denying that the precedents supported a general presidential "power to implement the legislative policy . . . by resorting to measures not embraced within the remedial and enforcement scheme provided by Congress"). "Perhaps in a time of emergency it might appear appropriate to conscript manpower for industry, to levy additional taxes to finance the legislative program, to impose more severe penalties on those who violate the laws. But it would hardly be contended that presidential prerogative would extend to these areas of legislative authority." *Id.* at 181.

without express statutory authority.[237] While Black rightly protested that one violation of the Constitution could not justify another,[238] Frankfurter appropriately acknowledged that long-accepted practice could establish a "gloss" on the Constitution itself.[239] The Court had often relied on the understanding of other branches to support the constitutionality of challenged actions.[240]

Many of the examples Vinson cited to establish such an understanding, however, missed the mark. In suppressing the Whiskey Rebellion and in blockading the confederacy, Washington and Lincoln had relied on express statutory authority to use armed force to suppress insurrection.[241] Adams's issuance of an extradition warrant served to implement a treaty.[242] The Louisiana Purchase was accomplished by treaty under the explicit terms of article II.[243] The Emancipation Proclamation was a battlefield measure of the Commander in Chief, applying only to slaves behind enemy lines, and Black acknowledged that the President had broad powers "in a theater of war."[244] Even Franklin Roosevelt's dramatic closing of the banks in 1933 was explicitly based on purported statutory authority, not on powers derived from the Constitution itself.[245] A handful of recent seizures not clearly supported by statute, as Frankfurter argued, hardly constituted long-standing acquiescence in the existence of general emergency authority.[246]

Because four of the majority Justices believed that Congress had forbidden the seizure, the question of presidential authority to employ means of law enforcement neither authorized nor forbidden was not definitively answered. *Youngstown* nonetheless stands as an eloquent reminder that the President must obey the law and that in general he may act only on the basis of statute.

---

[237] 343 U.S. at 683-700 (Vinson, C. J., dissenting).

[238] *Id.* at 588-89. *See also* Kauper, *supra* note 218, at 179 ("[P]rior self-serving assertions of presidential power . . . can hardly serve as adequate authority for defining the President's constitutional position.").

[239] 343 U.S. at 610 (Frankfurter, J., concurring) ("Deeply embedded traditional ways of conducting government cannot supplant the Constitution or legislation, but they give meaning to the words of a text or supply them."). *See also* W. TAFT, *supra* note 220, at 135-36 (reporting a long-standing practice of having postal treaties concluded by the Postmaster General).

[240] *See, e.g.,* McCulloch v. Maryland, 17 U.S. (4 Wheat.) 316, 401 (1819); Martin v. Hunter's Lessee, 14 U.S. (1 Wheat.) 304, 351-52 (1816); Stuart v. Laird, 5 U.S. (1 Cranch) 299, 309 (1803); THE FIRST HUNDRED YEARS at 77, 91-92, 160-61. *See also* p. 371 *infra* (discussing Ray v. Blair, 343 U.S. 214 (1952)).

[241] *See* Prize Cases, 67 U.S. (2 Black) 635 (1863), THE FIRST HUNDRED YEARS at 273-76.

[242] *See* 10 ANNALS OF CONG. 613-14 (1800) (quoted in *Youngstown,* 343 U.S. at 684). John Marshall, then a member of Congress, argued that until Congress acts, "it seems the duty of the Executive department to execute the contract by any means it possesses." *Id.* at 614.

[243] Treaty for the Cession of Louisiana, April 30, 1803, United States-France, 18 Stat. 232. *See* U. S. CONST. art. II, § 2 ("The President . . . shall have Power, by and with the Advice and Consent of the Senate, to make Treaties. . . .").

[244] *Sawyer,* 343 U.S. at 587; *see* Proclamation of Sept. 22, 1862, in 6 J. RICHARDSON, A COMPILATION OF THE MESSAGES AND PAPERS OF THE PRESIDENTS 96 (1900).

[245] 343 U.S. at 647-48 n.16 (Jackson, J., concurring); *see* ROSENMAN, THE PUBLIC PAPERS AND ADDRESSES OF FRANKLIN D. ROOSEVELT 4 (1933); Culp, *Executive Power in Emergencies,* 31 MICH. L. REV. 1066, 1078 & n.54 (1933) (expressing doubts about the adequacy of the statute invoked).

[246] 343 U.S. at 613 (contrasting United States v. Midwest Oil Co., 236 U.S. 459 (1915), where the Court deferred to a long-standing practice of withdrawing public lands from sale despite a statute making them available for purchase).

# Conclusion to Part Six

The opinions of Reed, Burton, Vinson, Minton, and Clark tended to be colorless in both substance and style, and they set the dominant tone of the period.[1] Black and Douglas, joined by Murphy and Rutledge until their deaths in 1949, regularly argued in dissent for greater protection of those interests singled out by Justice Stone in the *Carolene Products* case: those guaranteed by specific provisions of the Bill of Rights, the integrity of the political process, and the rights of discrete and insular minorities.[2]

Most interesting in terms of both style and substance were the relatively unpredictable Jackson and Frankfurter. The latter, who shared Jefferson's view that each Justice should write an opinion in important constitutional cases,[3] left us a legacy of no fewer than thirty-five concurring and forty-two dissenting opinions during the Vinson years, affording an unusually comprehensive picture of his views.[4] His voting pattern was equally striking, for though justifiably known as an apostle of judicial restraint,[5] he managed to dissent with some frequency from decisions rejecting claims based upon the first, fourth, and fifth amendments; once he even dissented from a decision broadly construing the federal tax

[1] For generally unflattering vignettes of these five Justices, see BERNARD SCHWARTZ, SUPER CHIEF: EARL WARREN AND HIS SUPREME COURT 56-73 (1983).

[2] United States v. Carolene Prods. Co., 304 U.S. 144, 152-53 n.4 (1938), p. 244 *supra. See* C. PRITCHETT, CIVIL LIBERTIES AND THE VINSON COURT 20 (1954) ("[T]he Court over which Vinson presided, if tested by the proportion of nonunanimous decisions handed down, was more divided than any in Supreme Court history.").

[3] *See* American Communications Ass'n v. Douds, 339 U.S. 382, 418 (1950). For Jefferson's views, see THE FIRST HUNDRED YEARS at 196 n.11.

[4] *See* Frank, *The United States Supreme Court: 1947-48,* 16 U. CHI. L. REV. 1, 51 (1948) (complaining that "more often the special opinion seemed expression for its own sake, without anything really worth saying").

[5] *See, e.g., Beauharnais v. Illinois, Dennis v. United States,* and *West Virginia State Bd. of Educ. v. Barnette.*

power.[6] In many of these cases he was joined by Jackson, who also wrote a series of highly original and spicy separate opinions.[7]

One of these was a dissent, joined only by Justice Douglas, in the undeservedly neglected case of *Ray v. Blair,* where the majority upheld an Alabama statute requiring candidates in party primaries for presidential electors to support whomever their party convention might select.[8] Quoting from the Federalist Papers, Jackson unimpeachably insisted that the whole purpose of the Electoral College was to interpose the independent judgment of the elector between the people and the choice of a President.[9] The majority relied on the fact that the system had never worked as intended; as early as 1826 a Senate committee had lamented that electors had bartered away that judgment in exchange for votes from the very beginning.[10] Protesting that "powers or discretions granted to federal officials by the Federal Constitution" cannot be "forfeited . . . for disuse," Jackson persuasively added that there was a difference between allowing and requiring them to do so.[11]

*Ray v. Blair* is a sobering reminder of the limited capacity of law to affect human behavior.

---

[6] *See, e.g.,* Everson v. Board of Educ., 330 U.S. 1 (1947) (establishment of religion); Zorach v. Clauson, 343 U.S. 306 (1952) (same); American Communications Ass'n v. Douds, 339 U.S. 382 (1950) (freedom of speech and association); On Lee v. United States, 343 U.S. 747 (1952) (search and seizure); United States v. Rabinowitz, 339 U.S. 56 (1950) (search and seizure); Harris v. United States, 331 U.S. 145 (1947) (search and seizure, self-incrimination); Shapiro v. United States, 335 U.S. 1 (1948) (self-incrimination); Shaughnessy v. United States *ex rel.* Mezei, 345 U.S. 206 (1953) (right to hearing); United States v. Kahriger, 345 U.S. 22 (1953) (federal tax power). *See* Frank, *The Supreme Court of the United States: 1949-50,* 18 U. Chi. L. Rev. 1, 46 (1950) ("[A]fter years of appearing at most a moderate on issues of civil rights, [Frankfurter] has again been made into a 'liberal' by the majority's turn to the right."); Jaffe, *The Judicial Universe of Mr. Justice Frankfurter,* 62 Harv. L. Rev. 357, 400-01 (1949) (arguing that the extreme deference exhibited in the *Barnette* dissent did not reflect Frankfurter's own prior or subsequent position).

[7] *See, e.g.,* his concurrences in *Kahriger,* 345 U.S. at 34-36; *Youngstown,* 343 U.S. 634-55; *Dennis,* 341 U.S. at 561-79; *Railway Express,* 336 U.S. 111-17; *Woods,* 333 U.S. 146-47. *See* the favorable assessment in Kurland, *Justice Robert H. Jackson—Impact on Civil Rights and Civil Liberties,* 1971 U. Ill. L.F. 551.

[8] 343 U.S. 214 (1952) (Reed, J.).

[9] *Id.* at 231, 232 & n.* (Jackson, J., joined by Douglas, J., dissenting) (citing The Federalist No. 68, at 441-42 (A. Hamilton) (Earle ed. 1937)) ("'It was equally desirable, that the immediate election should be made by men most capable of analyzing the qualities adapted to the station, and acting under circumstances favorable to deliberation. . . .'"). Compare Roger Sherman's objections to a proposed amendment that would have recognized the people's right "to instruct their Representatives" in Congress:

> This cannot be admitted to be just, because it would destroy the object of their meeting. I think, when the people have chosen a representative, it is his duty to meet others from the different parts of the Union, and consult, and agree with them to such acts as are for the general benefit of the whole community. If they were to be guided by instructions, there would be no use in deliberation. . . .

1 Annals of Cong. 763-64 (J. Gales ed. 1789).

[10] 343 U.S. at 228 & n.15 (quoting S. Rep. No. 22, 19th Cong., 1st Sess. 4 (1826)) ("'Electors, therefore, have not answered the design of their institution. They are not the independent body and superior characters which they were intended to be. . . . They have degenerated into mere agents. . . .'"). This report can hardly be viewed as a ringing endorsement of the practice in question.

[11] 343 U.S. at 233-35.

# Part Seven

## Chief Justice Warren
## 1953–1969

# Introduction to Part Seven

The sixteen-year tenure of Earl Warren as Chief Justice of the United States is commonly praised or condemned as an age of unrelieved judicial activism in which one "liberal" principle after another was discovered in or written into the Constitution.[1] This perception is nurtured by the fact that virtually the first act of the Court after Warren's appointment was the unanimous repudiation of the hoary separate-but-equal doctrine in *Brown v. Board of Education*,[2] which ushered in a new era in U.S. race relations. Moreover, as foretold by Justice Stone a generation before,[3] the Warren Court did in the last analysis afford greatly enhanced protection to the specific provisions of the Bill of Rights, to the integrity of the political process, and to the rights of discrete and insular minorities.

For several years, however, after a promising beginning, the Warren Court demonstrated a marked reluctance to stand up for those whom other organs of government elected to treat as disloyal, upholding one repressive measure after another over the dissents of Black, Douglas, Warren, and the newly appointed William J. Brennan.[4] In criminal procedure as well, despite occasional ground-breaking decisions, the revolution was slow in coming. In both fields the decisive event was the replacement of Justice Frankfurter by Arthur Goldberg in 1962, which transformed an activist minority into a majority.[5]

---

[1] *See, e.g.,* Kurland, *Foreword: "Equal in Origin and Equal in Title to the Legislative and Executive Branches of the Government,"* 78 HARV. L. REV. 143 (1964) (describing the preceding years as "a period during which the Justices have wrought more fundamental changes in the political and legal structure of the United States than during any similar span of time since the Marshall Court . . .").

[2] 347 U.S. 483 (1954).

[3] United States v. Carolene Products Co., p. 244 *supra.*

[4] Brennan, a state-court judge from New Jersey, was appointed by President Dwight Eisenhower to replace Minton in 1956. Eisenhower also appointed John M. Harlan, Potter Stewart, and Charles E. Whittaker—all federal court-of-appeals judges—to succeed Jackson, Reed, and Burton. See note 6 *infra.*

[5] Goldberg, who had been Secretary of Labor under President John F. Kennedy, was Kennedy's second appointment to the Court. The first was Byron R. White, a Colorado lawyer who had served briefly as Kennedy's

Frankfurter was in the vanguard of the assault on racial injustice and religious establishment, and he had lost a few important battles for judicial restraint in other fields. Apart
from questions of race and religion, however, most of what we think of as the legacy of
the Warren Court dates, not coincidentally, from the hour of Frankfurter's departure. It
therefore seems appropriate to consider separately the two halves of the Warren period.[6]

---

Deputy Attorney General and who succeeded Whittaker in early 1962. President Lyndon Johnson made two
appointments when Goldberg and Clark left the Court: the noted Washington lawyer Abe Fortas in 1965, and
Solicitor General Thurgood Marshall—the NAACP's lead lawyer in earlier days and the first black Justice—in
1967. *See* note 6 *infra*.

[6]        JUSTICES OF THE SUPREME COURT DURING THE TIME OF CHIEF JUSTICE WARREN

| Justice | Term | 1953 | 55 | 57 | 59 | 61 | 63 | 65 | 67 | 69 |
|---|---|---|---|---|---|---|---|---|---|---|
| Hugo L. Black | (1937-71) | | | | | | | | | |
| Stanley F. Reed | (1938-57) | | | | | | | | | |
| Felix Frankfurter | (1939-62) | | | | | | | | | |
| William O. Douglas | (1939-75) | | | | | | | | | |
| Robert H. Jackson | (1941-54) | | | | | | | | | |
| Harold H. Burton | (1945-58) | | | | | | | | | |
| Tom C. Clark | (1949-67) | | | | | | | | | |
| Sherman Minton | (1949-56) | | | | | | | | | |
| Earl Warren | (1953-69) | | | | | | | | | |
| John M. Harlan | (1955-71) | | | | | | | | | |
| William J. Brennan, Jr. | (1956-  ) | | | | | | | | | |
| Charles E. Whittaker | (1957-62) | | | | | | | | | |
| Potter Stewart | (1958-81) | | | | | | | | | |
| Byron R. White | (1962-  ) | | | | | | | | | |
| Arthur J. Goldberg | (1962-65) | | | | | | | | | |
| Abe Fortas | (1965-69) | | | | | | | | | |
| Thurgood Marshall | (1967-  ) | | | | | | | | | |

SOURCE: G. GUNTHER, CASES AND MATERIALS ON CONSTITUTIONAL LAW app. B. (11th ed. 1985). *See
generally* B. SCHWARTZ, SUPER CHIEF: EARL WARREN AND HIS SUPREME COURT (1983); G. EDWARD WHITE,
EARL WARREN: A PUBLIC LIFE (1982); G. DUNNE, HUGO BLACK AND THE JUDICIAL REVOLUTION (1977); H.
THOMAS, FELIX FRANKFURTER: SCHOLAR ON THE BENCH (1960); L. BAKER, FELIX FRANKFURTER (1969).

# 12

# The First Warren Court

## I.  BLACKS

### A.  Segregation

There had always been an air of unreality about the notion of "separate but equal" facilities for blacks and whites.[1] Those who lived with the system knew perfectly well, as Chief Justice Taney had declared in a related context in the *Dred Scott* case, that its purpose and effect were to keep blacks in an inferior position.[2] The modern Supreme Court had reflected the facts of life by striking down segregation requirements with increasing frequency on the ground that particular black facilities were deficient.[3] *Brown v. Board of Education*[4] merely confirmed what every schoolchild had known before the first Justice Harlan had told him: given their historical context, separate schools could not be equal.[5]

There was, of course, some difficulty in translating what everyone knew into accept-

---

[1] For the origins of the separate-but-equal thesis see THE FIRST HUNDRED YEARS at 387-90 (discussing Pace v. Alabama, 106 U.S. 583 (1883)); Plessy v. Ferguson, p. 40 *supra*.

[2] *See* Scott v. Sandford, 60 U.S. 393, 413, 416 (1857) ("Again, in 1822, Rhode Island, in its revised code, passed a law forbidding persons who were authorized to join persons in marriage, from joining in marriage any white person with any negro, Indian, or mulatto. . . . [T]he strongest mark of inferiority and degradation was fastened upon the African race. . . .").

[3] *See* pp. 249-50, 359 *supra*.

[4] 347 U.S. 483 (1954).

[5] *See* Plessy v. Ferguson, 163 U.S. 537, 557 (1896) (Harlan, J., dissenting) ("The thing to accomplish was, under the guise of giving equal accommodation for whites and blacks, to compel the latter to keep to themselves. . . ."). *See also* Black, *The Lawfulness of the Segregation Decisions*, 69 YALE L.J. 421, 424, 428 (1960):

> [I]f a whole race of people finds itself confined within a system which is set up and continued for the very purpose of keeping it in an inferior station, and if the question is then solemnly propounded whether such a race is being treated "equally," I think we ought to exercise one of the sovereign prerogatives of philosophers—that of laughter. . . . [C]onfronted with such a problem,

able judicial terms. The essence of the Chief Justice's position was contained in a quotation from the Kansas court: "[T]he policy of separating the races is usually interpreted as denoting the inferiority of the negro group. A sense of inferiority affects the motivation of a child to learn. Segregation with the sanction of law, therefore, has a tendency to [retard] the educational and mental development of negro children. . . ."[6] Apart from apparent weaknesses in the sociological studies cited to illustrate these injurious effects,[7] one astute observer pointed out the difficulty of attributing them to the state without an inquiry into legislative motivation not easy to square with judicial practice: "Is it . . . defensible to make the measure of validity of legislation the way it is interpreted by those who are affected by it?"[8] The bold response that the Court's conclusion was analogous to the "experiential judgment that official inquiries into private associations inhibit the freedom to join"[9] is provocative but perhaps not conclusive; an alternative approach might be to argue that, in light of the background of racial discrimination against which separate schools were established, the perception of blacks that segregation was disparaging could not be dismissed as baseless. In any event, the Court's narrow ground of decision made it unnecessary to consider the more sweeping and equally attractive argument the Justices themselves had suggested in *Shelley v. Kraemer:* that when a state excluded children from particular schools on account of their race it denied *both* blacks and whites the equal protection of the laws.[10]

The conceptual difficulties of *Brown* paled beside those presented by the companion case of *Bolling v. Sharpe,*[11] where the Court concluded that segregation was forbidden in the District of Columbia. Whatever the equal protection clause meant, it plainly applied only to the states. But the Court was in no mood to let imperfections in the Constitution

---

legal acumen has only one proper task—that of developing ways to make it permissible for the Court to use what it knows. . . .

*Cf.* Bailey v. Drexel Furniture Co., 259 U.S. 20, 37 (1922) ("[A] court must be blind not to see that the so-called tax is imposed to stop the employment of children."), pp. 173-74 *supra.*

[6] 347 U.S. at 494.

[7] *Id.* at 494-95 n.11. *See, e.g.,* Yudof, *School Desegregation: Legal Realism, Reasoned Elaboration, and Social Science in the Supreme Court,* 42 LAW & CONTEMP. PROBS. 57 (1978); Goodman, *De Facto Segregation: A Constitutional and Empirical Analysis,* 60 CAL. L. REV. 275 (1972); and other sources cited in G. GUNTHER, CASES AND MATERIALS ON CONSTITUTIONAL LAW 639 n.2 (11th ed. 1985). But see Black, *supra* note 5, at 430 n.25 ("That such treatment is generally not good for children needs less talk than the Court gives it.").

[8] Wechsler, *Toward Neutral Principles of Constitutional Law,* 73 HARV. L. REV. 1, 33 (1959). For the Court's general reluctance to investigate legislative motives see note 241 *infra* and accompanying text (discussing McGowan v. Maryland).

[9] A. BICKEL, THE LEAST DANGEROUS BRANCH 57 (1962). *See* text accompanying notes 382-83 *infra* (discussing NAACP v. Alabama).

[10] *See Shelley,* 334 U.S. at 22 ("It is . . . no answer to these petitioners to say that the courts may also be induced to deny white persons rights of ownership and occupancy on grounds of race or color. Equal protection of the laws is not achieved through indiscriminate imposition of inequalities."). *See also* THE FIRST HUNDRED YEARS at 388-89. The sparse references to school segregation in Congress around the time the fourteenth amendment was proposed do not seem to foreclose either this or the Court's interpretation. *See* Bickel, *The Original Understanding and the Segregation Decision,* 69 HARV. L. REV. 1 (1955). Nor does Wechsler's concern for associational rights, *supra* note 8, at 34, seem persuasive: a tendency toward compulsory association inheres in even segregated public schooling, while the Constitution requires equal treatment of the races. *See* Black, *supra* note 5, at 429.

[11] 347 U.S. 497 (1954).

stand between it and the desirable result: "In view of our decision that the Constitution prohibits the states from maintaining racially segregated public schools, it would be unthinkable that the same Constitution would impose a lesser duty on the Federal Government."[12] The decisions upholding the shameful treatment of Japanese-Americans during World War II had suggested how the Court might pin its conclusion on the Constitution. "As this Court has recognized," wrote the Chief Justice in *Bolling*, "discrimination may be so unjustifiable as to be violative of due process."[13]

Substantive due process was back, and in a most troublesome form; holding that equality was implicit in due process suggested that the equal protection clause added nothing at all. In addition, it was difficult to see how segregation of public schools deprived anyone of "liberty" within the meaning of the fifth amendment. In best Lochnerian terms, Chief Justice Warren defined liberty to embrace "the full range of conduct which the individual is free to pursue."[14] But the Constitution does not require the government to provide anyone with an education, and the statute setting up the schools could hardly be said to deprive pupils of the very interest it created.

When the segregation cases had first been argued, no fewer than four Justices had expressed reservations about discarding the separate-but-equal doctrine.[15] Acutely aware of the inflammatory potential of a decision setting aside one of the fundamental precepts of Southern society, both Frankfurter and Warren had worked hard to avoid a division that might further impede public acceptance of the decision.[16] Part of their strategy for achieving unanimity was to separate the question of constitutionality from that of remedy, leaving the knotty problem of enforcement for a later day.[17]

The next year, following reargument on the remedial question, the Court issued a second opinion.[18] The "transition to a system of public education freed of racial discrimination," the Chief Justice argued, faced "a variety of obstacles," involved many "complexities," and required "solution of varied local school problems."[19] Since the lower courts were in a better position to assess differing "local conditions," all but one of the cases were remanded with instructions to admit the plaintiffs to public schools on a nondiscriminatory basis "with all deliberate speed."[20] Mere "disagreement" with the *Brown* decision, the opinion added, was not to delay its implementation;[21] but the euphemistic allusion to the "variety of obstacles" to the obvious remedy of immediate admission left little doubt that the Court was fully cognizant of the practical limitations on its authority.[22]

---

[12]*Id.* at 500.

[13]347 U.S. at 499 (citing Korematsu v. United States and Hirabayashi v. United States, pp. 285-92 *supra*).

[14]347 U.S. at 499.

[15]*See* B. SCHWARTZ, SUPER CHIEF: EARL WARREN AND HIS SUPREME COURT 74-77 (1983) (naming Vinson, Reed, Jackson, and Clark).

[16]*See id.* at 78-106; Hutchinson, *Unanimity and Desegregation: Decisionmaking in the Supreme Court,* 68 GEO. L.J. 1948-58 (1979).

[17]*See Brown,* 347 U.S. at 495.

[18]Brown v. Board of Education (*Brown II*), 349 U.S. 294, 299 (1955).

[19]*Id.* at 299-300.

[20]*Id.* at 299, 301. The Delaware judgment, which had ordered immediate admission, was affirmed but also remanded "for such further proceedings as [the state] Court may deem necessary in light of this opinion." *Id.*

[21]*Id.* at 300.

[22]*See* Bickel, *The Decade of School Desegregation: Progress and Prospects,* 64 COLUM. L. REV. 193, 201 (1964) ("The system would have worked no differently in any event, no matter what the form of the Supreme

This impression was reinforced by the Justices' lame refusal, not long afterward, to entertain a challenge to miscegenation laws although the case appeared to fall within the Court's mandatory jurisdiction on appeal.[23] Moreover, as every student knows, the Court's fears proved anything but groundless. When the Little Rock school board adopted a modest plan for gradual desegregation in response to *Brown,* Arkansas Governor Orval Faubus called out the National Guard to keep black pupils from entering the building.[24] Although an injunction got rid of the Guardsmen, unruly crowds encouraged by the Governor's opposition continued to frustrate implementation of the plan until President Eisenhower sent in the army.[25]

Emboldened by executive support, the Court in *Cooper v. Aaron* reaffirmed its earlier assertion that hostility to desegregation was no excuse for delay: "[L]aw and order are not here to be preserved by depriving the Negro children of their constitutional rights."[26] This conclusion seemed a significant improvement on *Feiner v. New York,*[27] which had seemed to suggest that public hostility might justify silencing an unpopular speaker. It was insufficient, of course, to put an end to a program of massive and ingenious resistance to desegregation that was to last until after the new Chief Justice had left the Court.[28] Two years after *Cooper,* for example, the Court was called upon to reject the aberrant notion that the state could insulate school segregation from judicial control by "interposing" itself between the court and the local school district—as if the Constitution did not explicitly bind the states themselves.[29]

A considerable tempest was engendered by the Court's remark in *Cooper* that because "the federal judiciary is supreme in the exposition of the law of the Constitution," the *Brown* decision was "the supreme law of the land."[30] It was true that the school district in

---

Court's decree"); G. DUNNE, HUGO BLACK AND THE JUDICIAL REVOLUTION 312 (1977) ("[N]otwithstanding the Chief Justice's brave rhetoric that 'constitutional principles cannot be allowed to yield simply because of disagreement,' the plain fact was that constitutional principles were being allowed to yield precisely for that reason."). For further commentary on the "all deliberate speed" decision see sources cited in G. STONE, L. SEIDMAN, C. SUNSTEIN, & M. TUSHNET, CONSTITUTIONAL LAW 468 (1986); Elman, *The Solicitor General's Office, Justice Frankfurter, and Civil Rights Litigation, 1946-60: An Oral History,* 100 HARV. L. REV. 817, 825-27 (1987) (reporting that Justice Black was "scared to death—and he scared everybody else on the Court—of the political turmoil in the South that would follow" and arguing that although delayed enforcement was "unprincipled" and "wrong" it "offered the Court . . . a way to end racial segregation without inviting massive disobedience"). *See also id.* at 828, 832, 843-44, 848-49 (revealing a distressing series of *ex parte* contacts on pending matters between Frankfurter and Elman, a former law clerk then in the Solicitor General's office: "In *Brown* I didn't consider myself a lawyer for a litigant. I considered it a cause that transcended ordinary notions about propriety in a litigation." *Id.* at 842.).

[23] Naim v. Naim, 350 U.S. 986 (1956). *See* the revealing account in Hutchinson, *supra* note 16, at 62-67, and the memorandum of Justice Frankfurter reprinted in *id.* at 95-96 (arguing that "moral considerations far outweigh the technical considerations" respecting the obligatory nature of appeals: "The moral considerations are, of course, those raised by the bearing of adjudicating this question to the Court's responsibility in not thwarting or seriously handicapping the enforcement of its decision in the segregation cases.").

[24] *See* Cooper v. Aaron, 358 U.S. 1, 8-11 (1958).

[25] *See id.* at 11-12.

[26] *Id.* at 16. In view of the immense public importance of the *Cooper* case, the Court took the unusual step of having all nine Justices sign its opinion. See B. SCHWARTZ, *supra* note 15, at 289-301 (reporting that it was Justice Brennan who drafted the opinion).

[27] *See* pp. 348-50 *supra.*

[28] *See generally* McKay, *"With All Deliberate Speed,"* 31 N.Y.U. L. REV. 991 (1956).

[29] Bush v. Orleans Parish School Board, 364 U.S. 500 (1960) (per curiam).

[30] 358 U.S. at 18.

*Cooper* had not been a party to *Brown* and that, as Lincoln argued, there must be some latitude for asking the Supreme Court to overrule its prior decisions.[31] That is a far cry from justifying Governor Faubus's defiance of a principle he had every reason to know the Court would reaffirm; if everyone waited for a court order directed to him personally, the system would collapse entirely.[32]

*Brown*'s emphasis on the adverse effects of segregation on *education* made it unsatisfying that the Court proceeded in a series of later decisions to strike down segregation of such facilities as beaches and buses with no more than a cite to *Brown*.[33] Perhaps the Justices thought, not unreasonably, that segregation of these facilities caused feelings of inferiority as well;[34] perhaps they were tacitly moving toward the more absolute position put forth in *Shelley*. Justifications were not wanting, but it might have been better to give them.[35]

## B.  Political Power

The early Warren Court's solicitude for the rights of blacks was not confined to segregation cases. Several important decisions of the period served also to protect the rights of blacks to further their own interests through political action.

When the boundaries of Tuskegee, Alabama, were redrawn to exclude virtually all blacks from the city, it was the normally restrained Justice Frankfurter who wrote to find a racially based denial of the right to vote in municipal elections.[36] In contrast to the school segregation cases, the boundary had not been drawn explicitly on racial grounds. However, as in cases involving invariably all-white juries and grandfather clauses for voters,[37] the facts left no room for any other explanation of the state's decision.[38] A more serious obstacle to the Court's conclusion was Justice Whittaker's objection that the fifteenth

---

[31] *See* 2 THE COLLECTED WORKS OF ABRAHAM LINCOLN 494 (Basler ed. 1953); 3 *id.* at 255; 6 MESSAGES AND PAPERS OF THE PRESIDENTS 5, 9-10 (Richardson ed. 1897).

[32] *See* Wechsler, *The Courts and the Constitution,* 65 COLUM. L. REV. 1001, 1008 (1965); Bickel, *supra* note 22, at 259-64.

[33] *E.g.,* Mayor of Baltimore v. Dawson, 350 U.S. 877 (1955) (beaches); Holmes v. Atlanta, 350 U.S. 879 (1955) (golf courses); Gayle v. Browder, 352 U.S. 903 (1956) (buses); New Orleans City Park Improvement Ass'n v. Detiege, 358 U.S. 54 (1958) (parks); Turner v. City of Memphis, 369 U.S. 350 (1962) (restaurants). *See* Wechsler, *supra* note 8, at 22 ("[T]he question . . . appears to me to call for principled decision.").

[34] *See* Brest, *Foreword: In Defense of the Antidiscrimination Principle,* 90 HARV. L. REV. 1, 9 (1976) (arguing that "the stigmatic injury inflicted by discrimination" explains both *Brown* and its extension to other facilities "without the need to invoke controversial social science evidence").

[35] Following the example it had set in Shelley v. Kraemer, pp. 358-60 *supra,* the Court continued to construe broadly the equal protection clause's explicit limitation to "state" as opposed to private discrimination. *See* Pennsylvania v. Board of Directors of City Trusts, 353 U.S. 230 (1957) (per curiam) (holding that a city acting as trustee could not exclude blacks from Girard College in accordance with terms of privately created trust); Burton v. Wilmington Parking Auth., 365 U.S. 715 (1961) (Clark, J.) (holding the state responsible for discrimination by privately owned restaurant on public property). *See* Lewis, Burton v. Wilmington Parking Authority—*A Case without Precedent,* 61 COLUM. L. REV. 1458, 1459 (1961) (finding the latter opinion "singularly uninstructive" as to the reasons for its decision).

[36] Gomillion v. Lightfoot, 364 U.S. 339 (1960).

[37] *See* Neal v. Delaware, 103 U.S. 370 (1880), *The First Hundred Years* at 386-87); Guinn v. United States, pp. 106-07 *supra.*

[38] *See* Ely, *Legislative and Administrative Motivation in Constitutional Law,* 79 YALE L.J. 1205, 1279 (1970) ("[O]ne knows—yes, knows—that the selection in *Gomillion* was racial rather than random.").

amendment guaranteed only "the same right to vote as is enjoyed by all others within the same . . . political division"[39]—to which Justice Frankfurter responded, if at all, simply by declaring that, if the allegations of the complaint were proved, the new boundary would "obviously discriminate against colored citizens."[40] Most troublesome for Frankfurter was his own long-standing position that the constitutionality of legislative apportionment was a nonjusticiable "political question."[41] The Tuskegee case was different, he argued, because it involved total deprivation rather than mere dilution of the vote, because the inequality resulted from affirmative legislative action rather than inaction, and because it was directed at a specific racial minority;[42] but all these distinctions seemed to go more to the merits than to the propriety of a judicial determination.[43]

No less significant for black political power was the great opinion written by the recently appointed Justice John Marshall Harlan—a grandson of the sturdy *Plessy* dissenter—in *NAACP v. Alabama* in 1958.[44] In the course of litigation over an asserted obligation to qualify to do business in Alabama, the state court had ordered the National Association for the Advancement of Colored People to produce a list of its Alabama members. The Supreme Court unanimously concluded that this order infringed the members' constitutional rights. "It is hardly a novel perception," wrote Harlan, "that compelled disclosure of affiliation with groups engaged in advocacy may constitute [an] effective . . . restraint on freedom of association. . . ." NAACP members had been subjected to "economic reprisal, loss of employment, [and] threat of physical coercion"; disclosure might well "induce members to withdraw from the Association and dissuade others from joining it because of fear of exposure of their beliefs. . . ."[45] Since by the time of decision the

---

[39]*Id.* at 349 (Whittaker, J., concurring on the ground that fencing blacks out of Tuskegee was "an unlawful segregation of races . . . in violation of the Equal Protection Clause" and citing *Brown*). For further development of Whittaker's objection see Lucas, *Dragon in the Thicket: A Perusal of* Gomillion v. Lightfoot, 1961 SUP. CT. REV. 194, 210-13.

[40]364 U.S. at 342.

[41]*See* pp. 330-32 *supra* (discussing Colegrove v. Green).

[42]364 U.S. at 346.

[43]*See* Lucas, *supra* note 39, at 233-34; Pollak, *Judicial Power and "the Politics of the People,"* 72 YALE L.J. 81, 84 (1962) ("Surely the fact that the constitutional mandate is plainer and less equivocal in an instance of anti-Negro discrimination than in others doesn't make such a claim *more justiciable* than other equal protection claims; it simply makes a *justiciable* law suit easier to win."). To the extent that Frankfurter's political-question principle was based on the absence of judicially manageable standards for decision, however, the clarity of the ban on racial discrimination was relevant to justiciability as well. *See infra* pp. 412-14 (discussing Baker v. Carr).

[44]357 U.S. 449.

[45]*Id.* 462-63. Prominently cited in support of the Court's conclusion was American Communication Ass'n v. Douds, pp. 355-57 *supra,* a decision often condemned as hostile to political freedoms, where the Court in upholding a non-Communist oath for union officials had made clear that indirect burdens on speech and association were subject to serious constitutional scrutiny. The NAACP's standing to assert its members' rights was upheld on the appealing basis that "[t]o require that it be claimed by the members themselves would result in nullification of the right at the very moment of its assertion." 357 U.S. at 459, *citing* Barrows v. Jackson, p. 359, note 157 *supra. See generally* Sedler, *Standing to Assert Constitutional* Jus Tertii *in the Supreme Court,* 71 YALE L.J. 599 (1962).

The early Warren Court was not always so sensitive to the need for a forum to vindicate federal rights. *See, e.g.,* International Longshoremen's Union v. Boyd, 347 U.S. 222 (1954) (Frankfurter, J., over two dissents) (holding premature a suit for declaratory and injunctive relief respecting the right of alien workers to reenter the contiguous states after a projected trip to Alaska). *Cf.* United Public Workers v. Mitchell, p. 355, note 147 *supra.* More understandable was the refusal in Poe v. Ullman, 367 U.S. 497 (1961), over four dissents, to determine

NAACP had agreed to comply with the qualification statute, the Court found no compelling justification for such impairment of the interest in association.[46]

The Court also embarked before 1962 on what was to prove a long series of guerrilla skirmishes to prevent punishment of those who engaged in the widespread tactic of sit-ins to protest segregation of private restaurants. *Garner v. Louisiana*,[47] decided by a unanimous Bench badly divided over the reasons for its conclusion, illustrates both the Justices' determination to protect this novel form of political pressure and the difficulties of justifying their action.

Sitting at a lunch counter reserved for members of another race, as Harlan argued in a concurring opinion, was under the circumstances a form of expression—"as much a part of the 'free trade in ideas' . . . [as] a public oration delivered from a soapbox."[48] The difficulty was that the demonstrators had chosen to express their views on someone else's property, and there was little reason to think they had a right to do so against the wishes of the owner.[49]

The Justices sidestepped this difficulty in *Garner* by finding alternative bases for setting aside the convictions. The defendants had been found guilty of disturbing the peace; seeing no evidence of conduct that was "outwardly boisterous" or "likely to cause a public

---

the validity of a law forbidding the use of contraceptives; a long history of nonenforcement led the majority to conclude there was no realistic threat of prosecution. *See id.* at 507-08 (opinion of Frankfurter, J., for four Justices); *id.* at 509 (Brennan, J., concurring); A. BICKEL, *supra* note 9, at 143-56 (finding an actual controversy but making the novel argument that to enforce the law after such a period of "desuetude" would offend the due process clause for want of fair warning).

[46]357 U.S. at 463-65. In the same vein were Bates v. Little Rock, 361 U.S. 516, 525 (1960) (Stewart, J.) (finding "no relevant correlation between the power of . . . municipalities to impose occupational license taxes and the compulsory disclosure and publication of the membership lists of the local branches of the N[AACP]"); Shelton v. Tucker, 364 U.S. 479, 490 (1960) (Stewart, J., over dissents by Frankfurter, Harlan, Clark, and Whittaker) (holding that a requirement that public-school teachers disclose all their organizational affiliations went "far beyond what might be justified in the exercise of the State's legitimate inquiry into the fitness and competency of its teachers"); and Louisiana *ex rel.* Gremillion v. NAACP, 366 U.S. 293, 296 (1961) (Douglas, J.) (upholding a preliminary injunction against enforcement of a law requiring the association to disclose its members, without discussing the state's interest: "[W]here it is shown . . . that disclosure of membership lists results in reprisals against and hostility to the members, disclosure is not required."). *Cf.* Talley v. California, 362 U.S. 60, 64-65 (1960) (Black, J., over a dissent by Clark joined by Frankfurter and Whittaker) (holding a ban on anonymous handbills "subject to the same infirmity" as the disclosure requirements invalidated in NAACP v. Alabama and in *Bates:* "Persecuted groups and sects from time to time throughout history have been able to criticize oppressive practices and laws either anonymously or not at all."). For general discussions of the role of free association in constitutional adjudication see Fellman, *Constitutional Rights of Association,* 1961 SUP. CT. REV. 74; Emerson, *Freedom of Association and Freedom of Expression,* 74 YALE L.J. 1 (1964).

[47]368 U.S. 157 (1961).

[48]*Id.* at 201 (citing Stromberg v. California, pp. 255-57 *supra,* which had held the display of a red flag a form of protected expression). "We would surely have to be blind not to recognize," said Harlan, "that petitioners were sitting at these counters, where they knew they would not be served, in order to demonstrate that their race was being segregated in dining facilities in this part of the country." *Id.*

[49]*See* 368 U.S. at 202 (Harlan, J., concurring) ("This is not to say, of course, that the Fourteenth Amendment reaches to demonstrations conducted on private property over the objection of the owner. . . ."). This conclusion had been implicit in Justice Black's suggestion in Martin v. Struthers, pp. 317-18 *supra,* that the state could enforce a householder's decision to exclude solicitors seeking to bring protected messages to his door. *Cf.* Kovacs v. Cooper, pp. 343-45 *supra* (upholding a ban on the use of loud amplification equipment on public streets as a reasonable regulation of the manner of communication).

disturbance," the majority concluded that due process had been denied.[50] Retorting that it was not unreasonable to fear a disorderly reaction to sit-ins in Louisiana in 1960,[51] Douglas based his concurrence on the argument that state licensing and state customs made the state responsible for the segregation of private lunch counters.[52] Harlan, straining to find that two of the sit-ins in question had been conducted with the "implied consent" of the owners, argued that such communicative conduct could not be prohibited without "a legislative judgment as to whether that conduct presents [a] clear and present . . . danger to the welfare of the community. . . ."[53] The battle was far from over, but there was no doubt whose side the Justices were on.[54]

The otherwise unbroken string of black victories was significantly interrupted only by *Lassiter v. Northampton County Board of Elections*,[55] where even Justice Douglas had to concede that there was such a palpable relation between the ability to read and intelligent use of the ballot[56] that a literacy test could not be pronounced on its face either an evasion of the fifteenth amendment[57] or an unreasonable discrimination against uneducated citi-

---

[50] 368 U.S. at 173-74 (Warren, C. J.). *See* Thompson v. Louisville, 362 U.S. 199 (1960) (Black, J.) (holding that conviction on a charge unsupported by evidence offended the due process clause). For doubts as to the validity of this superficially appealing principle see Henkin, *Foreword: On Drawing Lines*, 82 HARV. L. REV. 63, 67 (1968) ("If a conviction supported by 'no evidence whatever' violates due process, why not a conviction where the evidence is flimsy, or which is against the weight of the evidence, or perhaps even where the evidence does not support guilt beyond a reasonable doubt?").

[51] 368 U.S. at 176-77 (Douglas, J., concurring). *See also id.* at 193-96 (Harlan, J., concurring).

[52] 368 U.S. at 177-85. *Cf.* Civil Rights Cases, 109 U.S. 3, 26-62 (1883) (Harlan, J., dissenting), THE FIRST HUNDRED YEARS at 398-401.

[53] 368 U.S. at 203 (Harlan, J., concurring). *See also id.* at 196-207 (adding that the overbreadth and vagueness of the statute made it inapplicable even in the absence of the owner's consent).

[54] For an approving view of the Court's evasive tactics in *Garner see* A. BICKEL, *supra* note 9, at 175-83. *See also* Taylor v. Louisiana, 370 U.S. 154, 156 (1962) (per curiam) ("Here, as in *Garner* . . . the only evidence to support the [breach of the peace] charge was that petitioners were violating a custom that segregated people in waiting rooms according to their race, a practice not allowed in interstate transportation facilities by reason of federal law.").

[55] 360 U.S. 45 (1959).

[56] *Id.* at 51-54.

[57] *See* Ely, *supra* note 38, at 1278 (defending the decision) ("[I]t would take either a record of the sort which will never exist or a judge hell-bent on invalidation to conclude in the face of a rational and otherwise permissible explanation for a choice that he knew it was unconstitutionally motivated."). *Contrast* Gomillion v. Lightfoot, text at notes 35-43 *supra;* Guinn v. United States, pp. 106-07 *supra* (invalidating grandfather clause). The issue of discrimination in the administration of the literacy test in *Lassiter*, Justice Douglas emphasized, 360 U.S. at 50, had not been properly presented. *Cf.* Neal v. Delaware, 103 U.S. 370 (1880), and Yick Wo v. Hopkins, 118 U.S. 356 (1886) (both striking down racial discrimination in the administration of facially neutral laws), THE FIRST HUNDRED YEARS at 386-87.

*See also* United States v. Raines, 362 U.S. 17 (1960) (upholding Congress's power to authorize the United States to seek injunctions against fifteenth amendment violations). It was not relevant, Justice Brennan concluded in *Raines,* whether the statute was subject to unconstitutional application in cases not involving racial discrimination; the nonseverability principle applied in United States v. Reese, 92 U.S. 214 (1876), THE FIRST HUNDRED YEARS at 393-95, was explicitly limited. *See* 362 U.S. at 22-24 (explaining *Reese* as a case in which the severance of valid from invalid applications would "create a situation in which the statute no longer gave an intelligible warning of the conduct it prohibited" and distinguishing instances in which "it can fairly be said that [the statute] was not intended to stand . . . only in a fraction of the cases it was . . . designed to cover" or in which "an otherwise valid provision or application [was] inextricably tied up with an invalid one"); Sedler, *supra* note 45, at 601-08.

zens generally.[58] The Court had made a good start toward assuring black access to political power, but full enfranchisement of blacks would require the cooperation of other branches.[59]

## II.  REDS

### A.  Skirmishing

Despite their general timidity in confronting McCarthyism during the Vinson years, the Justices had shown some spirit in striking down an overbroad loyalty requirement in *Wieman v. Updegraff.*[60] The Court's first encounters with that beast after the changing of the guard in 1953 suggested that, while assiduously minimizing broad confrontations with other federal branches, the Court was prepared to do a good deal of sniping around the edges to limit abuses in the effort to control subversion.[61]

Not infrequently the Court managed to afford relief without reaching any constitutional question.[62] *Peters v. Hobby,* which raised the due process issue of the right of a federal employee dismissed for disloyalty to confront his accusers,[63] held that the Loyalty Review Board had acted beyond the authority given it by Executive Order by reviewing a finding

---

[58] *Cf.* Harper v. Board of Elections, pp. 424-25 *infra,* which was soon to strike down on analogous grounds a law conditioning the right to vote on payment of a poll tax.

[59] In sharp contrast to the solicitude the early Warren Court exhibited for equal treatment of blacks was the unanimous decision in Hoyt v. Florida, 368 U.S. 57 (1961) (Harlan, J.), upholding the exemption of women from jury duty unless they had specifically indicated their willingness to serve. The dictum in Strauder v. West Virginia, 100 U.S. 303, 310 (1880), THE FIRST HUNDRED YEARS at 383-85, that a state could confine jury duty to males, had "gone unquestioned for more than eighty years in the decisions of the Court"; "[e]ven were it to be assumed that this question is still open to debate," the question presented was narrower. "[W]oman is still regarded as the center of home and family life," and a state might fairly excuse her "unless she herself determines that such service is consistent with her own special responsibilities." 368 U.S. at 60-62.

[60] *See* pp. 357-58 *supra.*

[61] In Galvan v. Press, 347 U.S. 522 (1954), decided exactly one week after Brown v. Board of Education, the Court over the dissents of only Black and Douglas reaffirmed the earlier decision in Harisiades v. Shaughnessy, p. 357 *supra,* permitting deportation of a long-resident alien for mere past membership in the Communist party. The obvious distaste with which Justice Frankfurter reached this result on the basis of precedent alone made even this opinion seem evidence of a more protective attitude:

> If due process bars Congress from enactments that shock the sense of fair play, . . . one is entitled to ask whether it is not beyond the power of Congress to deport an alien who was duped into joining the Communist Party, particularly when his conduct antedated the enactment of the legislation under which his deportation is sought.

347 U.S. at 530. The definitive account of the subversive-speech cases of the Warren period is H. KALVEN, JR., A WORTHY TRADITION: FREEDOM OF SPEECH IN AMERICA (1988).

[62] *See* R. MCCLOSKEY, THE AMERICAN SUPREME COURT 198 (1960) ("[T]here is a middle way between over-assertiveness and abdication. . . . National laws must be *interpreted* by the federal courts. . . ."). Frankfurter had shown the way in United States v. Rumely, 345 U.S. 41, a 1953 decision acknowledging "wide concern. . . . over some aspects of the exercise of the congressional power of investigation," *id.* at 44, and avoiding serious first amendment problems, *see id.* at 56-58 (Douglas and Black, JJ., concurring), by narrow interpretation of a House resolution authorizing an inquiry into "lobbying."

[63] *See* 349 U.S. 331, 350-52 (1955) (Douglas, J., concurring).

of loyalty that had not been appealed.[64] *Pennsylvania v. Nelson* held that Congress had preempted state authority to punish efforts to overthrow the federal government.[65] *Yates v. United States* construed the Smith Act to punish only advocacy of *action* to overthrow the government, not advocacy of overthrow as an abstract principle.[66] *Kent v. Dulles* concluded that a statute providing for issuance of passports "under such rules as the President shall designate and prescribe" did not authorize a regulation denying passports to Communists.[67] In other cases, however, it proved impossible to avoid constitutional issues altogether; and these cases are our principal concern.

## 1.   Slochower v. Board of Education

In *Slochower v. Board of Education,* in 1956, Justice Clark wrote for five Justices to hold that a city could not constitutionally dismiss a college teacher for refusing to incriminate himself before a congressional committee.[68] One may be tempted today to view this decision as a straightforward application of the doctrine of unconstitutional conditions: even though there is no constitutional right to public employment, to deny municipal jobs because of the exercise of a constitutional right may effectively deny the right itself.[69] As of 1956, however, the Court had never held that the fifth amendment privilege against self-

---

[64]*Id.* at 331, 339-48 (Warren, C. J., over a dissent by Reed and Burton). *See also id.* at 350 (Black, J., concurring) (expressing "grave doubt" whether Congress had authorized the President to institute the loyalty program and "doubt" that such a delegation would pass constitutional muster and adding, with a cite to the steel seizure case, Youngstown Sheet & Tube Co. v. Sawyer, pp. 365-69 *supra,* that "of course the Constitution does not confer lawmaking power on the President"). See G. DUNNE, *supra* note 22, at 332 (observing that *Peters* "unveiled the Fabian tactic that was to be the standard ploy in the judicial protectorate of the politically accused— a deft thrust that gained its result by seizing on some peripheral procedural issue and avoiding more substantive issues").

[65]350 U.S. 497 (1956) (Warren, C. J., over a dissent by Reed, Burton, and Minton).

[66]354 U.S. 298, 324-25 (1957) (Harlan, J.) ("The essential distinction is that those to whom the advocacy is addressed must be urged to *do* something, now or in the future, rather than merely to *believe* in something."). Justices Black and Douglas adhered to their position that the entire act infringed freedom of speech and association. *See id.* at 339 (Black and Douglas, JJ., dissenting in part). *Cf.* Dennis v. United States, 341 U.S. at 581 (dissenting opinion), pp. 353-54 *supra.* Clark's dissent, 354 U.S. at 344-50, did not take issue with Harlan's reading of the advocacy requirement. For detailed consideration of *Yates* see H. KALVEN, *supra* note 61, at 211-22 (celebrating the decision as "a bloodless revolution in the reading of the First Amendment" in the guise of statutory construction and "a brilliant example of legal craftsmanship and judicial statesmanship on the side of the angels").

[67]357 U.S. 116, 123, 129 (1958) (Douglas, J., over a dissent by Clark that Burton, Harlan, and Whittaker joined) ("Where activities or enjoyment, natural and often necessary to the well-being of an American citizen, such as travel, are involved, we will construe narrowly all delegated powers that curtail or dilute them."). *See also id.* at 125, 129 (adding important concerns of constitutional dimension):

> The right to travel is a part of the "liberty" of which the citizen cannot be deprived without due process of law. . . . If that "liberty" is to be regulated, it must be pursuant to the law-making functions of the Congress [citing Youngstown Sheet & Tube Co. v. Sawyer, pp. 365-69 *supra*]. And if that power is delegated, the standards must be adequate to pass scrutiny by the accepted tests [citing Panama Refining Co. v. Ryan, p. 216 *supra*].

[68]350 U.S. 551 (1956). Reed, Burton, Minton, and Harlan dissented, *id.* at 559-67. The questions concerned past membership in the Communist party, *id.* at 553.

[69]*See* pp. 355-57 *supra* (discussing American Communications Ass'n v. Douds).

incrimination applied to the states, and it did not so hold in *Slochower.*[70] It is therefore far from obvious how the Court could have reached the conclusion to which it came.

One promising approach would have built upon Justice Miller's famous interpretation of the privileges or immunities clause in the *Slaughter-House Cases:* no state may punish the exercise of privileges given by federal law—in this case the right not to incriminate oneself before Congress.[71] Justice Harlan, however, said this argument had not been made below,[72] and the majority disclaimed reliance on it.[73] Justice Clark invoked due process instead: "Since no inference of guilt was possible from the claim before the federal committee, the discharge falls of its own weight as wholly without support."[74]

The opinion is eloquent in defense of the privilege. "[A] witness may have a reasonable fear of prosecution," Justice Clark explained, "and yet be innocent of any wrongdoing. The privilege serves to protect the innocent who otherwise might be ensnared by ambiguous circumstances."[75] But the state court had expressly disavowed any inference of guilt from the exercise of the privilege; the dissenters thought the state could properly consider unfit for public service those unwilling "to cooperate with public authorities when asked questions relating to official conduct."[76]

More troubling than the question whether the dismissal was reasonable was the difficulty of determining of what "liberty or property" Slochower had been deprived. Two earlier decisions cited to show that discharges of public employees "must conform to the requirements of due process"[77] were readily distinguishable as involving alleged infringement of freedom of speech and association, which had long been recognized as "liberties" protected by the fourteenth amendment.[78] Clark did not suggest that Slochower's firing offended his "liberty" not to incriminate himself before Congress; nor did he say, though he may have thought, that the job itself constituted either "liberty" or "property." That Slochower was a tenured professor who could be discharged only for "cause"[79] would tend in light of later decisions to support the latter conclusion,[80] but the explicit statutory

[70] *See* Knapp v. Schweizer, 357 U.S. 371, 374 (1958) (Frankfurter, J.) ("Petitioner does not claim that his conviction of contempt for refusal to answer questions put to him in a state proceeding deprived him of liberty or property without due process of law in violation of the Fourteenth Amendment; that such a claim is without merit was settled in *Twining v. New Jersey* [p. 59, note 34 *supra*]."). The inapplicability of the privilege to the states was reaffirmed as late as 1961 in Cohen v. Hurley, 366 U.S. 117, 127-28 (Harlan, J., over four dissents).

[71] *See* Slaughter-House Cases, 83 U.S. 36 (1873), THE FIRST HUNDRED YEARS at 342-50.

[72] 350 U.S. at 567 (Harlan, J., dissenting).

[73] *See id.* at 555.

[74] *Id.* at 559.

[75] *Id.* at 557-58.

[76] *Id.* at 565-66 (Harlan, J., dissenting). *See also id.* at 561-64 (Reed, J., dissenting). Clark responded that the city was in no position to make such an argument since the questions Slochower had refused to answer had been posed by a federal committee whose inquiry had nothing to do with fitness to teach. *Id.* at 558.

[77] *Id.* at 555-56 (*citing* Adler v. Board of Education and Garner v. Los Angeles Board of Public Works (both noted at p. 357 *supra*), in both of which the challenged conditions had been found reasonable).

[78] The third decision cited for this proposition was Wieman v. Updegraff, pp. 357-58 *supra*, where the facts had lent themselves to the conclusion that a dismissal for simple membership in the Communist party infringed freedoms of speech and association. That the *Wieman* opinion had simply found such membership an arbitrary basis for the state's action without mentioning these freedoms makes *Wieman* something of a precedent for *Slochower* but subjects it to similar criticism.

[79] *See* 350 U.S. at 554.

[80] *See, e.g.,* Perry v. Sindermann, p. 505, note 3 *infra*.

provision making invocation of the privilege a ground for terminating his employment would appear to have limited any property right the state had conferred.[81] Not only did the majority appear to base its conclusion on an unexplained revival of substantive due process unrelated to the infringement of interests elsewhere enumerated in the Bill of Rights; in disregard of its express limitation to life, liberty, and property, the whole Court seemed to treat the due process clause as if it were a general guarantee against arbitrary state action.

The 1957 decisions in *Schware v. Board of Examiners* and *Konigsberg v. State Bar of California* applied the principles of *Wieman* and *Slochower* to admission to the practice of law: neither past membership in the Communist party nor refusal to say whether one had been a member could justify the inference that an applicant was of bad moral character.[82] Though its theory was due process rather than associational freedom, the Court seemed to be taking a firm stand against excessive zeal in keeping subversives out of positions of power. Two well-known contemporaneous decisions, moreover, testified to a similar attitude toward the troubling subject of legislative investigations.

## 2. Watkins v. United States

Established in 1938, the House Un-American Activities Committee was authorized to investigate "un-American propaganda" with an eye to possible legislation.[83] In the course of an inquiry in 1954, Watkins refused to say whether he knew certain persons to have been members of the Communist party, and he was convicted of contempt.[84] The Supreme Court, over the dissent of Justice Clark, reversed.[85]

Chief Justice Warren's opinion bristles with brave generalities about the constitutional limits of legislative investigation. As the early decision in *Kilbourn v. Thompson*[86] had held, investigations could be conducted only "in furtherance of a legitimate task of Congress"; the House had "no general authority to expose the private affairs of individuals" or to act as "a law enforcement or trial agency."[87] Moreover, congressional investigations were subject to the restrictions found in the Bill of Rights: "Witnesses cannot be com-

---

[81] *Cf.* text at notes 14-15 *supra* (discussing Bolling v. Sharpe).

[82] *Schware*, 353 U.S. 232, 243-47 (1957) (Black, J., without dissent) (membership); *Konigsberg*, 353 U.S. 252, 270-71 (1957) (Black, J.) (refusal to answer). *See also id.* at 271-72 (assumed past membership does not prove present advocacy of forcible overthrow of government). In the latter case Harlan, joined by Clark, dissented on the ground that it was reasonable to find that by refusing to answer the examiners' questions Konigsberg had failed to carry his burden of proof, *id.* at 276-312; Frankfurter would have remanded for a determination whether the constitutional questions had been properly presented and decided below, *id.* at 274-76. In contrast to *Wieman* and *Slochower,* the statutes in these cases did not themselves make mere membership or refusal to answer a ground for disqualification. Both *Schware* and *Konigsberg* may therefore be analogized to the procedural principle soon to be enunciated in Thompson v. Louisville, *supra* note 50, that a finding unsupported by evidence is inconsistent with due process.

[83] *See* Watkins v. United States, 354 U.S. 178, 201-02 (1957).

[84] *See id.* at 181-86.

[85] 354 U.S. 178 (1957). *See also id.* at 217-33 (Clark, J., dissenting). Burton and Whittaker, *id.* at 216, did not participate.

[86] 103 U.S. 168 (1881), *cited* in 354 U.S. at 194, THE FIRST HUNDRED YEARS at 436-38.

[87] 354 U.S. at 187.

pelled to give evidence against themselves. They cannot be subjected to unreasonable search and seizure. Nor can the First Amendment freedoms of speech, press, religion, or political belief and association be abridged."[88]

To compel a witness to testify "about his beliefs, expressions or associations," said the Court, "is a measure of government interference. And when those forced revelations concern matters that are unorthodox, unpopular, or even hateful to the general public, the reaction in the life of the witness may be disastrous." Third parties identified by witnesses "are equally subject to public stigma, scorn and obloquy," and the "effect is even more harsh when [as in *Watkins*] it is past beliefs, expressions or associations that are disclosed and judged by current standards rather than those contemporary with the matters exposed."[89] Thus "[t]he critical element is the existence of, and the weight to be ascribed to, the interest of the Congress in demanding disclosures. . . ."[90]

All of this sounds very much like what the Court would soon say in connection with the Alabama court's demand for a list of members of the NAACP.[91] Justice Clark seemed singularly insensitive to first amendment purposes in protesting in dissent that "the right of free belief has never been extended to include the withholding of knowledge of past events or transactions" and that "one cannot invoke the constitutional rights of another."[92]

At this point, however, the majority opinion becomes mushy, as, without resolving the question he had just posed, the Chief Justice began to ruminate over the relationship between the House and its committees. It is "the responsibility of the Congress . . . to insure that compulsory process is used only in furtherance of a legislative purpose," and thus the House itself must "spell out" the committee's authority "with sufficient particularity." The imprecision of the authorizing resolution's references to "un-American" activities and to "the form of government as guaranteed by our Constitution" made it impossible for a court to determine whether a particular question was authorized or pertinent to a sufficient legislative purpose. "Protected freedoms should not be placed in danger in the absence of a clear determination by the House or Senate that a particular inquiry is justified by a specific legislative need."[93]

Here the Court seemed to be suggesting that the House had unconstitutionally delegated its own authority by failing to provide sufficiently specific standards to guide the committee's inquiry.[94] Despite the Court's generally lenient attitude toward the nondelegation doctrine since the late 1930s,[95] there was recent authority for limiting delegations

---

[88] *Id.* at 188.

[89] *Id.* at 197.

[90] *Id.* at 198.

[91] *See* text at notes 44-46 *supra* (discussing NAACP v. Alabama).

[92] 354 U.S. at 231 (Clark, J., dissenting). Both Barrows v. Jackson, p. 359, note 177 *supra,* and NAACP v. Alabama, text at notes 44-46 *supra,* had permitted litigants to assert the constitutional rights of those not in a position to assert them for themselves.

[93] 354 U.S. at 200-06.

[94] Justice Clark, objecting that resolutions authorizing congressional inquiries were traditionally and necessarily vague, made forceful use of earlier statements by both Frankfurter and Black (who had made quite a reputation as a zealous investigator when in the Senate, *see* G. DUNNE, *supra* note 22, at 151-60), as to the need for broad investigative authority. *See* 354 U.S. at 217-25.

[95] *See, e.g.,* Yakus v. United States, Fahee v. Mallonee, and Lichter v. United States, pp. 300-01 and 366, note 219 *supra.*

to executive officers when freedom of expression was at stake.[96] Without quite reaching its apparent destination, however, the opinion changed course once again.

After twenty pages of discussing issues he did not mean to decide, Chief Justice Warren finally came to the point: like anyone else threatened with criminal sanctions, Watkins was entitled to fair notice of what he was required to do. He could not know whether he was obliged to answer the question without knowing the subject of the inquiry. Neither the resolution itself nor the chairman's statement that the committee was interested in "subversion and subversive propaganda" had given adequate notice of that subject or of "the manner in which the propounded questions are pertinent thereto." Thus Watkins had not been "accorded a fair opportunity to determine whether he was within his rights in refusing to answer, and his conviction [was] necessarily invalid under the Due Process Clause of the Fifth Amendment."[97]

The principle of fair warning was a familiar one,[98] but it was hard to dispute Clark's contention that it should have been obvious that the names of past members of the Communist party were relevant to an inquiry into subversion.[99] The majority seemed to be working hard to find some way of protecting Watkins without having to tell Congress that questions of this nature could never be asked at all.

Like the analogous practice of construing statutes narrowly to avoid constitutional questions, the tactic the Court pursued in *Watkins* can be criticized. If the Justices take liberties with other legal principles in order to avoid confrontation on the ultimate issue of power, they risk preventing Congress from doing what it has a perfect right to do. Moreover, the Court has no business sermonizing on issues it does not decide. The reasons for this include not only the technical limitations of its jurisdiction[100] and the confession of that notorious offender John Marshall that only "[t]he question actually before the court" is likely to be "investigated with care,"[101] but—more important for present purposes—the avoidance of unnecessary controversy. The process of *decisium interruptum* in *Watkins* combined the worst features of both possible worlds: by its animadversions on broad questions of legitimate purpose, first amendment freedoms, and delegation of congressional authority, the Court seemed to invite the very conflict with Congress that its narrow basis of decision was intended to avoid—without the advantage of settling any of those important issues.

---

[96]*E.g.,* Schneider v. State, p. 262 *supra;* Cantwell v. Connecticut, p. 266 *supra.* For an approving view of the delegation argument in *Watkins* see A. BICKEL, *supra* note 9, at 159-63.

[97]354 U.S. at 207-15. Frankfurter, while joining the Court's opinion, added a brief concurrence to make clear that this was the sole basis of the holding, *id.* at 216-17.

[98]See, e.g., United States v. L. Cohen Grocery, p. 109, note 123 *supra,* and cases cited in *Watkins,* 354 U.S. at 208 n.46.

[99]354 U.S. at 227-30. *Accord* H. KALVEN, *supra* note 61, at 485.

[100]*See* U. S. CONST. art. III, § 2 (extending the judicial power only to the decision of "cases" and "controversies"); 28 U.S.C. § 1254 (1982) (review of "cases" in the Courts of Appeals).

[101]Cohens v. Virginia, 19 U.S. 264, 399-400 (1821) (retracting one of the many dicta tossed out in Marbury v. Madison, 5 U.S. 137 (1803)); *see* THE FIRST HUNDRED YEARS at 100-01. *See also* Gunther, *The Subtle Vices of the "Passive Virtues"—A Comment on Principle and Expediency in Judicial Review,* 64 COLUM. L. REV. 1, 22 (1964) ("[I]t does a disservice to the Court's internal process as well as to public respect to encourage 'trial balloon' passages free of the responsibilities of principled constitutional adjudication.").

## 3.  Sweezy v. New Hampshire

On the same day the Court struck down a federal contempt citation for failure to answer questions about political associations in *Watkins,* it invalidated a state one in *Sweezy v. New Hampshire.*[102] This time, however, the majority was unable to agree on a single opinion.

The four Justices most known for their activism were content to rely on an obscure and questionable theory that left the legislature free, as in *Watkins,* to try again.[103] As in *Watkins,* Chief Justice Warren flirted extensively with arguments of free expression and association,[104] only to take refuge at last in the asserted imprecision of the investigator's instructions to inquire into "subversive organizations":

> The lack of any indications that the legislature wanted the information the Attorney General attempted to elicit from petitioner must be treated as the absence of authority. It follows that the use of the contempt power, notwithstanding the interference with constitutional rights, was not in accordance with the due process requirements of the Fourteenth Amendment.[105]

One would have thought, as Justice Frankfurter objected in his concurrence, that whether the investigator had acted within his authority was a question of state law— unless the Chief Justice was implying an unexplained return to the historic notion that due process permitted government action only in accordance with law.[106] Closer inspection suggests that Warren was attempting to equate the absence of authority with the absence of any legitimate interest in acquiring the requested information:

> No one would deny that the infringement of constitutional rights of individuals would violate the guarantee of due process where no state interest underlies the state action. Thus, if the Attorney General's interrogation of petitioner were in fact wholly unrelated to the object of the legislature in authorizing the inquiry, the Due Process Clause would preclude the endangering of constitutional liberties. We believe that an equivalent situation is presented in this case.[107]

The weakness in this line of reasoning is that it appears to assume that only the legislature can enunciate an interest in acquiring information, while the Court had repeatedly

---

[102] 354 U.S. 234 (1957). The day on which *Watkins* and *Sweezy* were decided came to be known in some circles as "Red Monday." *See* G. DUNNE, *supra* note 22, at 340.

[103] 354 U.S. at 235-55 (opinion of Warren, C. J., joined by Black, Douglas, and Brennan).

[104] *Id.* at 245-51.

[105] *Id.* at 254-55.

[106] *See id.* at 256-57 (Frankfurter, J., concurring); Pollak, *Mr. Justice Frankfurter: Judgment and the Fourteenth Amendment,* 67 YALE L.J. 304, 314 (1957); THE FIRST HUNDRED YEARS at 272 & n.268 (discussing Scott v. Sandford, 60 U.S. 393 (1856)).

[107] 354 U.S. at 254.

insisted that the Constitution did not require any particular distribution of state powers.[108] Specifically disclaiming any intention to invoke "the doctrine of separation of powers," Warren seemed to contradict himself as he concluded with one of the least informative and most conclusory sentences in the entire set of Reports: "Our conclusion does rest upon a separation of the power of a state legislature to conduct investigations from the responsibility to direct the use of that power insofar as that separation causes a deprivation of the constitutional rights of individuals and a denial of due process of law." [109]

The normally reserved Frankfurter and Harlan jumped in boldly to conclude that questions posed to an educator about his lectures and his associates in the Progressive party infringed his academic and political freedoms.[110] The balance they struck was encouraging, but *Watkins* had seemed an equally appropriate place to strike it;[111] the Justices appeared to be weighing very carefully just how far the country would let them go.


## B.   Surrender

In 1958, not long after the Justices had handed down the decisions just noted, Senator Jenner of Indiana introduced a bill that would have deprived the Supreme Court of jurisdiction to review cases involving congressional investigations, the federal employee security program, and state measures for control of subversion or admission to the bar.[112] This bill did not become law. Yet the Court, distinguishing its earlier decisions with a very fine scalpel, began regularly upholding measures for subversive control.


### 1.   Public employment, bar admission, and investigation

The new phase commenced with the 1958 decisions in *Beilan v. Board of Education*[113] and *Lerner v. Casey.*[114] In both cases, as in *Slochower,* municipal employees had been discharged for refusing to say whether they were members of the Communist party. In contrast to *Slochower,* however, and to *Konigsberg,* where a similar refusal had been held insufficient to justify denial of admission to the bar, the dismissals were upheld by a vote of five to four.

*Slochower* and *Konigsberg* had found it arbitrary to infer disloyalty or bad character from a refusal to answer questions about Party membership. That did not mean, said the

---

[108] *See id.* at 256-57 (Frankfurter, J., concurring) (citing Dreyer v. Illinois, 187 U.S. 71 (1902)).

[109] 354 U.S. at 255. *See* Sutherland, *Foreword: The Citizen's Immunities and Public Opinion,* 71 HARV. L. REV. 85, 91 (1957) ("[T]he exact way in which the fourteenth amendment was violated does not emerge from the opinions.").

[110] 354 U.S. at 257-67. Clark and Burton dissented; Whittaker did not participate. *See id.* at 267-70, 255.

[111] Academics are not the only people who enjoy freedom of expression and association, and self-preservation seems as legitimate an interest of a state as of the nation. H. KALVEN, *supra* note 61, at 496-97, suggests that the reason Warren and those who joined his opinion did not adopt Frankfurter's approach was the latter's warning, 354 U.S. at 266, that Communists might be more dangerous than progressives and thus subject to more questioning: "The other four Justices, I suspect, are unwilling to make such a concession; they are not ready to give up altogether on the First Amendment possibilities even in the Communist cases."

[112] S. 2646, 85th Cong., 2d Sess. (1958). This bill raised formidable constitutional questions. *See* THE FIRST HUNDRED YEARS at 304-05 (discussing *Ex parte* McCardle, 74 U.S. 506 (1869)).

[113] 357 U.S. 399 (1958) (Burton, J.).

[114] 357 U.S. 468 (1958) (Harlan, J.).

majority in *Beilan* and *Lerner,* that such a refusal could never be the basis for discharge. While membership in the Party could not itself be made a basis of dismissal under *Wieman,* it was relevant in determining the fitness of an employee for his position; the city might reasonably consider the refusal to answer such questions proof of insubordination, unreliability, or lack of candor.[115] The same philosophy was applied to the question of bar admission as a second appeal in *Konigsberg* produced a change in the result: though it had been arbitrary to find Konigsberg of bad character because of his refusal to say whether he was a Communist, it was reasonable to find he had obstructed the inquiry into his qualifications.[116]

At first glance it may seem perverse to allow dismissal or exclusion for refusal to say whether one is a Communist but not for being one.[117] The distinction is not wholly implausible, however, if one believes that questioning as to simple membership may lead to information that may be a basis for disqualification—such as active participation in a plot to overthrow the government.[118] The distinction of *Slochower* and *Konigsberg I,* moreover, was consistent with the narrow opinions in those cases, which had carefully emphasized that the questions resolved in the later decisions did not have to be decided.[119] The effect on freedom of association, however, was the same whether the state based its action on an inference of disloyalty or on an unwillingness to cooperate, and it was considerable: in either case the applicant must disclose his association or forgo his career.[120] The interest in trustworthy lawyers and public workers sounds weighty in the abstract, but to find it sufficiently threatened by mere refusal to say whether one was a Communist to justify the

---

[115] *See Beilan,* 357 U.S. at 405-09 (distinguishing *Konigsberg* as based upon "inferences impermissibly drawn from the refusal"); *Lerner,* 357 U.S. at 475-78. Nelson v. Los Angeles County, 362 U.S. 1 (1960) (Clark, J.), extended the reasoning of *Beilan* and *Lerner* to the refusal of a county employee to testify before a *federal* investigating committee, although the fact that the city had not itself asked the question in *Slochower* had been a basis for distinguishing that case from *Beilan.* The critical question, the Court now said, was whether the failure to reveal associations had been taken to show disloyalty or lack of candor. Black, Douglas, and Brennan dissented in all three cases, Warren in all but *Nelson,* in which he took no part.

[116] Konigsberg v. State Bar of California, 366 U.S. 36 (1961). *Accord In re* Anastaplo, 366 U.S. 82 (1961). Justice Harlan, who had voted to uphold the state actions in both *Slochower* and *Konigsberg I* on this basis, wrote both *Konigsberg II* and *Anastaplo.* Black, Douglas, Brennan, and Warren dissented in both cases; only Justice Burton thought both *Konigsberg* cases rightly decided.

[117] *See* H. KALVEN, *supra* note 61, at 569-70.

[118] *See Konigsberg II,* 366 U.S. at 46-47; Gerende v. Board of Supervisors, p. 357 *supra.*

[119] *See Slochower,* 350 U.S. at 558 ("On such a record the Board cannot claim that its action was part of a bona fide attempt to gain needed and relevant information"); *Konigsberg I,* 353 U.S. at 259 ("[Konigsberg] was not denied admission to the California bar simply because he refused to answer questions").

[120] In none of the decisions discussed did any Justice suggest a distinction between bar admission and government employment, or among various types of government jobs. Obviously the strength of the government's interest increases, as Vinson had suggested in *Douds,* 339 U.S. at 390-91, 409, 412, pp. 355-57 *supra,* as the position becomes one of greater influence over sensitive installations—an uncooperative or disloyal general is of more concern than a street sweeper with the same defects. Exclusion from the bar is arguably a more severe interference with protected interests than denial of public employment, since it forecloses most productive uses of an expensive education. *Cf.* Speiser v. Randall, 357 U.S. 513 (1958) (Brennan, J., over a dissent by Clark), where the Court recognized that a state had less interest in denying a Communist veterans'. benefits than in excluding him from a sensitive government job but relied on the fact that an oath requirement obliged the veteran to establish his own innocence to strike it down. This concern had bothered Alexander Hamilton in the 1790s and the Supreme Court in the post–Civil War loyalty oath cases. *See* THE FIRST HUNDRED YEARS at 292-96 (discussing Cummings v. Missouri, 71 U.S. 277 (1867), and *Ex parte* Garland, 71 U.S. 333 (1867)).

harsh results in these cases suggested that the principle of *NAACP v. Alabama* did not run very deep; it did not seem to take much of an impact on state concerns to overcome the interest in associational privacy.

This conclusion was reinforced by *Barenblatt v. United States,* a five-to-four 1959 decision cutting through the underbrush left by *Watkins* and *Sweezy* to resolve against the interest in association the ultimate question those decisions had left open. In the context of legislative investigations too, the Court now decided, a witness could constitutionally be required to say whether he was a member of the Communist party.[121]

Everything about Justice Harlan's *Barenblatt* opinion is refreshing except the result. Of course the question was authorized, pertinent, and known to be so;[122] of course there was no way to disprove the existence of a legitimate legislative purpose in posing it.[123] There was nevertheless a strong argument that the concomitant burden on freedom of association was unacceptable.[124]

---

[121] 360 U.S. 109 (1959) (Harlan, J.). *Accord* Wilkinson v. United States, 365 U.S. 399 (1961) (Stewart, J.); Braden v. United States, 365 U.S. 431 (1961) (Stewart, J.). Black, Douglas, Warren, and Brennan dissented in all three cases. There was no suggestion that the context made this conclusion either more or less difficult to reach than those in the bar admission or public employment cases. Arguably punishment for contempt was the most difficult to justify. In the first place, the harm to associational interests may be greater in the investigation context, since the jobholder or bar applicant has at least the unpalatable option of giving up his career. Furthermore, the state may have a more acute interest in keeping dangerous or untrustworthy individuals out of positions of power than in obtaining the information they can contribute to a legislative inquiry—though if many refused to answer such questions the enactment of general legislation to protect against future subversion might be impeded.

*See also* Uphaus v. Wyman, 360 U.S. 72, 79-81 (1959) (Clark, J., over the usual dissents) (upholding punishment for the refusal of a camp director said to have Communist connections to disclose the names of persons who had attended his camp):

> [T]he Attorney General had valid reason to believe that the speakers and guests at World Fellowship might be subversive persons within the meaning of the New Hampshire Act. . . . [T]he governmental interest in self-preservation is sufficiently compelling to subordinate the interest in associational privacy of persons who, at least to the extent of the guest registration statute, made public at the inception the association they now wish to keep private.

[122] *See* 360 U.S. at 116-25.

[123] *Id.* at 127-28. *But see id.* at 153-66 (dissenting opinions) (arguing that the committee's sole reason for asking the questions was to expose the witness's associations).

[124] *See id.* at 144-45 (Black J., dissenting); H. KALVEN, *supra* note 61, at 500. Harlan distinguished *Sweezy,* where he and Frankfurter had found the state's interest insufficient, on the facts:

> [T]he questioning of Sweezy, who had not been shown ever to have been connected with the Communist Party, as to the contents of a lecture he had given at the University of New Hampshire, and as to his connections with the Progressive Party, . . . was too far removed from the premises on which the constitutionality of the State's investigation had to depend. . . . This is a very different thing from inquiring into the extent to which the Communist Party has succeeded in infiltrating into our universities, or elsewhere, persons and groups committed to furthering the objective of overthrow.

360 U.S. at 129. Justice Black took the occasion to announce his famous view that the first amendment should be read literally to forbid *all* laws limiting the content of speech, *id.* at 140-44. Some of the difficulties of this approach have been discussed in connection with Schenck v. United States, pp. 115-20 *supra; see also* A. BICKEL, *supra* note 9, at 84-98. One is also led to wonder how Justice Black found textual justification for the balancing test he conceded, 360 U.S. at 140-44, was appropriate in passing upon time, place, and manner regulations; his theory would appear to suggest either that all such restrictions are valid because they do not regulate "speech" or invalid because they do.

## 2. Registration

The developments just traced culminated in Justice Frankfurter's opinion for the Court in *Communist Party v. Subversive Activities Control Board* in 1961.[125] The Subversive Activities Control Act of 1950, proclaiming the existence of "a world Communist movement" dedicated to establishing "a Communist totalitarian dictatorship," required all "Communist-action organizations" to register with the Attorney General. Registration entailed disclosing the names of members and contributors. Registered organizations were required to identify themselves in connection with any information they disseminated by mail, over the airwaves, or in interstate or foreign commerce. Members aware of the registration requirement were barred from employment by the federal government, by a labor union, or in any defense facility, and from applying for or using passports; alien members were generally ineligible for citizenship and subject to deportation or exclusion.[126]

Not surprisingly, the Communist party of the United States was ordered to register under this statute. The Party appealed, and it lost. Justice Frankfurter's opinion, one of his last, epitomizes his judicial philosophy: it begins by scrupulously avoiding the unnecessary decision of constitutional questions and ends by deferring to the considered judgment of Congress.

The asserted invalidity of such provisions as those disqualifying Party members from obtaining passports or government jobs, Frankfurter concluded, could not affect the outcome of the case, because the statute contained a severability clause. In any event, he added, these challenges were premature; the only issue properly presented was the constitutionality of the registration requirement itself.[127]

Conceding that "compulsory disclosure of the names of an organization's members may in certain instances infringe constitutionally protected rights of association" and that "the public opprobrium and obloquy which may attach to an individual" upon disclosure was no less in the case of the Communist party than in that of the NAACP,[128] Frankfurter distinguished *NAACP v. Alabama,* as Harlan had done in *Barenblatt,* on the basis of the greater governmental interest in combating subversion. After "detailed investigations," Congress had expressly found that Communist-action organizations posed a "threat . . . not only to existing government in the United States, but to the United States as a sovereign, independent nation." Congress's judgment as to "how that threat may best be met consistently with the safeguarding of personal freedom" was "not to be set aside merely because the judgment of judges would, in the first instance, have chosen other methods." The Court had allowed Congress to require disclosure in other situations, such as lobbying, in which secrecy was itself a source of the perceived evil:

> Where the mask of anonymity which an organization's members wear serves the double purpose of protecting them from popular prejudice and of enabling them to cover over a foreign-directed conspiracy, infiltrate into other groups, and enlist the support of persons who would not, if the truth were revealed,

---

[125] 367 U.S. 1 (1961).
[126] *See id.* at 4-19.
[127] *Id.* at 70-81.
[128] *Id.* at 90, 102.

lend their support, . . . it would be a distortion of the First Amendment to
hold that it prohibits Congress from removing the mask.[129]

All of this may remind the reader of the great Court-packing controversy of the 1930s,
in which the Justices changed their tune abruptly after President Roosevelt threatened to
dilute their votes.[130] One need not conclude, however, that the Court of the 1950s caved
in under pressure from the other branches. The timing was odd, for one thing; the Court's
reversal, if it was one, began more than three years after the Senate itself had repudiated
Senator McCarthy.[131] Moreover, although the earlier decisions may have given rise to exaggerated hopes, they had all been narrowly drawn to allow room for ultimate deference
to the other branches. The Court may well have been practicing a variant of what Bickel
termed the "passive virtues"—making sure that the appropriate policymaker had really
made the decision that associational interests must be subordinated, seeing to it that individuals were given adequate procedural protections, but bowing at last to the unmistakable mandate of the democratic process.[132] Indeed, however tempted one may be to dismiss the Court's performance in these cases as both cowardly and intellectually dishonest,
it may also in the last analysis have done more than either Kamikaze attack or immediate
surrender would have done to preserve ultimate constitutional values.

## III.  SINNERS

### A.  Smut

The Warren Court is known as a staunch defender of first amendment values, but its treatment of alleged subversives is not the only evidence that at least in its early years that
body was far from absolutist in its protection of the right to speak. The obscenity cases
are another prominent example.

### 1.  Criminal prosecution

In the course of upholding a conviction for the utterance of "fighting words" in *Chaplinsky
v. New Hampshire,* Justice Murphy had stated flatly that obscenity too, because of its "low

---

[129]*Id.* at 93-105 (citing, inter alia, United States v. Harriss, 347 U.S. 612 (1954) (upholding a registration
requirement for lobbyists, which seemed to present less danger of deterring protected freedoms)). Warren, Black,
Douglas, and Brennan dissented on various grounds, but none said a mere registration requirement offended the
first amendment. *See* 367 U.S. at 115-202. For detailed and trenchant criticism of the decision see H. KALVEN,
*supra* note 61, at 264-87.

[130]*See* pp. 235-44 *supra.* Some observers analogized Frankfurter's voting pattern in the subversive cases to
that of Justice Roberts in the New Deal crisis. *See* G. DUNNE, *supra* note 22, at 351-52 (adding that by decisions
such as *Barenblatt* and *Uphaus* "the Court itself contributed to the lessening of tensions" but concluding that
"*turnabout* is too strong a word"). Kurland, while acknowledging that "*Barenblatt* . . . and *Uphaus* . . . make it
look as though the Court tempered its sails to the prevailing winds," thought other decisions showed there had
been "no such retreat as that which the Court indulged in 1937." P. KURLAND, POLITICS, THE CONSTITUTION
AND THE WARREN COURT 30 (1970).

[131]McCarthy was officially censured by the Senate in 1954. S. Res. 301, 83d Cong., 2d Sess. (July 30, 1954),
100 CONG. REC. 16,392 (Dec. 2, 1954).

[132]*See* A. BICKEL, *supra* note 9, ch. 4 (applauding the Court for the "process of avoidance and admonition"
employed in such cases as *Watkins* but criticizing the ultimate "legitimation" of "action which it could not very
easily forbid" in *Barenblatt*). *Cf.* note 154 *infra* (discussing Times Film Corp. v. City of Chicago).

value," was no part of the constitutionally protected freedom.[133] The Court turned this dictum into holding in *Roth v. United States*.[134]

The long coexistence of obscenity laws with constitutional guarantees of freedom of speech, Justice Brennan argued, was persuasive evidence that obscenity had never been regarded as protected. Nor did obscenity fall within the constitutional purpose "to assure unfettered interchange of ideas for the bringing about of political and social changes"; "implicit in the history of the First Amendment is the rejection of obscenity as utterly without redeeming social importance."[135]

Even a dedicated first amendment buff can hardly weep over denial of access to filthy pictures as such. If it is difficult to find compelling society's asserted interest in denying such pleasures as obscene publications may afford,[136] it is equally difficult to lose sleep over their loss; as Justice Brennan said, smut is hardly at the core of the first amendment.[137]

More troubling is the risk that in prohibiting obscenity the government may suppress other communications that the Constitution values more highly. Obscenity does not define itself; as Douglas and Black insisted in dissent, "the test that suppresses a cheap tract today can suppress a literary gem tomorrow."[138] Unwilling to buck history by outlawing

---

[133] *See* pp. 314-15 *supra*. *But see* Monaghan, *Obscenity, 1966: The Marriage of Obscenity Per Se and Obscenity Per Quod*, 76 YALE L.J. 127, 132 (1966) (noting that because "the classes of speech other than obscenity referred to by Mr. Justice Murphy seem positively harmful . . . , they provide weak scaffolding for any theory that obscenity is beyond the First Amendment simply because it is worthless").

[134] 354 U.S. 476 (1957).

[135] *Id.* at 482-85. For doubts as to the validity of the Court's theory of "worthless" speech see Kalven, *The Metaphysics of the Law of Obscenity*, 1960 SUP. CT. REV. 1, 10-17 (fearing "unhappy repercussions on the protection of free speech generally").

[136] The Court made no effort to argue that the prohibition was reasonably designed to prevent sexual misbehavior stimulated by obscene publications; arguments that obscenity led to such behavior had been seriously disputed. *See* 354 U.S. at 486; *id.* at 510-11 (Douglas, J., dissenting); Lockhart & McClure, *Literature, the Law of Obscenity, and the Constitution*, 38 MINN. L. REV. 295, 385-86 (1954); Monaghan, *supra* note 133, at 130, 139 (noting arguments that obscenity actually provides "a harmless escape for sexual frustrations" and finding the *Roth* opinion unsatisfactory: "[W]hy could speech be repressed where there was no solid basis for believing that it caused immediate harm?"). *See also* Henkin, *Morals and the Constitution: The Sin of Obscenity*, 63 COLUM. L. REV. 391 (1963) (arguing that the real reason for obscenity laws was not so much prevention of antisocial behavior as "traditional notions . . . of 'decency' and 'morality'" of religious origin that were not legitimate bases for governmental action under either substantive due process or the establishment clause).

[137] The latter-day argument that certain pornographic publications not meeting the traditional narrow definition of obscenity may be forbidden because they induce men to think less well of women is more problematic; as the Seventh Circuit has pointed out, it is particularly troublesome to forbid communications because of the ideas they convey. American Booksellers Ass'n v. Hudnut, 771 F.2d 323 (7th Cir. 1985), *aff'd mem.*, 475 U.S. 1001 (1986). *But cf.* Beauharnais v. Illinois, pp. 350-52 *supra* (upholding a group libel law). Views as to the position of women in society, no less than those as to the position of blacks, are at the heart of the amendment's purpose of the "interchange of ideas for the bringing about of political and social changes" and therefore generally protected even if "hateful to the prevailing climate of opinion," *Roth*, 354 U.S. at 484. *Cf.* Kingsley Int'l Pictures Corp. v. Regents of the University of New York, *infra* note 140. In one respect the case for prohibition is even weaker in the case of pornography than in that of group libel. The publication punished in *Beauharnais* made disparaging remarks about blacks as a class; the pornography ordinances are based upon the fear that readers will infer that women generally behave like the individuals depicted.

[138] 354 U.S. at 514. *See also id.* at 495 (Warren, C. J., concurring) ("The history of the application of laws designed to suppress the obscene demonstrates convincingly that the power of government can be invoked under them against great art or literature, scientific treatises, or works exciting social controversy."). *Cf.* McCulloch v. Maryland, 17 U.S. 316, 431 (1819) ("[T]he power to tax involves the power to destroy. . . .").

obscenity laws entirely, Justice Brennan attempted to deal with the danger of overbroad application by enunciating limiting standards. "[S]ex and obscenity," he emphasized, were "not synonymous"; sex itself, like other "vital problems of human interest and public concern," could be freely discussed. The test for obscenity was narrow: "whether to the average person, applying contemporary community standards, the dominant theme of the material taken as a whole appeals to purient interest." [139] Much would depend on how this standard was applied; the Justices were to spend a good deal of their time watching dirty movies. [140]

## 2. Prior restraints

On the same day *Roth* was decided, but over four dissents, the Court in *Kingsley Books v. Brown* upheld a state's authority to *enjoin* the distribution of obscene literature and to destroy it. [141] Dissenting, Douglas invoked the principle of *Near v. Minnesota:* the mere fact that obscenity could be punished after the fact, as *Roth* held, did not mean it could be subjected to previous restraints. [142] For the majority, Frankfurter observed in a footnote that it was not clear the state would hold the distributor in contempt for violating the injunction if on appeal the material was found not obscene. [143] Nevertheless, there were disturbing accents in his vigorous disparagement of the traditional distinction between subsequent punishment and prior restraint. [144]

The worst fears of those who read *Kingsley* were realized when the Court upheld a system of outright prior censorship in *Times Film Corp. v. Chicago,* [145] where the city had

---

[139] 354 U.S. at 487-89. Justice Harlan, dissenting in part, objected that the statutes in question did not embody this standard, distinguished sharply between state and federal authority over the subject, and insisted that the Court should not have decided the case in the abstract without "making its own independent judgment upon the character of the material upon which these convictions were based." *Id.* at 496-508. *See also* Monaghan, *supra* note 133, at 129-30 (praising *Roth* as "a liberal bulwark" because of this narrow definition: "No serious, complex work may be suppressed as obscene.").

[140] *See* the amusing account in BOB WOODWARD & SCOTT ARMSTRONG, THE BRETHREN: INSIDE THE SUPREME COURT 192-204 (1979). LADY CHATTERLEY'S LOVER, the Court soon decided, could not be proscribed on the ground that it " 'portrays adultery as proper behavior' " ("What New York has done . . . is to prevent the exhibition of a motion picture because that picture advocates an idea. . . . Yet the First Amendment's basic guarantee is of freedom to advocate ideas. The State, quite simply, has thus struck at the very heart of constitutionally protected liberty."). Kingsley Int'l Pictures Corp. v. Regents of the University of New York, 360 U.S. 684, 687-88 (1959) (Stewart, J.). For reviews of later efforts to apply the *Roth* standard see Monaghan, *supra* note 133; Magrath, *The Obscenity Cases: The Grapes of Roth,* 1966 SUP. CT. REV. 7, 77 (likening the Court to a "Tower of Babel"); Krislov, *From Ginzburg to Ginsberg: The Unhurried Children's Hour in Obscenity Litigation,* 1968 SUP. CT. REV. 153; Katz, *Privacy and Pornography: Stanley v. Georgia,* 1969 SUP. CT. REV. 203.

[141] 354 U.S. 436 (1957). *See also id.* at 445-48 (Warren, C. J., and Black, Douglas, and Brennan, JJ., variously dissenting).

[142] *Id.* at 446-47. *See Near,* pp. 257-59 *supra.*

[143] 354 U.S. at 443 n.2. He did not deny that the order to destroy the offending publications interfered with their distribution, pending a final determination of their constitutional status; even a stay of the order would not remove that effect unless the materials remained in the distributor's possession.

[144] *See id.* at 445 (distinguishing *Near* as involving an injunction against "future issues of a publication because its past issues had been found offensive," that was issued not because the publication was found to contain obscenity but because it contained "matters deemed to be derogatory to a public officer").

[145] 365 U.S. 43 (1961).

forbidden exhibition of *all* motion pictures until they were approved by the police commissioner. For years it had been said that freedom of expression outlawed *only* this type of restraint;[146] now the Court said it was not forbidden at all.

A few years earlier, citing *Near,* Justice Clark had observed in striking down another movie censorship requirement that "[t]his Court recognized many years ago that such a previous restraint is a form of infringement upon freedom of expression to be especially condemned."[147] In *Times Film,* without so much as a passing reference to the special dangers of licensing, the same Justice emphasized statements in *Kingsley* and elsewhere that the protection against previous restraints was not absolute[148] and concluded that the Constitution conferred no right "to exhibit, at least once, any and every kind of motion picture."[149] Obscenity, he noted, had been held outside the first amendment in *Roth;* it was "not for this Court to limit the State in its selection of the remedy it deems most effective to cope with such a problem. . . ."[150]

That obscene films are unprotected, however, does not make it acceptable to suspend the exhibition of *all* films until they are found not to be obscene. "The delays in adjudication," as the Chief Justice pointed out for the four dissenters, "may well result in irreparable damage, both to the litigants and to the public."[151] The question was not whether there was a right to show an obscene movie once; it was whether the interest in suppressing such evils as obscenity justified delaying the showing of films that were not obscene.[152]

Justice Clark insisted that "we are dealing only with motion pictures" and that each method of expression " 'tends to present its own peculiar problems.' "[153] As Warren pointed out, however, Clark gave no reason for thinking movies any different from newspapers for this purpose, and it is not easy to find one.[154]

## B.  Crime

The Warren Court is also known for its aggressive expansion of the rights of those accused of crime. Like its advances in the field of expressive and associational freedoms, most of this expansion came only after Justice Frankfurter retired; but there were a few notable exceptions.

---

[146]*See, e.g.,* Patterson v. Colorado, 205 U.S. at 462 (citing Blackstone), pp. 58-59 *supra.*

[147]Joseph Burstyn, Inc. v. Wilson, 343 U.S. at 503, p. 351, note 110 *supra.*

[148]*See* 365 U.S. at 47-49 (quoting, among other decisions, *Near, Burstyn,* and *Kingsley Books*).

[149]365 U.S. at 46.

[150]*Id.* at 49-50.

[151]*Id.* at 73 (Warren, C. J., joined by Black, Douglas, and Brennan, JJ., dissenting).

[152]*See id.* at 55 (Warren, C. J., dissenting).

[153]*Id.* at 49-50 (quoting *Burstyn,* 343 U.S. at 503).

[154]365 U.S. at 75-78 (Warren, C. J., dissenting). *But see* A. BICKEL, *supra* note 9, at 140 ("[M]ovies, like the theater, address themselves to groups of people in public places."). Bickel, agreeing that the Court could not have held all movie censorship unconstitutional, argued that it should have denied certiorari to avoid "legitimating" the practice and thus "encourag[ing] Comstockian tendencies," *id.* at 133-40. The suggestion appears less palatable if phrased differently: the Court should deter public officials from lawful conduct by perpetuating the erroneous belief that it is unconstitutional.

## 1. Courts-martial

The Supreme Court had consistently acknowledged that there were categories of military offenses historically excluded from the constitutional requirements of indictment and jury trial before an independent judge.[155] *Ex parte Milligan,* just after the Civil War, had drawn one limit to the permissible military jurisdiction.[156] In a series of decisions of considerable doctrinal interest, the early Warren Court announced additional restrictions.

Justice Black wrote for a majority of six in *Toth v. Quarles* to invalidate the court-martial of an ex-serviceman for a crime committed while in service abroad.[157] Unlike the Court in *Milligan,* however, he did not hold that the military trial offended the judge and jury guarantees of article III and the sixth amendment. Rather he concluded that the statute providing for such trial did not fall within Congress's power "to make rules for the government and regulation of the land and naval forces." [158] "[G]iven its natural meaning," wrote Black, "the power granted . . . would seem to restrict court-martial jurisdiction to persons who are actually members or part of the armed forces." [159] Like the implicit authority of each House to punish contempt of its own processes,[160] the explicit authority to govern the military comprised " '*the least possible power adequate to the end proposed*' ";[161] it was "impossible to think that the discipline of the Army is going to be disrupted, its morale impaired, or its orderly processes disturbed, by giving ex-servicemen the benefit of a civilian court trial when they are actually civilians." [162]

One can quibble over the seriousness of the difficulties that would attend civilian trial of ex-servicemen for crimes committed while in service overseas.[163] One can argue that *Toth* was after all a case "*arising* in the land or naval forces" and thus within the military jurisdiction explicitly recognized by the fifth amendment,[164] or that history, which had been given great weight in earlier decisions involving military trials, tended to support

---

[155] *See* Dynes v. Hoover, 61 U.S. 65, 79 (1858) (dictum) (offense by serviceman on active duty); *Ex parte* Quirin, pp. 280-81 *supra* (enemy saboteurs charged with offenses against laws of war). *See generally* Henderson, *Courts-Martial and the Constitution: The Original Understanding,* 71 HARV. L. REV. 293 (1957); Wiener, *Courts-Martial and the Bill of Rights: The Original Practice II,* 72 HARV. L. REV. 266 (1958).

[156] 71 U.S. 2 (1866), THE FIRST HUNDRED YEARS at 288-92.

[157] 350 U.S. 11 (1955). Reed, Burton, and Minton dissented, *id.* at 23-45.

[158] U.S. CONST. art. I, § 8.

[159] 350 U.S. at 15.

[160] Anderson v. Dunn, 19 U.S. 204, 230-31 (1821), discussed in THE FIRST HUNDRED YEARS at 184-86, *cited in* 350 U.S. at 23 n.23.

[161] 350 U.S. at 23 (quoting Anderson v. Dunn, *supra*).

[162] 350 U.S. at 22.

[163] *See id.* at 28 (Reed, J., dissenting) ("This case itself would make a good example of the difficulty of a federal district court trial."). *Cf.* Kinsella v. Krueger, 351 U.S. 470, 479-80 n.12 (1956), *vacated on rehearing sub nom.* Reid v. Covert, 354 U.S. 1 (1957) (detailing the difficulties involved in a civilian trial of military dependents for foreign crimes). "It also seems a reasonable choice," Justice Reed added in *Toth,* "that uniform treatment by courts-martial trial of all accused of crimes punishable by the Military Code is preferred for morale and disciplinary purposes to courts-martial trial only for those who remain in the service." 350 U.S. at 28.

[164] U.S. CONST. amend. 5 ("No person shall be held to answer for a capital, or otherwise infamous crime, unless on a presentment or indictment of a grand jury, except in cases arising in the land or naval forces, or in the militia, when in actual service in time of war or public danger."). *See* 350 U.S. at 35-42 (Reed, J., dissenting); *Ex parte* Milligan, 71 U.S. at 123 (declaring that this exemption also applied to the right to jury trial).

continuing jurisdiction after the accused had been discharged.[165] Most controversial, however, was Justice Black's grudging approach to the question of interpreting an express grant of congressional authority.

Construing the provision for regulating the armed forces to confer "the least possible power adequate to the end proposed," as Justice Reed observed in dissent, was not easy to reconcile with *McCulloch v. Maryland,* where the Court had rejected just such a test of indispensability of federal legislation in favor of the familiar criterion of means "plainly adapted" to the achievement of a "legitimate" end.[166] It was in glaring contrast to the virtual carte blanche the Court had given Congress in recent years in determining the necessity and propriety of measures enacted on the purported authority of such provisions as the commerce clause.[167]

Justice Black's "compelling reason" for restrictive construction of article I in *Toth* was to avoid encroaching on the constitutional guarantees of jury trial and an independent judge.[168] In commerce clause cases, of course, the Court had shown no comparable solicitude to avoid diminishing the reserved powers of the states. In any event, the jury and judge guarantees could perfectly well have stood on their own; a measure otherwise necessary and proper to the exercise of federal power can always be struck down if the means Congress has chosen are "prohibited by the Constitution."[169]

*Kinsella v. Krueger* and *Reid v. Covert* presented a variation on the same theme: the constitutionality of a court-martial of servicemen's wives for offenses committed abroad. One might have thought a negative answer followed a fortiori from *Toth,* for the defendant in that case had at least been a soldier when the crime was committed.[170] Yet when the cases were first heard the Court over three dissents and a "reservation" of judgment by Frankfurter upheld the military jurisdiction.[171] Ever since Marshall's days, said Justice Clark, it had been settled that "Congress may establish legislative courts outside the territorial limits of the United States proper" and that "[t]he procedure in such tribunals need not comply with the standards prescribed by the Constitution for Article III courts."[172] Since a serviceman's wife in these circumstances "may be tried before a legislative court

[165] *See* 350 U.S. at 29-31 n.11, 32-33 (Reed, J., dissenting) (quoting from an advisory opinion by the judges of the three English law courts in 1760 affirming such jurisdiction and from an 1863 act of Congress so providing). For the weight given history in earlier cases involving military trials see the decisions cited in note 155 *supra.*

[166] 17 U.S. 316, 414, 421 (1819), THE FIRST HUNDRED YEARS at 162. *See* 350 U.S. at 31 (Reed, J., dissenting) (The statute "bears a reasonable relation to the 'Government and Regulation' of the armed forces; it is appropriate and plainly adapted to that end. *McCulloch v. Maryland.* . . .").

[167] *See* pp. 236-38 *supra* (discussing, *e.g.,* Wickard v. Filburn, where the Court upheld federal limitation of grain planted for a farmer's own use.). *Cf.* McDermott v. Wisconsin, 228 U.S. 115 (1913) (upholding a federal law providing for seizure of misbranded goods *after* transportation in interstate commerce).

[168] 350 U.S. at 15-16.

[169] McCulloch v. Maryland, 17 U.S. 316, 421 (1819).

[170] *See Reid,* 354 U.S. 1, 32 (1957), *on reh'g* (opinion of Black, J.).

[171] Kinsella v. Krueger, 351 U.S. 470 (1956); Reid v. Covert, 351 U.S. 487 (1956). *See also id.* at 481-85 (Frankfurter, J., insisting on additional time to make up his mind), 485-86 (Warren, Black, and Douglas, dissenting in both cases).

[172] 352 U.S. at 475 (citing, *e.g.,* American Ins. Co. v. Canter, 26 U.S. 511 (1828), THE FIRST HUNDRED YEARS at 119-22); *In re* Ross, 140 U.S. 453 (1891); and the Insular Cases, *e.g.,* Dorr v. United States, 195 U.S. 138 (1904) (discussed at pp. 59-65 *supra*).

established by Congress, we have no need to examine the power of Congress 'To make Rules for the Government and Regulation of the land and naval Forces' under Article I. . . ."[173]

This was not a convincing way to distinguish *Toth,* since there too the alleged crime had been committed, and the defendant was to be tried, outside the United States.[174] More important, as Justice Harlan pointed out when the *Krueger* and *Covert* decisions were reversed on reargument,[175] the asserted inapplicability of article III and the sixth amendment was not enough to make the court-martial of military dependents constitutional; such a trial must first be found necessary and proper to the exercise of some power granted to Congress.[176] The cases upholding the creation of "legislative" courts in the territories, as both Black and Frankfurter noted, had been based on Congress's explicit authority "to make all needful rules and regulations respecting the territory . . . of the United States," and neither Japan nor England, where the alleged offenses in *Covert* and *Krueger* had been committed, met that description.[177] Echoing the arguments they had made in *Toth,* Justice Black and three other Justices concluded that no court-martial of civilian dependents could be justified by the power "to make rules for the government and regulation of the land and naval forces."[178] Harlan, rehearsing the difficulties of civilian trials spelled out by Justice Clark for the two dissenters,[179] concluded that "the court-martial of civilian dependents abroad has a close connection to the proper and effective functioning of our overseas military contingents."[180] Nevertheless both Frankfurter and Harlan relied on the awesome gravity of capital punishment to conclude that civilian dependents could not be court-martialed for *capital* offenses—the former because military jurisdiction in such cases "cannot be justified by Article I, considered in connection with the specific protections of Article III and the Fifth and Sixth Amendments,"[181] the latter because under such circumstances "the Constitution guarantees . . . a trial in an Article III court, with indictment . . . and jury trial."[182]

[173] 351 U.S. at 476.

[174] *See Toth,* 350 U.S. at 13.

[175] Reid v. Covert, 354 U.S. 1 (1957) (disposing of *Krueger* in the same opinion). Justice Minton, who had been with the original majority, had retired; his successor, Justice Brennan, voted with the three earlier dissenters and with Justice Frankfurter to set the convictions aside. The change in outcome was not attributable solely to the change in membership, however, for Justice Harlan had switched his vote.

[176] *See id.* at 66 (Harlan, J., concurring).

[177] *See* U.S. CONST. art. IV, § 3; 354 U.S. at 13-14 (Black, J.); *id.* at 53 (Frankfurter, J., concurring). Justice Clark later made the remarkable assertion that he had indeed based the initial decision on article IV's authority to make rules for the " 'Territories,' " Kinsella v. Singleton, 361 U.S. 234, 237 (1960).

[178] 354 U.S. at 19-20 (Black, J., joined by Warren, Douglas, and Brennan) ("The term 'land and naval Forces' refers to persons who are members of the armed services and not to their civilian wives, children and other dependents.").

[179] *See id.* at 87-88 (Clark, J., joined by Burton, J., dissenting) (stressing the cost and impracticability of transporting witnesses to United States or empaneling juries abroad). Whittaker, the newly appointed successor to Reed, did not participate. *Id.* at 41.

[180] *Id.* at 72.

[181] *Id.* at 49 (Frankfurter, J., concurring).

[182] *Id.* at 74-78 (Harlan, J., concurring). Thus both concurring Justices, like Justice Black and his three companions, rejected the untenable notion that the Constitution has no application outside the United States and its possessions. "That approach is obviously erroneous," Black explained, "if the United States Government, which has no power except that granted by the Constitution, can and does try citizens for crimes committed abroad."

Justice Clark, dissenting, saw no relevant constitutional distinction between capital and noncapital cases.[183] The severity of the sanction, however, arguably fit into *Toth*'s general test of the reasonableness of the provision as a means of achieving Congress's legitimate end.[184] Three years later, over the objections of Frankfurter and Harlan, Clark wrote for the majority to extend the principle from which he had dissented to noncapital cases; ' having lost a fair fight, he was stoutly prepared to take the consequences.[185]


## 2. *Transcripts*

No less troublesome from a doctrinal standpoint was *Griffin v. Illinois*, which held over four dissents that the state could not make the inability of an indigent convict to purchase a transcript of his trial a bar to entertaining his appeal.[186] A state that permits appellate review, wrote Justice Black for four members of the majority, may not "do so in a way that discriminates against some convicted defendants on account of their poverty."[187] Justice Frankfurter, concurring separately, agreed: if the state "has a general policy of allowing

---

*Id.* at 12. *See also* THE FIRST HUNDRED YEARS at 119-22 (discussing American Ins. Co. v. Canter, 26 U.S. 511 (1828)). Arguments to uphold the trials in *Covert* on the basis of Congress's authority to make rules respecting "other property" of the United States, which could easily have included the U.S. bases on which the events had occurred, or of various powers over foreign affairs, *see In re* Ross, *supra* note 172 (upholding the creation of "consular courts" in foreign countries as necessary and proper to effectuation of a treaty), would have been subject to the same reservations in light of the tenure and jury provisions. *See also Covert*, 354 U.S. at 16 (repudiating loose language in Missouri v. Holland, 252 U.S. at 433, pp. 100-01 *supra*, that could have been read to suggest that the treaty power was not limited by the Constitution at all: "[T]he reason treaties were not limited to those made in 'pursuance' of the Constitution [in the supremacy clause of article VI] was so that agreements made . . . under the Articles of Confederation . . . would remain in effect.").

[183] 354 U.S. at 89.

[184] *See* text at notes 161-62 *supra* and accompanying text. *See also Covert*, 354 U.S. at 44 (Frankfurter, J., concurring) ("The issue in these cases involves regard for considerations not dissimilar to those involved in a determination under the Due Process Clause."). *Cf.* Korematsu v. United States, 323 U.S. at 243 (Jackson, J., dissenting) (suggesting that the severity of a deprivation was relevant in determining whether it was an appropriate means of preventing sabotage), pp. 289-92 *supra;* THE FIRST HUNDRED YEARS at 323-25 (discussing the legal tender controversy).

[185] Kinsella v. Singleton, 361 U.S. 234 (1960) (invalidating court-martial of civilian dependent for noncapital offense). Much of the discussion in this opinion concerned the reach of the grant of authority to regulate the armed forces, *id.* at 246-48; yet the bottom line was that the defendant was "protected by the specific provisions of Article III and the Fifth and Sixth Amendments," *id.* at 249. *See also id.* at 249-59 (Harlan, J., joined by Frankfurter, dissenting); Grisham v. Hagan, 361 U.S. 278 (1960) (Clark, J.), and McElroy v. Guagliardo, 361 U.S. 281 (1960) (Clark, J.) (extending the principles of *Covert* and *Singleton*, respectively, to forbid both capital and noncapital court-martial of civilian employees of the armed forces abroad). Whittaker, joined by Stewart, mustered impressive historical evidence to support his dissenting conclusion that civilian employees were "so intertwined with those forces . . . as to be in every practical sense an integral part of them," *id.* at 259-77. Clark responded, *id.* at 286-87, that if civilian trials proved cumbersome, such employees could be made members of the service—raising the question why title rather than function ought be determinative. Some implications of the court-martial decisions of the Warren years are explored in Bishop, *Court-Martial Jurisdiction over Military-Civilian Hybrids: Retired Regulars, Reservists, and Discharged Prisoners*, 112 U. PA. L. REV. 317 (1964).

[186] 351 U.S. 12 (1956). *See also id.* at 26-29 (Burton and Minton, JJ., joined by Reed and Harlan, dissenting); *id.* at 29-39 (Harlan, J., dissenting).

[187] *Id.* at 18.

criminal appeals, it cannot make a lack of means an effective bar to the exercise of this opportunity."[188]

Black invoked both equal protection and due process;[189] Frankfurter seemed to stress equal protection.[190] The focus of both opinions was clearly on discrimination. Frankfurter could not resist the temptation to quote Anatole France: " 'The law, in its majestic equality, forbids the rich as well as the poor to sleep under bridges, to beg in the streets, and to steal bread.' "[191]

These analogies are arresting, and they reveal the fragility of the majority's position. Did Frankfurter mean to suggest that it was unconstitutional to forbid the poor to steal bread—or, as Justice Harlan protested in dissent, to require them to pay tuition at state universities? Illinois had treated the poor exactly as it had treated everyone else; no one could obtain a transcript without paying for it. "All that Illinois has done," said Harlan, "is to fail to alleviate the consequences of differences in economic circumstances that exist wholly apart from any state action." It was anomalous, he concluded, to find in "a constitutional admonition to the States to treat all persons equally" a command to "give to some what it requires others to pay for."[192]

There is a concept of equality, as the invocation of Anatole France shows, that focuses on the practical impact rather than the form of government action, that insists that government action produce equal *results* between affected classes.[193] This is the philosophy that finds racial discrimination in the administration of identical tests that more whites than blacks pass, that finds progressive taxation constitutionally *required*, that forbids uniform prices for the sale of government services. Neither government practice nor judicial decision had reflected such a philosophy before *Griffin*, and there is no basis on which to attribute it to the framers of the fourteenth amendment.[194] The Court had contradicted it in upholding both poll taxes and literacy tests for voting: the fifteenth amendment did not require the state to equalize the percentages of black and white voters.[195] It was not clear how *Griffin* could be reconciled with this constitutional tradition.[196]

---

[188]*Id.* at 24.

[189]*See id.* at 18 ("[A]t all stages of the proceedings the Due Process and Equal Protection Clauses protect persons like petitioners from invidious discrimination.").

[190]*See id.* at 25 (suggesting that on remand the state court might find within existing state law "means of according to petitioners their constitutional rights not to be denied the equal protection of the laws").

[191]*Id.* at 23 (quoting JOHN COURNOS, A MODERN PLUTARCH, 27; quotation from France's novel LE LYS ROUGE (1894)).

[192]351 U.S. at 34-35 (Harlan, J., dissenting).

[193]*See* Currie, *Positive and Negative Constitutional Rights*, 53 U. CHI. L. REV. 864, 880-84 (1986), and authorities cited.

[194]*See* Winter, *Poverty, Economic Equality, and the Equal Protection Clause*, 1972 SUP. CT. REV. 41, 86 ("The Amendment was not designed to reduce inequality in the society generally or to serve as a device by which government might be compelled to take steps to bring about economic equality.").

[195]Breedlove v. Suttles, p. 251, note 46 *supra;* Lassiter v. Board of Elections, pp. 384-85 *supra.*

[196]For the proposition that "a law nondiscriminatory on its face may be grossly discriminatory in its operation," 351 U.S. at 17 n.11, Black cited only Guinn v. United States, pp. 106-07 *supra,* and a later related decision, where the Court had struck down grandfather clauses for voting "as discriminatory against Negroes." The Court had done so, however, not on the ground that the law disenfranchised more blacks than whites, but because the only purpose the law seemed to serve was racial discrimination. *See also* Michelman, *Foreword: On Protecting the Poor through the Fourteenth Amendment*, 83 HARV. L. REV. 7, 24-26 (1969) (attempting to assimilate *Griffin* to a general due process obligation "to ensure that everyone's just wants are fulfilled"—an

There was an equally troublesome problem with the alternative argument that, like a trial without an attorney,[197] an appeal without a transcript was inconsistent with due process of law. As Harlan conceded, the absence of a constitutional right to appeal did not mean that appeals could be arbitrarily denied.[198] Nor was there any doubt that Griffin was being deprived of liberty or property; criminal conviction is the predicate for imprisonment or fine. Equal protection arguments aside, however, it was not obvious why it was more unfair to require an appellant to pay for a transcript than to deny his appeal altogether.[199] As in *Slochower, Watkins,* and *Sweezy,* the Court in *Griffin* seems to have felt called upon to remedy an injustice. As in those cases it seems to have done so without excessive regard for the law.

## 3. Citizenship

The first clause of the fourteenth amendment, enacted to overrule the exclusion of blacks from citizenship in the *Dred Scott* case,[200] provides that "[a]ll persons born or naturalized in the United States, and subject to the jurisdiction thereof, are citizens of the United States and of the State wherein they reside." It does not say under what circumstances, if any, citizenship may be terminated. From an early date there had been arguments that citizenship was a privilege that could be relinquished voluntarily.[201] The Warren Court was confronted on several occasions with the more troubling question of the constitutionality of statutes depriving Americans of citizenship without their consent.

Two cases decided on the same day in 1958 provided an arresting introduction to the problem. By two five-to-four votes the Court held that citizenship could be taken away for voting in a foreign election[202] but not for deserting the army in time of war.[203]

Chief Justice Warren, joined by Black and Douglas, argued that the fourteenth amendment denied Congress authority ever to deprive persons of their citizenship.[204] A bare

---

equally novel doctrine raising the equally difficult question whether mere inaction can be said to "deprive" anyone of life, liberty, or property). *See* pp. 139-43 *supra* (discussing Truax v. Corrigan); Currie, *supra* note 193, *passim.*

[197] Powell v. Alabama, pp. 246-47 *supra.* Even this proposition had yet to be fully accepted by the Warren Court. *See* note 237 *infra* and accompanying text.

[198] *Cf.* Wieman v. Updegraff, pp. 357-58 *supra* (government employment).

[199] *See* 351 U.S. at 36-39 (Harlan, J., dissenting).

[200] *See* Afroyim v. Rusk, 387 U.S. 253, 282-85 (1967) (Harlan, J., dissenting), and sources cited; Scott v. Sandford, 60 U.S. 393 (1857), THE FIRST HUNDRED YEARS at 263-66.

[201] "Upon that principle," wrote Attorney General Black in 1859, "this country was populated." 9 Op. Atty. Gen. 356, 359. Congress expressly recognized such a right by statute in 1868, and "impressment of naturalized American seamen of British birth was a cause of the War of 1812." *See* Perez v. Brownell, 356 U.S. 44, 66-69 (1958) (Warren, C. J., dissenting). As Roche has shown, however, most early authority favoring a right of voluntary expatriation dealt with persons who wished to cast off foreign nationality in order to become U.S. citizens; when the case was reversed, the tendency was to reaffirm the common law position that citizenship entailed duties that could not be shucked off without official assent. *See* Roche, *The Expatriation Cases: "Breathes There the Man, with Soul so Dead . . . ?",* 1963 SUP. CT. REV. 325, 328-30 (citing, inter alia, Shanks v. Dupont, 28 U.S. 242, 246 (1830)).

[202] Perez v. Brownell, 356 U.S. 44 (1958).

[203] Trop v. Dulles, 356 U.S. 86 (1958).

[204] *See Perez,* 356 U.S. at 62-78 (Warren, C. J., dissenting); *Trop,* 356 U.S. at 91-93 (Warren, C. J., for four Justices). In order to get around earlier decisions, Warren took a generous view of what constituted "voluntary" expatriation. *See* 356 U.S. at 69-73 (discussing Savorgnan v. United States, 338 U.S. 491 (1950) (acquisition of

majority was to agree with him a few years later after a furious battle over the relevant history.[205] For the moment, however, Warren made little effort to set forth the arguments for his conclusion, and the majority dismissed it with the conclusory statement that "there is nothing in the terms, the context, the history or the manifest purpose of the Fourteenth Amendment to warrant drawing from it a restriction upon the power otherwise possessed by Congress to withdraw citizenship."[206]

The provision respecting foreign elections, Justice Frankfurter wrote for the Court in *Perez v. Brownell*, was a permissible exercise of Congress's broad implicit powers over foreign relations.[207] Congress could reasonably have believed that American citizens who "participate in the political or governmental affairs of another country" might "cause serious embarrassment to the government of their own country" and "jeopardiz[e] the successful conduct of international relations."[208] Loss of citizenship was an appropriate means to the legitimate end of avoiding such embarrassment, since "it is the possession of American citizenship . . . that makes the act potentially embarrassing. . . . The termination of citizenship," said Frankfurter, "terminates the problem."[209]

Like analogous arguments made in modern commerce clause cases, this reasoning was straightforward and deferential.[210] The usually restrained Justice Whittaker, however, found Congress's fears greatly exaggerated. Aliens had been allowed to vote in this country until 1928; when a foreign country permitted Americans to vote, "such legalized voting . . . cannot reasonably be said to be fraught with danger of embroiling our Govern-

---

foreign citizenship), and Mackenzie v. Hare, 239 U.S. 299 (1915) (marriage to foreigner)). *But see Perez*, 356 U.S. at 44-45 (opinion of Frankfurter, J., for the Court) (noting that in both cases Congress had prescribed denationalization "irrespective of—and, in those cases, absolutely contrary to—the intentions and desires of the individuals"). No such argument, Warren continued, *id.* at 77, could justify the provision in *Perez* ("Voting in a foreign election may be a most equivocal act, giving rise to no implication that allegiance has been compromised."). The ostensible concurrence of Justice Whittaker in *Trop* in these views, which he had expressly disavowed in *Perez*, 356 U.S. at 84 (memorandum of Whittaker, J.) ("I agree . . . that Congress may expatriate a citizen for an act which it may reasonably find fraught with danger of embroiling our Government in an international dispute or of embarrassing it in the conduct of foreign affairs"), can be explained as intended to indicate agreement with the alternative ground of Warren's *Trop* opinion (discussed at note 214 *infra*).

[205] Afroyim v. Rusk, 387 U.S. 253 (1967) (Black, J., over a Harlan dissent joined by Clark, Stewart, and White after Frankfurter had retired) (overruling *Perez*). The "undeniable purpose of the Fourteenth Amendment to make citizenship of Negroes permanent and secure," Black wrote, "would be frustrated by holding that the Government can rob a citizen of his citizenship without his consent. . . ." *Id.* at 263. Harlan responded that just before proposing the amendment Congress had passed two bills to deprive persons of citizenship, that sponsors of the citizenship provision had described it as merely declaratory, and that Senator Howard, chief spokesman for the amendment, had asserted in debate that a citizen could not ease to be a citizen "except by expatriation or the commission of some crime by which his citizenship shall be forfeited." *Id.* at 279-86. *See* Roche, *supra* note 201, at 343, agreeing with Harlan.

[206] *Perez*, 356 U.S. at 58 n.3.

[207] *See id.* at 57: "Although there is in the Constitution no specific grant to Congress of power to enact legislation for the effective regulation of foreign affairs, there can be no doubt of the existence of this power in the law-making organ of the Nation" (citing United States v. Curtiss-Wright Export Corp., p. 231, note 140 *supra*).

[208] 356 U.S. at 59 (adding that "[t]he citizen may by his action unwittingly promote or encourage a course of conduct contrary to the interests of his own government" and that "the people or government of the foreign country may regard his action to be the action of his government, or at least as a reflection if not an expression of its policy").

[209] *Id.* at 60.

[210] *See* note 167 *supra*.

ment in an international dispute or of embarrassing it in the conduct of foreign affairs. . . ."[211] 

Whittaker's close scrutiny of the means chosen by Congress to effectuate its legitimate end was reminiscent of that employed by Black, Frankfurter, and Harlan in the court-martial cases.[212] Justice Brennan, the only member of the Court to vote with the majority in both citizenship cases, applied a similarly sharp instrument to excise the desertion provision in *Trop v. Dulles*. In contrast to voting in foreign elections, there was nothing about wartime desertion that made loss of citizenship a peculiarly appropriate response, and denationalization was too severe to be an appropriate sanction for the simple commission of crime.[213] Warren, joined this time by Whittaker as well as Black and Douglas, added that in his view the loss of citizenship was a cruel and unusual punishment.[214] With this diversity of views it seemed clear that we had not heard the last of these issues.

## 4. Other cases

In *Robinson v. California*, in 1962, the Justices discovered in the prohibition of cruel and unusual punishment invoked by Warren in *Trop* a partial substitute for the discredited doctrine of substantive due process: *any* punishment was cruel and unusual when the defendant had done nothing wrong.[215] The purported offense was to "be addicted to the use of narcotics." Drawing a rather strained analogy to "mak[ing] it a criminal offense for a person to be mentally ill, or a leper," the majority argued that "[e]ven one day in prison would be a cruel and unusual punishment for the 'crime' of having a common cold."[216] No Justice contended, however, that Robinson had become an addict involuntarily;[217] Justice White plausibly wondered whether the Court would strike down a law against the *use* of narcotics as well.[218] More fundamentally, the language of the clause (here for the first

---

[211] 356 U.S. at 85 (memorandum of Whittaker, J., dissenting).

[212] *See* notes 155-85 *supra* and accompanying text.

[213] 356 U.S. at 105-14 (Brennan, J., concurring).

[214] *Id.* at 93-104.

[215] 370 U.S. 660 (1962) (Stewart, J.).

[216] *Id.* at 666-67.

[217] Indeed, as Justice Clark noted in dissent, *id.* at 684, there was no contention that even by the time of his conviction Robinson had lost the ability to control his own actions. *See* Greenawalt, *"Uncontrollable" Actions and the Eighth Amendment: Implications of* Powell v. Texas, 69 COLUM. L. REV. 927, 948 (1969) ("[C]haracterization of alcoholism as a disease does not necessarily establish that moral fault is absent in its acquisition," or even in its continuance: "It is conceivable that a sick person will be able to choose freely whether to undertake a cure or not.").

[218] 370 U.S. at 688-89 (White, J., dissenting). *See* Greenawalt, *supra* note 217, at 929 ("If it is unconstitutional to punish someone for suffering from a disease, can it be constitutional to punish him for acts that are caused by the disease?"). Fears about the scope of the decision were allayed only a little by the five-to-four vote in Powell v. Texas, 392 U.S. 514 (1968), to uphold conviction of an alleged alcoholic for drunkenness in a public place; there was no opinion for the Court, and Justice White cast the deciding vote, *id.* at 548-54, on the ground that even if the defendant could not help drinking there was no proof he could not avoid being in a public place. For interesting discussions of *Robinson*'s implication that mens rea may be a constitutional requirement see Greenawalt, *supra* note 217, *passim;* Henkin, *supra* note 50, at 67-72. *See also* Lambert v. California, 355 U.S. 225, 228 (1957) (Douglas, J.) (striking down on due process grounds an ordinance punishing any person formerly convicted of crime who failed to register with the police within five days after entering the city: "Engrained in our concept of due process is the requirement of notice."). *See* Packer, *Mens Rea and the Supreme Court,* 1962

time and without explanation applied to the states)[219] suggests it was concerned with the issue of appropriate punishment for those properly convicted, not with whether conviction was proper at all.[220] "If this case involved economic regulation," Justice White protested, "the present Court's allergy to substantive due process would surely save the statute. . . . I fail to see why the Court deems it more appropriate to write into the Constitution its own abstract notions of how best to handle the narcotics problem. . . ."[221]

Justice Frankfurter did not participate in *Robinson*,[222] but he lost a significant battle in his last Term when Justice Clark joined the four usual activists in *Mapp v. Ohio* to hold that state courts, like federal courts, were required to exclude evidence that was the product of an unreasonable search or seizure.[223] Just twelve years before, Frankfurter had written the contrary decision in *Wolf v. Colorado*.[224] *Wolf* itself had conceded that the prohibition of such searches and seizures applied to the states.[225] Now Clark, who had joined Frankfurter's opinion in *Wolf*, accepted Justice Murphy's dissenting argument in the earlier case that the constitutional prohibition could not be effectively enforced without forbidding the use of evidence unlawfully obtained.[226] Not content to rest the decision on the need for deterrence of illegal police practices alone, Clark closed by invoking " 'the imperative of judicial integrity' " and an apt quotation from Brandeis's *Olmstead* dissent: " 'If the Government becomes a lawbreaker, it breeds contempt for law.' "[227] Clark's two rationales, which worked in parallel to support the *Mapp* conclusion, were to

---

SUP. CT. REV. 107, 123, 152 (analogizing to the void-for-vagueness principle of United States v. L. Cohen Grocery Co., p. 109, note 123 *supra*, and adding that "[s]trict liability in the criminal law is irrational, in the substantive due process sense of that word"). *But see Lambert*, 355 U.S. at 230 (Frankfurter, J., joined by Harlan and Whittaker, dissenting) ("The present laws of the United States and of the forty-eight States are thick with provisions that command that some things not be done and others be done, although persons convicted under such provisions may have had no awareness of what the law required or that what they did was wrongdoing.").

[219] Louisiana *ex rel.* Francis v. Resweber, cited by Douglas in a concurrence as having established that proposition, 370 U.S. at 675, had expressly reserved the question. *See* 329 U.S. 459, 462 (1947).

[220] *See* Greenawalt, *supra* note 217, at 973 ("The historical origin of the eighth amendment suggests a relatively narrow scope, limited to inhuman and barbarous methods of inflicting punishment."). *Cf.* United States v. Morgan, 346 U.S. 502, 506 (1954) (interpreting Rule 35 of the Federal Rules of Criminal Procedure, which permits postconviction correction of "an illegal sentence": "Sentences subject to correction under that rule are those that the judgment of conviction did not authorize."). Long before *Robinson*, however, the Court had taken a small step in the direction of *Robinson*'s reinterpretation by finding "cruel and unusual" a punishment grossly disproportionate to the offense. Weems v. United States, p. 57 *supra*.

[221] 370 U.S. at 689 (White, J., dissenting).

[222] *See id.* at 668.

[223] 367 U.S. 642 (1961) (Clark, J., with Harlan, Frankfurter, and Whittaker dissenting and Stewart not reaching the question) (overruling Wolf v. Colorado, pp. 363-64 *supra*).

[224] *Wolf*, 338 U.S. at 28.

[226] Justice Black, who had joined *Wolf*, concurred specially in *Mapp*, 367 U.S. at 661-66, adding the fifth vote for the majority on the distinct ground that the admission of such evidence offended the privilege against self-incrimination, *see* THE FIRST HUNDRED YEARS at 444-47, discussing Boyd v. United States, 116 U.S. 616 (1886)—which as Harlan pointed out the Court had recently said was inapplicable to the states. 367 U.S. at 686 (citing Cohen v. Hurley, note 236 *infra*). For a tentative and skeptical attempt to determine whether the exclusionary rule actually deterred unconstitutional behavior see Oaks, *Studying the Exclusionary Rule in Search and Seizure*, 37 U. CHI. L. REV. 665 (1970). *See also* Allen, *Federalism and the Fourth Amendment: A Requiem for Wolf*, 1961 SUP. CT. REV. 1, 40; Karst, *Legislative Facts in Constitutional Litigation*, 1960 SUP. CT. REV. 75.

[227] 367 U.S. at 659 (citing Olmstead v. United States, 277 U.S. at 485, pp. 168-69 *supra*).

pull in opposite directions in later cases concerning the proper scope of the exclusionary rule.[228]

There were comparable departures in civil procedure as the Court in *Beacon Theatres v. Westover*[229] and *Dairy Queen, Inc. v. Wood*[230] concluded in effect that whenever legal and equitable claims were presented in a single proceeding, the former should be tried first in order that jury consideration not be foreclosed by the judge's prior decision. Since at the time the seventh amendment was adopted a plaintiff with multiple claims could often determine the order in which claims were tried by deciding whether to file first in law or in equity,[231] there was a strong argument that permitting the defendant in such cases to demand prior determination of the legal claim would be to extend the right of jury trial rather than merely "preserve[]" it, as the amendment prescribes.[232] Justice Black responded that the adequacy of legal remedies had to be reassessed in light of modern rules permitting joinder of legal and equitable claims in a single proceeding, and that equitable trial of common issues was no longer necessary to avoid multiple litigation.[233] The validity of this line of reasoning depends upon Justice Black's interesting premise that what the seventh amendment "preserve[s]" is not jury trial in those specific cases triable at law in 1791 but rather the general principle of jury trial in cases in which there is an adequate legal remedy.[234]

If the decisions just discussed suggest an increasing tendency toward innovation, however, in other cases the early Warren Court was still quite reserved in its interpretation of the fourth, fifth, and sixth amendments. *Frank v. Maryland,* taking a narrow view of the history of the fourth amendment, held that municipal officers could search homes for health reasons without obtaining warrants, though the purpose of the warrant requirement seemed as applicable to such searches as to those made in the investigation of crime.[235] *Cohen v. Hurley* allowed disbarment of an attorney for refusing to incriminate himself in a state investigation on the ground that even after *Slochower* the fifth amendment privilege was inapplicable to the states.[236] Numerous decisions continued to apply *Betts v. Brady's*

---

[228] *See* pp. 552-53 *infra.*

[229] 359 U.S. 500 (1959) (Black, J.). Stewart, Harlan, and Whittaker dissented, and Frankfurter took no part.

[230] 369 U.S. 469 (1962) (Black, J., without dissent).

[231] *See* F. JAMES & G. HAZARD, CIVIL PROCEDURE § 8.7 (3d ed. 1985); *cf.* American Life Ins. Co. v. Stewart, 300 U.S. 203 (1937), reaching a comparable conclusion in the context of a legal counterclaim to a suit for injunction.

[232] *See* F. JAMES & G. HAZARD, *supra* note 231, at 436.

[233] *See Beacon,* 359 U.S. at 506-11.

[234] *See* McCoid, *Procedural Reform and the Right to Jury Trial,* 116 U. PA. L. REV. 1, 13 (1967).

[235] 359 U.S. 360, 365 (1959) (Frankfurter, J.) (also invoking state practice) ("[I]t was on the issue of the right to be secure from searches for evidence to be used in criminal prosecutions or for forfeitures that the great battle for fundamental liberty was fought."). *But see id.* at 381 (Douglas, J., joined by Warren, Black, and Brennan, dissenting) ("[T]he Fourth Amendment . . . was designed to protect the citizen against uncontrolled invasion of his privacy."). *Cf.* Trustees of Dartmouth College v. Woodward, 17 U.S. 518, 644 (1819) ("It is not enough to say, that this particular case was not in the mind of the Convention, when the article was framed. . . . It is necessary to go farther, and to say that, had the particular case been suggested, the language would have been so varied, as to exclude it. . . ."). *Frank* and related decisions are criticized in Beaney, *The Constitutional Right to Privacy in the Supreme Court,* 1962 SUP. CT. REV. 212, 242-46.

[236] 366 U.S. 117, 127-28 (1961) (Harlan, J., over dissents by Warren, Black, Douglas, and Brennan). *Slochower* was distinguished, *id.* at 125, as it had been in *Beilan* and *Lerner,* on the ground that in *Cohen* no inference of guilt had been drawn from the refusal to respond.

case-by-case approach to determining the need for assigned counsel in state prosecutions.[237] Warren, Black, Douglas, and Brennan objected vigorously in all these cases,[238] but the dike was not to burst while Felix Frankfurter was on the Court.


## IV. SAINTS

In contrast to his restrained position on freedom of expression and criminal procedure, Justice Frankfurter was an energetic enforcer of the separation of church and state.[239] The most important religion decisions of the Warren period were handed down, with his support, during his tenure. These rulings got the Court into additional political trouble, but there was little in them that had not been implicit in earlier decisions.

*McGowan v. Maryland* and its companion cases, in upholding laws limiting Sunday employment, sensibly confirmed that the mere coincidence of religious and secular commands was no forbidden establishment; that murder is a sin does not mean it cannot also be made a crime.[240] Finding that Sunday closing laws served the legitimate secular purpose of providing a uniform day of rest, the Court was unimpressed by arguments as to impermissible religious motives of the legislators—as it had generally been whenever the challenged law served a constitutionally allowable goal.[241]

*Braunfeld v. Brown,* decided the same day, rejected the claim that application of Sunday laws to persons whose religion forbade them to work on another day abridged the free exercise of their religion.[242] This conclusion seemed in accord both with the history of the battle for religious freedom and with decisions ever since the polygamy case of *Reynolds*

---

[237]*E.g.,* Cash v. Culver, 358 U.S. 633 (1959); McNeal v. Culver, 365 U.S. 109 (1961); Carnley v. Cochran, 369 U.S. 506 (1962) (all finding counsel required). *See Betts,* pp. 320-22 *supra.*

[238]*See* notes 235, 236 *supra;* McNeal v. Culver, 365 U.S. at 117-19 (Douglas and Brennan, JJ., concurring); Carnley v. Cochrane, 369 U.S. at 517-24 (Black, Douglas, and Warren, concurring) (all urging that *Betts* be overruled).

[239]*See* pp. 339-43 *supra* (discussing Everson v. Board of Education and Zorach v. Clauson).

[240]366 U.S. 420, 433-53 (1961) (Warren, C. J.) (also rejecting equal protection objections to various exemptions from the ban on the ground that the exemptions could reasonably be found "necessary either for the health of the populace or for the enhancement of the recreational atmosphere of the day," *id.* at 426). Justice Frankfurter, *id.* at 459-559[!], added a separate concurrence saying the same thing in a great many more words. Justice Douglas dissented alone: "No matter how much is written, no matter what is said, the parentage of these laws is the Fourth Commandment. . . ." *Id.* at 572. *See also* Two Guys from Harrison-Allentown, Inc. v. McGinley, 366 U.S. 582 (1961); Braunfeld v. Brown, 366 U.S. 599 (1961); Gallagher v. Crown Kosher Super Market, 366 U.S. 617 (1961) (likewise upholding Sunday laws against establishment clause attack).

[241]*See* 366 U.S. at 469 (Frankfurter, J., concurring) (citing, *e.g.,* McCray v. United States, p. 30 *supra* (upholding tax on margarine); Ely, *supra* note 38, at 1124-27). *Cf.* Lassiter v. Board of Elections, pp. 384-85 *supra* (upholding literacy test for voting); *contrast* decisions concluding that laws serving no legitimate purpose must have been enacted for an illegitimate one, *e.g.,* Gomillion v. Lightfoot, pp. 381-82 *supra* (municipal boundaries redrawn so as to exclude virtually all blacks), and cases cited. It was embarrassing that the statutes in question spoke in terms of "Sabbath breaking" and "the Lord's day"; invoking the state court's interpretation, the Chief Justice concluded that "the statutes' present purpose" was secular. 366 U.S. at 445, 449. *See also id.* at 497-98 (Frankfurter, J., concurring) ("[T]he continuation of seventeenth century language does not of itself prove the continuation of the purposes for which the colonial governments enacted these laws. . . .").

[242]366 U.S. 599 (1961). There was no opinion for the Court. Warren wrote for himself, Black, Clark, and Whittaker; Frankfurter, joined by Harlan, concurred specially; Douglas, Brennan, and Stewart dissented. *See id.* at 616 (Stewart, J., dissenting) ("Pennsylvania has passed a law which compels an Orthodox Jew to choose between his religious faith and his economic survival.").

*v. United States.* Discrimination being at the heart of the prohibition, the Court had never held it entitled the religious to special exemptions from otherwise valid laws.[243]

*Torcaso v. Watkins,* in an eloquent opinion by Justice Black, held that a state could not limit public offices to persons willing to profess a belief in God.[244] With respect to federal offices, article VI explicitly forbade such a requirement.[245] Black's declaration in *Torcaso* that "neither a State nor the Federal Government . . . can constitutionally pass laws or impose requirements which aid all religions as against nonbelievers,"[246] which was a paraphrase of *Everson,*[247] seemed to suggest the unsurprising conclusion that the state oath offended the establishment principle, which had been in issue in *Everson.* Yet Black squarely based the decision on the equally compelling proposition that the oath requirement "unconstitutionally invades the appellant's freedom of belief and religion. . . ."[248] Thus *Torcaso* removed any remaining doubt that the free exercise clause protected nonbelievers too, and for a very good reason. The underlying purpose of preventing coercion and strife respecting matters of conscience, as the Court implied, precludes discrimination against those who have no religion at all.[249]

It was Justice Black again who wrote for eight Justices in the famous case of *Engel v. Vitale* in 1962 to hold that a state could not compose prayers to be read aloud in public schools.[250] This decision aroused a storm of controversy, and there were some who wondered whether the Court was wise to expend so much capital on such a case on the heels of its battles over segregation and subversion.[251] On the merits, however, the result should arguably have been obvious ever since the establishment clause was first held applicable to the states. As Justice Black said, there could be "no doubt that New York's program of daily invocation of God's blessings . . . is a religious activity."[252] Under the precedents it was plainly immaterial for establishment purposes that pupils were not compelled to par-

---

[243] *See* THE FIRST HUNDRED YEARS at 439-42 (discussing *Reynolds,* 98 U.S. 145 (1879)); pp. 267-68 *supra* (discussing the flag-salute cases); P. KURLAND, RELIGION AND THE LAW (1962). Both Warren and Frankfurter, however, seemed to leave the door open for special religious exemptions in some cases. The Chief Justice, 366 U.S. at 607, declared that an indirect effect on religion was permissible provided that the state could not "accomplish its [secular] purpose by means which do not impose such a burden"; Frankfurter, *id.* at 520, said the question was whether the secular goals of the law were important enough "to outweigh the restraint upon the religious exercise of Orthodox Jewish practicants which the restriction entails."

[244] 367 U.S. 488 (1961) (Black, J.). There were no dissents; Frankfurter and Harlan concurred in the result. *Id.* at 496.

[245] *See* U.S. CONST. art. VI ("[N]o religious test shall ever be required as a qualification to any office or public trust under the United States.").

[246] 367 U.S. at 495.

[247] *See* Everson v. Board of Education, 330 U.S. at 15-16 (pp. 339-42 *supra*), *quoted in Torcaso,* 367 U.S. at 492-93.

[248] *Id.* at 496. *See also id.* at 495 & n.11 (adding that the requirement also discriminated against adherents of religions not based upon belief in the existence of God).

[249] *See* W. KATZ, RELIGION AND AMERICAN CONSTITUTIONS 6 (1964) ("[I]f religious belief is to be free, freedom of religion must include freedom of religious disbelief.").

[250] 370 U.S. 421 (1962).

[251] *See, e.g.,* Sutherland, *Establishment according to Engel,* 76 HARV. L. REV. 25, 38-39, 50-51 (1962). *See also* Brown, *Quis Custodiet Ipsos Custodes?—The School-Prayer Cases,* 1963 SUP. CT. REV. 1, 15-33 (questioning the standing of school children to object to the public reading of prayers in class despite the Court's commonsense observation that those exposed to the exercise were "directly affected" by it, Abington School Dist. v. Schempp, 374 U.S. 203, 224 n.9 (1963)).

[252] 370 U.S. at 424.

ticipate and that the prayer was intended to be "non-denominational."[253] Even the incongruous *Zorach* decision, upholding a released-time program that appeared to put the weight of the state behind private religious instruction, had conceded that the states themselves could not teach religion.[254] The last thing we needed, the Court seemed to be saying, was for the government to tell us how to pray.

Justice Stewart dissented alone, professing to perceive no establishment of religion in "letting those who want to say a prayer say it."[255] In this he seemed to miss the point entirely; no one was arguing that the schools had a duty to prevent children from praying on their own.[256] Nor did the long-standing practice of providing chaplains for soldiers or prisoners cast serious doubt on the Court's conclusion; since it was the government that had deprived them of any other "effective opportunity . . . to satisfy [their] religious needs,"[257] the free exercise clause arguably demanded that some such provision be made. Stewart's references to officially sponsored prayers in Congress and in the Court's own proceedings[258] were more embarrassing. Unless one is willing to take the long existence of such practices as refuting *Everson*'s entire principle that government may not promote religion, the best answer to Stewart may be contained in the familiar maxim de minimis non curat lex[259] or in the Court's perception that such ceremonial exercises may have lost much of their religious significance.[260]

## V. PASSAGE

On March 26, 1962, Justice Frankfurter lost his greatest judicial battle. Only Justice Harlan joined him in agonized dissent as *Baker v. Carr* repudiated his position that judges could not determine the constitutionality of the apportionment of legislative seats within a state.[261] Frankfurter expanded at great length on the nonjusticiability arguments he had made for three Justices in *Colegrove v. Green*,[262] but Clark and Stewart joined the predictable Brennan, Warren, Black, and Douglas in seeing no reason why arbitrary limitations on voting power should be immune from judicial scrutiny.[263]

[253] *Id.* at 430.

[254] *See* pp. 339–43 *supra* (discussing Everson v. Board of Education, McCollum v. Board of Education, and Zorach v. Clauson). *See also* Katz, *Freedom of Religion and State Neutrality,* 20 U. CHI. L. REV. 426, 438 (1953) ("Devotional exercises in public schools, however simple and nonsectarian, are difficult to reconcile with a rule of neutrality."); Pollak, *Foreword: Public Prayers in Public Schools,* 77 HARV. L. REV. 62, 66-67 (1963) (noting that the test of religious purpose and effect enunciated in the second prayer case, Abington School Dist. v. Schempp, note 251 *supra,* cast doubt on *Zorach* itself).

[255] 370 U.S. at 445.

[256] *See* Kurland, *The Regents' Prayer Case: "Full of Sound and Fury, Signifying . . . ,"* 1962 SUP. CT. REV. 1, 17.

[257] *See* Pollak, *supra* note 254, at 74-77.

[258] 360 U.S. at 446-50.

[259] *See* W. KATZ, *supra* note 249, at 23-24.

[260] *See* 370 U.S. at 435 n.21; Abington School Dist. v. Schempp, 374 U.S. 203, 303-04 (1963) (Brennan, J., concurring).

[261] 369 U.S. 186 (1962). *See also id.* at 266-330 (Frankfurter, J., dissenting). Justice Whittaker, who was about to leave the Court, did not vote, *id.* at 237.

[262] *See* pp. 330-32 *supra.*

[263] *See* 369 U.S. at 251-64 (Clark, J., concurring); *id.* at 265-66 (Stewart, J., concurring).

The persistent notion that certain "political questions" are nonjusticiable has been traced to such hoary decisions as *Marbury v. Madison*[264] and *Luther v. Borden*.[265] Neither opinion, however, can fairly be said to stand for anything more than the unexceptionable proposition that the courts may not interfere with a decision that the law has committed to some other branch of government.[266] Later decisions, building upon *Luther*, had concluded in essence that only Congress could enforce article IV's provision guaranteeing each state "a Republican Form of Government,"[267] and *Coleman v. Miller* had held that only Congress could determine certain questions relating to the amendment process.[268] In each instance the Justices had employed language suggesting a general principle that "political" questions were nonjusticiable, but each decision was readily explainable on more conventional grounds.[269]

For better or worse, the existence of a general political-question doctrine was widely accepted when *Baker* was decided, and Justice Brennan's majority opinion chose to define it restrictively rather than to reject it:

> Prominent on the surface of any case held to involve a political question is found a textually demonstrable constitutional commitment of the issue to a coordinate political department; or a lack of judicially discoverable and manageable standards for resolving it; or the impossibility of deciding without an initial policy determination of a kind clearly for nonjudicial discretion; or the impossibility of a court's undertaking independent resolution without expressing lack of the respect due coordinate branches of government; or an unusual need for unquestioning adherence to a political decision already made; or the potentiality of embarrassment from multifarious pronouncements by various departments on one question.[270]

The *Baker* opinion was widely perceived to have significantly narrowed the political-question doctrine as it had previously been understood.[271] At the very least, the decision to entertain challenges to apportionment practices that had existed since the dawn of the Republic[272] was yet another dramatic indication of the Warren Court's increasing activism in pursuit of Justice Stone's fundamental constitutional values. Moreover, although Frankfurter had not spoken for a majority in *Colegrove*, eyebrows understandably rose at Justice Brennan's conclusion that a long series of later summary decisions rejecting similar challenges was consistent with *Baker*.[273] But it is also arguable that in the course of all this

---

[264] 5 U.S. 137 (1803).

[265] 48 U.S. 1 (1849).

[266] *See* THE FIRST HUNDRED YEARS at 67 n.19, 252-57.

[267] U.S. CONST. art. IV, § 4. *See, e.g.*, Pacific States Tel. & Tel. Co. v. Oregon, *supra* p. 93, note 20.

[268] *See supra* p. 272, note 7.

[269] *See* Henkin, *Is There a "Political Question" Doctrine?*, 85 YALE L.J. 597 (1976).

[270] 369 U.S. at 217.

[271] *See, e.g.*, McCloskey, *Foreword: The Reapportionment Cases*, 76 HARV. L. REV. 54, 59-61 (1962); *see also* the comprehensive review of the political-question field in Scharpf, *Judicial Review and the Political Question: A Functional Analysis*, 75 YALE L.J. 517 (1966).

[272] *See* 369 U.S. at 301-23 (Frankfurter, J., dissenting) (impressively marshaling the history).

[273] *See id.* at 234-37; *id.* at 278-80 (Frankfurter, J., dissenting); P. KURLAND, *supra* note 130, at 149 ("[I]t is difficult to believe that the Court thought it could find an audience ingenuous enough to accept the assertion.").

Justice Brennan lent unfortunate dignity to an untenable concept that had existed before only in stray language in assorted opinions that could be justified on more defensible grounds. I leave criticism of the decision itself to those who take issue with it;[274] I cannot reconcile the dissenters' broad political-question doctrine with *Marbury v. Madison*.[275]

Within a few months Justice Frankfurter was gone. His narrow view of the judicial function, born of the excesses of the *Lochner* period, had long served as a brake on expansive interpretation of political freedoms and of the rights of the accused. His retirement opened the way for completion of the revolution in civil rights and liberties that Justice Stone had proclaimed in 1938.

---

For detailed examination of the precedents see Lucas, *Legislative Apportionment and Representative Government: The Meaning of* Baker v. Carr, 61 MICH. L. REV. 711, 713-41 (1963).

[274] *See, e.g.,* Neal, Baker v. Carr: *Politics in Search of Law,* 1962 SUP. CT. REV. 252, 327 ("an example of the role of fiat in the exercise of judicial power"); A. BICKEL, *supra* note 9, at 183-97.

[275] 5 U.S. 137, 178 (1803) (stressing the need for judicial review in order to keep legislatures within constitutional limitations), THE FIRST HUNDRED YEARS at 66-74. *See also* Henkin, *supra* note 269 *passim;* Wechsler, *supra* note 8, at 7-9 (arguing that "all the [political-question] doctrine can defensibly imply is that the courts are called upon to judge whether the Constitution has committed to another agency of government the autonomous determination of the issue raised").

# 13

# The Real Warren Court

When Felix Frankfurter retired in August 1962, the Supreme Court under Earl Warren had already made a name for itself as a defender of racial equality and the separation of church and state. Over repeated dissents by the Chief Justice and Justices Black, Douglas, and Brennan, however, the majority had declined to stand up effectively for victims of the popular crusade against subversion, and it had generally resisted efforts to extend the procedural protections of the Bill of Rights to state prosecutions.[1]

From the moment Arthur Goldberg took Frankfurter's place in 1962 there was a dramatic shift, for the new Justice joined the four former dissenters to form a dependable majority for greater protection of civil liberties and fair procedure. In the seven years that remained before Warren's retirement, the Court completed the task it had begun in the days of Chief Justice Hughes, making dramatic advances in the fields of equality, free speech, and fair trial.[2]

## I. RACE

The struggle for black equality had been an increasing priority for the Court since the 1930s, and the 1954 decisions outlawing school segregation had been the crowning achievement of the early Warren period.[3] Despite his general reluctance to interfere with legislative judgments, Justice Frankfurter had been a leader in this battle; his successor fit comfortably into this tradition.

---

[1] See chapter 12 *supra*.

[2] See P. KURLAND, POLITICS, THE CONSTITUTION AND THE WARREN COURT 98 (1970) ("To the extent that the Warren Court has opened new frontiers, it has been in the development of the concept of equality as a constitutional standard.").

[3] See pp. 249-51, 322-25, 358-60, 377-85 *supra*.

## A.   Government Abuse

Without further elucidation, the Court in a series of brief opinions reaffirmed its essentially unexplained conclusion that the principle of *Brown v. Board of Education* forbade state-ordered racial segregation of such facilities as restaurants,[4] courtrooms,[5] and parks.[6] A new theory emerged, however, when the Court extended *Brown* to invalidate laws forbidding interracial cohabitation and marriage in *McLaughlin v. Florida*[7] and *Loving v. Virginia.*[8] No longer was it necessary to find that the law made blacks worse off than whites, wrote Justice White in *McLaughlin;* all racial classifications were " 'constitutionally suspect,' " and there was no "overriding statutory purpose" to justify singling out interracial cohabitation.[9] *Shelley v. Kraemer* had suggested a way to reconcile this conclusion with a text forbidding only inequality,[10] but neither opinion bothered to take it.[11]

In one of his first opinions for the Court, Justice Goldberg gave vent to the Court's impatience with continued delays in enforcing the *Brown* decree itself: "*Brown* never contemplated that the concept of 'deliberate speed' would countenance indefinite delay in elimination of racial barriers in schools, let alone other public facilities not involving the same physical problems or comparable conditions."[12] Public parks, the Court concluded, must be desegregated forthwith: "Desegregation of parks and other recreational facilities does not present the same kinds of cognizable difficulties inhering in elimination of racial classifications in schools, at which attendance is compulsory, the adequacy of teachers and facilities crucial, and questions of geographic assignment often of major significance."[13] By 1965 the Court unanimously declared that it was too late to ask more time even in the school context: "Delays in desegregating school systems are no longer tolerable."[14]

---

[4]*E.g.,* Peterson v. Greenville, 373 U.S. 244 (1963) (Warren, C. J.); Lombard v. Louisiana, 373 U.S. 267 (1963) (Warren, C. J.).

[5]Johnson v. Virginia, 373 U.S. 61 (1963) (per curiam).

[6]Wright v. Georgia, 373 U.S. 284 (1963) (Warren, C. J.); Watson v. Memphis, 373 U.S. 526 (1963) (Goldberg, J.).

[7]379 U.S. 184 (1964) (White, J.).

[8]388 U.S. 1 (1967) (Warren, C. J.).

[9]379 U.S. at 188–94. *See also Loving,* 388 U.S. at 11: "At the very least, the Equal Protection Clause demands that racial classifications, especially suspect in criminal statutes, be subjected to the 'most rigid scrutiny'" (citing Korematsu v. United States, 323 U.S. at 216 (upholding the deportation of citizens of Japanese descent from the West Coast), pp. 289-92 *supra,* where this exacting standard had been enunciated and ignored). Justice Stewart (joined by Douglas in the first case) went further: "I think it is simply not possible for a state law to be valid under our Constitution which makes the criminality of an act depend upon the race of the actor." *McLaughlin,* 379 U.S. at 198 (Stewart, J., concurring); *Loving,* 388 U.S. at 13 (Stewart, J., concurring).

[10]Blacks were disfavored with respect to marrying or living with whites, and vice versa. Thus the laws under attack discriminated against members of both races, and two wrongs do not generally make a right. *See Shelley,* 334 U.S. at 22 ("Equal protection of the laws is not achieved through indiscriminate imposition of inequalities."), pp. 358-60 *supra. See also* THE FIRST HUNDRED YEARS at 387-90 (discussing Pace v. Alabama, 106 U.S. 583 (1883), which was overruled in *McLaughlin*).

[11]The Court in *Loving* went on to hold that the miscegenation law also deprived "all the State's citizens of liberty without due process of law," 388 U.S. at 12. Not cited was Lochner v. New York, pp. 47-50 *supra,* on whose theory this unnecessary conclusion was based.

[12]Watson v. Memphis, 373 U.S. 526, 530 (1963).

[13]*Id.* at 532.

[14]Bradley v. School Board, 382 U.S. 103, 105 (1965) (per curiam) (also holding alleged faculty segregation relevant to the adequacy of a desegregation plan); Rogers v. Paul, 382 U.S. 198, 199 (1965) (per curiam) (order-

In other cases the problem was not when but how to comply with the constitutional ban on state segregation. Rather than desegregate its public schools, Prince Edward County, Virginia, had closed them entirely while providing subsidies for racially segregated private schools. In *Griffin v. County School Board* the Court held this course unconstitutional. "Whatever nonracial grounds might support a State's allowing a county to abandon public schools," wrote Justice Black, "the object must be a constitutional one, and grounds of race and opposition to desegregation do not qualify as constitutional." By "closing the Prince Edward schools and meanwhile contributing to the support of the private segregated white schools that took their place," public authorities had "denied petitioners the equal protection of the laws." [15]

Justice Black himself identified the soft spot in this reasoning shortly after Warren's retirement in holding that a city's alleged desire to avoid integration did not invalidate a decision to close its swimming pools altogether. "[N]either the Fourteenth Amendment nor any Act of Congress purports to impose an affirmative duty on a State . . . to operate swimming pools," and the record "shows no state action affecting blacks differently from whites." [16] Similarly, the mere closing of the schools in *Griffin* left whites and blacks alike without public education; though there may have been no doubt about its motivation, it did not treat blacks and whites differently on the basis of race.

Justice Black also attempted to make something in *Griffin* of the fact that public schools were open in other Virginia counties while they were closed in Prince Edward. [17] Virginia counties decided for themselves whether or not to operate public schools, however; [18] no single government had decided to treat various counties differently, and home rule was a long-standing democratic principle. [19]

More promising was Justice Black's explanation in the later case that *Griffin* had been based on the state's subsidy of segregated private schools, which had played a secondary role in the *Griffin* opinion. "[T]he *Griffin* case," wrote Black, "simply treated the school program for what it was—an operation of Prince Edward County schools under a thinly disguised 'private' school system actually planned and carried out by the State and the county to maintain segregated education with public funds." [20] Though there would be

---

ing immediate admission of black pupils to the only school in which certain courses were offered). For a progress report on the first ten years after *Brown* see Bickel, *The Decade of School Desegregation: Progress and Prospects*, 64 COLUM. L. REV. 193 (1964) (concluding, at 209, that "[t]he resistant minority has been politically reduced to manageable numbers and to a manageable temper, and it is now time for . . . enforcement in earnest").

[15] 377 U.S. 218, 231-32 (1964).

[16] Palmer v. Thompson, 403 U.S. 217, 220, 225 (1971) (over dissents by Douglas, Brennan, White, and Marshall). For the argument that even in this situation the state had discriminated against blacks by stigmatizing them, see *id.* at 265-68 ("[T]he closed pools stand as mute reminders to the community of the official view of Negro inferiority."). *Accord* Brest, Palmer v. Thompson: *An Approach to the Problem of Unconstitutional Legislative Motive*, 1971 SUP. CT. REV. 95, 133.

[17] 377 U.S. at 230-31.

[18] *Id.* at 229-30.

[19] *See* Cox, *Foreword: Constitutional Adjudication and the Promotion of Human Rights*, 80 HARV. L. REV. 91, 93 (1966) (classifying the *Prince Edward* case with Griffin v. Illinois, pp. 403-05 *supra* (where the Court had required provision of a free transcript for an indigent's appeal) as evidence of a tendency to interpret the equal protection clause to "impose affirmative obligations upon the states"); Kurland, *Foreword: "Equal in Origin and Equal in Title to the Legislative and Executive Branches of the Government*," 78 HARV. L. REV. 143, 157 (1964): "[W]hat the violation [in *Prince Edward*] consisted of is not made clear."

[20] *Palmer*, 403 U.S. at 222.

difficulties in distinguishing subsidies from the state's mere refusal to punish private actors for discrimination,[21] precedents under the religion clauses lent some support to Black's new theory. If subsidies made the state responsible for religious instruction given by private schools,[22] they might make it responsible for segregation of those schools as well.[23]

*Green v. County School Board* struck down yet another response to the *Brown* decision, the so-called freedom-of-choice plan permitting pupils in formerly segregated schools to attend whichever school they chose.[24] It was not enough, wrote Justice Brennan, that children were no longer excluded from any school on grounds of race. *Brown* had demanded "transition to a unitary, nonracial system of public education"; the board must take steps "to convert promptly to a system without a 'white' school and a 'Negro' school, but just schools."[25]

Did the Court mean to suggest that the Constitution required the state to assure that blacks and whites were represented in each school in proportion to their percentages of the district's population? That would have been revolutionary; the mere failure to equalize black and white representation had never been equated with state discrimination on grounds of race.[26] The Court would ultimately confirm that it had meant no such thing,[27] and its repeated references in *Green* to remedying past discrimination[28] furnish a more traditional explanation. Since every child who did not express a choice remained in the school to which the invalid segregation law had assigned him,[29] inertia worked to perpetuate the effects of earlier unconstitutional action. Just as an injunction against future tres-

---

[21] *See, e.g.,* Norwood v. Harrison, 413 U.S. 455 (1973) (state may not lend textbooks to pupils in segregated private schools); Gilmore v. Montgomery, 417 U.S. 556 (1974) (city need not exclude segregated groups from use of public park). *See also* Lewis, *The Meaning of State Action,* 60 COLUM. L. REV. 1083, 1103 (1960) ("It is assumed that the state's general common law and statutory structure under which its people carry on their private affairs . . . is not such state assistance as would transform private conduct into state action. . . .").

[22] *See, e.g.,* McCollum v. Board of Education, pp. 342-43 *supra* (striking down a program of private religious instruction on public property). *See also* the later decisions on state aid to parochial schools discussed at pp. 528-35 *infra.*

[23] *But see* Freed & Polsby, *Race, Religion, and Public Policy:* Bob Jones University v. United States, 1983 SUP. CT. REV. 1, 12-17 (noting the difficulty of reconciling this conclusion with the general principle that the equal protection clause forbids only *deliberate* state discrimination; *see* pp. 488-93 *infra* (discussing Washington v. Davis)):

> If one were seriously to pursue the notion that "state action," in the constitutional sense, ought to reach conduct that is any way touched or facilitated by the tax laws, one would lose the capacity for a pluralistic society made possible by observing the distinction between public and private institutions.

Not only the reasoning but also the discussion of remedies in *Griffin,* moreover, suggests that the Court's original theory was broader. An injunction against further subsidies to segregated schools would have ended state responsibility for continued segregation; yet over two dissents the Court expressly advised the district judge he could order the public schools reopened as well. *See* 377 U.S. at 232-34.

[24] 391 U.S. 430, 434 (1968).

[25] *Id.* at 436, 442. *Accord* Raney v. Board of Education, 391 U.S. 443 (1968) (Brennan, J.).

[26] *See, e.g.,* Lassiter v. Northampton Board of Elections, pp. 384-85 *supra* (upholding literacy test for voting).

[27] *See* Washington v. Davis, pp. 488-93 *infra* (holding a test for applicants for police force not invalid simply because failed by higher percentage of blacks than whites).

[28] *See* 391 U.S. at 437-41.

[29] *See id.* at 434.

passes is inadequate to redress those committed in the past, rejection of "freedom of choice" could be defended as necessary to eliminate the effects of past de jure segregation.[30]

More difficult to defend on this ground was the companion decision in *Monroe v. Board of Commissioners*, striking down a plan that redrew district boundaries on neighborhood lines assumed to be racially neutral and then permitted transfer to other districts at a pupil's request:

> [T]he "free-transfer" option has permitted the "considerable number" of white or Negro students in at least two of the zones to return, at the implicit invitation of the Board, to the comfortable security of the old, established discriminatory pattern. . . . [I]f it cannot be shown that such a plan will further rather than delay conversion to a unitary, nonracial, nondiscriminatory school system, it must be held unacceptable.[31]

One might have thought that by redrawing district lines on a nonracial basis the city had eliminated the effects of its past illegal practice; resegregation seemed attributable to individual choice rather than state direction.[32]

*Griffin* and *Monroe* were symptomatic of a general tendency toward looseness during the later Warren years in attributing racially discriminatory actions to the states. In *Evans v. Newton*,[33] for example, the Court found a city still responsible for segregation of a park after it had resigned as trustee: "The momentum it acquired as a public facility is certainly not dissipated ipso facto by the appointment of 'private' trustees."[34] Justice Douglas attempted to buttress this conclusion by assuming that the city continued to maintain the park, although there was apparently nothing in the record to support the assumption.[35] He also added, in a startling extension of the company town principle enunciated in *Marsh v. Alabama*,[36] that "[t]he service rendered even by a private park of this character is municipal in nature."[37] As Justice Harlan noted in dissent, the same theory would make private schools the "state" for fourteenth amendment purposes.[38] Harlan seemed to hit the nail on the head: "This decision . . . is more the product of human impulses, which I fully share, than of solid constitutional thinking."[39]

Harlan's fears seemed confirmed when the public-function theory was extended to an

---

[30] *See* Brest, *Foreword: In Defense of the Antidiscrimination Principle*, 90 HARV. L. REV. 1, 33 (1976) (calling *Green* for this reason "the Court's last easy school desegregation case").

[31] 391 U.S. 450, 458-59 (1968) (Brennan, J.).

[32] Far easier to strike down were provisions permitting voluntary transfer only from a school in which the pupil seeking transfer was in a racial minority: "Classifications based on race for purposes of transfers between public schools . . . violate the Equal Protection Clause." Goss v. Board of Education, 373 U.S. 683, 687 (1963) (Clark, J.).

[33] 382 U.S. 296 (1966).

[34] *Id.* at 301.

[35] *See id.* at 318 (Harlan, J., dissenting).

[36] *See* pp. 324-25 *supra*.

[37] 382 U.S. at 301.

[38] *Id.* at 321-22 (Harlan, J., dissenting). Justice Stewart joined Harlan's dissent; Black and White also dissociated themselves from Douglas's reasoning. *See id.* at 302-12 (White, J., concurring on the basis that state law encouraged private segregation); *id.* at 312-15 (Black, J., dissenting).

[39] *Id.* at 315.

ordinary shopping center in *Amalgamated Food Employees Union v. Logan Valley Plaza* in 1968, written by the newly appointed Justice Thurgood Marshall.[40] Justice Black, author of the doctrine, dissented vigorously, as he had in *Evans*.[41] Justice White dissented too,[42] while Harlan thought the question should not be decided;[43] it was not long (though it was after Warren's retirement) before *Logan Valley* was overruled.[44]

Most distressing of all these decisions, perhaps, was *Reitman v. Mulkey*,[45] where Justice White (over dissents by Harlan, Black, Clark, and Stewart) came perilously close to holding that a state could not repeal fair-housing laws once it had enacted them. The state court had found that a constitutional amendment forbidding the enactment of such laws "authorized" and "encouraged" private segregation[46]—as any repeal would do—and the Supreme Court found no reason to upset its finding.[47] Though the opinion expressly disclaimed any intention of outlawing mere repeal,[48] it flailed ineffectively in search of a distinction. Not long afterward the Court explained with some plausibility that imposing special procedural obstacles to the enactment of laws limiting private discrimination placed the potential beneficiaries of such laws at a disadvantage.[49]

Surveying the many liberties the Warren Court had taken in this area, one prominent observer concluded that "the 'state action' doctrine is in trouble" and applauded the result: "If one race is . . . substantially worse off than others with respect to anything with which law commonly deals, then 'equal protection of the laws' is not being extended to that race unless and until every prudent affirmative use of law is being made toward remedying the inequality."[50] It was noteworthy, however, that the Court carefully avoided any explicit endorsement of this radical principle; even its most extreme results were carefully couched in terms of asserted unequal treatment by the state itself.[51]

In sharp contrast to the Court's overall zeal to root out any hint of official racial discrimination was its apparent approval, in refusing to investigate a prosecutor's motive for challenging a potential juror in *Swain v. Alabama,* of peremptory exclusion on the basis of race.[52] Twenty years later, with the concurrence of the author of this suggestion, the Court

---

[40] 391 U.S. 308 (1968).

[41] *Id.* at 327-33.

[42] *Id.* at 337-40.

[43] *Id.* at 333-37.

[44] Hudgens v. NLRB, 424 U.S. 507 (1976) (Stewart, J., over two dissents).

[45] 387 U.S. 369 (1967).

[46] *Id.* at 375.

[47] *Id.* at 376, 379.

[48] *Id.* at 376-78.

[49] *See* Hunter v. Erickson, 393 U.S. 385 (1969) (White, J., over Black's dissent) (striking down a city charter provision requiring referenda on fair-housing ordinances). This thesis had been made explicit before *Hunter* by Charles Black, *Foreword: "State Action," Equal Protection, and California's Proposition 14*, 81 HARV. L. REV. 69, 74-83 (1967).

[50] Black, *supra* note 49, at 84-91, 97. *Accord* Karst & Horowitz, Reitman v. Mulkey: *A Telophase of Substantive Equal Protection,* 1967 SUP. CT. REV. 39 (finding the seeds of such a duty implicit in *Reitman* and earlier decisions); Miller, *Toward a Concept of Constitutional Duty,* 1968 SUP. CT. REV. 199.

[51] *See also* pp. 139-43 *supra* (discussing the analogous problem whether a state deprives persons of property within the meaning of the due process clauses by failing to protect them against trespass); Currie, *Positive and Negative Constitutional Rights,* 53 U. CHI. L. REV. 864, 886-88 (1986).

[52] 380 U.S. 202, 212, 220-21 (1965) (White, J., over a Goldberg dissent on other grounds joined by Warren and Douglas).

appropriately abandoned it: "[T]he Equal Protection Clause forbids the prosecutor to challenge potential jurors solely on account of their race or on the assumption that black jurors as a group will be unable impartially to consider the State's case against a black defendant."[53] *Swain* was an aberration; in general the later Warren Court was if anything too eager to find that the state had impermissibly discriminated on grounds of race.

## B. Self-help

After Frankfurter's departure the Court continued to promote the power of blacks to assert their own interests as well. *Gomillion v. Lightfoot* had already protected their right to participate in municipal elections,[54] *NAACP v. Alabama* their freedom of association.[55] *NAACP v. Button*, decided a few months after Frankfurter left the bench, protected their right to sue.[56]

The NAACP challenged a package of Virginia statutes condemning on the basis of the long-standing antipathy to fomenting litigation the association's practice of encouraging and underwriting suits challenging segregation in public schools. The state was wrong, the majority concluded, in equating organized civil rights litigation with ambulance chasing. As "a means for achieving the lawful objectives of equality of treatment . . . for the members of the Negro community," such litigation was "a form of political expression." Indeed "under the conditions of modern government, litigation may well be the sole practicable avenue open to a minority to petition for redress of grievances."[57] As construed by the state court, the statute made it a crime for one person to "advise[] another that his legal rights have been infringed and refer[] him to a particular attorney or group of attorneys." It thus tended to "smother[] . . . discussion looking to the eventual institution of litigation on behalf of the rights of members of an unpopular minority."[58] In finding no compelling interest to justify this serious limitation of expression and association,[59] the opinion despite its disclaimers[60] raised interesting questions as to why attorneys should ever be forbidden to urge people to assert their legal rights.[61]

Other forms of expression in pursuit of racial equality continued to be protected as

---

[53] Batson v. Kentucky, 476 U.S. 79, 89 (1986) (over two dissents). For doubts as to the appropriateness of this appealing decision see Pizzi, Batson v. Kentucky: *Curing the Disease But Killing the Patient*, 1987 SUP. CT. REV. 97.

[54] *See* pp. 381-82 *supra*.

[55] *See* pp. 382-83 *supra*.

[56] 371 U.S. 415 (1963) (Brennan, J.).

[57] *Id.* at 430-31.

[58] *Id.* at 434.

[59] *Id.* at 438-45.

[60] *See id.* at 439-44 (arguing that traditional laws against barratry, champerty, and maintenance were directed at malicious lawsuits or those filed for pecuniary gain).

[61] The three remaining Justices who had typically joined Frankfurter in restrained application of first amendment freedoms dissented, protesting that the state's interests were substantial and that the Court was applying a double standard. *See* 371 U.S. at 448-70 (Harlan, J., joined by Clark and Stewart, dissenting). Had Whittaker and Frankfurter still sat, the result might well have been otherwise. *See also* Brotherhood of Railroad Trainmen v. Virginia, 377 U.S. 1 (1964) (Black, J.), and United Mine Workers v. Illinois State Bar Ass'n, 389 U.S. 217 (1967) (Black, J.) (extending the *Button* decision to unions seeking to assure legal representation for injured members):

well. Without embracing *Shelley v. Kraemer*'s unsettling implication that a restaurant owner could not call the police to enforce a private policy of discrimination,[62] the Justices found one excuse after another for setting aside every sit-in conviction that was brought before them.[63] *Edwards v. South Carolina* and *Cox v. Louisiana* established that the ever-

---

It cannot be seriously doubted that the First Amendment's guarantees of free speech, petition and assembly give railroad workers the right to gather together for the lawful purpose of helping and advising one another in asserting the rights Congress gave them in the Safety Appliance Act and the Federal Employers' Liability Act.

*Trainmen*, 377 U.S. at 5. Clark and Harlan dissented in the first case ("[p]ersonal injury litigation is not a form of political expression, but rather a procedure for the settlement of damage claims"), *id.* at 10, and Stewart did not sit, *id.* at 8. Harlan dissented in the second case as well, *Mine Workers*, 389 U.S. at 225-34. *See* P. KURLAND, *supra* note 2, at 165-66 (arguing that if the states "had not attempted to utilize the ordinary powers over conduct of the bar to wage war on desegregation," the *Trainmen* decision might never have been reached).

[62] *See* pp. 358-60 *supra* (discussing *Shelley*). Justice Douglas was willing to take this position. *See* Lombard v. Louisiana, 373 U.S. 267, 274-83 (1963) (Douglas, J., concurring); Bell v. Maryland, 378 U.S. 226, 255-60 (1964) (Douglas, J., dissenting). Black, Harlan, and White, *see Bell*, 378 U.S. at 327-28 (dissenting opinion), squarely rejected it: "It would betray our whole plan for a tranquil and orderly society to say that a citizen, because of his personal prejudices, . . . is cast outside the law's protection and cannot call for the aid of officers sworn to uphold the law and preserve the peace." Douglas, Goldberg, and Warren also endorsed the arguments against discrimination by the restaurateur himself that the first Justice Harlan had made in the Civil Rights Cases, 109 U.S. 3 (1883), THE FIRST HUNDRED YEARS at 398-401. *See Lombard*, 373 U.S. at 274-83 (Douglas, J., concurring); *Bell*, 378 U.S. at 286-318 (Goldberg, J., joined by Warren and in part by Douglas, concurring).

[63] Peterson v. Greenville, 373 U.S. 244 (1963) (Warren, C. J.), attributed a manager's decision to call the police to an ordinance requiring segregation. Justice Harlan, concurring on the facts, feared that the Court's opinion effectively deprived the owner of the right to discriminate in any state whose law required him to, *id.* at 252. Lombard v. Louisiana, 373 U.S. 267 (1963) (Warren, C. J.), found the same controlling significance in an informally stated municipal policy of segregation, over a Harlan dissent, *id.* at 253-55, concluding that the policy statements left owners free to do as they pleased. *See* Lewis, *The Sit-in Cases: Great Expectations*, 1963 SUP. CT. REV. 101, 106, 112 (noting the irony of the Court's "tendency to make a segregation law operate as an antidiscrimination law" but concluding that "[i]f private choice in the sit-in context is left untouched by the Fourteenth Amendment, the Court is justified in taking those steps procedurally available to it to insure that the choice preserved is as private as it can be"). Shuttlesworth v. Birmingham, 373 U.S. 262 (1963) (Warren, C. J.), forbade conviction for aiding and abetting a sit-in that was itself constitutionally protected, though Harlan (concurring in part of other grounds, *id.* at 258-61) found ample evidence of incitement to sit-ins that had not been found protected. Griffin v. Maryland, 378 U.S. 130 (1964) (Warren, C. J.), held the state responsible for discrimination in a private amusement park because the employee who told the petitioners to leave had been made a deputy sheriff, over a dissent by Harlan, Black, and White, *id.* at 138, arguing that the state's involvement "was no different from what it would have been had the arrests been made by a regular policeman" at the owner's request. Barr v. Columbia, 378 U.S. 146 (1964) (Black, J.), held that the mere presence of blacks at a segregated lunch counter could not be taken as evidence of a breach of the peace. Robinson v. Florida, 378 U.S. 153 (1964) (Black, J.), found that a state rule requiring segregated washrooms in restaurants involved the state in segregation of food service itself. Bell v. Maryland, 378 U.S. 226 (1964) (Brennan, J., over a dissent by Black, Harlan, and White), remanded for determination whether passage of a state law forbidding discrimination in restaurants immunized earlier trespasses from prosecution. Bouie v. Columbia, 378 U.S. 347 (1964) (Brennan, J., over the same three dissents), held that a statute forbidding "entry upon the lands of another" after notice not to enter did not give fair warning to persons convicted of *remaining* in a restaurant after having been told to leave. Hamm v. Rock Hill, 379 U.S. 306 (1964) (Clark, J.), put an end to the whole business by holding that enactment of the federal Civil Rights Act forbidding discrimination in public accommodations precluded prosecution for trespasses committed before its passage. Justice Stewart joined the three *Bell* dissenters in disagreeing with *Hamm*, *id.* at 326-27, while both Black and Harlan doubted Congress's power to legalize past trespasses—the latter noting the difficulty of showing that past convictions had any effect on present interstate commerce, *id.* at 320, 325. *See* Paulsen, *The Sit-in Cases of 1964: "But Answer Came There None,"* 1964 SUP. CT. REV. 137; P.

present risk of violence did not justify forbidding peaceful demonstrations.[64] Three Justices even argued in *Brown v. Louisiana* that freedom of speech embraced the right to sit or stand in a public library to protest segregation in library services.[65] Justice Black, vigorous defender of civil liberties though he was, objected that "the First Amendment . . . does not guarantee to any person the right to use someone else's property, even that owned by government and dedicated to other purposes, as a stage to express dissident ideas."[66] Harlan, Clark, and Stewart agreed with Black, and White joined them in *Adderley v. Florida* to hold that the first amendment gave no right to demonstrate on jailhouse grounds.[67] "The State," wrote Black for the Court, "no less than a private owner of property, has power to preserve the property under its control for the use to which it is lawfully dedicated."[68] The public forum doctrine of *Schneider v. State*[69] had opened such public property as streets and parks to speakers on grounds of history and necessity, but it had its limits. "Traditionally," said Justice Black, "state capitol grounds are open to the public. Jails, built for security purposes, are not."[70]

The historical approach taken in *Adderley* has been criticized on the ground that, as a later decision would suggest, the extent of the right to speak on government property ought to be determined by a balance of opposing interests.[71] The difficulty with this argument is that it further elides the basic distinction between government interference with the exercise of a right and government failure to subsidize that exercise. The public forum doctrine was rationalized with this distinction by the notion of a traditional public easement in streets and parks that transformed what might otherwise have been viewed as a refusal to subsidize into governmental interference with private rights. That this conclusion may have been motivated in part by the perception that freedom of speech is worthless without a meaningful opportunity to reach one's audience does not justify abandoning

---

KURLAND, *supra* note 2, at 162 ("It would be helpful if these and other similar cases could be labeled 'good for use in sit-in cases only.'").

[64] *See Edwards*, 372 U.S. 229 (1963) (Stewart, J., over a dissent by Clark arguing that the particular demonstration had posed a serious danger of disorder); *Cox*, 379 U.S. 536, 544-51 (1965) (Goldberg, J.). *See also* Cox v. Louisiana (II), 379 U.S. 559 (1965) (Goldberg, J.) (recognizing the state's power to forbid demonstrations near a courthouse intended to influence courts in the discharge of their duties); Cameron v. Johnson, 390 U.S. 611, 616 (1968) (Brennan, J.) (upholding a statute forbidding picketing that "obstruct[ed] or unreasonably interfere[d] with free ingress or egress to or from . . . courthouses"). For the view that the two *Cox* decisions represented an unhealthy retreat from earlier broad notions of the right to speak in public places see Kalven, *The Concept of the Public Forum:* Cox v. Louisiana, 1965 SUP. CT. REV. 1.

[65] 383 U.S. 131, 141-43 (1966) (opinion of Fortas, J., joined by Warren and Douglas) (adding that there was no evidence of breach of the peace). Brennan, *id.* at 143-50, joined in voiding the conviction on the ground that the statute was unconstitutionally broad, White, *id.* at 150-51, on the ground that "petitioners were asked to leave the library because they were Negroes."

[66] 383 U.S. at 166 (Black, J., dissenting). *Cf.* Bell v. Maryland, 378 U.S. 226, 318-46 (1964) (Black, J., joined by Harlan and White, dissenting) (denying that freedom of speech included the right to intrude on *private* property for communicative purposes).

[67] 385 U.S. 39 (1966).

[68] *Id.* at 47.

[69] *See* pp. 263-66 *supra*.

[70] 385 U.S. at 41. Douglas, Warren, Brennan, and Fortas, *id.* at 48-56, dissented.

[71] *See* Stone, *Fora Americana: Speech in Public Places*, 1974 SUP. CT. REV. 233, 245-56 (quoting with approval from Grayned v. Rockford, 408 U.S. 104, 116 (1972), which had involved public streets: "'The crucial question is whether the manner of expression is basically incompatible with the normal activity of a particular place at a particular time.'").

the distinction itself; if it did the government might have to make money as well as real estate available to those too impecunious to communicate effectively on their own.[72]

Additional barriers to black voting fell too. Unable to perceive any legitimate reason for a state law requiring ballots to disclose the race of each candidate, the Court struck it down as serving an impermissible purpose.[73] Similarly, without questioning the validity of literacy tests in the abstract, the Justices invalidated a requirement that persons seeking to register "give a reasonable interpretation" of any section of the state or federal Constitution "when read to [them] by the registrar."[74] Not only was there abundant evidence that this requirement had been administered so as to discriminate against blacks. The district court had found that the provision itself "vested in the voting registrars a virtually uncontrolled discretion as to who should vote," and it offended the fifteenth amendment "to subject citizens to such an arbitrary power."[75]

More novel was the split decision in *Harper v. Virginia Board of Elections* invalidating the traditional requirement that poll taxes be paid as a condition of voting.[76] Whatever one's suspicions, the state's legitimate interest in collecting the revenue[77] made it difficult to dismiss this requirement, as the earlier grandfather clauses had been dismissed, as a mere subterfuge to disenfranchise black voters.[78] Nor, despite the analogy to the question of free transcripts in *Griffin v. Illinois*,[79] did Justice Douglas's hints that the poll tax discriminated against the poor[80] ring true; as Justice Harlan had protested in that case, the state imposed identical conditions on rich and poor alike.[81] Yet Douglas was convincing in concluding that voting was a "fundamental right" in light of the precedents[82] and that

---

[72] *See* pp. 263-66 *supra* (discussing Schneider v. State).

[73] Anderson v. Martin, 375 U.S. 399, 403 (1964) (Clark, J.). *See also id.* at 402 ("The vice lies . . . in the placing of the power of the State behind a racial classification that induces racial prejudice at the polls."). *Cf.* Guinn v. United States, pp. 106-07 *supra* (invalidating grandfather clause found to serve no purpose other than exclusion of black voters).

[74] Louisiana v. United States, 380 U.S. 145, 149 (1965) (Black, J.).

[75] *Id.* at 150, 153. Cf. Cox v. Louisiana (I), 379 U.S. 536, 555-58 (1965) (Goldberg, J.), which in addition to its holding respecting the right to demonstrate, *see* note 64 *supra* and accompanying text, reaffirmed the longstanding doctrine, *see* pp. 261-62 *supra* (discussing Schneider v. State), that executive officials could not be given unbridled discretion to determine who was entitled to use streets and parks for speech purposes.

[76] 383 U.S. 663 (1966). Black, Harlan, and Stewart dissented, *id.* at 670-86. The twenty-fourth amendment had outlawed poll taxes as a condition of voting in federal elections in 1964; *Harper* struck them down as a condition of voting in state elections as well.

[77] *See id.* at 674 (Black, J., dissenting) (adding that it was also rational for the state to believe that "voters who pay a poll tax will be interested in furthering the State's welfare when they vote.") Justice Harlan echoed the latter argument, *id.* at 684-85.

[78] *See id.* at 666 n.3 ("While the 'Virginia poll tax was born of a desire to disenfranchise the Negro,' . . . we do not stop to determine whether on this record the Virginia tax in its modern setting serves the same end."). *Cf.* Guinn v. United States, pp. 106-07 *supra*.

[79] *See* pp. 403-05 *supra*.

[80] *See* 383 U.S. at 668 ("Wealth, like race, creed, or color, is not germane to one's ability to participate intelligently in the electoral process. Lines drawn on the basis of wealth or property, like those of race, . . . are traditionally disfavored.").

[81] *See Griffin*, 351 U.S. at 34-36 (Harlan, J., dissenting).

[82] *See* 383 U.S. at 667 (quoting from Reynolds v. Sims, 337 U.S. 533, 561-62 (1964), pp. 429-32 *infra*) ("'Undoubtedly, the right of suffrage is a fundamental matter in a free and democratic society'"); 383 U.S. at 670 (citing Skinner v. Oklahoma, p. 288 *supra* (right of reproduction)).

the state's interests were not sufficiently compelling to justify making payment of taxes a condition of its exercise.[83]

## C. Government Support

Before Chief Justice Warren retired, the Court had thus done a great deal in the name of the Constitution to protect the right of blacks to help themselves[84] as well as to shield them from governmental abuse. There are limits, however, to what the Constitution itself could fairly be said to do; and beyond those limits lay additional racial discrimination. Affirmative government support was needed if blacks were to be treated fairly, and legislatures had begun to provide it. The Court found no constitutional obstacles to their doing so.

Upholding state laws forbidding racial discrimination in private employment was easy; economic due process had gone out of the vocabulary a quarter century before.[85] Sustaining federal prohibition of discrimination in hotels, restaurants, and other "public accommodations" under the commerce power required the Court only to construct more of those embarrassing for-want-of-a-nail causal chains that had been familiar since the revolution of the 1930s;[86] the Court's subsequent endorsement of the first Harlan's theory that private discrimination was a "badge of slavery" that Congress could forbid without regard to state action[87] was as unnecessary as it was doubtful.[88]

*Katzenbach v. Morgan* presented a more interesting question. New York law limited the vote to persons literate in English, but Congress had prohibited application of such

[83] *See* 383 U.S. at 670 ("[T]he right to vote is too precious, too fundamental to be so burdened or conditioned."). For the revelation that the Court was about to uphold the poll tax in *Harper* until Justice Goldberg circulated a vigorous draft dissent, see Schwartz, *More Unpublished Warren Court Opinions*, 1986 SUP. CT. REV. 317, 318-35.

[84] *See also* New York Times Co. v. Sullivan, *infra* pp. 438-39; Bond v. Floyd, *infra* pp. 439-40.

[85] Due process was not even mentioned when the Court unanimously rejected a commerce clause objection to applying a state antidiscrimination law to the hiring of an interstate airline pilot in Colorado Anti-Discrimination Commission v. Continental Air Lines, 372 U.S. 714 (1963) (Black, J.). Hall v. DeCuir, 95 U.S. 485 (1878), THE FIRST HUNDRED YEARS at 411, which had held a state could not forbid segregated seating of passengers on an interstate ship, was distinguished on the grounds that hiring even for an interstate job was "a much more localized matter than the transporting of passengers from State to State" and that the invalidity of laws *requiring* racial discrimination obviated the risk of inconsistent state regulations that *Hall* had found decisive. For the decline of substantive due process see pp. 236, 239-40 *supra*.

[86] Heart of Atlanta Motel v. United States, 379 U.S. 241, 253 (1964) (Clark, J.) (citing testimony that the difficulty of finding lodging "had the effect of discouraging travel on the part of a substantial portion of the Negro community"); Katzenbach v. McClung, 379 U.S. 294, 299-300 (1964) (Clark, J.) (arguing that "[t]he fewer customers a restaurant enjoys the less food it sells and consequently the less it buys" from other states); Daniel v. Paul, 395 U.S. 298, 304-05 (1969) (Brennan, J., over a dissent by Black) (assuming that some of a restaurant's customers were interstate travelers and taking judicial notice of the fact that it bought food from other states). *See* P. KURLAND, *supra* note 2, at 138-39 (criticizing *McClung*: "Since people tend to eat . . . wherever they happen to be, it is not quite clear how interstate commerce would be enhanced by this compelled nondiscrimination."). For earlier examples of similar reasoning see pp. 236-38 *supra* (discussing, inter alia, Wickard v. Filburn).

[87] Jones v. Alfred H. Mayer Co., 392 U.S. 409, 437-44 (1968) (Stewart, J., over a dissent by Harlan and White not reaching the constitutional question). *See also* The Civil Rights Cases, 109 U.S. 3, 32-43 (1883) (Harlan, J., dissenting).

[88] *See* THE FIRST HUNDRED YEARS at 400-01; 6 C. FAIRMAN, HISTORY OF THE SUPREME COURT OF THE UNITED STATES ch. 19 (1971).

limitations to those who had completed six years of schooling in Puerto Rico. Without deciding whether the state law denied equal protection to individuals literate in Spanish, seven Justices voted to uphold the federal statute under § 5 of the fourteenth amendment.[89]

Section 5, as Harlan insisted in dissent, empowers Congress only to enforce the fourteenth amendment itself, not "to define the *substantive* scope of the Amendment." Absent a violation of the amendment's own provisions, he contended, there was nothing for Congress to enforce; and the Court did not say that the requirement of English literacy was unconstitutional.[90] A series of immaculate nineteenth-century decisions culminating in the *Civil Rights Cases* had confirmed Harlan's basic point that § 5 did not authorize Congress simply to add to its prohibitions,[91] and there was unfortunate language in the majority opinion suggesting a degree of deference to a congressional determination of the reach of the amendment that seemed difficult to reconcile with this position:

> [I]t is enough that we perceive a basis on which Congress might predicate a judgment that the application of New York's English literacy requirement to deny the right to vote to a person with a sixth grade education in Puerto Rican schools . . . constituted an invidious discrimination in violation of the Equal Protection Clause.[92]

What Harlan may have slighted was the possibility that the ban on literacy requirements restricted to English might be an appropriate means of enforcing the prohibitions on racial discrimination found in the Constitution itself. The New Deal Court had by no means been the first to hold that the regulation of activities that were not themselves

---

[89] 384 U.S. 641 (1966) (Brennan, J.). A companion case in which the state law itself had been upheld was remanded for reconsideration in light of *Morgan*. Cardona v. Power, 384 U.S. 672 (1966) (Brennan, J.). Harlan and Stewart, *id.* at 659-64, dissented in *Cardona* on the ground that the requirement of literacy in English was valid, Douglas and Fortas, *id.* at 675-77, on the ground that it was not. Assuming that literacy was still a permissible requirement, Douglas argued that there was no reason to discriminate against those literate in Spanish: given the "widespread organs of public communications" in Spanish "which regularly report and comment on matters of political interest and public concern" in New York City, "intelligent use of the ballot should . . . be as much presumed where one is versatile in Spanish as it is where English is the medium." Harlan, still disagreeing with *Harper*'s conclusion that measures affecting voting rights were subject to unusually strict scrutiny, responded that those literate only in Spanish remained at a disadvantage in understanding the issues: "The range of material available . . . is much more limited. . . . ."

[90] 384 U.S. at 665-71 (Harlan, J., joined by Stewart, dissenting). *See* U.S. CONST. amend. 14, § 5 ("The Congress shall have power to enforce, by appropriate legislation, the provisions of this article."). For an approving view of Harlan's position see Bickel, *The Voting Rights Cases,* 1966 SUP. CT. REV. 79, 97.

[91] *See* THE FIRST HUNDRED YEARS at 393-401 (discussing United States v. Reese, 92 U.S. 214 (1876) (fifteenth amendment does not authorize Congress to forbid voting discrimination on grounds other than race); United States v. Harris, 106 U.S. 629 (1883) (fourteenth amendment does not authorize Congress to outlaw private denial of equal protection); Civil Rights Cases, 109 U.S. 3 (1883) (Congress may not outlaw private race discrimination)). *See also* United States v. Cruikshank, 92 U.S. 542, 555 (1876) (dictum) ("The only obligation resting upon the United States is to see that the States do not deny the right. . . . The power of the national government is limited to the enforcement of this guaranty.").

[92] *See* 384 U.S. at 656. *See also* Cox, *supra* note 19, at 106-07 (praising this argument because of Congress's better ability to assemble the information necessary to make such a judgment and suggesting that on the basis of this passage Congress might outlaw not only literacy tests but de facto segregation too as well as prescribing a code of criminal procedure for state courts); Burt, *Miranda and Title II: A Morganatic Marriage,* 1969 SUP. CT. REV. 81.

commerce might be necessary and proper to the regulation of interstate trade.[93] In the 1920s, moreover, a Court that could hardly be described as sympathetic to government intervention had allowed Congress to regulate both medicinal and industrial uses of alcohol under the eighteenth amendment's authority to "enforce" its ban on intoxicating liquors "for beverage purposes."[94] "The opportunity to manufacture, sell and prescribe intoxicating malt liquors for 'medicinal purposes,'" Justice Sanford had written for a unanimous Court, "opens many doors to clandestine traffic in them as beverages under the guise of medicines; aids evasion, and, thereby and to that extent hampers and obstructs the enforcement of the Eighteenth Amendment."[95]

A few months after Warren's retirement, Harlan himself accepted this line of reasoning in voting with the majority to uphold a congressional ban on all literacy tests as a means of evading the fifteenth amendment's prohibition of racial discrimination in voting:

> Despite the lack of evidence of specific instances of discriminatory application or effect, Congress could have determined that racial prejudice is prevalent throughout the Nation, and that literacy tests unduly lend themselves to discriminatory application. . . . This danger of violation of § 1 of the Fifteenth Amendment was sufficient to authorize the exercise of congressional power under § 2.[96]

Justice Brennan, citing the commerce clause and Prohibition decisions, thought the same principle applied to the English literacy provision in *Morgan*. Congress's action, he wrote, "may be viewed as a measure to secure for the Puerto Rican community residing in New York nondiscriminatory treatment by government—both in the imposition of voting qualifications and the provision or administration of governmental services, such as public schools, public housing and law enforcement."[97] Harlan's only objection was the absence of an adequate legislative record to support the majority's conclusions.[98] Thus despite the highly controversial language elsewhere in the majority opinion the decision found adequate justification on wholly conventional grounds.

The most startling affirmance of congressional authority to enforce the Civil War amendments, however, had come a few weeks earlier in *South Carolina v. Katzenbach*, where the Court upheld the so-called preclearance requirement of the Voting Rights Act

---

[93] *See, e.g.*, United States v. Coombs, 37 U.S. 72 (1838) (theft of shipwrecked goods), THE FIRST HUNDRED YEARS at 234; Houston E. & W. Tex. Ry. v. United States, pp. 94-96 *supra* (rates for intrastate carriage competing with interstate). For the more extreme New Deal decisions see pp. 236-38 *supra*.

[94] *See* pp. 179-81 *supra* (discussing James Everard's Breweries v. Day (medicinal use of malt liquor), Selzman v. United States (sale of denatured alcohol), and Lambert v. Yellowley (medicinal use of wine and liquor)).

[95] *Everard*, 265 U.S. at 561-62. *See also Selzman*, 268 U.S. at 469 (Taft, C. J.) ("It helps the main purpose of the Amendment . . . to hedge about the making and disposition of the denatured article every reasonable precaution and penalty to prevent the proper industrial use of it from being perverted to drinking it.").

[96] Oregon v. Mitchell, 400 U.S. 112, 216 (1970) (Harlan, J., concurring in part).

[97] 384 U.S. at 652 (adding that "enhanced political power will be helpful in gaining nondiscriminatory treatment in public services for the entire Puerto Rican community" and noting "some evidence suggesting that prejudice played a prominent role in the enactment of the requirement," *id.* at 652-54).

[98] *Id.* at 669. For criticism of the suggestion that Congress must make a record to support its legislation *see* Cox, *supra* note 19, at 105; for the argument that Congress had gone too far see Bickel, *supra* note 14, at 98-101.

of 1965.[99] Impatient with the traditional reactive approach to combating voting discrimination, Congress had taken the unprecedented step of forbidding *any* change in the election laws in areas with a history of such discrimination without prior approval by the Attorney General or by a federal court.[100] Justice Black thought this provision infringed what remained of state sovereignty:

> [I]f all the provisions of our Constitution which limit the power of the Federal Government and reserve other power to the States are to mean anything, they mean at least that the States have power to pass laws and amend their constitutions without first sending their officials hundreds of miles away to beg federal officials to approve them.[101]

Black mentioned only the tenth amendment, which he had earlier agreed took nothing from Congress that other provisions had given it,[102] and the guarantee of a republican form of government, which the Court had consistently refused to enforce.[103] Long-standing principles of implicit intergovernmental immunity, however, lent him a measure of support. If Congress could neither tax states nor enforce their constitutional obligation to hand over fugitives,[104] it was easy to argue that it could not subject their legislation to prior federal approval.

Without adequately distinguishing the tax and extradition cases, the Court had held since the 1930s that Congress could regulate the states' own activities under the commerce and war powers.[105] Obstruction of the state's lawmaking process, to be sure, was arguably a greater threat to its sovereignty than regulation of its railroads or timber sales.[106] Unless the state's immunity was absolute, however, there was a strong case for finding it inapplicable in *Katzenbach*. As the Chief Justice demonstrated, there was a long history of state ingenuity in finding new ways of evading the fifteenth amendment's command. The invalidation of the grandfather clause had been followed by the white primary, the poll tax, the

---

[99] 383 U.S. 301 (1966) (Warren, C. J.).

[100] Voting Rights Act of 1965, § 5, 79 Stat. 437, 42 U.S.C. § 1973, *quoted in* 383 U.S. at 342-43.

[101] *Id.* at 359 (Black, J., dissenting in part).

[102] *See* United States v. Darby, 312 U.S. at 124 (The Tenth Amendment "states but a truism that all is retained which has not been surrendered."), p. 238 *supra*.

[103] *See, e.g.*, Pacific States Tel. & Tel. Co. v. Oregon, p. 93, note 20 *supra*.

[104] *See* New York v. United States, p. 304, note 171 *supra* (reaffirming the general principle of tax immunity while upholding a federal tax on state sale of mineral water); Kentucky v. Dennison, 65 U.S. 66 (1861) (extradition), THE FIRST HUNDRED YEARS at 249. *See also* THE FIRST HUNDRED YEARS at 165-68, 355 (discussing the origins of tax immunity).

[105] *See, e.g.*, United States v. California, p. 234, note 156 *supra* (Safety Appliance Act applicable to state-owned railroad); Case v. Bowles, p. 303, note 171 *supra* (wartime price regulation applicable to state timber sales). The Court reaffirmed these precedents soon after *Katzenbach* in Maryland v. Wirtz, 392 U.S. 183 (1968) (Harlan, J., over two dissents) (upholding extension of Fair Labor Standards Act to public schools and hospitals).

[106] *Cf.* District of Columbia v. Train, 521 F.2d 971, 994 (D.C. Cir. 1975) (Congress may not require states to regulate private pollution). *See* D. CURRIE, AIR POLLUTION: FEDERAL LAW AND ANALYSIS § 4.29 (1981). In the cases cited above, however, the Court expressly declined to rest its decision on the proprietary nature of the state's activities. *See also* Federal Energy Regulatory Commission v. Mississippi (upholding a federal statute imposing certain procedures on state energy agencies), p. 567, note 53 *infra*.

literacy test, and the gerrymander; if the states remained free to impose new stratagems until the courts could invalidate them, the amendment might never be enforced.[107]

Startling? Yes. Untenable? Maybe not. Even the punctilious Harlan agreed that a century was long enough to wait.[108]

## II.  THE GREENING OF EQUALITY

What the real Warren Court did for blacks was dramatic enough, but for the most part it seemed the logical outgrowth of earlier decisions such as *Brown v. Board of Education* and *NAACP v. Alabama.* More novel was the contemporaneous expansion of the scope of equal protection outside the field of race.

Since the decline of economic rights in the 1930s, there had been little use of equal protection in nonracial matters. Occasional decisions had shown particular solicitude for aliens and for the "basic" right of reproduction,[109] but the Court had been quite unresponsive to serious allegations of both nepotism and sex discrimination.[110] Without questioning those precedents directly, the later Warren Court took a strikingly more active view of its responsibility to police the justifications for nonracial distinctions, most notably in the field of voting.

Even before Frankfurter's retirement, and over what may have been his most impassioned dissent, *Baker v. Carr* had broken down the artificial barrier of nonjusticiability in suits challenging the equality of legislative apportionments.[111] *Baker,* however, had said little to suggest that the Court would be particularly exacting in scrutinizing the justification put forward in defense of districts containing unequal numbers of voters. Justice Brennan had appropriately taken the narrowest possible road to upholding the Court's

---

[107]*See Katzenbach,* 383 U.S. at 310-15; Guinn v. United States, pp. 106-07 *supra* (invalidating grandfather clause); Nixon v. Herndon, pp. 138-39 *supra* (invalidating statute excluding blacks from primary); Nixon v. Condon, pp. 250-51 *supra* (invalidating white primary ordained by party committee found to be agent of state); Grovey v. Townsend, p. 251 *supra* (upholding white primary ordained by party itself); Lane v. Wilson, p. 249 *supra* (invalidating provision imposing short period for registration of persons disenfranchised by invalid grandfather clause); Breedlove v. Suttles, p. 251, note 46 *supra* (upholding poll tax); Smith v. Allwright and Terry v. Adams, pp. 322-25 *supra* (invalidating white primaries ordained by party and preprimary organization); Gomillion v. Lightfoot, pp. 381-82 *supra* (invalidating racial gerrymander); Lassiter v. Northhampton Board of Elections, pp. 384-85 *supra* (upholding literacy test); Harper v. Board of Elections, pp. 424-25 *supra* (invalidating poll tax); Oregon v. Mitchell, p. 427 *supra* (upholding congressional ban on literacy tests). *See also Katzenbach,* 383 U.S. at 335 ("Congress had reason to suppose that these States might try similar maneuvers in the future in order to evade the remedies for voting discrimination contained in the Act itself.").

[108]The suit in South Carolina v. Katzenbach had been brought by the state in defense of its sovereign prerogatives; Massachusetts v. Mellon, pp. 183-86 *supra,* had seemed to establish that a state had no standing to protect its "political" as contrasted with proprietary interests. Justice Black protested in dissent that South Carolina was seeking a forbidden "advisory opinion," 383 U.S. at 357-58; Warren responded in conclusory terms that a state unable to enforce its laws had "a concrete and immediate 'controversy' with the Federal Government." *Id.* at 335. For criticism of the Court's conclusion on this issue see Bickel, supra note 90, at 84-90.

[109]*See* Oyama v. California and Takahashi Fish & Game Comm'n, p. 360 *supra* (aliens); Skinner v. Oklahoma, p. 288 *supra* (sterilization of thieves).

[110]Kotch v. Board of Pilot Comm'rs, p. 360 *supra* (nepotism in selection of pilots); Goesaert v. Cleary, p. 361 *supra,* and Hoyt v. Florida, p. 385, note 59 *supra* (sex discrimination in employment and jury service).

[111]*See* pp. 412-14 *supra.*

authority: "[I]t has been open to courts since the enactment of the Fourteenth Amendment to determine . . . that a discrimination reflects *no* policy, but simply arbitrary and capricious action."[112]

As an original matter there was reason to doubt whether the equal protection clause had been meant to apply to either voting or nonracial distinctions,[113] but the Court had rejected both limitations.[114] Once these obstacles were out of the way, it was not difficult to conclude that voting, like reproduction in *Skinner v. Oklahoma*,[115] was a fundamental interest with respect to which inequality required a compelling rather than a merely rational excuse.[116] Justice Stone had pointed the way in *Carolene Products* by suggesting strict scrutiny of all measures impinging on the democratic process itself; as he suggested, the integrity of that process is the basis of the respect courts normally accord to legislative determinations.[117]

This settled, the Court was unable to find a compelling reason for effectively giving some citizens more votes than others. "[T]he Equal Protection Clause," wrote Chief Justice Warren in the ground-breaking case of *Reynolds v. Sims,* "requires that the seats in both houses of a bicameral state legislature must be apportioned on a population basis."[118]

---

[112]*Baker,* 369 U.S. at 226. *See also id.* at 254 (Clark, J., concurring) ("Tennessee's apportionment is a crazy quilt without rational basis."); *id.* at 265 (Stewart, J., concurring) ("[T]he Court does not say or imply that 'state legislatures must be so structured as to reflect with approximate equality the voice of every voter.' "); Bickel, *The Durability of* Colegrove v. Green, 72 YALE L.J. 39, 39 (1962) ("A crack in the judicial gate that should not have been closed in *Colegrove v. Green* has now been pried open, but the gate has not swung on its hinges.").

[113]*See* THE FIRST HUNDRED YEARS at 342-51, 383-85. Justice Harlan renewed the argument that the fourteenth amendment did not apply to voting, but the Court ruled against him. *See* Reynolds v. Sims, 377 U.S. 533, 593-608 (1964) (dissenting opinion); Carrington v. Rash, 380 U.S. 89, 97-98 (1965) (dissenting opinion). For the argument that history was not so decisive as Harlan made it see Van Alstyne, *The Fourteenth Amendment, the "Right" to Vote, and the Understanding of the Thirty-ninth Congress,* 1965 SUP. CT. REV. 33.

[114]*See* THE FIRST HUNDRED YEARS at 390-92; Nixon v. Herndon, pp. 138-39 *supra.*

[115]*See* p. 288 *supra.*

[116]*See* Reynolds v. Sims, 377 U.S. 533, 561-62 (1964).

[117]*See* United States v. Carolene Products Co., 304 U.S. 144, 152-53 n.4 (1938), p. 244 *supra. See also Reynolds,* 377 U.S. at 562 ("Especially since the right to exercise the franchise in a free and unimpaired manner is preservative of other basic civil and political rights, any alleged infringement of the right of citizens to vote must be carefully and meticulously scrutinized."). *Cf.* Ely, *The Chief,* 88 HARV. L. REV. 11, 12 (1974) ("The Chief used to say that if *Reynolds v. Sims* had been decided before 1954, *Brown v. Board of Education* would have been unnecessary.").

[118]377 U.S. at 568. Clark and Stewart, *id.* at 587-89, concurred on the narrower ground that the apportionment in question was arbitrary; Harlan, *id.* at 589-625, dissented. *Accord* WMCA, Inc. v. Lomenzo, 377 U.S. 633 (1964) (Warren, C. J.); Maryland Comm. for Fair Representation v. Tawes, 377 U.S. 656 (1964) (Warren, C. J.); Davis v. Mann, 377 U.S. 678 (1964) (Warren, C. J.); Roman v. Sincock, 377 U.S. 695 (1964) (Warren, C. J.); Lucas v. Forty-Fourth General Assembly, 377 U.S. 713 (1964) (Warren, C. J.).

Two cases decided shortly before *Reynolds* had helped pave the way to its conclusion. Gray v. Sanders, 372 U.S. 368, 379 (1963) (Douglas, J.), held that a state could not give different weight to votes from different counties in elections for statewide office: "Once the geographical unit for which a representative is to be chosen is designated, all who participate in the election are to have an equal vote. . . ." Justice Harlan alone dissented, arguing that even in this context "a State might rationally conclude that its general welfare was best served by apportioning more [power] . . . to agricultural communities than to urban centers, lest the legitimate interests of the former be submerged in the stronger electoral voice of the latter." *Id.* at 386-87. Wesberry v. Sanders, 376 U.S. 1 (1964) (Black, J.), extended the "one person, one vote" principle enunciated in *Gray, see* 372 U.S. at

Given the Court's premises, there is a considerable appeal to this conclusion.[119]

The majority had no difficulty in rejecting the phony analogy of the equal representation of states in the United States Senate; as Warren noted, that was a compromise necessary to the formation of a union among independent sovereign states.[120] Justice Stewart's objection that the principle of majority rule could not be infringed when the challenged apportionment had been approved by a majority of the voters[121] was equally unconvincing: "A citizen's constitutional rights can hardly be infringed simply because a majority of the people choose that it be."[122] The best argument against the Court's one person, one vote standard was that in order to constitute a microcosm of the populace a legislature must contain representatives from each geographical area; a rural county has little voice in disputes with its more populous urban neighbor if they must elect a common spokesman.[123] The Court was unimpressed, and I think justifiably so; acceptance of this argument would have entailed a serious compromise of the important principle of equality.[124]

*Reynolds* was followed by a series of decisions clarifying the reach of its rather straightforward conclusion. There was nothing wrong with multimember districts as such,[125] with the appointment of members of a school board,[126] or with a requirement that one city councilman elected at large reside in each of several boroughs of unequal population;[127] the Constitution demanded only that each voter in an election have an equal voice. For similar reasons there was no requirement that the apportionment base include "aliens, transients, short-term or temporary residents, or persons denied the vote for con-

---

381, to the drawing of districts for congressional elections, but it did so on the basis of a creative construction of article I, § 2's provision that members of the House of Representatives shall be "chosen by the People of the several States": in light of the Convention's insistence that House seats be apportioned according to population, election "by the people" meant that "as nearly as practicable one man's vote in a congressional election is to be worth as much as another's." 376 U.S. at 7-8, 10-18. Justice Harlan, joined on this issue by Stewart, rightly objected that the Convention had been concerned only that seats be distributed *among the several states* according to population and that not even as among the states did the Constitution require absolute equality, *id.* at 20-51. *See* Kelly, *Clio and the Court: An Illicit Love Affair,* 1965 SUP. CT. REV. 119, 135 ("Mr. Justice Black . . . mangled constitutional history."). Justice Clark, 376 U.S. at 18-19, agreeing with the majority that the District Court should have reached the merits, argued that apportionment on a strict population basis was not required.

[119] Many, of course, took issue with the Court's conclusion. *See, e.g.,* McCloskey, *Foreword: The Reapportionment Cases,* 76 HARV. L. REV. 54, 73 (1962) (arguing just after *Baker* that it would be "Lochneresque" to prescribe one person, one vote); P. KURLAND, *supra* note 2, at 150-57, finding among other things an "unbending simplicity" in the opinions that was "not untypical of the Court's work"; Neal, *Baker v. Carr: Politics in Search of Law,* 1962 SUP. CT. REV. 252, 275-86.

[120] *See Reynolds,* 377 U.S. at 572-75.

[121] *See Lucas,* 377 U.S. at 759 (Stewart, J., dissenting).

[122] *Id.* at 737.

[123] *See id.* at 756-57, 762 (Stewart, J., dissenting); Bickel, supra note 112, at 41 ("The need is for 'government responsive to the will of the full . . . constituency, without loss of responsiveness to lesser voices, reflecting smaller bodies of opinion, in areas that constitute their own legitimate concern.' ").

[124] For detailed refutation of the arguments against *Reynolds* see Auerbach, *The Reapportionment Cases: One Person, One Vote*—One Vote, One Value, 1964 SUP. CT. REV. 1.

[125] Fortson v. Dorsey, 379 U.S. 433 (1965) (Brennan, J.).

[126] Sailors v. Board of Education, 387 U.S. 105 (1967) (Douglas, J., without dissent).

[127] Dusch v. Davis, 387 U.S. 112 (1967) (Douglas, J., without dissent).

viction of crime."[128] On the other hand, the equality principle applied not only to state and federal legislatures but to the election of county commissioners as well.[129]

Owing in no small part to the simplicity of the Court's standard, Justice Frankfurter's fears of the unenforceability of reapportionment decrees proved groundless, and the apportionment cases turned out to be a signal success. As one commentator observed, "it is not easy to think of any other major Supreme Court decisions to which significant adjustment was so easily accomplished. . . . [F]our years after the key decisions, the task of revision was essentially complete."[130]

Other cases of the Warren years predictably carried the principle of equality in elections beyond the apportionment context. *Carrington v. Rash* held that military personnel who had become domiciled in a state could not be excluded from voting there.[131] *Harper v. Board of Elections* held that voting could not be conditioned on payment of a poll tax.[132] *Kramer v. Union Free School District* and *Cipriano v. City of Houma* held that the right to vote for school board members or on the issuance of municipal bonds could not be limited to property taxpayers or parents with children in the schools.[133] *Williams v. Rhodes*[134] and *Moore v. Ogilvie*[135] struck down discriminatory requirements mak-

---

[128] Burns v. Richardson, 384 U.S. 73, 90-97 (1966) (Brennan, J.) (also upholding an apportionment on the basis of registered voters because "on this record it was found to have produced a distribution of legislators not substantially different from that which would have resulted from the use of a permissible population basis").

[129] Avery v. Midland County, 390 U.S. 474 (1968) (White, J., over dissents by Harlan, Stewart, and Fortas). *See also* Swann v. Adams, 385 U.S. 440 (1967) (White, J.) (striking down a state legislative apportionment under which one district contained 15.09 percent fewer and another 10.56 percent more voters than if the apportionment had been made strictly according to population); Kirkpatrick v. Preisler, 394 U.S. 526 (1969) (Brennan, J., with Harlan, Stewart, and White dissenting) (striking down a congressional apportionment in which "the most populous district was 3.13% above the mathematical ideal, and the least populous was 2.84% below"). The voluminous commentary includes Dixon, *The Warren Court Crusade for the Holy Grail of "One Man-One Vote,"* 1969 SUP. CT. REV. 219 (criticizing *Kirkpatrick*); Black, *Inequalities in Districting for Congress,* 72 YALE L.J. 13, 14-22 (1962) (arguing for less strict scrutiny of state than of congressional legislative reapportionments on grounds both of federalism and of remedy).

[130] McKay, *Reapportionment: Success Story of the Warren Court,* 67 MICH. L. REV. 223, 229 (1968).

[131] 380 U.S. 89 (1965) (Stewart, J., over a dissent by Harlan).

[132] *See* pp. 424-25 *supra.*

[133] *Kramer,* 395 U.S. 621 (1969) (Warren, C. J., over a dissent by Stewart, joined by Black and Harlan); *Cipriano,* 395 U.S. 701 (1969) (per curiam). *See Kramer,* 395 U.S. at 632 ("The classifications in [the statute] permit inclusion of many persons who have, at best, a remote and indirect interest in school affairs and, on the other hand, exclude others who have a distinct and direct interest in the school meeting decisions."). *Cipriano* was made easier by the fact that the bonds were to be paid out of utility revenues rather than property taxes: "[T]he benefits and the burdens of the bond issue fall indiscriminately on property owner and nonproperty owner alike." 395 U.S. at 705. *Contrast* McDonald v. Board of Election Commissioners, 394 U.S. 802 (1969) (Warren, C.J.) (upholding the denial of absentee ballots to persons incarcerated while awaiting trial after reaching the strained conclusion that strict scrutiny was not required because the record did not exclude the possibility that inmates might be permitted to vote in person).

[134] 393 U.S. 23 (1968) (Black, J.) (striking down a requirement that new political parties present petitions signed by 15 percent of voters in the last gubernatorial election in order to place candidates for presidential elector on the ballot). Justice Harlan concurred on first amendment grounds; Justices Stewart and White dissented on the merits; Chief Justice Warren argued the case should be remanded for "a clearer determination" by the trial court, *id.* at 70. *See* Casper, Williams v. Rhodes *and Public Financing of Political Parties,* 1969 SUP. CT. REV. 271.

[135] 394 U.S. 814 (1969) (Douglas, J., over a Stewart dissent joined by Harlan) (invalidating a requirement that independent candidates for presidential elector obtain at least two hundred signatures from each of the fifty

ing it difficult for new parties or urban voters to get their candidates on the ballot.[136]

Two important developments in equality outside the voting field also occurred just before the end of the Warren period. In *Shapiro v. Thompson*,[137] over dissents by Warren, Black, and Harlan, the Court struck down requirements of one-year residency before an applicant could qualify for welfare benefits: "[I]n moving from State to State or to the District of Columbia appellees were exercising a constitutional right, and any classification which serves to penalize the exercise of that right, unless shown to be necessary to promote a *compelling* governmental interest, is unconstitutional."[138] In so holding, the Court added yet another "fundamental" interest to those whose limitation, like that of reproduction and voting, had been subjected to heightened judicial scrutiny.

Finally, in *Levy v. Louisiana*,[139] the Court over three dissents invalidated a law denying an illegitimate child a right of action for wrongful death of its mother.[140] In explaining this conclusion, Justice Douglas professed to apply the lowest level of scrutiny, finding no rational basis for the distinction the statute drew.[141] Justice Harlan's dissent, however, plausibly suggested that the Court was actually applying a far more demanding standard than in ordinary rational-basis cases: "[F]or many of the same reasons why a State is empowered to require formalities in the first place, a State may choose to simplify a particular proceeding by reliance on formal papers rather than a contest of proof."[142] Thus, as *Shapiro* extended the list of fundamental interests, *Levy* appeared to enlarge the compan-

---

counties and overruling McDougall v. Green, p. 361 *supra*). *Moore* also made a substantial dent in the case-or-controversy requirement of article III by holding the challenge not mooted by occurrence of the election in which the plaintiffs had sought to run: "[T]he burden . . . on the nomination of candidates . . . remains and controls future elections. . . . The problem is therefore 'capable of repetition, yet evading review'. . . . The need for its resolution thus reflects a continuing controversy. . . ." 394 U.S. at 816. Justice Stewart dissented from this conclusion as well, *id.* at 819: "In the absence of any assertion that the appellants intend to participate as candidates in any future Illinois election, the Court's reference to cases involving 'continuing controversies' between the parties is wide of the mark." *Cf.* Golden v. Zwickler, 394 U.S. 103, 109-10 (1969) (Brennan, J.) (unanimously dismissing a challenge to the distribution of anonymous handbills because the Congressman on whose behalf the plaintiff wished to distribute literature had left the House to become a judge) ("[I]t was wholly conjectural that another occasion might arise when Zwickler might be prosecuted for distributing the handbills referred to in the complaint. . . . The constitutional question . . . must be presented in the context of a specific live grievance."). For further criticism of the *Moore* approach to mootness as illuminated by subsequent decisions see Currie, *The Supreme Court and Federal Jurisdiction: 1975 Term*, 1976 Sup. Ct. Rev. 183, 187-90.

[136] *But cf.* Fortson v. Morris, 385 U.S. 231 (1966) (Black, J., over four dissents) (finding no objection to a provision empowering the state legislature to select a governor from the two candidates receiving the highest popular vote when neither had obtained a majority).

[137] 394 U.S. 618 (1969) (Brennan, J.).

[138] *Id.* at 634. *See also* United States v. Guest, 383 U.S. 745 (1966) (Stewart, J.) (upholding Congress's power to punish *private* interference with this right because the Constitution secured it "against any source whatever, whether governmental or private," *id.* at 759-60 n.17). As the Court conceded and Harlan emphasized in dissent, *id.* at 762-74, the favorable precedents had all involved *state* interference with travel. For the origins of the elusive right to travel see The First Hundred Years at 355 (discussing Crandall v. Nevada, 73 U.S. 35 (1868)).

[139] 391 U.S. 68 (1968) (Douglas, J., over dissents by Harlan, Black, and Stewart).

[140] *See also* Glona v. American Guaranty and Liability Co., 391 U.S. 73 (1968) (Douglas, J., over the same dissents) (striking down a law denying the mother a right of action for wrongful death of her illegitimate child).

[141] *See Levy,* 391 U.S. at 71, 75.

[142] *See id.* at 80 (Harlan, J., dissenting).

ion category of suspect classifications that also required enhanced examination by the judges. The two decisions thus seemed to open the door to further expansions of equal protection in the years to come.[143]

## III.  FREE SPEECH

### A.  Curbing the Witch Hunters

From the beginning the Court under Warren had vigorously protected rights of expression and association in pursuit of racial equality.[144] From virtually the moment Justice Goldberg was seated it began to make up for its earlier timidity in defending the corresponding rights of persons suspected of subversion.

Earlier decisions had held the government could require disclosure of Communist but not of NAACP associations.[145] *Gibson v. Florida Legislative Investigation Committee,* decided in 1963, lay at the intersection of these two lines of authority, for the committee had asked an NAACP officer whether certain suspected Communists were among its members.[146]

Justice Goldberg cast the decisive vote to hold that the question need not be answered, and he wrote the Court's opinion. To the majority the case was governed by *NAACP v. Alabama*. Disclosure would have a chilling effect on membership; there was no evidence "of any substantial relationship between the N.A.A.C.P. and subversive or Communist activities"; the committee had not established "the compelling and subordinating state interest which must exist if essential freedoms are to be curtailed or inhibited."[147]

Harlan, Clark, Stewart, and White, who dissented, found it impossible to distinguish precedents upholding other inquiries into Communist activities. The government, Harlan argued, had an obvious interest in investigating Communist infiltration into nonsubversive organizations, and the NAACP's own effort to rid itself of subversives justified the committee's decision to look for infiltrators there.[148] "The net effect of the Court's decision," Justice White added, was "to insulate from effective legislative inquiry and preventive legislation the time-proven skills of the Communist Party in subverting and eventually controlling legitimate organizations."[149]

---

[143]*See* Kurland, *supra* note 19, at 144 (calling attention to the "emerging primacy of equality as a guide to constitutional decision"). In striking down a one-year residency requirement enacted by Congress for the District of Columbia, moreover, the Court in *Shapiro* invoked due process: " '[W]hile the Fifth Amendment contains no equal protection clause, it does forbid discrimination that is "so unjustifiable as to be violative of due process."' " 394 U.S. at 642 (citing Bolling v. Sharpe, pp. 378-79 *supra*). *See also* pp. 285-92 *supra* (discussing the Japanese-American cases).

[144]*See* pp. 382-84, 421-24 *supra*.

[145]*See* pp. 382-83, 392-96 *supra*.

[146]372 U.S. 539 (1963). The officer had voluntarily answered these questions on the basis of his own personal knowledge but declined to look into membership records to fill out his answers. Justice Harlan, dissenting, thought this partial willingness to testify diminished the claim of associational privacy, *id.* at 582; the majority seemed to give it no weight at all. *See generally* H. KALVEN, A WORTHY TRADITION: FREEDOM OF SPEECH IN AMERICA 514-21 (1988).

[147]372 U.S. at 544, 554-55. Black and Douglas, who joined Goldberg's opinion, added concurrences that went even further. *See id.* at 558-76.

[148]*Id.* at 578-81.

[149]*Id.* at 585.

If *Gibson* might be understood on the narrow ground that Justice Goldberg thought the black aspect of the case more prominent than the red, other decisions could not be so lightly dismissed. *DeGregory v. New Hampshire*, for example, held that a state legislative committee had no sufficient reason for inquiring into Communist activities more than six and a half years in the past.[150] "The information being sought was historical," wrote Douglas, "not current. . . . There is no showing whatsoever of present danger of sedition against the State itself, the only area to which the authority of the State extends."[151] Harlan's dissent, which Stewart and White joined, suggested how far the Court had come since *Barenblatt:*

> New Hampshire . . . should be free to investigate the existence or nonexistence of Communist Party subversion . . . without first being asked to produce evidence of the very type to be sought in the course of the inquiry. . . . I cannot say as a constitutional matter that inquiry into the current operations of the local Communist Party could not be advanced by knowledge of its operations a decade ago.[152]

Later the same Term, in *Elfbrandt v. Russell*,[153] an even more closely divided Court threw out an oath provision effectively barring knowing members of the Communist party from public employment because the provision was not limited to those who shared the Party's unlawful aims: "Those who join an organization but do not share its unlawful purposes and who do not participate in its unlawful activities surely pose no threat, either as citizens or as public employees."[154] In reaching this conclusion the Court took a step beyond *Wieman v. Updegraff*,[155] which had held state employment could not be denied to members lacking even knowledge of the Party's unlawful aims, and relied on *Scales v. United States*,[156] where the Smith Act provision punishing membership in a organization with knowledge of its subversive purposes had been construed to require intent to accomplish those purposes. Distinguishing *Scales* as involving neither the Constitution nor the qualifications for public employment, Justices White, Clark, Harlan, and Stewart dissented in *Elfbrandt*,[157] arguing that the Court was overruling a flock of decisions upholding similar provisions excluding knowing members from public positions,[158] which the majority did not even bother to mention.[159]

---

[150] 383 U.S. 825 (1966) (Douglas, J.).

[151] *Id.* at 829-30.

[152] *Id.* at 830.

[153] 384 U.S. 11 (1966) (Douglas, J.).

[154] *Id.* at 17.

[155] *See* pp. 357-58 *supra.*

[156] 367 U.S. 203 (1961).

[157] 384 U.S. at 19-20.

[158] *See* p. 357 *supra.*

[159] *See also* Keyishian v. Board of Regents, 385 U.S. 589, 606 (1967) (Brennan, J., over the same four dissents) (striking down a similar requirement applicable only to teachers: "Mere knowing membership without a specific intent to further the unlawful aims of an organization is not a constitutionally adequate basis for exclusion from such positions as those held by appellants."). The same provision had been upheld in Adler v. Board of Education, p. 357 *supra;* but "constitutional doctrine which has emerged since that decision has rejected its major premise." 385 U.S. at 605. In the same opinion the Court struck down yet another subversive-advocacy provision as "plainly susceptible of sweeping and improper application," *id.* at 599.

Loyalty oaths in general encountered heavy weather during the later Warren years. *Baggett v. Bullitt*,[160] for example, found a requirement that public employees forswear all "aid" or "teach[ing]" of revolutionary acts unconstitutionally vague and a requirement that they promise to promote respect for the flag both vague and overbroad. *Whitehill v. Elkins*[161] eliminated a provision requiring teachers to swear they were "not engaged one way or another in an attempt to overthrow the Government of the United States, or the State of Maryland . . . by force or violence," even though, as three dissenters pointed out, the state had tailored its oath precisely to what the Court had said would be permissible in an earlier case;[162] other statutes, the majority concluded, suggested that the oath was unconstitutionally broad. "The only thing that does shine through the opinion of the majority," said Justice Harlan, "is that its members do not like loyalty oaths."[163]

*United States v. Robel* capped the protection of subversive speech by reaching the stunning conclusion that Congress had gone too far even in banning innocent members of the Communist party from defense employment.[164] "It is made irrelevant to the statute's operation," the Chief Justice wrote, "that an individual may be a passive member of a designated organization, that he may be unaware of the organization's unlawful aims, . . . that he may disagree with" them, or that he "may occupy a nonsensitive position in a defense facility." Thus the statute "contains the fatal defect of overbreadth because it seeks to bar employment both for association which may be proscribed and for association which may not be proscribed consistently with the First Amendment rights."[165]

Other decisions of the period reached similar results on the basis of other constitutional provisions. *Aptheker v. Secretary of State*[166] breathed new life into substantive due process by holding that revoking the passports of Communists not shown to share the Party's goals infringed their right to travel, despite Justice Black's more convincing argument that it chilled their first amendment freedoms.[167] *United States v. Brown*, narrowly distinguish-

---

[160] 377 U.S. 360 (1964) (White, J., over two dissents).

[161] 389 U.S. 54, 55 (1967) (Douglas, J.).

[162] *See id.* at 63 (Harlan, J., joined by Stewart and White, dissenting) (citing Gerende v. Board of Supervisors, p. 357 *supra*).

[163] *Id. See generally* Israel, Elfbrandt v. Russell: *The Demise of the Oath?*, 1966 Sup. Ct. Rev. 193. *See also* Dombrowski v. Pfister, 380 U.S. 479 (1965) (Brennan, J., over two dissents arguing for abstention) (striking down a registration requirement for members of "subversive" or "Communist-front" organizations, partly on vagueness and overbreadth grounds).

[164] 389 U.S. 258 (1967).

[165] *Id.* at 266. White and Harlan dissented; Marshall did not participate; Brennan, *id.* at 272-82, concurred on the ground that the broad delegation of authority to define defense employment made the statute unconstitutionally vague and created an unacceptable risk of arbitrary application. *See also* Lamont v. Postmaster General, 381 U.S. 301, 307 (1965) (Douglas, J., without dissent) (invalidating a ban on the delivery of mail constituting "communist political propaganda" from abroad unless requested by the addressee: "[A]ny addressee is likely to feel some inhibition in sending for literature which federal officials have condemned as 'communist political propaganda.'").

[166] 378 U.S. 500 (1964) (Goldberg, J.).

[167] *See id.* at 517-19 (Black, J., concurring); H. KALVEN, *supra* note 146, at 381 ("The vice [in *Aptheker*] is not the interference with travel; it is the interference with freedom of political association. . . ."). *Cf.* United States v. Robel, text at notes 163-65 *supra*. Dissenting, Clark, Harlan, and White objected that the parties to the proceeding were leading functionaries of the Communist party whose knowledge and acceptance of its aims were clear, 378 U.S. at 521-25. The majority responded by extending the overbreadth doctrine for the first time beyond the first amendment: "[S]ince freedom of travel is a constitutional liberty closely related to rights of free speech

ing a leading decision of the Vinson period, pronounced a provision forbidding members of the Communist party to serve as union officers a bill of attainder.[168] *Albertson v. Subversive Activities Control Board* concluded, reasonably enough, that a requirement that individual members of the Party register with the government compelled them to incriminate themselves.[169]

These cases raised no novel issues. Several of the decisions, however, were rendered over dissents by Clark, Harlan, Stewart, and White, and more than one of them seemed

---

and association, we believe that appellants in this case should not be required to assume the burden of demonstrating that Congress could not have written a statute constitutionally prohibiting their travel." *Id.* at 517.

In Zemel v. Rusk, 381 U.S. 1 (1965) (Warren, C. J.), the Court found a limit to the right recognized in *Aptheker,* holding that Congress could refuse to validate a passport for travel to Cuba after diplomatic relations with that country had been terminated: "[T]he restriction which is challenged in this case is supported by the weightiest considerations of national security. . . ." *Id.* at 16. Douglas and Goldberg, *id.* at 23-26, dissented on right-to-travel grounds; Black, *id.* at 20-23, on the refreshing though nearly forgotten ground that Congress had unconstitutionally delegated legislative authority by empowering the President and Secretary of State to grant or deny passports in their unfettered discretion: "The Congress was created on the assumption that enactment of this free country's laws could be safely entrusted to the representatives of the people in Congress, and to no other official or government agency." For similar sentiments see Arizona v. California, 373 U.S. 546, 626 (1963) (Harlan, J., dissenting).

[168] 381 U.S. 437 (1965) (Warren, C. J.). "A bill of attainder," the Court had said in Cummings v. Missouri, 71 U.S. 277, 323 (1867), THE FIRST HUNDRED YEARS at 292-96, "is a legislative act which inflicts punishment without a judicial trial." Thus the Court had tended to uphold laws disqualifying persons with specified characteristics from certain positions if there was reason to think they posed a danger of future harm, viewing them as prophylactic rather than punitive. *Compare, e.g.,* Hawker v. New York, 170 U.S. 189 (1898) (upholding a ban on medical practice by convicted felons), *with Cummings, supra* (finding no connection between past support for the Confederacy and fitness for the ministry). American Communications Ass'n v. Douds, pp. 355-57 *supra,* had applied this distinction in upholding a provision conditioning the right of unions to utilize the services of the National Labor Relations Board upon filing of an affidavit that none of its officers was a Communist: Congress had acted out of a reasonable fear that Communists might use their authority as union officers to bring about political strikes interfering with interstate commerce. See 339 U.S. at 388, 413:

> [I]n the previous decisions the individuals involved were in fact being punished for *past* actions; whereas in this case they are subject to possible loss of position only because there is substantial ground for the congressional judgment that their beliefs and loyalties will be transformed into *future* conduct.

Dissenting in *Brown,* Justice White understandably thought *Douds* governed. *See* 381 U.S. at 462-78 (White, J., joined by Clark, Harlan, and Stewart, dissenting). For the majority, Warren noted that the provision in *Brown* disqualified not only current Communists but everyone who had been a Party member in the preceding five years, *id.* at 458, but he cast doubt on *Douds* by arguing as in *Aptheker, supra* note 166, that the inclusion of *innocent* party members made the provision broader than its alleged purpose required, 381 U.S. at 456, and seemed to call into question the basic distinction between punishment and prophylaxis by observing that punishment served preventive as well as retributive goals, *id.* at 458. Yet the Chief Justice stressed that he did not mean "Congress cannot weed dangerous persons out of the labor movement"; the vice was that it had attempted to do so by "specify[ing] the people upon whom the sanction . . . is to be levied" rather than by prescribing "rules of general applicability." *Id.* at 461. *Cf.* United States v. Lovett, 328 U.S. 303 (1946) (striking down a law forbidding further salary payments to three named government employees). It was not clear what this left of such decisions as *Hawker, supra;* as in *Aptheker,* the Court might have been better advised to rely on the first amendment.

[169] 382 U.S. 70, 77 (1965) (Brennan, J., for a unanimous Court) ("Form IS-52a requires an admission of membership in the Communist Party. Such an admission . . . may be used to prosecute the registrant under the membership clause of the Smith Act. . . ."). The implications of this decision are explored in Mansfield, *The Albertson Case: Conflict between the Privilege against Self-Incrimination and the Government's Need for Information,* 1966 SUP. CT. REV. 103.

inconsistent with recent precedent. Taken together they suggested that Frankfurter's departure had produced a sea change in the degree of protection the Court was prepared to afford to allegedly subversive expression.

## B.  Other Cases

Of comparable importance was the substantial measure of additional protection afforded to political speech generally by *New York Times Co. v. Sullivan.*[170] An advertisement in the *Times* soliciting funds for civil rights causes had pointed to a series of incidents arising out of civil rights advocacy in Montgomery, Alabama. "[T]ruckloads of police armed with shotguns and tear gas" were said to have "ringed the Alabama State College Campus"; the students' "dining hall was padlocked in an attempt to starve them into submission"; "Southern violators" had not only arrested and prosecuted Dr. Martin Luther King but had "bombed his home."[171] The city's Commissioner of Public Affairs, whose duties included supervision of the police, sued for libel, and won in the state courts, on the ground that the advertisement falsely accused him of complicity in the asserted acts.

The state court had rejected a constitutional challenge to the judgment on the ground that "[t]he First Amendment . . . does not protect libelous publications."[172] That had indeed been the historical understanding, confirmed by Justice Murphy's dictum in *Chaplinsky v. New Hampshire*[173] and relied on by Justice Frankfurter in upholding a group-libel law in *Beauharnais v. Illinois.*[174]

Emphasizing that " 'mere labels' " were not determinative,[175] Justice Brennan analyzed the matter in terms of the purposes rather than the history of the first amendment. "The constitutional safeguard . . . 'was fashioned to assure unfettered interchange of ideas for the bringing about of political and social changes desired by the people.' "[176] The advertisement was "an expression of grievance and protest on one of the major public issues of our time" and thus fell within this protective purpose.[177] Posterity had condemned Congress's effort in the Sedition Act to punish "false writing against the government" as an unconstitutional deterrent to criticism of official action; to permit libel suits by individual officials on the basis of the same criticism would have an even more inhibiting effect.[178]

The upshot was that a public official charged with official misconduct could recover damages for injury to his reputation only if the offending statement was known to be false

---

[170] 376 U.S. 254 (1964).

[171] *See id.* at 257-58.

[172] *See id.* at 264. The state court had added that the Constitution did not limit *private* interference with speech, but its argument was out of place; it was the state that had made libelous speech a tort. *See id.* at 265; *contrast* Shelley v. Kraemer, pp. 358-60 *supra,* where the state's policy had been the neutral one of enforcing private agreements whether or not discriminatory.

[173] *See* pp. 314-15 *supra.*

[174] *See* pp. 350-52 *supra.*

[175] 376 U.S. at 269.

[176] *Id.* at 269 (quoting from Roth v. United States, 354 U.S. 476, 484 (1957)).

[177] 376 U.S. at 271.

[178] *Id.* at 273-79. *See id.* at 277 ("What a State may not constitutionally bring about by means of a criminal statute is likewise beyond the reach of its civil law of libel.").

or was made with "reckless disregard of whether it was false or not."[179] The decision that defamation might be constitutionally protected was something of a shock, but the Court was right that the risk of paying damages to every official implicitly maligned by criticism of government could significantly dampen expression that lay at the heart of the first amendment's protection.[180]

Contemporaneous decisions protected additional aspects of political speech. *Mills v. Alabama* struck down a law forbidding attempts on election day to persuade citizens how to vote. "[A] major purpose of th[e First] Amendment," said Justice Black, "was to protect the free discussion of governmental affairs," and the law "silences the press at a time when it can be most effective."[181] *Bond v. Floyd* held that a state legislature could not refuse to seat a member for having made statements critical of the Vietnam War and of the military draft:

> Legislators have an obligation to take positions on controversial political questions so that their constituents can be fully informed by them, and be better able to assess their qualifications for office; also so they may be repre-

[179] *Id.* at 279-80. This standard was taken from decisions of some state courts recognizing a similar common law privilege, *e.g.*, Coleman v. MacLennan, 78 Kan. 711, 98 P. 281 (1908) (discussed in 376 U.S. at 280-82). Analogizing to the absolute common law immunity of government officials from liability for libels committed in the course of their duties, *see* Barr v. Matteo, 360 U.S. 564 (1959), and arguing that the Sedition Act itself required a showing of malice, three Justices would have gone even further: the risk that a statement might be found malicious was sufficient to deter much honest criticism of government. *See* 376 U.S. at 293-97 (Black, J., joined by Douglas, concurring); *id.* at 297-305 (Goldberg, J., also joined by Douglas, concurring). Adding that the Court must independently examine the record to determine whether the constitutional standard had been properly applied, the Court found insufficient proof either of malice or that the statements reflected on the Commissioner as an individual, *id.* at 284-92): "[Impersonal] criticism of government" may not be "transmut[ed] . . . into personal criticism . . . of the officials of whom the government is composed." *See also* Garrison v. Louisiana, 379 U.S. 64 (1964) (Brennan, J.) (holding the same standards applicable to a *criminal* prosecution for libel of a public official); Rosenblatt v. Baer, 383 U.S. 75 (1966) (Brennan, J.) (remanding a private libel action for a determination whether the plaintiff was a "public official" within *Sullivan*); Time, Inc. v. Hill, 385 U.S. 374 (1967) (Brennan, J.) (applying the same standards to an action for invasion of privacy based upon allegedly false representation of an incident in which the plaintiffs had been the victims of crime: "[T]he subject of the . . . article, the opening of a new play linked to an actual incident, is a matter of public interest," *id.* at 388, and because the information conveyed was not defamatory, "the additional state interest in the protection of the individual against damage to his reputation" was not involved, *id.* at 391); Curtis Publishing Co. v. Butts, 388 U.S. 130 (1967) (no opinion for the Court) (in which five Justices concluded that the *Sullivan* standard should be applied to defamation of "public figures" such as the athletic director at a state university and a prominent ex-General who had embarked upon politics). Both in *Rosenblatt*, 383 U.S. at 88-91, 94-95, and in *Butts*, 388 U.S. at 170-72, Black and Douglas seemed to argue that *all* judgments for libel were unconstitutional. *See* the detailed discussion in Kalven, *The Reasonable Man and the First Amendment: Hill, Butts, and Walker*, 1967 SUP. CT. REV. 267 ("Only a concerned Court would have worked so hard on such a problem," *id.* at 308).

[180] *See generally* Kalven, *The* New York Times *Case: A Note on "the Central Meaning of the First Amendment,"* 1964 SUP. CT. REV. 191. For a less approving view see P. KURLAND, *supra* note 2, at 64 ("[W]hat [the decision] means is a greater protection for the defamer and a diminution of the very small protection that was available to the defamed.").

[181] 384 U.S. 214, 218-19 (1966). *See also id.* at 220 (rejecting the argument that the prohibition was justified because there was no time to refute arguments made on election day: even if this goal could justify a restriction on speech, the law in question did not achieve it, for it left no opportunity to reply to statements made on the day *preceding* the election).

sented in governmental debates by the person they have elected to represent them.[182]

*Pickering v. Board of Education* concluded that a public school teacher could not be fired for criticizing actions taken by the board and the superintendent of schools,[183] *Tinker v. Des Moines School District* that pupils could not be forbidden to wear black armbands to school to protest the Vietnam War.[184] *Street v. New York* forbade punishment for words that "cast contempt" on the American flag: "We have no doubt that the constitutionally guaranteed 'freedom to be intellectually diverse or even contrary,' and the 'right to differ as to things that touch the heart of the existing order,' encompass the freedom to express publicly one's opinions about our flag, including those opinions which are defiant or contemptuous."[185]

The Court drew the line at the symbolic burning of draft cards in *United States v. O'Brien*.[186] The Chief Justice began by doubting whether the burning of a draft card qualified as "speech" at all even if done, as in *O'Brien*, as a protest against the Vietnam War and the draft: "We cannot accept the view that an apparently limitless variety of conduct can be labeled 'speech' whenever the person engaging in the conduct intends thereby to express an idea."[187] He went on to hold the act punishable even on the assumption that speech was involved, finding the ban on willful destruction of registration cards "essential" to furthering "important or substantial governmental interest[s] . . . unrelated to the suppression of free expression."[188]

---

[182] 385 U.S. 116, 136-37 (1966) (Warren, C. J.). *See also id.* at 133-35 (noting that the statements in question could not constitutionally be punished as criminal).

[183] 391 U.S. 563 (1968) (Marshall, J.) (applying the *Sullivan* test of falsity and actual malice).

[184] 393 U.S. 503 (1969) (Fortas, J.). *See id.* at 505 (agreeing with the trial court that "the wearing of an armband for the purpose of expressing certain views is the type of symbolic act that is within the Free Speech Clause"); *id.* at 510-11 (noting that school authorities had discriminated on the basis of content by allowing the wearing of political campaign buttons); *id.* at 514 (finding no proof that the wearing of armbands was or was reasonably foreseen to be disruptive). Justice Black put the other side of the question strongly in dissent, arguing that schools were not the place for demonstrations and that "the armbands did exactly what the elected school officials and principals foresaw they would, that is, took the students' minds off their classwork and diverted them to thoughts about the highly emotional subject of the Vietnam war." *Id.* at 517-18. *See also id.* at 526 (Harlan, J., dissenting) (arguing that the plaintiffs should be required to show that the restriction "was motivated by other than legitimate school concerns").

[185] 394 U.S. 576, 593 (1969) (Harlan, J.). Four dissenters, insisting that Street had been convicted not for his words but for burning a flag, argued there was no constitutional right to do so even as a political protest, *id.* at 594-617 (Warren, Black, White, and Fortas, JJ., dissenting). *Cf.* United States v. O'Brien, text at notes 186-93 *infra*.

[186] 391 U.S. 367 (1968) (Warren, C. J., over a dissent by Douglas asking reargument on the unpresented question of the constitutionality of a peacetime draft—" a course of action that, to say the least, would have been spectacular"; Alfange, *Free Speech and Symbolic Conduct: The Draft-Card Burning Case*, 1968 SUP. CT. REV. 1, 14).

[187] 391 U.S. at 376. *See also id.* at 382 (distinguishing Stromberg v. California, pp. 255-57 *supra*, where the Court had held the display of a red flag for communicative purposes protected: "Since the statute there was aimed at suppressing communication it could not be sustained as a regulation of noncommunicative conduct."). It is not clear why the state's calling an action speech should be either necessary or sufficient to make it so for first amendment purposes.

[188] 391 U.S. at 376-77. For an approving view of the Court's insistence on a more searching standard of review when it is the message itself to which the government objects see Ely, *Flag Desecration: A Case Study in the Roles of Categorization and Balancing in First Amendment Analysis*, 88 HARV. L. REV. 1482 (1975).

In light of the purposes of the first amendment, a respectable argument can be made that any act intended to convey information or opinion should qualify as speech.[189] Indeed the act in question was a particularly dramatic means of calling attention to O'Brien's message. As Justice Harlan would soon suggest in an unusually sensitive opinion upholding the right to display the distasteful slogan "Fuck the Draft" on the back of a jacket, "I really think the draft is a bad idea" is hardly the rhetorical equivalent of either the expletive employed in the later case or the burning of a draft card in *O'Brien*.[190] On the other side of the balance, moreover, the interests cited in support of the prohibition—from reminding the bearer of his registration number to facilitating immediate induction in an imaginable emergency—seemed less than overpowering.[191] If other decisions of the time suggested that the Court might have balanced the competing interests in *O'Brien* differently,[192] however, the setback was relatively minor, for the restriction there upheld was a regulation of the *manner* of speaking that left open a variety of alternative means of conveying the speaker's message.[193]

---

[189] See pp. 255-57 *supra* (discussing Stromberg v. California); Henkin, *Foreword: On Drawing Lines*, 82 HARV. L. REV. 63, 79 (1968) ("[I]t would be surprising if those who poured tea into the sea and who refused to buy stamps did not recognize that ideas are communicated, disagreements expressed, protests made other than by word of mouth or pen."). *O'Brien* itself, as well as the loudspeaker cases, demonstrates that this conclusion would by no means rule out the possibility of prohibiting a particular means of communication on the basis of some overriding governmental concern. *Cf.* Kovacs v. Cooper, pp. 343-45 *supra* (upholding a ban on the use of "loud" amplification equipment in the streets).

[190] See Cohen v. California, 403 U.S. 15, 26 (1971) ("We cannot sanction the view that the Constitution, while solicitous of the cognitive content of individual speech, has little or no regard for that emotive function which, practically speaking, may often be the more important element of the overall message sought to be communicated."). The newly appointed Justice Harry Blackmun, joined by Black and the newly appointed Chief Justice Warren Burger, dissented on the merits, *id.* at 27-28; White, *id.* at 28, agreed with them that the case should be remanded for clarification of an issue of state law. *See also* Henkin, *supra* note 189, at 81 ("[F]or any persons concerned to express what O'Brien sought to express, there were few if any alternative forms of communication of comparable effectiveness.").

[191] See 391 U.S. at 378-80 (adding that draft cards made it easy to demonstrate compliance with the registration requirement or to correct errors in official records and reminded the registrant of his duty to keep the draft board informed of changes in his situation). *See also* Alfange, *supra* note 186, at 42-45 (adding that Selective Service officials had expressed no concern over the burning of cards and that the prohibition was at best an incomplete means of achieving its supposed goals); Henkin, *supra* note 189, at 81 ("One might also ask just how disruptive the burning of draft cards is and whether Congress had effective alternatives to safeguard the administration of the Selective Service program.").

[192] See Alfange, *supra* note 186, at 2.

[193] The Court expressly declined to investigate whether, as asserted, Congress had passed the law in an effort to suppress dissent rather than to serve the legitimate interests identified in the opinion. *See* 391 U.S. at 382-85. Reluctance to probe legislative motives in constitutional cases went back as far as Fletcher v. Peck, 10 U.S. 87 (1810); the Court had generally been willing to find illegitimate purposes only when revealed on the face of legislation or when the challenged practice seemed to serve no legitimate end. *See* THE FIRST HUNDRED YEARS at 128-36, 292-96 (discussing *Fletcher*) (refusing to decide whether a land grant had been the result of bribery), Cummings v. Missouri, 71 U.S. 277 (1877), and *Ex parte* Garland, 71 U.S. 333 (1867) (striking down post-Civil War loyalty oath requirements)); Guinn v. United States, pp. 106-07 *supra* (striking down grandfather clause for voting); the Child Labor Tax Case, pp. 173-74 *supra* (striking down federal tax on firms employing children); McGowan v. Maryland, p. 410 *supra* (upholding Sunday law). The opinion's recitation of legitimate administrative goals served by the draft card law suggests this was not the case in *O'Brien*. *See* Ely, *Legislative and Administrative Motivation in Constitutional Law*, 79 YALE L.J. 1205, 1339 (1970). *But see* the opinion of Judge Aldrich below, 376 F.2d 538, 541 (1st Cir. 1967) (concluding that Congress's purpose must have been

*Brandenburg v. Ohio,* in 1969, closed the Warren period with a fitting summary of the Court's work in this area by combining the most protective features of Justice Holmes's test for political speech and of that of Judge Learned Hand in striking down a criminal-syndicalism law like the one upheld in *Whitney v. California:*

> [L]ater decisions have fashioned the principle that the constitutional guarantees of free speech and free press do not permit a State to forbid or proscribe advocacy of the use of force or of law violation except where such advocacy is directed to inciting or producing imminent lawless action and is likely to incite or produce such action.[194]

There were no dissents;[195] freedom of expression had finally come of age.[196]

## IV. LEGISLATORS, JUDGES, AND PREACHERS

As suggested by *Bond v. Floyd*'s allusion to the right of voters to be "represented . . . by the person they have elected to represent them,"[197] freedom of expression is not the only interest threatened by exclusion of an elected legislator from his office. A similar concern for the integrity of the democratic process underlay the arresting 1969 decision in *Powell v. McCormack*[198] that the House of Representatives could not exclude a duly elected Congressman for alleged misuse of public money. The House's authority under article I, § 5 to determine the "Qualifications of its own Members," wrote Chief Justice Warren, was limited to requirements—such as age, citizenship, and residence—"expressly prescribed in the Constitution."[199]

This conclusion was amply supported by the historical materials impressively as-

---

illegitimate since these goals were already served by regulations requiring possession of draft cards). Other evidence of improper purpose in *O'Brien,* in any event, was troubling. *See, e.g.,* the House Report, *quoted in* 391 U.S. at 387 ("The House Committee . . . shares in the deep concern expressed throughout the Nation over the increasing incidences in which individuals . . . openly defy and encourage others to defy the authority of their Government by destroying or mutilating their draft cards."). *See* Alfange, *supra* note 186, at 15, 38 (concluding that the legislative history showed an intention to inhibit protest "with indisputable clarity"). Whether the burning of the card could validly have been the basis of a prosecution for incitement to draft evasion the Court did not consider. *See* pp. 115-24 *supra* (discussing Schenck v. United States and related cases).

[194] 395 U.S. 444, 447 (1969) (per curiam). *See* pp. 119-20 *supra* (discussing the Holmes and Hand formulations); pp. 160-61 *supra* (discussing *Whitney*).

[195] Black and Douglas, concurring separately, would have gone further, arguing that "the 'clear and present danger' doctrine should have no place in the interpretation of the First Amendment." 395 U.S. at 449-57.

[196] For an admiring summary of the speech cases of the Warren years see Kalven, *"Uninhibited, Robust, and Wide-Open"—A Note on Free Speech and the Warren Court,* 67 MICH. L. REV. 289 (1968).

[197] *See* pp. 439-40 *supra.*

[198] 395 U.S. 486 (1969) (Warren, C. J.).

[199] *Id.* at 522. *See also id.* at 520 n.41 (noting that it was unnecessary to decide whether the House could exclude a member who met the requirements of age, citizenship, and residence but who was disqualified by conviction following impeachment, U.S. CONST. art. I, § 3, by concurrently holding another "Office under the United States," art. I, § 6, or by taking part in a rebellion, amend. 14, § 3; who declined to take the oath prescribed by article VI; or who was selected under a regime that did not satisfy article IV's guarantee of a republican form of government). Luther v. Borden, 48 U.S. 1, 42 (1849), had emphatically given an affirmative answer to the last example; the reasoning in *Powell* suggests the House could exclude on the other listed grounds as well.

sembled in the Chief Justice's opinion.[200] In a passage from the Convention records also quoted in *Bond*,[201] Madison had objected to a proposal to give Congress power to establish additional qualifications for its members, on the ground that it would enable members of a dominant faction to frustrate the democratic process by excluding persons with whom they disagreed.[202] Later the same day, after Madison had argued that "the right of expulsion . . . was too important to be exercised by a bare majority of a quorum," the Convention agreed to his motion that a two-thirds vote be required to "expel a Member," as article I, § 5 now requires.[203] "Had the intent of the Framers emerged from these materials with less clarity," the Court justly concluded, "we would nevertheless have been compelled to resolve any ambiguity in favor of a narrow construction of the scope of Congress' power to exclude members-elect." For a "fundamental principle of our representative representative democracy is, in Hamilton's words, 'that the people should select whom they please to govern them.'"[204]

Perhaps the most important and striking aspect of the *Powell* decision was its further narrowing of the already restrictive criteria for nonjusticiable "political questions" laid down a few years earlier in the reapportionment case of *Baker v. Carr*.[205] Several of those criteria were watered down to the point of triviality, and with good reason: because "it is the responsibility of this Court to act as the ultimate interpreter of the Constitution," a judicial interpretation of its provisions could neither involve "an 'initial policy determination of a kind clearly for nonjudicial discretion,'" demonstrate "a 'lack of the respect due [a] co-ordinate branch of government,'" nor "result in 'multifarious pronouncements by various departments on one question.'"[206] Moreover, the Court's analysis of the merits had shown that there was no want of "judicially . . . manageable standards" for interpreting the provision in question.[207]

The more sobering argument was that the provision in question had excluded judicial authority by making each House the "Judge" of its members' qualifications, in the interest of legislative independence. Without denying that article I might prevent a court from reviewing "the House's factual determination that a member did not meet one of the standing qualifications,"[208] the Chief Justice dismissed this objection as well:

> In order to determine whether there has been a textual commitment to a co-ordinate department of the Government, we must interpret the Constitution. . . . [W]e must first determine what power the Constitution confers

---

[200] *See* 395 U.S. at 522-47.

[201] *See Bond*, 385 U.S. at 135-36 n.13.

[202] *See* 2 M. FARRAND, RECORDS OF THE FEDERAL CONVENTION OF 1787, at 249-50 (rev. ed. 1937), *quoted in Powell*, 395 U.S. at 533-34.

[203] 2 M. FARRAND, *supra* note 202, at 254, *quoted in Powell*, 395 U.S. at 536. *See also id.* at 541-47, demonstrating that both the House and the Senate had consistently confirmed their inability to exclude members who met the constitutional qualifications until their judgment was distorted by the animosities aroused by the Civil War.

[204] *Id.* at 547 (quoting 2 DEBATES ON THE FEDERAL CONSTITUTION 257 (J. Elliot ed. 1876)).

[205] *See* pp. 412-14 *supra*.

[206] 395 U.S. at 548-49 (quoting *Baker*, 369 U.S. at 211, 217).

[207] 395 U.S. at 549 (quoting *Baker*, 369 U.S. at 217).

[208] 395 U.S. at 521 n.42.

upon the House . . . before we can determine to what extent, if any, the exercise of that power is subject to judicial review.[209]

Since the power of each House to judge the elections and qualifications of its members had often been cited with the impeachment clauses as a prime example of the commitment of issues to the final decision of other branches,[210] this conclusion seemed to signal a marked decline in the fortunes of the political-question doctrine.[211]

Of a piece with the expansive view of the judicial function taken in *Powell* was that reflected by the 1968 decision in *Flast v. Cohen*,[212] where over Harlan's dissent the Court struggled to uphold the standing of a taxpayer to challenge federal expenditures allegedly offending the establishment clause, despite the contrary implications of *Massachusetts v. Mellon*.[213] There were two requirements, said the Chief Justice, for taxpayer standing: the challenge must be to an "exercise[] of congressional power under the taxing and spending clause of Art. I, § 8," and it must be based on "specific constitutional limitations" rather than (as in the earlier case) on a simple absence of congressional authority.[214]

These criteria oddly bore little resemblance on their face to those regularly employed to determine standing in other cases,[215] but they can largely be explained in compatible terms. The requirement that an expenditure be the subject of challenge assures at least a plausible claim that the taxpayer is injured by the action of which he complains; *Flast* implicitly rejects *Mellon*'s suggestion that any reduction of the victorious litigant's tax bill is too speculative to satisfy the case or controversy requirement of article III. Moreover, the reason the establishment clause was found to be a "specific limitation" on the tax power was that one of its purposes had been to protect taxpayers from having to support religion. Thus Flast could be said to be asserting his own constitutional right not to be taxed for religious purposes, while "Mrs. Frothingham [in the earlier case] was attempting to assert the States' interest in their legislative prerogatives. . . ."[216]

The general principle that litigants may not assert the rights of others was well established, but it had long been subject to exception in situations in which the owner of the right was unable to defend it himself,[217] as *Mellon* had held the states were.[218] Moreover, cases such as *Wickard v.Filburn*[219] and *Youngstown Sheet & Tube Co. v. Sawyer*[220] had

---

[209] *Id.* at 518-22 (citing *Baker,* 369 U.S. at 211).

[210] *See, e.g.,* Wechsler, *Toward Neutral Principles of Constitutional Law,* 73 HARV. L. REV. 1, 8 (1973).

[211] Applying the questionable distinction laid down in Kilbourn v. Thompson, 103 U.S. 168 (1881), THE FIRST HUNDRED YEARS at 436-38, *Powell* also rejected the argument that the speech and debate clause of article I, § 6 insulated House employees as well as members from suits challenging their official actions: "Freedom of legislative activity and the purposes of the Speech and Debate Clause are fully protected if legislators are relieved of the burden of defending themselves." 395 U.S. at 505. This distinction would not much longer survive. *See* Gravel v. United States, p. 587, note 197 *infra* (more persuasively concluding that, because Congress could not function without employees, an aide's immunity was as broad as a member's).

[212] 392 U.S. 83 (1968) (Warren, C. J.).

[213] *See* pp. 183-86 *supra.*

[214] 392 U.S. at 102-05.

[215] *See, e.g.,* Barrows v. Jackson, *supra* p. 359, note 177.

[216] *See* 392 U.S. at 103-05.

[217] *See, e.g.,* Barrows v. Jackson, p. 359, note 177 *supra.*

[218] *See* pp. 183-85 *supra.*

[219] *See* p. 238 *supra.*

[220] *See* pp. 365-69 *supra.*

consistently permitted other affected litigants to make arguments of federalism and separation of powers; it was not obvious why the rule should be any different for taxpayers.[221] The distinctions drawn in *Flast* thus were not entirely satisfying. But in opening up the traditionally forbidden areas of legislative apportionment, internal congressional practices, and federal spending to judicial oversight, *Baker, Powell,* and *Flast* exemplified the aggressive attitude of the later Warren Court toward the question of judicial review.

With respect to the religion clauses themselves, *Abington School Dist. v. Schempp*[222] predictably extended *Engel v. Vitale*[223] to invalidate state-sponsored Bible reading and recitation of the Lord's Prayer in public schools on the unsurprising ground that the state was not permitted to conduct religious exercises:[224] "[T]o withstand the strictures of the Establishment Clause there must be a secular legislative purpose and a primary effect that neither advances nor inhibits religion."[225] *Epperson v. Arkansas*[226] laid an old controversy to rest[227] by striking down a law forbidding the teaching of evolution on similar grounds: "No suggestion has been made that Arkansas' law may be justified by considerations of state policy other than the religious views of some of its citizens."[228] *Board of Education v. Allen,*[229] however, confirmed *Everson's* salutary reminder that neutrality toward religion was not the equivalent of hostility:[230] just as parochial school pupils could be included in a program of public transportation, they could also be included in a state program for the loan of secular textbooks.[231]

Most significantly, in *Sherbert v. Verner*[232] the Court for the first time clearly held that religious freedom required exemption of religious believers from a nondiscriminatory secular rule. The law in question declared ineligible for unemployment compensation anyone

---

[221] *See* Henkin, *supra* note 189, at 73–76. In any event, the Court's gratuitous exclusion of attacks on "incidental expenditure[s] . . . in the administration of an essentially regulatory statute" (392 U.S. at 102) has no such justification; the source of the power to spend money collected by taxation seems irrelevant both to the taxpayer's injury and to the purposes of the establishment clause.

[222] 374 U.S. 203 (1963) (Clark, J., over a dissent by Stewart).

[223] *See* pp. 411–12 *supra.*

[224] *See* 374 U.S. at 224:

> Surely the place of the Bible as an instrument of religion cannot be gainsaid, and the State's recognition of the pervading religious character of the ceremony is evident from the rule's specific permission of the alternative use of the Catholic Douay version as well as the recent amendment permitting nonattendance at the exercises. None of these factors is consistent with the contention that the Bible is here used either as an instrument for nonreligious moral inspiration or as a reference for the teaching of secular subjects.

[225] *Id.* at 222.

[226] 393 U.S. 97, 107 (1968) (Fortas, J.).

[227] *See* Scopes v. State, 154 Tenn. 105, 289 S.W. 363 (1927).

[228] 393 U.S. at 107.

[229] 392 U.S. 236 (1968) (White, J., over three dissents).

[230] *See* pp. 339–42 *supra* (discussing *Everson*).

[231] *See* 392 U.S. at 242 (citing *Everson*) ("[T]he Establishment Clause does not prevent a state from extending the benefits of state laws to all citizens without regard for their religious affiliation. . . ."). *But see* Freund, *Public Aid to Parochial Schools,* 82 HARV. L. REV. 1680, 1683 (1969) ("[B]uses . . . are not ideological. . . . Can the same be said of textbooks chosen by a parochial school for compulsory use, interpreted with the authority of teachers selected by that school, and employed in an atmosphere deliberately designed through sacred symbol to maintain a religiously reverent attitude?"). For an approving view of both *Epperson* and *Allen* see Ely, *supra* note 193, at 1318, 1321–22.

[232] 374 U.S. 398 (1963) (Brennan, J., over two dissents).

unwilling to work on Saturday; the Court held it could not be applied to persons whose religion forbade Saturday labor. The numerous precedents refusing to carve such exceptions in the past were explained on the ground that "[t]he conduct or actions . . . regulated have invariably posed some substantial threat to public safety, peace or order."[233] Invoking a long line of cases involving freedom of expression, Justice Brennan noted that "to condition the availability of benefits upon this applicant's willingness to violate a cardinal principle of her religious faith effectively penalizes the free exercise of her constitutional rights"[234] and distinguished *Braunfeld v. Brown*,[235] which had just refused to recognize an exception for Sabbatarians from laws limiting work on Sunday, on the basis of the "strong state interest [in that case] in providing one uniform day of rest for all workers."[236]

The principle that indirect burdens on constitutionally protected rights were subject to serious judicial scrutiny was unimpeachable, but its application in *Sherbert* posed a difficult problem. As Justice Stewart pointed out in his concurring opinion, precedents such as the school prayer decisions seemed to suggest that singling out religious people for preferential treatment would itself offend the Constitution;[237] it could hardly be that the free exercise clause required what the establishment clause forbade. Stewart's way out of the dilemma was to repudiate the prayer cases, but in light of the purposes of the two clauses it is at least as plausible to conclude that it was *Sherbert* that was wrongly decided.[238]

## V.  FAIR TRIAL

### A.   The Bill of Rights

What *Gibson* did for freedom of association immediately after Frankfurter's departure, *Gideon v. Wainwright* did during the same Term for criminal procedure. This time, moreover, the vote was unanimous. *Betts v. Brady*, one of the landmarks of the Frankfurter era, had limited to cases of special need a state defendant's right to assigned counsel.[239] *Gideon* broke down the barrier. "[I]n our adversary system . . . ," Justice Black declared, "any

[233] *Id.* at 403.

[234] *Id.* at 404-06 (citing, inter alia, American Communications Ass'n v. Douds, pp. 355-57 *supra*, and Speiser v. Randall, *supra* p. 393, note 120).

[235] *See* pp. 410-11 *supra*.

[236] 374 U.S. at 408. For a subtle exploration of this attempted distinction see Giannella, *Religious Liberty, Nonestablishment, and Doctrinal Development, Part* I, 80 HARV. L. REV. 1381, 1400-03 (1967). *See also* Ely, *supra* note 193, at 1319-22 (finding the two decisions irreconcilable and terming *Sherbert* an "aberration" that "should not be followed").

[237] 374 U.S. at 413-17 (Stewart, J., concurring). *See also id.* at 422 (Harlan, J., joined by White, J., dissenting) (citing Kurland, *Of Church and State and the Constitution*, 29 U. CHI. L. REV. 1 (1961)).

[238] *See* THE FIRST HUNDRED YEARS at 439-42 (discussing Reynolds v. United States, 98 U.S. 145 (1879)); pp. 266-68 *supra* (discussing Cantwell v. Connecticut and the flag-salute cases); P. KURLAND, RELIGION AND THE LAW (1962). For an excellent exposition of the inconclusive history see McConnell, *The Origins and Historical Understanding of Free Exercise of Religion*, 103 HARV. L. REV. 1409 (1990) (arguing in support of religious exemptions); for an early effort to develop standards for the balancing of interests required by *Sherbert* see Clark, *Guidelines for the Free Exercise Clause*, 83 HARV. L. REV. 327 (1969). The religion decisions of the period are summarized in Kauper, *The Warren Court: Religious Liberty and Church-State Relations*, 67 MICH. L. REV. 269 (1968).

[239] *See* pp. 320-22 *supra*.

person haled into court, who is too poor to hire a lawyer, cannot be assured a fair trial unless counsel is provided for him."[240]

Like *Gibson* in the political field, *Gideon* precipitated a rapid succession of aftershocks that left the contours of criminal procedure radically altered by the time Warren left in 1969. To begin with, while the Court never accepted Justice Black's argument that the fourteenth amendment made the entire Bill of Rights applicable to the states,[241] it might almost as well have. Successive decisions read one provision after another of the fifth and sixth amendments into due process: the privilege against self-incrimination,[242] the right to confront adverse witnesses,[243] the right to a speedy trial,[244] the right to call witnesses for the defense,[245] the right to trial by jury,[246] the prohibition against double jeopardy.[247] Since the question in each of these cases was the subjective one whether the right in question as "fundamental," there is not much to say about them at the analytical level. Yet it is not easy either to deny their practical importance or—if one concedes that the Court posed the right question—to quarrel with their appealing conclusions. It was less clear, as Harlan observed in the jury case, that every detail of each federal right was so fundamental as to be an element of due process: "I should suppose it obviously fundamental to fairness that a 'jury' means an 'impartial jury.' I should think it equally obvious that the rule, imposed long ago in the federal courts, that 'jury' means 'jury of exactly twelve,' is not fundamental to anything. . . ."[248] Nevertheless the majority flatly declared in the double-jeopardy case that completed the Warren Court's incorporation odyssey that "[o]nce it is decided that a particular Bill of Rights guarantee is 'fundamental to the American scheme

---

[240] 372 U.S. 335, 344 (1963) (Black, J.). For the argument that the Court might have done better to downplay the effect of changing personnel on the decision by emphasizing the lessons of intervening experience and precedent, see Israel, Gideon v. Wainwright: *The "Art" of Overruling*, 1963 SUP. CT. REV. 211. In Douglas v. California, 372 U.S. 353, 357 (1963) (Douglas, J., over three dissents), the Court relied not on *Gideon* but on Grffffin v. Illinois, pp. 403-05 *supra*, to hold that the state must also appoint counsel on appeal, even if its independent examination of the record suggested that counsel would be of no assistance: "[W]here the merits of *the one and only appeal* an indigent has as of right are decided without benefit of counsel, we think an unconstitutional line has been drawn between rich and poor."

[241] *See* Adamson v. California, pp. 321-22 *supra* (Black, J., dissenting).

[242] Malloy v. Hogan, 378 U.S. 1 (1964) (Brennan, J.). *See id.* at 6-7 (invoking decisions requiring state courts to exclude coerced confessions: "[T]he American system of criminal prosecution is accusatorial, not inquisitorial, and the Fifth Amendment privilege is its mainstay."). Harlan and Clark, dissenting, *id.* at 14-33, conceded that due process forbade "imprisoning a person *solely* because he refuses to give evidence which may incriminate him under the laws of the State," but argued against holding the states to standards governing the federal privilege; White and Stewart, *id.* at 33-38, thought the questions not incriminating under the federal standard. *See also* Murphy v. Waterfront Commission, 378 U.S. 52 (1964) (Goldberg, J.) (holding a federal court could not receive incriminating testimony that a state had compelled).

[243] Pointer v. Texas, 380 U.S. 400 (1965) (Black, J.). *See* Griswold, *The Due Process Revolution and Confrontation*, 119 U. PA. L. REV. 711 (1971).

[244] Klopfer v. North Carolina, 386 U.S. 213 (1967) (Warren, C. J.).

[245] Washington v. Texas, 388 U.S. 14 (1967) (Warren, C. J.).

[246] Duncan v. Louisiana, 391 U.S. 145 (1968) (White, J.). Separate opinions by Black and Harlan retraced the entire debate over incorporation of the Bill of Rights in the fourteenth amendment. *See id.* at 162-71 (Black, J., joined by Douglas, concurring); *id.* at 171-93 (Harlan, J., joined by Stewart, dissenting).

[247] Benton v. Maryland, 395 U.S. 784 (1969) (Marshall, J.). Virtually the only criminal-procedure provision remaining inapplicable to the states was that guaranteeing indictment by a grand jury. *See* Hurtado v. California, 110 U.S. 516 (1884), THE FIRST HUNDRED YEARS at 366-68.

[248] *Duncan*, 391 U.S. at 181-82 (Harlan, J., dissenting).

of justice,' . . . the same constitutional standards apply against both the State and Federal Governments." [249]

At the same time it extended most procedural provisions of the Bill of Rights to the states, the Court significantly expanded the scope of those provisions themselves. *Griffin v. California*[250] and *Garrity v. New Jersey*[251] persuasively concluded that the privilege against self-incrimination would be undermined if its invocation could give rise either to an inference of guilt or to deprivation of the right to earn a living. *Marchetti v. United States*,[252] overruling *United States v. Kahriger*,[253] held that individuals could not be required to admit crimes in filing tax returns.[254] *Camara v. Municipal Court*,[255] overruling *Frank v. Maryland*,[256] held that the prohibition of unreasonable searches applied to those conducted under housing and fire laws.[257] *Katz v. United States*,[258] overruling *Olmstead v. United States*,[259] held that it extended to electronic surveillance. All these decisions seemed sound enough as an original matter, but it was seldom that so many important precedents had been overruled in so short a time.

There was a considerable appeal to the Court's conclusion in *Massiah v. United States*[260] and *Escobedo v. Illinois*[261] that questioning an indicted or incarcerated suspect behind his lawyer's back infringed his right to counsel; as Justice Goldberg said in *Escobedo*, the presence of a lawyer at trial would be essentially worthless if the defendant had improvidently confessed beforehand.[262] At the same time, as Justice White said in dissent,

---

[249] *See* Benton v. Maryland, 395 U.S. at 795, *supra* note 247.

[250] 380 U.S. 609 (1965) (Douglas, J., over two dissents) (forbidding comment on a defendant's refusal to incriminate himself).

[251] 385 U.S. 493 (1967) (Douglas, J., over four dissents) (forbidding the use of testimony induced by threat of discharge). *See also* Spevack v. Klein, 385 U.S. 511 (1967) (no opinion of the Court) (forbidding disbarment of an attorney for invoking the privilege, over the same four dissents); Gardner v. Broderick, 392 U.S. 273 (1968) (Fortas, J.), and Uniformed Sanitation Men v. Commissioner of Sanitation, 392 U.S. 280 (1968) (Fortas, J.) (holding public employees could not be fired for invoking the privilege or for refusing to waive immunity from prosecution but adding, *id.* at 278, 284, as Fortas had suggested in casting the tie-breaking vote in *Spevack*, 385 U.S. at 519-20, that they could have been fired for refusing to answer questions relating to performance of their official duties if protected against use of their testimony in criminal proceedings). *See generally* McKay, *Self-Incrimination and the New Privilege*, 1967 Sup. Ct. Rev. 193.

[252] 390 U.S. 39 (1968) (Harlan, J.).

[253] *See* p. 363, note 197 *supra*.

[254] *Accord* Grosso v. United States, 390 U.S. 62 (1968); Haynes v. United States, 390 U.S. 85 (1968) (both also written by Harlan). Chief Justice Warren dissented in all three cases. *Cf.* Albertson v. SACB, p. 437 *supra*.

[255] 387 U.S. 523 (1967) (White, J., over dissents by Clark, Harlan, and Stewart).

[256] *See* p. 409 *supra*.

[257] *Accord* See v. Seattle, 387 U.S. 541 (1967) (White, J., over the same three dissents). The majority also concluded, however, that warrants for such searches could be issued without a showing of probable cause to believe they would turn up persons or materials to be seized, *Camara*, 387 U.S. at 534-39. This modification of the traditional standard seemed to take back much of what the decisions had given. *See* LaFave, *Administrative Searches and the Fourth Amendment: The Camara and See Cases*, 1967 Sup. Ct. Rev. 1, 20 (minimizing the significance of the warrant requirement and defending the Court's refusal to require probable cause because of the need to ensure an "acceptable level of enforcement" and the "relatively minor invasion of personal privacy and dignity" in administrative searches).

[258] 389 U.S. 347 (1967) (Stewart, J., over a dissent by Black).

[259] *See* pp. 168-69 *supra*.

[260] 377 U.S. 201 (1964) (Stewart, J., over dissents by White, Clark, and Harlan).

[261] 378 U.S. 478 (1964) (Goldberg, J., over four dissents).

[262] *See Escobedo*, 378 U.S. at 487-88.

the Court's reasoning seemed to contradict the long-standing principle that voluntary confessions were admissible, since there was no good reason to limit it to suspects who had been jailed or indicted.[263] Furthermore, the Warren Court itself—before Frankfurter's retirement, and by a vote of five to four—had recently reached the contrary conclusion.[264]

In any event, it seems difficult to find compulsion to incriminate oneself in mere questioning of a suspect in custody, as a bare majority found in the famous case of *Miranda v. Arizona*.[265] "Unless adequate protective devices are employed to dispel the compulsion inherent in custodial surroundings," wrote Chief Justice Warren after an extensive review of interrogation practices, "no statement taken from the defendant can truly be the product of his free choice."[266] As White protested in yet another dissent, this was yet another departure: "[I]t has never been suggested, until today, that such questioning was so coercive and accused persons so lacking in hardihood that the very first response to the very first question following the commencement of custody must be conclusively presumed to be the product of an overborne will."[267]

The most promising argument for *Miranda* may be the need for a broad prophylactic rule in light of the difficulty of proving actual coercion.[268] The Constitution itself may be said to embody rules of this nature—witness the much-cited requirement that the President be at least thirty-five years old.[269] Not long after Warren's retirement, moreover, the Court would hold that Congress could ban literacy tests as a means of enforcing the fifteenth amendment prohibition of racial discrimination in voting because of the difficulty of proving discriminatory application.[270] Indeed the Court too could be said to have laid down prophylactic rules as a matter of constitutional interpretation. *McCulloch v. Maryland*,[271] for example, had expressly refused to undertake the difficult inquiry whether the state tax it struck down actually impeded the operation of the national bank; *Schneider v. State*[272] had outlawed a standardless permit requirement because of the difficulty of determining whether it had been discriminatorily applied.[273] On the other hand, in *Lassiter v. Northampton Board of Elections*[274] the Court had declined to condemn literacy tests as such in the absence of congressional action. The fifteenth amendment forbids only racial

---

[263] *See Massiah*, 377 U.S. at 208 (White, J., dissenting); *Escobedo*, 378 U.S. at 495-97 (White, J., dissenting).

[264] *See Massiah*, 377 U.S. at 210 (White, J., dissenting) (citing Crooker v. California, 357 U.S. 433 (1958), and Cicenia v. Lagay, 357 U.S. 504 (1958)).

[265] 384 U.S. 436 (1966) (Warren, C. J., over dissents by Clark, Harlan, Stewart, and White).

[266] *Id.* at 458. *See also* Schulhofer, *Reconsidering* Miranda, 54 U. CHI. L. REV. 435, 446 (1987) ("Custodial interrogation brings psychological pressure to bear for the specific purpose of overcoming the suspect's unwillingness to talk, and it is therefore inherently compelling within the meaning of the fifth amendment.").

[267] *See* 384 U.S. at 535 (White, J., dissenting). *See also id.* at 533 ("Insofar as appears from the Court's opinion, it has not examined a single transcript of any police interrogation, let alone the interrogation that took place in any one of these cases which it decides today."); *id.* at 457 (opinion of the Court) (conceding that "we might not find the defendants' statements to have been involuntary in traditional terms").

[268] *See* Schulhofer, *supra* note 266, at 453.

[269] U.S. CONST. art. II, § 1.

[270] Oregon v. Mitchell, p. 427 *supra*.

[271] 17 U.S. 316, 430 (1819), THE FIRST HUNDRED YEARS at 165-68.

[272] *See* pp. 262-63 *supra*.

[273] *See generally* Strauss, *The Ubiquity of Prophylactic Rules*, 55 U. CHI. L. REV. 190 (1988).

[274] *See* pp. 384-85 *supra*.

discrimination; the fifth amendment forbids only compulsion. As a state case, *Miranda* was not strictly speaking governed by the self-incrimination provision, but the analogy of the literacy test is nonetheless troubling.[275]

Until the states came up with equally effective means to dispel the inherent coercion of custodial questioning, the Court added, they would have to follow a prescribed set of rules:

> Prior to any questioning, the person must be warned that he has a right to remain silent, that any statement he does make may be used as evidence against him, and that he has a right to the presence of an attorney, either retained or appointed. The defendant may waive effectuation of these rights, provided the waiver is made voluntarily, knowingly and intelligently. If, however, he indicates in any manner and at any stage of the process that he wishes to consult with an attorney before speaking there can be no questioning. Likewise, if the individual is alone and indicates in any manner that he does not wish to be interrogated, the police may not question him. The mere fact that he may have answered some questions or volunteered some statements on his own does not deprive him of the right to refrain from answering any further inquiries until he has consulted with an attorney and thereafter consents to be questioned.[276]

It is difficult to see how this exercise in judicial legislation can be reconciled with the constitutional requirement that the Court decide only the case before it.[277]

Other examples of the sweeping changes wrought in criminal procedure by the real Warren Court could be added,[278] and one more deserves mention in the text. *In re Gault*, the greatest opinion of Justice Abe Fortas's brief career, finally established that even children were entitled to a fair trial.[279]

---

[275] *See also Miranda*, 384 U.S. at 535 (White, J., dissenting) (arguing that, even if a prophylactic rule was necessary, less intrusive measures would satisfy the constitutional goal); *id.* at 505 (Harlan, J., dissenting) (doubting the efficacy of the rule: "Those who use third-degree tactics and deny them in court are equally able and destined to lie as skillfully about warnings and waivers.").

[276] *Id.* at 444-45.

[277] *See id.* at 504 (Harlan, J., dissenting) (referring to "the Court's new constitutional code"). A committee report elaborating on this code appears in *id.* at 467-79.

[278] *See, e.g.,* Kennedy v. Mendoza-Martinez, 372 U.S. 144 (1963) (Goldberg, J., over four dissents) (citizenship cannot be withdrawn for absence from country to evade draft without procedural safeguards of criminal trial); Estes v. Texas, 381 U.S. 532 (1965) (Clark, J., with Stewart, White, Black, and Brennan dissenting and Harlan concurring specially) (due process forbids televising trial); United States v. Wade, 388 U.S. 218 (1967) (Brennan, J., over three partial dissents) (counsel is required when a defendant is identified at police lineup); Bloom v. Illinois, 391 U.S. 194 (1968) (White, J., over two dissents) (requiring a jury trial to impose two-year sentence for contempt of court); Witherspoon v. Illinois, 391 U.S. 510 (1968) (Stewart, J., over three dissents) (jury from which persons with scruples against death penalty are excluded may not inflict it); O'Callaghan v. Parker, 395 U.S. 258 (1969) (Douglas, J., over three dissents) (no court-martial of serviceman for offense not connected to service).

[279] 387 U.S. 1 (1967) (over a Stewart dissent). *See generally* Paulsen, *The Constitutional Domestication of the Juvenile Court,* 1967 SUP. CT. REV. 233; Paulsen, Kent v. United States: *The Constitutional Context of Juvenile Courts,* 1966 SUP. CT. REV. 167.

## B.   Prospective Overruling

Not every decision of this period, of course, was favorable to the asserted procedural right,[280] and some observers even perceived a certain tendency toward retrenchment in the last few years of Warren's tenure.[281] Moreover, recognizing the revolutionary scope of the changes it was making, the Court invented a new theory to limit the impact of its new rules on earlier convictions: not all decisions announcing new procedural protections would be applied to persons previously convicted.

Without such a limitation, the Court said, the consequences would have been disastrous:[282] virtually every convict in the country would have had to be retried, though the necessary evidence in many cases had disappeared—for under questionable recent decisions it was never too late to relitigate constitutional challenges to ancient convictions on habeas corpus.[283]

The jurisprudential basis for nonretroactivity, however, was shaky. Courts have no authority to amend the Constitution, only to interpret it; a decision that the Constitution forbids certain conduct today means it forbade the same conduct the day before. Without some degree of retroactivity, indeed, there would be no controversy within the meaning of article III, for the decision would not affect the outcome of the case.[284]

The nonretroactivity doctrine first surfaced in *Linkletter v. Walker,*[285] where the Court declined to apply to a conviction that had become final before *Mapp v. Ohio*[286] the new le announced in that case forbidding the use of evidence obtained by unlawful search or

---

[280]*See, e.g.,* Schmerber v. California, 384 U.S. 757 (1966) (Brennan, J., over four dissents) (upholding compulsory blood testing of a driver involved in an accident); United States v. Hoffa, 385 U.S. 293 (1966) (Stewart, J., with Warren dissenting on nonconstitutional grounds) (criticized in Stone, *The Scope of the Fourth Amendment: Privacy and the Police Use of Spies, Secret Agents, and Informers,* 1976 AM. B. FOUND. RESEARCH J. 1193) (holding infiltration of a conspiracy by a government informer not an unreasonable search); Warden v. Hayden, 387 U.S. 294 (1967) (Brennan, J., over a dissent by Douglas) (overruling the decision in United States v. Boyd, 116 U.S. 660, 623 (1886), THE FIRST HUNDRED YEARS at 444-47, that a search for "mere evidence" was unreasonable); Gilbert v. California, 388 U.S. 263 (1967) (Brennan, J., over three partial dissents) (holding that the taking of a handwriting sample neither required a suspect to incriminate himself nor infringed his right to counsel); Terry v. Ohio, 392 U.S. 1 (1968) (Warren, C. J., over another Douglas dissent) (upholding the protective search of a suspect stopped for questioning despite the absence of probable cause), *see* LaFave, *"Street Encounters" and the Constitution,* 67 MICH. L. REV. 39 (1968); North Carolina v. Pearce, 395 U.S. 711 (1969) (Stewart, J., with three Justices disagreeing) (permitting an increase in the sentence originally imposed after a successful appeal in the absence of a vindictive purpose), criticized in Van Alstyne, *In Gideon's Wake: Harsher Penalties and the "Successful" Criminal Appellant,* 74 YALE L.J. 606 (1965).

[281]*See, e.g.,* Israel, *Criminal Procedure, the Burger Court, and the Legacy of the Warren Court,* 75 MICH. L. REV. 1319 (1977); Kamisar, *The Warren Court (Was It Really So Defense-Minded?), The Burger Court (Is It Really So Prosecution-Oriented?), and Police Investigatory Practices,* in V. BLASI, THE BURGER COURT: THE COUNTER-REVOLUTION THAT WASN'T 62, 63-68 (1983).

[282]*See* Linkletter v. Walker, 381 U.S. 618, 637 (1965); Tehan v. Shott, 382 U.S. 406, 418-19 (1966); Stovall v. Denno, 388 U.S. 293, 300 (1967).

[283]*See* Brown v. Allen, p. 364 *supra.*

[284]*See* Stovall v. Denno, 388 U.S. 293, 301 (1967). *See also* Mishkin, *Foreword: The High Court, the Great Writ, and the Due Process of Time and Law,* 79 HARV. L. REV. 56, 60-61 (1965) ("[I]t is the basic role of courts to decide disputes after they have arisen. That function requires that judicial decisions operate (at least ordinarily) with retroactive effect."). For an early defense of nonretroactivity see Levy, *Realist Jurisprudence and Prospective Overruling,* 109 U. PA. L. REV. 1 (1960).

[285]381 U.S. 618 (1965). *See also id.* at 640-53 (Black and Douglas, JJ., dissenting).

[286]*See* pp. 408-09 *supra.*

seizure. Justice Clark's basic argument could have been phrased as an interpretation of the exclusionary rule itself: the reason for excluding such evidence was to deter unlawful searches and seizures, and it was too late to deter those that had already occurred.[287] This argument plainly went too far; it had also been too late to deter the prior search in *Mapp* itself.[288] In any event, Clark made clear that he was setting forth a test for the retroactive application of new criminal-procedure decisions in general, not merely interpreting the exclusionary rule;[289] and later decisions found additional rules that were not to be given full retroactive application either.

*Linkletter* removed any doubt that, like so many other constitutional questions for the Warren Court, the extent of retroactivity depended upon "weigh[ing] the merits and de-merits" of the contemplated action.[290] The case for retroactive application of an exclusion-ary rule, Clark added, was weaker in the case of an unreasonable search than in that of a coerced confession; for only in the latter case were there doubts as to the reliability of the evidence obtained.[291] Justice Stewart expanded on this theme in denying full retroactive effect to the decision in *Griffin v. California*[292] forbidding comment on a defendant's re-fusal to incriminate himself: unlike denial of the right to counsel, comment on the exercise of the fifth amendment privilege created no substantial risk of convicting the innocent.[293]

Whether or not this decision did justice to the purposes of the privilege,[294] denial of the right to counsel when the victim of a crime is asked to identify a suspect would seem to fall on the other side of the line. As the Court had stressed in holding counsel constitution-ally required, the risk of mistaken identification raised doubts as to the correctness of the conviction.[295] Nonetheless only Black and Douglas, who had dissented in *Linkletter* itself,

---

[287] 381 U.S. at 636-37. *See also* Bender, *The Retroactive Effect of an Overruling Constitutional Decision: Mapp v. Ohio*, 110 U. PA. L. REV. 650, 653 (1962) ("[T]he purposes of the new law do not seem to be meaning-fully served by applying it to the past.").

[288] *See* Mishkin, *supra* note 284, at 75-76; *id.* at 73-74 (adding that the argument of justifiable reliance was weak in *Linkletter* because the unconstitutionality of the search had been clear at the time it was made).

[289] *See* 381 U.S. at 629:

> Once the premise is accepted that we are neither required to apply, nor prohibited from applying, a decision retrospectively, we must then weigh the merits and demerits in each case by looking to the prior history of the rule in question, its purpose and effect, and whether retrospective operation will further or retard its operation.

[290] *Id.* at 628.

[291] *Id.* at 638.

[292] *See* p. 448 *supra*.

[293] Tehan v. Shott, 382 U.S. 406, 415-16 (1966). Black and Douglas dissented for the reasons they had given in *Linkletter;* Warren and Fortas did not participate. *Id.* at 419. *See also* Johnson v. New Jersey, 384 U.S. 719 (1966) (Warren, C. J., over the same two dissents) (denying retroactive application, for similar reasons, to the limits on questioning of suspects announced in Escobedo v. Illinois and Miranda v. Arizona, pp. 448-50 *supra*).

[294] *See Griffin*, 380 U.S. at 613 (quoting from an earlier decision: "It is not every one who can safely venture on the witness stand though entirely innocent of the charge against him."); *Tehan*, 382 U.S. at 414-15 n.12 (acknowledging that "the privilege . . . is often 'a protection to the innocent' "); Slochower v. Board of Educa-tion, 350 U.S. at 555, 557-58 (holding it arbitrary to dismiss an employee for invoking the fifth amendment, because "[t]he privilege serves to protect the innocent who otherwise might be ensnared by ambiguous circum-stances": "[N]o inference of guilt was possible from the claim before the federal committee. . . ."), pp. 386-88 *supra*. For thorough discussion of the issues of retroactivity of *Griffin* and *Escobedo* see Mishkin, *supra* note 284, at 92-101.

[295] *See* United States v. Wade, 388 U.S. at 228 ("The vagaries of eyewitness identification are well-known; the annals of criminal law are rife with instances of mistaken identification."), *supra* note 278.

objected when the Court in *Stovall v. Denno* denied retroactivity to the identification rule. The danger of convicting the innocent, said Justice Brennan, was not so great as if counsel had been denied at trial, and it was outweighed by the disruptive effect of retroactivity on the administration of justice.[296]

Justice Harlan had joined the early decisions denying retroactivity in order, as he put it, to limit the harm done by what he considered erroneous interpretations of the Constitution.[297] In 1969, however, emphasizing the unfairness of making affirmance or reversal turn upon which defendant appealed first, Harlan pleaded for abandonment of the nonretroactivity doctrine altogether, suggesting a partial return to traditional limitations on habeas corpus jurisdiction to reduce the adverse effects on ancient convictions.[298] It is not easy to disagree with his conclusion.

The controversy over retroactivity was a troublesome sideshow that raised fundamental jurisprudential problems. It should not distract attention from the major revolution worked by the later Warren Court, often over four dissents, in the fairness of criminal procedure.[299]

---

[296] 388 U.S. 293, 297-300 (1967). The determinative criteria, Justice Brennan declared, were "(a) the purpose to be served by the new standards, (b) the extent of the reliance by law enforcement authorities on the old standards, and (c) the effect on the administration of justice of a retroactive application. . . ." *Id.* at 297. *See also* DeStefano v. Woods, 392 U.S. 631 (1968) (per curiam, over the same two dissents) (denying retroactivity to the jury-trial decisions in Duncan v. Louisiana, 392 U.S. at 633, p. 447 *supra,* despite the concession that "the right to jury trial generally tends to prevent arbitrariness and repression"). Additional difficulties in administering the nonretroactivity concept are discussed in Kitch, *The Supreme Court's Code of Criminal Procedure: 1968-1969 Edition,* 1969 SUP. CT. REV. 155, 183-94.

Black's dissent in *Stovall,* 388 U.S. at 302-06, added a protest against the majority's concession, *id.* at 301-02, that apart from the right to counsel such an identification procedure might be so unfair in some cases as to offend due process:

> No one has ever been able to point to a word in our constitutional history that shows the Framers ever intended that the Due Process Clause of the Fifth or Fourteenth Amendment was designed to mean anything more than that defendants charged with crimes should be entitled to a trial governed by the laws, constitutional and statutory, that are in existence at the time of the commission of the crime and the time of the trial.

*Id.* at 305. *Cf.* Adamson v. California, 332 U.S. at 68-125 (Black, J., dissenting), p. 362, note 194 *supra.*

[297] *See* Desist v. United States, 394 U.S. 244, 258 (1969) (Harlan, J., dissenting).

[298] *Id.* at 256-69 (Harlan, J., dissenting) (reflecting a suggestion made by Mishkin, *supra* note 284, at 77-87). The Court had vacillated about whether nonretroactivity should insulate from attack all errors committed before the announcement of a new rule (except in the case announcing it) or only those in cases in which avenues of direct review of the conviction had already been exhausted. *Compare, e.g., Linkletter* and *Tehan* (holding only collateral review precluded) *with Johnson, Stovall,* and *Desist* (holding direct review precluded as well). As Justice Brennan said in *Desist,* 394 U.S. at 253, the arguments against retroactivity seemed equally applicable in both situations. *Accord* Mishkin, *supra* note 284, at 74.

[299] For an approving summary of developments in criminal procedure during this period see Pye, *The Warren Court and Criminal Procedure,* 67 MICH. L. REV. 249 (1968). Significant advances were likewise made in the fairness of procedure in noncriminal matters. *See, e.g.,* Willner v. Committee on Character and Fitness, 373 U.S. 96 (1963) (Douglas, J.) (presaging an explosion in administrative procedure by holding an applicant for what was once regarded as the "privilege" of bar admission (and thus not "property" within the due process clause) entitled to a hearing on the issue of his character and fitness); Sniadach v. Family Finance Corp., 395 U.S. 337 (1969) (Douglas, J., over a dissent by Black) (holding that the traditional practice of *ex parte* wage garnishment deprived an alleged debtor of property without due process); Jenkins v. McKeithen, 395 U.S. 411 (1969) (no opinion for Court) (holding fair procedures required before a person could be branded as a criminal).

# Conclusion to Part Seven

These were heady times. While Earl Warren was Chief Justice, and especially after the retirement of Justice Frankfurter in 1962, the Supreme Court remade constitutional law in the mold Justice Stone had cast in 1938, giving broad protection to the political process, to discrete and insular minorities, and to interests protected by the Bill of Rights.[1] In so doing the Court made this country a decidedly better place.

Chief Justice Warren, the former Republican Governor of California, became the symbol of the aggressive Court over which he presided.[2] Appropriately, he wrote for the Court on many of the major occasions on which the Justices challenged the authority of other branches of government: *Brown v. Board of Education (I) and (II), Loving v. Virginia, Watkins v. United States, Reynolds v. Sims, South Carolina v. Katzenbach, Miranda v. Arizona, Powell v. McCormack*. Before Frankfurter's retirement Warren often dissented,[3] but he generally left the writing of dissenting opinions to Black, Douglas, and Brennan. After the votes of these four were augmented by that of Goldberg (and later by those of Abe Fortas and Thurgood Marshall), it was Justice Brennan who—along with the Chief Justice—most closely embodied the spirit of the Warren Court.[4] Already the author of

[1] *See* United States v. Carolene Products Co., 304 U.S. at 152-53 n.4, p. 244 *supra*.

[2] *See* Ely, *The Chief*, 88 HARV. L. REV. 11 (1974) (citing Warren as "one of the greatest single forces for right the nation has ever known"); Pollak, *The Legacy of Earl Warren*, 88 HARV. L. REV. 8, 8 (1974) (noting Warren's "catalytic" role in *Brown*'s "recommitment to the promise declared at Gettysburg [and] codified in the Fourteenth Amendment") ("[O]n a scale not matched by any other judge, he brought a measure of redemption to his country.").

[3] For documentation of the increasing professional and personal division between Warren and Frankfurter see Schwartz, *Felix Frankfurter and Earl Warren: A Study of a Deteriorating Relationship*, 1980 SUP. CT. REV. 115.

[4] *See* Hutchinson, *Hail to the Chief: Earl Warren and the Supreme Court*, 81 MICH. L. REV. 922, 924, 930 (1983):

> To the extent that the Court over which Warren presided has any intellectual legacy that is accessible to those trained in doctrine and not in ethics, it is Brennan who is responsible. . . . [I]f any

important opinions in *Speiser v. Randall* and *Baker v. Carr*, Brennan added such landmark decisions as *NAACP v. Button, New York Times v. Sullivan, Sherbert v. Verner,
Katzenbach v. Morgan,* and *Shapiro v. Thompson.* After 1962, moreover, Brennan almost
always voted with the majority in constitutional cases.[5] In this he differed significantly
from both Douglas and Black, Warren's other stauch allies during the dark years—for the
former was repeatedly prepared to go even further than the majority, while the latter was
increasingly left behind.

Douglas dissented, for example, when the Court declined to strike down an apportionment attacked on racial grounds in *Wright v. Rockefeller,* a ban on travel to Cuba in *Zemel
v. Rusk,* an English literacy requirement in *Cardona v. Power,* a search for "mere evidence" in *Warden v. Hayden,* a conviction for draft card burning in *United States v.
O'Brien,* a bench trial for contempt in *United States v. Barnett,*[6] and a blood test for
suspected drunk drivers in *Schmerber v. California.* In numerous other cases he concurred
on grounds broader than the majority thought it necessary or desirable to take. He argued
in *Garner v. Louisiana* and *Reitman v. Mulkey* that the state was responsible for private
segregation; in *Gideon v. Wainwright* that the entire Bill of Rights applied to the states; in
*Brandenburg v. Ohio* that dissident speech could not be punished even if it created a clear
and present danger of harm.

Owing in substantial part to his offhand approach to opinion writing, Douglas left
behind surprisingly few memorable statements for the Court. His opinion in *Elfbrandt v.
Russell,* for example, while establishing an important new point of first amendment doctrine, "does not pause to argue the fundamental point it unearths about the relationship of
partial sanctions to direct sanctions."[7] His most famous effort, the contraceptive case of
*Griswold v. Connecticut,* which remains to be discussed,[8] comes across as one of the most
hypocritical opinions in the history of the Court. "Critics have sometimes charged," wrote
one admiring observer, "that [Douglas] was result oriented and guilty of oversimplifica-
tion; those who understand how he thought, and who share his compassion, conscience,
and sense of fair dealing, see him as courageous and farsighted."[9] There is no necessary
contradiction between these two views.

Justice Black, on the other hand, objected to the Court's tendency to blame states for
what he viewed as private action in *Evans v. Newton, Reitman v. Mulkey, Hunter v. Erickson,* and *Amalgamated Food Stores v. Logan Valley;* to its freewheeling use of due process
to strike down pretrial garnishment, death-qualified juries, and a ban on contraception;
and to its aggressive employment of equal protection outside the fields of race and reapportionment to invalidate poll taxes, discrimination against illegitimates, and durational

---

single justice deserves to be identified with the constitutional revolution engineered by the Supreme Court in the last generation, it is William J. Brennan and not Earl Warren.

[5] The rare exceptions included Adderley v. Florida, where the Court held there was no right to demonstrate
on jailhouse grounds, and Powell v. Texas, where the majority concluded an alcoholic could be punished for
public drunkenness.

[6] 376 U.S. 681 (1964).

[7] *See* H. KALVEN, A WORTHY TRADITION: FREEDOM OF SPEECH IN AMERICA 357 (1988). Typically, Justice
Brennan improved upon Douglas's arguments in the subsequent *Keyishian* case.

[8] *See* pp. 458-59 *infra.*

[9] *See* Ginsburg, *Reflections of Justice Douglas's First Law Clerk,* 93 HARV. L. REV. 1403, 1406 (1980).

residency requirements for welfare. Moreover, despite his New Deal background, Black was even moved on occasion to dissent from decisions of the later Warren years that he thought interfered with rights reserved to the states (*South Carolina v. Katzenbach, Daniel v. Paul*) or infringed the largely forgotten contract clause.[10] Finally, despite his well-deserved reputation as a vigorous if not absolutist defender of free expression, it was Black who cast the decisive vote in *Adderley v. Florida* to limit the growth of the public forum doctrine permitting speech on public property. For the Court, Black wrote such memorable decisions as *Torcaso v. Watkins, Engel v. Vitale, Gideon v. Wainwright,* and the Prince Edward County school case; but as in earlier days he made his indelible mark largely in dissent.[11]

The leading spokesman for the old order was not so much Frankfurter, who had laid down the guiding principles in earlier years, as the admirable John Marshall Harlan, who engaged Black in a prodigious continuing debate over subversive speech while he still had five votes and who dissented vigorously from much of what happened thereafter. Harlan wrote for the Court to deny claims of free expression in such cases as *Lerner v. Casey, Barenblatt v. United States, In re Anastaplo,* and *Konigsberg v. California (II).* The list of his over 150 dissenting votes in constitutional cases ranges from dissident-speech cases such as *Gibson, DeGregory, Elfbrandt,* and *Keyishian v. Board of Regents* and criminal matters such as *Griffin v. Illinois, Mapp v. Ohio, Miranda v. Arizona,* and *Duncan v. Louisiana* to *NAACP v. Button, Katzenbach v. Morgan, Reitman v. Mulkey, Shapiro v. Thompson, Levy v. Louisiana,* and a whole range of cases involving reapportionment and other election issues. He went along, however, with *Watkins v. United States, Sweezy v. New Hampshire, Gideon v. Wainwright, In re Gault,* and *Katz v. United States* as well as—perhaps more surprisingly—with *Griswold v. Connecticut;* he wrote eloquently in defense of freedom of association in *Yates v. United States* and *NAACP v. Alabama.* "I believe," wrote the eminent Judge Henry J. Friendly, "that there has never been a Justice of the Supreme Court who has so consistently maintained a high standard of performance or, despite differences in views, has enjoyed such nearly uniform respect from his colleagues, the inferior bench, the bar, and the academy."[12]

In early years Harlan was generally joined in his restrained position not only by Frankfurter—whose most notable statements during the Warren years were his inordinately detailed and deferential opinions for the majority in *Communist Party v. Subversive Activities Control Board,* concurring in *McGowan v. Maryland,* and dissenting in *Baker v. Carr*[13]—but also by the colorless Reed, Minton, Burton, and Clark, who had shown similar voting patterns during the time of Chief Justice Vinson.[14] The first three of these Justices, all of whom disappeared by 1958, wrote nothing of significance for the Court

[10] *See* El Paso v. Simmons, 379 U.S. 497 (1965).

[11] *See,* in addition to the cases already noted, Barenblatt v. United States, Uphaus v. Wyman, *In re* Anastaplo, Communist Party v. Subversive Activities Control Board, and Zemel v. Rusk. On the question of consistency between Black's earlier and later opinions see Snowiss, *The Legacy of Justice Black,* 1973 SUP. CT. REV. 187.

[12] Friendly, *Mr. Justice Harlan, As Seen by a Friend and Judge of an Inferior Court,* 85 HARV. L. REV. 382, 384 (1971). *See generally* Bourguignon, *The Second Mr. Justice Harlan: His Principles of Judicial Decision-making,* 1979 SUP. CT. REV. 251.

[13] Frankfurter also wrote for the Court to strike down a racial gerrymander in Gomillion v. Lightfoot and for himself and Harlan in eloquent defense of academic freedom in *Sweezy.*

[14] The great Robert Jackson died prematurely in 1954 after casting a reportedly hesitant vote to strike down separate but equal schools in *Brown* and thus played little part in the Warren period.

except for Burton's benighted opinion in *Beilan v. Board of Education;* all three dissented when the Court stood up against civilian court-martial in *Toth* and self-incrimination in *Slochower.* Clark, who dissented from most decisions protecting subversive speech[15] and from much of the criminal-law revolution,[16] was the most interesting and unpredictable of this group. Not only did he go along with most of the reapportionment and race decisions and write to strike down school prayers in *Abington School District v. Schempp;* he also was the author of both *Slochower* and *Mapp v. Ohio.*[17]

After the departure of Reed, Burton, and Minton, Harlan was often joined not only by Frankfurter and Clark but also by Potter Stewart and the undistinguished Charles Whittaker[18] or (in criminal and security matters) by Byron White, who succeeded Whittaker in 1962. Stewart and White were among the more interesting members of the Warren Court. Stewart cast the decisive vote to reject first amendment claims in several major cases involving alleged subversion[19] and later dissented—as did White—when the new majority began upholding such claims[20] or extending the rights of the accused.[21] Unlike White, moreover, who was with the activist majority in most equal protection cases, Stewart also dissented from *Evans v. Newton, Reitman v. Mulkey, Harper v. Board of Elections, Katzenbach v. Morgan,* and *Levy v. Louisiana,* as well as from *Griswold v. Connecticut,* where only Black agreed with him. On the other hand, Stewart as well as White was with the Court in *Reynolds v. Sims* and *Shapiro v. Thompson,* and he wrote for the majority in such aggressive decisions as *Robinson v. California, Massiah v. United States,* and *Witherspoon v. Illinois,* in all of which White dissented.

In most cases, in my opinion, the Warren Court reached its revolutionary conclusions within the confines of fair interpretation of the relevant constitutional provisions[22]—often, indeed, fulfilling the promise of provisions that earlier decisions had given an excessively cramped application. At the same time, despite (or in part because of) their willingness to face widespread opposition in such matters as segregation, reapportionment, and school prayers, the Justices exhibited a realistic awareness of the practical limits of judicial power by refusing, despite serious doubts based upon article I's vesting in *Congress* of the power "to declare war," to grant certiorari in cases questioning the constitutionality of the undeclared hostilities in Vietnam.[23]

---

[15] *E.g., Watkins, Sweezy, Yates, Speiser, Aptheker, Elfbrandt, Keyishian, Gibson.*

[16] *E.g., Robinson, Massiah, Escobedo, Miranda,* and the court-martial and citizenship cases.

[17] Rumor had it that Clark had once been burned as a young lawyer by a court's refusal to exclude unlawfully obtained evidence, but one observer termed him an "underrated" judge who exhibited a considerable capacity for growth. *See* B. SCHWARTZ, SUPER CHIEF: EARL WARREN AND HIS SUPREME COURT 58 (1983).

[18] Whittaker, who sat from 1957 until 1962, wrote two opinions of interest: a concurrence challenging Frankfurter's facile reasoning in Gomillion v. Lightfoot and a sensitive dissent from the loss of citizenship in Perez v. Brownell. *See* B. SCHWARTZ, *supra* note 17, at 215-16 (noting Whittaker's "lack of intellectual capacity and inability to reach decisions" and concluding that, though "serious and hardworking," he "may have been the worst Justice of the century").

[19] *E.g., Barenblatt, Uphaus,* and *Anastaplo.*

[20] *See Elfbrandt, Keyishian, Gibson,* and *DeGregory.*

[21] *E.g., Escobedo, Miranda,* Griffin v. California, and United States v. Wade.

[22] *See also* Ely, *The Wages of Crying Wolf: A Comment on* Roe v. Wade, 82 YALE L.J. 920, 943 (1973) (concluding that, "by and large," the Warren Court "attempted to defend its decisions in terms of inferences from values the Constitution marks as special").

[23] *E.g.,* Mora v. McNamara, 389 U.S. 934 (1967). *See* Henkin, *Foreword: On Drawing Lines,* 82 HARV. L. REV. 63, 88-91 (1968) (concluding that this course "may well have been the better part of valor"). *Cf.* pp. 379-

Not surprisingly, however, the activism of the Warren years spawned occasional excesses. In such cases as *Bolling v. Sharpe, Reitman v. Mulkey, Watkins v. United States, Slochower v. Board of Regents, Griffin v. Illinois, Miranda v. Arizona,* and *Robinson v. California,* the Court's zeal may have got the better of its judgment. The most egregious example, however, is the famous 1965 decision in *Griswold v. Connecticut,* where even Justice Harlan succumbed to the temptation to strike down a law forbidding the use of contraceptives.[24]

Of course the law was utterly unreasonable.[25] The difficulty was that it seemed to offend nothing in the Constitution. The most obvious argument was substantive due process, which had begun to rear its ugly head again in occasional Warren Court opinions.[26] Harlan[27] and White, in separate concurrences,[28] candidly relied on due process, as both Douglas and Harlan had done when an earlier challenge was rejected as nonjusticiable.[29] Writing for the Court in *Griswold,* however, Douglas, who had done as much as any of his brethren to bury that discreditable doctrine entirely,[30] pulled out all the stops in an effort to find alternative handholds for his conclusion.

Despite Douglas's mystical references to "penumbras" and "emanations,"[31] it is difficult to take seriously his suggestion that the use of contraceptives had anything to do with freedom of expression, unreasonable searches, self-incrimination, or the quartering of troops.[32] Justice Goldberg's reliance on the ninth amendment[33]—which the Court, significantly, had never employed to strike down anything since its ratification in 1791— seemed to misread the history of that provision. As Justice Black said, "[t]hat Amendment was passed, . . . as every student of history knows, to assure the people that the Constitution in all its provisions was intended to limit the Federal Government to the powers granted expressly or by necessary implication."[34] Even Justice Douglas, who mentioned the ninth amendment in passing in *Griswold,*[35] later acknowledged that it "obviously does not create federally enforceable rights."[36]

---

80, 385-96 *supra* (discussing Naim v. Naim, the "all deliberate speed" formula, and the early subversion cases). For an argument that the war was unconstitutional see Van Alstyne, *Congress, the President, and the Power to Declare War: A Requiem for Vietnam,* 121 U. PA. L. REV. 1 (1972).

[24] 381 U.S. 479 (1965) (Douglas, J.).

[25] *See id.* at 505-06 (White, J., concurring).

[26] *E.g., Slochower,* Bolling v. Sharpe, Loving v. Virginia, and Shapiro v. Thompson.

[27] *See* 381 U.S. at 499-502 (Harlan, J., concurring).

[28] *See id.* at 502-07 (White, J., concurring).

[29] *See* Poe v. Ullman, 367 U.S. 497, 515-22 (1967) (Douglas, J., dissenting); *id.* at 539-55 (Harlan, J., dissenting).

[30] *See* Olsen v. Nebraska, pp. 239-40 *supra.*

[31] *See* 381 U.S. at 484.

[32] *Id.* at 482-86. For criticism of this suggestion see *id.* at 528-29 (Stewart, J., dissenting); Posner, *The Uncertain Protection of Privacy by the Supreme Court,* 1979 SUP. CT. REV. 173, 190-96.

[33] *See* 381 U.S. at 486-99 (Goldberg, J., joined by Warren and Brennan, concurring).

[34] *Id.* at 520 (Black, J., dissenting). *See also id.* at 529-30 (Stewart, J., dissenting); Kelly, *Clio and the Court: An Illicit Love Affair,* 1965 SUP. CT. REV. 119, 149-55; THE FIRST HUNDRED YEARS at 48-49 n.128, and authorities cited.

[35] *See* 381 U.S. at 484.

[36] Doe v. Bolton, 410 U.S. 179, 210 (1973) (Douglas, J., concurring). Goldberg himself ultimately backed off from his suggestion: "In sum, the Ninth Amendment simply lends strong support to the view that the 'liberty' protected by the Fifth and Fourteenth Amendments . . . is not restricted to rights specifically mentioned in the first eight amendments." *Griswold,* 381 U.S. at 493. Thus there appeared to be a majority not only for Douglas's opinion of the Court but also for the substantive due process theory.

"Whenever you get such a potpourri of constitutional provisions as suggested . . . in *Griswold*," one observer wrote, "the feeling must grow that the answer was not found in the Constitution at all."[37] Only Justice Stewart joined stern old Hugo Black in protesting that this sort of thing was no more justifiable in a good cause than it had been in the *Dred Scott* case or in *Lochner v. New York*.[38] The *Griswold* dissent showed that Black had been in earnest when he insisted in *Adamson v. California* that the Bill of Rights was not only incorporated in the fourteenth amendment but limited its meaning:[39] judges are no more entitled to invent new limitations than to ignore those the Constitution contains.[40]

On the whole, however, it was an inspiring time; a time of triumph for liberty, democracy, and equality, and for the human spirit; a time to be proud of the Supreme Court, of the Constitution, and of the United States.[41]

---

[37] P. KURLAND, POLITICS, THE CONSTITUTION AND THE WARREN COURT 93 (1970).

[38] *See* 381 U.S. at 507-27 (Black, J., dissenting); *id.* at 527-31 (Stewart, J., dissenting). *Cf.* Scott v. Sandford, 60 U.S. 393, 450-52 (1857), THE FIRST HUNDRED YEARS at 271-72; Lochner v. New York, pp. 47-50 *supra*.

[39] *See* p. 362 *supra*.

[40] Chief Justice Warren aptly and admiringly described Black as a constitutional "fundamentalist." Warren, *A Tribute to Hugo L. Black,* 85 HARV. L. REV. 1, 1 (1971). *See also* Freund, *Mr. Justice Black and the Judicial Function,* 14 U.C.L.A. L. REV. 467 (1967); G. DUNNE, HUGO BLACK AND THE JUDICIAL REVOLUTION 398 (1977). *Griswold* is discussed in detail in a symposium in 64 MICH. L. REV. 97-288 (1965).

[41] *See* Cox, *Chief Justice Earl Warren,* 83 HARV. L. REV. 1, 1 (1969) ("It will be recognized a century hence . . . that the responsibility of government for equality among men, the openness of American society to change and reform, and the decency of the administration of criminal justice received both creative and enduring impetus from the work of the Warren Court"). For a less admiring assessment see P. KURLAND, *supra* note 37, at 143-45, 165-68 (finding it "difficult to quarrel with the merits" of such principles as nonsegregated education and equal apportionment but criticizing the Court for both an "absence of workmanlike product" and a tendency to equate the undesirability of legislation with its unconstitutionality and quoting Molière:

Et c'est une folie à nulle autre seconde
De vouloir se mêler de corriger le monde.

*Le Misanthrope,* act I, scene 1).

# Part Eight

Chief Justice Burger
1969–1986

# Introduction to Part Eight

After sixteen years as Chief Justice, Earl Warren stepped down in 1969. Those years had dramatically altered the constitutional landscape. Revolutionary advances in racial equality, expression and religion, criminal procedure, and the integrity of the electoral process had made the speculations of *Carolene Products* a reality.

Now the Chief who had presided over this sea change was gone, and so in a trice were three of his colleagues. Abe Fortas, whom President Lyndon Johnson had hoped to elevate to Warren's center seat, departed unceremoniously under the only ethical cloud yet to shadow a sitting Justice,[1] and the veteran giants Hugo Black and John Harlan were forced off by illness.[2] Harlan had dissented from much of the revolution, but in Warren, Black, and Fortas the juggernaut had lost three of its engines. Thus when Republican Richard Nixon found himself with four vacancies to fill in his first three years in the White House, there were hopes and fears of another reversal in the Supreme Court's direction.

The appointment of Warren Burger as Chief Justice, followed by those of Harry Blackmun, Lewis Powell, and William Rehnquist as Associates, seemed to lend strength to these expectations. The first two were Republican judges from Minnesota, the third a Southern Democrat who had been President of the American Bar Association, and the fourth Nixon's own Deputy Attorney General.[3] Other Republican Presidents fanned the fire by replacing the zealous William O. Douglas with John Paul Stevens in 1975 and the moderate Potter Stewart with Sandra Day O'Connor in 1981—for the Court's first

---

[1] *See* B. MURPHY, FORTAS: THE RISE AND RUIN OF A SUPREME COURT JUSTICE (1988).

[2] *See* KURLAND, *1970 Term: Notes on the Emergence of the Burger Court*, 1971 SUP. CT. REV. 265, 319-21 ("[W]hatever one felt about the conclusions they reached, it has to be conceded that these were the intellectual leaders of the Court. . . . There is none left behind on the Court after the departure of Black and Harlan to carry out the same traditions of greatness.").

[3] *See* Kurland, *1971 Term: The Year of the Stewart-White Court*, 1972 SUP. CT. REV. 181, 185 (reporting on the basis of early voting patterns that "the Minnesota Twins have expanded into the Nixon quartet").

woman member was widely believed a judicial conservative. By this time only three members of the Warren Court remained: William Brennan and Thurgood Marshall, who had been dedicated members of the Warren coalition, and Byron White, whose record was mixed. A solid majority of six owed their appointments to Presidents Nixon, Ford, and Reagan.[4]

If there was to be a counterrevolution, however, it was slow in coming.[5] The most notable decisions of the Court under Burger were those that appeared to *extend* the work of the Warren period, not to restrict it. It was the Burger Court, not its predecessor, that first protected abortion and commercial speech and legitimated busing and affirmative action; that first curbed sex discrimination, political patronage, and aid to parochial schools; that constitutionalized administrative procedure and even called a temporary halt to capital punishment.

In none of these fields did the Court go as far as at least two of its members wished. In several instances, moreover, the Court later pulled back somewhat from the implications of its initial decisions. In addition, almost from the first the new Justices demonstrated a tendency to nibble away one case at a time at the edifice of criminal procedure that the Warren Court had erected, while a series of decisions upholding the constitutionality of plea bargaining suggested that it hardly mattered what procedures were required in the uncommon event of a trial. Finally, the Court under Burger manifested a revived concern for the separation of federal powers—a basic constitutional precept that had been largely ignored since the otherwise unlamented days before Franklin Roosevelt.

It was a time as dramatic for the departures that did not occur as for those that did.

JUSTICES OF THE SUPREME COURT DURING THE TIME OF CHIEF JUSTICE BURGER

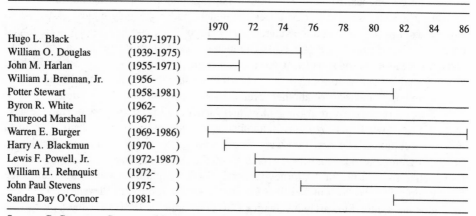

| | | 1970 | 72 | 74 | 76 | 78 | 80 | 82 | 84 | 86 |
|---|---|---|---|---|---|---|---|---|---|---|
| Hugo L. Black | (1937-1971) | | | | | | | | | |
| William O. Douglas | (1939-1975) | | | | | | | | | |
| John M. Harlan | (1955-1971) | | | | | | | | | |
| William J. Brennan, Jr. | (1956-  ) | | | | | | | | | |
| Potter Stewart | (1958-1981) | | | | | | | | | |
| Byron R. White | (1962-  ) | | | | | | | | | |
| Thurgood Marshall | (1967-  ) | | | | | | | | | |
| Warren E. Burger | (1969-1986) | | | | | | | | | |
| Harry A. Blackmun | (1970-  ) | | | | | | | | | |
| Lewis F. Powell, Jr. | (1972-1987) | | | | | | | | | |
| William H. Rehnquist | (1972-  ) | | | | | | | | | |
| John Paul Stevens | (1975-  ) | | | | | | | | | |
| Sandra Day O'Connor | (1981-  ) | | | | | | | | | |

SOURCE: G. GUNTHER, CASES AND MATERIALS ON CONSTITUTIONAL LAW app. B (11th ed. 1985).
[5] *See generally* THE BURGER COURT: THE COUNTER-REVOLUTION THAT WASN'T (V. Blasi ed. 1983).

# 14

# Privacy and Equality

## I.  THE NEW MORALITY

### A.  Abortion, Part I

Best known perhaps of all Burger Court decisions is *Roe v. Wade,* the 1973 case in which the Court invalidated a Texas law forbidding abortion except to save the life of the mother.[1]

By all rights the case ought never to have been decided. When the suit was filed, Jane Roe was a pregnant woman precluded by the statute from obtaining the abortion she desired.[2] Not surprisingly, by the time her case reached the Supreme Court she was no longer pregnant.[3] There remained the possibility that she might have another unwanted pregnancy, but the Court found such a scenario too speculative to support a justiciable controversy.[4] Given this conclusion, it should have followed that the case was moot; Ms. Roe had no more interest in attacking the law than if she had never been pregnant at all.

Pregnancy, however, never lasts long enough to permit Supreme Court review. If classical mootness principles were applied, said the Court, the issue might escape decision entirely. Invoking precedents of the aggressive Warren period, the Justices found the mat-

---

[1]410 U.S. 113, 117–18 (1973).

[2]Id. at 120.

[3]The suit was filed in March 1970, the Court's decision rendered in January 1973. The normal human gestation period, the opinion noted, was 266 days. *See id.* at 124-25.

[4]*See id.* at 127-29 (rejecting on this ground the challenge of a nonpregnant woman and her husband) ("Their alleged injury rests on possible future contraceptive failure, possible future pregnancy, possible future unpreparedness for parenthood, and possible future impairment of health. Any one or more of these several possibilities may not take place. . . ."). This analysis was rather miserly, since the complaint was that the risk of future harm interfered with present enjoyment of the plaintiffs' marriage by deterring sexual relations—a contention the Court dismissed as "the bare allegation" of an "indirect" injury, *id.* at 128. *Cf.* Laird v. Tatum, 408 U.S. 1,

ter justiciable.[5] Not so many years before, the Court had insisted that judicial review was not an end in itself but a mere by-product of deciding disputes;[6] now it was prepared to overlook the absence of a dispute in order to assure that a statute not "evade" review.[7]

On the merits, it may be difficult for those who have come of age since the 1960s to appreciate what a revolutionary decision *Roe* was. Whole generations had grown up accepting without question the constitutionality of laws against abortion; like narcotic drugs, homosexual relations, and cohabitation out of wedlock, abortion was beyond the pale. The analogies in the preceding sentence tell much of the story: the legal revolution within the Court reflected a social revolution outside its walls.

The legal seeds of the abortion decision had been sown long before in the notorious *Dred Scott* and *Lochner* decisions, which had established that substantively unreasonable laws deprived persons of life, liberty, or property without due process of law.[8] Twice repudiated by a nation weary of the reactionary limitations imposed by those decisions, the doctrine had sent forth tentative shoots in support of popular liberal causes during the Warren years—though the bad reputation of substantive due process had led the judges as often as not to cloak their conclusions under such unconvincing alternative labels as "penumbras," cruel and unusual punishment, and the ninth amendment.[9]

Compared with these antecedents, *Roe v. Wade* had the virtue of candor, for the decision was pegged squarely on due process.[10] Whatever one may think of the result in policy terms, however, it is subject to the same analytical counterarguments as its illiberal fore-

---

13-14 (1972) (Burger, C. J., over dissents by Douglas, Marshall, Brennan, and Stewart) (dismissing challenges to government surveillance alleged to chill present political activity by terming "speculative" the government's later use of the information acquired). A doctor facing present and future abortion prosecutions in *Roe* was thrown out on the nonconstitutional ground of deference to pending state criminal proceedings. 410 U.S. at 125-27. For cogent criticism of the last disposition see Laycock, *Federal Interference with State Prosecutions: The Need for Prospective Relief*, 1977 SUP. CT. REV. 193.

[5] 410 U.S. at 125 (citing *inter alia*, Moore v. Ogilvie, p. 433, note 135 *supra*, and terming the issue " 'capable of repetition, yet evading review' "). Even on this relaxed test, the Court's conclusion was misplaced. A companion decision upheld the standing of doctors to attack an abortion law although they had been neither prosecuted nor threatened with prosecution; even without Roe's challenge such a statute would not have escaped review. Doe v. Bolton, 410 U.S. 179, 188-89 (1973) (Blackmun, J.).

[6] *See* Massachusetts v. Mellon, p. 184 *supra*.

[7] Both views seem erroneous. The power of judicial review was conferred, as Marshall made clear in Marbury v. Madison, as a critical check on the usurpation of authority by the political branches of government; but article III makes perfectly plain that it can be exercised only in a judicial "case" or "controversy."

[8] *See* Scott v. Sandford, 60 U.S. 393 (1857), THE FIRST HUNDRED YEARS at 263-73; Lochner v. New York, pp. 57-60 *supra*. *See also* O'Meara, *Abortion: The Court Decides a Non-Case*, 1974 SUP. CT. REV. 337, 357 (commenting on *Roe*) ("*Lochner v. New York . . .* [is] back in the saddle again.").

[9] *See, e.g.,* Robinson v. California (cruel and unusual punishment), pp. 407-408 *supra*, and the various opinions in Griswold v. Connecticut, pp. 458-59 *supra*. More candid was the use of due process in Aptheker v. Secretary of State, p. 436 *supra*, to strike down a limitation on international travel that might more conventionally have failed on first amendment grounds, and as an unnecessary alternative ground for the relatively easy equal protection decision striking down miscegenation laws in Loving v. Virginia, p. 416 *supra*. Readily distinguishable in realist terms despite the analogous difficulties of their reasoning are both Bolling v. Sharpe, pp. 478-79 *supra*, and the numerous decisions applying such Bill of Rights guarantees as free speech and religion to the states; in both the Court employed due process as a handle to equate the limitations on state and federal action, not to create additional rights elsewhere guaranteed against neither.

[10] *See* 410 U.S. at 153, 164.

bears: that "process" means procedure, that "liberty" means freedom from imprisonment, and that "due process of law" means according to the law of the land.[11]

Even if one accepts the continuing vitality of substantive due process, *Roe* was a striking decision. It was one thing to invalidate a ban on contraception that virtually the whole country regarded as absurd and anachronistic;[12] it was quite another to conclude that a woman had a constitutional right to destroy what many sincere people considered a living human being. If, as Holmes had argued, the question was whether reasonable people could differ as to the appropriateness of the challenged law,[13] *Roe* seemed a textbook case for deference to the legislative judgment.[14]

For the majority, however, that was not the test. Earlier decisions, wrote Justice Blackmun, had recognized a constitutional right of "privacy" that embraced a variety of "fundamental" personal rights, and "a woman's decision whether or not to terminate her pregnancy" was among them.[15] Such a right could be confined only to promote a " 'compelling' " governmental interest, and even then the regulation must be "narrowly drawn" to accomplish its goal.[16] Although at some point during pregnancy the state's interests in maternal health and in the life of the fetus became "compelling," the statute before the Court swept too broadly; the state could not limit abortions to those necessary to save the life of the mother.[17]

Justice Stone's footnote in *Carolene Products* had brought into the open the fact that the Court was giving some constitutionally protected interests more protection than others.[18] Stone's list of what would later have been called fundamental rights, however, was limited to those enumerated in the Bill of Rights or related to the political process. Free-

---

[11] *See* THE FIRST HUNDRED YEARS at 272; pp. 57-60 *supra* (discussing *Lochner*); Griswold v. Connecticut, 381 U.S. 479, 510-18 (1965) (Black, J., dissenting). *See also* Posner, *The Uncertain Protection of Privacy by the Supreme Court,* 1979 SUP. CT. REV. 173, 199 (arguing that *Roe* "raise[s] . . . the question whether we have a written constitution").

[12] Griswold v. Connecticut, *supra* note 11.

[13] *See* Lochner v. New York, 198 U.S. 45, 76 (1905) (Holmes, J., dissenting).

[14] *See* 410 U.S. at 173 (Rehnquist, J., dissenting); Doe v. Bolton, 410 U.S. 179, 222 (1973) (White, J., dissenting from both *Doe* and *Roe*).

[15] 410 U.S. at 152-53.

[16] *Id.* at 155.

[17] *See id.* at 154, 162-64. The Court proceeded to set out what resembled a detailed code to govern the permissibility of restrictions on abortion. During the first three months of pregnancy, a woman's choice was to be essentially unrestricted. During the next three months, after the medical risk of an abortion equaled or exceeded that of childbirth, the state might impose restrictions necessary to effectuate its "compelling" concern for maternal health. During the last three months, when the unborn child might be capable of surviving outside the womb, the state could proscribe abortion altogether ("except when . . . necessary to preserve the life or health of the mother") in order to protect its life. *Id.* at 162-65. The dissenters rightly protested that it was not clear all of these questions were properly before the Court and added that the opinion read more like a statute than a judicial decision. *See id.* at 172-74; Doe v. Bolton, 410 U.S. at 222-23. For additional criticism of the Court's three categories as well as of the basic decision itself see Epstein, *Substantive Due Process by Any Other Name: The Abortion Cases,* 1973 SUP. CT. REV. 159.

[18] United States v. Carolene Prods. Co., p. 244 *supra.* The term "fundamental rights" had first appeared as a tool for determining which interests came within the due process clauses at all. See THE FIRST HUNDRED YEARS at 366-68 (discussing Hurtado v. California, 110 U.S. 516 (1884)); pp. 246-49 and 252-53 *supra* (discussing Powell v. Alabama and early decisions applying first amendment principles to the states). Since the 1930s similar formulations had often been employed to characterize interests deserving of unusual protection. *See, e.g.,* the decisions cited in notes 19-23 *infra.*

dom of speech satisfied both these standards,[19] and decisions on religion and elections suggested it was enough to meet either one.[20] The alleged right to an abortion, however, fell short of both.

There was much practical wisdom in Justice Stone's criteria. That the Framers took the trouble to enumerate a right in the first eight amendments is pretty good proof of its importance. Moreover, so long as the political process functions smoothly and—as Stone also insisted—minorities are given special protection against discrimination, other rights may arguably be expected to take care of themselves.

As Justice Blackmun noted in *Roe,* however, occasional later cases seemed to call for special protection of interests that did not fit within Justice Stone's categories. As early as 1942, in *Skinner v. Oklahoma,* the Court had expressly applied "strict scrutiny" in striking down a law requiring sterilization of certain offenders because "the right to have offspring" was "one of the basic civil rights of man."[21] In 1965 *Griswold v. Connecticut* had required a close fit between ends and means in invalidating a law forbidding married persons to use contraceptives.[22] Moreover, in holding a miscegenation law unconstitutional in *Loving v. Virginia* in 1967, the Court had described marriage as "one of the vital personal rights essential to the orderly pursuit of happiness by free men."[23]

None of these decisions was a fully satisfactory precedent for strict scrutiny under the due process clause. *Skinner* was an equal protection case; *Griswold* went to great lengths to demonstrate that due process was not in issue; *Loving* left the level of scrutiny unstated while branding the basis of the law "unsupportable."[24] There was enough in those cases, however, to show that *Roe* was not wholly without support in finding an interest entitled to special protection although it met neither of Justice Stone's criteria.[25]

[19] *See* Thornhill v. Alabama, 310 U.S. 88, 95 (1940) (declaring freedom of expression "essential to effective exercise of the power of correcting error through the processes of popular government"), pp. 269-70 *supra.*

[20] *See* Sherbert v. Verner, 374 U.S. 398, 406 (1963) (requiring a "compelling interest" to justify intervention in the "highly sensitive area" of religious freedom listed in the first amendment); Reynolds v. Sims, 377 U.S. 533, 561-62 (1964) (scrutinizing a claim of legislative malapportionment "carefully and meticulously" because voting rights were "preservative of other basic civil and political rights"), p. 430 *supra*; Aptheker v. Secretary of State, 378 U.S. 500, 514 (1964) (relating foreign travel to intelligent participation in the political process in concluding that "here, as elsewhere, precision must be the touchstone of legislation so affecting basic freedoms").

[21] 316 U.S. 535, 536, 540-41 (1942), p. 288, note 64 *supra.*

[22] 381 U.S. 479, 485 (1965) ("Such a law cannot stand in light of the familiar principle . . . that a 'governmental purpose to control or prevent activities constitutionally subject to state regulation may not be achieved by means which sweep unnecessarily broadly and thereby invade the area of protected freedoms.'"), pp. 458-59 *supra. See also id.* at 482 (distinguishing judicial review of "laws that touch economic problems, business affairs, or social conditions"); Eisenstadt v. Baird, 405 U.S. 438, 453 (1972) (Brennan, J., over a dissent by Burger) (striking down on equal protection grounds a law forbidding distribution of contraceptives to unmarried persons) ("If the right of privacy means anything, it is the right of the *individual,* married or single, to be free from unwarranted governmental intrusion into matters so fundamentally affecting a person as the decision whether to bear or beget a child.").

[23] 388 U.S. 1, 12 (1967), p. 416 *supra.* Shapiro v. Thompson, p. 433 *supra,* had held the right of interstate travel "fundamental" for equal protection purposes because it was implicitly guaranteed elsewhere in the Constitution—an argument plainly inapplicable to abortion.

[24] 388 U.S. at 12. The due process point in *Loving* was a brief afterthought in an opinion already anchored in the more traditional ground of a suspect racial classification, *id.* at 7-12.

[25] Although the equal protection clause forbids discrimination with respect to matters not qualifying as "life, liberty, or property" for due process purposes, there is no obvious reason why the test of which protected interests are "fundamental" should differ under the two clauses.

But if a right could be "fundamental" without being listed in the Bill of Rights or relating to self-government, what made it so? *Skinner* and *Loving* had described procreation and marriage as "fundamental to . . . very existence and survival."[26] Nothing so dramatic could be said of abortion, but Justice Blackmun picked up on the implication that what made a right fundamental was its importance: requiring a woman to carry an unwanted fetus might among other things endanger her health or saddle her with a child she was in no position to support.[27]

There is considerable intuitive appeal to this approach. If the ultimate question is whether the challenged limitation is reasonable, it should be more difficult to justify a serious injury than a trivial one.[28] In equal protection cases, however, the Court had already held that the importance of welfare benefits to the recipient was not enough to make them "fundamental."[29] Two months after *Roe*, despite the strong language of *Brown v. Board of Education*, the Court said the same of education.[30] Indeed it seems obvious that something besides the severity of the restriction must go into any determination whether an interest is entitled to special constitutional protection. A law against armed robbery may make the difference between wealth and poverty for an enterprising individual, but one would hardly subject it to strict scrutiny on that ground alone.

In justifying judicial solicitude for the right of married couples to practice contraception, Justice Douglas, in *Griswold*, had noted that marriage was "older than the Bill of Rights," "intimate," and "noble."[31] Justice Blackmun did not argue that abortion was either time-hallowed or elevating.[32] In associating abortion with procreation, contracep-

---

[26] *See Skinner,* 316 U.S. at 541; *Loving,* 388 U.S. at 12.

[27] 410 U.S. at 153. *See also* Ely, *The Wages of Crying Wolf: A Comment on* Roe v. Wade, 82 YALE L.J. 920, 923 (1973) ("Having an unwanted child can go a long way toward ruining a woman's life.").

[28] *See* p. 291 *supra* (discussing the Japanese-American cases). *Cf.* Mathews v. Eldridge, p. 545 *infra* (holding the seriousness of a deprivation one of three significant factors in determining what procedures are required to deprive a person of life, liberty, or property).

[29] Dandridge v. Williams, 397 U.S. 471, 484-87 (1970) (Stewart, J., over three dissents) (conceding that the case "involves the most basic economic needs of impoverished human beings" but upholding a welfare provision disadvantaging large families after finding it "rationally based and free from invidious discrimination"). *Contrast id.* at 520-22 (Marshall, J., joined by Brennan, J., dissenting) ("[T]his Court has already recognized . . . that when a benefit . . . is necessary to sustain life, stricter constitutional standards, both procedural and substantive, are applied. . . .").

[30] San Antonio Independent School Dist. v. Rodriguez, 411 U.S. 1, 30 (1973) (Powell, J., over four dissents) (upholding state's failure to make up for discrepancies in school spending attributable to variations in tax base of various districts) ("The importance of a service performed by the State does not determine whether it must be regarded as fundamental for purposes of examination under the Equal Protection Clause."). *Contrast Brown,* 347 U.S. 483, 493 (1954) (terming education "perhaps the most important function of state and local governments" and adding that "it is doubtful that any child may reasonably be expected to succeed in life if he is denied the opportunity of an education"). In arguing that "fundamental rights" included only those listed elsewhere in the Constitution, Justice Powell was unable to account for the voting cases, note 20 *supra,* and he neglected entirely the attractive *Carolene Products* category on which they were based. Indeed, as Justice Marshall insisted in dissent, there was a strong argument that education too fell within this category, for, as *Brown* had emphasized, education is "required in the performance of our most basic responsibilities" and thus "the very foundation of good citizenship." *See Brown,* 347 U.S. at 493; *Rodriguez,* 411 U.S. at 113 (Marshall, J., dissenting) ("Education serves the essential function of instilling in our young an understanding of and appreciation for the principles and operation of our governmental processes.").

[31] *Griswold,* 381 U.S. at 486.

[32] Blackmun did conclude that, "[a]t least with respect to the early stage of pregnancy, . . . the opportunity to make this choice was present in this country well into the 19th century." 410 U.S. at 140-41. That was a far cry

tion, and marriage under *Griswold*'s umbrella of "privacy," however, he did seem to emphasize that it was intimate; like the rights protected in earlier cases, abortion had something to do with the highly personal subject of reproduction.[33] The fact that abortion impedes rather than promotes reproduction, as noted, might suffice to distinguish two of the three precedents. The contraception case, however, suggests that this distinction is not determinative.

Without importing moral judgments into the calculus, it might thus have been difficult after *Griswold* to deny that a woman's interest in deciding whether or not to have an abortion was a "fundamental" one.[34] Her concern in each case was to avoid unwanted pregnancy and children. The principal difference between contraception and abortion lay in the strength of the state's countervailing interest, which the Court treated as relevant only to the other side of the balance: whether the law was narrowly tailored to serve a "compelling" state concern.[35]

The state's central interest in the abortion case was not simply in protecting "potential" life, which had also been implicated in the contraceptive case. As the destruction of an existing fetus differs from killing a newborn baby, it differs from preventing formation of the embryo as well.[36] Determining whether the state's interest in such a case is "compelling" is as subjective as determining whether the woman's right is "fundamental."

Debating such questions is like arguing whether chocolate ice cream tastes better than vanilla. Moreover, as Justice Marshall protested in equal protection cases,[37] the Court's

---

from finding that abortion was a cherished common law right, and he did not rely on history in explaining why it was fundamental. *See also id.* at 174-75 (Rehnquist, J., dissenting) ("By the time of the adoption of the Fourteenth Amendment in 1868, there were at least 36 laws enacted by state or territorial legislatures limiting abortion."). "The only conclusion possible from this history," said one observer, "is that the drafters did not intend to have the Fourteenth Amendment withdraw from the States the power to legislate with regard to this matter." O'Meara, *supra* note 8, at 337-38. For the decline of history as a limitation on the content of the due process clause see pp. 246-47 *supra* (discussing Powell v. Alabama).

[33]Other examples cited by Justice Blackmun to establish the existence of a preferred right of "privacy," however, left something to be desired. The strict protection afforded to reading habits in the home, Stanley v. Georgia, 394 U.S. 557, 564 (1969), and to confidentiality in the phone booth, Katz v. United States, 389 U.S. 347, 350 (1967), derives in the first instance from their inclusion in the speech and search provisions of the Bill of Rights. The rights to instruction in private schools and in foreign languages established under the quite different standards of the *Lochner* era, *see* Pierce v. Society of Sisters and Meyer v. Nebraska, pp. 153-54 *supra*, could be explained as useful in preparing citizens to play an effective role in the political process—if they had anything to do with "privacy" at all. The right of "associational privacy" recognized in such cases as NAACP v. Alabama, pp. 382-83 *supra*, which were not relied on in *Roe*, seems to fit into both of Stone's categories. For a detailed argument that "privacy" was an inapt term for rights such as that recognized in *Roe*—and that the Court at the same time "evinced little regard for the protection of privacy" in its more familiar senses of secrecy and seclusion—*see* Posner, *supra* note 11, at 190-216.

[34]*But see* Ely, *supra* note 27, at 929-30 (explaining *Griswold* as based essentially on the fourth amendment concern that a ban on the use of contraceptives could not be enforced without "outrageous . . . prying" into privacy of the home).

[35]*Griswold*'s reference to the nobility of marriage and the analogy of armed robbery suggests that moral considerations might also be relevant in determining whether an interest is "fundamental," or indeed whether it qualifies as a protected "liberty" at all. The majority in *Roe*, however, gave no indication that it thought so.

[36]*See* Ely, *supra* note 27, at 927 ("Abortion is too much like infanticide on the one hand, and too much like contraception on the other, to leave one comfortable with any answer.").

[37]*See, e.g.,* Dandridge v. Williams, 397 U.S. 471, 517-30 (1970) (Marshall. J., dissenting); San Antonio Independent School Dist. v. Rodriguez, 411 U.S. 1, 98-110 (1973) (Marshall, J., dissenting).

rigid two-step process may tend to distort the outcome of the balancing process if it does not merely camouflage a preconceived result. Weighing the policy of the abortion law impartially against the woman's interest in control of her own body might fairly have produced a result differing from that in the contraceptive case.[38] Branding the woman's right "fundamental" stacked the deck against the state before its interest was even considered.

## B. Abortion, Part II

*Roe v. Wade* was decided before the Justices appointed after Warren's retirement constituted a majority, but it was not the product of "liberal" holdovers alone. Indeed the Kennedy stalwart Byron White, who had lent his vote to many of the Warren Court's accomplishments including *Griswold,*[39] was the only Justice to join the newly appointed Rehnquist in dissent. Blackmun's opinion for the Court was joined not only by Stewart and the dependable Douglas, Brennan, and Marshall, but by Powell and Burger as well.[40] The decision would have been impossible without the vote of at least one of the supposedly conservative new arrivals; in fact it attracted three of them.

The companion case of *Doe v. Bolton* struck down provisions requiring that abortions be approved by a second physician, endorsed by a special committee, and performed in a hospital.[41] Later decisions of the Burger period invalidated laws requiring a husband's consent or that of the parent of a pregnant child,[42] a twenty-four-hour waiting period to protect against impulsiveness,[43] and a warning of the medical perils of abortion.[44] As the decisions became more extreme and two of the Justices who had joined *Roe* left the Court,

---

[38] Indeed a somewhat different evaluation of the same opposing interests—together with a greater willingness to find that constitutional provisions phrased as limitations on government imposed positive duties to protect the individual—led another respected court not long after *Roe* to reach the diametrically opposite conclusion that a similarly worded provision not only permitted but *required* that abortion generally be made a crime. 39 BVerfG 1, 65 (Federal Constitutional Court of West Germany 1975). *See* pp. 139-43 *supra* (discussing Truax v. Corrigan).

[39] *See* Griswold v. Connecticut, 381 U.S. 479, 502-07 (1965) (White, J., concurring).

[40] *See* 410 U.S. at 115. Justice Stewart, who had joined Black in dissent in *Griswold,* 381 U.S. at 527-31, explained that he concurred in *Roe* on the basis of that decision. 410 U.S. at 167-71 (Stewart, J., concurring). Chief Justice Burger added rather plaintively that "the Court today rejects any claim that the Constitution requires abortions on demand." Doe v. Bolton, 410 U.S. at 208 (Burger, C. J., concurring).

[41] 410 U.S. 179 (1973). Once again White and Rehnquist alone dissented, *id.* at 221-23.

[42] Planned Parenthood v. Danforth, 428 U.S. 52, 67-75 (1976) (Blackmun, J.). *See* Tribe, *Foreword: Toward a Model of Roles in the Due Process of Life and Law,* 87 HARV. L. REV. 1, 40 (1973) ("To give men the unreviewable power to sentence women to childbearing and childraising against their will is to delegate a sweeping and unaccountable authority over the lives of others.").

[43] City of Akron v. Akron Center for Reproductive Health, 462 U.S. 416, 449-51 (1983) (Powell, J.).

[44] Thornburgh v. American College of Obstetricians, 476 U.S. 747 (1986) (Blackmun, J.). Substantive due process decisions of the Burger period not concerning abortion include Moore v. City of East Cleveland, 431 U.S. 494 (1977) (Powell, J., over three dissents on the merits) (striking down a zoning ordinance that barred a grandmother from living with her grandchildren); Carey v. Population Services Int'l, 431 U.S. 678 (1977) (Brennan, J., over a Rehnquist dissent) (invalidating limitations on the distribution of contraceptives); and Youngberg v. Romeo, 457 U.S. 307 (1982) (Powell, J.) (holding inmate of state mental institution had substantive rights to safety, freedom from unnecessary restraints, and some degree of training). *See also* Cleveland Board of Education v. LaFleur, 414 U.S. 632, 642-43 (1974) (Stewart, J., over two dissents and an unrelated concurrence) (concluding, notwithstanding a later passage suggesting that the decision was based upon the procedural objec-

the number of dissenters increased to four;[45] but they remained in dissent.[46] With the concurrence of three of the Justices who had joined *Roe,* however, the Court drew an important limit to the right it had recognized: though the state could not outlaw abortion, it did not have to subsidize it.[47]

No Justice argued that the state deprived women of the right to abortions simply by refusing to fund them.[48] It is true that an abstract legal right may be worthless to people too poor to exercise it.[49] Moreover, there had been occasional suggestions in earlier decisions that provisions such as the due process clause might impose certain affirmative duties on the state to protect the interests of its citizens.[50] None of them, however, had gone so far as to establish a constitutional right to welfare payments. A decision that the fifth and fourteenth amendments required government payment for abortions would have been a startling departure from the history as well as the text of the Constitution.[51]

The argument that dissenting Justices did make in *Maher v. Roe* and in *Harris v. McRae* was that the state had unfairly placed its thumb on the scales by electing to subsi-

---

tion of an irrational conclusive presumption, *see* pp. 546-47, note 289 *infra,* that compulsory leave for teachers after the fourth or fifth month of pregnancy bore "no rational relationship to the valid state interest of preserving continuity of instruction").

[45]Burger joined White and Rehnquist in voting to uphold the spousal and parental consent requirements in *Danforth,* 428 U.S. at 92-95, and Stevens agreed with them as to the latter, *id.* at 101-05. O'Connor joined White and Rehnquist in voting to sustain the waiting period in *Akron,* 462 U.S. at 472-74. Burger, White, and Rehnquist voted to sustain the information provision in *Thornburgh,* 476 U.S. at 782-814; O'Connor, who reserved final judgment because the case had reached the Court on motion for interlocutory relief, *id.* at 814-15, observed that "[t]his is the kind of balanced information I would have thought all could agree is relevant to a woman's informed consent." *See id.* at 830.

[46]White and Rehnquist repeated their arguments against *Roe* itself in *Thornburgh. See* 476 U.S. at 786-97 (White, J., joined by Rehnquist, J., dissenting). O'Connor, who had argued in *Akron* that *Roe's* rigid trimester approach was mistaken and that strict scrutiny was not required of any measure that did not " 'unduly burde[n]' " the abortion right, emphasized in both cases that the question of overruling *Roe* had not been presented. *See Akron,* 462 U.S. at 452-66; *Thornburgh,* 476 U.S. at 827-28.

[47]Maher v. Roe, 432 U.S. 464 (1977) (Powell, J., over dissents by Brennan, Marshall, and Blackmun); Harris v. McRae, 448 U.S. 297 (1980) (Stewart, J., over dissents by Brennan, Marshall, Blackmun, and Stevens). Burger, Stewart, and Powell voted with the majority in both cases, as did White and Rehnquist.

[48]This argument is made in Tribe, *The Abortion Funding Conundrum: Inalienable Rights, Affirmative Duties, and the Dilemma of Dependence,* 99 HARV. L. REV. 330 (1985).

[49]*See Maher,* 432 U.S. at 483 (Brennan, J., dissenting) ("The stark reality . . . is that indigency makes access to competent licensed physicians not merely 'difficult' but 'impossible.' ").

[50]*See, e.g.,* pp. 139-43 *supra* (discussing Truax v. Corrigan); pp. 263-66 *supra* (discussing the public forum doctrine); Currie, *Positive and Negative Constitutional Rights,* 53 U. CHI. L. REV. 864 (1986).

[51]*See Maher,* 432 U.S. at 469 ("The Constitution imposes no obligation on the States to pay the pregnancy-related medical expenses of indigent women, or indeed to pay any of the medical expenses of indigents."). Easily distinguishable are such Burger Court decisions as Estelle v. Gamble, 429 U.S. 97, 103-05 (1976) (Marshall. J.), and Bounds v. Smith, 430 U.S. 817, 821-28 (1977) (Marshall, J.), requiring the state to provide prisoners with medical care and law books, for by locking up the complainants the state had deprived them of the ability to obtain such items for themselves. It is this analogy that made plausible the argument in Columbia Broadcasting System v. Democratic National Committee, 412 U.S. 94 (1973), that the FCC had an affirmative duty to require broadcasting stations to accept political advertising: by granting exclusive licenses without imposing such a requirement, the government had effectively deprived the complainants of all use of the airwaves. Three Justices argued that there was state action, three concluded that there was not, and three left the issue unresolved. *See also* pp. 345-48 *supra* (discussing Public Utilities Comm'n v. Pollak).

dize childbirth but not abortion. In so doing, they argued, the state had effectively denied the right to an abortion "by bringing financial pressures on indigent women that force them to bear children they would not otherwise have."[52]

The perception that selective denial of government benefits might infringe constitutional rights had a long and honorable history. First emerging in the 1870s to preclude states from conditioning the privilege of doing business on surrender of the right to litigate in federal court,[53] it had been applied by *Lochner*-era judges to prevent indirect subjection of corporations to unconstitutional taxation or regulation.[54] After the New Deal revolution it had surfaced again in decisions outlawing indirect interference with such rights as freedom of expression, free exercise of religion, and the privilege against self-incrimination.[55] After one glaring aberration,[56] the Burger Court faithfully applied the same principle to hold that the government could not condition government employment on political conformity[57] or financial support for broadcasters on total abstinence from editorials.[58] Justice Roberts's vain effort to prevent conditional grants from undermining the limitations on federal regulatory authority in the 1930s[59] only proved the point. As Justice Sutherland had so powerfully explained in 1926, if government could freely condition its considerable largesse on the surrender of constitutional rights, little would be left of the Constitution.[60]

Neither Justice Powell in *Maher* nor Justice Stewart in *Harris* fully explained why this principle did not condemn a law subsidizing childbirth but not abortion. As in the earlier cases, the government's offer to pay for the surrender of a constitutional right significantly increased the cost of asserting it and thus tended to discourage its exercise. Despite the Court's disclaimers, *Maher*'s effort to demonstrate that the differential subsidy did not

---

[52]*Maher*, 432 U.S. at 484 (Brennan, J., joined by Marshall and Blackmun, JJ., dissenting). *See also* the argument of the same three Justices in *Harris*, 448 U.S. at 333-34 ("By funding all of the expenses associated with childbirth and none of the expenses incurred in terminating pregnancy, the Government literally makes an offer that the indigent woman cannot afford to refuse."). The equal protection argument that the state had no compelling reason for discriminating against those who chose to exercise the fundamental right to an abortion, *see Harris*, 448 U.S. at 338 (Marshall, J., dissenting); *id.* at 349-57 (Stevens, J., dissenting), seems to raise essentially the same questions.

[53]*E.g.*, Insurance Co. v. Morse, 87 U.S. 445 (1874), THE FIRST HUNDRED YEARS at 413 n.74.

[54]*E.g.*, Western Union Tel. Co. v. Kansas, p. 46/126 *supra* (taxation); Frost & Frost Trucking Co. v. Railroad Comm'n, p. 146/60 *supra* (regulation).

[55]*E.g.*, Keyishian v. Board of Regents, p. 435, note 159 *supra* (speech and assembly); Sherbert v. Verner, pp. 445-46 *supra* (free exercise of religion); Garrity v. New Jersey, p. 448 *supra* (self-incrimination). *See generally* pp. 355-58 *supra* (discussing American Communications Ass'n v. Douds).

[56]Wyman v. James, 400 U.S. 309 (1971) (Blackmun, J., over three dissents) (permitting Congress to condition receipt of welfare benefits on consent to home visits by caseworkers).

[57]Elrod v. Burns, 427 U.S. 347 (1976); Branti v. Finkel, 445 U.S. 507 (1980) (Stevens, J.). In *Elrod* there was no opinion for the Court; in each case there were three dissents. *See* pp. 505-06 *infra*.

[58]FCC v. League of Women Voters, 468 U.S. 364, 399-401 (1984) (Brennan, J., over four dissents).

[59]*See* pp. 227-31, 238 (discussing United States v. Butler and subsequent cases).

[60] *Frost*, 271 U.S. at 594 ("If the state may compel the surrender of one constitutional right as a condition of its favor, it may, in like manner, compel a surrender of all. It is inconceivable that guaranties embedded in the Constitution of the United States may thus be manipulated out of existence."). For a contrary view see Garvey, *Freedom and Equality in the Religion Clauses*, 1981 SUP. CT. REV. 193, 198-203 (arguing that availability of a selective subsidy actually enhances the potential recipient's freedom of action).

impinge upon any fundamental right seemed to call into question either the unconstitutional-condition decisions or *Roe* itself.[61]

One of Justice Powell's counterexamples, however, suggested that there might be something to be said for the Court's conclusion. Surely, as he contended, the existence of a constitutional right to private education did not preclude a state from affecting a pupil's choice by subsidizing public but not private schools.[62] A later decision rendered with the agreement of the *Maher* and *Harris* dissenters made the point once again: the fact that certain competing uses of the complainants' resources were exempt from federal taxation did not require Congress to extend similar benefits to lobbying.[63]

Were these appealing conclusions consistent with the decisions on which the dissenters in *Maher* and *Harris* relied? Justice Rehnquist attempted to explain the distinction in the lobbying case. "The Code," he argued, "does not deny TWR the right to receive deductible contributions to support its non-lobbying activity, nor does it deny TWR any independent benefit on account of its intention to lobby. Congress has merely refused to pay for the lobbying [itself] out of public moneys."[64] Justices Blackmun, Brennan, and Marshall, who had dissented in *Maher* and *Harris,* agreed. The "organization's right to speak is not infringed," they argued, "because it is free to make known its views on legislation . . . without losing tax benefits for its nonlobbying activities."[65]

*Maher* and *Harris,* as the Justices who had dissented in those cases recognized,[66] were in this respect more like the lobbying case than like conditioning public employment on surrender of the right to speak. For the government had only refused to subsidize abortion itself; it had not made surrender of the right a condition of receiving other benefits such as food stamps or a government job.

This distinction seems significant in terms of the relevant constitutional policies. On the one hand, the government's interest is most directly impaired if it must pay for activities of which it does not approve. On the other hand, the government's influence is greatly expanded if it can condition its subsidy not only on using money itself for an approved purpose but also on surrendering other rights for which no subsidy is requested. There is an analogy here to antitrust principles respecting tie-ins and abuse of patent monopolies: a producer may be under no obligation to sell you his product, but he may not use his market power in one field to obtain a preferential position in another.[67] Conversely, while a state may not condition the payment of wages on becoming a Democrat or a Methodist,[68] it may condition them on the performance of services.

---

[61] *See* 432 U.S. at 474 ("An indigent woman who desires an abortion suffers no disadvantage as a consequence of Connecticut's decision to fund childbirth. . . . [T]he Connecticut regulation does not impinge upon the fundamental right recognized in *Roe.*").

[62] 432 U.S. at 476-77 (citing Pierce v. Society of Sisters, p. 154 *supra*).

[63] Regan v. Taxation with Representation, 461 U.S. 540 (1983) (Rehnquist, J.). *See also id.* at 551-54 (Blackmun, J., joined by Brennan and Marshall, concurring).

[64] *Regan,* 461 U.S. at 545.

[65] *Id.* at 553 (Blackmun, J., concurring). *See also id.* at 552 & n.* (drawing a distinction between "merely deny[ing] a subsidy for lobbying activities" and "depriv[ing] an otherwise eligible organization of its tax-exempt status . . . for all its activities" because of its lobbying).

[66] *Regan,* 461 U.S. at 552 n.*.

[67] *See, e.g.,* International Salt Co. v. United States, 332 U.S. 392 (1947); Jefferson Parish Hosp. Dist. v. Hyde Park, 466 U.S. 2, 9-15 (1984).

[68] *See* Elrod v. Burns, *supra* note 57.

Thus both precedent and common sense suggest it may be more questionable for the government to refuse to subsidize unrelated activities of a person of whose conduct it disapproves than to refuse to subsidize the conduct itself. Nevertheless the distinction is not an unfailing guide for determining whether a particular condition is permissible. On the one hand, there may be cases in which the grant of the benefit itself so enhances the government's interest that it may attach conditions that go beyond those necessary to avoid subsidizing the exercise of a constitutional right. We may not deny Communists veterans' benefits, but we may not be required to give them access to military secrets.[69] On the other hand, there are occasions on which the decision to subsidize competing activities seems difficult to distinguish from penalizing the protected conduct itself. The state may not make auditoriums available for all but religious assemblies,[70] for example, or finance only Republican political campaigns.[71]

The crucial question then is whether paying for childbirth and not abortion is more like these last cases than like subsidizing public and not private schools. The governing criteria are elusive, but the decisions seem to suggest that the most suspect cases are those in which a selective subsidy distorts the marketplace of ideas by discriminating according to the content of communications.[72]

## C.   Homosexual Relations

The social revolution that began in the 1960s entailed a widespread relaxation of attitudes respecting not only abortion but other sexual and reproductive matters as well. Laws forbidding homosexual relations, like those forbidding abortion, had been familiar elements of the legal landscape for many years. It was only a matter of time until they too came to be tested under the constitutional principles of *Roe v. Wade.* In *Bowers v. Hardwick,* in 1986, the time arrived.[73]

The argument that laws against homosexual activity impinged upon a "fundamental right" was not difficult to make after *Roe.* Like abortion, homosexual relations are of great importance to those who wish to engage in them; to forbid what may be the only sexual activity an individual finds satisfying is to inflict serious detriment indeed. Moreover, as the contraceptive cases recognized, sexual relations involve an intimate aspect of "privacy." Thus the interest in engaging in homosexual relations is arguably as "fundamental" as the interest protected in *Roe v. Wade,* and laws interfering with it should arguably be subjected to similarly strict scrutiny.

The argument could be made even more appealing, as Justices Blackmun, Brennan, Marshall, and Stevens demonstrated, by broadening the definition of the right in question:

[69] *See* pp. 355-58 and 393, note 120 *supra* (discussing American Communications Ass'n v. Douds and Speiser v. Randall).

[70] Widmar v. Vincent, 454 U.S. 263 (1981) (Powell, J.), pp. 531-32 *infra.*

[71] *See Harris,* 448 U.S. at 336 n.6 (Brennan, J., dissenting). *But see* the special case of Buckley v. Valeo, p. 512 *infra.*

[72] *See Widmar,* 454 U.S. at 277 (noting that the case involved "a content-based exclusion of religious speech"); *Regan,* 461 U.S. at 551 (Blackmun, J., concurring) (emphasizing that the provision denying a tax exemption was neutral as to the viewpoint expressed by a particular lobbyist). *See also id.* at 548 (quoting an earlier lobbying decision: "The case would be different if Congress were to discriminate invidiously in its subsidies in such a way as to '"ai[m]" at the suppression of dangerous ideas.'"").

[73] 478 U.S. 186 (1986).

"Only the most willful blindness could obscure the fact that sexual intimacy is 'a sensitive, key relationship of human existence. . . .'"[74] Justices Blackmun, Brennan, Marshall, and Stevens, however, were in dissent. Giving no weight to the importance or intimacy of the individual's interest, Justice White for the majority emphasized history and current practice: "Proscriptions against [sodomy] have ancient roots. . . . [W]hen the Fourteenth Amendment was ratified, all but 5 of the 37 States in the Union had criminal sodomy laws, . . . and today, 24 States and the District of Columbia continue to provide criminal penalties. . . ."[75] This was no way to distinguish *Roe;* the same had been true of abortion.

The precedents, said Justice White, had not established a general right of sexual privacy; they had all concerned "family, marriage, or procreation."[76] As an exercise in taxonomy, there was perhaps not much to criticize about this reasoning. However, it could as easily be said that none of the cases before *Roe* had concerned abortion. What was lacking from Justice White's opinion was any explanation of why the interests involved in past cases were more entitled to protection than the interest at issue in *Bowers*.

On the other side of the ledger, it was even arguable that the state had less of an interest in suppressing sodomy than in restricting abortion. In the abortion case the woman's interest could be protected only by permitting destruction of an unborn child; the statute in *Bowers* outlawed conduct in private between consenting adults.[77]

Justice White said only that laws might appropriately be based on "notions of morality": "[I]f all laws representing essentially moral choices are to be invalidated under the Due Process Clause, the courts will be very busy indeed."[78] "Morals" had indeed been a traditional head of the police power,[79] and the long history of condemnation of homosexual activity was enough to give one pause.[80] Both abortion and miscegenation, however, had also been long pronounced immoral.[81] As the dissenters observed, unless an objective reason for the epithet could be enunciated there was a danger that "immorality" might be a cover for prejudice.[82]

---

[74] *See id.* at 204-06 (Blackmun, J., joined by Brennan, Marshall, and Stevens, JJ., dissenting). *See also id.* at 199 (quoting Olmstead v. United States, 277 U.S. 438 (1928) (Brandeis, J., dissenting):

> This case is no more about "a fundamental right to engage in homosexual sodomy" . . . than *Stanley v. Georgia* . . . was about a fundamental right to watch obscene movies, or *Katz v. United States* . . . was about a fundamental right to place interstate bets from a telephone booth. Rather, this case is about "the most comprehensive of rights and the right most valued by civilized men," namely, "the right to be let alone."

[75] 478 U.S. at 192-94.

[76] *Id.* at 190-91.

[77] *See id.* at 212-13 (Blackmun, J., dissenting) (distinguishing public sexual activity on this ground). *See also id.* at 209-10 n.4 (distinguishing adultery and incest as more likely to harm innocent persons).

[78] *Id.* at 196.

[79] *See, e.g,* Mugler v. Kansas, 123 U.S. 623, 661-62 (1887) (upholding a ban on the manufacture of beer) ("[W]e cannot shut out of view the fact, within the knowledge of all, that the public health, the public morals, and the public safety, may be endangered by the general use of intoxicating drinks."). *See generally* E. FREUND, THE POLICE POWER 192-219 (1904).

[80] *See* 478 U.S. at 197 (Burger, C. J., concurring) ("To hold that the act of homosexual sodomy is somehow protected as a fundamental right would be to cast aside millennia of moral teaching.").

[81] *See id.* at 210-11 & n.5 (Blackmun, J., dissenting); *id.* at 216 (Stevens, J., dissenting).

[82] *See id.* at 212 (Blackmun, J., dissenting) (quoting O'Connor v. Donaldson, 422 U.S. 563, 575 (1975) ("'[M]ere public intolerance or animosity cannot constitutionally justify the deprivation of a person's physical liberty.'"))

More objective arguments in support of the sodomy law may be imagined, although the Court did not make them. A state might conceivably prefer heterosexual to homosexual relations in the interest of propagating the race. Onan, after all, was punished for merely casting his seed on the ground.[83] Even assuming a legitimate fear of underpopulation, however, it is hard to believe that banning sodomy significantly increases births.

Forbidding homosexual relations after the discovery of AIDS might also serve the important interest in limiting the transmission of disease.[84] The fact that *heterosexual* intercourse facilitates the spread of syphilis, however, would hardly justify making it criminal. The last example may of course be distinguished, but it illustrates the established principle that there must be some reasonable proportion between the end and the means.

The opinion in *Bowers* thus seems cavalier in its treatment of both the question whether the individual's interest was "fundamental" and the strength of the state's countervailing concern. This is not to say it is necessarily wrong; one thing the case reaffirms is the subjectivity of both sides of the calculation. Perhaps the decision indicates only that, *Roe* notwithstanding, there are limits to which judges can be expected to transcend the values of the society in which they were raised.[85]

There is one passage in the *Bowers* opinion, however, that may suggest a more significant conclusion. "The Court is most vulnerable and comes nearest to illegitimacy," wrote Justice White, "when it deals with judge-made constitutional law having little or no cognizable roots in the language or design of the Constitution."[86] This refreshing observation affords some basis for the hope that five Justices may have seen the dangers of the approach taken in such cases as *Griswold v. Connecticut* and *Roe v. Wade.*[87]

The reader, however, is not advised to hold his breath. Two hundred years of Supreme Court history have confirmed that it is not easy for judges to deny themselves the power to remedy what they perceive as injustice.

## II.   THE WAGES OF SLAVERY

### A.   Busing and Related Remedies

The Warren Court had outlawed racial segregation of public schools and held that neither subsidization of segregated private institutions nor freedom of choice was an adequate

---

[83] *See Genesis* 38:9.

[84] The dissenters noted that the state had made such an argument, but observed that there had been no opportunity to present evidence on the subject: "The connection between the acts prohibited . . . and the harms identified . . . is a subject of hot dispute, hardly amenable to dismissal under Federal Rule of Civil Procedure 12(b)(6)." 478 U.S. at 208-09 & n.3 (Blackmun, J., dissenting).

[85] The Court expressly reserved the question whether the distinction between homosexual and heterosexual sodomy was consistent with equal protection, for the issue had not been raised. 478 U.S. at 196 n.8. Sunstein has forcefully argued that *Bowers* did not foreclose the discrimination issue, since the due process clause was designed basically to entrench tradition and the equal protection clause to revise it. *See* Sunstein, *Sexual Orientation and the Constitution: A Note on the Relationship between Due Process and Equal Protection,* 55 U. CHI. L. REV. 1161 (1988). Even accepting the premise of this argument, however, it seems most unlikely that a Court convinced that a law against homosexual relations was amply supported by considerations of "morality" would find a classification in the same law based on those same considerations unjustified.

[86] 478 U.S. at 194. *Cf.* Ely, *supra* note 27, at 949 ("[B]efore the Court can get to the 'balancing' stage, . . . it is under an obligation to trace its premises to the charter from which it derives its authority.").

[87] See the penetrating criticism of the entire "fundamental rights" approach in Ely, *Foreword: on Discovering Fundamental Values,* 92 HARV. L. REV. 5 (1978).

response to the problem.[88] It was the Burger Court that first held transportation of pupils to schools outside their neighborhoods to be an appropriate remedy.

"The objective today," wrote the Chief Justice for a unanimous Court in *Swann v. Charlotte-Mecklenburg Board of Education* in 1971, "remains to eliminate from the public schools all vestiges of state-imposed segregation."[89] Past experience had shown that racially neutral pupil-assignment plans were not always sufficient to achieve this goal.[90] In *Swann* itself, the Court concluded, there was sufficient evidence to support the finding that "assignment of children to the school nearest their home . . . would not produce an effective dismantling of the dual system."[91] Accordingly, it was permissible for the court to make new assignments in such a way as "to accomplish the transfer of Negro students out of formerly segregated Negro schools and transfer of white students to formerly all-Negro schools."[92] It followed that pupils might be transported by bus if necessary to the schools to which they had been assigned: "Bus transportation has been an integral part of the public education system for years. . . ."[93]

Two companion cases raised the troubling question whether remedies such as those approved in *Swann* were consistent with the principle of racial neutrality that they were meant to enforce. The Georgia Supreme Court had concluded that assignments designed to reduce racial disparities offended the equal protection clause " 'by treating students differently because of their race.' "[94] A North Carolina statute enacted for the express purpose of prohibiting busing expanded on this theme by paraphrasing the *Brown* decision itself: "No student shall be assigned or compelled to attend any school on account of race, creed, color or national origin. . . ."[95]

The Court was unimpressed. To have ignored race in devising a remedy for racial segregation, Chief Justice Burger wrote, "would have severely hampered the board's ability to deal effectively with the task at hand."[96] The North Carolina statute, he added,

> exploits an apparently neutral form to control school assignment plans by directing that they be "color blind"; that requirement, against the background of segregation, would render illusory the promise of *Brown v. Board of Education.* . . . Just as the race of students must be considered in determining whether a constitutional violation has occurred, so also must race be considered in formulating a remedy.[97]

The argument of neutrality in this context, as the Court said, was seductive but untenable. The states had violated the fourteenth amendment, and the Constitution required that the wrong be undone. That could be accomplished only by putting the victims of

---

[88] *See* pp. 377-81, 416-19 *supra*.

[89] 402 U.S. 1, 15 (1971).

[90] *Id.* at 28 (adding that "discriminatory location of school sites or distortion of school size" had contributed to this difficulty).

[91] *Id.* at 30.

[92] *Id.* at 27.

[93] *Id.* at 29-31.

[94] *See* McDaniel v. Barresi, 402 U.S. 39, 41 (1971) (quoting the state court's opinion).

[95] *See* North Carolina State Board of Education v. Swann, 402 U.S. 43, 44 n.1 (1971).

[96] *McDaniel*, 402 U.S. at 41.

[97] Board of Education v. Swann, 402 U.S. at 45-46.

unconstitutional action in the same position as if there had been no violation. If that meant reassigning a pupil according to race, this was only to assure that in the last analysis race was not determinative. To order a thief to compensate his victim is not to take his property without compensation; it would pervert the noble principle of racial neutrality to hold that the Constitution forbade the courts to remedy its own infraction.

"Absent a constitutional violation," Chief Justice Burger warned, "there would be no basis for judicially ordering assignment of students on a racial basis."[98] Nor did the decision mean that either school authorities or courts were "required to make year-by-year adjustments of the racial composition of student bodies once the affirmative duty to desegregate has been accomplished and racial discrimination through official action is eliminated from the system"; "[t]he constitutional command to desegregate schools does not mean that every school in every community must always reflect the racial composition of the school system as a whole."[99] The courts had no general warrant to improve society; their sole function was "to correct past constitutional violations."[100]

It was entirely appropriate that the Chief Justice was the author of the opinion. The explosiveness of the issues had been amply demonstrated by the response to earlier desegregation decisions.[101] Busing itself, though the opinion made it seem a perfectly natural response, was to generate a firestorm of opposition in the North to rival that of Southerners to the initial decision in *Brown*.[102] It bears repeating that the highly controversial decision approving busing was not that of the "radical" Warren Court but of a Bench including both Burger and Blackmun, and that it was unanimous. It was also a singularly lucid and measured response to a difficult problem.[103]

Later decisions wrestled with the task of applying the twin principles of *Swann:* that the effects of official school segregation must be eliminated, and that the courts' sole function was to rectify past unconstitutional action. *Keyes v. School Dist. No. 1,* in 1973, showed that cracks had already developed in the united front previously presented. Because the trial judge had found deliberate segregation only in one part of the city of Denver, the court of appeals had held he could not order integration of the entire school system. In an opinion by Justice Brennan, the Supreme Court remanded for additional findings: because deliberate segregation of one area was likely to affect other parts of the city, a citywide remedy might nevertheless be required.[104]

Neither of the two Justices appointed since *Swann* joined Brennan's opinion. Rehnquist

---

[98] *Swann,* 402 U.S. at 28.

[99] *Id.* at 31-32, 24. This qualification was confirmed in Pasadena City Board of Education v. Spangler, 427 U.S. 424, 436-37 (1976) (Rehnquist, J.) (Having once corrected the perceived constitutional violation, "the District Court was not entitled to require the [district] to rearrange its attendance zones each year so as to ensure that the racial mix desired by the court was maintained in perpetuity."). Marshall and Brennan, *id.* at 441-44, dissented on the ground that the effects of the unconstitutional action had not yet been cured.

[100] *See* 402 U.S. at 25.

[101] *See, e.g.,* Cooper v. Aaron, pp. 380-81 *supra.*

[102] *See* Keyes v. School Dist. No. 1, 413 U.S. 189, 250 (1973) (Powell, J., concurring) ("The problem . . . has profoundly disquieted the public wherever extensive transportation has been ordered.").

[103] *See also* United States v. Scotland Neck City Board of Education, 407 U.S. 484, 490 (1972) (Stewart, J.) (unanimously invalidating the division of one school district into two upon finding that it "would have the effect of impeding the disestablishment of the dual school system"); Wright v. Council of the City of Emporia, 407 U.S. 451 (1972) (Stewart, J.) (same, over the dissent of the four new Justices as to the effect of the division).

[104] 413 U.S. 189, 191-95, 198-205. For consideration of additional portions of the opinions bearing on the distinction between de jure and de facto segregation see p. 489, note 174 *infra.*

dissented entirely, stressing among other things that the effects of deliberate segregation might conceivably be confined to the area in which it had been practiced.[105] The majority had conceded this; but it made such a result seem so intuitively improbable as to make clear it thought a citywide remedy appropriate in most cases.[106]

Justice Powell concurred in the remand, but his long opinion was in large part a vigorous indictment of busing, which he described as "[t]he single most disruptive element in education today": "A community may well conclude that the portion of a child's day spent on a bus might be used more creatively in a classroom, playground, or in some other extracurricular school activity."[107] Equity's traditional concern for " 'reconciling . . . public and private needs,' " Powell insisted, should make courts hesitant to order extensive busing even to correct the consequences of unconstitutional action.[108] More fundamentally, he argued, busing should never be used unless it was "necessary to redress the constitutional evil."[109] The latter principle was unassailable, but Justice Powell erred in suggesting that the *Swann* opinion had offended it;[110] the Chief Justice had made the same point in *Swann*.[111]

The principle that the Court's only task is to remedy past wrongs was the basis of decision in the next important school case to reach the Court, *Milliken v. Bradley* in 1974.[112] Finding that public schools in the city of Detroit had been deliberately segregated by race, the district court had directed the development of a desegregation plan covering not only Detroit but fifty-three suburban districts as well.[113] By the narrowest of margins the Court reversed. There was no finding, the Chief Justice insisted, that suburban schools had been deliberately segregated or that their racial composition had been affected by segregation of the schools in Detroit.[114] Thus "the remedy," as Justice Stewart put it in a concurring opinion, "was not commensurate with the constitutional violation found."[115]

The dissenters echoed the trial court's finding that there were too few whites in Detroit to permit effective desegregation without including the suburbs. A plan confined to the

---

[105] *See id.* at 255-57 (adding, *id.* at 258, a strong criticism of the "drastic extension" that had occurred when a prohibition on racial assignment was, as he saw it, transformed into an affirmative requirement of "racial mixing" in Green v. County School Board, pp. 418-19 *supra*).

[106] Absent the determination in a "rare" case that a district had effectively been "divid[ed] . . . into separate, identifiable and unrelated units," said Justice Brennan, "proof of state-imposed segregation in a substantial portion of the district will suffice to support a finding by the trial court of the existence of a dual system." 413 U.S. at 203.

[107] 413 U.S. at 253, 248.

[108] *Id.* at 251 (quoting Brown v. Board of Education, 349 U.S. 294, 300 (1955)).

[109] 413 U.S. at 249.

[110] *See id.* at 225 ("[T]he extension of the affirmative-duty concept to include compulsory student transportation went well beyond the mere remedying of that portion of school segregation for which former state segregation laws were ever responsible."). *See also id.* at 222-23.

[111] *See Swann,* 402 U.S. at 27-31. The vehemence of Justice Powell's opinion suggested that lower courts had carried the busing principle far beyond the extent to which *Swann* had found it justifiable. That would not have been surprising. What the racial makeup of the schools would have been without a long history of deliberate segregation was largely a matter of guesswork; the temptation to aim for a proportional racial mix in all schools must have been strong.

[112] 418 U.S. 717 (1974).

[113] *See id.* at 725-36.

[114] *See id.* at 744-52. Stewart, Blackmun, Powell, and Rehnquist joined Chief Justice Burger's opinion; Douglas, Brennan, White, and Marshall dissented.

[115] *Id.* at 754. *See also id.* at 757.

city itself, Justice Marshall argued, "would leave many of the Detroit city schools 75% to 90% Negro." Moreover, the result of such a plan would be to drive additional whites out of the city entirely and to reestablish "the all-Negro schools which were the hallmarks of Detroit's former dual system. . . ."[116]

The difficulty with this reasoning was in showing that the relative scarcity of whites in Detroit was attributable to the acts of which the plaintiffs complained. The Constitution did not require, as Justice Marshall suggested, that "Negro and white children in fact go to school together";[117] it required that the effects of any governmental separation of the races be set aside. The trial court had in fact suggested that government action had contributed to residential segregation throughout the metropolitan area,[118] and Justice Marshall argued that school segregation in Detroit "inevitably" increased the racial disparity between the city and its suburbs.[119] If supported by evidence, a finding to this effect might well have justified a remedy reaching beyond the city limits. Justice Stewart, however, stated without contradiction that there was nothing in the record to show that official action was responsible for the overall ratio of blacks to whites in Detroit's school population.[120] If he was right, there was no basis for concluding that this ratio would have been any different if the Constitution had never been violated, and thus no justification for attempting to alter it by judicial action.[121]

Later decisions continued to struggle with the challenging task of tailoring the remedy to the wrong in school segregation cases. There seemed no substantive reason to quarrel with the Court's conclusion that it was appropriate to order the institution of programs to remedy educational deficiencies resulting from operation of the segregated system in Detroit.[122] There did seem to be reason to doubt that the ratio of blacks to whites would have been the same throughout a city in the absence of unconstitutional action, as the majority seemed to imply in approving an order requiring that every school in Columbus, Ohio, "be brought roughly within proportionate racial balance."[123]

Justice Powell took the latter decision as the occasion for another major essay on the general topic of desegregation, arguing at some length that compulsory integration was a

[116]*Id.* at 801 (Marshall, J., joined by Douglas, Brennan, and White, dissenting). *See also id.* at 779 (White, J., joined by Brennan, Douglas, and Marshall, dissenting) ("[T]he maximum remedy available within [the city] will leave many of the schools almost totally black. . . .").

[117]*Id.* at 802.

[118]*See id.* at 724.

[119]*Id.* at 805.

[120]*See id.* at 756 n.2.

[121]*See also id.* at 728 n.7 (opinion of the Court) (noting that the court of appeals had disclaimed reliance on residential segregation " 'except as school construction programs helped cause or maintain' " it); *id.* at 799 n.19 (Marshall, J., dissenting) (terming it irrelevant whether the state was "responsible for the increasing percentage of Negro students in Detroit").

[122]Milliken v. Bradley (II), 433 U.S. 267 (1977) (Burger, C. J.). For the more troublesome issue of sovereign immunity raised by the inclusion of state officials in this order see pp. 575-76 *infra.*

[123]Columbus Board of Education v. Penick, 443 U.S. 449, 455n. 3 (1979) (White, J., over dissents by Powell and Rehnquist). *See also id.* at 480-81 (Powell, J., dissenting) (noting that much disparity in the makeup of schools resulted from "familiar segregated housing patterns . . . for which no school board is responsible"); Kitch, *The Return of Color Consciousness to the Constitution:* Weber, Dayton, *and* Columbus, 1979 SUP. CT. REV. 1, 6 (arguing that the remedy in *Columbus* assumed the unconstitutionality of neighborhood schools). Powell's dissent applied also to the companion case of Dayton Board of Education v. Brinkman (II), 443 U.S. 526 (1979) (White, J.), where Burger and Stewart joined the dissenters on the ground that the court of appeals had erred in setting aside a contrary trial-court finding. *See Columbus,* 443 U.S. at 468-79. On an earlier appeal

self-defeating remedy unlikely to advance the goal of "ethnic and racial diversity in the classroom." [124] Powell was as eloquent on this side of the question as Marshall had been on the other. [125] As powerful as their arguments might have been if directed elsewhere, both seemed to lose sight of the fact that the function of the courts was neither more nor less than to redress violations of the Constitution. [126]

## B.   Affirmative Action

The impetus behind the fourteenth amendment, as the Supreme Court recognized from the outset, was the need to protect blacks from discrimination. [127] That the text does not specifically mention blacks suggests that its framers had the foresight to perceive that other racial groups might someday be in need of similar protection, [128] and it was not long before the equal protection clause was employed to strike down discrimination against Chinese. [129]

One of the Court's first equal protection opinions, moreover, made clear that the Justices understood the clause to protect whites from discrimination too. In *Strauder v. West Virginia*, in 1880, the Court had invoked the analogy of the hypothetical exclusion of whites to support its conclusion that blacks could not constitutionally be excluded from juries. If a law "exclud[ed] all white men from jury service," Justice Strong had written, "we apprehend no one would be heard to claim that it would not be a denial to white men of the equal protection of the laws." [130]

Justice Strong was discussing discrimination by "States where the colored people con-

---

in *Dayton* the Court had unanimously held that the trial court's finding of isolated incidents of deliberate segregation did not justify the court of appeals in ordering a city-wide remedy. Dayton Board of Education v. Brinkman (I), 433 U.S. 406 (1977) (Rehnquist, J.).

[124] *See Columbus,* 443 U.S. at 483-86 (Powell, J., dissenting) (pointing to the familiar phenomena of "white flight" to the suburbs and increased white attendance at private schools).

[125] *See Milliken (I),* 418 U.S. at 783 (Marshall, J., dissenting) ("[U]nless our children begin to learn together, there is little hope that our people will ever learn to live together.").

[126] Entirely consistent with this principle, however, was the decision in Crawford v. Board of Educ., 458 U.S. 527, 535 (1982) (Powell, J., over a dissent by Marshall), that a state could forbid its courts to order busing except to remedy past equal protection violations: the provision "does not inhibit enforcement of any federal law or constitutional requirement." *Contrast* Washington v. Seattle School List., 458 U.S. 457, 467 (1982) (Blackmun, J., over four dissents) (striking down a similar provision directed at school boards because it "subtly distort[ed] governmental processes in such a way as to place special burdens on the ability of minority groups to achieve beneficial legislation"). *See Crawford,* 458 U.S. at 545-47 (Blackmun, J., joined by Brennan, concurring) (distinguishing the two cases); Sunstein, *Public Values, Private Interests, and the Equal Protection Clause,* 1982 SUP. CT. REV. 127, 145-66 (exploring the distinction); *see also* p. 420 *supra* (discussing Reitman v. Mulkey and Hunter v. Erickson).

[127] *See, e.g.,* Slaughter-House Cases, 83 U.S. 36, 70-71 (1873) (concluding that "the one pervading purpose" of all three Civil War amendments was "the freedom of the slave race, the security and firm establishment of that freedom, and the protection of the newly-made freeman and citizen from the oppressions of those who had formerly exercised unlimited dominion over him"); Strauder v. West Virginia, 100 U.S. 303, 306-07 (1880).

[128] *See* Slaughter-House Cases, 83 U.S. at 72 (discussing the thirteenth amendment) ("We do not say that no one else but the negro can share in this protection. . . . If Mexican peonage or the Chinese coolie labor system shall develop slavery of the Mexican or Chinese race within our territory, this amendment may safely be trusted to make it void.").

[129] Yick Wo v. Hopkins, 118 U.S. 356 (1886), THE FIRST HUNDRED YEARS at 387.

[130] 100 U.S. 303, 308 (1880). *See* THE FIRST HUNDRED YEARS at 383-85.

stitute a majority of the entire population."[131] He did not address the distinct question of discrimination against whites by states in which they held political power. As Justice Stone suggested in *Carolene Products,* "discrete and insular minorities" were clearly in greater need of constitutional protection;[132] a majority might generally be expected to look out for itself.[133]

Leaving aside the troublesome question whether for this purpose "whites" should be viewed as a single category,[134] however, the principle that individuals should be judged on their own merits[135] is as valid for one race as for another. Whiteness as well as blackness is an immutable, offensive, and usually irrelevant basis of classification. The first Justice Harlan's noble aphorism that the Constitution was "color-blind," while uttered in the context of a measure disadvantageous to politically powerless blacks, had embodied this perception.[136] Outside the racial context, moreover, the reapportionment cases had affirmed that equality was an individual right that could not be given away by a majority to which one belonged.[137] There was thus much to be said for the conclusion that, as its unqualified terms suggested, the framers of the amendment had drawn from the tragic experience of blacks the refreshing lesson that *no one* should be disadvantaged on account of race.[138]

The need to devise remedies for past discrimination against blacks, however, placed great strains on the notion of a color-blind Constitution. Since blacks had been disadvantaged before, it was argued, only preferential treatment could make them whole.

If a black person has been denied a job on account of race, it seems quite appropriate to order him hired. It is no ground for objection that in consequence the white person who has benefited from discrimination may lose his job, since he should not have got it in the first place.[139] In theory, at least, the Court's approval of a race-conscious remedy for school segregation in *Swann* had been consistent with this pattern. For in principle the

---

[131] 100 U.S. at 308.

[132] United States v. Carolene Products Co., p. 244 *supra.*

[133] *See* Ely, *The Constitutionality of Reverse Racial Discrimination,* 41 U. CHI. L. REV. 723, 727 (1974) ("[I]t is not 'suspect' in the constitutional sense for a majority . . . to discriminate against itself.").

[134] Affirmative action plans often subordinated the interests of working-class whites to those of their black competitors; whites not competing for jobs in the relevant industry did not necessarily share the interests of those whom they voted to disadvantage. *See* Regents of the University of California v. Bakke, 438 U.S. 265, 295 (1978) (opinion of Powell, J.) ("[T]he white majority itself is composed of various minority groups, most of which can lay claim to a history of prior discrimination. . . .").

[135] *See* Weber v. Aetna Cas. & Sur. Co., 406 U.S. 164, 175 (1972) (invoking "the basic concept of our system that legal burdens should bear some relationship to individual responsibility or wrongdoing," in striking down a provision discriminating against illegitimate children).

[136] *See* Plessy v. Ferguson, p. 40 *supra.*

[137] Lucas v. Forty-fourth General Assembly, p. 431 *supra.*

[138] *See* Fullilove v. Klutznick, 448 U.S. 448, 523, 525 (1980) (Stewart, J., dissenting); Posner, *The DeFunis Case and the Constitutionality of Preferential Treatment of Racial Minorities,* 1974 SUP. CT. REV. 1, 22 ("[T]he distribution of benefits and costs by government on racial or ethnic grounds is impermissible."). The obvious fact that a rule forbidding government to take race into account "reflects a decision to give special treatment to race," *see* Strauss, *The Myth of Colorblindness,* 1986 SUP. CT. REV. 99, 117, proves neither that the rule is incoherent, nor that it is misguided, nor that the Framers had something else in mind.

[139] Even in this situation, however, it has been argued that money damages against the wrongdoer might be preferable because they would compensate the victim without injuring an innocent party. *See* Brest, *Foreword: In Defense of the Antidiscrimination Principle,* 90 HARV. L. REV. 1, 38-39 (1976).

order was supposed to benefit the victims of prior unconstitutional action by those ordered to correct it, and those whom the order disadvantaged were understood to have been the beneficiaries of such action.[140] The difficulty was that the remedies devised for past discrimination often went beyond these paradigm cases. Blacks were to be preferred to whites *as a class* without proof that the individuals involved had been victims or beneficiaries of past discrimination by anyone, much less by those from whom corrective action was sought. To say that whites were to be disadvantaged now because blacks had been disadvantaged before seemed rather like saying that two wrongs made a right; there was an uncomfortably loose fit between the end and the means.[141]

It was this problem of overinclusiveness that divided the Court in the ground-breaking case of *Regents of the University of California v. Bakke* in 1978.[142] Partly in the interest of making up for past discrimination, the university had reserved sixteen places in its entering medical-school class for members of specified racial minorities. The disparate impact of this deliberate racial classification was patent: blacks could compete for all hundred positions, whites for only eighty-four.[143]

Four Justices thought that was all right. "In light of the sorry history of discrimination and its devastating impact on the lives of Negroes," wrote Justice Marshall, "bringing the Negro into the mainstream of American life should be a state interest of the highest order."[144] In achieving this overriding purpose, these Justices argued, some inexactness in the ends-means relation could be tolerated.[145] Four others thought discrimination even for this worthy goal forbidden by statute and did not reach the constitutional question.[146] The decisive vote was cast by Justice Powell, who took a middle position: race could be taken

---

[140] *See* pp. 478-82 *supra* (discussing Swann v. Charlotte-Mecklenburg Board of Education); *Bakke,* 438 U.S. at 300-05 (opinion of Powell, J.). *See also id.* at 362-66 (opinion of Brennan, White, Marshall, and Blackmun, JJ.) (taking a broad view of the significance of decisions like *Swann*).

[141] There had been no such difficulty with the 1866 Freedman's Bureau Act, which Justice Marshall, *see Bakke,* 438 U.S. at 397, invoked as precedent for preferential treatment of minorities; like its predecessor, that act extended its benefits not to blacks as such but to "refugees and freedmen," *i.e.,* to victims of past wrongs. *See* Act of July 16, 1866, ch. 200, 14 Stat. 173, 174; Act of Mar. 3, 1865, ch. 90, 13 Stat. 507. Justice Marshall argued with much force that it was unlikely any significant number of blacks had escaped harm from public or private racial discrimination, 438 U.S. at 400, but that was a far cry from saying either that the university had inflicted it or that Bakke himself had been its beneficiary. *See id.* at 310 (opinion of Powell, J.). The costs of the Freedmen's Bureau were borne by taxpayers in general, not by hapless individuals who happened to compete with members of the favored class. The more recent act of Congress indemnifying citizens of Japanese descent who were interned during the Second World War, *see* pp. 293-94, note 98 *supra,* is distinguishable on the same grounds. *See also* Posner, *supra* note 138, at 16 & n.33.

[142] 438 U.S. 265 (1978).

[143] *See* 438 U.S. at 272-76, 289, 319-20 (opinion of Powell, J.). It should not matter for this purpose that, as Justice Brennan insisted, *id.* at 357, 374-75, white applicants could not be said to have been "stigmatized" by this discrimination. The absence of stigma might reasonably justify a lower level of scrutiny, *see* p. 485 *infra,* but it does not prevent the reservation of seats for members of minority groups from being unequal. Brown v. Board of Education, pp. 377-78 *supra,* held that the psychological harm done by branding a race as inferior was sufficient to render separate facilities for blacks and whites unequal even when they were physically equivalent, not that it was the only form of inequality.

[144] 438 U.S. at 396.

[145] *See id.* at 325, 362-79 (Brennan, White, Marshall, and Blackmun, dissenting in part).

[146] *See id.* at 408-21 (Stevens, joined by Burger, Stewart, and Rehnquist, dissenting in part).

into account in the interest of diversifying the student body, but the university's rigid quota went too far.[147]

There was much discussion in *Bakke* of the requisite level of scrutiny. Justice Powell insisted that no racial classification could be sustained unless it was "precisely tailored to serve a compelling governmental interest";[148] Brennan, White, Marshall, and Blackmun thought it enough that the measure was "substantially related" to "important governmental objectives."[149] No matter; the crucial fact was that five Justices accepted the principle of affirmative action.[150]

Two years later, in *Fullilove v. Klutznick,* not five but six Justices voted to uphold a federal statute setting aside 10% of public-works funds for minority-owned contractors.[151] Among these six were three Justices appointed since the retirement of Chief Justice Warren.[152] Blackmun's affirmative vote was no surprise; like Brennan, White, and Marshall, he had voted to uphold the quota in *Bakke.* Chief Justice Burger, who provided the fifth

[147]*See id.* at 311-20. For cogent criticism of the diversification argument as embodying the same type of racial stereotyping that underlies much antiblack discrimination see Posner, *supra* note 138, at 7-15.

[148]438 U.S. at 299. *See also* Fullilove v. Klutznick, 448 U.S. 448, 537 (Stevens, J., dissenting) ("Racial classifications are simply too pernicious to permit any but the most exact connection between justification and classification."). Four Justices endorsed Powell's compelling-interest standard in Wygant v. Jackson Board of Education, 476 U.S. 267, 273-74 (1986) (Powell, J., joined by Burger, Rehnquist, and (on this issue) O'Connor). Stevens's dissenting opinion in *Wygant, id.* at 313-20, like White's fifth vote to strike down the preference in question, *id.* at 294-95, conspicuously refrained from any such pronouncement. After Burger's retirement a majority insisted that even "benign" racial classifications be strictly scrutinized: "Racial classifications are suspect." City of Richmond v. J. A. Croson Co., 488 U.S. 469, 500 (1989) (O'Connor, J.).

[149]438 U.S. at 356-62 (emphasizing that although race was "an immutable characteristic," whites as a class lacked "any of 'the traditional indicia of suspectness. . . .'"). For a good argument to sustain minority preferences on the basis of intermediate scrutiny see Greenawalt, *Judicial Scrutiny of "Benign" Racial Preferences in Law School Admissions,* 75 COLUM. L. REV. 559 (1975).

[150]The issue of affirmative action in education had reached the Court once before in DeFunis v. Odegaard, 416 U.S. 312 (1974) (per curiam), where a majority dismissed the case as moot because the victim of alleged discrimination had been admitted pursuant to court order and assured by school authorities that he could continue until his impending graduation. Two earlier decisions of the Burger period, however, were of particular significance as precursors of *Bakke.* Morton v. Mancari, 417 U.S. 535 (1974) (Blackmun, J.), had unanimously upheld a federal statute giving American Indians a preference in filling positions in the Bureau of Indian Affairs; United Jewish Organizations v. Carey, 430 U.S. 144 (1977) (no majority opinion), had allowed a state to take race into account in drawing legislative districts in order to avoid diluting the strength of black and Puerto Rican voters. *Mancari* was distinguishable on the grounds that the Constitution itself, art. I, § 8, singled out Indians for special treatment, *see* 417 U.S. at 551-52, and that (as an original matter) the equal protection clause applied only to the states. In *Carey* Justice Brennan limited his concurrence to "the carefully conceived remedial scheme embodied in the Voting Rights Act," reserving the general question of "'reverse discrimination'" for another day, 430 U.S. at 175; all but one of the remaining majority Justices found no racial discrimination at all because (in a matter to which individual accomplishment was irrelevant) whites were not underrepresented as a result of the plan. *See id.* at 166 (White, J., joined on this issue by Stevens and Rehnquist); *id.* at 179-80 (Stewart, J., joined by Powell, concurring). For the bearing of decisions ordering race-conscious remedies for school segregation and related wrongs see pp. 483-84 *supra.*

[151]448 U.S. 448 (1980). The statute in issue appears in *id.* at 454.

[152]Powell and White joined Burger's opinion announcing the judgment of the Court, 448 U.S. at 453, and Powell added a concurrence of his own, *id.* at 495; Blackmun and Brennan joined Marshall's concurring opinion, *id.* at 517. Rehnquist, Stewart, and Stevens, all of whom had voted to strike down the quota in *Bakke* on statutory grounds, dissented, *id.* at 522-54.

vote, had taken no position on the constitutional issue in the earlier case. What was most interesting was Justice Powell's effort to distinguish *Bakke*, where he had been on the other side.

Before a governmental body may provide for affirmative action, wrote Justice Powell, it must "have the authority to act in response to identified discrimination," and it "must make findings that demonstrate the existence of illegal discrimination." Neither requirement, he argued, had been met in *Bakke*, for "the Regents . . . were entrusted only with educational functions, and they made no findings of past discrimination." [153] *Fullilove*, in his opinion, was different: Congress had the requisite authority and had made the necessary finding. [154]

Whether the Regents had "authority" to remedy discrimination was in one sense the very constitutional issue the Court was attempting to decide. In any other sense it was a question of state law which the Justices had no business resolving in a case coming from state court. That Congress had legitimately found past discrimination in *Fullilove*, moreover, established only that a compelling interest existed, not that the remedy chosen was appropriately tailored to achieving it. After finding a compelling interest in diversification of the student body in *Bakke*, Justice Powell had nevertheless held a numerical quota an unconstitutional means of promoting it; in *Fullilove* too a stated percentage of available benefits had been set aside for minority group members alone.

Nevertheless, said Justice Powell, the measure was temporary; the set-aside was "pegged at a reasonable figure" in light of the overall proportion of minority members in the general population; and a waiver provision provided against unfairness "in areas of the country where minority group members constitute a small percentage of the population." Since the provision was estimated to leave the 96% of contractors who were not members of such groups free "to compete for 99.75% of construction funds" in the country as a whole, "the effect of the set-aside is limited and so widely dispersed that its use is consistent with fundamental fairness." [155]

In *Wygant v. Jackson Board of Education*, [156] just before Chief Justice Burger's retirement, the Court by a five-to-four vote invalidated a provision in a collective-bargaining agreement providing that, in any event of a reduction of the work force, "at no time will there be a greater percentage of minority personnel laid off than the current percentage of minority personnel employed. . . ." [157] As in *Bakke* and in *Fullilove*, there was no majority opinion. Justice Powell, joined by Burger and Rehnquist, found *Fullilove* distinguishable

---

[153] 448 U.S. at 498 (Powell, J., concurring) (citing his opinion in *Bakke*, 438 U.S. at 309-10).

[154] 448 U.S. at 499-506.

[155] *Id.* at 513-15. The discrepancy between the 10 percent figure in the statute and the 0.25 percent figure in Powell's argument is attributable to the fact that federal funds accounted for only 2.5 percent of the total sum spent on construction in the United States. *See id.* at 484-85 n.72 (opinion of Burger, C. J.). The Chief Justice's long opinion, joined by White and Powell, likewise invoked the waiver provision and stressed that the statute had been attacked on its face: it was "conceivable" that a particular application of the law might "bestow[] a benefit on businesses identified by racial or ethnic criteria which cannot be justified on the basis of competitive criteria or as a remedy for the present effects of identified prior discrimination," but "[w]e are not presented here with a challenge involving a specific award of a construction contract or the denial of a waiver request; such questions of specific application must await future cases." *Id.* at 486-88.

[156] 476 U.S. 267 (1986).

[157] *See id.* at 269-71 (opinion of Powell, J.).

because "[d]enial of a future employment opportunity is not as intrusive as loss of an existing job."[158] That was true enough; as with the other differences of degree that Justice Powell had relied on in *Bakke* and in *Fullilove*, one could disagree as to whether it was significant enough to be decisive.[159] A more serious difficulty was that the new distinction seemed to mean *Bakke* had been wrongly decided. For in contrast to the white teachers laid off in *Wygant*, Bakke had been denied admission to the university in the first instance, not expelled after commencing his studies.[160]

Thus, as the Burger years came to a close, a little affirmative action was permissible, but not too much. Whatever one thinks about his hairline distinctions as a legal matter, it may be that Justice Powell—a pivotal figure in these cases—proved to be a pretty good practical politician, for he managed to leave room for extraordinary action to meet a critical national problem while insisting that racial distinctions were almost never to be tolerated.[161] Without a decision more or less like *Fullilove* it is arguable that we might never have made substantial progress toward making amends for past discrimination.[162]

Nevertheless it seems less than clear that the Court's conclusion that racial distinctions are sometimes permissible will work in the long run to the benefit of those it was intended to help. Forty years earlier the same principle had led the Supreme Court to uphold the deplorable decision to drive U.S. citizens of Japanese descent from their homes on the

---

[158] *Id.* at 282-83.

[159] *See id.* at 307 (Marshall, J., dissenting) ("[A] hiring policy achieves no purpose at all if it is eviscerated by layoffs."); *id.* at 319 n.14 (Stevens, J., dissenting) ("In either event, the adverse decision forecloses 'only one of several opportunities' that may be available. . . .").

[160] *See Bakke*, 438 U.S. at 276-77; *Wygant*, 476 U.S. at 283 n.11 (distinguishing DeFunis v. Odegaard, *supra* note 150, on this ground). Justice O'Connor, who agreed with earlier portions of Powell's opinion, 476 U.S. at 274-78, suggesting that the district had not been shown to have engaged in prior discrimination and rejecting the "role model" theory noted below, concurred on the ground that the layoff provision was designed to assure a mix of teachers "tied to the percentage of minority students in the school district, not to the percentage of qualified minority teachers within the relevant labor pool," and thus bore "no relation to remedying employment discrimination." *Id.* at 294. The fifth vote to strike down the layoff provision was provided not by Justice Stevens, who had thought the affirmative action provisions in both *Bakke* and *Fullilove* illegal, but by Justice White, who had voted to uphold them. White's brief opinion seemed to draw the same distinction that Powell drew: "Whatever the legitimacy of hiring goals or quotas may be, the discharge of white teachers to make room for blacks, none of whom has been shown to be a victim of any racial discrimination, is quite a different matter." 476 U.S. at 295 (White, J., concurring). Stevens's dissent, *id.* at 313-20, relied on an interest less obviously present in *Fullilove*—the importance of providing black teachers as living proof that "diverse ethnic, cultural, and national backgrounds . . . do not identify essential differences among the human beings that inhabit our land." His vote against the program in *Bakke*, where the related argument for a diverse student body had been made, was based on a statute not invoked before the Supreme Court in *Wygant*. Marshall, Brennan, and Blackmun, *id.* at 295-312, also dissented.

[161] *Cf.* Tribe, *Perspectives on* Bakke: *Equal Protection, Procedural Fairness, or Structural Justice?*, 92 Harv. L. Rev. 864, 864-65 (1979) (suggesting a different sort of political adroitness: "The headlines could cry, 'Bakke Wins Admission,' while the lawyers and admissions officers would quietly read the subtitle: 'affirmative action upheld.' ").

[162] Posner, *supra* note 138, at 32, argued that the same goal could have been accomplished, with some "inconvenience," by redefining the preferred groups as "the underprivileged, the deprived, etc." *But see Bakke*, 438 U.S. at 377 (opinion of Brennan, White, Marshall, and Blackmun) ("A case-by-case inquiry into the extent to which each individual applicant has been affected, either directly or indirectly, by racial discrimination, would seem to be, as a practical matter, virtually impossible. . . .").

ground that some of them might be disloyal during the war with Japan.[163] It may be that politically powerless minorities are most secure if racial classifications are forbidden entirely.[164]

## C. The "De Facto" Problem

*Fullilove v. Klutznick* held that government was sometimes *permitted* to prefer blacks to whites. *Washington v. Davis* held that it was not generally *required* to do so.[165]

In choosing among applicants for its police force, the District of Columbia relied in part on a written examination " 'designed to test verbal ability, vocabulary, reading and comprehension.' " There was no claim that in adopting or administering the test the District had purposefully distinguished between whites and blacks. It was argued, however, that the test was racially discriminatory because it had a disproportionate *impact* on the races: a higher percentage of whites than blacks passed the test.[166]

The Court rejected the argument. "[O]ur cases," wrote Justice White, "have not embraced the proposition that a law or other official act, without regard to whether it reflects a racially discriminatory purpose, is unconstitutional *solely* because it has a racially disproportionate impact."[167] The equal protection clause (and its federal due process equivalent) thus prohibited discrimination *on grounds* of race; they did not require that blacks receive a proportional share of government jobs.[168]

With regard to voting, the fifteenth amendment makes this conclusion abundantly clear: "The right of citizens of the United States to vote shall not be denied or abridged . . . on account of race, color, or previous condition of servitude."[169] The fourteenth amendment is not so plain. Until the Warren years, however, there had never been a sug-

---

[163] *See* pp. 285-92 *supra* (discussing the *Hirabayashi* and *Korematsu* cases).

[164] *See* Van Alstyne, *Rites of Passage: Race, the Supreme Court, and the Constitution*, 46 U. CHI. L. REV. 767, 778 (1979) ("In the past, the consequences of admitting race-based laws . . . have been overwhelmingly dismal.").

[165] 426 U.S. 229 (1976).

[166] *Id.* at 234-37 (quoting the district court opinion).

[167] *Id.* at 239.

[168] No Justice took issue with this conclusion. Justice Stevens, concurring, while suggesting that "the line between discriminatory purpose and discriminatory impact is not nearly so bright, and perhaps not quite as critical," as the majority implied, agreed that "a constitutional issue does not arise every time some disproportionate impact is shown." *Id.* at 254-55. Brennan and Marshall, dissenting on statutory grounds, expressly left the constitutional question open, *id.* at 257 n.1. *Accord* Village of Arlington Heights v. Metropolitan Housing Development Corp., 429 U.S. 252, 264-68 (1977) (Powell, J.) (adding a useful essay on the evidence that might be relevant in determining whether official action was based on race). *See also* City of Mobile v. Bolden, 446 U.S. 55 (1980), where four Justices concluded that the harsh effect of an at-large election on black candidates did not make it racially discriminatory, four Justices found purposeful discrimination, and Marshall (joined by Brennan) argued that the intent requirement of Washington v. Davis was inapplicable to a case involving the fundamental right to vote—an argument that seems to confuse the question whether there is racial discrimination with the question whether strict scrutiny is required.

[169] *See* City of Mobile v. Bolden, 446 U.S. at 61-65 (opinion of Stewart, J., for four Justices), *supra* note 168. *But see id.* at 134 (Marshall, J., dissenting) ("The right to vote is of such fundamental importance in the constitutional scheme that the Fifteenth Amendment's command that it shall not be 'abridged' on account of race must be interpreted as providing that the votes of citizens of all races shall be of substantially equal weight."). Justice Brennan agreed with Marshall. *Id.* at 94.

gestion in the cases that the governing standards differed under the two provisions. As Justice White noted in *Davis*, the jury cases of the 1880s had established from the beginning that blacks need not be proportionally represented on juries; it was enough that they had not been excluded because of their race.[170] Similarly, the Warren Court itself, finding no evidence that race had been taken into account, had held that enormous discrepancies in the racial composition of legislative districts raised no constitutional problem.[171]

Justice White's treatment of recent precedents, however, was not entirely complete. *Griffin v. Illinois* and *Harper v. Virginia Board of Elections*, in requiring that the state provide indigent defendants with free transcripts and in striking down a law conditioning the vote on payment of a poll tax, had suggested that laws neutral on their face might discriminate against the poor.[172] Perceptive Justices protested at the time, and there were better grounds for both decisions; but the opinions were difficult to reconcile with *Washington v. Davis*. The school segregation decisions, moreover, while literally adhering (as White said) to the requirement of discriminatory purpose,[173] had gone to such lengths to achieve racial mixing on the basis of minor de jure infractions that it could be argued with considerable force that their actions spoke more loudly than their words.[174] Finally, as

---

[170] *E.g.*, Virginia v. Rives, 100 U.S. 313, 322 (1880) (Allegations that blacks "had never been allowed to serve as jurors in the county . . . fall short of showing . . . discrimination" because "the jury . . . may have been impartially selected."). *See* THE FIRST HUNDRED YEARS at 383-87; *Davis*, 426 U.S. at 239-40.

[171] *See id.* at 240 (citing Wright v. Rockefeller, 376 U.S. 52 (1964)). *See Wright* at 57 ("[T]he concentration of colored and Puerto Rican voters in one area in the county made it difficult, even assuming it to be permissible, to fix districts so as to have anything like an equal division of these voters among the districts."). *See also id.* at 59 (Douglas, J., dissenting) ("Neighborhoods in our larger cities often contain members of only one race; and those who draw the lines of Congressional Districts cannot be expected to disregard neighborhoods in an effort to make each district a multiracial one.").

[172] *See* pp. 403-05, 424-25 *supra*. *See also* Shelley v. Kraemer, pp. 358-60 *supra*, where the state had been held responsible for racial discrimination by private parties although there was no suggestion that its policy of enforcing covenants respecting real property was other than neutral with respect to race.

[173] *See* 426 U.S. at 240 (inappositely quoting the *definition* of de jure segregation in *Keyes*, pp. 479-80 *supra*, 413 U.S. at 205, 208. More to the point was Chief Justice Burger's unequivocal statement in *Swann*, pp. 478-79 *supra*, 402 U.S. at 24: "If we were to read the holding of the District Court to require, as a matter of substantive constitutional right, any particular degree of racial balance or mixing, that approach would be disapproved and we would be obliged to reverse."

[174] Despite urging from concurring Justices, the majority in *Keyes* expressly reserved the question whether the mere existence of racial disparities between schools was enough to establish a violation. *See* 413 U.S. at 212; *id.* at 214-17 (Douglas, J., concurring); *id.* at 217-23 (Powell, J., concurring in part). Nevertheless the Court paved the way to desegregation of an entire city by concluding that a court could find that intentional segregation of one neighborhood both affected others and raised a presumption that racial disparities elsewhere had been deliberately caused—a presumption, Justice Brennan argued, that could not be rebutted simply by showing a neutral justification for the challenged action. *Id.* at 198-213. The Burger Court itself, which in reliance on *Davis* unanimously rejected the notion that de facto segregation was unconstitutional, Dayton Board of Education v. Brinkman (I), 433 U.S. 406, 413 (1977) (Rehnquist, J.), was not free in this area from the appearance of remedying that which was not unconstitutional along with that which was. *See* Columbus Board of Education v. Penick, p. 481 *supra*. The school cases, it should be added, were complicated by the probable effect of other governmental actions (such as deliberate housing segregation) on the "de facto" composition of the schools. *See* pp. 480-81 *supra* (discussing Milliken v. Bradley).

Justice Powell, who joined Douglas in *Keyes* in arguing that de facto segregation was unconstitutional, was the Court's most vociferous opponent of busing. The apparent tension between his two positions may be more understandable if one considers his past association with the Richmond School board. Northern schools, he

Justice White acknowledged, the Court had unanimously held in 1972 that the Civil Rights Act of 1964 limited de facto as well as de jure discrimination: "[A]bsence of discriminatory intent does not redeem employment procedures or testing mechanisms that operate as 'built-in headwinds' for minority groups and are unrelated to measuring job capability." [175] What he did not say—and what the Chief Justice in the earlier case had tucked away in a footnote—was that the statute itself forbade only actions adversely affecting an individual "because of . . . race." [176]

Thus as a matter of precedent *Washington v. Davis* was not quite so easy as Justice White would have us believe. A historical analysis, which he did not undertake, might have lent more support to his position. The evil that prompted adoption of the fourteenth amendment, as the *Slaughter-House Cases* told us, was that blacks had been deprived of equal opportunity by law because they were black;[177] the most obvious purpose of the amendment was to give them a fair chance. The most obvious way to do so was to remove the cause of the evil by making race an impermissible basis of classification—an approach that also conforms with the widespread perception that it is immoral and offensive to judge individuals on the basis of race.

That removing de jure barriers to black advancement might leave blacks on the average worse off than whites has become increasingly evident over the years. It was the perception that past discrimination left its victims with significant disabilities that gave rise to powerful arguments for the constitutionality of departures from the generally accepted principle of racial neutrality for the laudable purpose of redressing past wrongs.[178] It would not have been inconceivable for the framers of the fourteenth amendment to have not only permitted but required such departures in order to achieve a more complete remedy for the evils of slavery.

It is important to bear in mind, however, that to do so would have been to depart significantly from the appealing principle of neutrality. It is no excuse for denying employment that the applicant is black; it may be a very good excuse that he cannot read.[179] To require a proportional distribution of jobs without regard to possession of the relevant skills could so jeopardize important interests in the efficient provision of services that it should not lightly be presumed the amendment had any such purpose.[180] To require careful scrutiny of measures having a differential impact on the races, however, would have no

---

complained, were still segregated because the de facto/de jure distinction had been "accepted complacently by many of the same voices which denounced the evils of segregated schools in the South," though "the evil of operating separate schools is no less in Denver than in Atlanta." *Id.* at 218-19.

[175] Griggs v. Duke Power Co., 401 U.S. 424, 432 (1971) (Burger, C. J.).

[176] *See id.* at 426 n.1. Some reliance was placed on the supposed negative implications of a proviso insisting that there was nothing wrong with acting upon a properly motivated "professionally developed ability test" in light of its unconvincing legislative history. *See id.* at 434-36.

[177] Slaughter-House Cases, 83 U.S. 36, 70 (1873) ("Among the first acts of legislation adopted by several of the States in the legislative bodies which claimed to be in their normal relations with the Federal government, were laws which imposed upon the colored race onerous disabilities and burdens, and curtailed their rights. . . .").

[178] *See* pp. 482-88 *supra.*

[179] *See Davis,* 426 U.S. at 245-46 ("[I]t is untenable that the Constitution prevents the Government from seeking modestly to upgrade the communicative abilities of its employees. . . .").

[180] *See* Brest, *supra* note 139, at 5 (arguing that "the antidiscrimination principle" reaffirmed in *Davis* "prevents and rectifies racial injustices without subordinating other important values").

such consequence; it would merely require (as under the 1964 Civil Rights Act) a strong showing that the challenged criterion was actually necessary to achieve its asserted goal.[181] It is one thing, however, for Congress to enact such a requirement in order to prevent unnecessary discriminatory impacts on blacks; it is quite another to read such a requirement into the Constitution.

For the historical record seems to suggest that the fourteenth amendment did no such thing. Shortly after its adoption, the Supreme Court paraphrased its provisions in such a way as to indicate that the aim was equal opportunity rather than equal results: "What is this but declaring that the law in the States shall be the same for the black as for the white . . . ?"[182] The fifteenth amendment, adopted to extend to the political field the revolution of which the fourteenth was a part, expressly required only neutrality, although the need for remedial measures was no less strong with respect to voting than it was in other fields.[183] Finally, both the civil rights act on which the fourteenth amendment was based and the clause of the amendment that was probably meant to ban most racial discrimination were phrased in terms of rights, privileges, and immunities[184]—suggesting once again the limited goal of permitting blacks to compete on equal terms.[185]

---

[181] See also Binion, "Intent" and Equal Protection: A Reconsideration, 1983 SUP. CT. REV. 397 (arguing for "serious scrutiny" under the fourteenth amendment of classifications with disproportionate effects on racial and analogous groups).

[182] Strauder v. West Virginia, 100 U.S. 303, 307 (1880).

[183] See Gaston County v. United States, 395 U.S. 285, 289 (1969) (quoting Attorney General Katzenbach's testimony before a Senate committee) (" 'To subject every citizen to a higher literacy standard [for voting] would, inevitably, work unfairly against Negroes—Negroes who have for decades been systematically denied educational opportunity equal to that available to the white population.' "). Nevertheless, absent proof that literacy tests were employed in order to prevent blacks from voting, the Court properly held that they did not abridge the right to vote on grounds of race. Lassiter v. Northampton Board of Elections, pp. 384-85 supra. Gaston County forbade use of a literacy test on the basis of the Voting Rights Act of 1965, which—responsive to the problem identified by the Attorney General—was triggered by the use of tests used "for the purpose or with the effect" of racial discrimination. See 395 U.S. at 286-87 (emphasis added).

[184] The statute, Act of Apr. 9, 1866, ch. 31, § 1, 14 Stat. 27, provided among other things that all citizens "shall have the same right . . . to make and enforce contracts, to sue, be parties, and give evidence, to inherit, purchase, lease, sell, hold, and convey real and personal property, and to full and equal benefit of all laws and proceedings for the security of person and property, as is enjoyed by white citizens. . . ." See THE FIRST HUNDRED YEARS at 347-50.

[185] The remarks of prominent advocates of the amendment support this interpretation. See, e.g., CONG. GLOBE, 39th Cong., 1st Sess., pt. 3, p. 2459 (Rep. Stevens):

> This amendment . . . allows Congress to correct the unjust legislation of the States, so far that the law which operates upon one man shall operate equally upon all. Whatever law punishes a white man for a crime shall punish the black man precisely in the same way and to the same degree. Whatever law protects the white man shall afford "equal" protection to the black man. Whatever means of redress is afforded to one shall be afforded to all. Whatever law allows the white man to testify in court shall allow the man of color to do the same. These are great advantages over their present codes. Now different degrees of punishment are inflicted, not on account of the magnitude of the crime, but according to the color of the skin. . . .

See also id. at 2766 (Senator Howard); id., pt. 4, at 2961 (Rep. Poland). To the argument that the Court did not feel bound by the specific intentions of the Framers in invalidating "separate but equal" schooling in Brown v. Board of Education, pp. 377-78 supra, see also THE FIRST HUNDRED YEARS at 387-90, it may be replied that both the evidence of congressional understanding and substantive doubts about the suitability of the suggested departure are far stronger in the case of de facto discrimination.

Without holding that either the fourteenth amendment or the fifteenth was meant to limit de facto discrimination as such, a plausible argument could be made that heightened scrutiny of measures having disproportionate effects on blacks was necessary to prevent frustration of the conceded goal of outlawing deliberate discrimination. The history of the fifteenth amendment reveals a series of evasive actions whose purpose and effect were widely believed to be to disenfranchise as many blacks as possible; only in the most egregious cases could the Court convincingly demonstrate the existence of an illegitimate intent.[186] Congress's ultimate answer, in part, was a prophylactic rule barring literacy tests altogether, which avoided the impracticability of policing their misuse.[187] The Court itself had done something similar in laying down a set of prophylactic rules to prevent involuntary confessions in *Miranda v. Arizona;*[188] arguably it should have done so in *Washington v. Davis* as well.[189]

*Miranda* itself, of course, is not above criticism; however appealing a ban on confessions that were not themselves coerced may be, it was not easy to find such a ban even in the open-ended due process clause. It would be harder still to find a ban on voting requirements not based on race in the fifteenth amendment, which expressly forbids only those that are; and history suggests that the difference in phrasing between the two equality provisions may have been accidental. That Congress was within its rights in outlawing literacy tests, moreover, does not prove that the Court would have been. It is one thing to

---

[186]*Compare* Guinn v. United States, pp. 106-07 *supra* (striking down a grandfather clause that served no conceivable purpose save racial discrimination), and Gomillion v. Lightfoot, pp. 381-82 *supra* (invalidating an improbable city boundary that fenced out most blacks without apparent reason), *with* Lassiter v. Northampton County Board of Elections, pp. 384-85 *supra* (upholding a literacy test because of the obvious relation between "ability to read and write" and "intelligent use of the ballot"). In fourteenth amendment cases too, as Justice White noted in *Davis,* a disproportionate racial impact will suffice to prove discriminatory purpose in the absence of a plausible alternative explanation. *See, e.g.,* Neal v. Delaware, 103 U.S. 370, 397 (1881) (uniform absence of blacks from juries); Yick Wo v. Hopkins, 118 U.S. 356, 374 (1886) (uniform denial of laundry licenses to Chinese). *See Davis,* 426 U.S. at 241-42; THE FIRST HUNDRED YEARS at 385-87.

[187]*See* p. 427 *supra* (discussing Oregon v. Mitchell). *See also* City of Rome v. United States, 446 U.S. 156, 177 (1980) (Marshall, J., over three dissents) (upholding a provision forbidding certain changes in election laws without any showing that they offended the fifteenth amendment) ("Congress could rationally have concluded that, because electoral changes by jurisdictions with a demonstrable history of intentional racial discrimination in voting create the risk of purposeful discrimination, it was proper to prohibit changes that have a discriminatory impact.").

[188]*See* pp. 449-50 *supra. Cf.* McCulloch v. Maryland, 17 U.S. 316, 430 (1819) (holding the state could not tax the national bank at all because of the difficulty of drawing the line between legitimate and abusive taxation) THE FIRST HUNDRED YEARS at 165-68. In apparent recognition of the fact that powerless minorities may be as helpless to protect themselves from de facto discrimination as from de jure, the Court has occasionally struck down state laws neutral on their face because of their discriminatory effects on interstate commerce; but the cases are hardly consistent. *Compare, e.g.,* Hunt v. Washington Apple Adv. Comm'n, 432 U.S. 333 (1977) (Burger, C. J.) (striking down a law requiring additional labeling of apples) *with* Exxon Corp. v. Governor of Maryland, 437 U.S. 117 (1978) (Stevens, J.) (upholding a law forbidding gasoline refiners to operate service stations), and Commonwealth Edison Co. v. Montana, 453 U.S. 609 (1981) (Marshall, J.) (upholding a substantial tax on the severance of coal). For dramatization of the problem, see the discussion of a hypothetical New York tax on cotton, tobacco, or rice in Woodruff v. Parham, 75 U.S. 123, 145-46 (1869) (Nelson, J., dissenting), THE FIRST HUNDRED YEARS at 337.

[189]*See* City of Mobile v. Bolden, 446 U.S. 55, 135 (1980) (Marshall, J., dissenting) "An approach based on motivation creates the risk that officials will be able to adopt policies that are the products of discriminatory intent so long as they sufficiently mask their motives through the use of subtlety and illusion."). *See also* Strauss, *The Ubiquity of Prophylactic Rules,* 55 U. CHI. L. REV. 190 (1988).

conclude that such a ban is necessary to enforce the amendment;[190] it is quite another to say that literacy tests as such discriminate on grounds of race.

Where does all this leave us? History seems to suggest that, as the Court held in *Davis,* the equal protection clause forbids only deliberate discrimination. If the difficulties of proving discriminatory intent are thought to present a serious obstacle to the enforcement of this prohibition, the precedent of the literacy test shows that Congress is not without power to enact a broader prophylactic rule. If neutrality itself proves insufficient to overcome the effects of past discrimination that was not itself unconstitutional, the Constitution may of course be amended again—at some cost, it should be added, to the salutary principle that race should be irrelevant to public policy.

## D.   Men, Women, and Children

[T]he civil law, as well as nature herself, has always recognized a wide difference in the respective spheres and destinies of man and woman. . . . The paramount destiny and mission of woman are to fulfill the noble and benign offices of wife and mother. . . . And the rules of civil society must be adapted to the general constitution of things. . . .[191]

Justice Bradley's words, uttered in 1873 to justify excluding women from the practice of law,[192] have the ring of a voice from another planet. Yet they governed our constitutional jurisprudence until surprisingly recently. In 1948 the Court unanimously upheld a law limiting the employment of women as bartenders;[193] in 1961 it held that women could be excused from jury service.[194] We have come a long way since 1873. So far as the Constitution is concerned, however, the journey did not begin until 1971.

The case was *Reed v. Reed,*[195] the author Chief Justice Burger. The question was whether Idaho could discriminate against women in appointing administrators of decedents' estates. The answer was no; the distinction between men and women bore no "rational relationship" to any identifiable state objective. "To give a mandatory preference to members of either sex over members of the other, merely to accomplish the elimination of hearings on the merits, is to make the very kind of arbitrary legislative choice forbidden by the Equal Protection Clause. . . ."[196] Justice Bradley would presumably have found the state's preference for male administrators entirely consistent with the woman's place in the home; it seemed pretty clear that his philosophy had lost its grip on the Supreme Court.

There was nothing in the text of the opinion, however, to suggest that classifications on

---

[190] *See* U. S. CONST. amend. XV, § 2 ("The Congress shall have power to enforce this article by appropriate legislation."). The fourteenth amendment (§ 5) contains a similar provision. For the broad interpretation of these provisions by analogy to the necessary and proper clause of article I see pp. 425-29 *supra.*

[191] Bradwell v. State, 83 U.S. 130, 141-42 (1873) (Bradley, J., concurring).

[192] The majority concluded that law practice was not a privilege or immunity of national citizenship and thus not protected by the applicable clause of the fourteenth amendment. *See* THE FIRST HUNDRED YEARS at 351.

[193] Goesaert v. Cleary, p. 361 *supra.*

[194] Hoyt v. Florida, p. 385, note 59 *supra.*

[195] 404 U.S. 71 (1971).

[196] *Id.* at 76.

the basis of sex were subject, like those based on race, to any unusual degree of scrutiny. "Arbitrary" and "rational relationship" are the language of maximum deference to legislative judgment, and the only precedent invoked was a 1920 decision striking down a distinction between domestic and foreign corporations.[197]

The result nevertheless gave reason to believe that, as in the case of classifications based on illegitimacy,[198] the Court was in fact applying a more exacting standard.[199] Without regard to Bradley's discredited views, it was probably still true in 1971, as the appellee argued, that "men [were] as a rule more conversant with business affairs than . . . women."[200] Similarly, the government was no doubt correct in arguing two years later in *Frontiero v. Richardson* that, "as an empirical matter," many more wives than husbands were dependent on their spouses.[201] Not all wives, of course, were either strangers to business or dependent on their husbands. Not all persons over fifty are too feeble to catch criminals either, yet the Court had no difficulty in upholding a law providing for the mandatory retirement of uniformed police officers at that age.[202] Generalization is what laws are all about; legislatures lay down imperfect rules in order to avoid the substantial costs of case-by-case determination.[203] In striking down a law requiring servicewomen but not servicemen to prove that their spouses were actually dependent in order to qualify for

---

[197] F. S. Royster Guano Co. v. Virginia, p. 104, note 86 *supra* (cited in 404 U.S. at 76, 77).

[198] *See* p. 433 *supra* (discussing Levy v. Louisiana and Glona v. American Guar. & Liab. Ins. Co. (striking down the exclusion of illegitimates from statutory remedies for wrongful death)). After initially appearing to retreat from *Levy* and *Glona* by upholding a law severely limiting the right of illegitimate children to inherit from their fathers, Labine v. Vincent, 401 U.S. 532 (1971) (Black, J., over four dissents), the Burger Court continued to subject classifications based on illegitimacy to what it ultimately described as "heightened" though not the "most exacting" scrutiny. *See* Pickett v. Brown, 462 U.S. 1, 8 (1983) (citing Mathews v. Lucas, 427 U.S. 495, 506 (1976)). Justice Powell set the tone in reaffirming *Levy* and *Glona* in the context of workers' compensation. Illegitimates were not to be disadvantaged on the ground that their parents had erred: "penalizing the illegitimate child is an ineffectual—as well as an unjust—way of deterring the parent." Weber v. Aetna Cas. & Sur. Co., 406 U.S. 164, 170, 175 (1972) (over the lone dissent of Rehnquist). Later decisions extended this reasoning to forbid exclusion of illegitimates from child support, Gomez v. Perez, 409 U.S. 535 (1973) (per curiam, with two votes to dismiss as improvidently granted), welfare benefits, New Jersey Welfare Rights Org. v. Cahill, 411 U.S. 619 (1973) (per curiam, over another Rehnquist dissent), and even inheritance, Trimble v. Gordon, 430 U.S. 762, 767 n.12, 776 n. 17 (1977) (Powell, J., over four dissents) (casting grave doubts on the apparently contrary decision in *Labine*). Outside the area of immigration, which the majority seemed to view as special, *see* Fiallo v. Bell, 430 U.S. 787 (1977) (Powell, J., over three dissents) (holding illegitimates need not be treated as children of their fathers for purposes of preferences under the immigration law), the Court tended to uphold provisions disadvantaging illegitimates only when it found them reasonably designed to assure a satisfactory determination of dependency, Mathews v. Lucas, *supra* (Blackmun, J., over three dissents) (upholding a requirement that certain illegitimates show actual dependency in order to qualify for survivors' benefits), or paternity, Lalli v. Lalli, 439 U.S. 259 (1978) (over four dissents) (permitting a state to condition an illegitimate's inheritance from his father on a judicial determination of paternity during the father's lifetime). *Contrast* Mills v. Habluetzel, 456 U.S. 91 (1982) (Rehnquist, J.), and Pickett v. Brown, 462 U.S. 1 (1983) (Brennan, J.) (unanimously striking down requirements that illegitimate child sue to establish right to paternal support within one or two years of birth, respectively).

[199] *See* Getman, *The Emerging Constitutional Principle of Sexual Equality,* 1972 Sup. Ct. Rev. 157, 158-63.

[200] *See* Brief for Appellee at 12.

[201] *See* 411 U.S. 677, 688-89 (1973).

[202] Massachusetts Board of Retirement v. Murgia, 427 U.S. 307 (1976) (per curiam, with only Marshall dissenting). *See id.* at 315 ("Since physical ability generally declines with age, mandatory retirement at 50 serves to remove from police service those whose fitness for uniformed work presumptively has diminished with age.").

[203] *See Murgia,* 427 U.S. at 314.

supplemental benefits, *Frontiero,* like *Reed,* suggested that the Court was far less tolerant of generalizations based on sex than of those based on other criteria such as age.[204]

Conceding that minimal scrutiny could not explain the result in either *Reed* or *Frontiero,* Justice Brennan, joined by Douglas, White, and Marshall, frankly argued in the latter case that the rational-basis test did not apply. Like race, sex was "an immutable characteristic" that "frequently bears no relation to ability to perform or contribute to society." To impose legal disabilities on the basis of sex was thus difficult to square with " 'the basic concept of our system that legal burdens should bear some relationship to individual responsibility. . . .' "[205] Like race, moreover, sex had often been misused as a basis of classification: "There can be no doubt that our Nation has had a long and unfortunate history of sex discrimination."[206] "[W]e can only conclude," Brennan concluded, "that classifications based upon sex, like classifications based upon race, alienage, or national origin, are inherently suspect, and must therefore be subjected to strict judicial scrutiny."[207]

Four other Justices managed to concur in *Frontiero* without deciding whether Brennan was right,[208] and for a while the issue remained unresolved.[209] In 1976, in *Craig v. Boren,* a majority agreed on an intermediate position: sex was a more suspect basis of classification than most, but not so suspect a basis as race.[210] "To withstand constitutional challenge," wrote Justice Brennan for the Court, "previous cases establish that classifications by gender must serve important governmental objectives and must be substantially related to achievement of those objectives."[211] Traffic safety, the Court conceded, was indisputably an "important" goal. The fact that more males than females drove while drunk, however, was no justification for setting the drinking age higher for men than for women. "[T]he relationship between gender and traffic safety," said Brennan, was "far too tenuous to satisfy *Reed*'s requirement that the gender-based difference be substantially related to achievement of the statutory objective."[212]

---

[204] *See* Gunther, *In Search of Evolving Doctrine on a Changing Court: A Model for a Newer Equal Protection,* 86 HARV. L. REV. 1, 34 (1972) ("It is difficult to understand [the *Reed*] result without an assumption that some special sensitivity to sex as a classifying factor entered into the analysis.").

[205] 411 U.S. at 686 (quoting Weber v. Aetna Cas. & Sur. Co., note 198 *supra*).

[206] 411 U.S. at 684.

[207] *Id.* at 688.

[208] *See id.* at 691-92 (Powell, J., joined by Burger and Blackmun, concurring) (professing to find the distinction irrational); *id.* at 691 (Stewart, J., concurring on the Delphic ground that the classification was "invidious"). Justice Rehnquist dissented alone for reasons given by the court below, *id.* at 691.

[209] *See, e.g.,* Kahn v. Shevin, 416 U.S. 351, 353 (1974) (Douglas, J., over three dissents) (upholding a provision extending tax relief to widows but not to widowers because "the financial difficulties confronting the lone woman . . . exceed those facing the man"); Schlesinger v. Ballard, 419 U.S. 498, 508 (1975) (Stewart, J., over four dissents) (upholding a provision giving navy women longer than their male colleagues to achieve promotion or be retired because "Congress may . . . quite rationally have believed that women line officers had less opportunity for promotion than did their male counterparts. . . ."); Weinberger v. Wiesenfeld, 420 U.S. 636, 651 (1975) (Brennan, J.) (finding it "irrational" to deny to the surviving spouse of a female worker Social Security benefits made available to the surviving spouse of a male); Stanton v. Stanton, 421 U.S. 7, 14 (1975) (Blackmun, J.) (finding "nothing rational" in terminating child support earlier for girls than for boys). These decisions are discussed in Ginsburg, *Gender in the Supreme Court: The 1973 and 1974 Terms,* 1975 SUP. CT. REV. 1.

[210] 429 U.S. 190 (1976).

[211] *Id.* at 197.

[212] *Id.* at 199-204. *See also id.* at 204-09, where the Court rejected the argument that the twenty-first amendment, by forbidding "transportation or importation" of intoxicating beverages into a state in violation of its laws,

Several Justices objected. Justice Stewart branded the classification irrational.[213] Chief Justice Burger saw no reason to judge gender-based distinctions by anything other than the ordinary deferential standard.[214] Justice Rehnquist argued that a history of discrimination against women did not justify heightened scrutiny of classifications that disfavored men.[215] Justice Stevens attacked the entire principle of varying levels of scrutiny.[216] Justices Blackmun and Powell, however, joined Brennan, Marshall, and White in insisting that no distinction on grounds of sex could be sustained simply by showing that it had a "rational basis."[217] No longer were there only two degrees of deference to decisions of other governmental bodies; "intermediate" scrutiny had been added to the arsenal.[218]

Later decisions, while provoking sharp disagreement whether or not the *Craig* test had been met, confirmed that the Court was applying an intermediate standard in sex discrimination cases. In contrast to classifications in terms of such characteristics as age, those based on overbroad generalizations about differences between men and women tended to be struck down, as they had been in *Reed, Frontiero,* and *Craig.* Thus, for example, the Court held that a state could not provide alimony only for women,[219] require only the mother's consent for adoption of an illegitimate child,[220] or give husbands exclusive control of community property.[221] At the same time, however, the Court seemed to find it

---

had made the equal protection clause inapplicable. As the Court said, the history of the provision showed it had been adopted in order to obviate commerce clause objections such as those upheld in Leisy v. Hardin, pp. 32-33 *supra;* intimation of a broader effect in earlier cases were explained away in *Craig. See also* Shapiro, *Mr. Justice Rehnquist: A Preliminary View,* 90 HARV. L. REV. 293, 304-05 (1976) (criticizing the suggestion in California v. LaRue, 409 U.S. 109 (1972), that the amendment permitted limitations on expression in establishments serving liquor that would otherwise be forbidden).

[213] 429 U.S. at 215 (Stewart, J., concurring).

[214] *Id.* at 216-17 (Burger, C. J., dissenting).

[215] *Id.* at 217-28 (Rehnquist, J., dissenting).

[216] *Id.* at 211-14 (Stevens, J., concurring).

[217] *See id.* at 214 (Blackmun, J., concurring in part); *id.* at 210-11 (Powell, J., concurring) (*"Reed* and subsequent cases involving gender-based classifications make clear that the Court subjects such classifications to a more critical examination than is normally applied when 'fundamental' constitutional rights and 'suspect classes' are not present.").

[218] As in the case of race, the Court held that not every measure having disparate impacts upon men and women was to be treated as classifying on the basis of sex: "[T]he Fourteenth Amendment guarantees equal laws, not equal results"; what the Constitution forbids is "purposeful discrimination." Personnel Administrator v. Feeney, 442 U.S. 256, 273-74 (1979) (Stewart, J.) (sustaining a veterans' preference that disadvantaged a higher percentage of women than of men seeking government jobs, over two dissents arguing that the disparate impact of the law established an unrebutted prima facie case of deliberate sex discrimination). *See also* Geduldig v. Aiello, 417 U.S. 484, 496-97 n.20 (1974) (Stewart, J., over three dissents) (declining to treat the exclusion of pregnancy from a disability insurance program as an instance of sex discrimination). *See generally* pp. 488-93 *supra* (discussing Washington v. Davis).

[219] Orr v. Orr, 440 U.S. 268 (1979) (Brennan, J., over three dissents not reaching the merits).

[220] Caban v. Mohammed, 441 U.S. 380 (1979) (Powell, J., over four dissents).

[221] Kirchberg v. Feenstra, 450 U.S. 455 (1981) (Marshall, J., without dissent). In reaffirming *Frontiero's* conclusion that men could not be required to prove actual dependency to qualify for benefits automatically available to women, Califano v. Goldfarb, 430 U.S. 199 (1977) (Brennan, J., over four dissents); Wengler v. Druggists Mut. Ins. Co., 446 U.S. 142 (1980) (White, J., over a dissent by Rehnquist), the Court went beyond contemporaneous decisions respecting illegitimacy, a basis for classification the Court also said was subject to intermediate scrutiny; for though generalizations about the tendency of illegitimate children to live with their mothers were held not to justify excluding them entirely from provisions for paternal support, the states were allowed to require a showing of actual dependence on the father. *See* note 198 *supra.*

easier to sustain affirmative action programs for women than for blacks, though the relative severity of past discrimination in the two cases suggested precisely the opposite conclusion. In sharp contrast to the strict insistence on a precise relation between means and ends in *Bakke* and *Wygant*, for example, the Court in *Califano v. Webster* approved a provision giving women a significant advantage in the computation of retirement benefits simply because it served in the Court's view "to compensate women for past economic discrimination."[222]

The decision in *Michael M. v. Superior Court* to uphold a law punishing only males for statutory rape, moreover, suggested the Court would be relatively tolerant of distinctions that could fairly be traced to inherent physical differences between men and women rather than to generalizations about their social roles. "Only women," said Justice Rehnquist, "may become pregnant." Since girls were thus more likely than boys to be harmed by premature sexual intercourse, it was reasonable for the state to protect only girls; since the risk of pregnancy deterred girls more than boys from engaging in sexual activity, it was reasonable to limit additional sanctions to the male participant.[223]

In most striking contrast to the strict scrutiny employed in race cases, however, was the 1981 decision in *Rostker v. Goldberg*, upholding a statute requiring only men to register for a possible military draft.[224] Since women were ineligible for combat duty, said Justice Rehnquist for the majority, it was perfectly reasonable not to draft them; "registration serves no purpose beyond providing a pool for the draft."[225] As the dissenters argued, this reasoning permitted a considerable inexactness in the fit between ends and means, since women in noncombat roles would free up men for fighting.[226] Moreover, although no one challenged the exclusion of women from combat itself,[227] that policy seemed of questionable validity if the Court really meant what it had said in recent cases about overbroad generalizations based on gender, for physical strength was neither confined to males nor necessary for dropping bombs.

The *Rostker* opinion was heavily larded with expressions of the exaggerated degree of deference the Burger Court commonly afforded to military decisions.[228] That it did not signify a general retreat to toothless scrutiny of gender classifications was underlined by the 1982 decision in *Mississippi University for Women v. Hogan*, holding that the state

---

[222] 430 U.S. 313, 318 (1977) (per curiam). *See also Craig*, 429 U.S. at 198 n.6 (explaining the *Kahn* and *Ballard* decisions, note 209 *supra*, on the basis of the "laudatory [sic] purposes" of the laws there upheld "as remedying disadvantageous conditions suffered by women in economic and military life"). It was this perception that led Justice Brennan in the *Wiesenfeld* and *Goldfarb* cases, *supra* notes 209 and 221, to insist that requirements disadvantaging male beneficiaries discriminated against their wage-earning wives. *See Wiesenfeld*, 420 U.S. at 645 ("Section 402(g) clearly operates . . . to deprive women of protection for their families which men receive as a result of their employment"); *Goldfarb*, 430 U.S. at 207-09. *See* pp. 482-88 *supra* (discussing the race cases).

[223] 450 U.S. 464, 471-73 (opinion of Rehnquist, J., joined by Burger, Stewart, and Powell). Blackmun concurred separately, *id.* at 481-87; Brennan, White, Marshall, and Stevens dissented, *id.* at 488-502.

[224] 453 U.S. 57 (1981).

[225] *See id.* at 75-79.

[226] *See id.* at 83-86 (White, J., joined by Brennan, dissenting); *id.* at 86-113 (Marshall, J., also joined by Brennan, dissenting).

[227] *See id.* at 77 n.13.

[228] *See* 453 U.S. at 64-72. *Cf.* Parker v. Levy, p. 516-17, note 70 *infra;* Goldman v. Weinberger, p. 533 *infra. Contrast Ex parte* Milligan, 71 U.S. 2 (1866) (holding unconstitutional the military trial of civilians during the Civil War), THE FIRST HUNDRED YEARS at 288-92.

had acted unconstitutionally in excluding an otherwise qualified male from a public school of nursing.[229] The Court stressed that it was not passing upon the permissibility of "separate but equal" schools for men and women;[230] the holding was only that the state had provided less adequate facilities for one sex than for the other. At the same time, as the dissenters pointed out, other state nursing schools in Mississippi were open to men as well as women; the rejected applicant was disadvantaged only by having to "driv[e] a considerable distance from his home."[231]

The decisive vote against sex discrimination in *Hogan* was cast by the newly appointed Justice O'Connor, who in other matters often voted with the more restrained Justice Rehnquist. Not content to reaffirm that gender distinctions were subject to heightened scrutiny, she conspicuously declared that such classifications must satisfy "at least" the criteria set forth in *Craig*, adding that "we need not decide whether classifications based upon gender are inherently suspect"—as three of the four Justices who joined her opinion had argued in *Frontiero*.[232]

Thus, despite contrary rumblings from some of the Justices, heightened scrutiny for gender classifications survived the Burger period that had produced it. It was of course true, as Justice Stevens protested in *Craig*, that there was "only one Equal Protection Clause."[233] The sex discrimination cases, however, were by no means the first to suggest that some types of classifications were more difficult to justify than others. The vocabulary of strict and less strict scrutiny may have been Procrustean, as Justice Marshall never tired of contending,[234] but it was candid. Not only classifications based on the "suspect" factor of race but also those affecting "fundamental" rights, as we have seen, had been subjected to enhanced scrutiny.[235] If there were to be two levels of scrutiny based on functional considerations, there might as well be three—or indeed as many as those considerations required.

The case for heightened scrutiny of discrimination with respect to fundamental rights has been adumbrated above: since the ultimate question is whether the distinction is reasonable, a serious detriment should be harder to justify than a trivial one.[236] The case for

---

[229] 458 U.S. 718 (1982).

[230] *Id.* at 720 n.1.

[231] *See id.* at 723-24 n.8; *id.* at 735-36 (Powell, J., joined by Rehnquist, J., dissenting). Burger and Blackmun, *id.* at 733-35, dissented as well. *See also id.* at 728-29 (opinion of the Court) (rejecting the argument that an additional school for women could be justified as compensating for earlier discrimination against their sex: there was no showing that women had previously been disadvantaged when it came to nursing).

[232] *Id.* at 724 & n.9.

[233] *See Craig,* 429 U.S. at 211 (Stevens, J., concurring). Actually, as *Frontiero* reaffirmed, there were now two: the one the Framers had written into the fourteenth amendment and the one the Justices had read into the fifth. *See* pp. 285-92 *supra* (discussing the *Hirabayashi* and *Korematsu* cases); Bolling v. Sharpe, pp. 378-79 *supra.* Stevens might more accurately have argued that each of these amendments contained only one such clause.

[234] *See* note 37 *supra. See also Rostker,* 453 U.S. at 69-70 (Rehnquist, J., for the Court) ("We do not think that the substantive guarantee . . . or certainty in the law will be advanced by any further 'refinement' in the applicable tests as suggested by the Government. Announced degrees of 'deference' to legislative judgments, just as levels of 'scrutiny' which this Court announces that it applies to particular classifications . . . , may all too readily become facile abstractions used to justify a result.").

[235] *See, e.g.,* Korematsu v. United States, p. 291 *supra;* pp. 482-85 *supra* (discussing the affirmative action cases); pp. 467-70 *supra* (discussing equal protection and due process antecedents to Roe v. Wade).

[236] *See* pp. 291, 467-70 *supra.*

strict scrutiny of "suspect" classifications is more complex. A long history of discrimination makes for mistrust of distinctions based on race.[237] The fact that race is seldom relevant to any legitimate governmental purpose both increases suspicion and reduces the risk that strict scrutiny may frustrate legitimate governmental goals. Finally, strict scrutiny of many racial classifications followed ineluctably from Justice Stone's insistence on the special need to safeguard the interests of "discrete and insular" minorities: special judicial protection is indispensable for people who cannot protect themselves.[238]

On the basis of this calculus there was much to be said for the Court's decision to place sex discrimination in an intermediate position. As Justice Brennan noted in *Frontiero,* sex as well as race is immutable, has often been employed invidiously, and is often irrelevant to any legitimate purpose. It is not, however, so likely to be irrelevant as race. Sexual differences are not only relevant but crucial to the fundamental question of reproduction. It would thus seem most peculiar, for example, to hold "suspect" a law distinguishing between the sexes for purposes of marriage.[239] More generally, one of the most important reasons for requiring strict scrutiny of racial classifications is absent in the case of gender: since the adoption of the nineteenth amendment, neither women nor men can fairly be considered a politically helpless minority.[240]

Whether the Constitution really empowers the judges to make calculations of this sort is another story. There ought indeed to be a constitutional provision requiring a good reason for distinctions on ground of sex, for all the reasons Justice Brennan suggested. A perfectly appropriate provision to that effect was proposed but not ratified during the Burger period.[241] The pendency of that proposal was not, as three Justices suggested,[242] a

[237] *Cf.* Pickett v. Brown, 462 U.S. 1, 8 (1983) (Brennan, J.) (stressing this factor in subjecting discrimination against illegitimate children to heightened scrutiny); Mathews v. Lucas, 427 U.S. 495, 504-06 (1976) (Blackmun, J.) (refusing to subject such distinctions to "our most exacting scrutiny" because "discrimination against illegitimates has never approached the severity of pervasiveness of the historic legal and political discrimination against women and Negroes").

[238] *See* United States v. Carolene Products Co., p. 244 *supra. See also* San Antonio Independent School Dist. v. Rodriguez, 411 U.S. 1, 28 (1973) (Powell, J., over four dissents) (summarizing the relevant criteria in rejecting the contention that classifications alleged to be on the basis of wealth were subject to enhanced scrutiny):

> The system of alleged discrimination and the class it defines have none of the traditional indicia of suspectness: the class is not saddled with such disabilities, or subjected to such a history of purposeful unequal treatment, or relegated to such a position of political powerlessness as to command extraordinary protection from the majoritarian political process.

[239] *Contrast* Loving v. Virginia, p. 416 *supra* (invalidating prohibition of interracial marriage).

[240] The case for scrutinizing classifications disfavoring women more strictly than those disfavoring men parallels that respecting differential levels of scrutiny for blacks and for whites: in both cases the history of discrimination runs only in one direction. In one important respect, however, the case for differential scrutiny is weaker in the case of sex than in that of race. Blacks remain a relatively small percentage of the population; the law of averages tends to ensure that there are about as many women as men.

[241] "Equality of rights under the law shall not be denied or abridged by the United States or by any State on account of sex." *See* H.R.J. Res. 208, 92d Cong., 2d Sess., 86 Stat. 1523 (1971). The apparently flat prohibition on sex as a basis of classification promised to present interesting interpretive problems. Supporters of the proposal tended to deny that it would allow same-sex marriages, for example, suggesting it merely equated sex with race by requiring truly strict scrutiny. The Court undoubtedly took some of the wind out of their sails by interpreting the fourteenth amendment to accomplish much of what they sought to achieve. What the Court giveth, however, the Court may conceivably take away; sexual equality is a fundamental principle of justice that belongs explicitly in the Constitution.

[242] *See Frontiero,* 411 U.S. at 691-92 (Powell, J., joined by Burger and Blackmun, concurring).

sufficient reason for refusing to decide what the existing Constitution required. Nevertheless the case of sex discrimination points up the fragility of the Court's initial decision to extend equal protection beyond the racial classifications that the Court once agreed the clause was all about.[243] No doubt it was a little late by the time the gender cases were decided to limit the clause once again to race, but that does not make any less regrettable the Court's original failure to justify turning what might have been a firm guarantee against racial discrimination into a flexible tool for striking down any laws found unreasonable by five unelected judges.

## E.   Strangers and Brothers

Among the more striking aspects of the Supreme Court's work was the solicitousness with which, from a very early date, it had scrutinized measures discriminating against persons who were not citizens of the United States. To be sure, aliens were a classic example of a "discrete and insular" minority[244] likely to be treated with hostility and politically unable to protect themselves. On the other hand, as Justice Rehnquist argued in an important 1973 dissent, "the very Amendment which the Court reads to prohibit classifications based on citizenship establishes the very distinction which the Court now condemns. . . ."[245] The first clause of the fourteenth amendment, which declares most persons born in the United States to be citizens, would hardly be necessary if the equal protection clause guaranteed noncitizens identical treatment. Indeed there is historical evidence to suggest that it was not the equal protection clause but the privileges or immunities clause of the same amendment that was designed to extend the nondiscrimination principle of article IV's similarly worded provision beyond citizens of other states, and that clause is explicitly limited to "citizens of the United States."[246]

Already in 1915, however, the Court had struck down a limitation on the private employment of aliens;[247] in 1948 it had invalidated a law excluding them from commercial fishing;[248] and the same year it had even cut back significantly on their exclusion from the traditionally sensitive area of land ownership.[249] It was the Burger Court, in the 1971 case of *Graham v. Richardson,* that carried this line of authority to the extreme of declaring alienage as suspect a classification as race[250]—a characterization so implausible that it would soon have to be revised.

"Aliens like citizens," wrote the newly appointed Justice Blackmun in *Graham* for all Justices save Harlan, "pay taxes and may be called into the armed forces. . . . There can be no 'special public interest' in tax revenues to which aliens have contributed on an equal basis"; thus it was unconstitutional to deny welfare benefits to otherwise eligible foreign-

---

[243] Slaughter-House Cases, 83 U.S. 36, 71, 81 (1973); Strauder v. West Virginia, 100 U.S. 303, 308-09 (1880). *See* THE FIRST HUNDRED YEARS at 347-50, 390-92.

[244] *See* Graham v. Richardson, 403 U.S. 365, 372 (1971).

[245] Sugarman v. Dougall, 413 U.S. 634, 652 (1973) (Rehnquist, J., dissenting).

[246] *See* THE FIRST HUNDRED YEARS at 347-50 (discussing the Slaughter-House Cases).

[247] Truax v. Raich, p. 109, note 123 *supra.*

[248] Takahashi v. Fish & Game Commission, p. 360 *supra.*

[249] Oyama v. California, p. 360 *supra.*

[250] 403 U.S. 365, 371-72 (1971) (Blackmun, J.) ("[T]he Court's decisions have established that classifications based on alienage, like those based on nationality or race, are inherently suspect and subject to close judicial scrutiny.").

ers.[251] Two years later, *In re Griffiths*[252] and *Sugarman v.Dougall*[253] added that states could not exclude aliens wholesale from law practice or civil service either.[254] Despite the argument that an attorney's power to influence the development of law required both undivided loyalty and a firm understanding of our social and political institutions,[255] the decision in the lawyer's case did not seem a very great extension of precedents holding that aliens could not be excluded from other private employment.[256] The civil service decision, however, appeared quite startling in view of the explicit constitutional provisions requiring elected federal officeholders to be citizens[257] and the obvious notions of self-government that underlie them.[258]

Confronted with a similar *federal* requirement in *Hampton v. Mow Sun Wong* in 1976,[259] the Court seemed to go out of its way to avoid following the implications of the approach it had taken in *Sugarman*. As the Court noted, the powers of Congress over aliens are greater than those of the states.[260] Like all others, however, these powers are limited by the Bill of Rights, which had long been held to include a requirement of equality.[261] Acknowledging that Congress in limiting the rights of aliens might legitimately act on the basis of naturalization or foreign-policy concerns that a state could not properly consider,[262] Justice Stevens reserved the question whether Congress or the President might

[251]*Id.* at 376. In a second holding joined by Harlan, *id.* at 383, Blackmun added that the denial of benefits conflicted with federal statutes regulating the status of lawfully admitted aliens. *Id.* at 376-83. *See also* Nyquist v. Mauclet, 432 U.S. 1 (1977) (Blackmun, J.) (striking down a provision denying certain resident aliens state scholarships although, as Rehnquist argued for two of the four dissenters, *id.* at 20, any resident alien could qualify simply "by declaring his intention to become a citizen as soon as possible").

[252]413 U.S. 717 (1973) (Powell, J.).

[253]413 U.S. 634 (1973) (Blackmun, J.).

[254]Justice Rehnquist objected not only to the results in both cases but also to the heightened level of scrutiny employed, *see Sugarman*, 413 U.S. at 649-64; Chief Justice Burger, who did not challenge the level of scrutiny, joined him in dissent in the lawyer's case alone, *Griffiths*, 413 U.S. at 730-33.

[255]*See Griffiths*, 413 U.S. at 724 (reporting the arguments of counsel); *Sugarman*, 413 U.S. at 663-64 (Rehnquist, J., dissenting).

[256]*See* Truax v. Raich, *supra* note 247; Takahashi v. Fish & Game Commission, *supra* note 248. *See also* Examining Board v. Flores de Otero, 426 U.S. 572 (1976) (Blackmun, J., over a Rehnquist dissent) (holding Puerto Rico could not limit the practice of civil engineering to United States citizens).

[257]*See Sugarman*, 413 U.S. at 651-52 (Rehnquist, J., dissenting) (citing U. S. CONST. art. I, §§ 2, 3 (Representatives and Senators) and art. II, § 1 (President)); *see also* amend. XII (Vice-President).

[258]Even the privileges and immunities clause of art. IV, which expressly guarantees equal treatment of citizens of other *states*, has always been understood not to require that they be allowed to participate in government. *See* Supreme Court of New Hampshire v. Piper, 470 U.S. 274, 282 n.13 (1985) (citing Simson, *Discrimination against Nonresidents and the Privileges and Immunities Clause of Article IV*, 128 U. PA. L. REV. 379, 387 (1979)).

[259]426 U.S. 88 (1976) (Stevens, J.).

[260]*See id.* at 100-01 (stressing "the paramount federal power over immigration and naturalization"). *See* pp. 14-16 *supra* (discussing the Chinese Exclusion Case).

[261]*See, e.g.,* Bolling v. Sharpe, pp. 378-79 *supra; Hampton*, 426 U.S. at 100-03.

[262]*See* 426 U.S. at 100. *See also id,* at 103-04 (recounting the interests asserted by the government); Mathews v. Diaz, 426 U.S. 67, 84-85 (1976) (Stevens, J.) (unanimously upholding the disqualification of most aliens from a federal program of medical insurance despite Graham v. Richardson, *supra*). For criticism of the suggestion in *Diaz* that the level of scrutiny was lower in the case of federal than of state alienage classifications see Rosberg, *The Protection of Aliens from Discriminatory Treatment by the National Government*, 1977 SUP. CT. REV. 275, 294:

The existence of these special federal interests may explain why the federal government can demonstrate a compelling need for a particular classification even though a state could not. But it does

validly have limited federal jobs to citizens[263] and found a narrower basis for striking down the limitation.

The provision in question had been adopted neither by the President nor by Congress, but by the Civil Service Commission. "That agency," wrote Stevens, "has no responsibility for foreign affairs, for treaty negotiations, for establishing immigration quotas or conditions of entry, or for naturalization policies." Due process required that the decision "be justified by reasons which are properly the concern" of the deciding agency; but "the interests which the petitioners have put forth as supporting the Commission regulation . . . are not matters which are properly the business of the Commission."[264]

Four dissenters understandably found it difficult to perceive the basis of this conclusion.[265] If the commission had not been authorized to adopt the regulation, there would have been no need to resort to due process to strike it down; the commission had only those powers granted by law. Moreover, as the Court acknowledged, the commission had been so empowered, for an executive order expressly authorized it "to establish standards with respect to citizenship."[266] Nor did the majority suggest either that this delegation was overly broad under the lenient standards that had long prevailed[267] or that only Congress could make it.[268] If the commission had been validly authorized to limit federal jobs to citizens, it was not obvious why the regulation was entitled to any less respect than a comparable act of Congress.

The key appeared to lie in distinguishing between the results the commission was authorized to achieve and the interests it was permitted to consider in reaching its decision. The regulation could not be struck down on nonconstitutional grounds because the commission had been empowered to make citizenship a condition of employment; but the regulation could not be constitutionally supported because the commission had not been authorized to consider the only interests that might justify its decision.

This argument may have represented a rather grudging interpretation of the commission's authority,[269] but as constitutional theory it seems entirely plausible. As Stevens suggested in distinguishing congressional from state regulation of aliens, an interest the enacting body is not entitled to consider cannot be even a legitimate interest under the circumstances, much less the compelling one strict scrutiny demands.

There remained some awkwardness in concluding that the disqualified applicants had been deprived of either liberty or property,[270] as was necessary to any due process viola-

---

not in any obvious way explain why the burden of justification on the federal government should be different from the burden on a state.

[263] 426 U.S. at 114.

[264] *Id.* at 114-16.

[265] *See id.* at 117-27 (Rehnquist, J., joined by Burger, White, and Blackmun, dissenting).

[266] *See id.* at 111 (quoting Ex. Ord. No. 10,577, § 2.1 (a), 3 C.F.R. 218, 219 (1954-58 Comp.)); *id.* at 113 (concluding that apart from constitutional questions, "the Commission may either retain or modify the citizenship requirement without further authorization from Congress or the President").

[267] *See* 426 U.S. at 122-24 (Rehnquist, J., dissenting); pp. 300-01 and 366, note 219 *supra* (discussing post–New Deal delegation decisions).

[268] *Cf.* Youngstown Sheet & Tube Co. v. Sawyer, pp. 365-69 *supra*.

[269] It might well have been concluded that in granting power to require citizenship the President had authorized the agency to take into account all relevant considerations.

[270] *See* 426 U.S. at 102 ("[I]neligibility for employment in a major sector of the economy . . . is of sufficient significance to be characterized as a deprivation of an interest in liberty.").

tion. Decisions respecting the right to a hearing had settled that only an "entitlement" created by law or contract could establish a protected interest in government employment, and the only relevant provision in *Hampton* was that making aliens ineligible.[271] This difficulty, however, had been ignored in earlier cases respecting federal discrimination;[272] liberty and property had to be defined differently for various due process purposes if the Court was to succeed in making the equal protection clause fully applicable to the United States.

In striking down the blanket exclusion of aliens from civil service in *Sugarman*, Justice Blackmun had conceded that the state's interest in self-government was substantial. While disqualifying aliens from such positions as typist and sanitation worker, however, the provision in that case had permitted them to hold a number of positions far more closely connected with the formulation of policy. In concluding that the statute was poorly tailored to achieving its end, the Court was able to suggest that more carefully drafted limitations on aliens in public service might well pass muster.[273]

Later cases confirmed this suggestion. "The essence of our holdings to date," wrote Chief Justice Burger in *Foley v. Connelie,* "is that although we extend to aliens the right to education and public welfare, along with the ability to earn a livelihood and engage in licensed professions, the right to govern is reserved to citizens."[274] This distinction, he explained, was "no more than recognition of the fact that a democratic society is ruled by its people."[275] Accordingly, the Court concluded, states were permitted to deny aliens the right to serve as police officers[276]—or even, as a later case more controversially established, as teachers in public schools.[277] *Sugarman,* it turned out, had been a narrow decision.

One of the more interesting features of this series of cases was the Court's explicit conclusion that some distinctions involving aliens were subject to stricter scrutiny than others. Questions of affirmative action aside,[278] one might have thought that alienage either was or was not a suspect classification. Yet Justice Blackmun had hinted otherwise in *Sugarman* itself in discussing the hypothetical exclusion of aliens from "functions that

---

[271]*See id.* at 118 (Rehnquist, J., dissenting); Board of Regents v. Roth, pp. 540-41 *infra.*

[272]*See, e.g.,* Bolling v. Sharpe, pp. 378-79 *supra.*

[273]*See* 413 U.S. at 641-43, 647-49.

[274]435 U.S. 291, 297 (1978). One sentence in Burger's opinion, *id.* at 295, appeared to explain the decisions protecting aliens entirely on the federalism ground that had been an alternative basis for the holding in *Graham,* see p. 500 *supra,* terming the exclusion of aliens in those cases "seemingly inconsistent with the congressional determination to admit the alien to permanent residence." Later decisions of the Burger period did not pick up on this suggestion.

[275]*Foley,* 435 U.S. at 296.

[276]*Id.* at 297-30 (over dissents by Marshall, Stevens, and Brennan). *See also* Cabell v. Chavez-Salido, 454 U.S. 432 (1982) (White, J.) (probation officers), where Blackmun joined Marshall, Stevens, and Brennan in dissent.

[277]Ambach v. Norwick, 441 U.S. 68, 76 (1979) (Powell, J.) (stressing "[t]he importance of public schools in the preparation of individuals for participation as citizens, and in the preservation of the values on which our society rests"). *But see id.* at 84 (Blackmun, J., joined by Brennan, Marshall, and Stevens, dissenting) ("It seems constitutionally absurd . . . [that] a Frenchman may not teach French or, indeed, an Englishwoman . . . the grammar of the English language."). To place the armed might of the state in foreign hands, *cf. Foley, supra,* seems an altogether different proposition, notwithstanding the dissenters' argument, 435 U.S. at 311, that ordinary state troopers make little policy.

[278]*See* the discussion of affirmative action in the context of race at pp. 482-88 *supra.*

go to the heart of representative government,"[279] and the Chief Justice developed this theme in *Foley*. While the decisions had required "close scrutiny" when aliens were excluded from private professions or government benefits, Burger concluded, only a "rational relationship" between ends and means was required to limit their participation in "democratic decision making."[280]

At first glance this double standard seems puzzling. Noncitizens are just as impotent to attain political goals as economic ones; one could argue that the legitimacy of the state's interest in reserving government to citizens should satisfy strict scrutiny rather than obviating it.[281] On the other hand, as in the case of de facto racial discrimination, the strong possibility that a justification may be found makes the disparate treatment of aliens much less suspicious in the area of governance than in that of sustenance, and mistrust of government motives has been an important factor in determining the appropriate scrutiny level. A similarly discriminating approach might commend itself in testing sex distinctions in the area of procreation or marriage.

That the decisions respecting policemen and teachers had not dissipated the Court's solicitude for aliens outside the special field of self-government was dramatically illustrated by the 1982 decision in *Plyler v. Doe* that Texas could not refuse to educate aliens who were illegally in the country.[282] With all due respect, this conclusion seemed to be carrying solicitude pretty far. Public funds are limited, and those who have no business even being in the state have a poor claim upon them. I may have a right to keep a burglar out of my house, the Court seemed to be saying, but once he gets inside I must invite him to dinner.[283]

---

[279] *Sugarman*, 413 U.S. at 647. *See also id.* at 648 ("[O]ur scrutiny will not be so demanding where we deal with matters resting firmly within a State's constitutional prerogatives.").

[280] *Foley*, 435 U.S. at 294-96.

[281] *See id.* at 303 n.1 (Marshall, J., dissenting).

[282] 457 U.S. 202 (1982) (Brennan, J.).

[283] *See id.* at 250 (Burger, C. J., joined by White, Rehnquist, and O'Connor, dissenting) ("By definition, illegal aliens have no right whatever to be here, and the state may reasonably, and constitutionally, elect not to provide them with governmental services at the expense of those who are lawfully in the state."). *See also id.* at 251 (listing a variety of federal benefit programs excluding illegal aliens); DeCanas v. Bica, 424 U.S. 351, 356 (1976) (Brennan, J., without dissent) (upholding against federalism objections a state law limiting employment of illegal aliens that was not even questioned on equal protection grounds: "California's attempt . . . to prohibit the knowing employment . . . of persons not entitled to lawful residence in the United States . . . is certainly within the mainstream of . . . police power regulation"). For discussion of the many difficulties raised by the *Plyler* opinion see Hutchinson, *More Substantive Equal Protection? A Note on* Plyler v. Doe, 1982 SUP. CT. REV. 167.

# 15

# Other Limitations

## I. SPEECH

The central problem of protecting dissident expression had been pretty well taken care of by the time Chief Justice Warren retired. *Brandenburg v. Ohio* had established that both incitement and a clear and present danger were necessary before political speech could be criminally punished,[1] and a series of cases involving government benefits and investigations had afforded substantial protection against the indirect suppression of unpopular views.[2] The Burger Court added an important footnote to this development in striking down the traditional system of political patronage in *Elrod v. Burns* and *Branti v. Finkel.*[3]

---

[1] *See* p. 442 *supra.*

[2] *See* pp. 434-38 *supra.* Three cases that reached the Court shortly after Burger's appointment raised once again the troublesome question of the extent to which an applicant for bar admission could be questioned about possibly subversive associations. By three votes of five to four, the Court concluded that the applicant could be asked about *knowing* membership in an organization advocating violent overthrow of the government, Law Students Civil Rights Research Council v. Wadmond, 401 U.S. 154 (1971), but not about membership alone, Baird v. State Bar of Arizona, 401 U.S. 1 (1971); *In re* Stolar, 401 U.S. 23 (1971). There was much to be said for the position of Black, Douglas, Brennan, and Marshall that, since nothing less than knowing membership by a person who shared the organization's goals would disqualify the applicant, *cf.* Keyishian v. Board of Regents, p. 435, note 159 *supra*, nothing less need be disclosed. There was also much to be said for the position of Blackmun, Burger, Harlan, and White that (as the early Warren Court had suggested, Konigberg v. State Bar of California (II), p. 393 *supra*) mere membership could be inquired about as a basis for further investigation. There seemed to be very little to be said for the intermediate position of Justice Stewart, who cast the deciding vote in all three cases, except that he had been among the four dissenters in *Keyishian. But see* H. KALVEN, A WORTHY TRADITION 574-86 (1988) (interpreting *Wadmond* to incorporate the *Keyishian* test because the state also inquired about specific intent and arguing that Black's objection that knowledge and intent were the subjects of separate questions "seems to elevate punctuation to constitutional status"). *See also* Kleindienst v. Mandel, 408 U.S. 753 (1972) (Blackmun, J., over three dissents) (reaffirming congressional authority to exclude an alien who advocated "world communism").

[3] *Elrod*, 427 U.S. 347 (1976) (no opinion for the Court); *Branti*, 445 U.S. 507 (1980) (Stevens, J.) (both over three dissents). *See also* Perry v. Sindermann, 408 U.S. 593 (1972) (Stewart, J.) (teacher may not be fired for

Apart from relatively few positions in which unquestioned loyalty was indispensable, the Court convincingly concluded, there was no justification for the damage done to first amendment interests by conditioning public employment on adherence to a particular political party.[4]

Less encouraging, however, was the 1986 decision in *Davis v. Bandemer,* where over the dissent of only Powell and Stevens the Court upheld a patent political gerrymandering of legislative districts.[5] Despite *Baker v. Carr,* three Justices voted to find the issue nonjusticiable for want of "judicially manageable standards."[6] Four others, conceding that any discrimination against Democrats in the case before them was intentional,[7] found insufficient proof that the discriminatory effect of the scheme was severe enough to establish a denial of equal protection.[8] Why it mattered that the undeniable detriment might

---

speech that could not be punished directly); Civil Service Commission v. National Ass'n of Letter Carriers, 413 U.S. 548 (1973) (White, J., over three dissents) (reaffirming the constitutionality of the substantial but neutral limitations on political activity of federal employees imposed by the Hatch Act, *see* United Public Workers v. Mitchell, p. 355 *supra*).

[4] Two 1982 decisions reaching dramatically opposite results posed the difficult question of the extent to which the first amendment protected the right to bring economic pressure to bear on innocent third parties for political ends. International Longshoremen's Ass'n v. Allied International, Inc., 456 U.S. 212 (1982) (Powell, J.), unanimously held that the Constitution did not preclude an action for damages against a union that had boycotted shipowners carrying Soviet cargoes as a protest against the entry of Soviet troops into Afghanistan: "We have consistently rejected the claim that secondary picketing by labor unions . . . is protected activity under the First Amendment. . . . There are many ways in which a union and its individual members may express their opposition to Russian foreign policy without infringing upon the rights of others." *Id.* at 226-27. NAACP v. Claiborne Hardware Co., 458 U.S. 886 (1982) (Stevens, J.), decided only a few weeks later, unanimously held that the first amendment protected the right of a civil rights organization to boycott merchants in an effort largely to influence government policies respecting racial equality: "The right of the States to regulate economic activity could not justify a complete prohibition against a nonviolent, politically motivated boycott designed to force governmental and economic change and to effectuate rights guaranteed by the Constitution itself." *Id.* at 914. As the lower court had said, *see id.* at 915, the political nature of the boycott in *Claiborne* distinguished the numerous decisions, *see* pp. 311-13 and 350, note 101 *supra,* upholding prohibition of secondary activity for economic ends— if one was prepared to concede that political speech was entitled to greater protection than speech about labor-management relations. It did not, however, distinguish the *Longshoremen's* case, which was dismissed as illustrating the principle that "[s]econdary boycotts and picketing by labor unions may be prohibited," *id.* at 912—as if members of labor unions were second-class citizens where political speech was concerned. A little more reassuring (but only a little) was the wholly independent footnote reserving the question whether a "narrowly tailored statute" proscribing "certain types of secondary pressure" would have required a different result: "No such statute is involved in this case." 458 U.S. at 915 n.49.

[5] 478 U.S. 109 (1986). The district court had found, and no member of the Court denied, that the General Assembly had deliberately drawn district lines to favor Republican candidates "by 'stacking' Democrats into districts with large Democratic majorities and 'splitting' them in other districts so as to give Republicans safe but not excessive majorities. . . ." The result was that in the next election Democrats won nearly 52 percent of the vote but only 43 percent of the seats. *See id.* at 116-17, 134 (opinion of White, J.).

[6] *See id.* at 144-61 (O'Connor, J., joined by Burger and Rehnquist, concurring). *See also* Schuck, *The Thickest Thicket: Partisan Gerrymandering and Judicial Regulation of Politics,* 87 COLUM. L. REV. 1325, 1330 ("Judicial regulation of partisan gerrymandering would be a cure worse than the disease.").

[7] 478 U.S. at 128-29 (opinion of White, J., joined by Brennan, Marshall, and Blackmun). *See also id.* at 116-17 n.5 (quoting the testimony of the Speaker of the House) ("We wanted to save as many incumbent Republicans as possible.").

[8] *See id.* at 129-37 (opinion of White, J.) (concluding that such discrimination was forbidden "only when the electoral system is arranged in a manner that will consistently degrade a voter's or a group of voters' influence on the political process as a whole" and finding the results of a single election not decisive) ("The District Court

have been even greater, however, was not clear; presumably a state could not tax members of one party more heavily than members of another even if the discrepancy was small. *Reynolds v. Sims* had rightly subjected mere geographical malapportionment to strict scrutiny on the ground that voting was a fundamental right;[9] the patronage cases should have made clear that an apportionment discriminating against those of a particular political persuasion was doubly suspect.[10]

The most celebrated first amendment controversy of the Burger years, the so-called Pentagon Papers case, resulted in another victory for free expression but added nothing of doctrinal interest.[11] Two newspapers had obtained copies of a classified study entitled "History of U.S. Decision-Making Process on Viet Nam Policy," and the government sought to enjoin its publication on grounds of national security. Over three dissents, the Court in *New York Times Co. v. United States* reaffirmed the "'heavy presumption'" against prior restraints and concluded that the government had not met its burden of justification.[12] Neither the brief unsigned order nor the individual opinions filed by each of the nine Justices revealed what the study contained; the decision showed only that the Court meant what it had said about the difficulty of justifying prior restraints.[13]

The two hundred–odd freedom of speech cases to reach the Burger Court afforded the Justices a number of opportunities to consider the constitutionality of measures that lim-

---

did not find that because of the 1981 Act the Democrats could not in one of the next few elections secure a sufficient vote to take control of the assembly."). For criticism of this grudging approach see Alfange, *Gerrymandering and the Constitution: Into the Thorns of the Thicket at Last,* 1986 SUP. CT. REV. 175.

[9] *See* p. 430 *supra*.

[10] Justice White made no effort to offer a rational basis for the discrimination, much less a compelling one. His argument that the Constitution did not require "proportional representation," 478 U.S. at 130, misses the point entirely; the Constitution does not require that blacks be proportionally represented on juries either, but that is no excuse for excluding them from jury service on account of race. *See* Strauder v. West Virginia, 100 U.S. 303 (1880); Virginia v. Rives, 100 U.S. 313 (1880), THE FIRST HUNDRED YEARS at 383-86.

[11] *See* Kurland, *The 1970 Term: Notes on the Emergence of the Burger Court,* 1971 SUP. CT. REV. 265, 285-89 ("In spite of its notoriety, the case is not likely to prove an important one in constitutional jurisprudence.)"; Henkin, *The Right to Know and the Duty to Withhold: The Case of the Pentagon Papers,* 120 U. PA. L. REV. 271, 271 (1971) ("'Great cases' . . . often make almost no law at all.").

[12] 403 U.S. 713, 714 (1971) (per curiam). *See* pp. 257-59 *supra* (discussing Near v. Minnesota).

[13] Black and Douglas, 403 U.S. at 714-24, seemed to say the publication of news could never be enjoined. Brennan, *id.* at 724-27, insisted there could be no temporary or permanent restraint until it was proved that "publication must inevitably, directly, and immediately cause the occurrence of an event kindred to imperiling the safety of a transport already at sea." Stewart, *id.* at 727-30, was unable to conclude that disclosure would "surely result in direct, immediate, and irreparable damage." White, *id.* at 730-40, conceded that publication might "do substantial damage to public interests" but agreed that the government had not met its "very heavy burden." Marshall, *id.* at 740-48, invoked the principles of Youngstown Sheet & Tube Co. v. Sawyer, pp. 365-69 *supra* ("It would . . . be utterly inconsistent with the concept of separation of powers for this Court to use its power of contempt to prevent behavior that Congress has specifically declined to prohibit."). Burger, Harlan, and Blackmun protested that the case should not be decided until a full record was developed below, *id.* at 748-63. Harlan, whose opinion the other dissenters joined, added that "the judiciary may not properly . . . redetermine for itself the probable impact of disclosure on the national security." *Id.* at 757. One commentator, while finding some comfort in the Court's ultimate refusal to approve a prior restraint against "the most massive security leak in American history," lamented that the controversy had destroyed an important "psychological barrier": "Prior restraints, for so long unheard of, are now relatively common. . . . Instead of stating that the First Amendment prohibits prior restraints, judges now go through a more complex . . . calculus attuned to the possibilities of action. . . ." Powe, Tornillo, 1987 SUP. CT. REV. 345, 389. *See also* Nebraska Press Ass'n v. Stuart, 427 U.S.

ited the time, place, or manner of communications without forbidding them entirely.[14] Relatively straightforward, though sometimes controversial, were decisions upholding content-neutral rules forbidding disruptive demonstrations near schools,[15] signs on utility poles,[16] and sleeping in parks.[17] Regulations that discriminated among speakers, not surprisingly, proved more difficult to defend. Limitations on the use of streets and parks based upon the viewpoint of the speaker, for example, distort the marketplace of ideas by favoring one side of the argument over another, and they had long been disfavored.[18] Justice Powell attempted to generalize this principle in *Erznoznik v. City of Jacksonville* in 1975: the first amendment "strictly limit[ed]" the power of government to limit even the time, place, or manner of communications on the basis of their content.[19]

The problem of content discrimination in this context, however, proved surprisingly difficult to capture in a single phrase. To begin with, not all content regulations were phrased in terms of viewpoint. Sometimes a regulation favored one subject of discussion over another. One city, for example, prohibited all picketing of schools or residences except that which was related to a labor dispute;[20] another allowed commercial but not polit-

---

539, 569 (1976) (Burger, C. J.) (unanimously upsetting an injunction against pretrial publicity on the narrow ground of insufficient proof that alternative measures could not have protected the right of fair trial); *id.* at 604 (Brennan, J., joined by Stewart and Marshall, concurring) (arguing that the risk of prejudicing a jury never justified prior restraints on the press); *id.* at 617 (Stevens, J., concurring) (agreeing with Brennan at least in the context of "information in the public domain").

[14] *See* pp. 263, 343-45 *supra* (discussing Schneider v. State and the loudspeaker cases).

[15] Grayned v. City of Rockford, 408 U.S. 104 (1972) (Marshall, J., over a Douglas dissent).

[16] City Council v. Taxpayers for Vincent, 466 U.S. 789 (1984) (Stevens, J., over three dissents).

[17] Clark v. Community for Creative Non-Violence, 468 U.S. 288 (1984) (White, J., over two dissents) (where the activity was assumed to qualify as speech, *see* pp. 440-41 *supra* (discussing United States v. O'Brien), because undertaken to dramatize the plight of the homeless). *See also* Heffron v. International Society for Krishna Consciousness, 452 U.S. 640 (1981) (White, J., over four partial dissents) (upholding a provision confining the solicitation of funds and the distribution of literature within a state fair to fixed locations); United States Postal Service v. Greenburgh Civic Ass'ns, 453 U.S. 114 (1981) (Rehnquist, J., over two dissents) (upholding a prohibition on depositing unstamped matter in residential mailboxes); Metromedia, Inc., v. City of San Diego, 453 U.S. 490 (1981) (where two Justices argued that a city could ban all billboards, two that it could not, and four, *see* note 24 *infra*, that the city had improperly discriminated in favor of commercial advertising); United States v. Grace, 461 U.S. 171 (1983) (White, J.) (striking down a ban on picketing and distribution of handbills on sidewalks surrounding the Supreme Court). A variant of this problem was presented by the threshold determination in Greer v. Spock, 424 U.S. 828 (1976) (Stewart, J., over dissents by Brennan and Marshall), that a military base, like a jail, Adderley v. Florida, p. 423 *supra*, was not a "public forum." The cases are analyzed in detail in Stone, *Content-Neutral Restrictions*, 54 U. Chi. L. Rev. 46 (1987). For the argument that *Greer* was part of a "pattern of downgrading free speech when it has appeared to conflict with proprietary rights" see Dorsen & Gora, *Free Speech, Property, and the Burger Court*, 1982 Sup. Ct. Rev. 195, 240. The problem of discrimination among speakers in *Greer* is noted in note 25 *infra*.

[18] *See, e.g.*, Hague v. CIO, p. 264, note 145 *supra;* Niemotko v. Maryland, p. 360 *supra*. Indeed the Court had gone so far as to strike down broad grants of discretionary power to executive officials on the ground that they posed a *risk* of discriminatory application. *E.g.*, Schneider v. State, p. 262 *supra*. *See generally* Police Dep't v. Mosley, 408 U.S. 92, 96 (1972) (dictum) ("[G]overnment may not grant the use of a forum to people whose views it finds acceptable, but deny use to those wishing to express less favored or more controversial views.").

[19] 422 U.S. 205, 209 (1975) (striking down, over three dissents, a ban on the display of nudity at drive-in theaters visible from public places). For a thorough discussion of viewpoint discrimination cases and the philosophy that underlies them see Stone, *Content Regulation and the First Amendment*, 25 Wm. & Mary L. Rev. 189 (1983).

[20] Police Dep't v. Mosley, note 18 *supra;* Carey v. Brown, 447 U.S. 455 (1980).

ical advertisements in its buses.[21] On occasion the Court said flatly that it was as bad to discriminate on the basis of subject matter as on the basis of viewpoint: "[G]overnment . . . may not select which issues are worth discussing or debating. . . ."[22] Without disparaging the need for close scrutiny of subject-matter distinctions, however, it is entirely plausible to view them as less destructive of first amendment values than those which condition speech upon government approval of the speaker's point of view.[23] In fact, despite its rhetoric, the Burger Court did not quite equate the two categories. While the regulation favoring labor picketing was struck down,[24] the exclusion of political speakers from a military base was upheld on the basis of the "objectively and evenhandedly applied" policy of insulating the military "from both the reality and the appearance of acting as a handmaiden for partisan political causes or candidates";[25] and four Justices made a similar argument in the inconclusive case in which the exclusion of political ads from buses was sustained.[26]

[21] Lehman v. City of Shaker Heights, 418 U.S. 298 (1974).

[22] *Mosley*, 408 U.S. at 96 (Marshall, J.). *See also* Consolidated Edison Co. v. Public Service Comm'n, 447 U.S. 530, 537 (1980) (Powell, J.) ("The First Amendment's hostility to content-based regulation extends not only to restrictions on particular viewpoints, but also to prohibition of public discussion of an entire topic.").

[23] *See* Young v. American Mini Theatres, 427 U.S. 50, 63-70 (1976) (opinion of Stevens, J.) (stressing the viewpoint neutrality of a measure requiring dispersal of theaters exhibiting sexually explicit films). For a thoughtful discussion of the problem see Stone, *Restrictions of Speech Because of Its Content: The Peculiar Case of Subject-Matter Restrictions*, 46 U. CHI. L. REV. 81 (1978).

[24] *Mosley*, 408 U.S. at 102 (Marshall, J., for a unanimous Court) (schools); *Carey*, 447 U.S. at 471 (Brennan, J., over three dissents) (residences) (both invoking the equal protection clause and the high degree of scrutiny required when a classification impinges on first amendment rights). *See also Consolidated Edison*, 447 U.S. at 544 (striking down a ban on the insertion of public-policy statements in utility bills despite the assumption the regulation was viewpoint neutral); *Metromedia*, 453 U.S. at 521 (opinion of White, J., for four Justices) (disapproving a preference for commercial over noncommercial billboards).

[25] Greer v. Spock, 424 U.S. 828, 839 (1976). *See also id.* at 838 n.10 ("The decision of the military authorities that a civilian lecture on drug abuse, a religious service by a visiting preacher at the base chapel, or a rock musical concert would be supportive of the military mission of Fort Dix surely did not leave the authorities powerless thereafter to prevent any civilian from entering Fort Dix to speak on any subject whatever.").

[26] *Lehman*, 418 U.S. at 303-04 (opinion of Blackmun, J.) (stressing the government's interests in maximizing revenue and avoiding "doubts about favoritism"), *supra* note 21. Justice Douglas, *Lehman*, *supra*, at 307-08, who cast the fifth vote to sustain the regulation, did not say the subject-matter distinction could be justified; noting that commercial advertisements were not in issue, he relied on the importance of protecting "captive" passengers from unwelcome messages. Brennan's dissent, joined by Stewart and Powell as well as Marshall, followed *Mosley* in equating subject matter with viewpoint discrimination: "That the discrimination is among entire classes of ideas, rather than among points of view within a particular class, does not render it any less odious." *Id.* at 316. For criticism both of Blackmun's conclusion as to the relative weight of the opposing interests and of Douglas's argument that the passengers were a captive audience see Stone, *Fora Americana: Speech in Public Places*, 1974 SUP. CT. REV. 233, 256-80. *See also* Perry Educ. Ass'n v. Perry Local Educators' Ass'n, 460 U.S. 37 (1983) (White J., over four dissents) (permitting a school district to limit use of its internal mail system to official business, including that of the union representing its employees but not of its rival).

Other "content" regulations considered during the Burger period posed even less of a danger to first amendment values than those discriminating between subjects of discussion in the sense of *Mosley, Lehman*, and *Greer. See, e.g.*, Young v. American Mini Theatres, 427 U.S. 50 (1976), in which a regulation dispersing sexually explicit entertainment throughout the city was sustained. As Stevens noted in an opinion joined by three other Justices, the regulation was indifferent to "whatever social, political, or philosophical message a film may be intended to communicate," *id.* at 70; it might have been better to view it, as well as the restrictions on nudity in *Erznoznik, supra* note 19, as an impartial limitation of the manner of communicating on any subject. *Cf.* pp. 314-15 *supra* (discussing Chaplinsky v. New Hampshire). Less convincing was Justice Rehnquist's later effort to

More troublesome still were cases involving such government facilities as auditoriums and schools, where it could plausibly be argued that the government had a legitimate interest in content discrimination for its own sake. Even in this context, there plainly were limitations.[27] Nevertheless, as Justice Rehnquist pointed out in a pair of thought-provoking dissents, one would think the government entitled to dedicate a theater to operas without having to show rock musicals[28] and to exercise a substantial degree of discretion in determining which books to make a part of its educational program.[29] The Court dealt rather cautiously and indecisively with these last issues during the Burger years;[30] we had every reason to expect to see them again.

The innovative work of the Burger period in the expression area was largely done in more exotic fields.

## A.  Political Spending

Without money one may speak, but one has difficulty being heard. Television broadcasts are expensive; even sound trucks and handbills cost something. It follows that, in the absence of regulation, there is a danger that people with lots of money may exercise a political influence disproportionate to their numbers and arguably in tension with democratic theory. It also follows, however, that any attempt to remedy this imbalance by limiting the employment of money for political purposes limits expression and thus raises troublesome first amendment issues.[31]

This was the dilemma the Court confronted in the great case of *Buckley v. Valeo* in

---

establish that a restriction on the location of "adult" theaters was not a content regulation because its purpose was not to suppress speech, City of Renton v. Playtime Theatres, Inc., 475 U.S. 41, 46-50 (1986); as Brennan noted in dissent, *id.* at 56-57, a neutral purpose might conceivably sustain the regulation, but it did not make it content-neutral.

[27] *See, e.g.,* Widmar v. Vincent, 454 U.S. 263 (1981) (Powell, J., over a single dissent) (holding a school auditorium could not be closed only to religious services); Board of Education v. Pico, 457 U.S. 853, 870-71 (1982) (opinion of Brennan, J.) ("If a Democratic school board, motivated by party affiliation, ordered the removal of all books written by or in favor of Republicans, few would doubt that the order violated the constitutional rights of the students. . . .").

[28] *See* Southeastern Promotions, Inc. v. Conrad, 420 U.S. 546, 572-73 (1975) (Rehnquist, J., dissenting).

[29] *See* Board of Education v. Pico, 457 U.S. 853, 908-20 (1982) (Rehnquist, J., dissenting).

[30] *Conrad, supra* note 28, which involved the refusal of a city auditorium for the performance of the musical *Hair,* was decided on the basis that the city had provided inadequate procedural protections for what the majority viewed as a prior restraint; *Pick* was remanded for a determination whether the school board had removed certain books from the library because of the books' ideology or their vulgar manner of expression.

[31] *See* Buckley v. Valeo, 424 U.S. 1, 19 (1976):

> A restriction on the amount of money a person or group can spend on political communication during a campaign necessarily reduces the quantity of expression by restricting the number of issues discussed, the depth of their exploration, and the size of the audience reached. This is because virtually every means of communicating ideas in today's mass society requires the expenditure of money.

*See also* Federal Election Comm'n v. National Conservative Political Action Comm., 470 U.S. 480, 493 (1985) (Rehnquist, J.) ("[A]llowing the presentation of views while forbidding the expenditure of more than $1,000 to present them is much like allowing a speaker in a public hall to express his views while denying him the use of an amplifying system.").

1976.[32] Uncomfortably aware of the competing interests, the Court neatly divided the baby: Congress might constitutionally limit contributions, but not spending, on behalf of candidates for public office.

Several Justices drew the relatively easy conclusion that Congress could limit both spending and contributions or neither, for the interest in limiting speech in order to equalize it seemed the same in both cases.[33] In defense of its middle position, the Court explained that direct contributions posed a greater danger of corruption and that the ability to make independent expenditures gave the citizen an adequate opportunity to express his opinion.[34]

As the Court conceded, this solution left the important interest in limiting the undue influence of wealth largely unsatisfied.[35] The opinion's insistence that the "concept that government may restrict the speech of some elements of our society in order to enhance the relative voice of others" was "wholly foreign to the First Amendment"[36] was surprisingly absolute, but the thrust of the argument was strong. As in the famous case of the hypothetical "checker-board ordinance" discriminating against blacks in order to promote integration,[37] it would not be difficult to conclude that although Congress's purpose was admirable, the means chosen for achieving it impinged too heavily on basic constitutional values.[38]

If this was true of the spending restrictions, it was arguably true of the contribution restrictions as well. The Court was right that, once the former limitation had been struck down, the latter left considerable room for the expression of individual opinion. By similar reasoning, however, the Court might have upheld the expenditure limit instead if it had begun its analysis at the other end. More important, the impact of either restriction alone on first amendment interests, though less severe than their cumulative effect, was far from

---

[32] 424 U.S. 1 (1976) (per curiam). *See generally* Polsby, Buckley v. Valeo: *The Special Nature of Political Speech*, 1976 SUP. CT. REV. 1. The designation "per curiam" is normally reserved for brief opinions disposing of trivial or noncontroversial matters; at 138 pages, this may have been the longest per curiam opinion in history. The Court did not say why it adopted this unusual expedient; perhaps various Justices drafted different portions of the opinion.

[33] *See* 424 U.S. at 235 (Burger, C. J.) (arguing that both limitations were invalid); *id.* at 261 (White, J.) (arguing that both were valid); *id.* at 290 (Blackmun, J.) (agreeing with Burger).

[34] *See id.* at 20-23, 45-47. *See also* California Medical Association v. Federal Election Comm'n, 453 U.S. 182 (1981) (over four dissents not going to the merits) (upholding a limitation on contributions to political action committees); Federal Election Comm'n v. National Conservative Political Action Comm., 470 U.S. 480 (1985) (Rehnquist, J., over three dissents) (invalidating a limitation on expenditures by political action committees); Citizens against Rent Control v. City of Berkeley, 454 U.S. 290, 297 (1981) (Burger, C. J., over a dissent by White) (invalidating a limitation on contributions to committees formed to support or oppose referenda on the ground that, as a lower court had earlier said, " '[t]he state interest in preventing corruption of officials, which provided the basis for . . . *Buckley*, . . . is not at issue here' ").

[35] "Contribution limitations alone would not reduce the greater potential voice of affluent persons and well-financed groups, who would remain free to spend unlimited sums directly to promote candidates and policies they favor in an effort to persuade voters." 424 U.S. at 26 n.26.

[36] *Id.* at 48-49. For an examination of the fate of enhancement arguments in other cases see Powe, *Mass Speech and the Newer First Amendment*, 1982 SUP. CT. REV. 243 (approving *Buckley*'s rejection of the principle).

[37] *See* Bittker, *The Case of the Checker-Board Ordinance*, 71 YALE L.J. 1387 (1962).

[38] *Cf.* Palmore v. Sidoti, 466 U.S. 429 (1984) (Burger, C. J.) (holding that protection of child from possible prejudice did not justify racial test for adoption).

trivial. Neither spending nor contributing is an adequate substitute for the other. If only others may convey my message, I have little control over what I say; if I cannot help the candidate to speak, I may be deprived of my most effective means of communication. In either case the loss in terms of first amendment values seems an uncomfortably high price to pay even for the substantial goals the legislation sought to attain.

Similarly controversial was the decision elsewhere in *Buckley* upholding provisions of the same statute authorizing federal financing of presidential campaigns. Government support as such, as the Court said, tends to promote rather than to inhibit political expression.[39] The difficulty was that Congress had played favorites in determining the beneficiaries of its largesse, for the lion's share went to parties that had received at least 25 percent of the previous vote.[40] Well-reasoned precedents suggested, and the patronage cases would soon confirm, that government impermissibly distorts the political process by taking sides in it.[41] It was not obvious how a statute providing essentially for paying the expenses of Democrats and Republicans could be reconciled with the principle of governmental neutrality.[42]

However, the law was phrased in terms of popular support, not ideology. Republicans and Democrats benefited only so long as they remained the dominant parties. Confining subsidies to parties with a substantial chance of winning, the Court argued, served important governmental interests both in not squandering public funds on "hopeless candidacies" and in avoiding "incentives to 'splintered parties and unrestrained factionalism.' "[43] Similar considerations had been held in some circumstances to justify the more extreme measure of exclusion from the ballot altogether.[44]

Beyond all this, it is even arguable that equal subsidies for great and small parties, far from being constitutionally required, would distort the political process much more seriously than the differential payments that Congress had actually provided. In realistic terms a political party is the representative of its adherents; to give the same financial support to a party of fifty thousand persons as to one of fifty million would be the antithesis of equality.[45]

---

[39] "[The financing provision] is a congressional effort, not to abridge, restrict, or censor speech, but rather to use public money to facilitate and enlarge public discussion and participation in the electoral process. . . . Thus [it] furthers, not abridges, pertinent First Amendment values." 424 U.S. at 92-93. Chief Justice Burger expressed reservations on this point, fearing that regulation might follow subsidization and drawing an analogy to government subsidy of religion. *See id.* at 248-50 (Burger, C. J., dissenting in part).

[40] Parties obtaining as much as 5 percent of the vote in either the current or the previous election were entitled to funding "based on the ratio of the vote received by the party's candidate . . . to the average of the major-party candidates." *See* 424 U.S. at 86-90.

[41] *See, e.g.,* the decisions involving Communists in public employment at pp. 434-38 *supra;* Elrod v. Burns and Branti v. Finkel, pp. 505-06 *supra.*

[42] *See* 424 U.S. at 293-94 (Rehnquist, J., dissenting in part) ("I find it impossible to subscribe to the Court's reasoning that because no third party has posed a credible threat to the two major parties in Presidential elections since 1860, Congress may by law attempt to assure that this pattern will endure forever."). *See also id.* at 251 (Burger, C. J., dissenting in part).

[43] *Id.* at 96.

[44] *See id.* at 96 (citing, inter alia, Jenness v. Fortson, 403 U.S. 431, 442 (1971) (upholding a requirement that independent candidates present petitions signed by at least 5 percent of eligible voters) ("There is surely an important state interest in requiring some preliminary showing of a significant modicum of support. . . .")).

[45] *See* McConnell, *Political and Religious Disestablishment,* 1986 B.Y.U.L. REV. 405, 456 (suggesting that the only neutral solution would be "a system of indirect subsidies, through tax deductions, credits, or vouchers").

## B.  Commercial Speech

*Buckley* dealt with an unusual type of limitation on speech, but the speech affected—that in support of candidates for public office—lay at the heart of the first amendment.[46] The further a communication lay from the central purpose of promoting informed self-government, the less likely the Court had been to hold it immune from government restriction. Obscenity, narrowly defined in hopes of avoiding interference with the expression of ideas, had been declared fair game on the ground that it was of no relevant value whatever.[47] The inroads the Court had made into the traditional libel law served essentially to

Also upheld in *Buckley* was a provision requiring disclosure of the names and addresses of all persons contributing more than $10 to a candidate's campaign, 424 U.S. at 60-84. Recognizing that "compelled disclosure . . . can seriously infringe on privacy of association and belief" (citing NAACP v. Alabama, pp. 382-83 *supra*), the Court found the interests served by disclosure substantial and the dangers to first amendment freedoms "highly speculative." 424 U.S. at 64, 70. The Chief Justice was less sanguine and more convincing. Conceding that there was reason to require disclosure of "contributions of such dimensions reasonably thought likely to purchase special favors," he concluded that the statute unnecessarily deterred small contributors: "Rank-and-file union members or rising junior executives may now think twice before making even modest contributions to a candidate who is disfavored by the union or management hierarchy. . . ." *Id.* at 236-37 (Burger, J., dissenting in part). *See also* Brown v. Socialist Workers '74 Campaign Committee, 459 U.S. 87 (1982) (Marshall, J., over three partial dissents) (finding a sufficient risk of deterring support for an unpopular minor party to invalidate a requirement that it disclose its contributors and suppliers). *See* Stone & Marshall, Brown v. Socialist Workers: *Inequality as a Command of the First Amendment*, 1983 SUP. CT. REV. 583, 613 (seeking to reconcile the exception from a generally applicable law established in *Brown* with the Court's general reluctance to permit laws favoring one point of view over another) ("The potential of disclosure to drive an unpopular 'minor' party out of existence is so severe that extraordinary measures are warranted to avoid that result."). For discussion of *Buckley*'s further holding with respect to the appointment and duties of the Federal Election Commission see p. 589 *infra*.

[46] *See* Thornhill v. Alabama, 310 U.S. 88, 95 (1940) ("Abridgement of freedom of speech and of the press . . . impairs those opportunities for public education that are essential to effective exercise of the power of correcting error through the processes of popular government."); First National Bank v. Bellotti, 435 U.S. 765, 776-77 (1978) (Powell, J.) (quoting *Thornhill* in striking down a limitation on the right of *corporations* to engage in political speech) ("It is the type of speech indispensable to decisionmaking in a democracy, and this is no less true because the speech comes from a corporation rather than an individual."). *See also* Whitney v. California, 274 U.S. 357, 375 (1927) (Brandeis, J., concurring); New York Times Co. v. Sullivan, 376 U.S. 254, 292 (1964); A. MEIKELJOHN, FREE SPEECH AND ITS RELATION TO SELF-GOVERNMENT (1948), *passim*.

[47] *See* pp. 396-99 *supra* (discussing, inter alia, Roth v. United States). Stanley v. Georgia, 394 U.S. 557 (1969) (Marshall, J., with three Justices concurring on other grounds), had cast considerable doubt on *Roth* while purporting to distinguish it in holding that the state could not make mere possession of obscene material a crime. *See id.* at 565 ("If the First Amendment means anything, it means that a State has no business telling a man, sitting alone in his own house, what books he may read or what films he may watch."). There was a powerful argument that the right to possess obscene material implied the right to acquire it. *See* H. KALVEN, *supra* note 2, at 47; *cf.* Carey v. Population Services Int'l, p. 471, note 44 *supra* (right to acquire contraceptives); Lamont v. Postmaster General, pp. 523-24 *infra* (right to receive foreign propaganda). Nevertheless, over only two dissents, the Burger Court reaffirmed *Roth* in United States v. Reidel, 402 U.S. 351 (1971) (upholding a statute forbidding the mailing of obscene matter ) ("To extrapolate from Stanley's right to have and peruse obscene material in the privacy of his own home a First Amendment right in Reidel to sell it to him would effectively scuttle *Roth,* the precise result that the *Stanley* opinion abjured."). *Id.* at 355.

In five decisions rendered on the same day in June 1973, the Burger Court essayed a comprehensive reexamination of the obscenity problem and brought forth a mouse. The principal case was Miller v. California, 413 U.S. 15 (1973) (Burger, C. J., over four dissents), in which the Court took violent issue with a test for obscenity propounded by three Justices in Memoirs v. Massachusetts, 383 U.S. 413, 418 (1966), only to replace it with one that seemed to differ only in minor particulars. *Compare Memoirs*, 383 U.S. at 418 (requiring that "(a) the dominant theme of the material taken as a whole appeals to a prurient interest in sex; (b) the material is patently

promote discussion of issues of public concern.[48] Even artistic expression had been protected not so much for its own sake as because of the difficulty of determining when it was a vehicle for commentary on public issues.[49]

In line with this understanding of the amendment's purpose, the Court had held flatly in *Valentine v. Chrestensen* in 1942 that "the Constitution imposes no . . . restraint on government" with respect to the street distribution of "purely commercial advertising."[50] This had been understood to mean that "commercial speech," like obscenity, was not protected at all.[51] The Warren Court had left this conclusion essentially undisturbed; the Burger Court threw it unceremoniously out the window.[52]

The leader in this innovation, as in the cases of abortion and unequal treatment of aliens,[53] was the recently appointed Justice Blackmun. *New York Times v. Sullivan* had already established that the mere fact that a political message appeared in the form of a paid advertisement did not strip it of constitutional protection; what mattered was the content of the communication.[54] Expanding on this line of reasoning, Justice Blackmun

---

offensive because it affronts contemporary community standards relating to the description or representation of sexual matters; and (c) the material is utterly without redeeming social value"), *with Miller*, 413 U.S. at 24 (requiring a determination "(a) whether 'the average person, applying contemporary community standards' would find that the work, taken as a whole, appeals to the prurient interest . . . ; (b) whether the work depicts or describes, in a patently offensive way, sexual conduct specifically defined by the applicable state law; and (c) whether the work, taken as a whole, lacks serious literary, artistic, political, or scientific value"). The reformulation of the "value" standard, as Justice Brennan noted, *see* Paris Adult Theatre v. Slaton, 413 U.S. 49, 97 (1973) (Brennan, J., dissenting), entailed a subtle shift in the theoretical basis for prohibiting obscenity; in upholding a ban on exhibiting obscene movies to consenting adults in *Slaton* (Burger, C. J., over four dissents), the Court focused not on the worthlessness of obscenity but on the state's interests in suppressing it. *See id.* at 57-61. *See generally* H. KALVEN, *supra* note 2, at 48-53 (concluding that "over time the Court has dramatically narrowed the jurisdiction of the censor in this volatile area").

[48] *See* pp. 438-39 *supra* (discussing New York Times v. Sullivan and subsequent decisions). Indeed the Burger Court held, over two dissents, that the *Sullivan* requirement of malice was inapplicable even when matters of public interest were at stake unless the person defamed was a "public official" or "public figure." Gertz v. Robert Welch, Inc., 418 U.S. 323 (1974) (Powell, J.) (arguing that public figures or officials had less claim for redress because they had "thrust themselves" into the limelight and less need for it because of their "greater access" to means of rebutting false charges). *But see id.* at 347-50 (over two different dissents) (holding that even in ordinary private defamation cases there must be some showing of "fault" and that "presumed or punitive damages" required a showing of malice).

[49] *See* Joseph Burstyn, Inc. v. Wilson, 343 U.S. 495, 501 (1952) (quoting Winters v. New York, 333 U.S. 507, 510 (1948)) (" 'The line between the informing and the entertaining is too elusive for the protection of that basic right [a free press]. Everyone is familiar with instances of propaganda through fiction. What is one man's amusement, teaches another's doctrine.' ").

[50] 316 U.S. 52, 54 (1942). *See* p. 314 *supra.*

[51] *See also* Breard v. Alexandria, p. 345 *supra* (upholding a ban on commercial door-to-door soliciting and distinguishing Martin v. Struthers, pp. 317-18 *supra,* on the ground that the speech in *Breard* was commercial).

[52] In its first brush with the problem, Pittsburgh Press Co. v. Pittsburgh Comm'n on Human Relations, 413 U.S. 376, 384-89 (1973) (Powell, J., over four dissents), the Burger Court, in permitting a state to ban advertisements for positions reserved for members of one sex in violation of a fair-employment law, adverted to the special nature of commercial speech but based its holding on the generally applicable principle that solicitation of illegal activity may be made a crime. *See* pp. 311-13 *supra* (discussing the picketing decisions); Village of Hoffman Estates v. Flipside, 455 U.S. 489, 496 (1982) (Marshall, J.) (promotion of illegal drug use).

[53] *See* pp. 465, 71, 500-04 *supra.*

[54] 376 U.S. 254, 266 (1964). *See also* pp. 438-39 *supra.* For the argument that *Sullivan* had changed the law by looking to content rather than motive see Schiro, *Commercial Speech: The Demise of a Chimera,* 1976 SUP. CT. REV. 45, 60-65.

concluded for all but two Justices in *Bigelow v. Virginia* that the state could not prohibit an advertisement soliciting customers for an out-of-state provider of abortions. Not only was the proposed operation entirely lawful, said the Court, but the advertisement "did more than simply propose a commercial transaction. It contained factual material of clear 'public interest' " respecting the availability of abortions.[55]

The disagreement of Justices Rehnquist and White with this characterization[56] highlighted a difficulty of line drawing in this area comparable to that which had led the Court to forgo any effort to distinguish political from artistic expression.[57] For the moment Justice Blackmun refrained from abandoning the commercial exception itself, but he gave warning that it might be in for heavy weather:

> To the extent that commercial activity is subject to regulation, the relationship of speech to that activity may be one factor, among others, to be considered in weighing the First Amendment interest against the governmental interest alleged. Advertising is not thereby stripped of all First Amendment protection. The relationship of speech to the market-place of products or of services does not make it valueless in the marketplace of ideas.[58]

The next Term, in *Virginia Pharmacy Board v. Virginia Consumer Council*, the implications of this passage were realized when the Court over Rehnquist's lone dissent struck down a law forbidding pharmacists to advertise the prices of prescription drugs.[59] Acknowledging that, unlike the advertiser in *Bigelow*, "[o]ur pharmacist does not wish to editorialize on any subject, . . . to report any particularly newsworthy fact, or to make generalized observations even about commercial matters,"[60] Justice Blackmun proceeded to dismantle the distinction he had worked so hard to construct in the earlier case.

> [N]o line between publicly "interesting" or "important" commercial advertising and the opposite kind could ever be drawn. . . . So long as we preserve a predominantly free enterprise economy, the allocation of our resources in large measure will be made through numerous private economic decisions. It is a matter of public interest that those decisions, in the aggregate, be intelligent and well informed. To this end, the free flow of commercial information is indispensable.[61]

---

[55] 421 U.S. 809, 822-23 (1975). This conclusion should have meant only that the publication of that information was protected, not (as the Court seems to have concluded, *id.* at 829) that the advertiser was free to attach to it a purely commercial solicitation.

[56] *See id.* at 831 (Rehnquist, J., joined by White, dissenting) ("[T]he advertisement appears to me, as it did to the courts below, to be a classic commercial proposition directed toward the exchange of services rather than the exchange of ideas.").

[57] *See* note 49 *supra*. A similar difficulty led Justice Brennan, author of the initial decision to accept laws prohibiting the delivery of obscene matter to consenting adults, to abandon his position entirely. *See* Paris Adult Theatre v. Slaton, 413 U.S. 49, 73-114 (1973) (Brennan, J., joined by Stewart and Marshall, dissenting).

[58] 421 U.S. at 826.

[59] 425 U.S. 748 (1976) (Blackmun, J.). The newly appointed Justice Stevens, *id.* at 773, took no part.

[60] *Id.* at 761. "The 'idea' he wishes to communicate," the opinion added, "is simply this: 'I will sell you the X prescription drug at the Y price.' " *Id.*

[61] *Id.* at 765. *See also id.* at 763 (noting that "the particular consumer's interest in the free flow of commercial information . . . may be as keen, if not keener by far, than his interest in the day's most urgent political debate").

Thus it was no longer necessary to show that the advertisement in question contained information of noncommercial interest to the public. Advertising itself was protected.

Later decisions applied the principle of *Virginia Pharmacy* to protect the posting of For Sale signs on real property,[62] the advertising of contraceptives[63] and legal services,[64] and advertisements promoting the use of electricity.[65] At the same time it held commercial speech not wholly without constitutional protection, however, the Court made clear that the protection afforded to advertising was not necessarily as broad as that afforded to other types of speech. *New York Times Co. v. Sullivan,* for example, had held that even false statements about the functioning of government were generally protected in order not to deter discussion of issues of public importance.[66] Prohibitions on false advertising, Justice Blackmun said in *Virginia Pharmacy,* posed less of a problem: since the advertiser was usually discussing his own product, he was better able than most speakers to verify the accuracy of his statements; and his economic interest in advertising made commercial speech "more durable than other kinds."[67]

Invoking these arguments, the Court later upheld a blanket prohibition on the use of trade names by optometrists, noting that there was "a significant possibility that trade names will be used to mislead the public."[68] For the same reasons, even as it held that a particular advertisement for legal services could not constitutionally be forbidden,[69] the Court held that the overbreadth doctrine did not apply to professional advertising. That doctrine, as Justice Blackmun said, was based on the fear of deterring protected speech, and the commercial speaker was less likely to be deterred.[70]

---

[62] Linmark Associates, Inc. v. Township of Willingboro, 431 U.S. 85 (1977) (Marshall, J.). The prohibition had been designed for the laudable purpose of limiting so-called white flight from a neighborhood perceived as in danger of becoming a minority ghetto.

[63] Carey v. Population Services International, 431 U.S. 678, 700-02 (1977) (Brennan, J., over two dissents); Bolger v. Youngs Drug Prods. Corp., 463 U.S. 60 (1983) (Marshall, J.) (striking down a ban on *unsolicited* contraceptive advertisements).

[64] Bates v. State Bar of Arizona, 433 U.S. 350 (1977) (Blackmun, J., over four dissents); Zauderer v. Office of Disciplinary Counsel, 471 U.S. 626 (1985) (White, J., over three dissents).

[65] Central Hudson Gas & Elec. Corp. v. Public Serv. Comm'n, 447 U.S. 557 (1980) (Powell, J., over a dissent by Rehnquist).

[66] *See* pp. 438-39 *supra.*

[67] *See* 425 U.S. at 771-72 & n.24. *See also id.* at 775–81 (Stewart, J., concurring).

[68] Friedman v. Rogers, 440 U.S. 1, 13 (1979) (Powell, J., over two dissents).

[69] *See* note 64 *supra.*

[70] Bates v. State Bar of Arizona, 433 U.S. 350, 379-81 (1977). *See generally* pp. 255-57 *supra* (discussing Stromberg v. California). See also *Virginia Pharmacy,* 425 U.S. at 772 n.24 (suggesting that the same considerations "may also make inapplicable the prohibition against prior restraints").

The overbreadth doctrine had a generally rough time during the Burger years. After being applied to strike down laws in Coates v. Cincinnati, 402 U.S. 611 (1971) (Stewart, J., over three dissents) (ordinance making it unlawful for three or more persons "to assemble . . . on any of the sidewalks . . . and there conduct themselves in a manner annoying to persons passing by"), and in Gooding v. Wilson, 405 U.S. 518 (1972) (Brennan, J., over two dissents) (law forbidding "opprobrious words or abusive language, tending to cause a breach of the peace"), the doctrine was limited to laws that were "substantially overbroad" in order not to interfere unduly with a state's interest in "enforcing the statute against conduct that is admittedly within its power to proscribe." Broadrick v. Oklahoma, 413 U.S. 601, 615 (1973) (White, J., over four dissents) (refusing to invalidate on their face provisions limiting political activity of civil service employees despite assumption that they impermissibly applied to the display of political buttons and bumper stickers). A year later, arguing that "[t]he fundamental necessity for obedience . . . may render permissible within the military that which would be constitutionally

In holding despite *Virginia Pharmacy* that an attorney could be disciplined for following accident victims to the hospital to solicit personal injury litigation, the Court in *Ohralik v. Ohio State Bar Ass'n* went beyond the arguments just noted to declare generally that commercial speech was entitled to "a limited measure of protection, commensurate with its subordinate position in the scale of First Amendment values. . . ."[71] The case was made more compelling by the overbearing tactics employed by the attorney, which gave credence to the state's concerns about overreaching, undue influence, and invasion of privacy.[72] At the same time, however, the basic distinction the Court was establishing between commercial and other speech was emphasized by its insistence that the case did not involve solicitation of civil rights litigation, which—as the Court dramatically reaffirmed the same day *Ohralik* was decided[73]—had been held constitutionally protected nearly twenty years before.[74]

No Justice objected to this general standard of reduced scrutiny for commercial speech when it was enunciated in *Ohralik*. When it was repeated in the course of striking down a total ban on promotional advertising by electric companies in *Central Hudson Gas & Elec. Corp. v. Public Serv. Comm'n,* however,[75] Justice Blackmun did object. The considerations that distinguished commercial from other speech, he argued, justified a more relaxed attitude toward the former when "deception or coercion" was in issue; they did not justify a generally subordinate position for commercial speech.[76] But it was no longer the greater "durability" of advertising alone that prompted less exacting scrutiny; it was the majority's perception that commercial speech was less important in terms of first amendment values.

On its face, the test laid down in *Central Hudson* seemed rather protective. Unless a commercial communication was "related to unlawful activities" or "misleading," wrote Justice Powell, it could be restricted only to the extent "necessary" to advance a "substantial" governmental interest "directly."[77] How little this formulation might mean in unsym-

---

impermissible outside it," the Court concluded that the policies underlying the overbreadth doctrine "must be accorded a good deal less weight in the military context." Parker v. Levy, 417 U.S. 733, 758, 760 (1974) (Rehnquist, J., over three dissents) (upholding provisions proscribing both "conduct unbecoming an officer and a gentleman" and "disorders and neglects to the prejudice of good order and discipline" because these proscriptions could constitutionally reach both the utterances in issue (which had urged enlisted personnel to disobey orders) and "a sufficiently large number of similar or related types of conduct so as to preclude their invalidation for overbreadth"). *Id.* at 761. *Cf.* Rostker v. Goldberg, p. 497 *supra;* Goldman v. Weinberger, p. 533 *infra* (both emphasizing the narrow application of other constitutional principles in the military context). That the overbreadth doctrine had not lost its bite, however, was shown by Schad v. Borough of Mt. Ephraim, 452 U.S. 61 (1981) (White, J., over two dissents), where the author of the restrictive opinion in *Broadrick* wrote for the Court to strike down an ordinance that was understood to forbid all live entertainment on the ground that it "prohibit[ed] a wide range of expression that ha[d] long been held to be within the protections of the First and Fourteenth Amendments," *id.* at 65—even though the "entertainment" for which the objecting party had been punished fell in the dubious category of nude dancing.

[71] 436 U.S. 447, 456 (1978).

[72] *See id.* at 461, 467. *See also id.* at 469-70 (Marshall, J., concurring).

[73] *In re* Primus, 436 U.S. 412 (1978) (Powell, J., over a dissent by Rehnquist).

[74] *See* NAACP v. Button, p. 421 *supra.*

[75] *Central Hudson*, note 65 *supra*, 447 U.S. at 562–63 (Powell, J.) ("The Constitution . . . accords a lesser protection to commercial speech than to other constitutionally guaranteed expression.").

[76] *Id.* at 578 (Blackmun, J., concurring).

[77] *Id.* at 564, 566.

pathetic hands, however, was shown in *Posadas de Puerto Rico v. Tourism Co.*, decided just before Burger's retirement, where by a five-to-four vote the Court upheld a prohibition of advertisements respecting lawful gambling.[78] There was no constitutional right to gamble, wrote Justice Rehnquist; "the greater power to completely ban casino gambling necessarily includes the lesser power to ban advertising of casino gambling. . . ."[79]

Not only did this line of reasoning cast doubt on the very decision whose standards the Court professed to be applying;[80] the argument itself was profoundly troubling. Decisions holding that the greater power did not necessarily include the lesser were legion, and *Posadas* should have been among them.[81] In the commercial field, as elsewhere, the Court had consistently stressed that the essential function of speech was to promote informed decision-making.[82] Thus so long as gambling remains lawful, there is a strong first amendment interest in the free flow of information relevant to the decision whether or not to gamble. "[D]epriving the public of the information needed to make a free choice," as Justice Blackmun warned in *Central Hudson*, "strikes at the heart of the First Amendment."[83] Once gambling is forbidden, this interest disappears; informed decision-making requires only knowledge of the law, not incitement to its violation.[84] Fortunately the Court's insistence in *Posadas* on the special nature of commercial speech should prevent the extension of its holding to other and more sensitive fields.

If the question is whether the Court's assessment of the competing interests in commercial speech cases makes sense, apart from *Posadas* I see little reason to quarrel with its conclusions. The more serious question is whether, in light of the generally accepted purposes of the first amendment, purely commercial speech should have been held to be protected at all.[85]

## C. The Right Not to Speak

*West Virginia Board of Education v. Barnette* had revealed a new dimension of the first amendment in 1943 in concluding that a state could not require schoolchildren to salute

---

[78] 478 U.S. 328 (1986). For a convincing demonstration that the law upheld in *Posadas* did not satisfy the *Central Hudson* criteria see Kurland, Posadas de Puerto Rico v. Tourism Co.: "'Twas Strange, 'Twas Passing Strange; 'Twas Pitiful, 'Twas Wondrous Pitiful," 1986 SUP. CT. REV. 1, 6-12.

[79] 478 U.S. at 345-46.

[80] *See Central Hudson*, 447 U.S. at 579 (Blackmun, J., concurring) (conceding that the state could have limited the use of electricity directly).

[81] *See* pp. 472-75 *supra* (discussing the abortion-funding cases).

[82] *See, e.g., Virginia Pharmacy*, 425 U.S. at 761-65; Bates v. State Bar of Arizona, 433 U.S. 350, 364 (1977); Linmark Associates, Inc. v. Township of Willingboro, 431 U.S. 85, 96 (1977); *Central Hudson*, 447 U.S. at 567. *Cf.* Thornhill v. Alabama, pp. 268-70 *supra*.

[83] 447 U.S. at 574-75 (Blackmun, J., concurring). *See also Posadas*, 478 U.S. at 348-51 (Brennan, J., joined by Marshall and Blackmun, dissenting); Kurland, *supra* note 78, at 2, 12-13. Justice Stevens, *id.* at 359-63, also dissented, but on narrower grounds. One might test the principle announced in *Posadas* by asking whether a legislature could make it a crime to advocate homosexual relations, or abortions during the third trimester, without forbidding the activities themselves. *See* pp. 465-71, 475-77 *supra* (discussing Bowers v. Hardwick and Roe v. Wade).

[84] *Cf.* Pittsburgh Press Co. v. Pittsburgh Comm'n on Human Relations, note 52 *supra*.

[85] *See Virginia Pharmacy*, 425 U.S. at 787 (Rehnquist, J., dissenting) (commenting on the argument that the amendment was primarily "'an instrument to enlighten public decisionmaking in a democracy'") ("I had understood this view to relate to public decisionmaking as to political, social, and other public issues, rather than the decision of a particular individual as to whether to purchase one or another kind of shampoo.").

the flag. Freedom of speech, wrote Justice Jackson, meant freedom to decide what to say, and compulsion as well as prohibition might infringe it.[86] The Court under Burger carried this appealing principle to new and sometimes controversial lengths.

The first case to present this issue after Burger's accession was *Miami Herald Publishing Co. v. Tornillo,*[87] which involved a Florida statute requiring a newspaper that had attacked a candidate for public office to print his reply. The argument in support of the law was similar to that soon to be rejected in *Buckley:* since candidates seldom had newspapers of their own, they could not adequately respond without some limitation of the publisher's freedom.[88]

The Court unanimously held the statute unconstitutional. Though nobody cited *Barnette,* the premise of the decision was *Barnette*'s principle that compulsion to speak limits expressive freedom.[89] "The Florida statute," Chief Justice Burger argued, "exacts a penalty on the basis of the content of a newspaper." Not only did compliance entail unreimbursed printing costs. Faced with the prospect of having to publish a reply, "editors might well conclude that the safe course [was] to avoid controversy," and "political and editorial coverage would be blunted or reduced."[90] Moreover, the statute interfered with "the exercise of editorial control and judgment" involved in "[t]he choice of material to go into a newspaper," and it was "yet to be demonstrated how government regulation of this crucial process can be exercised consistent with First Amendment guarantees of a free press. . . ."[91]

The first objection hardly goes to the heart of the matter; the measure would not have been significantly more acceptable if the candidate had been required to pay for printing his reply. More fundamental, as in *Barnette,* was the unpalatability of forcing people to say what they do not believe.[92] Nothing in the law, of course, forbade the publisher to make clear that the sentiments expressed in the reply were not his own.[93] Even under the most visible disclaimer, however, one might legitimately take offense at being required to propagate, for example, the obnoxious racial views of Adolf Hitler.

Nevertheless, in the closing days of the Warren period, the Court had upheld a strikingly similar provision applicable to radio and television broadcasting.[94] The physical

---

[86] 319 U.S. 624 (1943), pp. 318-20 *supra. See id.* at 634 ("To sustain the compulsory flag salute we are required to say that a Bill of Rights which guards the individual's right to speak his own mind, left it open to public authorities to compel him to utter what is not in his mind.").

[87] 418 U.S. 241 (1974).

[88] *See id.* at 247-54 (summarizing the arguments); *cf.* pp. 510-12 *supra* (discussing *Buckley*). For the background of the case see Powe, Tornillo, 1987 Sup. Ct. Rev. 345.

[89] *See* 418 U.S. at 256.

[90] *Id.* at 256-57.

[91] *Id.* at 258. *See* Powe, *supra* note 88, at 384 ("A fair press, as determined by a government mechanism, is not a free press.").

[92] Despite express reservations in a concurring opinion, *see* 418 U.S. at 258 (Brennan, J., joined by Rehnquist, concurring), the decision did seem to cast doubt on long-standing requirements that those found liable for defamation publish retractions—except to the extent that such rules related to speech that was somehow entitled to less protection than the political, *cf.* pp. 513-18 *supra* (discussing commercial speech), or merely made such publication a means of avoiding compensatory sanctions for the violation. The finding of an infringement of private right, of course, is itself an arguable basis for distinction.

[93] *See* Wooley v. Maynard, 430 U.S. 705, 722 (1977) (Rehnquist, J., dissenting).

[94] Red Lion Broadcasting Co. v. FCC, 395 U.S. 367 (1969) (White, J.). There were no dissents. Douglas, who did not participate, later said he would not have joined the decision. *See* Columbia Broadcasting System v.

scarcity of frequencies, Justice White had written, justified limitations on a broadcaster's freedom that would not be permissible in other contexts. If there was to be effective use of the airwaves, only a few broadcast licenses could be granted. It followed, said the Court, that a licensee might be required to "share his frequency with others," for otherwise those without licenses might never be heard at all.[95]

The argument that economic barriers to the establishment of additional newspapers created a comparable necessity for a right of reply in the newspaper industry was recited but not answered in *Tornillo*,[96] and the broadcasting case was not even cited. The fact that the obstacles to entry in the earlier case were legal rather than economic, however, affords a possible ground for distinction.

In the broadcasting case the government had made it unlawful for anyone to speak over the airwaves without permission of the fortunate few to whom it had issued licenses. On this basis two Justices argued with considerable force in *Columbia Broadcasting System v. Democratic National Committee* that the government was not only permitted but *required* to assure that nonlicensees be given access to broadcasting facilities, since otherwise the licensing requirement would deprive them entirely of their freedom to communicate over the air.[97] There was no such problem in *Tornillo;* as the abortion-funding decisions would soon confirm, government is not generally held to have deprived a person of constitutional rights by declining to remove economic impediments to their exercise.[98]

The Court afforded additional protection against compulsory speech in *Wooley v. Maynard,* where an overzealous prosecutor had gone after Jehovah's Witnesses who for religious reasons had obliterated the motto "Live Free or Die" from the license plates of their car.[99] "Here," wrote the Chief Justice, "as in *Barnette,* we are faced with a state measure which forces an individual . . . to be an instrument for fostering public adherence to an ideological point of view he finds unacceptable."[100] In contrast to the right-of-reply cases, there was no significant state interest to justify what the state was doing,[101] and the requirement was struck down.[102]

The burden of displaying the state's silly slogan may seem de minimis, but the parties

---

Democratic National Committee, 412 U.S. 94, 154 (1973) (Douglas, J., concurring). *Red Lion* was reaffirmed in CBS, Inc. v. FCC, 453 U.S. 367 (1981) (Burger, C. J.).

[95] 395 U.S. at 386-89.

[96] *See* 418 U.S. at 247-54.

[97] 412 U.S. 94, 170-204 (1973) (Brennan, J., joined by Marshall, J., dissenting). Burger, Stewart, and Rehnquist, *id.* at 114-21, rejected this position on the insufficient basis that "[t]he First Amendment does not reach acts of private parties in every instance where the Congress or the Commission has merely permitted or failed to prohibit such acts"; White, Blackmun, and Powell, *id.* at 146-48, thought the provisions upheld in *Red Lion* satisfied any duty the government might have to permit public access and did not reach the state-action question. An argument analogous to that made by the dissenters in *Columbia Broadcasting* has actually prevailed in construing a similar provision respecting broadcasting freedom in the West German Constitution. 12 BVerfG, 205 (1960) (Fernsehurteil); *see* Currie, *Positive and Negative Constitutional Rights,* 53 U. CHI. L. REV. 864, 870-71 (1986). *Cf.* decisions respecting the duty to provide medical treatment and legal research materials to prison inmates whom the government has disabled from procuring such necessities for themselves, noted at pp. 345-48 *supra* (discussing Public Utilities Commission v. Pollak).

[98] *See* pp. 472-75 *supra.*

[99] 430 U.S. 705 (1977).

[100] *Id.* at 715.

[101] *Id.* at 715-17.

[102] *See also* Pacific Gas & Elec. Co. v. Public Utilities Comm'n, 475 U.S. 1 (1986) (over three dissents) (striking down requirement that utility distribute views of organization representing interests of its customers).

in *Wooley* found the message as offensive as others might find a swastika or a Confederate flag. In such a context Justice Rehnquist's dissenting contention that the display " 'carries no implication . . . that [the owners] endorse . . . it' "[103] seems less than overwhelming.[104] Another of Justice Rehnquist's arguments, however, provided more nutritious food for thought. The requirement in *Wooley,* he contended, was indistinguishable from the erection of a billboard carrying the identical message; surely a taxpayer could not complain that spending his money on billboards made him an unwilling instrument for dissemination of the objectionable text.[105]

Rehnquist's example can be distinguished; it seems even less likely in the billboard

[103] 430 U.S. at 721-22 (Rehnquist, J., joined by Blackmun, dissenting) (quoting an opinion of the state supreme court).

[104] Rehnquist's view prevailed, however, in the subsequent case of Pruneyard Shopping Center v. Robins, 447 U.S. 74 (1980), where the Court unanimously held that a state could require the owner of a shopping center to permit opponents of a United Nations resolution condemning Zionism to distribute leaflets on its premises. "The views expressed by members of the public in passing out pamphlets," wrote Justice Rehnquist, "will not likely be identified with those of the owner," which in any event was "free to publicly dissociate [itself] from the views of the speakers." 447 U.S. at 87-88. As in *Wooley,* one may grant the Justice's premises without accepting his conclusion. It remains a significant intrusion on the owner's first amendment interests to say he must let Nazis use his property to disseminate their noxious doctrines, and there is no way consistent with the constitutional requirement of governmental neutrality to distinguish Nazis from anyone else. See 447 U.S. at 99 (Powell, J., joined by White, concurring) ("A minority-owned business confronted with leaflet distributers from the American Nazi Party or the Ku Klux Klan . . . could be placed in an intolerable position if state law requires it to make its private property available to anyone who wishes to speak.").

*Pruneyard* also appeared to involve a garden-variety taking of property without compensation, since the state law did not require the speaker to pay for occupying the owner's land. In rejecting this argument the Court seemed to say the state could take property without compensation so long as it did not take too much: "[A]ppellants have failed to demonstrate that the 'right to exclude others' is so essential to the use or economic value of their property that the state-authorized limitation of it amounted to a 'taking.' " 447 U.S. at 84. This reasoning, borrowed from the distinct problem area of determining when mere regulation amounted to a taking, see pp. 146-52 *supra* (discussing Pennsylvania Coal Co. v. Mahon), appeared quite out of place when applied to *Pruneyard;* it seems difficult to deny that any physical occupation of land is a taking. See Loretto v. Teleprompter Manhattan CATV Corp., 458 U.S. 419 (1982) (Marshall, J.) (finding compensation required for the installation of cable television facilities on real property, although, as the dissenters pointed out, see id. at 443, 445 (Blackmun, J., joined by Brennan and White, dissenting), the equipment in question occupied "only about one-eighth of a cubic foot of space on the roof of appellant's . . . building" and had been found not to "affect the fair return on her property").

Equally insensitive to taking clause values was Penn Central Transp. Co. v. New York City, 438 U.S. 104 (1978) (Brennan, J.), which relied on the absence of physical invasion to permit uncompensated limitation of development above Grand Central Station in New York City—not because such development would harm neighboring property, as in traditional zoning cases, but in order to require the owner to preserve a landmark building for the benefit of the public. One might as well say the city could require the owner to construct a fountain for the enjoyment of passers-by. See id. at 144-46 (Rehnquist, J., joined by Burger and Stevens, dissenting); p. 151 *supra* (discussing Justice Brandeis's views).

The related contract clause of article I, § 10, however, which had been largely read out of the Constitution during the 1930s, see pp. 211-13 *supra,* enjoyed a modest revival as the Court found two exercises of state power that even on the Court's homemade balancing test unjustifiably impaired the obligation of existing contracts. United States Trust Co. v. New Jersey, 431 U.S. 1 (1977) (Blackmun, J., over three dissents) (attempt to repeal the security the state had given for its own bonds); Allied Structural Steel Co. v. Spannaus, 438 U.S. 234 (1978) (Stewart, J., over three dissents) (retroactive modification of private pension plans). See generally Schwartz, *Old Wine in Old Bottles? The Renaissance of the Contract Clause,* 1979 SUP. CT. REV. 95 (approving the Court's historically surprising conclusion that stricter scrutiny was called for when the contracts interfered with were public rather than private because in the former case "the State's own self-interest is at stake," id. at 107-08).

[105] See 430 U.S. at 721 (Rehnquist, J., dissenting).

case than in *Wooley* or *Tornillo* that the citizen will be understood to have endorsed the unwelcome message. Even the billboard case, however, is not so easy as it might appear, for the well-known objections of Jefferson and Madison to taxation for religious purposes suggest that compulsory extraction of funds for the support of abhorrent ideas poses a problem differing only in degree from those of other forms of coerced expression.[106]

It would be a mistake to draw an exact parallel between speech and religion in this regard. In forbidding establishment of religion but not of politics, the first amendment seems to acknowledge that, while government has no legitimate interest in promoting religion, it may have an interest in promoting secular policy.[107] Nevertheless, once *Buckley* had held that a limitation on spending impinged upon first amendment interests, *Barnette* seemed to imply that compulsion to spend did too.[108] Thus it was not altogether surprising when the Court concluded in *Abood v. Detroit Board of Education* that government employees could not be required to support the political activities of unions that represented them.[109] Indeed, despite his billboard example, Justice Rehnquist agreed.[110]

Here again there would be difficult line-drawing problems in balancing legitimate government interests against those of the individual.[111] On the one hand, as *Abood* illustrates, the Court cannot close its eyes to the impact of government expenditures on the taxpayer's freedom. On the other hand, the example of that oversized billboard we call the Voice of America suggests that one cannot simply equate the taxpayer cases either with precedents under the establishment clause or with decisions like *Barnette* or even *Wooley,* which involved more personal affirmations of obnoxious views than does the mere payment of taxes.[112]

---

[106] *See* pp. 339-42 *supra* (discussing Everson v. Board of Education).

[107] *See* Garvey, *Freedom and Equality in the Religion Clauses,* 1981 SUP. CT. REV. 193, 214-17 ("[I]t would be fatuous to suggest that in designing public school curricula the state could not include civics courses which teach the virtues of democracy and the evils of fascism."). *See generally* M. YUDOF, WHEN GOVERNMENT SPEAKS: POLITICS, LAW, AND GOVERNMENT EXPRESSION IN AMERICA (1983); Schauer, *Is Government Speech a Problem?,* 35 STAN. L. REV. 373 (1983).

[108] *See* McConnell, *Political and Religious Disestablishment,* 1986 B.Y.U.L. REV. 405 (drawing a close analogy between religious and political matters in respect to government funding of private advocacy).

[109] 431 U.S. 209, 232-37 (1977) (Stewart, J.). At the same time, not surprisingly, the Court unanimously held that public employees *could* be required to pay for the services rendered by such a union as their bargaining agent, *id.* at 217-32. The majority made this conclusion appear easier than it was by invoking decisions upholding similar provisions in *private* employment contracts, *id.* at 217-23 (citing Railway Employees' Dept. v. Hanson, 351 U.S. 225 (1956), and International Ass'n of Machinists v. Street, 367 U.S. 740 (1961)). As Justice Powell observed in a concurrence insisting that the government had the burden of proving that no part of the employee's money was used for an improper purpose, 431 U.S. at 244-64, in the earlier cases the government had merely authorized such provisions, not required them. Unless the aberrant decision in Shelley v. Kraemer is understood more broadly than it usually is, *see* pp. 358-60 *supra,* the Constitution does not generally limit government enforcement of private contracts. *Cf.* Jackson v. Metropolitan Edison Co., 419 U.S. 345 (1974), *cited* by Powell in 431 U.S. at 251 (holding a state not responsible for a utility's practices although it had approved them).

[110] *See* 431 U.S. at 242-44 (Rehnquist, J., concurring).

[111] *See* Ellis v. Brotherhood of Railway Clerks, 466 U.S. 435 (1984) (White, J., over a partial dissent by Powell) (upholding a provision permitting dissenting employees to be assessed for the cost of union publications, conventions, and social activities); Chicago Teachers Union v. Hudson, 475 U.S. 292 (1986) (Stevens, J.) (finding that a union had employed inadequate procedures for preventing use of funds for purposes forbidden by *Abood*).

[112] For the related question whether differential governmental subsidies violate the rights of those who are *denied* them see pp. 472-75, 508-10 *supra* (discussing the abortion-funding and public-forum cases).

## D. Access to Information

The right to speak is of little value if one has nothing to say. As the Court seemed to recognize in holding legislative investigations protected by the speech or debate clause of article I, one cannot disclose information without having first acquired it.[113] To prevent news gathering would stifle the press as effectively as to forbid publication. A Court prepared to find such ancillary rights as association, anonymity, and spending implicit in freedom of expression[114] might therefore be expected to be sympathetic to a right to acquire information, and the Burger Court took several important steps in this direction.

*Branzburg v. Hayes,* in 1972, produced a tactical setback and a strategic victory.[115] Four dissenters argued that the first amendment gave journalists at least a qualified privilege to refuse to reveal information acquired in the course of their duties,[116] while the majority found the deterrent effect of grand-jury questioning on the collection of news justified by the compelling interest in combating crime.[117] Reasonable minds may differ as to the balance of interests in the particular case.[118] More significant was the majority's reminder that no one denied news gathering fell within the first amendment. "[W]ithout some protection for seeking out the news," Justice White observed, "freedom of the press could be eviscerated."[119]

The idea that freedom of speech implied freedom to hear was not entirely new. As early as 1943 the Court had said in an offhand way that freedom of expression necessarily embraced both the right to distribute literature and "the right to receive it."[120] In 1965 this

[113] Gravel v. United States, 408 U.S. 606, 615-16 (1972) (White, J.). Perhaps recollecting abuses by congressional committees in the past, *see* pp. 388-94 *supra,* the Court rather grudgingly added that the dissemination of such information to the general public as contrasted with its use within Congress was not protected: "[T]he courts have extended the privilege to matters beyond pure speech or debate in either House, but 'only when necessary to prevent indirect impairment of such deliberations.'" *Id.* at 625. *See also* Doe v. McMillan, 412 U.S. 306 (1973).

[114] *See, e.g.,* NAACP v. Alabama, pp. 382-83 *supra;* Talley v. California, p. 383, note 46 *supra;* Buckley v. Valeo, pp. 510-12 *supra. See generally* Lamont v. Postmaster General, 381 U.S. 301, 308 (1965) (Brennan, J., concurring) ("[T]he protection of the Bill of Rights goes beyond the specific guarantees to protect from congressional abridgment those equally fundamental personal rights necessary to make the express guarantees fully meaningful.").

[115] 408 U.S. 665 (1972) (White, J.).

[116] *See id.* at 725-52 (Stewart, J., joined by Brennan and Marshall, JJ., dissenting). *See also id.* at 711-25 (Douglas, J., dissenting) (arguing that reporters never need appear before grand juries).

[117] *See id.* at 690, 695, 700-01. In United States v. Nixon, 418 U.S. 683 (1974), the Court drew a similar balance in holding the interest in confidentiality of executive deliberations outweighed by the need to obtain tape recordings bearing upon pending criminal prosecutions. *See also* Zemel v. Rusk, 381 U.S. 1, 16-17 (1965), relied on by the majority in *Branzburg,* 408 U.S. at 684, where the Court held that the interest in acquiring information was outweighed by foreign-affairs considerations in upholding a ban on travel to Cuba.

[118] *See, e.g.,* Kurland, *1971 Term: The Year of the Stewart-White Court,* 1972 Sup. Ct. Rev. 181, 241-46 (finding the decision justified by the "shortage of hard facts" respecting the consequences of one or the other decision).

[119] 408 U.S. at 681. *See also id.* at 728 (Stewart, J., dissenting) ("News must not be unnecessarily cut off at its source, for without freedom to acquire information the right to publish would be impermissibly compromised.").

[120] Martin v. City of Struthers, 319 U.S. 141, 143 (1943) (Black, J.). Nothing turned on this conclusion in *Martin* itself, which upheld the right of the distributor to engage in door-to-door solicitation. *See* pp. 317–18 *supra.*

dictum had become holding as the Court unanimously concluded that a restriction on the delivery of "communist political propaganda" infringed the first amendment rights of the *addressee*.[121] Typically, Justice Douglas had not bothered to explain the existence of this right. Typically, Justice Brennan had done so in a concurring opinion: "The dissemination of ideas can accomplish nothing if otherwise willing addressees are not free to receive and consider them."[122]

To the extent that this argument implied that the right to hear was necessary to make the speaker's freedom a reality, it was very likely insufficient to justify the decision it was designed to support; for it had not been established that the first amendment protected the right to send materials into the United States on behalf of a foreign government.[123] In 1969, in rejecting broadcasters' objections to provisions requiring them to transmit certain messages not of their own choosing, the Court had enunciated a broader justification: a general right to receive information could be deduced from the understanding that a central purpose of the amendment was to promote informed decision-making.[124]

*Branzburg's* recognition of a right to learn *in order* to speak was a new twist that tied the protected interest to the language of the amendment as well as to its purpose, and it soon pursued an independent life of its own. Echoing *Branzburg's* acknowledgment that " 'news gathering is not without its First Amendment protections,' " another bare majority concluded in two 1974 decisions that the state need not allow the press to interview individual prisoners: "[N]ewsmen have no constitutional right of access to prisons or their inmates beyond that afforded the general public."[125] Four years later, though a majority

---

[121] Lamont v. Postmaster General, 381 U.S. at 305-07, note 114 *supra*.

[122] *Id.* at 308 (Brennan, J., joined by Harlan and Goldberg, JJ., concurring).

[123] *See id.* at 308 (Brennan, J., concurring). *See also* Kleindienst v. Mandel, 408 U.S. 753, 762-65 (1972) (Blackmun, J.) (recognizing a first amendment interest in listening to a foreigner who was held to have no protected interest in entering the country to speak); Procunier v. Martinez, 416 U.S. 396, 407-09 (1974) (Powell, J.) (holding that limits on communications by prisoners infringed the rights of those to whom the communications were directed, while reserving the question of "the extent to which an individual's right to free speech survives incarceration").

[124] Red Lion Broadcasting Co. v. FCC, 395 U.S. 367, 390 (1969) (White, J.) (repeating that " '[s]peech concerning public affairs . . . is the essence of self-government' ") ("It is the right of the viewers and listeners, not the right of the broadcasters, which is paramount. . . . It is the right of the public to receive suitable access to social, political, esthetic, moral, and other ideas and experiences which is crucial here."). *See also* Lewis, *A Public Right to Know about Public Institutions: The First Amendment as Sword*, 1980 SUP. CT. REV. 1, 2-3 ("If citizens are the ultimate sovereigns, . . . they must have access to the information needed for intelligent decision."). There were echoes of this approach in First National Bank v. Bellotti, 435 U.S. 765, 776 (1978) (Powell, J.), which struck down a limitation on corporate speech: "The First Amendment . . . serves significant societal interests. The proper question therefore is not whether corporations 'have' First Amendment rights . . . [but] whether [the provision] abridges expression that the First Amendment was meant to protect." The same approach may have been implicit in Justice Brennan's earlier insistence that dissemination without hearers "can accomplish nothing," *see* text at note 122 *supra*. For the decision-making principle on which Justice White's argument was based see pp. 269-70, 515 *supra* (discussing Thornhill v. Alabama and the commercial speech cases).

[125] Pell v. Procunier, 417 U.S. 817, 833-35 (1974). *See also* Saxbe v. Washington Post Co., 417 U.S. 843 (1974). Both opinions were written by Justice Stewart, who had dissented in *Branzburg*. The principal dissent, *see Saxbe*, 417 U.S. at 850-75, was written by Justice Powell, who had concurred specially in the earlier case, 408 U.S. at 709-10, to emphasize that news gathering was not wholly unprotected. *See* 417 U.S. at 862 ("What is at stake here is the societal function of the First Amendment in preserving free public discussion of governmental affairs."). *See also Pell*, 417 U.S. at 836-42 (Douglas, J., dissenting). Brennan and Marshall joined both dissenting opinions. On the relation between freedom of speech and freedom of the press see Blanchard, *The Institutional Press and Its First Amendment Privileges*, 1978 SUP. CT. REV. 225, 226 (noting that the Court had

found once again that the court below had gone too far in protecting the interest of the press, four of the seven Justices who took part actually concluded that the state had unduly limited press access to jail.[126]

These developments approached fruition in the 1980 case of *Richmond Newspapers, Inc. v. Virginia,* where seven of eight participating Justices agreed that the first amendment gave the press the right to attend a criminal trial.[127] There was no opinion for the Court, and not all the majority Justices expressly invoked the theory of the *Branzburg* dictum.[128] Justice Stevens, who had argued for a right of access to prisons, was nevertheless ecstatic: "Today, . . . for the first time, the Court unequivocally holds that an arbitrary interference with access to important information is an abridgment of the freedoms of speech and of the press. . . ."[129]

How broadly one could properly generalize the holding in *Richmond Newspapers,* however, was a matter of dispute.[130] The context, moreover, was an awkward one in which to apply the *Branzburg* principle. First of all, in light of the one-year-old holding in *Gannett Co. v. DePasquale,* it could plausibly have been argued that the sixth amendment had excluded any such claim by giving only the defendant and not the press the right to a public trial.[131] More generally, *Branzburg*'s unassailable dictum did not compel the con-

---

consistently rebuffed any effort to establish special protection for the institutional press) ("Freedom of the press is almost universally measured by the standard of what the general public could do in a like situation.").

[126] Houchins v. KQED, Inc., 438 U.S. 1 (1978). There was no opinion for the Court. *See id.* at 3-16 (opinion of Burger, C. J., joined by White and Rehnquist, JJ.) (denying that any right of access existed); *id.* at 16-19 (Stewart, J., concurring) (agreeing that the injunction had gone too far but adding that it was proper to order that the press be allowed more frequent access to areas open to the public and to bring recording equipment); *id.* at 19-40 (Stevens, J., joined by Brennan and Powell, dissenting on the ground that prison policy "unduly restricted the opportunities of the general public to learn about the conditions of confinement in Santa Rita jail"). *Id.* at 30. Marshall and Blackmun did not participate.

[127] 448 U.S. 555 (1980). Justice Powell, who had voted to require access to prisons in *Pell* and *Houchins,* did not participate, *id.* at 581; Justice Rehnquist, *id.* at 604-06, dissented.

[128] *See id.* at 576-77 (opinion of Burger, C. J., joined by White and Stevens) ("The explicit, guaranteed rights to speak and to publish concerning what takes place at a trial would lose much meaning if access to observe the trial could, as it was here, be foreclosed arbitrarily."); *id.* at 598 (Brennan and Marshall, JJ., concurring) (emphasizing "the importance of public access to the broader purposes of the trial process"); *id.* at 600 (Stewart, J., concurring) (arguing that public presence at a trial "serves to assure the integrity of what goes on"); *id.* at 604 (Blackmun J., concurring) (stressing the public's interest in knowing about trials).

[129] *Id.* at 583 (Stevens, J., concurring). *See also* Globe Newspaper Co. v. Superior Court, 457 U.S. 596, 604-05 (1982) (Brennan, J.) (striking down a rule automatically excluding the public during testimony of a rape victim) ("[T]o the extent that the First Amendment embraces a right of access to criminal trials, it is to ensure that th[e] constitutionally protected 'discussion of governmental affairs' is an informed one."). The principle of *Richmond Newspapers* was applied to the voir dire in Press-Enterprise Co. v. Superior Court, 464 U.S. 501 (1984) (Burger, C. J.), and to a preliminary hearing by a later decision of the same name, 478 U.S. 1 (1986).

[130] *See Globe Newspaper Co.,* 457 U.S. at 611 (O'Connor, J., concurring) ("I interpret neither *Richmond Newspapers* nor the Court's decision today to carry any implications outside the context of criminal trials."); Lewis, *supra* note 124, at 23 ("The question in each case should be whether the closing of a governmental institution to the public, the denial of access, prevents accountability."). *See also* Ares, Chandler v. Florida: *Television, Criminal Trials, and Due Process,* 1981 SUP. CT. REV. 157, 173-78 (raising the question whether after *Richmond Newspapers* freedom of the press required what Estes v. Texas, p. 450, note 278 *supra,* once held that due process forbade: permission to televise a criminal trial. That the presence of television cameras was sometimes permissible was established in *Chandler,* 449 U.S. 560 (1981) (Burger, C. J.)).

[131] 443 U.S. 368, 379-80 (1979) (Stewart, J., with Blackmun, Brennan, White, and Marshall dissenting) (holding that the sixth amendment gave the public no right to attend a pretrial proceeding) ("The Constitution

clusion that the first amendment guaranteed access to government facilities such as court-rooms or jails. That the state may not prohibit news gathering in general, as Chief Justice Burger had stressed in the second prison case, "affords no basis for the claim that the First Amendment compels others . . . to supply information. . . . Neither the First Amendment nor the Fourteenth Amendment mandates a right to access to government information or sources of information within the government's control." [132]

There was much to be said for the Chief Justice's position. The first amendment forbids government action "abridging" the freedoms of speech and press; as all Justices in the abortion-funding cases acknowledged, the government is not normally perceived to have abridged a right by merely failing to subsidize its exercise. [133] Freedom to seek information no more obligates others to provide it than freedom of contract requires others to enter a bargain. [134]

On its face, Burger's objection was no less applicable to courtrooms than to prisons. Persuasively invoking the analogy of the public forum, however, he distinguished the prison cases in *Richmond* on the ground that criminal trials were traditionally open to the public. [135]

Even in the prison cases, moreover, it was arguable that the Chief Justice's distinction was out of place. Unlike those hoping to peek into government files, the plaintiffs were not seeking government information; the government was preventing access to information that inmates were apparently willing to provide. It is true that the informants were on government property, and that a jail was not a public forum. [136] The inmates were in jail, however, because the government had put them there; its doing so could be said to have deprived journalists of contact with them without holding that the government was required "to supply information" within its control. [137]

---

nowhere mentions any right of access to a criminal trial on the part of the public; its guarantee, like the others enumerated [in the same amendment], is personal to the accused."). *See* U. S. CONST. amend. VI ("In all criminal prosecutions, *the accused* shall enjoy the right to a speedy and public trial." (emphasis added). The dissenters' best argument was that the similarly worded right of trial by jury had been held to permit the government to block an attempted waiver of the defendant's right, Patton v. United States, p. 246, note 8 *supra*. That conclusion, however, may itself be questioned on the grounds that persuaded the majority in *Gannett. See also* Lewis, *supra* note 124, at 1 (commenting on the contrast between *Gannett* and *Richmond*) ("Not since Gertrude has anyone posted with such dexterity from one set of sheets to another.").

[132] Houchins v. KQED, Inc., 438 U.S. 1, 11, 15 (1978) (opinion of Burger, C. J., joined by White and Rehnquist, JJ.).

[133] *See* pp. 471-72 *supra;* Currie, *Positive and Negative Constitutional Rights,* 53 U. CHI. L. REV. 864 (1986).

[134] *Cf.* Jones v. Alfred H. Mayer Co., p. 425, note 87 *supra,* where in construing a civil rights statute guaranteeing the equal right to own property the majority lost sight of this distinction; Runyon v. McCrary, 427 U.S. 160 (1976) (Stewart, J.) (making the same mistake with respect to the right to contract in another provision of the same statute). Four Justices in *Runyon* noted their disagreement with this interpretation as an original matter; two of them concurred on the basis of stare decisis.

[135] *See* 448 U.S. at 576-78 & n. 11. *See* pp. 263-66 *supra* (discussing the same issue in the context of the public forum). *See also* Cox, *Foreword: Freedom of Expression in the Burger Court,* 94 HARV. L. REV. 1, 23 (1980) ("[C]utting off opportunities previously and generally provided by the state may be treated as interference with the activity rather than as a refusal to facilitate such activity.").

[136] Adderley v. Florida, pp. 423-24 *supra.*

[137] *Cf.* p. 520 *supra* (discussing Columbia Broadcasting System v. Democratic National Committee). So to hold would merely satisfy the threshold requirement of invasive government action, not assure a right of access to prisons. The substantial interest in prison discipline would surely place limits on any such right; the Court

As Justice Stevens said in *Richmond Newspapers,* the Burger Court had made great strides in establishing a first amendment right of access to information. Nothing in the decisions, however, impaired Chief Justice Burger's basic point that the government's inability to prevent acquisition of information from willing speakers did not imply an affirmative duty to reveal the contents of government files.[138]

## II. RELIGION

### A. The Decline of Neutrality

Decisions before the retirement of Chief Justice Warren had done much to effectuate the twin guarantees against establishment and abridgement of religion.[139] With rare exceptions, moreover, these decisions had seemed consistent with, if not always based upon, a general theory that the attitude of government toward religion should be one of neutrality.[140]

In the first three years after Chief Justice Burger's appointment, the Court handed down three major decisions respecting the relationship between church and state. One of these decisions carried to new lengths the principle of religious freedom, another the principle against establishment. All three, however, seemed to cast doubt on the neutrality thesis as it had previously been understood.

### 1. Property taxes

Government, the Supreme Court had led us to believe, was not supposed to promote religion. The state was forbidden to sponsor religious instruction in public buildings, to compose prayers for public school recitation, or to conduct Bible readings in public classes.[141] It seemed to follow, as Justice Brennan acknowledged in his concurring opinion

---

conceded after *Richmond Newspapers* that there might be times when a courtroom could be closed to protect compelling interests such as the psychological well-being of minors. *See Globe Newspaper Co., supra* note 129, 457 U.S. at 607. Moreover, the availability of other means of access to information possessed by inmates reduces the adverse effect of closing the prison on the right to know. *See* Procunier v. Martinez, 416 U.S. 396 (1974) (Powell, J.) (striking down overbroad limitations on mail sent to and by prisoners). *But see* Kleindienst v. Mandel, *supra* note 123, 408 U.S. at 765 (acknowledging the relevance of alternative means of communication but stressing the "particular qualities inherent in sustained, face-to-face debate, discussion and questioning").

[138] The twin decisions entitled Press-Enterprise Co. v. Superior Court, 464 U.S. 501 (1984) (Burger, C. J.), and 478 U.S. 1 (1986) (Burger, C. J.), in holding the press entitled to transcripts of judicial proceedings that had been improperly closed to the public, contained nothing to suggest a general right of access to government files; the Court seemed to think access to the transcripts followed naturally from access to the proceedings themselves—perhaps as a remedy for the unlawful exclusion. Any expansion of the first amendment right of access to government information would present increasing opportunities for conflict with the first amendment right of privacy in speech and association recognized by such cases as NAACP v. Alabama, pp. 383-84 *supra.*

[139] *See* pp. 266-68, 315-20, 339-43, 410-12, 445-46 *supra.*

[140] *See generally* P. KURLAND, RELIGION AND THE LAW (1962). *But see* Garvey, *Freedom and Equality in the Religion Clauses,* 1981 SUP. CT. REV. 193, 219 ("The difficulty with Professor Kurland's formulation . . . is that, in an effort to reconcile the religion clauses, it substitutes 'equality' for 'freedom'. . . .").

[141] *See* Illinois *ex rel.* McCollum v. Board of Education, p. 342 *supra;* Engel v. Vitale, pp. 411-12 *supra;* Abington School Dist. v. Schempp, p. 445 *supra. See generally* Everson v. Board of Education, 330 U.S. 1, 15

in *Walz v. Tax Commission* in 1970, that a state could not subsidize private religious observances either.[142]

Nevertheless, over the solitary dissent of Justice Douglas,[143] the Court in *Walz* managed to uphold the long-standing practice of tax exemptions for property used for religious purposes.[144] Exemptions, the Chief Justice argued, were different from subsidies: "[T]he government does not transfer part of its revenue to churches but simply abstains from demanding that the church support the state."[145]

As Justice Brennan suggested, the fact that tax exemptions did not involve giving tax money directly to churches made less applicable Madison's concern for the taxpayer's freedom of conscience, on which the Court had so heavily relied in condemning state support of religion in *Everson v. Board of Education*.[146] The prayer cases, however, had shown that the objection to government support for religion was not confined to cases involving significant expenditures of taxpayer funds.[147] In economic terms it makes little difference to the property owner whether he is handed dollars or relieved of the burden of handing them to the government.[148] "A tax exemption," Justice Douglas insisted, "is a subsidy."[149] Thus despite its protestations, the majority in *Walz* seemed to have concluded that there were occasions when the state could promote religion after all.

## 2. Parochial schools

Although before *Walz* it had been understood that government was not supposed to support religion, the decisions also suggested that participation in religious activities did not disqualify individuals or organizations from receiving secular government help. Catholic hospitals were eligible for subsidies designed to improve medical care; parochial-school pupils could participate in state programs providing safe transportation and nonreligious books.[150] Indeed, as the Court had suggested in *Everson*, the *exclusion* of religious institutions from generally available benefits would have raised serious issues under the free exercise clause, which forbids the state to discriminate on religious grounds.[151]

---

(1947) ("Neither a state nor the Federal Government . . . can pass laws which aid one religion, aid all religions, or prefer one religion over another."), pp. 339-42 *supra*.

[142] 397 U.S. 664, 690 (Brennan, J., concurring) ("General subsidies of religious activities would, of course, constitute impermissible state involvement with religion.").

[143] *See id.* at 700-27.

[144] On the antiquity of tax exemptions for churches see *id.* at 676-78 (opinion of the Court); *id.* at 681-87 (Brennan, J., concurring) (both noting, inter alia, that Congress had enacted such an exemption for the District of Columbia in 1802).

[145] *Id.* at 675.

[146] *See Walz*, 397 U.S. at 690-91 (Brennan, J., concurring); *Everson*, 330 U.S. at 11-14.

[147] *See Doremus v. Board of Education*, p. 343, note 30 *supra* (holding that a taxpayer had no standing to challenge Bible reading such as that struck down on the merits in *Schempp* because there was no allegation that the practice increased the cost of schooling).

[148] *See Walz*, 397 U.S. at 699 (Harlan, J., concurring).

[149] 397 U.S. at 704 (Douglas, J., dissenting).

[150] *See Bradfield v. Roberts*, p. 56 *supra;* Everson v. Board of Education, pp. 339-42 *supra;* Board of Education v. Allen, p. 445 *supra*.

[151] *See Everson*, 330 U.S. at 16 ("[W]e must be careful, in protecting the citizens of New Jersey against state-established churches, to be sure that we do not inadvertently prohibit New Jersey from extending its general state law benefits to all its citizens without regard to their religious belief.").

It might seem to follow that a state was free to subsidize the teaching of secular subjects in parochial schools so long as none of the money was spent in teaching religion. It is true that every dollar received for teaching mathematics frees up a dollar for teaching religion.[152] Yet the religious is thus aided only to the extent its proponents elect to promote the secular; the religious institution is no better off than if it had given no worldly lessons at all.[153]

Insofar as higher education was concerned, the Burger Court drew this very conclusion.[154] Below the college level, however, wrote Chief Justice Burger for the Court in *Lemon v. Kurtzman* in 1971, religious and secular teachings were so closely intertwined that any attempt to separate them would impermissibly entangle the state in the administration of a religious body—an evil long associated with the establishment of religion.[155]

In defense of the Court's conclusion it might be said that religious bodies could qualify for support simply by separating their secular and religious instruction. Since the commingling of these subjects was itself likely to be the product of religious conviction,[156] however, this prospect did not seem to offer much consolation. The Court in *Lemon* seemed close to holding that sometimes the state not only might but must treat those who practiced their faith less favorably than those who did not.[157]

[152] *See* Tilton v. Richardson, 403 U.S. 672, 693 (1971) (Douglas, J., dissenting).

[153] *See* Lemon v. Kurtzman, 403 U.S. 602, 663 (1971) (White, J., dissenting) ("Our cases . . . recognize that legislation having a secular purpose and extending governmental assistance to sectarian schools in the performance of their secular functions does not constitute 'law[s] respecting an establishment of religion'. . . .").

[154] *See* Tilton v. Richardson, 403 U.S. 672 (1971) (upholding federal grants for the construction of buildings used for secular purposes); Hunt v. McNair, 413 U.S. 734 (1973) (Powell, J.) (upholding the issuance of state revenue bonds for the same purpose); Roemer v. Board of Public Works, 426 U.S. 736 (1976) (upholding general subsidies for nonsectarian uses). *See Roemer,* 426 U.S. at 746 (opinion of Blackmun, J.) ("[R]eligious institutions need not be quarantined from public benefits that are neutrally available to all."). In neither *Tilton* nor *Roemer* was there an opinion for the Court; there were four dissents in both cases, three in *Hunt.*

[155] 403 U.S. 602, 614-22 (1971) (over a dissent by White) (striking down provisions for state support of the salaries of teachers of secular subjects). *See also id.* at 657 (Brennan, J., concurring) (arguing that secular education in parochial schools "cannot be separated from the environment in which it occurs, for its integration with the religious mission is both the theory and the strength of the religious school"); *id.* at 624 (opinion of the Court) and 645-49 (Brennan, J.) (noting the absence of any long history of aid to parochial schools comparable to that which had helped to sustain the tax exemption in *Walz*). On government interference in church administration see *Everson,* 330 U.S. at 16 ("Neither a state nor the Federal Government can, openly or secretly, participate in the affairs of any religious organizations. . . ."). Entanglement formed the third prong of the general test that *Lemon* laid down for determining whether a measure was compatible with the establishment clause. *See* p. 531 *infra*. For an argument that the Court exaggerated the dangers of entanglement in *Lemon* see Giannella, *Lemon and Tilton: The Bitter and the Sweet of Church-State Entanglement,* 1971 SUP. CT. REV. 147, 170-75.

[156] *See* Grand Rapids School Dist. v. Ball, 473 U.S. 373, 379 (1985) (quoting a statement declaring one of the goals of Catholic education to be " '[a] God oriented environment which *permeates* the total educational program' " and a policy of the Christian schools that " 'the Word of God must be an all-pervading force in the educational program' ").

[157] *See* McConnell, *Unconstitutional Conditions: Unrecognized Implications for the Establishment Clause,* 26 SAN DIEGO L. REV. 255, 268 (1989) ("That some parents wish their children to receive education in a religious environment should not deprive them of their fair share of the public resources devoted to education"); Marty, *Of Darters and Schools and Clergymen: The Religion Clauses Worse Confounded,* 1978 SUP. CT. REV. 171, 181 ("Penalizing private schools that are religious because they are religious extends the First Amendment in the wrong direction. . . .").

## 3. Compulsory education

If, as the prayer cases had held, government was not even *permitted* to favor religion,[158] it might have seemed obvious that it was not *required* to do so. In its first substantive interpretation of the free exercise clause the Court had seemed to confirm this conclusion by holding that religious belief created no claim to exemption from a generally applicable law serving legitimate secular interests in suppressing polygamy.[159] With one conspicuous recent exception,[160] later cases had seemed to support this principle.[161]

It ought to have followed that religious convictions could not justify a refusal to go to school. In *Wisconsin v. Yoder,* however, Chief Justice Burger picked up the lone exception and ran with it, concluding for another all-but-unanimous Court that the state could not require Amish children to attend school beyond the eighth grade.[162]

Even on the assumption that issues of freedom of religion, like those of freedom of speech, are properly resolved by balancing opposing interests, this seemed an extreme decision in light of the state's often-acknowledged and powerful interest in education.[163] More important than the particular result, however, was the legitimacy the opinion gave to the theretofore shaky balancing approach.[164] Despite the countervailing thrust of the

---

[158] *See also* Torcaso v. Watkins, p. 411 *supra* (holding that a state could not limit public office to those willing to affirm a belief in God).

[159] Reynolds v. United States, 98 U.S. 145 (1879), THE FIRST HUNDRED YEARS at 439-42.

[160] *See* Sherbert v. Verner, p. 445-46 *supra* (holding a state could not apply a general rule making willingness to work on Saturday a condition of receiving unemployment benefits to persons whose refusal was based on religious grounds). *Sherbert* was reaffirmed in Thomas v. Review Board, 450 U.S. 707 (1981) (Burger, C. J.) (where the applicant was unemployed because of conscientious objection to the manufacture of arms). Like Justice Stewart in the earlier case, Justice Rehnquist protested that what the Court required in *Thomas* would be forbidden by the establishment clause as interpreted in such cases as Lemon v. Kurtzman. *See id.* at 726 (Rehnquist, J., dissenting). *Cf. Sherbert,* 374 U.S. at 414-17 (Stewart, J., concurring).

[161] *See, e.g.,* Hamilton v. Regents, p. 266, note 155 *supra* (allowing state university to exclude students who refused military education on religious grounds); Minersville School Dist. v. Gobitis, pp. 267-68 *supra* (holding Jehovah's Witnesses entitled to no exemption from flag-salute requirement later struck down as to *all* objectors); Prince v. Massachusetts, *supra* p. 319, note 81 (upholding conviction of religious objector for violation of child labor law); Braunfeld v. Brown, pp. 410-11 *supra* (upholding application of Sunday law to those with religious scruples against work on another day).

[162] 406 U.S. 205 (1972). Justice Douglas's partial dissent, *id.* at 241-49, was based on a possible divergence of views between pupils and their parents, which the majority insisted, *id.* at 231, had not been asserted in the case.

[163] *See, e.g.,* Brown v. Board of Education, 347 U.S. 483, 493 (1954); Plyler v. Doe, 457 U.S. 202, 221-23 (1982). Important to the Court's conclusion in *Yoder* was the perception that "an additional one or two years of compulsory formal education" promised "at best a speculative gain," 406 U.S. at 227—a perception that appeared to trivialize the obvious benefits of an education beyond the primary grades. *See also id.* at 238 (White, J., joined by Brennan and Stewart, concurring) ("This would be a very different case for me if respondents' claim were that their religion forbade their children from attending any school at any time."). On the other side of the balance, the Court was right that the impact of compulsory attendance on religious beliefs was severe, for (unlike a Sunday law, for example) the school law "affirmatively compel[led]" the Amish "to perform acts undeniably at odds with fundamental tenets of their religious beliefs." *Id.* at 218.

[164] *See* 406 U.S. at 220 (citing *Sherbert*) ("A regulation neutral on its face may, in its application, nonetheless offend the constitutional requirement for governmental neutrality if it unduly burdens the free exercise of religion.").

establishment clause, the Court seemed to be saying that government was sometimes not only permitted but required to accord special privileges on account of religion.[165]

## B. A Partial Recovery

By the time *Yoder* was decided in 1972, therefore, neutrality seemed to be in retreat on several fronts. When, however, after continued skirmishing over the precise limits of state aid to parochial schools,[166] the Justices turned to additional church-and-state questions in 1978, it gradually became apparent that they might not be so far from the positions of their predecessors as their first three decisions might have led one to believe. *Lemon* had distilled from earlier cases a three-pronged test for the validity of action challenged under the establishment clause: "First, the statute must have a secular legislative purpose; second, its principal or primary effect must be one that neither advances nor inhibits religion . . . ; finally, the statute must not foster 'an excessive government entanglement with religion.' "[167] It turned out that in many cases both this calculus and the balancing test employed for free exercise purposes in *Yoder* produced results consistent with the earlier conception of neutrality.

### 1. Easy cases

*McDaniel v. Paty*[168] and *Widmar v. Vincent*[169] reaffirmed that, notwithstanding *Lemon*, the state was generally not permitted, much less required, to discriminate against those who exercised their religious freedom. The first of these cases held that a minister could not be disqualified from serving as delegate to a constitutional convention, the second that religion could not be excluded from an auditorium open generally to other private uses.

---

[165] *See* Kurland, note 118 *supra*, at 181, 215-19. For a strong defense of the thesis that the first amendment sometimes permits and sometimes requires exceptions designed to accommodate religious beliefs see McConnell, *Accommodation of Religion*, 1985 SUP. CT. REV. 1. See also McConnell, *The Origins and Historical Understanding of Free Exercise of Religion*, 103 HARV. L. REV. 1409 (1990) (an excellent review of the inconclusive history revealing early support for religious exemptions).

[166] *See, e.g.,* Levitt v. Committee for Public Education, 413 U.S. 472, 479-81 (1973) (Burger, C. J., over White's dissent) (striking down state financing of tests prepared by teachers because "no attempt is made . . . to assure that internally prepared tests are free of religious instruction"); Committee for Public Education v. Nyquist, 413 U.S. 756 (1973) (Powell, J., over three dissents) (expressly rejecting the distinction that had been the basis of *Walz* in striking down not only direct subsidies for tuition and maintenance but also tax benefits for tuition payments on the ground that none was limited to secular activities); Meek v. Pittenger, 421 U.S. 349 (1975) (over a variety of partial dissents) (reaffirming that parochial students might be provided with secular books, *see* Board of Education v. Allen, p. 445 *supra*, but forbidding the provision of such items as maps and laboratory equipment to the schools themselves); Wolman v. Walter, 433 U.S. 229 (1977) (over the usual partial dissents) (holding that pupils could be provided with diagnostic and remedial services and standardized tests as well as books but not with other instructional materials of the sort involved in *Meek*). *See also* Committee for Public Education v. Regan, 444 U.S. 646 (1980) (White, J., over four dissents) (upholding reimbursement of schools for administering state-prepared tests). For discussion of the intricacies of these decisions see Morgan, *The Establishment Clause and Sectarian Schools: A Final Installment?*, 1973 SUP. CT. REV. 57.

[167] 403 U.S. at 612-13.

[168] 435 U.S. 618 (1978).

[169] 454 U.S. 263 (1981) (over a dissent by White).

In each case the Court squarely rejected the argument that discrimination was justifiable because *required* by the establishment clause. That the church was not supposed to run the state, said the Justices in *McDaniel,* did not require that its functionaries be excluded entirely from the government to which, like everyone else, they were subject.[170] "If the Establishment Clause barred the extension of general benefits to religious groups," Justice Powell added in *Widmar,* " 'a church could not be protected by the police and fire departments, or have its public sidewalk kept in repair.' "[171]

The Court could not agree on an opinion in *McDaniel,* and *Widmar* invoked freedom of expression rather than of religion. Nevertheless the message was unmistakable: the establishment clause did not require discrimination against religion, and other clauses of the same amendment forbade it.[172]

On the other side of the equation, *Stone v. Graham*[173] and *Grand Rapids School District v. Ball*[174] demonstrated that, despite *Walz,* government was still not supposed to promote religion either. Understandably unable to find any secular reason for posting the Ten Commandments in public classrooms, the Court in *Stone* pronounced the state's very purpose illegitimate: "It does not matter that the posted copies of the Ten Commandments are financed by voluntary private contributions, for the mere posting of the copies under the auspices of the legislature provides the 'official support of the State . . . Government' that the Establishment Clause prohibits."[175]

There was no want of secular purpose in *Grand Rapids,* where the state had sent public employees into parochial schools to teach secular subjects. Nevertheless, as the opinion observed, the case was the mirror image of *McCollum v. Board of Education,* which had held that private teachers could not offer religious instruction in public schools.[176] In either case, Justice Brennan wrote, the sharing of space created the appearance that religious and public instruction were part of " 'a joint enterprise.' "[177] Thus the shared-time programs failed not the first prong of the *Lemon* test but the second: "[T]he conclusion is inescapable that [they] have the 'primary or principal' effect of advancing religion."[178] There was

---

[170] *See* 435 U.S. at 628-29 (opinion of Burger, C. J., joined by Powell, Rehnquist, and Stevens); *id.* at 639-41 (Brennan, J., joined by Marshall, J., concurring); *id.* at 642-43 (Stewart, J., concurring). Justice White, *id.* at 643-46, based his concurrence on equally convincing equal protection grounds. *Contrast* Larkin v. Grendel's Den, Inc., 459 U.S. 116, 127 (1982) (Burger, C.J, over a Rehnquist dissent) (striking down a provision that gave only churches and schools a veto over the grant of liquor licenses on neighboring premises) ("The Framers did not set up a system of government in which important, discretionary governmental powers would be delegated to or shared with religious institutions.").

[171] 454 U.S. at 274-75 (quoting Roemer v. Board of Public Works, note 154 *supra*).

[172] *See* Marty, *supra* note 157, at 183 (viewing *McDaniel* as a welcome step toward reviving neutrality).

[173] 449 U.S. 39 (1980) (per curiam).

[174] 473 U.S. 373 (1985) (over four dissents).

[175] 449 U.S. at 42. Justice Rehnquist, dissenting, *id.* at 43-47, took the state at its word that the display served the secular purpose of informing pupils of a document that had "had a significant impact on the development of secular legal codes of the Western World," but the context was against him. *Cf.* Epperson v. Arkansas, p. 445 *supra* (finding no secular reason for forbidding the teaching of evolution in public schools). Justice Stewart also dissented, 449 U.S. at 43; Burger and Blackmun, *id.,* objected to deciding the case without plenary consideration.

[176] *See* p. 342 *supra*.

[177] *See* 473 U.S. at 392 (quoting Judge Friendly's opinion in a companion case below).

[178] *Id.* at 397.

room for argument as to the Court's application of principle to the facts but no doubt what the Court's principle was: as the prayer cases and *Stone* had made clear, government was not permitted to make any "endorsement" of religion.[179]

It remained to reaffirm that, despite *Yoder,* the free exercise clause did not generally require religious exemptions from generally applicable laws. This the Court did in *United States v. Lee,* which held that religious objections did not free Amish from payment of Social Security taxes,[180] and in the 1986 case of *Goldman v. Weinberger,* which held that religious scruples did not excuse compliance with military dress regulations.[181]

In comparison with the powerful interest in education that the Court had subordinated to religious freedom in *Yoder,* the air force's "considered professional judgment . . . that the traditional outfitting of personnel in standardized uniforms encourages the subordination of personal preferences and identities in favor of the overall group mission"[182] sounds trivial indeed in its application to the case. As Justice Brennan said in dissent, "[t]he contention that the discipline of the Armed Forces will be subverted if Orthodox Jews are allowed to wear yarmulkes with their uniforms surpasses belief."[183]

Justice Rehnquist attempted to blunt the impact of the decision by insisting that review of military regulations was "far more deferential" than review of those applicable to civilians.[184] This notion of special deference in military matters had been a pervasive theme during the Burger years,[185] but it seems fundamentally misguided. If military regulations are often easier to uphold than their civilian counterparts, the only tenable explanation is that the military context enhances the government's interest in adopting them.[186] But the government's interest was a puny one in *Goldman;* if balancing was the test, *Goldman* was a preposterous decision. The result can be defended only by viewing the case as another major step toward restoring the neutrality rule.

[179] *Id.* at 390.

[180] 455 U.S. 252, 260 (1982) (Burger, C. J.) ("The tax system could not function if denominations were allowed to challenge the tax system because tax payments were spent in a manner that violates their religious belief."). *See also id.* at 263 & n. 3 (Stevens, J., concurring) (noting that the decision cast doubt on *Yoder* and arguing that "there is virtually no room for a 'constitutionally required exemption' on religious grounds from a valid tax law that is entirely neutral in its general application").

[181] 475 U.S. 503 (1986).

[182] *Id.* at 508.

[183] *Id.* at 517 (Brennan, J., joined by Marshall, J., dissenting). Blackmun and O'Connor also dissented, *id.* at 524-28, 528-33, making the decision five to four. The other side of the balance similarly favored the claim of exemption; as Justice Brennan observed, Dr. Goldman "was asked to violate the tenets of his faith virtually every minute of every workday." *Id.* at 514.

[184] *Id.* at 507.

[185] *See, e.g.,* Rostker v. Goldberg, p. 497 *supra;* Parker v. Levy, pp. 516-17, note 70 *supra.*

[186] *See* 475 U.S. at 530 (O'Connor, J., joined by Marshall, J., dissenting) ("[W]hen the government attempts to deny a free exercise claim, it must show that an unusually important interest is at stake [and] that granting the requested exemption will do substantial harm to that interest. . . . There is no reason why these general principles should not apply in the military, as well as the civilian, context."). *See also* Brown v. Glines, 444 U.S. 348 (1980) (Powell, J.) (upholding a requirement of prior approval for circulation of petitions by service personnel on military bases on the basis of "the substantial governmental interest" in discipline, *id.* at 354-55, without mention of any special deference to the military).

## 2. *Mueller v. Allen*

Seeking a way to support parochial education without offending *Lemon,* Minnesota permitted deduction of tuition costs in computing a state income tax. The strategy succeeded; a divided Court upheld the deductions in *Mueller v. Allen* in 1983.[187]

As Justice Rehnquist said, there was no doubt that the deduction served the legitimate purposes of promoting and diversifying secular education.[188] Furthermore, because the *entire* cost of tuition was deductible, there was no need to separate the costs of religious and secular instruction and thus no entanglement like that which had proved fatal in *Lemon.*[189] The difficulty was that in the absence of such separation the tax benefit promoted not only secular but also religious activities. The contrast was striking: *Lemon* had forbidden the state to support even secular instruction; *Mueller* allowed it to support religious instruction as well.[190]

One basis for distinguishing earlier decisions striking down aid to parochial education, wrote Justice Rehnquist, was that in "all but one" of them assistance had been given to the schools directly. The tax benefits in *Mueller,* in contrast, were given to the pupils' parents; religion was aided only by virtue of the private decision to send children to parochial schools.[191] Even direct subsidies, however, are likely to depend on the number of pupils and thus on the same private choices. In conceding both that the practical effect of the deductions was "comparable" to that of a subsidy[192] and that the effect of a measure posing no problems of purpose or entanglement was determinative,[193] Rehnquist seemed to undermine his own position.[194]

The distinction between aid to parents and aid to schools, however, was an afterthought;[195] Justice Rehnquist had already explained the decision on the more attractive ground of neutrality. The state allowed deductions for all pupils, not just for those in parochial schools. Moreover, it allowed deductions for charitable and medical expenses as well.[196] The principle was clear: when the state affords benefits to the public generally, it need not discriminate against religious activities.[197]

---

[187] 463 U.S. 388 (1983).

[188] *Id.* at 395.

[189] *See id.* at 403.

[190] *See id.* at 416-17 (Marshall, J., joined by Brennan, Blackmun, and Stevens, dissenting).

[191] *Id.* at 399. The one acknowledged exception was Committee for Public Education v. Nyquist, 413 U.S. 756 (1973), which Rehnquist distinguished, 463 U.S. at 398, on the ground that the tax-benefit program there in question had not been available to children in *public* schools—who as Marshall pointed out in dissent, *id.* at 408-09, had no tuition expenses to deduct. Justice Rehnquist's distinction was also difficult to reconcile with Wolman v. Walter, 433 U.S. 229 (1977), which had struck down a provision for furnishing educational materials and equipment to pupils rather than to the schools themselves. Meek v. Pittenger, 421 U.S. 349 (1975), on the other hand, had appeared to draw the same distinction that *Mueller* drew in upholding aid to pupils but not to schools. These and other precedents are collected in note 166 *supra.*

[192] 463 U.S. at 399.

[193] *Id.* at 394 (quoting the three-pronged *Lemon* test, p. 531 *supra*).

[194] For a notable effort to defend the distinction between direct and indirect aid see McConnell, *supra* note 108, at 454-56 (suggesting, among other things, that it "serves as a low-cost proxy" for the "more subtle and important distinction" discussed immediately below).

[195] *See* 463 U.S. at 399 ("We also agree with the Court of Appeals that. . . .").

[196] *Id.* at 396-99.

[197] *See id.* at 398-99 ("[A] program . . . that neutrally provides state assistance to a broad spectrum of citizens is not readily subject to challenge under the Establishment Clause.").

This had been the teaching of *Everson,* where state-subsidized buses had been permitted to carry pupils to schools providing religious as well as secular instruction.[198] It was the lesson of *Widmar,* which, in holding that religious activities could not be excluded from a school auditorium, had made clear that they need not be.[199] It was reconfirmed in *Witters v. Washington Dept. of Services for the Blind,* which permitted a student to finance his preparation for the ministry out of a general state program of aid to the blind.[200] The same theory even provides an arguable justification for the otherwise troublesome exemption of religious property from taxation in *Walz:* as the Court noted in its opinion, similar benefits had been extended to other nonprofit organizations.[201] If the church burns, Justice Black had said in *Everson,* the state may put out the fire.[202]

The governing principle, in other words, was not that religion may not be supported; it was that religion may not be preferred. The policy of the religion clauses is furthered, not offended, by permitting religion to share equally in the benefits of government programs serving legitimate secular goals.

## C.   The Shadow of History

Like other cases of the period, *Mueller* thus helped clear the way for a return to the salutary position that the first amendment requires neither discrimination in favor of religion as in *Yoder* nor against it as arguably in *Lemon,* but rather neutrality. The ink was hardly dry on the *Mueller* opinion, however, when yet another strain appeared: a tendency to uphold state action that appeared to have no purpose or effect save the supposedly illegitimate one of promoting religion.

In *Marsh v. Chambers,* in 1983, the Court held that Nebraska could constitutionally pay a Presbyterian minister to open each session of the legislature with prayer.[203] No pretense was made that legislative prayers served anything but religious purposes; as Justice Brennan argued in dissent, the practice seemed to offend all three branches of the test laid down in *Lemon.*[204]

The Court's answer was history. The same Congress that had proposed the first amendment, the Chief Justice wrote, had appointed and paid a chaplain. "It can hardly be thought," he concluded, "that in the same week Members of the First Congress . . . intended the Establishment Clause . . . to forbid what they had just declared acceptable."[205] Justice Brennan responded bravely that Congress might indeed have been inconsistent, that it was the states and not Congress that had given the amendment legal force, and that the meaning of the clause might change over time.[206] The Chief Justice's history remained

---

[198] *See* pp. 339-42 *supra.*

[199] *See* pp. 531-32 *supra.*

[200] 474 U.S. 481 (1986) (Marshall, J., for a unanimous Court). Justice Powell, *id.* at 490-92, concurred specially to point out that the result was strongly supported by *Mueller,* on which Marshall (a dissenter in that case) had conspicuously omitted to rely.

[201] 397 U.S. at 671, 673. *See also id.* at 687, 689 (Brennan, J., concurring); *id.* at 696-97 (Harlan, J., concurring).

[202] *See Everson,* 330 U.S. at 17-18; pp. 339-42 *supra.*

[203] 463 U.S. 783 (1983).

[204] *See id.* at 795-801 (Brennan, J., joined by Marshall, J., dissenting).

[205] *Id.* at 786-91.

[206] *Id.* at 813-17 (Brennan, J., dissenting).

powerful evidence that the appointment of legislative chaplains was consistent with the first amendment.[207]

The *Marsh* opinion and the history on which it relied suggest more than the relatively trivial conclusion that legislatures may appoint chaplains. They cast more than a little doubt on *Everson's* basic theory that the clause forbids evenhanded government promotion of religion. If the state may sponsor prayers in the legislature, it is not obvious why it should not be able to do so in the schools. Possibly, as Justice Reed had belatedly argued in his dissent in *McCollum*,[208] the first amendment forbade only the establishment of a particular denomination after all.[209]

The year after *Marsh*, in *Lynch v. Donnelly,* the Court upheld the right of a city to erect a Christmas display that included a crèche depicting the newborn Christ.[210] Since, as Justice Brennan argued in dissent, it seemed as difficult to find a secular purpose or effect here as it had been in *Marsh*,[211] the result appeared to confirm the conclusion that there were cases in which the state might promote religion as such. As in *Marsh*, moreover, the Chief Justice adorned the Court's opinion with references to long-standing "governmental sponsorship" of religious manifestations—from Thanksgiving proclamations and the motto In God We Trust to the legislative chaplains in *Marsh* itself.[212]

At the crucial moment, however, the Court shied away from the apparent goal of its reasoning and explained its decision on more traditional if factually unconvincing grounds. "The display is sponsored by the city to celebrate the Holiday and to depict the origins of that Holiday," said the Chief Justice. "These are legitimate secular purposes."[213] If this unexpected turn suggested a new readiness to find secular purposes where ordinary mortals had difficulty detecting them, it also suggested that *Marsh's* historical approach was not to be given the weight that the opinion in that case had appeared to portend.

The Court confirmed the latter inference in *Wallace v. Jaffree,* which, despite the chaplain and crèche decisions, struck down an Alabama statute authorizing public schools to set aside one minute a day "for meditation or voluntary prayer."[214] There could be little doubt that a moment of silence served the legitimate secular goals of rest and contemplation.[215] The Sunday-law cases thus suggested that, even on the established test of secular purpose and effect, a law providing for silence without more would be upheld.[216]

---

[207] *Compare* the use of history to sustain tax exemptions of church property in *Walz,* note 144 *supra.*

[208] *See* p. 342 *supra.*

[209] Even on this view, as Justice Stevens observed in a separate dissent, there was difficulty in upholding the provision in *Marsh,* for a single Presbyterian minister had held the chaplain's post for sixteen years. 463 U.S. at 822-24 (Stevens, J., dissenting).

[210] 465 U.S. 668 (1984).

[211] *Id.* at 694-726 (Brennan, J., joined by Marshall, Blackmun, and Stevens, dissenting) (adding that the display offended the effect and entanglement aspects of the *Lemon* test as well).

[212] *See id.* at 673-78. The additional reference to the display of religious paintings in the National Gallery, *id.* at 676-77, seems out of place; no one ever doubted the government could employ religious works for secular educational purposes. *See id.* at 712 (Brennan, J., dissenting); Stone v. Graham, 449 U.S. 39, 42 (1980).

[213] 465 U.S. at 681. *See also id.* at 687-94 (O'Connor, J., concurring on the equally tenuous ground that the city could not be said to have endorsed religion). *Contrast* Grand Rapids School Dist. v. Ball, p. 532 *supra.*

[214] 472 U.S. 38 (1985).

[215] *See id.* at 70-74 (O'Connor, J., concurring).

[216] *See* McGowan v. Maryland, p. 410 *supra* (upholding a law limiting retail sales on Sunday). The parties in *Jaffree* abandoned any challenge to the validity of a separate provision setting aside time for "meditation" alone, 472 U.S. at 40-41 & n. 2.

The Alabama law, however, explicitly authorized schools to reserve time for "voluntary prayer." Especially since Alabama already had a law providing for a period of "meditation," the express reference to prayer suggested that the state "intended to characterize prayer as a favored practice."[217] Thus, Justice Stevens concluded, the statute was invalid for the same reason that had condemned earlier provisions for school prayers: "[T]he First Amendment requires that a statute must be invalidated if it is entirely motivated by a purpose to advance religion."[218]

In dissent, Justice Rehnquist protested, as *Marsh* had suggested, that a religious purpose was no longer fatal: "[N]othing in the Establishment Clause requires government to be strictly neutral between religion and irreligion."[219] Justice Stevens made no effort to distinguish *Marsh;* his opinion reads as though that case had never been decided.

It may be that the history in *Marsh* was thought to justify only the practice of legislative chaplains that Congress had expressly endorsed, not to establish a general principle permitting government support of religion. It may be that, as Justice Brennan suggested of the word "God" in the national motto and in the Pledge of Allegiance, legislative prayers were thought to have lost their religious significance.[220] It may be that, unlike schoolchildren, legislators were thought to need all the help they could get.[221]

The one thing that seems clear after *Jaffree* is that, as Justice Brennan had predicted, *Marsh* was a minor aberration and not—so far as the then members of the Court were concerned—the first stage of a revolution.[222] Chief Justice Burger's argument in *Marsh,* however, is no less thought provoking for having been ignored. As Justice Rehnquist said in his dissent in *Jaffree,*

> George Washington himself, at the request of the very Congress which passed the Bill of Rights, proclaimed a day of "public thanksgiving and prayer, to be observed by acknowledging with grateful hearts the many and signal favors of Almighty God." History must judge whether it was the Father of his Country

[217] *Id.* at 58-60. *But see* McConnell, *supra* note 165, at 46 (noting that the state had made no effort to influence how the children spent their minute of silence) ("The addition of the words 'or voluntary prayer' does no more than indicate that prayer is one of the permissible uses of the time.").

[218] 472 U.S. at 56. The Court buttressed its conclusion with explicit statements of the bill's sponsor both in the Senate Journal and in court that his purpose had been " 'to return voluntary prayer to our public schools.' " *Id.* at 43, 56-57. Even apart from the fact that the statements in question had been made after passage of the legislation, *see id.* at 86-87 (Burger, C. J., dissenting), it was most unusual for the Court—for reasons long ago adumbrated in Fletcher v. Peck, 10 U.S. 87, 129-30 (1810), THE FIRST HUNDRED YEARS at 129—to look beyond the text of the legislation and the absence of any conceivable legitimate purpose in searching for improper legislative motivation. *See also* Hunter v. Underwood, 471 U.S. 222, 228-33 (1985) (Rehnquist, J.) (relying on the presiding officer's announcement that the purpose of Mississippi's 1901 constitutional convention was to establish white supremacy in finding that a facially neutral and plausible provision disenfranchising persons convicted of crimes evincing "moral turpitude" was racially motivated and thus contrary to the fourteenth [*sic*] amendment).

[219] 472 U.S. at 113 (Rehnquist, J., dissenting) (reviewing the history of the provision in detail). Justice White, acknowledging that he had been "out of step with many of the Court's decisions dealing with this subject matter," suggested he would support a "basic reconsideration" of the precedents in light of Rehnquist's opinion. *Id.* at 91 (White, J., dissenting).

[220] *See Marsh,* 463 U.S. at 795-96, 818 (Brennan, J., dissenting) (retracting his earlier suggestion in Abington School Dist. v. Schempp, 374 U.S. 203, 299-300 (1963) (concurring opinion), that legislative prayers fell into this category).

[221] *See Jaffree,* 472 U.S. at 85 (Burger, C. J., dissenting).

[222] *See Marsh,* 463 U.S. at 795-96 (Brennan, J., dissenting).

in 1789, or a majority of the Court today, which has strayed from the meaning
of the Establishment Clause.[223]

## III.  ADMINISTRATIVE PROCEDURE

Due process had long been understood to mean, among other things, fair procedure.[224]
The text of the relevant provisions, however, made clear that due process was required
only when the government sought to deprive someone of "life, liberty, or property."[225]

Historically speaking, "life, liberty, and property" was a paraphrase of Magna Charta's
reference to destruction, imprisonment, and disseisin, the traditional punishments for
crime.[226] Before the end of the nineteenth century, however, the Supreme Court had departed from a strict historical interpretation by construing "liberty" to include freedom of
contract,[227] and later cases had held it included most of the substantive provisions of the
Bill of Rights as well.[228] By 1951 Justice Frankfurter could plausibly imply that "life,
liberty, or property" was merely a poetic way of describing everything that was of significant value: "[T]he right to be heard before being condemned to suffer grievous loss of any
kind . . . is a principle basic to our society."[229]

Frankfurter had not spoken for a majority, however, and other decisions had taken a
narrower view. Just the year before, for example, *United States ex rel. Knauff v. Shaughnessy* had held that an alien could be excluded from the country without hearing because
the admission of aliens was "a privilege granted . . . upon such terms as the United States
shall prescribe."[230] Similarly, in *Bailey v. Richardson,* where the lower court had flatly
proclaimed that "Government employ is not 'property,'" the Supreme Court affirmed by
an equally divided vote.[231] Liberty and property, the Court seemed to be saying, did not
include benefits the government had no constitutional duty to provide.[232]

---

[223] 472 U.S. at 113 (Rehnquist, J., dissenting).

[224] *See* pp. 246-49 *supra* (discussing Powell v. Alabama and related cases).

[225] U. S. CONST. amends. V, XIV.

[226] *See* Shattuck, *The True Meaning of the Term "Liberty" in Those Clauses in the Federal and State Constitutions Which Protect "Life, Liberty, and Property,"* 4 HARV. L. REV. 365 (1890).

[227] *See* Allgeyer v. Louisiana, pp. 45-47 *supra.*

[228] *See* pp. 252-53 *supra.*

[229] Joint Anti-Fascist Committee v. McGrath, 341 U.S. 123, 168 (1951) (Frankfurter, J., concurring) (arguing
that publication of the "Attorney General's list" of "subversive" organizations offended the due process clause of
the fifth amendment), p. 357, note 161 *supra.*

[230] 338 U.S. 537, 542 (1950) (Minton, J., over four dissents on statutory grounds). *See also* the extensive
early learning on the distinction between "vested rights" and mere "expectancies" (such as the possibility of
inheritance) that did not qualify as "property" for due process purposes. *E.g.,* Green v. Edwards, 31 R. I. 24, 77
A. 188, 197 (1910) (dictum); 2 T. COOLEY, CONSTITUTIONAL LIMITATIONS 752 (8th ed. 1927).

[231] 341 U.S. 918 (1951), *affirming* 182 F.2d 46 (D.C. Cir. 1950).

[232] In holding that access to a naval installation could be denied without a hearing in Cafeteria & Restaurant
Workers Union v. McElroy, 367 U.S. 886, 894 (1961), the Court professed to recede from this position: "This
question cannot be answered by easy assertion that, because she had no constitutional right to be there in the first
place, she was not deprived of liberty or property in the Superintendent's action." Nevertheless the same philosophy seemed to inform the conclusion (over four dissents) that due process had not been denied: "Where it has
been possible to characterize [the] private interest . . . as a mere privilege subject to the Executive's plenary
power, it has traditionally been held that notice and hearing are not constitutionally required." *Id.* at 895. *See also
id.* at 896 (adding that "[t]he Court has consistently recognized that . . . the interest of a government employee
in retaining his job can be summarily denied").

It was the Burger Court that first extended the concepts of property and liberty to afford procedural protection to interests that had previously been dismissed as mere "privileges."

## A.   Demise of the Privilege Doctrine

It all began with Justice Brennan's opinion for the Court in *Goldberg v. Kelly* in 1970, where the issue had not even been raised.[233] New York law permitted termination of individual welfare payments without a prior evidentiary hearing. The state did not deny that the due process clause was applicable,[234] but Justice Brennan hastened to confirm that it was. Welfare benefits, he argued, "are a matter of statutory entitlement for persons qualified to receive them. Their termination involves state action that adjudicates important rights."[235] It might therefore be "realistic . . . to regard welfare entitlements as more like 'property' than a 'gratuity.' "[236]

The obvious obstacle to this conclusion was the privilege doctrine. Since the government was not required to provide welfare benefits at all, the precedents seemed to establish that they were not "property."[237] But "[t]he constitutional challenge cannot be answered," said Justice Brennan, "by an argument that public assistance benefits are 'a "privilege" and not a "right." ' "[238] Decisions restricting the denial of such "privileges" as unemployment compensation, tax exemption, and public employment had shown that there were constitutional limitations on the power of government to withhold even that which it had no obligation to give; there was no reason, he concluded, to hold otherwise as to "the withdrawal of public assistance."[239]

That the government was subject to constitutional limitations in handing out privileges, however, did not prove they were "property." In two of the three decisions on which Justice Brennan relied, the denial of a privilege had been struck down because in effect it punished the individual for exercising a distinct constitutional right that was not a matter of governmental grace. *Sherbert v. Verner* had held that denying unemployment compensation to a Sabbatarian unwilling to work on Saturday infringed his freedom of religion,[240] *Speiser v. Randall* that veterans' tax exemptions could not be conditioned on affirmative proof of loyalty because "discriminatory denial of a tax exemption for engaging in speech is a limitation on speech."[241] *Shapiro v. Thompson*, which Justice Brennan quoted for the irrelevance of the right-privilege distinction in the context of welfare benefits, was if anything even less compelling; an equal protection case, it had turned upon a constitutional provision whose applicability did not depend on the existence of "liberty" or "property" at all.[242]

---

[233] 397 U.S. 254 (1970).

[234] *Id.* at 261-62.

[235] *Id.* at 262.

[236] *Id.* at 262 n.8.

[237] *See id.* at 275 (Black, J., dissenting) ("It somewhat strains credulity to say that the government's promise of charity to an individual is property belonging to that individual when the government denies that the individual is honestly entitled to receive such a payment."). Burger and Stewart also dissented, *id.* at 282-85, but neither made this point explicitly.

[238] *Id.* at 262 (quoting Shapiro v. Thompson, 394 U.S. 618, 627 n.6 (1969)).

[239] 397 U.S. at 262.

[240] *See* pp. 445-46 *supra.*

[241] *See* p. 393, note 120 *supra.*

[242] *Shapiro* invalidated a durational residency requirement for welfare benefits. *See* p. 433 *supra.*

There remained *Slochower v. Board of Higher Education,* where the Court had held a public employee could not be fired for invoking his constitutional privilege against self-incrimination.[243] By modern standards this might have been just another unconstitutional-condition case like *Sherbert* and *Speiser,* for the state may not deny privileges discriminatorily to punish the exercise of a constitutional right. This had not been the basis of *Slochower,* however; in finding the board had acted arbitrarily the Court seemed to have treated the job itself as property.[244]

The force of *Slochower* as a precedent on this issue, however, was impaired by the failure of the Court in that case even to discuss the question. If *Goldberg* was right that "privileges" might be "property," it could only be because the purposes of the due process clause embraced them.

To that issue Justice Brennan devoted an interesting footnote. "Much of the existing wealth in this country," he argued, "takes the form of rights that do not fall within traditional common-law concepts of property."[245] There was the same need for fair procedure to protect the new wealth as to protect the old, he seemed to be saying; as "commerce" had been held to include telegraphy, and copyrightable "writings," photographs,[246] "property" included government benefits to which the applicant was legally entitled.

## B.   Later Property Cases

The new test was promptly applied to protect such entitlements as drivers' licenses[247] and tenured public employment.[248] Justices Douglas and Marshall to the contrary notwithstanding,[249] however, *Goldberg* did not mean that the denial of a government job always triggered the due process requirement. Justice Brennan had emphasized in that case that the law created an "entitlement" to welfare benefits for those who met its criteria. What that meant was spelled out in *Board of Regents v. Roth* in 1972.[250]

In *Roth,* as in the companion case of *Perry v. Sindermann,* a college teacher had been refused reemployment without a hearing. In *Roth* itself, where the teacher's contract had expired, relief was denied. In *Perry,* where there was a plausible claim that informal agreements had given the teacher tenure, the case was remanded to determine that question.[251]

---

[243] *See* pp. 386-88 *supra.*

[244] *See also* Wieman v. Updegraff, pp. 357-58 *supra* (taking a similar tack in striking down an overbroad exclusion of alleged subversives from public employment); Bolling v. Sharpe, pp. 378-79 *supra* (striking down public school segregation in the District of Columbia on the basis of the fifth amendment's due process clause). In *Wieman* the issue of liberty or property was not addressed; in *Bolling* the Court said without explanation that liberty "extends to the full range of conduct which the individual is free to pursue. . . ." 347 U.S. at 499.

[245] 397 U.S. at 262 n.8 (citing Reich, *Individual Rights and Social Welfare: The Emerging Legal Issues,* 74 YALE L.J. 1245 (1965), and Reich, *The New Property,* 73 YALE L.J. 733 (1964)).

[246] Pensacola Tel. Co. v. Western Union Tel. Co., 96 U.S. 1 (1878); Burrow-Giles Lithographic Co. v. Sarony, 111 U.S. 53 (1884). *See* THE FIRST HUNDRED YEARS at 429-30, 435.

[247] Bell v. Burson, 402 U.S. 535 (1971) (Brennan, J.).

[248] Connell v. Higginbotham, 403 U.S. 207 (1971) (per curiam); Perry v. Sindermann, 408 U.S. 593 (1972) (Stewart, J.).

[249] Board of Regents v. Roth, 408 U.S. 564, 584 (1972) (Douglas, J., dissenting); *id.* at 588-89 (Marshall, J., dissenting).

[250] 408 U.S. 564 (1972). Justice Brennan, *id.* at 604-05, voted with Douglas and Marshall, *see* note 249 *supra,* in dissent.

[251] *See* note 248 *supra.*

Not every hope of a government benefit, Justice Stewart explained, constituted "property"; there must be, as in *Goldberg*, "a legitimate claim of entitlement." The Constitution did not create property interests but merely protected those created by some "independent source such as state law."[252] Stewart intimated that the distinction had something to do with the protection of legitimate expectations,[253] and the language of the Constitution seems to support him: the term "property" suggests that to which one has a legal claim.[254]

Benefits whose bestowal lay in the discretion of an administrator, therefore, did not qualify as "property."[255] In *Arnett v. Kennedy*, moreover, three Justices offered an interpretation of the entitlement test that threatened to disembowel it altogether. Although the statute in question gave a civil service employee the right not to be discharged without "cause," Justice Rehnquist argued, "the very section . . . which granted him that right . . . expressly provided also for the procedure by which 'cause' was to be determined. . . . [T]he property interest which appellee had in this employment was itself conditioned by the procedural limitations which had accompanied the grant of that interest."[256]

This argument, as Justice Marshall protested, was a new formulation of the privilege doctrine that *Goldberg* and later decisions had rejected, for each of those cases had held that due process required procedures beyond those the law had provided.[257] Property, the majority in *Kennedy* insisted, was a substantive concept independent of the procedures prescribed by state law. "While the legislature may elect not to confer a property interest in federal employment," said Justice Powell, "it may not constitutionally authorize the deprivation of such an interest, once conferred, without appropriate procedural safeguards."[258] The policy of the due process clauses, in other words, was that substantive legal rights should not be denied without adequate procedural protection; that the Consti-

---

[252] 408 U.S. at 577.

[253] "It is a purpose of the ancient institution of property to protect those claims upon which people rely in their daily lives. . . ." *Id.* at 577.

[254] *See also* Goss v. Lopez, 419 U.S. 565 (1975) (White, J., over four dissents) (finding entitlement to continued public education absent misconduct); Barry v. Barchi, 443 U.S. 55, 65 (1979) (White, J.) (finding entitlement to retain horse-training license during good behavior). For an argument that the due process clause itself should be read to create property rights see Tushnet, *The Newer Property: Suggestion for the Revival of Substantive Due Process*, 1975 SUP. CT. REV. 261.

[255] *See also* Bishop v. Wood, 426 U.S. 341, 344-46 (1976) (Stevens, J.), where the majority over four understandably warm dissents deferred to lower federal courts that had interpreted a provision authorizing dismissal of a policeman who "fail[ed] to perform work up to the standard of the classification held, or continue[d] to be negligent, inefficient, or unfit to perform his duties" to mean that he "held his position at the will and pleasure of the city"; O'Bannon v. Town Court Nursing Center, 447 U.S. 773 (1980) (Stevens, J., over a Brennan dissent) (finding residents of a nursing home to have no entitlement to continued government support of their institution). *See also* the suggestion in Rakoff, Brock v. Roadway Express, Inc., *and the New Law of Regulatory Due Process*, 1987 SUP. CT. REV. 157, 174-75, that the *Roth* distinction was "out of tune with the vast body of administrative law which considered control of administrative discretion as its *raison d'être*."

[256] 416 U.S. 134, 152, 155 (1974) (opinion of Rehnquist, J., joined by Burger and Stewart).

[257] *Id.* at 210-11 (Marshall, J., joined by Douglas and Brennan, dissenting from the holding that the procedure satisfied due process). *See also* Shapiro, *Mr. Justice Rehnquist: A Preliminary View*, 90 HARV. L. REV. 293, 322-24 (1976).

[258] 416 U.S. at 167 (Powell, J., joined by Blackmun, concurring). *See also id.* at 185 (White, J., concurring in part) ("While the State may define what is and what is not property, once having defined those rights the Constitution defines due process. . . ."). The three Justices who thought the statutory procedures insufficient, of course, took the same view. *See* note 257 *supra*.

tution was indifferent to whether a particular right was created did not mean it was silent as to the procedure for taking it away.[259]


## C. Liberty

The legal entitlement test, which had originated as an interpretation of "property," was soon applied to "liberty" as well. The procedure for revoking parole, the Chief Justice wrote in *Morrissey v. Brewer,* must satisfy due process because, among other things, "[t]he parolee has relied on at least an implicit promise that parole will be revoked only if he fails to live up to the parole conditions."[260] A legal entitlement thus might qualify as "liberty" as well as "property."[261]

The historical example of freedom from imprisonment, however, as well as more recent additions such as "liberty of contract" and "privacy,"[262] made it clear that liberty, unlike property, also embraced interests not created by independent sources of state or federal law.[263] Among these interests protected by the "liberty" provision itself, the Court held in *Ingraham v. Wright,* was the interest in "personal security": school children could not be paddled without due process of law.[264]

History, the Court concluded, provided a minimum test of liberty:

> The Due Process Clause . . . was intended to give Americans at least the protection against governmental power that they had enjoyed as Englishmen against the power of the Crown. . . . While the contours of this historic liberty interest in the context of our federal system of government have not been defined precisely, they always have been thought to encompass freedom from bodily restraint and punishment.[265]

---

[259] *Cf.* Curtis v. Loether, 415 U.S. 189 (1974) (Marshall, J.), which reaffirmed the long-standing applicability of the same principle in the area of jury trial: though Congress need not create a damage remedy for housing discrimination, if it does it must provide for trial by jury. For determined criticism of the Court's distinction see Easterbrook, *Substance and Due Process,* 1982 SUP. CT. REV. 85 (arguing, *id.* at 113, that "[t]he Court cannot logically be reticent about revising the substantive rules but unabashed about rewriting the procedures to be followed in administering those rules").

[260] 408 U.S. 471, 482 (1972) (Burger, C. J.).

[261] *See also* Wolff v. McDonnell, 418 U.S. 539, 557 (1974) (White, J.) (statutory entitlement to good-time credits absent misconduct); Greenholtz v. Inmates of Nebraska Penal and Correctional Complex, 442 U.S. 1, 12 (1979) (Burger, C. J.) (entitlement to release on parole if statutory conditions met); Vitek v. Jones, 445 U.S. 480, 489-90 (1980) (White, J.) (entitlement not to be transferred from prison to mental institution absent mental problem). *Contrast* Meachum v. Fano, 427 U.S. 215 (1976) (White, J., over three dissents) (no entitlement to remain in same prison since transfer decision discretionary).

[262] *See* Lochner v. New York, pp. 47-50 *supra;* Roe v. Wade, pp. 465-71 *supra.*

[263] *See also Roth,* 408 U.S. at 572 (quoting a long list of recognized liberties not created by other laws from Meyer v. Nebraska, pp. 153-54 *supra*).

[264] 430 U.S. 651 (1977) (Powell, J.).

[265] *Id.* at 672-74. *Contrast* Hurtado v. California, 110 U.S. 516 (1884) (holding that not all elements of common law procedure were encompassed within the concept of "due process"), THE FIRST HUNDRED YEARS at 366-68.

Several decisions appeared to suggest that the interest in reputation—which Blackstone had said was a part of the right to personal security[266]—was protected as well. "Where a person's good name, reputation, honor, or integrity is at stake because of what the government is doing to him," said the Court in *Wisconsin v. Constantineau,* "notice and an opportunity to be heard are essential." [267] Quoting this passage, *Roth* dismissed a due process argument based on infringement of a teacher's liberty by observing that "[t]he State, in declining to rehire the respondent, did not make any charge against him that might seriously damage his standing and associations in his community." "Had it done so," Justice Stewart concluded, "due process would accord an opportunity to refute the charge. . . ."[268]

It was therefore something of a surprise when, in *Paul v. Davis* in 1976, the Court held that reputation was not part of the "liberty" protected by the fourteenth amendment.[269] The plaintiff alleged that the police had injured him by including his name in a list of "active shoplifters" distributed to local merchants.[270] As Justice Brennan wrote for the dissenters, "the police here have officially imposed on respondent the stigmatizing label 'criminal' without the salutary and constitutionally mandated safeguards of a criminal trial." [271]

For the majority, Justice Rehnquist gave the precedents a narrow reading. *Constantineau,* he noted, had involved more than a mere injury to reputation; in "posting" the plaintiff as an excessive drinker the state had forbidden others to provide her with alcoholic beverages and thus deprived her of a preexisting "right to purchase or obtain liquor. . . ."[272] *Roth*'s suggestion that a government employee might be entitled to a hearing on allegations damaging to his reputation had been limited to statements made "in the course of declining to rehire him"; simple defamation by a state official did not suffice.[273] Finally, said Rehnquist, *Goss v. Lopez,* where the Court had required a rudimentary hearing before school suspension in part because of potential harm to the pupil's reputation, had also emphasized that the suspension had deprived the pupil of his legal right to attend school.[274]

None of this was inaccurate, but it was not highly persuasive. The *Constantineau* opinion had relied only on the injury to reputation, not on the lost right to acquire alcohol.[275]

---

[266] *See* Monaghan, *Of "Liberty" and "Property,"* 62 CORNELL L. REV. 405, 411-14 (1977).

[267] 400 U.S. 433, 437 (1971) (Douglas, J., over four dissents not reaching the merits) (striking down a statute providing for posting the names of persons to whom alcoholic beverages were not to be sold).

[268] 408 U.S. at 573 (adding that mere proof that "his record of nonretention in one job . . . might make him somewhat less attractive to some other employers would hardly establish the kind of foreclosure of opportunities amounting to a deprivation of 'liberty' ").

[269] 424 U.S. 693 (1976).

[270] *Id.* at 694-95.

[271] *Id.* at 718 (Brennan, J., joined by White and Marshall, JJ., dissenting). Justice Stevens, *id.* at 714, did not participate.

[272] *Id.* at 707-09.

[273] *Id.* at 709-10. Even in the context of a discharge from public employment, the Court later held, stigmatizing remarks did not infringe the employee's liberty unless they were made public. Bishop v. Wood, 426 U.S. 341, 347-49 (1976) (Stevens, J., over two dissents on this issue).

[274] *See* Goss v. Lopez, 419 U.S. 565 (1975), *discussed in* 424 U.S. at 710.

[275] *See* Shapiro, *supra* note 257, at 326.

Since the employee in *Roth* had no entitlement to his job, it was unclear why it mattered whether the defamatory remarks the Court had hypothesized were related to the loss of employment. In *Goss* the injury to reputation had been an alternative ground of decision wholly independent of the exclusion from school.[276] Most damaging, however, was the Court's inability to distinguish *Jenkins v. McKeithen,* which had held that due process forbade an executive agency to brand an individual as a criminal without a trial.[277] Justice Brennan highlighted the difficulty in his dissent in *Paul:*

> The logical and disturbing corollary of this holding is that no due process infirmities would inhere in a statute constituting a commission to conduct *ex parte* trials of individuals, so long as the only official judgment pronounced was limited to the public condemnation and branding of a person as a Communist, a traitor, an "active murderer," a homosexual, or any other mark that "merely" carries social opprobrium.[278]

Justice Rehnquist's principal response was that to hold reputation protected would constitutionalize the whole law of government torts:

> [I]t would be difficult to see why the survivors of an innocent bystander mistakenly shot by a policeman or negligently killed by a sheriff driving a government vehicle, would not have claims equally cognizable. . . . We think it would come as a great surprise to those who drafted and shepherded the adoption of th[e Fourteenth] Amendment to learn that it worked such a result. . . .[279]

Justice Brennan's riposte was crushing:

> [T]he Court's opinion confuses the two separate questions of whether reputation is a "liberty" or "property" interest and whether, in a particular context, state action with respect to that interest is a violation of due process. . . . There is simply no way in which the Court . . . could declare that the loss of a person's life is not an interest cognizable within the "life" portion of the Due Process Clause.[280]

---

[276] *See Goss,* 419 U.S. at 567-75.

[277] 395 U.S. 411 (1969). *See* 424 U.S. at 725-29 (Brennan, J., dissenting) (discussing *Jenkins*). The majority, *id.* at 706 n.4, said only that *Paul* did not involve, in the words of the dissenters in *Jenkins,* " 'an agency whose sole or predominant function . . . is to expose and publicize the names of persons it finds guilty of wrongdoing.' " Why this distinction was relevant to the question whether reputation was protected by the fourteenth amendment, Justice Rehnquist did not say. *See also* Shapiro, *supra* note 257, at 325 ("Since *Jenkins* was very much in point, it is startling that Justice Rehnquist addressed only the dissent in that case, and this only by reference in a footnote.").

[278] 424 U.S. at 721 (Brennan, J., dissenting).

[279] *Id.* at 698-99.

[280] *Id.* at 721 n.8, 717 n.2.

The reason not every accident involving a government truck was a violation of the Constitution, the Court would later explain, was that, in light of history, negligent harm was not a "deprivation" within the meaning of the due process provisions.[281] The reasoning in *Paul* left something to be desired.

## D. That Process Which Is Due

Once it was determined that the state had deprived a person of life, liberty, or property, it was necessary to decide whether the procedures by which the deprivation had been accomplished constituted "due process of law." Decisions since the 1930s, eschewing history as either a minimum or as a limitation, had basically concluded that what was required was what was fair.[282] The Burger Court explicitly held that the question of fairness was to be determined by yet another balancing test and applied it to resolve a number of issues of administrative procedure.

*Mathews v. Eldridge* set forth the governing standard.[283] What procedures due process required, wrote Justice Powell, turned upon "three distinct factors":

> First, the private interest that will be affected by the official action; second, the risk of an erroneous deprivation of such interest through the procedures used, and the probable value, if any, of additional or substitute procedural safeguards; and finally, the Government's interest, including the function involved and the fiscal and administrative burdens that the additional or substitute procedural requirement would entail.[284]

The procedures required by this test varied enormously from one situation to another. In *Goldberg v. Kelly*, for example, where the termination of welfare benefits endangered the recipient's very survival, the Court required many of the safeguards of a prior judicial trial.[285] In *Goss v. Lopez*, on the other hand, where an allegedly misbehaving pupil faced only a brief suspension from school, it was enough that the principal informed him of the grounds for the proposed suspension and gave him a chance to respond on the spot.[286]

---

[281] Daniels v. Williams, 474 U.S. 327 (1986) (Rehnquist, J., for a unanimous Court) (finding no due process violation in injuries caused by the alleged negligence of a prison guard).

[282] *See* pp. 246-49 *supra* (discussing Powell v. Alabama and subsequent cases); International Shoe Co. v. Washington, p. 330 *supra*.

[283] 424 U.S. 319 (1976).

[284] *Id.* at 335. For a useful attempt to be more specific see Friendly, *"Some Kind of Hearing,"* 123 U. PA. L. REV. 1267 (1975); for criticism of the *Mathews* formulation see Mashaw, *The Supreme Court's Due Process Calculation for Administrative Adjudication in* Mathews v. Eldridge: *Three Factors in Search of a Theory of Value*, 44 U. CHI. L. REV. 28 (1976); J. MASHAW, DUE PROCESS IN THE ADMINISTRATIVE STATE (1985), *passim*.

[285] 397 U.S. 254, 266-71 (1970) (notice, opportunity to present evidence, confrontation and cross-examination, right to counsel, record decision, impartial decision-maker). *Contrast* Mathews v. Eldridge, 424 U.S. 319, 340 (1976) (Powell, J., over two dissents) (holding that the procedures *Goldberg* had required were inapplicable to termination of disability payments: "Eligibility for disability benefits . . . is not based upon financial need"). *See* Rakoff, *supra* note 255, at 176 ("It was apparent on the face of *Mathews* that the court intended to cauterize *Goldberg*.").

[286] 419 U.S. 565, 577-84 (1974). *See* note 254 *supra*.

Indeed, in *Ingraham v. Wright* the Court went so far as to hold that schoolchildren could be corporally punished with no prior procedure whatever, although the subsequent tort remedy which the Court held sufficient afforded no redress for an honest mistake of fact.[287]

There were many decisions, and the details are of interest only to the litigants.[288] The significant fact is that it was the Burger Court that by its expansive interpretation of the terms "property" and "liberty" constitutionalized much of administrative procedure.[289]

---

[287] 430 U.S. 651, 674-82 (1977) (Powell, J.). "The logic of this theory," Justice White added for the four dissenters, "would permit a State that punished speeding with a one-day jail sentence to make a driver serve his sentence first without a trial and then sue for damages for wrongful imprisonment." Justice Stevens, who joined White's dissent, opined that the Court's theory might nevertheless provide a more satisfactory rationale for the denial of relief against state defamation in Paul v. Davis, pp. 543-45 *supra* ("It may also be true—although I do not express an opinion on the point—that an adequate state remedy for defamation may satisfy the due process requirement when a State has impaired an individual's interest in his reputation." *Id.* at 701.). The troublesome case of Parratt v. Taylor, 451 U.S. 527 (1981) (Rehnquist, J., over a partial Marshall dissent), applied similar reasoning to hold that a subsequent damage action afforded due process for the negligent loss of property belonging to a prisoner. It was not long before the Court (as Powell's concurrence had suggested in *Parratt*, 451 U.S. at 546-54) found a more satisfactory way of explaining why not every traffic accident involving a public employee was unconstitutional. *See* Daniels v. Williams, note 281 *supra*.

The majority in *Ingraham* also held that paddling of school children was not "cruel and unusual punishment[]" because the relevant constitutional provision protected only "those convicted of crimes." 430 U.S. at 664. To the four dissenters, the Court seemed to be saying that children could be beaten with sticks because they had done nothing wrong: "[I]f it is constitutionally impermissible to cut off someone's ear for the commission of murder, it must be unconstitutional to cut off a child's ear for being late to class." *Id.* at 684 (White, J., joined by Brennan, Marshall, and Stevens, dissenting).

[288] Worthy of brief mention are Richardson v. Perales, 402 U.S. 389, 406-07 (1971) (Blackmun, J., over three statutory dissents), which sensibly concluded that the important right to confront and cross-examine adverse witnesses in a disability proceeding was satisfied by the opportunity to subpoena doctors who had submitted written reports, and Withrow v. Larkin, 421 U.S. 35 (1975) (White, J.), which more disturbingly concluded that it was permissible for the same officials who had investigated charges of professional misconduct to pass upon them in a later proceeding. *See id.* at 56: "It is also very typical for the members of administrative agencies to receive the results of investigations, to approve the filing of charges or formal complaints instituting enforcement proceedings, and then to participate in the ensuing hearings. This mode of procedure . . . does not violate due process of law." *Contrast* the Labor Department study cited by Justice Jackson in construing the Administrative Procedure Act to forbid trial of a deportation case by an officer with investigatory responsibilities and the contingent duty of presenting the government's case in order to avoid a difficult due process question: "A genuinely impartial hearing, conducted with critical detachment, is psychologically improbable if not impossible, when the presiding officer has at once the responsibility of appraising the strength of the case and of seeking to make it as strong as possible." Wong Yang Sung v. McGrath, 339 U.S. 33, 44, 50-51 (1950).

[289] It was also the Burger Court that held due process forbade the state to charge indigents filing fees in divorce cases, Boddie v. Connecticut, 401 U.S. 371, 380-81 (1971) (Harlan, J., over a dissent by Black) (emphasizing that the fee requirement effectively closed to the plaintiffs "the only avenue open for dissolving their allegedly untenable marriages"), and to seize property on the mere allegation that it was wrongfully detained, Fuentes v. Shevin, 407 U.S. 67 (1972) (Stewart, J., for four of the seven participating Justices). After the appointment of Rehnquist and Powell, however, the Court began to limit these decisions. *See* United States v. Kras, 409 U.S. 434, 443-49 (1973) (Blackmun, J., over four dissents) (upholding a requirement that even indigents pay fees in bankruptcy cases because "bankruptcy is not the only method available to a debtor for the adjustment of his legal relationship with his creditors" and because no "fundamental interest" was affected); Ortwein v. Schwab, 410 U.S. 656 (per curiam, over four dissents) (upholding a filing fee in welfare cases); Mitchell v. W. T. Grant Co., 416 U.S. 600, 618 (1974) (White J., over four dissents) (upholding a provision for ex parte pretrial attachment and distinguishing *Fuentes* because of various requirements serving "to minimize the risk of error of a wrongful interim possession by the creditor"). *See also* North Georgia Finishing, Inc. v. Di-Chem, Inc., 419 U.S. 601 (1975) (White, J., over three dissents) (reaffirming *Fuentes* itself). It was also the Burger Court that invented the short-lived fiction that a statutory provision not precisely enough tailored to its purpose effectively rested on an

## IV. CRIME AND PUNISHMENT

What the Burger Court did for administrative procedure its predecessors had already done for criminal trials.[290] Criminal procedure was to be the one area of constitutional law in which the new Justices managed almost from the beginning to cut back on the achievements of the Warren period. At the same time, however, the Court managed in the criminal field yet another step beyond the work of its forebears: a startling moratorium on the long-standing practice of capital punishment.

### A. The Death Penalty

The eighth amendment, which the Court had held the fourteenth made applicable to the states,[291] forbade "cruel and unusual punishments." The fifth and fourteenth amendments, however, clearly contemplated death sentences by providing, among other things, that no person should be deprived of life without due process of law.[292] Consequently the Court had had no difficulty in concluding during the nineteenth century that death by shooting was not "cruel and unusual."[293] As late as 1947 the Court had not only assumed the constitutionality of the death penalty as such but had gone so far as to hold it permissible for a state to electrocute a convicted murderer after an earlier attempt to do so had failed.[294] Justices had often suggested, and the Court had sometimes held, that imposition of the death penalty heightened the need for various procedural safeguards.[295] Before 1969, however, no Justice had ever contended that the death penalty itself was impermissible.[296]

In *Furman v. Georgia,* in 1972, two Justices took that position.[297] Although it might have been constitutional in 1791, wrote Justice Brennan, capital punishment was cruel

---

irrational "irrebuttable presumption"—thus neatly turning what should have been an issue of disfavored substantive due process into a procedural one. *See, e.g.,* Cleveland Board of Educ. v. LaFleur, 414 U.S. 632, 644 (1974) (Stewart, J., over two dissents) (concluding that automatic provisions respecting maternity leave for teachers "amount to a conclusive presumption that every pregnant teacher who reaches the fifth or sixth month of pregnancy is physically incapable of continuing"). The truth of the matter was that the state had presumed nothing; the real issue was whether it was reasonable for the state to dispense with an inquiry into actual disability in the interest of administrative convenience. *See id.* at 651-57 (Powell, J., concurring on equal protection grounds); *cf.* Massachusetts Board of Retirement v. Murgia, p. 494 *supra.* For due process decisions of the period respecting personal jurisdiction and choice of law see pp. 581-82 *infra.*

[290] *See* pp. 246-49, 403-05, 446-50 *supra.*

[291] Robinson v. California, pp. 407-08 *supra.*

[292] The fifth amendment also requires indictment before prosecution for a "capital" offense and forbids placing a person twice in jeopardy of "life" as well as limb.

[293] Wilkerson v. Utah, 99 U.S. 130, 134-36 (1879), THE FIRST HUNDRED YEARS at 447 n.114. *See also In re Kemmler,* 136 U.S. 436, 447 (1890) (saying the same of electrocution while holding the ban on cruel and unusual punishments inapplicable to the states: "Punishments are cruel when they involve torture or a lingering death; but the punishment of death is not cruel, within the meaning of that word as used in the Constitution.").

[294] Louisiana *ex rel.* Francis v. Resweber, 329 U.S. 459 (1947). The four dissenters conceded the constitutionality of electrocution itself. *See id.* at 474 (Burton, J., joined by Douglas, Murphy, and Rutledge, dissenting).

[295] *See, e.g.,* Betts v. Brady, pp. 320-22 *supra* (right to counsel); Reid v. Covert, pp. 401-03 *supra* (right to civilian trial).

[296] *See also* Trop v. Dulles, 356 U.S. 86, 99 (1958) (opinion of Warren, C. J., joined by Black, Douglas, and Whittaker) (dictum) ("[T]he death penalty has been employed throughout our history, and, in a day when it is still widely accepted, it cannot be said to violate the constitutional concept of cruelty.").

[297] 408 U.S. 238 (1972).

and unusual in the 1960s because it no longer "comport[ed] with human dignity": "Death is an unusually severe and degrading punishment; there is a strong probability that it is inflicted arbitrarily; its rejection by contemporary society is virtually total; and there is no reason to believe that it serves any penal purpose more effectively than the less severe punishment of imprisonment."[298] Justice Marshall agreed: the death penalty was excessive, unnecessary, and "morally unacceptable to the people of the United States at this time in their history."[299]

The validity of this position depended not only upon the subjective conclusion that capital punishment was "morally unacceptable" or incompatible with "human dignity," but more fundamentally on the express premise of both Justices that what was "cruel and unusual" might change over time. On this issue both Brennan and Marshall quoted from Chief Justice Warren's opinion for four Justices in *Trop v. Dulles,* which had argued that expatriation was a cruel and unusual punishment: "The Amendment must draw its meaning from the evolving standards of decency that mark the progress of a maturing society."[300]

This had not been the dominant theme in earlier decisions,[301] but it was neither textually nor logically absurd. Granting that the Framers could have bound posterity to their own notions of which punishments were cruel and unusual, the question was whether they had done so. No one having come up with any historical evidence that cast light on this issue, the Justices were left to decide on their own.[302]

The four new appointees—Burger, Blackmun, Powell, and Rehnquist—concluded that capital punishment was still constitutional. Significantly, they conceded that what was "cruel and unusual" could change over time; but they were unable to find that society had so completely rejected the death penalty that it could be said to offend the constitutional standard.[303]

The remaining three Justices, in three separate opinions, took an intermediate position. Whether or not the death penalty might ever be constitutional, they argued, it could not be inflicted under the statutes then before the Court.[304]

---

[298] *Id.* at 305 (Brennan, J., concurring).

[299] *Id.* at 358-60 (Marshall, J., concurring).

[300] *See id.* at 269-70 (Brennan, J., concurring), 329 (Marshall, J., concurring) (both quoting *Trop,* 356 U.S. at 100, p. 407 *supra*). *See also* the dictum in Weems v. United States, 217 U.S. 349, 378 (1910) (quoted by Brennan, 408 U.S. at 270 n.10: "The clause . . . in the opinion of the learned commentators may be . . . progressive, and is not fastened to the obsolete but may acquire meaning as public opinion becomes enlightened by a humane justice."), p. 57 *supra*.

[301] *See* decisions cited in notes 293-94 *supra*. *See also* 1 T. COOLEY, CONSTITUTIONAL LIMITATIONS 694 (8th ed. 1927), *cited in Weems,* 217 U.S. at 375 (arguing it was probable that "any punishment declared by statute for an offense which was punishable in the same way at the common law could not be regarded as cruel or unusual in the constitutional sense").

[302] The issue was reminiscent of the question whether the equal protection clause forbade "separate but equal" facilities for different races. *See* THE FIRST HUNDRED YEARS at 387-90. In the case of capital punishment, however, it was far clearer that the Framers thought the practice constitutional at the time.

[303] *See* 408 U.S. at 375-96 (Burger, C. J., joined by Blackmun, Powell, and Rehnquist, dissenting); *id.* at 405-14 (Blackmun, J., dissenting); *id.* at 414-43 (Powell, J., joined by Burger, Blackmun, and Rehnquist, dissenting); *id.* at 465-70 (Rehnquist, J., joined by Burger, Blackmun, and Powell, dissenting).

[304] Justice Stewart, however, plainly rejected the argument that retribution was a constitutionally impermissible purpose: "When people begin to believe that organized society is unwilling or unable to impose upon

The central flaw, in the opinion of all three Justices, was that the statutes in issue left the decision whether to inflict the death penalty to the discretion of the judge or jury. This discretion, wrote Justice Douglas, "enable[d] the penalty to be selectively applied," and in practice it had been: " 'Application of the death penalty is unequal: most of those executed were poor, young, and ignorant.' "[305] "[O]f all the people convicted of rapes and murders in 1967 and 1968," Justice Stewart added, "the petitioners are among a capriciously selected random handful upon whom the sentence of death has in fact been imposed."[306] "[A]s the statutes before us are now administered," Justice White concluded, "the penalty is so infrequently imposed that the threat of execution is too attenuated to be of substantial service to criminal justice."[307]

Justice White thus thought the infliction of the death penalty in *Furman* pointless, while Douglas and Stewart found it unequal. The dissenters disputed the relevance as well as the correctness of these conclusions.[308] For White as well as Douglas and Stewart, however, the critical facts were the breadth of discretion and the manner in which it had been exercised. As Chief Justice Burger observed in dissent, the argument that juries could not be given discretion in capital cases had been rejected just the year before in *McGautha v. California:* "In light of history, experience, and the present limitations of human knowledge, we find it quite impossible to say that committing to the untrammeled discretion of the jury the power to pronounce life or death in capital cases is offensive to anything in the Constitution."[309] Justice Stewart noted that *McGautha* had considered only due process and equal protection objections;[310] the Chief Justice termed it "disingenuous to suggest" that *McGautha* had not been overruled.[311]

---

criminal offenders the punishment they 'deserve,' then there are sown the seeds of anarchy—of self-help, vigilante justice, and lynch law." 408 U.S. at 308 (Stewart, J., concurring).

[305]*Id.* at 250 (Douglas, J., concurring) (quoting from an empirical study of capital punishment in Texas). *See also id.* at 256 ("A law that stated that anyone making more than $50,000 would be exempt from the death penalty would plainly fall. . . . A law which in the overall view reaches that result in practice has no more sanctity than a law which in terms provides the same.").

[306]*Id.* at 309-10 (Stewart, J., concurring).

[307]*Id.* at 313 (White, J., concurring).

[308]*See id.* at 397, 399 (Burger, C. J., dissenting):

[T]he Eighth Amendment forbids the imposition of punishments that are so cruel and inhuman as to violate society's standards of civilized conduct. The Amendment does not prohibit all punishments the States are unable to prove necessary to deter or control crime. The Amendment is not concerned with the process by which a State determines that a particular punishment is to be imposed in a particular case. . . . Th[e] claim of arbitrariness is not only lacking in empirical support, but it also manifestly fails to establish that the death penalty is a 'cruel and unusual' punishment.

[309]402 U.S. 183, 207 (1971) (Harlan, J.), *quoted in Furman,* 408 U.S. at 399 (Burger, C. J., dissenting). Brennan, joined by Douglas and Marshall, *id.* at 248-312, had argued in *McGautha* that untrammeled discretion offended due process; White and Stewart had joined the majority's opinion.

[310]*See* 408 U.S. at 310 n.12 (Stewart, J., concurring). Justice White did not mention *McGautha;* Justice Douglas thought it inconsistent with the argument against discretion. *See id.* at 248.

[311]*Id.* at 400 (Burger, C. J., dissenting). *See* Polsby, *The Death of Capital Punishment? Furman v. Georgia,* 1972 Sup. Ct. Rev. 1, 26 ("Why Justices Stewart and White found the due process arguments unconvincing in *McGautha* but persuasive in *Furman* is an unusual riddle."). This would not be the last time the Burger Court would hold state action unconstitutional under one provision immediately after upholding it against arguments based on another. *See* pp. 525-26 *supra* (discussing public access to criminal proceedings).

Since discretion in sentencing was the almost universal practice, the result was that virtually every death penalty statute in the country was unconstitutional.[312] If discretion was the problem, however, it could be eliminated by making capital punishment mandatory in specified classes of cases. Yet when several states took the Court up on this suggestion, they were unpleasantly surprised. The existence of discretion had condemned the laws in *Furman;* the absence of discretion was fatal to their successors. A requirement that death always be imposed for first-degree murder, three swing Justices concluded, was Procrustean; by ignoring significant differences among cases in the prescribed category, the law imposed identical punishments for crimes of unequal gravity.[313] Heads I win, the Court seemed to be saying; tails you lose.

It turned out that there was a middle ground. A law that required consideration of specified aggravating and mitigating factors and assured consistency by providing for appellate review, the majority concluded in *Gregg v. Georgia,* avoided Scylla and Charybdis as well.[314]

For those who accept the death penalty, this solution had much to recommend it in policy—though it was not obvious what it had to do with the eighth amendment. It was the work, however, of a small and shifting minority of Justices. Two members of the Court voted consistently to strike down capital punishment in all cases, three just as consistently to uphold it. Douglas and White joined Stewart in voting against excessive discretion; Powell and Stevens joined him in condemning excessive rigidity. The Court's ultimate position had the full support of only one Justice.[315]

## B.    Criminal Procedure

*In re Winship,* decided only a few months after Chief Justice Warren had left the Bench, added one more important strand to the bundle of procedural rights the Court had con-

---

[312] *See id.* at 417 (Powell, J., dissenting).

[313] Woodson v. North Carolina, 428 U.S. 280, 282-305 (1976) (opinion of Stewart, J., joined by Powell and Stevens) (adding that society had condemned mandatory death sentences and that there was still a risk of unequal administration through jury nullification). Brennan and Marshall, *id.* at 305-06, adhered to their argument in *Furman* that the death penalty could never be imposed; White, Burger, Blackmun, and Rehnquist, *id.* at 306-24, dissented.

[314] 428 U.S. 153 (1976). As usual, there was no majority opinion. Only Brennan and Marshall, *id.* at 227-41, dissented. For the suggestion that in later decisions of the Burger period the Court came close to abandoning any effective control over the degree of discretion given to the judge or jury see Wiesberg, *Deregulating Death,* 1983 SUP. CT. REV. 305.

[315] *See also* Coker v. Georgia, 433 U.S. 584 (1977) (over two dissents), and Enmund v. Florida, 458 U.S. 782 (1982) (White, J., over four dissents) (applying the disproportionality test of Weems v. United States, p. 57 *supra,* to strike down capital punishment for rape and for felony murder respectively); Ford v. Wainwright, 477 U.S. 399 (1986) (Marshall, J.) (relying on history and current practice to hold it unconstitutional to execute an insane prisoner). When capital punishment was not involved, however, the Burger Court was initially rather lenient in determining whether the punishment fit the crime. *See* Rummel v. Estelle, 445 U.S. 263 (1980) (Rehnquist, J., over four dissents) (upholding a life sentence for three crimes amounting to "defrauding persons of about $230," *id.* at 307 (Powell, J., dissenting)); Hutto v. Davis, 454 U.S. 370 (1982) (per curiam, over three dissents) (upholding a forty-year sentence for possessing nine ounces of marijuana). In Solem v. Helm, 463 U.S. 277 (1983) (Powell, J., over four dissents), the Court struck down a sentence of life without parole for a habitual offender whose latest crime was the passing of a bad check for $100—suggesting a significant change of attitude on the part of Justice Blackmun, who had been with the majority in both *Rummel* and *Davis.*

structed on the basis of the due process clauses during his tenure: the prosecution was required to prove guilt beyond a reasonable doubt.[316] In other respects, however, it was plain from the beginning that the new Justices were not unduly sympathetic to further expansion of the procedural rights of the accused.

Despite broadsides fired by individual Justices, none of the major procedural protections enunciated by the Warren Court was expressly abandoned. It would be more accurate to say that the Burger Court engaged in a campaign of sapping and mining around the perimeter.[317] The cases are numerous and largely fact-bound; it would be tedious to review them in any detail. The mere fact that so many of them were taken[318]—not infrequently over dissents protesting that they involved nothing more than application of settled principles to the facts[319]—suggests that the new Justices were trying to send a new message to the state and lower federal courts. I shall illustrate these conclusions with examples drawn from two areas: the exclusion of evidence unlawfully seized and the limits on custodial interrogation.

*Mapp v. Ohio*, overruling contrary precedent, had concluded in 1962 that the constitutional ban on unreasonable searches and seizures could not effectively be enforced unless the fruits of its violation were excluded from evidence in state courts.[320] The Burger Court never mustered a majority to abandon *Mapp* itself, though on more than one occasion the Chief Justice called that decision into question.[321] Nevertheless five or more votes

---

[316] 397 U.S. 358, 363 (1970) (Brennan, J.) ("The reasonable-doubt standard . . . is a prime instrument for reducing the risk of convictions resting on factual error."). Justice Black, *id.* at 377-86, dissented on the familiar ground that the due process clause merely required government to act "according to law" and did not give the Justices a roving commission to determine what was fair, *see* pp. 362-63 *supra* (discussing Adamson v. California); Burger and Stewart, 397 U.S. at 375-76, disputed the applicability of the requirement to juvenile proceedings. *See In re* Gault, p. 450 *supra* (holding various procedures required in such proceedings); McKeiver v. Pennsylvania, 403 U.S. 528 (1971) (over three dissents) (holding jury trial not required). Mullaney v. Wilbur, 421 U.S. 684 (1975) (Powell, J.), made clear that the reasonable-doubt requirement applied to every element of the offense charged—in that case the absence of "heat of passion" sufficient to reduce the crime from murder to manslaughter. Patterson v. New York, 432 U.S. 197 (1977) (White, J.), however, held that the state could avoid the requirement simply by making the same element an affirmative defense—a disposition that, as Justice Powell argued for the three dissenters, *id.* at 223, bade fair to reduce the great principle recognized in *Winship* to a quibble over the phrasing of the relevant statute.

[317] *See* Alschuler, *Failed Pragmatism: Reflections on the Burger Court*, 100 HARV. L. REV. 1436, 1441-42 (1987); Kamisar, *The Warren Court (Was It Really So Defense-Minded?), The Burger Court (Is It Really So Prosecution-Oriented?), and Police Investigatory Practices*, in THE BURGER COURT: THE COUNTER-REVOLUTION THAT WASN'T 62, 68 (V. Blasi ed. 1983) (arguing that in its later years the Burger Court was "significantly less police-oriented" and that "fears that the Burger Court would dismantle the work of the Warren Court . . . seem to have been considerably exaggerated").

[318] For example, the Burger Court decided more than 130 cases involving searches and seizures alone.

[319] *See, e.g.,* California v. Beheler, 463 U.S. 1121, 1126-28 (1983) (Stevens, J., joined by Brennan and Marshall, dissenting); California v. Carney, 471 U.S. 386, 396 (1985) (Stevens, J., joined by Brennan and Marshall, dissenting).

[320] *See* pp. 408-09 *supra*.

[321] *See* Bivens v. Six Unknown Named Agents, 403 U.S. 388, 415 (1971) (Burger, C. J., dissenting) (terming the exclusionary rule "conceptually sterile and practically ineffective" but refraining from calling for its abandonment until Congress provided an alternative remedy); Stone v. Powell, 428 U.S. 465, 496-502 (1976) (Burger, C. J., concurring). In *Bivens*, over three dissents, the Court added a damage remedy to the arsenal of tools available to combat illegal searches or seizures by federal officers. For a generally approving critique see Dellinger, *Of Rights and Remedies: The Constitution as a Sword*, 85 HARV. L. REV. 1532 (1972).

could consistently be found to limit both the extent to which illegally obtained evidence had to be excluded and the occasions on which a search or seizure would be found unreasonable.

Balancing the benefits against the costs of excluding unlawfully obtained evidence, the Warren Court had limited the exclusionary rule in two significant respects: the rule would not be applied retroactively to invalidate convictions obtained before it was announced,[322] and only a victim of the illegal action had standing to object.[323] Any marginal additional deterrence that would have resulted from contrary holdings, the Court had suggested, was outweighed by the attendant burdens—which sometimes included the inability to convict a defendant whose guilt was not in doubt.[324]

The Burger Court picked up this theme and ran with it, over anguished dissents protesting that the rule was being put to death by inches. *United States v. Calandra* permitted illegally obtained evidence to be used before the grand jury.[325] *United States v. Janis*[326] and *INS v. Lopez-Mendoza*[327] allowed federal courts in civil proceedings to receive evidence that either state or federal officers had unlawfully obtained. *Stone v. Powell* held that federal habeas corpus did not lie to challenge the use of evidence resulting from an unlawful search or seizure if there had been a "full and fair hearing" on the issue in state court.[328] *United States v. Ceccolini* refused to suppress the testimony of a witness although it appeared to be the product of an illegal search and seizure.[329] *Rakas v. Illinois*[330] and *Rawlings v. Kentucky,*[331] contrary to the thrust of earlier decisions, held that neither an automobile passenger nor the alleged owner of drugs could object to a search of premises belonging to another.[332] *United States v. Havens* significantly expanded a preexisting exception permitting limited use of illegally obtained evidence for impeachment purposes.[333] Finally, *United States v. Leon* held that evidence need not be excluded when the officer conducting the search had relied in good faith on a defective warrant.[334] The theory

---

[322] Linkletter v. Walker, pp. 451-52 *supra*.

[323] Alderman v. United States, 394 U.S. 165 (1969).

[324] *See Linkletter,* 381 U.S. at 638-39 (contrasting coerced confessions); *Alderman,* 394 U.S. at 174-75.

[325] 414 U.S. 338, 350-52 (1974) (Powell, J., over three dissents).

[326] 428 U.S. 433, 453-54 (1976) (Blackmun, J., over three dissents) (evidence unlawfully obtained by state officer may be used in federal tax proceeding).

[327] 468 U.S. 1032, 1040 (1984) (O'Connor, J., over four dissents) (evidence unlawfully obtained by federal officer may be used in deportation proceeding).

[328] 428 U.S. 465, 493-95 (1976) (Powell, J., over three dissents).

[329] 435 U.S. 268, 280 (1978) (Rehnquist, J., over two dissents).

[330] 439 U.S. 128 (1978) (Rehnquist, J., over four dissents) (passenger).

[331] 448 U.S. 98 (1980) (Rehnquist, J., over two dissents) (owner of drugs).

[332] *Contrast* Jones v. United States, 362 U.S. 257, 261-67 (1960) (holding that a guest might object to the search of a house and dispensing with the requirement that a defendant claim ownership of seized drugs because to do so would establish his guilt).

[333] 446 U.S. 620, 627 (1980) (White, J., over four dissents) (effectively overruling Agnello v. United States, 269 U.S. 20, 35 (1925), which had held that such evidence could not be used to impeach evidence brought out on cross-examination). *See* W. LaFave & J. Israel, Criminal Procedure, § 9.6 (1985). *Cf.* Walder v. United States, 347 U.S. 62, 66 (1954) (allowing use to impeach *direct* testimony and distinguishing *Agnello*).

[334] 468 U.S. 897 (1984) (White, J., over three dissents). For criticism of the decision see Alschuler, *"Close Enough for Government Work" : The Exclusionary Rule after Leon,* 1984 Sup. Ct. Rev. 309, 322 (arguing inter alia, *id.* at 322, that *"Leon* all but immunized judicial decisions to issue search and arrest warrants from higher court review").

seemed to be that the threat of exclusion of illegally obtained evidence, as Justice White had argued earlier, would hardly deter an officer from doing what he believed to be lawful.[335]

Cases on the legality of particular searches grew like weeds, and in many of them a lower-court decision of unconstitutionality was reversed.[336] Welfare payments could be conditioned on consent to "home visits" that would otherwise be prohibited.[337] Sellers of liquor and firearms could be searched,[338] and mail from abroad could be opened,[339] without either a warrant or probable cause.[340] A house trailer could be searched without a warrant because it might otherwise disappear,[341] an impounded car although it obviously would not.[342] A vehicle could be stopped on mere suspicion that it contained illegal aliens,[343] a boat[344] (or a vehicle at an established checkpoint)[345] without any suspicion at all. The government could enter premises covertly to execute a warrant,[346] record all numbers called from a suspect's telephone,[347] and make arrests for violation of an unconstitutional ordinance.[348] Immigration agents could station themselves at the doors to a factory

[335] See 468 U.S. at 918-21; Stone v. Powell, 428 U.S. at 539-40 (White, J., dissenting), supra note 328. See also United States v. Peltier, 422 U.S. 531, 542 (1975) (Rehnquist, J., over four dissents) (refusing to apply a decision limiting border searches retroactively) ("If the purpose of the exclusionary rule is to deter unlawful police conduct then evidence obtained from a search should be suppressed only if it can be said that the law enforcement officer had knowledge, or may properly be charged with knowledge, that the search was unconstitutional. . . ."). But see Posner, Rethinking the Fourth Amendment, 1982 Sup. Ct. Rev. 49, 68 ("[R]ecognizing a good-faith exception . . . would swing the pendulum of the exclusionary rule from overdeterrence to underdeterrence by removing the incentive of law-enforcement agencies to take measures to minimize good-faith violations of the Fourth Amendment.").

[336] Reversal of decisions suppressing the fruits of searches and seizures was facilitated by two decisions narrowly interpreting the principle that the Court had no jurisdiction to review state-court judgments resting on adequate and independent state-law grounds. Delaware v. Prouse, 440 U.S. 648, 651-53 (1979) (White, J., over a Rehnquist dissent), held that a state's interpretation of its own constitution was not "independent" when based upon the premise that the state constitution meant the same as the federal; Michigan v. Long, 463 U.S. 1032, 1037-44 (1983) (O'Connor, J., over three dissents), abandoning numerous earlier decisions, held that when it was unclear whether a decision rested upon independent state grounds it should be presumed that it did not. See also id. at 1069-70 (Stevens, J., dissenting) (complaining that the Court was giving excessive attention to cases in which state courts had upheld claims of constitutional right).

[337] Wyman v. James, 400 U.S. 309 (1971) (Blackmun, J., over three dissents).

[338] Colonnade Catering Corp. v. United States, 397 U.S. 72 (1970) (Douglas, J.) (dictum) (liquor); United States v. Biswell, 406 U.S. 311 (1972) (White, J., over a dissent by Douglas) (firearms).

[339] United States v. Ramsey, 431 U.S. 606 (1977) (Rehnquist, J., over three dissents on statutory grounds).

[340] See also Donovan v. Dewey, 452 U.S. 594 (1981) (Marshall, J., over a dissent by Stewart) (upholding warrantless search of stone quarry).

[341] California v. Carney, 471 U.S. 386 (1985) (Burger, C. J., over three dissents). Cf. Carroll v. United States, pp. 165-67 supra (upholding warrantless search of an automobile on this ground).

[342] Chambers v. Maroney, 399 U.S. 42 (1970) (White, J., over a dissent by Harlan); South Dakota v. Opperman, 428 U.S. 364 (1976) (Burger, C. J., over four dissents focusing on the absence of a reasonable basis for the search in question).

[343] United States v. Cortez, 449 U.S. 411 (1981) (Burger, C. J.).

[344] United States v. Villamonte-Marquez, 462 U.S. 579 (1983) (Rehnquist, J., over two dissents on the merits).

[345] United States v. Martinez-Fuerte, 428 U.S. 543 (1976) (Powell, J., over two dissents).

[346] Dalia v. United States, 441 U.S. 238 (1979) (Powell, J., with two Justices arguing that the warrant must expressly authorize such an entry and three that there was no statutory authority for the practice).

[347] Smith v. Maryland, 442 U.S. 735 (1979) (Blackmun, J., over three dissents).

[348] Michigan v. DeFillippo, 443 U.S. 31 (1979) (Burger, C. J., over three dissents).

and interrogate workers as to their citizenship.[349] A prison cell might be searched at will,[350] a public school pupil's purse on reasonable suspicion.[351] A traveler suspected of importing drugs in her alimentary canal might even be detained at the border until she responded to nature's call.[352]

Similar things happened to the controversial rule of *Miranda v. Arizona,* where the Warren Court had held that a suspect in police custody could not be questioned until warned of his right to be silent and to have a lawyer.[353] Here too, as in the case of unreasonable search and seizure, the sanction for violation was exclusion of the product of illegal action. Not long after Warren's retirement, however, the Court permitted statements obtained in violation of *Miranda* to be used for impeachment purposes[354] and to track down otherwise unknown witnesses.[355] Later the Court added that the doctrine of the "fruit of the poisonous tree"—which generally required exclusion not only of the illegally obtained evidence itself but also of other evidence to which it had led—was not really applicable to *Miranda* violations at all.[356]

As in the case of search and seizure, not only the remedy for *Miranda* violations but also the substance of the rule itself was limited. The warning requirement was held inapplicable to a suspect who had come to the police station voluntarily.[357] Conversation between officers that seemed plainly designed to elicit an incriminating response was held not to constitute forbidden questioning.[358] Waiver of the right not to be questioned without an attorney did not need to be explicit.[359] Even if there was no waiver, moreover, the police could ask questions about the location of a murder weapon: the balance of interests favored the government when public safety was at stake.[360]

This is not to say that either *Miranda* or the exclusionary rule vanished entirely. An outdoor arrest was held not to justify searching a house,[361] nor a warrant to enter a tavern

---

[349] INS v. Delgado, 466 U.S. 210 (1984) (Rehnquist, J.). *See also id.* at 229 (Brennan, J., joined by Marshall, J., dissenting) ("Although none of the respondents was physically restrained by the INS agents during the questioning, . . . a reasonable person could not help but feel compelled to stop and provide answers to the INS agents' questions.").

[350] Hudson v. Palmer, 468 U.S. 517 (1984) (Burger, C. J., over four dissents).

[351] New Jersey v. T.L.O., 469 U.S. 325 (1985) (White, J., over three dissents).

[352] United States v. Montoya de Hernandez, 473 U.S. 531 (1985) (Rehnquist, J., over two dissents).

[353] *See* pp. 449-50 *supra.*

[354] Harris v. New York, 401 U.S. 222 (1971) (Burger, C. J., over four dissents).

[355] Michigan v. Tucker, 417 U.S. 433 (1974) (Rehnquist, J., over a dissent by Douglas).

[356] Oregon v. Elstad, 470 U.S. 298 (1985) (O'Connor, J., over three dissents).

[357] California v. Beheler, 463 U.S. 1121 (1983) (per curiam) (over three dissents not reaching the merits). *See also* Beckwith v. United States, 425 U.S. 341 (1976) (Burger, C. J., over a dissent by Brennan) (no warnings necessary when suspect not in custody).

[358] Rhode Island v. Innis, 446 U.S. 291 (1980) (Stewart, J., over three dissents). In Brewer v. Williams, 430 U.S. 387, 393, 399 (1977) (Stewart, J., over four dissents), in contrast, where the defendant had directed the police to the body of his victim after having been advised that "the parents of this little girl should be entitled to a Christian burial," the Court found an infringement of the right to counsel as interpreted in Massiah v. United States ("There can be no serious doubt . . . that Detective Leaming deliberately and designedly set out to elicit information from Williams just as surely as—and perhaps more effectively than—if he had formally interrogated him."). *See* p. 448 *supra.*

[359] North Carolina v. Butler, 441 U.S. 369 (1979) (Stewart, J., over three dissents).

[360] New York v. Quarles, 467 U.S. 649 (1984) (Rehnquist, J., over four dissents).

[361] Vale v. Louisiana, 399 U.S. 30 (1970) (Stewart, J., over two dissents).

a search of its patrons.[362] A warrant was required to tap a telephone for internal security purposes,[363] to open a footlocker taken from an automobile,[364] and to inspect a place of employment for unsafe working conditions.[365] Even automobiles could not be stopped randomly without reasonable suspicion[366] or searched without probable cause.[367] Puerto Rico could not search all travelers coming from the mainland;[368] police could not shoot all fleeing suspects;[369] a surgical operation to remove a bullet from a suspect went too far.[370] *Miranda* itself was not only enforced by forbidding questioning by the police after the suspect had requested a lawyer;[371] it was extended to require warnings before questioning by a psychiatrist as well.[372]

One need not agree with Justice Brennan's gloomy conclusion that both *Miranda* and *Mapp* were effectively dead[373] to perceive in the search-and-seizure and custodial-interrogation cases a tendency to limit at least the expansion of their principles if not the decisions themselves.[374] One senses a new concern lest additional procedural safeguards impair society's ability to combat crime. It is not a complete answer to point out that the Bill of Rights was adopted with full awareness of its costs; the extent of those costs may be relevant in determining what its guarantees mean. *Mapp* and *Miranda* still clung to life as Chief Justice Burger retired; but it would hardly be a surprise if one day they quietly or not so quietly disappeared.

## C.   Plea Bargaining

When the Burger Court whittled away at the edges of the procedural rights established during the 1960s, dissenting Justices protested like stuck pigs. When it concluded that defendants could be coerced into surrendering all their procedural rights at once, there was hardly any objection at all.

Most constitutional rights can be waived. The sixth amendment creates only a right to be represented by counsel, not a duty.[375] The fifth prohibits compulsory but not voluntary

---

[362] Ybarra v. Illinois, 444 U.S. 85 (1979) (Stewart, J., over three dissents).

[363] United States v. United States District Court, 407 U.S. 297 (1972) (Powell, J.).

[364] United States v. Chadwick, 433 U.S. 1 (1977) (Burger, C. J., over two dissents).

[365] Marshall v. Barlow's, Inc., 436 U.S. 307 (1978) (White, J., over three dissents).

[366] United States v. Brignoni-Ponce, 422 U.S. 873 (1975) (Powell, J.); Delaware v. Prouse, 440 U.S. 648 (1979) (White, J., over a dissent by Rehnquist).

[367] Almeida-Sanchez v. United States, 413 U.S. 266 (1973) (Stewart, J., over four dissents); United States v. Ortiz, 422 U.S. 891 (1975) (Powell, J.).

[368] Torres v. Puerto Rico, 442 U.S. 465 (1979) (Burger, C. J.).

[369] Tennessee v. Garner, 471 U.S. 1 (1985) (White, J., over three dissents).

[370] Winston v. Lee, 470 U.S. 753 (1985) (Brennan, J.).

[371] Edwards v. Arizona, 451 U.S. 477 (1981) (White, J.).

[372] Estelle v. Smith, 451 U.S. 454 (1981) (Burger, C. J.).

[373] *See* United States v. Leon, 468 U.S. 897, 928-29 (1984) (Brennan, J., dissenting); Oregon v. Elstad, 470 U.S. 298, 319 (1985) (Brennan, J., dissenting). *See* United Bhd. of Carpenters v. Vincent, 286 F.2d 127, 132 (2d Cir. 1960) (Friendly, J.) ("[D]issenting opinions are not always a reliable guide to the meaning of the majority; often their predictions partake of Cassandra's gloom more than of her accuracy.").

[374] *See* Stone, *The Miranda Doctrine in the Burger Court*, 1977 Sup. Ct. Rev. 99.

[375] *See* Johnson v. Zerbst, 304 U.S. 458, 465 (1938) (dictum) (right to counsel may be waived); Faretta v. California, 422 U.S. 806 (1975) (right to refuse assistance of counsel).

self-incrimination.[376] The fourth does not forbid searches to which the victim has consented.[377] There has never been any doubt that a defendant may waive his right to be tried at all, provided that his guilty plea is made knowingly and voluntarily.[378]

The crucial question was what kinds of pressures placed by the state on the defendant rendered a plea less than voluntary. There was a large body of precedent dealing with this very question in the context of out-of-court confessions, for it had been established ever since the 1930s that due process forbade the introduction into evidence of confessions involuntarily made.[379] In that context the concept of coercion had been held to include not only physical and psychological torture[380] but also—and most pertinently—the promise of leniency in return for a confession.[381] This precedent would appear to sound the death knell of most guilty pleas, for defendants do not generally give up their procedural rights for nothing; they are typically bribed to do so by promises of a more lenient sentence.

The Warren Court had taken two substantial steps toward outlawing such plea bargaining. In *Machibroda v. United States* the petitioner alleged that the prosecutor had promised him a sentence of not more than twenty years in exchange for a guilty plea.[382] "There can be no doubt," the Court concluded, "that, if the allegations contained in the petitioner's motion and affidavit are true, he is entitled to have his sentence vacated. A guilty plea, if induced by promises or threats which deprive it of the character of a voluntary act, is void."[383] Subsequently, in *United States v. Jackson,* the Court struck down on similar grounds a statute that provided for the death penalty only on recommendation of the jury: "The inevitable effect of any such provision is, of course, to discourage assertion of the Fifth Amendment right not to plead guilty and to deter exercise of the Sixth Amendment right to demand a jury trial."[384]

The Burger Court extracted the teeth from this salutary precedent in *Brady v. United States,* where the majority assumed that a guilty plea had been induced by the desire to avoid a risk of capital punishment under the provision invalidated in *Jackson* but upheld it anyway. "We decline to hold," wrote Justice White (who had not joined the Court's opinion in *Jackson*), "that a guilty plea is compelled and invalid under the Fifth Amendment whenever motivated by the defendant's desire to accept the certainty or probability of a lesser penalty. . . ."[385] Brennan, Douglas, and Marshall, concurring on the narrow ground

---

[376] *See* Minnesota v. Murphy, 465 U.S. 420 (1984).

[377] Schneckloth v. Bustamonte, 412 U.S. 218 (1973).

[378] *See* Brady v. United States, 397 U.S. 742, 747-48 (1970), and cases cited.

[379] *See* pp. 247-48 *supra*.

[380] Brown v. Mississippi, pp. 247-48 *supra;* Chambers v. Florida, 309 U.S. 227 (1940).

[381] Bram v. United States, 168 U.S. 532, 565 (1897).

[382] 368 U.S. 487, 489 (1962) (Stewart, J.). In light of later developments it should be noted that the prosecutor was also alleged to have warned the defendant not to tell his lawyer, *id.,* but the Court gave no visible weight to this allegation.

[383] *Id.* at 493.

[384] 390 U.S. 570, 581 (1968) (Stewart, J.).

[385] 397 U.S. 742, 751 (1970) (White, J.). The confession cases were distinguished, *id.* at 754:

> *Bram* dealt with a confession given by a defendant in custody, alone and unrepresented by counsel. In such circumstances, even a mild promise of leniency was deemed sufficient to bar the confession, not because the promise was an illegal act as such, but because defendants at such times are too sensitive to inducement and the possible impact on them too great to ignore and too difficult to assess.

that the plea had not been influenced by fear of the death penalty,[386] warned that the majority seemed indifferent to excessive pressures on the defendant's choice but came close to conceding the validity of ordinary plea bargaining:

> We are dealing here with the legislative imposition of a markedly more severe penalty if a defendant asserts his right to a jury trial and a concomitant legislative promise of leniency if he pleads guilty. This is very different from the give-and-take negotiation common in plea bargaining between the prosecution and the defense. . . .[387]

If the minority in *Brady* thought the influence of a statutory distinction in punishments more severe than that of an individual offer of leniency, a footnote in the majority opinion might have been read to suggest the opposite: "We here make no reference to the situation where the prosecutor or judge, or both, deliberately employ their charging and sentencing powers to induce a particular defendant to tender a plea of guilty."[388] Any hopes raised by this reservation, however, were gravely diminished by *Santobello v. New York,* where in holding that a prosecutor must live up to his part of a plea bargain the Court, with the express concurrence of Justice Douglas, proclaimed plea bargaining itself "an essential component of the administration of justice" that was "highly desirable" and therefore "to be encouraged." "If every criminal charge were subjected to a full-scale trial," wrote Chief Justice Burger, "the States and the Federal Government would need to multiply by many times the number of judges and court facilities."[389]

If any doubt remained, *Bordenkircher v. Hayes* extinguished it in 1978.[390] Hayes had been indicted for uttering a forged check, an offense punishable by not more than ten years in prison. Offering to recommend a five-year sentence in return for a guilty plea, the prosecutor threatened that if his offer was not accepted he would seek a further indictment under the Habitual Criminal Act, which carried a mandatory life term.[391] Four dissenters argued that this was the case *Brady* had specifically reserved and that decisions forbidding vindictive actions against defendants who had exercised the right to appeal required that the plea be set aside.[392] The majority disagreed.

---

[386] *Id.* at 814-16 (Brennan, J., joined by Douglas and Marshall, JJ., concurring and dissenting in Parker v. North Carolina, 397 U.S. 790 (1970)).

[387] 397 U.S. at 809. *Brady* was followed in North Carolina v. Alford, 400 U.S. 25, 31 (1970) (White, J.), where the record was clear that the fear of death had been the basis of the plea; Brennan, Douglas, and Marshall, *id.* at 39-40, dissented.

[388] 397 U.S. at 751 n.8. "[T]here is no claim," the Court added, "that the prosecutor threatened prosecution on a charge not justified by the evidence or that the trial judge threatened Brady with a harsher sentence if convicted after trial in order to induce him to plead guilty." Plea bargaining was conspicuously omitted from the Court's list, *id.* at 751, of allegedly innocuous practices from which, in the majority's opinion, Brady's situation could not be distinguished.

[389] 404 U.S. 257, 260-61 (1971). *See also id.* at 264 (Douglas, J., concurring) ("These 'plea bargains' are important in the administration of justice both at the state and at the federal levels and, as the Chief Justice says, they serve an important role in the disposition of today's heavy calendars.").

[390] 434 U.S. 357 (1978) (Stewart, J.).

[391] *Id.* at 358-59.

[392] *Id.* at 365-68 (Blackmun, J., joined by Brennan and Marshall, dissenting); *id.* at 368-73 (Powell, J., dissenting) (both citing, inter alia, North Carolina v. Pearce, 395 U.S. 711 (1969)).

Making the most of Justice Brennan's reference in *Brady* to "the give-and-take negotiation common in plea bargaining,"[393] the Court echoed *Santobello*'s encomium to that process as one that, " 'properly administered,' " could " 'benefit all concerned.' "[394] "To punish a person because he has done what the law plainly allows him to do," wrote Justice Stewart, "is a due process violation of the most basic sort." Plea bargaining, on the other hand, "flows from 'the mutuality of advantage' to defendants and prosecutors, each with his own reasons for wanting to avoid trial."[395] The " 'discouraging effect' " on a defendant's right to trial of "confronting [him] with the risk of more severe punishment" was " 'an inevitable . . . attribute of any legitimate system which tolerates and encourages the negotiation of pleas.' "[396]

The dissenters argued lamely that there was a difference between reducing a charge already made and threatening to seek an additional indictment.[397] No one challenged the majority's assertion that plea bargaining itself was constitutional. The entire Court appeared to agree that the state had the power to induce a defendant by promises of leniency to surrender his constitutional right to a trial.

Justice Stewart to the contrary notwithstanding, plea bargaining seems a classic instance of what he termed "the most basic sort" of unconstitutional action, for it punishes a defendant for asserting his constitutional right to be tried. It is no answer that the sentence imposed on an uncooperative defendant is within the statutory maximum; it has long been established that government discretion may not be so exercised as to deny an independent constitutional right.[398] To condition lenient sentencing on surrender of the right to a trial is like conditioning a government job on working for Democratic candidates[399] or a license to do business on taxation of out-of-state property.[400] It is true, as Chief Justice Burger said in *Santobello,* that it saves money to do without trials; but it seems fair to conclude that the cost of a trial was knowingly accepted by the Framers. Exercise of the constitutional right to be tried is no justification for inflicting more severe punishments on some individuals than on others who have committed identical crimes.[401]

The legalization of plea bargaining was no minor incursion on the procedural protections so painstakingly put together by the Framers. As Justice Douglas observed in *San-*

---

[393] 434 U.S. at 362-63 (quoting *Brady,* 397 U.S. at 809) (Brennan, J., concurring).

[394] 434 U.S. at 361-62 (quoting Blackledge v. Allison, 431 U.S. 63, 71 (1977)).

[395] 434 U.S. at 363. *See also Brady,* 397 U.S. at 752 (listing the advantages of a guilty plea to both parties).

[396] 434 U.S. at 364 (quoting from Chaffin v. Stynchcombe, 412 U.S. 17, 31 (1973)).

[397] 434 U.S. at 368 n.2 (Blackmun, J., joined by Brennan and Marshall, dissenting); *id.* at 371-72 (Powell, J., dissenting).

[398] This is not a case in which, as in the abortion-funding cases, the government merely chooses not to subsidize the exercise of a constitutional right. Even in that context, the discussion above suggests, there is sometimes a strong argument of unconstitutionality. *See* pp. 472-75 *supra.*

[399] Elrod v. Burns, pp. 504-05 *supra.*

[400] Western Union Co. v. Kansas, p. 46, note 126 *supra.*

[401] *See, e.g.,* Alschuler, *The Changing Plea Bargaining Debate,* 69 CAL. L. REV. 652 (1981); Langbein, *Torture and Plea Bargaining,* 46 U. CHI. L. REV. 3 (1978); Schulhofer, *Is Plea Bargaining Inevitable?,* 97 HARV. L. REV. 1037, 1106 (1984) ("[I]n America's fourth-largest city, no concessions of any kind are offered for guilty pleas in the great majority of felony cases."). *See also* Coffee, *"Twisting Slowly in the Wind": A Search for Constitutional Limits on Coercion of the Criminal Defendant,* 1980 SUP. CT. REV. 211 (exploring the implications of *Bordenkircher* for situations in which a defendant is pressured to surrender rights other than the right to trial).

*tobello,* the overwhelming majority of criminal cases were disposed of by plea bargaining.[402] Most defendants, in other words, are euchred out of the high-sounding rights the Court still insists they enjoy by the threat that they will be punished for asserting them; the continuing debates over the rights of the few hardy souls who insist on their constitutional rights have little impact on the real world.

[402] *See* 404 U.S. at 264 nn.1, 2 (noting that in 1964 and 1965 guilty pleas accounted for 95.5 percent of all convictions in New York, 90.2 percent in federal courts, and 74.0 percent in California).

# 16

# The Structure of Government

When asked which provisions of the Constitution protect individual liberty, one is likely to think first of the Bill of Rights. Without minimizing their importance, it should not be forgotten that the explicit guarantees of the first eight amendments were an afterthought. Some serious thinkers believed that no Bill of Rights was needed at all, for the structure of government had been carefully designed to protect liberty.[1] Democratic elections reduce the likelihood of oppression because the people are not likely to oppress themselves. Federalism reduces the power of any one government to infringe individual rights. Separation of legislative, executive, and judicial powers requires three independent branches to concur before a person may be deprived of life, liberty, or property.[2] Checks and balances such as the veto power, impeachment, and the requirement of Senate consent to treaties and appointments reinforce these safeguards by giving one branch the affirmative power to inhibit arbitrary action by another. Even unpopular minorities are protected by tying their fate to that of everyone else: if a dominant faction can limit the freedom of others only by restricting its own, it is unlikely to do so without a pretty convincing reason.[3] Only when all these indirect safeguards fail must we fall back on the direct guarantees of the Bill of Rights to protect liberties we deem so fundamental that government may *never* infringe them—as it may occasionally be tempted to do even in a democratic

---

[1] *See, e.g.*, THE FEDERALIST Nos. 51 (J. Madison), 84 (A. Hamilton); 2 M. FARRAND, RECORDS OF THE FEDERAL CONVENTION OF 1787, at 617-18 (rev. ed. 1937) (Mr. Sherman).

[2] *See* THE FEDERALIST No. 51 (J. Madison) ("In the compound republic of America, the power surrendered by the people is first divided between two distinct governments, and then the portion allotted to each subdivided among distinct and separate departments. Hence a double security arises to the rights of the people.").

[3] Provisions of the original Constitution reflecting this principle include the privileges and immunities clause of article IV, the requirement of just compensation for the taking of private property, and the commerce clause as interpreted to protect interstate commerce from discrimination. The equal protection clause and the various amendments limiting discrimination in voting are further embodiments of the same principle. *See generally* J. H. ELY, DEMOCRACY AND DISTRUST 81-88 (1980).

federation enjoying separation of powers, checks and balances, and explicit guarantees of equality.

Following the trail blazed by Justice Stone in *Carolene Products*,[4] the Supreme Court since the late 1930s had increasingly protected not only the specific guarantees of the Bill of Rights and the interests of politically powerless minorities but also the structural principle of democracy.[5] At the same time, however, the Court had conspicuously ignored the important structural guarantees of federalism and the separation of powers.[6] In so doing it had placed unnecessary strains on the specific guarantees of freedom and equality.[7]

Despite early encouraging signs, the Burger Court did little in the last analysis to revive the moribund principle of federalism. It did render several significant decisions reflecting a welcome resurgence of concern for checks and balances and the separation of powers.

## I. THE FEDERAL SYSTEM

### A. Enumerated Powers

*Oregon v. Mitchell,* in 1970, was the first decision in thirty years to hold that Congress had legislated on a matter reserved to the states.[8] In the late 1930s the Court had been frightened into upholding federal measures having only the most tenuous connection with powers explicitly entrusted to Congress, and it had continued to do so ever since.[9] Contrary to the plain purpose of the Constitution, it was difficult to think of anything so local as to be beyond Congress's ken. In *Mitchell* the Court found there was something left after all.

In amending the Voting Rights Act in 1970, Congress had among other things lowered the minimum voting age to eighteen years.[10] By two separate votes of five to four, the Court held this provision could be constitutionally applied to federal but not to state elections.

Justices Brennan, White, Marshall, and Douglas thought § 5 of the fourteenth amendment empowered Congress to prescribe the voting age in both federal and state elections

---

[4]United States v. Carolene Products Co., 304 U.S. 144, 152 n.4 (1938). *See* p. 244 *supra.*

[5]*See, e.g.,* pp. 429-33 *supra* (discussing the reapportionment cases); pp. 322-25, 424-25 *supra* (discussing barriers to voting by blacks).

[6]*See especially* pp. 236-38 *supra* (discussing the decline of limitations on congressional authority); p. 366, note 219 *supra* (discussing the decline of the nondelegation doctrine).

[7]*See* Nagel, *Federalism as a Fundamental Value: National League of Cities in Perspective,* 1981 SUP. CT. REV. 81, 88:

> [T]o see the purposes of judicial review almost entirely in terms of securing individual rights is to invert the priorities of the framers. . . . [The] structure itself was to be the great protection of the individual, not the "parchment barriers" that were later (and with modest expectations) added to the document.

[8]400 U.S. 112 (1970). The court-martial cases of the Warren years, pp. 400-03 *supra,* which had construed the grant of military authority narrowly, had done so out of a concern for fair trial, not for the division of power between nation and state. The last previous decisions holding that Congress had invaded state authority were those invalidating New Deal measures in the mid-1930s. *See* pp. 222-31 *supra.*

[9]*See* pp. 236-38, 309, 425 *supra.*

[10]*See* 400 U.S. at 117.

in order to enforce the equal protection clause: "Congress had ample evidence upon which it could have based the conclusion that exclusion of citizens 18 to 21 years of age from the franchise is wholly unnecessary to promote any legitimate interest the States may have in assuring intelligent and responsible voting."[11] Black, Harlan, Stewart, Burger, and Blackmun disagreed: Congress had no basis for rejecting a state's reasonable decision that only twenty-one-year-olds were mature enough to vote.[12]

Justice Black cast the decisive vote to sustain the requirement as to federal voters on the basis of Congress's authority to alter the "times, places and manner" of Senate and House elections as fixed by state law.[13] Not only did this provision conspicuously fail to cover presidential elections, for whose regulation Black lamely found "inherent" authority;[14] it also overlooked article I's explicit distinction between "times, places, and manner" of elections and "qualifications" of voters, which a separate provision remitted to state law with no reference to congressional alteration.[15]

Whatever the merits of Justice Black's argument, he was surely right that nothing in the provision on which he relied afforded the slightest support for congressional regulation of *state* elections. The majority thus seems quite correct in concluding, for a change, that Congress had exceeded its powers.

The *Mitchell* decision was promptly reversed in the manner for which the Constitution provides.[16] "The right of citizens of the United States, who are eighteen years of age or

---

[11]*Id.* at 280 (opinion of Brennan, J., joined by White and Marshall). *See also id.* at 141 (opinion of Douglas, J.). The equal protection clause was relevant to *federal* elections because of the role assigned to the states by article I, § 2, article II, § 1, and the seventeenth amendment in fixing the qualifications of federal voters.

[12]*See* 400 U.S. at 128-30 (Black, J.); *id.* at 200-09 (Harlan, J., also repeating his powerful historical argument, *see* p. 430, note 113 *supra,* that § 1 of the amendment did not apply to voting); *id.* at 293-96 (Stewart, J., joined by Burger and Blackmun). The decision elsewhere in *Mitchell* to uphold a congressional ban on literacy tests was easily distinguishable: Congress had reasonably found such a prohibition necessary and proper to prevent racial discrimination in their administration. *See* p. 427 *supra.*

[13]U.S. CONST. art. I, § 4 (excepting "places of choosing Senators"). *See* 400 U.S. at 119-24.

[14]400 U.S. at 124 n.7:

> [I]nherent in the very concept of a supreme national government with national officers is a residual power in Congress to insure that those officers represent their national constituency as responsively as possible. This power arises from the nature of our constitutional system of government and from the Necessary and Proper Clause.

*But see* art. II, § 1 ("Each State shall appoint, in such manner as the Legislature may direct, a Number of Electors. . . .").

[15]U.S. CONST. art. I, § 2, and amend. 17 ("[T]he electors in each State shall have the qualifications requisite for electors of the most numerous branch of the state legislature."). *See* 400 U.S. at 209-12 (opinion of Harlan, J.); *id.* at 287-91 (opinion of Stewart, J.); THE FEDERALIST No. 60 (A. Hamilton); Kurland, *1970 Term: Notes on the Emergence of the Burger Court,* 1971 SUP. CT. REV. 265, 277. Even Black's underlying argument that it would be surprising if the Framers had not given the central government the power to assure its own existence can be disputed: tying federal to state electoral qualifications may have been one of the intended checks on national power. *See* 2 M. FARRAND, note 1 *supra,* at 249-50 (Mr. Madison) (opposing a proposal to give Congress authority to set voter qualifications as dangerous to the Constitution). *See also* Mikva & Lundy, *The 91st Congress and the Constitution,* 38 U. CHI. L. REV. 449, 484 (1971) ("[A]t no time during congressional consideration of the 18-year-old vote issue was the possibility raised that there was greater power to affect voter qualifications for elections to national offices than for elections to state and local offices.").

[16]U.S. CONST. art. V ("The Congress, whenever two thirds of both Houses shall deem it necessary, shall propose amendments to this Constitution, . . . which . . . shall be valid . . . when ratified by the legislatures of three fourths of the several States. . . .").

older, to vote," says the twenty-sixth amendment, "shall not be denied or abridged by the United States or by any State on account of age." Praise for the amendment is entirely consistent with applause for the decision; it is the business of the country, not of the Court, to rewrite the Constitution.

## B. Intergovernmental Immunity

*Mitchell* was a refreshing reminder that there still were limits to the reach of congressional authority, but by upholding federal regulation of loan sharks,[17] of strip mining,[18] and of the quintessentially local business of real estate[19] the Burger Court made clear it did not mean to undo the New Deal revolution.[20] In one narrow field, however, the Court gave

---

[17] Perez v. United States, 402 U.S. 146, 154 (1971) (Douglas, J.) ("Extortionate credit transactions, though purely intrastate, may in the judgment of Congress affect interstate commerce."). *See also id.* at 157 (Stewart, J., dissenting):

> [U]nder the statute before us a man can be convicted without any proof of interstate movement, of the use of the facilities of interstate commerce, or of facts showing that his conduct affected interstate commerce. I think that the Framers of the Constitution never intended that the National Government might define as a crime and prosecute such wholly local activity through the enactment of federal criminal laws.

[18] Hodel v. Virginia Surface Mining & Reclamation Ass'n, 452 U.S. 264 (1981) (Marshall, J.); Hodel v. Indiana, 452 U.S. 314 (1981) (Marshall, J.). *See id.* at 326 ("Congress had a rational basis for finding that surface coal mining on prime farmland affects interstate commerce in agricultural products.").

[19] Russell v. United States, 471 U.S. 858 (1985) (Stevens, J., for a unanimous Court) (upholding federal prosecution for arson involving apartment building) ("The rental of real estate" is "an 'activity' that affects commerce."). *Id.* at 862. Respect for state authority survived, however, as a significant factor in determining the reach of federal statutes once enacted. *See, e.g.,* United States v. Bass, 404 U.S. 336, 349 (1971) (Marshall, J., over two dissents) (construing the words "in commerce" in a provision punishing a convicted felon who "receives, possesses, or transports in commerce" a firearm to apply not only to transportation but to possession as well) ("[U]nless Congress conveys its purpose clearly, it will not be deemed to have significantly changed the federal-state balance.").

[20] The Court also dealt somewhat lightly with the requirement of article I that both indirect taxes and bankruptcy laws be "uniform throughout the United States." *See* United States v. Ptasynski, 462 U.S. 74, 84-85 (1983) (Powell, J.) (upholding an exemption of certain Alaskan and offshore oil from a windfall-profits tax because the uniformity requirement permitted Congress to consider "geographically isolated problems"); Regional Rail Reorganization Act Cases, 419 U.S. 102, 158-61 (1974) (Brennan, J., over a dissent by Douglas) (employing the same reasoning in upholding a bankruptcy law applicable only to a statutorily defined region). *But see* Railway Labor Executives' Ass'n v. Gibbons, 455 U.S. 457 (1982) (Rehnquist, J.) (striking down a bankruptcy law applicable to a single railroad and adding that the commerce power could not be used to undermine the express uniformity requirement of the bankruptcy clause). *See* THE FIRST HUNDRED YEARS at 431-32 (discussing the Head Money Cases, 112 U.S. 580 (1884)); Baird, *Bankruptcy Procedure and State-Created Rights: The Lessons of* Gibbons *and* Marathon, 1982 SUP. CT. REV. 25, 30-36 (criticizing *Gibbons*).

Similarly, after sensibly holding that the mere fact that an airplane crashed in navigable waters did not bring a lawsuit arising out of the accident within the purposes of the admiralty jurisdiction, Executive Jet Aviation v. City of Cleveland, 409 U.S. 249 (1972) (Stewart, J.), the Court not only upheld admiralty jurisdiction over an action involving the collision of two pleasure boats, Foremost Ins. Co. v. Richardson, 457 U.S. 668 (1982) (Marshall, J., over four dissents), but (more doubtfully) upheld the power of Congress to provide for federal jurisdiction over a suit brought against one foreign country by a citizen of another because federal law governed the "threshold" question of sovereign immunity—notwithstanding the fact that immunity was a defense and its absence not a part of the plaintiff's claim. Verlinden B.V. v. Central Bank of Nigeria, 461 U.S. 480 (1983) (Burger, C.J.). *See* THE FIRST HUNDRED YEARS at 102-04 (discussing Osborn v. Bank of the United States, 22 U.S. 738 (1824)).

initial signs of recognizing the legitimacy of state as contrasted with federal interests, only to alter its course. That field was federal interference with the operation of state government.

Congress, five Justices concluded in *National League of Cities v. Usery* in 1976, lacked power to prescribe minimum wages for employees of state and local governments.[21] The majority did not deny that the activities of such employees bore a sufficient relationship to interstate commerce to bring them presumptively within the commerce power. Rather, said Justice Rehnquist for the majority, the regulation foundered on an "affirmative limitation" on that power analogous to due process and trial by jury: " 'Congress may not exercise power in a fashion that impairs the States' integrity or their ability to function effectively in a federal system.' "[22]

Justice Brennan, for three of the four dissenters, went up in smoke. "My Brethren," he exclaimed, "have today manufactured an abstraction without substance, founded neither in the words of the Constitution nor on precedent."[23] The tenth amendment, on which Justice Rehnquist had relied,[24] imposed no "affirmative limitation" on the powers elsewhere granted to Congress; by its express terms it merely declared the federal government one of delegated powers.[25] The Court's decision, Brennan concluded, suggested a return to that unfortunate "line of opinions dealing with the Commerce Clause and the Tenth Amendment that ultimately provoked a constitutional crisis for the Court in the 1930's."[26]

Justice Brennan was right about the tenth amendment.[27] He was wrong about those decisions of the 1930s, which had struck down federal statutes affecting private conduct; *National League of Cities* was explicitly based on the narrow principle of intergovernmental immunity. Moreover, while as Brennan said there was no support for this limitation in the words of the Constitution, there was an abundance of support for it in precedent. Implicit intergovernmental immunity went all the way back to *McCulloch v. Maryland*.[28]

"The power to tax," Chief Justice Marshall had recognized in that case, "involves the power to destroy."[29] Unwilling to infer that the Framers had meant to place the central government at the mercy of the states, the Court in *McCulloch* had concluded that the United States and its instrumentalities were immune from state taxation although no pro-

---

[21] 426 U.S. 833 (1976).

[22] *Id.* at 840-43 (quoting Fry v. United States, 421 U.S. 542, 547 n.7 (1975)). For an effort to defend the decision on the basis of values espoused by the Framers see Nagel, *supra* note 7. To extract from *National League of Cities* the basis for recognition of a constitutional right to basic government services, *see* Michelman, *States' Rights and States' Roles: Permutations of "Sovereignty" in* National League of Cities v. Usery, 86 YALE L.J. 1165 (1977); Tribe, *Unraveling* National League of Cities: *The New Federalism and Affirmative Rights to Essential Government Services,* 90 HARV. L. REV. 1065 (1977), is fanciful if not facetious; it transforms a decision designed as a shield for state autonomy into a sword for its destruction.

[23] 426 U.S. at 860.

[24] *See id.* at 842-43 (citing Fry v. United States, *supra* note 22).

[25] 426 U.S. at 861-63.

[26] *Id.* at 868 (citing Carter v. Carter Coal Co., pp. 223-25 *supra;* United States v. Butler, pp. 227-31 *supra;* and Hammer v. Dagenhart, pp. 96-98 *supra*).

[27] U.S. CONST. amend. X ("The powers *not delegated to the United States by the Constitution,* nor prohibited by it to the States, are reserved to the States respectively, or to the people." (emphasis added)). *See* pp. 96-98, 238 *supra* (discussing Hammer v. Dagenhart and United States v. Darby).

[28] 17 U.S. 316 (1819). *See* THE FIRST HUNDRED YEARS at 165-68.

[29] 17 U.S. at 431.

vision of the Constitution or statutes said so. Marshall had added in dictum that there was no need to read in a comparable state immunity from federal exactions, since the states could protect themselves through their representatives in Congress.[30] The enumeration of limited federal powers, however, reinforced by the tenth amendment, demonstrated that the Framers were not convinced of the adequacy of such political checks. In other respects, moreover, the case for state immunity was *stronger* than that for federal: since article VI makes federal law supreme, only the central government can protect itself by a statutory immunity provision.

Consequently it had not been long before implicit immunities cropped up on the state side as well. *Kentucky v. Dennison* had held that Congress could not impose affirmative duties on state officials under the extradition clause,[31] *Collector v. Day* that the salaries of state officers were immune from federal taxation.[32] *Hans v. Louisiana* had held that unconsenting states could not be sued by their own citizens in federal court,[33] *Coyle v. Smith* that Congress could not dictate the location of a state capital.[34] None of these immunities was based upon any specific language of the Constitution. *Hans* invoked persuasive evidence of explicit statements of influential Framers to buttress the tradition of sovereign immunity; the other decisions were firmly grounded in *McCulloch's* perception that the Founders could hardly have contemplated that one essential unit of their federal union would have the power to destroy another.

As Justice Brennan argued, more recent decisions had detracted from the force of this line of authority. Under the leadership of Justice Stone, the Court had restricted both state and federal tax immunities to exactions laid on the government itself or discriminating against it.[35] Most significantly, *Maryland v. Wirtz* in 1968 had squarely upheld an earlier version of the law struck down in *National League of Cities* itself as applied to workers in public hospitals and schools.[36] Indeed, ever since the 1936 decision in *United States v. California*[37] the Court had consistently denied that intergovernmental immunity limited Congress's regulatory powers at all.[38]

In this context, however, no one had suggested any good reason to distinguish regulation from taxes. As the Court had recognized in holding that a state could not require a license to drive a post office truck, the power to regulate is equally the power to destroy.[39]

---

[30] *See id.* at 428, 435. *See also National League of Cities,* 426 U.S. at 876-78 (Brennan, J., dissenting); J. CHOPER, JUDICIAL REVIEW AND THE NATIONAL POLITICAL PROCESS (1980).

[31] 65 U.S. 66 (1860), THE FIRST HUNDRED YEARS at 245-47.

[32] 78 U.S. 113 (1871), THE FIRST HUNDRED YEARS at 355.

[33] See pp. 7-9 *supra.*

[34] 221 U.S. 559 (1911). *See* p. 101, note 71 *supra.*

[35] *See* pp. 240-41 *supra.*

[36] 392 U.S. 183 (1968).

[37] 297 U.S. 175 (1936) (upholding federal requirement of automatic couplers on state-owned railroad), p. 234, note 156 *supra.*

[38] *See also* Case v. Bowles, 327 U.S. 92 (1946) (regulation of state timber sales), p. 303, note 171 *supra*; Fry v. United States, 421 U.S. 542 (1975) (wage freeze for state employees). The one short-lived exception was Ashton v. Cameron County Water Improv. Dist., 298 U.S. 513 (1936) (McReynolds, J., over four dissents), *overruled,* United States v. Bekins, 304 U.S. 27 (1938), where the Court perverted the doctrine to bar Congress from giving local governments the *benefit* of federal bankruptcy laws. *See* pp. 234-35, 240 *supra.*

[39] Johnson v. Maryland, 254 U.S. 51 (1920), p. 234, note 156 *supra.* In support of the distinction it might be argued that tax immunities are less damaging to federal interests than regulatory ones. If Congress may not tax

Nor could the *California* decision very well be taken as implicitly overruling the tax cases it professed to distinguish, since later decisions had expressly confirmed that there were still limits to federal power to tax the states.[40] In limiting federal authority to regulate state conduct, *National League of Cities* was not manufacturing a novel and unsupported "abstraction";[41] it was excising a questionable exception to the still respected and ever appealing principle that the Constitution does not permit one government to destroy another.

Justice Rehnquist acknowledged that Congress was free to regulate such state activities as railroading, which had once been fittingly called "proprietary."[42] The tax cases had typically recognized a similar exception.[43] What the Constitution protected, in other words, was the state's right to govern, not its advantage over commercial competitors. From the beginning, however, the tax decisions had declined to undertake the slippery inquiry whether a particular exaction actually impeded the operation of federal or state government; if the tax was laid on the government's nonproprietary activities, that was enough to condemn it.[44] Justice Rehnquist took a different tack with respect to federal regulation in *National League of Cities*.

Just the year before, in *Fry v. United States*, the Court had upheld the power of Congress to freeze the wages of state employees.[45] Rehnquist had dissented alone from *Fry*;[46] he was in no position to overrule it. The best he could do was to argue that it was distinguishable. The regulation upheld in *Fry* had been " 'an emergency measure to counter severe inflation that threatened the national economy' "; it had been a temporary provision merely preserving wage levels the states themselves had set; it had reduced state costs

---

the states, it may make up the deficit by taxing somebody else; if it cannot regulate state emissions or wages it cannot control pollution or inflation or guarantee a living wage. The balancing approach that would justify this distinction, however, had been rejected by *McCulloch* as inappropriate for judicial administration. *See* 17 U.S. at 430. Moreover, Justice Rehnquist had earlier argued with equal plausibility that the distinction cut precisely the other way: federal taxes interfered less with state policy choices than did federal regulation, because the state could make up for tax losses by taxing someone else. Fry v. United States, 421 U.S. 542, 554 (1975) (Rehnquist, J., dissenting). *See also* Alfange, *Congressional Regulation of the "States Qua States": From* National League of Cities *to* EEOC v. Wyoming, 1983 Sup. Ct. Rev. 215, 235-36 (arguing, despite the enormous scope that decisions of the past fifty years had given the commerce power, that the narrowness of federal regulatory authority made it less of a threat to state autonomy than the power to tax).

[40]*See, e.g.*, New York v. United States, 326 U.S. 572 (1946), p. 304, note 172 *supra*.

[41]*See* 426 U.S. at 860 (Brennan, J., dissenting). *See also* Field, Garcia v. San Antonio Municipal Transit Authority: *The Demise of a Misguided Doctrine*, 99 Harv. L. Rev. 84 (1985) (professing puzzlement as to the source of the immunity in *National League of Cities*, with only a passing acknowledgment of the analogies).

[42]This distinction supports United States v. California, though the Court there expressly declined to invoke it. It also accounts for Case v. Bowles, *supra* note 38, which Rehnquist unfortunately explained on the alternative basis that the limitation on state timber prices had been enacted under the war power and was thus peculiarly free from immunity concerns. *See* 426 U.S. at 854-55 n.18.

[43]*See* New York v. United States, *supra* note 40 (upholding federal tax as applied to state sales of mineral water); South Carolina v. United States, p. 25, note 128 *supra*.

[44]*See McCulloch*, 17 U.S. at 430 ("We are not driven to the perplexing inquiry, so unfit for the judicial department, what degree of taxation is the legitimate use, and what degree may amount to the abuse of the power.").

[45]421 U.S. 542 (1975) (Marshall, J.).

[46]*Id.* at 549-59.

rather than increasing them.[47] Yet another constitutional principle had become a balance of competing interests.[48]

Justice Blackmun, whose vote was essential to the decision, concurred explicitly on this basis: "I may misinterpret the Court's opinion, but it seems to me that it adopts a balancing approach, and does not outlaw federal power in areas such as environmental protection, where the federal interest is demonstrably greater and where state facility compliance with imposed federal standards would be essential."[49] Why the federal interest in environmental protection was greater than that in decent wages Justice Blackmun did not say.

For the next few years the Court struggled bravely with the unsatisfying scheme it had erected. Congress could regulate labor relations on state-owned railroads because railroading was not a "traditional" government function.[50] It could forbid actions by the states themselves in order to enforce the overriding policy of the fourteenth amendment.[51] It could ban age discrimination in state employment because the interference with state autonomy was minimal: "[A]ppellees remain free under the [statute] to continue doing *precisely what they are doing now,* if they can demonstrate that age is a 'bona fide occupational qualification'. . . ."[52] It could even, to an unclear extent, take actions that bordered on commandeering state agencies to aid in the enforcement of federal policy.[53]

In 1985, in *Garcia v. San Antonio Metropolitan Transit Authority,* Justice Blackmun changed his mind. Experience had shown that the test established in *National League of Cities* was not administrable; the states would have to rely on political checks for protection after all. The vote was still five to four, but *National League of Cities* was overruled.[54]

Justice Blackmun did not rule out state immunity altogether, even in commerce clause

---

[47] 426 U.S. at 852-53 (citing 421 U.S. at 548).

[48] For criticism of the Court's various bases of distinction as well as the decision itself see Alfange, *supra* note 39, *passim.*

[49] 426 U.S. at 856 (Blackmun, J., concurring).

[50] United Transportation Union v. Long Island R.R., 455 U.S. 678 (1982) (Burger, C.J., for a unanimous Court).

[51] City of Rome v. United States, 446 U.S. 156 (1980) (Marshall, J., over four dissents on unrelated grounds). *See id.* at 179 ("[P]rinciples of federalism that might otherwise be an obstacle to congressional authority are necessarily overriden by the power to enforce the Civil War Amendments 'by appropriate legislation.'" (citing Fitzpatrick v. Bitzer, pp. 573-74 *infra*).

[52] EEOC v. Wyoming, 460 U.S. 226, 240 (1983) (Brennan, J., over four dissents).

[53] FERC v. Mississippi, 456 U.S. 742 (1982) (Blackmun, J., over four dissents) (permitting Congress to require state public-utility commissions to consider specified regulatory options, to follow prescribed procedures in so doing, and to entertain claims based on certain federal regulations). The Court explained the last of these requirements in such a way as to bring it within Testa v. Katt, 330 U.S. 386 (1947), which had held that Congress could require state courts to entertain actions under federal law. *See* 456 U.S. at 760-61. The other requirements were more difficult to sustain. *See id.* at 775 (O'Connor, J., dissenting) (arguing that the challenged provisions "conscript state utility commissions into the national bureaucratic army"); D. Currie, Air Pollution: Federal Law and Analysis § 4.29 (1981 and supp. 1989) (citing lower-court decisions under the Clean Air Act) ("[E]ven in Maryland v. Wirtz the Court did not say Congress could require the states to enact and enforce laws regulating the conduct of others."). Some hope for continuing limits in this regard was held out by the Court's insistence that the statute required "only *consideration* of federal standards," 456 U.S. at 764 (emphasis in original); as the opinion seemed to imply, there is a marked difference between telling an agency to consider standards and telling it to adopt them.

[54] 469 U.S. 528 (1985) (Blackmun, J., over four dissents).

cases.[55] Indeed the climactic paragraph of the opinion seemed to suggest that what saved the minimum-wage provision in *Garcia* was the fact that it did not discriminate against public employers: "SAMTA faces nothing more than the same minimum-wage and over-time obligations that hundreds of thousands of other employers, public as well as private, have to meet."[56]

The nondiscrimination principle had been put on the table by a final paragraph of the *McCulloch* opinion and had seemed the logical goal of Justice Stone's decisions of the New Deal years.[57] It had also figured prominently in decisions of the Burger Court re-specting taxes indirectly burdening governments.[58] Though the Court remained unwilling for precedential reasons to apply the doctrine to taxes on the United States itself,[59] a non-discrimination rule might well be adequate to protect both state and national interests, for no popular government is likely to destroy another if it can do so only by ruining its own constituents.[60]

In contrast to *United States v. California, Garcia* made no reference to any distinction between regulation and taxation. Since everything the Court said seems equally applicable to taxes, the opinion opens the way for a corresponding restriction of state tax immunities, and arguably of federal immunities as well. Thus, whether *Garcia*'s allusion to the non-discrimination principle or its more sweeping invocation of state political power proves dominant in the long run, the intergovernmental-immunity decisions of the Burger period, which had begun by restoring a modicum of the federal principle, may have ended up eroding that principle still further.

## C.   Sovereign Immunity

The Constitution is silent about governmental immunity from taxation or regulation, but not about governmental immunity from suit. The eleventh amendment, adopted in 1795 to overrule the contrary decision in *Chisholm v. Georgia*,[61] expressly excised from the federal judicial power any suit brought against one state by a citizen of another or by a

---

[55]"These cases do not require us to identify or define what affirmative limits the constitutional structure might impose on federal action affecting the States under the Commerce Clause. See *Coyle v. Oklahoma*, 221 U.S. 559 (1911)." 469 U.S. at 556.

[56]*Id.* at 554.

[57]*See* THE FIRST HUNDRED YEARS at 167-68; pp. 240-41 *supra*.

[58]*See* United States v. County of Fresno, 429 U.S. 452 (1977) (White, J., over a dissent by Stevens) (uphold-ing state tax on value of housing furnished by United States to its employees); Memphis Bank & Trust Co. v. Garner, 459 U.S. 392 (1983) (Marshall, J.) (striking down state tax applicable to federal but not to state bonds); Washington v. United States, 460 U.S. 536 (1983) (Rehnquist, J., over four dissents) (upholding nondiscrimi-natory sales tax on federal contractor).

[59]*See* United States v. New Mexico, 455 U.S. 720, 733-34 (1982) (Blackmun, J.) (dictum) (reaffirming the "absolute federal immunity from state taxation"). In Massachusetts v. United States, 435 U.S. 444 (1978) (Bren-nan, J., over two dissents), the Court upheld application of a nondiscriminatory registration tax to aircraft oper-ated by the state in the indisputably governmental field of law enforcement, but on the narrow and persuasive ground that the tax could be viewed as a user fee to defray the cost of federal services.

[60]*See* the general discussion at p. 60 *supra*.

[61]2 U.S. 419 (1793), THE FIRST HUNDRED YEARS at 14-20.

foreigner.[62] In the light of this amendment, the Court later concluded that article III did not authorize a citizen to sue his own state either; unless it consented, a state could be sued only by the United States or by another state.[63] It had been a long time since the Court had had much to say about the states' judicial immunity, but it had a number of opportunities to do so during the Burger period.

## 1. Consent

Despite the apparently absolute language of the eleventh amendment, the Court had long held that, because the purpose of the amendment was to protect the states, the immunity it recognized was "a personal privilege which [the state] may waive at pleasure."[64] In accordance with its definition of waiver as the "intentional relinquishment . . . of a known right,"[65] however, the Court had tended to be reluctant to find a waiver unless the state had consented to suit in unmistakable terms. It was not enough for federal jurisdiction, for example, that a state had consented to be sued in its own courts;[66] even a provision allowing suit in "any court of competent jurisdiction" had been held to open only state courts and not federal.[67]

A 1959 decision construing a sue-and-be-sued clause in an interstate compact to waive immunity from federal process[68] had manifested a more receptive attitude toward express waivers, but nothing in that or any other decision gave any hint of what the Warren Court would do to the law of waiver in the 1964 case of *Parden v. Terminal Railway,*[69] where Justice Brennan explained that Alabama had consented to be sued in federal court for injuries to workers on a state-owned railroad although its law contained no waiver provision whatever:

> [B]y enacting the [Federal Employers' Liability Act,] . . . Congress conditioned the right to operate a railroad in interstate commerce upon amenability

---

[62] "The judicial power of the United States shall not be construed to extend to any suit in law or equity, commenced or prosecuted against one of the United States by citizens of another state, or by citizens or subjects of any foreign state."

[63] See pp. 7-9 *supra* (discussing Hans v. Louisiana and other decisions); Monaco v. Mississippi, 292 U.S. 313 (1934).

[64] See Clark v. Barnard, 108 U.S. 436, 447-48 (1883), THE FIRST HUNDRED YEARS at 427 n.163.

[65] Johnson v. Zerbst, 304 U.S. 458, 464 (1938) (right to counsel).

[66] Smith v. Reeves, 178 U.S. 436, 441-45 (1900).

[67] *E.g.*, Kennecott Copper Corp. v. State Tax Comm'n, 327 U.S. 573, 577-80 (1946). *See also* Great Northern Ins. Co. v. Read, 322 U.S. 47, 54 (1944) ("[W]hen we are dealing with the sovereign exemption from judicial interference in the vital field of financial administration a clear declaration of the state's intention to submit its fiscal problems to other courts than those of its own creation must be found."). *Kennecott*, like *Read*, involved a suit for the recovery of taxes claimed to have been illegally exacted. *See also* Atascadero State Hosp. v. Scanlon, 473 U.S. 234, 238 (1985) (Powell, J.) (generalizing the principle enunciated in *Kennecott*). *Cf.* the principle that statutes consenting to suit against the United States are to be strictly construed. *See, e.g.*, Library of Congress v. Shaw, 478 U.S. 310 (1986).

[68] In approving the agreement, said the Court, Congress had provided that nothing in it should "affect, impair, or diminish any right, power, or jurisdiction . . . of the United States," and the compact had been "made in an era when the immunity of corporations performing governmental functions was not in favor in the federal field." Petty v. Tennessee-Missouri Bridge Comm'n, 359 U.S. 275, 280-81 (1959).

[69] 377 U.S. 184 (1964) (Brennan, J., over four dissents).

to suit in federal court . . . ; by thereafter operating a railroad in interstate commerce, Alabama must be taken to have accepted that condition and thus to have consented to suit.[70]

Apart from the striking contrast with the Court's earlier decisions in this field, there were three weaknesses in this argument. Since the statute on which the Court relied made no reference to suits against states, it seemed doubtful either that Congress had meant to impose such a condition[71] or that the state had knowingly accepted it.[72] Moreover, the Court had established many years before that a state could not require a foreign corporation to relinquish its right to litigate in federal court as a condition of doing intrastate business; there were strict limits to government power to condition the grant of a privilege on surrender of a constitutional right.[73]

Nine years later, in *Employees v. Department of Public Health & Welfare,*[74] the Burger Court began a gradual retreat from *Parden.* The question was whether, during a period when the Fair Labor Standards Act validly applied to public school and hospital employees,[75] they could sue the state to enforce its provisions. The answer, over Brennan's solitary dissent, was no. Although, in contrast to *Parden,* the statute explicitly authorized suits against "employer[s]" and defined "employer" to include a state,[76] the majority in an opinion by Justice Douglas (who had dissented in *Parden*) concluded that Congress had not intended to condition the operation of state facilities on a waiver of immunity.

Because the United States was authorized to sue on behalf of injured employees, said Douglas, immunity from individual suit would not leave the beneficiaries of the statute, as in *Parden,* without remedy. Moreover, *Parden* had involved "a rather isolated state activity" in an "area where private persons and corporations normally ran the enterprise." In dealing with operations that were "not proprietary," as in *Employees,* the Court was not prepared "to infer that Congress . . . desired silently to deprive the States of an immunity they have long enjoyed under another part of the Constitution."[77]

---

[70] *Id.* at 192.

[71] *See id.* at 199 (White, J., joined by Douglas, Harlan, and Stewart, dissenting) ("Particular deference should be accorded that 'old and well-known rule that statutes which in general terms divest pre-existing rights or privileges will not be applied to the sovereign without express words to that effect.'") (citing United States v. United Mine Workers, 330 U.S. 258, 272 (1947), which had held the Norris-LaGuardia Act's limitations on labor injunctions inapplicable to suits by the United States).

[72] *See* 377 U.S. at 200 (White, J., joined by Douglas, Harlan, and Stewart, dissenting) (citing Johnson v. Zerbst, note 65 *supra*).

[73] *See e.g.,* Terral v. Burke Constr. Co., 257 U.S. 529, 532-33 (1922). *See also* Elrod v. Burns, pp. 505-06 *supra.* The dissenters in *Parden,* however, 377 U.S. at 198, conceded Congress's authority to impose such a condition.

[74] 411 U.S. 279 (1973).

[75] *I.e.,* after Maryland v. Wirtz had upheld the statute as applied to such employees and before National League of Cities v. Usery had (for the time being) held the contrary. *See* pp. 564-67 *supra.*

[76] *See* 411 U.S. at 289-90 (Marshall, J., concurring).

[77] *Id.* at 284-86 (adding that the statutory provision for double damages reinforced this conclusion):

> It is one thing, as in *Parden,* to make a state employee whole; it is quite another to let him recover double against a State. Recalcitrant private employers may be whipped into line in that manner. But we are reluctant to believe that Congress in pursuit of a harmonious federalism desired to treat the States so harshly.

Douglas's distinctions were neither implausible nor compelling.[78] The difference in tone, in any event, was patent, and two concurring Justices went even further. Marshall and Stewart, who thought Congress had meant to condition operation of the affected facilities on a waiver,[79] concluded that it lacked power to do so. Since the state had no real option to abandon "vital public services" it had been operating long before the statute was made applicable, wrote Marshall, it had not voluntarily consented to suit.[80]

The erosion of *Parden* continued in *Edelman v. Jordan,* where the Court held that a state had not waived its immunity by participating in a federally funded welfare program.[81] Without attempting to decide whether the case was more like *Employees* or *Parden,* Justice Rehnquist concluded that the "threshold" requirement for waiver was not met: "Both *Parden* and *Employees* involved a congressional enactment which by its terms authorized suit by designated plaintiffs against a general class of defendants which literally included States," and there was no such provision in *Edelman.*[82]

The case against waiver on *Parden*'s test seemed stronger in *Edelman* than in *Employees,* but Rehnquist went out of his way to disown the philosophy of *Parden* itself by observing caustically that "[c]onstructive consent is not a doctrine commonly associated with the surrender of constitutional rights."[83] Shortly after Chief Justice Burger's retirement the Court formally announced what Justice Brennan had perceived ever since the *Employees* decision. *Parden* was no longer the law; henceforth states would be held to have consented to suit only if they had actually consented.[84]

---

[78] The governmental-proprietary distinction, while common in a variety of contexts, *e.g.,* Bank of United States v. Planters' Bank, 22 U.S. 904 (1824) (immunity from suit), THE FIRST HUNDRED YEARS at 106-07; South Carolina v. United States, p. 25, note 128 *supra* (immunity from taxation); National League of Cities v. Usery, pp. 564-67 *supra* (immunity from regulation), had been given short shrift in more recent decisions on immunity from suit, *see Ex parte* New York, 256 U.S. 490 (1921) (upholding state immunity from suit arising out of its operation of tugboat), and rejected in holding the Fair Labor Standards Act applicable to the schools and hospitals in issue in *Employees,* Maryland v. Wirtz, 392 U.S. at 195-98. Nor was it obvious that the running of such enterprises was properly classified as governmental rather than proprietary; it involved not governance but the provision of services. The provision for private remedies, Justice Brennan argued, was a central part of the act, without which its purposes could not be achieved; the double-damage provision was not penal but designed to assure compensation for actual but unmeasurable losses resulting from failure to pay the prescribed minimum wage. *See* 411 U.S. at 304-08 (Brennan, J., dissenting).

[79] *See* 411 U.S. at 289-90 (Marshall, J., joined by Stewart, J., concurring). *See also id.* at 301-03 (Brennan, J., dissenting).

[80] *Id.* at 296-97.

[81] 415 U.S. 651 (1974).

[82] *Id.* at 672. Three of the four dissenters argued that the state had constructively waived its immunity. *See id.* at 685-87 (Douglas, J., dissenting); *id.* at 688-96 (Marshall, J., joined by Blackmun, dissenting).

[83] *Id.* at 673. *See also* Atascadero State Hosp. v. Scanlon, 473 U.S. 234, 238 n.1 (1985) (Powell, J., over four dissents) (reaffirming *Edelman* and adding that waiver would be found only where there was "an unequivocal indication that the State intends to consent to federal jurisdiction . . .").

[84] Welch v. State Department of Highways, 483 U.S. 468 (1987) (over four dissents).

## 2. Compulsion

Although *Parden* had plainly been based on the finding that Alabama had consented to suit by running a railroad,[85] there were passages in Justice Brennan's opinion that suggested consent was not necessary at all:

> By empowering Congress to regulate commerce, . . . the States necessarily surrendered any portion of their sovereignty that would stand in the way of such regulation. Since imposition of the FELA right of action upon interstate railroads is within the congressional regulatory power, it must follow that application of the Act to such a railroad cannot be precluded by sovereign immunity.[86]

Justice Marshall suggested the definitive answer to this contention in his concurring opinion in *Employees:* ever since *Hans v. Louisiana* it had been clear that suits against unconsenting states did not fall within the judicial power as defined by article III.[87] That being so, Congress can no more give the federal courts jurisdiction over them than over nondiverse, nonfederal suits between private parties.

Justice Brennan frankly argued that sovereign immunity did not limit the grant of judicial power and that *Hans* had not said it did.[88] When he first put this thesis forward in *Employees,* no other Justice agreed with him. Before the Burger years were over, however, he attracted three of his brethren to this position; despite its return to traditional notions of waiver, the supposedly conservative Burger Court was only one vote short of holding that the only constitutional immunities from suit were those explicitly prescribed by the eleventh amendment.[89]

Even as he disagreed with Brennan about Congress's power to subject states to suit in federal courts, moreover, Justice Marshall suggested in *Employees* that it could make them suable in courts of their own. Both the eleventh amendment and article III, he argued, limited only federal jurisdiction, and any remaining state-law immunity must yield to the exercise of congressional authority under the supremacy clause.[90] Federal subjection of a state to suit in its own courts, however, would be nearly as offensive to state sovereignty as in a federal one. It would thus seem appropriate to construe the substantive

[85] See 377 U.S. at 192 ("It remains the law that a State may not be sued by an individual without its consent. Our conclusion is simply that Alabama, when it began operation of an interstate railroad approximately 20 years after enactment of the FELA, necessarily consented to such suit as was authorized by that Act.").

[86] 377 U.S. at 192.

[87] See *Employees,* 411 U.S. at 290-92 (Marshall, J., joined by Stewart, J., concurring); pp. 7-9 *supra* (discussing *Hans*). *See also* 411 U.S. at 281 n.1 (opinion of Douglas, J., for the Court) (reading *Parden* itself to have recognized the existence of constitutional limitations on suits against states by their own citizens).

[88] See, e.g., *Employees,* 411 U.S. at 315-21 (Brennan, J., dissenting).

[89] See Atascadero State Hosp. v. Scanlon, 473 U.S. 234, 247-302 (1985) (Brennan, J., joined by Marshall, Blackmun, and Stevens, dissenting). The same opinion went on to suggest that the eleventh amendment itself might be inapplicable to federal-question cases despite its explicit reference to "any suit in law or equity." *See id.* at 290. Justice Brennan and his three compatriots expressly took this position shortly after Burger's retirement in Welch v. State Dept. of Highways, 483 U.S. 468, 509-17 (Brennan J., joined by Marshall, Blackmun, and Stevens, dissenting).

[90] 411 U.S. at 297-98.

provisions under which such a statute would be enacted, like article III in *Hans,* to respect the states' traditional immunity.[91]

The Burger Court never passed upon Justice Marshall's suggestion and never adopted Justice Brennan's. In 1976, however, in the unexpected boots of Justice Rehnquist, it took a sudden step in Brennan's direction in the surprising case of *Fitzpatrick v. Bitzer.*[92] Without reference to any supposed waiver, the Court concluded, Congress had authority to subject states to suit whenever it legislated to enforce the fourteenth amendment.[93] Congress's authority under § 5 of that amendment was "plenary," and other sections of the same amendment expressly embodied "limitations on state authority." Thus, in order to enforce the fourteenth amendment, Congress could "provide for private suits against States or state officials which are constitutionally impermissible in other contexts."[94]

This reasoning is less than overwhelming. One might have thought that § 5, like other "plenary" grants of power, was subject to explicit and implicit constitutional limitations; one would hardly read it to authorize the imposition of cruel and unusual punishment. That the fourteenth amendment limits state sovereignty does not distinguish it from the contract clause, which had long been held limited by sovereign immunity.[95] In any event, *Fitzpatrick* did not hold that the fourteenth amendment itself rendered sovereign immunity inapplicable; in the absence of statute the states still could not be sued for violation of its provisions.[96]

Moreover, lower courts to the contrary notwithstanding,[97] *Fitzpatrick* was emphatically not authority for congressional power to abolish state immunity from suit under any provision of the original Constitution. Emphasizing that adoption of the fourteenth amend-

---

[91] *Cf.* the other implicit state immunities that have been found from time to time to limit express grants of congressional power, discussed at pp. 563-68 *supra.*

[92] 427 U.S. 445 (1976).

[93] The statute in question, title VII of the Civil Rights Act of 1964, authorized federal courts to award damages against states for employment discrimination on grounds, inter alia, of sex. *See* 427 U.S. at 447-49.

[94] 427 U.S. at 456. Justice Brennan, *id.* at 457-58, concurred on the broader ground that the states had surrendered their immunity in ratifying the Constitution, *see* p. 572 *supra*; Justice Stevens, *id.* at 459-60, on the narrower ground that any judgment would be paid not from the state treasury but from "separate and independent pension funds." Since he conceded, *id.* at 460, that those funds would be reimbursed with state money, it is hard to see why this should make any difference.

[95] *E.g.,* Hans v. Louisiana, *supra* note 63. *Ex parte* Virginia, 100 U.S. 339 (1880), on which the Court relied, held only that Congress could provide criminal penalties against state officials who deprived individuals of their federal rights. Such suits have never been considered suits against states for purposes of sovereign immunity. *Cf.* Scheuer v. Rhodes, 416 U.S. 232, 237-38 (1974) (Burger, C.J.) (unanimously reaffirming that sovereign immunity did not preclude actions against state officers for damages payable out of their own pockets). *See* THE FIRST HUNDRED YEARS at 393-94 n.172, 423-24.

[96] *See e.g.,* Alabama v. Pugh, 438 U.S. 781 (1978) (holding a fourteenth amendment suit barred by immunity after *Fitzpatrick*). *See also* Quern v. Jordan, 440 U.S. 332, 338-46 (1979) (Rehnquist, J., over objections by Brennan and Marshall) (reaffirming after *Fitzpatrick* the holding in *Edelman,* 415 U.S. at 675-77, that 42 U.S.C. § 1983, which authorized relief against "any person" who deprived another of federal rights under color of state law, did not abrogate the state's immunity).

[97] *See, e.g.,* Jennings v. Illinois Office of Education, 589 F.2d 935, 942 (7th Cir. 1979) (upholding the authority of Congress under its war powers to provide for suits against states by veterans denied civilian reemployment and citing *Fitzpatrick* for the proposition that *every* power granted to Congress "includes the power to make the states amenable to damage actions in the federal courts"). *Accord* Peel v. Florida Dept. of Transportation, 600 F.2d 1070, 1080 (5th Cir. 1979) ("[A] state consents to private damage actions when *Congress* [sic] manifests a sufficient purpose to abrogate a state's immunity.").

ment had worked a "shift in the federal-state balance" and authorized intrusions into "spheres of autonomy previously reserved to the States,"[98] Justice Rehnquist explicitly argued in *Fitzpatrick* that Congress could do under the fourteenth amendment what it could *not* do elsewhere.[99] Nevertheless *Fitzpatrick* stands as a startling reminder that even the Burger Court was prepared to take considerable liberties with the constitutional immunities of the states.

## 3.  Evasion

In *Edelman v. Jordan,* which the Court decided in 1974,[100] a lower federal court had ordered a state officer to pay from the state treasury money that had been withheld from the plaintiffs in violation of a federal welfare law.[101] In an opinion by Justice Rehnquist, the Supreme Court reversed. A suit "seeking to impose a liability which must be paid from public funds in the state treasury," said Rehnquist, "is barred by the Eleventh Amendment."[102]

Since the suit was by an Illinois citizen and the state in question was Illinois, the eleventh amendment was not the source of this immunity.[103] Moreover, Rehnquist's generalization was overly broad, for it overlooked the Court's long-standing concession that mandamus would lie to compel an official to perform a duty imposed upon him by state statute.[104] At bottom, however, the Court's conclusion in *Edelman* reflected the unassailable proposition that a state's immunity would be meaningless if it could be evaded simply by suing an officer instead of the state itself.[105]

To say the least, however, the Court was not writing on a clean slate. For better or worse, a long series of decisions exemplified by *Ex parte Young* had held that in some circumstances a state officer could be sued even though the effect of the judgment was the same as if the state had been named as defendant.[106] Rehnquist's task was to demonstrate that *Edelman* differed significantly from *Ex parte Young*.

Like many cases in which suits against state officers had been permitted, *Young* had involved a request for injunction against future unconstitutional action—in that case the enforcement of allegedly confiscatory rate limitations. "The relief awarded in *Ex parte Young*," said Justice Rehnquist, "was prospective only"; but the order challenged in *Edelman* directed the payment of compensation for a past wrong.[107] It was true that even the injunction in *Young* had an effect on the state treasury, since it cost the state substantial

---

[98] 427 U.S. at 455.

[99] See id. at 456 ("We think that Congress may, in determining what is 'appropriate legislation' for the purpose of enforcing the provisions of the Fourteenth Amendment, provide for private suits against States or state officials which are constitutionally impermissible in other contexts.").

[100] 415 U.S. 651 (1974).

[101] See id. at 653-58.

[102] Id. at 663.

[103] For the proper explanation see Hans v. Louisiana, pp. 7-9 supra.

[104] See, e.g., Board of Liquidation v. McComb, 92 U.S. 531, 541 (1876), THE FIRST HUNDRED YEARS at 417, 422, 426.

[105] See THE FIRST HUNDRED YEARS at 104-06 (discussing Osborn v. Bank of the United States, 22 U.S. 738 (1824)).

[106] See pp. 50-54 supra (discussing Ex parte Young).

[107] 415 U.S. at 664, 668.

money penalties. Later decisions permitting injunctions against discrimination in the distribution of government benefits, Rehnquist added, had probably had even "greater impact" upon state funds. "But the fiscal consequences to state treasuries in these cases," he insisted, "were the necessary result of compliance with decrees which by their terms were prospective in nature. . . . Such an ancillary effect on the state treasury is a permissible and often an inevitable consequence of the principle announced in *Ex parte Young*. . . ."[108]

As Rehnquist said, apart from the question of mandamus to enforce state law the Court had always held that a state officer could not be ordered to pay money out of the state treasury.[109] What *Edelman* failed to explain, however, was why the Court's distinctions made any sense. In light of any conceivable policy underlying the immunity doctrine, it seems wholly immaterial whether the relief sought is prospective or retrospective and whether its effect is ancillary or direct. Moreover, there was a tension between the Court's two bases for distinguishing the injunctive cases that can be highlighted by hypothesizing an order compelling future compliance with a law requiring payments of state funds: such an order is prospective, but its impact on the treasury is direct.

The distinction between *Edelman* and *Young* can be understood only in the light of history. The theory the Court had constructed to explain why officers could be sued in cases like *Young*, as the opinion there said, was that the officer was "stripped of his official or representative character" whenever he attempted to do what the Constitution forbade.[110] Since the reason there was no immunity was that the suit was deemed to be against the officer personally, it followed that he could be sued only if he was personally liable, and so the Court had held in a series of nineteenth-century decisions culminating in *In re Ayers*.[111] The reason a state officer could not be required to pay off the state's bonds was thus that only the state was liable for breach of its contracts. Similarly, the reason the officer could not be sued in *Edelman* was that federal law imposed the duty to make welfare payments only on the state itself.

In losing sight of the origins of the distinction between *Ayers* and *Young*, *Edelman* made the law of immunity seem more absurd than it was. Moreover, it left the law in a very uncertain state, and later decisions of the Burger period added to the confusion.

In *Milliken v. Bradley*,[112] for example, in reliance on the loose language of *Edelman*, state officers were ordered to spend money from the state treasury to finance remedial programs to counteract the effects of past school segregation. This decree, the Court held without dissent, "fits squarely within the prospective-compliance exception reaffirmed by *Edelman*."[113]

Despite its references to prospectivity, however, *Edelman* had not established any blanket exception for prospective orders. Quite the contrary, it had begun by announcing an absolute bar to actions "seeking to impose a liability which must be paid from public funds

---

[108] *Id*. at 667–68.

[109] *See e.g.*, Ford Motor Co. v. Department of Treasury, 323 U.S. 459 (1945), *cited in Edelman*, 415 U.S. at 668–69 (rejecting a suit for refund of taxes allegedly unlawfully collected).

[110] *See Young*, 209 U.S. at 159–60.

[111] 123 U.S. 443, 502–03 (1887). *See* THE FIRST HUNDRED YEARS at 416–28.

[112] 433 U.S. 267 (1977) (Burger, C.J.).

[113] *Id*. at 289.

in the state treasury."[114] Far from following authority, *Milliken* seems to have been the first case outside the traditional mandamus area consciously to order payment of state funds.

The second problem was in applying the supposed distinction, for the order in *Milliken* was no more "prospective" than that condemned in *Edelman* itself. In both cases the money was to be paid in the future in order to right a past wrong. If that is enough to make the order "prospective," there is no such thing as a retrospective order; nobody is ever ordered to have paid in the past.

In an apparent reference to *Edelman*'s observation that the order there requested was "compensation" for the past wrong, the Court in *Milliken* seized upon the fact that in the latter case the money was not to be paid directly to the victims of discrimination.[115] But *Edelman* had not made direct monetary compensation requisite to a holding of immunity; it had condemned compensatory orders as one example of those ordering payment from government funds. The Court in *Milliken* gave no hint of why it thought the distinction material, and it appeared to have nothing to do with either precedent or any conceivably relevant policy.

The year after *Milliken,* in *Hutto v. Finney,*[116] the Court extended suability still further by upholding an order to pay attorneys' fees out of the state treasury on the ground that it was merely "ancillary" to the issuance of a negative and prospective injunction.[117] This ruling completely transformed the "ancillary" concept employed in the *Edelman* opinion. *Edelman* had spoken not of ancillary orders to pay money but of orders having ancillary effects on the treasury, and the rest of the opinion showed it was referring to orders that did not direct the payment of money at all.

The Court attempted to buttress its conclusion in *Hutto* by analogizing the fee order to a fine for violating an injunction and argued that such a fine might even be so framed as to "compensate[] the party who won the injunction for the effects of . . . noncompliance."[118] Unlike a fine, however, a fee award is given to the plaintiff to pay his attorneys; the fact that the money ordered to be spent in *Milliken* was not given to the plaintiffs had been, for better or worse, the reason for upholding the order in that case.[119] More fundamentally, the reason a fine against the officer who disobeyed an injunction would be permissible is that he would pay it himself. Like a damage award to be paid out of the officer's pocket,[120] the fine would not have the same effect as if the state had been ordered to pay it. The fee in *Hutto,* in contrast, was ordered to be paid out of the state treasury; and that, *Edelman* had said, could not be done.

Finally, *Quern v. Jordan*[121] in 1979 held that a federal court could order a state official to notify members of the class that had been denied retroactive relief in *Edelman* that they might seek back benefits by invoking state administrative procedures. Unlike the order in *Edelman,* Justice Rehnquist properly emphasized, the requirement of notice left it "en-

---

[114] *Edelman,* 415 U.S. at 663.
[115] 433 U.S. at 290 n.22.
[116] 437 U.S. 678 (1978) (Stevens, J., over a dissent by Rehnquist).
[117] *Id.* at 690-92.
[118] *Id.* at 691.
[119] *See* text at note 115 *supra.*
[120] *See* Scheuer v. Rhodes, note 95 *supra.*
[121] 440 U.S. 332 (1979).

tirely with the State" to determine whether or not retroactive benefits would be awarded.[122] Thus, the Court concluded, the order in *Quern* did not offend *Edelman's* strictures against requiring the payment of money from the state treasury.[123]

The trouble with this reasoning is that treasury payments did not exhaust the category of impermissible orders but were only one example of the more general principle that an officer could be ordered to perform only his own duties and not those of the state; federal law no more required the individual officer to give notice of state remedies than to pay out state money in *Edelman* itself.[124] The Court added that the order to give notice was "ancillary to the prospective relief already ordered,"[125] but, like the similar argument in *Hutto*, this was not what Justice Rehnquist himself had seemed to mean by an "ancillary effect" in *Edelman*.[126] Finally, in discussing the general principles of immunity, the *Hutto* opinion flatly declared that "the distinction between that relief permissible under the doctrine of *Ex parte Young* and that found barred in *Edelman* was the difference between prospective relief on one hand and retrospective relief on the other."[127] If taken seriously, this dictum would authorize suits to compel officers to pay future interest installments on state obligations, contrary to *Edelman's* flat statement that no money could be ordered paid from the state treasury, and despite the fact that it remains as difficult today as it was at the time of *Ayers* to justify holding an agent for breach of a contract to which only his principal is a party.

## 4. Expansion

In an action involving both federal- and state-law challenges, a federal district court entered an injunction requiring state officers to provide suitable community living arrangements for mentally retarded inmates of a public institution.[128] After the Supreme Court held that a federal statute on which the court below had partly relied provided no basis for the order,[129] the court of appeals reaffirmed the injunction on state-law grounds. In 1984, in *Pennhurst State School & Hospital v. Halderman*,[130] the Supreme Court reversed, five to four.

*Ex parte Young*, wrote Justice Powell for the majority, had been based on the necessity

---

[122]*Id.* at 348.

[123]The Court specifically noted that the officer "makes no issue of the incidental administrative expense connected with preparing and mailing the notice," *id.* at 347, which although described as "de minimis," *id.* at n.19, would appear to have created a serious objection in principle if it had been properly asserted.

[124]*Cf.* Hawaii v. Gordon, 373 U.S. 57 (1963) (holding an officer could not be compelled to convey government land).

[125]440 U.S. at 349.

[126]Nevertheless the fact that the notice requirement was "ancillary" to a prospective injunction proved to be the key to the *Quern* decision. In 1985, over four dissents, the Court held an identical order barred by immunity because the state's voluntary cessation of the offending conduct had left no room for prospective relief; there was nothing to which the notice order could be said to be "ancillary." Green v. Mansour, 474 U.S. 64 (Rehnquist, J.).

[127]440 U.S. at 337. *See also* Papasan v. Allain, 478 U.S. 265 (1986) (White, J.) (holding that an officer could be ordered not to violate the equal protection clause in distributing educational funds but, over four dissents, not to compensate the victims of past breaches of trust).

[128]*See* Pennhurst State School & Hosp. v. Halderman, 465 U.S. 89, 92-95 (1984).

[129]Pennhurst State School & Hosp. v. Halderman, 451 U.S. 1 (1981).

[130]465 U.S. 89 (1984).

of "permit[ting] the federal courts to vindicate federal rights"; there was no such necessity "when a plaintiff alleges that a state official has violated state law."[131] As Justice Stevens observed in dissent,[132] however, the Court had entertained state-law claims against state officers since long before *Young* itself, and it had never before suggested that *Young* was limited to federal claims.[133] Nor had the question invariably passed unnoticed. As early as 1887, for example, in expressly rejecting an eleventh amendment objection, the Court had said the litigation was "with the officer, not the State" because "the suit is to get a state officer to do what a statute requires of him."[134] In a case decided during the same term as *Young*, the Court had expressly said a suit charging an official only with what the opinion called "dereliction of duties enjoined by the statutes of the State" was "not a suit against the State."[135] Nine years later, in a case presenting both federal and state claims, the Court had proceeded directly to the latter after declaring that the question of sovereign immunity had been settled by decisions like *Ex parte Young;*[136] and eight Justices had reaffirmed the principle not two years before *Pennhurst.*[137] The majority's efforts to get around the precedents were unconvincing.[138]

Apart from precedent, the Court's explanation of *Ex parte Young* confuses the theory of that decision with its motivation. It is no doubt true that a desire to find an effective means of enforcing the Constitution influenced the Court in its narrow construction of the state's immunity in suits against officers.[139] But the theory the Court developed to accomplish that goal was not limited to federal claims. As *Young* itself said, the Constitution "stripped" the official of any authority the state may have attempted to give him to commit an act otherwise actionable;[140] he was left in the same position as if the state had given him no authority at all.[141]

---

[131] *Id.* at 105-06.

[132] *Id.* at 130-67 (Stevens, J., joined by Brennan, Marshall, and Blackmun, dissenting).

[133] Indeed, it had long been the Court's explicit rule that state-law claims in suits against state officers should be decided first in order to avoid unnecessary constitutional questions. Siler v. Louisville & N.R.R., 213 U.S. 175 (1909).

[134] Rolston v. Missouri Fund Commissioners, 120 U.S. 390, 411 (1887).

[135] Scully v. Bird, 209 U.S. 481, 490 (1908).

[136] Greene v. Louisville & I.R.R., 244 U.S. 499, 506-08 (1917).

[137] Florida Department of State v. Treasure Salvors, Inc., 458 U.S. 670, 696-97, 714 (1982). For the four dissenting Justices, this conclusion was dictum. *See also* Cory v. White, 457 U.S. 85, 91 (1982) (reaffirming that immunity barred interpleading officials of two states taxing a single estate because of the settled rule that state officials could not be sued "unless they are alleged to be acting contrary to federal law or against the authority of state law").

[138] As the majority noted, 465 U.S. at 110 n.19, *Greene* did not expressly say it was rejecting "the Eleventh Amendment" argument as to both state and federal grounds. However, it said nothing to support the unnatural inference that it meant to limit its discussion to the federal claim and then to enter an order on state-law grounds without determining its authority to do so. The majority's only response to *Scully* was that since it had allowed suit against an officer who had not violated state law it had been overruled by Larson v. Domestic & Foreign Commerce Corp., note 145 *infra*. But *Larson* contained nothing to impair *Scully's* clear holding that *Young* applied although the claim was not based on federal law. *Rolston* was distinguished, 465 U.S. at 109 n.18, on the unresponsive ground that the state statute in that case had imposed a " 'plain ministerial duty.' "

[139] *See, e.g.,* Osborn v. Bank of the United States, 22 U.S. 738, 847-48 (1824) (arguing that a contrary holding would cripple the enforcement of federal law).

[140] *See* p. 53 *supra*.

[141] There are many similar statements of the governing principle. *E.g.,* Cunningham v. Macon and Brunswick R.R., 109 U.S. 446, 452 (1883) ("To make out his defence he must show that his authority was sufficient in law

A closer look at the *Pennhurst* opinion, indeed, suggests that the questionable conclusion that *Young* was limited to federal claims may not have been the basis of the decision after all. For near the end of his opinion Justice Powell appended a footnote declaring that "it may well be wondered" whether it was really consistent with state immunity to permit suits against officers on the ground that they had acted "without any statutory authority."[142] One would have thought the extended passages devoted to showing that *Young* applied only to federal claims had already settled the issue about which the footnote "wondered."[143] But the footnote added explicitly: "We hold only that to the extent the doctrine is consistent with the analysis of this opinion, it is a very narrow exception" not satisfied on the facts of the *Pennhurst* case.[144]

In other words, the distinction between federal and state claims was unnecessary to the decision; there was a narrower ground on which the Court relied. That ground was the one taken in the 1949 decision of *Larson v. Domestic & Foreign Commerce Corp.*: even the *ultra vires* theory did not justify suing an officer who was acting within his authority.[145] As Justice Stevens again pointed out,[146] the trouble with this argument was that, in contrast to *Larson,* where the plaintiff had alleged merely a common law tort, the complaint in *Pennhurst* seemed to satisfy the *Larson* criterion by alleging that the officers had violated statutory requirements defining their official duties.[147] If *Larson* meant an officer could not be sued on grounds like those in *Pennhurst,* it seemed inconsistent with its own express affirmation that, "where the officer's powers are limited by statute," he could be sued for "actions beyond those limitations."[148]

---

to protect him."). *See Pennhurst,* 465 U.S. at 147 (Stevens, J., dissenting) ("Since a state officer's conduct in violation of state law is certainly no less illegal than his violation of federal law, in either case the official, by committing an illegal act, is 'stripped of his official or representative character.' ").

[142] 465 U.S. at 114 n.25.

[143] *See also id.* at 106 ("We conclude that *Young* and *Edelman* are inapplicable in a suit against state officials on the basis of state law."). In light of the footnote quoted above, this may only mean that the analysis is different in respect to state-law claims, not that the bar is absolute.

[144] *Id.* at 114 n.25.

[145] *See id.* at 106-17 (citing *Larson,* 337 U.S. 682, 689-95 (1949), *criticized in* Currie, *Sovereign Immunity and Suits against Government Officers,* 1984 SUP. CT. REV. 149, 156-59). This entire discussion gives every appearance of having been tacked on as an afterthought in response to Justice Stevens's overpowering dissent.

[146] *See* 465 U.S. at 153-58.

[147] Indeed, that is what both the district court and the court of appeals had held, 446 F. Supp. 1295, 1322-23 (E.D. Pa. 1977) ("both the Commonwealth and the counties have violated their statutory obligation to provide minimally adequate habilitation"); 673 F.2d 647, 651-56 (3d Cir. 1982). *Contrast Larson,* 337 U.S. at 691 ("Nor was there any allegation of a limitation in the Administrator's delegated power to refuse shipment in cases in which he believed the United States was not obligated to deliver."). Whether all relief granted in *Pennhurst* was consistent with the distinctions made in Edelman v. Jordan, pp. 574–75 *supra,* the Supreme Court did not have to determine.

[148] 337 U.S. at 689. *See* Shapiro, *Wrong Turns: The Eleventh Amendment and the* Pennhurst *Case,* 98 HARV. L. REV. 61, 74-76 (1984). The majority in *Pennhurst* argued that the defendants had not acted "beyond their delegated authority" because the statute "gave them broad discretion to provide 'adequate' mental health services" and the claim was that "petitioners have not provided such services adequately." 465 U.S. at 101-02 n.11. But the courts below had held the defendants had contradicted a statutory limitation on that discretion. *See* note 147 *supra.* Official immunity from damages in cases of violations of law, *see* 465 U.S. at 109 n.17, is not a good analogy; an official may be free from damage liability, for reasons inapplicable to injunctive cases, even when he has acted unconstitutionally and thus is clearly not treated as the state under the Court's own test. *See* Scheuer v. Rhodes, 416 U.S. 232 (1974).

Overall the Burger Court was more faithful than some of its predecessors to the unenlightened principle of sovereign immunity. This is as it should be, since that doctrine is a part of the Constitution. It seems unfortunate, however, that the Court weakened the doctrine in *Fitzpatrick* by permitting Congress to override immunity in order to enforce the fourteenth amendment and in *Milliken* and *Hutto* by ordering officers who were suable only on the theory that they were not the state to pay money that only the state had a duty to pay. Moreover, one cannot help wondering why the Court thought it would improve the acceptability of its decision in *Pennhurst* by going to such lengths to disguise the fact that it was taking a new tack that, as the ultimate interpreter of a less than pellucid provision, it had a perfect right to take.

## D.  Interstate Relations

To be contrasted with cases such as *Edelman* and *Pennhurst* was the 1979 decision in *Nevada v. Hall* that one state had no constitutional immunity from suit in the courts of another.[149] A workable federation requires harmonious relations among the states themselves as well as between states and nation, and article IV of the Constitution is devoted in substantial part to promoting them. None of its provisions, however, seemed even remotely to suggest that interstate immunity was among the protections afforded unless it was the requirement that each state give "full faith and credit" to the acts of others.[150] That clause, as the Court recognized in *Hall*, had been rather consistently construed over the past forty years not to require one state to subordinate its legitimate interests to those of another;[151] since the action had been brought by California residents to recover for injuries incurred on a California highway, California could hardly be held to lack a legitimate interest in requiring compensation.[152]

Justice Blackmun, in dissent, argued that interstate immunity was "implied as an essential component of federalism";[153] Justice Rehnquist analogized to such decisions as *McCulloch v. Maryland* and *Hans v. Louisiana*.[154] Distinguishing *Hans* as establishing a limit on *federal* jurisdiction, Justice Stevens seemed to hint at an argument that might serve to distinguish other federal-state immunities as well: in contrast to both *McCulloch* and *Hans*, *Hall* involved no grant of federal authority—and no other provision of the Constitution—in which the asserted immunity could be said to be fairly implied.[155]

---

[149]440 U.S. 410 (Stevens, J., over three dissents).

[150]The other provisions of article IV respecting interstate relations (apart from the superseded provision concerning fugitive slaves) are the privileges and immunities and extradition clauses. For the early history of these clauses see THE FIRST HUNDRED YEARS at 237-49.

[151]*See* 440 U.S. at 421-24 (citing, inter alia, Pacific Ins. Co. v. Industrial Acc. Comm'n, p. 242, note 194 *supra*). The one relatively recent exception was the 1947 case of Order of Commercial Travelers v. Wolfe, p. 365, note 216 *supra* (holding that the state where a deceased member of a fraternal benefit society lived could not apply its own law to invalidate a contract clause requiring a suit for insurance benefits to be brought within six months of his death).

[152]*See* 440 U.S. at 411, 424 ("California's interest is the . . . substantial one of providing 'full protection to those who are injured on its highways through the negligence of both residents and nonresidents.'").

[153]*Id*. at 430 (Blackmun, J., joined by Burger and Rehnquist, dissenting).

[154]*Id*. at 432-43 (Rehnquist, J., joined by Burger, dissenting).

[155]*See id*. at 420-21 ("Nor does anything in Article III authorizing the judicial power of the United States, or in the Eleventh Amendment limitation on that power, provide any basis, explicit or implicit, for this Court to impose limits on the powers of California exercised in this case."). *Hans* construed the grant of judicial power narrowly; Collector v. Day and National League of Cities v. Usery did the same for the tax and commerce

In other respects, however, the Burger Court gave modest support to the needs of federalism in its interstate aspects. *Allstate Ins. Co. v. Hague,* to be sure, seemed to carry the deferential attitude of earlier modern cases to extremes in 1981 by permitting a state to apply its own law to increase the insurance benefits payable for injuries inflicted by one nonresident on another outside its borders;[156] as the dissenters pointed out, none of the contacts on which the plurality relied (that the victim had worked in the forum state, that his widow had moved there after the accident, and that the insurer did business there) seemed to provide any legitimate basis for applying the law in question.[157] However, *Phillips Petroleum Co. v. Shutts* made clear four years after *Hague* that the Constitution still imposed limits on the authority of one state to meddle with the affairs of another by holding for the first time in many years that a state had offended both full faith and due process by applying its own law to a case in which it had no legitimate interest.[158]

Moreover, in the related field of jurisdiction over the person, the Burger Court was quick to insist that the fairness principle of *International Shoe Co. v. Washington*[159] was a two-way street. *International Shoe* had refused to allow the traditional requirement that the defendant be found within the state to preclude an exercise of jurisdiction that was consistent with "fair play and substantial justice." *Shaffer v. Heitner,* in 1977, appropriately added that the traditionally sufficient presence of intangible property within the state could not save an exercise of jurisdiction that did not comport with those standards.[160] Indeed, in *Kulko v. Superior Court,* decided the year after *Shaffer,* the Court carried its solicitude for out-of-state defendants to the point of denying the state of a child's residence jurisdiction to order the father who had sent her there to support her, despite the assumption that the forum had an interest sufficient to justify application of its law on the merits.[161] To suggest that due process placed more stringent limitations on

---

powers. *McCulloch* may be said to have found federal immunity from state taxation implicit in the grant of authority to establish the national bank.

[156] 449 U.S. 302 (1981).

[157] *See id.* at 339-40 (Powell, J., joined by Burger and Rehnquist, dissenting) ("The plurality focuses only on physical contacts *vel non,* and in doing so pays scant attention to the more fundamental reasons why our precedents require reasonable policy-related contacts in choice-of-law cases."). Justice Stevens concurred in the result without finding that the forum state had any interest in the case on the ground that application of forum law was neither unfair nor a threat to any other state's "sovereignty," *id.* at 320–32; Justice Stewart did not participate.

[158] 472 U.S. 797, 814-23 (1985) (Rehnquist, J., over a dissent by Stevens) (striking down the application of Kansas law with respect to the payment of interest on royalties under gas leases having no connection with that state). *See also* Sosna v. Iowa, 419 U.S. 393, 407 (1975) (Rehnquist, J., over three dissents) (demonstrating that the equal protection clause did not *require* one state to ride roughshod over the interests of another by upholding a one-year residency requirement for divorce under the law of the forum state) ("Iowa may quite reasonably decide that it does not wish to become a divorce mill. . . ."). *See* pp. 329-30 and 365, note 216 *supra* (discussing Williams v. North Carolina and related cases).

[159] *See* p. 330 *supra.*

[160] 433 U.S. 186 (1977) (Marshall, J., over a dissent by Brennan finding sufficient contacts to satisfy *International Shoe*). *See also* Rush v. Savchuck, 444 U.S. 320 (1980) (Marshall, J., over two dissents) (applying *Shaffer* to invalidate an outlandish attempt to assert quasi-in-rem jurisdiction over an out-of-state defendant on a claim unrelated to the forum state on the basis of the presence of an insurer); Helicopteros Nacionales de Colombia v. Hall, 466 U.S. 408 (1984) (Blackmun, J., over a dissent by Brennan) (holding that trivial contacts with the forum state did not support in personam jurisdiction over an unrelated claim).

[161] 436 U.S. 84, 98 (1978) (Marshall, J., over three dissents). *See also* World-Wide Volkswagen Corp. v. Woodson, 444 U.S. 286 (1980) (White, J., over three dissents) (denying the state where the occupants of a vehicle were injured jurisdiction over the out-of-state seller of the vehicle).

personal jurisdiction than on choice of law not only seemed to make the concession that a state's law might constitutionally be applied somewhat hollow; it also appeared to suggest that it mattered less to a defendant whether he was hanged than where the execution took place.[162]

Similarly, although it resuscitated the doubtful principle that article IV outlawed discrimination against outsiders only with respect to those privileges and immunities that were "fundamental,"[163] the Burger Court aggressively held that citizens of other states could not be subjected to discriminatory income taxes,[164] subordinated to local competitors for private jobs on the Alaska pipeline,[165] or excluded from the practice of law.[166] Indeed in *United Bldg. & Constr. Trades Council v. Mayor of Camden*[167] the Court went so far as to hold that the privileges and immunities clause required a *city* to show a reasonable justification for preferring its own residents in respect to public-works employment, although out-of-staters were arguably protected by the fact that persons residing elsewhere in the state—and thus with a say in its legislation—were subjected to the same disability. Moreover, *Zobel v. Williams* carried the principle behind the privileges and immunities clause a step beyond the provision itself by holding that equal protection forbade Alaska in distributing oil royalties to discriminate among *its own* citizens on the basis of the length of time they had resided in the state.[168]

There was a considerable overlap between the privileges and immunities clause, which forbade discrimination against citizens of other states, and the commerce clause, which had long been held to preclude most discrimination against interstate commerce itself.[169]

---

[162] *See* Silberman, Shaffer v. Heitner: *The End of an Era,* 53 N.Y.U.L. REV. 33, 88 (1978). *See also* Sedler, *Judicial Jurisdiction and Choice of Law: The Consequences of* Shaffer v. Heitner, 63 IOWA L. REV. 1031, 1033 (1978) ("[T]he constitutional dimensions of the exercise of long-arm jurisdiction and the application of the forum's substantive law should be fully co-extensive."). The Burger Court was not consistently unreceptive to assertions of long-arm jurisdiction, however. Two 1984 decisions holding that states in which allegedly defamatory materials were distributed could assert jurisdiction over out-of-state periodicals and their employees firmly rejected the notion that the first amendment imposed special limitations on personal jurisdiction when speech was concerned (Keeton v. Hustler Magazine, Inc., 465 U.S. 770; Calder v. Jones, 465 U.S. 783 (both by Rehnquist, J., for a unanimous Court)). *See also* Burger King Corp. v. Rudzewicz, 471 U.S. 462 (1985) (Brennan, J., over two dissents) (permitting suit against a franchisee for breach of contract in the injured party's state).

[163] Baldwin v. Montana Fish & Game Comm'n, 436 U.S. 371, 388 (1978) (Blackmun, J., over three dissents) (permitting discrimination against nonresident elk hunters) ("Equality in access to Montana elk is not basic to the maintenance or well-being of the Union."). Contrast the text of the provision itself: "The citizens of each state shall be entitled to *all* privileges and immunities of citizens in the several states" (emphasis added). For earlier appearances of this interpretation see THE FIRST HUNDRED YEARS at 240 n.20; for renewed criticism in light of the purposes of the clause see Varat, *State "Citizenship" and Interstate Equality,* 48 U. CHI. L. REV. 487, 509-16 (1981).

[164] Austin v. New Hampshire, 420 U.S. 656 (1975) (Marshall, J., over a dissent by Blackmun).

[165] Hicklin v. Orbeck, 437 U.S. 518 (1978) (Brennan, J.).

[166] Supreme Court of New Hampshire v. Piper, 470 U.S. 274 (1985) (Powell. J., over a dissent by Rehnquist). *Cf.* the decisions dealing with discrimination against aliens discussed at pp. 500-04 *supra.*

[167] 465 U.S. 208 (1984) (Rehnquist, J., over a dissent by Blackmun).

[168] 457 U.S. 55 (1982) (Burger, C. J., over a dissent by Rehnquist). *See also id.* at 78-81 (O'Connor, J., concurring) (arguing that the discrimination unduly burdened the article IV privilege of outsiders to settle within the state). *Accord* Hooper v. Bernalillo County Assessor, 472 U.S. 612 (1985) (Burger, C. J., over three dissents) (holding that a tax break for veterans could not be limited to pre-1976 residents).

[169] *See, e.g.,* Welton v. Missouri, 91 U.S. 275 (1876), THE FIRST HUNDRED YEARS at 404-05. The Burger Court reaffirmed this principle in Philadelphia v. New Jersey, 437 U.S. 617 (1978) (Stewart, J., over two dis-

The *Camden* decision, in finding that a preference for residents of a single city implicated the privileges and immunities clause, had had its equally debatable counterpart in the earlier decision in *Dean Milk Co. v. City of Madison* that the commerce clause precluded a city from requiring that all milk sold be processed within five miles of its boundary.[170] Only a few months before *Camden,* however, the Court in *White v. Massachusetts Council of Construction Employers* had rejected the argument that a similar preference for city residents on public-works projects offended the commerce clause.[171] It had done so in reliance on earlier Burger Court decisions establishing a spanking new exception to the general antidiscrimination principle: a state may freely discriminate against interstate commerce when it acts in a proprietary capacity.

This exception had its origin in 1976 in *Hughes v. Alexandria Scrap Corp.*, a rather complicated case upholding a state bounty effectively available only to local scrap processors.[172] The governing principle was stated as a bare conclusion: "Nothing in the purposes animating the Commerce Clause prohibits a State, in the absence of congressional action, from participating in the market and exercising the right to favor its own citizens over others."[173] Whether *Alexandria Scrap* was an appropriate case in which to describe the state as a market participant may be questioned. Moreover, the result might have been defended on the basis that local operators had a special claim to the benefit of their taxes. It is generally assumed, for example, that the privileges and immunities clause does not forbid charging outsiders more than taxpayers to attend a state university.[174] *Reeves v. Stake,* however, applied the proprietary principle unequivocally in holding that a state

---

sents) (striking down a virtual ban on the importation of waste for disposal within the state), and in Hughes v. Oklahoma, 441 U.S. 322 (1979) (Brennan, J., over two dissents) (overruling Geer v. Connecticut, p. 39, note 77 *supra,* in holding that a state could not forbid the shipment of minnows to other states despite the contention that the state as "owner" was free to dictate the terms on which wild animals could be taken and sold). *But see* Maine v. Taylor, 477 U.S. 131 (1986) (Blackmun, J., over a dissent by Stevens) (upholding a law forbidding importation of live baitfish on the ground that there were no less restrictive means to prevent introduction of out-of-state parasites and nonnative fish species that might upset the ecological balance). On the question of the extent to which legislation neutral on its face may be held to discriminate against interstate commerce because of its disparate effects see Hunt v. Washington Apple Adv. Comm'n, Exxon Corp. v. Governor of Maryland, and Commonwealth Edison Co. v. Montana, all noted at p. 492, note 188 *supra.* The general test for the validity of state laws affecting interstate commerce was reaffirmed in Pike v. Bruce Church, Inc., 397 U.S. 137, 142 (1970) (Stewart, J.), where the Court struck down as unduly burdensome a requirement that cantaloupes grown in Arizona be packed there: "Where the statute regulates evenhandedly to effectuate a legitimate local public interest, and its effects on interstate commerce are only incidental, it will be upheld unless the burden imposed on such commerce is clearly excessive in relation to the putative local benefits." *Cf.* Southern Pacific Co. v. Arizona, pp. 327-28 *supra. See also* Hellerstein, Hughes v. Oklahoma: *The Court, the Commerce Clause, and State Control of Natural Resources,* 1979 SUP. CT. REV. 51, 71 (concluding that decisions from *Pike* to *Hughes* "attest to the Court's achievement of an increased measure of doctrinal consistency in an important area of constitutional law").

[170] 340 U.S. 349 (1951).

[171] 460 U.S. 204 (1983) (Rehnquist, J., over two dissents).

[172] 426 U.S. 794 (Powell, J., over three dissents).

[173] *Id.* at 810.

[174] *See* Varat, *supra* note 163, at 523 ("Like other groups free to combine their members' efforts to produce collective benefits to be shared among the group, political communities, including states, have a prima facie justification for limiting distribution of their public goods to those who combined to provide them."). Since the economic effect of a subsidy may be similar to that of a regulation, however, this principle may arguably have less applicability in a commercial context. *See id.* at 541-45; J. JACKSON, WORLD TRADE AND THE LAW OF GATT 329-32 (1969).

favor local customers of a publicly owned cement plant even though no monetary subsidy appeared to be involved.[175]

The theory of these cases was that the commerce clause required that buyers and sellers be free to make their own business decisions, not that they deal fairly with outsiders.[176] Competitive forces, in other words, could be counted on to assure efficient behavior in the absence of legal restraints. In other constitutional contexts, however, such as intergovernmental or sovereign immunities, the distinction had cut in precisely the opposite direction: a state's interest was entitled to *less* respect when it was performing a proprietary rather than a governmental function.[177]

Moreover, the state is not an ordinary participant in the market. Its tax powers render it relatively immune to competitive restraints on inefficient behavior, and its subservience to local political forces creates the risk that even in a proprietary capacity it may not think first of maximizing its own profit.[178] It may be true that so long as the state has competitors a proprietary discrimination may be less damaging to outside interests than a regulatory one, but the principle seemed broad enough to permit discrimination by a state monopoly.[179] If the Court meant what it said, all a state had to do to destroy the common market the Framers had tried to establish—subject to the congressional check the Court had found insufficient in the context of state regulation—was to take over the business in question.[180]

In holding in *White* that the commerce clause did not forbid preferences for local residents in *private* employment on public works projects, moreover, the Court arguably offended the very distinction on which it professed to rely. For the majority it was enough that the rule "covers a discrete, identifiable class of economic activity in which the city is a major participant": "Everyone affected by the order is, in a substantial if informal sense, 'working for the city.'"[181] As Justice Blackmun noted in dissent, however, *Alexandria Scrap* and *Reeves* had upheld "unilateral refusals to deal" by the states themselves; *White*

---

[175] 447 U.S. 429 (1980) (Blackmun, J., over four dissents).

[176] *See id.* at 436-39.

[177] *See* p. 566 *supra*. For a useful discussion of the various contexts in which the distinction has been found relevant see Wells & Hellerstein, *The Governmental-Proprietary Distinction in Constitutional Law,* 66 VA. L. REV. 1073 (1980).

[178] *See Reeves,* 447 U.S. at 450 (Powell, J., dissenting) ("A State frequently will respond to market conditions on the basis of political rather than economic concerns."). *See also* Jackson, *supra* note 174, at 331, 333-34, 345 (noting that for this reason article XVII of the General Agreement on Tariffs and Trade imposes on state enterprises a general obligation in the international context not to discriminate against foreign purchasers or suppliers).

[179] The Court in *Reeves* conceded the possibility that there might be exceptions to the market-participant principle and specifically reserved the question whether a state might successfully "hoard resources" by acting in a proprietary capacity, 447 U.S. at 442-44, but it placed no explicit limits on its principle. *See also White,* 460 U.S. at 208 ("*Alexandria Scrap* and *Reeves* . . . stand for the proposition that when a state or local government enters the market as a participant it is not subject to the restraints of the Commerce Clause.").

[180] The Court's consistent refusal to rubber-stamp regulation of the use of state-owned highways suggests a way of avoiding this unpalatable conclusion. *See, e.g.,* Bibb v. Navajo Freight Lines, Inc., 359 U.S. 520 (1959) (invalidating requirement of specified type of mudguard); Raymond Motor Transportation, Inc., v. Rice, 434 U.S. 429 (1978) (striking down limitations on length of trucks); Hellerstein, *supra* note 169, at 76-77 n.150.

[181] *White,* 460 U.S. at 211 n.7.

permitted the state to impose discriminatory rules on private parties. For government "to dictate to another those with whom *he* may deal . . . is the essence of regulation."[182]

If proprietary discrimination was consistent with the purposes of the commerce clause, it was unclear why it was not consistent with the related policy of the privileges and immunities clause as well.[183] Let us be thankful at least that the Court concluded it was not; even at the price of inconsistency it is better to weaken one constitutional provision than two.

## II.  The Distribution of Federal Powers

### A.  Presidential Immunities

The most newsworthy decision of the Burger Court in the field of separation of powers was *United States v. Nixon,* which upheld an order directing the President of the United States to turn over tape recordings of his own conversations for possible use as evidence in a criminal trial.[184] The impact was dramatic: fatally compromised by the impending disclosures, the President resigned within days rather than face impeachment and removal. The unanimous decision was a tribute to judicial independence; three Justices voted without blinking to bring down the President who had appointed them.[185]

The basic question in *Nixon* was whether an order requiring the President to produce evidence was inconsistent with the separation of powers. Ever since *McCulloch v. Maryland* it had been understood that federalism required that one organ of government be to some extent protected from incursions by another;[186] the same reasoning seemed applicable to the separation of powers. Article I acknowledged this by providing that members of Congress should not be "questioned in any other place" respecting their speech or debate and by limiting the power to arrest them while Congress was in session.[187] No comparable provision was made for the President; but there was no express provision for the immunity in *McCulloch* either. It had long been clear that the Constitution implicitly provided immunities that were essential to its operation.[188]

---

[182]*Id.* at 218-19.

[183]*See Camden,* 465 U.S. at 220-21 (stating conclusorily that article IV's "concern with comity cuts across the market regulator–market participant distinction that is crucial under the Commerce Clause") ("It is discrimination against out-of-state residents on matters of fundamental concern which triggers the [Privileges and Immunities] Clause, not regulation affecting interstate commerce."). Justice Blackmun, who dissented in both *Camden* and *White,* thought the privileges and immunities clause the *less* restrictive of the two in respect to discrimination against nonresidents of a municipality: "The Commerce Clause entails a substantive policy of unimpeded interstate commerce that is impermissibly undermined by local protectionism even when intrastate commerce is penalized as well." *Camden,* 465 U.S. at 235 n.16.

[184]418 U.S. 683 (1974).

[185]Justice Rehnquist, who had served in the Justice Department during many of the events in question, did not participate. See *id.* at 716.

[186]*See* p. 571, note 78 *supra.*

[187]U.S. Const. art. I, § 6.

[188]*See* 418 U.S. at 705-06 n.16; P. Kurland, Watergate and the Constitution 134 (1978):

> The congressional privilege was a reaction to English experience of harassment of antiestablishment members of Parliament; there was no similar evidence that executive officials had

There were three parts to the immunity question in *Nixon*. First, was the President amenable to judicial process at all? If so, was the question whether he should produce documents in response to a subpoena committed to his unreviewable determination? If not, should he have turned over the tapes? The issues were distinct, but the Court did not always keep them separate in its opinion.[189]

Amenability to process entails judicial control and thus compromises the independence of other branches of government. Some such consideration seems to have underlain the express and implicit limitations the Constitution places on suits against unconsenting states in federal court.[190] On the other hand, judicial process is an important means of keeping officials within the legal limits of their authority and thus may be viewed as a vital element in the system of checks and balances. From the first this tension was resolved by holding there was no general immunity of executive officers from judicial orders; *Marbury v. Madison* emphatically declared that mandamus would lie to compel a cabinet officer to perform a nondiscretionary duty.[191]

In *Mississippi v. Johnson,* however, in 1867, the Court had come close to saying the President could not be subjected to judicial process at all.[192] It had done so, moreover, in a context particularly favorable to the opposite conclusion. The need for a judicial check was at its height because the action the President was threatening to take was allegedly unconstitutional; the risk of intimidating the President was reduced because the suit was for an injunction that would not affect his pocketbook.[193] The decision seemed difficult to reconcile with *Marbury,* for the risk of executive disobedience of a court order, which so troubled the Justices in *Johnson,* had been hardly less serious in *Marbury* itself.

Not surprisingly, when efforts were made to compel production of the so-called Watergate tapes, President Nixon invoked *Johnson*. In an earlier round the Court of Appeals for the District of Columbia pronounced that decision dead on the basis of the intervening *Steel Seizure Case*[194] and distinguished it on the basis of its own unconvincing argument that enjoining the President from enforcing an unconstitutional law would "interfere[] with the exercise of Executive discretion."[195] The Supreme Court evidently agreed that

---

been similarly imposed upon. . . . Many other official privileges have been sustained, even without statutory support, and in the absence of constitutional language.

[189] *See* Gunther, *Judicial Hegemony and Legislative Autonomy: The* Nixon *Case and the Impeachment Process,* 22 UCLA L. REV. 30 (1974).

[190] *See* pp. 568-80 *supra*.

[191] 5 U.S. 137, 162-73 (1803). *See* THE FIRST HUNDRED YEARS at 66-67 & n.16.

[192] 71 U.S. 475, THE FIRST HUNDRED YEARS at 299-301.

[193] *Cf.* Supreme Court of Virginia v. Consumers Union, 446 U.S. 719, 736-37 (1980) (holding that state judges acting in prosecutorial capacity in disciplinary proceedings could be sued for injunction although immune from damages). *But see id.* at 731-34 (holding the same judges immune from injunctions as well as damages when acting in rule-making capacity in order to spare them " 'the burden of defending themselves' ") (also citing Eastland v. United States Servicemen's Fund, 421 U.S. 491, 502-03 (1975), which had held members of Congress immune in an injunctive suit without considering the question).

[194] Youngstown Sheet & Tube Co. v. Sawyer, pp. 365-69 *supra* (upholding an injunction against unlawful action by the Secretary of Commerce in reliance on a presidential order, without considering the effect of *Johnson*).

[195] Nixon v. Sirica, 487 F.2d 700, 708-12 (D.C. Cir. 1973) (upholding an order requiring production of the tapes before a grand jury).

the President was not entirely immune from process, since it upheld the order to produce,[196] but it did not address the issue. It would have been helpful to know the reasons for its conclusion.[197]

The claim that the President must be the ultimate judge of the need for executive confidentiality was rejected on the ground that *Marbury* had held it was for the courts to determine what the Constitution meant.[198] It would have been entirely consistent with this principle, however, for the Court to accept the President's argument, for "there is nothing in [*Marbury*] that precludes a constitutional interpretation which gives final authority to another branch."[199] The question could properly be answered only by a comparison of the risks to executive authority of permitting the courts to make such decisions and of the risks to judicial authority of leaving the matter to the President.

The Court undertook a similar inquiry in determining the final question whether the requested materials should be produced. Because of the need for confidentiality, the Chief Justice concluded, the President (like the courts) did enjoy some constitutional protection against compulsory disclosure of internal communications,[200] but his privilege was not absolute. Full disclosure of relevant facts was essential to fair trial of those accused of crime; the President's "generalized interest in confidentiality . . . cannot prevail over the fundamental demands of due process of law in the fair administration of criminal justice."[201] The requested material was therefore to be turned over to the trial court for in camera determination as to which parts were appropriate for use at trial.[202]

---

[196] *See also* Nixon v. Fitzgerald, 457 U.S. 731, 753-54 (1982) (dictum) ("It is settled law that the separation-of-powers doctrine does not bar every exercise of jurisdiction over the President. . . ."). Chief Justice Marshall had issued a hotly contested subpoena duces tecum to President Jefferson in the course of Aaron Burr's treason trial in 1807. *See* United States v. Burr, 25 F. Cas. 30, 34 (C.C.D. Va. 1807).

[197] Eight years later, in Nixon v. Fitzgerald, 457 U.S. 731, 749 (1982) (Powell, J., over four dissents), the Court concluded that absolute presidential immunity from damages on account of official acts (even after his departure from office) was "a functionally mandated incident of the President's unique office, rooted in the constitutional tradition of the separation of powers and supported by our history." *See also* P. KURLAND, note 188 *supra*, at 135 (concluding that presidential immunity from criminal prosecution while in office was constitutionally required because "a necessary condition to the performance of his functions"). On the same day the President was held absolutely immune, however, the Court held that his assistants were not, Harlow v. Fitzgerald, 457 U.S. 800 (1982) (Powell, J., over a dissent by Burger)—although the analogous immunity of members of Congress had been held to extend to their aides because their help was essential to the members' performance (Gravel v. United States, 408 U.S. 606, 616-17 (1972) (White J.)).

[198] 418 U.S. at 703-05 ("We therefore reaffirm that it is the province and duty of this Court 'to say what the law is' with respect to the claim of privilege presented in this case.").

[199] Gunther, *supra* note 189, at 34. *See, e.g.*, Roudebush v. Hartke, 405 U.S. 15, 19 (1972) (Stewart, J.) (dictum) ("Which candidate is entitled to be seated in the Senate is . . . a nonjusticiable political question" (quoting the provision of article I, § 5 that "[e]ach House shall be the judge of the elections . . . of its own members")). *See also* THE FIRST HUNDRED YEARS at 254-55 (discussing Luther v. Borden, 48 U.S. 1 (1849)). *But see* Freund, *Foreword: On Presidential Privilege*, 88 HARV. L. REV. 13, 22 (1974) ("To support such an authority in a case where there was complicity between the President and the defendants would offend violently against the ancient precept that no man shall be judge in his own cause.").

[200] 418 U.S. at 705-08. *See* R. BERGER, EXECUTIVE PRIVILEGE: A CONSTITUTIONAL MYTH (1974) (taking the dim view of executive privilege suggested by the title); Sofaer, Book Review, 88 HARV. L. REV. 281, 284 (1974) (describing Berger's historical account as "one-sided" and "misleading").

[201] 418 U.S. at 713.

[202] *Id.* at 713-16.

Many questions were left open,[203] and one may agree or disagree with the balance the Court struck;[204] the decision remains a signal monument to the rule of law.

## B.   The Executive and Congress

Apart from incidental authority to manage its internal affairs and a few matters in which it functions as a check on other branches, Congress has been given only legislative powers. The debates on adoption of the Constitution leave no doubt that one of the reasons executive authority was withheld from Congress was to guard against the dangers of oppression that arise when the same persons both make and carry out the laws. "The accumulation of all powers legislative, executive, and judiciary in the same hands," as Madison said in *The Federalist*, "whether few or many, and whether hereditary, self appointed, or elective, may justly be pronounced the very definition of tyranny."[205] The limited enumeration of congressional powers and the explicit vesting of the executive power in the President plainly preclude Congress from administering spending programs, prosecuting offenses, or giving orders to armies in the field.[206]

The Framers were not content, however, merely to prevent Congress itself from exercising executive functions. "[A] dependence of the Executive on the Legislature," Madison insisted, would effectively make Congress "the Executor as well as the maker of laws."[207] It was on this ground that the President's salary was protected against congressional alteration and his election by the legislature (absent a deadlock in the electoral college) rejected.[208] Similar reasoning had informed the 1928 decision in *Springer v. Philippine Islands* that provisions of the Philippine Organic Act vesting legislative and executive power in separate branches forbade the legislature to play a role in the choice of

---

[203] *See id.* at 712 n.19 (noting that the case presented no issue of the availability of such materials for use by Congress or in civil litigation, and no claim that production would endanger "state secrets"). *See also* P. KUR-LAND, note 188 *supra*, at 55-58 (criticizing the decision of the court of appeals, Senate Select Comm. v. Nixon, 498 F.2d 725 (D.C. Cir. 1974), that the same materials could not be subpoenaed by a congressional committee for purposes of devising legislation: "There is no doubt that, for the federal courts in the District of Columbia, it was more important to punish criminals than to reveal the institutional deficiencies that were the origins of the constitutional crisis."). The third article of impeachment approved by the House Judiciary Committee against President Nixon was that he had refused to honor subpoenas issued in the impeachment inquiry itself. The claim of executive privilege seems at its weakest in this context, since to sustain it could seriously impair the principal constitutional check on abuse of presidential authority. *See* Cox, *Executive Privilege*, 122 U. PA. L. REV. 1383, 1436 (1974); Gunther, note 189 *supra*, at 34.

[204] *See, e.g.*, Freund, *supra* note 199, at 30-31, 35 (concluding that the decision "largely confirmed" the principles laid down by Chief Justice Marshall in the *Burr* case) ("[A] reversal would have marked a fundamental alteration in our standards of criminal justice.").

[205] THE FEDERALIST No. 47. This of course had been a central point for Montesquieu, whom Madison, 2 M. FARRAND, RECORDS OF THE FEDERAL CONVENTION OF 1787, at 34-35 (rev. ed. 1937), had explicitly invoked at the Convention: "When the legislative and executive powers are united in the same person, or in the same body of magistracy, there can then be no liberty; because apprehensions may arise, lest the same monarch or senate should enact tyrannical laws, to execute them in a tyrannical manner." L'ESPRIT DES LOIS 202 (1748).

[206] *See, e.g., Ex parte* Milligan, 71 U.S. 2, 139-40 (1866) (Chase, C. J., concurring).

[207] 2 M. FARRAND, *supra* note 205, at 34.

[208] *See id.* at 29-36, 52-59; THE FEDERALIST Nos. 71, 73. Morris and Madison even thought that the limited power of impeachment conferred by article II rendered the President too dependent on the legislature. 2 M. FARRAND, *supra*, at 53, 550-51. *See generally* 3 J. STORY, COMMENTARIES ON THE CONSTITUTION 279 (1833).

directors of public corporations.[209] The mere power to appoint administrators, the Court concluded, gave the legislature too much control over the execution of the laws.

In the case of the federal government, moreover, the Framers did not leave the matter of appointments entirely to implication. Article II marks the limit of legislative participation in the appointment process by requiring Senate confirmation of many nominations by the President as a check on executive abuse. In the case of "inferior Officers," Congress is expressly empowered to vest appointing power "in the President alone, in the Courts of Law, or in the Heads of Departments"—in almost anybody, that is, except itself.[210] Accordingly, the Court unanimously held in *Buckley v. Valeo* in 1976 that a Federal Election Commission whose members were appointed by House and Senate leaders or subject to House as well as Senate approval could not be empowered to promulgate regulations, to determine eligibility for campaign subsidies, or to seek judicial relief against violation of the law.[211] None of these activities, the Court rightly concluded, could fairly be said to be incidental to any legitimate legislative function.[212] Thus the conclusion that they could be exercised only by "officers of the United States" chosen in accordance with the appointments clause was bolstered by repeated "expressions of fear" during the Convention "that the Legislative Branch of the National Government will aggrandize itself at the expense of the other two branches."[213]

Congressional power to discharge those who administer the laws would give the legislature even greater control over the exercise of executive functions than would the power to appoint them. The President is given authority to appoint judges, but not to remove them; while the most carefully selected candidate may change his mind after appointment, "[a] power over a man's subsistence amounts to a power over his will."[214]

This noncontroversial proposition underlay the 1986 decision in *Bowsher v. Synar* that Congress could not empower the Comptroller General to make determinations of anticipated revenues and expenditures that would trigger spending reductions designed to en-

---

[209] 277 U.S. 189 (1928). *See* p. 196 *supra*.

[210] U.S. CONST. art. II, § 2:

> The President . . . shall nominate, and by and with the advice and consent of the Senate, shall appoint ambassadors, other public ministers and consuls, judges of the Supreme Court, and all other officers of the United States, whose appointments are not herein otherwise provided for, and which shall be established by law; but the Congress may by law vest the appointment of such inferior officers, as they think proper, in the President alone, in the courts of law, or in the heads of departments.

*See* Buckley v. Valeo, 424 U.S. 1, 127 (1976) ("While the Clause expressly authorizes Congress to vest the appointment of certain officers in the 'Courts of Law,' the absence of similar language to include Congress must mean that neither Congress nor its officers were included within the language 'Heads of Departments' in this part of [the clause].").

[211] 424 U.S. 1, 109-43 (per curiam).

[212] *Id.* at 137-41. *See, e.g., id.* at 138 ("A lawsuit is the ultimate remedy for a breach of the law, and it is to the President, and to the Congress, that the Constitution entrusts the responsibility to 'take Care that the Laws be faithfully executed.' "). On the other hand, "[i]nsofar as the powers confided in the Commission are essentially of an investigative and informative nature, falling in the same general category as those powers which Congress might delegate to one of its own committees, there can be no question that the Commission as presently constituted may exercise them." *Id.* at 137.

[213] 424 U.S. at 129.

[214] THE FEDERALIST No. 79 (A. Hamilton).

sure a balanced federal budget.[215] As Justice White insisted in dissent, Congress could discharge that official only upon a finding of "disability, . . . inefficiency, . . . neglect of duty, . . . malfeasance, . . . felony or . . . moral turpitude";[216] but that is a far cry from the limited control the Framers grudgingly afforded Congress by authorizing impeachment for "high Crimes and Misdemeanors."[217] Removal on a finding of "maladministration," Madison successfully argued at the Convention, would be "equivalent to a tenure during pleasure of the Senate";[218] as the Court noted, Congress had plainly intended to retain more control over the Comptroller General than over ordinary executive officers.[219] In accordance with article II's policy of unified executive power,[220] the impeachment clauses have been held not to forbid *presidential* removal of executive officials.[221] The debates demonstrate, however, that they were meant to limit the degree of *legislative* interference with the independent executive.

Indeed, as the Court recognized, the decision in *Bowsher* was inevitable after *Myers v. United States,* which had struck down a provision forbidding the President to discharge a postmaster without Senate approval.[222] Congressional control had been more attenuated in *Myers,* for the provision in that case did not permit the Senate to discharge the official on its own. The mere authority to preclude the President from firing his subordinate, the Court concluded, gave legislators more influence over the executive than was consistent with the constitutional plan. For Congress "to draw to itself, or to either branch of it, the power to remove or the right to participate in the exercise of that power," Chief Justice Taft wrote in terms amply sufficient to condemn the provision in *Bowsher,* "would be . . . to infringe the constitutional principle of the separation of governmental powers."[223]

---

[215] 478 U.S. 714 (Burger, C.J.). There was no serious doubt that the authority granted the Comptroller General was executive. It involved neither legislation nor adjudication, but rather was part of the process for carrying the law into effect. *See id.* at 732 ("Interpreting a law enacted by Congress to implement the legislative mandate is the very essence of 'execution' of the law."). *But see id.* at 736-59 (Stevens, J., joined by Marshall, concurring) (arguing that Congress had offended the Constitution by delegating to its own agent the power to make nationwide policy without meeting article I's requirements for the enactment of legislation).

[216] *See id.* at 728 (quoting the statute); *id.* at 759-76 (White, J., dissenting) (arguing that these provisions and the President's power to veto the joint resolution by which such discharge would be accomplished, subject of course to override by a two-thirds vote of both houses, made the Comptroller General effectively independent of Congress). Stevens and Marshall, who concurred in the result on other grounds, *see* note 215 *supra,* agreed with White on this issue. *See id.* at 737-41. Justice Blackmun, *id.* at 776-87, dissented on the ground that if the statutes gave Congress greater control over the Comptroller General than was compatible with his administration of the budget law, it was the provisions for congressional control that should be struck down.

[217] U.S. CONST. art. II, § 4. *See* 478 U.S. at 723.

[218] 2 M. FARRAND, *supra* note 205, at 550.

[219] *See* 478 U.S. at 727-32 (quoting H. MANSFIELD, THE COMPTROLLER GENERAL: A STUDY IN THE LAW AND PRACTICE OF FINANCIAL ADMINISTRATION 65 (1939): "Congress created the office because it believed that it 'needed an officer, responsible to it alone, to check upon the application of public funds in accordance with appropriations.' ").

[220] *See, e.g.,* 1 M. FARRAND, *supra* note 205, at 65 (Rutledge and Wilson); THE FEDERALIST Nos. 70, 72, 74 (A. Hamilton); 3 J. STORY, *supra* note 208, at 284-91, 340-41. The alternative these commentators were opposing was a collegial executive; no one even suggested that executive authority be dispersed among departments independent of one another.

[221] Myers v. United States, pp. 193-95 *supra.*

[222] *See* 478 U.S. 724-25 (citing *Myers*).

[223] *Myers,* 272 U.S. at 161. The holding that congressional control of the execution of law in *Bowsher* offended the separation of powers made it unnecessary for the Court to decide whether placing executive authority

A third attempt at congressional control of the executive was found wanting in *INS v. Chadha* in 1983.[224] In authorizing the Attorney General to suspend expulsion of a deportable alien on grounds of hardship, Congress had empowered either the Senate or the House to reverse his action by simple resolution.[225] Provisions for such a "legislative veto" of administrative action had proliferated like rabbits over the previous half century as antidotes to the practice of delegating broad policy-making discretion to administrators.[226] Only Justice White, however, thought such a provision constitutional.[227]

The control over executive action exerted in *Chadha* was far more direct than that in either *Buckley* or *Bowsher.* If Congress did not like the Attorney General's decision, it did not have to act circuitously by seeking to replace the officer; it had only to reverse the offending action itself.[228] If the legislative veto was itself an exercise of executive power— or of judicial power, as Justice Powell argued in his concurring opinion[229]—then it was obvious that neither the House nor the Senate could employ it. Congress has only the powers given it by the Constitution,[230] and the only nonlegislative powers given to either House—such as impeachment, consent to appointments and treaties, and purely internal matters like the election of legislative officers—were plainly inapplicable.[231] Nowhere is

---

in an officer independent of presidential control offended the distinct constitutional principle of a unified executive. For arguments that it did, see Currie, *The Distribution of Powers after* Bowsher, 1986 SUP. CT. REV. 19, 34-36, and Miller, *Independent Agencies,* 1986 SUP. CT. REV. 41. *See also* the discussion of Myers v. United States and of Humphrey's Executor v. United States, pp. 193-95, 220-22 *supra.*

A blow to the unified executive was struck two years after Burger's retirement in Morrison v. Olson, 487 U.S. 654 (1988) (Rehnquist, C.J., over a fine dissent by Justice Scalia), where the Court upheld a statute providing for judicial appointment of a special prosecutor not subject to effective presidential control. Apart from the obvious difficulty of reconciling the independence of such an official with the President's responsibility to "take care that the laws be faithfully executed," art. II, § 3, as construed in Myers v. United States, pp. 193-95 *supra,* the provision in article II, § 2 permitting nonpresidential appointment only of "inferior officers" seemed designed to ensure that persons the President had not chosen would be subject to control by those he had. Similar considerations of hierarchical control reinforce the institutional logic of the Court's initial position that § 2 authorized judicial and executive officers to appoint their own subordinates, not "inferior officers" generally. *See* Matter of Hennen, 38 U.S. 230, 257-58 (1939) (dictum) (arguing that the power "was no doubt intended to be exercised by the department . . . to which the official most appropriately belonged"); *Ex parte* Siebold, 100 U.S. 371, 397-98 (1880) (suggesting there was no such limitation but adding that the courts seemed as appropriate as any other body to appoint federal election supervisors); THE FIRST HUNDRED YEARS at 436 n.43. Humphrey's Executor v. United States, pp. 220-22 *supra,* which held that Federal Trade Commissioners could be insulated from presidential control, was distinguishable on its own flimsy ground, for the special prosecutor had no quasi-judicial or quasi-legislative tasks to which his plainly executive functions could be described as "ancillary." The basic principle underlying the special-prosecutor law was the need for a check on executive misconduct, but the Framers had provided one by their carefully crafted impeachment provisions.

[224] 462 U.S. 919 (1983) (Burger, C.J.).

[225] *See id.* at 923-28.

[226] *See id.* at 944-46; *id.* at 967-74 (White, J., dissenting).

[227] *See id.* at 967-1003 (White, J., dissenting).

[228] *Cf.* Hayburn's Case, 2 U.S. 409 (1792), THE FIRST HUNDRED YEARS at 6-9, where two circuit courts declared an act of Congress unconstitutional because subjecting judicial decisions to revision by an executive officer was incompatible with the judicial independence guaranteed by the tenure provision of article III.

[229] 462 U.S. at 959-67 (Powell, J., concurring). *See id.* at 964-65 ("On its face, the House's action appears clearly adjudicatory. The House did not enact a general rule; rather it made its own determination that six specific persons did not comply with certain statutory criteria.").

[230] The necessary and proper clause, of course, does not empower Congress to alter the constitutional allocation of federal powers.

[231] *See* 462 U.S. at 955-56 (opinion of the Court).

Congress given power to reverse executive policy except by legislating, and the legislative veto does not satisfy the Constitution's requirements for the enactment of legislation.

It is abundantly clear that neither the House nor the Senate was meant to make law on its own. Article I, § 7 provides for the enactment of laws by the concurrence of both Houses, subject to an overridable presidential veto. Apart from the obvious safeguard against ill-considered action provided by any bicameral legislature, the history reveals a deliberate decision to require the concurrence both of a popularly elected representative chamber and of one partly insulated by a six-year term from the fickle popular will and in which each state has an equal voice.[232] The President's veto was designed both as protection for the executive from legislative encroachments and as an additional safeguard "against the enaction of improper laws."[233] To permit a single House to reverse executive action by simple resolution plainly undermined these purposes.

Justice White argued in dissent that the effect of the legislative veto was the same as if the executive had proposed a private bill to grant Chadha resident status and a single House had rejected it.[234] But the Attorney General had not merely made a proposal that failed for want of legislative approval; as a result of the Attorney General's action Chadha would have become a permanent resident but for the affirmative intervention of a single House.[235]

Justice White also contended that it was no worse for Congress to delegate authority to its own Houses than to delegate it to an executive agency.[236] Apart from the fact that the provision for legislative veto in *Chadha* lacked the standards to limit the delegate's action that are necessary to sustain any delegation, however, the theory of the delegation cases is that filling in the details of congressional policy is a normal executive task.[237] There was a more fundamental difficulty with both of Justice White's arguments, however. The Con-

---

[232]*See, e.g.,* THE FEDERALIST Nos. 51, 62, 63; 1 M. FARRAND, *supra* note 205, at 48, 50, 233, 254, 544, 546.

[233]*See, e.g.,* THE FEDERALIST No. 73.

[234]462 U.S. at 994-98 (White, J., dissenting).

[235]*See id.* at 952 (opinion of the Court).

[236]*Id.* at 984-89 (White, J., dissenting).

[237]*See* pp. 16-19 *supra* (discussing earlier delegation cases). Far from abandoning limits on delegation to administrative officers, the work of the Burger period gave reason for modest hope that such delegations might be scrutinized more closely than they had been in the recent past. In 1974 the Court explicitly reaffirmed the nondelegation doctrine in narrowly interpreting an authorization to charge fees to the recipients of government services in order to avoid a question of its constitutionality, National Cable Television Ass'n v. United States, 415 U.S. 336, 342 (1974) (Douglas, J., over two dissents); in two subsequent cases Justice Rehnquist argued that the not very sweeping authority to carry out a congressional policy of all feasible protection from certain workplace health hazards went too far. Industrial Union Dept. v. American Petroleum Inst., 448 U.S. 607, 671-88 (1980) (concurring opinion); American Textile Manufacturers Inst. v. Donovan, 452 U.S. 490, 543-48 (1981) (dissenting opinion, joined by Burger).

The district court in Synar v. United States, 626 F. Supp. 1374, 1382-91 (D.D.C. 1986), was wholly consistent with this principle in concluding that the Gramm-Rudman Act's delegation of authority to the Comptroller General with respect to spending reductions did not go too far. Congress itself had made the basic policy decision that the federal budget must be balanced. As the court said, the statute left to the administrator only the task of estimating revenue and expenditures and plugging the numbers into a legislatively prescribed formula. Because the Supreme Court found the challenged provision invalid on other grounds, *see* pp. 589-90 *supra,* it did not review this conclusion. *See* Bowsher v. Synar, 478 U.S. 714, 736 n.10 (1986).

More troublesome at first glance were the Court's own decisions in United States v. Mazurie, 419 U.S. 544 (1975) (Rehnquist, J.), and Federal Energy Comm'n v. Algonquin SNG, Inc., 426 U.S. 548 (1976) (Marshall,

stitution is not to be judically amended by arguing that what the Framers did not authorize is no more dangerous than what they did.[238]

## C. The Courts

During the Burger years, in short, the Court was alert to protect the executive from legislative encroachment. It also took a modest but significant step toward protecting the independence of the judiciary.

Article III vests the judicial power of the United States in judges with irreducible salary and tenure during good behavior in order, as Hamilton made clear in *The Federalist*, that cases may be decided without fear of reprisal.[239] The Supreme Court had repeatedly enforced the tenure and salary provisions. When President Lincoln subjected civilians to trial by military commissions during the Civil War, the Court held that even war did not justify dispensing with their protection.[240] When Congress attempted to reduce the compensation of District of Columbia judges during the depression of the 1930s, the Court found our gravest economic crisis an insufficient excuse.[241] When litigants complained that judges of the Court of Claims and of the Court of Customs and Patent Appeals could not constitutionally be assigned to hear cases in article III courts, the Court rejected the argument only after concluding that those judges enjoyed tenure and irreducible salary, and Justice Harlan wrote expressly that the litigants had a right to an article III judge.[242]

Unfortunately the Court had not always been so attentive. Chief Justice Marshall himself had allowed the creation of courts without article III protections in the territories, and the Burger Court extended his conclusion to the District of Columbia, reasoning mistakenly that the absence of federalism concerns in those areas justified dispensing with the distinct requirements of the separation of powers.[243] *Ex parte Bakelite Corp.* in 1929 had swallowed the unconvincing argument that because Congress need not provide for judicial

---

J.), respectively upholding a standardless delegation to an Indian tribe to regulate the sale of liquor and an authorization to the President to "adjust . . . imports" in any way he deemed necessary to prevent them from endangering national security. Both delegations, however, were to entities that "possesse[d] independent authority over the subject matter." In such cases, as the Court said in *Mazurie*, the limitations on delegation had long been held "less stringent." 419 U.S. at 556-57 (citing United States v. Curtiss-Wright Export Corp., pp. 217-18, note 63 *supra*). *See also Algonquin*, 426 U.S. at 558-60 (arguing that a rather vague list of factors the President was required to consider, together with the statutory reference to national security, provided adequate standards).

[238] *But cf.* Elliott, INS v. Chadha: *The Administrative Constitution, the Constitution, and the Legislative Veto*, 1983 SUP. CT. REV. 125, 135-36, 176 (criticizing the *Chadha* opinion as "formalistic" and arguing that in light of the extraconstitutional rise of the administrative state, "[t]he task for the Court should have been to reinterpret the Constitution to create a harmonious new whole, just as that would have been the Court's task if a Fourth Branch had been created by constitutional amendment").

[239] THE FEDERALIST Nos. 78, 79. *See also* 2 M. FARRAND, *supra* note 205, at 34, 428-29; 3 J. STORY, *supra* note 208, at 425ff.

[240] *Ex parte* Milligan, 71 U.S. 2, 122 (1866), THE FIRST HUNDRED YEARS at 288-92.

[241] O'Donoghue v. United States, p. 216, note 56 *supra*.

[242] Glidden Co. v. Zdanok, 370 U.S. 530, 533 (1962) ("Article III . . . is explicit and gives the petitioners a basis for complaint."). Justice Harlan spoke only for three Justices, but the others seemed to agree with this conclusion. *See id.* at 585-89 (Warren, C.J., and Clark, J., concurring); *id.* at 589-606 (Douglas and Black, JJ., dissenting). *See also* United States v. Will, 449 U.S. 200, 224-26 (1980), where the Burger Court held Congress without power to deprive federal judges of salary increases that had already gone into effect.

[243] American Ins. Co. v. Canter, 26 U.S. 511, 546 (1828), THE FIRST HUNDRED YEARS at 119-22; Palmore v. United States, 411 U.S. 389, 403, 410 (1973). Earlier the Court had found the tenure and salary provisions applicable in the District of Columbia. O'Donoghue v. United States, *supra* note 241.

resolution of certain customs disputes it could entrust them to judges lacking the tenure and salary protections of article III.[244] A 1932 dictum in *Crowell v. Benson* had gone even further, basically suggesting that administrative decisions in workers' compensation cases need be subject only to appellate judicial review.[245]

In reliance on these precedents, Congress in 1978 attempted to vest jurisdiction over all civil proceedings related to bankruptcy in a new set of courts whose judges were appointed for terms of fourteen years. In *Northern Pipeline Construction Co. v. Marathon Pipe Line Co.*, in 1982, the Court held that article III precluded such nontenured judges from entertaining common law claims against debtors of a bankrupt estate.[246]

There was no majority opinion. Writing for four Justices, Justice Brennan appropriately found most of the precedents distinguishable on the basis of their own reasoning. The territorial and District of Columbia cases had relied on the special status of those "limited geographic areas" in which Congress exercised "the *full* authority of government."[247] *Bakelite*'s insistence that there was something special about matters "arising between the government and others" and which "do not require judicial determination" had no application to a contract claim between private parties.[248] Moreover, the jurisdiction of nontenured state judges over article III claims posed no threat to separation of powers because "Congress has no control over state-court judges,"[249] while the longstanding acceptance of courts-martial in appropriate cases had been based on the historically separate tradition of military justice.[250]

Most difficult to distinguish was *Crowell v. Benson*, which had come close to saying it was sufficient that there was a right of appeal to a court composed of tenured judges. Though technically the offending passage in *Crowell* was dictum,[251] a great many quasi-judicial agencies had grown up in accordance with it, and it was not likely the Court would abandon them entirely. Something might perhaps have been made of *Crowell*'s emphasis on the need for establishing a tribunal with distinctively nonjudicial procedures,[252] since the caseload and expertise problems urged in support of the nontenured judges in *Northern Pipeline* could have been satisfied as well by a specialized article III court.[253] Justice Bren-

---

[244] *See* pp. 191-93 *supra*.

[245] *See* pp. 214-15 *supra*.

[246] 458 U.S. 50. For more detailed consideration of this controversy see Currie, *Bankruptcy Judges and the Independent Judiciary*, 16 CREIGHTON L. REV. 441 (1983).

[247] *See* 458 U.S. at 76. *See also id.* at 64-65. Marshall had explicitly stated in the first territorial case that nontenured judges could not be empowered to exercise admiralty jurisdiction within the states. American Ins. Co. v. Canter, 26 U.S. 511, 546 (1828).

[248] 458 U.S. at 67-70.

[249] 458 U.S. at 64 n.15 (citing Krattenmaker, *Article III and Judicial Independence: Why the New Bankruptcy Courts Are Unconstitutional*, 70 GEORGETOWN L.J. 297, 304-05 (1981)). In any event, the opinion added, the Framers clearly thought there was a difference; for while leaving to Congress the extent to which state courts would decide article III cases they made quite clear that *federal* judges must hold office during good behavior.

[250] 458 U.S. at 66 (noting the explicit exemption of "cases arising in the land or naval forces" from the fifth amendment's grand-jury provision, which had figured prominently in the decisions). *See also* Dynes v. Hoover, 61 U.S. 65, 79 (1858); THE FIRST HUNDRED YEARS at 288-92 (discussing *Ex parte* Milligan); pp. 280-83 and 400-03 *supra* (discussing *Ex parte* Quirin and the court-martial decisions of the Warren period).

[251] The holding was that the trial court had properly held a trial de novo on the factual question whether a master-servant relationship had existed between the parties. 285 U.S. at 65. *See Northern Pipeline*, 458 U.S. at 82 n.34 (acknowledging that this part of the *Crowell* opinion "has been undermined by later cases" but adding that the Court had continued to require de novo review of certain constitutional questions).

[252] *See Crowell*, 285 U.S. at 46.

[253] *See* Currie, *supra* note 246, at 456-58; Krattenmaker, *supra* note 249, at 308-09.

nan did not follow this road, however, and neither of his two bases for distinguishing *Crowell* was entirely satisfactory.

First, said Justice Brennan, *Crowell* had "involved the adjudication of congressionally created rights." In creating a substantive right, Congress had "substantial discretion to prescribe the manner in which that right may be adjudicated"; it had no such discretion with regard to "the adjudication of rights *not* created by Congress," as in *Northern Pipeline*.[254] This argument was an extension of *Bakelite*'s notion that Congress might leave to nontenured judges whatever it could have resolved for itself, and it was subject to the same objection. The Constitution does not require Congress to create any federal right of action, but it leaves no doubt who is to decide "cases . . . arising under . . . the laws of the United States." In deciding an analogous question under the due process clause, Justice Brennan had been with the majority in reaching a conclusion inconsistent with his argument in *Northern Pipeline:* while a state is free to determine whether or not to create a property interest in public employment, once it has done so it may not take that interest away without due process of law.[255]

Moreover, as Justice White noted in dissent, it seemed most improbable that the underlying policy of separation of powers required greater independence in cases involving state law than in cases involving federal.[256] Accordingly it was not long before this distinction was expressly disapproved: "[T]here is no reason inherent in separation of powers principles to accord the state law character of a claim talismanic power in Article III inquiries."[257]

More faithful to article III, though hardly to precedent, was Justice Brennan's suggestion that *Crowell,* like the later decision in *United States v. Raddatz,* had allowed nontenured officials to resolve article III matters only because their decisions were subject to plenary judicial review: "[W]hile orders issued by the agency in *Crowell* were to be set aside if 'not supported by the evidence,' the judgments of the bankruptcy courts are apparently subject to review only under the more deferential 'clearly erroneous' standard."[258] Unfortunately this assertion is refuted by the very passages that Brennan was trying to distinguish, for the whole point of the *Crowell* opinion was that, with the exception of two narrow categories of "jurisdictional" facts, de novo review was not constitutionally required. Justice Brennan's reformulation might do much to restore the constitu-

[254] 458 U.S. at 78-84.

[255] *See* Arnett v. Kennedy, pp. 541-42 *supra. See also* Curtis v. Loether, p. 542, note 259 *supra* (holding that the seventh amendment gave a right to jury trial on a cause of action created by Congress). Less encouraging in the latter context was the decision in Atlas Roofing Co. v. Occupational Safety & Health Review Comm'n, 430 U.S.442 (1977) (White, J.), that a civil penalty action assumed to require a jury when tried in court could be decided without one by an administrative agency—a decision wholly unsupported by the precedents invoked and permitting Congress to circumvent the constitutional provision apparently at will in any proceeding brought by the government in its "sovereign capacity"—a distinction that appeared to set the policy of insulation from government decision precisely on its head. *See* pp. 191-93 *supra* (discussing an analogous distinction drawn for purposes of the article III requirement of an independent judge). *Atlas* is criticized in detail in Kirst, *Administrative Penalties and the Civil Jury: The Supreme Court's Assault on the Seventh Amendment,* 126 U. Pa. L. Rev. 1281 (1978).

[256] 458 U.S. at 98 (White, J., joined by Burger and Powell, dissenting).

[257] Commodity Futures Trading Commission v. Schor, 478 U.S. 833, 853 (1986).

[258] 458 U.S. at 85. *Cf.* United States v. Raddatz, 447 U.S. 667 (1980) (upholding the adjudicatory authority of nontenured magistrates subject to de novo court review). In such a case the purposes of article III are satisfied; full power to decide is reserved to an independent judge.

tional plan if it is taken to modify the *Crowell* dictum, but it might as easily be abandoned in later cases as a historical error.

Determining just how far *Northern Pipeline* went in assuring judicial independence was made more difficult by the fact that Justices Rehnquist and O'Connor, one of whose votes was necessary to the result, wrote separately to emphasize the narrowness of the decision. Unfortunately they did not say whether they agreed with Justice Brennan's reasons for concluding that the claim before them could not be decided by a nontenured bankruptcy judge; they said only that "[n]one of the cases has gone so far. . . ."[259]

Two subsequent decisions of the Burger period limited the progress made in *Northern Pipeline*. *Thomas v. Union Carbide Agricultural Products Co.* upheld a provision requiring arbitration of disputes over the allocation of pesticide-registration costs among various manufacturers, although the arbitrator's decision was subject to judicial review only for "fraud, misrepresentation, or other misconduct."[260] *Commodity Futures Trading Comm. v. Schor* allowed nontenured members of a federal commission to pass upon a state-law counterclaim to a complaint seeking reparations for violations of federal law.[261]

Fortunately, the reasoning of both decisions was narrow. For better or worse, *Thomas* assimilated the provision for compulsory arbitration to *Bakelite*'s long-standing and limited category of matters which (like claims against the United States) " 'could be conclusively determined by the Executive and Legislative Branches.' "[262] *Schor* in turn relied heavily upon the fact that both parties had agreed to the commission's jurisdiction: the objecting party had "waived any [personal] right" to an article III trial, and "separation of powers concerns" were "diminished" because "the decision to invoke this forum is left entirely to the parties."[263] It may be, as several of our most thoughtful judges have argued, that the requirement of an independent tribunal serves purposes beyond protection of the immediate parties;[264] but in any event the Court's reasoning preserves the parties' all-important right to insist on trial before a tenured judge.[265]

---

[259] 458 U.S. at 91.

[260] 473 U.S. 568 (1985) (O'Connor, J.).

[261] 478 U.S. 833 (1986) (O'Connor, J., over two dissents).

[262] 473 U.S. at 588. What was new was the addition of the cost dispute to that category ("Congress, without implicating Article III, could have authorized EPA to charge follow-on registrants fees to cover the cost of data and could have directly subsidized FIFRA data submitters for their contributions of needed data") and the express elimination of the additional requirement that the Government be a party, which had never made sense in terms of the relevant considerations: independence is most essential when the government is a party. *See* 473 U.S. at 590.

[263] 478 U.S. at 848-50, 854-55.

[264] *See* Geras v. Lafayette Display Fixtures, Inc., 742 F.2d 1037, 1051-52 (7th Cir. 1984) (Posner, J., dissenting); Lehman Bros. v. Clark Oil & Ref. Corp., 739 F.2d 1313, 1318-19 (8th Cir. 1984) (Lay and Arnold, JJ., dissenting); Pacemaker Diagnostic Clinic v. Instromedix, Inc., 725 F.2d 537, 549 (9th Cir. 1984) (Schroeder, J., dissenting). Arbitration, Judge Posner argued, was not analogous to decision by a nontenured magistrate: arbitrators' decisions have less impact on third parties; arbitrators "are not public officials"; "[t]heir decisions carry no official imprimatur"; and "they do not rule on questions of law at all." 742 F.2d at 1052. Justices Brennan and Marshall, dissenting in *Schor*, also argued that "consent is irrelevant to Article III analysis." 478 U.S. at 867. The majority agreed that consent could not cure "structural" objections "to the extent" they are "implicated in a given case," *id.* at 850-51, but went on to find that the voluntary nature of the commission's jurisdiction reduced structural as well as personal objections.

[265] *See* Fallon, *Of Legislative Courts, Administrative Agencies, and Article III*, 101 Harv. L. Rev. 915 (1988) (concluding after *Thomas* and *Schor* that the Court was employing an "ad hoc balancing test," *id.* at 917, and that the best that could be hoped for was a right of "appellate" review by an article III court, such as *Crowell* had established in "private right" cases).

# Conclusion to Part Eight

More than twelve hundred constitutional cases were decided during Warren Burger's seventeen years as Chief Justice, and there was a decided tendency toward long opinions. The 1968 Term had produced three volumes of the official reports; most of the Burger terms produced five. The volumes became noticeably thicker as well. A more subtle change occurred in 1976, when the printed portion of each page was quietly widened from three and three-fourths to four and one-eighth inches, increasing the number of words per page by a full 10 percent.[1]

The Burger years brought to the Court many important controversies—abortion, homosexuality, affirmative action, sex discrimination, aid to parochial schools, and capital punishment, to name only a few. But the significance of some of the issues does not explain the verbal hemorrhage; most of the opinions can be reduced to half a dozen pages for casebook purposes without perceptible loss of substance. The typical opinion of the Burger period recounts the background of both the individual case and the relevant field of law in cloying and dispensable detail. There is a self-indulgent tone not only in this excessive length but also in the proliferation of individual opinions punctiliously concurring in Parts I, II-B, and all but the last sentence of III-C of Justice So-and-so's opinion;[2] there comes a point where differences of opinion are best suppressed in the interest of coherence.[3]

There was much talk during the Burger years of adventurous and questionable schemes

---

[1] *Compare* 428 U.S. with 429 U.S., *passim.*

[2] There were roughly three concurring opinions for every four for the majority; decisions without concurring opinions were not common.

[3] *See* Easterbrook, *Agreement among the Justices: An Empirical Note*, 1984 SUP. CT. REV. 389 (concluding that the proliferation of opinions in recent years did not reflect increasing disagreement over matter of principle); Cox, *Foreword: Freedom of Expression in the Burger Court*, 94 HARV. L. REV. 1, 72 (1980) ("Continuous fragmentation could well diminish not only the influence of the Court but the ideal of the rule of law."). For a more tolerant view see Easterbrook, *Ways of Criticizing the Court*, 95 HARV. L. REV. 802, 804-11 (1982).

to rescue the Court from its workload,[4] but the problem seemed much exaggerated. Not only would the Justices be less burdened if they wrote fewer and shorter opinions. Of the 5,000 or so applications for review presented to the Court each year, only about 150 were accepted, and that was too many; in every term the Court took a significant number of cases that raised no important legal issues. Sifting the incoming flood for the occasional nugget should take no more than a few minutes of a law clerk's time per case. Scant harm is done if a deserving case slips through the sieve; if an issue is important enough to warrant the Court's attention, it will soon crop up again.[5]

The opinions themselves tended to be competent, faceless, and dull. The rise of the bright and industrious law clerk had virtually eliminated the possibility of truly egregious opinions such as those composed by Justices Clifford and McKenna in bygone days,[6] but it also had largely deprived individual Justices of personality. Almost any opinion by Jackson, Black, or Frankfurter had been a literary experience. Apart from a few pungent phrases by Rehnquist and a number of idiosyncratic opinions by Stevens, most opinions of one Justice during the Burger period read very much like those of any other—except, of course, for their contrasting conclusions.

Moreover, despite the significance and controversial nature of the issues, the opinions of the Burger Court often lack analytical interest as well. Over the years the Court had interpreted one constitutional provision after another to require a balancing of the costs and benefits of a challenged action; one can rapidly have one's fill of debating whether the government's interest in doing $A$ outweighs the burden thereby imposed on $B$.[7]

The big story of the Burger years, however, was the counterrevolution that did not come. With the announced intention of changing the Court's direction, Republican Presidents had appointed six Justices by 1981. Nevertheless, though the remaining pillars of the Warren Court dissented from decisions of the Burger period with great frequency,[8] outside the criminal-procedure field the major accomplishments of the Warren revolution were not merely preserved but in many respects actually extended.[9]

[4]See FEDERAL JUDICIAL CENTER, REPORT OF THE STUDY GROUP ON THE CASELOAD OF THE SUPREME COURT (1972) (recommending establishment of a new national court of appeals to resolve minor intercircuit conflicts and to sift certiorari petitions for the Supreme Court); U.S. COMMISSION ON REVISION OF THE FEDERAL COURT APPELLATE SYSTEM, STRUCTURE AND INTERNAL PROCEDURES: RECOMMENDATIONS FOR CHANGE (1975) (urging creation of a national court of appeals to make nationally binding decisions in cases referred by the Supreme Court or by another court of appeals). For criticism of the respective proposals see Brennan, *The National Court of Appeals: Another Dissent,* 40 U. CHI. L. REV. 473 (1973); Black, *The National Court of Appeals: An Unwise Proposal,* 83 YALE L.J. 883 (1974); G. CASPER & R. POSNER, THE WORKLOAD OF THE SUPREME COURT (1976); Casper & Posner, *The Caseload of the Supreme Court: 1975 and 1976 Terms,* 1977 SUP. CT. REV. 87.

[5]See Kurland & Hutchinson, *The Business of the Supreme Court, O.T. 1982,* 50 U. CHI. L. REV. 628, 650 (1983) ("The Supreme Court is in a crisis, but it is largely a crisis of its own making.").

[6]See generally Currie, *The Most Insignificant Justice: A Preliminary Inquiry,* 50 U. CHI. L. REV. 466 (1983).

[7]See Aleinikoff, *Constitutional Law in the Age of Balancing,* 96 YALE L.J. 943, 987 (1987) ("Balancing is undermining our usual understanding of constitutional law as an interpretive enterprise. In so doing, it is transforming constitutional discourse into a general discussion of the reasonableness of governmental conduct.").

[8]Marshall and Brennan each dissented over four hundred times, i.e., in over a third of the cases; Douglas dissented at least 165 times in a third of the period. Only Justice Stevens, with over two hundred dissents in eleven years, rivaled these percentages of disagreement.

[9]See, e.g., the decisions on abortion, school segregation, affirmative action, sex and alienage discrimination, freedom of speech, administrative procedure, and capital punishment discussed in the three preceding chapters. Significantly, the most frequent dissenter apart from the Justices mentioned in note 8 *supra* was the implacably

This was certainly not the fault of Justice Rehnquist. When the Court rejected arguments for privacy, affirmative action, sexual equality, separation of church and state, or fair trial, he was with the majority;[10] when it upheld such claims he was often to be found in dissent.[11] Both Burger and O'Connor, moreover, commonly voted with him. Once in a while, however, he was abandoned by the Chief Justice in a speech case, by O'Connor on a matter of religion, and by one or the other on an equal protection issue. Most significantly, Burger voted to allow both affirmative action in *Fullilove* and abortion in *Roe*.[12] Despite an early tendency to vote with Rehnquist and Burger on a variety of topics,[13] Justice Blackmun was from the beginning the Court's principal spokesman for privacy, commercial speech, and the rights of aliens, and a firm supporter of affirmative action as well.[14] After 1978, indeed, he seldom differed with Brennan and Marshall except in criminal matters, and even there he was no longer a dependable vote for the other side.[15] Justice

---

conservative Rehnquist, who took issue with the majority in nearly one-quarter of the cases. This is not to say that the Burger Court was more liberal than its predecessor; given the same cases to decide, the Warren Court would surely have gone even further.

[10] *See, e.g.,* Harris v. McRae and Bowers v. Hardwick (privacy); Regents of the Univ. of Calif. v. Bakke and Wygant v. Jackson Bd. of Educ. (affirmative action); Michael M. v. Superior Court and Rostker v. Goldberg (sex discrimination); Mueller v. Allen and Lynch v. Donnelly (establishment of religion); United States v. Leon and Hudson v. Palmer (search and seizure); Harris v. New York, New York v. Quarles, and Allen v. Illinois (self-incrimination). *See also* Milliken v. Bradley (I), Ambach v. Norwick, and Lalli v. Lalli (denying claims for relief from discrimination on grounds of race, citizenship, and illegitimacy); Branzburg v. Hayes, Miller v. California, and Goldman v. Weinberger (rejecting claims of freedom of expression or religion); Gregg v. Georgia (upholding capital punishment); National League of Cities v. Usery, Edelman v. Jordan, and Pennhurst State Hosp. v. Halderman (upholding state immunity from regulation and suit). Neither Brennan, Marshall, nor Douglas voted with the majority in any of these cases.

[11] *See, e.g.,* Roe v. Wade, Planned Parenthood v. Danforth, and Thornburgh v. American Coll. of Ob-Gyn (privacy); Fullilove v. Klutznick (affirmative action); Frontiero v. Richardson, Craig v. Boren, Califano v. Goldfarb, and Mississippi Univ. for Women v. Hogan (sex discrimination); Grand Rapids School Dist. v. Ball and Wallace v. Jaffree (establishment of religion); Almeida-Sanchez v. United States (search and seizure); and Brewer v. Williams (right to counsel). *See also* his dissent from findings of discrimination in Dayton Board of Education v. Brinkman and Batson v. Kentucky (race), Weber v. Aetna Cas. & Sur. Co. and Trimble v. Gordon (illegitimacy), In re Griffiths, Sugarman v. Dougall, and Plyler v. Doe (aliens); from the upholding of free expression claims in Elrod v. Burns, Virginia Consumer Council v. Virginia Pharmacy Ass'n, Wooley v. Maynard, and Board of Education v. Pico; from the invalidation of capital punishment in Furman v. Georgia, North Carolina v. Woodson, and Enmund v. Florida; and from the denial of governmental immunity in Garcia v. San Antonio Mass Transit Authority. Neither Brennan, Marshall, nor Douglas dissented in any of these cases. *See* Shapiro, *Mr. Justice Rehnquist: A Preliminary View,* 90 HARV. L. REV. 292, 293 (1976) ("[W]hile he is a man of considerable intellectual power and independence of mind, the unyielding character of his ideology has had a substantial adverse effect on his judicial product.").

[12] Before O'Connor's appointment, Burger had voted with Rehnquist in all the cases listed in notes 10 and 11 except *Roe, Fullilove, Frontiero, Sugarman, Weber, Virginia Pharmacy,* and *Wooley.* After O'Connor was appointed she agreed with Rehnquist in all the listed cases except *Hogan, Batson, Wallace,* and *Goldman,* and Burger agreed with him in every one.

[13] *See, e.g., Michael M.* and *Goldfarb* (sex discrimination), *Milliken* (race), *Lalli* and *Trimble* (illegitimacy), *Almeida-Sanchez, Harris,* and *Brewer* (criminal procedure), *Branzburg, Miller,* and *Wooley* (speech), and *Gregg, Furman,* and *Woodson* (capital punishment).

[14] *See, e.g.,* Roe v. Wade, *Virginia Pharmacy,* Sugarman v. Dougall, and *Bakke.*

[15] Post-1978 decisions listed in notes 10 and 11 in which Blackmun voted with Rehnquist include only *Hogan* (sex discrimination) and the criminal cases of *Leon, Quarles,* and *Enmund.* Blackmun voted with Brennan and Marshall in the search and incrimination cases of Hudson v. Palmer and Allen v. Illinois.

Stevens, in turn, was almost as predictable an ally of Brennan and Marshall as his predecessor Douglas had been, with the important exception of affirmative action.[16] Thus not only before the departure of Black and Douglas but in later years as well there were four reliable "liberal" votes on many important noncriminal issues.

Justice White usually provided a fifth in equal protection cases,[17] as Justice Stewart (until his 1981 retirement) not infrequently did in matters of free expression.[18] When all else failed, yet another of the new appointees came to the rescue on several important occasions. Although Justice Powell frequently sided with Rehnquist even in five-to-four cases,[19] he was with Brennan and Marshall in both *Roe* and *Fullilove* and cast the decisive vote for their position in a smattering of decisions most notably respecting abortion.[20]

In short, only part of the explanation for the Burger Court's failure to reverse the Warren revolution lies in the fact that it was not until 1975 that the new Justices constituted a majority. Equally important is the fact that at least three of them (Blackmun, Stevens, and Powell) turned out to be not as "conservative" as those who selected them may have hoped they would be.

The liberal margin of victory during the Burger years, however, was at best narrow. The fact that Justice Powell's departure in 1987 left the Court with only four members who had supported affirmative action in *Fullilove* or who had ever voted for abortion helps to explain the furor that surrounded President Reagan's efforts to replace him with yet another widely known conservative.[21] The traditional inertia of precedent tempered the

[16] In the cases listed in notes 10 and 11, Stevens voted with Rehnquist only to deny the claim of religious freedom in *Goldman*, to uphold the requirement of parental consent in *Danforth*, and to strike down affirmative action in *Bakke* and *Fullilove*. In other matters of both privacy and affirmative action (see *McRae*, *Thornburgh*, *Bowers*, and *Wygant*) he voted with Brennan, Marshall, and Blackmun.

[17] White voted with Brennan and Marshall in every equal protection case listed in notes 10 and 11 except *Wygant*, *Ambach*, and *Plyler;* in *Goldfarb*, *Hogan*, *Dayton*, and *Trimble* he cast the decisive vote. White voted with Rehnquist in the privacy and religion cases listed and in most criminal matters (but not in *Rakas*, *Furman*, or *Enmund*). In speech cases, he was with Rehnquist in *Branzburg* and *Miller*, with Brennan in *Elrod*, *Virginia Pharmacy*, *Wooley*, and *Pico*. He voted to uphold state immunity from suit (*Edelman*, *Pennhurst*) but not from Federal regulation (*National League of Cities*, *Garcia*). White also had a uniquely permissive attitude regarding experimentation with the structure of government. *See* his dissents in *Northern Pipeline*, *Chadha*, and *Bowsher*.

[18] Stewart cast the decisive vote to uphold free speech claims in Baird v. State Bar of Arizona, Cohen v. California, and Plummer v. City of Columbus, as well to upset a number of criminal judgments (*e.g.*, *Almeida-Sanchez*, *Brewer*, *Furman*, and *Woodson*). He voted with Brennan in all the other speech cases listed in notes 10 and 11 as well as in the privacy cases of *Roe* and *Danforth*. In other listed cases, however, he was with Brennan only in lopsided equal protection cases (*Frontiero*, *Craig*, *Griffiths*, *Sugarman*, and *Weber*).

[19] Powell cast the indispensable fifth vote for Rehnquist's position in *McRae* and *Bowers*, *Bakke* and *Wygant*, *Michael M.* and *Hogan*, *Ambach*, *Milliken*, and *Lalli*, *Branzburg*, *Miller*, and *Goldman*, *Mueller* and *Lynch*, *Hudson*, *National League of Cities*, *Edelman* and *Pennhurst*. He also voted with Rehnquist in *Dayton*, *Elrod*, *Pico*, *Leon*, *Quarles*, and the capital punishment cases.

[20] *E.g.*, *Danforth* and *Thornburgh* (abortion), *Goldfarb*, *Plyler*, and *Trimble* (equality), *Grand Rapids* (establishment), *Almeida-Sanchez* and *Brewer* (search and seizure and right to counsel). He also joined Brennan and Marshall in *Wallace* (moment of silence) and in the relatively noncontroversial cases of *Frontiero*, *Craig*, *Sugarman*, *Batson*, and *Weber* (discrimination), *Virginia Pharmacy* and *Wooley* (speech). For contrasting assessments see Gunther, *A Tribute to Justice Lewis F. Powell, Jr.*, 101 HARV. L. REV. 409, 410 (1987) (praising Powell as "a judge who takes the law seriously"), and Kahn, *The Court, the Community, and the Judicial Balance: The Jurisprudence of Justice Powell*, 97 YALE L.J. 1, 5 (1987) (accusing him of formless balancing that confused the role of judge with those of legislator, juror, and citizen).

[21] *See* Totenburg, *The Confirmation Process and the Public: To Know or Not to Know*, 101 HARV. L. REV. 1213 (1988). Chief Justice Burger, the sixth vote in both *Roe* and *Fullilove*, had left the Court in 1986.

probability of radical change, and past performance suggested that Justice White could be counted on to vote with Brennan, Marshall, Blackmun, and Stevens in most equal protection cases. In other areas, however, there was reason to predict a decreased judicial sympathy for many achievements of the Warren Court as a highly ideological Republican administration replaced Burger and Powell with two more Justices of its own choosing.[22] With three of the Court's often outnumbered liberals fast approaching the ends of their careers, there seemed a real possibility as the Court's second century came to a close that the counterrevolution that had been staved off during the Burger years might finally come to pass.

[22] Reagan elevated Rehnquist to Chief Justice, appointing Antonin Scalia and Anthony Kennedy to fill the two vacancies. Both were widely understood to be conservative, and their initial votes did nothing to dispel doubts that they would turn out to be staunch compatriots of Brennan and Marshall.

# Epilogue

At the age of seventy-eight, Chief Justice Burger left the Supreme Court to organize a birthday party for the Constitution. There was ample cause for celebration. Exemplary in most respects when adopted, the Constitution had not only survived two difficult centuries but had improved materially in the process. In the story of its success the Supreme Court had played a considerable role.

When the Constitution emerged from Philadelphia in 1787, it set forth only the "great outlines" of our system of government.[1] Whether its lofty goals would be realized depended to a substantial degree upon the wisdom and integrity of those who would interpret it. Thanks to the doctrine of judicial review, that meant it depended in no small part upon the Justices of the Supreme Court.

Judicial review has been defended from the beginning on the common-sense ground that other branches of government cannot be trusted to determine the limits of their own authority. Yet the argument that it is not prudent to appoint rabbits to guard cabbages applies to judges as well as to legislators and executives—the more so since federal judges are not even subject to the popular check of elections. At the same time, judicial authority to enforce the Constitution is limited by the case or controversy requirement and by sovereign immunity. Other branches also have a variety of weapons for attacking the courts—from impeaching refractory judges to packing the courts with compliant ones to restricting their jurisdiction. Moreover, as Hamilton observed, the judiciary wields neither the sword nor the purse;[2] it cannot enforce its decisions if other branches choose to ignore them. Thus we are perennially confronted with the question whether the judges are either too weak or too strong: is judicial review an effective means of keeping other branches within their powers, and are there adequate controls on excesses by the judges themselves?

The record of the first two hundred years graphically reveals both the weaknesses and the dangers of judicial review. In a number of crises, on the one hand, the Court has

[1] *See* McCulloch v. Maryland, 17 U.S. 316, 407 (1819).
[2] THE FEDERALIST No. 78.

proved unable or unwilling to prevent other branches from exceeding their authority. When Congress effectively reduced the Southern states to colonies after the Civil War, the judges lacked the audacity to intervene.[3] When Congress in the 1930s assumed extensive powers the Constitution had apparently reserved to the states, the Court was intimidated into submission.[4] When freedom of expression was endangered by popular hysteria during the First World War, the Court went along without a murmur; when the problem recurred after the Second World War, it protested cautiously and then withdrew from the field.[5] The Justices dragged their feet in ordering desegregation in the face of popular opposition[6] and ran from the opportunity to stand up for congressional prerogatives during the Vietnam War.[7] Even favorable decisions of the Supreme Court failed to effectuate the voting rights of blacks until other branches of the federal government finally added their weight to the scale.[8]

On other occasions, moreover, the judges have so exercised their power of judicial review as to deprive the people of what seemed the legitimate fruits of the democratic process. On the threshold of the Civil War the Court impeded a political solution by a cramped interpretation of Congress's power to legislate for the territories.[9] Before and during the Great Depression the Court repeatedly throttled efforts to ameliorate social ills with the due process weapon it had essentially fashioned out of whole cloth.[10] A generation later, in the eyes of many, it repeated the error with its controversial abortion and contraception decisions.[11]

Judicial review has thus paradoxically proved weak and dangerous at the same time. On the one hand, the judges have not always had the strength to enforce the Constitution in opposition to the spirit of the times. On the other, they have occasionally substituted their own principles for those laid down by the sovereign people.

Judicial review might be made more effective by allowing states or taxpayers to challenge federal expenditures, by abolishing sovereign immunity, by expressly forbidding court packing, by insulating jurisdiction from congressional control. Some or all of these reforms might be desirable, but they would enhance the Court's power to do mischief as well. The sanction of constitutional amendment would remain; but even an amendment must be interpreted, and John Calhoun's famous argument against Supreme Court review of state judgments suggests how much can be done by a court with final interpretive authority.[12]

The key to both the effectiveness of judicial review and control of the judges may lie in the fact that the Court's only power is the power to persuade. Judicial decisions are re-

---

[3] *See* THE FIRST HUNDRED YEARS at 296-376.

[4] *See* pp. 235-38 *supra.*

[5] *See* pp. 115-24, 385-96 *supra.*

[6] *See* pp. 379-80 *supra.*

[7] *See* p. 457 *supra.*

[8] *See* pp. 428-29 *supra.* It remains true, as Robert McCloskey wrote some years ago, that "[a]t no time in its history ha[s] the Court been able to maintain a position squarely opposed to a strong popular majority." R. MCCLOSKEY, THE AMERICAN SUPREME COURT 196 (1960).

[9] Dred Scott v. Sandford, 60 U.S. 393, 452; THE FIRST HUNDRED YEARS at 263-73.

[10] *See* pp. 45-50, 143-46 *supra.*

[11] *See* pp. 458-59, 465-72 *supra.*

[12] "If the appellate power from the state courts to the U. States court provided for by the 25th Secn. [of the Judiciary Act of 1789] did not exist, the practical consequences would be, that each government would have a negative on the other, and thus possess the most effectual remedy, that can be conceived against encroachment."

spected in the last analysis only because the people believe in the Court,[13] and there is much the Justices can do to help promote public confidence in their decisions. They can educate the public in the values of liberty and democracy, as Holmes and Brandeis did in their powerful first amendment opinions. They can earn respect by keeping their own house free from scandal, as they have done with remarkable success since the beginning. Most important, they can preserve the good will of the public by prudence in the exercise of their awesome authority.

This is not to say that the Court should practice judicial restraint in the sense of extreme deference to the views of other branches. This philosophy would severely curtail the checking function that judicial review was intended to serve. Nor is it to endorse the notion of differing levels of scrutiny under various provisions; I see no warrant for concluding that some parts of the Constitution are less deserving of enforcement than others. It is to say that the Justices must be careful never to exceed the limits of their own authority. To strike down a law on grounds lacking support in the Constitution is unacceptable not only because it is illegitimate, but also because it weakens public confidence in the Court and thus impairs its ability to enforce the Constitution.

Whether on occasion prudence may also entail finding ways to minimize direct confrontation with hostile public opinion is a more difficult question. One does not like to think of the Court avoiding intervention when it is most needed. Yet one cannot but wonder whether political suicide is in the long run likely to be the best means of defending the Constitution. Would democracy, federalism, and liberty be more secure today if the Court had stood up to Congress on Reconstruction, to Roosevelt on the New Deal, to McCarthy on political persecution? Or would the Court have been packed, stripped of jurisdiction, or simply defied—to the lasting detriment of judicial review and of the Constitution? I do not suggest that there are easy answers to these questions. I do suggest that considerations such as these may not be wholly irrelevant to a judge whose goal is to see that the Constitution is respected.[14]

The record of the first two centuries suggests that most of the time the Justices have appreciated both the demands and the limits of their power. Despite its weaknesses and dangers, on balance judicial review has served us well. In the first place, decisions unjustifiably restricting the democratic process have been relatively rare. Most of them were based on the largely abandoned doctrine of substantive due process, and it would not be surprising if the modern vestige of that doctrine were also to disappear in the next few years. Wrong decisions as well as right ones have a way of yielding ultimately to the spirit of the times; the courts are truly, as Hamilton wrote, "the least dangerous branch."[15]

---

Letter by Calhoun to Senator Littleton W. Tazewell of Virginia, August 25, 1827, in the Calhoun Papers, Library of Congress.

[13]*Cf.* L. HAND, THE SPIRIT OF LIBERTY 189-90 (3d ed. 1960).

[14]Some ways of avoiding destructive confrontations are more acceptable than others. The worst is to capitulate on the merits and legitimate unconstitutional action, as may have happened in the New Deal and McCarthy cases. Labeling an issue nonjusticiably "political," as Justice Frankfurter would have done with reapportionment, avoids judicial complicity in the wrong but abandons all hope of judicial correction. What may be more promising—and what the Court finally got, with minor exceptions, not long after Chief Justice Burger's retirement—is complete control over its docket, to ensure that it can decline jurisdiction not only when the issue is too trivial to warrant the Court's attention but also while it is too hot to handle, as it did in the Vietnam crisis.

[15]THE FEDERALIST No. 78.

The inability of the judges to prevent *every* violation of the Constitution is no argument against judicial review; pretty clearly there would have been even more violations without it. Most of the time the Justices have stood up for the Constitution, and the country has gone along. Prisoners are no longer regularly beaten to extract confessions;[16] residents of metropolitan areas are no longer denied an equal say in government;[17] state-sponsored racial segregation no longer exists.[18] Above all, time and time again the Court has protected freedom of expression from ham-handed governmental invasion.[19] This alone is enough to justify judicial review; the harm done by occasionally overzealous judges seems trivial in comparison.[20]

There were great moments in the Court's second century: the first Harlan's defense of a color-blind Constitution in *Plessy v. Ferguson;*[21] the Confederate veteran White's indignant rejection of the grandfather clause in *Guinn v. United States;*[22] Holmes and Brandeis's timeless pleas for freedom of expression in *Abrams, Gitlow,* and *Whitney;*[23] Jackson's sober insistence on cutting square corners with an accused traitor in *Cramer v. United States;*[24] Black's eloquent affirmation of the separation of powers in the *Steel Seizure Case;*[25] Warren's noble brief for racial justice in *Brown v. Board of Education.*[26] There were great careers as well: those of Holmes, the inimitable stylist who devoted thirty years to the task of opposing judicial usurpation; of Stone, who modernized entire fields of law and wrote the agenda for the second half of the century; of Black and Frankfurter, whose epic debate over how best to avoid the arrogance of the past spanned more than twenty years; of the second Harlan, who set a standard of intellectual integrity and trenchant analysis that won the admiration of his colleagues even when they disagreed with him; of Brennan, who fought an impassioned and often successful thirty-year battle for liberty, democracy, and equality.

Holmes and Brandeis, Cardozo and Hughes, Stone and Jackson, Frankfurter and Black: with Marshall, Story, Curtis, and Miller from an earlier century, these are names that belong in the pantheon. The United States has been fortunate in its Constitution, in its judges, and in its people; may it be as fortunate during the next two hundred years.

---

[16] *See* Brown v. Mississippi, pp. 247-48 *supra.*

[17] *See* Reynolds v. Sims, pp. 429-32 *supra.*

[18] *See* Brown v. Board of Education, pp. 377-78 *supra.*

[19] *See* pp. 252-70, 309-20, 434-42, 505-27 *supra.*

[20] *See generally* Choper, *Consequences of Supreme Court Decisions upholding Individual Constitutional Rights,* 83 MICH. L. REV. 1 (1984) (dramatically documenting the practical impact of a large number of Supreme Court decisions). Even when, as in the depths of the McCarthy period, popular passion raised doubts whether the Constitution could be fully enforced, the Court bought precious time by guerrilla resistance while appealing to the nation to return to its senses in eloquent opinions that suggested far more than they could prudently decide. The fact that only a few years passed before the Court was able to breathe new life into the bruised constitutional provisions tends to confirm one of the basic premises of the Constitution itself: that although periodic crises may distort their judgment, in the long run the people really believe in democracy, freedom, and the rule of law.

[21] *See* p. 40 *supra.*

[22] *See* pp. 106-07 *supra.*

[23] *See* pp.121-24, 154-62 *supra.*

[24] *See* pp. 294-99 *supra.*

[25] *See* pp. 365-69 *supra.*

[26] *See* pp. 377-78 *supra.*

# Appendix A
# Justices of the Supreme Court
# 1888–1986

1880 90 1900 10 20 30 40 50 60 70 80 90

Samuel F. Miller (1862-1890)
Stephen J. Field (1863-1897)
Joseph P. Bradley (1870-1892)
John M. Harlan (1877-1911)
Stanley Matthews (1881-1889)
Horace Gray (1881-1902)
Samuel Blatchford (1882-1893)
Lucius Q. C. Lamar (1888-1893)
*Melville W. Fuller (1888-1910)
David J. Brewer (1889-1910)
Henry B. Brown (1890-1906)
George Shiras (1892-1903)
Howell E. Jackson (1893-1895)
*Edward D. White (1894-1921)
Rufus W. Peckham (1895-1909)
Joseph McKenna (1898-1925)
Oliver W. Holmes, Jr. (1902-1932)
William R. Day (1903-1922)
William H. Moody (1906-1910)
Horace H. Lurton (1909-1914)
Charles Evans Hughes (1910-1916)
Willis Van Devanter (1910-1937)
Joseph R. Lamar (1910-1916)
Mahlon Pitney (1912-1922)
James C. McReynolds (1914-1941)
Louis D. Brandeis (1916-1939)
John H. Clarke (1916-1922)
*William H. Taft (1921-1930)
George Sutherland (1922-1938)
Pierce Butler (1922-1939)

Edward T. Sanford        (1923-1930)

*Harlan F. Stone          (1925-1946)

*Charles Evans Hughes    (1930-1941)

Owen J. Roberts          (1930-1945)

Benjamin N. Cardozo      (1932-1938)

Hugo L. Black            (1937-1971)

Stanley F. Reed          (1938-1957)

Felix Frankfurter        (1939-1962)

William O. Douglas       (1939-1975)

Frank Murphy             (1940-1949)

James F. Byrnes          (1941-1942)

Robert H. Jackson        (1941-1954)

Wiley B. Rutledge        (1943-1949)

Harold H. Burton         (1945-1958)

*Fred M. Vinson           (1946-1953)

Tom C. Clark             (1949-1967)

Sherman Minton           (1949-1956)

*Earl Warren              (1953-1969)

John M. Harlan           (1955-1971)

William J. Brennan, Jr.  (1956-    )

Charles E. Whittaker     (1957-1962)

Potter Stewart           (1958-1981)

Byron R. White           (1962-    )

Arthur J. Goldberg       (1962-1965)

Abe Fortas               (1965-1969)

Thurgood Marshall        (1967-    )

*Warren E. Burger         (1969-1986)

Harry A. Blackmun        (1970-    )

Lewis F. Powell, Jr.     (1972-1987)

William H. Rehnquist     (1972-    )

John Paul Stevens        (1975-    )

Sandra Day O'Connor      (1981-    )

* Denotes Chief Justice.

# Appendix B
# The Constitution of the United States

We the People of the United States, in Order to form a more perfect Union, establish Justice, insure domestic Tranquility, provide for the common defence, promote the general Welfare, and secure the Blessings of Liberty to ourselves and our Posterity, do ordain and establish this Constitution for the United States of America.

## ARTICLE I

SECTION 1. All legislative Powers herein granted shall be vested in a Congress of the United States, which shall consist of a Senate and House of Representatives.

SECTION 2. The House of Representatives shall be composed of Members chosen every second Year by the People of the several States, and the Electors in each State shall have the Qualifications requisite for Electors of the most numerous Branch of the State Legislature.

No Person shall be a Representative who shall not have attained to the Age of twenty-five Years, and been seven Years a Citizen of the United States, and who shall not, when elected, be an Inhabitant of that State in which he shall be chosen.

Representatives and direct Taxes shall be apportioned among the several States which may be included within this Union, according to their respective Numbers, which shall be determined by adding to the whole Number of free Persons, including those bound to Service for a Term of Years, and excluding Indians not taxed, three fifths of all other Persons. The actual Enumeration shall be made within three Years after the first meeting of the Congress of the United States, and within every subsequent Term of ten Years, in such Manner as they shall by Law direct. The Number of Representatives shall not exceed one for every thirty Thousand, but each State shall have at Least one Representative; and until such enumeration shall be made, the State of New Hampshire shall be entitled to chuse three, Massachusetts eight, Rhode Island and Providence Plantations one, Connecticut five, New-York six, New Jersey four, Pennsylvania eight, Delaware one, Maryland six, Virginia ten, North Carolina five, South Carolina five, and Georgia three.

When vacancies happen in the Representation from any State, the Executive Authority thereof shall issue Writs of Election to fill such Vacancies.

The House of Representatives shall chuse their Speaker and other Officers; and shall have the sole Power of Impeachment.

SECTION 3. The Senate of the United States shall be composed of two Senators from each State, chosen by the Legislature thereof, for six Years; and each Senator shall have one Vote.

Immediately after they shall be assembled in Consequence of the first Election, they shall be divided as equally as may be into three Classes. The Seats of the Senators of the first Class shall be vacated at the Expiration of the second Year, of the second Class at the Expiration of the fourth Year, and of the third Class at the Expiration of the sixth Year, so that one-third may be chosen every second Year; and if Vacancies happen by Resignation, or otherwise, during the Recess of the Legislature of any State, the Executive thereof may make temporary Appointments until the next Meeting of the Legislature, which shall then fill such Vacancies.

No Person shall be a Senator who shall not have attained to the Age of thirty Years, and been nine Years a Citizen of the United States, and who shall not, when elected, be an Inhabitant of that State for which he shall be chosen.

The Vice President of the United States shall be President of the Senate, but shall have no Vote, unless they be equally divided.

The Senate shall chuse their other Officers, and also a President pro tempore, in the absence of the Vice President, or when he shall exercise the Office of President of the United States.

The Senate shall have the sole Power to try all Impeachments. When sitting for that Purpose, they shall be on Oath or Affirmation. When the President of the United States is tried, the Chief Justice shall preside. And no Person shall be convicted without the Concurrence of two thirds of the Members present.

Judgment in Cases of Impeachment shall not extend further than to removal from Office, and disqualification to hold and enjoy any Office of honor, Trust or Profit under the United States: but the Party convicted shall nevertheless be liable and subject to Indictment, Trial, Judgment and Punishment, according to Law.

SECTION 4. The Times, Places and Manner of holding Elections for Senators and Representatives, shall be prescribed in each State by the Legislature thereof; but the Congress may at any time by Law make or alter such Regulations, except as to the Place of Chusing Senators.

The Congress shall assemble at least once in every Year, and such Meeting shall be on the first Monday in December, unless they shall by Law appoint a different Day.

SECTION 5. Each House shall be the Judge of the Elections, Returns and Qualifications of its own Members, and a Majority of each shall constitute a Quorum to do Business; but a smaller number may adjourn from day to day, and may be authorized to compel the Attendance of absent Members, in such Manner, and under such Penalties as each House may provide.

Each House may determine the Rules of its Proceedings, punish its Members for disorderly Behavior, and, with the Concurrence of two thirds, expel a Member.

Each House shall keep a Journal of its Proceedings, and from time to time publish the same, excepting such Parts as may in their Judgment require Secrecy; and the Yeas and Nays of the Members of either House on any question shall, at the Desire of one fifth of those Present, be entered on the Journal.

Neither House, during the Session of Congress, shall, without the Consent of the other, adjourn for more than three days, nor to any other Place than that in which the two Houses shall be sitting.

SECTION 6. The Senators and Representatives shall receive a Compensation for their Services, to be ascertained by Law, and paid out of the Treasury of the United States. They shall in all Cases, except Treason, Felony and Breach of the Peace, be privileged from Arrest during their Attendance at the Session of their respective Houses, and in going to and returning from the same; and for any Speech or Debate in either House, they shall not be questioned in any other Place.

No Senator or Representative shall, during the Time for which he was elected, be appointed to any civil Office under the Authority of the United States, which shall have been created, or the Emoluments whereof shall have been encreased during such time; and no Person holding any Office under the United States, shall be a Member of either House during his Continuance in Office.

SECTION 7. All Bills for raising Revenue shall originate in the House of Representatives; but the Senate may propose or concur with Amendments as on other Bills.

Every Bill which shall have passed the House of Representatives and the Senate, shall, before it become a Law, be presented to the President of the United States; If he approve he shall sign it, but if not he shall return it, with his Objections to that House in which it shall have originated, who shall enter the Objections at large on their Journal, and proceed to reconsider it. If after such Reconsideration two thirds of that House shall agree to pass the Bill, it shall be sent, together with the Objections, to the other House, by which it shall likewise be reconsidered, and if approved by two thirds of that House, it shall become a Law. But in all such Cases the Votes of both Houses shall be determined by Yeas and Nays, and the Names of the Persons voting for and against the Bill shall be entered on the Journal of each House respectively. If any Bill shall not be returned by the President within ten Days (Sundays excepted) after it shall have been presented to him, the Same shall be a Law, in like Manner as if he had signed it, unless the Congress by their Adjournment prevent its Return, in which Case it shall not be a Law.

Every Order, Resolution, or Vote to which the Concurrence of the Senate and House of Representatives may be necessary (except on a question of Adjournment) shall be presented to the President of the United States; and before the Same shall take Effect, shall be approved by him, or being disapproved by him, shall be repassed by two thirds of the Senate and House of Representatives, according to the Rules and Limitations prescribed in the Case of a Bill.

SECTION 8. The Congress shall have Power To lay and collect Taxes, Duties, Imposts and Excises, to pay the Debts and provide for the common Defence and general Welfare of the United States; but all duties, Imposts and Excises shall be uniform throughout the United States;

To borrow money on the credit of the United States;

To regulate Commerce with foreign Nations, and among the several States, and with the Indian Tribes;

To establish an uniform Rule of Naturalization, and uniform Laws on the subject of Bankruptcies throughout the United States;

To coin Money, regulate the Value thereof, and of foreign Coin, and fix the Standard of Weights and Measures;

To provide for the Punishment of counterfeiting the Securities and current Coin of the United States:

To establish Post Offices and post Roads;

To promote the Progress of Science and useful Arts, by securing for limited Times to Authors and Inventors the exclusive Right to their respective Writings and Discoveries;

To constitute Tribunals inferior to the supreme Court;

To define and punish Piracies and Felonies committed on the high Seas, and Offenses against the Law of Nations;

To declare War, grant Letters of Marque and Reprisal, and make Rules concerning Captures on Land and Water;

To raise and support Armies, but no Appropriation of Money to that Use shall be for a longer Term than two Years;

To provide and maintain a Navy;

To make Rules for the Government and Regulation of the land and naval Forces;

To provide for calling forth the Militia to execute the Laws of the Union, suppress Insurrections and repel Invasions;

To provide for organizing, arming, and disciplining the Militia, and for governing such Part of them as may be employed in the Service of the United States, reserving to the States respectively, the Appointment of the Officers, and the Authority of training the Militia according to the discipline prescribed by Congress;

To exercise exclusive Legislation in all Cases whatsoever, over such District (not exceeding ten Miles square) as may, by Cession of particular States, and the acceptance of Congress, become the Seat of the Government of the United States, and to exercise like Authority over all Places purchased by the Consent of the Legislature of the State in which the Same shall be, for the Erection of Forts, Magazines, Arsenals, dock-Yards, and other needful Buildings;—And

To make all Laws which shall be necessary and proper for carrying into Execution the foregoing Powers, and all other Powers vested by this Constitution in the Government of the United States, or in any Department or Officer thereof.

SECTION 9. The Migration or Importation of such Persons as any of the States now existing shall think proper to admit, shall not be prohibited by the Congress prior to the Year one thousand eight hundred and eight, but a tax or duty may be imposed on such Importation, not exceeding ten dollars for each Person.

The privilege of the Writ of Habeas Corpus shall not be suspended, unless when in Cases of Rebellion or Invasion the public Safety may require it.

No Bill of Attainder or ex post facto Law shall be passed.

No capitation, or other direct, Tax shall be laid, unless in Proportion to the Census or Enumeration herein before directed to be taken.

No Tax or Duty shall be laid on Articles exported from any State.

No Preference shall be given by any Regulation of Commerce or Revenue to the Ports of one State over those of another; nor shall Vessels bound to, or from, one State, be obliged to enter, clear, or pay Duties in another.

No Money shall be drawn from the Treasury, but in Consequence of Appropriations made by Law; and a regular Statement and Account of the Receipts and Expenditures of all public Money shall be published from time to time.

No Title of Nobility shall be granted by the United States; And no Person holding any Office of Profit or Trust under them, shall, without the Consent of the Congress, accept of any present, Emolument, Office, or Title, of any kind whatever, from any King, Prince, or foreign State.

SECTION 10. No State shall enter into any Treaty, Alliance, or Confederation; grant Letters of Marque and Reprisal; coin Money; emit Bills of Credit; make any Thing but gold and silver Coin a Tender in Payment of Debts; pass any Bill of Attainder, ex post facto Law, or Law impairing the Obligation of Contracts, or grant any Title of Nobility.

No State shall, without the Consent of the Congress, lay any Imposts or Duties on Imports or Exports, except what may be absolutely necessary for executing its inspection Laws: and the net Produce of all Duties and Imposts, laid by any State on Imports or Exports, shall be for the Use of the Treasury of the United States; and all such Laws shall be subject to the Revision and Controul of the Congress.

No State shall, without the Consent of Congress, lay any duty of Tonnage, keep Troops, or Ships of War in time of Peace, enter into any Agreement or Compact with another State, or with a foreign Power, or engage in War, unless actually invaded, or in such imminent Danger as will not admit of delay.

## ARTICLE II

SECTION 1. The executive Power shall be vested in a President of the United States of America. He shall hold his Office during the Term of four Years, and, together with the Vice-President, chosen for the same Term, be elected, as follows.

Each State shall appoint, in such Manner as the Legislature thereof may direct, a Number of Electors, equal to the whole Number of Senators and Representatives to which the State may be entitled in the Congress: but no Senator or Representative, or Person holding an Office of Trust or Profit under the United States, shall be appointed an Elector.

The Electors shall meet in their respective States, and vote by Ballot for two persons, of whom one at least shall not be an Inhabitant of the same State with themselves. And they shall make a List of all the Persons voted for, and of the Number of Votes for each; which List they shall sign and certify, and transmit sealed to the Seat of the Government of the Untied States, directed to the President of the Senate. The President of the Senate shall, in the Presence of the Senate and House of Representatives, open all the Certificates, and the Votes shall then be counted. The Person having the greatest Number of Votes shall be the President, if such Number be a Majority of the whole Number of Electors appointed; and if there be more than one who have such Majority, and have an equal Number of Votes, then the House of Representatives shall immediately chuse by Ballot one of them for President; and if no Person have a Majority, then from the five highest on the List the said House shall in like Manner chuse the President. But in chusing the President, the Votes shall be taken by States, the Representation from each State having one Vote; a quorum for this Purpose shall consist of a Member or Members from two thirds of the States, and a Majority of all the States shall be necessary to a Choice. In every Case, after the Choice of the President, the Person having the greatest Number of Votes of the

Electors shall be the Vice President. But if there should remain two or more who have equal Votes, the Senate shall chuse from them by Ballot the Vice-President.

The Congress may determine the Time of chusing the Electors, and the Day on which they shall give their Votes; which Day shall be the same throughout the United States.

No person except a natural born Citizen, or a Citizen of the United States, at the time of the Adoption of this Constitution, shall be eligible to the Office of President; neither shall any Person be eligible to that Office who shall not have attained to the Age of thirty-five Years, and been fourteen Years a Resident within the United States.

In Case of the Removal of the President from Office, or of his Death, Resignation, or Inability to discharge the Powers and Duties of the said Office, the same shall devolve on the Vice President, and the Congress may by Law, provide for the Case of Removal, Death, Resignation or Inability, both of the President and Vice President, declaring what Officer shall then act as President, and such Officer shall act accordingly, until the Disability be removed, or a President shall be elected.

The President shall, at stated Times, receive for his Services, a Compensation, which shall neither be encreased nor diminished during the Period for which he shall have been elected, and he shall not receive within that Period any other Emolument from the United States, or any of them.

Before he enter on the Execution of his Office, he shall take the following Oath or Affirmation:—"I do solemnly swear (or affirm) that I will faithfully execute the Office of President of the United States, and will to the best of my Ability, preserve, protect and defend the Constitution of the United States."

SECTION 2. The President shall be Commander in Chief of the Army and Navy of the United States, and of the Militia of the several States, when called into the actual Service of the United States; he may require the Opinion in writing, of the principal Officer in each of the executive Departments, upon any subject relating to the Duties of their respective Offices, and he shall have Power to Grant Reprieves and Pardons for Offenses against the United States, except in Cases of Impeachment.

He shall have Power, by and with the Advice and Consent of the Senate, to make Treaties, provided two-thirds of the Senators present concur; and he shall nominate, and by and with the Advice and Consent of the Senate, shall appoint Ambassadors, other public Ministers and Consuls, Judges of the supreme Court, and all other Offices of the United States, whose Appointments are not herein otherwise provided for, and which shall be established by Law: but the Congress may by Law vest the Appointment of such inferior Officers, as they think proper, in the President alone, in the Courts of Law, or in the Heads of Departments.

The President shall have Power to fill up all Vacancies that may happen during the Recess of the Senate, by granting Commissions which shall expire at the End of their next Session.

SECTION 3. He shall from time to time give to the Congress Information of the State of the Union, and recommend to their Consideration such Measures as he shall judge necessary and expedient; he may, on extraordinary Occasions, convene both Houses, or either of them, and in Case of Disagreement between them, with Respect to the Time of Adjournment, he may adjourn them to such Time as he shall think proper; he shall receive Ambassadors and other public Ministers; he shall take Care that the Laws be faithfully executed, and shall Commission all the Officers of the United States.

SECTION 4. The President, Vice President and all civil Officers of the United States, shall be removed from Office of Impeachment for, and Conviction of, Treason, Bribery, or other high Crimes and Misdemeanors.

## ARTICLE III

SECTION 1. The judicial Power of the United States, shall be vested in one supreme Court, and in such inferior Courts as the Congress may from time to time ordain and establish. The Judges, both of the supreme and inferior Courts, shall hold their Offices during good Behaviour, and shall, at stated Times, receive for their Services, a Compensation, which shall not be diminished during their Continuance in Office.

SECTION 2. The judicial Power shall extend to all Cases, in Law and Equity, arising under this Constitution, the Laws of the United States, and Treaties made, or which shall be made, under their Authority;—to all Cases affecting Ambassadors, other public Ministers and Consuls;—to all Cases of admiralty and maritime Jurisdiction;—to Controversies to which the United States shall be a Party;—to Controversies between two or more States;—between a State and Citizens of another State;—between Citizens of different States;—between Citizens of the same State claiming Lands under Grants of different States, and between a State, or the citizens thereof, and foreign States, Citizens or Subjects.

In all Cases affecting Ambassadors, other public Ministers and Consuls, and those in which a State shall be Party, the supreme Court shall have original Jurisdiction. In all the other Cases before mentioned, the supreme Court shall have appellate Jurisdiction, both as to Law and Fact, with such Exceptions, and under such Regulations as the Congress shall make.

The trial of all Crimes, except in Cases of Impeachment, shall be by Jury; and such Trial shall be held in the State where the said Crimes shall have been committed; but when not committed within any State, the Trial shall be at such Place or Places as the Congress may by Law have directed.

SECTION 3. Treason against the United States, shall consist only in levying War against them, or in adhering to their Enemies, giving them Aid and Comfort. No Person shall be convicted of Treason unless on the Testimony of two Witnesses to the same overt Act, or on Confession in open Court.

The congress shall have Power to declare the Punishment of Treason, but no Attainder of Treason shall work Corruption of Blood, or Forfeiture except during the Life of the Person attained.

## ARTICLE IV

SECTION 1. Full Faith and Credit shall be given in each State to the public Acts, Records, and judicial Proceedings of every other State. And the Congress may by general Laws prescribe the Manner in which such Acts, Records and Proceedings shall be proved, and the Effect thereof.

SECTION 2. The Citizens of each State shall be entitled to all Privileges and Immunities of Citizens in the several States.

A Person charged in any State with Treason, Felony, or other Crime, who shall flee from Justice, and be found in another State, shall on demand of the executive Authority of the State from which he fled, be delivered up, to be removed to the State having Jurisdiction of the Crime.

No Person held to Service or Labour in one State, under the Laws thereof, escaping into another, shall, in Consequence of any Law or Regulation therein, be discharged from such Service or Labour, but shall be delivered up on Claim of the Party to whom such Service or Labour may be due.

SECTION 3. New States may be admitted by the Congress into this Union; but no new State shall be formed or erected within the Jurisdiction of any other State; nor any State be formed by the Junction of two or more States, or parts of States, without the consent of the Legislatures of the States concerned as well as of the Congress.

The Congress shall have Power to dispose of and make all needful Rules and Regulations respecting the Territory or other Property belonging to the United States; and nothing in this Constitution shall be so construed as to Prejudice any Claims of the United States, or of any particular State.

SECTION 4. The United States shall guarantee to every State in this Union a Republican Form of Government, and shall protect each of them against Invasion; and on Application of the Legislature, or the executive (when the Legislature cannot be convened) against domestic Violence.

## ARTICLE V

The Congress, whenever two-thirds of both Houses shall deem it necessary, shall propose Amendments to this Constitution, or, on the Application of the Legislature of two-thirds of the several States, shall call a Convention for proposing Amendments, which, in either Case, shall be valid to all Intents and Purposes, as part of this Constitution, when ratified by the Legislatures of three-fourths of the several States, or by Conventions in three-fourths thereof, as the one or the other Mode of Ratification may be proposed by the Congress: Provided that no Amendment which may be made prior to the Year One thousand eight hundred and eight shall in any Manner affect the first and fourth Clauses in the Ninth Section of the first Article; and that no State, without its Consent, shall be deprived of its equal Suffrage in the Senate.

## ARTICLE VI

All Debts contracted and Engagements entered into, before the Adoption of this Constitution, shall be as valid against the United States under this Constitution, as under the Confederation.

This Constitution, and the Laws of the United States which shall be made in Pursuance thereof; and all Treaties made, or which shall be made, under the Authority of the United States, shall be the supreme Law of the Land; and the Judges in every State shall be bound thereby, any Thing in the Constitution or Laws of any State to the Contrary notwithstanding.

The Senators and Representatives before mentioned, and the Members of the several State Legislatures, and all executive and judicial Officers, both of the United States and of the several States, shall be bound by Oath or Affirmation, to support this Constitution; but no religious Test shall ever be required as a Qualification to any Office or public Trust under the United States.

## ARTICLE VII

The Ratification of the Conventions of nine States shall be sufficient for the Establishment of this Constitution between the States so ratifying the Same.

ARTICLES IN ADDITION TO, AND AMENDMENT OF, THE CONSTITUTION OF THE UNITED STATES OF AMERICA, PROPOSED BY CONGRESS, AND RATIFIED BY THE LEGISLATURES OF THE SEVERAL STATES, PURSUANT TO THE FIFTH ARTICLE OF THE ORIGINAL CONSTITUTION.

## AMENDMENT I

*(Amendments I-X were ratified 15 December 1791)*
Congress shall make no law respecting an establishment of religion, or prohibiting the free exercise thereof; or abridging the freedom of speech, or of the press; or the right of the people peaceably to assemble, and to petition the Government for a redress of grievances.

## AMENDMENT II

A well regulated Militia being necessary to the security of a free State, the right of the people to keep and bear Arms shall not be infringed.

## AMENDMENT III

No Soldier shall, in time of peace be quartered in any house, without the consent of the Owner, nor in time of war, but in a manner to be prescribed by law.

## AMENDMENT IV

The right of the people to be secure in their persons, houses, papers, and effects, against unreasonable searches and seizures, shall not be violated, and no Warrants shall issue, but upon probable cause, supported by Oath or affirmation, and particularly describing the place to be searched, and the persons or things to be seized.

## AMENDMENT V

No person shall be held to answer for a capital, or otherwise infamous crime, unless on a presentment or indictment of a Grand Jury, except in cases arising in the land or naval forces, or in the Militia, when in actual service in time of War or public danger; nor shall any person be subject for the same offence to be twice put in jeopardy of life or limb; nor shall be compelled in any criminal case to be a witness against himself, nor be deprived of life, liberty, or property, without due process of law; nor shall private property be taken for public use, without just compensation.

## AMENDMENT VI

In all criminal prosecutions, the accused shall enjoy the right to a speedy and public trial, by an impartial jury of the State and district wherein the crime shall have been committed, which district shall have been previously ascertained by law, and to be informed of the nature and cause of the accusation; to be confronted with the witnesses against him; to have compulsory process for obtaining witnesses in his favor, and to have the Assistance of counsel for his defence.

## AMENDMENT VII

In suits at common law, where the value in controversy shall exceed twenty dollars, the right of trial by jury shall be preserved, and no fact tried by a jury, shall be otherwise reexamined in any Court of the United States, than according to the rules of the common law.

## AMENDMENT VIII

Excessive bail shall not be required, nor excessive fines imposed, nor cruel and unusual punishments inflicted.

## AMENDMENT IX

The enumeration in the Constitution, of certain rights, shall not be construed to deny or disparage others retained by the people.

## AMENDMENT X

The powers not delegated to the United States by the Constitution, nor prohibited by it to the States, are reserved to the States respectively, or to the people.

## AMENDMENT XI

*(Ratified February 7, 1798)*

The Judicial power of the United States shall not be construed to extend to any suit in law or equity, commenced or prosecuted against one of the United States by Citizens of another State, or by Citizens or Subjects of any Foreign State.

## AMENDMENT XII

*(Ratified June 15, 1804)*

The Electors shall meet in their respective states and vote by ballot for President and Vice-President, one of whom, at least, shall not be an inhabitant of the same state with themselves; they shall name in their ballots the person voted for as President, and in distinct ballots the person voted for as Vice-President, and they shall make distinct lists of all persons voted for as President, and of all persons voted for as Vice-President, and of the number of votes for each, which lists they shall sign and certify, and transmit sealed to the seat of the government of the United States, directed to the President of the Senate;—The President of the Senate shall, in presence of the Senate and House of Representatives, open all the certificates and the votes shall then be counted;—The person having the greatest number of votes for President, shall be the President, if such number be a majority of the whole number of Electors appointed; and if no person have such majority, then from the persons having the highest numbers not exceeding three on the list of those voted for as President, the House of Representatives shall choose immediately, by ballot, the President. But in choosing the President, the votes shall be taken by states, the representation from each state having one vote; a quorum for this purpose shall consist of a member or members from two-thirds of the states, and a majority of all the states shall be necessary to a choice. And if the House of Representatives shall not choose a President whenever the right of choice shall devolve upon them, before the fourth day of March next following, then the Vice-President shall act as President, as in the case of the death or other constitutional disability of the President.—The person having the greatest number of votes as Vice-President, shall be the Vice-President, if such number be a majority of the whole number of Electors appointed, and if no person have a majority, then from the two highest numbers on the list, the Senate shall choose the Vice-President; a quorum for the purpose shall consist two-thirds of the whole number of Senators, and a majority of the whole number shall be necessary to a choice. But no person constitutionally ineligible to the office of President shall be eligible to that of Vice-President of the United States.

## AMENDMENT XIII

### *(Ratified December 6, 1865)*

SECTION 1. Neither slavery nor involuntary servitude, except as a punishment for crime whereof the party shall have been duly convicted, shall exist within the United States, or any place subject to their jurisdiction.

SECTION 2. Congress shall have power to enforce this article by appropriate legislation.

## AMENDMENT XIV

### *(Ratified July 9, 1868)*

SECTION 1. All persons born or naturalized in the United States, and subject to the jurisdiction thereof, are citizens of the United States and of the State wherein they reside. No State shall make or enforce any law which shall abridge the privileges or immunities of citizens of the United States; nor shall any State deprive any person of life, liberty, or property, without due process of law; nor deny to any person within its jurisdiction the equal protection of the laws.

SECTION 2. Representatives shall be apportioned among the several States according to their respective numbers, counting the whole number of persons in each State, excluding Indians not taxed. But when the right to vote at any election for the choice of electors for President and Vice-President of the United States, Representatives in Congress, the Executive and Judicial officers of a State, or the members of the Legislature thereof, is denied to any of the male inhabitants of such State, being twenty-one years of age, and citizens of the United States, or in any way abridged, except for participation in rebellion, or other crime, the basis of representation therein shall be reduced in the proportion which the number of such male citizens shall bear to the whole number of male citizens twenty-one years of age in such State.

SECTION 3. No person shall be a Senator or Representative in Congress, or elector of President and Vice-President, or hold any office, civil or military, under the United States, or under any State, who, having previously taken an oath, as a member of Congress, or as an officer of the United States, or as a member of any State legislature, or as an executive or judicial officer of any State, to support the Constitution of the United States, shall have engaged in insurrection or rebellion against the same, or given aid or comfort to the enemies thereof. But Congress may by a vote of two-thirds of each House, remove such disability.

SECTION 4. The validity of the public debt of the United States, authorized by law, including debts incurred for payment of pensions and bounties for services in suppressing insurrection or rebellion, shall not be questioned. But neither the United States nor any State shall assume or pay any debt or obligation incurred in aid of insurrection or rebellion against the United States, or any claim for the loss or emancipation of any slave; but all such debts, obligations and claims shall be held illegal and void.

SECTION 5. The Congress shall have power to enforce, by appropriate legislation, the provisions of this article.

## AMENDMENT XV

### (Ratified February 3, 1870)

SECTION 1. The right of citizens of the United States to vote shall not be denied or abridged by the United States or by any State on account of race, color, or previous condition of servitude.

SECTION 2. The Congress shall have power to enforce this article by appropriate legislation.

## AMENDMENT XVI

### (Ratified February 3, 1913)

The Congress shall have power to lay and collect taxes on incomes, from whatever source derived, without apportionment among the several States, and without regard to any census or enumeration.

## AMENDMENT XVII

### (Ratified April 8, 1913)

The Senate of the United States shall be composed of two Senators from each State, elected by the people thereof, for six years; and each Senator shall have one vote. The electors in each State shall have the qualifications requisite for electors of the most numerous branch of the State legislatures.

When vacancies happen in the representation of any State in the Senate, the executive authority of such State shall issue writs of election to fill such vacancies: *Provided,* That the legislature of any State may empower the executive thereof to make temporary appointments until the people fill the vacancies by election as the legislature may direct.

This amendment shall not be so construed as to affect the election or term of any Senator chosen before it becomes valid as part of the Constitution.

## AMENDMENT XVIII

### *(Ratified January 16, 1919)*

SECTION 1. After one year from the ratification of this article the manufacture, sale, or transportation of intoxicating liquors within, the importation thereof into, or the exportation thereof from the United States and all territory subject to the jurisdiction thereof for beverage purposes is hereby prohibited.

SECTION 2. The Congress and the several States shall have concurrent power to enforce this article by appropriate legislation.

SECTION 3. This article shall be inoperative unless it shall have been ratified as an amendment to the Constitution by the legislatures of the several States as provided in the Constitution, within seven years from the date of the submission hereof to the States by the Congress.

## AMENDMENT XIX

### *(Ratified August 18, 1920)*

SECTION 1. The right of citizens of the United States to vote shall not be denied or abridged by the United States or by any State on account of sex.

SECTION 2. Congress shall have power to enforce this article by appropriate legislation.

## AMENDMENT XX

### *(Ratified January 23, 1933)*

SECTION 1. The terms of the President and Vice President shall end at noon on the 20th day of January, and the terms of Senators and Representatives at noon on the 3d day of January, of the years in which such terms would have ended if this article had not been ratified; and the terms of their successors shall then begin.

SECTION 2. The Congress shall assemble at least once in every year, and such meeting shall begin at noon on the 3d day of January, unless they shall by law appoint a different day.

SECTION 3. If, at the time fixed for the beginning of the term of the President, the President elect shall have died, the Vice President shall become President. If a President shall not have been chosen before the time fixed for the beginning of his term, or if the President elect shall have failed to qualify, then the Vice President elect shall act as President until a President shall have qualified; and the Congress may by law provide for the case wherein neither a President elect nor a Vice President elect shall have qualified, declaring who shall then act as President, or the manner in which one who is to act shall be selected, and such person shall act accordingly until a President or Vice President shall have qualified.

SECTION 4. The Congress may by law provide for the case of the death of any of the persons from whom the House of Representatives may choose a President whenever the right of choice shall have devolved upon them, and for the case of the death of any of the persons from whom the Senate may choose a Vice President whenever the right of choice shall have devolved upon them.

SECTION 5. Sections 1 and 2 shall take effect on the 15th day of October following the ratification of this article.

SECTION 6. This article shall be inoperative unless it shall have been ratified as an amendment to the Constitution by the legislatures of three-fourths of the several States within seven years from the date of its submission.

## AMENDMENT XXI

### *(Ratified December 5, 1933)*

SECTION 1. The eighteenth article of amendment to the Constitution of the United States is hereby repealed.

SECTION 2. The transportation or importation into any State, Territory, or possession of the United States for delivery or use therein of intoxicating liquors, in violation of the laws thereof, is hereby prohibited.

SECTION 3. This article shall be inoperative unless it shall have been ratified as an amendment to the Constitution by conventions in the several States, as provided in the Constitution, within seven years from that date of the submission hereof to the States by the Congress.

## AMENDMENT XXII

### *(Ratified February 27, 1951)*

SECTION 1. No person shall be elected to the office of the President more than twice, and no person who has held the office of President, or acted as President, for more than two years of a term to which some other person was elected President shall be elected to the office of the President more than once. But this Article shall not apply to any person holding the office of President when this Article was proposed by the Congress, and shall not prevent any person who may be holding the office of President, or acting as President, during the term within which this Article becomes operative from holding the office of President or acting as President during the remainder of such term.

SECTION 2. This article shall be inoperative unless it shall have been ratified as an amendment to the Constitution by the legislatures of three-fourths of the several States within seven years from the date of its submission to the States by the Congress.

## AMENDMENT XXIII

### *(Ratified March 29, 1961)*

SECTION 1. The District constituting the seat of Government of the United States shall appoint in such manner as the Congress may direct:

A number of electors of President and Vice President equal to the whole number of Senators and Representatives in Congress to which the District would be entitled if it were a State, but in no event more than the least populous State; they shall be in addition to those appointed by the States, but they shall be considered, for the purposes of the election of President and Vice President, to be electors appointed by a State; and they shall meet in the District and perform such duties as provided by the twelfth article of amendment.

SECTION 2. The Congress shall have power to enforce this article by appropriate legislation.

## AMENDMENT XXIV

### (Ratified January 23, 1964)

SECTION 1. The right of citizens of the United States to vote in any primary or other election for President or Vice President, for electors for President or Vice President, or for Senator or Representative in Congress, shall not be denied or abridged by the United States or any State by reason of failure to pay any poll tax or other tax.

SECTION 2. The Congress shall have power to enforce this article by appropriate legislation.

## AMENDMENT XXV

### (Ratified February 10, 1967)

SECTION 1. In case of the removal of the President from office or of his death or resignation, the Vice President shall become President.

SECTION 2. Whenever there is a vacancy in the office of the Vice President, the President shall nominate a Vice President who shall take office upon confirmation by a majority vote of both Houses of Congress.

SECTION 3. Whenever the President transmits to the President pro tempore of the Senate and the Speaker of the House of Representatives his written declaration that he is unable to discharge the powers and duties of his office, and until he transmits to them a written declaration to the contrary, such powers and duties shall be discharged by the Vice President as Acting President.

SECTION 4. Whenever the Vice President and a majority of either the principal officers of the executive departments or of such other body as Congress may by law provide, transmit to the President pro tempore of the Senate and the Speaker of the House of Representatives their written declaration that the President is unable to discharge the powers and duties of his office, the Vice President shall immediately assume the powers and duties of the office as Acting President.

Thereafter, when the President transmits to the President pro tempore of the Senate and the Speaker of the House of Representatives his written declaration that no inability exists, he shall resume the powers and duties of his office unless the Vice President and a majority of either the principal officers of the executive department or of such other body as Congress may by law provide, transmit within four days to the President pro tempore of the Senate and the Speaker of the House of Representatives their written declaration that the President is unable to discharge the powers and duties of his office. Thereupon Congress shall decide the issue, assembling within forty-eight hours for that purpose if not in session. If the Congress, within twenty-one days after receipt of the latter written declaration, or, if Congress is not in session, within twenty-one days after Congress is required to assemble, determines by two-thirds vote of both Houses that the President is unable to discharge the powers and duties of his office, the Vice President shall continue to discharge the same as Acting President; otherwise, the President shall resume the powers and duties of his office.

## AMENDMENT XXVI

### *(Ratified July 1, 1971)*

SECTION 1. The right of citizens of the United States, who are eighteen years of age or older, to vote shall not be denied or abridged by the United States or by any State on account of age.

SECTION 2. The Congress shall have power to enforce this article by appropriate legislation.

# Table of Cases

Table of Cases

# Index